The Rise
OF THE

West

A HISTORY OF THE HUMAN COMMUNITY

by WILLIAM H. McNEILL

DRAWINGS BY BÉLA PETHEÖ

THE UNIVERSITY OF CHICAGO PRESS

Chicago & London

I seek to understand, and if I can
To justify the ways of man to man.

THIS BOOK IS DEDICATED

TO

THE COMMUNITY OF SCHOLARS CONSTITUTING

THE UNIVERSITY OF CHICAGO

1933–1963

THE UNIVERSITY OF CHICAGO PRESS, CHICAGO 60637

The University of Chicago Press, Ltd., London

Published 1963. Eighth Impression 1975
Printed in the United States of America

ISBN: 0-226-56142-9 (clothbound); 0-226-56144-5 (paperbound)
Library of Congress Catalog Card Number: 63-13067

Preface

This book was conceived in 1936, commenced in 1954, and completed in 1962. The footnotes list most of the works consulted in the course of its composition, but I have made no systematic effort to record the sources of ideas and information accumulated beforehand. The consequence is a lopsidedness of citation, for the passages of the book which concern European history, where my professional interests have lain, almost entirely lack the apparatus of scholarship. A more serious lopsidedness inheres in the text itself, for I have assumed a decent familiarity with Western history and, in dealing with our own past, have chosen to emphasize matters which have been usually underrated, while passing over more familiar ground with a casual reference or even with no mention whatever. This unfits the book for schoolroom use and, hopefully, keys it to the historically literate, adult public of the Western world. Heirs of other civilizations will also, I hope, find stimulus in the following pages but will probably discover passages of needlessly obvious exposition alternating with untoward obscurities.

Discrepancies between the reader's familiar knowledge and an author's presuppositions will always introduce such disproportions, and a book that attempts to deal with so large a subject as the history of the world invites misunderstanding on an unusually massive scale. Yet it is only when others take aspects of what an author has thought and said in order to develop, twist, and reinterpret his ideas to fit their own predilections and answer their own problems that the cold type of a printed page leaps to life; and, if this happens often enough, a single book such as this may become a real force in the cultural history of mankind. Without irony, therefore, I hope my book may be richly and repeatedly misunderstood.

The Rise of the West is designed to be like a three-legged stool, for the text, the photographs, and Béla Petheö's maps and charts are intended to support and mutually reinforce one another. In principle, and perhaps also in practice, an attentive perusal of any one of the three constituents of the

v

work should offer its own limited yet coherent insight into the history of the human community, whereas the combination of all three is designed to multiply the force and enrich the meaning of any one taken by itself.

* * *

In some sense, everyone I have met as well as all I have ever read enters into this book. Those who have had a closer and more intimate relation with the pages that follow include the students who have served as my assistants during its composition: Hsio Yen Shih, Albert S. Hanser, George W. Smalley, and Jean A. Whitenack, to whose editorial eye and indefatigable typing I am particularly indebted. Colleagues and friends who have read and criticized all or part of the manuscript are: Robert M. Adams, Robert J. Braidwood, Michael Cherniavsky, Pinhas Delougaz, Mircea Eliade, Louis Gottschalk, Robert M. Grant, David Grene, Stephen Hay, Marshall G. S. Hodgson, Bert F. Hoselitz, Walter Johnson, Donald Lach, Christian W. Mackauer, J. A. B. van Buitenen, Karl J. Weintraub, and John A. Wilson of the University of Chicago; Edward Bastian of Earlham College; Pratulchandra Gupta of Jodavpur University, Calcutta; Peter Hardy of London University; Bryce Lyon of the University of California; Walter Porges of Pierce College, California; Earl Pritchard of the University of Arizona; Arnold J. Toynbee of the Royal Institute of International Affairs; G. E. von Grunebaum of the University of California, Los Angeles; Y. C. Wang of the University of Kansas; Martin Wight of Sussex University; and my father, John T. McNeill of Union Theological Seminary, New York. All these have contributed in greater or lesser degree to the improvement of this volume, but none is in the least responsible for whatever errors of fact or of interpretation remain to disfigure its pages.

A Ford Faculty Fellowship, 1954–55, allowed me leisure and gave me courage to begin the composition of this book, and a munificent grant from the Carnegie Corporation of New York permitted me to devote six months of each year from 1957 to 1962 to concentrated work upon the task. Without such help the book might never have been undertaken and could most certainly not yet have come to completion.

Last, the University of Chicago provided the genial matrix within which my thoughts and investigations arose and have now taken tangible form, while the narrower circle of my family gracefully tolerated the cuckoo in the nest this book has been to them these eight years past. I am very grateful to both.

WILLIAM H. McNEILL

September 25, 1962

Contents

PART II
EURASIAN CULTURAL BALANCE
500 B.C.–1500 A.D.

PART III

THE ERA OF WESTERN DOMINANCE, 1500 A.D.
TO THE PRESENT

Illustrations

xiii

PLATES

PART I

The Era of Middle Eastern Dominance to 500 B.C.

CHAPTER I

In the Beginning

In the beginning human history is a great darkness. The fragments of man-like skeletons which have been discovered in widely scattered parts of the earth can tell us little about the ascent of man. Comparative anatomists and embryologists classify the animal species *Homo sapiens* among the primates with apes, monkeys, and baboons; but all details of human evolution are uncertain. Shaped stones, potsherds, and other archeological remains are sadly inadequate evidence of vanished human cultures, although comparison of styles and assemblages, together with the stratification of finds, allows experienced archeologists to infer a good deal about the gradual elaboration of man's tool kit and to deduce at least some of the characteristics of human life in times otherwise beyond our knowledge. But the picture emerging from these modes of investigation is still very tentative. Not surprisingly, experts disagree, and learned controversy is rather the rule than the exception.

The various skulls and other bones which have been recovered from scattered parts of the Old World make clear that not one but several hominid (manlike) forms of life emerged in the Pleistocene geological epoch.[1] The use of wood and stone tools was not confined to the modern species of man, for unmistakable artifacts have been discovered in association with Peking man in China and, more doubtfully, with other hominid remains in Africa and

---

[1] Classification based on the few skeletal fragments yet known is hazardous; but recent finds, especially in Africa, make plausible a threefold generic classification, as follows:

Early Pleistocene (1,000,000 to 500,000 years ago)	Australopithecine
Middle Pleistocene (500,000 to 100,000 years ago)	Pithecanthropi
Late Pleistocene (From 100,000 years ago)	Homo

Within these genera, subgenera and species occur: e.g., *Homo* subdivides into *Homo neanderthalensis*, *Homo rhodesiensis*, *Homo sapiens*, and others. Cf. John Grahame Douglas Clark, *World Prehistory: An Outline* (Cambridge: Cambridge University Press, 1961), pp. 16–25; S. L. Washburn and F. Clark Howell, "Human Evolution and Culture," in Sol Tax (ed.), *Evolution after Darwin* (Chicago: University of Chicago Press, 1960), II, 35–46.

southeast Asia. Peking man also left traces of fire in the cave mouth where he lived, while in Europe, Neanderthal man knew both tools and fire.

Enough hominid and human remains have been discovered in Africa to suggest that the major cradle of mankind was in that continent.[2] The savanna which today lies in a great arc north and east of the rain forests of equatorial Africa offers the sort of natural environment in which our earliest human ancestors probably flourished. This is big-game country, with scattered clumps of trees set in a sea of grass and a climate immune from freezing cold. While weather patterns have certainly changed drastically in the past half-million years or so, it is probable that in the ages when glaciers covered parts of Europe, a shifting area of tropical savanna existed somewhere in Africa, and possibly also in Arabia and part of India. Such a land, where vegetable food could be supplemented by animal flesh, where trees offered refuge by night or in time of danger, and where the climate permitted human nakedness, was by all odds the most suitable for the first emergence of a species whose young were so helpless at birth and so slow to mature as to constitute a weighty burden upon the adults.

Indeed, the helplessness of human young must at first have been an extraordinary hazard to survival. But this handicap had compensations, which in the long run redounded in truly extraordinary fashion to the advantage of mankind. For it opened wide the gates to the possibility of cultural as against merely biological evolution. In due course, cultural evolution became the means whereby the human animal, despite his unimpressive teeth and muscles, rose to undisputed pre-eminence among the beasts of prey. By permitting, indeed compelling, men to instruct their children in the arts of life, the prolonged period of infancy and childhood made it possible for human communities eventually to raise themselves above the animal level from which they began. For the arts of life proved susceptible of a truly extraordinary elaboration and accumulation, and in the fulness of time allowed men to master not only the animal, but also the vegetable and mineral resources of the earth, bending them more and more successfully to human purposes.

*　　*　　*

Cultural evolution must have begun among the prehuman ancestors of modern man. Rudimentary education of the young may be observed among many types of higher animals; and the closest of man's animal relatives are all social in their mode of life and vocal in their habits. These traits presumably provided a basis upon which protohuman communities developed high skill as hunters. As the males learned to co-ordinate their activities more and more effectively through language and the use of tools, they became able to kill large game regularly. Under these circumstances, we may imagine that, even after they had gorged themselves, some flesh was usually left over for the

[2] Cf. John Desmond Clark, *The Prehistory of Southern Africa* (Harmondsworth: Penguin Books, 1959), pp. 24–130 and *passim;* L. S. B. Leakey, "The Origin of the Genus Homo," *Evolution after Darwin,* II, 17–31; Robert Ardrey, *African Genesis* (London: Collins, 1961), offers a popular but well-informed account.

females and children to eat. This made possible a new degree of specialization between the sexes. Males could afford to forego the incessant gathering of berries, grubs, roots, and other edibles which had formerly provided the main source of food and concentrate instead upon the arts of the hunt. Females, on the contrary, continued food-gathering as before; but, freed from the full rigor of self-nutrition, they could afford to devote more time and care to the protection and nurture of their infant children. Only in such a protohuman community, where skilled bands of hunters provided the principal food supply, was survival in the least likely for infants so helpless at birth and so slow to achieve independence as the first fully human mutants must have been.[3]

How modern types of men originated is one of the unsolved puzzles of archeology and physical anthropology. It is possible that the variety of modern races results from parallel evolution of hominid stocks toward full human status in widely separated and effectively isolated regions of the Old World;[4] but the very fragmentary evidence at hand may be interpreted equally well to support the alternative hypothesis that *Homo sapiens* arose in some single center and underwent racial differentiation in the course of migration to diverse regions of the earth.[5]

Homo sapiens appeared in Europe only after the last great glacial ice sheets had begun to melt back northward, perhaps 30,000 years ago. There is reason to believe that he came from western Asia, following two routes, one south and the other north of the Mediterranean.[6] The newcomers were skilled hunters, no doubt attracted to European soil by the herds of reindeer, mammoths, horses, and other herbivores that pastured on the tundra and in the thin forests which then lay south of the retreating glaciers. Neanderthal man, who had lived in Europe earlier, disappeared as *Homo sapiens* advanced. Perhaps the newcomers hunted their predecessors to extinction; perhaps some other change—epidemic disease, for example—destroyed the Neanderthal popula-

[3] Biologically considered, the distinguishing mark of humanity was systematic developmental retardation, making the human child infantile in comparison to the normal protohuman. Some adult human traits are also infantile when compared to those of an ape: e.g., the overdevelopment of brain size in relation to the rest of the body, underdevelopment of teeth and brow-ridges. But developmental retardation of course meant prolonged plasticity, so that learning could be lengthened. Thereby the range of cultural as against mere biological evolution widened enormously; and humanity launched itself upon a biologically as well as historically extraordinary career.

[4] Cf. Wilhelm Volz, "Die geographischen Grundlagen der menschlichen Rassenbildung," *Saeculum*, II (1951), 10–45. The author distinguishes five great habitable regions of the Old World—Europe and western Asia, eastern Asia, Africa south of the Sahara, southeast Asia, and India—and suggests that in each of these major regions a distinct racial type arose during the last Ice Age.

[5] Cf. Carleton S. Coon, *The Story of Man* (New York: Alfred A. Knopf, Inc., 1954), pp. 41, 73, 195–215; William W. Howells, "The Distribution of Man," *Scientific American*, CCIII (September, 1960), 113–27.

[6] Skeletons exhibiting a mixture of Neanderthal and modern characteristics have been discovered in caves on the slopes of Mount Carmel in Palestine. This may be interpreted to mean that the European type of modern man developed in the Middle East from Neanderthal-like types at a time when the ice sheets isolated the Neanderthal population of Europe from the rest of protomankind. Cf. F. Clark Howell, "The Place of Neanderthal Man in Human Evolution," *American Journal of Physical Anthropology* (n.s.), IX (1951), 409–12. But if one believes that modern men evolved earlier elsewhere, this same evidence may be considered as the result of interbreeding between *sapiens* and Neanderthal populations. The puzzle remains unsolved.

tions. Nor can one assume the absence of interbreeding, although skeletons showing mixed characteristics have not been found in Europe. In the Americas, by contrast, *Homo sapiens* appears to have entered a previously uninhabited land, although the date of his arrival (10000–7000 B.C.?) and even the skeletal characteristics of the first American immigrants remain unclear.

In regions of the world where the glacial retreat brought less drastic ecological changes, there appears to have been almost no development of tool assemblages.[7] Indeed, during the late Paleolithic era, human inventiveness may in fact have been called into play mainly along the northern fringes of the Eurasian habitable world, especially in its more westerly portion.[8] Here a comparatively harsh climate and radically fluctuating flora and fauna presented men with conditions to challenge their adaptability. Therefore, the apparent pre-eminence of European Paleolithic materials may not be solely due to accidents of discovery.

Seemingly from the date of their first arrival in Europe, *Homo sapiens* populations had a much enlarged variety of tools at their command. Implements of bone, ivory, and antler supplemented those of flint (and presumably of wood) which Neanderthal men had used. Bone and antler could be given shapes impossible for flint. Such useful items as needles and harpoon heads could only be invented by exploiting the characteristics of softer and more resilient materials than flint. The secret of working bone and antler lay in the manufacture of special stone cutting tools. Tools to make tools were seemingly first invented by *Homo sapiens;* and possession of such tools offers a key to much of our species' success in adapting itself to the conditions of subarctic Europe.[9]

On the analogy of hunting peoples who have survived to the present, it is likely that Paleolithic men lived in small groups of not more than twenty to sixty persons. Such communities may well have been migratory, returning to their caves or other fixed shelter for only part of the year. Very likely leadership in the hunt devolved upon a single individual whose personal skill and prowess won him authority. Probably there existed a network of relationships among hunting groups scattered over fairly wide areas or, at the least, a delimitation of hunting grounds between adjacent communities. Exogamous marriage arrangements and intergroup ceremonial associations may also have existed; and no doubt fighting sometimes broke out when one community trespassed upon the territory of another. There is also some evidence of long-distance trade,[10] although it is often impossible to be sure whether an object

[7] Hallam L. Movius, Jr., "Paleolithic Archaeology in Southern and Eastern Asia, Exclusive of India," *Cahiers d'histoire mondiale*, II (1954–55), 257–82, 520–53; J. G. D. Clark, *World Prehistory: An Outline*, pp. 45–50.

[8] In the Far East, the loess deposits of north China seem to have been laid down during the glacial ages and attest a long era of cold desert in that region. As long as such conditions prevailed, there was, of course, insufficient moisture to maintain an abundant fauna such as that upon which European hunters of the late Paleolithic periods were able to prey.

[9] Cf. C. S. Coon, *The Story of Man*, pp. 78–83.

[10] J. G. D. Clark, *Prehistoric Europe: The Economic Basis* (New York and London: Methuen & Co., 1952), pp. 241–81.

PALEOLITHIC HAND AX

This chipped flint, perhaps as much as 500,000 years old, was found in England on the banks of the Thames. It is $5\frac{1}{2}$ inches long, and the butt is blunt enough to fit into a man's palm. To a modern eye, the ax seems to have aesthetic as well as utilitarian value. Even if beauty had no place in its maker's thoughts, we may admire the evident skill with which he chipped the raw stone to produce such a balanced and symmetrical weapon.

Carleton Coon, The Story of Man, Plate V. Alfred A. Knopf, Inc. Photograph by Reuben Goldberg.

brought from afar came to its resting place as a result of an exchange or had
been picked up in the course of seasonal or other migrations.

Rude sculpture, strange signs, and magnificent animal frescoes in the recesses of a few caves in France and Spain[11] offer almost the only surviving
evidence of Paleolithic religious ideas and practices. Interpretation of the remains is uncertain. Ceremonies, very likely ritual dances in which the participants disguised themselves as animals, probably occurred in the dark depths.
Perhaps the purpose of such ceremonies was to bring the hunters into intimate
relation with their prospective quarry—to propitiate the animal spirits, and
perhaps to encourage their fecundity. Possibly caves were used for these
rituals because the dark recesses seemed to permit access to the womb of
Mother Earth, whence men and animals came and whither they returned; but
this is merely speculation.[12]

The prominence of animal figures in cave art may serve to remind us how
precarious was the success of Paleolithic hunters. Their existence depended
on game, which in turn depended on a shifting ecological balance. About ten
thousand years ago, the glaciers, which for a million years had oscillated over
the face of Europe and North America, began their most recent retreat. Open
tundra and sparse forest of birch and spruce followed the ice northward,
while heavier deciduous forests began to invade western Europe. The herds
followed their subarctic habitat northward, while new animals, which had to
be hunted by different methods, arrived to inhabit the thick new forests.

About 8000 B.C., therefore, a new style of human life began to prevail in
western Europe.[13] There is evidence of the arrival of new populations, presumably from the east. Whether these invaders mingled with their predecessors, or whether the older inhabitants followed their accustomed prey northward and eastward, leaving nearly uninhabited ground behind them, is not
known.[14] In any case, the newcomers brought to Europe some fundamental
additions to the Paleolithic tool kit: bows and arrows, fish nets, dugout canoes, sleds, and skis, as well as domesticated dogs, used presumably as assistants in the hunt.

The remains from this so-called Mesolithic period (*ca.* 8000–4500 B.C.)
are on the whole less impressive than those of the Paleolithic age which had
gone before. Flints are characteristically smaller; and rock paintings, found
mostly in Spain, are less strikingly beautiful. Yet it would be wrong to assume

[11] *Izvestia*, September 24, 1961, announced the discovery of animal frescoes like those of France and
Spain in a cave in the Ural Mountains.

[12] Cf. Gertrude Rachel Levy, *The Gate of Horn: A Study of the Religious Conceptions of the Stone Age
and Their Influence upon European Thought* (London: Faber & Faber, Ltd., 1948), pp. 3–70, for an interesting attempt to elucidate the religion of the cave.

[13] A similar shift occurred simultaneously and for the same reason in the eastern woodlands of
North America: intrusive forests eliminated some old food resources and offered new ones, com-
pelling human populations to change their style of life accordingly. Cf. Gordon R. Willey, "Historical
Patterns and Evolution in Native New World Cultures," *Evolution after Darwin*, II, 120.

[14] Large parts of Siberia were inhabited, as late as the third millennium B.C., by men who resembled
physically the Paleolithic hunters of western Europe. Cf. Karl Jettmar, "Zur Herkunft der türkischen
Völkerschaften," *Archiv für Völkerkunde*, III (1948), 13. This suggests that some, at least, of the old
population of western Europe followed the herds as the climate changed.

Archives photographiques, Paris.

PALEOLITHIC CAVE PAINTING

This black bull is one of numerous similar figures painted on the walls of a cave near Lascaux in south-central France. It was probably made by Magdalenian hunters who inhabited the region about 16,000 years ago. Why they descended into the bowels of the earth and painted such pictures in the dark depths can scarcely now be known. Accurate observation, seizing upon a characteristic pose even when, as in this example, such details as horns and ears are optically incorrect, lends a remarkable force to these paintings. In a modern observer, this image evokes a sense of animal strength, latent, admirable, yet potentially threatening. Such feelings may actually correspond in some faint measure to the emotional ambiguities which linked ancient hunters to their prey and which such paintings must have somehow expressed for their makers.

that human culture in Europe had undergone a decline. Even though to the casual eye an arrowhead or a fishhook is less impressive than a harpoon, nonetheless the bow and arrow and the fishing line may be a good deal more effective in winning food. Nor does the fact that almost no traces of Mesolithic religious life survive imply that religion ceased to occupy men's minds, or even that older religious traditions had been forgotten. We must simply rest in ignorance.

During the Paleolithic and Mesolithic ages man had already become master of the animal kingdom in the sense that he was the chief and most adaptable of predators; but despite his tools, his social organization, and his peculiar capacity to enlarge and transmit his culture, he still remained narrowly dependent on the balance of nature. The next great step in mankind's ascent toward lordship over the earth was the discovery of means whereby the natural environment could be altered to suit human need and convenience. With the domestication of plants and animals, and with the development of methods whereby fields could be made where forests grew by nature, man advanced to a new level of life. He became a shaper of the animal and vegetable life around him, rather than a mere predator upon it.

This advance opened a radically new phase of human history. The predator's mode of life automatically limits numbers; and large-bodied predators, like early men and modern lions, must perforce remain relatively rare in nature. Thus larger populations, with all the possibilities of specialization and social differentiation which numbers permit, could only be sustained by human communities that found ways of escaping from the natural limits imposed by their predatory past. This constituted perhaps the most basic of all human revolutions. Certainly the whole history of civilized mankind depended on the enlargement of the human food supply through agriculture and the domestication of animals. The costs were real, however; for the tedious labor of tilling the fields was a poor substitute for the fierce joys, sharp exertions, and instinctive satisfactions of the hunt. The human exercise of power thus early showed its profoundly double-edged character; for a farming folk's enlarged dominion over nature, and liberation from earlier limits upon food supply, meant also an unremitting enslavement to seed, soil, and season.

Archeological discovery cannot yet tell us much about this fundamental transformation of human life. Even proto-men may unwittingly have begun to affect the distribution and speciation of certain plants that attracted their attention. Hunters probably valued especially those plants from which dyes, narcotics, stimulants, or poisons could be derived. Perhaps the first efforts to control the growth and reproduction of plants centered rather upon these than upon the later staples of ordinary agriculture.[15]

Domestication of plants was a process rather than an event. Genetic combinations and recombinations, cross-breeding between cultivated and wild

[15] Cf. Edgar Anderson, "The Evolution of Domestication," *Evolution after Darwin*, II, 74–83.

varieties, and selection by human action—both conscious and unconscious[16]—meant, in effect, an unusually rapid biological evolution of certain types of plants toward a more effective symbiosis with man. In some cases, domestication proceeded so far that the very survival of the plant depended on human actions—as with maize. Reciprocally, human survival came in time to depend no less absolutely upon the crops.

It is probable that agriculture was invented more than once. The fact that the crops of pre-Columbian America were botanically quite different from those of the Old World has persuaded most students of the question that agriculture developed independently in the Americas.[17] Even within the Old World, agriculture probably originated in at least two different areas. The principal evidence for this is the basic contrast which until recently divided Eurasian agriculture into two distinct styles. Field agriculture, depending on reproduction by seed, dominated Europe and the Middle East, where grains constituted the principal crop. On the other hand, garden farming, involving propagation of crops by transplantation of offshoots from a parent plant, prevailed in much of monsoon Asia and the Pacific islands, where root crops were of major importance.[18] Such differences are fundamental and may stem from independent discoveries of the possibility of raising vegetable food by deliberate human action. Yet the contrast may also arise merely from an intelligent exploitation of varying local flora under conditions imposed by diverse climates.[19]

The grain-centered agriculture of the Middle East provided the basis for the first civilized societies. Careful work by archeologists permits us to know something of the natural conditions which made the development of that agriculture possible. Radiocarbon dating suggests we should look for the beginnings of Middle Eastern agriculture at about 6500 B.C., when the icecap had vanished from Continental Europe, and the earth's climatic zones were probably distributed more or less as at present. In western and central Europe

[16] Forest or brush fires started by men drastically affected local plant assemblages, opening forest lands to annual grasses, for example. Some of these grasses may have been ancestral to the cultivated grains of Middle Eastern agriculture.

[17] This is not, however, a universal opinion; for some think that voyaging across the Pacific or migration across Bering Strait from Asia to America may have allowed the importation of the *idea* of agriculture, even though new crops, based on the American flora, had to be or soon were brought under cultivation. Cf. Carl O. Sauer, *Agricultural Origins and Dispersals* (New York: American Geographical Society, 1952).

[18] Wet rice culture, which predominates on the Asian mainland and in some of the Pacific islands, only partially conforms to this description of "garden culture." Reproduction is by seed, but the practice of transplanting seedlings assimilates its cultivation to that of root crops. Rice may therefore at first have figured as a weed in root patches and only later been recognized as a valuable crop in its own right. Cf. André G. Haudricourt and Louis Hedin, *L'homme et les plantes cultivées* (Paris: Librairie Gallimard, 1943), pp. 91, 153.

[19] The divergence in the Old World between a predominantly root-growing style of agriculture depending on vegetative reproduction and a more northerly grain-centered style depending on reproduction by seed was duplicated in the Americas. Maize, beans, and squashes were the staples of North American agriculture; sweet potatoes, potatoes, and various other roots were staples of the South American highlands and of the Caribbean islands. Does this reflect simply an adjustment to climatic conditions? Or does it imply that agriculture was twice invented in the Americas, too? Or twice imported?

this meant the appearance of heavy forests and the corresponding human shift from Paleolithic to Mesolithic tool kits. Farther south, desiccating trade winds had already begun to form the Saharan, Arabian, Gedrosian, and Thar deserts in regions that had previously been important centers of human population. Between lay a zone of transition, where the trade winds blew only part of the year, while in winter cyclonic storms from the Atlantic brought life-giving precipitation. This was the zone of Mediterranean climate, within which lies most of the Middle East. Here the vegetable cover was thinner than in the better watered lands to the north; but before men and their domesticated animals had denuded the landscape, the plains supported a scattered growth of trees, among which grasses luxuriated in the spring, withered in the summer drought, and revived with the winter rains. By contrast, rain-catching hillsides and mountain slopes were often thickly wooded on their windward side.

Such a varied landscape was eminently suited to mankind.[20] Food resources unavailable in the deciduous northern forest offered themselves for human exploitation in the Middle East. The seed-bearing grasses ancestral to modern cultivated grains probably grew wild eight or nine thousand years ago in the hill country between Anatolia and the Zagros Mountains, as varieties of wheat and barley continue to do today. If so, we can imagine that from time immemorial the women of those regions searched out patches of wheat and barley grasses when the seeds were ripe and gathered the wild harvest by hand or with the help of simple cutting tools. Such women may gradually have discovered methods for assisting the growth of grain, e.g., by pulling out competing plants; and it is likely that primitive sickles were invented to speed the harvest long before agriculture in the stricter sense came to be practiced.

A critical turn must have come when collectors of wild-growing grain came to understand that allowing a portion of the seed to fall to the ground at harvest time assured an increased crop in the following year. Perhaps this idea was connected with concepts of the spirit of the grain, propitiation of that spirit, and the reward that befitted a pious harvester who left part of the precious seed behind. A second breakthrough occurred with the discovery that by scattering seed on suitably prepared ground, women could create grain fields even where the grasses did not grow naturally. Yet the laborious practice of breaking ground with a digging stick and covering the seed to keep it from birds may well have spread slowly, even after the prospective rewards for such labor were well understood; for hunting communities seldom remained long enough in one locality to engage in extended tillage.

Nonetheless, the development of agriculture in the Middle East was rapid as compared to the earlier progress of mankind. The spread of grain fields so enlarged human food resources that men began decisively to transcend their

---

[20] It resembled the savanna lands which were probably man's earliest cradle, differing only in possessing a climate in which seasonal variations of temperature were more pronounced. The resemblance arises from the fact that the tropical savanna lies on the southern as the Mediterranean climatic zone lies on the northern flank of the trade winds, which oscillate across the face of the earth with the sun, visiting each region in turn with their parching breath.

predatory past, escaping the limits upon number and density of population that had hitherto made humankind relatively rare in the balance of nature.[21] No date can confidently be assigned to this tremendous departure; and indeed, no completely satisfactory archeological evidence for the transition has yet come to light. But assuming that as new food-producing methods proved their advantage, they spread far and wide among the wild-grain gatherers of the Middle East; and assuming further that enlarged food resources resulted in comparatively rapid population growth, then it is probable that this earliest agriculture did not much antedate 6500 B.C. Village sites, created by the necessity for a more sedentary existence when fields had to be cultivated and guarded against browsing animals, have not been found dating from before about 6250 B.C. (plus or minus 200 years), but become increasingly numerous for later periods.[22]

Middle Eastern agriculture must at first have been conducted on a small scale, and was women's work. Hunting remained the task of the menfolk; but by discovering even rudimentary agriculture, women rudely upset a delicate ecological balance. Human hunters became too numerous; game animals within range of the pullulating grainfields must quickly have been almost exterminated.[23] As this happened, agriculture gradually displaced hunting from the center of community life. Men, whose bows had lost much of their usefulness, may have been persuaded to take on part of the work of the fields—fencing to keep out animals, harvesting in the precious days when the grain must be gathered before it scattered its seeds irreparably on the earth; and at last, as food for the year came to depend mainly on the size of the cultivated plot, men may in some communities have taken spade or hoe reluctantly in hand to work the fields side by side with their womenfolk.

But there was another possibility. Men could tame some of the beasts upon which they were accustomed to prey. It was logical for intelligent hunters confronted with a dwindling game reserve to protect their potential victims from rival predators and to conserve the herds for their own future use. This still falls short of full-scale domestication, however, which implies exploitation of the living animal for its milk, wool, and even its blood.

No one really knows how or by what stages a hunting-collecting way of life retreated before agriculture and stock raising. Perhaps the first fully domesticated animals were used to decoy their wild fellows within the reach of hunters; and other uses for them may have been discovered only gradually, as the numbers of wild herds decreased. No doubt the innovators failed to foresee how domestication of animals would transform their familiar customs.

---

[21] Cf. the calculations of Edward S. Deevey, Jr., "The Human Population," *Scientific American*, CCIII (September, 1960), 195–204, which suggest that human population multiplied about sixteen times between 8000 and 4000 B.C. as a consequence of the agricultural revolution.

[22] Here I follow R. J. Braidwood's data and arguments, as most recently set forth in "The Agricultural Revolution," *Scientific American*, CCIII (September, 1960), 130–48.

[23] There is some ground for believing that the human hunters of North America extinguished several potentially domesticable animal species, e.g., the horse, in relatively recent times. Cf. J. G. D. Clark, "New World Origins," *Antiquity*, XIV (1940), 128.

Reason presumably had little scope in this transformation, for the whole relationship of man to animals was saturated in magical conceptions. Ritual
slaughter of captured beasts played a part in the religions of some hunting
peoples; and perhaps protecting and nurturing herds of potential victims in
the hope of assuring better hunting through more regular and sumptuous
sacrifices seemed the only proper answer to an increasing shortage of wild
game.

All that can be said with certainty is that men in the Middle East did succeed in domesticating goats, sheep, pigs, and cattle at an early stage of their
agricultural development, and were able thereby to secure a continued and
perhaps even an enlarged supply of meat and other animal products. Conceivably, domestication of animals may have begun even before agriculture caused human population to increase beyond the level that could be
maintained by predation; but even if so, domesticated flocks and herds can
have had only a very limited importance before hunters found their accustomed prey becoming scarcer. As long as hunting continued to bring in the
usual amount of food, why abandon a way of life inculcated by the practice
of untold generations and sanctified by firm religious and moral values?[24]

Discoveries in the Middle East suggest that once agriculture had begun to
transform human life, the range of material equipment at the disposal of the
new farming communities rapidly increased. The apparent suddenness with
which new accouterments appear in the archeological strata may partly be
due to gaps in the record. Yet the new routines of daily life must have called
for new tools and methods; and the human response to such new needs may
have been relatively rapid. Presumably the drastic transformation implicit in
the shift from hunting to agriculture and stock-raising temporarily freed
men's inventive capacities from the bonds of custom. Normal resistance to
innovation was reduced for a time, until a series of brilliant inventions and
adaptations of old methods provided the basis for a new and satisfactory way
of life, which then in its turn formed a stable, customary pattern: that of the
Neolithic village community.

Archeology permits us to know something of the technical and material
side of this social mutation. Tillage and stock raising were associated with
brewing, weaving, and the manufacture of pottery and polished stone tools.
Some pre-pottery sites have been discovered where traces of agriculture are
discernible; and no doubt some centuries were needed before the mature as-

[24] This is a telling consideration against the idea developed by the "Vienna school" of ethnologists,
to the effect that domestication of animals occurred first among hunters in northern Eurasia (beginning
probably with reindeer), while domestication of plants first took place somewhere south of the great
mountain backbone of that continent. According to this theory, the style of agriculture that established
itself in the Middle East and in Europe, which combines plant with animal husbandry, arose as a consequence of the intermingling of these older and originally independent styles of life. For a recent statement of this view, cf. Carl J. Narr, "Hirten, Pflanzen, Bauern: Produktionsstufe," in Fritz Valjavec (ed.),
Historia Mundi (Bern: Francke, 1953), II, 66–100. The most serious objection to the theory, however,
is the absence of datable archeological evidence in its support; and it is logically incorrect to assume
that the way of life characteristic of contemporary primitive herdsmen of Siberia and of primitive
gardeners in southeast Asia is *necessarily* older than the more complex economy of the ancient Middle
East.

semblage of what archeologists call "Neolithic" tools had been worked out and adopted by the primitive farming communities of the Middle East.

Once a community had come to rely on cereal foods, its members automatically became far more firmly rooted to a given spot than had been the case in the days of hunting economy.[25] Throughout the growing season, at least part of the community had to protect the fields from browsing animals; and even during the rest of the year the difficulty of transporting harvested grain, together with the need to work old fields and clear new ones, must have kept the women of the community tied to a fixed location for nearly the whole circle of the seasons.

With the establishment of permanent settlements, it became possible to accumulate bulky, heavy, and fragile household goods. Clay pots, for example, became suitable substitutes for the lighter and less fragile containers made from animal skins, gourd shells, and woven willow withes that had been used previously. The first departure from older types was minimal. Much early pottery suggests that it had been copied in clay from basket and gourd shapes; and it is tempting to imagine that the first pots were made when it became necessary to coat such earlier containers with a fireproof and waterproof layer of clay in order to cook newfangled cereal porridge. Meat, after all, could be roasted on a wooden spit; but to cook cereals required a container both fire- and waterproof: required, in short, a pot.

The earliest known traces of cloth come from Neolithic sites. This does not prove that cloth was previously unknown, for clothmaking, like potmaking, had its Paleolithic antecedents in basketry. But until flax came into cultivation and hair and wool from domesticated animals became available, the supply of fiber must have been too scant to allow much clothmaking, even if the skills of spinning and weaving were familiar. Agriculture and the domestication of animals, however, so enlarged the supply of fiber that woven cloth became an important adjunct to the new way of life.

Polished stone tools, particularly axes, constitute the hallmark of every Neolithic site. Flint, chipped and flaked in a fashion to produce sharp cutting edges, had been perfectly adequate for the arrowheads, knives, and scrapers needed by hunters; but flint was too brittle for stripping the bark and branches from trees or cutting them down. Usable axes could only be made from tougher kinds of stone, which could not be shaped by traditional methods of flint-knapping. The solution to this difficulty was found by transferring to the harder medium of stone the methods of rough-hewing and polishing which had long been in use for shaping bone and horn implements. Polished stone axes and other tools therefore became characteristic of agricultural settlements; and the conspicuous difference between them and the older flints caused archeologists to name such remains "Neolithic" long before the connection between the technique of tool manufacture and the changed requirements of the community was understood.

The first agriculturalists were not fully sedentary. Soil repeatedly cropped

[25] This has led some modern students to suppose that the first agricultural communities probably arose among fisher folk, whose way of life already in Mesolithic times allowed a settled existence.

lost its fertility after a few years, so that if harvests were to be maintained, old fields had to be abandoned and virgin soil broken in from time to time. The sort of land that lent itself to primitive agriculture was thickly wooded ground where the tree cover prevented heavy undergrowth. In such areas, once the trees had been killed by stripping their bark, the soil beneath lay relatively open and might easily be worked with digging stick, spade, or hoe by going around the stumps. After a season or two of cropping such soil, fertility could be renewed by burning the dried limbs and tree trunks and scattering their ashes. By contrast, natural grassland offered stubborn resistance to wooden digging sticks; and it was almost impossible to prevent the native grasses from growing up through the grain and crowding it out. Hence the earliest agriculturalists, like eighteenth-century American pioneers, preferred the woodlands and clung at first to the slopes and foothills of the Middle East where trees grew naturally. It was probably this style of slash-and-burn agriculture, involving a semi-migratory pattern of life, which was practiced by the "mature" Neolithic villages of the ancient Middle East, as it still is today by primitive farmers in tropical rain forests and in subarctic birch and spruce forests on the fringes of the agricultural world.[26]

As agriculture evolved in the Middle East, mixed economies, combining cereal-cropping with stock-raising, became characteristic. No doubt some communities put more emphasis upon the one or the other activity. At lower altitudes along the margins of the woodlands, where grasslands shaded off into desert, the domestication of animals made possible a predominantly pastoral mode of life; and just as Abraham set out from Ur of the Chaldees with his flocks and herds and human followers,[27] so many another group must also have done, both before and after his time.

Since pastoral peoples leave few traces for archeologists, it is uncertain when a distinct divergence between pastoral and agricultural modes of life first developed. The occupation of the steppe and desert was gradual. Indeed, the full potentiality of pastoral nomadism was not realized until men learned to ride horseback habitually—not before about 900 B.C.; while the earliest peoples who followed their flocks onto the grasslands also cultivated favorable patches of ground, so that the difference between the two ways of life was at first rather of emphasis than of kind.

In all probability, pastoralism was divorced fully from agriculture only by communities that had remained hunters until the migratory expansion of stock-raising farmers brought the new style of life to their attention, perhaps by usurping some part of their accustomed hunting grounds. Clearly, hunters would find the labor of the fields little to their liking; whereas the arts of the herdsman fitted smoothly and easily into traditions of the hunt. Hence, if for any reason hunters had to modify familiar routines, it is not difficult to believe that they might accept domesticated animals eagerly but repudiate crop tillage as unworthy of free men. It was therefore toward the margins of the earliest centers of agricultural life—in the steppes of Europe and central Asia

[26] J. G. D. Clark, *Prehistoric Europe: The Economic Basis*, pp. 91–98.
[27] Genesis, 11:31.

NEOLITHIC PAINTED POT

This handsome pot was discovered at a Neolithic site in the province of Kansu, China. Its curvilinear decoration resembles Neolithic pottery styles of the Ukraine and lower Danube region so closely that many archeologists believe that the technique of making such pots must have had a common origin, and been carried east and west by semi-migratory cultivators of cereal grains.

and in northern Arabia, where natural grasslands made cultivation difficult at best—that pastoralism found its principal home.[28]

The occupation of the grasslands by pastoral peoples meant that two divergent styles of human life, partially interdependent and capable of endless interaction, came to exist side by side in the Middle East. As they still do today, pastoralists must from the earliest times have brought their animals to feed on the grain stubble. No doubt from the beginning they entered into trade relations with farming populations, for the surpluses produced by farmer and by herdsman naturally complement each other; and the more mobile life of the pastoralist made it easy and natural for him to act as carrier of such special and precious goods as hard stone for axes, shells for decoration, and valued perishables which have not left archeological traces. Finally, the perennial warfare between peasant and herdsman, symbolized in the biblical story of Cain and Abel, must have brought recurrent violence into the lives of Neolithic peoples.

Communities of hunters, whose way of life was essentially uniform throughout wide areas, and whose skills were exquisitely adapted to the existing environment, could find little stimulus to social change from contact with neighboring human groups. But with the development of agriculture and pastoralism, ways of life were no longer uniform. A new and fertile stimulus to fresh departures had arrived on the human scene. Once men had started re-creating their environments to suit themselves, older limits to social change were removed, and the spectacular ascent to our contemporary level of skill in manipulating the forces of nature began.

*   *   *

For farmer and herdsman alike, the cycle of the seasons assumed an importance unmatched in the older hunting life. Storms and drought, recurring irregularly though within a loosely predictable seasonal pattern, set the basic rhythm of life for communities dependent upon grain fields and pastures. Probably the seasons in the Middle East were much the same then as now—sometimes irregular, but nonetheless sharply marked. This area today is characterized by winter rains, followed by luxuriant growth of vegetation in spring, and succeeded in turn by the parched drought of summer heat. The rains, brought by the southernmost edge of cyclonic storms coming in from the Atlantic, are not always dependable. Years of abundant rainfall bring good harvests and rich pastures; years when rain is scant mean famine for man and beast.[29]

Of necessity, therefore, the caprices of weather and season provided the central themes of Middle Eastern Neolithic religion. The generative and destructive aspects of earth, rain, and sun pressed themselves upon the farmers' attention; and religious ceremonies underwent a corresponding development

---

[28] Cf. Karl Jettmar, "Les plus anciennes civilisations d'éleveurs des steppes d'Asie centrale," *Cahiers d'histoire mondiale*, I (1954), 775–76.

[29] To be sure, the Middle East was not always as dry as it is today; but much of the region's desiccation may be due to human agency—destroying natural cover, hastening erosion, and speeding run-off. Yet even if precipitation was higher in the sixth or fifth millennium B.C., the variability of rainfall would have presented an ever recurrent problem for the earliest farmers.

in the hope of persuading or compelling the forces of nature to act in accordance with human desires. Older pieties, centered upon animal and vegetable spirits, persisted; and rites that had been designed to propitiate or to increase the fecundity of these spirits blended easily with new, or newly important, cults of earth, sky, and sun to produce the Middle Eastern "fertility religions."

A widespread shift in human relations brought about by the transition from hunting to agriculture seems also to have affected Neolithic cults. In proportion as women became the major suppliers of food for the community, their independence and authority probably increased; and various survivals in historic times suggest that matrilineal family systems prevailed in many Neolithic communities. Correspondingly, the spread of agriculture was connected everywhere with the rise of female priestesses and deities to prominence.[30] The earth itself was apparently conceived as a woman—the prototype for the Great Mother of later religions—and the numerous female figurines which have been unearthed from Neolithic sites may have been intended as representations of the fruitful earth goddess.[31] In addition, stone axes (which cleared the trees to make fields), sacred fire (which fertilized the plots and kept the hearth alive), and sacred mountains, trees, and stones seem to have played varying parts in Neolithic religious observances. Indeed, one may imagine that just as a new tool kit developed by appropriate elaboration of older elements, so also the intellectual, emotional, and moral aspects of the new agricultural society soon became rationalized by myth, ritualized by practice, and suffused with a sense of the sacred.

Although the foci of religious practice, symbols, and ritual were thus rather drastically displaced, there was no fundamental break with the older animism of the Paleolithic and Mesolithic hunters. In one respect, however, the Neolithic pattern of life and religion did mark an important departure, ritually expressed in the worship of the moon, and practically in the necessity of time-reckoning. The waxing and waning of the moon offered primitive peoples their only obvious calendar. Moreover, since the horns of cattle resemble the crescent moon, primitive cultivators came to associate cow and moon goddesses with the difficult art of reckoning the seasons, in variously complicated ways whose details we cannot hope to unravel.[32]

The importance of measurement and calculation in the agricultural routine of the Middle East profoundly affected the subsequent development of human society and thought. To hunters, neither temporal nor spatial measurement matters much. Life consists of alternate feast and famine, somewhat mitigated by freezing or drying surplus meat or accumulating modest stores of wild-growing seeds and roots. But the time until the next kill is incalculable, nor is it feasible to preserve and store food against a definite period of

[30] Cf. Robert Briffault, *The Mothers* (London: Allen & Unwin, Ltd., 1927), III, 45 and *passim;* Pia Laviosa-Zambotti, *Ursprung und Ausbreitung der Kultur*, trans. Ferdinand Siebert (Baden-Baden: Verlag für Kunst & Wissenschaft, 1950), pp. 164–68.

[31] In contrast, male deities date only from later times, when political and other changes had drastically altered the social structure of the earliest Neolithic village communities. Gertrude Rachel Levy, *Gate of Horn*, pp. 86–88.

[32] The association between cattle, the moon, and fertility may have developed only after the invention of the plow, which gave cattle a central role in tillage.

foreseeable shortage. All this is different for the cultivator. For him the seasons set a basic rhythm of existence, with fixed and foreseeable times of plenty and of dearth. Rationing grain consumption to last until harvest, reserving surplus against a year of drought, and calculating what is needed for seed, how much land to dig, and when to dig it—all these and similar acts of foresight and measurement were necessary to the primitive agriculturalist. Basic to all such calculation was a method of foreknowing the seasons—how long it would be till seed time and harvest came round once more. Hence under Middle Eastern conditions the arts of measurement were an indispensable and absolutely vital part of the agriculturalist's equipment.

Rough measurement of dimensions, accurate enough to allow men to estimate how much seed to save for sowing a given plot of ground, probably offered little difficulty to the earliest farmers. Rule of thumb served. A basketful of seed per field, basket and field being about "so" big, would do. Not until men undertook large-scale irrigation and monumental architecture were more accurate spatial measurements needful. But the measurement of time presented a formidable problem; for under Middle Eastern conditions the arrival of the winter rains does not announce itself from year to year in any unambiguous way. Erratic summer or autumn showers might easily lead a hungry farmer to plant the irreplaceable seed too soon, so that his grain would sprout only to wither in a renewed drought. The fact that the phases of the moon do not fit exactly into the solar year vastly complicated the problem. Only when men had learned to watch and interpret correctly the seasonal movements of moon, sun, and stars could they know for certain under which cycle of the moon to plant their crops. The supreme importance of measuring the seasons accurately, and the difficulty of doing so, provided a basic stimulus to intellectual and scientific development in the Middle East.[33] Not until the rise of Sumerian and Egyptian civilization was the problem fully solved by the development of reliable calendars.

It is worth noting that the problems of time measurement in monsoon Asia were far less serious. Except in fringe areas, the monsoon announces itself unmistakably, and the growing season begins with the return of the rains. There can be no problem of planting too soon or too late; and an accurate calendar is simply not needed. Perhaps it is not fantastic to suggest that the notorious indifference of Indian civilization to time was connected with this fundamental difference in the agricultural cycle. Contrariwise, the preoccupation of the earliest Middle Eastern farmers with time measurement may well have imparted a fundamental cast to Western and Moslem minds, rooted as they are in the Mediterranean–Middle Eastern past.

In agricultural communities, male leadership in the hunt ceased to be of much importance. As the discipline of the hunting band decayed, the political institutions of the earliest village settlements perhaps approximated the anarchism which has remained ever since the ideal of peaceful peasantries all round the earth. Probably religious functionaries, mediators between helpless

[33] Cf. O. Neugebauer, *The Exact Sciences in Antiquity* (Princeton, N.J.: Princeton University Press, 1952), p. 161.

GOD

PRIEST

June

October

DROUGHT

REAPING PLANTING

February

THE CIRCLE OF THE YEAR

mankind and the uncertain fertility of the earth, provided an important form of social leadership. The strong hunter and man of prowess, his occupation gone or relegated to the margins of social life, lost the unambiguous primacy which had once been his; while the comparatively tight personal subordination to a leader necessary to the success of a hunting party could be relaxed in proportion as grain fields became the center around which life revolved.

Among predominantly pastoral peoples, however, religious-political institutions took a quite different turn. To protect the flocks from animal predators required the same courage and social discipline which hunters had always needed. Among pastoralists, likewise, the principal economic activity—focused, as among the earliest hunters, on a parasitic relation to animals—continued to be the special preserve of menfolk. Hence a system of patrilineal families, united into kinship groups under the authority of a chieftain responsible for daily decisions as to where to seek pasture, best fitted the conditions of pastoral life. In addition, pastoralists were likely to accord importance to the practices and discipline of war. After all, violent seizure of someone else's animals or pasture grounds was the easiest and speediest way to wealth and might be the only means of survival in a year of scant vegetation.

Such warlikeness was entirely alien to communities tilling the soil. Archeological remains from early Neolithic villages suggest remarkably peaceable societies. As long as cultivable land was plentiful, and as long as the labor of a single household could not produce a significant surplus, there can have been little incentive to war. Traditions of violence and hunting-party organization presumably withered in such societies, to be revived only when pastoral conquest superimposed upon peaceable villagers the elements of warlike organization from which civilized political institutions without exception descend.

With all its technical limitations, the ancient Middle Eastern style of agricultural life offered substantial advantages over the older hunting existence. If life was less exciting, food was more nearly assured, and more people could survive on a given area of land. Such advantages meant that agriculture was bound to spread outward from its center of origin, establishing itself wherever cultivation was easiest. In Europe at least, this meant a preference for light soils, especially loess and chalk hillsides, where natural drainage was good and the soil could be worked easily.

The advance of the agricultural tide through Europe proceeded by two routes, one north, the other south of the Mediterranean. The more northerly and more massive of these movements carried the so-called "Danubian" cultivators into central and western Europe between 4500 and 4000 B.C. The southerly stream of pioneer farmers and herders traversed north Africa and crossed the Straits of Gibraltar to meet and mingle with the Danubian flood. Older hunting populations of Europe were not destroyed. They survived in forest fastnesses for centuries after farmers had occupied hilltops and slopes. Probably considerable mixing of populations occurred; and hunters may sometimes have borrowed the newcomers' techniques and assimilated themselves to the agricultural mass.[34]

A very similar agricultural expansion occurred in Kazakhstan and central Siberia, perhaps a thousand years after pioneer farmers had penetrated western Europe. By about 2500 B.C., hunting economies in those regions had begun to give way to societies dependent on herding and agriculture, whose pottery shows clear affinities with that of the Middle East. In addition, these peoples had small quantities of bronze; and in metalliferous regions some of their settlements engaged in mining.[35]

In other parts of the earth, almost nothing is known about the spread of Neolithic agriculture. In India, no clear evidence has yet been found of a period in which men tilled the ground with only stone and wood tools, though Neolithic tool types persisted for millennia after the introduction of metal.[36] There seems little doubt, however, that agriculture and animal husbandry of the Middle Eastern type spread at least into northwest India and provided the basis for Indus civilization.[37] In China, on the other hand, direct archeological evidence of a Neolithic age has been found in the valley of the Yellow River. Pottery styles discovered on sites of ancient Chinese villages sufficiently resemble those familiar from sites of the western steppe—south Russia and eastern Iran—to suggest some relationship between the Neolithic cultures of the two regions. The comparatively late date tentatively assigned to Chinese Neolithic discoveries—about 2400 B.C.—allows ample time for semi-migratory agriculturalists starting from the hill regions of the Middle East sometime after 6500 B.C. to have occupied favorable ground along the river banks and on wooded mountainsides all across central Asia, mingling perhaps with local populations at every stage until the easternmost pioneers carried elements of Middle Eastern agricultural techniques into the Yellow River Valley. At the same time, Chinese Neolithic remains show traits that can best be explained by assuming the existence of a primitive agricultural society to the south of the Yellow River. The most telling of these is the presence of rice, which is believed to have originated as a cultivated crop in monsoon Asia.[38] It looks,

---

[34] C. F. C. Hawkes, *The Prehistoric Foundations of Europe to the Mycenaean Age* (London: Methuen & Co., Ltd., 1940), pp. 87–134. M. Richard Pittioni, "Zur Urgeschichte des Bauerntums," *Anzeiger der oesterreichischen Akademie der Wissenschaften*, Phil.-Hist. Klasse, No. 21 (1957), pp. 326, 341; J. G. D. Clark, *World Prehistory*, pp. 119–29.

[35] Karl Jettmar, "Zur Herkunft der türkischen Völkerschaften," pp. 14–15.

[36] Stuart W. Piggott, *Prehistoric India to 1000 B.C.* (Harmondsworth: Penguin Books, 1950), p. 37; Robert Eric Mortimer Wheeler, *Early India and Pakistan to Ashoka* (London: Thames & Hudson, 1959), pp. 80–92; D. H. Gordon, *The Prehistoric Background of Indian Culture* (Bombay: N. M. Tripathi, Ltd., 1958), pp. 26–33.

[37] This judgment is based on the affinity between pottery and art motifs of the Indus civilization and those of Iran, Syria, and even Crete. Cf. Heinz Mode, *Indische Frühkulturen und ihre Beziehungen zum Westen* (Basel: Benno Schwabe & Co. Verlag, 1944), p. 131 and *passim;* Willibald Kirfel, "Vorgeschichtliche Besiedlung Indiens und seine kulturellen Parallelen zum alten Mittelmeeraum," *Saeculum*, VI (1955), 166–79.

[38] Cf. J. Gunnar Andersson, *Children of the Yellow Earth* (London: Kegan Paul, Trench, Trubner & Co., Ltd., 1934), pp. 184–87; C. W. Bishop, "Long-Houses and Dragon-Boats," *Antiquity*, XII (1938), 411–24; W. Eberhard, "Eine neue Arbeitshypothese über den Aufbau der frühchinesischen

therefore, as though techniques of grain agriculture which originated in the Middle East met and mingled in north China during the third millennium B.C. with another style of cultivation deriving from monsoon Asia. This strengthens the hypothesis that agriculture originated in two separate areas of the Old World.

*   *   *

Long before the wielders of digging sticks, hoes, and spades had reached the full limits of their expansion in Eurasia, other and more developed forms of agricultural life had arisen in the Middle East. Perhaps a growing shortage of cultivable land compelled or encouraged technical innovation and improvement. As primitive farming populations multiplied, sooner or later a time had to come when all suitable soil within reach of a given community had already been cropped to exhaustion. It then became necessary either to migrate—as some communities probably did—or to return at more and more frequent intervals to the tillage of land whose fertility had already been depleted by annual cropping.

The problem this presented to peoples accustomed to slash-and-burn agriculture was solved by two basic inventions. One was fallowing, the other the traction plow. The two were closely connected. Only the most back-breaking labor could maintain a substantial area of fallow in good tilth without the use of animal power. But once someone had hit upon the idea of hitching a modified spade behind one or more animals and exploiting the beasts' strength to break the ground, it became relatively easy for an ordinary family to cultivate more land than was needed to feed its members. By leaving unsown a part of the land so cultivated, and plowing it several times during the growing season to keep down weeds and conserve moisture, the fertility of the fields could be maintained indefinitely, though at a level far below the luxuriance of virgin land freshly cleared from the forest.

How and when the traction plow was invented is not clear. It was in use in the Middle East sometime before 3000 B.C.; for crude plows are familiar from the earliest Sumerian and Egyptian records, which date from about that

Kultur," *Tagungsberichte der Gesellschaft für Völkerkunde*, No. 2 (Leipzig, 1936); Folke Bergman, *Archaeological Researches in Sinkiang* (Stockholm: Bokförlags Aktiebolaget Thule, 1939), pp. 14–26.

Recent work by Chinese archeologists has tended to minimize resemblances between the painted pottery culture of northwestern China and painted pottery of the Ukraine and western Asia. Earlier investigators may well have exaggerated the likenesses by seizing upon particular instances to the neglect of the total assemblages of artifacts recovered from the separate sites. Yet recent Chinese scholarship cannot entirely fail to be influenced both by national pride and by Marxian doctrines about prehistory which decry the significance of migration. For a non-committal discussion of recent discoveries, cf. Cheng Te-k'un, *Archaeology in China.* I: *Prehistoric China* (Cambridge: W. Heffer & Sons, 1959), pp. 73–87 and *passim*.

The sort of diffusion of agricultural and of pot-decorating techniques which probably took place does *not* require massive migration all across Asia. Local peoples, especially if confronted by some food crisis, might be expected to welcome the new food resource and borrow the techniques of hoe cultivation from their agricultural neighbors, only to take over, in relation to peoples lying still farther away from the initial center of dispersion, the role of agricultural pioneers.

time. But how much before then, and exactly where men first successfully hitched an animal to a spadelike device, cannot be said.[39]

It does not appear that the technical innovation was in itself very great. The so-called foot-plow had been devised very early indeed and must have spread over the earth with or close behind the earliest type of spade and hoe cultivation. The foot-plow is a simple modification of the familiar spade. It has a long, crooked handle, which allows the user to turn the soil by pressing down on the handle instead of by lifting. A peg near the bottom of the handle serves as a footrest, whereby a man may use his weight to drive the blade into the soil at a shallow angle approximating the horizontal.[40]

To convert such a device into a traction plow was a simple matter. All that was needed was a rope or thong to tie to the lower part of the handle, and an animal that could be attached to the other end of the rope. Cattle might be hitched simply by tying a knot around their horns; and some of the earliest plows pictured on Sumerian and Egyptian monuments were pulled in just this manner.[41] Cattle, particularly oxen, came therefore to serve as the primary draft animals, thus giving rise to a new association between horned beasts and the fertility of the fields.[42]

The first plows had no moldboard to turn a furrow. They simply scratched the earth, breaking the surface into loose lumps by driving a flat share some inches below the surface of the ground. Cross-plowing was characteristic, perhaps from the beginning. Hence squarish field shapes are almost always associated with light scratch plows of this primitive type.

The technical limitations of the first plows partly determined the patterns of human settlement. Being both small and light, these plows could not easily penetrate heavy soils, especially clays. Thus early European agriculturalists continued to prefer loess, chalk, and light loam soils even after plowing had become their normal mode of cultivation.

The harnessing of animal power for the labor of tillage was a step of obvious significance. Human resources were substantially increased thereby, since for the first time men tapped a source of mechanical energy greater than that which their own muscles could supply. The use of animal power also

---

[39] Paul Leser, *Entstehung und Verbreitung des Pfluges*, Anthropos Bibliothek, III, No. 3 (Münster: Aschendorf, 1931), 568–69.

[40] Cf. E. C. Curwen, *Plough and Pasture: The Early History of Farming* (New York: Henry Schuman, 1953), p. 71.

[41] Cf. Paul Leser, *Entstehung und Verbreitung des Pfluges*, pp. 551–60. Asses, the other domesticated beasts large enough to pull a plow and available to the first plowmen, could not be hitched so easily; yet it is interesting to know that it was customary in Ireland as late as the seventeenth century A.D. to hitch horses to the plow by tying willow withes into their tails. Charles Hughes, *Shakespeare's Europe: Unpublished Chapters in Fynes Moryson's Itinerary* (London: Sherratt & Hughes, 1930), p. 214.

[42] The argument advanced by Eduard Hahn, *Die Entstehung der Pflugkultur* (Heidelberg: Carl Winter, 1909), to the effect that the invention of the plow was a result of religious ritual aimed at promoting fertility, seems to put the cart before the horse—or rather, the plow before the ox! Religious ritual is inherently conservative and does not easily permit innovation; and surely it is more sensible to assume that the fertility rites connecting cattle with the fields were elaborated after the plow, not before it. I prefer to imagine that some man, tongue-lashed by his wife for not doing his share of work in the field, was the harassed genius who first devised means whereby he could both accomplish the needful cultivation and preserve his masculine dignity as master of the beasts!

established a much more integral relation between stock-breeding and agriculture. Mixed farming, uniting animal husbandry with crop cultivation, was to become the distinguishing characteristic of agriculture in western Eurasia. It made possible a higher standard of living or of leisure than was attainable by peoples relying mainly or entirely upon the strength of merely human muscles.

The spread of traction plowing served also to reverse the role of the sexes in agriculture. Hunting and tending animals had always been primarily a man's job; and when animals came into the field, men came with them. Women lost their earlier dominion over the grain fields; and as followers of the plow, men became once again the principal providers of food. Therewith they were able to reinforce or restore masculine primacy in family and society. By the time of the earliest written records, patrilineal families and male dominance were universal among plowing peoples in the Middle East, although enough traces of an earlier system remain to suggest that this had not always and everywhere been so. The rise of male deities and priests—established features of Sumerian and Egyptian religion—may also be connected with the new masculine role in agriculture. Political organization was probably less affected. Traces of a system of government based upon the informal decisions of an assembly of elders survived into historic times in Mesopotamia;[43] and this sort of "primitive democracy" seems a likely model for whatever government the earliest plowing villagers found needful.

The plowing style of agriculture spread from its point of origin in the Middle East much as the earlier spade and hoe culture had done. Evidence of plowed fields has been discovered in Denmark dating from about 1500

[43] Thorkild Jacobsen, "Primitive Democracy in Ancient Mesopotamia," *Journal of Near Eastern Studies*, II (1943), 159–72.

SHIFTS OF ECONOMIC ROLES BETWEEN THE SEXES

HUNTING AND GATHERING   HOE AGRICULTURE   PLOW AGRICULTURE

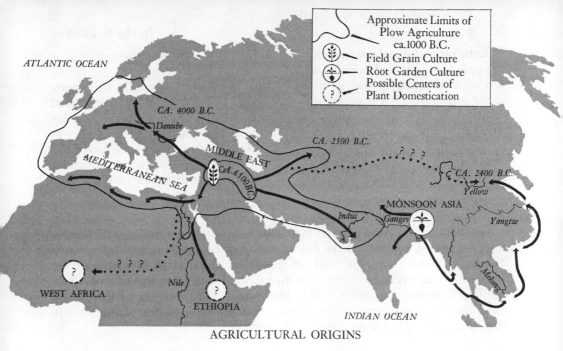

AGRICULTURAL ORIGINS

B.C.;[44] and circumstantial evidence suggests that the Aryans, who invaded northwestern India at about the same date, brought the plow into that subcontinent for the first time.[45] In China, however, the first definite evidence of plows dates from the Chou dynasty, perhaps as late as 350 B.C.[46]

Whether built around hoe, spade, or plow, Neolithic agriculture involved prolonged and heavy labor at certain times of the year. Particularly in the harvest season, the whole year's food supply depended upon intensive and steady effort, for which every man, woman, and child had to be mobilized. But in other seasons, for long stretches of time no very pressing work in the fields required attention. Such slack periods, when men were freed from the immediate necessity of finding food, offered hitherto unparalleled opportunities for the elaboration of human culture.

How the first farmers used the leisure thus laboriously won can be known only imperfectly. Song and dance, together with scarcely less evanescent arts like tattooing, dyeing of fabrics, wood carving and construction, feather and leather work, and all decoration of perishable materials, can only be guessed at. Pottery sherds, with a few statuettes and models made from fired clay, constitute by far the largest stock of surviving artifacts, while polished stone tools are the most conspicuous. A few bits of copper on village sites attest the beginnings of metallurgy. Such surviving fragments suffice at least to

[44] E. C. Curwen, "The Furrows in Prehistoric Fields in Denmark," *Antiquity*, XX (1946), 38–39.

[45] Stuart W. Piggott, *Prehistoric India*, p. 265.

[46] C. W. Bishop, "Origin and Early Diffusion of the Traction Plow," *Smithsonian Institution Annual Report of the Board of Regents*, 1937, pp. 531–47.

indicate the increased variety and complexity of Neolithic craftsmanship, as compared to what had been before.

Such craftsmanship had its limits. With the possible exception of experts in the supernatural, it is unlikely that anyone in Neolithic villages specialized full-time at any of the crafts which were normally pursued only in the interstices of the agricultural year. Thus a fully professional level of skill was not attainable in the village context. The attainment of such specialized skills was the distinguishing mark of the earliest civilized, urban societies, which appeared in the Middle East toward the close of the fourth millennium B.C.

*   *   *

Chronologically, the spread of Neolithic agriculture and village life through the Old World overlapped the rise of civilized societies in the valleys of the Tigris-Euphrates, the Nile, and the Indus rivers. As the peoples of these valleys became civilized, they came to exert powerful influences upon their neighbors, thereby affecting village life over wide stretches of Eurasia. We must therefore next turn to the history of the river valley civilizations and then trace among bordering peoples the repercussions of their rise.

CHAPTER II

The Breakthrough
to Civilization
in Mesopotamia

As suitable soil was reclaimed from the wooded slopes of the Middle East and the land became more fully occupied, the pressure of a multiplying population caused settlers to move outward in all directions. The valleys of the great rivers flowing southward from the mountains through grassland and desert to the sea both tempted and repelled such would-be settlers. Fish and water-fowl abounded; the alluvial soil was fertile and easily worked; and the date palm offered rich food to supplement a mainly cereal diet. But as one moved downstream to lower altitudes and latitudes, the life-giving rains weakened and all but disappeared. Seed could easily be sown on the soft muck left behind after the spring floods; but until a way was found for bringing water artificially to the growing grain, the young shoots could not survive the heat of the summer sun.

Yet soon after 4000 B.C., agricultural settlements equal in size and elaboration to any in the lands watered by natural rains began to appear in the valleys of the lower Tigris and Euphrates. The inference is obvious: pioneers must have learned to bring water artificially to their crops. At first, no doubt, such efforts were on a small scale. The techniques of irrigation may first have been tried out along the banks of lesser watercourses, in the regions where ordinary cropping failed as the streams emerged from the relatively well-watered hills and debouched into the Mesopotamian desert lowland.[1] But once the feasibil-

[1] Cf. Robert M. Adams, "Agriculture and Urban Life in Early Southwestern Iran," *Science*, CXXXVI (1962), 112–13.

ity of growing crops with an artificial water supply had been demonstrated, agricultural settlement in the great desert valleys of the lower Tigris-Euphrates opened a new range of possibilities to pioneer communities.

Settlement in lower Mesopotamia was at first probably concentrated on a narrow strip of land adjacent to the rivers. Irrigation here was a simple matter of cutting through the embankments formed by flood deposition along the river's edge, thus allowing the water to flow onto the lower-lying land beyond. Only when farmers pushed their fields farther from the rivers did a more complicated system of canals and dikes become necessary.

The new environment was strikingly different from the hill country where farming had first begun. The rivers with their tangle of swamps and bayous made fishing and the snaring of waterfowl an important activity. Also important, surprisingly, was stock-raising.[2] An indefinite reduplication of substantially identical village communities living at a comfortable distance from one another was therefore no longer possible when the narrow riches of the river valley gave rise to a comparatively dense population and compelled adjustment of diverging interests and outlook among fishers, herdsmen, and cultivators, all of whom had to live cheek by jowl with one another.

Such conditions called for larger social units than the ordinary Neolithic village afforded; and the recurrent frictions arising from divergent occupational interests within a comparatively very dense population required the emergence of a class of managers with authority to adjust particular conflicts. Two technical characteristics of early Mesopotamian agriculture made possible the effective solution of this political problem. First, the nearly flat and stone-free terrain of the lower Tigris-Euphrates Valley greatly facilitated plowing;[3] and this together with the rich alluvial soil made it easy to produce a grain surplus sufficient to support a managerial class. Second, annual flooding brought a fresh top dressing of silt to the fields each year, thus renewing the fertility of the land[4] and rendering migratory cultivation entirely unnecessary. Agricultural surplus produced by a sedentary population thus made possible the emergence of territorially defined communities managed by specialists in the supernatural. Kinship, the oldest basis of human society, came to be sup

[2] Away from the life-giving waters, the landscape of lower Mesopotamia faded rapidly into parched desert during most of the year; but when the winter rains fell, the desert blossomed luxuriantly, though briefly. At other times of year, limited amounts of perennial pasture could be found in the narrow transition zones between swamp and desert. Sheep, goats, and donkeys could also survive on straw when green pasture was altogether lacking.

[3] The difficulty of plowing on uneven or stumpy ground deprived the plow of most of its value for slash-and-burn cultivators. Hence it is possible that the invention of the plow did not occur until men began to cultivate the alluvium. If so, the diffusion of plowing, discussed above, was among the first consequences of the rise of civilization to reach the rest of the world. The evidence necessary to decide this point is lacking, however. Cf. Robert M. Adams, "Agriculture and Urban Life in Early Southwestern Iran," pp. 112–13.

[4] Through centuries, evaporation of the water used for irrigation accumulates salt in the soil. Eventually, this became a serious and in the end an insuperable problem in Mesopotamia; but measured by the scale of a single human life, salting was at first of no importance. Cf. Thorkild Jacobsen and Robert M. Adams, "Salt and Silt in Ancient Mesopotamian Agriculture," *Science*, CXXVIII (1958), 1251–58.

plemented and then supplanted by a new principle of social cohesion: mere propinquity.[5]

The local peculiarities of desert river banks do much to explain the direction of social evolution among the pioneer agricultural communities that penetrated the lower reaches of the Tigris-Euphrates Valley after about 4000 B.C. The larger geographical setting of this habitat also stimulated human ingenuity by both inviting and necessitating long-distance transport and communication on a comparatively massive scale. This meant that the stimulus of contacts with strangers was never long absent from the early settlers' horizon. Boats and rafts could move with ease along the rivers, lagoons, and bayous of the region itself, and sail along the shores of the Persian Gulf (and beyond) without encountering any but the natural difficulties of wind and waves. Overland, too, no geographical obstacles hindered pack trains on their way to the mountains that ringed the Mesopotamian plain to the north, east, and west. The fact that the alluvium of lower Mesopotamia lacked stone, timber, and metals supplied ample incentive for travels. In proportion as the valley dwellers required these commodities, they had either to organize expeditions to find, prepare, and bring back what they needed, or else to persuade neighboring peoples to exchange local stone, timber, or metals for the surpluses of the plains. As specialization progressed within the social structure of the valley peoples, such trade between hill and plain assumed an increasing scale and importance; and the emergent cities along the rivers became centers of communication and stimulus for the whole surrounding region.

Thus it became possible for relatively dense populations to sustain life in the river valleys of Mesopotamia; and the presence of such large populations in turn provided the massed labor power needed for erecting monumental structures, for extending the system of dikes and canals to new ground year by year, and for performing the tasks of long-distance transport required by the growing complexity of their style of life.

There were, of course, limits to the expansion of such communities. Water could not be made to flow uphill; hence rising slopes could not be irrigated, nor could low-lying areas be drained of stagnant swamp water. But except for the raised river banks, the lower reaches of the Tigris-Euphrates Valley constituted a remarkably flat plain. Artificial canals could therefore carry water several miles from the river bank, availing themselves of the almost imperceptible fall of land downstream. Yet such elaborate canals had serious drawbacks, since in a year of low floods the water might not suffice to reach the more distant fields. Far more dangerous were the years when the flood waters rolled with unusual force, for then main dikes and channels might be oblit-

[5] How this happened can only be guessed. The palpable fact that all who lived in the same locality were subject to the same divinities of flood and storm may have been given its logical application by subordinating all kindred dwelling in a particular part of the river bank to the gods' own accredited human agents, *i.e.*, to priests. But since territorial frontiers were much more adjustable than kinship lines, the new basis of social cohesion provided a far more flexible framework for human activity. It even proved capable of sustaining the complexities and mutabilities of full-blown civilization and eventually allowed men who had never seen one another before and who might live hundreds of miles apart still to treat one another as fellows, because they happened to reside within the boundaries of the same territorial state.

erated; and from time to time the mighty Euphrates itself changed course, leaving populated areas helpless against the coming drought unless the irrigation works could be remodeled in time. In general, the more elaborate Mesopotamian water engineering became, the heavier became the tasks of maintenance and the greater the chance of sporadic breakdown. By a cruel irony, therefore, populations dependent on dikes and canals exposed themselves to periodic disaster just in proportion as they pushed technical mastery of their style of gravity-flow irrigation to its technical limits.

The human environment also constituted a very important check upon the elaboration of Mesopotamian irrigation systems. A society dependent on water coming from a canal that could be blocked several miles upstream from the fields it served was extremely vulnerable to warlike attack. A position upstream was therefore always of supreme strategic importance in Mesopotamian politics and war, while downstream populations were always and inescapably at the mercy of whoever controlled their water supply.

Hence nature and man alike combined to limit the growth of irrigated agriculture in the lower Tigris and Euphrates valleys; but before the limit was attained, a new style of human life had emerged, characterized by a complexity, wealth, and general impressiveness that justify the epithet "civilized." Between about 3900 B.C. and 3500 B.C. the potentialities of irrigated agriculture in Mesopotamia were explored, settlements were established in the plain of Sumer in the far south, and the pioneering phase of agricultural and human adjustment to the new environment was successfully completed. Then about 3500 B.C. began a rapid elaboration of institutions, ideas, ceremonies, techniques, until by 3000 B.C. or thereabouts, when decipherable documents permit more accurate knowledge of this ancient society, something already old, established, and in a real sense mature emerges for inspection: the civilization of the Sumerians.

The question of who the Sumerians were and whence they came cannot be answered. Their tongue seems unrelated to any other known language, and their skeletons provide no unambiguous evidence of racial affinities. Sumerian religion and art gave special prominence to animals, suggesting that some element of the population had once been pastoral. Certain of their recorded traditions suggest that they arrived by sea from the south. But these hints do not allow us to assign any particular region as their original homeland.[6]

From the beginning of recorded history, a mixture of peoples occupied the valleys of Mesopotamia. We may imagine that, as the soil was tamed for agriculture, settlers pressed in from all sides, as they continued to do in historic times. The earliest accessible records show Sumerians existing side by side with speakers of Semitic languages.[7] Sumerians predominated in the

---

[6] A summary of the various theories that have been advanced is conveniently presented in A. Parrot, *Archéologie mésopotamienne: technique et problèmes* (Paris: Albin Michel, 1953), pp. 308–31.

[7] Pervasive bilingualism probably had far-reaching consequences for Mesopotamian intellectual development. As compared with the case of the Egyptians, for example, there is remarkably little word magic in Mesopotamian records. A distinction between word and concept and between word and thing

south, Semites farther north; but in many areas there was extensive inter-mixture.[8] Despite this commingling, it is usual to call the earliest civilization "Sumerian"; for the oldest written records were made in that tongue, and the first fully developed cities clustered in the southern part of the flood plain where Sumerian-speakers were most numerous.

Sumerian civilization was a city civilization. From one point of view, a Sumerian city was little more than an overgrown village, since most of its inhabitants were farmers. But in size and above all in structure, it differed fundamentally from Neolithic village communities, for the simple reason that the water engineering vital to survival required organized community effort. Instead of cultivating small family-sized fields, as Neolithic villagers almost certainly did, the Sumerians divided the irrigated land into large tracts "owned" by a god, and administered by priests on his behalf. One or more such temple communities constituted a city.

The practical effect of this land system was to group the Sumerians into work forces several hundred or perhaps even several thousand strong. With simple hand tools such gangs could undertake and maintain the large-scale irrigation works necessary fully to exploit the river waters. Details of how the work was organized cannot be reconstructed from the scanty available records; and variations may have existed from city to city of which no hint now survives. Clay tablets from Lagash show that the land of that city (and therefore also the harvest) was divided into three categories: (1) fields owned by the god and worked on his behalf; (2) fields rented out annually to individuals; and (3) fields awarded to individuals rent-free on a permanent basis and in lots of varying size.[9] From other cities we have no direct information.

It is nevertheless clear that priests regularly served as managers, planners, and co-ordinators of the massed human effort without which Sumerian civilization could not have come into existence or long survived. They supervised the allocation of land, maintained boundary markers, saw that a

---

was almost forced upon learned Mesopotamians by their familiarity with at least two quite unrelated languages; and the resultant penchant toward intellectual abstraction may have contributed to their remarkable mathematical sophistication.

[8] Thorkild Jacobsen, "The Assumed Conflict between Sumerians and Semites in Early Mesopotamian History," *Journal of the American Oriental Society*, LIX (1939), 485–95.

[9] Anna Schneider, *Die Anfänge der Kulturwirtschaft: Die sumerische Tempelstadt*, Staatswissenschaftliche Beiträge, Heft IV (Essen, 1920); A. Falkenstein, "La Cité-temple sumérienne," *Cahiers d'histoire mondiale*, I (1954), 791. Agricultural communities may also have survived in ancient Sumer apart from dependence upon any temple, as suggested by A. L. Oppenheim, "A Bird's-Eye View of Mesopotamian Economic History," in Karl Polanyi *et al.*, *Trade and Market in the Early Empires* (Glencoe, Ill.: Free Press, 1957), pp. 27–37. This does not change the fact that what was new and essential for the elaboration of Sumerian civilization was the temple community, with the specialization of socioeconomic roles which that social system allowed.

It is interesting to notice that the earliest Sumerian records available to modern scholars show no trace of tribal or kin-group organization. Territorial groupings and individual small-family units seem to be the rule. This suggests that the Sumerians had several centuries of agricultural life behind them before records began, during which time whatever tribal ties may once have existed among their ancestors had worn away, leaving village communities composed of small-family units as the social raw material from which the mature cities were constructed.

generous share of the harvest was stored in temple granaries, and directed the work gangs that annually cleared the canals and strengthened the dikes. The authority of the priestly colleges was thus very great; but their services to the community were correspondingly vital. The priests alone possessed the skills of calculating the seasons, laying out canals, and keeping accounts, without which effective co-ordination of community effort would have been impossible. Still more important as a basis of sacerdotal power was the supernatural aura enveloping those through whom the great gods deigned to communicate with men. Armed with such authority, the priests were free to develop their organizing capacities in both the practical and the religious spheres, until they succeeded in raising Sumerian society to the level of primitive civilization.

As temple communities established themselves in Sumer, it became normal for cultivators to produce a food surplus sufficient to maintain a corps of specialists who no longer had to work in the fields. This social differentiation, which lies at the basis of all civilization, is neither natural nor automatic. In contemporary primitive societies, men rarely care to produce more than they immediately require; yet in ancient Mesopotamia tens of thousands of farmers were persuaded to exert themselves to feed others. The implausible irrationality of such behavior arose out of older fears that had impelled men immemorially to offer a propitiatory share of their food to the jealous spirits who might otherwise withhold future nourishment from an ever hungry mankind. Sumerian theology, as later recorded, held that men had been created expressly to free the gods from the necessity of working for a living. Man was thus considered to be a slave of the gods, obliged to serve ceaselessly and assiduously under pain or direst punishment—flood or drought and consequent starvation. Such ideas no doubt had a long history before they were recorded in writing, and probably justified the earliest beginnings of the practice of concentrating grain and other goods in temple storehouses, where they were used by priests to minister to the gods' needs.

Each Sumerian temple was believed in a quite literal sense to be the house of a particular god. Priests and other attendants constituted the god's personal household.[10] Their primary task was to minister to their divine master's wants through ceremonies and sacrifices. A secondary duty was to act as mediator between the god and his human slaves: to discover the god's will, propitiate his anger, or determine the divinely approved time for any important human undertaking. As the wealth of the temples grew, the splendor and elaboration of sacred routines increased, until the adequate service of the god became a major economic enterprise, involving the professional attention not only of priests but of many types of craftsmen as well.

Such behavior was based on the assumption that the god had to be cajoled and propitiated, lest he send flood or drought or disease, or raise up some murderous enemy against his people. The frequency with which such disasters did in fact afflict the Mesopotamian cities obviously helped to engender an attitude of anxiety toward divinities who so often acted capriciously and

---

[10] Cf. F. R. Kraus, "Le Rôle des temples depuis la troisième dynastie d'Ur jusqu'à la première dynastie de Babylon," *Cahiers d'histoire mondiale,* I (1954), 519–21.

MESOPOTAMIAN PRIESTS OR DEITIES

These statuettes were discovered in the ruins of an ancient temple at Tell Asmar, Iraq. They date from the third millennium B.C. but come from a backwoods region of Mesopotamia. The comparatively crude technique of sculpture here exemplified lagged far behind developments in the more active centers of Sumerian civilization. These statues therefore preserve a more antique quality and offer an insight into the very genesis of Sumerian civilization. For the stiff awkwardness of these figures, with hands clasped in ritual gesture, perhaps of prayer, with enormous, upward-looking eyes and a general aspect of tense expectation, manages to suggest the eager anxiety with which the ancient Mesopotamians sought to serve the capricious gods and in doing so established the earliest civilization of the earth.

in ways beyond human understanding. To avoid unintentional transgression against the gods' good pleasure and to interpret aright the signs and portents which the gods might vouchsafe became matters of the very highest import. Only a learned and expert priesthood could perform such services for the rank and file.

Hence the very insecurity of life in the early Sumerian cities acted to guarantee priestly power and influence. Priestly control, in turn, permitted the proliferation of administrative and craft specialists, whose ability to concentrate full-time attention upon non-agricultural tasks opened the door for a rapid development of all sorts of skills and ideas. Yet the emergent social variety was articulated within a closely co-ordinated framework: the temple community.

It is not clear to what extent the rise of craft specialization benefited the peasants. Probably for a long time, priests and, somewhat later, soldiers were the principal merely human consumers of the products of craftsmen's workshops. Yet some exchange between peasant and craftsmen may have taken place in very early times. In a prosperous year, even after discharging his obligations to the god, a peasant might retain more food than he himself needed, and thus be able to barter grain or dates for professionally made tools or pots. Such exchange, however, remained definitely marginal to the temple economy, which directed and dominated Sumerian social effort.

The important point is this: For the first time in human history the Sumerian temple community technically permitted and psychologically compelled the production of an agricultural surplus and applied that surplus to support specialists, who became, as city dwellers have since remained, the creators, sustainers, and organizers of civilized life.

*   *   *

The rapidity with which the main lines of Sumerian civilization crystallized during the protoliterate period (*i.e.*, before 3000 B.C.) is most obvious in art, for the major forms and motifs of the Sumerian style were already developed and surprisingly "mature" before written records began. Probably the theological world-view which sustained the Sumerians and their successors in Mesopotamia through historic times took shape during the same formative period. The same is true in technology, where a cluster of great inventions—irrigation, wheeled vehicles, sailing ships, metallurgy, oven-baked and wheel-turned pottery—appears rather abruptly in the archeological record of the protoliterate period; whereas after the establishment of literacy, comparably important inventions cease. On the other hand, in the spheres of political administration and military organization, Mesopotamian life continued to evolve in historic times; for the rise of more militarized and secularized government drastically modified the temple-centered economic system of the earliest historic horizon.

Yet even the most stable aspects of ancient Mesopotamian culture reveal incessant minor fluctuations over the centuries. This is best illustrated through close examination of cylinder seals—miniature works of art used to impress marks of ownership on sealed jars. Thousands of them have survived from

CYLINDER SEAL IMPRESSION

This seal impression, found at Tell Asmar and dating from about the time of Sargon of Akkad, shows how skilful Mesopotamian seal engravers became. The scale of this art was minuscule: this photograph is about twice the size of the original. Moreover, not only were the figures cut in reverse into hard stone, but they were incised around the curved surface of a rather small cylinder. By rolling such a seal on wet clay, the figures could therefore be made to repeat in an indefinitely long series, as is here illustrated by the double appearance of the leaping antelope. This scene may have some mythological meaning, but whatever it was escapes modern knowledge.

all periods and offer an unparalleled body of material for the study of Mesopotamian art history. The earliest seals dating from the protoliterate period "achieve an astonishing perfection,"[11] and introduce motifs which were to last as long as such seals were made. Thereafter came a falling away of artistic level, perhaps as a result of wholesale production, or of the diversion of artistic inventiveness into other channels after the original problems of design and craftsmanship had been solved. Subsequently a series of fluctuations in style occurred, influenced partly by minor modifications in the technique of production and partly by sporadic enlargement of the repertory of motifs. But the art always stayed within fairly strict limits and continued to adhere to conventions established in the early period.

The history of other Sumerian arts, while less well documented than that of cylinder seals, appears to conform to the same pattern. Stylistic conventions crystallized early in both sculpture and jewelry manufacture; and later times saw only relatively minor fluctuations. Architecture showed greater variation. The size and elaboration of temple construction increased markedly until the ziggurat achieved its classical form in the time of the Third Dynasty of Ur (*ca.* 2050–1950 B.C.). In the earliest days of Sumerian city life, a temple was a simple rectangular house for the god, set on a raised platform which perhaps was intended to preserve it from flood. In later times, the temple was raised higher and higher by inserting additional stages between the ground level and the inner sanctuary; while various subsidiary sacred precincts were added at the base of the structure. Yet the fundamental temple plan remained unchanged.[12]

No series of documents comparable to the sequence of cylinder seals illuminates the development of Mesopotamian religion. In historic times (and presumably from the very beginning of Sumerian culture), the high gods of the land were conceived in human form, personifying the great forces of nature—sky, sun, earth, water, and storm. The cycle of the seasons was accounted for through the myth of a dying god of vegetation, whose periodic disappearance into the underworld caused plant life to wither, until his release permitted its resurgence. Other myths dealt with the creation of the world, the discovery of the arts of civilization, the genealogies of the gods, and the relation of man to the divine.[13]

The great festivals corresponded to the turning points of the agricultural year and were conducted with much pomp and circumstance by priestly professionals. Temples became impressive structures, rising high above the city, adorned with splendid decoration, sculpture, and precious materials. The

---

[11] Henri Frankfort, *Cylinder Seals* (London: Macmillan & Co., 1939), p. 15.

[12] Cf. Heinrich J. Lenzen, *Die Entwicklung der Zikurrat von ihren Anfängen bis zur Zeit der III. Dynastie von Ur* (Leipzig: Otto Harrassowitz, 1942); André Parrot, *Ziggurats et Tour de Babel* (Paris: Albin Michel, 1949); Charles Leonard Woolley, *The Development of Sumerian Art* (New York: Scribner's Sons, 1935); A. Parrot, *Sumer* (Paris: Librairie Gallimard, 1960).

[13] Cf. S. N. Kramer, *Sumerian Mythology: A Study of Spiritual and Literary Achievement in the Third Millennium B.C.* (Philadelphia: American Philosophical Society, 1944); and Thorkild Jacobsen's chapter in Henri Frankfort *et al.*, *Before Philosophy* (Harmondsworth: Penguin Books, 1941), pp. 137–99.

ALABASTER VASE

This vase may have been used in temple rituals. It was found at Uruk and dates from the protoliterate period. The carved relief probably depicts the New Year festival. At the top the goddess is shown receiving the gifts of her human slaves, whose destiny it is to serve her, just as it is the destiny of the plants and animals, shown at the bottom of the vase, to serve the wants and needs of mankind. In the center, men bearing gifts for the goddess complete the chain of being as the ancient Sumerians conceived it. The vase therefore portrays the essential structure of a Sumerian temple community.

common people were merely onlookers at the public ceremonies; but within each family dwelling a niche was reserved for images of lesser deities with whom the individual enjoyed an immediate relationship. Only in exceptional cases would a private person directly approach the great god of the temple.[14]

Both cult observance and theological doctrine probably took enduring form in the very early days of Sumerian city-building, proceeding *pari passu* with the consolidation of priestly management of the temple communities; for the one depended upon the other. Each city was conceived as the property of a particular god, and its inhabitants as his slaves. But each local god was subject to the collective will of all the gods, who assembled each New Year to determine destiny for the ensuing twelve months and who might overrule any one of their number. Hence, even if the slaves of a particular god pleased him in every possible respect, the will of rival gods might still permit a divine decree of disaster. In such cases, the Sumerians believed that Enlil, god of the storm, exercised an overriding sovereignty, crushing one or another city according to the collective will of the gods.[15] Thus Sumerian theology plausibly explained the vicissitudes of human life under the precarious condition of irrigation agriculture in the Tigris-Euphrates Valley and, through the doctrine that men were slaves to the gods, effectively inculcated obedience to the priests.

Conservatism in religion and even in art is a sentiment familiar enough to us; but technology has been a never-failing field of innovation in modern times. In Sumer it was not so. In the early days of settlement, when specialists were developing craft skills, the arts of irrigation, and techniques for managing the agricultural surplus, and when long-distance trade was expanding rapidly, a series of important inventions were either made or applied extensively for the first time. During these centuries of the protoliterate period, the basic technical equipment of ancient Mesopotamian civilization emerged. Thereafter only minor improvements occurred.

This technological arrest no doubt reflects the stabilization of the other aspects of life. Once the temple communities had become firmly established and capable of organizing the production, concentration, and distribution of wealth by means of inventions like writing, the plow, wheeled vehicles, sailing ships, and bronze tools and weapons, all essential wants were adequately

---

[14] Cf. Édouard Dhorme, *Les Religions de Babylonie et d'Assyrie* (Paris: Presses universitaires, 1945), pp. 174–282.

[15] Henri Frankfort *et al.*, *Before Philosophy*, pp. 229–31. In the later version of the myth, Marduk, god of Babylon, was accorded executive duties; but this is almost certainly a late substitution dating from the period of Babylonian supremacy.

It is tempting to see in these relationships among the gods reflection of an early stage of Sumerian political development, when major decisions were perhaps taken by assemblies of citizens. If this be the case, these myths must have taken shape before Sumerian political institutions had assumed their historic forms. Cf. Thorkild Jacobsen, "Primitive Democracy in Ancient Mesopotamia," *Journal of Near Eastern Studies*, II (1943), 159–72. Jacobsen also discovered certain vestigial remnants of "primitive democracy" in Hammurabi's time, which, if he reads the texts aright, greatly strengthen his thesis. Yet even if he is entirely correct in his inferences, "primitive oligarchy" might be as good or better a description of the political regime he deduces.

Jacobsen's interpretation of the Mesopotamian myths is not universally accepted. Other scholars believe that the pantheon took shape only after kingship had become established in Mesopotamia. Cf. Anton Moortgat, "Grundlagen und Entfaltung der sumerisch-akkadischen Kultur," in Fritz Valjavec (ed.), *Historia Mundi*, II (Bern, 1953), p. 239.

provided for. Life tended to settle toward a fixed and sacred routine; and no stimulus proved sufficient to overcome the force of social inertia.

Yet it would be false to assert that no technical changes occurred at all. In some fields, e.g., shipbuilding, paucity of information does not allow any judgment; but where material evidence abounds, minor changes within a fixed general frame are found to prevail. Thus at a very early date the Mesopotamians conceived the idea of using mud bricks of fixed size and shape for monumental building and continued this practice throughout their history. Yet the size and shape of particular buildings did alter; and the exact dimensions of the bricks from which they were built also changed, so that an important method of dating a building is to determine the exact size of the bricks employed in its construction.

In metallurgy, too, enough specimens survive to show that Sumerians were quite familiar with bronze in their earliest literate period. Yet at a later time, tools and weapons were made of more nearly pure copper. This apparent retrogression—copper is softer than its alloy, bronze—may have been due to shortage of tin; for there is reason to suppose that when bronze reappeared after Sargon's time (*ca.* 2350 B.C.), tin had to be sought as far afield as central Europe.[16] Despite all supply difficulties, metal tools and especially weapons became more abundant as time passed. More than anything else, this reflected the onset of chronic warfare among the Sumerian cities. War created an imperative demand for enlarged supplies of metal; since without metal helmets, spearheads, and shields, an army could scarcely stand against soldiery so equipped. But changes in the quantity of military equipment were not accompanied by any great changes in weapons design. Once again we see variation within the limits of a nearly fixed tradition.

*   *   *

The increased use of metal for warfare points up the fact that independent Sumerian city-states were quite unable either to maintain a tolerable order within the circle of civilized communities or to secure themselves against barbarian raiders. The further development of Mesopotamian civilization until about 1700 B.C. was largely a consequence of this radical political defect in the style of life which had emerged in Sumer by 3000 B.C.

The political instability of early Sumerian societies was in large degree a function of geography. Unlike Egypt, Mesopotamia enjoyed no natural defenses; and on every side the valley lay open to raiders. As soon as the cities of the plain had been made to flourish, they became tempting objects of plunder to the barbarous peoples of the country round about. Yet the early Sumerian temple communities, whose social discipline was directed toward lavish propitiation of the gods rather than war, were not in a favorable position to bring to bear their superiority of manpower against pastoral raiders, whose accustomed mode of life inculcated a military (or at least paramilitary) discipline and aptitude.

Intercity relations presented an equally serious problem. As long as communities were separated by stretches of unreclaimed swamp and desert, no

---

[16] R. J. Forbes, *Metallurgy in Antiquity* (Leiden: E. J. Brill, 1950), p. 251.

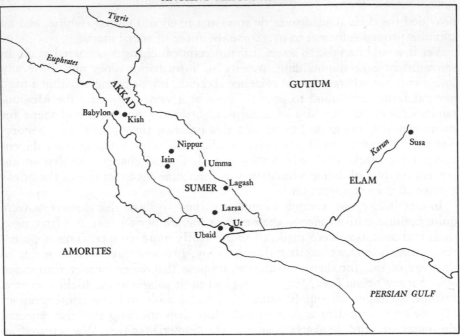

serious conflicts arose. Indeed, the striking homogeneity of protohistoric Sumerian culture clearly implies free contact and exchange of expertise among the priests of all the emergent cities. The religious prestige of the city of Nippur and the central importance early Sumerian theology accorded to its god, Enlil, probably reflected a time when the shrines of that city served as a periodic meeting center for priests from the various temples of Sumer.[17] But such presumably harmonious relationships changed radically as soon as most of the easily irrigable land of lower Mesopotamia came under cultivation, and the fields of one community came to abut directly upon those of another. Because there existed no authority to determine boundaries between cities, nor any legal way to allocate water in times of shortage, common boundaries gave rise to perennial friction and chronic war.

By 3000 B.C., intercity warfare was already frequent. The temple community had become altogether too small and too specialized an administrative unit to cope with the problems of communities dependent on a more or less contiguous irrigation system covering the lower reaches of the entire valley. The first consequence of this deficiency in priestly management was the rise of a semisecular kingship alongside the older temple administration. Just how this occurred is not known. Later tradition held that after the Flood the gods bestowed kingship upon the rulers of Kish; and several historic monarchs

[17] Cf. Thorkild Jacobsen, "Early Political Development in Mesopotamia," *Zeitschrift für Assyriologie*, N.F., XVIII (1957), 104–10; Bruno Meissner, *Babylonien und Assyrien* (2 vols.; Heidelberg: Carl Winter, 1920–25) II, 6–8; Henri Frankfort, *Kingship and the Gods* (Chicago: University of Chicago Press, 1948), pp. 216–17. Cf. the role of Delphi in early Greek history.

seem to have acknowledged the prestige of an ancient title by styling themselves "King of Kish," even after that city had lost all political weight.[18] Kish lay toward the northern limits of early Sumer, and in later times was inhabited predominantly by an Akkadian-speaking population. Perhaps the idea of "kingship"—as distinct from temple administration, which seems peculiarly Sumerian in origin—was introduced into Mesopotamia by the descendants of Semitic pastoral tribesmen, who in the environment of the irrigated flood plain might be expected to transform their traditional tribal leadership into territorial kingship.[19]

Whatever its ultimate origin, the institution of kingship stabilized itself in Sumer by superimposing military relationships upon an older religio-political system. The authority of a field commander over his army served as prototype for the king's authority over the city; and the rise of kingship may be conceived as a process whereby extraordinary powers delegated in time of war became normal in peacetime.[20] Kings arrogated to themselves supreme military and judicial authority and organized royal households analogous to the divine households of the temple communities. In so doing, they encroached upon the administrative authority of the priestly colleges; and no doubt the relation between king and priest was often an uneasy one. Perhaps accommodation usually occurred without prolonged dispute or open violence; but we are informed that Urukagina, king of Lagash (*ca.* 2400 B.C.), openly set himself against the priests, proposing to restore the good old days by protecting the poor and weak from priestly oppression. In time, however, royal usurpation became santified by myth and ritual, of which the central act was an annual ceremonial marriage between king and goddess of the city.

In proportion as war became chronic, kingship became necessary. Concentration of political authority in the hands of a single man seems to have become the rule in Sumerian cities by 3000 B.C. No doubt this change did something to improve local defense against barbarian raids, especially since it coincided with the construction of massive city walls. But the struggles among the cities themselves merely became sharper and probably absorbed an increasing proportion of the total energies of the Sumerians.

It appears that the evolution of interstate relations in the third millennium B.C. roughly paralleled the development of later state systems of which

[18] A. Falkenstein, "La Cité-temple sumérienne," p. 805.

[19] Some experts believe they can detect in art and architecture signs of an Akkadian impact upon earlier and more purely Sumerian styles and are inclined to attribute to the king of Kish an extensive empire reaching from the Persian Gulf to the middle Euphrates. Cf. Anton Moortgat, "Grundlagen und Entfaltung der sumerisch-akkadischen Kultur," pp. 235–39. Others, however, whose eyes are presumably no less sharp, fail to detect these changes—or, more accurately, see no reason to assign a large-scale Semitic irruption into the flood plain of the Tigris-Euphrates as a cause of those changes which can be detected. Cf. T. Jacobsen, "The Assumed Conflict between Sumerians and Semites," pp. 285–95.

[20] The survival of two distinct terms for "king" in the Sumerian literary tradition suggests that kingship may have had a double origin. Cf. Thorkild Jacobsen, "Appraisal of Breasted and Childe on Mesopotamia," in *Human Origins*, a general introductory course in anthropology, selected readings, series 2 (mimeographed; Chicago: University of Chicago Press, 1946), p. 252.

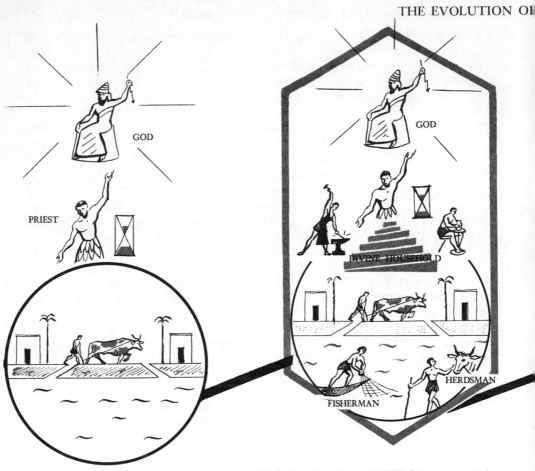

TEMPLE COMMUNITY CA. 3500–3000 B.C.

VILLAGE COMMUNITY CA. 5000 B.C.

a fuller historic record survives. One may guess that what started as local quarrels among adjacent communities in time provoked systems of rival alliances embracing most of the civilized cities of the plain. Surviving records suggest that from about 2500 B.C., Lagash and Umma were the protagonists around which rival alliance systems formed. By degrees, the full autonomy of at least the weaker cities was reduced. Particularly strong rulers often created petty "empires" by uniting several communities under their rule; but such structures were highly unstable and broke apart whenever opportunity offered. The city-states of classical Greece and of Renaissance Italy evolved within such a general pattern; and the scanty surviving evidence suggests that the cities of ancient Sumer did likewise.

In any case, imperial conquest began to give a new scope to Mesopotamian

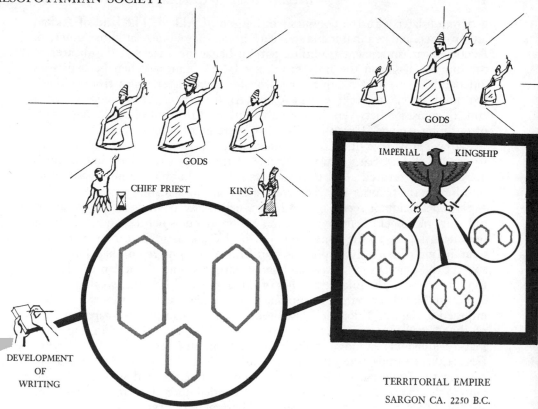

GODS

GODS

IMPERIAL KINGSHIP

CHIEF PRIEST   KING

DEVELOPMENT
OF
WRITING

TERRITORIAL EMPIRE

SARGON CA. 2250 B.C.

CITY STATE CA. 3000–2250 B.C.

politics in the second half of the third millennium B.C.[21] Lugalzaggisi of Umma is the first ruler known to have united most of the cities of Sumer under his lordship (*ca.* 2375 B.C.);[22] but a more enduring unification came a

[21] Most calculations of Mesopotamian chronology depend upon projection backward and forward from the reign of Hammurabi, whose dates, however, are unfortunately in dispute. Scholarly consensus once assigned Hammurabi a date near 2000 B.C.; but recent archeological discoveries in Syria and elsewhere have persuaded many scholars to accept a shortened chronology, putting Hammurabi either at the beginning or at the close of the eighteenth century B.C. In the face of such expert disagreement, it seems best to assign 1700 B.C. arbitrarily as a chronological peg with which to associate Hammurabi. For discussion of the issue see Sidney Smith, *Alalakh and Chronology* (London: Luzac & Co., 1940); Benno Landsberger, "Assyrische Königsliste und 'Dunkles Zeitalter,'" *Journal of Cuneiform Studies*, VIII (1954), 31–45, 47–73, 106–33; Arnold Toynbee, *A Study of History* (New York and London: Oxford University Press, 1954), X, 171–212; Friedrich Schmidtke, *Der Aufbau der babylonischen Chronologie* (Münster: Aschendorff, 1952); P. van der Meer, *The Chronology of Ancient Western Asia and Egypt* (Leiden: E. J. Brill, 1955); André Parrot, *Archéologie mésopotamienne: technique et problèmes*, pp. 332–445; Sabatino Moscati, "Nuovi Aspetti della Cronologia dell'Antico Oriente Anteriore," *Relazioni del X. Congresso Internazionale di Scienza Storiche*, II (1955), 167–98.

[22] A number of shadowy predecessors probably sought to assert some sort of military hegemony over all Mesopotamia even before the time of Lugalzaggisi of Umma, whose career happens to be illumined by a number of surviving inscriptions. Cf. Thorkild Jacobsen, "Early Political Development in Mesopotamia," pp. 122–36.

generation later with the conquests of Sargon of Akkad. The land of Akkad lay up-river, and its inhabitants spoke a Semitic tongue unrelated to Sumerian. According to an ancient tradition, Sargon began his career as cup-bearer to the king of Kish, on the northernmost edge of Sumer. When he began an independent career of conquest, he probably drew his strength from soldiery recruited among his fellow Akkadians. At that time, Akkad constituted a zone of transition between the high civilization of the south and the barbarism of outlying regions. Thus the Akkadians were in a favorable position to unite barbarian prowess with civilized technique to form a powerful military force; and in fact, Sargon was only one of the earliest of a long line of lords marcher who created empires by successfully exploiting a similarly strategic position on the frontier between civilization and barbarism.

Sargon's conquest seems not to have worked any profound changes in the old cities of Sumer. Temple communities continued as before; and local kings became tributary to the conquerer. But in Akkad, Sargon's career marks the culmination of a highly important transformation. The region had long been subject to Sumerian influence; and about Sargon's time, Sumerian civilization took firm root in the middle reaches of the Tigris and Euphrates valleys.

Yet in Akkad the temple communities never acquired the importance they enjoyed in Sumer. Tribal and clan leaders, rather than priests, managed most of the Akkadian agricultural and pasture land. In time, something approximating individual landownership evolved from this beginning, as old tribal ties weakened under the influence of settled life and urban conditions. Temples on the Sumerian model were established; but the god was merely one landholder among many, and sometimes depended upon the king for economic support. As a result, priests in central Mesopotamia never enjoyed the near monopoly of land management which they seem to have held in early Sumer.[23]

This difference can be understood in the light of the different road to civilization which the Akkadians pursued. We may imagine that Semitic-speaking tribesmen, whose lives traditionally centered around flocks and herds, exhibited no great enthusiasm for the hard and tedious labor of digging and diking which alone made agriculture possible in Mesopotamia. Yet in the course of the second half of the third millennium B.C., irrigated agriculture established itself in the land of Akkad, providing the economic base upon which high civilization was extended to that part of the Tigris-Euphrates flood plain. No doubt the obvious rewards of irrigation induced this change; but it occurred within the framework of a social system which had developed to suit the needs of pastoralism. Above all, this meant a society led by tribal chieftains, whose function it was to direct the co-operative effort needed to safeguard the flocks and move them from pasture to pasture. As irrigated agriculture took root in Akkad, this sort of traditional authority was extended

[23] Cf. F. R. Kraus, "Le Rôle des temples," pp. 524, 533–40; A. Falkenstein, "La Cité-temple sumérienne," pp. 804–14. I have been unable to discover how the kings of Sumerian cities secured their revenues. Very probably they took the easiest and most obvious course of confiscating part of the revenues of the temples, while leaving to the priests the day-to-day management of the land and labor force. Later, royal income from trade was sometimes significant. Cf. W. F. Leemans, *Foreign Trade in the Old Babylonian Period* (Leiden: E. J. Brill, 1960), pp. 55–56.

and transformed: chieftains began to mobilize and supervise the work gangs needed to build and maintain irrigation works. The major obstacle to this process must have been the shepherd's proud disdain for prolonged and strenuous labor; and it is possible that irrigation agriculture moved up-river only in proportion to the emergence of a class of impoverished tribesmen who, being no longer able to live off their flocks, found themselves constrained to dig and delve. Slaves taken in war may also have played a vital role in spreading irrigation agriculture northward.[24]

It was perfectly obvious to Akkadian apprentice irrigators that only by understanding how to deal both with the floods and with the gods could they hope for good harvests. Hence they borrowed both the arts of water engineering and the techniques of communicating with the gods from Sumerian priests. In so doing, they acquired the literary, artistic, and intellectual traditions of Sumer too, for these were part and parcel of priestcraft—needful adjuncts of successful dealings with the gods. Being eager pupils, the Akkadians absorbed also the Sumerian reverence for tradition, the source of all authority and skill. Consequently, the extension of civilization to Akkad did not cause basic changes in the older forms of Mesopotamian cultural expression.[25] Language was the one important exception; for the Akkadians kept their native Semitic speech, which by degrees became the usual medium of communication throughout all Mesopotamia. The cuneiform symbols used in writing Sumerian were adapted without difficulty to the Akkadian tongue.[26] At the same time, preservation of Sumerian for ritual use required the compilation of bilingual dictionaries, the discovery of which has vastly simplified for modern scholars the task of deciphering Sumerian texts.

The rise of the Akkadian language and the eclipse of the Sumerian proceeded gradually and was not completed until about five hundred years after Sargon's time. Similarly, the displacement of political and economic power northward, symbolized by Sargon's victorious career, was long in the making. We should not imagine a sudden and massive Akkadian invasion and conquest, but rather a steady infiltration and slow and gradual acculturation going back to the very beginning of Sumerian civilized development. As a result, soon after 2000 B.C., the cultural attainments of Akkad had reached a level more or less equal to that long established in Sumer. As this happened, the numerical preponderance of Semitic peoples—constantly reinforced by

[24] There is, however, no definite evidence to suggest that the Akkadians used an enslaved population on the land. Cf. A. Falkenstein, "La Cité-temple sumérienne," pp. 793, 811. In Sargon's time, war captives were enslaved, but so far as we know, this was the first time that slavery became an important institution in Mesopotamia.

[25] There is a large subjective element in any such judgment as this. The arbitrariness of the judgment is further increased by the fact that artistic remains (except always for seals) are very fragmentary, and surviving works of literature have a complex textual history, going back in fact (but how much?) to Sumerian sources. Some scholars see important shifts in art and literature in Sargon's time, e.g., Anton Moortgat, "Grundlagen und Entfaltung der sumerisch-akkadischen Kultur," pp. 254–56. But this judgment is as subjective as its opposite.

[26] The principle which allows "2" to symbolize "two," "zwei," "deux," etc., operated generally to make cuneiform symbols transferable from language to language.

seepage from the marginal grasslands—won for their languages the supremacy they still hold in Mesopotamia.[27]

The successful transplantation of Sumerian high culture up-river among the Akkadians marked an important stage in the expansion of civilization. The sociological barrier which had hitherto restricted civilized life to communities organized and led by priesthoods was for the first time transcended. Temple communities of the sort that had grown up with Sumerian civilization and served as its organizing center were inherently difficult to transplant to new land. Before priests could secure obedience among strangers, they had somehow to persuade a whole population to submit to supernatural sanctions and ideas alien to local religious tradition. This must have been difficult in itself; and even more restricting was the fact that the possessors of precious religious lore had every reason for keeping their skills and secrets to themselves. Why give to outsiders and potential enemies the advantage of one's own proven access to the supernatural?[28]

By contrast, any conqueror could follow the Akkadian example and use military force to organize labor for irrigation works. By this means, large-scale agriculture could expand up-river at a comparatively rapid rate. The Akkadian type of social organization was able to accumulate and utilize an agricultural surplus almost as effectively as the early Sumerian temple communities had done. Moreover, the looser and more varied texture of Akkadian society—combining tribal, individual, royal, and temple landholding, and dividing administration between king and priests—furthered the growth of Mesopotamian civilization in a way that the more nearly closed societies of the tightly knit Sumerian temple communities could never have done.

*   *   *

An imperial kingship, uniting all the cities of the plain and holding the border regions in awe, was clearly the solution to the political difficulties plaguing the Sumerian city-states. Yet Sargon's empire did not last for more than about a century. Attacks by barbarous Gutians from the region of the upper Tigris became serious toward the end of the reign of Sargon's grandson, Naram Sin; and soon thereafter, the imperial structure fell into jarring fragments.

Cherished local loyalties certainly played a part in disrupting Sargon's realm. Even more crucial was the empire's exposed geographical position, for on all sides potential enemies watched with hungry eyes for any sign of mili-

[27] Salting of the land, resulting from the evaporation of irrigation water (a serious modern problem in Iraq), undermined the agriculture of the south between 2400 and 1700 B.C., and eventually all but destroyed it. This decay probably gave powerful impetus to the eclipse of Sumerian culture and language. Cf. Thorkild Jacobsen and R. M. Adams, "Salt and Silt in Ancient Mesopotamian Agriculture," p. 1252.

[28] Merchants and merchant colonies operating on behalf of Sumerian temple communities were, however, capable of transmitting important elements of Sumerian civilization to barbarian communities. Such merchant groups may have played a part in civilizing the Akkadians of the middle reaches of the Tigris-Euphrates Valley, as they certainly did farther north in Ashur, the center around which the later Assyrian state formed. For the Sumerian imprint upon Ashur in pre-Sargonic times cf. A. T. Olmstead, *History of Assyria* (New York: Scribner's Sons, 1923), pp. 15–16.

NARAM SIN AS GOD AND CONQUEROR

Sargon's grandson and successor is here portrayed in the act of smiting his enemies in the Zagros Mountains, far to the northeast of the Mesopotamian heartland. The conical mountain as well as the veined pattern of the deciduous tree branches show how unfamiliar such landscape features were to Mesopotamian sculptors of the late third millennium B.C. Horns such as those Naram Sin is wearing were reserved for deities in Mesopotamian art. Hence the stele asserts, not merely the king's military might, but his divinity as well. This claim was later abandoned in Mesopotamia when alternative bases for imperial kingship were devised.

tary slackness. A third difficulty was inherent in the mere extent of Sargon's conquests, for the rudimentary administrative methods of the time did not permit effective control of broad territories. Naram Sin resorted to the practice of deposing local rulers and installing his own relatives in their places; and he tried to clothe his person with the mantle of divinity. But in Mesopotamia, as elsewhere, royal relatives were not always obedient to the head of the house; and deities deliberately manufactured to support high policy did not easily become living gods. In the absence of a developed bureaucracy, the practical limits of the central power must have been very narrow, perhaps scarcely extending beyond the range of the monarch's personal attention. Where the king was, there his power was real; elsewhere, the subordination of local chieftains, priests, or other notables was probably more theoretical than effectual.

Yet forces leading to imperial consolidation continued to exist. No sooner had central kingship failed than the old pattern of intercity war and diplomacy reasserted itself, creating new opportunities for political unification through conquest. In the course of this turmoil, the practical limits upon the power available to a vigorous monarch slowly receded; and as a result, successive imperial governments in Mesopotamia proved more effective than Sargon's had been. Yet political stability was never achieved for long. As the sinews of Mesopotamian empires grew stronger, the striking power of neighboring peoples and states increased proportionately. Barbarians who had acquired knowledge of civilized technologies and a taste for the fleshpots of Babylon were formidable neighbors for even the most warlike empire of the flood plains; and whenever the central authority weakened, such peoples stood ready to penetrate the civilized core area as raiders or as conquerors.

Interplay between these divisive and unifying tendencies produced an alternating rhythm in Mesopotamian political history. A conqueror from the margins of civilized life, like Sargon, might indeed establish an effective central authority; but after a few generations, the conquering group was likely to abandon its military habits in favor of the softer and more luxurious ways of the cities. In turn, relaxation of military discipline and decay of the warrior spirit opened a path for either revolt from within or fresh conquest from the margins. Domestic revolts often coincided with raids from several directions, so that with the decay of a great conqueror's power, periods of prolonged confusion might ensue before a new imperial unification of Mesopotamia emerged from the welter of competing states and peoples.

The histories of the Mesopotamian dynasties from Sargon to Hammurabi fit this scheme without difficulty. As the Sargonid empire decayed, the Gutians penetrated the flood plain from the northeast and set up a loosely centralized state which lasted for nearly a century. Revolt from within overthrew the Gutian power; and the so-called Third Dynasty of Ur ruled Sumer and Akkad for another hundred years (*ca.* 2050–1950 B.C.). This last period of Sumerian political independence saw a significant enrichment of Mesopotamian culture. Sculpture in stone achieved new refinement, and many oral traditions and myths were first recorded in writing. The kings of Ur seem to have developed more effective methods of administration than their predecessors had done. Inscriptions attest some sort of royal bureaucracy; and the temples apparently were controlled through appointment of royal relatives to priestly office.[29]

Weakened by successive conflicts with the semi-civilized Elamites to the east and barbarous Amorites to the west, the power of Ur was overthrown about 1950 B.C. For the following two and a half centuries, Mesopotamia was politically disunited. Power was at first loosely divided between rival dynasties established at Larsa and Isin respectively; but soon afterward, Amorite intruders established a third imperial state around Babylon. By this time, civilized social organization had spread widely beyond the limits of the Mesopotamian flood plain, so that powerful and relatively stable kingdoms bordered upon the old centers from which Mesopotamian civilization had sprung. The balance of power was therefore no longer a matter of internal alignment within Sumer and Akkad, but embraced larger units and a much expanded territory. Indeed, the old Sumerian cities seem to have become pawns on the diplomatic chessboard, while even the suzerains of Isin and Larsa came to depend upon support from Amorites and Elamites.

This balance of power, weighted against the cities of the plain, was overturned toward the end of the eighteenth century B.C. by the Amorite ruler, Hammurabi of Babylon (*ca.* 1700 B.C.). Hammurabi conquered both Isin and Larsa; and thus, like Sargon before him, united Mesopotamia and moved its political center one more step northward. But the dynasty of the new conqueror ruled unchallenged for less than a century before a familiar process repeated itself. Barbarous Kassites appeared from the north, harassed the Amorite power for more than a century, and then superseded it entirely (*ca.* 1525 B.C.). Yet the Kassite conquest was not merely a recapitulation of earlier barbarian victories. It was part of a larger movement of peoples which affected all parts of the civilized world, from Crete to Egypt and India, and thus marks a significant breakpoint in the history of ancient civilization.

*   *   *

If, from this confusion of events, we seek to discover the major lines of development in Mesoptamian civilization, clearly the central stimulus to new departure must be sought in the political-military sphere. The inhabitants of the flood plains knew small rest from danger and lived under almost unremitting pressure to improve their defenses against the threat or the actuality of war. The practical force of such pressure was to forward political centralization. It is therefore not surprising to find that by the time of Hammurabi, four aspects of Mesopotamian life had undergone far-reaching development in a direction calculated to sustain centralized and secular authority. These were: (1) the development of an imperial political theory and of a wider political loyalty as against the unmitigated localism which had characterized the first Sumerian age; (2) the development of a bureaucracy and of a professional army; (3) the improvement of administrative technique, especially through

---

[29] In particular, the temples seem to have become economically dependent upon royal grants. Cf. F. R. Kraus, "Le Rôle des temples," pp. 524–33. Presumably the lands once administered by temples in the Sumerian cities were confiscated, or declared royal, thus depriving the temples of their income, save as the king granted the priests some part of it anew.

the use of written communication; (4) the increase in intercity and inter-regional trade and the appearance of an independent merchant class. Each deserves our attention.

1) *Political theory and loyalty.* It was a basic principle of ancient Mesopotamian belief that rulership derived from the gods. Clearly, such a view could be used to justify any successful consolidation of power: the successful conqueror *ipso facto* proved himself the chosen instrument of the gods. Subsequently, a somewhat more elaborate political theory emerged, probably at the time of the native revolt against the Gutians (*ca.* 2050 B.C.). According to this theory, the "Land," *i.e.*, the civilized world of the river valleys, had always been united under a single monarch; and to support this conviction, old traditions and records were edited to produce a document known as the Sumerian King List.[30] This reworked historical record served the central government as a useful propaganda instrument; for clearly, if the "Land" had always been united under a supreme monarch, it was right and fitting that it should continue to be so.[31]

Some of the Mesopotamian high kings claimed divine status for their persons, most prominently under the Third Dynasty of Ur (*ca.* 2050–1950 B.C.). But this idea, perhaps an imitation of Egyptian practice, did not take permanent hold in Mesopotamia; and later rulers abandoned the claim to deification.[32] Nonetheless, the high kingship was vested with a strong religious aura through the personal participation of the king in temple rituals.

Satisfactory evidence for a transfer of political loyalty from the city-state to a larger whole is difficult to find. Yet with the loss of practical independence, with the rise of royal officials to supplement or replace local functionaries, and with the common experience of barbarian conquest, loyalty to the old city-states must slowly have decayed. There is good evidence that a powerful Babylonian self-consciousness existed in later times and endured even after Babylonia itself had lost political independence to the greater imperial structures of Assyria and Persia. The elevation of the Babylonian god Marduk to supremacy among the gods provides a symbol and measure of this larger loyalty, although no evidence clearly proves that such a change was in progress before Hammurabi's time.[33]

[30] Cf. Thorkild Jacobsen, *The Sumerian King List* (Chicago: University of Chicago Press, 1939), p. 140. As usual, scholars disagree. Some are prepared to assign a greater degree of historical accuracy to the theory of the antiquity of a high kingship uniting all "the Land," e.g., Anton Moortgat, "Grundlagen und Entfaltung der sumerisch-akkadischen Kultur," pp. 235–39. Nor, indeed, is it universally agreed that the King List and Sumerian literature at large were written down under the Third Dynasty of Ur. Some scholars think this occurred only some two centuries later, under the rulers of Isin. Cf. Adam Falkenstein und Wolfram von Soden, *Sumerische und akkadische Hymnen und Gebete* (Zürich: Artemis Verlag, 1953), pp. 11–13; F. R. Kraus, "Zur Liste der älteren Könige von Babylonien," *Zeitschrift für Assyriologie*, N.F., L (1952), 47.

[31] Henri Frankfort *et al.*, *Before Philosophy*, p. 210.

[32] Henri Frankfort, *Kingship and the Gods*, pp. 301–2.

[33] As early as the third millennium B.C., an inscription erected by Urukagina, king of Lagash (*ca.* 2400 B.C.), contrasted Sumerians with barbarous invaders from Gutium. The phrases of this tablet have been interpreted (orally in 1958) by Thorkild Jacobsen as evidence of the emergence of Sumerian in-group feeling, transcending the separate city loyalties which divided the land of Sumer into hostile fragments both before and after Urukagina's time.

2) *The development of bureaucracy and of a professional army.* Early rulers like Lugalzaggisi and Sargon lacked any sort of established officialdom to assist them in controlling their conquests. Sargon did, however, have at his disposal a great household, numbering, according to an inscription, no less than 5,400 men who "ate with him daily."[34] These were presumably mostly soldiers. No doubt it was difficult in time of peace to maintain such a force around the king's person; for only a well-articulated organization could bring together in one place the massive supplies of food, arms, and clothing so many men required. Sargon lacked such an organization; yet to disperse the troops and station them at a distance from his person was probably to risk losing real control over them. The obvious solution was to go annually on campaign, for in the field the army could hope to feed and supply itself from plunder. This is speculation; but it seems to explain the restless military activity which characterized the reigns of both Sargon and his grandson and successor, Naram Sin.

By the time of Hammurabi the dilemma had been solved.[35] Hammurabi's administrative machinery was sufficiently developed to permit him to scatter soldiers at various points far from his person and summon them for service when necessary. The system was far more economical than Sargon's; for it avoided the choice between either concentrating vast stores in one spot or living by incessant plunder. But it required an elaborate bureaucracy to keep records of the names, whereabouts, and obligations of thousands of fighting men.

The first step toward establishing a bureaucratic machine may be detected in Naram Sin's practice of supplanting local rulers and chief priests with his own relatives. From this primitive beginning, royal officialdom proliferated greatly, until by Hammurabi's time, royal judges, tax collectors, and garrison commanders served throughout the land. The royal household itself underwent considerable elaboration and specialization. The titles of many officials have come down to us, although their exact function and the hierarchy of government are not clear.[36] An energetic king like Hammurabi supervised even small details, as hundreds of his letters prove. Under less energetic monarchs, central control over local officials no doubt relaxed. The substance of the royal power might then disappear rapidly, and the land easily fall prey to fresh harassment from the borderlands.

3) *Improvement of administrative technique.* Central control of a bureaucracy and of soldiers who were widely dispersed as military landholders depended upon extensive use of written communication. Resort to writing in order to overcome distance is so familiar to us that it is difficult to conceive of a society in which such communication is not routine. Yet it was not always so; and the Mesopotamians seem to have been the first to adapt written signs for this purpose.

---

[34] Bruno Meissner, *Babylonien und Assyrien*, I, 84.

[35] Imperfect indications suggest that bureaucratic government was first really effective in the Ur III period.

[36] Bruno Meissner, *Babylonien und Assyrien*, I, 116–27.

Writing began in Sumer as a symbolic accountancy, used to keep records of goods brought into or dispatched from temple storehouses. Simple pictographs and a system of numerical notation served reasonably well for these purposes, except for difficulties which arose when it was necessary to denote personal names in order to credit or debit individual accounts. Perhaps it was the necessity of recording proper names which stimulated Sumerian scribes to assign phonetic values to certain pictographic symbols. In any case, a generalization of this principle eventually made possible the transcription of all ordinary connected speech into writing. Yet for a long time the potentialities of this technique were not fully exploited. Writing was used primarily for temple accounts, secondarily to record economic contracts between individuals, and scarcely at all for other purposes.

Apparently it was the needs of centralized government that caused the scope of writing to expand. Up to a certain point, a ruler might simply remember what had been agreed to between himself and his subordinates, even as in modern bureaucracies an arcanum of oral and unrecorded transactions remains at the very seat of power. But long before Hammurabi's time, government had become too complex for any one man to keep all its facets in his head. Written records, to which reference could subsequently be made, had become indispensable instruments of government. Records of landholding rights, of obligations toward individuals, of judicial decisions, and of administrative instructions all served to give coherence and scope to governmental action across wide distances and over long periods of time.[37] The development of writing capable of transcribing ordinary speech also permitted the establishment of uniform royal justice throughout the realm. Hammurabi's code is a famous example of what could be achieved, once a written substitute for orally transmitted law had been devised.[38]

4) *The growth of trade and a merchant class.* The daily lives of the peasant majority in Sumer and Akkad were probably but little affected by the establishment of a central political authority. From time immemorial, the routine of peasant life had remained much the same: sowing and reaping, cleaning the irrigation channels, and paying rents and taxes. Whether their social superiors were royal officials, temple priests, or private landlords presumably

---

[37] Cf. Ignace J. Gelb, *A Study of Writing* (Chicago: University of Chicago Press, 1952), pp. 61 ff.; Thorkild Jacobsen, "The Relative Roles of Technology and Literacy in the Development of Old World Civilization," *Human Origins*, selected readings for introductory general course in anthropology at University of Chicago (2d ed.; Chicago: University of Chicago Press, 1946), pp. 245–49.

[38] It is perhaps unnecessary to emphasize how greatly the administration of justice may enhance the power of central and distant government by bringing representatives of the monarchy directly into contact with the affairs of private persons and local groups. Moreover, the right of appeal to the king, in person or as represented by a royal judge, may make the central authorities the ultimate font of justice for the population at large, and undermine traditional local leaders of every sort, who administer a merely local law or custom. It is not certain, however, that the particular code promulgated by Hammurabi was ever extensively employed in the settlement of lawsuits. Records of legal proceedings which have been discovered and deciphered do not seem to conform to its provisions. Cf. Wilhelm Eilers, *Die Gesetzesstele Chammurabis* (Leipzig: J. C. Hinrichs, 1932), pp. 8–9. This does not imply, however, that uniform royal justice did not exist in ancient Babylonia, using other procedural rules than those recorded on Hammurabi's famous stele.

Musée du Louvre and Archives photographiques, Paris.

Directorate General of Antiquities, Government of Iraq.

SARGON OF AKKAD AND HAMMURABI OF BABYLON

The attribution of these two portraits to the two most famous monarchs of ancient Mesopotamia is merest guesswork. Yet this is how each man should have been portrayed. The cast bronze, with its magnificent detail of hair and beard, proud lips and air of confident self-assertion (an effect that even the plunderer's chisel, which rudely extracted the precious stones which once constituted "Sargon's" eyes, oddly fails to destroy and perhaps even enhances) reflects a more sanguine, optimistic age than that mirrored in the quieter, sadder, and perhaps wiser face of the granite "Hammurabi" on the right. Beard, headdress, and treatment of such details as the eyebrows show the continuity of artistic tradition that links the two statues. Yet the contrasting impact of the two works shows how much variation could occur within the limits of such conventions.

made little difference to the peasants, who themselves had slight personal contact with the royal courts or high officialdom.

But by the time of Hammurabi, a significant, if somewhat small intermediary social group had begun to form between the majority of the population and the official classes. These were the professional merchants, who carried on long-distance trade, partly on behalf of the government, partly on their own account. Under a strong ruler like Hammurabi, foreign trade seems to have been conducted mainly on behalf of the ruler, much as it had been conducted on behalf of the god in the old Sumerian temple communities.[39] Yet even under Hammurabi, private trade continued to exist, subject to the control of royal licenses.

Foreign trade was always a vital necessity to civilized populations in Mesopotamia, because basic raw materials had to be sought abroad. When simple seizure was impracticable, the workshops of Mesopotamia were in a position to offer various fine products in exchange.[40] No ruler dared be indifferent to such trade; for without metal, stone, and timber, he could neither maintain an army nor build temples to the gods. Some of Sargon's campaigns may have been designed to assure access to foreign goods; and slaves captured in war were perhaps an important element of his household and government. Hammurabi's code, similarly, shows both how the king sought to control and tax the merchants of his kingdom, and how the royal law, which took mercantile contracts within its purview, protected the merchant group. Indeed, the availability of a uniform law and of royal officials to enforce it must have been an inestimable advantage to men whose occupation required them to trade in various localities.

Surviving records suggest that professional merchants engaging in large-scale trade were relatively few, even in times when the government allowed them greater independence than Hammurabi did.[41] Nevertheless, by the very nature of their activity, merchants, great and small, gradually transformed the older basis of social organization. For every merchant who traded abroad, scores of artisans were needed to produce exportable goods or to work up the imported raw materials. Moreover, within Babylonian society itself, merchants distributed and redistributed local products. No doubt the royal government and the temples were always the major consumers of foreign goods; but a variety of private persons—landowners, officials, or soldiers—also purchased craft products, while a well-developed market for grains, fish, and other foods existed to feed the city folk of ancient Babylonia.

As market relationships increased in significance, a new principle regulating social and individual effort emerged. Side by side with the older agrarian groupings—whether temple communities or landlord estates—arose a looser-

[39] W. F. Leemans, *The Old-Babylonian Merchant: His Business and Social Position* ("Studia et Documenta ad Iura Orientis Antiqui Pertinenta," III [Leiden: E. J. Brill, 1950]), pp. 113–21 and *passim*.

[40] W. F. Leemans, in *Foreign Trade in the Old-Babylonian Period*, has compiled a list of several score of articles of commerce, including a good many items of re-export for which Babylonian merchants served merely as middlemen.

[41] W. F. Leemans, *The Old-Babylonian Merchant*, pp. 49–69.

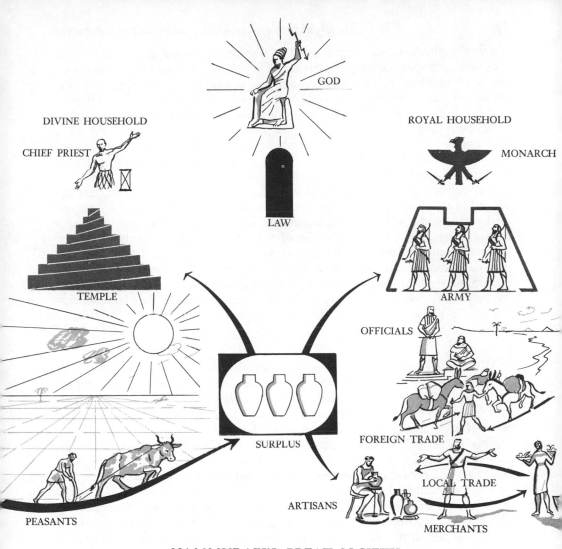

HAMMURABI'S GREAT SOCIETY

textured and geographically widely dispersed "great society" whose individual members were directly accessible to royal justice and taxation, and whose political outlook was less narrowly parochial than that which had prevailed when peasants, dependent artisans, and land-managing elites had constituted the whole of civilized society. Not the service of the gods, but the satisfaction of everyday human wants, became the dominating aim of this emergent "great society," although divinities of course continued to receive their traditional due. Decisions controlling relations among the participants in this "great society" rested partly with officials, judges, soldiers, and partly with ordinary merchants and artisans who could make a limited but important range of decisions independently (e.g., quality, price, assortment of goods).

No doubt all concerned usually acted on blindly traditional lines; yet each of the participants was capable of altering his actions according to his own calculations. Possibilities of indefinite growth and sustained social change were inherent in the comparatively wide dispersion of effective decision-making within such a "great society." Successful innovators could always find imitators; and no single authority could easily prevent the acceptance of new ways that might be powerfully recommended by the operation of an impersonal market—all the more because at first the conditions affecting the market's operation seemed entirely mystifying.[42]

Agriculture, of course, retained overwhelming preponderance—a fact reflected in the tenacity of old cultural forms, sustained as they were by organized priesthoods, who guarded traditional doctrine and ritual with a faithful conservatism. Nevertheless, the rise of the "great society" marked a major advance in the evolution of civilized social structure and stimulated important new departures in the forms of Mesopotamian cultural expression. In particular, the first appearance of written poetry and of higher mathematics belongs to the period when the lineaments of a secularizing great society were emerging in the Valley of the Two Rivers.

*   *   *

When the technique of writing became adequate to record ordinary discourse, it became possible to transcribe the old myths and ritual phrases which had previously been transmitted orally. This both crystallized ritual forms and facilitated the training of young men in sacred routines. Until about 1800 B.C., Mesopotamian written literature kept within these narrow and thoroughly conservative bounds; but between about 1800 and 1600 B.C., individuals arose who, like Homer and Hesiod in Greek times, took the old mythical materials and reworked them into new and lengthy works of art.

The two principal monuments of this literature are the *Epic of Gilgamesh* and the *Epic of Creation*. Each draws upon heterogeneous mythical materials to construct a story which presents a fairly coherent view of the nature of the world and man's place in it. The central theme of the *Epic of Gilgamesh* is the vanity of all human effort to escape death, even when the protagonist is a hero "two-thirds divine and one-third human." The *Epic of Creation* is an elaborate glorification of Marduk, lord god of Babylon. As justification for Marduk's claim to pre-eminence among gods and men, the author devoted about half of his poem to an account of creation and Marduk's part therein; while the second part consists of a liturgical listing of the names and powers of the god. In spite of passages that seem bizarre to a modern reader, the main

---

[42] Karl Polanyi's effort to define the nature of trade relationships in ancient Mesopotamia does not, if I understand his remarks aright, contradict the views here advanced. Long-distance trade conducted along monopoly lines on a commission basis is still a form of market relation: all parties to the exchange must agree to the *quid pro quo*, however equivalencies may be calculated and however firmly incrusted by customary or legal definition they may be. Prices fluctuating "rationally" in response to changes in supply and demand do not seem to me necessary characteristics of market relationships, nor does the term "market" as used here imply any such highly unstable relationship. Cf. Karl Polyani, "Marketless Trading in Hammurabi's Time," in Karl Polyani *et al.*, *Trade and Market in the Early Empires*, pp. 12–26.

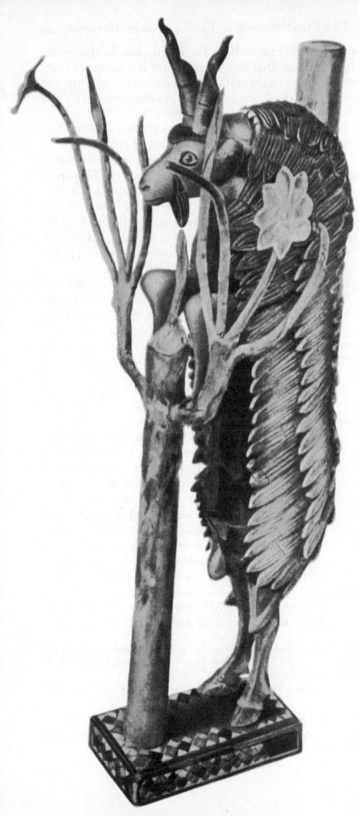

THE INQUIRING GOAT

This statuette, made of gold, lapis lazuli, mother-of-pearl, and silver, all inlaid upon an adhesive of asphalt, was discovered in the royal graves of the Third Dynasty of Ur and dates from about 2000 B.C. The motif of a goat climbing in a tree recurs quite frequently in Mesopotamian art. What the original use or symbolic meaning of this statuette may have been is not known. Few comparable examples of the goldsmith's and jeweler's craft survive, for the goat stands a full twenty inches tall. To a modern eye it suggests a lighter and more luxurious aspect of Mesopotamian civilization than is revealed by most surviving art and literature.

themes of these poems—death and creation—have remained close to the center of human thought and feeling from that day to this; and if one reads them with some small adjustment of mind to accommodate their mythical form and the occasional naïve crudity of incident, one may feel and extraordinary sense of kinship with the poets who conceived and wrote them.[43]

Both poems represent a denial of the adequacy of received religious doctrine. The *Epic of Gilgamesh* protests against the injustice of the gods in refusing to men the gift of eternal life; while the *Epic of Creation* consciously reshapes old myths to justify the exaltation of Marduk and his city. This spirit was further illustrated by a third poem, sometimes called the *Righteous Sufferer*.[44] In a fashion comparable to the Book of Job, it describes how a blamelessly pious man suffered inexplicable affliction at the hands of the gods in the form of foul disease. The author concludes that the ways of the gods are unfathomable to men; yet conventional piety is saved somewhat lamely at the very end by the restoration of the sufferer to health and happiness.

The author of the *Righteous Sufferer* clearly felt that the gods should deal justly with men, and not treat them arbitrarily. This belief is stated in a positive and optimistic way in a hymn to the sun god, Shamash, who is praised as the doer of justice among men, punisher of evildoers, and helper of the oppressed.[45] Shamash was the god who gave Hammurabi his laws, according to the carving at the top of the stele upon which that famous code was found; and the growth of the idea that the gods ought to be just may well be connected with the rise of an administratively effective royal justice among men.[46]

Yet such a view had no place in the older religious outlook; and when political disturbance once again broke down the legal machinery of Mesopotamia, the justice of the gods seemed far to seek. Under the circumstances, curiosity could only lead to impiety. Thus it is not surprising to discover that after about 1500 B.C., priests and scribes abandoned theological, cosmological, and moral speculations, and concentrated instead upon the compilation of bulky catalogues and word lists, which gradually developed into encyclopedias of received knowledge and doctrine. Learning supplanted literature; and the daring of the authors who had questioned or modified established religious interpretations was not repeated. Instead of using myths as the basis for new epics or for philosophical drama, as the Greeks were later to do, the ancient Mesopotamians rested content with what had already been achieved.

Such an outcome recapitulated the pattern of innovation followed by an early stabilization which had characterized early Sumerian art. The close association between priestly colleges and both artists and writers probably ex-

---

[43] A sampling of this literature, including translations of both the *Epic of Gilgamesh* and the *Epic of Creation*, may be found in James B. Pritchard (ed.), *Ancient Near Eastern Texts relating to the Old Testament* (Princeton, N.J.: Princeton University Press, 1955), pp. 60–119.

[44] An English translation may be found in S. H. Langdon, *Babylonian Wisdom* (London: Luzac & Co., 1923), pp. 35–66.

[45] An English translation may be found in Pritchard, *Ancient Near Eastern Texts*, pp. 387–89.

[46] This discussion of Mesopotamian literature draws heavily upon the elegant exposition by Thorkild Jacobsen, in Henri Frankfort *et al.*, *Before Philosophy*, pp. 187–99, 223–31.

plains the cessation of artistic and literary innovation just at the point when, to modern eyes, problems and possibilities became really interesting. We should, however, remember that when portraying gods and heroes—whether in words or with a sculptor's chisel—novelty necessarily verges on heresy. True doctrine is old doctrine; and proper piety demands reverent preservation of ancient ways and ideas. In addition, the school system of ancient Babylonia powerfully reinforced hieratic conservatism. Scribal schools were organized as craft guilds and soon became jealous corporations guarding both professional standards and professional privileges with an impartial rigor. Long years of apprenticeship were required to master the intricacies of the Akkadian and Sumerian languages and the cuneiform symbols, not to mention the mathematics and music which were also incorporated into the curriculum. By 1500 B.C., the task was lightened by a series of texts and compendia of received knowledge that gave aspiring scribes easy access to everything they were now expected to master. Whatever was excluded from this canon tended to be overlooked and forgotten, while all conflicts or uncertainties within the body of ancient Mesopotamian learning were glossed over by the skill of the epitomizers and textbook writers. The result was to assure that the long training required to achieve literacy could scarcely fail to produce in each successful pupil a thoroughly conventional mind.[47]

Given the institutional setting of ancient Babylonian learning, it is more surprising that a few individuals found inspiration to create the great epics than that such enterprise did not long endure. Both poems seem to be the product of a brief period of intellectual and sociological unsettlement, occurring about the time when Hammurabi extended his power over the ancient cities of Sumer and Akkad. The Amorite conquerors were then still close to their pastoral origins; and their native religious ideas and attitudes may have conflicted with those of the more civilized Akkadians and Sumerians. Moreover, the new prominence of Babylon logically implied the elevation of its god, Marduk, to a position of supremacy among the other gods of the land. But Marduk's usurpation required his priests to suppress professional scruples against tampering with old myths and sacred stories. In this they were eminently successful, as the *Epic of Creation*—a towering monument to their ruthless ambition and radical piety—amply attests.

No comparably transparent motive may be detected behind the composition of the *Epic of Gilgamesh* or the *Righteous Sufferer*. Nevertheless, in an age of political and social change, when Amorites were blending with more anciently civilized peoples, and when power, wealth, and religious supremacy were in process of removal to the new capital of Babylon, age-old religion was obviously disturbed. Like a sea of ice in the grip of spring tides, the crystallized expression of established religion heaved and cracked; inadequacies were felt in old formulations; and certain individuals were able to

---

[47] On Babylonian schools and the "canonization" of Babylonian literature, see Adam Falkenstein, "Die babylonische Schule," *Saeculum*, IV (1953), 125–37; S. N. Kramer, "Schooldays: A Sumerian Composition relating to the Education of a Scribe," *Journal of the American Oriental Society*, LXIX (1949), 199–215; Adam Falkenstein und Wolfram von Soden, *Sumerische und akkadische Hymnen und Gebete*, pp. 15–16.

employ the perfected technique of writing to record their dissent from received tradition.

But such irreverence, and the conditions which provoked it, were short-lived. Priestly and scribal conservatism quickly adjusted itself to the remodeling of earlier tradition, and sternly discouraged further modifications. Copying, not creating, was the truly pious and scholarly attitude; and copying was accordingly pursued, to the advantage of modern scholars, who have discovered multiple copies of the great epics, variously mutilated, but so similar as to permit use of one text to supply lacunae in another.

The development of Babylonian mathematics, so far as it is known, followed the same curve. Tablets from about the time of Hammurabi reveal the use of an elegant sexagesimal number system that made use of the place value principle familiar to us in our own "Arabic" numerals. Indeed, the only deficiency of Babylonian numerical notation of the eighteenth century B.C. as compared with our own was the absence of a sign for zero. The Babylonian system evolved from the numerical notation employed in keeping accounts; and its sexagesimal base resulted from the fact that the Babylonian weights for silver—by Hammurabi's time a very important measure of value—were arranged in multiples of sixty. About the same time, mathematics transcended purely utilitarian limits; and some of the tablets show a theoretical interest in and mastery over complex algebraic relationships. Methods were known for the solution of quadratic equations; and special cases of equations using higher exponents could also be solved. Numbers and their relations remained always in the center of Babylonian mathematics, in marked contrast to the geometrical emphasis of the Greeks.

Accidents of preservation and discovery may seriously distort our picture of Babylonian mathematical development. Nevertheless, it is remarkable that after the burst of creativity about the time of Hammurabi, no further development manifested itself until the Seleucid era (312–263 B.C.), when old Babylonian learning was stimulated afresh by contact with Greek science. The innovating age was apparently brief in mathematics, as in literature. After a few mathematical pioneers had achieved much, successive generations of Babylonian scribes seem to have rested smugly content with received computational procedures until, after more than a millennium, Greek geometry brought a new challenge to their attention.[48]

* * *

To sum up: two great landmarks define the Mesopotamian achievement down to 1700 B.C. First, through the temple community organization of peasant life, the ancient Sumerians were able to create conditions for the emergence of civilization. Based upon a religious world-view, but sustained also by the practical services which the priestly colleges performed for the peasantry,

[48] O. Neugebauer, *The Exact Sciences in Antiquity*, p. 19. On Babylonian mathematics cf. also M. E. M. Bruins, *Nouvelles découvertes sur les mathématiques babyloniennes* (Paris: Presses universitaires, 1951).

the temple community permitted the concentration of a considerable surplus of agricultural products and used this surplus to support priestly experts and a train of dependent craftsmen. Such specialization led to a rapid development of skill and to an early crystallization of artistic, intellectual, and technological traditions. By the end of the third millennium B.C., the temple communities of Sumer had been supplemented by other, lay types of agrarian social systems, within which landlords took over an economic role analogous to that of the priestly colleges, and were able to concentrate wealth in their own hands, not as agents of a divinity, but by virtue of military force or traditional prerogatives of social leadership.

Agrarian communities of either the temple or lay type remained always the fundamental cell of ancient Mesopotamian society. Such communities provided the frame within which the vast majority of the population lived and worked; and their age-long stability over generations, centuries, and millennia —subject always to recurrent disruption by flood, famine, or war, but equally capable of rapid regeneraton—gave Mesopotamian civilization its remarkable uniformity and extraordinary power of recuperation in the face of disaster.

The second great Mesopotamian achievement was the slow and partial development of a looser social unit, the "great society," which functioned like a fluid in the interstices between the separate agrarian communities and bound them into a larger whole. Its sanctions were partly religious, too, but less strongly so. In addition, law, administration, military force, and the impersonal relationship of the market all contributed to its organization. By comparison with the agrarian communities, the cohesion of this larger society was weak and liable to more drastic breakdown. The way of life of the "great society" directly affected only a small minority of the people who lived in the land, and never penetrated deeply into the daily round of the basic agrarian communities. Yet for all its initial weakness and instability, this type of social organization, especially in its secular aspects, was to provide the primary context for the further development of civilization in Mesopotamia itself and, even more conspicuously, beyond the borders of that ancient land.

* * *

The peoples of Mesopotamia did not live a life alone: they were constantly surrounded by aliens, who sometimes threatened attack and regularly offered goods in trade. The brilliance and impressiveness of Mesopotamian civilization were not lost upon these peoples. From the beginning, a process of diffusion can be detected, whereby neighboring nations imitated what had been done in Mesopotamia, or else, stimulated by Mesopotamian achievement, embarked upon social and cultural construction of their own. The next chapter will trace the stages of this process.

CHAPTER III

The Diffusion
of Civilization:
First Phase

A. INTRODUCTION

From very small and simple beginnings about 6500 B.C., agricultural villages of the Middle Eastern pattern multiplied and spread to new ground. This process continued throughout the fifth and fourth millennia, until by 3000 B.C. grain-growing agricultural communities extended into Europe, along the coast of North Africa, into India, and across the Iranian plateau toward central Asia. At the same time, a process of social differentiation was at work within this agricultural world which, in such extreme and specially favored cases as that of Mesopotamia, led to the rise of civilization.

Mesopotamia constituted the largest irrigable river valley near the original centers of Middle Eastern agriculture. This fact undoubtedly gave the region something of a head start on the way to civilization; and as the agricultural potentialities of the flood plain became manifest, the rise of civilization was accelerated by complex interplay among the culturally divergent groups that pressed inward upon the irrigated land. The first Mesopotamian farmers were never permitted to settle down securely into a fixed and unchanging routine. Instead, as we have just seen, the proximity and pressure of diverse alien peoples compelled them to amalgamate, elaborate, and invent ways of coping with their difficult but potentially very rich environment, until between 3500 and 3000 B.C. something recognizable as civilized society emerged among them.

But the attainment of civilization did not end the reactive social process. On the contrary, the appearance in the lower Tigris-Euphrates Valley of a society so skilled and elegant, so powerful and wealthy, and so much in need of imported goods, gave the process fresh impetus. Needing metals, wood, and stone from afar, the civilized populations had either to send out expeditions to cut trees from the mountain slopes, dig ore from the ground, and quarry stone from the cliffs; or they had to induce natives to perform such labor for them. In either case, intimate relations were established between men skilled in the arts of civilization and their ruder fellows. Wherever Mesopotamian traders or soldiers penetrated, they left a trail of social upheaval behind. As a result, those elements of the civilized way of life which appealed to local peoples and could be built into the context of their social structures, technologies, and geographical environments tended to spread far and wide.

In one sense, this diffusion of customs and techniques was nothing new. From the beginning of the human adventure, bands of men had borrowed and adapted ways of doing things from their neighbors. But civilized society had much to impart and relatively little to learn from peoples not yet civilized. With the onset of civilization, therefore, the social processes of borrowing tended to run in one direction, outward from the civilized center toward the periphery of the agricultural world. Thus during the latter part of the fourth millennium and throughout the third, two social frontiers were in motion across the face of the Old World: an agricultural frontier between Neolithic barbarism and Paleolithic savagery, and a civilized frontier between "urbanity" and barbarism.

But the spread of civilization could not proceed in quite the same manner as did the spread of agricultural villages. To carve new fields from virgin land did not require very special conditions, once the basic agricultural skills had been acquired. Suitable soil was distributed in wide belts, and new settlements could be set down at no great distance from old ones, forming a more or less continuous agricultural zone. This was not true of civilization, which in its first phase required very special geographical conditions in order to flourish, namely, an irrigable alluvium.

Irrigation was vital to early civilization partly because it put the production of a regular agricultural surplus easily within the reach of primitive farmers. Even more important, by requiring comparatively very massive coordination of social effort, irrigation facilitated the creation of a social engine for the concentration of surplus food in the hands of a managerial group. And once a body of managers had established its right to collect part of the farmers' surplus crop, growing numbers of men could be employed not only to dig canals, but also to elaborate the cult of the god, to undertake military enterprises, and to specialize as craftsmen, artists, or musicians: to create, in short, a civilization.

All this was impossible on land watered only by rain. Without the benefit of river silt and dependable moisture, it was difficult or impossible to raise any large surplus of food. Without the necessity of organized, large-scale collective effort on canals and dikes, it was equally difficult for a managerial group to establish control over whatever surplus may have been available.

Hence the diffusion of civilization began as a leap-frog movement, jumping across comparatively great distances from one irrigable river valley to the next. Since the major irrigable valleys were separated from one another by vast expanses of inhospitable ground, new civilizations, as they arose, enjoyed a fundamental independence of one another. Local social materials—customs, religious cults, political institutions—were the basic stuff from which new river valley civilizations had to be elaborated. Yet in the critical period of transition to civilization, before local solutions had been found to the problems inherent in the creation of a complex society, there was a period when foreign stimulus was vitally important, hastening and facilitating the rise of new styles of civilization in all the propitious places that lay within range of Mesopotamian influence.

A number of river valleys amenable to irrigation lay within the limits of the agricultural world of the fourth millennium. Some were relatively small, like the Karun River, which today flows into the lower reaches of the Tigris-Euphrates, but which in ancient times made its independent way to the Persian Gulf. This river, with others near it, offered the basis for the early rise of Elamite civilization; but it lay so close to the larger Tigris-Euphrates complex that the originally independent growth of Elam was soon submerged in the culture of Mesopotamia.[1] Similarly, a great spring of water near the banks of the Jordan River provided the basis for the early rise of the city of Jericho, an isolated and comparatively minute island of high culture in the surrounding sea of barbarism.[2] No doubt there were other small centers of irrigated agriculture in the Middle East which sustained small cities, whose inhabitants even in the fourth millennium were able to create for themselves at least the beginnings of a civilized style of life. But such isolated growths could not easily protect themselves from barbarian onslaught; and when in the second millennium B.C. the full power and glory of Mesopotamian and Egyptian civilization came to bear upon them, they were engulfed in the larger cosmopolitan society which slowly established itself in the Middle East.

On the margins of the Middle East, however, lay three larger river valleys well suited to accommodate massive civilized communities. Two of the rivers, the Nile and the Indus, were in fact tamed for human purposes about 3000 B.C.; and the civilizations on their banks soon rivaled that of Mesopotamia. The third peripheral river system, the Oxus-Jaxartes, was not, so far as anyone knows, the scene of any parallel early development;[3] but perhaps some archeologist may yet discover traces of a vanished and forgotten civilization in those valleys. After all, the discovery of Sumerian civilization dates back only to the 1890's; and Indus civilization was completely unknown before 1922.

The landlocked location of the Oxus-Jaxartes valleys, however, made them

---

[1] George G. Cameron, *History of Early Iran* (Chicago: University of Chicago Press, 1936), pp. 33–34; Clément Huart and Louis Delaporte, *L'Iran antique* (Paris: Albin Michel, 1943), pp. 74 ff.

[2] Kathleen M. Kenyon, "Jericho and Its Setting in Near Eastern History," *Antiquity*, XXX (1955), 184–94; Kathleen M. Kenyon, *Digging up Jericho* (London: E. Benn, 1957).

[3] Sergei P. Tolstow, *Auf den Spuren der altchoresmischen Kultur* (Berlin: Verlag Kultur & Fortschritt, 1953), pp. 73–100.

STONE KNIFE FROM EGYPT

This weapon was found at Gebel el-Arak, Egypt, and dates from late pre-dynastic times. The ivory handle, both sides of which are shown here, reveals definite Mesopotamian influence. On the left, fallen corpses mingle toward the hilt with ships of a design familiar from Mesopotamian seals; while at the handle's heel end a rather stately battle is underway. Sumerian seafarers visiting the Red Sea coast may often have engaged in such scuffles with local inhabitants. The other side of the handle repeats Mesopotamian motifs: the bearded man flanked by two rampant lions is a scene familiar in Mesopotamian art; so is the portrayal of a lion leaping upon the back of its prey, shown just below the boss. The over-all impression left by the carving is of a clever but still primitive local imitation of high Mesopotamian art.

far less accessible to Mesopotamian stimulus than were the Indus and the Nile. Even in the fourth millennium B.C., ships from the land of Sumer sailed through the Persian Gulf to Arabia and into the Red Sea, thus making contact with the ancient Egyptians;[4] and while no positive evidence indicates so early a sea link between Sumer and the Indus region, the same ship captains who reached the Red Sea surely could (and probably did) reach the mouths of the Indus. But no sea lanes smoothed the way between Mesopotamia and the Oxus-Jaxartes valleys. Since overland transport was inherently more expensive and more dangerous, perhaps the slender but electric tenacles extending outward from Sumer, which seem to have quickened civilization in the Nile and Indus valleys, failed to penetrate so far northeastward. If so, the future discovery of a forgotten early civilization in the Oxus-Jaxartes valleys becomes far less likely.

The inherent potentialities of irrigated agriculture in the Nile and Indus valleys permitted the rise of civilization in Egypt and India soon after 3000 B.C.; and sporadic contact with Sumerian skills accelerated the process. Yet only as the Egyptians and Indus peoples developed toward civilization from an inner momentum of their own did they become really accessible to Sumerian influence. Monumental architecture was all very well, but until the local societies had developed individuals interested in building great structures and able to command the necessary labor power, Sumerian technical models were meaningless. Similarly, even such a comparatively simple device as the potter's wheel—which, like monumental architecture, seems to have been imported into Egypt from Mesopotamia—could not establish itself until professional potters appeared in Egypt who were both interested in acquiring and able to develop the special skills required for making pottery on a fast-spinning wheel.

As Egypt and India developed their own unique styles of civilized life, they became fresh centers of social disturbance, acting upon the less-advanced peoples round about in much the same fashion as the civilization of Mesopotamia had done and continued to do. The range and intensity of cultural interplay between barbarian and civilized peoples therefore increased, and the pace of social evolution throughout the Middle East as well as in outlying regions accelerated, until a high barbarism, incorporating many of the detachable elements of river valley civilization, spread widely through Europe and Asia. Archeologists commonly call this phase of human history the Bronze Age, which for Europe may be dated between about 1800 and 1000 B.C.

The development of high barbarism fundamentally altered the balance of

[4] Pre-dynastic rock carvings portraying ships of Mesopotamian design have been found in the Wadi Hammamat, a dry valley that offers a natural line of communication between Upper Egypt and the Red Sea coast. Such ships may not have come directly from Sumer. Perhaps various intermediaries plied the Arabian and Red sea coasts; but insofar as they had themselves been affected by Sumerian civilization, this would not vitiate the reality of seaborne contact between Sumer and Egypt, however slender and sporadic it may have been. Cf. Helene J. Kantor, "The Early Relations of Egypt with Asia," *Journal of Near Eastern Studies*, I (1945), 174–213; Helene J. Kantor, "Further Evidence for Early Mesopotamian Relations with Egypt," *ibid.*, XI (1952), 239–50. Overland contact between Sumer and Egypt should not be ruled out, either. Cf. W. F. Albright, "Syrien, Phönizien und Palästina," in F. Valjavec (ed.), *Historia Mundi*, II, 339.

the world. Civilized peoples became more exposed than ever before to conquest by barbarians made newly formidable by their mastery of the techniques and weapons of civilized war. This basic transformation of what might be called the "social gradient" of Eurasia manifested itself soon after 1700 B.C. and may be considered as marking the end of the first phase of civilized history.

Let us then look briefly at the early Egyptian and Indian versions of river valley civilization and trace, as well as the sketchy data will permit, the influence these, together with Mesopotamian civilization, exerted upon the barbarian world.

B. THE CIVILIZATIONS OF THE NILE AND INDUS VALLEYS TO 1700 B.C.

1. ANCIENT EGYPT

Compared to the thousand-year gestation of Sumerian civilization, the maturation of Egyptian culture and society was precocious. But the tremendous successes of the early Egyptians in building a state, elaborating a religious system, devising a new art, and, generally, in shaping a unique and powerfully attractive style of civilized life weighed heavily upon later generations. Heirs of the first great period of Egyptian history felt it all but impossible to improve upon the models offered by their ancestors and found it difficult even to maintain the achievement of the past. Since the geographical position of the country assured a long immunity from serious foreign pressure, the peoples of Egypt found little outside stimulus to new departures; and despite a brilliant start, their civilization began in some important respects to lag behind the more turbulent, but also more persistent development of Mesopotamian society.

The most obvious precocity of Egyptian development was political. About 3100 B.C., when large parts of the Nile Valley were probably still unreclaimed marsh and desert, when local communities had scarcely begun to rise above the simplicity of neolithic villages, and when the intellectual and artistic traditions of Egypt were as yet unformed, the country was united under a single ruler, traditionally known as Menes.[5] Despite subsequent changes in dynasty, perhaps accompanied in some cases by brief periods of disorder, the political unification of the country remained a reality for about 900 years.

How could a king, lacking the administrative devices so painfully developed in Mesopotamia, hold a great state together from the beginning of Egyptian history?

Geography does much to explain this seeming anomaly. Deserts gave the land of Egypt clear-cut and easily defensible boundaries; while the Nile provided it with a natural backbone and nervous system. Frontier defense against outlanders was scarcely a serious problem for the king of Egypt. To be sure, infiltration of Libyans from the west and of Asiatics from the east sometimes

---

[5] Although exact dates are not known, early Egyptian chronology is subject to far less uncertainty than Mesopotamian. For convenience, I have adopted the round numbers tabulated in John A. Wilson, *The Burden of Egypt* (Chicago: University of Chicago Press, 1951), pp. vii–viii.

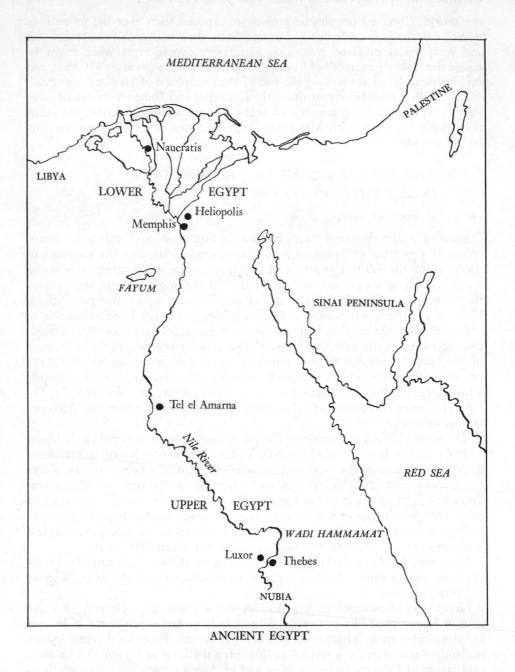

MEDITERRANEAN SEA

PALESTINE

LIBYA

● Naucratis

LOWER   EGYPT

● Heliopolis
Memphis ●

FAYUM

SINAI PENINSULA

● Tel el Amarna

Nile River

RED SEA

UPPER   EGYPT

WADI HAMMAMAT

Luxor ● ● Thebes

NUBIA

ANCIENT EGYPT

required military action along the fringes of the Delta; and frontier skirmishes against the Nubians in the south were not unknown. Yet such barbarian dangers were minor in the third millennium B.C. and could not seriously threaten the Pharaonic majesty. Hence one of the most disruptive factors in Mesopotamian political history was insignificant in the case of Egypt.

The early integration of the land into a single state depended directly upon the easy navigability of the Nile. The flow of the river carried boats northward; and by a lucky chance, the winds of Egypt blow dominantly from the north, so that movement upstream proceeded quite easily with the help of sails. By controlling shipping, the king automatically and easily regulated all major movements of goods and people, and therewith possessed the means for effective rule over Egypt.[6] By contrast, Mesopotamian rulers could avail themselves of no ready-made natural instrument for securing their centralized authority, but had slowly and painfully to develop law and bureaucratic administration as an artificial substitute for the natural articulation which geography gave to Egypt.[7]

Social factors reinforced the centralizing effects of Egypt's geography. Before 3100 B.C., no strong, wealthy, and self-conscious organizations comparable to Sumerian temple communities and city-states existed in Egypt. Local districts, the nomes, were recognized as administrative subdivisions of the kingdom from the earliest times; and the duality between Upper and Lower Egypt, between the narrow Valley of the Nile and the marshy flats of the Delta, remained always prominent in official nomenclature. These subdivisions were probably based upon political units which antedated the unification of the Two Lands; but the authority exercised locally by priests, chieftains, or priest-kings must have been undeveloped and flimsy in prehistoric Egypt as compared with the authority of comparable rulers in Sumer.[8]

[6] Hermann Kees, *Das alte Ägypten: eine kleine Landeskunde* (Berlin: Akademie Verlag, 1955), pp. 50–56.

[7] The Tigris and Euphrates are turbulent; and although rafts and light boats could go downstream in the seasons when the rivers were neither too high nor too low for safe navigation, it was impractical to proceed upstream. Hence overland portage, which on the broad flats of the flood plain was not limited to any exact route, was the normal method of carrying goods northward, as well as east- and westward.

[8] It is uncertain how far the development of irrigation had proceeded before the completion of Egypt's political unification; but there is reason to think that its major development came after and not before Menes' conquest. If so, then the still primitive and undeveloped character of local religio-political institutions becomes intelligible. Cf. J. A. Wilson, *The Burden of Egypt*, p. 31.

The methods of irrigation used in ancient Egypt were fundamentally different from those employed in Mesopotamia. The Egyptians did not construct canals artificially until imperial times. Instead, they relied upon the natural flood of the Nile River, trapping the waters behind solid dikes until the soil had been thoroughly soaked, then allowing the waters to run off downstream. Through this run-off process, the danger of salting the soil was avoided—a problem which harassed the Mesopotamians.

This type of "basin" irrigation involved far less digging than the Mesopotamian type; and the gentle, regular rise and fall of the Nile meant that maintenance work was light. This explains why the Egyptian peasants had time and manpower to spare for the pyramids; for under the conditions of early Egyptian cultivation, there were several months each year, after the harvest was in and before the Nile had risen, when there was little or nothing to do on the land. In Mesopotamia, by contrast, there was always work on dikes and canals to be done when seasonal tasks were not pressing. Cf. Charles Singer (ed.), *A History of Technology* (Oxford: Clarendon Press, 1955), I, 535–55; Hermann Kees, *Das alte Ägypten*, p. 22.

Otherwise, the concentration of supreme power in the royal household which prevailed in the Old Kingdom could not have been effected. Moreover, if tradition is correct in identifying the first king of Upper and Lower Egypt as a pastoralist conqueror from the south, then the truly extraordinary prerogatives of the later Pharaohs can be seen as resulting from the application to conquered agricultural populations of the necessarily broad powers assigned by any successful pastoral community to its leader.

A corollary of Egypt's precocious political unification was that, unlike Mesopotamia, the Valley of the Nile had no great cities to serve as matrices of high culture. Instead, early Egyptian civilization was the product of the royal household, which proliferated so widely as to become, in the specialization of its parts, a city in itself. Being able to command the labor of vast numbers of peasants throughout the country, the administrators and engineers of the royal household found it possible to carry through such extraordinary operations as the construction of the great pyramids, while royal craftsmen performed the scarcely less extraordinary feat of creating the sophisticated conventions of Egyptian sculpture and painting. Most amazing of all, they achieved these successes within a few centuries of the raw beginnings of civilization in the Nile Valley.

The basic social unit of Egypt remained the rural village. In the first centuries of Egyptian history, important social groupings intermediary between the villages and the royal household apparently did not exist. In later times, some of the principal temples may have employed groups of administrators, artisans, and servitors in something like the Mesopotamian fashion. But such centers never attained the basic importance for Egyptian life that their analogues had in Mesopotamia. Local magnates, many of them originally royal administrative officials, played a more significant role; and from the time of the First Intermediate Period through the Middle Kingdom (2200–1800 B.C.), such landed aristocrats and petty princes were able to interpose themselves between the villagers and the central royal authority. From the peasant point of view, this probably amounted to little more than an exchange of masters. The organization of their village life, and with it the fundamental texture of Egyptian society, did not change very much. Cities in the Mesopotamian sense of the word—that is, centers of artisan production and commerce existing independently of a ruling household—failed to take root on Egyptian soil before the imperial age, and even then remained few and, as it were, alien bodies within the fabric of Egyptian society.

Early Egypt was like a single temple community writ large. It is as though the first rulers of united Egypt had taken the social system of Sumer and improved upon it by enlarging the territorial base to include the entire navigable length of the lower Nile, thereby automatically solving the political problem which arose from conflict between adjacent states in the older land.

In at least two respects, the economic and social organization of Egypt resembled that of the early Sumerian temple community. First, the fundamental division of society was between a peasant mass and the household of a god. The fact that in Egypt the god was incarnate in a human ruler, whereas in

ROUGE PALETTE OF KING NARMER-MENES

These carvings contrast sharply with the imitative patterns of the Gebel el-Arak knife handle. What was later to become the distinctive style of Egyptian art is here well on its way to definition; yet this palette was probably made in the time of the First Dynasty, for it celebrates Menes' victories that united the Two Lands of Egypt into a single kingdom. The palette is also interesting because it seems to antedate the definition of hieroglyph shapes. Design elements from which the hieroglyphs later were constructed can be seen in such a figure as the falcon on the left. This part of the composition can in fact be read as a hieroglyph.

Comparison between the animal portrayals here and on the Gebel el-Arak knife handle (p. 67) is particularly instructive, for the Egyptian emphasis upon design and disinterest in realistic details of musculature or of gesture are immediately apparent. Likewise the principle of scaling the size of each figure to its importance is here well developed, as illustrated in the upper register on the right where the king is shown inspecting the decapitated corpses of his defeated enemies.

Mesopotamia the god was superhuman and spoke only through priests, should not obscure the real resemblance. Second, trade and all large-scale economic enterprises were managed and controlled by officials of the divine household. At intervals the Pharaohs dispatched expeditions of a semi-military character to Syria for timber, to Sinai for copper, to Nubia for gold, to Punt for myrrh; while within the country similar enterprises brought granite and other special stone from Upper Egypt and gathered taxes in kind into the royal treasuries. So far as these goods were not utilized directly by the god-king for the maintenance of his court or for the construction of his tomb and other buildings, they were distributed among the courtiers of the royal household. The earliest economic organization of the Sumerian temple communities was probably very similar. But whereas in Mesopotamia merchants and other secular entrepreneurs found scope for their activities in the interstices between the separate temple communities, in Egypt the monolithic organization of the Old Kingdom precluded any such development.

In the long run, monolithic cohesion may have hampered the growth of Egyptian civilization; but at first, it offered every advantage. The divine status of the Pharaoh imparted to the central government a stability never attained by the high kingship of Mesopotamia, for the doctrines of Egyptian religion gave the god-king a hold upon his subjects that had no parallel in a land whose rulers, however powerful, were not themselves divine.

In Egypt the king, being a god, was believed (as it were, by definition) to enjoy immortality. Proper precautions were needful to preserve his body and to provide a fitting house for his spirit; hence the pyramids. But in the time of the Old Kingdom, Egyptians believed that no ordinary man, not even the most pious priest or powerful official, could attain immortality on the strength of his own personality. Survival after death depended on securing a place in the retinue of the departed king. For this reason, the officials of the Old Kingdom took great pains to build their tombs as close to the royal sepulcher as the divine ruler would graciously permit; and wall inscriptions in such tombs emphasize the dead man's services to the god-king, perhaps in the hope that the immortal, though perhaps absent-minded, spirit of the departed Pharaoh would be stimulated thereby to remember how truly indispensable the dead official's services had been.

Survival after death seems always to have been of prime concern to the Egyptians. Insofar as they were truly convinced that their sole hope of immortality rested on the Pharaoh's good pleasure, it became easy for even a distant monarch to secure loyal and punctual obedience to his commands. Who would wittingly incur the god-king's wrath when penalties for disobedience were so drastic, and the rewards for good behavior seemed so sweet? Here, surely, lay the secret of the Old Kingdom. Instead of trying to control officials by law and frequent letters in Hammurabi's poor human fashion, the Egyptian Pharaoh could offer the reward of immortal life to those who obeyed him well.

Yet even in the best days of the Old Kingdom, a strong localism lurked just beneath the surface. The king and his household were raised high above the

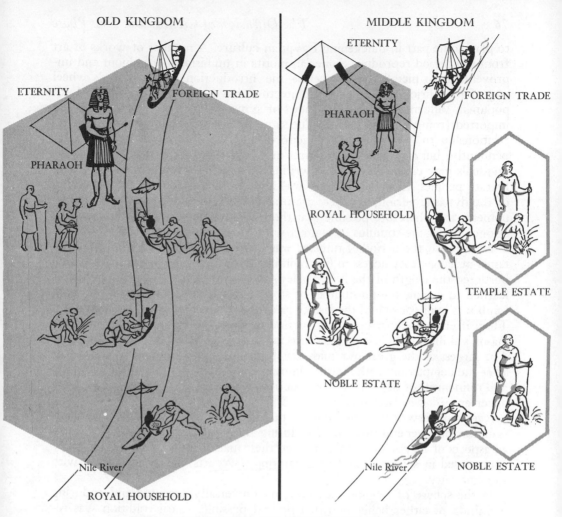

OLD KINGDOM

ETERNITY

PHARAOH

FOREIGN TRADE

Nile River

ROYAL HOUSEHOLD

MIDDLE KINGDOM

ETERNITY

PHARAOH

ROYAL HOUSEHOLD

FOREIGN TRADE

TEMPLE ESTATE

NOBLE ESTATE

Nile River

NOBLE ESTATE

THE EVOLUTION OF EGYPTIAN SOCIETY

peasantry; but that peasantry was very closely rooted to locality; and except for the royal administration, there was little to bind one locality to another. The best evidence of this submerged centrifugal localism may be found in Egyptian religion. The extraordinary confusion of the Egyptian pantheon reflected the existence, survival, and elaboration of diverse local cults, which originally bore little relationship to one another and could only imperfectly be harmonized, even after a single political authority had united the Two Lands. The truly extraordinary unity and stylistic coherence of Egyptian civilization was the creation of the royal household, not of the population at large; and in religion—the one sphere where local village attitudes emerge for our inspection—not coherence, but a desperate confusion confronts us.

Little is known about the history of Egypt under the first three dynasties (*ca.* 3100–2650 B.C.). During this period Mesopotamian influence continued to play some part in quickening Egyptian culture. A number of works of art from the period reproduce Sumerian motifs in unmistakable fashion; and improvements in metallurgy, as well as the introduction of the potter's wheel and of mud-brick monumental architecture, have also been traced to Mesopotamian influences. Perhaps the idea of symbolizing speech in writing was imported from the same source. The signs of Egyptian hieroglyphic bear no relationship to Mesopotamian cuneiform and were certainly devised independently; but a number of instances in recent times show that inventive individuals may create a system of writing *de novo* as a result of contact with literate peoples. Egyptian writing was already in existence at the beginning of the dynastic period; yet there are practically no traces of any prior development. It is therefore possible that the hieroglyphic script was invented all at once under the stimulus of contact with Mesopotamian literacy.[9]

In any case, the period of tutelage was short. Egypt differed from Mesopotamia in having easy access to fine building stone along the desert scarp which bordered the length of the Nile Valley; and before long, Egyptian architects learned to exploit the possibilities of stone construction. The first stone-built tomb was built for one of the last kings of the Third Dynasty (*ca*. 2700 B.C.). Thereafter, in an amazingly short period of time, the Egyptians mastered the mason's skills, until their architecture far surpassed Mesopotamian exemplars. The largest of the great pyramids was built only about a century and a half after the completion of the earliest known stone-built tomb; and the accuracy and refinement of detail in its construction, not to speak of its sheer size, were never exceeded in later times.[10]

Rapid mastery of the techniques of building with stone was only one manifestation of a general upsurge; for during the same critical centuries, nearly all aspects of Egyptian culture attained their mature style. This is most easily appreciated in sculpture and wall painting, two arts closely associated with stonemasonry.

In the sphere of religion, however, no universally accepted and enduring definition of either belief or ritual proved possible. Local tradition was refractory and could not be reformulated in a coherent way, even after the

---

[9] Cf. Ignace J. Gelb, *A Study of Writing* (Chicago: University of Chicago Press, 1952), pp. 72–81, 206–10, 214–15. Deliberate invention of a script unrelated to anything that has gone before appears to be not uncommon when a people—or rather a reflective individual—with no literate tradition comes into contact with literate culture. Several examples of such invention in the nineteenth and twentieth centuries are known to have occurred among Amerindians, and also among certain tribes in Africa and Siberia. Cf. David Diringer, *The Alphabet: A Key to the History of Mankind* (New York: Philosophical Library, 1948), pp. 150–57, for particulars.

[10] Somers Clarke and R. Engelbach, *Ancient Egyptian Masonry* (Oxford: Oxford University Press, 1930), pp. 5–11 and *passim*. Profound contrasts in the technology of stone and brick construction practically forced the Egyptians to free themselves from dependence on Mesopotamian architectural examples as soon as the decision to build in stone had been taken. Mud bricks must be made small in size to allow uniform air drying, whereas the vast labor of trimming stone to regular shapes makes it advantageous to build of blocks as large as can be moved. (The larger the block, the smaller its surface area in proportion to its volume, and therefore the less stonecutting required to achieve a given height of wall.) Other consequences followed from this size difference. Geometric decorative patterns, formed by exposing various faces of the bricks, were a main feature of Mesopotamian structures; but this was impossible when using vast stone blocks of irregular sizes. Compensatory possibilities opened, e.g., column and lintel construction, of which mud-brick architecture was not capable.

KHAFRE, LORD OF UPPER AND LOWER EGYPT

This seated diorite statue from Khafre's funerary temple in Giza shows the divine king both in his human form and as Falcon Horus. The sculptor overcame the inherent awkwardness of such an artistic undertaking magnificently, for the falcon's protecting wings bind the two figures indissolubly together; and the sublime severity of the Pharaoh's human face is reaffirmed by the aloof benevolence of the falcon's expression. Such sculpture symbolized, and in symbolizing perhaps helped also to strengthen and define, the all-important role of the god-king in ancient Egypt. This skilled and stylistically perfect work was executed under the Fourth Dynasty (2650–2500 B.C.), when the resources of all Egypt were drafted for the construction of the great pyramids. (Khafre's pyramid is exceeded in size only by that of his immediate predecessor, known to Herodotus as Cheops and to Egyptologists as Khufu.)

unification of the land under a single god-king had brought centralizing pressures to bear upon the primitive diversity of cult and theology. Yet an attempt to reconcile practice with logic seemed imperative, particularly in view of the Pharaoh's claim to rank as a divinity. The reigning monarch at first found his place among the gods of the land by assuming the title of Horus, falcon god of the sky, while identifying his royal (and presumptively immortal) predecessors with Osiris, ruler of the abode of the dead. Horus and Osiris may originally have stemmed from different parts of Egypt. Certainly their characteristics suggest that the one harked back to a nomadic and comparatively warlike past, while the other embodied a distinctly agricultural concern with the seasons and the renewal of vegetable life.[11] The identification of the reigning king with Horus, and of his predecessors on the throne with Osiris, was never surrendered in Egyptian history; but with the Fifth Dynasty (2500–2350 B.C.), the Pharaoh began also to term himself son of Re, god of the sun. This idea undoubtedly reflected the influence of the priesthood of the temple of Heliopolis; and indeed an old tradition declares that the Fifth Dynasty was founded by priests of Re from that temple.

To modern minds, jumbling son of Osiris, son of Re, and Falcon Horus into an incompatible trinity, and then identifying the resulting multiform divinity with the Pharaoh's person, is hard to comprehend; yet this sort of confusion pervaded all Egyptian religion. Doubtless most Egyptians felt no inconsistency in adhering to traditional and time-honored religious formulae and observances.[12] But in the years when Egyptian culture was struggling toward its historic definition, some reflective minds were troubled by the local discrepancies of myth and ritual and strove to construct speculative theological systems reconciling differences and explaining relationships among the various gods in a logically more satisfactory fashion.

Three such systems, emanating from powerful and important temples, are known to modern scholars, though some of the pertinent records are fragmentary. All three theologies attempted to establish lines of descent among the gods, starting from a first creator through successive divine pairs.[13] Priests of Ptah at Memphis probably originated the most interesting and most sophisticated of these attempts. At any rate, the "Memphite theology" assigned to the god Ptah the role of creator, and in general bears clear traces of propaganda on his behalf. The text describes Ptah's act of creation as a matter of conception in his heart, followed by an utterance of his lips. By these acts, he

[11] Cf. Joachim Spiegel, *Das Werden der altägyptischen Hochkultur* (Heidelberg: F. H. Kerle Verlag, 1953), pp. 87–96.

[12] Cf. Henri Frankfort's efforts to defend the consistency and unity of Egyptian religion as a manifestation of "mythopoetic thought" which saw "a multiplicity of approaches" to the manifestations of divine power, in his book, *Ancient Egyptian Religion* (New York: Columbia University Press, 1948), pp. 16–22 and *passim*. See also his chapters in Frankfort *et al.*, *Before Philosophy* (Harmondsworth: Penguin Books, 1941).

[13] Adolf Erman, *Die Religion der Ägypter* (Berlin and Leipzig: Walter de Gruyter & Co., 1934), pp. 88–96, offers a straightforward paraphrase; for more interpretive treatments, see John A. Wilson in *Before Philosophy*, pp. 59–70; Henri Frankfort, *Kingship and the Gods* (Chicago: University of Chicago Press, 1948), pp. 24–35; Hermann Junker, *Pyramidenzeit: Das Wesen der altägyptischen Religion* (Einsiedeln: Benziger Verlag, 1949).

was credited with creating not only the physical world but also the community of gods and men and the principles of social intercourse among mankind. Ptah's activity seems to have been modeled on the actual role of the Pharaoh in human affairs. After all, thoughts conceived and words uttered by the god-king summoned pyramids into being, endowed his faithful servants with immortal life, and threw barbarians into confusion.

Yet systematic efforts to rationalize Egyptian religious traditions did not prevail. Even though priests of Ptah in the royal capital of Memphis might exalt their god above all others, there were other priests devoted to other gods in other shrines, whose piety impelled them to resist any departure from local sacred tradition. In the end, therefore, the Egyptians chose the easier path of accepting the established variety of religious expression, rather than trying to remodel it. Official religion calmly juxtaposed doctrines that are logically quite incompatible; and well-worn usage was modified only when some new dynasty, loyal to its own gods and cults, rose to power. Thus when the rulers of Thebes in Upper Egypt fastened their control upon the land, a local Theban deity, Amon, came to power with them, and soon, through association with the sun god, became Amon-Re. But the older great gods were not thereby displaced: the Pharaoh continued to style himself Horus; Osiris still conferred immortality upon the dead in competition with Re; and all the variety of local usage persisted, even when partially disguised by the nominal assimilation of local deities to one or another of the high gods honored by the royal government.

The survival of religious multiplicity can only be understood as a consequence of the survival of local shrines and priesthoods, each enjoying at least a modicum of independence of the royal government. Certain documents suggest that, as time went on, the power of some of these priesthoods increased at the expense of the central government.[14] However, it was not so much the temple priesthoods as insubordinate officials who undermined and eventually destroyed the authority of the god-king.

The wonder is not that insubordination occurred but that it was so long delayed. When the Old Kingdom was at its height, under the Fourth and Fifth Dynasties (2650–2350 B.C.), a relatively small number of officials seems to have administered all of Egypt. Many of them were relatives of the Pharaoh; and all of them, as members of the god-king's household, were directly dependent upon the royal good pleasure for all the honors and perquisites which they could ever hope to enjoy, both in this life and in the next. But as time went on, the number of officials increased, and the mere growth of numbers must have weakened the psychological ties between the god-king and his servants. How could a petty official stationed far from court hope confidently for eternal life as a member of the royal retinue if the god knew him not? Perhaps even more significant, offices tended to become hereditary. This, of course, blocked the advancement of men of talent and ambition and sustained inefficient heirs in high office. As son succeeded father in outlying

[14] John A. Wilson, *The Burden of Egypt*, pp. 98–99.

districts, ties to local persons, places, and divinities must have grown stronger, until they vitiated the old automatic obedience.

As a result, the administrative machine gradually fell apart. Disintegration began under the Sixth Dynasty (2350–2200 B.C.); and soon thereafter, regional magnates and princelings assumed sovereign powers, several of them simultaneously claiming supreme royal authority without being able to enforce it upon their rivals.

This so-called First Intermediate Period (2200–2050 B.C.) was accompanied by artistic degeneration. The scale of monumental building was drastically reduced, while crudities of style and technique, with clearly perceptible local variations, manifested themselves.[15] All this is understandable in view of the fact that high art had earlier been a product of the royal household. In the sphere of thought and letters, however, this period of social distress provoked a notable enlargement of the Egyptian tradition. Scribes, whose place in the social hierarchy had been seriously disturbed by the decay of orderly government, took pen in hand to protest and deplore what had happened to the land of Egypt. Some surviving literary works from this period betray blank despair; others proclaim a crass hedonism; and still others seek a basis for restoration of social order by insisting upon the necessity of personal righteousness.[16]

The ethical ideals expressed by authors of this third group have sometimes excited the admiration of modern scholars;[17] but the moral principles propounded so impressively by these indignant scribes were never built into the religious system of Egypt. As the social disorder which provoked the literary outburst again receded, the ideals proclaimed in time of troubles faded away, leaving little enduring mark upon Egyptian civilization.[18] The elemental conservatism of the Egyptian religious establishment, which had previously defeated rationalizing efforts like those embodied in the Memphite theology, submerged this sort of literary reinterpretation of the basis of human life without even feeling the impact. In one respect only did the breakdown of the Old Kingdom work permanent alteration in religion: henceforth, the hope of immortality no longer depended entirely on association with the god-king, but lay open to lesser persons if the proper tombs, spells, and paraphernalia were provided.

Egyptian literature has a distinctly this-worldly cast.[19] Literary composi-

---

[15] Cf. William C. Hayes, *The Scepter of Egypt*, Part I: *From the Earliest Times to the End of the Middle Kingdom* (New York: Harper & Bros., 1953), pp. 135–48.

[16] Translations of this literature may be found in Adolf Erman, *The Literature of the Ancient Egyptians*, Aylward M. Blackman (trans.) (London: Methuen & Co., 1927), pp. 75–108.

[17] Cf. James Henry Breasted, *The Dawn of Conscience* (New York and London: Scribner's Sons, 1935), pp. 207 ff. Other scholars have read social revolution and class war into the same texts, without withdrawing their admiration: cf. Joachim Spiegel, *Soziale und weltanschauliche Reformbewegungen im alten Ägypten* (Heidelberg: F. H. Kerle Verlag, 1950), pp. 7–56.

[18] John A. Wilson, *The Burden of Egypt*, p. 124.

[19] The sacred traditions of Egypt were not written down. Hints of myth cycles exist in surviving texts; but the Greek, Plutarch, who lived in the second century A.D. when Egyptian civilization was already a thing of the past, appears to have been the first to record a connected narrative of one such myth—the story of Osiris, Isis, and Horus. Moderns know the story solely through Plutarch—a devi-

tion was the work of scribes employed in secular or semisecular tasks; and it was the world of men that attracted their attention. Thus rules of conduct, characteristically put into the mouths of high state officials, occupy a prominent place in the literature of the Old Kingdom. These rules were designed to instruct the young in the art of getting ahead by pleasing superiors and by behaving correctly toward inferiors. Fearing the gods in a Mesopotamian spirit simply did not enter the picture. Even in the time of troubles which followed the decay of the Old Kingdom, Egyptian scribes held insubordinate and overweening men, not the gods, responsible for disaster and disorder.

The worldliness of Egyptian literature no doubt indicates a fundamental contrast between the Mesopotamian and the Egyptian mental outlook in ancient times. The difference is partly attributable to Egypt's relative security, both from foreign attack and from natural disaster.[20] In a country where the gods were so dependable, where the river flood came regularly, and where no hostile barbarians appeared suddenly over the horizon, learned scribes could afford to ignore the gods, save on appointed ritual occasions. Spared undue concern for survival in this world, religious anxiety concentrated upon the attainment of immortality in the next; and literary composition might with a clear conscience be directed to merely mundane matters. Not so in Mesopotamia, where natural or military disaster was an ever-present threat, and where the gods were therefore conceived as wilfully capricious, by turn unpredictably dangerous or magnificently beneficent, but never negligible.

The gap which thus opened in Egypt between written literature and orally transmitted theological myth allowed Egyptian scribes much greater freedom than that which their Mesopotamian counterparts enjoyed. Hence, Egyptian literature antedated the Mesopotamian, and very early in its career gave rise to some thoroughly secular genres—stories, proverbs, dialogues, and love songs—which had little or no known parallel in Mesopotamia.[21]

No doubt the disorder which followed the breakup of the Old Kingdom brought much suffering to the people of Egypt; and certainly the ideal of a united land, obedient to a god-king, was never erased. At length, about the middle of the twenty-first century B.C., the local lord of Thebes in southern Egypt gained military ascendancy and united the country once more, thus inaugurating the so-called Middle Kingdom (2050–1800 B.C.).[22] This new dynasty (the Twelfth) restored something resembling the centralization of

---

ous and dubious source indeed for an element of Egyptian religion that is often assumed to have been central to the piety of the entire civilization. Mesopotamians, for their part, reduced their religious lore to writing only when the Sumerian language became a learned tongue whose meanings had to be explained. No comparable crisis of transmission ever gave Egyptian priests cause to record their sacred secrets.

[20] John A. Wilson, *The Burden of Egypt*, pp. 12–13.

[21] Cf. T. Eric Peet, *A Comparative Study of the Literatures of Egypt, Palestine and Mesopotamia* (London: Oxford University Press, 1931), p. 17 and *passim*.

[22] The Theban conquest paralleled the original conquest by Menes, in the sense that both came from the south and from relatively backward frontier areas. The two unifications illustrate the advantages of a marcher lord in a struggle for power among petty civilized states. Cf. the remarks above in connection with Sargon of Akkad.

the Old Kingdom; but the resemblance masked a real difference. Local magnates and priesthoods were not displaced. Their power remained, constituting an intermediary link between officials of the royal household and the peasants on the land. The central authority was less exalted, less absolute. The labor force of all Egypt was no longer drafted to build a tomb for the king; nor did official doctrine pretend that immortality could be achieved only by association with the divine king in afterlife.[23] It is symptomatic of the changed basis of Egyptian life that art styles continued to show minor but perceptible regional differentiation within the canon inherited from the Old Kingdom.[24] Yet some of the energetic kings of the Twelfth Dynasty did make their power supreme in all Egypt, although weaker men easily let the reins of authority slip.

By about 1800 B.C., Egypt had again lost political cohesion. The Egyptians therefore failed to present effective opposition to a new and strange phenomenon in their historical experience: foreign invasion in force. Beginning about 1730 B.C., a people known as Hyksos crossed the desert of Sinai and filtered into Egypt, easily conquering the northern portions of the country, and establishing an alien rule which lasted until about 1570 B.C.

The Hyksos became a stench in Egyptian nostrils. The priests and nobles of Egypt, long accustomed to consider themselves vastly superior to all other peoples, found themselves subjected to despised Asiatic barbarians, who desecrated their temples and set their most cherished traditions at naught. This experience worked a fundamental change in the Egyptian mentality. Even after a new king had come from the south to liberate the Two Lands from the hated Hyksos, the Egyptians no longer felt secure behind their desert barriers. They therefore brought their long isolation from the rest of the world to an end, and for the next thousand years joined as a great imperial state in the complex power struggles of the Middle East. With the expulsion of the Hyksos, therefore, the Egyptian rulers entered upon a cosmopolitan career in direct contact with and competition against the other great Middle Eastern river valley civilization, the Mesopotamian. We shall leave the Egyptians here, at the point where their unique style of life was about to enter a larger theater of action.

In sum: in certain respects the Egyptian achievement of the third millennium B.C. surpassed anything known elsewhere. Egyptian art and architecture strike modern sensibility far more powerfully than anything known from Mesopotamia. The ethical ideas advanced in certain literary works also excite a special resonance in modern minds.[25] Finally, we cannot but admire the precocious political unity of the Old Kingdom, so perfectly symbolized by the solidity, simplicity, and monumentality of the great pyramids.

Yet in another sense, Egypt fell behind the Mesopotamian achievement. Nothing like the Mesopotamian "great society" emerged in the Nile Valley.

[23] John A. Wilson, *The Burden of Egypt*, pp. 112–37.

[24] William C. Hayes, *The Scepter of Egypt*, Part I, p. 154.

[25] From a literary standpoint, however—judging entirely from available translations—it seems to me that the *Epic of Gilgamesh* surpasses anything surviving from Egypt.

SEAL IMPRESSIONS FROM THE INDUS CIVILIZATION

Linkage between Mesopotamia and the Indus civilization is demonstrated by the first two of these seal impressions, for the seal on the left was discovered in the ruins of the Sumerian seaport of Ur, whereas the second came from Mohenjo-daro, one of the twin Indus capitals, where many others of roughly similar style were also discovered. Clearly, the former had been brought to Ur from the Indus area, perhaps by some merchant. The third seal impression has a different interest. The three-faced figure, sitting cross-legged and surrounded by a tiger, elephants, and other wild beasts, precisely matches the pose later associated with the Hindu god Shiva in his role as Parupati, Lord of Beasts. Such continuity effectively demonstrates a survival of elements from the Indus culture in later Hinduism. Modern scholars cannot read the writing on these seals.

The extreme polarity between the god-king and his household on the one hand, and the rural villager on the other, remained characteristic even of the Middle Kingdom; and the tenuous intermediary links—local magnates and temple priesthoods—could not give to Egyptian society the inner resilience, variety, and capacity for growth that was latent in the Mesopotamian structure. Egypt lacked the structural supports for high kingship which political theory, written law, and a wealthy merchant class gave to Mesopotamia. Instead, the whole weight of the government—its scribes, masons, architects, artists, officials, and priests—rested directly upon the backs of a submissive peasantry. Little scope for further development could be found within such a society; and even the extended contact with foreigners which the New Kingdom brought in its train did not in the end lead the Egyptians to do more than reaffirm the validity of old ideas and to reject alien influence as completely as possible. Despite all the foreign entanglements of political empire, the Egyptians effectively maintained their spiritual isolation throughout ancient times. Until after their incorporation in the Roman Empire, they remained a people apart, peculiar unto themselves, preservers of an age-old tradition, makers of nothing new.

2. THE INDUS CIVILIZATION

The civilization of Egypt bore significant likeness to another civilization which arose at about the same time in India. Two great cities and numerous smaller towns and villages flourished on the banks of the Indus River and its tributaries between about 2500 and 1500 B.C. The inhabitants of these settlements knew the art of writing and the use of copper and bronze; they built monumental structures of burnt brick, and carved statues and seals in a distinctive style. In short, the material side of their civilization was equivalent to that of contemporary Mesopotamia or Egypt. But because of inadequate evidence, particularity the inability of modern scholars to read the Indus script, very little is known of the non-material aspects of this civilization, and nothing at all of its historical development.

The great cities of Mohenjo-daro and Harappa appear to us full-blown, with no traces of a gradual development from more primitive beginnings. Ground water has so far prevented archeologists from uncovering the lower levels of these sites; and the strata already excavated, which must represent the debris of many centuries, seem only to show decadence from the initial achievement.[26] The stratification of lesser sites also fails to reveal clear signs of development from primitive beginnings toward the full panoply of systematic city planning evidenced at Harappa and Mohenjo-daro.[27] Only the discovery in Mesopotamia of a few Indian seals in contexts that permit rough

[26] Stuart W. Piggott, *Prehistoric India to 1000 B.C.* (Harmondsworth: Penguin Books, 1950), pp. 167, 200–201.

[27] R. E. M. Wheeler, *The Indus Civilization: The Cambridge History of India*, Supplementary Volume (Cambridge: Cambridge University Press, 1953), pp. 8–14.

dating allows scholars to assign 2500–1500 B.C. as an approximate time span for this Indus civilization.[28]

The existence of trade relations between Mesopotamia and the Indus Valley from about 2500 B.C. (and probably several hundred years earlier) suggests that the Sumerians may have played a role in the earliest stages of Indus civilization analogous to the one they played in Egypt. Seaborne contact with Sumer may have provided ready-made models and ideas which the Indus peoples could adapt to the peculiarities of their local cultural tradition.[29] If so, the rise of Indus civilization was probably rapid—a matter of a few centuries at most.

The extraordinarily systematic layouts of Mohenjo-daro and Harappa justify other inferences. Both cities were built on a checkerboard pattern.[30] On the western edge of each was an elevated citadel, artificially raised above the plain. Both cities also possessed capacious granaries, regularly constructed on a fixed plan, as well as geometrically laid-out quarters presumably designed to house workmen. All this suggests a highly centralized administration, commanding large tribute in grain, and controlling labor gangs on a scale sufficient to build whole cities. It suggests, too, that the cities were laid out according to a master plan on previously unencumbered sites. Mohenjo-daro and Harappa were therefore probably constructed as twin capitals of an already consolidated and at least semicivilized state.[31]

Further, the remarkable uniformity of the remains suggests that the political structure of Indus civilization became highly centralized early in its history. The two capitals lay about 350 miles apart; and lesser towns have been found separated by as much as a thousand miles. The sixty-odd sites at which traces of this civilization have so far been observed lie either in the flood plain of the Indus and its tributaries or along the coast of the Arabian Sea as far south as the mouth of the Narbada River. Yet throughout this comparatively vast area,[32] no regional or local stylistic variations appear among the known archeological assemblages. Precocious political unification, analogous to that of Egypt, alone explains such uniformity.

[28] The discovery of some seals in Mohenjo-daro resembling types current in Mesopotamia about 3000 B.C. leads some scholars to argue for an earlier dating of the Indus remains. Cf. Heinz Mode, *Die indischen Frühkulturen und ihre Beziehungen zum Westen* (Basel: Benno Schwabe & Co., 1944), pp. 127–28. It is, however, hard to believe that such elaborate cities as those of the Indus region could have arisen so early. Objects such as the seals in question might have survived in active use for several centuries as valued curiosities; or they might have come to Mohenjo-daro from some area marginal to Mesopotamia, where old styles persisted later than in the active culture center itself.

[29] Heinz Mode, *Die indischen Frühkulturen*, pp. 86–87, 128–38; R. E. M. Wheeler, *Early India and Pakistan to Ashoka* (London: Thames & Hudson, 1959), pp. 100–104.

[30] A large part of the Harappa site was plundered in the nineteenth century to provide ballast for railways. Hence the layout of the city is not entirely clear, though it seems to match closely that of Mohenjo-daro.

[31] Mesopotamian cities, by contrast, had crooked and irregular streets and buildings. Cf. the contrast between the geometric layouts of Washington, D.C., Canberra, or Brazilia and the crooked irregularities of London, Paris, Lisbon.

[32] The civilized portion of Egypt stretched no more than 600 miles along the Nile; and the Mesopotamian flood plain, though broader, was somewhat less extended. Cf. R. E. M. Wheeler, *The Indus Civilization*, pp. 2–3.

How such a far-flung state may have been organized and held together is impossible to say. During the second half of the third millennium, when the Indus civilization was in full flower, its cities seem to have been constructed with small concern for security against military attack. City walls have not been discovered, while remains of weapons and armor are scarce, and lack some of the forms familiar in contemporary Mesopotamia.[33] Hence not a military empire, like Sargon's, but a priestly state, like the Egyptian Old Kingdom, seems the likely political pattern.

Except for the fairly numerous engraved seals, which sometimes rival the best Mesopotamian examples, artistic remains from Indus sites are pitifully scant. Moreover, the few objects which have been discovered present puzzling stylistic discrepancies.[34] Similar uncertainty surrounds Indus religion. Female figurines, often very crude and sometimes displaying exaggerated sexual traits, presumably attest fertility rites and the worship of some form of "Great Mother" goddess. Tree and phallus cults point in the same direction. But without access to the Indus script, it is not possible to reconstruct the mythology that gave meaning to the scattered images and symbols which survive.

Signs are not wanting that the vitality and social discipline of Indus civilization had seriously declined before the two capital cities were finally destroyed. At Mohenjo-daro, for instance, destructive flooding recurrently made it necessary to rebuild the whole town. Old streets and buildings were at first faithfully reconstructed in the old patterns; but in the last period of the city's life, rebuilt walls no longer observed the earlier street boundaries in every case; and smaller, jerry-built structures appeared where monumental buildings had stood before. Clearly, the social discipline which originally dictated and so long sustained the geometric precision of the city's ground plan had somehow weakened.

Causes for such decay can only be surmised. Perhaps desiccation or deforestation made floods more destructive and agriculture less productive than before.[35] But in the light of what we know about the decay of the Old Kingdom of Egypt, it is tempting to attribute the disruption of the Indus social order to internal political changes. If for any reason the hold of the central government upon the tributary population of the Indus plain relaxed, then the capital cities must immediately have suffered impoverishment and disorganization such as that evidenced at Mohenjo-daro.

Incursions from the hill country to the north and west may have played

[33] E.g., helmets and shields, which were standard equipment in Mesopotamian warfare from very early in the third millennium, have not been found. Cf. R. E. M. Wheeler, *The Indus Civilization*, pp. 52–56.

[34] Cf. D. H. Gordon, *The Pre-historic Background of Indian Culture* (Bombay: N. M. Tripathi, Ltd., 1958), p. 69. Even if, with Gordon, one rejects the authenticity of two stone torsos from Harappa and attributes them to much later Buddhist work that somehow got buried in deeper strata, there remains a rather startling contrast between stolid "portrait" heads and the spindly grace of a bronze dancing girl found at Mohenjo-daro.

[35] Cf. the cautious remarks in R. E. M. Wheeler, *The Indus Civilization*, p. 91.

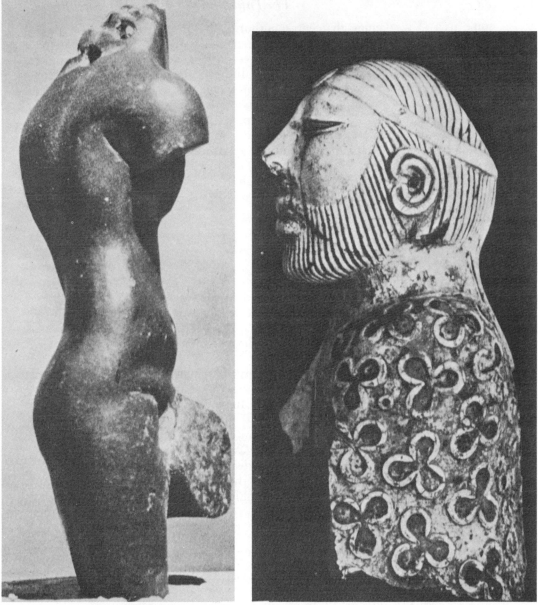

National Museum of India, New Delhi.

INDUS STATUETTES

The naked torso on the left and the crude, yet haughty figure on the right were found at Harappa and Mohenjo-daro respectively. No one would be likely to think they stemmed from the same art tradition, and some scholars have suggested that the torso may be an intrusion from much later Buddhist times. The imperfect records kept by the excavators make confirmation of this hypothesis and of the alternative view that the two figures may represent an archaic and fully developed phase of Indus sculpture equally impossible. The lithe grace of the one and the hauteur of the other remain to haunt and puzzle students of the Indus culture.

some part in weakening the central authority.[36] But the final *coup de grâce* probably came when warlike barbarians, speaking an Indo-European tongue ancestral to Sanskrit and calling themselves Aryans, descended from the hills to ravage and burn their way across the Indus Valley. With true barbarian fury, they reduced the Indus cities to smoking piles of rubble.

Harappa and Mohenjo-daro never recovered. The social order which had once sustained the life of those twin capitals disintegrated; and the site of Mohenjo-daro was subsequently occupied only by a handful of alien squatters. Yet while the capital cities and the apparatus of government were destroyed so utterly that all memory of the existence of Indus civilization vanished, humble villages survived. Presumably the continuities of village life transmitted to later generations the motifs of Indus religiosity which were to reappear so strikingly in later Hinduism.

*   *   *

It is worth asking why Indus civilization disintegrated under barbarian attack, whereas the civilizations of Mesopotamia and Egypt survived and eventually reasserted themselves when exposed to similar assault. Perhaps barbarian numbers were greater and the attack wilder and more ruthless in India than in Egypt or Mesopotamia. Or perhaps the Indus civilization was more fragile, without deep roots among the villagers subjected to the control of a ruling minority.

Existing information does not justify any judgment between these or other hypotheses. Yet a provocative hint may be found in the *Rig Veda*,[37] some elements of which—e.g., descriptions of how the war god Indra assaulted walled fortresses and ruthlessly destroyed his dark-skinned enemies—probably descend from the period of the Aryan conquest.[38] Various passages may be interpreted as showing that the early Aryans viewed the religious practices of the Indus peoples with a strong distaste, rising to holy horror at explicitly sexual sacred rites.[39] Moreover, as the *Rig Veda* itself makes clear, the invading Aryans possessed a relatively sophisticated theology and well-organized priesthood, both of which seem to have taken shape under the influence of contact with Sumerian and Babylonian religious ideas.[40]

[36] Stuart Piggott, *Prehistoric India*, pp. 208–21, points out an increase during the last phases of Indus life in cultural traits stemming from Baluchistan.

[37] Scholars agree that the *Rig Veda* incorporates the oldest surviving materials of Sanskrit literature.

[38] R. C. Majumdar (ed.), *The History and Culture of the Indian People: The Vedic Age* (London: Allen & Unwin, Ltd., 1951), pp. 225–28, 360.

[39] The interpretation of the relevant passages of the *Rig Veda* is disputed. Some Indian scholars believe that the phrases in question only condemn excessive lust and do not attack the customs of the pre-Aryan population. Cf. R. C. Majumdar, *History and Culture of the Indian People: The Vedic Age*, p. 187.

[40] Cf. V. Gordon Childe, *The Aryans: A Study of Indo-European Origins* (New York: Alfred A. Knopf, Inc., 1926), I, 80–81; Louis Renou and Jean Filliozat, *L'Inde classique: Manuel des études indiennes* (Paris: Payot, 1947), p. 516; Sir Charles Eliot, *Hinduism and Buddhism: An Historical Sketch* (London: Edward Arnold & Co., 1921), I, 60–61; James Hope Moulton, *Early Religious Poetry of Persia* (Cambridge: Cambridge University Press, 1911), pp. 37, 44–45. Merchants and metalworkers traveling from the mountain zone of the Middle East northward into the steppes certainly taught the

It is therefore likely that the Aryan invasion involved a collision between two rival religious system and priesthoods. Perhaps the conquerors set out systematically and with religious zeal to erase all traces of the hateful religion of their enemies. But if ancient Indus society was in fact priest-ruled, to destroy the priesthood was to destroy the social managers who had built and maintained the civilization. Furthermore, if the Indus society, like that of Egypt in the time of the Old Kingdom, lacked any mediate social stratum between the priest-kings in their magnificent citadels and a rudely egalitarian village peasantry, then the destruction of the priestly colleges would mean the abrupt evaporation of the Indus civilization, with no possibility of its revival. Only those fragmentary aspects of the old culture which were accessible to village use and understanding could then survive; and this, to all appearance, was exactly what did occur.[41]

C. THE TRANSPLANTATION OF CIVILIZATION TO RAIN-WATERED LANDS: ASIA MINOR AND CRETE

1. INTRODUCTORY

At the beginning of the third millennium B.C., the social organization and technical equipment available to Middle Eastern agriculturalists were still so primitive that civilized societies could arise only on irrigable land. By the close of the millennium this was no longer true, for shortly before 2000 B.C. a considerable number of stylistically distinct, though interrelated civilizations began to establish themselves beyond the narrow territorial limits of alluvial flood plains. This breakthrough allowed the whole scale of civilized development to multiply several times over. Any region with fairly good agricultural land now became a potential seat of civilized life; and the further expansion of civilized society became a matter of ebb and flow across broad,

---

primitive Indo-Europeans a great deal—e.g., the Indo-Europeans' term for copper derived from the Sumerian name for that metal. Religious as well as material lessons must also have been learned from representatives of what was, after all, a more sophisticated culture than that of the steppes, for resemblances between Indo-European and Mesopotamian pantheons are too great to be accidental. Cf. the manner in which Mohammed borrowed from Judaeo-Christian religious ideas, which he probably had encountered through mercantile contacts in his youth.

[41] Cf. the fate of the Amerindian civilizations when native priests and chieftains had been suppressed or converted by Spanish soldiers and Christian missionaries.

A similar destruction might have overtaken Egyptian civilization if the Nile Valley had been overrun by religiously hostile barbarians in the days when the Pharaoh's household constituted the sole bearer of the higher manifestations of Egyptian culture. But by the time the Hyksos did in fact overrun Egypt, subjecting priests and temples to barbarous desecration, a slender but vital intermediate social stratum, the scribes and "nobles" (*i.e.*, local magnates and landowners), shared with the royal household and the priestly colleges the tasks of sustaining Egyptian cultural traditions. These scribes and magnates survived under the Hyksos because the latter required their services as tax collectors and village administrators. But their survival implied the survival of ancient Egyptian cultural traditions, as was proven when a local magnate, the lord of Thebes, led a successful revolt against the Hyksos and restored the old patterns of Egyptian civilization. Cf. also the repeated emergence of Chinese culture from periods of barbarian conquest and the Russian cultural revival under the Mongols.

If we assume, therefore, that the Indus society lagged a little behind Egypt, and continued to be organized along lines analogous to those of the Egyptian Old Kingdom until the time of the Aryan invasion, the failure of the high tradition of Indus culture to survive becomes readily intelligible.

continuous land areas, rather than a leap-frog movement from river valley to river valley, as had at first been the case.

How did this transition from irrigated to non-irrigated land occur?

Only by giving free rein to the imagination can even a general answer to this question be supplied. As the common starting point for civilized life, we must assume a more or less egalitarian agricultural society grouped into autonomous village communities. With the spread of the plow, village agriculturalists became able to raise more food than they themselves required, even on land watered only by rain. Fallowing, the effectiveness of which depended on keeping weeds down by frequent plowings, simultaneously allowed permanent use of particular fields, and made the old, semi-migratory style of tillage obsolete. Farmers thus found themselves tied down to a single locality as never before. Simple villagers, if left to their own devices, quickly absorbed any food surplus that might result from such improvements in farming technique by increasing their numbers, until a denser population established a new equilibrium[42] with the enlarged food supply. Comparatively dense rural settlement could thus develop without giving rise to any great differentiation of social classes or to any important change in manner of life.[43]

But village communities living within range of the river valley civilizations were not left to their own devices. War and trade combined to bring the villagers into contact with the way of life of the flood plains; while simultaneously, pastoral peoples from the margins of the agricultural world constantly harassed and sometimes conquered them. Thus caught between hammer and anvil, the village communities of the ancient Middle East could not pursue the even tenor of their ways, but during the third millennium B.C. found themselves harshly subordinated to alien masters. It was this that made civilization contagious in rain-watered lands. Crude and often extreme social differentiation between landlord and peasant allowed landlords to accumulate wealth on a scale sufficient, under propitious circumstances, to maintain a corps of specialists able to generate or sustain an independent style of civilized life.

It is easy to see how pastoral conquest might lead to this result. The fighting discipline inherent in pastoral life gave herdsmen a tremendous military advantage against dispersed and peaceable farmers. Fighting men, accustomed to a parasitical dependence upon flocks and herds, found it easy and vastly advantageous to transfer their parasitism to humans, whenever they could find communities rich enough to survive their demands and defenseless enough to submit to them. Such communities came into existence beyond the limits of irrigation only after plow cultivation had stabilized and enlarged agricultural production on rain-watered lands. The emergence of loosely consolidated

---

[42] *I.e.*, until land shortages replaced earlier technical limitations upon productivity as the prime limit upon food supply.

[43] This was the case, for example, in early Latium, where the volcanic soil was particularly fertile. Cf. Tenney Frank, *An Economic History of Rome* (2d rev. ed.; Baltimore, Md.: Johns Hopkins Press, 1927), pp. 1–12.

states governed by warlike landowning aristocracies thus went hand in hand with the spread of the plow.[44]

Since civilized conquerors were less inclined than pastoralists to settle among remote agricultural populations, their invasions had a correspondingly less profound effect upon the physiognomy of local village life. Yet in either case, a class of 'local magnates, which laid claim to part of the villagers' produce, was created or consolidated. Military conquest issuing from the flood plains scarcely antedated the career of Sargon (*ca.* 2350 B.C.). Nonetheless, Sargon's armies probably reached the Mediterranean, and perhaps the Black Sea, traversed the passes of the Zagros Mountains to the east, and penetrated far up the Tigris Valley.[45] Wherever he went, the great king undoubtedly demanded tribute in kind and sent out agents to collect whatever goods the region might afford. Whoever organized the labor necessary to comply with Sargon's orders found himself in a position to extend and consolidate what might be called a "proto-industrial" form of social differentiation among the villagers. More important, the villagers became peasants, in the sense that their social universe was extended to embrace an imperfect participation in the great civilized world.[46]

The impact of trade upon village communities was more complex and must have varied considerably from case to case. Merchants unsupported by military power could only offer inducements for the production of goods they desired. The members of an autonomous, tight-knit village community may at first have resisted the blandishments of fine cloth and trinkets, preferring life as it had always been to working for strangers. But other villages, where good land was becoming short, may gladly have sent men to fell trees or dig ores in exchange for the merchants' goods. By enlarging local trade relations, long-distance merchants gradually made possible the establishment of peasant populations in hilly regions where local food supplies were inadequate, but where timber and ores, sheepskins and wool might be produced. Thus arose a differentiation between hill and plain, between villages of food deficit and those producing a surplus, which has remained fundamental to the life of the Middle Eastern and Mediterranean lands down to the present day.

As hill populations became dependent upon plains dwellers for some part of their food supply, a new disturbing force arose on the fringes of the agricultural world. Even distant political disorders might upset the complex circulation of goods upon which the very livelihood of the hillsmen depended. Whenever trade was disrupted, they were impelled to seize by force what they could no longer secure by exchange. If the plains communities were

[44] It is conceivable, indeed, that the spread of the plow was accelerated by aristocratic entrepreneurship, since farmers so equipped became much more valuable to their masters. I know of no evidence supporting this hypothesis, however.

[45] Great uncertainty prevails concerning the real extent of Sargon's conquests. Cf. Sidney Smith, *Early History of Assyria to 1000 B.C.* (London: Chatto & Windus, 1928), pp. 80–94.

[46] For a stimulating discussion of what it means to be a peasant, cf. Robert Redfield, *Peasant Society and Culture: An Anthropological Approach to Civilization* (Chicago: University of Chicago Press, 1956); and Robert Redfield, *The Primitive World and Its Transformations* (Ithaca: Cornell University Press, 1953).

unable either to retaliate or to restore some mutually profitable trade pattern, such raids might easily develop into full-scale conquest. Thus throughout subsequent history, hillsmen rivaled pastoral nomads as raiders and conquerors of the plains.

For communities already subjected to a conqueror, the expansion of trade served only to increase their subservence. No longer able freely to determine their own fate, unfree villagers could be compelled to produce raw materials at the bidding of foreign merchants who supplied their aristocratic masters with civilized luxuries in exchange. In other words trade increased the range of services which militarized aristocrats could profitably demand of their subjects. It also gave barbarian warriors a taste for the goods of civilization. Having once learned of the wealth and wonders of foreign parts, bands of booty- and glory-hungry fighting men were continually tempted to turn their arms against the core area of civilization itself. Soon after 2000 B.C., therefore, the civilized peoples of the Middle East found themselves exposed to attacks mounted from increasing distances by semi-barbarous overlords of outlying agricultural regions.

Thus the activities of civilized traders and conquerors, which had helped to fasten militarized and alien rule upon the agricultural villagers of the borderlands in the third millennium B.C., ended by recoiling upon the civilized communities themselves. By the second millennium B.C., civilized farmers, as well as more primitive villagers of the march lands, found themselves boxed in between nomads and hillsmen. Even more formidable were those ex-nomads or ex-hillsmen who, by exploiting peasant communities, freed themselves to devote all their energies to the pursuit of prowess and war. The social landscape of the Middle East thus became extraordinarily complex. Nomads, hillsmen, and warrior aristocrats confronted peasants, artisans, priests, merchants, and bureaucrats in a precarious yet inescapable symbiosis.

Increasingly, bands of militarized aristocrats dominated the social scene. Yet the position of any one band was inherently unstable. In the early phases of conquest, when such a group met unusual military success and succeeded in fastening its power upon an agricultural region, its semibarbarous members accepted a restless subordination to their leaders. But the captains of successful barbarian war bands (or their heirs) normally strove to escape from customary limits upon their personal authority by invoking the principles of absolute and bureaucratic rule that civilized communities had developed. Tension between monarchs and aristocrats was therefore usual; and when as a result of such tensions barbarian war-band discipline broke down, the path was cleared for new conquest, a new monarchy, new aristocrats, and new frictions between a centralizing ruler and his reluctant followers.

Despite all the apparent confusion, these superficial cyclic patterns of political conquest, consolidation, and disruption, forwarded slower and more enduring changes. The power and wealth of borderland rulers depended primarily upon rents, taxes, and the peasants' forced labor. These were supplemented in varying degrees by income from trade; for in addition to organizing the production and export of raw materials and trading on their own account, kings might exact payment for the protection of merchant caravans crossing their territories. In the course of time, artisan communities arose in the shadow of royal courts, producing partly for export and partly for local demand created by the royal household. In short, the social structure of the borderlands gradually assimilated itself to the ancient diversification of the Mesopotamian flood plain; and the arts and skills of civilization penetrated to new ground accordingly.

Another way to describe the process is to say that by about 2000 B.C., the "great society" of Mesopotamia had begun to develop a wide fringe of semicivilized communities which were only imperfectly incorporated into its body politic. This evolution interlocked city and village, herder and warrior, merchant and artisan, priest and peasant, more closely and across greater distances than before. Self-sufficient village communities such as those which had dotted the landscape in the fifth and fourth millennia could no longer survive, save in remotest refuge areas of the Middle East.

But economic, social, and cultural interdependence outran the limits of political consolidation. This confronted Middle Eastern society with a problem like that which had earlier distracted the Sumerian city-states; and in the course of time it was met in similar fashion. For just as in the third millennium B.C., when internecine struggles among the Sumerian cities found surcease only through imperial consolidation of the entire Mesopotamian flood plain, so in the second and first millennia B.C., conflicts among rival territorial states of the Middle East culminated in the erection of a much vaster imperial structure, the Persian empire, which united all the lands of the civilized Orient under a single administration.

2. ASIA MINOR

Any such sketch of the development toward civilization in the Mesopotamian borderlands must remain hazardous, for detailed information is very scant. Yet archeology permits us a few isolated glimpses of conditions in those regions. For example, cuneiform tablets written by Assyrian merchants tell something of the state of affairs in eastern Anatolia about 1900 B.C. That area was then divided into numerous petty principalities; and some of the princely capitals had begun to assume the characteristics of urban centers. The presence of regularly established merchant colonies, whose members corresponded with colleagues in their home city of Ashur—itself a remote outpost of Mesopotamian civilization—attests the existence of a rather highly developed long-distance trade. With that trade went a powerful current of cultural influence, so that when an imperial Hittite state arose in Anatolia (after 1800 B.C.), the art, religion, and writing of the court all exhibited close affinities with Mesopotamian models.[47] Yet imitation of Mesopotamian techniques and styles did not involve complete abandonment of native traditions. Rather, an amalgamation between barbaric and civilized elements produced

---

[47] The Hittite script preserved some of the peculiarities of Mesopotamian cuneiform of the Third Dynasty of Ur (*ca.* 2050–1950). This suggests that the natives of Asia Minor learned writing from Mesopotamian scribes of that age.

in due time a derivative, yet stylistically distinct Hittite culture and society.[48]

The Hittite civilization was only one of several which developed in the Mesopotamian borderlands about 2000 B.C. Hurrians, Canaanites, Assyrians, Kassites, Elamites—all evolved something approaching civilization;[49] and with the exception of the Canaanites, they all laid the groundwork for the rise of militarily formidable states. Even on the distant Aegean coast, the Trojans had built a small but wealthy city by 2000 B.C. and knew some of the amenities of civilization.[50] In all probability, the Trojans' wealth came mainly from exploitation of the local peasantry; but sea transport and trade perhaps also contributed something to the prosperity of the city. The Trojan style of life thus represents an intermediate form between the type of civilization developed by warrior aristocracies like the Hittite, and that based upon seafaring, of which Minoan Crete constitutes the chief example.

3. CRETE

Invasion from Asia Minor may have inaugurated the first phase of Minoan civilization.[51] A distinction between conquerors and conquered may therefore have prompted an initial social differentiation in Crete; but the comparative difficulty of attacking an island meant that the military prick toward civilization could not operate more or less continually as it did on the mainland. Instead, the Minoans arrived at civilization by another route, for it was wealth garnered from sea trade, and the stimulus of contacts with more advanced peoples resulting from that trade, that permitted the inhabitants of Crete to create the art and elegance revealed in the ruins of Knossos.

Mediterranean seafaring must have begun about 4000 B.C., when Neolithic settlements first appeared in Crete.[52] Cultural influences from the mainland continued at least sporadically to filter across the sea for a thousand years; and in strata dating from soon after 3000 B.C., signs of commerce with Egypt are unmistakable. How such commerce may have originated cannot be deduced from archeology; but the effect upon Crete of a growing trade with Egypt and other lands must have been to encourage social differentiation between commercial entrepreneurs on the one hand, and common people on

[48] These summary remarks on the background and origins of Hittite civilization are based on O. R. Gurney, *The Hittites* (Harmondsworth: Penguin Books, 1954); Margarete Riemschneider, *Die Welt der Hethiter* (Stuttgart: Gustav Kilpper Verlag, 1954); Eugène Cavaignac, *Le Problème Hittite* (Paris: Librairie Ernest Leroux, 1936).

[49] Perhaps also peoples in southern Arabia. Cf. Carl Rathjens, "Die Weihrauchstrasse in Arabien," *Tribus: Jahrbuch des Lindenmuseums*, N.F. II/III (1952–53), 290–95; Richard Le Baron Bowen, Jr., and Frank P. Albright, *Archaeological Discoveries in South Arabia* (Baltimore, Md.: Johns Hopkins Press, 1958), p. 87.

[50] Carl W. Blegen *et al.*, *Troy* (Princeton, N.Y.: Princeton University Press, 1950), Vol. I, Part I, pp. 41, 204–13.

[51] J. D. S. Pendlebury, *The Archaeology of Crete: An Introduction* (London: Methuen & Co., 1939), p. 53. Sir Arthur Evans, *The Palace of Minos* (London: Macmillan & Co., 1921), I, 66, suggested that there may have been an Egyptian settlement in Crete at the beginning of his Early Minoan I. These two books provide the principal basis for my remarks on Minoan civilization.

[52] Since no Paleolithic remains have been found on the island, Crete may have been uninhabited until colonized by Neolithic navigators.

E. Meyer, Reich und Kultur der Chetiter.

HITTITE BAS RELIEF

This scene depicts the king (*smaller figure on the right*) interceding on behalf of his people with the god of vegetation. Traces of Mesopotamian artistic influence are readily apparent in such matters as the style of the king's dress and the sculptural treatment of beard and hair. Yet the clumsy, squat solidity of the figures remains distinctively Hittite.

the other. Someone had to organize the felling of timber and the export of olive oil, which were probably the staples of Cretan overseas trade; and whoever did so was in a strategic position to enhance his own wealth and power.

The silent witness of physical objects fails to reveal the inner evolution of Minoan society; but archeological remains do indicate that by about 2100 B.C. a full-scale civilization (Middle Minoan I) had emerged on the island. The great palace of Minos was founded at about that time; bronze tools and weapons put in an appearance; the fast-spinning potter's wheel allowed the creation of magnificent pottery; and a form of pictographic writing came into use.

In view of the commerce that linked Crete with the Mediterranean littoral, it is not surprising that Cretan culture exhibited diverse affinities. The origins of Cretan religion seem to lie in Asia Minor; for the Great Mother goddess familiar from Minoan art, where she is symbolized by the double ax and associated with the sacred snake and bull, bears close kinship to deities worshipped in historic times in Anatolia. Cretan painting, on the other hand, shows definite traces of Egyptian influence. But after an initial stimulus from the land of the Nile, the Cretans were quick to establish an independent

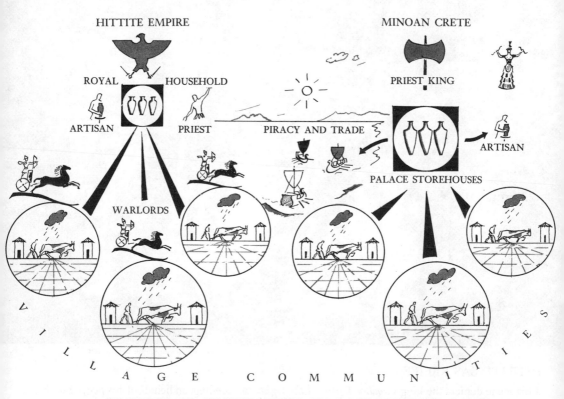

GROWTH OF CIVILIZATION ON RAIN-WATERED LAND

artistic style, whose vivid colors and vivacious naturalism powerfully attract modern taste.[53]

Until the early Minoan script has been deciphered, the structure of Cretan society must remain conjectural. The fact that the royal dwelling places were not frowning fortifications, but luxurious labyrinthine palaces centering around a hall used probably for religious ceremonial, suggests that priests rather than military chieftains dominated Cretan political life. Probably the wealth and power of the rulers of Knossos depended more upon foreign trade and religious prerogative than upon land rents and forced services. If such rulers controlled the trading fleets which plied between Crete, Egypt, the Levant, and the western Mediterranean,[54] they could have accumulated sufficient wealth to maintain the body of consummate craftsmen who built and decorated their palace-temple without having to oppress the peasantry of Crete with heavy rents and *corvées*. At any rate, something in the lightness, exuberance, and grace of Minoan art seems to reflect a freer, more lighthearted society than that of ancient Anatolia or Mesopotamia; but we cannot be certain.

Perhaps it is not fanciful to detect in the art of Minoan Crete some anticipation of the free spirit which was later to characterize Greek civilization. Memories of the "thalassocracy of Minos" remained alive in classical times;[55] and classical Greek religion inherited some of its deities and rites from Crete.[56] But though Minoan traditions thus percolated in attenuated form by way of the Greeks into the mainstream of later European history, it remains true that even at its apogee, Minoan civilization was something of a hothouse plant, requiring the special protection of an island location in order to exist and flourish. When warlike Indo-European tribesmen took to the sea as pirates and plunderers about the middle of the second millennium B.C., Minoan fleets failed to hold their own. Soon thereafter, the high civilization of Crete met a ruin scarcely less complete than that which almost simultaneously overtook the Indus civilization at the other extremity of the civilized world.

The Achaeans, who destroyed the thalassocracy of Minos, did not do so

---

[53] An interesting suggestion, which I think requires further proof, derives both Cretan and Indus naturalistic art forms from a Neolithic, or at least precivilized "painted pottery" culture, originating in northern Mesopotamia and Syria some centuries before the art forms of Sumerian and Egyptian civilization took shape. Cf. Heinz Mode, *Die indischen Frühkulturen*, pp. 137–38 and *passim*. Mode is able to point to interesting parallels between art motifs and religious symbols of the Indus and Minoan civilizations. Mother goddesses, the double ax, snakes, and bulls all occur in Indus art also. The naturalism of some statuettes from the Indus region parallels Cretan naturalism and, in at least one instance, seems startlingly to anticipate Greek classical style. The authenticity of the torso in question (reproduced on p. 87, *left*) is, however, in dispute.

[54] Minoan remains have been found as far off as Sardinia and on a scale to suggest that a merchant colony established itself in that distant island, drawn, no doubt, by the copper mines for which Sardinia remained famous throughout antiquity. Cf. C. F. C. Hawkes, *The Prehistoric Foundations of Europe* (London: Methuen & Co., 1940), p. 156.

[55] Thucydides, I, 4.

[56] Martin P. Nilsson, *The Minoan-Mycenaean Religion and Its Survival in Greek Religion* (2d rev. ed.; Lund: C. W. K. Gleerup, 1950).

deliberately.[57] But in preying upon merchant ships and trade centers, they perhaps disrupted the exchange of goods which had provided the economic sinews of Cretan civilization. Consequently, when some plundering band attacked and burned the city of Knossos about 1400 B.C., it could not be restored. Only with the establishment of a more militarized Greek thalassocracy in the seventh and sixth centuries B.C. did a second sea-based civilization arise in the Aegean.

D. THE IMPACT OF CIVILIZATION ON THE OUTER FRINGES OF THE AGRICULTURAL WORLD

We have just seen how the great river valley civilizations of Mesopotamia and Egypt, with the co-operation of hillsmen and pastoral conquerors from the margins of cultivation, called a constellation of subsidiary civilizations into being. But the transforming force of civilized styles of life did not halt here. More distant peoples, too, responded to the charms of those aspects of the civilized achievement that were accessible to them. And just as the land-based civilizations of the second millennium B.C. differed in important respects from the sea-based culture of Crete, so also overland propagation of civilized traits to the far fringes of the ecumene differed fundamentally from the pattern of their propagation by sea.

I. MEGALITHIC PROTOCIVILIZATION

A proper perspective requires us to view the rise of Cretan civilization as part of a much wider maritime development. Cretan ships were not the only ones to sail the quiet waters of the Mediterranean. Far to the west, a second and smaller island, Malta, became the main center of a far-flung maritime culture that extended, eventually, beyond the western Mediterranean out into the Atlantic. The evidences are of course archeological, and notoriously difficult of interpretation; for the only definite traces left by those early seafarers are the tombs and other megalithic monuments that dot the Atlantic coasts of Europe and Africa, from southern Sweden to the Sahara Desert.

Learned dispute has long raged as to the proper interpretation to be put upon these megaliths; for they show differences of type, and the dates of their construction are uncertain. Perhaps the original form was a rock-cut tomb of a type well known in the Aegean area; while simpler forms developed in western Europe, varying locally according to the wealth and skill of the builders. Malta appears to have been the metropolis upon which this westward megalithic dispersion in some sense depended. The island was an entrepôt for trade between the eastern and western Mediterranean; and several large tem-

---

[57] The decipherment of Minoan Linear B, showing it to record an archaic form of Greek, proves that Greek-speaking rulers gained control of Minoan cities during their last phases of bloom, without disrupting the civilization or even leaving any obvious traces of their presence in the non-literary archeological remains. Cf. Michael Ventris and John Chadwick, "Evidence for Greek Dialect in the Mycenaean Archives," *Journal of Hellenic Studies*, LXXIII (1953), 84–103; John Chadwick, *The Decipherment of Linear B* (Cambridge: Cambridge University Press, 1958).

THE SEA AND THE COURT OF MINOS

Both this sinuous octopus and the detail from a fresco on the walls of the palace of Minos in Knossos, Crete, were probably painted in the fifteenth century B.C. To a modern viewer, the lady's bold and wandering eye gives her a distinctly roguish expression. The conventions of Minoan art may, however, have protected the original viewers from any such reaction to the spectacle of an eye seen frontally set within a face in profile, for solemnity and things divine may have been the painter's real theme. Yet if one compares Hittite heaviness with the slender alertness prescribed by Minoan artistic convention the contrast surely mirrors a fundamental difference between a land-based military empire of the second millennium B.C. and the gayer, freer life sustained by riches raked from the sea.

ples and other structures suggest that it was also peculiarly holy.[58] At any rate, megalithic tombs in their various forms spread widely through the islands and coasts of the western Mediterranean and beyond to the Atlantic shores as far as France, Britain, and the Baltic lands. A style of life related to the megalithic survived until the fourteenth century A.D. in the remote Canary Islands.[59]

The expansion of this megalithic culture was probably associated with the spread of a religion that promised some form of life after death. This supposition alone seems adequate to account for the effort expended on tomb construction. We cannot know the doctrines of the religion which persuaded simple villagers of western Europe to cut and transport the enormous stone blocks from which the megalithic tombs were built; but fairly large numbers of men must have been needed to construct the more conspicuous monuments.[60] Stonemasonry and emphasis upon the afterlife suggest an ultimate linkage with Egyptian civilization, although undoubtedly other influences, notably from the Aegean, entered into the development of megalithic culture.[61]

The distribution of European megaliths, and what we can guess about their dates, requires us to imagine that from about 2500 B.C., seafarers familiar with some of the techniques and inspired by ideas related to those current in centers of Middle Eastern civilization planted themselves along the coasts of the western Mediterranean and the Atlantic, where they were able to transform some aspects of the lives of the simple farming and fisher folk inhabiting those parts. The megalithic movement seems to have been propagated peaceably. Very likely a small elite of priests and merchants colonized one site after another, much as their spiritual heirs, the Irish monks of early medieval centuries, were later to do; and in each new location were able (by offering immortality?) both to turn the minds of the local inhabitants into new channels and to organize their labor for new ends.

Megalithic monuments are by no means confined to the Mediterranean and Atlantic coasts. The shores of east Africa, southern India, southeastern Asia, and some of the Pacific islands also bear megalithic structures that are surprisingly similar to those of Europe. Just as in the West, coastal concentration of most such structures seems to attest a seaborne diffusion; and it is plausible to derive the movement ultimately from the Middle East. Yet whatever the

[58] Themistocles Zammit, *Prehistoric Malta: The Tarxjea Temple* (London: Oxford University Press, 1931); John Davies Evans, *Malta* (London: Thames & Hudson, 1959).

[59] Dominick Josef Wölfel, "Die kanarischen Inseln, die westafrikanischen Hochkulturen und das alte Mittelmeer," *Paideuma*, IV (1950), pp. 231–53; Leonardo Torriani, *Die kanarischen Inseln und ihre Urbewohner*, übersetzt von Dominick Wölfel (Leipzig: K. F. Koehler Verlag, 1940).

[60] It is also possible that the missionaries of megalithic religion mobilized local labor for mining (or perhaps timbering) enterprises and engaged in long-distance trade; for although the tombs themselves have yielded no metal objects—religious conservatism may have excluded metal from the afterworld—it is striking that the main concentrations of megalithic structures are all located at places where metals such as cooper, tin, or gold, or other precious substances like amber were to be found.

[61] Probably only a small elite had access to the arcana of megalithic religion and learning. At any rate, continuities of local pottery styles prove that the expansion of megalithic ideas and practices brought little or no change to the humbler aspects of daily life.

THREE EUROPEAN MEGALITHS

These photographs show something of the variety of structures commonly termed megalithic. The interior view of a Maltese temple at the top may represent what is left of a prehistoric "Mother Church," whence megalithic missionaries perhaps traveled across the seas to western Europe and Africa. The Irish dolmen, shown in the lower left, is a far more common type of megalith, though this specimen is more spectacular than most. On the other hand, standing circles of stones, yoked into pairs by massive architraves, as at Stonehenge, England, are comparatively rare.

kinship between Eastern and Western megaliths, there was one great difference between them: their date. The Recent archeological investigations seem to
show that the Indian megaliths cannot have been erected until well into the
first millennium B.C.; and if the megalith builders migrated eastward from
India, the graves and standing stones in southeastern Asia and the Pacific must
be of even later date.[62] It therefore appears that megalithic ideas and practices
were somehow delayed in their easterly movement for about 1,500 years,
though how this happened is quite unclear.[63]

Although the geographical scope of the megalithic movement may seem
surprising at first glance, in actuality coasting voyages in seas as calm as the
Mediterranean and the Indian Ocean offered no great difficulties to small
and primitive vessels that could be beached on almost any shore whenever
bad weather threatened. Overland travel was a different matter; and its difficulties restricted the landward scope of civilized influence to comparatively
modest ranges.

2. HIGH BARBARISM OF THE EURASIAN STEPPE

The deeper civilized probes into the surrounding sea of barbarian life appear
to have been inspired mainly by an insatiable greed for metals. Thus Nubian
gold may have prompted Egyptian penetration of the upper Nile Valley; and
perhaps similar quests for the metals of the Deccan led the Indus peoples into
that region. But the most significant direction of civilized expansion in the
third millennium B.C. was northward, into the western and central steppe.
From the very inception of civilization, the mountain zone that lay in a great
arc north and east of Mesopotamia had been an important source of metals;
and by 2500 B.C., overland trade routes crisscrossed the Armenian highlands
—perhaps the oldest and most highly developed center of ancient metallurgy—
and extended into Asia Minor and the Caucasus and Zagros Mountains.

The early diffusion of metallurgy was almost certainly the work of itin-

---

[62] Cf. Alphonse Riesenfeld, *The Megalithic Culture of Melanesia* (Leiden: E. J. Brill, 1950); Robert
Heine-Geldern, "Die Megalithen Südostasiens und ihre Bedeutung für die Klärung der Megalithen-
frage in Europa und Polynesien," *Anthropos*, XXIII (1928), 276–315; K. P. Srinivasan and N. R.
Banerjee, "Survey of South Indian Megaliths," *Ancient India*, IX (1953), 103–15; Christoph von
Fürer-Haimendorf, "Altindien," in Fritz Valjavec (ed.), *Historia Mundi*, II, 490–92. It is possible that
two distinct cultures and religious systems were at work in creating the Asian megaliths. Cf. R. E. M.
Wheeler, *Early India and Pakistan to Ashoka*, pp. 150–69.

[63] East Africa, or perhaps southern Arabia, would be likely places where megalith-builders might
have sojourned during that long period. Some religious upheaval or improvement in shipbuilding, connected perhaps with the acquisition of iron tools, might account for the resumption of expansion, this
time across wide ocean distances and not merely by means of coastal voyaging.

In addition to books cited separately, I have consulted the following on the megalith question:
C. F. C. Hawkes, *The Prehistoric Foundations of Europe*, pp. 159 ff.; V. Gordon Childe, *The Dawn of
European Civilization* (4th ed.; London: Kegan Paul, Trench, Trubner & Co., 1947), pp. 208–18, 293–
311, 316–20; C. Daryll Forde, "Early Cultures of Atlantic Europe," *American Anthropologist*, XXXII
(1930), 19–100; Ernst Sprockhoff, *Die nordische Megalithkultur* (Berlin and Leipzig: Walther de
Gruyter & Co., 1938), pp. 150–53; Harold Peake and Herbert J. Fleure, *The Way of the Sea* (New
Haven: Yale University Press, 1929), pp. 29–42.·For interesting attempts to reconstruct the ideas of
the megalithic religion, cf. Hermann Baumann, *Das doppelte Geschlecht: Ethnologische Studien zur Bi-
sexualität in Ritus und Mythos* (Berlin: Dietrich Reimer, 1955); and Horst Kirchner, *Die Menhire in
Mitteleuropa und der Menhirgedanke* (Wiesbaden: Franz Steiner Verlag, 1955).

erant prospectors and smiths who kept the secrets of their trade to themselves, carried special identifying marks on their persons, and were accorded a semi-sacred status by the strangers among whom they worked.[64] Nothing prevented such primitive craftsmen from traveling north as well as south of the metalliferous mountain zone; for barbarous tribesmen and chieftains of the steppe soon learned to welcome and honor strangers who knew the secrets of making such valuable objects as metal axes, knives, and brooches. The first archeological evidence of the diffusion of metallurgy northward into the steppe dates from about 2500 B.C., when chieftains of the Kuban Valley, just north of the Caucasus, began to acquire metal weapons and jewelry.[65] During the centuries which followed, a greater familiarity with the techniques of civilization, particularly those useful in war, continued to penetrate the western steppe.

The exact geographical and chronological stages of this process are unclear. Before the influence of civilized war and technology had become important in the region north of the Black Sea, invaders had begun to spill westward into forested Europe. These people are known to archeologists as the "battle axe" folk. Their distant, but nonetheless real relationship to the high cultures of the Middle East is well illustrated by the fact that when they began to invade central Europe, their distinguishing weapon was still of stone, though its shape was modeled on Sumerian metal prototypes.

Although the movement of steppe peoples into Europe was begun by "battle axe" folk, the pace of this expansion was greatly accelerated when later generations acquired the arts of bronze metallurgy. Accordingly, by about 1700 B.C., bronze-wielding barbarians who spoke Indo-European languages had reached the westernmost confines of Europe, where they met and subdued the peaceable megalith-builders of the Atlantic coast. Presumably the conquerors set themselves up as an aristocracy and made the earlier populations into dues-paying subjects. Certainly all traces of megalithic culture were not eradicated. Indeed, it seems likely that the greatest of all megalithic monuments, the standing circles of stone, were built to the specifications of the conquerors, being translations into stone of tree-trunk circles—a style of sacred architecture which may well have originated in northern and eastern Europe, and traveled west with the Indo-European tribesmen.[66]

The spread of these warrior cultures brought a great revolution to European life. In place of peaceable villagers and remote hunters and fishers, Europe was now dominated by warlike barbarians familiar with bronze metallurgy. In the linguistic sense, Europe was Europeanized, since the speech

---

[64] Cf. Ernst Herzfeld, *Iran in the Ancient East* (New York and London: Oxford University Press, 1941), pp. 156–61; R. J. Forbes, *Metallurgy in Antiquity* (Leiden: E. J. Brill, 1950), pp. 69–73.

[65] C. F. C. Hawkes, *The Prehistoric Foundations of Europe*, pp. 221–22; V. Gordon Childe, *The Dawn of European Civilization*, pp. 148–58.

[66] Harold Peake and Herbert John Fleure, *Merchant Venturers in Bronze* (New Haven: Yale University Press, 1931), pp. 37–40; C. F. C. Hawkes, *The Prehistoric Foundations of Europe*, pp. 314–16; V. Gordon Childe, *The Dawn of European Civilization*, pp. 321–29. Carbon-14 analysis of a bit of charcoal found at Stonehenge in southwestern England and believed to be "early" gave a date of 1747 B.C. ± 275, which would agree well enough with this hypothesis.

of the warrior peoples eventually supplanted the earlier languages of the Continent.[67] In a profounder sense, too, the warrior ethos of the Bronze Age gave European society a distinctive and enduring bias. Europeans came to be warlike, valuing individual prowess more highly than any other civilized people (save only the Japanese) found it fitting to do; and these attitudes, stemming ultimately from the style of life befitting warrior-herdsmen of the western steppe, have remained a basic part of the European inheritance down to the present day.

The higher barbarism of Bronze Age Europe was only indirectly linked to the centers of Middle Eastern civilization, for the tangled and difficult mountains of Anatolia and the Caucasus tended to limit the northward diffusion of civilized techniques to metal weapons and other easily portable objects and skills. Farther east, however, where the Iranian plateau abuts upon the middle reaches of the Eurasian steppe, no such mountain barrier restricted the diffusion of Mesopotamian civilization. From the fourth millennium B.C., agricultural communities had clustered on the better-watered patches of this plateau; and agriculture probably increased in importance there during the second millennium.[68] On the grasslands around and between these agricultural settlements lived barbarian pastoralists, linguistically akin to the warriors of the western steppe. Through the mediation of agricultural communities in their midst, these pastoralists became increasingly exposed to influences radiating from the distant Mesopotamian culture center. In this setting, not long before 1700 B.C., a critically important fusion of civilized technique with barbarian prowess seems to have occurred, for it was here, in all probability, that the light two-wheeled war chariot, soon to become the supreme arbiter of the battlefield in all Eurasia, was invented, or perhaps merely perfected.

The steppe peoples domesticated horses about 3000 B.C., using them at first only as food animals.[69] The idea of hitching horses (or horselike "onagers") to wheeled vehicles was of Mesopotamian origin and had been familiar in early Sumerian times. But Sumerian four-wheeled wagons that could turn only by slipping their wheels sidewise were too slow and cumbersome to have any value on the battlefield, however impressive in processions or useful for haulage they may have been. Basic improvements in design were necessary before horse-drawn vehicles could attain the speed and maneuverability that made the perfected war chariot so formidable. In particular, light, spoked wheels turning around a fixed axle and a type of harness that allowed the horses to bear part of the weight of the vehicle were needed to make the two-wheeled chariot practicable.

In perfected form, the new style of armament comprised three distinct elements: the chariot itself, a powerful compound bow, and the practice of

[67] Except for the Basque pocket in the Pyrenees.

[68] Karl Jettmar, "The Altai before the Turks," Museum of Far Eastern Antiquities, Stockholm, *Bulletin*, XXIII (1951), 142–43; Ernst Herzfeld, *Archaeological History of Iran* (London: Oxford University Press, 1935), pp. 6–9.

[69] Franz Hančar, *Das Pferd in prähistorischer und früher historischer Zeit* (Wiener Beiträge zur Kulturgeschichte und Linguistik), XI (1955), pp. 542–44 and Table 12.

making simple quadrilateral earthwork fortifications in open country. From the barbarian side, the basic innovation was the use of horses as draught animals; and no doubt this idea, together with the techniques of carpentry and leatherwork required to produce spoked wheels, pierced hubs, and an appropriate harness derived from Mesopotamian sources.[70]

The compound bow, too, may not have been altogether new in the second millennium B.C.;[71] but its suitability for chariot warfare gave it a new importance. A wooden bow, strengthened with bone and sinew in such a fashion as to increase its resilience, could be shortened without sacrifice of strength, thus allowing a warrior standing in the cramped confines of a chariot to shoot without difficulty over the top of the chariot's protective parapet. It thus became possible for a company of charioteers to gallop at will across the field of battle, shooting as they went. Even the best disciplined and best equipped infantry of the second millennium B.C. could scarcely stand under a rain or arrows launched from the security of mobile chariots; and when the hapless infantrymen had been disarrayed by volleys of arrows, a massed chariot charge could be relied upon to decide the battle. Such tactics were all but irresistible.

Armies of the older type could hope for success only by attacking the charioteers when they had dismounted and unharnessed their horses. To guard against surprise in such circumstances, the chariot warriors who overran the Middle East adopted the practice of constructing simple field fortifications on a quadrilateral plan.[72]

As they adopted these new techniques of war, the barbarian horse-raisers of the central steppe region became formidable indeed. The fact that their pastoral way of life involved a social tradition combining intense admiration for individual prowess with a political organization under authoritative tribal chieftains still further enhanced their military effectiveness.

The new technology of battle quickly transformed the entire social balance of Eurasia. No people or state in the civilized world could withstand horse chariotry. Rapid and extensive conquests and a widespread churning of

[70] Gradual evolution from solid to spoked wheels can be discerned from Mesopotamian remains; but the development of a light, maneuvrable, two-wheeled chariot appears to have occurred rather abruptly. It is plausible to believe that such a solution to the problem of speed and maneuverability occurred only when the potentialities of chariot warfare had been glimpsed by horse-owning warrior aristocrats of the Mesopotamian borderlands, who were in a position to put skilled wheelwrights to work designing a vehicle for carrying warriors rather than goods. Cf. Franz Hančar, *Das Pferd in prähistorischer und früher historischer Zeit*, pp. 548–51; Joseph Wiesner, *Fahren und Reiten in Alteuropa und im alten Orient* (*Der alte Orient*, Band 38; Leipzig: 1939), pp. 19–22; Richard LeFèvre de Noëttes, *L'Atellage et le cheval de selle à travers les âges* (Paris: Éditions A. Picard, 1931), pp. 21–35.

[71] There is some doubtful evidence that compound bows were known as early as the time of Naram Sin (*ca.* 2300 B.C.). Cf. Hans Bonnet, *Die Waffen der Völker des alten Orients* (Leipzig: J. C. Hinrichs, 1926), pp. 138–39; W. F. Albright, "Mitannian Maryannu, 'Chariot-Warrior' and the Canaanite and Egyptian Equivalents," *Archiv für Orientforschung*, VI (1930–31), 219. On the other hand, the compound bow seems to have been at home among hunters of Mongolia from very early times, where the shortage of suitable wood makes the invention of bone and sinew strengthening all the more likely. Cf. Karl Jettmar, "Hunnen und Hsiung-Nu—ein archäologisches Problem," *Archiv für Völkerkunde*, VI/VII (1951–52), 174–75. In any case, large-scale use of compound bows was new in the Middle East in the second millennium B.C., and came in with the charioteers.

[72] W. F. Albright, "Mitannian Maryannu," p. 219.

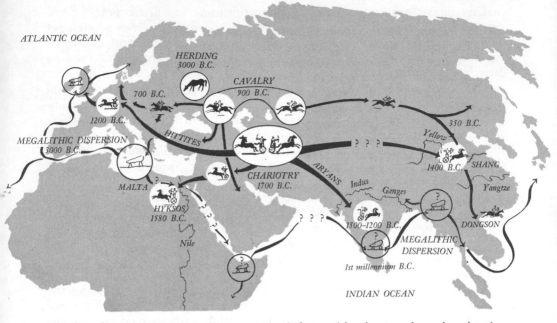

peoples all across the continent resulted from this abrupt alteration in the balance of power. As barbarian war bands conquered, they everywhere altered the life of the peoples they subdued, sometimes drastically, in other cases only superficially. Civilized societies ceased to enjoy military superiority vis-à-vis their barbarian neighbors. The social gradient no longer ran smoothly from the heights of Middle Eastern civilization outward to the periphery of the agricultural world, as had been the case in the third millennium B.C., but was complicated by sporadic reverse movements which brought massive waves of semi-civilized conquerors into the ancient centers of civilization. As a result, such barbarian conquerors as the Kassites in Mesopotamia, the Hyksos in Egypt, and the Mitanni in Syria all rested their power upon a command of the newfangled techniques of chariot war.

To be sure, the Indo-European conquest of the European Far West proceeded without benefit of chariots. The tribesmen from the steppe who subdued the peaceable villages and weak hunting tribes of the European peninsula had no need of the latest and best techniques of warfare. In any case, they probably lacked artisans sufficiently skilled to make spoked wheels, harnesses, and the other accouterments needed for chariot fighting. In the course of time, the new superweapon did filter into Europe, but more as a ceremonial and symbolic device to show the dignity and greatness of its possessor than as a practicable instrument of the battlefield. Chariot tactics based on archery required open ground; and such ground was rare in the heavily forested regions of western and northern Europe.[73]

[73] Rock drawings of chariots in southern Sweden have been dated to about 1300 B.C. Cf. Charles Singer (ed.), *A History of Technology* (Oxford: Clarendon Press, 1955), p. 722. When chariots pene-

Likewise in the more northerly regions of Asia, there is no sign that the chariot style of warfare ever established itself.[74] To be sure, early in the second millennium B.C. steppe warriors of a culture closely related to that of the Pontic steppe penetrated as far east as the upwaters of the Yenisei River and established an aristocratic type of society in the heart of Siberia. But here, just as in the remoter and more northerly parts of Europe, there was little to attract booty-hungry marauders. As soon as the riches of the Middle East and of India had been pre-empted, war bands equipped with the deadly but expensive chariots might rather be expected to turn their attention to the belt of small but densely settled agricultural oases extending across central and southern Asia from Iran and the Oxus-Jaxartes valleys through Chinese Turkestan to the Yellow River.

Archeological research in Turkestan is as yet insufficiently developed to show whether traces of conquering charioteers lie buried in the oases of that region.[75] But in the Yellow River Valley, the horse and chariot, together with bronze armor and weapons, the compound bow, and rectangular fortifications, were all present and well developed by about 1300 B.C.[76] Such similarity to the Middle Eastern style of warfare and equipment seems too great to be accidental. Warrior bands originating along the margins of the Iranian plateau, or perhaps farther east in the Altai, must have moved step by step, from oasis to oasis, across Chinese Turkestan to the Yellow River Valley, and there conquered the Neolithic peasantry inhabiting that region.[77]

---

trated into the European West, bows and the tactics based upon their use did not accompany the new weapons of war. Instead, the Homeric heroes and their later counterparts in Celtic lands fought with spears and other hand-to-hand weapons, often dismounting from their chariots to do so. Archery indeed is portrayed by Homer as not quite sporting –indulged in only by such questionable heroes as Paris of Troy.

It is fairly certain that chariotry reached Greece and the rest of Europe via Asia Minor. Cf. Wiesner, *Fahren und Reiten*, pp. 34–35. It seems that the tremendous prestige which the chariot won in the antique world led the fighting men of the European continent to adopt it, without, however, adjusting their weapons and conventions of combat to take advantage of the chariot's mobility. Homer's war tactics are absurd; his chariots serve little more than decorative purposes; but his report of Mycenaean warfare is not necessarily unhistorical. Warriors accustomed to hand-to-hand combat, and committed to a code of honor that required personal exposure of life and limb, might well have behaved as Homer says, employing the potent engine of Asian warfare as a symbol of personal wealth and importance that was practically useful only as a convenience in getting to and from the field of battle.

[74] Karl Jettmar, "Archäologische Spuren von Indogermanen in Zentralasien," *Paideuma*, V (1950–54), 237–39. Cf. also Roman Ghirshman's summary of S. V. Kisselev, *Drevniaia Istoria Iuzhnoi Sibiri* (2d ed.; Moscow, 1951), "Histoire ancienne de la Sibérie du sud," in *Artibus Asiae*, XIV (1951), 169–89.

[75] The results of the surveys which were made up to 1934 are conveniently summarized, with a catalogue of new finds, in Folke Bergman, *Archaeological Researches in Sinkiang* (Stockholm: Bokförlags Aktienbolaget Thule, 1939). I have failed to locate reports of more recent work.

[76] Herrlee Glessner Creel, *The Birth of China* (London: Jonathan Cape, Ltd., 1936), pp. 141–57; H. G. Creel, *Studies in Early Chinese Culture* (Baltimore, Md.: Waverly Press, 1937), pp. 133–254; Cheng Te-K'un, *Archaeology in China*, II, *Shang China* (Cambridge: W. Heffer & Sons, 1960), pp. 243–49.

[77] The art and pottery of the Shang capital at Anyang also provide isolated but quite unmistakable hints of connection with the Mesopotamian culture-area, though the main tradition is independent. Cf. Li Chi, *The Beginnings of Chinese Civilization* (Seattle: University of Washington Press, 1957), pp. 25–29.

In the course of this triumphant ride through Asia, which stretched across 200 years or more, far-reaching linguistic and ethnic changes probably took place among the charioteers. Members of a victorious band, settling temporarily in some newly won oasis, no doubt took local women to wife, and perhaps sent their sons onward to the next oasis only after a generation's pause. Hence it is not necessary to imagine that speakers of Indo-European tongues ever conquered China. Nor, if the conquerors came by the oasis route, can their numbers have been large; for the oases of the Tarim Basin are too small to support more than a handful of charioteers with their horses and complicated gear. Indeed, the smallness of the oases and the difficulty of finding room for younger sons within their fixed boundaries must have offered a powerful motive for continued adventures eastward.

In the absence of the necessary archeological studies, reconstruction of the link between western Asia and China must remain tentative. The connection between western Asia and India is far clearer; for between about 1500 and 1200 B.C., successive waves of Aryan charioteers and bowmen moved southward from eastern Iran to the Indus Valley,[78] where, as we have already seen, they used their military superiority to destroy the Indus civilization.

Such far-ranging conquests meant that the process by which the Mesopotamian borderlands had earlier been brought within the circle of civilization was re-enacted, with appropriate local variations, throughout the whole breadth of Eurasia, from the Atlantic to the Pacific. Social differentiation between conquerors and conquered meant that wealth might be concentrated in a fashion to sustain the arts of civilization anywhere in the Eurasian agricultural world. But in fact it was only in a few specially favored places that any such development followed in the wake of chariot conquests. In the short run, the militarization of society incident to the dramatic expansion of the steppe warriors often had destructive effects, as it did in India. Endemic warfare, habitual violence, and the frequently brutal exploitation of dependent peasantries did not necessarily offer a propitious base for the rise of new civilizations, though the militarism associated with steppe conquest did succeed in giving a new tone to human life in all those parts of Eurasia where population was dense enough to make conquest worthwhile. Only the remoter fastnesses of the southeast Asian jungles and the Arctic north escaped the impact of the militarized barbarism of the second millennium B.C.

Militarization of Eurasian society checked the development of the seaborne type of protocivilization. Horse-loving warriors, with their narrow military code of honor, could neither understand nor respect the merchant's way of life, seeing in mercantile cargoes only a rich and easily won booty. In such circumstances, some of the early prehistoric lines of seaborne commerce snapped and broke. Long voyages were no longer safe from local plunderers and had to be abandoned. Only in the Bay of Bengal and the southwest

[78] In general, the earlier date seems called for if one attributes the destruction of Indus civilization to the Aryans; whereas the close linguistic affinity between the *Rig Veda* and the *Avesta* seems to call for a later departure from Iran. If it is assumed that heroic songs and hymns dating from the earliest wave of invasion were recast into the dialect of the later invaders, and thus mingled with other and later sacred literature to produce the *Rig Veda*, the difficulty can be overcome.

Pacific did peaceable long-distance sea travel retain its earlier character and importance into the first millennium B.C.; for the coasts of southeast Asia continued to be occupied by pacific societies, as yet untouched by the militarism of civilized-pastoralist styles of life.

In northern and central Eurasia, however, the military-political balance came to center upon the land; and the seaways lost their earlier importance. Behind the clash and tumult of battle, a vastly complicated, incessant and inescapable cultural interaction proceeded in a blind but effective manner. Sharp collision among divergent peoples generated and sustained social change in a fashion that soon stamped the more pacific populations of southeast Asia as archaic. Constant exposure to formidable military challenge from outside prevented any community from settling down for long to a fixed routine of life. Despite the frequent local setbacks caused by war and devastation, an ever recurrent strain toward improvement of the power-wielding and power-generating dimension of civilized life was thereby assured.

CHAPTER IV

The Rise of a Cosmopolitan Civilization in the Middle East 1700–500 B. C.

A. INTRODUCTION

Beginning about 1700 B.C., a wave of barbarian invasions initiated far-reaching changes in the political and cultural map of the Middle East; and shortly thereafter, the development of chariot warfare imparted an extraordinary impetus to the barbarian advance.

In 1700, numerous petty kingdoms and city-states shared sovereignty over Syria and Palestine, while Egypt had been sunk in anarchy ever since the decay of the Twelfth Dynasty. None of these lands proved able effectively to resist the incursions of plundering bands of tribesmen from the southern deserts and the northern hill country. Such bands may originally have been ethnically and linguistically homogeneous; but before long, groups of widely differing origins coalesced. As a result, the ethnic and cultural affinities of the Hyksos peoples, who first infiltrated Egypt and Palestine and then established a more regular political authority there about 1680 B.C., remain a puzzle to this day.

It was not long before the pressure of similar plunderers was felt in Mesopotamia, too. Hammurabi's centralized administration could not prevent sporadic barbarian raids from the hills. These raids became serious shortly after his death and continued for more than a century, until the barbarian Kassites established a loose hegemony over most of Mesopotamia about 1525 B.C. The

Kassite monarchs, like the Hyksos, commanded a mixed body of warriors; and at least two linguistic elements were represented within their ranks.

Generally speaking, three groups of invaders collaborated in overrunning the ancient centers of Middle Eastern civilization. From the desert grasslands of the south came speakers of Semitic tongues; out of the hills came Hurrians and Kassites; and from the more distant steppe came speakers of Indo-European languages. On the strength, presumably, of their mastery of the techniques of chariot warfare, Indo-European warriors appear to have organized and led the hill peoples in their assault upon the civilized societies of the plains. At any rate, both the Kassite state in central Mesopotamia and the new-sprung

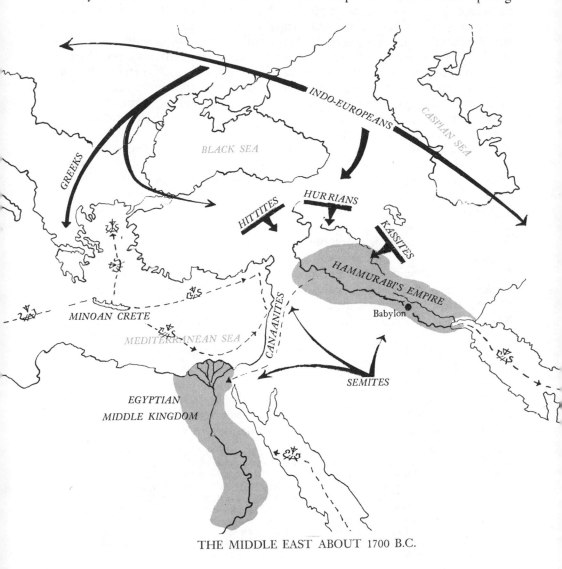

THE MIDDLE EAST ABOUT 1700 B.C.

empire of the Mitanni in the upper Euphrates Valley were ruled over by kings who honored gods with Indo-European names. Less definite evidence indicates the presence of an Indo-European strain among the Hyksos also. In general, Indo-Europeans seem to have been few in number. As a small ruling stratum, they soon adopted the languages of their followers, whether Hurrians, Kassites, or Semites. Consequently, only tenuous traces of their separate linguistic identity survive.[1]

Prolonged exposure to barbarian raids and conquest temporarily rolled back the geographical limits of civilized life in the Middle East. Mesopotamia and Egypt survived the shock best, thanks to their relatively massive populations and imposing cultural traditions; but beyond the limits of the flood plains, where civilization was less firmly rooted, barbarian attack occasionally disrupted civilized life entirely. Some cities were so thoroughly destroyed that their sites became desolate; in other cases, semibarbarous populations came to live amid the ruins of more developed communities. Yet for all their violence and rapine, fundamentally the barbarians sought not to destroy but to enjoy the sweets of civilization. By degrees, as the new conquerors settled down and undertook the defense of what they had won, city life and the patterns of civilized society revived. By the fifteenth century B.C., powerful and civilized states, most of them ruled by descendants of the barbarian invaders of earlier generations, divided the fertile agricultural areas of the ancient Orient and carried on a lively diplomatic, commercial, and cultural intercourse. Old geographical and cultural barriers had been broken through; and a cosmopolitan civilization, incorporating both Egypt and Mesopotamia into a larger whole, began to emerge in the Middle East.

This change in the scale of human organization and action recapitulated, upon a much larger geographical and social scale, the earlier development of Mesopotamian society. The first units of civilized political and social organization in Mesopotamia had been temple communities, grouped into a number of independent city-states. Then, following the creation and disintegration of Sargon's empire (*ca.* 2350 B.C.), the city-states were eclipsed by larger political and social groupings. Imperial or tribal-national agglomerations, in and adjacent to the Mesopotamian flood plain, became the principal units of political and military enterprise; and new social and occupational groups arose to bind these enlarged political units into a loosely integrated "great society." By the fifteenth century B.C., however, the Mesopotamian plain and its borderlands no longer constituted a more or less self-contained theater of political and social action. Instead, the entire agricultural area of the Fertile Cres-

[1] Cf. T. Säve-Söderbergh, "The Hyksos Rule in Egypt," *Journal of Egyptian Archaeology*, XXXVII (1951), pp. 53–71; Robert M. Engberg, *The Hyksos Reconsidered* (Chicago: University of Chicago Press, 1939); E. A. Speiser, "Ethnic Movements in the Near East in the Second Millennium B.C.," *Annual of the American Schools of Oriental Research*, XIII (1931–32), 13–54; Ignace J. Gelb, *Hurrians and Subarians* (Chicago: University of Chicago Press, 1944); Albrecht Götze, *Hethiter, Churriter und Assyrer* (Oslo: H. Aschehoug & Co., 1936); Theodore Burton-Brown, *Early Mediterranean Migrations* (Manchester: Manchester University Press, 1959), pp. 63–76. A comparison of the inferred role of Indo-European tribesmen between 1700 and 1400 B.C. with the well-known role of Normans in European history between 900 and 1200 A.D. is perhaps helpful. In both cases, we may believe that a marked aptitude for war was combined with an equally marked cultural adaptability.

cent—from Egypt through Palestine and Syria to Mesopotamia—took over the role of civilized core area which had once been played separately by Mesopotamia and (on a lesser scale) by Egypt; while the borderlands widened to include both the semifertile desert fringe to the south and the highlands and adjacent steppe zones to the north. Moreover, to the east and west, the plateaus of Iran and Anatolia entered prominently into the balance of power for the first time.

The barbarian invasions of the eighteenth to sixteenth centuries B.C. drastically modified Egypt's isolation from the rest of the world. To be sure, Egypt remained always a special land, never for long disloyal to its ancient gods and cultural traditions; and the distinctive forms of Mesopotamian religion and art likewise remained a living reality in the Land of the Two Rivers. Yet despite the survival of these cultural contrasts and the creation or modification of numerous local civilized traditions, nonetheless an approximate uniformity of social structure gradually but unmistakably manifested itself in the Middle East. In another idiom, we may say that between about 1500 and 500 B.C., a "great society" arose throughout the length and breadth of the Fertile Crescent, complete with professional administrators, soldiers, merchants, and craftsmen, and co-ordinated by law and by the market.

By the latter date, the Persian empire had succeeded in providing a single political framework for this cosmopolitan society. Just as Sargon of Akkad had united the world of Sumerian city-states, and Hammurabi the world of Mesopotamian tribal-national states, so Cyrus the Great in his turn united the Middle Eastern national and imperial states. More successfully than any of its predecessors, the Persian empire both pacified the core area of Middle Eastern civilized life and built a wide protective glacis out into the barbarian borderlands.

* * *

We have seen that the political history of Mesopotamia from Sargon to Hammurabi shows an irregular alternation between periods of imperial consolidation and periods of barbarian irruption and internal fragmentation. On a larger geographical and chronological scale, a similar rhythm continued to manifest itself thereafter. Accordingly, the political history of the Middle East between 1700 and 500 B.C. may be schematized as follows:

a) As the great wave of barbarian chariot invasions subsided about 1500 B.C., "native reactions" against the intruders gained headway. In Egypt, the expulsion of the Hyksos by a native dynasty led to the creation of the Egyptian empire (1465–1165 B.C.). This state became the dominant power of the age, extending from Nubia to the Euphrates (until the Hittites rolled back the Egyptian frontier from northern Syria). In the north and east, native reaction was less pronounced, for Mitannian, Kassite and Hittite rulers accepted the cultural traditions of their subjects to a large degree, in that sense ceasing to be alien. Nevertheless, native kings of Assyria, who threw off the Mitannian overlordship (*ca.* 1380 B.C.), rapidly raised their state to the rank of a first-class power, strong enough to destroy the Mitanni empire about

1270 B.C., and to subordinate the Kassite kingdom. The Assyrians thus emerged as imperial rivals to the distant Hittites and Egyptians.

b) Soon after 1200 B.C., a new wave of barbarian invasion burst upon the civilized peoples of the Middle East and destroyed the three-cornered balance of power that had developed between the Egyptian, Assyrian, and Hittite empires. Once again, hill, desert, and steppe peoples mingled in these movements. This second wave of invasion was less devastating than its predecessor; for neither Egypt nor Assyria was ever entirely overwhelmed. Yet the power and impetus of the assault was sufficient to break apart the three great empires and to change the linguistic and ethnic map considerably. It was during this period of wandering that such familiar tribes and nations as the Hebrews, Philistines, Aramaeans, Phrygians, Dorians, Chaldaeans, and Medes found their historic homes.

c) As these invasions subsided soon after 1100 B.C., a second native reaction gained headway, this time centering primarily in Assyria. Through almost incessant and peculiarly bloodthirsty campaigns, the Assyrians gradually extended their power, until their empire at its height (745–612 B.C.) came close to uniting the entire civilized area of the Middle East into a single body politic. Yet the success of the Assyrian armies in conquering Babylonia and Egypt brought a nemesis of its own, for these anciently civilized lands proved culturally indigestible. Both Babylonians and Egyptians, being acutely aware of their ancient greatness, despised the Assyrians as upstarts and never acquiesced for long in what they felt to be a humiliating political dependency. As a result, recurrent rebellion in Babylonia and endemic disorder in Egypt and Palestine presented the Assyrians with a problem they were never able to solve.

Hence the Assyrian empire rested on insecure foundations. Perhaps Assyrian manpower was insufficient to permit the maintenance of garrisons and corps of officials throughout the entire Middle East; or perhaps the effort to do this spread Assyrian resources dangerously thin. At any rate, the classic combination of barbarian assault (Medes from Iran and Scythians from the northern steppes) with domestic revolt (centering in Babylonia) brought the Assyrian power suddenly to ruin (612–606 B.C.). Nineveh, the capital, was left desolate; and the Assyrian nation disappeared forever as a political entity.

d) After a brief interlude, during which the Medes, the Chaldaeans, and the Egyptians divided the legacy of fallen Assyria, still another semi-barbarous conqueror upset the rather precarious balance of power among these three peoples. Cyrus the Persian emerged about 550 B.C. from the southwestern part of the Iranian plateau, and within an amazingly short period overran most of the Middle East. When his son and successor, Cambyses, conquered Egypt in 525 B.C., the Persian empire extended from the Nile to the Oxus.

Persian hegemony did not eliminate separatist feeling in Egypt and Babylonia; and serious revolts in both areas broke out more than once. But the Persians probably had at their disposal a larger pool of military manpower than the Assyrians had ever had, and, in every case, they were able to repress

THE CHARIOT IN ACTION

Artists of three precariously civilized states, located on the northern periphery of the ancient Orient, here record the spectacle offered by the master weapon of the age—the light, two-wheeled chariot—when used in hunting rather than for the more serious purposes of war. At the top, a gold dish, found at Ras Shamra, Syria, is probably of Mitannian origin. In the center, Hittite charioteers, who were still learning some of the fine points of chariot management from their Mitannian neighbors in the fourteenth century B.C., seem to find it hard to bring their horses to a full gallop, whereas the Mycenaean seal impression at the bottom portrays a high-tailed gallop so reckless as to forget the harness and defy the law of gravity.

Henri Frankfort, Art and Architecture of the Ancient Orient.

Musée du Louvre, Paris.

National Museum, Athens. Photo by Carl Albiker.

rebellion. Moreover, their Assyrian predecessors had already done much to break down local resistance to imperial dominion; and even the pride of Egypt and Babylon faltered after repeated military failure. As a result, Persian military strength, supported by trade and cultural interchange, and reinforced by important improvements in methods of administration and communication, gave their empire relative stability.

With this achievement, the political evolution of the ancient Orient came to a logical, if not to a historical, conclusion. The anciently civilized world was united under one administration; the barbarian world was effectively overawed. But on their northwest frontier, the Persians faced a problem that turned out to be beyond their power to solve. Even before Cyrus' time, a cluster of petty Greek city-states had begun to create a civilization which, while drawing upon the Orient for many of its elements, was nevertheless profoundly different in quality. This civilization soon became a lodestar for barbarian peoples in Macedonia, Thrace, and southern Russia, and indeed, began to be admired even in Persia. As early as 479 B.C., unexpected Greek victories in the battles of Salamis and Plataea forced the Persians onto the defensive. A century and a half later, Hellenized Macedonians and their Greek allies broke into the Persian empire and destroyed it (334–330 B.C.), thus bringing a new and very powerful cultural force to bear upon the age-old civilization of the Middle East.

The rise of Greek civilization from the status of a peripheral offshoot of the Middle East to equality with and superiority over that ancient center marked a fundamental turning point in civilized history. The era of Middle Eastern dominance thereby came to an end; and a complicated cultural interplay began among the major civilized communities of Europe, the Middle East, India, and China. Something like a balance of cultures arose in Eurasia, a balance which was to last until after 1500 A.D., when Europe began to assert a new dominance over all the peoples and cultures of the world.

Any termination date assigned to the era of Middle Eastern pre-eminence must of course be arbitrary. But 500 B.C. offers a convenient round number, representing the high point of Persian power and prestige on both the Greek and Indian frontiers of the ancient Oriental world, before the Ionian revolt of 499 B.C. challenged the Great King's might. By 500 B.C. also, the civilizations of Greece, India, and China had attained many of their distinguishing characteristics. Greek art and philosophy had put in an appearance; while Confucius in China and Buddha in India were then bringing to expression much that remained distinctive of Chinese and Indian civilization.

B. MILITARY-POLITICAL CHANGES

During the period 1700–500 B.C., the balance of power between civilized states and their barbarian neighbors remained central to the military-political history of the Middle East. This balance was never simple. Generally speaking, weight of numbers, regular discipline, and larger resources of wealth and skills told in favor of civilized peoples; but domestic revolt, chronically provoked by disaffection against oppressive and sometimes culturally alien rulers or officials, at times more than canceled these advantages. Moreover, the barbarians sporadically showed a superior flexibility in inventing or exploiting new techniques of war. This happened in the seventeenth century B.C., when peoples from the northeastern margins of the Mesopotamian world perfected chariot warfare; and a similar enhancement of barbarian striking power through the adoption of iron (more properly, steel) weapons helped to provoke the second wave of invasion (1200–1000 B.C.).

The techniques of smelting iron ores came into common use about 1400 B.C. in northeastern Anatolia; but for a long time the new art remained secret and local.[2] Then, following the destruction of the Hittite empire (perhaps by Phrygian invaders) about 1200 B.C., the ironsmiths of Asia Minor, who had been subjects of the Hittites, seem to have scattered far and wide. Thereafter, ironworking began to assume general importance in both the Middle East and Europe, so that in these regions semi-steels replaced bronze as the primary metal for both weapons and tools between 1200 and 1000 B.C.[3]

The imperfect steels of antiquity were seldom intrinsically superior to bronze and always suffered from the disadvantage of liability to rust. The importance of iron metallurgy lay in the fact that iron ores were abundant in nature and therefore comparatively cheap, so that common farmers could afford steel plowshares, sickles, and scythes. Such tools significantly lightened the labor and increased the productivity of agriculture. In particular, heavy and stony soils which had been scarcely cultivable with plowshares made of wood or stone could now be tilled successfully. The new availability of such steel tools therefore enlarged both the geographical scope and the productivity of the agriculture upon which urban life and civilization ultimately rested.[4]

More immediately obvious was the effect of the new metallurgy upon warfare. As steel weapons and armor became cheap enough for commoners to afford, the importance of brute numbers increased correspondingly. Protected by metaled corselets, shields, and helmets, ordinary infantrymen became able

---

[2] R. J. Forbes, *Metallurgy in Antiquity* (Leiden: E. J. Brill, 1950), pp. 418–19. The technique of iron manufacture was fundamentally different from that of bronze. The new metal could not be cast like bronze without producing a uselessly brittle product. Instead, it had to be treated red hot, by a combination of hammering and quenching, to produce a tempered blade; and in addition, carbonization to produce at least a semi-steel was necessary if the end product was to equal bronze in durability and hardness. This was done by allowing the semi-molten iron to come into direct contact with the fuel (charcoal), which was an impure carbon. This was radically different from the smelting of copper and tin in crucibles, preparatory to pouring the liquid metal into molds. Hence it was not simply a new metal, but an entirely new technique of metallurgy that had to be invented. R. J. Forbes, *Metallurgy in Antiquity*, pp. 404–14.

[3] Professor Cyril Smith has suggested (orally, December, 1961) that perhaps the rapid spread of ferrous metallurgy in these centuries was due to the introduction of techniques, as yet not understood, whereby ancient smiths could control the amount of carbon that penetrated the metal, thus producing a usably uniform steel product with a hardness and flexibility as good or better than anything obtainable in bronze. Might not the introduction of charcoal as the standard fuel for iron smelting provide just such an improved and standardized product?

[4] V. Gordon Childe, *What Happened in History* (Harmondsworth: Penguin Books, 1943), pp. 175–76.

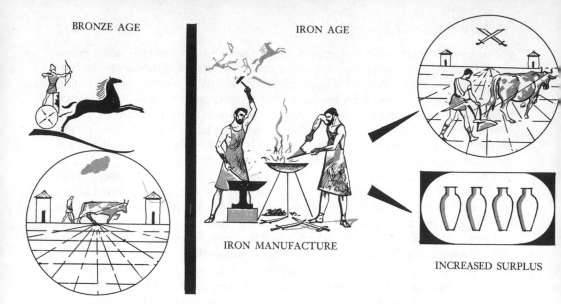

BRONZE AGE   IRON AGE

IRON MANUFACTURE

INCREASED SURPLUS

FROM BRONZE TO IRON

to withstand the arrows of even the noblest charioteers and to reply in kind. Consequently, battle could no longer be decided by maneuvering a few score chariots. Massed infantry became the decisive factor.

The relatively homogeneous barbarian tribes, among which every man was an effective soldier, were the first to exploit the full possibilities of the new metal in war. Civilized communities found it more difficult to utilize the new military technology. Haughty aristocrats, the rulers of the civilized world, seldom deigned and did not usually dare to arm the bulk of the population. Thus civilized military strength was vitiated by the sharp social division between warrior aristocrats and an unmilitary subject population, which in many cases was so alienated from its masters as to be actively or passively disloyal. It is therefore not strange that relatively crude and barbarous tribes were able to overwhelm the chariot-chivalry of the Hittites in Anatolia and of the Mycenaeans in Greece, reducing both areas to neo-barbarism.

Nearer the center of the Middle East, however, the structure of civilized life proved to be more solid. Both the Egyptians and the Assyrians lost their imperial possessions to barbarian invaders, but staved off conquest of their home territories. Thus the two principal core regions of Middle Eastern civilization retained political autonomy, while the ethnic, linguistic, and political map altered drastically along the margins of the Fertile Crescent, and particularly in its more exposed middle section joining Egypt with Mesopotamia.

*   *   *

These technical considerations go far to explain the success of the barbarian invasions that punctuated the political history of the ancient Orient toward the close of the second millennium B.C. But the countermovements of "native reaction" must be attributed in large measure to psychological factors. Tax gatherers and rent collectors are never likely to win the active sympathy of their victims; and one may assume that barbarian overlords were seldom popular among their subjects. Moreover, differences of culture between rulers and ruled gave native leaders an ever-ready handle for mobilizing popular discontent. Observation of the improved techniques of warfare which had initially made barbarian conquest possible allowed such leaders to learn from their oppressors and thereby to enhance the striking force of their rebellion. While native military posture improved in this fashion, a complementary process undermined the strength of the alien masters of the land; for as barbarian warriors and their descendants accustomed themselves to the luxuries of civilization, they tended to lose military cohesion and valor. Thus the stage was set for a successful "native reaction."

The history of Egypt under the Hyksos offers a clear example of this double process. The later Hyksos rulers took on the outward trappings of Egyptian civilization; while the native rebels won decisive victory only after they had borrowed the technique of chariot warfare from their hated alien masters and made it their own. By the time the restored Egyptian Pharaohs had taken the offensive into Palestine and Syria and established their rule as far as the Euphrates, the striking arm of the new-model Egyptian army was a mercenary and professional force of charioteers, recruited largely from the barbarian fringes of the Egyptian world, and paid from booty and from taxes levied on the subject populations.[5]

Building upon the age-old centralization of Egyptian administration, the Pharaohs thus created a military organization superior to anything possible for barbarian war leaders or their descendants. The Pharaoh's charioteers were hired men who could be concentrated into garrison fortresses at strategic points in the empire and kept in a high state of readiness. Such a force had an inherent edge over rival armies which had to be assembled for campaign by summoning the descendants of victorious barbarian warriors from their estates. But at the same time, under a Pharaoh who failed to maintain personal ascendancy over the troops, the danger of rapid disintegration of discipline was real. Such disintegration occurred in fact under the Pharaoh Ikhnaton (1380–1362 B.C.), who devoted himself to religious reform to the exclusion of the military enterprise necessary to preserve the empire.

Following the military disasters of Ikhnaton's reign, reorganization of the army was begun by the Pharaoh Haremhab (1349–1319 B.C.)—himself, significantly, a professional soldier who had usurped the throne. The warlike Pharaohs of the Nineteenth Dynasty (1349–1200 B.C.) used this reorganized force to reconquer Palestine and part of Syria. Yet the old supremacy was irremediably gone. From 1280 B.C. onward, Egypt was on the defensive against the increasingly severe raids of "Sea Peoples"—militant wanderers of mixed ori-

---

[5] On the Egyptian army, cf. Adolf Erman, *Aegypten und aegyptisches Leben im Altertum*, neu bearbeitet von Hermann Ranke (Tübingen: J. C. B. Mohr Verlag, 1923), pp. 649–57; George Steindorff and Keith C. Seele, *When Egypt Ruled the East* (rev. ed.; Chicago: University of Chicago Press, 1957), pp. 90–93.

gins issuing from the north and west, and armed, at least toward the end of the millennium, with cheap and abundant iron weapons. The Egyptians were hard pressed to hold back these raids and after 1165 B.C. lost all their territories beyond the Nile Valley itself. The finely tempered professional chariot army which had built the empire was now outmoded; and since the Nile Valley lacked iron ores, it was difficult for the Egyptians to take advantage of the new military technology. Actually, they scarcely made the attempt. Egypt abandoned imperial ambitions and clung, as far as possible, to a policy of isolation behind her protecting deserts.[6]

The Assyrians were better situated to lead a "native reaction" against the barbarians who had so nearly overwhelmed civilized states in the twelfth and eleventh centuries B.C. Iron ores were easily available in the mountains of northern Mesopotamia; and the Assyrian monarchs of the first millennium B.C. found it easy to equip their soldiers with the new metal. Indeed, they took advantage of the relative abundance of iron ore to increase the size of their armies beyond anything previously known. In time of emergency, the Assyrian kings called out the entire male population of their homeland, thus massing the superior numbers of a settled population against barbarian war bands.

At first the soldiers were recruited from the hardy peasantry of Assyria proper; and a native nobility provided semi-professional officers for such forces. But as the empire increased in size and campaigns came to be waged on more and more distant frontiers, the number of native Assyrians proved inadequate to fill the ranks. It therefore became royal policy to enlarge the Assyrian armies by incorporating conquered forces wholesale and by making levies upon domestic slaves and conquered populations. Such practices carried seeds of disaster. By the time of Assyria's downfall (612 B.C.), the army was largely composed of aliens and subject peoples, who felt no deep loyalty to their lords and masters.

What Assyrian armies of the late imperial age may have lacked in rude national spirit was made up for by skilful, systematic organization and discipline. During the period of Assyria's most rapid expansion (middle eighth century B.C. and after), the army was divided into four basic branches: light infantry, heavy infantry, cavalry (introduced about 875 B.C.), and the old-fashioned chariotry. Of these, infantry were by far the most numerous and were organized into regular units. The Assyrian army was further divided into an elite corps, a standing force on garrison duty, and a "reserve" in the form of discharged veterans and others to whom land was assigned in return for the obligation of military service in time of emergency. The officer corps constituted a distinct social group in the Assyrian state; and the higher officers seem to have been recruited exclusively from a rather small circle of military families. Appointments and promotions from one command to another were regularly made in the name of the king; and the inauguration of a new reign characteristically involved a general reshuffle of the high military officers.

[6] John A. Wilson, *The Burden of Egypt* (Chicago: University of Chicago Press, 1951), pp. 239–54, 258–60, 274.

THE TWO FACES OF ASSYRIA

These sculptural representations of two Assyrian kings, Ashur-nasir-appl (883–859 B.C.) on the left and Sargon II (722–705 B.C.) on the right, illustrate respectively the religious conservatism and the ruthless administrative rationality characteristic of the Assyrian empire. Ashur-nasir-appl is shown in the ritual posture assumed by the earliest Sumerian statuettes (p. 35), and like them waits anxiously for the verdict of the gods, mediated to him through a priesthood whose arts descended unbroken from most ancient Sumer. Sargon II's fierce profile also had artistic antecedents deep in the Mesopotamian past (cf. p. 55 [*left*]); but the tradition of military enterprise and imperial consolidation which he carried forward everywhere disrupted old habits, customs, and pieties. Tension between stark conservatism and radical rationality, between priest and king, temple and palace, had been central to all the recorded history of Mesopotamia. The Assyrians merely carried the ancient polarity to a new, and in the end insupportable, extreme: a feature of their empire here powerfully suggested in stone.

Almost nothing is known of Assyrian battle tactics. No regular formation seems to have been kept on the battlefield: open order presumably gave more freedom to bowmen and offered only a dispersed target for enemy missiles. The sculptured battle scenes that once decorated the royal palaces suggest that bow-wielding infantry constituted the principal offensive arm. Each archer was protected by a heavy-armed shield bearer, who carried a spear for hand-to-hand combat. Cavalry and chariotry had a marginal though highly honorific place, being employed mainly for pursuing a broken foe. The Assyrians developed a variety of heavy engines for battering down or surmounting walls and were particularly skilful at besieging fortified places. In addition, such feats as opening roads for chariots through rough terrain, ferrying men and equipment across rivers, and marching with an unexampled rapidity over long distances to catch their enemies unprepared were matters of routine, which reflected the general excellence of Assyrian military organization.

In general, Assyrian army organization and administration seem surprisingly modern. Certainly European-style armies of the last three hundred years resembled the Assyrian in many respects, as did the imperial armies of Rome and Persia.[7] To have matured such a basic instrument of statecraft as the mass infantry army was surely a great achievement with which we must credit the bloodthirsty Assyrians, however much we may shrink from the use they made of it.[8]

C. ADMINISTRATIVE SYSTEMS

The ebb and flow of peoples and armies across the agriculturally fertile parts of the Middle East between 1700 and 500 B.C. resulted in sporadic improvement of the administrative devices capable of holding a large state together. Such advances were, however, interrupted by long periods of pronounced setback, so that it was not until the time of the Assyrian and Persian empires that Hammurabi's administrative methods were noticeably improved upon.

[7] Persian military organization was closely modeled on Assyrian prototypes. The Persian army, like the Assyrian, was organized into decimal units, regularly graded in size from squads of ten to army corps of 60,000 men, with Persian officers in command of all the larger units. The Persian kings enrolled an even more varied list of subject nationalities in their imperial forces than the Assyrians had done. Cf. Herodotus' catalogue of Xerxes' invading force of 480 B.C., VII, 60–88, which appears to be based on an official Persian source.

In one respect, the Persians went beyond Assyrian precedent, for they conscripted Egyptian, Phoenician, and Greek ships and sailors to form a navy. Aided by a larger reserve of military manpower than the Assyrians had possessed, the Persians were therefore able to extend their conquests farther than any of their predecessors had done. On the Persian military establishment, see A. T. Olmstead, *History of the Persian Empire* (Chicago: University of Chicago Press, 1948), pp. 237–47; *Cambridge Ancient History* (Cambridge: Cambridge University Press, 1926), IV, 270–76.

[8] On Assyrian military organization, see Bruno Meissner, *Babylonien und Assyrien* (Heidelberg: Carl Winter, 1920), I, 89–114; Johannes Hunger, *Heerwesen und Kriegsführung der Assyrer auf der Höhe ihrer Macht* (Leipzig: J. C. Hinrichs, 1911). The re-establishment of infantry as the backbone of military operations obviously opened the possibility for a more democratic form of government; but only the Greeks, on the margins of the Oriental world, were in a position to remodel their institutions in this direction. In the Orient proper, the monarchical, bureaucratic tradition was too strong to be shaken by the change in battle order which came to pass at the beginning of the first millennium B.C. as a result of the introduction of iron.

The charioteers who overran the Middle East between 1700 and 1500 B.C. set up loosely centralized "feudal" states. Successful war-band leaders simply divided the land they had conquered among their chief followers. The whole spirit of barbarian organization made any other policy inconceivable; for a king who sought to preserve for himself the public power and personal prerogative which such a monarch as Hammurabi had exercised would have seemed a tyrant and usurper in the eyes of his fellow warriors. Hence the administrative machine upon which Hammurabi had founded his power was partly dismantled or allowed to decay.

At first, no doubt, the conquerors assumed that their tribal and war-band traditions would suffer no great change. Military enterprise would continue on the familiar basis: when a campaign seemed desirable, the king would summon his mighty men, who would come from their estates, complete with arms and chariots, ready for the next adventure. But landed magnates, secure in the possession of broad acres, were easily seduced from heroism both by new ideas and by new luxuries available to them as landlords and rulers of civilized populations. Such men might not always welcome the prospect of another campaign nor spontaneously obey the royal command. Defection in the countryside increased concurrently with royal ambition; for a king ruling urban populations familiar with traditions of centralized bureaucratic government was always tempted to try to restore the autocratic authority enjoyed by his predecessors in the land. Hence the settling down of a victorious war band amid a civilized population inevitably resulted in tension between king and nobles. Just how the balance of power between central and local authority worked itself out varied with personalities and circumstances.

Details are rarely available from surviving records. Stone stelae found in Babylonia indicate that something of the old royal prerogative remained. Inscriptions record how various Kassite monarchs granted immunity from royal jurisdiction and taxation to a noble, or more rarely, to a town. These grants of immunity were fairly numerous; and the weakness of the Kassite state in international struggles makes it appear that little was left of the substance of central royal power.[9]

Farther north, on the margins of civilization, the barbarian type of feudal government had more success. Between about 1600 and 1400 B.C., the kings of the Mitanni constructed a vast, if loosely centralized state which exercised a general suzerainty over northern Mesopotamia, Syria, and perhaps also over part of Anatolia. In these regions, where urban life was comparatively weak, and where constant effort was required to stand off fresh barbarian attacks issuing from the hills and steppes to the north, warlike spirit and war-band discipline probably decayed less rapidly than was the case in Kassite Babylonia. When the power of the Mitanni weakened and finally crumbled (*ca.* 1380–1270 B.C.), another feudal and imperial state, the Hittite empire, grew to greatness along the northwest frontier of Middle Eastern civilized society. Thus it appears that the decay of barbarian prowess and of war-band discipline came earliest to the Kassites, then to the Mitanni, and least rapidly of all

[9] Bruno Meissner, *Babylonien und Assyrien,* I, 127–29.

to the remoter Hittites, who in the fourteenth century B.C. were still acquiring the fine points of chariot management from Mitannian specialists.[10]

The principal heir to these barbarian empires was imperial Egypt; yet the conquering Pharaohs did not introduce any important administrative improvements. Within Egypt itself, the god-king's age-old absolute monopoly of power was ostensibly restored after the expulsion of the Hyksos; but the realities of administration, even in the Nile Valley, interestingly resembled the decentralization characteristic of the barbarian monarchies of the day. In particular, the wealth and privileges of a few great temples tended to create an ecclesiastical *imperium in imperio;* and the standing army constituted another and quite novel instrument of power which sometimes played a decisive part in palace intrigue and coups d'état. Thus privileged priests and professional soldiers changed the inner realities of Egyptian government at home, even though the old forms and formulae were preserved intact.

Beyond Egyptian borders, Nubia to the south was incorporated into the administrative structure of the Egyptian state; but to the north, in Palestine and Syria, the Pharaohs followed barbarian precedent and left local princes and potentates *in situ,* requiring of them only payment of tribute and the dispatch of armed contingents to join the royal Egyptian army on campaigns. Direct Egyptian administration of these provinces was limited to the military sphere; for garrison commanders were stationed at strategic points under the orders of Pharaonic officials.[11] Nothing resembling Hammurabi's legal code or even his bureaucratic hierarchy of administrative officials bound Egypt's Asian provinces into a closer unity. Perhaps the native Egyptian system of administration, dependent as it was on the Nile and on the theological principles which made the Pharaoh a god on earth, could not be transplanted to foreign lands, where neither geography nor religious and cultural traditions were propitious. Except in Nubia, the attempt seems not to have been made. The Egyptian empire in Asia never amounted to more than a loose hegemony over a collection of disparate local principalities.

*   *   *

The barbarian states established in the twelfth and eleventh centuries B.C. differed in important respects from their predecessors of the eighteenth to sixteenth centuries. The abundance of iron had democratized warfare, so that extensive aristocratic empires no longer accorded with military realities.[12]

---

[10] Cf. the analysis of developments in the second millennium in Albrecht Götze, *Hethiter, Churriter und Assyrer,* pp. 101–12 and *passim.*

[11] Cf. J. A. Wilson, *Burden of Egypt,* pp. 181–85; Steindorff and Seele, *When Egypt Ruled the East,* pp. 103–5.

[12] The reassertion of political localism was much facilitated also by the abundance of deposits of iron ore, which made it impossible for a handful of strategically placed monopolists to control the metal trade. When tin had to be sought at great distances, it was relatively easy matter for kings and nobles to control the merchants who imported such rarities; but when literally hundreds of sources of metal lay within much shorter range, even of those parts of the Middle East which themselves had no iron ore, the metal trade, together with warfare, was democratized. Local tribesmen and farmers could no longer be overawed by aristocrats whose arms were now little better than their own; and large

Instead, the tribes and bands of freebooters who penetrated the Middle East between 1200 and 1100 B.C. characteristically established smaller states, in which petty landholders and free peasants countered the pressures toward political centralization by clinging stubbornly, though in the end vainly, to the rude egalitarian tradition which measured a man's worth by the strength of his arm and the firmness of his courage in battle.

Among these newer states, only the Hebrew polity is well enough known to allow us to understand something of its development. Before the time of Saul (*ca.* 1020 B.C.), the Hebrews were led but scarcely ruled by "judges," and the separate tribes were only loosely united in a religious amphictyony, whose occasional meetings were presided over by priests of the sanctuary at Shiloh.[13] The situation in Palestine was perhaps unusual in that the invading Hebrews had only a very slender military advantage over the Canaanites whom they attacked. Their settlements tended therefore to center upon high ground and agriculturally marginal districts in southeast Palestine; while the richer coastal plains fell to the better-equipped Philistines, among whom iron was more abundant than it was among the Hebrews.[14]

In regions where invaders enjoyed a greater military superiority, they characteristically set themselves up as a privileged class, sometimes, like the Philistines, living in towns and leaving the work of the fields to enserfed natives. In Syria and southern Mesopotamia, the Aramaean and Chaldaean conquerors seem to have followed this system, as did the Dorians in Greece. City-states or petty tribal confederations therefore tended to replace the imperial and feudal pattern of government which had characterized the age of chariot warfare. These small political units were inherently unstable; for struggles between adjacent states and peoples led rather rapidly to the concentration of more and more authority in the hands of individual war leaders who, in proportion as they were successful, built up larger and larger states and developed at least the rudiments of a professional army and administrative bureaucracy.

The biblical narrative of the rise of the Hebrew kingdom under Saul, David, and Solomon (1020–925 B.C.) provides vivid insights into some details of this process among the ancient Israelites. Popular resistance to the taxes and *corvée* imposed by the royal administration can be seen in the biblical account of David's "sin" of numbering the people.[15] The denunciation of David's personal conduct by the prophet Nathan[16] illustrates the collision between the traditional moral code and the temptations besetting a powerful monarch

---

territorial states could not thrive when even relatively small groupings among local populations could mount a military force roughly equivalent to anything that could be brought against them. Cf. Fritz M. Heichelheim, *Wirtschaftsgeschichte des Altertums* (Leiden: A. W. Sijthoff, 1938), I, 205–7.

[13] W. F. Albright, *From the Stone Age to Christianity* (Baltimore, Md.: Johns Hopkins Press, 1940), pp. 214–17.

[14] Cf. Judges, 1:19: "And the LORD was with Judah, and he took possession of the hill country, but he could not drive out the inhabitants of the plain, because they had chariots of iron." Revised Standard Version.

[15] II Samuel, 24:1–10.   [16] II Samuel, 12:1–13.

supported by a professional body of mighty men, including, as the name of Uriah the Hittite reminds us, foreign mercenaries as well as Israelites. By Solomon's time, an assimilation of government and cult to the civilized patterns of Phoenicia and northern Syria was in full swing. But in proportion as the Hebrew kingdom became civilized, its rulers drew away from the old, popular traditions and standards of conduct. This fissure, which widened with time, provoked the great prophets of the eighth century to denounce, in the name of Yahweh and pure religion, the unrighteous innovations of the kings and their servants.

No doubt the evolution of the Hebrew kingdom was unique in some respects; certainly the evolution of prophetic religion was unparalleled elsewhere. But such neighboring states as Damascus, Tyre, Hamath, Aleppo, and Carchemish probably developed from tribal groupings or local city-states into small kingdoms in more or less the same manner. The political evolution of the Iron Age thus recapitulated that of Sumer and Akkad in the third and second millennia. But this time the pace was enormously accelerated, since handy models of centralized administration were preserved in such decadent but still impressive states as Egypt and Babylon. An ambitious, energetic local king had always close at hand a ready-made pattern of civilized government toward which to aspire. Wholesale borrowing of the elements of Hammurabi's bureaucratic system was vastly easier than the original invention had been, so that a single generation could achieve a degree of political integration comparable to that attained in ancient Mesopotamia only after an entire millennium of development.

Political consolidation and bureaucratization did not, of course, come to a halt with the emergence of a series of centralized but geographically petty states in the Middle East. On the contrary, the military-political pressures which had previously favored centralized royal administration continued to operate, and did so on an ever-expanding geographic scale. By the time the Assyrian state had become a territorially vast empire, its administrative integration therefore equaled and in some respects surpassed Hammurabi's achievement.

From the time of Tiglath-Pilesar III (745–727 B.C.), the territory near the center of Assyrian power was subdivided into artificial provinces, administered by royal officials who supervised the collection of taxes, mobilized manpower for royal *corvée* or military service, settled legal disputes, and maintained regular communication with the royal palace. On the margins of the empire, where it was more difficult to bring the central power to bear, the Assyrians transformed local rulers into vassals; but, as later in the Roman empire, there was a strong tendency to convert such vassal states—sooner or later—into regularly administered provinces.

As befitted the heirs of so much of ancient Babylonian culture, the Assyrians early developed a body of written law. Some of the Assyrian laws clearly were modeled on Hammurabi's famous code; others reflect somewhat harsher and more primitive conditions and attitudes. These laws seem to have been applied throughout the provinces of the empire, thus giving a common legal system to a very substantial portion of the Middle East. In the vassal states, however, local law and practice continued in all their diversity.

Another important bond uniting the Assyrian empire was trade. In the days of their imperial greatness, the Assyrians themselves were not a very active mercantile people. Instead, Aramaeans dominated the inland trade, and Phoenicians the trade overseas. Clearly, even imperfect pacification of a large civilized area facilitated commerce; and the extension of Assyrian law to a large part of the empire presumably had a similar effect. But more important than either was the Assyrian system of arterial roads, built to serve military needs. In some places these roads were paved with stone, wide enough for chariots to pass; but because the movement of armies and of goods proceeded by substantially identical means, an important consequence of the construction of these roads was greatly to facilitate long-distance transport and trade.

In spite of the efforts of Assyrian monarchs and their officials to assure the stability of the empire, local revolts were a constant menace. Assyrian frightfulness, so proudly boasted in many royal inscriptions, did not eliminate the danger; it may even have had the effect of making resistance, once embarked upon, more desperate. Yet two administrative devices which the Assyrians used to minimize the possibility of successful revolt had important consequences for the history of the Middle East. One was the planting of military colonies in the midst of restive populations. Such colonies perhaps originally provided an outlet for land-hungry Assyrian peasants; but before the empire had reached its height there were no more surplus Assyrian peasants to be found. As a result, new military colonies comprised people of mixed antecedents and brought many diverse cultural strands into close association. The Assyrians' second precautionary measure was wholesale transplantation of rebellious peoples from their native lands to some distant part of the empire. Such resettlement obviously shook traditional patterns of social cohesion profoundly and insured a mingling of diverse peoples and traditions on a scale much greater than would otherwise have been the case.

Policies such as these, together with the polyglot character of the Assyrian army, the rise of trade, and the spread of the Aramaean language and alphabet as a lingua franca, fostered the rapid development of a cosmopolitan culture in the Middle East. This culture drew upon many divergent local traditions, but submerged local differences to a greater or lesser degree in a rough common denominator. This incipient cosmopolitanism was perhaps the most enduring achievement of the Assyrian empire; but the administrative and military structure within which the cultural evolution occurred was itself no mean accomplishment and provided subsequent empires of the Middle Eastern and Mediterranean lands with persuasive models upon which to pattern their own governments.[17]

The Persians profited from their imitation of Assyrian administrative methods, although it was not until the reign of Darius the Great (522–486 B.C.)

[17] The above remarks on Assyrian administration are based on Meissner, *Babylonien und Assyrien*, I, 130–46; A. T. Olmstead, *A History of Assyria* (New York and London: Scribner's Sons, 1923), pp. 606–11; *Cambridge Ancient History*, III, 92–99, 108.

that the Persian governmental structure settled into enduring molds. Cyrus and Cambyses had little time for anything but war and did not establish uniform administration in the territories they conquered. Indeed, Cyrus undid a part of the Assyrians' work by permitting, even encouraging, the restoration of local religious institutions which his imperial predecessors had trampled underfoot. Probably he owed much of his easy success to this policy, which permitted him to play the role of liberator, not only toward the Jews whom he released from exile in Babylon, but toward other peoples as well.

Yet the logic of empire soon forced the Persians to return to Assyrian precedent. Darius, whose hereditary claim to the throne was in dispute, could not base his authority simply on the traditional role of national war leader, as Cyrus and his son Cambyses[18] had tried to do. Instead, he elaborated a regular bureaucracy, organized his army into a uniform hierarchy, and promulgated a code of law. In so doing, he borrowed directly from Assyrian and Babylonian precedent. Darius did, however, initiate one significant improvement: from time to time he sent out special inspectors, "the King's eyes," to report on the state of the provinces and on the loyalty and competence of local officials.[19]

By the end of Darius' reign, and more plainly during that of his son and successor Xerxes (486–465 B.C.), the Persian kings were impelled to follow Assyrian precedent even further. Cyrus' policy of granting wide autonomy to temple priesthoods and other local religio-political institutions offered a ready-made instrument of power and a focus of discontent which ambitious native leaders might use to organize revolt. At the end of Darius' reign, Egypt rose; and almost immediately thereafter, a similar rebellion occurred in Babylonia. Xerxes revenged himself by destroying the great temple of Marduk and by dispersing the ancient priesthood which had long constituted the chief bulwark preserving the ancient Babylonian civilization. Egypt suffered no comparably drastic punishment until 343 B.C., when, following yet another revolt, the Persians thoroughly plundered the chief temples of that ancient land and scattered their priesthoods.

These disruptions of the temple organizations of Babylonia and Egypt by the Persians mark the effective extinction of the old separatist traditions of Babylonian and Egyptian civilization. To be sure, the ancient priesthoods revived; but in Mesopotamia, at least, continuity had been irretrievably broken. In subsequent generations, Babylonian priests no longer could blindly maintain their former sublime hauteur on the strength of immemorial antiquity. Instead they began to react to the world about them by undertaking an active reassessment of their cultural heritage. In particular, complex assimilation between Zoroastrian and Babylonian religious themes and ideas began to alter both partners to the fusion, even before the tide of Greek influence

[18] Cambyses (530–521 B.C.) discovered the hidden thorn in his father's policy of religious toleration when his disregard of Egyptian religious sensibilities nearly provoked revolt in that province; but his premature death postponed for a generation the collision between Persian imperial interests and Egyptian xenophobia.

[19] On Persian administration, cf. A. T. Olmstead, *History of the Persian Empire*, pp. 119–34, 185–94; *Cambridge Ancient History*, IV, 184–201.

brought by Alexander (334–323 B.C.) inundated the ancient Orient and inaugurated a new cultural era in Mesopotamia.

The ancient Egyptian culture, on the other hand, did not break out of its protective shell quite so soon. Even under the Ptolemies (323–30 B.C.), despite the presence on Egyptian soil of important Hellenized populations, Egyptian priests and peasants seem to have gone their way much as before. It was scarcely before Roman times that signs of any culturally fruitful interaction between the autochthonous Egyptian and the cosmopolitan Hellenistic-Oriental traditions began to emerge. Thereupon, the Egyptians, like the Mesopotamians before them, began to lose their ancient cultural identity and gradually merged into the larger civilization around them, reacting to the same cultural influences as the rest of the Oriental world, and beginning once again to exhibit a capacity for growth and innovation.

D. SOCIAL STRUCTURE

If we attempt a bird's-eye view of Middle Eastern social structure between 1700 and 500 B.C.—a view embracing all the varied terrain from the borders of Egypt to the Iranian plateau and from Anatolia to the Persian Gulf—the general impression is one of leveling up and leveling out. Cities took root in areas that at the beginning of this period were inhabited only by tribal or village communities; principles of social cohesion and organization which had been confined to Mesopotamia and immediately adjacent areas spread to embrace the Middle East as a whole. In short, the "great society" of Hammurabi's age survived the setbacks incident to barbarian irruption and revived more vigorous than ever, spreading its tentacles throughout the entire ancient Orient.

Peasant villages remained, as they had from Neolithic times, the fundamental social unit within which a majority of human beings lived their lives. In the hill country, such communities presumably remained relatively free and but little affected by political and cultural developments in the plains. Equally, the tribal life of the desert fringe remained unchanged from what it had been in the third millennium B.C. These two barbarian reservoirs therefore maintained a spirit of proud and primitive egalitarianism which contrasted strongly with the psychological alienation from their social superiors characteristic of the downtrodden peasantry of civilized plains, where long before 1700 B.C. landlords had established their claim to direct the labor of the cultivators and to share in the harvest. The invasions of the next few centuries brought no change in this relationship, though the linguistic and cultural affiliations of the landlord group fluctuated with the ebb and flow of military and political events.

The coming of iron and the renewed barbarian invasions of the twelfth and eleventh centuries B.C. had a deeper impact on the lives of Middle Eastern peasants. This time the barbarian invaders came not as a conquering aristocracy, ensconced in chariots and eager to lord it over dependent agriculturalists, but as massed tribesmen, armed with steel weapons, and prepared to preserve as best they could the rude egalitarian life of their ancestors. The effect was to create in some parts of the Middle East free and independent peasantries, acknowledging only a somewhat vague tribal or personal submission to war leaders and judges.

How widely the Iron Age migrations led to the establishment of free peasantries in the Middle East cannot be said with certainty. In Babylonia and Egypt, the traditional dependency upon priestly, royal, or private landlords apparently survived without much alteration; and even in such backward communities as Israel, the demands made by local war leaders for taxes, military service, and forced labor had begun by 1000 B.C. to undermine the independent status and personal freedom of the peasantry. Political and military factors were supplemented by a process of economic differentiation, which operated powerfully wherever money became important.[20] This was so because money and the commercial habit of mind invited usury; and usury was able to disrupt free agricultural communities very quickly. In a bad season, independent peasants might fall into irremediable debt, losing first their land and then their personal freedom to men who had somehow accumulated a store of money or of seed grain. The biblical prohibitions of usury and the prophetic denunciations of the rich must be understood against this background.[21]

By the time the Assyrian empire had risen to domination over most of the Middle East, large estates and a dependent peasantry apparently prevailed once more. However, Assyrian law offered some protection to the dependent peasant (for example, interest on crop loans began only after the agreed date of repayment had passed); and even slaves had some rights before the law, as well as obligations for military service to the state.[22] Perhaps some faint survival of a freer and more egalitarian age lingered in these legal provisions; but in general, the peasant communities of the Middle East seem to have relapsed into something very like their half-free status of the second millennium B.C.

Yet just as the peasants of the Assyrian and Persian empires continued to enjoy the advantage of metal plowshares and sickles as an inheritance from the invasions of the Iron Age, so also their return to a dependent status did not exclude them from a modestly enlarged participation in the market economy of the Middle Eastern "great society." Reversion to the conditions of the second millennium was therefore not complete; for even after landlords,

[20] Coinage in the familiar European sense was first invented in Lydia, probably during the seventh century B.C.; but long before that time, metal cast into standard weights and sometimes stamped with signs to indicate weight and purity had been used in Babylonia and Assyria. In Hammurabi's time, silver "shekels" had been the prevailing standard of value, although the older standard, gurs of barley, was also used. In Assyrian times, metal currency of standard weights came into general use. Copper was cast as well as silver to give smaller units of value, thus greatly facilitating small-scale local exchange. Except for the disk shape of Lydian coins and the fact that in Assyria the state apparently did not monopolize coinage, there seems to be no important difference between Assyrian and later Lydian, Greek, and Persian money. Cf. A. T. Olmstead, *History of Assyria*, pp. 536–38.

[21] E.g., Amos, 2:6–8; 8:4–6.

[22] A. T. Olmstead, *History of Assyria*, pp. 510–24; *Cambridge Ancient History*, III, 98–99.

tax collectors, and usurers had taken their shares, at least some peasants had a surplus to sell on the market. This, in turn, allowed them to buy tools and other products of artisan workshops. The fact that metal tools made agricultural work easier and more productive helped to secure a modest surplus to the peasants. Conversely, since the smelting and shaping of metal tools involved special equipment and skills beyond the capacity of any ordinary farmer, the new necessity of buying such tools required the peasants to find such a surplus.

It is impossible to know how widespread local trade between peasants and artisans may have been. No doubt it varied from time to time and from locality to locality. In general, the more produce the peasants were forced to surrender in the economically unrequited form of rents, taxes, and interest, the less they could dispose of through urban markets. But inasmuch as town life grew stronger throughout the first millennium B.C., it is probable that, by and large, local peasant populations continued to command small surpluses which they could exchange with the artisans and storekeepers of the towns. Without such local circulation of goods between town and country, and without a growing specialization between urban craftsmen and peasant farmers, towns would have remained primarily the administrative and religious centers they had tended to be in the second millennium B.C. The fact that the size and number of urban centers increased implies that craftsmen began to serve not only aristocratic landlords, but the larger community of peasants and humble urban folk as well.

The importance of such specialization should not be exaggerated. By far the greater part of Middle Eastern peasant life continued to be spent within the small, tight-knit circle of the village community, where market relations did not prevail, and where townsmen were always alien and scarcely to be trusted, even when they knew the secrets of such useful arts as metallurgy or pottery-making. Yet the fact remains that peasant communities, whose origin antedated the first appearance of civilized societies by some two thousand years, were now firmly, if marginally, incorporated within the "great society" which had slowly formed itself around the major urban seats of civilization. Farmers were no longer sufficient unto themselves, as they had been in the fourth millennium B.C.; nor were they simply the victims of their social superiors, supporting the culture of their masters by their own involuntary privation or forced labor, as they had been in the late third and through most of the second millennium B.C. Instead, the peasants themselves began to enter modestly but significantly into the "great society," exchanging part of their surpluses for iron implements and other goods that were useful or necessary to their improved methods of farming. The effect was to allow the humblest class of society to benefit modestly but really from urban-rural differentiation and specialization.

This pattern of local exchange provided the Middle East with a new economic base level. Even when political or military events interrupted long-distance trade and forced local regions back upon their own resources, the social and economic structure allowed for a division of labor between town

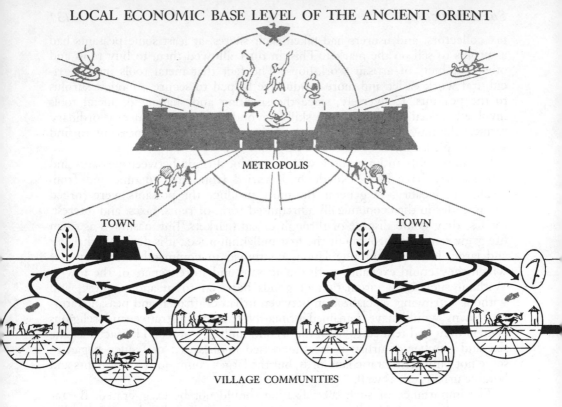

METROPOLIS

TOWN   TOWN

VILLAGE COMMUNITIES

and country, between artisan and peasant. Under these conditions, urban life could never entirely disappear; and with urban life went the potentiality of civilized high culture, even though the finest flowers of urbanity were still reserved for a privileged few who enjoyed greater wealth and leisure than a mere craftsman could ever achieve. Styles of cultural expression of course continued to fluctuate; and the originality and refinement of Middle Eastern high culture varied greatly through the centuries. But economic specialization between town and country supplied an enduring social matrix within which civilized life, even if temporarily interrupted, could re-establish itself relatively smoothly and quickly. Through all its subsequent vicissitudes, the Middle East never lost this fundamental local basis for civilization.

The achievement throughout the fertile regions of the Middle East of a socio-economic base level attuned to the support of artisan experts constituted a fundamental advance in human history. In the third millennium B.C., civilization had been unattainable upon merely rain-watered land. In the second, civilization had begun to spread beyond the confines of river flood plains; but in the regions where irrigation was impossible, it remained a tender and weakly rooted plant, dependent always upon a precarious concentration of wealth in the hands of a small number of rulers, landlords, or merchants. By contrast, in the first millennium B.C., the overthrow of a particular political regime, the destruction of a given body of cultured landowners, or the interruption of an existing pattern of long-distance trade no longer implied the disappearance of urban life, and with it, the collapse of the economic specialization and social complexity needed to sustain civilization. Civilization had become endemic in the Middle East, for the first time fully acclimated to rain-watered land.

* * *

The market economy which thus infiltrated the ancient Middle Eastern villages operated on various levels. At the base lay the local trade between simple artisans and peasants. At a second level stood the artisans and traders of the numerous provincial towns, who served local landowners, priests, and other dignitaries by supplying them with local manufactures and occasional imported luxuries. At the top were a few metropolitan commercial and manufacturing centers, whose network of trade relationships extended throughout the civilized world and beyond.

At the heart of this network lay the cities of Mesopotamia, connected to one another and to the ports by caravan routes, which the Assyrian and Persian governments often improved into regular roads. Babylon was the greatest metropolis of the area; but many of the other ancient Mesopotamian urban centers continued to flourish into the first millennium. Under Kassite and Assyrian rule, some of them possessed royal charters which guaranteed a very considerable autonomy, with various special rights extending even to lands outside their walls. Citizens, for example, were entirely exempt from service in the Assyrian armies; and local magistrates and priests continued to govern urban affairs without much interference from imperial officials. Even after being incorporated first into the Assyrian and then into the Persian empire, such communities remained in fact tributary city-states, entirely immune from ordinary provincial administration.

Other great cities, similarly privileged by imperial governments, existed on every side of the ancient Mesopotamian center. As long as Assyrian rule endured, the imperial capitals of Ashur and Nineveh were important seats of commerce and industry. Damascus in Syria became a major way station on the route between Phoenicia and Babylonia; and Carchemish, farther north on the upper Euphrates, played a similar role in trade with Anatolia. To the southeast, Susa had been an important commercial city long before it became one of the capitals of the Persian empire, although other Persian towns, such as Ecbatana, Pasargadae, and Persepolis, seem to have been little more than administrative headquarters. The same was true of most of the cities of inland Anatolia, although Sardis, capital of Lydia, was a prominent commercial and industrial center as well as a fortress and palace city. Along the coasts of Anatolia, a number of commercial towns began to flourish after about 900 B.C.; and a century and a half later, commerce also became important across the Aegean in mainland Greece.

On the eastern shore of the Mediterranean, the cities of Phoenicia became major commercial and industrial centers after about 1000 B.C. Tyre and

Sidon took leading roles in colonizing the western Mediterranean; and a vigorous shipping brought the wealth of all the Mediterranean lands to their harbors. Sailors from Phoenicia ventured as far as Britain and visited the Atlantic coast of Africa as well.[23] Phoenician trade thus followed patterns established earlier by Minoan and Mycenaean seafarers, linking the barbarian backwoods of the Mediterranean with the workshops of civilized communities.

In Egypt, the first cities to be more than palace or temple communities appeared under the empire (1465–1165 B.C.).[24] Memphis, at the apex of the Delta, and Thebes, in Upper Egypt, were the greatest of these; but in both of them strong hieratic and royal elements continued to dominate commercial and secular life. In the Delta itself, more purely commercial cities arose, of which Naucratis was the most prominent. But it is significant that Naucratis is known by its Greek name, for it was both founded and to a considerable degree populated by Greeks. As a rule, native Egyptians no longer engaged in foreign trade but left such enterprise to foreigners.

No doubt the southern seas, uniting Egypt, Mesopotamia, and India, continued to be traversed by merchant vessels in the second and first millennia B.C. The Aryan conquest of India probably interrupted all but sporadic sea commerce between that subcontinent and the Middle East for some centuries;[25] but after the Persian conquest of part of the Indus Valley, Darius took an active interest in opening up sea communication with this distant province. His success appears to have been slight, although definite data about the early commercial history of the seas and gulfs surrounding Arabia are quite lacking.[26] The introduction of camels, which allowed commerce between Egypt and Mesopotamia to move more easily overland across the desert than around the long shoreline of the peninsula, probably forwarded the decay (or per-

[23] It is even possible that a Phoenician ship circumnavigated Africa about 600 B.C. Cf. Herodotus, IV, 42.

Cloth dyed with Tyrian purple was a staple Phoenician export, together with such other manufactured luxuries as wine, bronze art objects, and glassware. Imports from the Mediterranean and Atlantic coasts consisted mostly of raw materials and slaves. G. Contenau, *La Civilisation Phénicienne* (Paris: Payot, 1926), pp. 298–308.

[24] J. A. Wilson, *Burden of Egypt*, pp. 204–5.

[25] A few references in the *Rig Veda* seem to imply knowledge of seagoing ships and trade with distant lands; but this was presumably very small in quantity and not of much importance. Cf. R. C. Majumdar (ed.), *The History and Culture of the Indian People: The Vedic Age* (London: Allen & Unwin, Ltd., 1951), pp. 396–97.

One should not forget that the Indian and southwestern Pacific oceans saw a far-ranging "megalithic" cultural expansion during the first millennium B.C., affecting southern India, southeastern Asia, some of the islands of the southwest Pacific, and extending as far northward as Japan. See above, pp. 98–102.

[26] A Greek ship captain, Scylax, was dispatched by Darius to explore the Indus River and the sea routes linking it with his other dominions; and the Great King thought it worthwhile to complete a canal between the Nile and the Red Sea in order to permit shipping to pass from the Mediterranean to the southern seas. How much active commerce followed from these efforts is unclear. Darius' canal, at least, was soon allowed to silt up; and though it is reported that cities existed in India, they may have been religious and administrative, rather than commercial and industrial centers. Cf. A. T. Olmstead, *History of the Persian Empire*, pp. 144–47.

haps only stagnation) of navigation in Arabian waters during the first millennium B.C.[27]

As always, trade involved complex currents of cultural influence. Within the Middle Eastern civilized area, the effect was to wear down local differences in culture. Beyond, in the half-barbarous worlds of India and Greece, and in the still more barbarous lands of the western Mediterranean, the effect was to stimulate local peoples to imitate, adapt, and alter what they found admirable in Middle Eastern civilization, and to create their own styles of civilized life, peripheral to but essentially independent of the older civilizations.

Thus the law and administration of the Assyrian and Persian empires, together with the ships and caravans of city merchants, combined to create throughout the Middle East a "great society" comparable to that which had existed in Hammurabi's time within the narrower confines of Mesopotamia. Only a small part of the total population had any direct part in this "great society," for long-distance trade and the activities of the central government touched only a small minority. Hence the metropolitan economy and imperial political structures showed a certain fragility, in contrast to the far more stable pattern of local exchange between peasant and artisan which assured the survival of at least a modest urbanization even in the face of political or economic disaster.

E. CULTURAL CONSERVATION AND ADVANCE

From 1700 to 500 B.C., Middle Eastern culture exhibited complex interplay between conservative, archaizing efforts and cosmopolitan impulses toward syncretism and innovation. The conservative spirit had strongest hold in Babylonia and Egypt, for the priests of these lands had much to preserve and found it hard to believe that anything new could deserve their attention. Syncretism was most apparent in Syria and Palestine, where the Egyptian and Mesopotamian cultural provinces met and overlapped. Such syncretism involved the combination of native traditions with Mesopotamian or Egyptian motifs of art and thought; and the results often lacked stylistic cohesion. Toward the farther margins of the civilized world, however, where native tradition was stronger and the influence of civilized models less oppressive, important cultural advances occurred.

I. BABYLONIA

The Kassite conquest, followed by a long period of Assyrian dominance and eventual annexation, worked remarkably little change in Babylonian culture.

[27] The introduction of the camel as a common beast of transport soon after 1000 B.C. enlarged the mobility of desert nomads considerably and made it possible for both trade and warlike enterprise to surmount hitherto insuperable geographical obstacles, especially in northern and central Arabia. Camels seem to have been domesticated in small numbers soon after 2000 B.C.; but it was nearly a thousand years later before the refractory beasts became common enough to have serious importance for human society. Cf. Joseph P. Free, "Abraham's Camels," *Journal of Near Eastern Studies*, III (1944), 187–93; Reinhard Walz, "Zum Problem des Zeitpunkts der Domestikation der altweltlichen Cameliden," in *Zeitschrift der deutschen morgenlandischen Gesellschaft*, CI (1951), 29–51; Reinhard Walz, "Neue Untersuchungen zum Domestikationsproblem der altweltlichen Cameliden," *loc. cit.*, CIV (1954), 47–50.

Some retrogression may perhaps be inferred from the scanty materials surviving from Kassite times; but the general impression is of an intensely conservative preservation of the ancient cultural forms.

Babylonian cultural conservatism was partly due to the fact that the very considerable geographic expansion attained by Mesopotamian styles of life before 1700 B.C. thereafter constituted an effective cushion for the core area against exposure to communities of entirely alien culture. Before conquerors from outlying regions could penetrate to the ancient cities of the flood plain, they inevitably acquired a considerable tincture of Mesopotamian civilization as it had been naturalized in the borderlands. Kassites and Assyrians came, therefore, not as utter strangers within the gates, but as rural cousins, prepared on the whole to welcome a more thoroughgoing initiation into the mysteries of high Babylonian civilization. This fact contributed powerfully to Babylonia's cultural stability after 1700, for the artists, writers, and priests of Babylonia itself did not have to come to terms with any radically new world-view, nor with any alien high art or impressive literary tradition. They could afford to cling reverently and complacently to the old models handed down from ancient and better times.

Deeply conservative priestly colleges and scribal schools continued to provide the chief institutional framework for Babylonian cultural activity. Priestly authority actually increased as political autonomy declined, for military and political disaster could always be interpreted as the result of divine anger and provided a telling argument for an even more assiduous service of the gods. Hence, as political sovereignty fell into the hands of strangers, Babylonian collective feeling tended to concentrate increasingly upon the priestly colleges, especially upon that of Marduk.

Public religion remained much as it had been in Hammurabi's day. Ritual hardened into fixed forms, so that when the priests of Babylon had worked out suitable versions of prayers, hymns, and litanies for every ceremonial occasion, variant forms were allowed to lapse into forgetfulness. In this process, older religious literature seems to have been systematically purged of concepts which had become offensive to the orthodoxy of Marduk. For example, Sumerian hymns referring to rulers as divinities were either deliberately suppressed or merely forgotten.[28] Later Babylonian religion also placed increasing emphasis upon the supreme god of the pantheon, Marduk. But the inheritance from ancient Sumer and Akkad was too strong to allow the emergence of anything that may properly be called monotheism. At most, there was a trend in that direction.

Of course, no absolute crystallization of cultural forms occurred. In the realm of art, the scant remains of the Kassite period show innovations in palace architecture, involving the use of columns and molded bricks to produce figures in low relief. But old traditions of religious architecture were painstakingly preserved; and no significant changes in sculptural styles can be detected. Where the hand of the priest prevailed, frozen stability, tempered

[28] Cf. Adam Falkenstein and Wolfram von Soden, *Sumerische und akkadische Hymnen und Gebete* (Zürich: Artemis Verlag, 1953), pp. 16–18.

only by an occasional crudity of workmanship, was the rule; new artistic departures were confined to court and palace.[29]

Yet religion itself was not immune from innovation, despite the unchanging façade of traditional ceremonies conducted on behalf of the community. In earlier times, private concerns had been left to minor gods with whom the head of each household dealt directly. Such petty deities were probably conceived as intercessors with the high gods who ruled the cosmos. In Kassite and Assyrian times, however, private persons undertook to assure a more effective communication with the divine rulers of the world by addressing themselves directly to the high gods, using divination procedures which had formerly been reserved for matters of public and community concern. Marduk and the rest of the pantheon were thus in a sense democratized, in a sense universalized, and in a sense debased through being asked to pay attention to the petty affairs of individuals. Priests profited most, for they acquired new social functions and sources of income by undertaking to mediate between private persons and the high gods;[30] yet this new role did not in the least diminish their age-old prerogative as leaders of public ceremonies.

Presumably only the upper classes of society were affected by these changes; at any rate, only the wealthy could afford the fees requisite for satisfying personal religious anxieties. Nevertheless, this individualization of Babylonian religious practice implies that at least some persons were conscious of serious defects in the older collective religion. In the megalopolitan environment of Babylon, individuals could no longer identify themselves entirely with the fate of the social groups to which they belonged: native city, occupational associations, and even family ceased to have unchallenged sway over men's affections. But insofar as a more individualized viewpoint gained ground, it weakened and undermined the values and ideals of Mesopotamian civilization. For if the past and future welfare of a man's family and city ceased to serve as an adequate criterion of effective relationships with the gods, what consolation could a helpless mortal find in the doctrines of traditional Babylonian religion?

It is therefore not surprising that a few literary works of the first millennium B.C. express spiritual weariness, pessimism, and hopeless protest against the ways of the world. An example is the acrostic poem, sometimes called the Babylonian Ecclesiastes. It takes the form of a dialogue, in which the first speaker laments his own miseries and inveighs against the follies and injustices of men generally. He charges the gods with having absconded from

---

[29] Henri Frankfort, *The Art and Architecture of the Ancient Orient* (Harmondsworth: Penguin Books, 1954), pp. 62–64.

[30] In this, the priests imitated the example which had been set by royal judges in and before the age of Hammurabi. When royal jurisdiction ceased to concern only collectivities, but was made to apply to individuals as well, the practical power and influence of royal government increased enormously. So also did income from fees and fines. Exactly the same considerations apply to the expansion of priestly functions into the private sphere: the priests' authority over men's acts and thoughts was enhanced and their income enlarged by fees and perquisites provided by private persons seeking divine help or guidance.

the world they had created, for they had given equivocal or variable answers to his queries and failed utterly to protect pious and good men from undeserved disaster. The interlocutor at first offers conventional pious responses, explaining the inscrutability of divine intentions and urging patience, but at the end seems to be won over to the view that there is no justice on earth or in heaven.[31] One cannot tell, of course, how widespread such a spirit may have been in Babylonia during the first millennium B.C.; but the mere fact that such a poem was written and preserved suggests that a real decay had set in beneath the unchanging surface of traditional routine and ceremonial. Clearly, the author of this poem (together with those who read and copied it) found little comfort in traditional religion, or satisfaction in daily life.

Others, however, sought reassurance by trying to restore aspects of the vanished greatness of the past. Several Assyrian kings, especially Ashurbanipal (668–626 B.C.), searched out ancient tablets and had them copied or preserved in great palace libraries; and Nabonidus (555–539 B.C.), the last king of Babylon before the Persian conquest, organized excavations on old temple sites with the intention of rediscovering ancient ground plans so that he could construct exact replicas. The effort put into such antiquarian enterprises suggests a sense of inadequacy, as though Ashurbanipal and Nabonidus hoped to regain a vanished confidence by preserving the knowledge or restoring the physical structures of an age believed to have qualities lacking in their own times.

Thus the characteristic feature of Babylonian cultural history after 1700 B.C. seems to be an outward fossilization, combined with secret inner decay.

2. EGYPT

During the same centuries, the traditions of antique Egyptian civilization withstood a much fiercer challenge than any issuing from world-weary Mesopotamian sophisticates. The end result was much the same: conscious archaism striving to disguise an inner uncertainty. But before Egyptian culture reached this impasse, the rulers, priests, artists, and scribes of Upper and Lower Egypt for the first time had to take seriously into account the achievements of other peoples. Breakdown of the former smug isolation resulted in a stormy flirtation with alien ways, followed by·emphatic revulsion against all things foreign.

In the time of the Old and Middle Kingdoms, geographical barriers to foreign contacts had permitted the inhabitants of the Nile Valley to regard themselves as infinitely superior to all other peoples.[32] The Hyksos conquest rudely challenged this belief; and after their expulsion Egypt's imperial adventure into Asia made it impossible simply to neglect foreign ideas and prac-

---

[31] A translation may be found in James B. Pritchard, *Ancient Near Eastern Texts relating to the Old Testament* (Princeton, N.J.: Princeton University Press, 1955), pp. 438–40. Cf. a second poem in which a slave urges his master to "teach the god to run after you like a dog," by withholding sacrifices! *Idem*.

[32] Trade with neighboring areas brought the Egyptians into contact with regions of distinctly less developed culture than their own. Minoan Crete was perhaps an exception; but if such trade was conducted largely in Cretan ships after about 2100 B.C., as seems likely, the Egyptians presumably learned little and cared less about Cretan achievements in their island homeland.

tices. With the expansion of trade under the empire, new-sprung cities attracted nests of foreigners to the soil of Egypt itself, while the imperial Egyptian armies were recruited largely from among neighboring barbarian peoples.

Under these conditions, the inherited pattern of Egyptian society exhibited a disturbing fragility. A particularly critical weakness lay in the theoretically unlimited prerogatives of the god-king; for the same enormous powers which traditionally had maintained the old pieties and decorum might equally well be used to confound them. Moreover, as conquerer and defender of strange lands, and as commander in chief of an army composed largely of foreign mercenaries, the Pharaoh was constantly exposed to foreign novelties. The danger of his turning apostate was therefore real.

The Pharaoh Amenhotep IV (1380–1362 B.C.), who renamed himself Ikhnaton, did in fact exploit his traditional prerogatives to become a royal revolutionary of the most radical sort. As a convert to the new (or newly revived and revised) religion of the sun-disk, Aton, he undertook to suppress all rival pieties, and to make the worship of Aton and of himself as son of Aton the sole religion of the empire.[33] The revolutionary Pharaoh closed the old temples and obliterated the name of Amon, the mightiest of the old gods, from public inscriptions, perhaps in the hope of destroying Amon's power through destroying his name. But by exhibiting the spirit of a fanatic, Ikhnaton subjected the thread of traditional obedience which gave him his power to an almost intolerable strain;[34] and in the end, he provoked an unreasoning counter-fanaticism among adherents of traditional religion.

Atonist doctrine conceived the power of the deified sun-disk as extending equally to all peoples, whether within or without the borders of the Egyptian empire. Such universalism may have reflected a radically rational reaction to the religious diversity of mankind—a diversity which had come to Egyptian attention with all the force of a new revelation when their armies and officials began, under the empire, to move familiarly in distant lands and among alien peoples. Pious and devout minds, disturbed by such religious variety, may well have been struck by the undoubted presence of the sun in every part of the world, shining with majesty and overwhelming brightness upon all men. Here, clearly, was a true god, manifest and indubitable, unique, universal, and beneficent. By comparison, other so-called deities appeared to be false, distorted, man-made.[35] Yet there is no reason to suppose that more than a

[33] Ikhnaton tried to revive the Old Kingdom doctrine that life after death lay within the gift of the Pharaoh and could not be attained otherwise. The whole Aton movement may have originated as a reassertion and reform of the ancient worship of the Heliopolitan sun god Re. If so, a putative return to ancient purity justified radical departure from the immediate past. Thus, as in the much later age of the European Reformation, revolution espoused archaism the more effectually to reject the present.

[34] No revolt broke out during Ikhnaton's lifetime. Even military disaster on the frontiers of the empire provoked no effective protest in Egypt. Such passivity reflected the peculiar anguish of the conservative position; for by a supreme irony, in a social universe that turned upon obedience to a god incarnate, the old pieties could only be upheld by obeying the Pharaoh in their repudiation!

[35] The further fact that solar worship already existed in Egypt, and that priests of Re at Heliopolis knew of a time when such an important god as Amon of Thebes had not even been heard of, probably helped the Aton religion to get started and may have provided hints as to how the worship of the true god should be conducted.

handful of Egyptians fully believed in Atonism, or that such views would have attained much importance without the support of the Pharaoh's power. Certainly the movement collapsed utterly after Ikhnaton's death and left few traces behind.

The Aton movement was revolutionary in art and literature, as well as in religion. The reformers' key concept was *maat*, or truth-justice, of which Aton was believed to be the embodiment. This concept was not new in Egyptian thought; but the Atonist application of it to art and letters was often startlingly at variance with older tradition.

The Atonist understanding of *maat* transformed religious architecture, since it was thought incompatible with *maat* to worship in the secret recesses of closed temples, as the priests of Amon always did. Only an open courtyard, where the rays of the sun could be sensed directly, was acceptable to Aton; and the architecture of Ikhnaton's new capital city was conceived according-ly. In sculpture and painting, Atonism inspired a freer and more naturalistic style. To portray nature and man in accordance with *maat* required an un-flinching—even exaggerated—portrayal of the abnormalities of Ikhnaton's per-son. But it is characteristic of the limitations of the Atonist movement that Ikhnaton's slack musculature and bony face became a new standard for portraiture, so that his courtiers were often painted to resemble him. The Atonists' most profound break with Egyptian artistic tradition was perhaps their rejection of the ideal of monumentality and timelessness. The artists of Ikhnaton's age sought to capture human emotion and the feeling of a fleeting moment. Accordingly, Ikhnaton and his family were sometimes portrayed in startlingly informal poses, which scarcely fitted Pharaoh's role as god incarnate.

As applied to literature, *maat* signified a closer conformity to everyday speech. The result was a rapid evolution in the vocabulary and syntax of hieroglyphic Egyptian. Yet many of the old patterns of speech persisted: the hymns praising Aton continued to use traditional phrases and epithets, and the written language retained most of the old grammatical forms. Nonethe-less, a new spirit may be sensed in such a masterpiece as the Hymn to Aton, celebrating the universal power and beneficence of the sun-disk. Joy in the beauty of nature, and the absence of references to the multiple names and mythical activities of the god distinguish this from traditional Egyptian hymns.[36]

Ikhnaton's reforms affected spheres of activity other than religion and aesthetics, although these are the only aspects of the Atonist movement readi-

[36] Attribution of universal and supreme power to a single god can be paralleled in several other Egyptian hymns of the imperial age. The easy path of syncretism (and perhaps a natural tendency to flatter the god one worshipped) had led men to exalt the power of Amon-Re or of some other god to encompass the whole world, without necessarily or even probably implying that other divinities did not simultaneously have jurisdiction and power in their own spheres. By denying divinity to any but Aton and the Pharaoh, Atonism may have gone a step further toward monotheism than earlier Egyptian religion had done; but "monotheistic" phrases, which if taken literally imply the existence of only one god, can easily be found in religious texts of the imperial period both before and after Ikhnaton's heresy. A sampling of such texts may be found in J. B. Pritchard, *Ancient Near Eastern Texts*, pp. 365–69. The Hymn to Aton is translated in the same volume, pp. 370–72.

WHAT IS TRUTH?

The upper picture, discovered on a casket in Tutankhamen's (1362–1349 B.C.) tomb, shows the imperial Pharaoh scattering destruction among his enemies with delicate elegance. The bas-relief below portrays domestic bliss as known to the Pharaoh Ikhnaton (1380–1362 B.C.). Contrasts between the two scenes reflect the force of the Aton revolution. Thus Ikhnaton is shown sitting under the protective rays of Aton, the sun-disk, upholder of *Maat;* whereas Tutankhamen has the Falcon Horus decoratively hovering over his head (cf. p. 77). Ikhnaton's family is portrayed in a fashion designed to insult traditional concepts of the pharaonic dignity, whereas Tutankhamen's casket presents the Pharaoh re-enacting, though without any conviction, an ancient and completely traditional military role (cf. p. 73). Despite such deliberate contrasts, these works of art share a refined and highly mannered style, and both suggest weakness and moral uncertainty.

ly accessible to modern scholars. Probably the religious collision between adherents of Amon and of Aton involved also a fierce struggle between oligarchy and absolutism. The priests of Amon were closely linked with a number of great noble families, whose members had enjoyed a near monopoly of high state office for generations. In challenging Amon and his priesthood, Ikhnaton necessarily defied also the power and privileges of these families. His supporters seem to have been mainly social upstarts and soldiers, so that it is possible to interpret the Atonist movement as a struggle between army and priesthood for primacy in the state. Insofar as foreign elements dominated the army and had a foothold in the Pharaonic household, the struggle lay also between "subversive" foreigners and privileged natives.[37]

In another idiom, one may describe Ikhnaton's reforms as a convulsive effort to bring Egyptian life and thought into tune with the emergent cosmopolitan world of the Middle East. The illogic of traditional Egyptian religion, the stiff monumentality of Egyptian art, and the rigidities of Egyptian social structure were all bound to appear increasingly parochial and archaic to men who had experienced the variety of life and belief prevalent in the great world beyond Egyptian borders.

Yet, like the rationalizing Memphite theology of more than a thousand years before, the whole Atonist movement soon collapsed. Some efforts at compromise with the old order seem to have been made during Ikhnaton's last years; and his successor Tutankhamon made still further concessions. But once the fanaticism of the Atonist reform had been abandoned, no compromise could stand; for the priests and nobles, whose privileges had been so rudely attacked, would not rest until all traces of what they viewed as revolutionary foreign subversion had been eradicated from the land of Egypt.[38] The army appears to have made its peace with the reaction easily enough. At any rate, when the army commander Haremhab usurped the throne (1349 B.C.), he devoted his attention to salvaging what he could of the empire in Asia and let home affairs fall entirely into the hands of the priests of Amon and their allies.

Thenceforward, although the Pharaoh was still officially a god, he was a god in leading strings, and the priests of Amon held the strings. No important enterprise could be undertaken without consulting the oracle of Amon, so that the priests, who interpreted the oracle, acquired enormous influence. The army remained as a countervailing force in the state; and friction between priests and soldiers recurred from time to time. But on the whole it was the priests who prevailed. Official effort thenceforth successfully sought to preserve old forms and repress all innovations, particularly any that smacked of foreignness.

[37] John A. Wilson, *The Burden of Egypt*, pp. 206–8.

[38] New bands of stonecutters were dispatched to erase the name of Aton wherever it could be found, just as Amon's name had earlier been obliterated. Ikhnaton's palaces and temples were destroyed, and his new capital abandoned, never to be reoccupied. Thus archeologists had the great advantage of a relatively undisturbed site when they began to dig at Tel Amarna, where Ikhnaton's capital once stood.

THE BURDEN OF EGYPT

The variety of Egyptian art is demonstrated by these three sharply differentiated portraits. Moreover, the confident smile of Amenhotep III (1417–1379 B.C.) (*upper left*), distorted in the next generation into the brooding visage of his son and successor, Ikhnaton (1380–1362 B.C.) (*upper right*), and succeeded within less than a century by the deliberately archaistic portrait of Rameses II (1292–1225 B.C.) (*lower left*), effectively symbolizes the transformation of Egyptian outlook incident to Ikhnaton's attempted religious revolution. A smug conviction of Egypt's imperial superiority to all the world may be read into Amenhotep's portrait, whereas Ikhnaton's face bespeaks his doctrinaire espousal of transcendental truths, and the withdrawn aloofness of Rameses' pose expresses the Egyptians' deliberate withdrawal into their parochial past—a withdrawal which became increasingly emphatic as their empire waned.

The cultural changes accompanying the Atonist upheaval could not be so easily eradicated; and perhaps the counterrevolutionaries who overthrew Atonism did not desire to eradicate them all. Extremism in art was abandoned; and a partial return to the older conventions occurred. But something remained of the more varied and freer styles which had run riot under Ikhnaton; and the "new" hieroglyphic continued in use for literary and monumental purposes. In general, the level of artistic achievement declined. Gigantism in statuary and architecture supplanted careful craftsmanship, especially in the age of Rameses II (1301–1234 B.C.), when the glories of empire were ostentatiously revived, even though Egypt had now lost her former undisputed hegemony in Asia and had to share power with rival Hittite and Assyrian empires.

After the final loss of all imperial possessions in Asia (*ca.* 1165 B.C.), Egypt underwent little perceptible change. As the country sank toward the status of a second-rate power and trade passed more and more into foreign hands, Egyptians increasingly turned in upon themselves and looked to the past. Archaism found expression in the deliberate (and sometimes very skilful) imitation of Old Kingdom styles in architecture, sculpture, and painting. Yet, less conspicuously—as it were beneath the surface—important changes did occur in Egyptian culture. Some surviving inscriptions suggest the rise of a more personal piety and express personal gratitude or penitence toward some particular god. Immortality was democratized, for the only prerequisite for a blissful afterlife came to be ready reference to suitable charms and magic formulae which, when written down and inclosed in a man's coffin, provided the departed soul with all necessary protection from the perils of the underworld.[39] In these developments we may see analogues to the more individualistic outlook upon the world which simultaneously found expression in Babylonia. But traditional piety suffered far weaker challenge in Egypt than in Mesopotamia. Egyptian doctrine offered the consolation of blissful immortality for the world-weary, as Babylonian religion did not; and this hope sustained individual Egyptians even in difficult times.

3. THE INTERMEDIATE REGIONS

The period from 1700 to 1200 B.C.—the age of the charioteer and of feudal empires—saw a mingling of Mesopotamian, Egyptian, and Aegean cultural influences throughout the coastal regions of the Levant. This was an international age, when kings exchanged rich presents, sealed alliances by giving their daughters in marriage, and corresponded regularly with one another in Akkadian cuneiform. Even the haughty Egyptians conducted their diplomacy and maintained archives in Akkadian.

Farther inland, where powerful royal courts provided lavish patronage, semi-autonomous art styles and literature arose. Excavations at the Hittite capital in Anatolia, for example, have revealed a distinctive, heavy-set, and slightly clumsy sculptural style, derived unmistakably from Mesopotamian prototypes. But Hittite sculptors never passed beyond the stage of a rude,

[39] Cf. J. B. Pritchard, *Ancient Near Eastern Texts*, pp. 34–36, 380–81.

vigorous, and in its own way charming apprenticeship. They were still wrestling with the technical problems of stonecutting and had only begun to emancipate themselves from foreign models when the invasions of the twelfth century B.C. destroyed the power of their royal patrons. Thereafter, Hittite art dissolved into inferior provincial styles.[40] Hittite literature, too, was largely dependent on Mesopotamian models for inspiration, and used cuneiform script. Yet Hittite scribes wrote in their own languages and recorded a number of myths pertaining to their native gods.[41]

About the culture of Mitanni little can be said until the capital of that realm has been located and excavated; but a few admirable pieces of sculpture have been recovered which, especially in the realistic treatment of animals, show affinities with later Assyrian art.[42]

No comparable stylistic independence manifested itself nearer the center of the Middle East. Syrian art of the second millennium B.C. offers a curiously disharmonious blend of Egyptian, Aegean, and Mesopotamian elements, in which neither skilful workmanship nor stylistic integrity is apparent.[43] Syrian literature of the period attained rather more distinction. Inscribed tablets discovered at the site of ancient Ugarit (near modern Beirut) record epic cycles dealing with gods, kings, and heroes. These poems are reminiscent of certain Mesopotamian myths; yet in details they show much that was peculiar to Syria, and their prosody anticipates many characteristics of later Hebrew psalmody.[44]

In the fourteenth century B.C., when these tablets were inscribed, the town of Ugarit was a cosmopolitan trading center. At least six foreign scripts were simultaneously in use: Akkadian, Sumerian, Hittite, Hurrian, Egyptian, and Cypriote. Local scribes must have found it quite impossible to master the intricacies of so many styles of writing, each of which involved the use of several score or even several hundred signs. The need for a simplified system of writing was evident; and the scribes of Ugarit were favorably situated to invent one. Exposed to multiple foreign influences, and lacking any antique and well-consolidated local literary tradition, they were free to experiment with radical simplification when confronted with the humdrum task of recording commercial contracts and other utilitarian documents in the local Semitic tongue. As a result, the Ugaritic scribes reduced the repertory of signs required to record their native tongue to a mere thirty. This process was far

---

[40] Cf. the convenient collection of photographs in Margarete Riemschneider, *Die Welt der Hethiter* (Stuttgart: Gustav Killper Verlag, 1954).

[41] Translation may be found in J. B. Pritchard, *Ancient Near Eastern Texts*, pp. 120–28.

[42] Cf. Albrecht Götze, *Hethiter, Churriter, und Assyrer*, pp. 183–85.

[43] Cf. Henri Frankfort, *The Art and Architecture of the Ancient Orient*, pp. 139–63.

[44] The tablets discovered at Ugarit have a particular interest for modern scholars, because they are the fullest—indeed almost the only—evidence for the nature of the Canaanite fertility religion, which in subsequent centuries competed with the worship of Yahweh among the Hebrews. For translations see J. B. Pritchard, *Ancient Near Eastern Texts*, pp. 129–55; and Cyrus H. Gordon, *Ugaritic Literature: A Comprehensive Translation of the Poetic and Prose Texts* (Rome: Pontificium Institutum Biblicum, 1949). For discussion, cf. G. A. S. Kapelrud, *Baal in the Ras Shamra Texts* (Copenhagen: G. E. C. Gad, 1952).

from unique to Ugarit, for throughout the middle length of the Fertile Crescent, similar systems of simplified writing were adapted to various languages during the same period.[45]

Such simplified scripts made possible the spread of literacy among much wider segments of society than before. This was a fundamental change, involving important shifts in the structure and rigidity of society at large. As long as years of effort were required to master the art of writing, the successful student was likely to cherish complexity as an end in itself. How else could the wisdom of the past be accurately preserved? How else keep interlopers from mastering the powerful secrets of things human and divine? Only the rarest graduate of such training could retain much capacity for freshness of thought or any desire to question the received ideas which were so inextricably bound up with the complicated signs he had spent years in mastering.

None of these rigidities applied to men who acquired literacy with a comparatively modest expenditure of effort, as a useful tool in the transaction of everyday business. Like the ancient Sumerian cuneiform, which had begun as symbolic accountancy, the simplified scripts of the second millennium B.C. for a long period were used solely for commercial and other practical purposes. Until the tenth century B.C., texts with literary pretensions clung to the hallowed complexities of the older styles of writing.

A second change in the mechanics of literacy became important toward the end of the second millennium B.C.—the use of papyrus sheets and animal skins, perhaps also of other perishable materials like wax tablets and wooden boards, as common materials upon which to write.[46] Egypt led the way in this development. Papyrus sheets had been manufactured and used for writing from the time of the Old Kingdom;[47] and a special cursive form of hieroglyphic had been developed to suit the natural movements of a pen. The perishability of papyrus makes it difficult to judge how rapidly cursive scripts spread beyond Egypt. Nevertheless, chance inscriptions on bits of pottery show that by 1300 B.C., cursive writing in simplified scripts was familiarly employed in

---

[45] Thirty signs could be mastered about as easily as a modern alphabet, the only difference being that vowels were not directly indicated, but had to be supplied by the reader from his knowledge of the language. This was not much more difficult than to interpret the vagaries of English spelling.

In more outlying regions—Elam, northern Mesopotamia, and Anatolia—scripts also moved in the direction of simplification, eliminating many word signs and relying mainly upon syllabic symbols. Only in the heartlands of Mesopotamia and Egypt did the full complication of the older scripts survive. Cf. Ignace J. Gelb, *A Study of Writing* (Chicago: University of Chicago Press, 1952), pp. 120–47. Efforts to pin down more exactly the place and time when the earliest "proto-Semitic alphabet" was invented are still inconclusive. Cf. David Diringer, "Problems of the Present Day on the Origin of the Phoenician Alphabet," *Cahiers d'histoire mondiale*, IV (1957), 40–58. Diringer considers Palestine or Syria during the Hyksos period (1730–1580 B.C.) as the most likely place of origin of the Semitic alphabet.

It has long been customary to regard these Semitic scripts as alphabetic. This view has been challenged by I. J. Gelb in *A Study of Writing*. Gelb believes that they were really syllabic and that a true alphabet was first invented by the Greeks. Cf. Marcel Cohen, *La Grande invention de l'écriture et son évolution* (Paris: Imprimerie nationale, 1958), I, 138–43.

[46] Clay tablets remained in use in Mesopotamia until the first century A.D.; but long before then, less bulky, but more perishable materials had come to predominate even in Mesopotamia itself and had completely displaced the incised cuneiform in regions peripheral to Mesopotamia.

[47] Stephen R. K. Glanville, *The Legacy of Egypt* (Oxford: Clarendon Press, 1942), p. 137.

Palestine and Syria. The casual use of potsherds to record entirely ordinary matters certainly suggests that literacy had percolated some distance down the social scale.[48]

But it would be wrong to suppose that in the second or even in the first millennium B.C., the simplification of writing abruptly transformed the life or thought of the Middle East. Phoenician and Aramaean merchants no doubt used writing in their affairs—but so had the Babylonians a thousand years before. For the most part, literacy continued to be the special preserve of conventionally minded priests and scribes. Yet not entirely so; and in the long run, even a few exceptional cases were quite enough to alter fundamentally the cultural physiognomy of the Middle East. For when writing was used to record the thoughts of prophetic and rebellious individuals, whose minds ran far beyond established and authorized limits, a powerful and versatile enzyme was loosed within the body of traditional piety and learning. Prophecies and protests, criticism of prevailing customs, and radical assertion of new standards of righteousness could create only temporary and local disturbances so long as their impact was confined to the range of a man's voice and the memory of his immediate hearers. But when such outpourings were reduced to writing, the fiery poetry of an Amos, Jeremiah, Isaiah, or Zoroaster acquired an unimaginably reinforced vibrancy, capable of affecting the lives of untold millions all round the world in ways quite unforeseen and unintended by the men who preached and prophesied so vehemently. Had writing remained the monopoly of a privileged clique, the angry words of prophets who so freely attacked established practices would never have been written down. Hence the democratization of learning implicit in simplified scripts must be counted as one of the major turning points in the history of civilization.

* * *

The barbarian invasions of the thirteenth to eleventh centuries B.C. brought few lasting changes to the cultural scene of the Middle East. Syria remained the melting pot of the region; and when the cities of Phoenicia arose to dominate the sea trade of the Mediterranean, the workshops of Tyre and Sidon turned out metalwork showing a rather ill-digested assortment of motifs and styles differing little from those which had flourished on the same ground two or three centuries before. Just as in earlier times, the major new art styles were the products of royal courts.

As early as the thirteenth century B.C., Assyrian art showed characteristics which were to endure throughout the later imperial period. A fine mastery of animal forms, especially of lions, and a free use of space between figures to concentrate attention on the protagonists may be seen in some early seal engravings. Later, when the Assyrian kings sought to celebrate their greatness by constructing vast palaces and even by founding entirely new cities, sculptors successfully transferred this miniature tradition to full-sized friezes, cut shallowly into stone. These friezes were a species of historical record. Occa-

---

[48] W. F. Albright, *From Stone Age to Christianity*, pp. 192–93.

sional inscriptions identified particular incidents from military campaigns or hunting expeditions; and unusual scenery served as a reminder of particular deeds the sculptor sought to celebrate. Some of the scenes effectively reproduced the fury and confusion of the battlefield; but the masterpieces of Assyrian art are portrayals of the hunt that marvelously convey both the pride of the hunter and the power and pathos of the wounded beasts. Assyrian palace sculpture was a secular art. As such, it was independent of old Mesopotamian religious tradition; no pious precedents or ancient models limited the artists' achievements, which were, accordingly, of the very highest order.[49]

Yet the limits of Assyrian cultural innovation were very narrow. Literary records show that the mighty kings of the sculptured friezes were simultaneously prisoners of priests who, in their capacity as guardians of ancient ritual and interpreters of oracles, minutely circumscribed the monarchs' daily actions.[50] Indeed, Assyrian priests appear to have been nearly as powerful in the state as were their contemporaries in Babylonia and just as intent upon maintaining a past which, if not dead, was surely dying.[51]

Priestly authority was evidenced by the fact that the Assyrians, though builders of the most rationalized, powerful state the world had yet seen, nonetheless sought piously and faithfully to preserve every jot and tittle of the religion and learning they had inherited from Sumer and Babylonia. In fact, much of the literature and religious doctrine of these ancient lands is known to us only through Assyrian copies, which were systematically accumulated by royal scribes and librarians. New composition was scant. Only the royal annals, constituting an elementary sort of history, went beyond antique literary precedent, incidentally permitting modern scholars to reconstruct Assyrian chronology with an exactitude not matched for earlier periods. For the rest, Assyrian literature, learning, and religion shared fully in the stark conservatism of contemporary Babylonia.

When the Chaldaean rulers of Babylon shared with the Medes the lordship of the Middle East, that ancient capital enjoyed a brief period of renewed greatness. The city's restored imperial power was faithfully reflected in art; for Nebuchadnezzar (604–562 B.C.), like his Assyrian predecessors, constructed monumental buildings on a lavish scale and built himself a magnificent palace. The lower courses of the walls of Nebuchadnezzar's palace, which alone survive, are decorated with colorful glazed tiles molded to form figures in low relief. How faithful these friezes may be to older Babylonian

---

[49] Motifs from other art traditions—for example, the Egyptian winged sun-disk as an emblem of divinity—were used occasionally, though they were thoroughly absorbed into a new, vigorous, and realistic style.

I have depended mainly on Henri Frankfort, *Art and Architecture of the Ancient Orient*, pp. 65–105, and my own eyes, for these remarks on Assyrian art.

[50] Henri Frankfort, *Kingship and the Gods* (Chicago: University of Chicago Press, 1948), pp. 253–55.

[51] In the imperial age, the worship of Ashur seems scarcely to have differed from the worship of Marduk and was clearly modeled on the Babylonian cult.

KINGS OF MEN AND OF BEASTS

Milton's sympathy for Satan seems here to find precedent in the pains anonymous Assyrian sculptors took to portray the power and pathos of the leonine victims of their royal masters' hunts. Such expeditions were both surrogates and training for war, as the appearance of two infantry soldiers at the top may remind us.

models cannot be said, since the exterior finish of earlier examples of mud-brick monumental building has not survived.[52]

Persian art, of which the palace of Darius at Persepolis is the most impressive surviving example, was more austere. Important affinities with Assyrian palace art are evident; yet the old motifs and devices were transformed into something new. The distinctiveness of this art depended partly on the Persians' use of new elements, like the columns that tower so impressively over the ruins at Persepolis.[53] More importantly, Persian imperial artists sought to portray the power and dignity of the Great King, not by recording particular deeds of prowess, as the Assyrians had done, but by symbolizing the abstract relationship of sovereign to subject in static but sometimes marvelously harmonious compositions. Artists from Ionia and various other parts of the empire worked on the palace at Persepolis; yet despite their diverse backgrounds, the over-all effect is one of decorative dignity and balance, pervaded by a spirit peculiarly Persian.[54]

Unlike the Assyrians, the Persians in their imperial age were by no means the passive heirs of an old religious and literary tradition. Assyrian culture, after all, dated from the third millennium, when the town of Ashur had first come into existence as an outpost of Sumerian civilization; and until the downfall of their empire, the Assyrians maintained a reverence for Babylon and the south, whence their culture derived. By contrast, when the Persians conquered the Oriental world, they were just emerging from barbarism. Their language may not have been reduced to writing until the time of Cyrus; and the earliest Persian script—a simplified cuneiform—seems never to have become the vehicle for any important literary composition.

One reason for the Persians' limited literary achievement in the age of the Achaemenids (550–330 B.C.) was the wide use they made of Aramaic for written communication. A Semitic language introduced into the civilized world in the twelfth century B.C., Aramaic had clothed itself in a simplified script similar to the Phoenician, and in the time of the Assyrian empire had replaced Akkadian as the lingua franca of the Middle East. Lacking a body of scribes who knew Persian, the Achaemenids found Aramaic by far the most convenient language for administering their far-flung territories and tended to confine their mother tongue to its traditional oral employments among themselves.

Persian literary tradition therefore does not go back to the court of the Achaemenids, but to the religious movement associated with the name of Zoroaster. Yet the *Avesta*, the sacred scripture of Zoroastrianism, was not written down in its present form until sometime between the fourth and sixth centuries A.D. Before that time, the body of sacred writings had gone through a complicated evolution, the stages of which are almost entirely obscure.

---

[52] The fantastic animals that constitute the chief element in Nebuchadnezzar's friezes, as well as the hieratic, processional character of the composition, seem thoroughly in the spirit of ancient Sumer.

[53] Such columns may represent the translation of tree trunks used in a native and primitive architecture into stone.

[54] Henri Frankfort, *Art and Architecture of the Ancient Orient*, pp. 215–33.

Vorderasiatisches Museum, Staatliche Museen zu Berlin.

THE WALLS OF BABYLON

These spirited lions adorned the walls of Nebuchadnezzar's palace at Babylon. The early destruction of his empire and palace preserved this portion of the wall by burying it beneath the rubble of the upper stories. Multicolored glazed brick facings had long been a feature of Mesopotamian architecture, but only such an accident as befell Nebuchadnezzar's palace allows modern eyes to again experience the gaudy brilliance that must once have shimmered where dusty mounds of crumbling brick are all that now remain.

Only one small fragment of the *Avesta*, the *Gathas*, seems to have been composed during or before the sixth century B.C.[55] The *Gathas* probably derive from poems that were originally declaimed in public by Zoroaster; but their language is so crabbed and full of grammatical uncertainties that modern translators find difficulty in determining the sense of some passages and cannot transmit their original literary force.[56]

In any case, the importance of Zoroaster's poems was religious rather than literary. In this they were true to their times; for the transformation of religious sensibilities which came fully into focus in the sixth century B.C. far overshadowed all other cultural achievements of the ancient Middle East.

4. ZOROASTRIANISM AND JUDAISM

From Sumerian times, the cultural life of the Middle East had been polarized between sacred and secular, temple and palace, priest and courtier. Throughout the second millennium B.C., the important cultural achievements were secular, while religion remained a stronghold of conservatism and immobility. The opposite was true of the first millennium B.C., when religious innovations were made that in time eclipsed the proudest artistic attainments of the imperial courts. For the religious doctrines and world-view attached to the names of Zoroaster and the Hebrew prophets survived long after the great palaces of Nineveh and Susa had fallen into ruin and the very names of their royal builders had been forgotten.

In Egypt and Mesopotamia, to be sure, we have already seen that rigid conservatism continued to be the rule in all matters touching upon religion. Toward the margins of the civilized world, however, no deep commitment to ancient formulae paralyzed thought; and in certain regions, where rival cultural traditions mingled, reflective minds were stimulated to grapple anew with the great questions of human fate and destiny. One such region was eastern Persia, where Mesopotamian and Indian influences met, and Zoroastrianism arose. A second was Israel, where Mesopotamian and Egyptian civilizations confronted each other, and Judaism took shape. Still a third, less important and less well known than the others, was in Asia Minor, where Mesopotamian and Aegean cultures mingled, and the cult of Orpheus appears to have originated. The history of Orphism is so obscure that it seems best not to undertake its discussion, beyond mentioning the fact that purificatory rites to assure life beyond death lay close to the center of the religion.[57] Zoroastrianism and Judaism, on the contrary, deserve more extended treatment.

---

[55] Jack Finegan, *The Archaeology of World Religions* (Princeton, N.J.: Princeton University Press, 1952), pp. 75–76, 110, 113. The remainder of the *Avesta* originated at a later date; and the whole corpus evolved toward its present form during the Parthian (250 B.C.–229 A.D.) and more particularly during the Sassanian (229–651 A.D.) epochs of Persian history.

[56] James Hope Moulton, *Early Religious Poetry of Persia* (Cambridge, 1911), pp. 80–85. An English translation of the *Gathas* may be found in J. H. Moulton, *Early Zoroastrianism* (London: Williams & Norgate, 1913), pp. 344–90.

[57] Cf. the probable character of the megalithic religion, as discussed above, pp. 98–102.

THE PILLARS OF PERSEPOLIS

Even in its ruined and fragmentary condition, the palace of Darius appears grand and imposing. The stately serenity of the sculptured friezes contrasts strongly both with the high-pitched violence characteristic of Assyrian palace art (p. 149) and with the colorful patternings of Nebuchadnezzar's glazed brick. Even when Darius' sculptors chose to fill an awkward corner with the familiar Mesopotamian motif of a lion attacking his prey (shown here on the stair front and enlarged), their composition took on a heraldic quality, giving a new and distinctively Persian accent even to borrowed art forms (cf. p. 67). The winged figure on the lower left is a representation of Zoroaster's supreme divinity, Ahura Mazda. The sculptor's effort to portray Ahura Mazda, itself a divagation from strict Zoroastrianism, drew upon ancient Mesopotamian (perhaps ultimately Egyptian) motifs of the winged sun-disk.

The origins of Zoroastrianism are in dispute. Remote forefathers of the Medes and Persians of the imperial period presumably professed some ancestral form of the religion attested in the *Rig Veda,* involving the worship of vaguely personified natural forces, and of spirits who presided over particular arts and places.[58] As the Persians began to settle down to a more sedentary, agricultural mode of life, and as cultural influences from Mesopotamia became more intense, severe strains must have been put upon their older system of religion and ethics which had developed under more purely pastoral conditions. Perhaps this opened a way for the reception of Zoroastrianism among the Iranians of the Achaemenid period.[59]

Almost everything about Zoroaster's historic career is uncertain. When he lived and where he preached are subject to wide differences of opinion; and even the relationship between Zoroastrianism and the religion of the Achaemenid monarchs is in dispute. On one point only is there a fairly general consensus: that Zoroaster's thought, and in many cases his own words, are preserved in the *Gathas.* However, the numerous obscurities and unsystematic character of these poems make it difficult to interpret his message.

Yet Zoroaster had a message. In one of his poems he refers to a conversion experience, in which Ahura Mazda (*i.e.,* Lord of Wisdom) first instructed him in the truths of religion.[60] The central item of this instruction may be suggested by a quotation:

I will speak of that which the Holiest declared to me as the word that is best for mortals to obey: he, Mazdah Ahura [said], "They who at my bidding render him [Zoroaster] obedience shall all attain unto Welfare and Immortality by the actions of the Good Spirit."
. . . In immortality shall the soul of the righteous be joyful, in perpetuity shall be the torments of the Liars. All this doth Mazdah Ahura appoint by his Dominion.[61]

Obedience to Zoroaster and to Ahura Mazda involved modest cultic observances in which the recitation of hymns and prayers played a central part, while bloody sacrifice was expressly forbidden. But the ceremonial aspect of the religion, which became pervasive in later times, was not stressed in the *Gathas.* Emphasis was put instead upon practical action in this world. Zoroaster summoned his hearers to fight, with weapons if necessary, against up-

---

[58] Roughly comparable religious conceptions were probably common to many of the Indo-European tribes and may have developed out of some still earlier form of barbarian religiosity as a result of indirect contact with the pantheon of ancient Sumer, whose gods of storm, sun, and sky bear a telltale likeness to the Aryan, Greek, and other Indo-European divinities.

[59] Eduard Meyer, *Geschichte des Altertums* (Stuttgart: J. C. Cotta, 1910), III, 101, applied the epithet "agricultural" to Zoroaster's religion; and it is clear that the prophet had nothing good to say of pastoral nomads who raided the sedentary communities on the eastern outskirts of Iran (where Zoroaster perhaps lived). Sometimes, indeed, Zoroaster seemed to equate the forces of evil with nomad raiders.

[60] Yasna 43:11.

[61] Yasna 45:5–7. This and subsequent quotations are taken from the translation of the *Gathas* in Moulton, *Early Zoroastrianism,* pp. 344 ff.

holders of the Lie, *i.e.*, against adherents of unreformed pagan religion and the forces of evil in general.

Zoroaster's conception of Ahura Mazda was abstract and lofty:

> He that in the beginning thus thought, "Let the blessed realms be filled with lights," he it is that by his wisdom created Right. . . . I conceived of thee, O Mazdah, in my thought that thou, the First, art [also] the Last—that thou art father of Good Thought . . . and art the Lord to judge the actions of life.[62]

Yet Zoroaster did not believe the world was a place where truth and goodness reigned secure in accordance with the will of Ahura Mazda. Instead, he envisaged the universe as the scene of a cosmic struggle between good and evil. The practical force of Zoroaster's preaching was to urge men to espouse good and to live lives informed by the half-personified angelic spirits—Good Thought, Right, etc.—which Mazda had created to assist him in the struggle against the Lie. To the man who chose the good and acted uprightly, Zoroaster promised prosperity in this life and immortality hereafter. He seems also to have prophesied a Day of Judgment, when final victory would come to the forces of Ahura Mazda, whereupon a freshet of molten metal would purify the earth, and the forces of evil go down to torment everlasting.

An element in Zoroaster's message that seems oddly out of harmony with his abstract theology was the special place he accorded to cattle. No doubt this feature of his thought derived from primitive times, when the lives of the Persian tribesmen had revolved around their herds.[63] But such survivals were exceptional. For the most part, Zoroaster broke deliberately and consciously with the religious observances of his day. Various passages of the *Gathas* denounce pagan cult practices such as blood sacrifice and ritual drunkenness;[64] but Zoroaster never suggested that in making such denunciation he was merely purifying an old religious tradition. He had nothing but hatred for the gods of the old Persian pantheon: they ranked among the evil spirits who served the Lie. He saw himself as the founder of a new religion, inspired directly by Ahura Mazda, and guided by Good Thought and the other angels.[65]

Although Zoroaster's religion never spread significantly beyond the limits of the Persian nation, nothing in his teaching made such a history inevitable. On the contrary, he intended his message for all mankind. In one passage, for example, the prophet implored Ahura Mazda to impart the divine plan for

---

[62] Yasna 31:7–8.

[63] In one of Zoroaster's poems, for example, the Ox-soul petitions Mazda for protection against violence done to cattle on earth by men and devils. Mazda offers Zoroaster's preaching as a means of redressing the wrongs which the Ox-soul has suffered. The Ox-soul is at first not satisfied with "the ineffectual word of an impotent man . . . when I wish for one that commands mightily"; but is pacified when Zoroaster prays for good dwellings and peace for the oxen: "O Ahura, now is help ours: we will be ready to serve those that are of you." Yasna 29:1–11. This may be interpreted as a metaphorical statement of Zoroaster's conception of his mission: to protect peaceable husbandmen and their herds against nomadic raiders. Nonetheless, passages of the *Gathas* like this seem to echo a very distant past, for the Ox-soul reminds one of the animal spirits of Paleolithic art.

[64] Yasna 32:12, and 44:20, for example.

[65] In his complete rejection of the old faith, as well as in certain other aspects of his thought—e.g., the material and outward forms in which he envisioned the rewards of obedience to Ahura Mazda—Zoroaster closely resembled Mohammed.

the world in order "with the tongue of thine own mouth that I may convert all living men."[66] Not the nation, as with the earlier Jewish prophets, but the individual man was the religious unit for Zoroaster; and he treated the entire world as a stage upon which the divine drama was to be played out.

These universalist aspects of Zoroaster's teaching strongly suggest that he lived at a time when tribal bonds were loosening, when knowledge of the great world had penetrated to the Persian highlands, and when the myths and ritual of traditional religion had lost their power to satisfy sensitive and inquiring minds. The general sophistication, ethical elevation, abstraction, and universality of Zoroastrian doctrine seem to require a late date: perhaps the sixth century B.C., when the Medes and Persians had already come deeply under the disturbing influence of Mesopotamian civilization and had been at least slightly exposed to the individualist and universalist tendencies of contemporary civilized thought.[67]

If Zoroaster preached in the time of Cyrus, when Persian power was rapidly expanding over almost the entire civilized world, the new religion must still have had the force of fresh revelation when Darius and Xerxes attributed their authority to the will of Ahura Mazda. How widely the Persian populace accepted Zoroastrianism cannot be said; perhaps at first it was the creed only of restricted aristocratic and court circles. If so, the survival of the new religion was extremely precarious; for among the Achaemenids only Darius the Great and his successor Xerxes used definitely Zoroastrian language in their monumental inscriptions. In later times, Median priests, the magi, who professed some of the doctrines Zoroaster had so emphatically rejected, came to play a significant role at court. Later, under the influence of Mesopotamian ideas, further modifications of Persian court religion occurred. King Artaxerxes II (404–359 B.C.), for instance, set up cult statues in temples—a practice repugnant both to Zoroastrian and to magian principles.

Yet these changes did not involve the outright repudiation of Zoroastrianism, nor of Ahura Mazda. Rather, a series of compromises grafted some of the ancient gods onto Zoroastrian theology in a rather anomalous fashion.[68] Mithra, for example, a sun god and member of the old Persian pantheon, came to be conceived as mediator between mankind and the transcendent and unembodied Ahura Mazda; while Anahita, originally connected with rivers and water, was incongruously incorporated into Zoroastrianism as a fertility goddess.

Despite all historical obscurities, there can be no doubt that religious ideas underwent a rapid and impressive development among the Persians during their first imperial age. Zoroaster strove to bring into religious focus the new world opening before his people; and in this he was strikingly successful.

[66] Yasna 31:3.

[67] Zoroaster's doctrines had certainly been formulated before Darius came to the throne in 522 B.C., since one of Darius' early inscriptions echoes Zoroastrian terminology in an unmistakable fashion. This gives a firm *terminus ante quem* for Zoroaster's activity, but no more than that.

[68] The process may be compared with the development of Christology and Mariolatry within the Christian tradition.

However much his doctrines were elaborated, systematized, and debased by later generations, they remained alive to men's minds. Zoroaster's teachings deeply affected the religious ideas, and tinctured the conduct, of the Persians who ruled the civilized world. This fact alone sufficed to bring his ideas to the attention of the medley of peoples within the empire. Zoroastrianism was thus bound to influence other religious traditions, notably Judaism; and through Judaism it has played a far wider part in the world's history than would be suggested by the comparatively modest number of those who through subsequent ages have looked directly to Zoroaster as the founder of their faith.[69]

* * *

The influence of Zoroastrianism upon Judaism is difficult to assess. Certainly the differences between the two religions were significant. The gradual evolution of Judaism contrasted with the abrupt revelation of Zoroastrianism; for instead of a single towering figure who eclipsed all others, the Hebrews had many prophets, scattered across six centuries of time. Although both Zoroaster and the Hebrew prophets were deeply affected by their respective national pasts, Zoroaster explicitly rejected the Persian religious inheritance, while the Hebrew prophets appealed always to a purer ancestral religion which they believed themselves to be restoring. Finally, the national careers of the Persian and Hebrew peoples could scarcely have diverged more sharply; for while the Persians gained the world, the Hebrews lost their Promised Land. Thus the Hebrew prophets had to wrestle with crushing national disaster and human suffering far greater than anything Zoroaster had to explain.

But numerous similarities between the two religions are also evident. In matters of doctrine, for example, the Pharisaic expectation of a fiery Day of Judgment, when evil would be banished and God's power made manifest, closely resembled Zoroastrian eschatology, as did the belief in an immortality combining reward for the righteous with punishment for the wicked. To what extent these conceptions arose in Judaism as a consequence of the general religious spirit of the age, and to what extent the borrowing from Zoroastrianism was direct, though perhaps unconscious, cannot be determined. In some details—belief in angels, for instance—there seems little doubt of direct Zoroastrian influence.[70]

Congruences of doctrine such as these were supported by striking resemblances in the social and psychological backgrounds of Zoroastrianism and prophetic Judaism. Zoroaster probably preached to communities in the process of adjusting ancestral customs to an agricultural and civilized style of life,

[69] In addition to the books cited above, I have consulted the following on Zoroastrianism: Ernst Herzfeld, *Archaeological History of Iran* (Oxford: Oxford University Press, 1935), pp. 40–43; Ernst Herzfeld, *Zoroaster and His World* (2 vols.; Princeton, N.J.: Princeton University Press, 1947); H. S. Nyberg, *Die Religionen des alten Iran* (Leipzig: J. C. Hinrichs, 1938); A. T. Olmstead, *History of the Persian Empire; Cambridge Ancient History*, IV, 205–21; Maneckji N. Dhalla, *History of Zoroastrianism* (New York: Oxford University Press, 1938); R. C. Zaehner, *The Dawn and Twilight of Zoroastrianism* (New York: G. P. Putnam's Sons, 1961).

[70] Cf. J. H. Moulton, *Early Zoroastrianism*, pp. 286–331; W. F. Albright, *From Stone Age to Christianity*, pp. 275–80.

but whose assimilation of civilized ways was complicated by the availability of two rival models, one Mesopotamian and one Indian. The social background of the Hebrew prophets was essentially the same. Their people, too, had shifted from nomadry to agriculture within recent memory, while the rival attractions of Mesopotamian and of Egyptian styles of civilized life deprived both these profoundly impressive cultures of the prestige of unquestionable authority. These are probably ideal circumstances for intellectual invention. Confronted by new conditions at home and by variant models from abroad, sensitive minds find neither simple reaffirmation of established views nor passive borrowing of foreign ideas to be really satisfactory. Reflective reinterpretation is called for, combining elements old and new, autochthonous and foreign, personal and traditional, into emotionally persuasive and logically beautiful wholes. Both Zoroaster and the Hebrew prophets met this challenge so successfully that ideas and attitudes they originated have never since ceased to influence men's minds.

*   *   *

Biblical tradition asserts that Abraham, the ancestor of the Hebrew people, migrated about 1950 B.C.[71] from the Sumerian metropolis of Ur northward to Harran, and thence to Palestine. This story may have a sound basis; and it is possible that the God of Abraham originated as a family deity, one of the small gods of ancient Sumer.[72]

The distinctive beginning of Hebrew religion, however, must be dated from the time of the exodus from Egypt. Only a part, perhaps a small part, of the Hebrew people had sojourned in Egypt, departing for the desert sometime in the thirteenth century B.C. under the leadership of Moses. Their abrupt change in mode of life from forced labor on public works to wandering in the wilderness—reversion though it undoubtedly was to an ancestral nomadic pattern—required explicit lawgiving. The years in Egypt must have eroded ancient customs; and Moses' followers were probably of varied origins, lacking any single traditional leadership and organization.

It was natural, indeed inevitable, that Moses' lawgiving should take religious form, and there is no reason to doubt the essential accuracy of the biblical account of how, after making good the escape from Egypt, Moses ascended Mount Sinai to commune with Yahweh and returned with a simple code of law—the Ten Commandments. The people's formal acceptance of the Commandments constituted their covenant with Yahweh, whom they recognized henceforth as their divine guardian and supreme authority.[73]

[71] This date is based upon calculation from biblical genealogies.

[72] Cf. Leonard C. Woolley, *Abraham: Recent Discoveries and Hebrew Origins* (New York: Scribner's Sons, 1936); Jack Finegan, *Light from the Ancient Past: The Archaeological Background of Hebrew-Christian Religion* (Princeton, N.J.: Princeton University Press, 1946), pp. 57–61. The date for Abraham's migration from Ur, as derived from biblical genealogies, coincides closely with the end of the Third Dynasty of Ur. Such a coincidence lends verisimilitude to the biblical story.

[73] Exodus, 18:13—20:17; 24:1–8. The biblical narrative is, of course, a very complicated mosaic, skilfully put together from divergent traditions and written records. I do not mean to imply that the Decalogue of Exodus, 20:2–17 exactly reproduces Moses' laws, though it may. Certainly the "laws of

When the tribe that Moses had thus re-formed took its place in Palestine side by side with other Hebrew tribes, the religion of Yahweh and the Mosaic law offered a valuable rallying point for the larger community. The other tribes, having recently come from the desert, presumably lacked written law, regular priestly organization, or definite revealed religion. Under the conditions of the conquest and early settlement of Palestine, they soon began to feel the need for such supplements to traditional tribal organization and custom, and, finding a suitable system ready at hand among a kindred and neighboring people, readily adopted the religion of Yahweh and made it their own.[74]

The turn to agriculture involved a basic shift in mode of life, with profound political and religious repercussions. Politically, the need for defense against both nomadic neighbors to the east and the formidable Philistines to the west led in the eleventh century to the rise of the Hebrew monarchy. Religiously, the worship of Yahweh increasingly gave way to fertility cults, which had been indigenous to Canaan before the arrival of the Hebrew tribesmen. After all, Yahweh was a god of the desert and of war, and when life came to depend on agriculture, it seemed logical to resort to those divinities—the Baals—which had of old proved their efficacy by promoting the fertility of the fields.

Yahweh's role as the national war god kept his worship alive, for there was frequent need to call upon his aid in battles against neighboring peoples. The military enterprise by which Saul established the monarchy therefore had the incidental effect of exalting the cult of Yahweh; and even though David,[75]

Moses" which intervene between chapters 18 and 24 originated, for the most part, much later, reflecting an age when the Hebrews had settled down to agriculture.

Whether or not Moses was a monotheist, *i.e.*, whether he taught that Yahweh was the only true God, and that all other gods were false idols; or whether Mosaic religion in its early days merely asserted that Yahweh was the sole God to be worshipped by his covenanted people, defending, protecting, and judging them as other gods and pantheons supervised the affairs of other nations, is a difficult and much disputed question. A suggestion by W. F. Albright, *Archaeology and the Religion of Israel* (Baltimore, Md., 1946), pp. 117–18, seems persuasive, though scarcely conclusive. Albright points out that Moses, who probably had contact with Egyptian religious thought of the thirteenth century, may well have conceived of a single, universal God ruling all peoples. This was certainly the direction in which Egyptian religious expression had moved under the empire. Then, when the cosmopolitanism of the Bronze Age gave way to the localism of the Iron Age as large-scale interchange among distant regions and peoples declined in the twelfth and eleventh centuries, Albright suggests that this universalistic religious outlook was clouded over and largely supplanted by the idea that Yahweh, the God of Israel, was merely one among other national gods, each looking after his own. On this hypothesis, the reassertion of unambiguous monotheism by the Hebrew prophets of the eighth and subsequent centuries came only when conditions of international intercourse and politics once again raised up mighty empires and brought alien peoples into increasingly intimate contact with one another, so that the fate of any one nation was seen to depend upon the acts and fortunes of a wide variety of other peoples and states.

[74] On this hypothesis, the God of Abraham and the God of Moses can have had little or no original connection. The story of the patriarchs, as preserved in the first books of the Old Testament, may be a revision and reinterpretation of traditions current among the Hebrews who had *not* been in Egypt, aimed at harmonizing such stories with the revealed authority of Mosaic religion.

[75] David probably built an imperial cult in Jerusalem largely on the pre-existing Jebusite and other foreign models, as a supplement to his own personal relationship to Yahweh. Cf. Ivan Engnell, *Studies in Divine Kingship in the Ancient Near East* (Uppsala: Almqvist & Wiksell Boktryckeri, A.B., 1943), pp. 173–77; and H. H. Rowley (ed.), *The Old Testament and Modern Study* (Oxford: Clarendon Press, 1951), pp. 189–200, 294.

Solomon,[76] and their successors in the divided kingdoms of Israel and Judah proved hospitable to foreign worships, the religion of Yahweh remained vigorously alive. In particular, Yahweh by common consent took precedence over all other gods in time of public emergency.

Civilization in all its aspects penetrated among the Hebrew people in the days of the monarchy. To be sure, the Mosaic prohibition of graven images inhibited the development of art;[77] but the Hebrews' literary achievements more than made up for this defect. Old traditions, perhaps largely oral, were organized into narrative histories—the stories of the patriarchs, of Moses and Joshua, and of the judges of Israel. Even more impressive was the vivid and informed contemporary, or near-contemporary, account of David and his mighty men.[78] The reputation of David as a singer and of Solomon as a wise man no doubt attest the cultivation of lyric poetry and gnomic literature under the monarchy; but it is difficult to tell which of the surviving psalms and proverbs may be attributed to this early age.

The historical writing of the Hebrews was infused with the religion of Yahweh, whose hand was seen guiding events. The special role of Yahweh as God of Battles meant that his power manifested itself most distinctly in the military and political sphere. The biblical account of the exodus from Egypt is a striking example of the view that God revealed himself through history. He might indeed show himself as a pillar of smoke by day and of fire by night; but he had revealed himself most tellingly by freeing his people from Pharaoh's bondage.

As a deity directing the course of history, Yahweh was unique in the Middle East. Other war gods were at the same time nature gods—characteristically, as in most ancient Sumer, gods of the storm. Their worship thus easily merged into fertility rites, since the storm not only thundered and destroyed, but also brought rain and new life to vegetation. Not so Yahweh. His worship stood in isolation, emphatically opposed to the religion of the fields. Under the circumstances, old wounds stemming from the initial conflict between a desert God of Battles and the village deities of Canaan could never be entirely healed.

The prophets became the pre-eminent spokesmen for the religion of Yahweh in early Hebrew society. In the time of Saul and David, prophecy was an ecstatic and group phenomenon. Dancing and singing induced trances which were interpreted as signs of direct communion with God; and the men who experienced such trances inspired a reverence which gave them a quasi-sacrosanct status. Their advice was solicited by the community at large whenever matters of import, in which God might be presumed to have an interest, had to be decided.

As spokesmen for Yahweh, the prophets championed his claims to exclu-

[76] I Kings, 11:8.

[77] When Solomon set out to build a temple to Yahweh in Jerusalem, he had no native tradition to fall back upon, and so imported Phoenician workmen and combined Phoenician, Egyptian, and Babylonian elements in his building. W. F. Albright, *Archaeology and the Religion of Israel*, pp. 142–55.

[78] Preserved in II Samuel, 9–20.

sive worship and denounced the cults of Baal. Equally, as spokesmen for the old religion of the desert, they came into conflict with all the newfangled ways of settled society. On the strength of their outward holiness, and sustained by inner conviction, they even dared to attack the monarchy and the unrighteousness of the wealthy and powerful.[79] Thus the prophets served also as specially privileged representatives and spokesmen of the humbler classes in the growingly stratified society of the day.

During the eighth century B.C., the prophetic tradition underwent a great transformation. In place of bands of ecstatic holy men, there arose individual prophets, who felt themselves inspired by Yahweh to denounce social abuses and religious corruption. They did so in fiery poetry. Amos (*ca.* 750 B.C.) was the earliest of these literary prophets whose works have been preserved; but he was quickly followed by Hosea and the first Isaiah. Thereafter, the literary prophetic tradition continued almost unbroken until the time of the author of the Book of Daniel (*ca.* 150 B.C.). These individual prophets inherited at least a share of the mantle of holiness borne by their predecessors. The words of a prophet could never be neglected, not even by kings and priests whose actions the prophet might denounce. The poor and oppressed, whose thoughts and feelings were often given form and direction by the prophets' utterances, no doubt listened eagerly and took seriously the pronouncements made so emphatically in the name of Yahweh, even when immediate events did not always bear out the prophetic foreboding of disaster.

The major theme of the early literary prophets was simple. Yahweh was a just but stern God, who demanded righteous conduct of men and punished those who flouted his commandments. But the Israelites had betrayed their covenant with Yahweh, forgetting his laws and worshipping false gods. In consequence, disaster was bound to come: a Day of Yahweh, when the sins of the people would be visited upon them and the awful majesty of God revealed to all mankind. The prophets were vague as to exactly what form the Day of Yahweh would take; but many of their prophecies envisioned military and political disaster to the kingdoms of Israel and Judah.

One implication of this view was that Yahweh controlled the destiny not only of his chosen people, but of all mankind. If the Assyrians, for example, overwhelmed the Israelites, it was Yahweh who had summoned the Assyrian armies to punish Israel's sins. Thus the prophets expanded the idea that God revealed himself through history to make him supreme over all the world. In defending and exalting the power of Yahweh, they swept aside the claims of all other divinities and cults and proclaimed monotheism in its clearest and most emphatic form.

But the prophets proclaimed God's justice and mercy as well as his power, arguing that his motive for intervention in human affairs was to safeguard the right and punish evildoing. This juxtaposition of universal power and abso-

[79] Cf. the story of Nathan and David, which serves well to express the prophetic position against the monarchy, even though it is probably not historical. The story of Elijah and his slaughter of the priests of Baal illustrates how powerful and effective the prophets could be when they set out to defend the religion of Yahweh in opposition to the monarch and his court. Still later, Jeremiah and the first Isaiah carried on the tradition of prophetic opposition to constituted political authorities.

lute righteousness brought to a logical culmination the trends toward religious universalism and ethical individualism apparent in other religions of the Middle East during the same centuries. But other peoples, bound by their traditional recognition of a plurality of gods, could not accept monotheism without breaking away from their religious inheritance. Religious thinkers of Israel and Judah were here at an advantage; for the fact that Yahweh had always been a jealous God, hopelessly antagonistic to local fertility cults and demanding an exclusive worship, made the transition to radical monotheism easy. With only a modest reinterpretation of their national religious past, Israel and Judah became uniquely free to develop the full implication of the monotheistic currents of thought already running strongly throughout the Middle East. The Hebrew prophets of the eighth and later centuries exploited their strategic opportunity to the full.

Logic indeed required monotheism. Neither Yahweh nor any other deity or deities could retain a merely local sovereignty in an age when the fate of nations and peoples depended upon the actions of distant Assyria and Egypt. It is improbable that the Hebrew prophets would have asserted their view of God's universal power so clearly and emphatically if such political conditions had not existed. But although the times thus set their mark upon the development of the Hebrew religion, the form of prophetic utterances and the passion with which they were expressed depended upon individual human experience in the context of the Hebrew national religious past.

Interaction between religious and political development was clearly illustrated by the next important stage through which nascent Judaism passed. Political disaster struck in 721 B.C., when the Assyrians overwhelmed the kingdom of Israel and carried many leading families into exile. Under the impress of this apparent fulfilment of prophecy, a party of religious reform arose within the still surviving kingdom of Judah. Nearly a century later, this party came to power when King Josiah (638–609 B.C.) launched an energetic campaign to purify the religion of Yahweh and to repress all traces of other cults. The reformers concentrated the worship of Yahweh at the Temple in Jerusalem and entrusted the rites to priests who sought to conform to the best precedents of ancient and uncorrupted religion. This effort required the collection and codification of all available religious records; and to this enterprise posterity probably owes both the Book of Deuteronomy and the fixation of large parts of the Old Testament into their present form.[80]

But despite the Deuteronomic reforms, Judah was not spared the fate of Israel. King Josiah was barely able to maintain his independence; and almost immediately after his death, the kingdom acknowledged Babylonian overlordship. Then, after a rising inspired in part by prophetic assurances of divine help, King Nebuchadnezzar captured and destroyed Jerusalem (586 B.C.) and deported a large part of the city's population to Babylonia.

---

[80] It is interesting to observe that this energetic research into old religious records and their systematic editing and preservation exactly corresponded in time with the fullest expression of religious archaism in both Egypt and Mesopotamia. Cf. W. F. Albright, *From Stone Age to Christianity*, pp. 241–44.

The failure of Yahweh to prevent this disaster presented the heirs of the prophetic tradition with a new and formidable challenge. The Deuteronomic reforms had clearly failed to appease God's wrath. What more did God require? What really was his plan? If the religion of Yahweh were to survive, convincing answers to such questions had to be found; for men could not be expected to remain faithful to a God who had inexplicably abandoned them in their hour of need.

In this ultimate crisis, the prophets Ezekiel and the second Isaiah boldly undertook, from their exile in Babylon, to justify the ways of God to man. Ezekiel demanded a still more rigorous obedience to the commands of Yahweh and foresaw as a reward the eventual re-establishment of a united kingdom of Israel and Judah. The fall of Jerusalem he attributed to the survival of pagan and unholy practices even after King Josiah's reforms; and he outlined a still stricter pattern for the future. The second Isaiah, whose eloquent poetry was composed during the lifetime of Cyrus the Great, saw in the Persian victories over Babylon a sure sign that the day was at hand when the sins of Israel would be forgiven and the glory of God become manifest to all the nations. In his view, the sufferings of the Jews were not simply punishment for their disobedience, but part of a far grander divine plan; for when Israel, purged and repentant, had been restored in glory, true religion and just government would be established everywhere. Instead of a petty and persecuted people, exposed to the scorn of more fortunate nations, the children of Israel would take their rightful place as a light to the gentiles and establishers of justice to the ends of the earth.[81]

Such extravagant hopes were of course never fulfilled; but Ezekiel and the second Isaiah wove a new emotional tone into Judaism. Prophecy in the early days had been largely denunciatory; and the Day of Yahweh had loomed ahead as a time of dreadful doom. Now there was hope—ever delayed but never forgotten—of a Day when, after appropriate and drastic purification, mankind would actually witness the establishment of the Kingdom of God on earth. With eyes fixed confidently on such a future, hardship and disappointment became comparatively easy to bear. Paradoxically, the really pious might even enjoy suffering: indeed, the worse, the better; for in proportion as present afflictions increased in severity, the day of final redress seemed surer and more imminent.

Such eschatological hope was not incompatible with careful elaboration of rules for ritual purity. In the megalopolitan environment of Babylon, such rules were in fact a psychologically very useful substitute for the customary patterning of life in small, homogeneous communities. As a result, the exile community's ritual observances allowed its members to maintain a strong self-consciousness and distinct ethos in the very midst of Babylonia. Moreover, after Cyrus the Persian had overthrown the imperial might of Babylon, and a few Jews began to trickle back to Jerusalem, ritual prescriptions, as elaborated by Ezekiel and others, provided a ready-made blueprint for the new corporate life.

[81] Isaiah, 42:1–9; 49:1–13.

At first the returned exiles, or a party among them, pinned their hope for the restoration of the Kingdom of David upon a layman who claimed descent from the royal house; but this movement soon ran afoul of the Persian authorities and was repressed. Thereafter, the Temple became the principal focus and sole unifying factor for the struggling and precarious Jewish community of Palestine. Not until Nehemiah (*ca.* 444 B.C.) and Ezra (*ca.* 397 B.C.) had reorganized the worship of Yahweh at Jerusalem did the community of returned exiles really begin to flourish. Yet this partial success in no way matched the vast expectation built upon the Day of Yahweh; and the hope of its coming remained powerful and ever present, ready to flare into political revolt against alien authority whenever a promising candidate for the role of Messiah—the Lord's anointed—should appear.

Two other aspects of the work of Ezekiel and the second Isaiah need only be mentioned. Ezekiel emphasized, as no predecessor had done, the relation of the individual to God—a response, no doubt, to the weakening of local community solidarity among the exiles in the great cities of Babylonia. This individualization of religious responsibility and observance was pregnant for the future, as was also the second Isaiah's emphasis upon God's fatherly loving-kindness and the patience with which He bore offenses against His will. The stern judge and fiercely jealous God of earlier prophecy was thereby supplemented by a more kindly conception of the Godhead, which merged

THE DEVELOPMENT

ATONISM

MOSAIC MONOTHEISM

with the older conceptions in a logically incompatible but psychologically most persuasive fashion.

Thus by 500 B.C., the religion of Yahweh had undergone far-reaching transformations that fitted it to survive as a world religion. Judaism was no longer the cult of a tribe, as in the days of Moses, but a law and doctrine claiming universal validity for itself and total error for all rivals. Moreover, under the exigencies of exile, the worship of Yahweh had survived even without the focus of the Temple at Jerusalem, and without a definite territorial home. Wherever the faithful might gather, prayers, psalms, and reading from the sacred scriptures kept the doctrines and hopes of the Jewish religion alive in the minds and hearts of its adherents. Judaism retained a strong emphasis upon the concept of a chosen people, united to God by a special covenant which set them apart from all others; yet within this collective and corporate frame there developed a belief in direct personal accountancy to God for individual moral and ritual acts.

Both universalism and individualism in religion were thus accommodated within the national framework which had been inherited from primitive tribal times. As a result, it became possible for men of widely differing modes of life and cultural milieux to remain faithful to the religion of their fathers. Although certain pagan customs were forbidden to the pious, the wide dispersion of later times inevitably led Jews to imitate all sorts of local habits.

OF MONOTHEISM

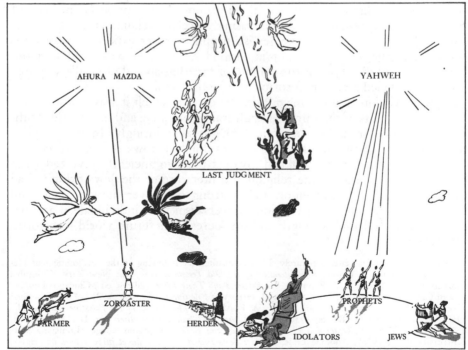

AHURA MAZDA

YAHWEH

LAST JUDGMENT

ZOROASTER

FARMER

HERDER

PROPHETS

IDOLATORS

JEWS

ZOROASTRIANISM

PROPHETIC JUDAISM

But such assimilation no longer implied apostasy. Religion had become a separable element in the total cultural complex; and Jews might maintain their faith while in most things taking on the coloring of the society in which they happened to find themselves.

Here was a new phenomenon: a religion which lived a life of its own, largely independent of geographical locality and of secular culture. This is familiar enough in our time and may even seem natural. But by the standard of earlier ages, when religion and the total style of life had been part and parcel of one another—and therefore inseparable from a particular social community living in a more or less fixed geographical location—the new sociological character of Judaism was indeed strange and novel.[82]

The emotional power, poignancy, and literary distinction of the Old Testament need scarcely be emphasized. The poetry of the second Isaiah has seldom been equaled; the same is true of many of the psalms and of such a literary masterpiece as the Book of Job. From an intellectual point of view, revelation manifesting itself in dogmatic assertion and violent denunciation may seem a poor substitute for reasoning; and if modern scholars correctly interpret the intent of prophetic pronouncements, this adverse judgment was also borne out practically, since political prophecies were consistently wrong. Yet the prophets of Israel and Judah struggled hard to solve the dilemma confronting the religious thought of all western Asia: how to justify the apparent injustices and suffering which the Divine imposed even upon righteous men. In Mesopotamia, as we have seen, no solution to this problem was found; and a spirit of religious disillusion gained ground. In Egypt, after the Atonist reform had been repudiated, an increasingly archaic religious formalism prevailed. But in the minds of the Jewish prophets, eager expectation took the place of despair; disappointment intensified rather than weakened religious conviction; and the hope for the coming of the Messiah and of God's kingdom on earth provided a powerful solace in time of trouble.

This conviction, and the magnificent poetry in which it was clothed, have become basic parts of the European cultural inheritance; and one cannot withhold admiration from the men who wrought so enduringly. In an age when the civilization of the Middle East was leveling out toward a flaccid cosmopolitanism, and when dry rot had invaded the two anciently civilized lands of Babylonia and Egypt, the religion and literature of the Jews exhibited an extraordinary power and vigor. In its strong hold over human minds and hearts, uniquely combining religious universalism with individualism and nationalism, lay Judaism's strength and the secret of its future world-transforming career.

[82] In addition to books cited separately, I have consulted the following on the development of Hebrew religion: Julius A. Bewer, *The Literature of the Old Testament* (rev. ed.; New York: Columbia University Press, 1938); J. M. P. Smith, *The Prophets and Their Times* (2d rev. ed.; Chicago: University of Chicago Press, 1941); A. T. Olmstead, *History of Palestine and Syria to the Macedonian Conquest* (New York, London: Scribner's Sons, 1931); W. F. Albright, *The Archaeology of Palestine* (2d rev. ed.; Harmondsworth: Penguin Books, 1956); Eduard Meyer, *Geschichte des Altertums*, II, 187–362; III, 157–221; Eric Voegelin, *Order and History*, I: *Israel and Revelation* (Baton Rouge: Louisiana State University Press, 1956); Adolphe Lods, *Histoire de la littérature hebraïque et juive depuis les origines jusqu'à la ruine de l'état juif* (Paris: Payot, 1950).

CHAPTER

The Formulation of Peripheral Civilizations in India, Greece, and China 1700–500 B.C.

A. INTRODUCTION

The centuries following the barbarian invasions of the Bronze Age saw the gradual formulation of three new civilizations in Eurasia.

In India and Greece, on the fringes of the anciently civilized world, the new civilizations derived something from Indus or Minoan predecessors in the land, something from the barbarian invaders who had conquered those predecessors, and something also from contact with the ancient culture of the Middle East. Yet the diverse roots and disparate elements of which Indian and Greek civilization were composed did not prevent, but rather encouraged profound originality. By degrees, therefore, the growing uniformity of the Middle East came to be flanked, in India and in Greece, by new, fresh, and different styles of life. At the same time, a third new civilization emerged on the eastern extremity of Eurasia. China was more isolated than either India or Greece from any but barbarian contacts, but its isolation was never complete. China too, however remotely and sporadically, became a participant in Eurasian processes of social interaction after about the middle of the second millennium B.C.

167

For each of these newly formulated civilizations, the barbarian expansion of the eighteenth and subsequent centuries B.C. marked a sort of beginning point. All three were called into being through interaction between chariot invaders and indigenous agriculturalists. It is therefore no mere coincidence that many of the characteristic traits of each of these civilizations emerged concurrently. The sixth century B.C. witnessed the careers of Buddha and Confucius, as well as the first expression of rationalistic philosophy in Greece. By 500 B.C., the master social institutions of India and of Greece—the caste system (probably) and the city-state (certainly)—were already well developed. Perhaps because of China's comparative isolation, the institutions of that country developed more slowly, so that the familial and imperial bureaucratic framework of mature Chinese civilization came clearly into focus only with the establishment of the Han dynasty (202 B.C.).

To be sure, subsequent enrichment and elaboration within Indian, Greek, and Chinese civilization worked cumulatively great changes. Nonetheless, by 500 B.C. the fundamental direction of growth had been fixed in both India and Greece, while China lagged only slightly behind in defining the character and bent of her civilization.

Until about the same date, the Middle East retained a recognizable cultural primacy within the ecumene. Archaic Greece learned much from the Orient, before the Persian Wars and the flowering of Greek culture itself reduced Greek susceptibility to the wonders and wisdom of the East. The effect of Middle Eastern civilization upon India is more conjectural; but such important skills as alphabetic writing and iron metallurgy almost certainly reached India from the older center.

China's case was different, but only in degree. Wide areas of steppe, mountain, and desert offered formidable obstacles to communication between the Yellow River Valley and the Middle East. Regular and direct contact across Asia began only in the first century B.C., when powerful military empires based in China and in Iran opened the Silk Road across the oases of central Asia. The sea, which offered a relatively easy highway connecting the Middle East with both Greece and India, seemingly failed to link China with India and the Middle East before the first century A.D. Hence, when Chinese civilization was in its formative and most impressionable stage, only those elements capable of transmission by rude and warlike barbarians could pass from western to eastern Asia. Bronze weapons and horse-drawn chariots were such elements; subtler matters such as alphabetic writing failed to surmount the barbarian and geographic barriers. By the time these barriers were broken through in the second century B.C. so that the Chinese could learn about alphabetic writing, their language and learned tradition were too deeply committed to an ideographic script to permit change.

From its inception, therefore, Chinese civilization was much less affected by the Middle Eastern model than were the civilizations of either India or Greece. In a sense, therefore, the cultural development of Eurasia after 1500 B.C. was twofold rather than fourfold. Middle Eastern, Indian, and Greek civilization constituted a single, loose geographical continuum, with zones of transition between the three principal segments, while Chinese civilization stood apart and isolated in the Far East. Yet in view of subsequent history, it seems best to regard the styles of life which emerged in India and in Greece about 500 B.C. as distinct, though interrelated civilizations, comparable in magnitude and historic importance to their Middle Eastern prototype and to the distant Chinese offshoot.

Here we may see a double pulse beat of history on the largest scale. In the age of river valley civilization, Mesopotamian stimulus had hastened the development of the Egyptian and Indus civilizations until they arrived at an inner perfection and balance which inhibited further borrowing from outside. There ensued about a thousand years of approximate equilibrium, between roughly 2700 and 1700 B.C., during which time the civilizations of Mesopotamia, Egypt, and the Indus developed separately in accordance with their own inner momenta. This world balance was slowly modified during the closing centuries of the third millennium B.C. and the opening centuries of the second millennium B.C. by the rise of civilized communities on rain-watered land, most notably in the lands bordering Mesopotamia. But the definitive upset of the old river valley civilizations came only after 1700 B.C., when barbarians from the steppes, armed with the latest technological improvements, burst upon the old centers of civilization.

As we saw in the last chapter, a cosmopolitan civilization slowly emerged in the Middle East from the confusion and destruction of the invasions. During the same centuries, toward the margins of the Eurasian agricultural world in northern India, Greece, and northern China, other civilized patterns of life were taking form; and just as ancient Egypt and the Indus culture had received critically significant stimuli from sporadic contacts with Mesopotamia, so also in the years 1700–500 B.C., the deep-rooted, vastly impressive civilization of the Middle East contributed important stimuli to the peoples of India, Greece, and China as they struggled toward civilization. By 500 B.C., however, the basic characteristics of each of these peripheral civilizations had become apparent. Thereafter, just as had happened in the third millennium B.C.,

RELATIONS BETWEEN OLD WORLD CIVILIZATIONS

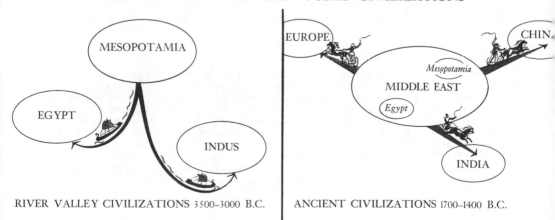

RIVER VALLEY CIVILIZATIONS 3500–3000 B.C.   ANCIENT CIVILIZATIONS 1700–1400 B.C.

an effective, if precarious political and cultural equilibrium established itself across the ecumene. The geographic scale was much enlarged; and temporal rhythms lengthened, for this time the equilibrium of cultures lasted roughly two thousand years, until the modern expansion of Europe definitively upset the by then immemorial balance of the world.

B. THE FORMULATION OF INDIAN CIVILIZATION

The history of India before 500 B.C. is veiled in obscurity. The archeological record is full of gaps; and until recently scholarly study of the literary materials deriving from the period has been rather narrowly philological. The hymns and ritual texts of the *Vedas* and related literature shed remarkably little light on matters about which the historian would like information. To be sure, royal genealogies and heroic tales survive in epic poems and books of "tradition"; but these were not fixed in their present form until after the beginning of the Christian era. Whatever authentic core of secular history may be embedded in them is heavily overlaid with priestly piety and confounded by a total absence of chronology.

Indeed, the almost unrelieved chronological mistiness of early Indian history constitutes the greatest single obstacle to historical investigation. The Vedic canon probably achieved its present form after 600 B.C.;[1] but it is impossible to know precisely when its various portions were composed. Since Vedic literature was oral, it descended by rote memorization from master to pupil generation after generation.[2] Only when painstaking preservation of the ancient verbal forms began to seem essential to the potency of the ritual did the Vedic language freeze into a fixed mold. Hence the *Rig Veda*, which constitutes the basis of the entire Vedic literature, is almost uniform in language. No linguistic criterion exists by which earlier and later compositions can be distinguished.[3] Thus, however satisfying to the philologist, the *Vedas* are a dismal morass for the historian.

Nevertheless, some landmarks of early Indian history are discernible. The immediate aftermath of the Aryan invasions was a heroic age comparable to the Mycenaean period of Greek history. To be sure, no Indian Mycenae has yet been unearthed and probably never will be, since there is no suggestion in the written sources that the Aryans built fortifications of stone or brick.

[1] R. C. Majumdar (ed.), *The History and Culture of the Indian People: The Vedic Age* (London: Allen & Unwin, Ltd., 1951), p. 227.

[2] When curious Western scholars in the eighteenth century began to inquire into Vedic traditions, their first step was to secure a Brahmin priest to dictate the sacred texts to a scribe. This was not necessarily or even probably the first time the texts had been reduced to writing; but there was absolutely no "manuscript tradition" of the sort familiar to European medievalists. Indian sages regarded written transmission as far less satisfactory than oral communication; and since it was an inferior vehicle, they felt that writing was not worthy of their most sacred texts. Since only oral acquaintance and memorization could give the student the full meaning and value, written texts were not normally used by the learned men who kept the Vedic literature alive.

[3] Certain grammatical shifts do, however, mark off the final book of the *Rig Veda* from the rest and show that it must have crystallized into its present form at a somewhat later date.

But the great epic of India, the *Mahabharata*, centers around the story of a war between two rival coalitions of noble charioteers. Their warfare, quite in the manner of the *Iliad*,[4] was an affair of heroic individual combat, in which the gods occasionally became incarnate to advise or assist their favorites. The passages of the *Mahabharata* which describe this sort of warfare may be taken as a literary reflection of an aristocratic, warlike, and barbarous age; but the specific events which presumably provided a basis for the epic elaboration of the poem cannot be identified. Moreover, the long evolution which occurred before the text achieved its present form makes the *Mahabharata* completely untrustworthy as a source of historical detail.[5]

The nobly born charioteers who dominated war and politics in the heroic age had lost their supremacy by the sixth century B.C. Presumably iron weapons were the major instrument of their destruction,[6] if we may extrapolate from the analogous evolution of tactics and social structure in the Middle East and Europe. At any rate, by the sixth century B.C., warfare in India had come to hinge upon infantry and cavalry forces, with chariots relegated to a purely honorific place in the battle array.

Just as in the Middle East, this military change opened the way for new political developments. Early Buddhist works reveal traces of aristocratic and republican polities comparable to the primitive city-states of Greece. Such communities flourished in the hill country at the foot of the Himalayas and appear to have been quite numerous. But in the broad plains of the major rivers, particularly in the Ganges Valley, centralized monarchical states began to dominate the scene from about the eighth century B.C. War and conquest, administrative consolidation, fortification of strategic points, and perhaps also the construction of large-scale irrigation works all contributed to the extension of royal power. By the sixth century B.C., these monarchies had

---

[4] Tactics were, however, more rational in India, for the bow was the principal weapon, and discharge of arrows from moving chariots was apparently the standard manner of fighting a battle. The Aryans, after all, had come to India from eastern Iran, near the center where chariot techniques had probably first developed.

[5] The *Mahabharata* existed in some form or other as early as 400 B.C.; but its present recension, which includes a tremendous bulk of priestly piety, presumably deposited around an original core of more secular poetry, dates from between 200 and 400 A.D. It is rather as though Homer had been reworked by the Christian Fathers into an allegory and handbook of Christian doctrine, leaving only traces of the original spirit of the poem. Cf. N. K. Sidhanta, *The Heroic Age of India: A Comparative Study* (New York: Alfred A. Knopf, Inc., 1930), pp. 48–49. Various efforts to date the Bharata war have been made, giving anything between 1400 and 900 B.C., depending on assumptions made as to the reliability of various royal genealogies contained in the *Puranas*, and on calculations of average length of reign. Cf. F. E. Pargiter, *Ancient Indian Historical Tradition* (London: Oxford University Press, 1922), pp. 179–83; Majumdar, *History and Culture of the Indian People*, pp. 268–69.

[6] Herodotus, VII, 65, reports that the Indian troops in Xerxes' army had their arrows tipped with iron. This is the earliest firmly dated reference to Indian use of iron; but there is no doubt that the metal had been familiar to the Indians long before 480 B.C. The *Atharva Veda* mentions swords of black metal which must be iron; and if one assumes that this text was in its present shape, more or less, by 800 B.C., this would put iron back to the ninth century. Cf. Narayanchandra Bandyopadhyaya, *Economic Life and Progress in Ancient India: Hindu Period* (2d ed.; Calcutta: University of Calcutta Press, 1945), I, 156–59; D. H. Gordon, "The Early Use of Metals in India and Pakistan," *Journal of the Royal Anthropological Institute of Great Britain and Ireland*, LXXX (1950), 55–78.

either absorbed or established their hegemony over most of the small republican states of northern India.[7]

This political evolution was accompanied by a transfer of the centers of Indian life eastward from the valley of the Indus to the Ganges plains. Details of the Aryan infiltration and conquest of eastern and southern India are entirely unknown; and even the major outlines of the process, not to mention its dates, are obscure. Probably there was little to attract conquerors to the rank jungle of the Ganges Valley until the availability of iron axes and other tools facilitated both the felling of trees and subsequent tillage of root-encumbered soil. In all probability, therefore, clearing of the jungle for agriculture got under way on a large scale only about 800 B.C.[8] Two hundred years later, the upper and middle Ganges Valley had become India's most active center of cultural activity and the seat of its most powerful kingdoms.

The rise of Gangetic kingdoms like Kosala and Magadha in the seventh and sixth centuries B.C. thus seems a typical case of marcher lords exploiting a position near the margins of civilized society to build larger and more autocratic states than was possible in the older centers, where aristocratic feuds and priestly pretensions agreed in obstructing royal administration. In addition, powerful climatic forces contributed to the precocious political consolidation of the Ganges plain. The monsoon brought enough water to make rice by far the most productive and therefore the staple crop of the region. But rice required irrigation for maximum productivity; and irrigation, in turn, required canals and embankments, which could only be constructed by the labor of large numbers of men organized for the task by some superior authority. From about the sixth century B.C., the kings of the Ganges area seem to have assumed direction of local irrigation systems, thereby enormously enhancing their authority by giving it secure roots in the daily lives and needs of the cultivators.[9]

In the Indus area, by contrast, irrigation was little developed. Not rice, but wheat and barley, were the main crops. These were cultivated by comparatively primitive methods; for a field exhausted through repeated cropping was simply fallowed for a period of years until its fertility had recovered sufficiently to start the cycle over again. Under such circumstances, populations in the Indus region must have remained comparatively sparse, and states correspondingly small and ill-consolidated. Hence the emergent urbanism of the

---

[7] On Indian political development see Majumdar, *History and Culture of the Indian People*, pp. 425–33, 482–88; *Cambridge History of India* (Cambridge: Cambridge University Press, 1922); Paul Masson-Oursel *et al.*, *Ancient India and Indian Civilization* (London: Kegan Paul, Trench, Trubner & Co., 1934), pp. 88–105; Hermann Goetz, *Epochen der indischen Kultur* (Leipzig: Verlag Karl Hiersemann, 1929), pp. 83–88; T. W. Rhys Davids, *Buddhist India* (New York: G. P. Putnam's Sons, 1903), pp. 1–34.

[8] Cf. Walter Ruben, *Einführung in die Indienkunde* (Berlin: Deutscher Verlag der Wissenschaften, 1954), p. 103.

[9] The earliest sure evidence of royal supervision of irrigation works dates only from the time of Chandragupta (*ca.* 321–297 B.C.); but small-scale irrigation was known even in Rig Vedic times; and the elaborateness of Chandragupta's irrigation administration seems to require a considerable time for development. Cf. *Cambridge History of India*, I, 417, 475; Majumdar, *History and Culture of the Indian People*, p. 399; N. Bandyopadhyaya, *Economic Life and Progress*, pp. 130–31.

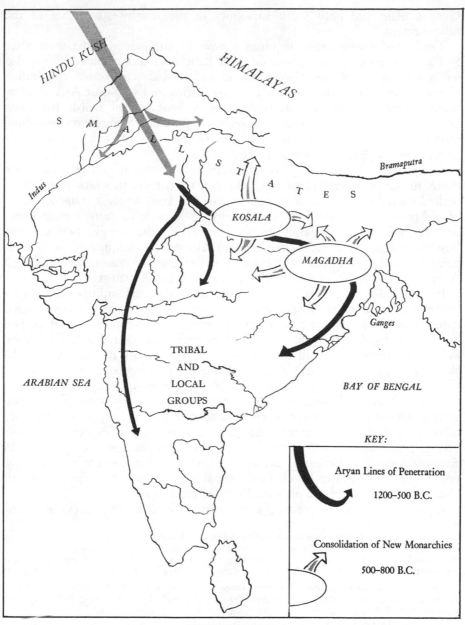

ANCIENT INDIA

Ganges plain had only weak analogues in the northwestern part of the subcontinent.[10]

Trade and manufacture acquired a new importance in India soon after 800 B.C., when overseas commerce with Babylonia was resumed. Ships also navigated the Indus and Ganges rivers and probably traversed the Indian Ocean to visit the barbarous lands of east Africa and southeast Asia. Professional merchants and caravan leaders—or at least special words for these occupations—existed; but such an important lubricant to commerce as coined money was apparently not introduced until the sixth century B.C., as a by-product of the Persian conquest of the Punjab.[11]

As tribal bonds gave way to territorial subordination and as agriculture came to supplant cattle tending, old Aryan tribal-aristocratic solidarities melted away. Through local conquests, royal grants, or some transformation of old tribal obligations, free Aryan warriors became liable to various rents and services.[12] The consequence was to reduce the margin between the humbler members of the Aryan community and the subjugated pre-Aryan peoples, until by degrees only vestigial differences of custom distinguished Aryan commoners from their fellow peasants of pre-Aryan stock.[13]

Paradoxically enough, this leveling may have provided an important stimulus to the development of one of India's distinctive and peculiar institutions: caste. The Aryan invaders were rather acutely color-conscious and looked down upon the dark-skinned peoples whom they encountered in India. Hence as Aryan commoners sank toward the social status of the despised dark-skinned peoples, they probably clung all the more energetically to beliefs and practices that continued to mark them off from non-Aryans.[14]

At least three additional elements entered into the formation of the caste system. One was the concept of ceremonial purity, which involved elaborate taboos against bodily contact with impure persons, and especially against eating food which such persons had touched. This was much emphasized in Sanskrit texts; and Buddhist literature shows that the concept was already familiar in or soon after Buddha's time.[15] It was ceremonial purity, above all else, which marked off the priestly, Brahmin caste from others.

Equally important in creating caste consciousness was the survival of in-

---

[10] An adventitious factor enhancing the military power of Ganges kings was their easier access to elephants. This counterbalanced the better supply of horses available to the Indus region from north of the mountains; for, as Alexander of Macedon later discovered, war elephants effectively terrified untrained horses and made them useless on the battlefield. Cf. Rhys Davids, *Buddhist India*, pp. 266–67.

[11] Cf. N. Bandyopadhyaya, *Economic Life and Progress*, pp. 169–90, 220–29, 253, 255–63; Majumdar, *History and Culture*, pp. 396–98; 461–62; *Cambridge History of India*, I, 135–37, 198–219. Necklaces of gold and silver had served as a medium of exchange before coinage reached India.

[12] As in the Middle East, debt may have played a part in reducing the lower classes to dependence on landowners; but I know of no evidence for this.

[13] *Cambridge History of India*, I, 128–29.

[14] Analogous attitudes toward Negroes among the "poor whites" of the southern United States are well known.

[15] Richard Fick, *Die soziale Gliederung im nordöstlichen Indien zu Buddhas Zeit* (Kiel: C. F. Haeseler, 1897), pp. 24–39.

group feeling among pre-Aryan populations. As the Aryans consolidated their hold upon India, no doubt the indigenous populations were compelled to adjust older customs in deference to the powerful newcomers, and in many cases were forced to pay some form of tribute. But former social cohesions, whether based primarily upon tribal or upon village communities, did not thereby disappear. On the contrary Aryan prejudice put special obstacles in the way of intermarriage with the darker-skinned natives, and this permitted the subordinated groups to retain their separate identities as protocastes.[16]

Finally, a third element of the system was the theory, first clearly expressed in the Vedic commentaries known as *Brahmanas*, that all society was divinely divided into four castes: first the *Brahmins*, whose proper function was to perform sacrifices and other religious ceremonies; then the *Kshatriyas*, who fought and ruled; next the *Vaisyas*, who engaged in various gainful occupations; and at the bottom of the scale the *Sudras*, who performed the humblest tasks, especially those which bore a religious stigma. The first three of these castes were Aryan, the fourth non-Aryan. Brahminical literature emphasized both the hereditary character of membership in these four castes and the hierarchical relationship among them.

Practice never corresponded to such a theory of caste. Rulers and warriors did not accept subordination to the *Brahmins* with good grace; and individuals occasionally shifted from one caste to another.[17] Numerous subcastes and intercastes conformed awkwardly, if at all, to the theoretical fourfold pattern. Yet the theory, however inexact as a description of social practice, exerted an influence nonetheless and may be responsible for the emphasis on social precedence among the castes which became a very prominent part of the system in later times.[18]

Instead of four castes, today in India there are thousands, if caste is defined as a social group whose members intermarry and will eat together. Many castes, moreover, are organized more or less formally and discipline their members by invoking the penalty of exclusion against anyone who violates the caste's traditions.[19] A man's caste defines his social universe. Standards of personal conduct, as well as attitudes and expectations in dealings with others, are fixed by caste and by the more or less definite hierarchic relationships among separate castes within the larger society. The result is to combine some of the advantages of living in a small primary group with the fact of membership in a much larger, looser, impersonal society.

Like nearly everything else in India's past, the history of the caste principle is obscure. By what date castes had definitely emerged cannot be said with certainty. It is clear that many modern castes are very recent, forming basical-

---

[16] *Cambridge History of India*, I, 129. In the frontier areas of Assam and elsewhere, tribal groups coming within the matrix of Indian society still continue to form new castes. Cf. J. H. Hutton, *Caste in India: Its Nature, Function and Origins* (Cambridge: Cambridge University Press, 1946), pp. 101, 186.

[17] Majumdar, *History and Culture*, pp. 451–52, 507–10; Fick, *Die soziale Gliederung*, pp. 1–8.

[18] J. H. Hutton, *Caste in India*, pp. 155–56, 164.

[19] *Ibid.*, pp. 41–96.

ly around occupational groups.[20] Moreover, successive invaders of India have tended to fit into the system, sometimes quite unconsciously. The Anglo-Indian population, for example, constituted something very like a caste, despite the fact that the individuals who went to India from England had no sense of caste (in the Indian meaning of the term) before going there. Indeed, once the idea of caste came to seem the natural and inevitable organization of human intercourse, the system exhibited an indefinite elasticity. Old castes might split into two or more new ones; occupational groupings, perhaps originally of very heterogeneous origins, might speedily become new castes through being treated as such by the people around them. Indeed, any group of "outsiders" would soon be compelled to conform to the prevailing caste restrictions on marriage and meal-taking simply because the exclusive habits of their neighbors automatically forced them in upon themselves.

The complex caste system of modern India existed only in outline by 500 B.C. Its seeds were certainly present that early; probably they dated from the first contact between Aryans and non-Aryans (if indeed pre-Aryan society was not itself divided on castelike lines).[21] The period between 700 and 500 B.C., when cities were first becoming important in India, was probably critical for the caste principle. Individuals of varying origins mingling in urban environments were probably then able to change their status far more freely than in later times. Perhaps not until some time after 500 B.C. was victory for the caste principle assured in the urban context, whereas sharply defined caste rules probably prevailed in the countryside by the time of Buddha.[22]

The basic importance of castes (or of protocastes) to the structure of Indian society at large had important political consequences. The rather fragile quality exhibited by Indian states and empires in historic times is in part attributable to the fact that men's primary loyalties lay, not with a territorial entity, but with a territorially indeterminate caste. The fierce dedication to the collective body social made manifest in a territorial state, which has characterized so much of European history, was impossible in a society where

[20] A caste of automobile attendants was in the process of formation a few years ago.

[21] Megasthenes, a Greek ambassador to the court of Chandragupta at the end of the fourth century B.C., mentions seven caste-like groups into which he said Indian society was divided and reported that intermarriage between the different groups was forbidden. A translation of Megasthenes' remarks may be found with commentary in N. K. Dutt, *Origin and Growth of Caste in India* (London: Kegan Paul, Trench, Trubner & Co., Ltd., 1931), pp. 280–94. Similarly, Buddhist literature mentions many caste groups. Cf. Fick, *Die soziale Gliederung, passim.*

[22] The peasant village community of the Middle East was in many respects comparable to an Indian caste. A man was born into the village and seldom left; a sharp line was drawn between members of the village and outsiders; a strictly defined series of expectations and attitudes defined the relationships between the members of the community; and their relationships with outsiders were governed by a scarcely less well-defined code. But in the urban communities of the Middle East, such in-groups tended to break down. Middle Eastern urban guilds and occupational associations of one sort or another perhaps sometimes approximated to a caste. But restrictions on intermarriage and on commensality were never institutionalized, either in the village or in the city; and a man could always leave his hereditary status behind more easily than in India, where caste came to be regarded as indelible, natural, necessary.

Perhaps it was the racial and cultural variety of the Indian population, together with notions of ceremonial defilement related to that diversity, which reinforced the village or forest tribe's in-group feeling and allowed such communities to survive as castes in the urban environments of India.

castes constituted the primary social grouping. As long as a man's strongest self-identification lay with his caste, government officials and rulers were at best troublesome outsiders and at worst oppressors, whose demands and activities had only superficial contact with the vital relationships of ordinary life.

Under these circumstances, government and politics clearly had less scope in India than in the Middle East or in Europe. The power of the state over men's thoughts and passions—though not necessarily over their persons—was distinctly less. War and politics therefore became the comparatively insignificant concern of a few specialists in violence—matters which could be passed over in literature all the more easily because they were little heeded in everyday life. The peculiar and tantalizing defects of Indian literary tradition for the historian who demands a political and chronological framework become more intelligible when one views the matter in this light.

*   *   *

It would be a mistake to think of the castes of India as autonomous or isolated social groups. The daily process of mixing and mingling among members of different castes obviously required mutual adjustment of a very complex sort. Moreover, certain common assumptions and views about the nature of things united the castes into a real cultural whole. Without such community of viewpoint, there would be as many ways of life as castes, and Indian civilization would not exist. But there *is* an Indian civilization, and what holds it together and gives it unity is religion. Even in the twentieth century a holy man exercised power in India on a scale no ancient king or conqueror ever surpassed; but Gandhi's modern success built upon the earlier work of the innumerable holy men who shaped the traditions of Indian civilization in ancient times. The activities of rulers, warriors, merchants, and artisans—groups which played an important role in the cultural development of the Middle East and dominated that of the Greeks—counted for comparatively little in the land of Buddha and Gandhi.

To be sure, this difference may be partly illusory, for almost everything known about early Indian civilization derives from documents transmitted by priests and monks. But this is itself indicative of the special role religion and the pursuit of holiness came to play in Indian life. Lay literature once flourished in India, as the kernel of the *Mahabharata* shows; but secular traditions were either lost and forgotten or else absorbed into religious literature. Indeed, the absorptive power of Indian religion could scarcely be more tellingly demonstrated than by the strange structure of the *Mahabharata*, for like the oysters of the Malabar coast, secreting pearls around intrusive grains of sand, religious poets of ancient India responded to the vainglory of heroic warfare by clothing its original brutality with a garment of religious instruction and allegory, thereby quite obscuring the poem's ostensible theme of fratricidal war.

How was the rough warrior spirit of Aryan tribesmen, who gloried unabashed in the strength of their arms, in the destruction of their foes, and in the number of their cattle, so transformed that priests and holy men could succeed in setting the whole tone of Indian intellectual life and plausibly lay claim to first rank in society? Why, in other words, did the Aryan ethos evolve in a direction so different from that which prevailed in Europe?

In such matters, an element of mystery should always be acknowledged; but two factors do help to explain the special direction of Indian cultural evolution. One is climate. The decisive formulation of Indian culture and attitudes toward life took place not in northwestern India, where climatic conditions generally resembled those of the Middle East, but in the Gangetic plain, where the monsoon dominated the cycle of the year. Different possibilities lay open in such a climate than in the drier and severer climate of the Mediterranean zone. For example, a bulky and deeply influential body of literature originated in forest retreats, where holy men lived ascetically—often without clothing of any sort—and sought religious knowledge and illumination. The ascetic extremes to which such men drove themselves would have led to speedy death in a colder climate; and the wisdom they transmitted to eager pupils could not have been pursued in a region where snow fell in winter or where temperatures came near the freezing point. Second, the pre-Aryan populations of India were not without cultural traditions of their own, though the specific forms and institutions of those cultures are unknown. Much that was peculiar to Indian civilization may nevertheless have resulted from a reassertion of pre-Aryan traditions, modified, to be sure, by adjustment to Aryan attitudes and institutions, and elaborated by free invention to form a new whole.[23]

Absolute dates cannot be satisfactorily assigned to the religious history of ancient India before the time of Buddha (d. *ca.* 485 B.C.). The divergent religious outlooks which may be discerned in the surviving literature presumably found expression at various times among different social groups in different parts of India. Moreover, as schools of thought took form, they did not simply supersede older doctrine and ritual but instead provoked a very complex process of interaction and adjustment between older and newer religious points of view. Amid such uncertainties and confusion, it has long been customary for scholars to distinguish four "stages" of Indian religion. This device seems acceptable, so long as logical presentation is not confused with any clear-cut chronological succession.

The collection of hymns known as the *Rig Veda* is the oldest stratum of

---

[23] As an example of what appears probable, consider the status of the Brahmin priesthood. The Brahmins claimed to rank first among the castes, and in the more extreme statements Brahmins equated themselves with the gods. Such high pretensions may have descended from the real social status which priests of the Indus civilization had once enjoyed. Becoming familiar with the status actually enjoyed by priests among the native populations, Aryan priests may have been stimulated to enlarge their own claims to social dignity, power, and wealth. Intellectual weapons with which to support such claims very likely lay ready at hand in the conception of priestly magical powers current among the pre-Aryan peoples.

F. E. Pargiter, *Ancient Indian Historical Tradition* (London: Oxford University Press, 1922), pp. 303–11, even argues that leading Brahmin families derived from pre-Aryan peoples. Pargiter's opinion is based upon examination of the *Puranas* and depends on his identification of Aryan and non-Aryan kingdoms in their confused accounts of a distant past.

surviving Indian literature. The gods of the *Rig Veda* were rather ill-defined personifications of natural forces and phenomena—especially of the sun, thunder, dawn, fire, and the sacred intoxicant *soma*. The cult, while susceptible of extreme elaboration in details, was fundamentally simple, centering around an altar fire set up out-of-doors and involving the sacrificial slaughter of animals and the dedication of such substances as *soma* and *ghee* (melted butter). The gods were powerful, sometimes capricious, but their separate personalities were not very distinct. Many hymns use terms which may equally well be understood abstractly as invoking a god or concretely as referring to physical objects used in the cult. Perhaps the absence of any artistic representations of the gods contributed to this vagueness. In any case, later generations were able to alter old conceptions of divinity without explicitly rejecting the language of the Vedic hymns. Such plasticity was already apparent in parts of the *Rig Veda*, which presaged the metamorphic pluralism of later Indian religion by freely identifying leading gods of the pantheon with one another.[24]

Since the earliest form of the Vedic religion was ill-fitted to sedentary farmers, when the Aryans settled down to a life in which agriculture played an ever larger role and warlike enterprise ceased to have central importance, pre-Aryan religious ideas presumably came more vividly to their attention. At any rate, the Vedic gods were whittled down until they became mere servants at the beck and call of priests skilled in elaborately defined ritual word and act. This transformation is hinted at in the *Vedas* themselves, for their existing form reflects the use of the hymns in liturgical ceremonies;[25] but explicit statement of the altered doctrine is reserved for a body of Vedic commentary known as *Brahmanas*. In the *Brahmanas* the gods of the *Rig Veda* fade into insignificance. The tendency to amalgamate disparate divinities is carried further, especially through the prominence accorded the god Prajapati, who now appears as lord of all creatures and creator of the universe. The act of sacrifice itself came to be conceived as a re-creation of Prajapati, and hence as a microcosmic re-creation of the universe itself. It followed that the priests who performed the sacrifice were greater than the gods—an assertion freely and emphatically made in the texts.[26]

The Brahmin priests who asserted these high claims formed a closed and

---

[24] Sir Charles Eliot, *Hinduism and Buddhism: An Historical Sketch* (3 vols.; London: Edward Arnold & Co., 1921), I, 56–58.

[25] M. Winternitz, *A History of Indian Literature* (2 vols.; Calcutta: University of Calcutta Press, 1927–33), I, 158–63.

[26] It is perhaps worth quoting two definitions: "The Brahmin descended from a Risi (i.e., a seer and author of Vedic hymns) indeed is all deities"; and "The Brahmin is the highest deity." These come from *Satapatha Brahmana*, XII, 4, 4–6, and the Law of Manu, IX, 319, respectively, as quoted in M. Winternitz, *A History of Indian Literature*, I, 200.

Cf. the words of Pope Innocent III: ". . . simple minded priests are not to be spoken ill of, even by scholars, for the priestly ministry should be honored in them. To this end the Lord commanded in the Law, 'Thou shalt not speak ill of the gods' [Exodus 22:28] meaning the priests, who are called by the name of gods because of the eminence of their rank and the dignity of their office." *Letter to the Faithful at Metz*, trans. Saul Levin from J. P. Migne (ed.), *Patrologiae Cursus Completus*, CCXIV (Paris: 1890), p. 697.

privileged caste, to which only sons of Brahmins could belong. A Brahmin was expected to exhibit a becoming personal conduct, to memorize at least one of the *Vedas,* and to learn the meaning of sacrifice as set forth in the *Brahmanas.* In return for priestly services, the Brahmins claimed exemption from lay control, taxation, or molestation of any sort, and expected generous fees and gifts. A priest claiming to incorporate all the gods in himself could certainly expect no less.

Two aspects of this development deserve special emphasis. First, a Brahmin was a learned man and acquired his learning by sitting at the feet of a teacher who knew the exact verbal formulae of sacred texts. The entire instruction was oral, depending on memorization; and individuals famous for the scope and accuracy of their learning naturally acquired a bevy of eager pupils, thus constituting an informal school.

Second, the emergence of schools provided an institutional setting that encouraged, indeed demanded, fuller explanation and additional commentary upon sacred texts, whose intelligibility suffered as the colloquial language evolved. The *Brahmanas* were the earliest product of such schools. They embodied the wildest sort of speculation, uninhibited by historical or philological knowledge or by well-defined traditional concepts of theology. Indeed, the invention of new ideas and fantastic explanations of old rites was restricted only by the ingenuity and verbal agility of the inventors; and it would doubtless be a mistake to confuse the wild exuberance of their doctrines with popular religion or with actual practice in society. There is good reason to think that the Brahmins did not enjoy the unchallenged supremacy and social dignity to which they laid claim. Aristocratic chieftains, kings, and warriors might respect them, might even fear their magical powers, but could not easily be persuaded to yield to the extravagant claims of upstart priests.[27]

Further evidence that reality fell short of the Brahmins' pretensions may be detected in the development of Indian religion itself. The sacerdotalism and ritualistic bias of the Brahmin schools did not long hold the field uncontested. Ascetic withdrawal to secluded jungle retreats, where individuals might seek holiness and religious enlightenment by any means that recommended itself to them, may have been a part of the Indian scene from pre-Aryan times. Whether or not this was the case, asceticism became an important social institution in India before the sixth century B.C. Ascetics of unusual holiness attained wide repute and attracted disciples in much the same fashion as especially learned Brahmins attracted students. Thus a second and more or less consciously rival school system arose, in which the effort to discover religious truth emancipated itself from any direct relationship to the ancient Vedic texts. The literary precipitate of these forest schools is the treatises known as *Upanishads.* Their doctrines mark a third stage of Indian religion.

---

[27] For traces of conflict between the warrior and priestly classes in ancient Indian society, see Majumdar, *History and Culture,* pp. 280–82; Pargiter, *Ancient Indian Historical Tradition,* p. 176; Hutton, *Caste in India,* p. 135.

Though the *Upanishads* are unsystematic in form and vary considerably in doctrine, even the earliest of them develop a number of distinctive themes. They reject sacrifice and priestly offices, declaring the goal of religious life to be "enlightenment," attainable through mastery of an esoteric knowledge rather than through correct performance of ritual acts. Such knowledge might be assisted by instruction and by ascetic practices; but it culminated in a mystic experience essentially incommunicable by words.

So far as words could go, however, the *Upanishads* endeavored to penetrate. Many of the doctrines which were to become central for later Hinduism here emerge clearly for the first time: in particular, the concepts of *Brahman*, *Atman*, and *Karma*. These terms cannot be precisely translated, for their nearest English equivalents inevitably carry the connotations of European religious and philosophic thought. Thus we may describe *Brahman* as the universal spiritual reality behind sense appearances, and equate *Atman* with the human soul. Yet such approximations to the Sanskrit meanings imperfectly prepare us for the assertion "That art Thou," *i.e.*, that *Brahman* and *Atman* are the same.[28] Similarly, *Karma* means "act," or "sin"—though of a special sort, involving intellectual as well as moral shortcoming.

The goal sought by holy and wise men was mystic ecstasy, through which the identity between *Brahman* and *Atman* could be experienced. *Karma* was the obstacle, distracting or obstructing *Atman* from the attainment of mystical communion with *Brahman*. Moreover, *Karma* was heritable, for souls were believed to be immortal, carrying with them into each new incarnation the accumulated *Karma* of earlier lives. Self-discipline, ascetic exercises, and verbal instruction all might aid *Atman* to slough off its individual share of *Karma* and open up the path to ultimate escape from the encumbrances of a material body with its carnal desires. *Atman* would then realize its identity with *Brahman* fully, completely, and eternally. Thus the final and perfect end of religious striving might be attained without the aid of priests, sacrifices, rituals, or indeed, without overt action of any sort.[29]

Such doctrines consciously challenged the Brahminical emphasis upon sacrificial ritual and caste prerogative. Yet with characteristic adaptability, the Brahmins did not long treat the *Upanishads* as heretical. Although these

[28] Numerous allegories in the *Upanishads* illustrate the meaning of "That art Thou," e.g., this dialogue between King Aruni and his son Svetaketu:

"These rivers flow east and west, they are drawn from the sea east and west, and flow into the sea again. They become sea and only sea. They know not there that one is this river and another that. And so with all these living things. They come out of the real, and do not know that they come out of it, and therefore they become in this life, as it may be, lion, or wolf, or boar, or worm, or moth, or gnat, or mosquito. All this world is animated by the supersensible. This is real, this is Self. THAT ART THOU, Svetaketu." From *The Upanishads*, trans. Swami Prabhavananda and Frederick Manchester (Mentor Pocket ed.; New York: New American Library of World Literature, 1957), p. 90.

[29] In attempting this summary of the doctrines of the *Upanishads*, I have consulted Winternitz, *A History of Indian Literature*, I, 247–67; Eliot, *Hinduism and Buddhism*, I, 71–86; S. Radhakrishnan, *Indian Philosophy* (2 vols.; New York: Macmillan Co., 1927), I, 137–267; Arthur Berriedale Keith, *The Religion and Philosophy of the Vedas and Upanishads* (Oxford: Oxford University Press, 1925), II, 440–600.

treatises were never accorded the same sacrosanct status as the *Vedas*, they nevertheless became a recognized and important part of the religious canon of Hinduism. Paradoxically, the inherent obscurity and esoteric character of their doctrines made them easier for Brahmins to accept. The *Upanishads* could directly affect only an intellectual elite; and the Brahmins made a place for such persons in their scheme of things by advancing the idea that an ascetic and priestless pursuit of holiness was appropriate for a man at the close of his life, after he had honored the priests and fulfilled normal family obligations during his active years. Only when Buddhists and Jains popularized views related to those set forth in the *Upanishads* and proclaimed them to be the sole standard of religious life did compromise between the Brahmins and these new sectaries become impossible.

The shift in philosophic outlook which first found sophisticated and extended expression in the *Upanishads* was a radical one. Vedic religion had had quite earthly aims in view, holding out prosperity, long life, and health as the rewards to be expected from good relations with the gods. The *Brahmanas* differed only slightly, supplementing material rewards with the promise that meticulously performed sacrifices might secure reincarnation in an immortal body. But the *Upanishads* disdained mere earthly pleasures, and proclaimed personal annihilation in the universal *Brahman* to be the supreme reward of the religious life.

It is rash to speculate on reasons for such a change when so little is known about ancient Indian society. Ascetic practices and the belief that miraculous powers might be attained through appropriate ascetic discipline may have been pre-Aryan. Yet drastic disruption of older and more naïve value systems seems needed to account for the *Upanishads*. Such disruption was not far to seek in the seventh and sixth centuries B.C., when the free, aristocratic mode of life, expressed politically in the tribal republics and petty states of northern India, crumbled under the pressures of urbanism and of absolute, centralized, and bureaucratized monarchy.[30] In such circumstances, what could a man of noble family and high expectations do in a world where his traditional social status had vanished? Some no doubt joined the victors and became servants of the rising monarchies; but especially stubborn or sensitive souls must have found a new sort of freedom and a substitute style of life in the asceticism of

[30] As a rough parallel, consider what might have happened to the world of the *kalos kagathos* of Athens in the sixth century B.C. if a foreign power, e.g., Persia, had intervened in Athenian affairs, raised upstarts and foreigners to positions of authority, and undermined the social and economic position of the noble families by acts of deliberate policy. Such an eventuality would have introduced a numbing paralysis into the Athenian polis; and Athenian culture would certainly have sought other directions than it in fact did. When in the fourth century B.C. a much less crippling blow did come to the aristocracy of Athens, one of the bluest bloods of all, Plato, reluctantly espoused a transcendentalism not entirely dissimilar from the ideals of the *Upanishads* or of Buddhism. Cf. Plato's account of his political frustration in *Epistle VIII*.

On conflict between an Indian aristocracy and officialdom, see Majumdar, *History and Culture*, p. 432. There is a tradition, probably well founded, that a king attacked and destroyed the aristocratic clan into which the Buddha was born during Gautama's own lifetime. T. W. Rhys Davids, *Buddhist India*, p. 11.

forest retreats, where their metaphysical and psychological speculation about the nature and meaning of mystic trances gave birth to the *Upanishads*.[31]

This spiritual resolution of worldly frustration became in due course a distinctive emphasis pervading Indian civilization and marking it off from its neighbors and contemporaries in the Middle East and Europe. Before the sixth century B.C., Indian development had not diverged so widely from what was happening elsewhere. The adjustment of the invading Aryans' warrior ethos to an aristocratic and agricultural mode of life had analogues in the Middle East and Europe. But when the aristocrats of the Ganges area came under attack from centralized and absolute monarchies, their response was unique, for on the basis of what were probably indigenous pre-Aryan ascetic techniques they formulated essentially new mystic ideals. Given literary expression in the *Upanishads*, these ideals soon attracted the allegiance of uprooted city dwellers, for whom an escape from the personal frictions and uncertainties of new-sprung urbanism had become urgent. Fed by individuals fleeing from the burgeoning cities, jungle retreats offered an institutional frame within which ascetic mysticism of the utmost sophistication could thus elaborate itself. Court and bazaar collaborated with jungle fastness to give shape to a new and distinctive religious world-view, able alike to satisfy the mind with philosophical subtlety, and the heart with mystic rapture.

The tendencies of thought and feeling apparent in the *Upanishads* were popularized by two important religious leaders who lived in the latter part of the sixth century B.C.—Mahavira, the founder (or reformer) of the Jain religion, and Gautama Buddha. Their exact dates are uncertain, but the two men were contemporaries; and probably both were active before and for some time after 500 B.C.[32] Their lives and preaching started large-scale and highly important religious movements, constituting the fourth of our stages of religious development in India.

The challenge which Jains and Buddhists offered to Brahmin ritualism won wide response. Indeed, two centuries after Buddha's death, India seemed on the verge of becoming a Buddhist land. Brahminism survived and eventually turned the tables only by transforming itself into what may conveniently be termed Hinduism, incorporating in the process many of the attitudes and ideals

---

[31] In later centuries, the primary technique for inducing mystic trances was breath control, whereby the adept so repressed his breathing as to reduce the oxygen supply in the blood to a point at which normal consciousness lapsed. Without any special training, an ordinary man, by holding his breath to the limit of conscious control, can induce dizziness; but practice can produce far more spectacular visual and psychological results through more prolonged oxygen starvation of the brain. It is possible, even probable, that breath control was the fundamental technique at the bottom of Upanishadic and pre-Aryan asceticism in India.

The cultural and historical consequences of these facts of physiology have been enormous. Not only Indian, but Moslem, Christian, and even Chinese Buddhist religiosity has been in varying degrees infused with mystic-ascetic ideals rooted in (or at least reinforced by) visions induced by oxygen starvation.

[32] Buddha probably died within a few years of 485 B.C. Mahavira's dates are more obscure, his death falling anywhere between 527 and 477 B.C., according to different traditions and systems of dating. Cf. Winternitz, *History of Indian Literature*, II, Appendix I; Jack Finegan, *Archaeology of World Religions* (Princeton, N.J.: Princeton University Press, 1952), pp. 197–99, 248.

which had first been voiced in the *Upanishads* and made popular by the Jains and Buddhists.

With the promulgation and organization of Jainism and Buddhism, the distinctive world-view characteristic of Indian civilization crystallized along enduring lines. By the end of the sixth century B.C., all the elements of what has happily been termed the "federation of cultures popularly known as Hinduism"[33] were already present; and later changes never transgressed this fundamental frame.

[33] The phrase comes from N. K. Bose, "Caste in India," *Man in India*, XXXI (1951), 113.

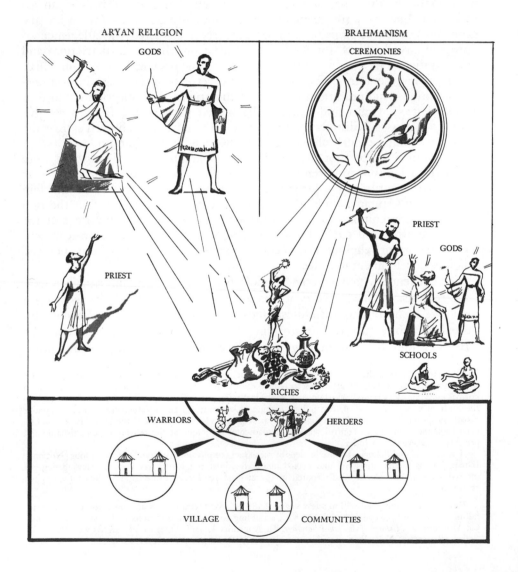

The complexities of Jain and Buddhist doctrine need not concern us here. The original ideas of Mahavira and Buddha can be distinguished only with difficulty from those elements later added to their message; yet there is no reason to suppose that, in their first years, either Buddhism or Jainism underwent any such fundamental reshaping as occurred in the case of Christianity when it left its Jewish cradle.

Much was common to Jainism and Buddhism. Both faiths held out the hope of salvation without resort to priest or sacrifice; both centered around groups of specially energetic seekers after enlightenment, or "monks," who attracted to themselves a body of laity whose obligations were less onerous. Both took

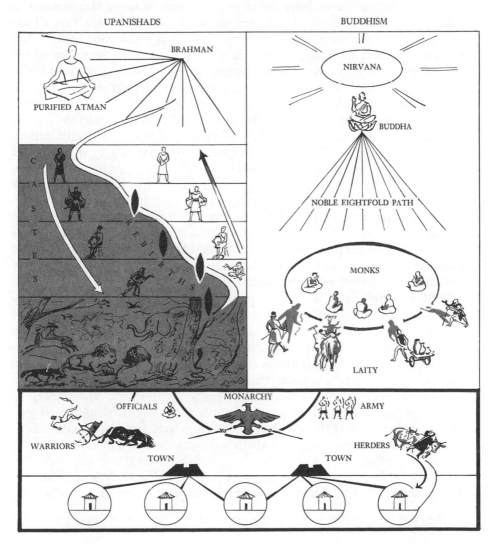

UPANISHADS

BUDDHISM

BRAHMAN

NIRVANA

PURIFIED ATMAN

BUDDHA

CASTES

REBIRTHS

NOBLE EIGHTFOLD PATH

MONKS

LAITY

OFFICIALS

MONARCHY

ARMY

WARRIORS

HERDERS

TOWN

TOWN

AND WORLD VIEWS

reincarnation to be a basic principle of the universe, and both sought an escape from the circle of births and deaths through correct knowledge and conduct. Both were atheistic.

But in details, doctrinal differences loomed large. The Jains considered *Atman* to be a permanent entity and praised asceticism, even to the point of starving to death, as the principal means of freeing the soul from *Karma* and gaining release. Buddha, on the contrary, denied the permanence of *Atman*, as of everything else in the world. After trying extreme asceticism in his early years, he decided that self-torture was vain and recommended instead a middle way—a quiet, moderate life of contemplation, religious discussion, and self-control—as the true path to religious enlightenment.

Buddhist doctrine eventually developed so many intricate complexities as to baffle any mere beginner. Yet Gautama Buddha's central idea, that all existence involved suffering, and that correct knowledge and good habit of life can annihilate that suffering, seems simple enough. And his definition of the way to attain release is not unduly obscure, for the "Noble Eightfold Path" to Enlightenment consists of systematic cultivation of right views, right aspirations, right speech, right conduct, right livelihood, right effort, right-mindedness, and right rapture. To be sure, Buddha did not attempt precise explanation of what was meant by "right" in these phrases. He taught, rather, by example, so that early Buddhist literature consisted largely of stories of Buddha's (often miraculous) deeds and sayings.

What made Buddha's career so significant for Indian and world history was not the doctrines he espoused, which in any case underwent great alteration in subsequent generations;[34] but his practical organization of the pursuit of holiness. There was nothing deliberate about the process. Rather, as his followers confronted particular problems from day to day, Buddha was called upon for an opinion, and in this piecemeal fashion he laid down a body of precedent, which later generations made binding.

Buddha himself lived a wandering life, but he normally spent the rainy season in one place. Even during his lifetime, pious laymen made grants of land or buildings where he and his monks might spend this period; and from this beginning arose the monastic establishments which have ever since remained the principal organizational focus of Buddhism. At first, admission to the circle of followers was arranged after an interview with Buddha himself; but as numbers grew, monks residing at a particular monastic center accepted novices into their ranks by means of a simple ceremony. Discipline was voluntary and informal. The monks assembled regularly for mutual edification; and on such occasions errant individuals were expected to confess their shortcomings in public.

The early Buddhist monasteries probably modeled their discipline and governance upon the aristocratic republican clan practices of an earlier pe-

[34] Popular Buddhism probably never corresponded very closely to the abstract, impersonal vision of the universe which scholars attribute (on rather slender grounds) to Buddha himself.

riod.[35] There was no fixed hierarchy of authority. Decisions were taken at assemblies of all the monks; and particular individuals were chosen for special tasks by a sort of informal election. Thus despite the political circumstances which made the older aristocratic republics no longer viable, Buddha was able to salvage the freedom and fellowship he had known in his youth within the new frame of a corporation of seekers after holiness and truth. In so doing, he democratized the community of free men, for any earnest seeker was welcomed to the Buddhist ranks regardless of ancestry. Moreover, by removing the basis of association to a religious plane, he and his followers effectively escaped the clutches of the growing monarchies which were destroying the type of aristocratic political community Buddha had known in his childhood.[36]

In founding a corporation of seekers after religious enlightenment and peace, Buddha did not seem to be breaking new ground. Holy men with their disciples had long been a prominent feature of the Indian social scene, and there is no reason to think that Buddha expected the groups that formed around him to perpetuate themselves. But the very size of the following he attracted, the remarkable force of his personality, and above all, the practical rules he laid down to define the daily conduct of each member of the community combined to maintain the cohesion of his followers, generation after generation.[37]

Thus, probably without any deliberate intent, a sort of church was called into being. It was at first a church without the hierarchical organization and public cult which are so intimately associated with all Christian churches, although these elements were sometimes added to Buddhist communities later.

No doubt Indian society, with its federal caste structure, was peculiarly hospitable to the creation of a social organization directed toward religious ends and divorced as far as might be from mundane politics. Yet the remarkable nature of such an institution should not be overlooked. Private pursuit of sanctity apart from the framework of normal life would have seemed inconceivable to Buddha's Greek contemporaries, for whom religion and the state were all but inseparable. The persistent frictions between church and state in Europe illustrate the difficulty European minds have always had in separating the religious from the other spheres of life. Nothing comparable troubled subsequent Indian history. Buddhists, or any other religious sect, could fit into the Indian scene as one more caste; and Indian governments were prepared to give all such social groups very wide autonomy.

The Buddhist way of life, maintained through the monastic organization,

---

[35] This insight I owe to Ernst Waldschmidt, "Indien in vedischer und frühbuddhistischer Zeit," in Fritz Valjavec (ed.), *Historia Mundi*, II, 545.

[36] If pious stories are to be believed, Buddha had been born a prince of an aristocratic clan republic. Despite the collision between such polities and the rising monarchies, some of the Gangetic kings were active patrons of early Buddhist establishments. Presumably supernatural benefits weighed heavily with such rulers; but the monastic communities obviously had a value as a safety valve also, since discontented individuals might find an utterly non-political release from political frustration by becoming monks.

[37] Cf. the role of St. Benedict of Nursia for the monasticism of Latin Christendom.

attracted the loyalty of millions and turned their conduct into new paths. Thereby the transitory master-disciple relationship that had linked Buddha and his followers was institutionalized and perpetuated.[38] As a result, the insight and personality of a single man was immeasurably magnified. The particular vision of the world which had gradually taken form among Indian religious recluses became dominant in all India, while modified forms found lodgment in China, Japan, Burma, Siam, and Tibet.

The long and varied career of Buddhism became possible, of course, only through the crystallization of traditional versions of Buddha's teachings into a body of authoritative literature. Several different Buddhist canons are in existence, each differing substantially from the others. The Pali canon, current in Ceylon, may be the closest to Buddha's own message; but although most scholars accept some passages of this canon as fairly exact versions of Buddha's sermons, it is impossible to be sure where history ends and embroidery begins. The figure of Gautama Buddha came very early to be invested with a supernatural aura; and later ages revered him as a god and savior, in flat contradiction to the original force of his doctrine.[39]

In many respects, Indian culture was still in process of formulation when Buddha and Mahavira died. No visual art, for example, is known to antedate the Buddhist era; and since Brahmanism required neither temples nor statues in its worship, it is possible that artistic skill was confined to woodworking and the decoration of other perishables. Equally, the political organization of the country was unstable; large parts of the countryside were still covered with jungle; and southern India lived a life of its own, about which practically nothing is known. It must be remembered that not Buddhism, but a remodeled and popularized Brahminical religion—Hinduism—eventually prevailed in India, so that the religious development of the country by no means came to a standstill with Buddhism.

In other words, Indian civilization in the fifth century B.C. was a living, growing thing with a long history ahead of it. Yet the directions of growth and some of its limits had been defined by the time Buddha died. The master institution of caste and the major outlines of the religious world-view which were to govern all subsequent Indian history down to the present had emerged. Indian civilization, in short, had achieved its distinctive formulation.

C. THE FORMULATION OF GREEK CIVILIZATION

Far more is known about early Greek history than about the simultaneous emergence of civilization in India. From about 1500 B.C., approximate dates

---

[38] The modern industrial corporation bears a similar relationship to the older individual enterprises or partnerships of European economic history. The practical consequences of corporate business enterprise are, in their way, no more striking than the practical results which followed upon the invention of popular religious corporations, of which the Buddhist (and Jain) "churches" appear to have been the earliest examples.

[39] I have consulted the following for this summary of Buddha's life and teaching: Eliot, *Hinduism and Buddhism*, I, 127–345; Winternitz, *A History of Indian Literature*, II, 1–423; T. W. Rhys Davids, *Buddhism: Its History and Literature* (New York: G. P. Putnam's Sons, 1896); S. Radhakrishnan, *Indian Philosophy*, I, 581–611.

can be assigned to the major turning points of Greek development; and by the sixth century B.C.—perhaps the most critical of all centuries for the formation of both Greek and Indian civilization—events and individuals begin to stand forth with a clarity and precision unparalleled south of the Himalayas.

This contrast is in part attributable to the fact that the Aegean world was in much closer contact with the anciently civilized Orient than was India. Thus it is often possible to date Greek archeological finds by means of objects imported from the Middle East, and in some cases Egyptian and Hittite written sources record dealings with the Aegean peoples. It is these Middle Eastern bench marks, rather than anything left by the Greeks themselves, that allow a relatively exact chronology for Greek history in the second millennium B.C.

A more fundamental reason for our superior knowledge of Greek affairs is that the ancient Greeks themselves, far more than their Indian contemporaries, took an interest in history and were at some pains to record it. "Man is a political animal," said Aristotle; and his definition was particularly apt for Greek antiquity, when the polis, or city-state, embraced almost all human concerns within its institutional frame. By contrast, Indian thinkers, preoccupied by the infinities within and beyond humankind, were almost entirely indifferent to the temporal and accidental aspects of ordinary life. As a consequence, Indian literature records remarkably little about social conditions or political events, whereas the Greeks invented both secular history and political theory.

In proportion as the Greeks' cultural values revolved around individual and collective life in the everyday world, history assumed an importance for them which it could never have for Indian sages. Despite this fact, a connected narrative of events becomes possible only in the fifth century B.C.; and even then, Athens and Sparta tend to pre-empt the stage to the exclusion of other Greek states. For the earlier period, only the major outlines of Greek history can be discerned and important uncertainties remain.

1. POLITICAL AND SOCIAL DEVELOPMENT

No indisputable archeological or literary evidence marks the first arrival of Greek-speaking tribesmen in the Balkan Peninsula. Probably the first such groups reached Greece soon after 2000 B.C.[40] For several centuries, however, life on the Greek mainland and in the Aegean islands remained backward in comparison to the civilization of Crete.

About 1600 B.C., a more advanced style of life took root on the Greek mainland, centering in a few great strongholds, like that of Mycenae. This civilization was strongly influenced from Minoan Crete; and many of its earlier surviving art objects are indistinguishable from contemporary Cretan products. Nonetheless, there is reason to suppose that other aspects of mainland life were different from those prevailing in Crete. In particular, Mycenaean towns were dominated by strong fortifications; and archeological remains

---

[40] The appearance of Greek-speaking warriors in Greece was part of a much wider migration of peoples which eventually spread bronze metallurgy and the so-called Indo-European languages over all Europe. See above, pp. 102–8.

give a prominence to weapons and armor which is not paralleled in Crete. Clearly, warriors, rather than priest-kings, ruled at Mycenae.[41]

The establishment of civilization on the Greek mainland required a considerable degree of political and economic centralization. Vast numbers of men must have toiled to erect the mighty fortifications of Mycenae, not to mention those of lesser sites. It is not possible to say how such centralization was first effected. Perhaps conquerors, knit together by battle-tested war-band discipline, overran the country, and parceled out great "fiefs" among the victorious captains; or perhaps some more gradual consolidation of power located a precarious hegemony in the hands of the lords of Mycenae.

In any case, one of the major props of Mycenaean social structure was the aristocratic character of the warfare of the age. Chariots of war were introduced into Greece about the middle of the second millennium B.C.; and details of construction and harnessing suggest that the Mycenaean chariots were modeled on Syrian prototypes.[42] Perhaps bands of venturesome warriors from across the sea (possibly the Pelops of mythology) implanted the new technology of war among the Greeks; or alternatively, artisans capable of building chariots may have been captured in raids on the Levantine coast. However this may be, the result of the new technology was to create or to confirm the power of an aristocracy, whose members alone could afford the elaborate equipment necessary for chariot warfare.

Thus Mycenaean development was analogous to the Middle Eastern. Like the Kassite, Mitanni, Hittite, and Hyksos states, the Mycenaean also rested upon a chariot aristocracy recruited from among barbarian tribesmen. And just as these Middle Eastern conquerors had borrowed and adapted the culture of their civilized subjects and neighbors, so the Mycenaeans also turned to the civilized example closest at hand—the Cretan—and rapidly acquired the outward trappings of that civilization.[43]

However, there was one important difference between Mycenaean and Hittite, Kassite, or Mitanni society. The latter peoples were landsmen pure and simple; but the lords of Mycenae commanded fleets which plied the seas as traders and pirates. The range of Mycenaean shipping was wide. Contact with Asia Minor, Cyprus, the Levant, and Egypt was extensive; and Mycenaean remains have been discovered as far afield as Sicily, Sardinia, and more doubtfully, in Spain and Britain.[44] Whether Mycenaean seamanship was directed primarily to trade or to piracy is difficult to judge; and no doubt the distinction between the two was often blurred. Nevertheless, as long as the

---

[41] On relations between Crete and Mycenae, see Helene J. Kantor, *The Aegean and the Orient in the Second Millennium B.C.* (Archaeological Institute of America, Monograph No. 1 [Bloomington, Ind.: Principia Press, 1947]).

[42] Eugen von Mercklin, *Der Rennwagen in Griechenland* (Leipzig: Druck von Radelli und Hilte, 1909), pp. 1–2.

[43] It may be that Cretan craftsmen, captured in war or attracted by princely patronage, executed many of the early works of art discovered on mainland sites; for Mycenaean art shows no significant independence of Cretan styles until after the ruin of Knossos about 1400 B.C.

[44] *Cambridge Ancient History*, II, 459; Pierson Dixon, *The Iberians of Spain and Their Relations with the Aegean World* (Oxford: Oxford University Press, 1940), pp. 18–21.

THE GATEWAY TO MYCENAE

This was the main entrance to Agamemnon's fortress, perched high on a precipitous hilltop, looking down on the fertile plain of Argos, and controlling a pass through the mountains that led northward to the Gulf of Corinth. The rampant lions repeat a motif long familiar in Mesopotamian art (p. 67). The massiveness of the fortification, as well as details of design—right-handed warriors approaching this gate were forced to expose their unshielded side to missiles launched from the rampart on the extreme right of this photograph—reflects the warlike character of Mycenaean society.

Egyptian empire remained militarily vigorous, *i.e.*, until the fourteenth century B.C., there is no evidence that Mycenaean fleets engaged in anything but peaceable trade along the Levantine coast; and perhaps the Greek memory of the "thalassocracy of Minos" reflects an age when an organized and powerful Cretan fleet kept piracy in the Aegean under control. However, after about 1400 B.C., the Cretan fleet dispersed, and large-scale piracy and sea raiding came strongly to the fore. Knossos itself may have been the victim of a seaborne atack launched from the mainland. Similarly, Mycenaean seamen were among the leagued "Peoples of the Sea" who attacked Egypt toward the end of the thirteenth century B.C.[45] The *Iliad* of Homer probably represents the memory of still a third such venture, directed northward against Troy at the gate of the Dardanelles, traditionally (and perhaps accurately) dated 1184 B.C.

In all probability, wealth garnered overseas was the cement holding the Mycenaean empire together. Only with gold and other valuables at his disposal could the high king of Mycenae reward his allies and followers with the liberality they expected; and only through judicious largess could such a ruler maintain an armed force sufficient to overawe any potential dissidence among vassal princes. But when disorders within the Egyptian and Hittite empires began to disturb trade and thus to reduce Mycenaean wealth, the kings may have been impelled to take by force what they could no longer acquire through more peaceful means.[46]

Yet in the long run, wholesale resort to force undermined the high king's position. Every town sacked meant less wealth to support the apparatus of political centralization. An unsuccessful expedition, such as that sent against Egypt in the early twelfth century B.C., must have discouraged princes and sub-kings from answering any future summons to war. At such a juncture after a disastrous raid, when the high king's resources were straitened, his disappointed followers and domestic rivals would be likely to revolt. Such civil disorder would make it relatively easy for rude outer barbarians—the Dorians of subsequent Greek history—to invade the land and destroy the

---

[45] The definitive repulse of these sea raids occurred about 1190 B.C., when the Pharaoh's army and navy defeated mutually supporting land and sea forces that had advanced from the north. The remnant of the defeated attackers settled in Palestine, where they became the Philistines of biblical history and gave their ethnic name to the land. Cf. A. R. Burn, *Minoans, Philistines and Greeks, B.C. 1400–900* (London: Kegan Paul, Trench, Trubner & Co. Ltd., 1930).

[46] This may be conceived as a special case of the more generalized and simpler relation between hill and plain in the Middle East and Mediterranean areas, as analyzed above. The difference lay in the fact that no simple food deficit impelled Mycenaean "vikings" on their raids. Instead, it lay in their need for prestige and luxury goods with which to maintain the power and dignity of the high king of Mycenae by appropriate distribution of gold, bronze, and slaves among his followers. Not simple villages, but the urban centers of high civilization were therefore the only suitable targets. Just as the hill villages were marginal to the plains, so too the state of Mycenae was marginal to the richer, more securely civilized states of the Middle East. Perhaps the full panoply of an Agamemnon could not be maintained on the basis of resources directly under his control but depended upon wealth derived from foreign lands through trade or war. In other words, the political centralization of the Mycenaean age may have been possible only through a parasitic relationship upon older, richer civilized communities—Crete in the first phase, and the whole Levant coast in the later phase of the Mycenaean age. Cf. the relation of steppe empires to civilized society, from the time of the Hsiung-Nu (third century B.C.) until the eighteenth century A.D., when Chinese armies collaborated with the smallpox virus to destroy the last stronghold of steppe power, the Kalmuk confederacy.

Mycenaean power. Thus we may surmise that, once launched on a path of predation, the high kings of Mycenae strove mightily but in the end vainly against the disintegration of their power.

At any rate, soon after 1200 B.C., Dorian Greeks descended from the north, plundered the great citadels, and destroyed the kingdom.[47] Large-scale migrations connected with these invasions lasted until about 1000 B.C., and no doubt involved much mixing and many secondary and tertiary displacements of population. The Dorians themselves settled chiefly in the old centers of Mycenaean power, perhaps because there they found the best farm land and the most tempting booty. As a result the fertile parts of the Peloponnesus, Crete, and southwestern Asia Minor became Dorian, while less favored regions remained in the possession of other Greeks, whose forefathers had penetrated into the land before the Dorians came. Attica, for example, became "Ionian"; so did a group of cities located across the Aegean in the central section of the Asia Minor coast. These cities, founded by refugees from the Greek mainland during the period of the Dorian invasions, quickly took the lead in developing the rudiments of a new style of life which eventually flowered into classical Greek civilization.

Ionia's precocity was in part due to the intimacy of contact with the civilized Orient which resulted from the region's geographic location. Perhaps traces of Mycenaean high culture also survived more strongly across the Aegean. The Ionic (or perhaps Aeolic-Ionic) origin of the Homeric epics is good evidence for such survival; for these poems clearly incorporate echoes of the Mycenaean age and represent a final flowering of a bardic tradition which had its roots in pre-Dorian times.[48]

Another stimulus to Ionian development arose from the necessity of organizing an effective basis of social and political cohesion in an alien and potentially hostile environment. Refugees, drawn perhaps from diverse localities and with differing family traditions, were compelled to start life anew; and the break with the past was especially effective just because a sea voyage had interrupted continuities of social tradition.[49] Thus the Greek settlers of Ionia enjoyed (or suffered from) an unusual plasticity of circumstance when it came to establishing a social and political framework within which to live. Their response was to create the foundations of what later became the master institution of Greek civilization, the polis.[50]

---

[47] The Dorian invasion was accompanied or swiftly followed by the introduction of iron tools and weapons into Greece, with social consequences similar to those we have already traced in the Orient, *i.e.*, democratization of warfare and localization of political authority.

[48] Cf. Martin P. Nilsson, *Homer and Mycenae* (London: Methuen & Co., 1933); Denys L. Page, *History and the Homeric Iliad* (Berkeley and Los Angeles: University of California Press, 1959); M. I. Finley, *The World of Odysseus* (New York: Viking, 1954).

[49] Cf. A. J. Toynbee's acute remarks about the effect of overseas movements upon the social plasticity of migrants in *A Study of History* (London: H. Milford, Oxford University Press, 1934), I, 84–100.

[50] Developments in Ionia and adjacent parts of the Asia Minor coast are as obscure as anything on the mainland of Greece during the "Dark Age" which followed the Dorian invasions. The Ionian league of historic times may have evolved from an Ionic kingship existing in the early days of settlement. Archeological investigation, in particular at "Old Smyrna," shows fairly conclusively that the first Greek settlers in Ionia gathered together for protection against hostile natives, usually on penin-

The polis constituted the fundamental cell of both Greek and Roman civilized life. Physically, it consisted of a town or city with an area of farm and pasture land round about. Politically, it was a community governed by magistrates and laws. Psychologically, it was a self-sufficient in-group to which a privileged part of the total population—the adult male citizens—belonged and from which not only aliens, but also slaves, women, and children were excluded. In its mature form, the Greek polis commanded an almost total dedication on the part of its citizens. Economics and politics, together with religion, art, literature, and philosophy, came to be pursued largely within its framework.

The mountainous terrain of Greece no doubt favored the establishment of small political units. But geography was scarcely determinative; for many of the historic Greek poleis united separate plains (e.g., Athens and Sparta), while in other cases, contiguous expanses of fertile ground were broken up into a number of separate political units (e.g., the cities of Boeotia and Achaea).[51] Not geography, therefore, but social conditions and institutions gave the polis its distinctive character.

As population movements associated with the Dorian invasions died away, agriculture became more settled in the Greek world. No longer were fields cropped to exhaustion, only to be abandoned when the tribe moved onward. Instead, fallowing made it possible to farm suitable soils indefinitely; and in proportion as this simple technical improvement was introduced, each family household could settle down and make good its claim to permanent possession of a definite piece of land. Tribal ties weakened correspondingly, as tribal leaders transformed themselves into landed aristocrats; and society tended to disintegrate into its ultimate household units.[52]

---

sular and other easily defensible sites. The need for mutual protection thus compelled them to gather into what soon became towns; while the recurrent need to stand off inland populations probably continued to prick the Ionians on toward an ever tighter and more effective military-political organization within the urban or polis frame. By comparison, the mainland Greeks lagged behind in developing urbanism and the polis type of political organization. The mainlanders started from a more dispersed pattern of settlement and were organized by tribal and family links. In Ionia, on the contrary, kinship relations had been broken up in course of flight across the sea; and when every man was needed to aid in defense against the native inhabitants, some new and inclusive political frame, that would take the place of traditional kinship ties, had to be invented. The territorial unit of the polis was the Ionian answer. On early Ionia, cf. the illuminating discussion in Carl Roebuck, *Ionian Trade and Colonization* (New York: Archaeological Institute of America, 1959), pp. 24–41.

[51] The republics of northern India in the sixth century B.C. and some of the city-states of the Middle East which flourished in the early part of the first millennium B.C. much resembled the early Greek poleis. But these communities were cut off in their youth by the rise of great territorial monarchies, whereas the Greeks were able, in the Persian Wars of 493–79 B.C., to stand off that threat successfully. Their peripheral relation to the center of Middle Eastern civilization, and the dependence of the Persians on seaborne supplies, made such an outcome possible. No comparable geographic advantages came to the rescue of the Indian and Middle Eastern proto-poleis in their hour of need. In this sense, perhaps, geography had more to do with the success of the Greek polis organization than I have allowed in the text.

[52] In some regions of mainland Greece there may have been a weak survival of Mycenaean public organization and administration, as there surely was in Ionia. This was perhaps the case in Attica, where legend had it that Theseus first united the land in Mycenaean times and that one of his royal successors, Codrus, rallied the forces of all Attica to repel Dorian attack. A similar echo of the Mycenaean inheritance appeared in the Argive claim to primacy in the Peloponnesus.

ANCIENT GREECE

But certain problems remained which independent households could not effectively solve. One was the maintenance of personal security. In the early days, crimes were generally revenged by the victim himself or by his relatives; but the resultant blood feuds easily got out of hand, and became damaging to all concerned. Here lay perhaps the most fertile ground for the growth of public functions, for the parties to a quarrel were sometimes willing to settle their dispute by adjudication. Tribal kings had traditionally been charged with the task of judicial pacification, since otherwise the cohesion of the kindred could not long endure. This aspect of traditional leadership did not entirely decay with the cessation of large-scale migration, although it is not clear how regularly a distant king was able to enforce his decisions upon recalcitrant families. A device that lent extra weight to royal decisions was to associate a council of important men with the king to decide the rights and wrongs of particularly important cases. A discontented and potentially defiant litigant then had to face the forces, not merely of the king, but of influential nobles as well, and would be correspondingly reluctant to resort to arms.

A second public function was leadership in war. The nature of Greek military organization between 1000 and 600 B.C. is obscure; but it is clear that, by the latter date, cavalry played the decisive role in Greek warfare. Horsemen had many advantages: they could move rapidly to surprise an enemy and charge with a momentum difficult for straggling infantry to oppose. But only men of considerable agricultural wealth could become cavalrymen, for natural grass was so scant in Greece that horses had to eat grain through most of the year. Thus, in proportion as cavalry became decisive in battle, noble landowners increased their influence in public affairs.

The balance of forces in early Greek society was therefore such as to encourage noble families to band together and limit royal authority. This was done initially by appointing members of the nobility as assistants to the king for a fixed term. Moreover, because such primitive magistrates could not always be trusted to serve the interests of the landowners as a whole, a general council of the nobility began to meet more often and to take a more active part in important decisions. Details of this process no doubt differed considerably from state to state; but by the eighth century B.C., noble aristocracies had usurped most of the royal powers in all the more developed parts of Greece. In Athens, for example, the kingship ceased to be hereditary; and the "king" himself became merely a magistrate, appointed for a fixed term, and charged primarily with religious functions. Other magistrates were entrusted with judicial and military business, while the aristocratic Council of the Areopagus exercised a general supervision over public affairs.

Noble families active in government tended to take up residence near the seat of administration, which thus gradually assumed the character of a town. Such a center, normally chosen for its defensive strength, also attracted artisans and merchants, though these groups were at first of little importance. Town life was therefore originally aristocratic, not mercantile or industrial. This fact gave an enduring stamp to Greek city life. Even in the most active commercial and industrial centers of later centuries, the aristocratic ideal of public and private life was never effectively challenged.[53]

In the countryside as well, the power of the nobility increased with the passage of time. From the time when the Greeks first settled down to permanent agriculture, tribal leaders had presumably occupied larger tracts of land than had their humbler followers. By the seventh century B.C., in many parts of Greece population pressure had become a serious problem. Farms were subdivided, so that in bad years a poor farmer might be obliged to borrow

---

[53] This distinguishes Greek cities from the towns which arose in northern Europe during the high Middle Ages. The social leaders and magistrates of medieval towns were merchants who developed an ethos that stood in more or less conscious opposition to the ideals of the landed aristocracy. Since the higher manifestations of culture were in ancient as in more recent times largely the product of town populations, this difference in the original character of ancient as against modern towns subtly but profoundly colored the whole civilization of the two eras. Industriousness, for example, was never a virtue in Greek or Roman eyes; and artisan trades always carried a certain taint of indignity.

THE PHALANX

The first of these Greek vases dates from the late seventh century B.C., when the phalanx was still a new invention, while the lower and less damaged specimen was painted two generations afterward. The upper photograph shows two ranks of the phalanx charging at full speed, yet keeping step perfectly, while cavalrymen guard the flanks at each end of the line. In a real battle, the rear ranks of the phalanx crowded close behind the front line, converting the formation into a single moving mass of disciplined humanity. The vase painter had to separate the ranks and showed only two, for reasons of design. Details of the hoplites' equipment—helmet, shield, spear, and greaves—may be seen more clearly in the photograph below.

seed or food from his richer neighbors. In return, he pledged his land or his liberty, which became forfeit if the loan were not repaid. Noble landowners, themselves protected by their wider lands against want even in years of poor harvest, were thus in an excellent position to make such loans and profit from them.[54] As a result, bitter class conflict broke out in many cities; but as long as the nobility maintained both economic and military preponderance, the poor obtained little redress of their grievances.

An important change in military tactics checked, for a few centuries, the drift of Greek society toward the Middle Eastern pattern of polarization between a leisured aristocracy and an oppressed, poverty-stricken populace. In the second half of the seventh century, and more especially in the sixth, the hoplite—a heavily armed and armored infantryman—replaced the horseman as the decisive element on the battlefield. When massed together into a phalanx —a regular formation trained to charge and maneuver in unison—hoplites could prevail even against cavalry and were able to sweep loosely organized infantry from the field. Although regular military formations were nothing new in Greek or Middle Eastern warfare,[55] the combination of heavier armor, closer order, and above all, the rhythmic co-ordination of mass movement in the phalanx, raised the effectiveness of Greek infantry to hitherto unequaled levels.

In its mature form, the phalanx comprised eight ranks, each so closely formed that every man's shield helped to cover the neighbor to his left in the line. Whether this arrangement prevailed from the beginning is not clear. But by the early sixth century, the charge of a well-trained and well-armored phalanx, its thousands of men acting as one and keeping pace by means of the rhythmic shouts of the paean, proved itself all but irresistible.[56] Cavalry could not oppose the advance of such a unit nor break its front. Only by taking the phalanx on the flank or in the rear could horsemen still play an effective role in battle.

Profound social consequences flowed from this change. The ultimate basis of aristocratic primacy was, of course, removed when the farmer-hoplite became the decisive factor on the battlefield. Far more important was the psychological effect of the prolonged drill needed to train the members of the phalanx to maintain formation in the field and to execute maneuvers quickly and smoothly in the face of an enemy. In the ranks each man was the equal of his fellows. Each hoplite's life depended upon the stalwart behavior of his neighbor in the battle line. Differences of wealth or social status ceased to matter, while strength, courage, and discipline were at a premium. All this no doubt fostered a sense of solidarity and equality among the citizen-soldiers of

---

[54] These developments probably coincided chronologically with the introduction of cavalry into Greek warfare, which give the nobility an additional source of power.

[55] E.g., Achilles had his Myrmidons (*Iliad*, II, 683–85); and the Assyrians built their army around regular infantry units.

[56] The new efficiency of well-trained and heavily armored infantry was probably first demonstrated during the long war between Chalcis and Eretria which occupied the middle years of the seventh century B.C. Thereafter, the new formation spread rapidly to other Greek cities, for once the phalanx had proven its power, no city could afford to be without one.

the phalanx. Moreover, as graduates of the close-order drill of a modern army will readily admit, oft-repeated drill exercises, involving rhythmic movements of large masses of men to the accompaniment of singing and music, acts like a powerful hypnotic, fostering a quite subrational sense of well-being and social solidarity.

As a natural extension of the sentiments generated within the phalanx, a new standard of behavior gained ground among the Greeks. Aristocratic display became bad form, un-Greek, barbarian. The measure of a good man and citizen came to be the modest life of an independent farmer, owning enough land to live decently, able to equip himself with spear, shield, and helmet, and ready to play his part manfully on the battlefield. As this ideal won increasing acceptance, the amassing of private wealth lost much of its attractiveness; and by the close of the sixth century, even wealthy aristocrats had begun to live and dress simply. Competitive conspicuous consumption which had been characteristic of the nobility in the seventh century was diverted into new channels, as men of wealth began to take pride in financing public buildings and services with a munificence they no longer dared or cared to lavish upon themselves. Thus, a lively spirit of egalitarianism and civic solidarity began to distinguish Greek from foreign ways of life.[57]

The introduction of the phalanx had far-reaching political as well as social consequences. Other things being equal, the larger the phalanx, the stronger and more secure the polis. Hence a system of society permitting wealthy landowners to acquire the small farms of their fellow citizens and reduce the poorer agricultural class to penury or slavery became intolerable. Each such downward shift in status meant a smaller phalanx, a weaker city, and insecurity for all. Consequently, both Sparta and Athens (the only two states about which we are tolerably well informed) took steps in the late seventh and early sixth centuries B.C. to insure themselves against the decay of their phalanxes.

Sparta's response to the problem of organizing and maintaining an efficient phalanx took the drastic form of the so-called Lycurgan constitution. Probably introduced toward the end of the seventh century B.C., the sole aim of this constitution was to make the Spartan phalanx as strong and numerous as possible. It set up a rigorous system of obligatory military training lasting throughout every citizen's active life. The Spartans suppressed all outward marks of differences in rank or wealth—indeed officially they termed themselves *Homoroi*, or Equals. All able-bodied citizens became, in effect, professional soldiers, a garrison planted in the midst of a subject population of disfranchised freemen and serfs who were compelled to work the land and support the citizenry. As a result of full-time training all the year round, the Spartan phalanx became by far the best in Greece. Yet the insidious fear of corrupting citizens by exposing them to the temptations of a freer life abroad, together with the even more paralyzing fear of revolt in the rear, deterred the Spartan leaders from using their military superiority to support a consist-

---

[57] The Greeks of the classical age felt this to be at the heart of the gap between Hellene and barbarian. Cf. Thucydides, I, 6, and Herodotus, VI, 207.

ent imperial policy vis-à-vis other Greek cities. Instead they settled for the establishment of a loose league of cities under their own rigidly conservative leadership.

Athens' reaction to the threatened decay of her phalanx was drastic enough but did not involve conscripting all citizens into a barracks life. Instead, the Athenians appointed Solon as special magistrate with extraordinary powers. to revise the laws. Solon forbade debt-slavery for the future; and by canceling outstanding debts, he restored the small farmers to their land and to the status of free citizens. In this fashion, some of the grosser economic inequalities within the Athenian citizen body were removed; and the strength of the phalanx was restored.[58]

The phalanx, therefore, was the school which made the Greek polis. It checked the incipient growth of an aristocratic luxury and substituted an ideal of moderation in all outward things. It confirmed, if it did not actually create, the ideal of self-identification with and dedication to the polis. Finally, it greatly broadened the class of citizens who took an active part in polis affairs, for the hoplites who defended their city on the battlefield could scarcely be excluded from participation in civil affairs. Nor were they. Solon's laws, for example, gave the class of hoplites the right to act as a court of appeal from judicial decisions of the aristocratic magistrates; and in Sparta the Lycurgan constitution gave the assembly of citizen-hoplites power to elect all magistrates. In this fashion, the right to a voice in public affairs, formerly restricted to nobles, was broadened to include all citizens having the means to equip themselves as members of the phalanx. The "hoplite franchise" remained a conservative ideal for many Greek cities throughout the fifth century and later.

Nevertheless, not all citizens were able to equip themselves with the necessary sword, spear, helmet, and shield. Many were too poor, for metal was still comparatively expensive. There were also fairly large numbers of men drifting about the Greek world who had no polis or who had left their homes to live as foreigners, without polis rights. As population grew, the relative importance of these groups tended to increase, so that even before the hoplite franchise became a familiar ideal heavy new pressures were building up within the body politic at commercial centers like Athens, Corinth, or Miletus.

Men without sufficient land for farming were forced to seek other means of livelihood. They found two major outlets: trade and manufacture, or emigration overseas. The two were complementary; for newly established colonies often imported goods from the homeland, and after a few years began themselves to produce grain and other surpluses for export. Both trade and emigration increased in importance about the middle of the eighth century. Ionian cities, especially Miletus, took the lead in colonization; but towns such as Corinth, Chalcis, and Eretria followed closely behind. The colonial movement lasted approximately from 750 B.C. to 550 B.C. Thereafter, Carthaginian

[58] Practical results were evident when the Athenians in the next generation were able to seize the island of Salamis from their Megarian neighbors.

and Etruscan opposition closed the western Mediterranean to further Greek colonial enterprise, while at the same time, the growing commercial prosperity of some of the older Greek cities permitted even the landless to earn a tolerable living closer to home.

The commercial pattern which arose during these two centuries remained of fundamental significance throughout both Greek and Roman history. Formerly, Greek farmers had produced most household necessities themselves, selling only what was needed to purchase specialized goods like metal tools and weapons; but now, in important parts of Greece, agriculture itself was put on a commercial basis. While grain remained basic, more and more effort was devoted to the preparation of two comparatively precious and easily transportable products: wine and olive oil. Wine was of course a valued convivial intoxicant. Olive oil was more versatile, being not only an important element in the fat-poor Mediterranean diet but also a substitute for soap, and the only easily available fuel for lamps. Under these circumstances, it is not strange that barbarian peoples were willing to pay handsomely with grain, metals, timber, or other raw materials for the wine and oil of Greece.

Despite the obvious advantages of grape and olive culture, its diffusion was slow. Even in regions where no climatic barrier prevented the planting of grape vines or olive trees, the unfamiliar procedures (pruning, grafting) and back-breaking labor required for their cultivation served to hinder the spread of olive groves and vineyards. Even more crucial was the fact that several barren years had to elapse between the time of planting and and the first fruition. Many farmers could not afford to forego an annual harvest, even when they clearly understood the increased rewards to be had from grapes or olives. In Attica, for example, the new style of commercial agriculture became widespread only after about 560 B.C., when the tyrant Peisistratus introduced a policy of granting state loans on very favorable terms to farmers who planted their land with grapes or olives.

The transition to commercial agriculture brought enormous advantages to pioneering cities like Miletus, Eretria, or Athens. In effect, by exporting oil and wine, these cities secured in exchange vastly more grain (and other commodities) than they could ever produce locally. Moreover, grape-olive agriculture increased the total area of productive soil in Greece; for olive trees, and to a lesser extent, grape vines, could flourish on rough and stony slopes where grain grew indifferently, if at all. Consequently, commercial agriculture could support far larger populations than subsistence agriculture had ever done; and the development of a distinctively new type of urban economy became possible.

The transition to grape-olive agriculture reinforced the democratizing tendencies inherent in phalanx tactics and accentuated the divergences between Greek and Middle Eastern social patterns. The commercial cities of the Middle East had long exported manufactured goods like cloth and metal objects in exchange for metals, timber, or other raw material. Food for these cities came from the immediate hinterland, much of it in the economically unrequited form of rents or taxes. Thus the agriculturalists of the Middle

East constituted a peasantry only marginally entangled in the urban commercial nexus. The peasant majority of such a society always tended to regard city dwellers as aliens and oppressors—often with good reason. In Greece, on the contrary, the farmers who produced the wine and oil essential to urban commerce regarded themselves and were regarded by others as the ideal type of citizen. They took a leading part in political life, bore the brunt of phalanx warfare, and purchased the products of city workshops as freely as any urban resident.

As a result, market relationships penetrated much farther down the social scale in Greece than in the Middle East and united a far greater proportion of the total population into a cohesive, self-conscious, and proud political unit. A passive peasantry, accepting any political change with indifference, seeing only a change of masters that could bring no benefit to themselves, was characteristic of the Orient. In Greece, on the contrary, the rural population was vitally and actively concerned in all the affairs of the state. Herein lay much of the secret of Greek military effectiveness against Oriental foes, and although Herodotus may have overdrawn his contrast between Persian soldiers driven by the lash into battle and Greeks fighting of their own free will, his picture nonetheless contains an element of truth.

Commerce was of minor importance to the majority of Greek cities. Most of them, like Sparta, remained primarily agricultural centers, where the hoplite franchise, with its corresponding social attitudes, remained the norm of political and personal life. Those cities which, like Athens, became commercial and industrial centers experienced further political convulsions, for as a considerable commercial and artisan class arose, it pressed for a fuller share in polis affairs. Many urban dwellers, especially artisans and sailors, were without sufficient property to qualify as hoplites. Their discontents, often united with the restlessness of small farmers whose plots of land were too small to support a decent life, produced an epidemic of tyranny in Greek cities during the seventh and sixth centuries.

A tyrant was a man who gained power through coup d'état and ruled extra-legally. Most tyrants favored the poor at the expense of the rich, and sometimes confiscated large estates and distributed the land among the propertyless. Nonetheless, tyrannical regimes were seldom secure. The taint of illegality was hard to live down; and the hoplite class, which constituted the military backbone of the state, was likely to resent the loss of its control over public affairs. Hence tyrannies were never formidable in war; and tyrants characteristically required a mercenary bodyguard to protect themselves from their subjects. This internal weakness helps to account for the passivity with which the Greek cities of Asia Minor, where tyrannies were especially numerous, submitted first to the Lydian and then to the Persian empires. In Greece proper, however, the Spartans made it their business in the latter years of the sixth century to overthrow tyrannies whenever they conveniently could. Such was the prowess of the Spartan phalanx that when the Persian Wars began, no tyrants remained in European Greece.

Yet Sparta's action against the tyrants did not reverse or undo the social conditions that had provoked their rise. Two courses lay open to the commercially active cities of Greece: either political repression of the poor through some form of oligarchic government with a limited citizen franchise, or a radical plunge toward a more broadly based democracy than the hoplite franchise allowed. Corinth took the first path; but the oligarchs of that isthmus city depended on Spartan military support to keep themselves in office and paralyzed effective action within their own polis by dividing the citizens into two irreconcilable factions. Athens took the opposite course. After the overthrow of the Peisistratid tyranny in 510 B.C., constitutional evolution drove ahead toward radical democracy. Even landless citizens won a voice in public affairs through the right to participate in the popular assembly and law courts; but until after 483 B.C., when Themistocles arranged for a great expansion of the Athenian fleet, this political order remained precarious in the extreme, more a byplay of aristocratic personal rivalry than a reflection of the internal balance of Athenian society. But when Athens came to possess a great fleet, manned by citizen rowers, the landless Athenian whose only property was a strong back became able to play his part in the military affairs of the city. As a rower in the triremes, he contributed as much as the hoplites themselves to the military security and wealth of Athens. Thereby his right to be heard in the assembly was confirmed. Indeed, in the fifth century, the rowers of Athens and the urban demos from which they came tended to crowd the farmer-hoplites to the margins of the political stage.

If the phalanx was the basic school of the Greek polis, the fleet was the finishing school for its democratic version; and if the family farm was the economic basis for the limited democracy of the hoplite franchise, the merchant fleet with its necessary complement of workshops, warehouses, and markets provided the economic sinews for radical democracy.

Nonetheless, Greek democracy was never total. Slaves, who were very numerous in some cities, lacked all political rights; women were likewise disfranchised; and resident aliens were admitted to citizenship only in very exceptional circumstances. Indeed, the idea that the citizenry constituted a closed and hereditary group, united fundamentally by ties of kinship, was not abandoned in Greece until long after 500 B.C. The citizen body remained always a privileged corporation, quite distinct from the adult male inhabitants of the polis territory.

Aristocratic ideals continued to dominate even the radically democratic polis. A good citizen had to be a man of some leisure; otherwise he could not attend to the public business of the law courts, assembly, and religious festivals, or train himself adequately to bear arms for his polis. Manual labor was not incompatible with respectable citizenship, so long as it left ample time for political activities. This ideal of citizenship was a direct inheritance from the aristocratic ethos of an earlier age. In effect, the humbler social classes, eager to imitate their betters, deftly put the old aristocratic ideal on a polis basis by substituting the collective aggrandizement of the city for the individual aggrandizement sought so eagerly by Homer's heroes.

A rural community of independent small farmers constituted the Greek

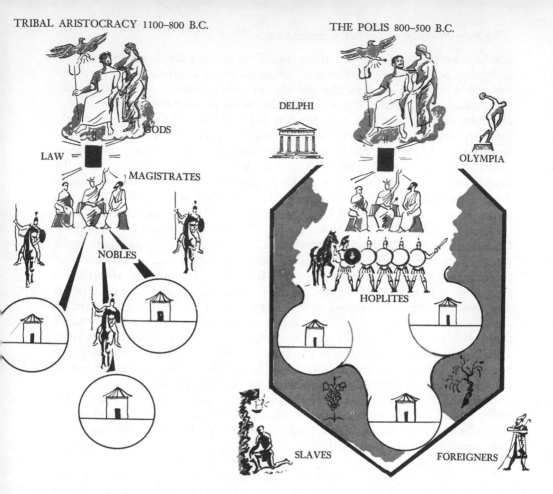

EVOLUTION

political ideal at least as late as the fourth century B.C. The Athenians themselves tended to regard the commercial-industrial activities of their city as an
unfortunate departure from the best. Probably the pinnacle of ambition for
the average citizen-rower of the Athenian fleet was to make a rich haul of
booty on some fortunate expedition and then buy a farm, on which to live
out his life as a free man and citizen should. Neither artisan occupations nor
the pecuniary cunning of the market place ever commanded social respect in
ancient Greece;[59] and in the sixth and fifth centuries even landholding was
suspect unless the owner used his wealth unstintingly for public purposes.

[59] Greek agriculture was markedly seasonal; and for several months in the year there was little
work to be done on the land. Hence it was quite possible to combine the life of a farmer with the leisure
proper to a citizen; whereas an artisan, especially if he worked for wages, could ill afford to surrender
even a day's pay in order to participate in polis affairs. Partly as a result, artisan occupations were very
largely assigned to slaves and foreigners; and by the latter part of the fifth century the Athenian demos
depended upon state employment as rowers, jurors, and the like to a surprising degree. Cf. *Old Oligarch*,
I, 2–3.

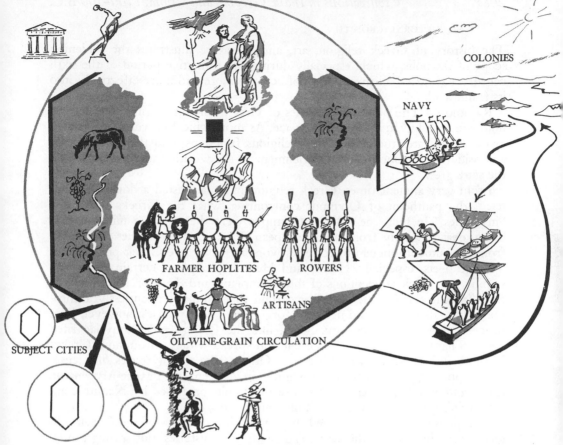

COLONIES

NAVY

FARMER HOPLITES   ROWERS

ARTISANS

SUBJECT CITIES

OIL-WINE-GRAIN CIRCULATION

OF GREEK SOCIETY

The mature Greek polis exercised an extraordinarily pervasive influence upon the lives of its citizens. Politics tended to coincide with life itself, and little indeed was left private. Democratic Athens found it quite natural to demand that the citizens' time, wealth, and wholehearted devotion be lavished upon public affairs, while Sparta outdid any modern totalitarian regime in the demands and regulations it imposed upon its citizens. Yet this invasion of privacy seems to have been accepted willingly enough, perhaps because, to a degree unparalleled in modern times, the citizens did in fact constitute the state. Each individual citizen could rightly feel that the polis was not an alien, outside entity, but an integral extension and collective magnification of his personal life and powers. Under these circumstances, experience could be widely shared without losing its intimate intensity, thereby unveiling new dimensions of human character and unleashing fresh springs of collective energy to produce the extraordinary flowering of classical Greek culture.

2. CULTURAL GROWTH

The history of Greek religion, art, and literature illustrates the widening scope of the polis, which, especially during the formative period of the sixth century B.C., fitted all these realms of activity more and more effectively into its framework.

RELIGION.   The public ceremonies of Greek religion originated as household rites conducted in the royal palace. As monarchical power was whittled away, magistrates took over royal religious functions; and these underwent a considerable elaboration and enrichment as the wealth and organization of the state grew.

From very ancient times, Greek religion had manifested a double character:[60] the pantheon of Olympus confronting what the Greeks called the "mysteries." In fact, the gods of Olympus were themselves a mixed assemblage, derived partly from Indo-European sky and nature deities and partly from the autochthonous protectresses worshipped by pre-Greek populations. Yet the poets, especially Homer and Hesiod, brought a certain order and stability to Greek conceptions of the Olympians; and the supreme artistry of the *Iliad* and the *Odyssey* made it certain that Homer's relentlessly anthropomorphic theology could never be forgotten. The mysteries, however, bore little relation to this theology. Some, like the Orphic and Dionysiac rites, seem to have originated in the Orient and spread widely throughout Greece in the eighth or seventh centuries B.C. Others, like the mysteries of Eleusis, were apparently indigenous, originating in Mycenaean or pre-Mycenaean times, and may have been related to fertility cults professed by Neolithic agriculturalists as early as the third millennium B.C.

The polis successfully resolved the crying discrepancies of the Greek religious scene by uniting the Olympians with the mysteries, not through intellectual synthesis, but through ceremonial invention. Public ceremonies honoring Olympian deities were juxtaposed with publicly supported mystery celebrations; and at least in some cases, the two were effectively merged. The Panathenaic procession aptly symbolized this linkage. Conceived (or at least reorganized) by the tyrant Peisistratus as a ceremony honoring Athena, his city's special patron among the Olympians, the procession nevertheless started from the sacred precinct at Eleusis, where the mysteries of the Great Mother were celebrated and ended on the Acropolis, in the heart of the Athenian polis. Similarly, the plays presented as part of the Dionysiac festivals at Athens drew their subject matter from the general stock of Greek myths and legends, although these were originally quite alien to Dionysiac worship. Hence in act, if not in theory, the polis reconciled the diverse and mutually incompatible strands of which Greek religion was composed.

Yet not all of Greek religion fitted into the polis framework. The splendid public festivals did not supersede family rites, especially among the wellborn; and there was a private, personal side to the mysteries—the promise of salva-

[60] Cf. Raffaele Pettazzoni, "Introduction to the History of Greek Religion," in his *Essays on the History of Religion*, trans. H. S. Rose (Leiden: E. J. Brill, 1954), pp. 68–80.

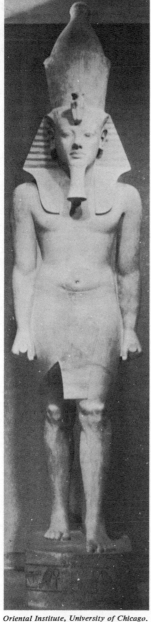

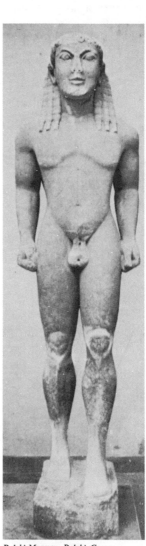

Oriental Institute, University of Chicago.   Delphi Museum, Delphi, Greece.

THE GREEK APPRENTICESHIP

These two statues illustrate the importance of Egyptian models in stimulating the earliest Greek sculptors. On the left is a statue of Tutankhamen (1362–1349 B.C.) in a pose that had been traditional to Egyptian art for more than a thousand years when it was made. When the Greeks began to try to carve full-sized human figures, Egyptian sculpture was by far the most impressive art style accessible to them. The consequence is here plainly to be seen. Details of the pose, and even the odd treatment of the hair of the statue on the right, which dates from about 590 B.C., clearly derive from the ancient and well-established Egyptian tradition. Greek nakedness, however, would have shocked the Egyptians, and reflected the customs of the gymnasium.

tion and life beyond the grave[61]—which never fitted smoothly into the public religion of the state. At the other extreme, certain important religious institutions had a pan-Hellenic character and did something to unite the separate cities of Greece into a larger community. Foremost of these was the Delphic oracle, whose astute priests played a prominent part in regulating inter-polis relations during the sixth century, and who were particularly conspicuous in forwarding the colonization movement.[62] The quadrennial games at Olympia, supplemented by similar contests at Corinth and elsewhere, also had a pan-Hellenic religious character. Here, under the aegis of the gods, individual prowess of the old-fashioned aristocratic sort still found scope; and some survival of the supra-polis aristocratic solidarity of the eighth and seventh centuries could still be experienced by participants and spectators, who assembled from all over the Greek world.

It is difficult to assess the importance to individual minds and hearts of those aspects of Greek religion and cult which were never assimilated to the polis framework. But whatever may have been the scope of private piety, familial rites, and pan-Hellenic festivals, these were not the bases upon which the major cultural monuments of ancient Greece were raised. It was religion as digested by the polis that built the Greek temples and stimulated Athenian drama; and it was these aspects of Hellenism which survived to win the admiration of subsequent generations. In this sense, at least, the significance of public religion far surpassed that of any of the faiths and rites that successfully resisted the jurisdiction of the polis.

ART.   The earliest Greek sculptors flourished under aristocratic patronage. Some statues were seemingly intended to be images of particular persons,[63] serving thus to glorify both the god to whom the statue was dedicated and the noble who commissioned the work. Nor is it merely fanciful to see in the elaborate costume and aloof "archaic smile" of the maidens of the Acropolis a mirror of the grace and elegance of aristocratic life in the days before it was simplified and endowed with a severer seriousness by deliberate conformity to the polis norm.

But Greek monumental art was gradually absorbed into the framework of the polis. The full flowering of public art came only after 500 B.C.; yet monumental temples were begun in many parts of the Greek world in the sixth century. Such undertakings were always public in character; and in most cases the temples were designed to house the patron god or goddess of the polis. Sculptors found a new, or greatly expanded, task in decorating the walls and pediments of such temples, and of course also had to carve cult statues for the interiors.

Thus during the generations when Greek sculptors and architects were

[61] Cf. the presumed character of megalithic religion, discussed above.

[62] The oracle suffered a serious loss of prestige when it backed the Persians in 480 B.C.; and its authority never entirely recovered.

[63] Gisela A. M. Richter, *Kouroi: A Study of the Development of the Greek Kouros from the Late Seventh to the Early Fifth Century B.C.* (New York: Oxford University Press, 1942), pp. 3–4; W. Deonna, *Dédale, ou la statue de la Grèce archaïque* (Paris: E. de Boccard, 1930), I, 56–59.

Musée du Louvre, Dépôt du Musée d'Auxerre.

Acropolis Museum, Athens.

THE FORMULATION
OF THE GREEK STYLE

These three female figures illustrate the emancipation of Greek sculpture from its Egyptian prototypes and the emergence of a technically accomplished, aesthetically superb, and authentically Greek style. The earliest of these statues dates from the seventh century and still shows the mark of Egypt. The so-called Hera of Samos at the right (*ca.* 575 B.C.) already exhibits a sinuous harmony of line that has no Egyptian analogue. The combination of decorative drapery with naturalistic human figures which was to become a leading feature of Greek sculpture is not yet in evidence but emerges clearly in the third statue here represented, carved toward the close of the sixth century B.C. The rich drapery and aloof, archaic smile on this "Acropolis Maiden" from Athens bespeaks the aristocratic epoch of Greek development during which it was created.

mastering the techniques and establishing the conventions of their art, they were increasingly employed on behalf of the state. This fact had a profound influence upon Greek art styles. Realistic portraiture, of the sort which was later to distinguish Roman sculpture, was definitely not in demand. The Greek sculptor's task was instead to create a generalized representation of idealized humanity and of humanized divinity. Moreover, the sacred character of monumental public building required strict adherence to traditional architectural models.[64] These limitations upon their inventiveness led architects to concentrate upon the fine details of decoration, proportion, and symmetry which give Greek temples their exquisite beauty. The architects of early Greece could scarcely have attained such artistic restraint and perfection if they had been free to invent new ground plans and façades, as their contemporaries who built the palaces of Nineveh and Persepolis were free to do.

The polis character of Greek art distinguished it from its Oriental forerunners and from its Roman successor; yet not all the characteristics of Greek sculpture and architecture can be explained in this way. Archaic Greek sculpture quite obviously imitated Egyptian models; but as the Greeks mastered techniques of stone carving, they emancipated themselves from Egyptian conventions in favor of much greater naturalism and plasticity. The increasingly public character of Greek art did not demand this. Perhaps the thoroughly human picture of the gods enshrined in Homer urged the artists toward naturalism; perhaps, too, the opportunity to observe and study the motions of naked human bodies in the gymnasia challenged sculptors to create anatomically accurate works. But this is conjecture; and the reasons for the direction of Greek artistic evolution (as of any other great art style) remain essentially mysterious.[65]

[64] Many of the details of Greek architecture can only be explained as imitation in stone of earlier wooden construction. Beam ends and other features which once had a functional role were faithfully preserved in stone as conventional decorative elements.

[65] Minoan painting and sculpture, too, had been strikingly naturalistic. Yet it is scarcely conceivable that there was any continuity of art tradition from Minoan-Mycenaean to classical Greek times, for the two were separated by a geometric period, when pottery—the sole form of Greek art surviving from the post-Dorian age—was decorated in totally unnaturalistic fashion.

If one can assume that the primal effort behind all art is accurately to remind the viewer of visual experience—and I am not sure this assumption is valid—then perhaps the parallelism between Minoan and classical Greek art can be understood as follows: Any early effort to exploit a new medium or technique to create an accurate reminder of visual experience is bound to fall short because of deficiencies of skill. In a society having little contact with other styles of art, it is altogether likely that these early awkward efforts will become objects of imitation in their own right; and what had begun as an imperfectly successful effort to produce a reminder of reality may then establish the conventions of a non-naturalistic art tradition.

But peoples in contact with a number of mutually divergent non-naturalistic or imperfectly naturalistic art styles may find it less easy to erect any one of them into an object of imitation in its own right. Such peoples may therefore be encouraged to prolong the effort to imitate nature until technical abilities accumulate and a highly naturalistic art style emerges. Both Crete and Greece were in contact with art styles from all around the Mediterranean littoral; and in due course, the artists of both societies achieved a technical virtuosity that permitted them to achieve highly naturalistic effects.

Yet the initial assumption is open to question. Some art traditions, certainly, delighted in the fantastic distortion of visual reality—e.g., the Scythian animal style. Perhaps, therefore, one should only say that insofar as an accurate reminder of visual experience becomes the artistic goal, artists in contact with diverse art traditions are more likely than artists isolated from such contact to persist in their effort toward naturalism until technical mastery of the medium has been achieved.

LITERATURE. The *Iliad* and the *Odyssey*, the earliest and greatest of all surviving Greek poems, had nothing to do with the polis; and the same is true of Hesiod's work. Yet these poems, especially Homer's, were to play an enormous role in later Greek culture. The *Iliad*'s aristocratic and heroic ideal, combining fierceness and joy in action with a strong sense of the tragic certainty of death and the inescapability of fate, became a basic element in the Greek conception of the human condition. Homer's heroes struggled for personal glory and gain; the Greeks of the classical period substituted, in theory if not always in practice, the glory and gain of the polis; but with this modification, Homer's ideals remained almost unchallenged.

Greek lyric poetry was also largely the creation of the aristocratic age and was little influenced by the discipline of the polis. The tone of the early poets was often intensely personal, sometimes autobiographical; and the self-assertiveness of unbridled aristocracy infuses many of their verses. On the other hand, the poet Tyrtaeus employed his art to glorify the Spartan polis and to provide marching songs for the newly organized phalanx; and he asserted in the most extravagant terms the ideal of self-sacrifice for the state. In a similarly political, but characteristically more moderate spirit, the Athenian lawgiver Solon used poetry to express the concepts of justice and law which guided him in reforming the Athenian constitution.

In general, however, poetry was not profoundly influenced by the polis, largely because poetic forms (except for the drama) matured before the polis acquired a really strong emotional hold. Yet it proved possible to adapt poetry to the purposes of the city-state, a process no doubt facilitated by the fact that the polis ideal incorporated so much of the aristocratic ethos of an earlier age. The relationship was reciprocal; for poetry's charms were the mightiest of all the forces promoting the survival of the aristocratic ideal in the democratized world of the polis. Nurtured on Homer, Greeks of the classical era could not fail to be influenced by the heroic vision which his poems so powerfully expressed.

Prose literature was but little developed in Greece before 500 B.C. With the exception of Hecataeus, whose collections of geographic information and tales of wonder and far places have not survived, the only prose compositions of note from this period are those of the philosophers.

PHILOSOPHY. By the sixth century B.C., at least two flaws in Homer's view of the universe had begun to trouble the Greeks. One was the ambiguous relationship between Fate and the gods of Olympus. In some Homeric passages, Zeus is declared all-powerful, while in others he is said to be bound by Fate. A second anomaly was the all-too-human frailties which Homer attributed to the Olympians. The Greeks of the classical period, whose own standards of justice had risen with the establishment of regular laws and institutions, were not satisfied with Homer's portrait of deities who bickered among themselves, cheated and deceived one another as well as humankind, and indulged a variety of morally dubious impulses.

Homer's theological deficiencies were part of a more general disorder which prevailed within the religious tradition of sixth-century Greece, as a result of the imperfect blending of divergent and incompatible myths. Moreover, the Greeks lacked an authoritative, organized priesthood which might have repaired or obscured such inconsistencies. Public religious ceremonies were conducted by elected magistrates who, as practical politicians, were unlikely to be speculatively inclined. Consequently there was no regularly constituted authority empowered to explain the nature of the world, especially its supernatural aspects, to the ordinary citizen. This task, so far as it was undertaken at all, was left instead to isolated individuals.

In the archaic age, poets had boldly undertaken to explain whatever needed explaining. They were thought to be seers, inspired by a divine force; and an aura of respect, if not of awe, surrounded them. Yet as compared to Oriental priests, the Greek poets labored under two serious handicaps in seeking to bring order and system to the world of gods and men. First, the verbal grace and perfection of their poetry facilitated memorization but inhibited emendation. This meant that the ideas of earlier generations could not easily be modified to suit later ages without explicitly rejecting poetic authorities. Successive generations of Oriental priests could, in a spirit of perfect piety, reinterpret, transform, and embroider old religious materials in accordance with contemporary knowledge or taste; but thinkers like Xenophanes and Heraclitus, knowing exactly what Homer and Hesiod had said, felt impelled to denounce as lies the assertions of their predecessors, while the Milesian philosophers avoided such lese majeste by tacitly ignoring the entire poetic tradition. Second, the Greek poets did not belong to an organized, self-perpetuating college; and as individuals, they had no easily validated monopoly of truth. An Oriental priest, intoning sacred ritual and myth, could point to a long line of predecessors from whom his knowledge and authority derived; the Greek poet had only his individual inspiration, reason, and imagination.

Thus Greeks of inquiring mind and reflective temper confronted no very impressive or well-organized system of myth and doctrine which could give them an intellectual and emotional orientation to the world. Yet when they began to trade and travel in the Orient, they encountered impressive theological and cosmological systems, together with much useful knowledge. The Greek response was to wonder articulately about the nature of things, *i.e.*, to invent philosophy. Thales of Miletus (*ca.* 585 B.C.), the traditional founder of Greek philosophy, is supposed to have learned geometry in Egypt and put it to practical use. His view that water was the primary substance reminds one of the ancient Babylonian cosmology, which made water the first element of creation. Indeed, the doctrines attributed to Thales might be described as a restatement of Babylonian mythology, with the important difference that Thales omitted the deities who lay at the heart of the Oriental cosmology.

But if Greek philosophy began as an attempt to mend the poets' intellectual fences on the strength of helpful hints from the Orient, it was not long before the philosophers, like contemporary Greek sculptors, emancipated themselves from dependence upon any foreign stimuli and gave free rein to their own speculation.

The school of philosophy which arose in Ionia toward the close of the sixth century directed curiosity toward the natural world and sought to reduce physical phenomena to a comprehensive regularity. This effort carried forward the intellectual tradition which had led Homer (or his nameless predecessors) to organize and define the Olympian pantheon; for Thales, Anaximander, and Anaximenes in effect eliminated Homer's anthropomorphic gods and sought instead to analyze the nature and meaning of Homer's Fate.[66] So far as surviving fragments of their books allow us to judge, the intellectual method of the Milesian philosophers was not far removed from that of earlier poets. Simple assertion rather than reasoned argument was their usual habit; but Anaximander, at least, may have begun to develop more rigorous rules of reasoning.[67]

Ionian philosophers departed fundamentally from the Oriental world-view by rejecting vitalistic principles. Despite local diversities in Middle Eastern intellectual traditions, all agreed that the processes of nature depended on the

[66] Cf. F. M. Cornford, *From Religion to Philosophy: A Study in the Origins of Western Speculation* (London: Edward Arnold, 1912), p. 144.

[67] John Burnet, *Early Greek Philosophy* (4th ed.; London: A. and C. Black, Ltd., 1930), pp. 53–54.

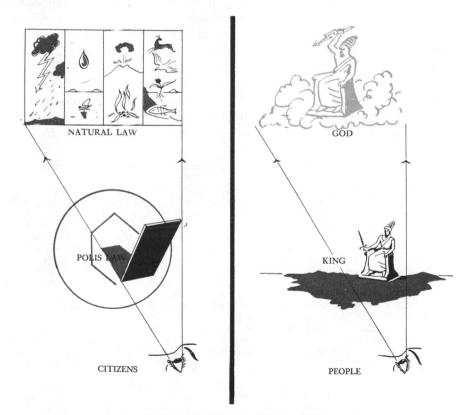

GREEK VS. ORIENTAL WORLD VIEWS

acts and wills of superhuman living beings. The universe was interpreted in the image of man: things were believed to happen because some god or spirit, susceptible to impulses like those which men experience, made them happen that way. But the Ionian philosophers neglected the gods and conceived of the universe as lawful and therefore intelligible. They did not deny the existence of spirits or souls, but thought that souls, like other things, were subject to natural laws.[68]

Ever since, emphasis upon laws of nature as the key to the universe has colored the intellectual traditions of all the peoples influenced by the ancient Greeks. Christian and Moslem scientists, philosophers, and theologians have always had to take account of the Ionian concept of a nature subject to law; and they have nearly always agreed that natural law insulated the universe, at least partially, from the arbitrary acts of an unpredictable divine will.

No doubt many factors helped to induce this fundamental departure from age-old patterns of human thought. Contact with Oriental and barbarian societies acquainted the Ionians with the diversity of existing religious doctrines; and though they had outgrown Homer's theology, they retained his concept of an impersonal and inexorable Fate, brooding over and ultimately controlling both gods and men. But the really decisive factor takes us right back to the polis. In sixth-century Ionia, human affairs were regulated quite successfully by impersonal, uniform, necessary, and—hopefully—just laws. Obviously, the laws of nature, which the Ionian philosophers thought they could detect in the universe at large, bore a striking resemblance to the laws of the polis, which surely, though invisibly, governed their own individual lives. The beginnings of Greek philosophy, therefore, may be viewed as a naïve but enormously fruitful projection upon the cosmos of the busy, ordered world of the polis.

Earlier thinkers, both Greek and barbarian, had likewise projected their so-

---

[68] The atheism of Buddha and the systematic refusal of Confucius to speculate upon divinity (or on life after death) bore a certain similarity to the movement of thought among their contemporaries in Ionia. All three turned their backs upon the gods, but in contrasting ways. The Ionians were curious to know how the world worked and tried to discover laws of nature. Buddha was totally uninterested in physical laws and strove to withdraw from the world which the Ionians found so attractive. Confucius took still another path, for he was interested only in human affairs, and sought to find a "law" or norm of conduct in the traditions and rites of a remote ancestral past. He did not seek a basis for social principles in the nature of things, as the Ionians' successors were to do in the fourth century, when Greek philosophers had ceased to take the world of the polis for granted. Thus the Confucian Way (*Tao*), Buddhist Nirvana, and Greek laws of nature were very different from one another, in spite of the fact that all three agreed in rejecting the Middle Eastern reliance upon gods (or God) to explain the world and man's place in it.

It is an impressive tribute to the enduring persuasiveness of the Middle Eastern view that both Indian and Western thought soon returned to a theological interpretation of the world. In doing so, neither the Indians nor the Greek philosophers' Christian and Islamic heirs entirely obscured their non-theistic heritages. Rather they combined old and new interpretations of the world in varying ways (Buddhism even made the atheistic Gautama into a divinity), with a greater or lesser sense of the logical tensions implicit in such a compromise. Similarly, in China, Confucian this-worldliness, with its cool and utilitarian tone, did not hold the field uncontested. Almost at once, Taoism arose to offer a vitalistic (though not quite theistic in the Western sense) doctrine in opposition to Confucianism; and Buddhism reinforced this strand of Chinese thought some seven or eight centuries later.

cial environment upon the cosmos.[69] But in nearly all earlier societies, men had been narrowly subjected to the vagaries of nature, or to the arbitrary will of social superiors, or most often, to both at once. As long as the food of the community depended upon capricious weather, while the common welfare hung upon the good pleasure of some perhaps distant overlord, and life itself was constantly exposed to the chance arithmetic of raid and pestilence, any view of the universe which did not emphasize the irregular and unpredictable nature of things was evidently absurd. But in a prosperous and independent city like Miletus, the lives and welfare of the citizens depended primarily upon their own co-ordinated activity, regulated by law. Local crop failures lost part of their terror when ships, trading afar, could bring grain to the city as needed. No distant monarch held the fate of the Milesians in the hollow of his hand. Even the chances of war depended largely upon the training and discipline of the citizen soldiers. The polis thus interposed a cushion between its members and the whims of nature, wove a strait jacket around the arbitrary impulses of magistrate and ruler, and, through military training, even succeeded in reducing the risks of war to a minimum. A citizen of such a city was as free as man can be from subjection to any alien will; yet his life was rigorously bound by law. Thus it is scarcely surprising that a few speculatively inclined citizens imagined that the universe might be similarly governed. Yet this implausible guess gave a distinctive bent to all subsequent Greek (and European) thought. This was remarkable enough; far more remarkable is the fact that behind all the variety of particular occurrences, laws of nature do in fact seem to exist.[70]

If the Ionians basically affirmed the polis by projecting its framework upon the universe, the Pythagorean school, which flourished mainly in Italy and Sicily, may be thought of as a direct antitype, being centrally inspired by a rather desperate private revolt against the all-encompassing, yet inadequate public life of the polis. Pythagoras himself abandoned his native Samos and settled in Croton in southern Italy (*ca.* 525 B.C.), where he established a society or order of select fellow spirits who sought holiness and the salvation of their souls. Pythagoras was therefore a religious reformer rather than a lover of wisdom for its own sake. But the distinction was not clear, since he seems to have taught that the pursuit of knowledge was the best path to the purification of the soul. In pursuance of this belief, he and his followers made important contributions to mathematical studies, though they did not neglect to seek purification by fasting and other asceticisms.[71]

[69] Homer's predecessors, for example, had obviously modeled the governance of Olympus upon Agamemnon's rather erratic government of Mycenae. In exactly the same fashion, Sumerian priests (or their predecessors) of the fourth millennium B.C. had modeled the Mesopotamian pantheon upon the "primitive democracy" (or oligarchy) of overgrown villages of the Tigris-Euphrates flood plain.

[70] A guess so lucky and so perfectly timed occurred only once in human history. Even the sanguine founders of the Ionian school would be surprised at the manner in which their natural laws, which so rashly projected the local and evanescent circumstances of a few Greek towns upon the universe, have developed into the natural science of recent centuries.

[71] Pythagoras may have known something about the contemporary religious and philosophical thought of India. This would, of course, explain why some of the doctrines of the *Upanishads* strikingly

The Pythagorean tradition carried over into philosophy the basic dualism of Greek religion. For just as Ionian philosophy was in a sense a rationalistic reform of Olympian theology, Pythagoreanism may be described as a reform movement within the Orphic cult. Moreover, the two reforms moved along parallel lines, for Pythagoras' most important innovation was the emphasis he put upon knowledge and science as a path to salvation, which of course implied a corresponding reduction in the value put upon raw emotional manifestations such as had earlier characterized Orphism and the other mystery cults of Greece.

Pythagoras wrote nothing himself; and his teaching was long kept secret within the order he founded, so that trustworthy information about his ideas is hardly to be expected. But it is plain that the Pythagorean pursuit of personal holiness was basically incompatible with the demands made by the Greek polis upon its citizens. Withdrawal from the normal frame of society in order better to pursue a religious and intellectual life—a practice taken for granted in India—was intolerable in the context of a Greek city. As a result, the history of the Pythagorean Order was stormy. Either the Order dominated the polis, as it seems to have done for a few years in Croton when Pythagoras first established himself there; or the polis counterattacked and dispersed the Order, as apparently happened near the end of Pythagoras' life. Similar conflicts with civic authorities continued to plague the Pythagoreans for a century, until suspicious citizens and jealous magistrates finally succeeded in breaking up the last of the Pythagorean communities.

The looser texture of Indian political and social organization could accommodate such groups without apparent difficulty; but the very totality of the polis' control over its citizens' lives forbade any similar accommodation in the Greek social context. We may, indeed, regard the history of the Pythagorean Order as the first recorded conflict between church and state in European history.

Yet the tensions between the Order and the dominant ideals of ancient Greece did not deprive the Pythagoreans of profound influence upon subsequent Greek thought. The striving for individual salvation and holiness, the effort toward some sort of communion with divinity, the desire for an immortality more personal than any assured by the collective survival of the community—all these dimensions of human longing were inadequately provided for within the polis. Pythagoras attempted to correct this shortcoming by rationalizing and refining Orphism, and making philosophy-religion into a way of life. He was before his time; for philosophy as a way of life came into its own only in Hellenistic and Roman times, when the polis framework had lost much of its psychological validity. Yet philosophers in the two centuries after him—the Eleatics and Empedocles in Italy, and Plato in Athens

---

resemble what little is known about Pythagoreanism. It is a fact that in Pythagoras' youth the city of Samos had close commercial relations with Egypt; and there is some reason to think that a colony of Indian merchants lived permanently in Memphis, Egypt from about 500 B.C. Overland contact, via the Persian court, which ruled both Greek and Indian provinces, was also entirely possible. Cf. Nilakanta Sastri, "Ancient Indian Contacts with Western Lands," *Diogenes*, No. 28 (1959), pp. 44–57.

—were affected by Pythagorean doctrines, and thus kept philosophy from a complete assimilation to the polis framework. Partly for this reason, perhaps, philosophy became one of the principal growing points of Greek culture in the age when the parochial rigidity of the separate poleis began to inhibit the further development of Greek civilization.

* * *

By 500 B.C., the Greeks had succeeded in organizing a new and remarkably attractive style of life. The ruling institution, the polis, was firmly rooted; and most of the characteristic forms of Greek cultural expression had already found a place within its framework. It remained for the Greeks of the fifth century to work out to their logical conclusion and technical perfection the principles which their predecessors of the sixth century had established.

Thereby the mold within which later classical civilization would flourish was set. Certain of the most fundamental characteristics of that mold were indeed to remain basic to all subsequent European culture. Greek thought, art, literature, and institutions have always remained a sort of norm for Western civilization, which successive ages have variously modified, but never entirely abandoned.

The most fundamental peculiarity of European society—the absolute primacy of the territorial state over all competing principles of social cohesion—has its origins in the Greek polis, where it was carried to an extreme which has seldom been approached since. Even Christianity, sprung from Oriental roots, became in good part Greek; for the early Christians drew upon the traditions of the mystery religions which the Greeks had partially suppressed and partially brought within the scope of public religion. Christianity, to be sure, was a reassertion of a dimension of human personality which the Greek polis had done its best to neglect: the aspiration for individual salvation and an individual relationship with God. Yet even here, the imprint of the polis could not be eradicated; for the Church, like the Pythagorean Order before it, tended always to become a state within a state. The rise of the Church therefore created a duality of political allegiance as between the city of God and the city of this world; but each derived its claims to the total man from the claims which were first advanced by the city-states of ancient Greece.

D. THE BEGINNINGS OF CHINESE CIVILIZATION TO 500 B.C.

The quickening stimuli that Middle Eastern ideas and techniques gave to the nascent civilizations of India and Greece could extend only sporadically all the way across Asia to China. The importance of local and indigenous cultural traditions in shaping the Chinese style of life was proportionately greater. This is not surprising. Inhospitable deserts, high mountains, and a distance of three to four thousand miles separated the portion of the Yellow River Valley where Chinese civilization began from the anciently civilized regions of the Middle East. Reinforcing these geographical obstacles was the social barrier interposed after about 1700 B.C. by warlike barbarians, whose heroic prowess and unthinking violence interdicted all ordinary travel from oasis to oasis across central Asia just at the time when Chinese civilization began to take form.

Nevertheless, Chinese development did not proceed in a vacuum. We have already seen how Neolithic farming techniques, originating in the Middle East about 6500 B.C., apparently spread across Asia to meet and mingle in the Yellow River valley with a different style of agriculture coming from monsoon Asia. Another definite link with western Asia is indicated by the appearance in China (ca. 2000 B.C.) of a type of painted pottery showing many technical and stylistic affinities with a similarly painted pottery found at Neolithic sites in the Middle East and in eastern Europe.[72]

Despite such contacts, Chinese culture always exhibited a strong autochthony. It was symptomatic of their deep-seated cultural independence that the Chinese never adopted the Middle Eastern type of extensive field agriculture, but clung instead to their own intensive garden style of cultivation. The ox-drawn plow, permitting a single man to till a comparatively large area, had been invented in the Middle East before 3000 B.C.; but there is no firm evidence of such a plow in China until the fourth century B.C.[73] No doubt the special nature of the soil and rainfall patterns of north China had much to do with the Chinese failure to adopt plow cultivation. The loess and alluvium of the Yellow River Valley were easily worked with hoe and spade, while a sometimes scant and always erratic rainfall put a premium on artificial irrigation and drainage and made extensive dry farming (for which alone the plow was suited) comparatively precarious.[74] Whatever the full reasons, the mas-

[72] It is possible that the people who brought this style of pottery to China were refugees, fleeing before the assault of the "battle-axe folk" who began their widespread expansion shortly before 2000 B.C. Cf. Ludwig Bachhofer, *A Short History of Chinese Art* (London: B. T. Batsford Ltd., 1947), p. 19.

[73] C. W. Bishop, "Origin and Early Diffusion of the Traction Plow," *Annual Report of the Board of Regents of the Smithsonian Institution*, 1937, pp. 531–47. Even though the Chinese may in fact have used plows for some time before the fourth century B.C., it is clear that the basic pattern of Chinese agriculture was never affected by what in the Middle East and in Europe amounted to a second agricultural revolution.

[74] It is also likely that the Chinese were long denied any acquaintance with the possibilities inherent in plow cultivation by the fact that the agricultural communities of the central Asian oases that lay between themselves and the Middle East had absolutely no use for labor-saving devices that required them to find forage for such large animals as oxen. The ability to till more land means nothing in a community where there is only a tiny patch of arable soil available per agricultural head; and this was probably the case in the central Asian oases within a few generations of their initial settlement by neolithic hoe cultivators.

In a sense the Yellow River Valley was merely the largest and most easterly of these central Asian oases. The plow might have been useful there in pioneering days, when much arable land was still uncultivated; but by the time knowledge of the plow did reach China (perhaps by more northerly routes through the steppe) the style of Chinese agriculture had already been set. On early Siberian plows, dated as early as the fifth century B.C. by their discoverers, cf. Tamara Talbot Rice, *The Scythians* (London: Thames & Hudson, 1957), p. 125.

The plow (and water buffalo rather than oxen) did eventually come to play a considerable role in Chinese agriculture; but animal power remained merely a useful auxiliary which could be dispensed with. The agriculture of western Eurasia, by contrast, depended absolutely (or very nearly so) upon animal traction. Related to this difference was the fact that the Chinese, unlike the peoples of western and northern Eurasia, eschewed the consumption of animal milk and milk products.

On the advantages and disadvantages of animal power in agriculture, cf. the very interesting observations of Fred Cottrell, *Energy and Society* (New York: McGraw-Hill, 1955), pp. 20–23.

sive fact that the rhythm of daily life for most Chinese differed widely from the agricultural rhythms familiar to Middle Eastern, European, and to most Indian peasants constituted (and continues to constitute) an incalculably pervasive, yet seldom obvious difference between the civilized communities of the Far East and those of western Eurasia.

Early Chinese history is known only in rude outline. Archeologists have discovered that three principal Neolithic cultures, distinguished from one another most conspicuously by their pottery styles, divided the ground of north China in the early part of the second millennium B.C. Of these, the so-called Black Pottery culture, which appears to be directly ancestral to later Chinese civilization, developed rather large villages protected by elaborate earthen walls. Black Pottery village sites suggest a populous and nearly egalitarian society, drawing sustenance from an intensive garden style of agriculture, but lacking most of the high skills that required professional specialization.[75]

The manner in which this society emerged to civilization can only be surmised. Historical tradition later declared the Hsia Dynasty to be the first merely human government of China; but archeological investigation has not yet turned up anything that can be identified with this legendary period. The case is otherwise with the second dynasty of Chinese tradition, the Shang (traditional dates 1766–1122 B.C., or, according to a second and probably more nearly accurate chronology, 1523–1028 B.C.). The city of Anyang, the last of three capitals assigned to that dynasty by Chinese tradition, has been painstakingly excavated. Its material remains, dating from between *ca.* 1300 and 1000 B.C., show a striking combination of elements descended from the Black Pottery culture, together with a full development of the distinctive techniques which in the Middle East were characteristically associated with invaders from the steppe: horse-drawn chariots, bronze weapons and accouterments, the compound bow, and a quadrilateral city layout reminiscent of charioteers' encampments. The inference is irresistible: charioteers must have overrun China also, and like their counterparts in Mesopotamia and Egypt, then proceeded to assimilate a large part of the culture of their subjects.[76]

---

[75] Cf. J. G. Andersson, "Researches into the Prehistory of the Chinese," Museum of Far Eastern Antiquities, Stockholm, *Bulletin*, XIV (1943), 7–298; Li Chi, *The Beginnings of Chinese Civilization* (Seattle: University of Washington Press, 1957); Cheng Te-K'un, *Archaeology in China*. I: *Prehistoric China* (Cambridge: W. Heffer & Sons, 1959). Some scholars believe that the Black Pottery culture had affinities westward, though this is more commonly rejected. Cf. Max Loehr, "Zur Ur- und Vorgeschichte Chinas," *Saeculum*, III (1952), 46–52; H. G. Creel, *Birth of China*, pp. 44–49.

[76] I have called the inference irresistible, but many Chinese experts do in fact resist it with considerable emotional energy, e.g., H. G. Creel, *The Birth of China*, pp. 50–51; and less strongly, Cheng Te-K'un, *Archaeology in China*, II, *Shang China* (Cambridge: W. Heffer & Sons, 1960), 243–49.

The undoubted continuity between Neolithic and Shang remains in China does not in the least detract from the likelihood of conquest by warriors who commanded techniques of chariot warfare which had first been developed along the steppe margins of Mesopotamian civilization. Nor does the discovery of semi-bronze objects and objects cast in simple and imperfect shapes prove that Chinese artisans in provincial towns invented bronze metallurgy independently of Middle Eastern examples.

One difficulty does exist in deriving historic Chinese civilization from a superimposition of chariot conquerors upon the Black Pottery folk, for the art style of Shang bronzes seems to bear little or no relation to either presumptive component of Shang society. Cf. Max Loehr, "Zur Ur- und Vorgeschichte Chinas," pp. 54–55, and Cheng Te-K'un, *Archaeology in China*, II, 236. But if one assumes that Shang bronze masters reproduced in metal motifs which had originated in wood carving, this difficulty vanishes, since wooden objects from Chinese Neolithic sites have not survived.

SHANG AND CHOU EMPIRES

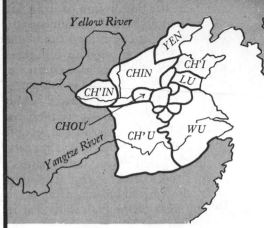

THE WARRING STATES

The age of the Shang was an aristocratic one, when noble warriors exploited a more or less helpless peasantry, and fought and hunted under the suzerainty of a royal overlord. Much of the north China plain was still swamp, annually inundated by the floods of the Yellow River; and it is certain that barbarian tribes existed within striking distance of the Shang dominions. Probably the intensive agriculture upon which the society depended was concentrated near the edges of the north China plain where it abutted on higher ground, and in the valleys of tributaries of the middle reaches of the Yellow River. Mountains and swamps separated one cultivated region from another; and it is difficult to believe that the ruler of Anyang exercised more than a vague supremacy over the lords of other districts.[77]

The site of Anyang revealed definite quarters of the city where craftsmen plied their trades; but there was no trace of money, aside from cowry shells, which may have served as a measure of value.[78] Only the presence of a number of objects which must have come from afar—cowry shells, jade, etc.—shows that long-distance trade existed. Nothing concerning the social status of the craftsmen can be deduced from the archeological evidence; but the artisan and merchant classes were probably of small importance, narrowly dependent on the noble landowners for whom they produced exquisite bronzes and other objects of luxury.[79]

The structure of Shang society which emerges from these sketchy indications appears therefore essentially similar to that of the early civilizations on the rain-watered lands of western Asia. Yet the content of Shang culture was

[77] Cheng Te-K'un, *Archaeology in China*, II, 195–212; O. Franke, *Geschichte des chinesischen Reiches* (Berlin and Leipzig: Walter de Gruyter & Co., 1930), I, 89–93; Henri Maspero, *La Chine antique* (Paris: E. de Boccard, 1927), pp. 36–55.

[78] H. G. Creel, *Birth of China*, pp. 68–69, 90–94.

[79] Cheng Te-K'un, *Archaeology in China*, II, 109–76.

Museum of Far Eastern Antiquities (Ostasiatiska Museet), Stockholm.

Museum of Far Eastern Antiquities (Ostasiatiska Museet), Stockholm.

Museum of Far Eastern Antiquities (Ostasiatiska Museet), Stockholm.

Smithsonian Institution, Freer Gallery of Art, Washington, D.C.

THE EMERGENCE OF THE CHINESE ART STYLE

These four containers illustrate the continuity between Neolithic and civilized art in China. On the left are two pots from Neolithic sites. The shape of the one and the geometric pattern of decoration used on the other reappear in the specimens on the right, which date from the period of the Shang dynasty. The isolation of China from foreign cultures with any high art tradition capable of stimulating the Chinese to change their ways is reflected in the unilinear, undeviating character of the development here illustrated. Clearly, the prehistoric Chinese artists worked within a limited repertory of motifs to achieve the delightful elegance and precision of detail characteristic of Shang art.

Chinese—that is to say, the forms of expression employed by the Shang in religion, art, and writing were ancestral to the ideas, motifs, and techniques which flourished throughout the entire history of Chinese civilization.

The religion of the Shang was a mixture of ancestor and nature worship. Gods connected with the great forces of nature—rivers, wind, earth, etc.—are mentioned in Shang inscriptions, together with a number of other divinities whose names do not clearly reveal their functions or powers. But these nature gods bulk far less large in the written remains than do the spirits of the ancestors, who were asked for advice on a large number of questions, and whose power to give or withhold benefits from their descendants was believed to be considerable.[80]

Shang art, as represented by the numerous bronze vessels recovered from Anyang and other sites, shows great technical virtuosity. Elaborate designs, often zoomorphic, were cast with an accuracy and precision of line which excites the admiration of modern collectors. Shang decorative art was both highly conventionalized and highly sophisticated, probably deriving its forms of animal representation from an older, indigenous woodcarving tradition. The ultimate origins of specific motifs are in dispute;[81] but there is no doubt that the vessel shapes of some of the Shang ritual bronzes were derived from the Black Pottery tradition of north China.

The symbols used by Shang diviners to record their oracles were closely related to the modern Chinese script. Indeed, all the devices and principles employed in later Chinese writing are to be found in the Shang texts, although sometimes in undeveloped forms.[82] The basis of the script was ideographic, and the ideographs show no relation to any other known system of writing. Stratified finds also demonstrate an evolutionary elaboration of the script. This suggests that Chinese writing had an independent origin; yet it seems

[80] The relative unimportance of nature gods in Shang inscriptions may reflect the limited purpose of the surviving records, which were written on shell and bone as a register of oracular interrogations. Aspects of Shang religion not connected with this type of oracle taking escape our knowledge. On Shang religion, cf. Creel, *Birth of China*, pp. 174–216; Cheng Tê-K'un, *Archaeology in China*, II, 213–25.

[81] A characteristic feature of Chinese bronzes is the use of animal "masks" split in two along a median line, so that such elements as ears and horns appear in bilateral symmetry, separated from one another save by a mouth or other uniting part. This suggests a translation to the rounded surface of a bronze vessel of something like the wooden totem poles of the American Indians of the Pacific Northwest. A simultaneous portrayal of the side aspects of a totem pole would produce a pattern not unlike those on Shang bronzes. Stylistic resemblances between Chinese bronzes and the art of American Indians have often been observed. It seems possible that a common heritage from inhabitants of the Pacific coast of Asia accounts for these similarities. Cf. Osvald Siren, *A History of Early Chinese Art: The Prehistoric and Pre-Han Periods* (London: Ernest Benin, Ltd., 1929), p. 20 and Plate 21. There are also important parallels between Chinese motifs and those of Scythian art; cf. Gregory Borovka, *Scythian Art* (New York: Frederick A. Stokes Co., 1928), pp. 82–89; and it is possible that the Shang brought the "animal style" of decoration with them from the steppes. So Ludwig Bachhofer, *A Short History of Chinese Art*, p. 28, suggests; but one may argue the reverse, that Scythian style borrowed from the Chinese, as does Creel, *Birth of China*, p. 121. I find most plausible the theory that a very ancient style of wood carving, indigenous to eastern and northern Asia, was developed in different directions by the Chinese, the Scythians, and the Amerindians of the Pacific coast. But in these matters, opinion must remain tentative.

[82] Creel, *Birth of China*, pp. 159–60.

likely that the germinal idea—the notion that language could be reduced to visual symbols—reached China from western Asia.[83]

Whatever the truth may be (and since germinal ideas do not leave archeological traces, we are unlikely ever to know), the fact remains that Chinese writing, as developed among the Shang and their heirs, was unique. As such, it epitomizes the general character of this earliest known Chinese culture. Whatever stimuli came from the Middle East, and whatever techniques conquerors brought to China, the use made of such imports was thoroughly Chinese in character. Unlike the Hittites or the pre-classical Greeks, the Chinese did not imitate more developed styles in art, nor did they profit from exposure to sophisticated foreign ideas. No doubt the reason was that China's neighbors offered no impressive models for imitation. The early Chinese were therefore thrown back upon comparatively crude local resources. But by elaborating materials handed down from their Neolithic predecessors, and by combining these with certain motifs derived from neighboring peoples of the steppe, they built up Chinese civilization, bit by bit.

* * *

The Shang no doubt represent an important phase in the development of Chinese civilization. But the classical period of China's history, when the ideas which would remain basic to Chinese life for over two thousand years first took definite form, came only after the Shang had been overthrown. Shortly before 1000 B.C.,[84] invaders from the Wei Valley in modern Kansu established a new dynasty, the Chou, which lasted, with many vicissitudes, until 256 B.C. The period of its rule falls into two contrasting parts. For over two centuries, the Chou capital remained in western China; and effective imperial authority probably extended over most of the north. However in 771 B.C., barbarians sacked the capital, killed the reigning emperor, and shattered the central power.[85] To be sure, a scion of the imperial house established his throne in Loyang, near the main centers of Chinese civilization; but the power of the new line (known as the Eastern Chou in distinction from the earlier or Western Chou) was merely nominal. Effective rule over China passed into the hands of various princely houses.

[83] Cf. the argument for "stimulus diffusion" of the art of writing to Egypt, above.

A Russian scholar, S. P. Tolstov, claims to have discovered a script in the Oxus-Jaxartes area related to Indus and Elamite scripts and of roughly comparable antiquity. If his deductions are correct, then chariot conquerors of China could easily have known that writing was possible. Cf. Karl Jettmar, "Zur Herkunft der türkischen Völkerschaften," *Archive für Völkerkunde*, III (1948), 18. Also I. J. Gelb, *A Study of Writing*, pp. 217–220; David Diringer, *The Alphabet: A Key to the History of Mankind* (New York: Philosophical Library, 1948), pp. 98–106.

[84] Two discordant chronologies for early Chinese history have been preserved in the literary tradition, giving 1123 B.C. and 1051 B.C. respectively for the beginning of the Chou dynasty. Modern scholars favor the later date, or one even closer to 1000 B.C.; but there is no unanimity on this point. After 841 B.C., the two traditional chronologies agree, and modern scholarship finds little to quarrel with in its detail—a truly remarkable tribute to Chinese historical-mindedness and to the continuity of the Chinese literary tradition over nearly three thousand years.

[85] The collapse of the Western Chou was perhaps connected with a general unsettlement of political-military relationships which occurred in all northern and central Eurasia as a consequence of the development of cavalry tactics and of a full-blown horse nomadry. See below, pp. 234–39.

When the Chou conquerors first overran the centers of Shang civilization, they were rough and ready warriors, trained in a hard school of frontier fighting against the outer barbarians who surrounded the Chinese world. Indeed, the Chou used barbarian tribes as allies in their conquest of China. Yet, like many another marchland people, the Chou had been tinctured by Shang culture even before they conquered Shang territory; and under their rule, Chinese civilization continued uninterruptedly to elaborate itself.

It was under the Chou, for example, that Chinese literature first took shape. Yet, while there is no doubt that many of the themes later incorporated into the Chinese classics originated in early Chou times, literature is a treacherous guide for anyone seeking to understand the age. It was not until after Confucius' time that the classics were given their present forms; and until then, Chinese literati had no compunction about expanding, interpreting, deleting, and altering old texts. Indeed, the only existing literary work which seems to have assumed something like its present form before 500 B.C. is the *Book of Poetry*, a collection of slightly more than three hundred poems of sharply varying character. Some seem to be simple peasant songs; some emanated from noble households and celebrate remarkable feats of prowess; some are satires against nobles and princes; many are love songs or laments for personal sorrow. How the collection was put together or for what purposes is not clear;[86] but apt quotation from the *Book of Poetry* soon became one of the marks of an educated man. Moreover, in later ages the poems were freely interpreted, sometimes in far-fetched allegorical fashion, to make them mean more than appeared on the surface.

More authentic, if limited, evidence of the development of Chinese culture is offered by the unbroken series of bronze ritual vessels that survive from Shang and Chou times. These, at least, have not been edited or recast by later generations. Throughout the Shang period, shapes and decorative patterns became progressively more ornate; but soon after the Chou conquest a more severe style came in. At first utilizing only some of the motifs and shapes of Shang art, the Chou style in turn underwent a gradual elaboration, until once again overripe decoration prepared the way for another reaction toward decorative simplicity.[87]

It is striking how this art history seems to match what is known of the political and social history of ancient China. As Shang bronzes became more and more elaborate, Shang society became more and more effete. The plainer style introduced under the early Chou, with its reduced repertory of motifs and types of vessels, corresponded to a pruning and simplification of manners in general and of older religious practices and cults in particular. Again, the peak of elaboration of Chou bronzes coincided approximately with the overthrow of the Western Chou (771 B.C.). During the following centuries, when political power was divided among a large number of petty states, several different styles competed for pre-eminence in China, each seeming to strive

---

[86] Confucius was traditionally declared to have selected and ordered these poems; but this is doubtful. Cf. H. G. Creel, *Confucius: The Man and the Myth* (New York: John Day Co., 1949), p. 102.

[87] Bachhofer, *A Short History of Chinese Art*, pp. 28–54.

Victoria and Albert Museum, London.

Smithsonian Institution, Freer Gallery of Art, Washington, D.C.

Smithsonian Institution, Freer Gallery of Art, Washington, D.C.

ANCIENT CHINESE BRONZES

These three bronze containers illustrate the fluctuation in decorative style that occurred within the comparatively narrow limits of traditional shapes, defined, presumably, by fixed ceremonial uses to which these bronzes were put. The contrast between the pair at the left shows the simplification of decorative elements which followed the Chou conquest of China. The vessel shown at the top right is of a later date, when decorations had again begun to proliferate.

for a new simplicity and proportion. This was achieved only after 550 B.C., at a time when, in a completely different sphere of culture, Confucius was also bringing order and symmetry to Chinese moral ideas. Here, as so often, the history of art corresponds in a mysterious and subtle way to shifts and pulses in social and political development.[88]

The early Chou seem to have given Chinese ideas and institutions a number of decisive turns which remained normative for later generations. Certain it is that they brought a somewhat new emphasis to Chinese religion; and possibly they initiated important developments in political theory. But in neither religion nor politics, any more than in art, did the Chou break radically with Shang precedent. Rather they selected and recast older materials, modestly interjecting some new notions that unobtrusively held the composite structure together.

The political theory which prevailed in China until the overthrow of the Manchu Dynasty in 1911 A.D. perhaps originated with the Chou. According to this theory, Tien (or Heaven) conferred a mandate upon whoever was appointed to exercise political authority, but the mandate might be withdrawn at any time in the same mysterious way in which it had been initially conferred.[89] This idea had two important corollaries. First, since Heaven encompassed all lands, an emperor appointed by Heaven was, in the nature of things, a universal monarch—or ought to be. The notion that all peoples, Chinese and barbarian alike, should defer to a single "Son of Heaven" became the fundamental article of all later Chinese political thought and made a divided China seem always a moral as well as a political enormity. This frame of mind enormously facilitated imperial consolidation under successive dynasties and kept the country far more consistently united than the naked balance of military forces could ever have done. On the other hand, belief in the unique superiority of the Chinese emperor, while tenable in dealing with limitrophic barbarians, greatly complicated relations with more civilized and powerful rulers when in later times the Chinese were forced to treat with them.

The second corollary of Chou political theory was that the emperor, as the appointee of Heaven, held his place only so long as he conformed to the will of Heaven. Generations of Chinese thinkers were therefore at pains to interpret what was, after all, a matter of highest import to the rulers of the country. In general, they concluded that Heaven was pleased by sacrifices and other rites accurately and sumptuously performed. But Heaven was also pleased by moral conduct and good government. The emperor's failure in either respect might bring disaster to the country—flood or famine or pestilence—and in extreme cases might even provoke Heaven to withdraw its mandate and overthrow the emperor's dynasty forever.

Such a theory of government, while justifying usurpation or successful rebellion, also set limits upon the naked military power of a conqueror. Even

---

[88] Bachhofer points out these parallels; I merely paraphrase his exposition.

[89] It is tempting to accept Creel's suggestion that the theory which made the emperor's right to rule depend on the decree of Heaven was a propaganda instrument used by the usurping Chou to justify their ascent to supreme power at the expense of the Shang. Creel, *The Birth of China*, pp. 367–75.

after 771 B.C., when the reality of central power disappeared, the theory lingered on as an ideal. Reinforced by the Confucians, it served in due course to consolidate and at the same time to limit the power of all the emperors of later Chinese history.

A complicated cosmological system supplemented the political aspects of this theory. Earth became an image of Heaven, which was the abode of the ancestral spirits and of all good order. The emperor, "Son of Heaven," was the link connecting the two realms; and just as the Heavens revolved around the polestar, so terrestrial things ought to revolve around the emperor. Building upon this core, scholars worked out elaborate correspondences between celestial and terrestrial phenomena, in a fashion reminiscent of the astrological theorizing of the West.[90] But the new emphases thus imparted to older Chinese religion did not supersede ancestor worship nor displace old gods of earth, rivers, and mountains.[91] The older cults remained more or less as before, although human sacrifices and other crudities of Shang piety were abandoned.

The Chou state was a feudal monarchy. The victorious emperor parceled out conquered territory among his relatives and allies; and they in turn divided their lands among noble followers, each of whom commanded a train of dependents. For security in an alien and at first hostile land, these noble households erected fortified enclosures, some of which later developed into cities. Each spring the inhabitants went out to cultivate fields assigned to them and camped out in open air. When harvest was in, they returned to spend the winter months behind the security of earthen walls.[92] Conquered populations were held to tribute payments, but probably continued to live under their own village leaders and institutions, more or less apart from the conquerors.

At first it was possible for the Chou emperor to repossess the land of a disobedient noble family; but gradually the occupation of land came to be so intertwined with religious apprehensions that neither the emperor nor anyone else quite dared to interfere. If powerful ancestral spirits did in fact guard the lands of the great noble families, no prudent man would lightly brave their wrath by extinguishing the legitimate line. This belief may have checked the virulence of local warfare and blood feud among the nobility; and although it severely limited the emperor's practical authority, similar reverence applied to the imperial line effectually guarded the Chou against usurpation.

Two customs operated during the first two centuries of Chou rule to check

[90] Whether Chinese astronomy owed anything to Babylonia is a disputed point. Cf. Joseph Needham, *Science and Civilization in China* (Cambridge: Cambridge University Press, 1954), I, 151–52. In some respects, the Chou betray a contact with Babylonian ideas, for they introduced the seven-day week to China, replacing a ten-day week which the Shang had observed. C. W. Bishop, *Origin of the Far Eastern Civilizations* ("Smithsonian Institution War Background Studies," No. 1 [1942]), p. 23. But the doctrine of correspondence between earth and Heaven seems to be attested in Shang oracle records. Cf. Cheng Te-K'un, *Archaeology in China*, II, 225.

[91] It is noteworthy that Chou divinities tended to be male, whereas goddesses had played a prominent part in Shang piety. Bishop, *Origin of the Far Eastern Civilizations*, p. 41. Changes in the sex of divinities are not, however, as rare as one might suppose.

[92] This interpretation of the so-called "well-field" system I take from Wolfram Eberhard, *Conquerors and Rulers: Social Forces in Medieval China* (Leiden: E. J. Brill, 1952), pp. 6–9.

the centrifugal tendency inherent in a feudal system. First of all, each noble had the duty to serve his immediate superior in war and to assist him in rites and ceremonies conducted at his court. More unusual was the practice of sending the eldest sons of the chief nobles to a school in the capital, where the heir to the throne was also educated. At the imperial school, successive emperors could gain intimate acquaintance with some of their chief vassals; and long residence, in youth, at the capital must have strengthened the vassals' sense of solidarity with the reigning house. Lesser nobles and younger sons were sent to similar schools set up in the provinces. All followed a fixed curriculum: archery and chariot driving; rites and ceremonial, writing and arithmetic. The period of training lasted ten years, long enough to put a fairly uniform stamp upon the Chou aristocracy.[93]

After the end of the Western Chou dynasty in 771 B.C., more than a dozen Chinese princes divided effective (though not theoretical) sovereignty over the country. The political history of the following centuries well illustrates the advantages of a frontier position; for without exception, the states which became powerful were located on the margins of the Chinese world. By conquering the barbarians round about and bringing them within the circle of Chinese culture, such states grew so large that they easily overshadowed the military strength of their more anciently civilized neighbors toward the center, where territorial expansion was effectively blocked by balance-of-power diplomacy. Even when imperial authority had faded to nothing, the Chinese retained a strong sense of their community as against outer barbarians. This found political expression in efforts to substitute for the imperial unity a "concert of princes" to keep the peace among the various Chinese states. These efforts were not without a measure of success during the eighth and seventh centuries B.C.; and even when wars did break out between Chinese states, they failed to wreak heavy damage, owing to the development of an elaborate code of chivalry which forbade wholesale destruction of a vanquished enemy.

But by the sixth century B.C., this balance of power and code of chivalry showed unmistakable signs of disruption. The success of the "concert of princes" had always depended on recognition of the primacy of one or another among the states; and when, as happened more than once, a newcomer challenged that primacy, a bout of general war regularly ensued. The system therefore broke down decisively during the sixth century, when four powerful frontier states simultaneously laid claim to primacy in the Chinese world. A complicated struggle followed, fought mainly on the territories of the weaker states in the center. Warfare became chronic, and its intensity began to increase as old chivalric courtesy decayed.

[93] Henri Maspero, *La Chine antique*, pp. 131–32. If we compare this Chinese feudalism with the feudalism of medieval Europe or with the analogous organization of Hammurabi's empire in Babylonia, the prominent place occupied by literacy and religious training in the Chinese system stands out as unique. This was necessary because separate religious corporations, like the Mesopotamian priesthoods or the medieval Church, did not exist in China. As a result, the nobility could not specialize solely in warfare. Every Chinese noble had to be his own priest when it came to making sacrifices to his ancestors.

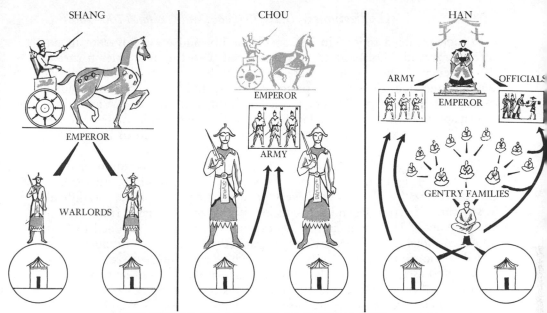

SHANG   CHOU   HAN

EMPEROR

WARLORDS

EMPEROR

ARMY

ARMY   EMPEROR   OFFICIALS

GENTRY FAMILIES

EVOLUTION OF CHINESE SOCIETY 1500 B.C.–220 A.D.

Yet prolonged internal disorder forwarded rather than hindered a rapid geographical expansion of Chinese culture. Refugees and adventurers, uprooted by wars at home, spread Chinese ideas and attitudes to neighboring barbarians. Through this process, the Shantung Peninsula and the coastal plain northeast of it were brought fully within the circle of Chinese civilization; and a comparable extension occurred all along the northern and western borders of China. The greatest territorial expansion, however, was to the south, where the valley of the Yangtze and the coastal regions on either side of its delta were gradually organized after the Chinese fashion. Barbarians thus taken within the fold made important contributions to Chinese culture. Chinese poetry, for example, owes much to the state of Ch'u, located in former barbarian territory to the south;[94] and certain new religious ideas, later taken up by the Taoists, probably derive from the same region.

But if the breakdown of the old political order brought benefits of a sort to the fringes of the Chinese world, it was far otherwise for the small states which clustered in the old centers of Chinese civilization along the middle and lower reaches of the Yellow River. From the sixth century B.C. onward, these states were reduced more and more to the status of pawns, subject to recurrent invasions and diplomatic bludgeonings at the hands of the ruder, but also stronger, frontier principalities. The emperor's domain, centered at Loyang, was no better off than its neighbors, despite imperial pretensions to supreme authority. Amid this political chaos, it was natural for the educated classes to hark back to the good old days, when imperial power had been a reality. This nostalgia was one of the roots from which Confucius' thought grew.

[94] Arthur Waley, *The Temple and Other Poems, with an Introductory Essay on Early Chinese Poetry* (New York: Alfred A. Knopf, Inc., 1923), p. 12.

In such troubled times, old-fashioned morality and good government nowhere prevailed. Oaths and treaties concluded with the most solemn rites in the presence of the ancestors were repeatedly broken; all sorts of violence and intrigue flourished at the princely courts; and the most unscrupulous ruffians often fared best. Where, in such a world, was Heaven? Why did the august spirits of the ancestors allow their names to be taken in vain? And how should a man behave when all traditional landmarks seemed to be tumbling down?

This was the problem Confucius faced in his lifetime (traditional dates, 551–479 B.C.); and the answers he gave were to prove fundamental for later Chinese civilization. Yet, as with every great teacher of mankind, it is difficult to separate fact from legend or to distinguish his own doctrine from the embellishments of later generations. No existing book can be assigned to Confucius' authorship; and his sayings, as handed down by his disciples, were added to and edited in later times. Consequently, even the *Analects*, universally accepted as the most nearly authentic exposition of Confucius' teaching, cannot be taken *in toto* as representative of his thought.[95]

Nevertheless, some points are clear. Confucius certainly looked back to the good old days with the warmest feeling: these remained for him the standard of how things should be. As he is quoted in the *Analects:* "I have transmitted what was taught me without making up anything of my own, I have been faithful to and loved the Ancients."[96] But how should a man who loved the ancients behave in a world that loved them not? This was Confucius' central problem; and because traditional morality was in decay, the practical force of his doctrine was a good deal more than transmitting "what was taught to me without making up anything of my own." For Confucius emphasized only some of the old ideals of aristocratic conduct, while rejecting or ignoring others, to make a compound that was in many respects new.

Confucius' most important departure from the old aristocratic point of view was his rejection of the idea that nobility was inborn. Nobility (or perhaps better, gentility) was for him a matter of education and conduct. It followed that men of low birth might, with training and natural aptitude, become gentlemen.[97] The marks of gentility were goodness, wisdom, and courage—virtues requiring moderation both of outward conduct and inner emotion, as well as knowledge of traditional rites and manners, performance of promises, faithfulness to superiors, and dissociation from those who lacked

[95] H. G. Creel, *Confucius: The Man and the Myth*, pp. 7–11, summarizes the problem. Cf. Arthur Waley, *The Analects of Confucius* (London: Allen & Unwin, Ltd., 1938), pp. 13–26.

[96] VII, 1. This and subsequent quotations from the *Analects* are taken from Arthur Waley's translation.

Confucius believed that his basic ideas and ideals were no more than a restatement of the principles which had inspired Tan, the Duke of Chou. According to tradition, the Duke, a brother of the first Chou conqueror, assumed the imperial power during the minority of the heir to the throne in order to suppress rebellion and then used his position to establish new institutions and to regularize the government before returning authority to his nephew. There is some reason to believe that Confucius was not altogether wrong in regarding himself as the spiritual heir of the Duke of Chou, who may in fact have had considerable personal influence on the development of Chou institutions.

[97] *Analects*, IV, 5; VI, 4; VII, 7; IX, 7.

such traits.[98] Such a man ought to find satisfaction in the mere cultivation of his virtues. "He that is really good can never be unhappy. He that is really wise can never be perplexed. He that is really brave is never afraid."[99] But the true sphere and proper career for a gentleman was to govern. Like Plato after him, Confucius was plagued all his life by the unwillingness of rulers and politicians to adopt his precepts or to appoint him to ministerial office, where he might personally put his principles into practice. He consoled himself as best he might with the thought that virtue was its own reward, capable of surmounting even poverty.[100] But neither Confucius nor his followers ever surrendered the conviction that the full expression of a gentleman's virtue could be attained only by governing.[101]

Confucius summed up his teaching in the word *Tao*.[102] The full meaning of this term is difficult to comprehend, for though Confucius often used it, he scarcely explained it. Clearly, *Tao* meant the practice of all the virtues becoming a gentleman. Beyond that, Confucius seems to have believed that conduct in accord with *Tao* somehow cut with the grain of the universe, or in more nearly Chinese language, conformed to the will of Heaven. Perhaps he conceived *Tao* on the model of decorous relations prevailing within a well-ordered noble family and wished to transfer the familial pattern to the entire political world.[103]

Confucius' doctrine clearly departed in important respects from older aristocratic mores. He decried violence and paid little attention to military training, which had been in the forefront of traditional education. Decorum, a concept dear to him, forbade resort to force in all ordinary circumstances; and he seems to have believed in the feasibility of governing "by ritual and yielding,"[104] *i.e.*, by giving way gracefully to others, all according to rules of precedence and propriety laid down by the code of good manners. Indeed, any other manner of governing, he believed, would invite endless retaliation, intrigue, and violence—the very ills that deformed the politics of his age.

Confucius modified older tradition in another way by rejecting the simple faith that lavish and correct sacrifices would assure the favor of ancestral spirits and success in the world. He taught that virtue was its own reward; and he had to admit, sorrowfully, that its possession was no guaranty of worldly success. Was not he himself denied the political power needed to put his

---

[98] *Analects*, IV, 17, 18; VI, 25; VII, 24, 36; VIII, 8, 16; IX, 24.

[99] *Analects*, IX, 28. Cf. IV, 14.

[100] *Analects*, IV, 8, 9.

[101] *Analects*, VII, 32.

[102] *Tao* may be translated as "Way"; and if one lends this English word the necessary overtones, it may serve. The term had great importance in other Chinese schools of thought—so much so that one such school, sharply critical of Confucianism, is called Taoist.

[103] Creel, *Confucius: The Man and the Myth*, p. 125. Confucius himself, so far as the *Analects* permit one to judge, did not emphasize filial piety very greatly. Perhaps he assumed it as a datum, whereas later Confucians found it necessary to make this aspect of Tao explicit. At any rate, the heirs of the Confucian tradition put great emphasis upon filial piety as the foremost of the virtues.

[104] *Analects*, IV, 13; cf. XII, 1.

principles into practice? Concerning the spirits and their action among men he was always reticent. There is no reason to suppose that he doubted their existence or their power; but he systematically refused to discuss theological or metaphysical questions. Traditional sacrifices and religious rites were part of the life of a gentleman and should not be neglected; but that was as far as he chose to go. The world of men and morals came first; speculation about Heaven or the nature of life after death he simply put aside.[105] Such an attitude bypassed the religious doubts which existed in his time and left a gap in the Confucian armory which the Taoists were later to exploit with their own bold, fantastic brand of metaphysical theorizing. But Confucius' reticence in these matters accorded well with the practical end he always kept in view: to instruct gentlemen who would be prepared to govern well.

Confucius regarded his own career as a failure. He never exercised power; and a merely private life, however replete with virtue, could only amount to a poor second in his eyes. Yet from the long-range point of view, his power proved greater and far more lasting than any mere monarch's; for his ideas catalyzed the institutional and intellectual definition of Chinese civilization. In the two-and-a-half centuries after his death (479 B.C.), Confucians continued to exist in China, sometimes in office, often not; but only after China had been unified once again through highhanded violence did the emperors of the first Han dynasty (202–9 B.C.) entrust Confucians with the administration of the state. From that day until our own,[106] the Confucian civil service never for long lost its grip on China.

Confucius' followers brought many changes to his doctrines before this extraordinary vindication of his hopes came to pass; yet the imprint of the Master was by no means erased. His ideal of the gentleman, governed by a traditional yet individual ethic, averse from theological speculation, devoted to decorum, reluctant to resort to violence, and aiming always at *Tao*, was never eclipsed. Such gentlemen, however imperfectly they embodied the Confucian ideal, ruled China for over two millennia and through most of that time gave a remarkable stability and coherence to Chinese culture and politics. Few indeed are the men to whom posterity has raised so majestic a monument.

E. CHANGES IN THE BARBARIAN WORLD TO 500 B.C.

The consolidation of a cosmopolitan civilization in the Middle East and the growth of vigorous new civilizations in Greece, India, and China multiplied and varied the influences playing upon the barbarian world. Much of the early history of India, Greece, and China is in fact a history of the conversion of barbarians to their respective styles of civilized life. By 500 B.C., southern India, central and southern China, and almost the entire coastline of the Mediterranean and Black seas had either been won for civilization or set in motion toward it.

[105] *Analects*, V, 12; VII, 20; XI, 11. For remarks upon the likenesses and contrasts between the doctrines of Confucius, Buddha, and early Greek philosophers, see above, p. 214 n.

[106] It is well to remember that Mao Tse-tung began life as a student of the Confucian classics and met Marxism only as a mature man of 27.

Only in the Mediterranean and Black Sea area is it possible to follow in some detail the steps of civilized expansion. Three peoples—Phoenicians, Etruscans, and Greeks—were primarily responsible for planting the seeds of civilization in these regions. Between about 800 and 550 B.C., most of the Mediterranean and Black Sea coastline was brought within the spheres of influence of one or another of these peoples; and a lively trade connected all portions of the Mediterranean littoral with the more developed civilizations of its eastern shores. Not infrequently, colonization followed trade. Phoenician and Greek colonies were modeled upon the city-states of their homelands; and the Etruscan cities, which may (or may not) have been founded by a people fleeing from Asia Minor, bore a loose resemblance to Greek and Phoenician settlements.[107] With the establishment of these communities, such civilized accomplishments as literacy, a high art, and monumental building found lodgment on previously barbarian territories; while trade relations with the interior brought some acquaintance with the ways of civilization to the European and African hinterlands.

Beyond the immediate radius of civilized societies as they existed in 500 B.C., five great reservoirs of savage or barbarian life remained. Three were in the Old World: (1) Africa south of the Sahara and the Abyssinian massif; (2) the monsoon forests of southeast Asia, together with the adjacent islands of Indonesia; (3) the steppe and forest zones of northern Eurasia. Beyond lay the two great ocean-insulated islands of the earth: (4) Australia, and (5) the Americas.

Archeological investigation of these regions has progressed unevenly; and it is still perhaps too soon to pass judgment upon the influences, if any, which reached them from the rising centers of Eurasian civilization during the first millennium B.C. Australia, certainly, remained a world apart; and until long after 500 B.C., sub-Saharan Africa was apparently almost unaffected by the social storm centers which had arisen to the north. Only a geographically modest penetration of Egyptian influence into Nubia—the modern Sudan—has so far been attested by archeology.[108] The situation in southeast Asia before 500 B.C. is also unclear. The earliest written accounts of the region date from the second century A.D., when Chinese diplomats and conquerors came into touch with a series of partially Hinduized states in northern Burma, Annam,

---

[107] Cf. M. Pallottino, *Gli Etruschi* (Rome: Casa Editrice Carlo Colombo, 1939), pp. 43–72, 129–54. Luisa Banti, *Die Welt der Etrusker* (Stuttgart: Gustav Kilper Verlag, 1960), pp. 132–35.

[108] H. Alimen, *Préhistoire de l'Afrique* (Paris: Éditions N. Boubée & Cie, 1955); Sonia Cole, *The Prehistory of East Africa* (Harmondsworth: Penguin Books, 1954), pp. 271–85; Diedrich Westermann, *Geschichte Afrikas* (Cologne: Greven, 1952), pp. 3–20. It should be pointed out, however, that prehistoric chronology in Africa is almost entirely guesswork. It is possible, for example, that "megalithic" influences were at work both along the east coast, especially in the region of Cape Gardafui, and in west Africa long before 500 B.C. Cf. Dominik Josef Wölfel, "Die kanarischen Inseln: die westafrikanischen Hochkulturen und das alte Mittelmeer," *Paideuma*, IV (1950), 231–53. Carthaginian trading along the Atlantic coast of Africa probably extended as far as the Rio del Oro, although explorers certainly penetrated farther. Placer gold was the magnet which drew Carthaginian ships so far; and "silent" trade, whereby each of the trading parties retired after displaying its goods in order to avoid direct contact with the other, prevailed. Cf. B. H. Warmington, *Carthage* (London: Robert Hale, Ltd., 1960), pp. 59–66.

and Cochin China. How long before that date Indian influence had been felt in southeast Asia remains uncertain.[109] Archeological finds suggest that before any very close contact with either Indian or Chinese civilization took place, wealth accumulated by means of a widespread sea trade provided the basis for an independent protocivilization centered on the south China coast and in northern Viet-Nam.[110]

Yet whatever any future archeological discoveries may add to present-day knowledge of prehistoric southeast Asia and sub-Saharan Africa, it is all but certain that these areas, like Australia and the Americas, remained cultural backwaters. World-shaking changes, affecting the whole pattern of civilized evolution in Eurasia, did not derive thence. The case was far otherwise with the Eurasian steppe and forest belt. In the eighteenth century B.C., bronze-wielding charioteers had emerged from this region with dramatic consequences for civilized peoples everywhere. Almost a thousand years later, in the ninth-eighth centuries B.C., a second disturbance in the balance of military forces between steppe and civilized peoples occurred, though this time the change was not so drastic and the geographical range of steppe conquerors was correspondingly more modest.

The critical fact was this: steppe tribesmen began to ride on horseback habitually and learned to control their mounts in a fashion to allow free use of both hands, at least for limited periods of time. It thus became possible for them to launch a shower of arrows from horseback, even at full gallop.

Exactly when and where the new style of cavalry warfare was first employed can only be surmised. Riding had been tried, but only occasionally, as early as the third millennium B.C.; but the great success of horse chariotry, together with the real difficulties of controlling a horse without saddle, bridle, or stirrups, had made so simple a method of exploiting the speed of the horse quite unimportant. The appearance of centaur motifs on Mesopotamian seals in the thirteenth century suggests that riding had become more common among steppe peoples by that date; but the full perfection of horsemanship, and its real importance for steppe life and for the military establishments of

---

[109] Megalithic monuments in southern India, southeast Asia, and in some of the islands of the western Pacific perhaps attest some sort of connection among these diverse regions during the first millennium B.C.

[110] D. G. E. Hall, *A History of South East Asia* (New York: St Martin's Press, 1955), pp. 7–9; C. W. Bishop, "Long-Houses and Dragon-Boats," *Antiquity*, XII (1938), 411–24; Wolfram Eberhard, *Kultur und Siedlung der Randvölker Chinas*, pp. 326–31; G. Coedès, *Les États hindouisés d'Indochine et d'Indonésie* (Paris: E. de Boccard, 1948), pp. 25–26. This protocivilization of southeast Asia, termed the Dongson culture after the site of its principal archaeological remains, suggests comparison with the early civilization of Crete. However, Dongson culture never achieved a long life or full development like that of Cretan civilization, largely perhaps because its mainland position brought it early into crushing contact with the expanding military and cultural power of Han China. Cf. the fate of the abortive Viking civilization of Scandinavia, as analyzed by A. J. Toynbee, *A Study of History*, I, 340–60. A sea-roving tradition was however maintained in Borneo and other Indonesian islands, eventuating, among other things, in the colonization of Madagascar at about the beginning of the Christian era. Cf. George Peter Murdock, *Africa: Its Peoples and Their Culture History* (New York: McGraw-Hill, 1959), pp. 45, 212–16. The Polynesian dispersal of the first millennium A.D. may have derived from the same roots.

THE CAVALRY REVOLUTION

This Assyrian bas-relief, carved on the walls of Ashurbanipal's (668–625 B.C.) palace at Nineveh, is a spirited and comparatively quite early artistic portrayal of a cavalryman, shown here engaged in the hunt rather than in war. The imperfect adjustment of Assyrian accouterments to the new style of locomotion is evident in the survival of a skirtlike costume, ill fitted for sitting astride a horse. Obviously, the absence of stirrups put the rider very much at the mercy of his mount. Only well-trained horses could be trusted to maintain their speed and direction while the rider dropped the reins in order to bend his bow.

civilized peoples, dates only from the ninth century B.C.[111] The center from which the perfected style of horsemanship radiated was in all probability the same from which chariotry had spread some nine hundred years earlier—the Iranian aperture on the steppe.[112]

Riding was only a part of the total adjustment necessary to full mastery of the steppe. Nomads also had to develop easily portable gear, clothing suitable for riding astride (*i.e.*, trousers), and a diet largely (or even entirely) independent of agricultural products. Only then did they become fully free to follow their herds across the grasslands, moving perhaps hundreds of miles annually in pursuit of the best available pasture.

The perfection of horse nomadry therefore required rather drastic changes in the lives of the scattered communities which had earlier inhabited the European and central Asian steppe. But this was only preliminary to a transformation of the entire Eurasian military and social balance, for the new nomadry created, incidentally as it were, a numerous and formidable steppe cavalry, eager and able to subject civilized defenses to heavier and more continuous strain than ever before.

Mastery of the arts of riding obviously gave the steppe herdsmen a new military advantage. Every nomad had to possess horses, and every man with a mount under him and a bow in his hand became a potential first-line soldier. The elusive speed of a galloping horse made it safe enough to dispense with metal armor and other expensive accouterments. Hence the skills and materials (stone arrowheads are very serviceable for killing a man) available to every nomad tribe became fully adequate to sustain successful raids against even the most up-to-date civilized military establishment. For the first time, therefore, the whole depth and breadth of the Eurasian steppe became a breeding ground for warriors capable of attacking civilized communities with every prospect of success.[113]

Steppe cavalry could travel faster and farther than any other type of troops, penetrating passes and crossing rivers with comparative ease. A nomad "army" was in fact no more than the male members of a tribe, or tribal confederation, moving as they always moved, but relieved of the encumbrance of women, children, and flocks. When opposed by less mobile enemies, such horsemen could raid and run almost with impunity. Only collision with forces of similar type, or a shortage of fodder for their horses, put limits on their depredations.

The history of the first millennium B.C. reflects the military advantages thus accruing to the men of the steppe. The Middle East, through its proximity to the center from which the new style of nomadry diffused, was naturally

---

[111] Franz Hančar, *Das Pferd in prähistorischer und früher historischer Zeit*, pp. 551–63; William Ridgeway, *The Origin and Influence of the Thoroughbred Horse* (Cambridge: Cambridge University Press, 1905), pp. 94, 98, argues that the long delay before riding became normal was because early types of domesticated horses were not strong enough in the back to carry a man for any length of time.

[112] Franz Hančar, *Das Pferd*, p. 555; Karl Jettmar, "Archaeologische Spuren von Indogermanen in Zentralasien," *Paideuma*, V (1950–54), 236–37.

[113] Cf. how cheap steel made barbarian foot-soldiery effective in the thirteenth century B.C., as analyzed above, pp. 117–19. A useful summary and overview of steppe history from the Cimmerians to the Huns is available in E. D. Phillips, "New Light on the Ancient History of the Eurasian Steppe," *American Journal of Archaeology*, LXI (1959), 269–80.

the first to feel the assault. Indeed, it is Assyrian records of massive nomad invasions, beginning toward the close of the eighth century B.C.,[114] that permit us to deduce the change which had come to steppe life. At that time, bands of horsemen, known to the Greeks as Cimmerians, issued from the steppes of southern Russia and raided far and wide in Asia Minor. They may have been driven to take this offensive by pressure from other tribes, the Scythians, who from their homeland in central Asia[115] pressed westward shortly before 700 B.C. and seized the richer Russian grasslands from the Cimmerians. Scythian raiders, in turn, followed the Cimmerians southward and took a leading part in the coalition of forces that overthrew the Assyrian empire in 612 B.C. Hence the revolution of life on the Eurasian steppe played a critical role in the collapse of Assyria and the rise of the Persian empire.[116]

The imperial heirs of the Assyrians, the Medes and the Persians, were not spared the problem of safeguarding Middle Eastern civilized communities from the newly formidable nomad harassment. Despite the general excellence of their military establishment, the Achaemenid rulers found the task by no means easy, as Cyrus' death on his eastern frontier (530 B.C.) and Darius' difficult European campaign against the Scythians (512 B.C.) may remind us. The Iranian gateway to the steppe was especially vulnerable; and it was only by employing steppe cavalry as mercenaries in the imperial service that the Achaemenids were able to check nomad depredation along the northern and eastern fringes of their empire.[117]

In barbarian Europe, the rise of horse nomadry had equally spectacular consequences. Early in the sixth century B.C., the Scythians created a powerful, if loosely consolidated "empire" in southern Russia, and expanded their power as far west as the plain of Hungary. Like their Persian kinsmen and counterparts, they imposed themselves as a ruling stratum upon earlier inhabitants. But unlike the Persians, the Scythians themselves continued to live a seminomadic life under tribal discipline.[118]

Farther west, Celtic tribesmen were the first to master the arts of riding; and their expansion from southern Germany over most of northwest Europe was facilitated by their resort to cavalry tactics. The Celts, however, did not take over the full complement of the steppe nomads' war equipment: not the bow, but a long two-handed sword became their characteristic weapon.[119]

---

[114] Herodotus' garbled account is also valuable.

[115] Karl Jettmar, "The Altai before the Turks," Museum of Far Eastern Antiquities, Stockholm, *Bulletin*, XXIII (1951), 154–55.

[116] M. Rostovtzeff, *Iranians and Greeks in South Russia* (Oxford: Clarendon Press, 1922), pp. 35–44.

[117] Karl Jettmar, "The Altai before the Turks," pp. 156–57.

[118] Rostovtzeff, *Iranians and Greeks*, pp. 35–44.

[119] On Celtic expansion see Henri Hubert, *Les Celtes et l'expansion celtique jusqu'à l'époque de la Tène* (Paris: La Renaissance du livre, 1932); for the value of cavalry to the Celts, cf. William McGovern, *The Early Empires of Central Asia* (Chapel Hill: University of North Carolina Press, 1939), pp. 46–48. Why the steppe type of cavalry did not penetrate into western Europe, and why the Celts preferred swords to bows, is unclear. Perhaps the wooded and often marshy terrain of western Europe was at least partly responsible; for in a leafy forest, bows are of limited use, and one must come closer to grips with an enemy. But old and quite irrational tradition may have played a part, also. Cf. the remarks on Homeric warfare above, p. 107 n.

To the east, the progress of the cavalry revolution is more obscure. Tribes that had mastered the newly perfected style of horse nomadry had small incentive to push eastward, where pastures and climate alike became less hospitable. Therefore, the techniques of horse nomadry probably spread toward Mongolia quite slowly, as one tribe after another borrowed elements of the new style of life from westerly neighbors.[120] The process probably required about four hundred years to come to completion, for the first Chinese records indicating the presence of the new cavalry techniques among the barbarians along the northwestern frontier date only from the fourth century B.C.[121]

The appearance of shifting clusters of black felt tents on the steppes of Mongolia put China under the same sort of military strain that the Middle East had experienced three centuries before. The state of Ch'in, in northwestern China, bore the brunt. At first the nomad raids were not organized on a scale sufficient to overwhelm Chinese resistance; but they did lead the rulers of Ch'in to adopt the new cavalry tactics themselves and to build their army around horse archers. This new-style force checked barbarian raids and incidentally proved capable of overwhelming all rival Chinese states, thus permitting the ruler of Ch'in to emerge in 221 B.C. as the emperor of a united China.[122]

Nevertheless, the establishment of full-blown horse nomadry in Mongolia during the fourth century B.C. may not have been the first time that the Far East felt the impact of cavalry warfare. The evidence for this is archeological and involves many uncertainties, in particular, the much debated problem of the "Scythian" or "animal" style of art. The facts are these: Scythian art motifs, as known from southern Russia and western Asia, show Chinese affinities, while Chinese art in the late Chou period shows some "Scythian" traits. Furthermore, in an area along the south China coast and extending into northern Viet-Nam, a fair number of objects which show striking similarities to materials from the distant Black Sea steppes have been dug up or have come to museums from unauthenticated sources.[123]

---

[120] Karl Jettmar, "Zur Herkunft der türkischen Völkerschaften," *Archiv für Völkerkunde*, III (1948), 16–17; K. Jettmar, "The Altai," 148–50; B. Rubin, "Das neue Bild der Geschichte Eurasiens," *Jahrbücher für Geschichte Osteuropas*, N.F. II (1954), 106–7.

The well-known spread of horsemanship northward among the Amerindians of the Great Plains from the sixteenth to the eighteenth centuries A.D. presents an exact parallel. In the American case, it is certain that the diffusion of horse nomadry proceeded, not by conquest, but by borrowing; and here, too, the movement traversed a climatic gradient, penetrating successively into less hospitable regions. The gradient, however, was less marked in North America than in Eurasia, since in America only temperatures and the length of the growing season decrease as one moves northward through the Great Plains, whereas as one proceeds eastward across the Eurasian steppe toward Mongolia, the far more critical factor of precipitation drops also.

[121] W. McGovern, *Early Empires of Central Asia*, pp. 100–101.

[122] The rise of Ch'in offers a classic instance of how a lord marcher may profit from his exposed position. From a different point of view, both the Ch'in and the Persian empires may be conceived as "native reactions" against the threat created by the newly perfected horse nomadry.

[123] Gregory Borovka, *Scythian Art*; M. I. Rostovtzeff, *The Animal Style in South Russia and China* (Princeton, N.J.: Princeton University Press, 1929); Ludwig Bachhofer, *A Short History of Chinese Art*, p. 46; Robert Heine-Geldern, "Das Tocharerproblem und die pontische Wanderung," *Saeculum*, II (1951), 225–55; Karl Jettmar, "The Altai before the Turks," 148–56.

How this evidence should be interpreted is doubtful. Possibly Scythian tribesmen of the Altai region, after mastering the new techniques of riding, exploited their position on what was then (eighth century B.C.) the easternmost edge of the new style of horse nomadry to launch raids across the oases of Chinese Turkestan, following the probable route of the charioteer conquerors of the preceding millennium. The collapse of the western Chou dynasty in 771 B.C. may in part have been due to just such a sudden, brief irruption. At about the same time, other bands of horsemen may have penetrated via Szechuan as far as the south China coast.[124]

On this hypothesis, it was only a generation or two after they had raided China that the Scythians turned their horses' heads westward and emerged into history through their collision with literate peoples of the Middle East. Such a delay might be accounted for by the likelihood that movement to the west was at first obstructed by other militarily formidable horse nomads, from whom, indeed, the Scythians had probably acquired the arts of riding. Only after such neighbors had been overcome in battle or else folded into an enlarged war confederation could the Scythians launch themselves westward. But when they did, they quickly discovered the wider and richer grasslands of southern Russia. Having defeated the Cimmerian occupants of the region, we may then suppose that the Scythians shifted the main center of their population to the Ukraine, abandoning China to its own devices, and leaving only a small rearguard behind in central Asia.

* * *

Startling as it may seem, the political upheavals and the interchange of techniques and art motifs following in the wake of Scythian raids and invasions may not have been confined to the Old World. A number of lines of evidence suggest that men crossed the Pacific several centuries before the Christian era, despite the enormous distances involved. Parallels between various archeological items from Peru and Mexico and others from the coasts of southeast Asia seem best explained by this hypothesis.[125] The botanical

---

[124] This reconstruction rests upon a query by Jettmar in his article, "The Altai before the Turks," and is of course highly speculative. Only when Chinese Turkestan and western China have been explored archeologically can this hypothesis, and the equally speculative reconstruction of the route taken by charioteers of the preceding millennium, be either proven or disproven. The occupation of the oases of the Tarim Basin, at China's very back door, by speakers of Indo-European languages—"Tocharian"—may date from Scythian times. Cf. René Grousset, *L'Empire des steppes*, p. 79. If so, the survival of this tongue into historic times would constitute one tangible bit of evidence to support the interpretation here advanced.

[125] According to the chronology of Robert Heine-Geldern, "Die asiatische Herkunft der sudamerikanischen Metalltechnik," *Paideuma*, V (1954), 347–423, trans-Pacific migration of art motifs and technological methods became particularly important soon after our putative horsemen from the steppe reached the south China coast, that is, in or shortly after the seventh century B.C. Perhaps a semi-barbarous "Dongson" society brought together an old local skill in seafaring with the bold venturesomeness of a handful of warriors derived but recently from Central Asia, who had learned the art of horseback riding only a short time previously. In such an amalgam, habits and social patterns would

character and distribution of certain domesticated plants on both shores of the Pacific also suggest that seeds or cuttings must have been carried across the ocean by human agency at an early time.[126]

Since Europeans were unable to cross the Atlantic until 1000 A.D. and failed to make permanent lodgment on the opposite shore for five hundred years thereafter, the idea that Asians traversed the immensely wider Pacific in the pre-Christian era at first appears absurd. Yet two considerations make this hypothesis far less improbable. First, the conquest of Europe by barbarian warriors in the Bronze Age had the effect of nearly destroying the skills of older megalithic seafarers; and a population skilled in seamanship did not arise again in western Europe until the age of the Scandinavian Vikings.[127] Nonetheless, the fact that both the Azores and Canary Islands were inhabited by Stone Age populations when European discoverers intruded upon them in the fourteenth century A.D. indicates that quite primitive peoples, whose culture appears to have been "megalithic," had been able—by accident or intent—to voyage far into the Atlantic, and for all anyone can tell, may even have sent refugees or storm-tossed mariners all the way to the New World.[128]

Second, the navigability of the oceans differs greatly from one area to another. Europe abuts upon one of the most stormy and tide-beset seascapes of the entire earth; and Western ideas of ocean travel are shaped by memories of the North Atlantic crossing. But in lower latitudes, especially in the wide ocean reaches where the trade winds blow with nearly uniform force and direction throughout the year, ocean voyaging becomes an entirely different experience. Very small and primitive vessels—rafts, canoes, coracles—can safely venture upon such pacific waters; and with a suitable combination of

---

be unusually plastic; and a period of unparalleled sea ventures may have constituted one aspect of the response in such circumstances.

It is not necessary to accept Heine-Geldern's contention that a two-way traffic was established across the Pacific. If even a single boatload of seamen crossed the Pacific—perhaps driven by a storm until it appeared wiser to sail on than to attempt to beat back against the wind in a vessel incapable of doing so very effectively—this might be enough to account for the resemblances which appear to link the Americas with southeast Asia. To be sure, a band of castaways could have such an importance only under special circumstances. Yet if the Amerindians of Mexico or Peru had developed their cultures to such a point that superior techniques (e.g., copper-bronze metallurgy) and (magically potent) art motifs familiar to a venturesome boat's crew from Asia could be successfully incorporated into the local social structure, then the slightest and most transient contact might suffice to stimulate Amerindians to make revolutionary changes in their pre-existing techniques and art styles.

[126] George F. Carter, "Plant Evidence for Early Contacts with America," *Southwestern Journal of Anthropology*, VI (1960), 161–82; George F. Carter, "Plants across the Pacific," Society for American Archaeology, *Memoirs*, No. 9 (1953), 62–72.

[127] A survival of megalithic seafaring tradition in Ireland underlay the sea journeying of the Irish in the early Christian centuries. The discovery and first settlement of Iceland was the most dramatic fully authenticated achievement of these centuries. Mythical accounts of "St. Brendan's isle" may reflect contact with other Atlantic islands or even with America.

[128] Aztec myths about culture-bringers from the West may derive from trans-Atlantic ventures of such a people. On the cultural affinities and evidence concerning the state of the Canary Islanders when Europeans first reached them, cf. Dominik J. Wölfel, "Die kanarischen Inseln: die westafrikanischen Hochkulturen und das alte Mittelmeer," *Paideuma*, IV (1950), 231–53.

Osvald Siren, Art ancien.

CHINESE AND AMERINDIAN ART

The three objects shown here on the left are of Chinese provenance, while those on the right come from Central America. Such resemblances seem too close to be accidental. Similar (though not always so close) parallels abound. Some sort of trans-Pacific movement seems necessary to account for these likenesses.

SCYTHS

Nineveh (612)

Monsoon Pressure Center

Chang'an (717)

Dongson

INDIAN OCEAN

PACIFIC OCEAN

ATLANTIC OCEAN

Main Currents
Trade Winds
Cyclonic Storms

sails, steering paddle, and keel, simple craft can travel indefinitely across the wind as well as before it.[129]

In the Atlantic, however, the trade winds prevail in the latitude of the Sahara Desert (indeed they create it), where until recent centuries only scant and primitive populations, incapable of developed seamanship, could exist.[130] But in the Pacific, the trade winds abut in winter upon the fertile south China coast, to be replaced in summer by the monsoon, which blows with comparable equability, though from an opposite direction. Thus southeast Asia offered a base from which long-range navigation might easily proceed; and as we have seen, evidence indicates that the arts of seamanship were well-developed along the south China coast centuries before the region was incorporated into the Chinese culture area.

If we measure not statute miles, but the practical difficulties which the central Pacific and the North Atlantic presented to early mariners, it appears that the wider ocean was by far the lesser barrier. Contact across the Pacific was technically possible; and it is likely that mariners deriving from Asia (perhaps via intermediate island stages, as later among the Polynesians) lent

[129] Even the North Atlantic was not entirely impenetrable to primitive craft. Several Eskimo kayaks crossed from Greenland to Scotland in the seventeenth century with men aboard. Cf. Ian Whitaker, "The Scottish Kayaks and the 'Finnmen,'" *Antiquity*, XXVIII (1954), 99–104. Similar and well-authenticated tales of Japanese fishermen surviving a storm-tossed trip across the north Pacific in modern times prove that Asia and America were not rigidly separated even by the stormy northern oceans. Cf. Andrew Sharp, *Ancient Voyagers in the Pacific* (Wellington, N.Z.: Polynesian Society, 1956), p. 60. Gentler waters were correspondingly more penetrable to ancient and primitive craft. Sharp's convincing argument that Polynesians deliberately ventured on no more than two- to three-hundred-mile interisland hops does not imply that longer voyages were not entered upon whenever navigation failed and the intended island speck failed to appear from the vastness of the ocean. On the contrary, Sharp is at pains to record the numerous proven cases in which such long voyages did occur by misadventure during the few decades when Europeans were just penetrating Oceania and native seafaring continued in the traditional manner.

[130] Only after modern Europeans had penetrated into Saharan waters did the Spanish discovery of America occur. Columbus knew enough about Atlantic trade winds and currents to head south to the Azores, where he picked up the trades which took him westward. Cf. S. E. Morison, *Admiral of the Ocean Sea* (Boston: Little Brown & Co., 1942), I, 265–70.

impetus to the elaboration of civilization in the New World. Yet though the isolation of the Americas was probably not complete, early transoceanic contacts were far too limited and sporadic to allow the Amerindians to borrow extensively from the more advanced cultures of the Old World. As a result, the Andean and Mexican civilizations developed belatedly and never attained a mastery of their environment that could rival the levels attained by their contemporaries in Eurasia.[131]

* * *

The civilizations of Greece and India were both effectively sheltered from the direct impact of steppe cavalry. High mountains and the political barrier interposed by the Persian and Seleucid empires kept India immune from harassment until the second century B.C., when a steppe people known as Shakas crossed the Hindu Kush and set up a series of short-lived states in northwest India. Similarly, mountain barriers and formidable barbarian tribes like the Thracians protected Greece and the Mediterranean littoral. Indeed, the Far West was spared nomad invasion until the fourth century A.D.; but for a millennium previously, fighting along the Danube frontier had brought civilized Europe into sporadic contact with horsemen of the steppe.

The influence of the steppe was felt in Mediterranean Europe only in this indirect way from the time of Darius' invasion of Scythia in 512 B.C. until the Roman defeat at Adrianople in 378 A.D. The marginal character of that influence is indicated by the European failure to adjust their military tactics to counter those of the nomads. Cavalry played only a modest part in both Greek and Roman warfare; and archery was little used. Instead, a disciplined infantry maneuvering in massed formations remained central to the European military art from the seventh century B.C. to the fourth century A.D.[132]

The peoples of the steppe, who had such far-ranging effects upon the civilized communities of Eurasia from the eighth century B.C. onward, were themselves susceptible to many of the charms of civilization, though only insofar as these were compatible with the conditions of nomadic life. Thus

---

[131] On the question of early trans-Pacific contacts, cf. the collection of articles in M. W. Smith, *Asia and North America: Trans-Pacific Contacts*, Society for American Archaeology, *Memoir*, No. 9 (1953). The likelihood of such contacts has been repudiated by most American anthropologists and espoused mainly by German ethnologists like Heine-Geldern or Walter Krickeberg, *Altmexikanische Kulturen* (Berlin: Safari Verlag, 1956), pp. 568–75. Neither party to the dispute, which has often generated considerable emotional heat, seriously considered the conditions of trans-Pacific movement—winds, currents, seamanship, and the limits and capacities of primitive navigation. Thor Heyerdahl, *American Indians in the Pacific* (Stockholm: Bokförlaget Forma, 1952), added this dimension to the debate; but the technical discussion of Polynesian seamanship in Andrew Sharp, *Ancient Voyagers in the Pacific*, pp. 60–61 and *passim*, pretty well disproves Heyerdahl's thesis of a one-way traffic from America westward into the Pacific.

[132] Alexander's use of cavalry shock tactics is perhaps an exception to this. Macedonian warfare in his generation had been shaped in part by struggles in the north against Thracians and others, incident to pushing the frontier of Macedon to the Danube. This, of course, brought the Macedonians into direct contact with steppe peoples; yet Alexander's cavalry tactics were not those of horse archery. Perhaps one may say that he adopted for his cavalry the basic tactical idea of the phalanx: to charge at speed and bear down opposition by sheer momentum. Alexander's cavalry was in fact a phalanx mounted on horseback.

metal weapons, cloth, and gold always met with a ready reception, whereas monumental building and higher mathematics did not.

Roughly speaking, civilized goods and influence could penetrate the steppe in two ways. A powerful nomad confederacy might hold even a distant civilized community to ransom and extort a tribute of whatever products attracted nomad taste. But this was essentially a parasitic relationship; and when such a confederacy broke apart, the flow of goods came abruptly to a halt.[133]

Peaceable commerce could penetrate nomad society rather more deeply. The possibilities of such a relationship were well illustrated by the diffusion of Greek tastes and styles into Scythia, where the upper classes were able to indulge their appetite for Greek wine, oil, and other products by compelling their subjects to produce grain which the Greeks needed at home. Moreover, in time, through mixing with Greeks of the colonial cities on the Black Sea coast, at least some of the noble Scythians acquired a very respectable smattering of Greek culture.[134]

The Scythians also served as intermediaries between the civilized lands of the south and the remoter barbarian hinterland to the north and east. By the seventh century B.C., a fairly well-established trade route probably ran from the mouth of the Don River across southern Siberia to the Altai Mountains, whence, presumably, came the gold in which Scythian tombs are peculiarly rich. Other traders may have carried Altai gold to northwest China.[135] This sort of long-distance overland trade was probably sporadic and small in volume; yet it had the effect of transforming the great central Eurasian sea of grass into a conductor of influences among the settled communities located on its edges. This conductivity, however, was always limited to ideas and objects which illiterate nomads could carry with them over long distances.

Not all parts of the Eurasian steppe were equally susceptible to civilized influences. In Mongolia and adjacent areas, agriculture was all but impossible; shortage of water and the resultant sparsity of vegetation enforced a rigorously nomadic and pastoral life. Indeed, the adjustment among the nomadic inhabitants to the demanding geographic conditions of the region became so exact that little scope for further elaboration was left to them. However, on the western extremity of the steppe, rainfall was comparatively abundant; agriculture could be successfully practiced in many localities; and a far more variegated and complex society was possible. Accordingly, it was on the European steppe that nomads were chronically capable of appropriating civilized habits of life; whereas farther east, the population perforce preserved an almost pure nomadism; and the goods of civilization came to them only as tribute, if at all.

[133] Cf. Wolfram Eberhard, "Der Prozess der Staatenbildung bei mittelasiatischen Nomadenvölker, *Forschungen und Fortschritte*, XXV (1949), 52–54.

[134] Cf. Herodotus IV, 78–80, where he tells how a Scythian king was slain by his subjects for being too Greek in his tastes and style of life.

[135] G. F. Hudson, *Europe and China* (London: Edward Arnold & Co., 1931), pp. 27–45; Gregory Borovka, *Scythian Art*, p. 29; Karl Jettmar, "The Altai before the Turks," 145–48, 154–56; George Vernadsky, *Ancient Russia* (New Haven: Yale University Press, 1943), pp. 56–74.

Yet the geographical severities of life in Mongolia were not without their compensations. Hardened by their harsh environment, the nomads of the eastern steppe came regularly to enjoy a margin of military superiority over their western neighbors, who were likely to lose the taste for war in proportion as they became increasingly enamored of the comforts of settled life. The result was a long series of nomad movements from east to west, beginning with the Scythian invasion of southern Russia toward the end of the eighth century B.C., coming to a climax with the great Mongol expansion of the thirteenth century A.D. and ending only in the eighteenth century, when Kalmuks fleeing from Chinese arms found refuge in Russia. During the two-and-a-half millennia between these extremes, ever-recurring, but basically similar nomad movements constituted one of the main threads of Eurasian political history. Tribe after tribe pushed west and south, displacing less war-like rivals, winning richer pastures for their flocks, or establishing themselves as overlords of settled agricultural populations. Dozens of others doubtless perished in the attempt.

*   *   *

Only after horse nomadry had diffused to the eastern margin of the Asian grasslands did the east-west socioeconomic gradient of the Eurasian steppe come fully into operation. This occurred more than a century after 500 B.C.; and the civilization of China did not assume definite and characteristic form until even later. The year 500 B.C., which I have taken as a symbol of the end of one era of world history and the beginning of another, is therefore not perfectly apt. But if we blur its fictitious sharpness, the date nonetheless marks a fundamental transformation. After about that time, the cultural leadership of the Middle East became a thing of the past; the dominance of Europe lay still far in the future; and for two thousand years between, the four major civilizations of Eurasia pursued their separate ways, often affected by what transpired beyond the frontier, sometimes borrowing cultural elements from one another, and repeatedly afflicted by nomad attacks. Yet from about 500 B.C. to 1500 A.D., despite ever-present challenges from outside, each civilization developed in the main according to an inner logic and momentum of its own.

An analysis of the age of Eurasian cultural balance will therefore constitute the second part of this book.

PART **II**

Eurasian
Cultural Balance
500 B.C.–1500 A.D.

General Introduction

Civilizations may be likened to mountain ranges, rising through aeons of geologic time, only to have the forces of erosion slowly but ineluctably nibble them down to the level of their surroundings. Within the far shorter time span of human history, civilizations, too, are liable to erosion as the special constellation of circumstances which provoked their rise passes away, while neighboring peoples lift themselves to new cultural heights by borrowing from or otherwise reacting to the civilized achievement. Yet it is only within the frame of geological paleontology and universal history that mountains and civilizations rise and pass away. On shorter time scales, they constitute enduring landmarks. How enduring civilizations are becomes clear if we impose this simile upon the cultural map of Eurasia as it existed in 500 B.C. and compare the results with the same map two thousand years later.

At the opening of the fifth century B.C., there existed four distinct regions of high culture in Eurasia. The most massive of these was the ancient and partially eroded plateau of the Middle East, where the debris of older cultures had leveled out into the somewhat tired cosmopolitanism of the Persian empire. Abutting upon this ancient center were two younger, more jagged ranges, one centering around the Aegean, with outlying spurs in Italy and Sicily, the other occupying the Indus and Ganges valleys of northern India. Far to the east and more nearly isolated lay the Chinese cultural highland, still rising toward the characteristic forms of its maturity.

Two thousand years later, the physiognomy of Eurasia was recognizably the same. The four major areas of high culture were still there, each considerably enlarged in territorial extent and altered internally in important respects, but in fundamental structure conforming to lines apparent two millenia previously. This persistence across some eighty generations testified to the reality of a loose but real cultural balance within Eurasia, and appropriately defines an era of world history.

The balance was always precarious, especially in the Middle East, where three of the four Eurasian civilizations abutted upon one another, while the barbarian reservoir of the steppe lay just to the north. In this fulcral region the major historical dramas of our two-thousand-year period played themselves out. First Hellenism, under Alexander and his successors, took the offensive, and for a time even seemed to threaten Oriental civilization with obliteration. Hellenism was simultaneously winning far more enduring successes in Europe, where, under the Roman empire, an increasingly cosmopolitan, though still basically Hellenic civilization extended tentacles even to remotest Britain.

Before the expansion of Hellenism in the modified and mixed forms characteristic of the Roman empire came to a halt, reaction against it gained ground in the Middle East and led to an important infiltration of Oriental attitudes and ideas into the old heartland of Hellenism itself. Simultaneously, a powerful, though markedly less militant expansion of Indian civilization began to transform the Eurasian cultural balance. The propagation of Buddhism through central Asia and northeastward into China and Japan was one aspect of this expansion; another was the massive reception of Indian culture among the comparatively primitive societies of southern India and southeast Asia.[1]

With the beginning of the Moslem era, "Oriental reaction" took on a new vigor and velocity. Indeed, the Moslem reformulation of Middle Eastern civilization marked a reassertion of that region's ancient cultural primacy in Eurasia. Between 632 A.D., when Mohammed died, and about 1500 A.D., when western Europe decisively overtook and outflanked Islam, the Moslem world expanded steadily, though intermittently and not without local setbacks, at the expense of both Christendom and of Hinduism. Moreover, Moslems converted the African savanna and most of the Eurasian steppe, penetrated China via the caravan routes of central Asia, and simultaneously, by overseas ventures, spread local versions of Islamic culture into east Africa, southeast Asia, Indonesia, and the Philippines.

More than once, therefore, in the years from 500 B.C. to 1500 A.D., the ebb and flow of the frontiers between Middle Eastern, Indian, and Hellenic civilization threatened to upset the fourfold cultural balance of Eurasia. Yet the dynamism first of Hellenism, then of Indian civilization, and finally of Islam never quite succeeded in destroying that balance; nor did the blending of elements derived from the separate but adjacent civilizations of western Eurasia ever obscure the essential continuity of the three separate traditions.

The vast mass of China lay outside the fulcral area of the ecumene. In addition, between about 600 and 1000 A.D., civilized styles of life began to take distinctive new forms in Japan, western Europe, and Russia. Due to their marginal locations, these four societies escaped the full impact of the disturb-

---

[1] The dual front of this Indian expansion closely resembled the earlier duality of Hellenic expansion. Thus, the Indian imprint upon China and Japan resembled the Hellenic imprint on the Orient—superficial even when fertile in provoking new departures; whereas the imprint of both societies upon their barbarian flank—Hellenism westward into Europe via the Mediterranean, and India southward and eastward via the Bay of Bengal—was far deeper, since local cultural models were but weak rivals for such attractive civilizations to overbear. The parallel may be completed by pointing to the fact that just as weak echoes of Hellenism (in Buddhist garb for the most part) reached China, so also echoes of Indian styles of piety seem to have been incorporated into the Hellenic world disguised in Christian dress.

ances generated in the main cultural storm centers of the age; yet none was entirely isolated, and each of them clearly tended to expand geographically. Thus, the Chinese style of life pushed southward and inland and developed colonial regions in Korea, Annam, Tibet, and Turkestan. Japanese culture, itself semi-dependent on China, spread northwestward through the Japanese archipelago. During the same period, western European civilization moved eastward across the Elbe, northward to Scandinavia, westward to the Celtic fringes of Atlantic Europe, and southward into Spain and Italy. Crusading Europeans even attempted, though with only transitory success, to establish a colonial sphere overseas in the Levant and along the Aegean and Black Sea coasts. Russian expansion was less spectacular, for the initial centers of piracy and trade around which the Russian state developed were, from the very beginning, widely scattered along the Russian rivers. Russian expansion during these centuries therefore consisted of massive but unobtrusive pioneering, in the course of which agriculturalists penetrated from initial lodgments on the river banks into the wide forest spaces of the east European plain.

These processes coincided with the continued expansion and territorial consolidation of the Moslem and Indian civilizations nearer the center of the continent. As a result, the geographical gaps between the separate Eurasian civilizations narrowed or even closed, and the density of contact among them tended clearly, if sporadically, to increase. After the second century B.C., for example, Chinese and Indian penumbras overlapped in the area formerly (and appropriately) called Indochina; and a few centuries thereafter, as we have just seen, a Moslem strand was added to the cultural interchanges passing through the southern oceans.

Two other highways linked the major civilizations of Eurasia: (1) the ancient path from oasis to oasis through central Asia, along which regular caravans began to pass in the second century B.C. when for the first time a chain of imperial states organized, policed, and taxed the so-called Silk Road between China and the Levant; and (2) the newer but nonetheless ancient route across the open grassland of the steppe, where nomad tribesmen sometimes plundered and sometimes traded with their southerly civilized neighbors.

Traffic along these different routes varied from time to time, and so did the significance of the cultural interchange resulting from such traffic. In general, except for the shifting of cultural frontiers in the fulcral area as a result of military action, borrowing among the civilizations of Eurasia was selective and spontaneous and of comparatively minor significance. As long as each of the four major civilizations remained roughly on a level with the others, civilized men rarely saw reason to abandon the traditions of their fathers in favor of outlandish novelty. Only when foreign conquest or internal decay severely threatened their established institutions did the bearers of any of the four main civilized traditions exhibit more far-reaching receptivity to alien ways.

The northernmost highway between the civilizations of Eurasia, running through the steppe, was of rather more importance than the others in promoting cultural change. This was because nomads continued to offer a serious military threat to all the agricultural populations within reach of their bow-shot, until after the middle of the seventeenth century. Any local weakness opened a path for raiding or conquest, even at comparatively very long range. Thus eastern Europe, China, the Middle East, and northwest India were overrun repeatedly; and even the remote and forested European Far West from time to time felt the sting of unusually far-ranging steppe warriors like those who followed Attila the Hun.

Nomad conquest was seldom of great significance in itself, since the barbarians hastened to adopt as much as they could of the culture of their civilized subjects. Yet nomad infiltration and repeated conquest did sometimes provoke far-reaching changes. This was particularly true in the Middle East, where Turkish domination transformed Islamic society after about 1000 A.D. and provoked a fresh burst of military expansion that carried the faith of Mohammed deep into both Europe and India. In addition, steppe peoples sometimes created new cultural compounds by mingling elements drawn from separate civilized traditions. Thus the nomad empire of Genghis Khan brought China more firmly and intimately than before into the circle of Eurasian civilizations; while the Ottoman Turks in Europe and the Moguls in India more or less consciously commingled Islamic with indigenous cultural traditions on a wholesale scale.

The Eurasian cultural balance, 500 B.C to 1500 A.D., was therefore land-centered. Each civilization, in addition to staving off internal disruption and civilized rivals, had perpetually to maintain a frontier guard against nomad harassment. Contacts by sea remained comparatively unimportant.

*   *   *

About the beginning of the Christian era, civilized societies took form in Peru and Mexico. As compared with their Eurasian contemporaries, these late growths remained always puny, analogous in many interesting ways to the cultures that flourished in Mesopotamia, Egypt, and the Indus Valley in the third millennium B.C. In the larger context of world history, therefore, the Amerindian civilizations developed too late to stand a chance against European aggression. In this sense, Amerindian civilizations were abortive and enter only passively and as victims into the story of the rise of the West.

The same may be said of the pre-Moslem cultures of Africa. By the seventh century A.D. or thereabouts, several societies were moving toward protocivilization in the west African savanna south of the Sahara; and a little later, others followed suit along the highland spine of east Africa. These cultures were never independent of the main civilizations of Eurasia; and they never attained a level permitting them to stand for long against the Moslem and European assaults that converged upon them after the fifteenth century.

As for the other habitable continent, Australia, it apparently remained entirely insulated from the circle of interacting civilizations until the eighteenth century A.D.

The problem of how to present what is inherently a very complex story in an intelligible form, while doing no more than minimal injustice to facts, is far more formidable in this middle section of *The Rise of the West* than it was in the first or will be in the third section, which deal with periods when the grain of world history ran predominantly outward from a single cultural center.

During the era of Eurasian cultural balance, no such simplicity existed. Each of the four major civilizations developed more or less freely along its own lines. Cultural influences and mutual stimulus ran criss-cross through the barbarian world and between the major civilizations. How can one reduce such a complex pattern to the single thread of verbal discourse?

My solution has been to describe first and at greatest length the major center or centers of disturbance to the cultural balance of Eurasia in successive periods of time, and then to turn attention to marginal areas, describing their development more summarily. Such a procedure may magnify the role of the Middle East and of its twin adjuncts, the eastern Mediterranean and northern India; for it was here that the frontiers of rival civilizations marched with one another in such a fashion that changes, when they became unusually rapid or extensive, threatened to upset the fourfold cultural balance of the Old World. Perhaps, in the longest view of human history, these disturbances within the fulcral area of Eurasian civilization were less important than the inexorable, if not entirely uninterrupted, encroachment of civilizations upon barbarism. It was this encroachment which built up the mass and internal variety of the separate civilizations of the world and increased the frequency of contact among them, preparing the way for the spectacular unification of the globe which has occurred during the past three or four centuries.

Yet to put the expansion of separate civilizations in the forefront and organize world history around this theme would create other difficulties. In particular, whenever the geographical spheres of two or more civilizations collided or overlapped, an awkward choice between repetition and distortion would regularly present itself. Moreover, to emphasize the separateness of each civilization and treat their contacts and collisions as subordinate (or even accidental) would obscure a major source—perhaps, even in this age, *the* major source—of social change within the separate civilizations themselves, *i.e.*, the stimulus of alien contact.

Therefore, Part II is organized along lines that seem merely the less unsatisfactory of two unsatisfactory alternatives· that is, to keep the balance of cultures always in mind and treat of its successive disturbances as exemplified in the separate histories of separate civilized societies.

CHAPTER VI

The Expansion of Hellenism 500-146 B.C.

The Greek style of civilized life, as organized and expressed within the master institution of the polis, occupied a very small geographical area at the beginning of the fifth century B.C. Even within the narrow limits of Greece itself, a landlocked region such as Arcadia was only doubtfully civilized; and Thessaly was but a twilight zone, to the north and west of which lay Greek-speaking barbarism. Several hundred years later, a much modified Hellenism had spread through all the Mediterranean coastlands and penetrated Europe as far as the Tweed, Rhine, and Danube. Elements of this same Hellenism had been imposed upon the anciently civilized Middle East and had filtered into India, while faint but recognizable echoes were beginning to reverberate in distant China.

This was a remarkable career for a style of life which had been geographically so restricted in 500 B.C. Indeed, the disturbance of the Eurasian cultural balance wrought by an expanding Hellenism may be regarded as the central historical fact of the years between 500 B.C. and 200 A.D. Yet the processes of expansion involved both intermixture with other traditions and a far-reaching sociological transformation of Hellenism itself, with the result that after the fourth century B.C., some of its initial *élan* began to abate.

When the original polis shell had been left behind, a new Hellenic cosmopolitanism arose, incorporating and indeed developing further the devices of social co-ordination which had first evolved in the "great society" of ancient Mesopotamia. The political and sociological structure of Greek civilization thus gradually assimilated itself to more ancient Oriental patterns. As this happened, many of the distinguishing emphases of Hellenic culture lost their

254

vigor, to be replaced more and more by ideas and attitudes akin to, and sometimes demonstrably derived from, the older Oriental civilization of the Middle East.

The definitive Roman conquest of Greece (146 B.C.) conveniently marks the midpoint in the career of Hellenism. Oriental reaction had not yet gathered headway; and Hellenism's farthest penetration of both the Far West and the Far East was then still in the future. Yet the spirit went out of Greek civilization when the eagles of Rome finally destroyed all but the pretense of local polis sovereignty. In the original hearth of classical culture there remained only empty, echoing political forms, a depopulated countryside, together with an impoverished urban demos and a polite, gentlemanly high culture, more concerned with fashioning a tolerable way of life for men who had little left to live for than with truth, beauty, freedom, or any of the other ideals which once had found such reckless and exquisite expression among the Greeks.

It seems appropriate, therefore, to break off this chapter halfway through Hellenism's career, at the point where its initial intense cultural individuality dissolved back into more normal but less attractive sociological and intellectual patterns.

A. THE FLOWERING OF GREEK CULTURE
500–336 B.C.

1. INTRODUCTION

When Xerxes, son of Darius, mounted the Persian throne in 485 B.C., he inherited two important military-political problems. One, and the more pressing, was revolt in Egypt, which his armies put down only after severe fighting. The second was to secure his westernmost frontier, along the Aegean coast, against chronic instability resulting from the refusal of a backward part of the Greek world, lying across that sea, to recognize Persian overlordship. Moreover, Xerxes had a military tradition to sustain: his predecessors, Cyrus, Cambyses, and Darius, had all been mighty conquerors, and Darius had already committed Persian prestige to the project of bringing the Greeks to heel. Therefore, as soon as he had crushed the Egyptians, Xerxes marshaled his armies and fleets for the conquest of Greece.

Many Greeks, including the well-informed and sapient priests of Delphi, concluded that the petty communities of Greece stood no chance against the might of Persia. Yet a ragged coalition of scarcely more than twenty Greek cities, hindered by divided counsels and hesitant strategy, succeeded against all reasonable expectation in driving the Persians back. In the years that followed, Greeks under Athenian leadership took the offensive and in a series of campaigns lasting until 448 B.C. freed all the Greek (and some non-Greek) cities of the Aegean from Persian control.

The effect upon the Greeks was as extraordinary as the victory itself. Sparta, previously the leading power of Greece, withdrew into conservative immobility, having glimpsed the dangers to her domestic social order inherent in empire.[1] Athens, however, chose an exactly opposite course, risking everything, refusing nothing. Before the Persian Wars, Athens had not ranked among the most powerful and prosperous of Greek cities. After the wars, and largely because of them, Athens became the focus of all that was most active in Greek civilization. Economically, Athenians dominated the trade of the eastern Mediterranean and Black Sea regions; politically, they formed and led a formidable confederation of cities, which successfully combated the Persians and seemed for a time on the verge of dominating the entire Greek world; culturally, their literature and art eclipsed anything achieved elsewhere in Greece and gave to all Hellenism a perfected expression which gradually became standard wherever Greek was spoken. Indeed, the career of Athens during the half-century between the expulsion of Persia from Europe and the outbreak of the Peloponnesian War in 431 B.C. was probably the most sharply concentrated "golden age" in history.[2]

The key to Athens' extraordinary career lay in her fleet. This had been created shortly before the Persian Wars, when Themistocles persuaded the Athenian assembly to finance naval construction with money accruing to the polis from newly discovered Attic lodes of silver. Two hundred triremes of the latest design allowed Athens to play the decisive role in the war, for the defeat of the Persian navy at Salamis (480 B.C.) forced the larger part of the Persian army to withdraw into Asia for lack of supplies.[3] The Athenian fleet, moreover, made it possible to carry the war across the Aegean and liberate the Greek cities of Asia Minor from Persian domination. In addition, through its control of the Aegean and adjacent waters, the fleet attracted the goods of the eastern Mediterranean to Athens' port of Piraeus.

The fleet had two further consequences for the Athenian polis. First, it made Athens securely democratic and incurably aggressive. In the fleet, the poorest citizens played the main role, since the rowers who drove the ships into battle needed no equipment but trained muscles.[4] Consequently, the democratic

---

[1] Cf. the career of the Spartan King Pausanius, who, having commanded the Greek forces at the battle of Plataea (479 B.C.), dreamed of exploiting the victory by building a kingdom for himself, but whose plans in fact miscarried so that he died miserably of starvation when the Spartans walled up the temple in which he had taken sanctuary.

[2] Fewer than a quarter of a million persons took part in Athens' "golden age." Adult male citizens of Athens probably numbered between 35,000 and 50,000 on the eve of the Peloponnesian War, and the total population of Attica was probably between 250,000 and 350,000, of which somewhat less than half were slaves and disfranchised foreigners. Cf. Julius Beloch, *Die Bevölkerung der griechisch-römischen Welt* (Leipzig: Duncker & Humblot, 1886), pp. 99–101; A. W. Gomme, *The Population of Athens in the Fifth and Fourth Centuries B.C.* (Oxford: Basil Blackwell, 1957), Appendix: "The Citizen Population of Athens during the Peloponnesian War."

[3] Cf. George B. Grundy, *The Great Persian War* (London: John Murray, 1901), for a fascinating reconstruction of Herodotus' sometimes confused narrative.

[4] Training was, however, of the utmost importance, for only by pulling in time and obeying commands rhythmically and in unison could a ship outstrip and outmaneuver its opponents. Since Athenian naval tactics treated the vessel itself as a projectile and sought always to ram the enemy athwartships, everything depended on the speed and maneuverability of each ship and upon accurate co-ordination of the movement of separate ships into effective fleet formations.

The training and rhythmic exertion of rowing was generally comparable to the rhythm and training required by the phalanx. As a matter of fact, ships' crews required a somewhat higher discipline, for

forms of Athenian government were enormously strengthened when Athenians too poor to equip themselves as hoplites acquired a vital military role as rowers. Moreover, the aggressiveness of the Athenian polis was enhanced when rowers' pay and plunder became, for a surprisingly large proportion of the Athenian citizenry, a necessary or at least highly desirable addition to family resources.[5] Against this background, Athens' ruthless and incessant naval enterprise, which kept the entire Greek world in turmoil from 480 to 404 B.C., becomes intelligible.

Second, as Athenian citizens encountered foreign places and strange customs in the course of their ventures overseas, and as strangers crowded in upon the city which had become the mercantile mistress of the eastern Mediterranean, traditional beliefs and attitudes underwent rapid erosion. Familiar institutions and the established articulation of society as between noble and commoner, farmer and landless man, free and slave, were transformed, and new ideas about human life and man's place in the universe found ready lodgment when so many familiar landmarks were obviously shifting.

Yet for half a century, until the hardships and eventual defeat of the Peloponnesian War (431–404 B.C.) took the bloom off Athenian self-confidence and brought into the open conflicts which in more prosperous days had remained submerged, the abandonment of old ways and attitudes must have seemed to many Athenians more of a liberation than a loss. The niggling poverty of citizens who lacked sufficient land to live upon was relieved by the new wealth from imperial plunder, from tribute, and from trade. There seemed no limits to what the Athenians could achieve. The dedication of each citizen to the task of forwarding the greatness and glory of Athens seemed a satisfactory and sufficient ideal for human striving, spacious enough to develop and employ the best talents of all citizens of every rank and condition. In short, for a few brief but vibrant decades, Athens' successes demon-

---

each rower, facing backward, had to act blindly as part of a machine and could not pause to see where the ship might be going, or what danger threatened. The discipline of the rowing benches also lacked the direct appeal to instinctive ferocity inherent in hand-to-hand battle. Yet in spite of these differences, which all tended to emphasize the importance of subordination to a captain and steersman, the rowers' training, like that of the hoplite, clearly tended to identify individual aspiration with communal success.

There was, however, one vital novelty. As long as the phalanx was the only important arm of the polis, military training and sentiments of polis solidarity tended to coincide. When a second military arm arose, a potential fissure opened between hoplites and rowers. As long as the Athenian fleet operated mainly overseas, and its victories did not directly affect the farmers who constituted the backbone of the phalanx, this fissure was unimportant. Only when, in the course of the Peloponnesian War, the aggressiveness of Athens, concentrated mainly in its fleet, provoked disaster for the farmer-hoplites through the occupation of Attica by enemy forces did the tension between propertied hoplite and propertyless rower become acute.

[5] Rapid increase in population left the small Athenian farmer no choice but to look abroad for supplemental income, since a farm adequate in one generation could not begin to support the families of several sons. Aristotle, *Constitution of Athens*, 24, calculates that at the time of the Peloponnesian War the public payroll amounted to 20,000. Not all the rowers were citizens; yet if one takes the range of 35,000–50,000 as the likely total of Athenian citizens in 431 B.C., when their numbers were at the maximum, it becomes obvious how generally the Athenian demos had come to depend on annual naval expeditions to piece out the family budget. The intensity of population pressure is further illustrated by the fact that some 10,000 families emigrated from Attica to colonies (cleruchies) between 479 and 431 B.C.

strated to the satisfaction of nearly all Athenians that the inherited legal structure and ethical values of their polis constituted an adequate frame for their
lives. Yet within this still unquestioned framework, new contacts with the
wide and variegated world provoked reflective minds to speculation, challenging them to interpret afresh and for themselves the nature of the universe
and of man. With emotions tied securely to a familiar social frame, and with
minds freed from commitment to any particular view, the Athenians were
thus ideally situated for cultural creativity. The admiration of all subsequent
ages attests the use they made of their opportunity.

2. POLITICAL EVOLUTION, 500–336 B.C.

The political history of the Greek city-states in the fifth and fourth centuries
B.C. offers a classic example of how dispersed sovereignty, operating within a
balance-of-power system, may evolve through a series of unstable alliances
toward the hegemony of a single marchland state.[6]

The sovereign polis won its greatest successes in the Persian Wars. The surprising outcome of Xerxes' invasion (480 B.C.) no doubt proved to many—as
it did to the historian Herodotus (*ca.* 484–435 B.C.)—that under the gods, free
men organized into city-states need fear no military danger from without and
could be trusted to develop a more perfect individual manhood and a more
glorious collective greatness than could possibly arise in a politically authoritarian society.[7] Yet a paradox lay just beneath the surface, for it soon became
evident that the energetic pursuit of the greatness of one polis involved the
eclipse of the freedom and greatness of its neighbors. Even in the sixth century, Sparta's hegemony in the Peloponnesus had raised the question of what
legitimate limits there might be to the freedom of each polis in foreign (*i.e.,*
interpolis) affairs. This question became acute after 466 B.C., when Athens
began to convert what had started as a voluntary league for defense against
Persia into an empire of tribute-paying subjects.[8]

Thus Athenian imperialism very quickly and drastically pointed up an elemental flaw in the polis ideal as inherited from the sixth century. Nor did
Athens' defeat solve the dilemma; for although Sparta and her allies entered

---

[6] A probable analogue to this development in the early history of Mesopotamia has been pointed out
above. I have no doubt that this constitutes a recurrent pattern in interstate politics, of which the world
has probably not yet seen the last. The Greek instance, nevertheless, can rightly claim a certain pride
of place, since the discursive charm of Herodotus' pages, the severe restraint of Thucydides' history,
and the practiced oratory of Demosthenes allow us to penetrate more fully and vividly into the critical
phases of this pattern of political evolution in Greece than is possible for any comparable development
in other times and places. This lends the study of classical Greek history a peculiar intellectual excitement and makes it, even for the relatively unimaginative mind, what Lord Acton wished all history to
be, "not a burden on the memory, but an illumination of the soul." John Emerich Edward Dalberg,
Lord Acton, *Lectures on Modern History* (London: Macmillan & Co., 1906), p. 317. Cf. A. J. Toynbee's
comments on the peculiar immediacy of classic Greece for modern minds in *The Tragedy of Greece*
(Oxford: Clarendon Press, 1921), pp. 8–15.

[7] This theme pervades Herodotus' book, but cf. particularly Demaratus' speech to Xerxes, VII,
102–4.

[8] Athens thus became, perhaps even in Athenian eyes, a "tyrant city," violating the freedom of the
Greeks which their fathers had defended so brilliantly at Salamis and Plataea. Cf. Pericles' words as
reported by Thucydides, ii, 63.

the Peloponnesian War (431–404 B.C.) with the professed purpose of restoring the freedom of the Greeks, the practical result was far different. After 404 B.C., victorious Sparta intervened in the affairs of other cities even more highhandedly than Athens had done; and Thebes and Macedon later did likewise. In truth, the separate sovereignty of scores of small city-states was no longer practicable in an age when great fleets and armies could be created and maintained by tribute and plunder. Yet even in the third and second centuries B.C., despite locally successful efforts at federal government, Greek particularism proved too strong to allow either stable union within or firm control from without. Only the crushing military superiority of Rome brought interpolis warfare to an end.

The Peloponnesian War hastened both the spread of Greek culture and its debilitation. What had started in 431 as a local war on the Greek mainland spread over a much wider area during the course of the fighting, as each side sought allies wherever it could. The Athenian empire was only brought down after Sparta had enlisted the military might of Persia against Athens. Other peripheral areas—Sicily and southern Italy, Thrace, Macedon, and Epirus—were also drawn into the war, sometimes becoming the scene of combat, often supplying mercenaries or providing strategic bases. Thus the courts of Persian satraps and of Thracian kings, the tribal councils of wild Epirotes, and the city assemblies of Sicily and southern Italy all blended into a single diplomatic-military balance of power, centered upon the Aegean. And since that same Aegean was the seat and center of the highest expression of Hellenic culture, strangers whom the war threw into contact with that civilization were all impressed by it in one way or another. Persian grandees like Cyrus the Younger, mercenary slingmen from barbarous Acarnania, Sicilian Greeks who enslaved the remnants of the Athenian expeditionary force and, according to legend, freed those who could recite the verses of Euripides: all these and others like them learned to know and admire aspects of the Athenian cultural achievement.

Yet within the heartland of Greek civilization, the Peloponnesian War was drastically disruptive of polis life. In many city-states, sentiments of solidarity among the citizens were strained, even destroyed, by the hardships and opportunities of the war. What happened cannot be better described than in Thucydides' own words:

. . . the whole Hellenic world was convulsed; struggles being everywhere made by the popular chiefs to bring in the Athenians, and by the oligarchs to introduce the Lacedaemonians [*i.e.*, Spartans]. In peace there would have been neither the pretext nor the wish to make such an invitation; but in war, with an alliance always at the command of either faction for the hurt of their adversaries and their own corresponding advantage, opportunities for bringing in the foreigner were never wanting to the revolutionary parties. . . .

Thus every form of iniquity took root in the Hellenic countries by reason of the troubles. The ancient simplicity into which honor so largely entered was laughed down and disappeared; and society became divided into camps in which no man trusted his fellow.[9]

[9] R. Crawley's translation, iii, 82, 83.

The Greek city-states never entirely recovered from such shattering experiences. In Athens after the war, an underlying suspicion and mutual dislike divided the few from the many, the rich from the poor;[10] and similar sentiments pervaded other Greek cities.

The old Periclean concept of citizenship, with its demands upon the whole man, could not be maintained. Individualism, political passivity, and the sense of personal alienation from the community all gained ground. The career of Xenophon (*ca.* 430–355 B.C.), an Athenian who ventured into the heart of Asia as a mercenary in the service of Cyrus the Younger and subsequently retired to an estate in the Peloponnesus, exemplifies the loosening of polis ties characteristic of the fourth century. The despairing epilogue to his history of Greece perhaps reflects a widespread weariness and confusion of mind among a generation for whom the old polis ideal could no longer seem valid and to whom no alternative moral or political order seemed conceivable. With regard to the battle of Mantinea (362 B.C.),[11] Xenophon wrote:

> The result of the battle was the exact opposite of that which everybody had expected . . . either side claimed the victory although neither could show the slightest gain in territory, allies or empire beyond what they had possessed before the battle. On the contrary, there was more unsettlement and disorder in Hellas after the battle than before it—but I do not propose to carry my narrative further and will leave the sequel to any other historian who cares to record it.[12]

In Athens, the only Greek polis about which we are tolerably well informed, the fourth century saw a growing specialization of the functions which in the fifth century had been united in the citizen body. Professional soldiers and generals increasingly took over military matters, as they had begun to do during the Peloponnesian War itself. Professional orators and demagogues gained control of the assembly. Financial specialists assumed the often difficult task of balancing the state budget.

Appeals to a bygone past and to the old glories of Athens still roused some echo among the Athenians; but even the eloquence of Demosthenes (d. 322 B.C.) did no more than fan a brief glow in dying embers. The tight-knit, parochial community of 500 B.C. had been transformed into a much looser, more cosmopolitan, and markedly less vigorous society. The extraordinary human energies that had been called into life during Athens' brief period of splendor could never be harnessed again. Yet the forms of cultural expression

---

[10] Landless citizens and those whose family farms were near the minimal size necessary for subsistence must have found it very difficult to endure the loss of income from military and imperial service which had helped to support their fathers in the fifth century. But population losses during the Peloponnesian War were heavy, and perhaps this helped to make it possible for the survivors to make do. Precautions were subsequently taken, e.g., by exposure of infants, to prevent the rapid population growth which had characterized the comparatively affluent days of imperial greatness. Cf. A. H. M. Jones, "The Social Structure of Athens in the Fourth Century B.C.," *Economic History Review*, VIII (1955), 141–55.

[11] *I.e.*, the battle which stalemated the brief Theban supremacy over Greece, and where Xenophon's son was killed.

[12] *Hellenica*, vii, 5. A. J. Toynbee (trans.), in *Greek Historical Thought* (New York: New American Library, 1953).

which emerged in Athens during the fifth century B.C. did live on as models for subsequent generations, thus giving to Hellenic civilization its permanent stamp and an extraordinary, perennial attractiveness.

3. THE PERFECTING OF GREEK CULTURAL FORMS

TRAGEDY. Although "goat songs," honoring the popular but somewhat disreputable god, Dionysus, were sung in a number of Greek cities in the archaic age, only Athens saw the development of a high art from this crude ritual. The individual genius of a handful of poets, together with the wealth which permitted elaborate staging, made this development possible. Equally important—and a good deal rarer in human history—was the wide-reaching rapport between playwright and public arising from the intensely cohesive character of Athenian society—a cohesion which the Dionysiac festival, like other public religious ceremonies, both expressed and renewed by the ritual act of the dramatic performance itself.

The religious character of their art gave the tragedians a conventional subject matter: what we call myth, but what the Greeks themselves regarded as ancient history, preserved by the poets in unsystematic and sometimes contradictory versions. The ritual from which tragedy developed also established important dramatic conventions: the chorus, masked actors, together with stylized music and choreography. Inability to reconstruct these latter aspects of Greek drama has led modern scholars to emphasize the playwrights' ideas; but the chief impact of the performance upon the original audiences must have arisen from the rhythms of music and dance, and the visual spectacle created by masked actors moving in front of painted stage sets.[13] Athenian tragedy was in fact enriched during the fifth century by a number of innovations along these lines. Sophocles, for example, is reputed to have introduced stage scenery painted to produce a three-dimensional illusion; and a new style of solo singing was associated with some of Euripides' later plays.[14] A parallel development, about which we happen to be adequately informed, was the increase in the number of actors simultaneously appearing on the stage and the corresponding decline in the importance of the chorus.

Such elaborations altered the Athenian tragic performances very substantially in the course of the fifth century; yet the highly conventionalized tradition remained essentially unbroken. Even the intellectually restless Euripides (484 or 480–406 B.C.) continued to draw the subject matter of his plays from the common stock of myths and retained the chorus and other inherited devices. In the early and middle years of the century, the traditional frame of Attic tragedy had allowed Aeschylus (525–456 B.C.) and Sophocles (495–406 B.C.) to speak their minds freely, while titillating the interest of their audiences with the alterations they brought to received convention. They were able thereby to liberate and deepen the tragic art, without shattering the

---

[13] Modern grand opera stripped of its music, costume, and scenery offers an approximate parallel to the Greek drama as we know it.

[14] D. W. Lucas, *The Greek Tragic Poets* (London: Cohen & West, 1950), pp. 41, 48.

ritual, religious links between themselves and their audiences. Apparently neither Aeschylus nor Sophocles felt any compunction about adjusting and reinterpreting incidents from familiar myths to suit their dramatic purposes, though traditional views of the relationships between gods and men remained central to the work of both. The moral and theological implications of their tragedies, which so exercise modern scholars, presumably remained incomprehensible to the majority of the audience; but this element was present to spice the occasion for the intellectually acute, while the familiar (if interestingly turned) plots of traditional and well-known stories, together with rhythm, song, and spectacle, delighted the ordinary citizen.

With Euripides, however, the tragic conventions began to chafe just because his intellectual world had drawn apart from that of most of his fellow citizens, so that he could no longer express his opinions freely and completely within traditional forms.[15] He relieved his feelings by sprinkling his plays with caricatures of gods and heroes, conceived in a spirit of mockery verging upon sacrilege.

With the opening of a gap between the intellectual elite and the rest of the citizenry, the possibility of tragedy as practiced by the great fifth-century playwrights of Athens disappeared. When the most sensitive minds could no longer share the ideas and attitudes of the community at large by enriching and reinterpreting popular notions in the light of their own personal experience and reflection, the public theater ceased to provide an adequate vehicle for the enunciation of high and serious ideas. Hence in the fourth century new tragedies ceased to be produced, and revivals of the classic works occupied the stage instead. Contemporary poets concentrated on comedy, a dramatic form disdaining serious ideas and emphasizing wit, spectacle, character, and suspense plots of a sort which continued to attract the interest of all classes of the Athenian public.[16] Exploration of religious and moral ideas, which had previously been conducted in public by poets and playwrights, was transferred to the private competence of closeted philosophers.

PHILOSOPHY.   Athenian philosophy fell heir to tragedy. No one can read Plato's early dialogues and fail to recognize their dramatic quality. Indeed, the dialogue form[17] is only an outward manifestation of Plato's deep affinity with the drama, for he carried into the fourth century the discussion of the sort of political and ethical problems with which the great tragedians of the fifth had wrestled. Plato's intellectual seriousness was possible because, unlike Euripides, he no longer had to please a mass audience, but could address himself to a self-

[15] Despite his posthumous popularity, which eclipsed that of his great predecessors, tradition holds that in his own day Euripides was not very well received by the Athenian public. His ideas, no doubt, were too iconoclastic, too far removed from the ancestral stock of piety and respectable convention to have popular appeal.

[16] The striking contrast between the scurrilous political lampoons of "Old Comedy" and the almost complete absence of political personalities and topics from the comedy which came in after the Peloponnesian War also illustrates the decline of the polis as an all-embracing—or nearly all-embracing—frame for personal existence, and the development of a far more spacious private sphere of life than any that had been recognized in Pericles' day.

[17] Plato did not invent the dialogue. He did, probably, put it to new uses. Cf. Leon Robin, *La Pensée hellénique, des origines à Épicure* (Paris: Presses Universitaires, 1942), p. 111.

selected intellectual elite. Such an audience was by its nature emancipated from the limits of any particular polis. Wherever there were sensitive and thoughtful minds, familiar with the Attic tongue, Plato's dialogues could count upon a sympathetic reception.

Athens had not been a center of early Greek thought. But about the middle of the fifth century, the city became a leading resort of a new kind of teacher, the sophist. Sophists instructed pupils in the skills and knowledge needed for getting ahead in a democratic polis. Their great contribution to the development of Greek philosophy—a contribution which they shared with the Eleatics of Italy—was the discovery that language was susceptible of analysis and manipulation, according to self-evident logical rules.[18] To be sure, the precise nature of the sophists' teaching is difficult to determine since only small scraps of their works survive, and Plato gave them all a bad name. Only by observing the impact of sophistic style and method upon men like Thucydides and Euripides, and by a feat of the imagination running beyond what can be proven from any surviving source, can one begin to grasp the initial sophistic impact upon the bright young men of Athens who came of age between 450 and 431 B.C.

The sophists undertook to teach the arts whereby an ambitious man, even of ignoble birth, might learn to influence the assembly and lead the people by virtue of a proper use of words. But, beyond that, the sophists claimed to have a method of verbal reasoning according to precise rules of argument, whereby a man might hope to unravel all the mysteries of the universe, given the necessary acuity and an appropriate store of information. To hear and understand the radical ramifications of the famous phrase, "Man is the measure of all things," from the mouth of Protagoras (*ca.* 480–410 B.C.) himself; to discover the parochial limits of traditional Athenian concepts of the gods, the world, and men's place in it; personally to grasp after new truths to replace the unexamined superstitions of the past: all this must have been in the highest degree exciting, and, at first, liberating. The acute and passionate mind of Thucydides is the best evidence available to us of how such teachings exposed new dimensions of human reality to view and inspired a new rigor and subtlety in the definition of truth about human affairs.

Yet by the end of the fifth century, the disruptive consequences of verbal rationalism had become clearly apparent. The sophists had called the bases of polis life into question. If law was a conspiracy of the weak against the strong, and if morality was no more than a man-made convention, as some of the sophists held, then clearly the sentiments of self-dedication and sacrifice for the good of the polis—so strenuously inculcated by former generations—were the merest self-delusion. A real man would see through such fictions and conduct himself in such a way as to indulge his own "natural" impulses so far

---

[18] The Eleatics—Parmenides (b. *ca.* 514 B.C.) and his disciple Zeno (*ca.* 480–430 B.C.)—tied themselves into a series of spectacularly logical knots. One may doubt whether the paradoxes to which their reasoning led were ever accepted as an entirely adequate statement of truth, even by the originators themselves. Nevertheless, their self-conscious intellectual method made the simple assertions of the earlier Ionians and of Pythagoras seem crudely inadequate.

as it was safe to do so, without regard for common goals or public good. Such doctrines appealed especially to the Athenian upper classes, who were required to contribute substantial sums year after year for the maintenance of the fleet and yet were outvoted by the demos when it came to making political and military decisions. The sophists' doctrines therefore provided the oligarchs with a convenient justification for the violence and chicanery they used to overthrow the democracy in 411 B.C. and again in 404 B.C.

Democracy was soon restored; but the problem of finding some system of values to replace the old naïve identification of self and polis remained. The upper classes, distrustful of the populace and distrusted by it, could no longer accord uncritical loyalty to the city and its leaders. Nor was a political career open to anyone who would not flatter the people and truckle to popular prejudices. How then could the good life be achieved? And how should the individual and the community be governed? These were the questions to which Plato (427–347 B.C.) addressed himself and from which he never escaped. He remained always a polis man, an Athenian, wistfully watching the course of events from the sidelines. By birth (he claimed descent from Athens' kings) and education he felt himself qualified to govern, but by temperament he was incapable of compromising his principles in order to win political influence.

Socrates (469–399 B.C.) had in some measure anticipated Plato's alienation from the Athenian polis. He spent his mature years criticizing, with devastating verbal agility, the ignorance and presumption of the democratic leaders of Athens; and in the end they retaliated by executing him for corrupting the youth and for impiety. Yet Socrates served his city as hoplite and as magistrate; his acts, if not his opinions, fitted the standards of the day, as those of Plato never could.

Plato's portrayal of his revered master is so compelling that our conception of the historical Socrates is perhaps permanently and irreparably colored by it. Certainly, Xenophon's account and Aristophanes' burlesque contrast oddly with Plato's portrait. Probably Socrates' own contemporaries were in doubt as to what his ideas really were, since he specialized in exploding other men's pretensions to wisdom and was loath to commit himself to positive affirmations. Nevertheless, in general, it is clear that Socrates was a radical conservative. In politics, he was conservative in holding, like any oligarch, that Athens should be ruled by wise men and good; he was radical in defining wisdom and goodness as compounded of more than aristocratic birth and gentlemanly education. Intellectually, he was conservative in believing that right and wrong were absolutes, not man-made conventions. Yet he was radical in his attempt to subject these absolutes to rational definition and demonstration. Similar paradoxes informed his religion: conservative in his reverence for oracles and outward forms of piety—"A cock to Asclepius"[19]—he yet heard voices and experienced trances and rejected belief in the traditional gods of his country.

[19] *Phaedo*, 118.

In all these respects, Socrates' conservatism was superficial, his radicalism profound. Plato carried the same paradox further; and the radicalism of his cure for the ills of the Athenian polis, as set forth in the *Republic* and even in the tamer version of his old age, the *Laws*, was so thoroughgoing that one does not always recognize the conservative character of the ideal polis to which his radical speculations led. Yet the tripartite and mainly hereditary class division of the *Republic* corresponded closely to the division of sixth-century Greek society between slaves and foreigners who labored, citizens who fought for the polis, and an aristocracy that guided the state.

Although the political problem always remained central for Plato personally, other aspects of his philosophy attracted more attention in later times and may even have done so in his own day. Perhaps he founded the Academy in the hope of training a new generation of statesmen, acquainted with truth and therefore able to reform Athens and other Greek states.[20] Yet in his maturer years, in such dialogues as the *Timaeus, Philebus, Theaetetus*, and *Parmenides*, it looks as though the frustrated politician had begun to find a dim substitute for political action by making intellectual speculation and synthesis an end in itself. In any event, more than any man before him, Plato brought together diverse intellectual strands from different parts of the Greek world. He did so with a consummate artistry that few have ever equaled and gave to subsequent Greek and indeed to all European philosophy its central themes and problems, as well as much of its working vocabulary.

Succeeding generations naturally emphasized particular aspects of Plato's thought at the expense of others. Later antiquity seized upon the recurrent dualism of passages in which Plato posed antitheses between soul and body, Ideas and their objects, knowledge and opinion, Being and Becoming. In this version, Platonism entered early and deeply into the Christian tradition, within which subsequent European civilization matured. Consequently, the transcendent world of Ideas, though for Plato himself probably never an altogether satisfactory concept and one he seemingly rejected in later life,[21] became the heart of historical Platonism, and as such influenced the minds of men through many centuries. In this (probably distorted) fashion, Plato deserves to rank only a little behind the greatest teachers of mankind—Buddha, Confucius, Christ, and Mohammed.[22]

---

[20] Cf. David Grene, *Man in His Pride: A Study in the Political Philosophy of Thucydides and Plato* (Chicago: University of Chicago Press, 1950), p. 100. The parallel between the career of Confucius and of Plato is striking. In life, both were frustrated politicians, who after their deaths became the revered teachers of an imperial bureaucracy.

The speculative element was of course larger in Plato, as one would expect from the character of earlier Greek thought. Yet his practical success, though less enduring than Confucius', was nevertheless real. Four or five centuries after Plato's death, it became usual for the rulers of the Hellenized world to train themselves for office by acquiring a smattering of philosophy, which though not usually Platonic in a direct sense, nonetheless derived from the Platonic mold. Before they began to rule China, Confucians may well have departed from the authentic teachings of their master fully as much as Stoics did from those of Plato.

[21] *Parmenides*, 129–37.

[22] Resemblances between elements of Platonic and of Buddhist doctrine—e.g., otherworldliness, treating the world of sense as a veil between man and a transcendental truth—raise the question whether

The very richness, complexity, and subtlety of Plato's thought meant that his writings appealed to a limited audience of the well-educated and intellec-tually acute. In and especially after Plato's day, the philosophers' audience consisted mainly of landowners who, having lost their traditional role as polis leaders, frequently found themselves at loose ends. Such persons could not rest content with old pieties. The intellectual enlightenment which sophism had brought to the Greek world made such a course impossible. Philosophy, therefore, was called upon, more and more insistently and at the same time insidiously, to serve as a substitute way of life and code of conduct for gentle-men who had lost both their ancestral social function and their forefathers' religous convictions. In such a milieu, the tension between the impulse to fol-low reason wheresoever it might lead and the will to believe in a humanly hospitable universe was never far from the surface.

The tension between these opposites explains much of the subsequent his-tory of Greek philosophy. At first, confidence in reason and a voracious urge to absorb, organize, understand, and interpret wider and wider bodies of information dominated. The skepticism of Plato's successors in the Academy, and the grandiose system-building of Plato's pupil Aristotle, competed and collided, yet shared a common confidence in reason as the only satisfactory guide to the mysteries of the world. The absorption of fresh information speedily led to specialization: the separation of science from philosophy, and of philology, rhetoric, and criticism from other branches of learning. The residue, professionally labeled philosophy, gradually lost touch with these related fields. Consequently, philosophers insulated themselves from the stim-ulus which new data had provided to their predecessors. Their professional concerns began to shrink toward the promulgation of a code of gentlemanly ethics, buttressed by whatever supporting metaphysical, physical, or episte-mological doctrine seemed necessary. As this happened—a process substan-tially complete by the second century B.C.—Greek philosophy became a mere surrogate for religion—and not even a very satisfactory surrogate, because of the denial of emotion which characterized all the Hellenistic schools.

But before philosophy thus distilled itself into noble and not unheroic codes of ethics, the work of Aristotle (384–322 B.C.) had insinuated a corpus of learning and of robust common sense into Greek thought which rivaled the achievement of Plato himself. Unlike his great teacher, Aristotle was not a polis man; he was a professional thinker. The course of Athenian political development was for him an interesting subject of study; it did not seriously

---

there was any historical contact between Indian and Greek speculative traditions before the Hellenistic age. No positive evidence exists to support such a hypothesis. But cf. E. J. Urwick, *The Message of Plato* (London: Methuen & Co., 1920), pp. 15–42; K. A. Nilakanta Sastri, "Ancient Indian Contacts with Western Lands," *Diogenes*, No. 29 (1959), pp. 49–50. Absence of any surviving record of the wander-ings of some Indian sage into the Greek world, or of the return of some curious Greek from India with reports of Indian philosophical and religious speculation, does not in itself prove that contacts may not have occurred. On the other hand, one may argue that the disinherited aristocrats, Buddha and Plato, not unnaturally directed their thoughts along roughly parallel lines, since both grew up in approximately similar circumstances, when local republican government and aristocratic society were being disrupted by new social and political forces.

engage his emotions. After all, he was not an Athenian and had little more than accidental ties to the Thracian city of his birth, Stagira. Thus Aristotle began his work where Plato had most reluctantly ended—aloof from any polis, pursuing knowledge as an end in itself.

The scope and architectonic grandeur of Aristotle's work command admiration. He came close to summing up all the knowledge of his time; and his sturdy rationalism makes some of Plato's flights of fancy seem childish. And yet he has none of Plato's scintillation, none of Plato's poetry: one seems to confront not a man so much as a thinking machine. Ironically, the immensity of Aristotle's achievement (together with the flat and often crabbed prose of his surviving works) made his subsequent influence less than Plato's. Within his own system of terms, Aristotle had given nearly all the answers. Disciples could only admire the works of the master, while filling in crevices he had left unexplored, as Theophrastus did with his history of plants. Live issues and burning problems had all received Aristotle's cool and reasonable answers; nothing really important was left for his disciples to do; and in the course of a few centuries, having nothing to discuss, they simply dispersed, allowing Aristotle's works to fall into an undeserved neglect.

In sum: the initial liberation of Greek speculation took place within the polis frame, first with the Ionians, then acquiring new impetus and a widened variety of problems from the work of the Eleatics and sophists. With Socrates and Plato, philosophical speculation began to transcend the polis frame; with Aristotle, it spread its wings to survey the whole world, unhampered and but little influenced by the polis community from which it had sprung. This suprapolis intellectual tradition, however, soon encapsulated itself within a new, if loosely defined, community: the community of intellectually inclined gentlemen of the Hellenistic world. Philosophers, losing all real hope of transforming or much affecting public affairs, concentrated attention more and more upon personal life and manners.

Philosophy's golden age was the period of its emergence from the polis framework, when the techniques of logical argument had already been perfected and a copious diet of new information presented itself for assimilation. Yet as information became too abundant, specialization and skepticism developed. Reacting against such a fraying-out of the philosophic tradition, men sought after the modest certainty of practical codes of conduct. Hence the brave system-building of the first generations of philosophers became restricted to less and less ambitious intellectual formulations, in which ethical prescription played the central role, while the ideal of truth as an end in itself shriveled into the cold and wizened rationalism of the Hellenistic schools.

HISTORY AND RHETORIC.   The investigations of Herodotus of Halicarnassus (d. *ca.* 425 B.C.) into things human and divine took so different a turn from those of the poets and philosophers who preceded him that he established a new literary genre: history. Through wide-ranging travel, both in the Greek world and in the Orient, Herodotus gained an extensive knowledge of the stories men told of the past. His discursive account of the Persian Wars preserves, with consummate literary art, much of what he heard.

Like the first Ionian philosophers, Herodotus was interested in the natural world, but more in its variety and wonders than in the philosophers' uniformities and regularities. Like the tragic poets, he dealt with the gods and their ways toward men, but he was fascinated more by the varying views of divinity held by men in different lands than by the poets' problem of affirming religious truth. But Herodotus did relish a good moral and took care to point out how excessive human pride and presumption sometimes brought supernatural punishment.

The epic quality of his narrative is reminiscent of Homer; and like Homer, Herodotus rises above narrow partisanship. His confidence in the value of the Greek way of life allowed him both to give the barbarians their "due meed of glory" and to point out instances of the "childishness of the Hellenes" in contrast to the immemorial wisdom of the East. Herodotus' vision of the Persian Wars as at bottom a struggle between freedom and slavery made his book an optimistic affirmation of the polis world in which he lived and allowed him to express his admiration for the Athenians above all other Greeks. It is a striking tribute to the "Father of History" that this interpretation of the facts, despite its transparent bias, still dominates scholarship.

Although Thucydides' lifetime (d. *ca.* 400 B.C.) overlapped that of his great predecessor, he breathed a very different intellectual atmosphere. An Athenian aristocrat and at one time a general of the Athenian polis, Thucydides grew up in close contact with the new currents of thought that ran so strongly in fifth-century Athens. The rhetorical and logical discipline of the sophist movement formed both his style and the rigorous criterion of relevancy he applied to his theme—the history of the Peloponnesian War. His careful observation of facts, and the effort he made to discern the real causes of the convulsions that the Peloponnesian War brought to the Greek world, may represent a conscious effort to transfer the methods of Hippocratic medicine to the body politic. The acuity of Thucydides' diagnoses and the plausibility of his effort to view particular events as instances of more general phenomena excite unending admiration and make his book what he himself declared it to be: "Not a prize essay for the moment, but a possession forever."[23]

Unlike Herodotus, Thucydides was himself a polis man through and through. No one can read his account of the disastrous Sicilian expedition without feeling extraordinary pangs of pity and fear as the career of imperial Athens moves step by step toward its inexorable tragic climax. Indeed, Thucydides probably came to see the fate of his native city as a tragedy in the full Aristotelian sense—a fall brought on by a tragic flaw, namely the Athenians' excessive greed—and dignified to tragic proportions by the magnitude of the effort on both sides.[24] This dramatic conception, even more than its penetrating analysis and skilled rhetoric, gives Thucydides' history an extraordinary emotional and intellectual power.

[23] I, 22.

[24] Cf. F. M. Cornford, *Thucydides Mythistoricus* (London: Edward Arnold & Co., 1907).

In a sense, both Thucydides' life and his book constituted a reluctant farewell to the tight little polis world. It is not sure whether he ever returned to Athens after his political rivals, making him the scapegoat for an important military defeat, exiled him from Attica in 425 B.C.; while his book records and analyzes the squalid disintegration of polis loyalties under the stresses of the Peloponnesian War, the consequences of this disintegration for historical writing became apparent in the work of Xenophon (431–354 B.C.), who undertook to carry on Thucydides' narrative. As a man of letters, more interested in a good turn of phrase and an effective moral than in the stubborn complexity of human affairs, Xenophon presaged the subsequent degeneration of historical writing into a branch of rhetoric.

* * *

As long as Greek cities continued to enjoy at least a modicum of their old sovereignty, rhetoric played an important part in political life. In fourth-century Athens, for example, decisions were still made by the people assembled. In the law courts also, rhetoric had a conspicuous place; for juries voted condemnation or acquittal on the strength of the protagonists' speeches. But with the general fragmentation and professionalization of life in the fourth century, speech-making and speech-writing became more and more the province of specially trained orators, for whom eloquence and glib plausibility tended to become ends in themselves. To be sure, Isocrates (436–338 B.C.) and Demosthenes (384–322 B.C.) attempted to make rhetoric serve high political and ethical ends. But by the third century, when political affairs were no longer decided through public speeches, but in the secret councils of kings and generals, eloquence and gracefulness of delivery strove by sheer virtuosity to disguise an unfortunate absence of meaning. Rhetoric became art for art's sake, style an end in itself; and words, instead of serving as guides to action or as windows upon the truth, were valued for themselves.

MONUMENTAL ART. In the fifth century B.C., Greek monumental art was almost entirely public. Architects stayed within conventional forms and contented themselves with refining proportions and perfecting details of workmanship. Yet no one who has visited the Athenian Acropolis, seen the Parthenon, and admired the elegant decoration of the Erechtheum will feel that these details were trivial. Opulent precision produces its own powerful impact upon the observer, and this the Greek architects of the fifth century achieved with unique— or almost unique—success.

Sculptors, on the other hand, departed freely from earlier models, developing a technical mastery of anatomy and of composition—whether of a single free-standing statue or of sculptural groups in pediments and friezes—that has never been excelled. Although the vicissitudes of time have destroyed most of the original sculpture of the fifth and fourth centuries B.C., enough survives[25]

---

[25] The handful of original fifth-century statues available for modern inspection is supplemented by innumerable copies made in later centuries and distributed over the Greco-Roman world by Alexandrian and other art dealers. The artistic quality of these copies varies widely. Tracing "families" of existing

to permit scholarly reconstruction of the history of Greek art. As in other fields, Athens produced the greatest excellence, but sculptors of other cities, particularly those of Argos and Sicyon, were worthy rivals.

Phidias of Athens (d. *ca.* 432 B.C.) was acclaimed by later generations as the greatest of Greek sculptors. His masterpieces, the cult statues of Athena in the Parthenon and of Zeus at Olympia, are totally lost to us, since the gold and ivory of which they were made assured their early destruction. Yet literary descriptions tell something of his work; and the surviving friezes of the Parthenon were carved under Phidias' supervision, probably according to his designs. Phidias' statues of the gods were traditional in the sense that they retained all the appropriate mythological attributes and symbols;[26] yet we are told that the majesty and beauty of his cult statues at Athens and Olympia added something to received religion,[27] giving visual form to deities more serene, mighty, and universal than had been conceived in traditional mythology. Thus Phidias, like the tragedian Sophocles, was able to reinterpret tradition in a fashion to satisfy the more critical and sophisticated minds of his own age and powerfully to impress men who came long after, for whom the anthropomorphic religion of early Greece had become no more than a pleasing myth.

The sculptors of the fourth century B.C. turned the gods into beautiful, but more nearly human, figures—graceful, sometimes sensuous, but lacking the aura of majesty that had surrounded Phidias' cult statues. The Hermes of Praxiteles (*ca.* 385–320 B.C.), one of the very few original statues from the hand of a great sculptor to survive essentially intact, illustrates the change: an alteration in the sculptor's attitude toward divinity analogous to Euripides' irreverent treatment of the Olympians. In the fourth century, indeed, sculpture became a self-conscious art pursuing virtuosity and dramatic effect with consummate skill. Yet all their skill scarcely compensated sculptors for the loss of their former role as public mediators between gods and men.

SUMMARY.   The great age of classical Greece came to a close in 338 B.C., when the battle of Chaeronea first clearly demonstrated the crushing military superiority of Macedon. Thereafter, the ideal of sovereignty for each separate polis, long honored more in the breach than in the observance, sank to the level of nostalgic, though still powerful sentiment. The autonomy of the individual city-state ceased to be a practical option, save in fleeting moments when the ever shifting constellation of great powers permitted a temporary recrudescence of polis particularism.

This transformation of the Greek scene had a blighting effect upon many facets of cultural activity. No ordinary individual could hope to affect the

---

statues back to a classical original and reconstructing what it may have been like on the basis of variant copies constitutes the stock in trade of classical art historians. The absence of originals opens the field to an almost unfettered ingenuity.

[26] An anecdote about Phidias makes him declare, before commencing his statue of Zeus at Olympia, that he intended to embody the Zeus portrayed in words by Homer. Cf. E. A. Gardiner, *A Handbook of Greek Sculpture* (rev. ed.; London: Macmillan & Co., 1909), p. 262.

[27] Quintilian (first century A.D.), *Inst. Orat.* XII, 10, 9.

TWO ASPECTS OF CLASSICAL GREECE

The Maenad, dancing in ecstasy to honor Dionysios, suggests a side of classical Greek civilization persistently in tension with the Olympian ideal here expressed by Praxiteles' famous Hermes. For a short while, as classical civilization reached its creative apogee, the polis was able to hold both these aspects of Greek culture together. But when the vase was painted, soon after 500 B.C., the success of the polis in taming the raw emotional outbursts of Dionysiac worship was still unsure, whereas by the time Praxiteles carved his statue of Hermes (*ca.* 350 B.C.), any real belief in the gods of Olympus had evaporated among the cultivated classes of Greece. The two photographs therefore also reflect Greek cultural evolution from an undisciplined intensity toward a genteel, lovely, and just a bit effete style of life.

confused and changeable political-military balance of the third and second centuries B.C. As a result, both the lively sense of freedom, and its corollary, recognition of personal responsibility to the community, were weakened or even erased. The ever widening intellectual gap between the educated classes and the majority of citizens reinforced the depressing psychological effect of the loss of polis independence. The very complexity and richness of Greek thought and letters, so much admired by later generations, reserved their full enjoyment to those with the leisure to pursue higher education. Thus through an irony perhaps inherent in all great human achievement, the very success with which Greeks of the fifth and fourth centuries developed the culture they had inherited in rudimentary form from their ancestors both expressed the weakening and hastened final destruction of the social nexus that had stimulated and sustained their creativity.

This sociological parasitism should not detract from our admiration, indeed reverence, for the magnitude of the Greek cultural achievement. A tiny handful of men gave definition to the intellectual, literary, and artistic forms of later classical antiquity and profoundly affected the European civilization which in recent centuries has come to dominate the entire globe. This, surely, was no small thing, but the very brilliance of the fifth and fourth centuries weighed heavily on later generations. Such persuasive models were difficult to improve upon and quite impossible to forget.

In the short run, however, these limitations were not felt. There were then new worlds still to conquer, unexampled wealth yet to win, fresh glories to strive after, and distant horizons to explore. These exciting possibilities arose from the extraordinary geographical expansion that came to Hellenism in the time of Alexander of Macedon and his successors.

B. HELLENIC EXPANSION INTO BARBARIAN EUROPE

The irruption of Macedon into the Greek heartland was itself a by-product of the spread of certain aspects of Hellenic civilization northward from the Aegean, for only after King Philip (ruled 356–336 B.C.) organized his army on Greek models was Macedon's numerical superiority effectively brought to bear upon the Greek political stage. Yet the spread of Hellenism northward and inland to backward regions like Macedonia required adjustment to a social and economic milieu radically different from that within which Greek culture had arisen and flourished.

In the fifth century B.C., the higher manifestations of Greek culture were fully shared only by cities on or very near the coast. Athens, like her predecessor Knossos and her successor Venice, was married to the sea. Without substantial income from overseas, the civil strife and nagging poverty of the sixth century could have been relieved only by emigration; and Athens could never have become the magnet she in fact became for men of talent and skill from all over the Greek world.

This was so because technical factors severely restricted the capacities of the classical world for producing wealth. Except on irrigated land, dense populations could not survive on the basis of merely local food production.

Only by a collective exploitation of advantageous terms of trade—oil and wine for grain[28]—or by the more direct exploitation of weaker communities through the forcible extraction of tribute and booty, could a substantial number of citizens maintain the modest yet satisfactory level of material existence required for participation in Greek cultural life.

Lack of cheap enough transport meant that no large urban communities could support themselves inland. Therefore, only by recapitulating the process of social differentiation whereby civilized societies had first arisen on rain-watered land in the second millennium B.C. could the fine fruit of Greek urbanity find lodgment in regions far from the sea. Foreign conquerors or local tribal leaders turned rent collectors did, however, find it possible to concentrate locally produced wealth into their hands. This they used first to purchase Greek luxuries and eventually to support a few local craftsmen and professional specialists (often grouped into a provincial town) who could supply goods and services in the style first developed within the busy collectivity of a maritime polis.

The Greek colonies were major intermediaries in the diffusion of metropolitan luxuries. Merchants of the colonial cities were ready and eager to extend their dealing inland, wherever metals, timber, grain, or other valuables could be had. The production of such items was generally organized by barbarian chieftains or landlords, who soon developed a taste for Greek wine, oil, and manufactures. Such exchanges are attested by the discovery of Greek vases in such dispersed localities as Bulgaria and south Russia, central Italy, and southern France. In some cases trade stimulated a deeper interest in Greek culture on the part of the barbarians; but when the element of fear or compulsion was absent, most men were ready to change their ideas or habits only superficially.

Greek civilization, however, was not propagated solely by peaceable means. In the fifth and early fourth centuries B.C., Greek military organization and tactics enjoyed a clear superiority over all rivals. Even before the Peloponnesian War, Persian satraps paid their unruly neighbors the ultimate compliment of hiring them as mercenary troops.[29] But it was the kings of Macedon who most successfully adopted Greek military methods, not by hiring Greek soldiers—Macedon lacked the ready cash for that—but by conscripting Macedonian peasants into a royal phalanx equipped and trained after the Greek fashion.[30] By combining the mass of such a phalanx with the striking power of the traditional cavalry force recruited from among the Macedonian nobility, King Philip created an army unequaled in Greece or anywhere else.

[28] The advantage lay in the fact that the amount of land and labor required to produce a given quantity of wine or oil was less, usually very much less, than the amount of land and labor required to raise the quantity of grain for which they could be exchanged.

[29] H. W. Parke, *Greek Mercenary Soldiers* (Oxford: Clarendon Press, 1933), pp. 14–15.

[30] The Macedonian foot soldiers carried a longer spear than had been customary among the Greeks, giving their phalanx a longer reach. Thus, Philip did not simply borrow military methods; he improved as he borrowed. Cf. F. E. Adcock, *The Greek and Macedonian Art of War* (Berkeley: University of California Press, 1957), pp. 50–51 and *passim*. Philip also employed a few Greek mercenaries, mainly for garrison duty. Cf. Parke, *Greek Mercenary Soldiers*, pp. 155–64.

The Hellenization of Macedonia was not entirely military. As early as the fifth century, the Macedonian royal house laid claim to Greek descent and even brought a number of Greek literary figures, including Euripides, to court. Philip himself came into intimate contact with the politics, war, and culture of metropolitan Greece in the three years of his youth which he spent as a hostage in Thebes; and he employed Aristotle as tutor for his son, Alexander. Indeed, the royal court appears to have been the prime agency through which Hellenic high culture penetrated Macedonia.

At first Greek influence constituted a potential danger to the Macedonian monarchy, for the Greeks had long ago reduced their kings to the merest figureheads or discarded them entirely. Accordingly, at the beginning of the fourth century, a group of Macedonian towns, reinforced by an immigrant Greek element,[31] attempted to supersede the Macedonian monarchy by a league of cities organized on the Greek model. Spartan military intervention caused the failure of this enterprise (379 B.C.); and thereafter the Macedonian towns remained submissive to their king.

During the rest of the fourth century, Hellenization went hand in hand with the strengthening of the Macedonian monarchy. Residence at court and service in the royal army gave young Macedonian noblemen a taste for the graces and luxuries of Greek life. This experience—perhaps even more than mere pay and booty—attached the Macedonian aristocracy to the royal house; for having once glimpsed a much more attractive life, young noblemen were forever alienated from the fierce rural clannishness which in earlier times had made the Macedonian nobles utterly unruly.[32] The powerful seductiveness of Hellenizing court culture constituted the real secret of Philip's extraordinary political success, for it provided him with a loyal nobility to lead his remodeled armies.

Hellenization of the Macedonian peasantry and common soldiery was not possible, either in Philip's day or for a long time after. Their very success in battle inspired the Macedonian rank and file with a strong disdain for effete Greeks. Until Roman times, when military failures humbled Macedonian pride, the inland regions of the country, whence came the soldiers of the phalanx, remained the seat of a nearly egalitarian society, in which genuine cities could not flourish. Private wealth sufficient to maintain a Hellenized gentleman in appropriate style scarcely existed in Macedonia, where the aristocrats' traditional social leadership did not extend to the collection of heavy rents. Only the king, with his income from booty and from the exploitation of forests and mines, could sustain a Hellenized circle around his person. Conversely—and this was what really tied the aristocracy to the monarch—a partially Hellenized Macedonian gentleman could live the life of his choice only by serving the king.

[31] Stanley Casson, *Macedonia, Thrace and Illyria: Their Relations to Greece from the Earliest Times down to the Time of Philip, Son of Amyntas* (Oxford: Oxford University Press, 1926), pp. 80–86.

[32] Cf. the use the Hapsburgs made of the Baroque culture of Vienna—expressed not only in the Counter Reformation and in monumental art, but in courtly pageantry, sweet music, and elegant mistresses—to tame the rustic Hungarian nobility in the seventeenth and eighteenth centuries.

Macedon was not, of course, the only barbarian state that rose to political importance by assimilating aspects of Hellenism. The Odrysian kingdom in Thrace was moving in a similar direction when Philip's conquest cut short its development; Epirus soon followed in Macedon's footsteps; and on the shores of the Black Sea, both the Bosphoran kingdom around the Sea of Azov and Bithynia in northern Asia Minor saw the rise of Hellenizing dynasties in the fourth century B.C.

In the central Mediterranean, the existence of three rival high cultures, the Greek, the Carthaginian, and the Etruscan, complicated but in no wise hindered the diffusion of civilization. Conflict centered mainly in Sicily, where Greek cities struggled indecisively with imperial Carthage for more than two centuries, until the Romans intervened with crushing superiority in the First Punic War (264–241 B.C.) and made Sicily into the first Roman province. A subsidiary theater of conflict existed briefly along the western face of Italy, where Etruscans and Greeks confronted one another. But a Greek naval victory at Cumae (*ca.* 473 B.C.) compelled the Etruscans to withdraw from Campania and probably made the liberation of Rome from Etruscan control finally secure. Thereafter, the Latin League under Roman leadership interposed an effective native buffer between the Greeks and their Etruscan rivals.[33]

Etruria, Carthage, and the Greek cities of southern Italy and Sicily maintained a lively trade, both among themselves and with the various more backward communities of the western Mediterranean coast. Nor did these western outposts of the civilized world fail to maintain a quite intimate relation with the eastern Mediterranean. Both Carthage and Etruria, particularly the latter, became familiar with Greek art styles and sometimes imported Greek artists or imitated their achievements locally. After the middle of the fourth century, Carthage, like Persia, came to appreciate the qualities of Greek mercenaries. By the third century, Carthaginian aristocrats were familiar with the Greek language and apparently had accepted some Greek ideas into their otherwise conservative and rather brutal religion. Yet for all their appreciation of certain aspects of Greek civilization, neither Etruria nor Carthage can properly be described as members of the Hellenistic family of nations. In

[33] The early growth of Roman power from these small beginnings was very slow. When Alexander attacked Persia, the Romans controlled only Latium and Campania in west central Italy. As befitted a largely peasant society, the splendors and luxuries of civilization, whether Etruscan or Greek, were then still foreign to the future capital of the Mediterranean world. This was not because of lack of exposure, but from choice. Rome's political independence had been secured (509 B.C.) by rejecting civilization in its Etruscan version, as represented by the monarchy. But champions of the good old ways, however aristocratic their families, could not easily turn around and ape the civilized habits of rejected royalty. Thus a rude egalitarianism of economic circumstance, a vigorous hunger for enough land to give each family a plot of ground, and an aristocratic leadership which was effective just because it left the backward socio-economic structure of the community undisturbed distinguished republican Rome from neighboring peoples. The socially divisive effects of the penetration of civilization through a process of rapid social differentiation weakened Rome's rivals and prepared the way for the very rapid pace of the last stages of Roman expansion in Italy and beyond. An artificially and deliberately prolonged childhood thus allowed the Roman body politic to become larger and more robust than more precociously civilized societies, like the Etruscan, Carthaginian, and even the Macedonian, could ever hope to become.

Etruria, a native style persisted beneath a Hellenizing exterior,[34] and the aristocratic republic of north Africa remained true to its Phoenician cultural inheritance, even after Phoenicia itself had entered upon a Hellenizing phase.[35]

Thus while Hellenism was definitely the most active cultural strand in the central Mediterranean area between 500 and 336 B.C., victory over its rivals was far from complete; while on the political-military level, it had difficulty in holding its own.

The shifting political and cultural balances of the western Mediterranean had no very great effect upon Greece proper until the very end of the third century B.C. But in the economic field, the diffusion of techniques associated with high Greek civilization worked powerfully to the disadvantage of the core area of the Aegean. In Thrace and along the Black Sea coast, Greek colonies gradually acquired manufacturing skills which in the fifth century had been concentrated in cities like Athens or Corinth. In the West, Greek and Etruscan cities did likewise. Still more disastrous to Greece was the development of wine and oil production in Sicily, southern Italy, and the Carthaginian territories of north Africa, and of viticulture in central Italy, Thrace, Bithynia, and the Crimea.

As these changes occurred, bit by bit the trade patterns which previously had concentrated wealth in a few Aegean commercial cities broke down. More peripheral regions began to enjoy the favorable terms of trade that wine and oil continued to command as against grain. As this occurred, radical economic decay set in at the center.[36] Depressed living conditions for the lower classes at home fed the mercenary armies which became a growingly conspicuous feature of the Greek scene; and the bitter civil strife that paralyzed so many Greek cities from the fourth century onward was a normal, if deplorable, response to vanishing prosperity.

The consequences of the expansion of Hellenism and of Hellenic techniques were therefore not entirely happy for the communities which had first formulated Greek civilization. Internal disturbances, ceaseless and often brutal interpolis wars, and depressed living conditions smoothed a path for Macedonian hegemony. Yet when Alexander used that hegemony to turn the energies of Hellenic society outward—when he opened the vast and varied world of the Orient to Greek and Macedonian enterprise—the effect upon metropolitan Greek society was like the bursting of a dam. Following Alexander's footsteps, thousands, perhaps hundreds of thousands, of Greeks emigrated to seek their fortunes in the East. The resultant Hellenic imprint upon the Orient was far deeper than could have been achieved by merely military conquest.

[34] The Greek imprint upon Etruria must be measured largely by artistic remains, because the Etruscan script has not yet been deciphered. Cf. the masterly exposition in Gisela M. A. Richter, *Ancient Italy: A Study of the Interrelations of Its Peoples as Shown in Their Arts* (Ann Arbor: University of Michigan Press, 1955), pp. 1–33.

[35] Stéphane Gsell, *Histoire ancienne de l'Afrique du Nord. IV: La civilisation carthaginoise* (Paris: Hachette, 1920), pp. 190–93, 484–86, and *passim;* B. H. Warmington, *Carthage* (London: Robert Hale Ltd., 1960), pp. 134–35.

[36] M. Rostovtzeff, *The Social and Economic History of the Hellenistic World* (Oxford: Clarendon Press, 1941), I, 104–25, has assembled sketchy but convincing indications in support of this generalization.

C. THE HELLENIZATION OF THE ORIENT
500–146 B.C.

I. MILITARY AND POLITICAL

In barbarian Europe the full impact of Hellenic high culture could not be felt until comparatively slow and painful processes of economic and social differentiation had prepared a milieu within which the amenities of civilization could be appreciated and paid for. No such obstacle delayed the eastward diffusion of Greek culture. In the Orient, a differentiated society was already age-old; and a wealthy and cultivated class of rulers, landlords, and merchants were ready to use Greek products and skills whenever they seemed clearly superior to local equivalents. As early as the fourth century B.C., Greek wine and oil and miscellaneous manufactures were consumed in rather large quantities in Egypt and the Levant,[37] although more inland regions were as yet largely untouched by such commerce. Greek wares were for the most part not sufficiently valuable in proportion to their bulk to travel far from the seas and waterways, though stray sherds of Attic vases dating from the fourth century have been picked up in Iran. But, generally speaking, Hellenic commercial penetration of the vast inland regions of the Persian empire occurred only after Alexander's conquests led to the establishment of Greek settlements far into Asia.

Greek mercenaries powerfully seconded Greek merchants as agents spreading the civilization of Greece to the Orient. Yet the military and political relationships resulting from the mobilization of Persian gold to employ Greek soldiers were very complicated. On the one hand, the willingness of Greeks to fight for Persian pay allowed the satraps of Asia Minor to become arbiters of Greek politics during and after the Peloponnesian War. But at the same time, the prestige of Greek fighting men was so high that every Persian grandee and even the Great King himself sought to secure his power by hiring a bodyguard of Greeks. This meant that the rebellions which frequently distracted the Persian empire during the fourth century B.C. began to take on the quality of Greek civil wars, in which opposing mercenary phalanxes decided the day, while supporting Oriental troops played only a secondary and often quite undistinguished part. Consequently, when Alexander attacked Persia, the most formidable troops and the most skilful commander he had to overcome were Greek.[38]

Seen in this light, Alexander's meteoric career seems less an interruption than the logical culmination of a long-standing process of interpenetration

---

[37] Wholesaling and specialization prevailed in this trade to a rather surprising degree. At a site named Al-Mina on the Syrian coast, archeologists have discovered warehouses where Attic pottery imports (together with local products) were separately stored according to type—lamps, wide-mouthed jars, narrow-mouthed jars, etc., each in a separate room. This suggests a rather large wholesale operation. Cf. M. Rostovtzeff, *The Social and Economic History of the Hellenistic World*, I, 85 ff.

[38] H. W. Parke, *Greek Mercenary Soldiers*, pp. 23–41, 57–62, 105–12, 165–69, 177–85. Persian officials often exhibited a not undeserved suspicion of the trustworthiness of Greek mercenary captains. This greatly hampered the Persian resistance to Alexander in Asia Minor, and perhaps even assured his initial victory at the Granicus.

Soprintendenza alle Antichità della Compania, Naples.

THE EXPANSION OF HELLENISM

On the right, the statue of Mausolus, satrap of Caria in southwestern Asia Minor (377–353 B.C.), shows a barbarian dressed and memorialized in a thoroughly Greek manner. As a matter of fact, the most famous Greek sculptors of the day were employed by Mausolus' widow to decorate the magnificent tomb she planned for her husband: whence the English term "mausoleum." Such peaceful penetration of Greek civilization into new lands was supplemented by Alexander's conquest, depicted on the left. The scene shows Alexander at the Battle of Issus (333 B.C.) driving home his cavalry charge against King Darius III, who turns his chariot to flee at the approach of the fierce Macedonian.

between Greece and the Orient. When he attacked Persia in 334 B.C., he professed to do so as a champion of Hellenism; and he carried with him a contingent of troops raised from the cities of the Hellenic confederacy, of which he was president. He restored local sovereignty to the Greek cities of Asia Minor; and in territories farther afield, where the Greek imprint was slight or non-existent, he consciously and consistently played the role of champion of Greek civilization. Frequently he celebrated games in the Greek fashion; and his army itself constituted a sort of mobile Greco-Macedonian state as it marched and countermarched across the face of western Asia. More significant for the future was Alexander's policy of founding Greek cities, endowed with Greek institutions and special privileges, along the frontiers of his empire. The largest number of these cities clustered in the eastern marchlands of Iran, where protection against raiders from the steppe was a standing problem; but of all his cities, Alexandria by Egypt, located at the opposite, southwesternmost extremity of his empire, flourished best.

After Darius III, the last of the Achaemenids, was assassinated by his faithless followers in 330 B.C., Alexander modified his role as self-appointed defender of Hellenism by claiming to be the legitimate successor of the Persian kings as well. As such, he sought to associate Persians with Macedonians and Greeks as ruling elements in his empire; and he dramatized this policy by marrying a Persian noblewoman himself and by arranging a mass marriage of 10,000 of his soldiers with Persian women at Susa after the return from India.

At the age of 33, less than twelve years after starting his invasion of Persia, Alexander died. He thus was spared defeat—not defeat in battle, for he had little to fear on that score, but defeat of his views as to how to deal with the multitudinous and varied peoples he had conquered. For not even an Alexander could long have retained his popularity with the Egyptians and Babylonians, who had welcomed him as a liberator from Persian oppression, while at the same time reconciling the antagonistic pride of the Persian and Macedonian nations and somehow securing the co-operation of the Greeks.

The generals who fought over and eventually divided Alexander's empire were in no position to follow his policies toward the subject peoples. Usurpers without hereditary claims to rule, aliens among their subjects, they depended entirely upon the loyalty and obedience of the Macedonian rank and file for their power. To ignore the soldiers' prejudices was to risk desertion or mutiny, which could destroy the most promising career overnight. And the Macedonian soldiery disliked Greeks, despised Orientals, and wished the impossible: that the familiar rude institutions and manners of the Macedonian backwoods should be maintained, while each individual soldier acquired booty and wealth on a scale previously undreamt.

The successful Macedonian rulers were therefore men who kept the Macedonian soldiers happy by paying them liberally and by affecting a royal style of life that emphasized the bluff manners of the camp. Except in the homelands, the dislike between Greeks and Macedonians soon faded. There was room for both in the new Hellenistic monarchies, for Macedonian kings desperately needed Greek administrative skill and economic energy in order to exploit the resources of their new kingdoms efficiently and thus acquire the means to support the soldiers upon whom their power all too nakedly depended.

After 281 B.C., when a modicum of stability emerged from the struggles between Alexander's generals, his empire was divided among three great states: the Seleucid kingdom in western Asia; the Ptolemaic kingdom in Egypt; and in Europe an Antigonid Macedonia, reconstituted within somewhat narrower limits than those of Alexander's day. The Greek cities occupied an uneasy position, nominally free in most cases, but usually allied with and in varying degrees subject to one or another of the three great Hellenistic monarchies.

The administrative systems of the major states conformed closely to older precedent. In Macedonia, Hellenization of the upper classes proceeded steadily, and some Greek-style towns developed; but the countryside remained in the possession of a free or very nearly free peasantry until after the Roman conquest.[39] The government of Ptolemaic Egypt became a more rationally and perhaps more ruthlessly efficient version of the ancient Pharaonic system. The Ptolemies monopolized key agricultural products, issued seed (of improved varieties) to the peasants, controlled and extended the irrigation works, and taxed the population with an unexampled thoroughness. In the Seleucid realm, a much looser administrative system prevailed, built upon a reorganization of the old Persian satrapies. Nothing like the Ptolemies' detailed control over villages and individuals was possible in those vast and varied territories. A wide diversity of local organizations—semi-princely landowners, temple states, and city-states—dominated local administration and paid varying tributes to the central authorities. The Persians, and before them the Assyrians, had ruled in much the same fashion.

Nonetheless the Macedonian conquest had a significant effect upon the texture and outward forms of Oriental social life. The swarm of hungry Greeks and sturdy Macedonians who emigrated from their crowded homelands brought Hellenic styles of life massively to the attention of Oriental peoples. The inherent attractiveness of Hellenic civilization was enhanced by the leading positions Greeks occupied in Hellenistic society. As security against potential native revolt, the Macedonian rulers of Egypt and Asia deliberately staffed their administrations as far as possible with men of Greek background. But not all immigrants secured official posts; many served as merchants or professional men—doctors, teachers, athletes, actors, architects, and the like.

To lessen the cost of maintaining standing armies, while simultaneously appeasing the land hunger of peasant-soldiers who had left home to make their fortunes, both the Ptolemies and the Seleucids adopted the policy of settling large numbers of soldiers in special military colonies, where in return for a plot of farm land they were obligated to return to active service upon

[39] The population of Macedonia may have been considerably reduced by the emigration of young men who went off to make their fortunes in the East. At any rate, the Antigonid armies were uniformly smaller than those of Philip and Alexander had been; and mercenaries played a larger role in them than before.

call. In the Seleucid realm, though not in Egypt, such military colonies sometimes developed into full-fledged Greek-style cities. The king allowed and often encouraged them to create standard Greek polis institutions: elective magistrates, a council, and an assembly of the citizens.

The inhabitants of these and other Hellenistic cities were a mixed lot. In the cities that really took root and flourished, probably a majority of the inhabitants were always of non-Hellenic origin. But the privileges of citizenship were usually reserved for those who, whether by descent or education, had a plausible claim to rank as Greeks or Macedonians. Since these privileges were worth acquiring, it quickly became fashionable among the native upper classes of such ancient centers as Antioch or Susa to learn Greek ways and adopt Greek styles. These cities, therefore, and scores of others, new and old, became islands of Hellenism in an Oriental sea, where a more or less plausible facsimile of the life of a Greek polis prevailed, at least among those of the upper class who enjoyed full citizen rights.[40]

*   *   *

Before the Macedonian conquest, the central core of Middle Eastern civilization had embraced Mesopotamia, Syria, and Egypt, with outliers in Iran and Anatolia. Alexander in effect merged the Aegean coastlands and Asia Minor with the older core; while northern India on the east and the central Mediterranean lands to the west became the outliers of the new Hellenistic-Oriental civilization.

Cultural diversity of course continued to prevail. The immixture of Greek cultural forms and institutions simply added another and very lively strand to the already tangled variety of the Middle East. Hellenization of the upper classes in Oriental countries never perhaps went very deep. Still, Greece and the Orient had become one as never before. Events in Egypt or Syria, in Iran or Anatolia, in Greece proper or Macedonia intimately influenced one another. With the passage of time, Rome and Carthage as well as the states of northern India were more and more caught up in the political-military-economic web whose most active centers lay around the shores of the Aegean and the eastern Mediterranean.

Within this core area, a long series of wars and frequent diplomatic realignments gave Hellenistic politics a disheartening complexity. The Ptolemies and Seleucids struggled sporadically for control of southern Syria and Palestine; Macedonia and Egypt staged a similar contest for control of the Aegean seaboard. At first, the centralized efficiency of the Egyptian administration, with the ample funds provided by its tax system, gave the Ptolemies an edge over their less wealthy and less efficient rivals. Toward the end of the third cen-

---

[40] Handsome public buildings—gymnasia, theaters, temples—together with more utilitarian structures like city walls, water supply systems, or harbor improvements became characteristic of every self-respecting Hellenistic city. Layout was often systematically planned on a rectilinear pattern, with two main streets at right angles dividing the city into four quarters, while the main cluster of public buildings was located at the central intersection. But assembly, magistrates, law courts, and council were as much a part of a city as was the outward show.

tury, however, radical decay set in in Egypt when bureaucratic corruption and slackness began to throttle the wealth which the first Ptolemies had nurtured so skilfully and exploited so ruthlessly.

The more loosely consolidated Seleucid state also suffered internal disorders. Early in its history, outlying provinces asserted independence. Pergamum in western Asia Minor, Parthia southeast of the Caspian Sea, and Bactria in the far northeast all broke away during the third century; and in the middle of the second, the Jewish state of the Maccabees followed suit. Yet the Seleucid realm exhibited a resiliency absent from Ptolemaic Egypt. Two of the later Seleucid rulers, Antiochus III (227–187 B.C.) and Antiochus IV (175–163 B.C.)[41] temporarily recovered vast eastern territories, although neither of them was able to resist Roman preponderance on the one flank or eliminate the stubborn, if loosely organized, Parthian harassment on the other.[42]

The careers of the lesser states make details of Hellenistic political history unusually complicated. Buffers arose in Greece, Asia Minor, and Judea, where the spheres of influence of the three major monarchies collided.[43] To the north of the Hellenic world, a string of petty frontier kingdoms—Epirus, Bithynia, and Pontus—evolved much as Macedon had done in the fifth and fourth centuries, acclimating Greek culture to royal courts and native aristocracies. The kingdom of Pergamum, because of its central location in northwestern Asia Minor, was more deeply Hellenized, embracing several important Greek cities within its boundaries, and enjoying, under the energetic rule of the Attalids, a generally high level of prosperity.

With the weakening of the Seleucid kingdom, another series of frontier states came into existence in Asia. Of these, Galatia and Cappadocia in Asia Minor remained largely barbarous until Roman times; but the kingdom of Parthia, established about 247 B.C. by Iranian-speaking tribesmen from the steppes near the Caspian Sea, became the scene of an interesting symbiosis between Hellenized cities and a loosely "feudal" monarchy. In general, the Parthian rulers appeared to have favored the cities: one early ruler even called

---

[41] The career of Antiochus III (the Great) is well known, primarily from Polybius; that of Antiochus IV Epiphanes, the evil genius of the Book of Maccabees, is far more obscure. Only the piecing together of coin inscriptions and scattered references permits the inference that it was his agent and relative who overthrew the independent Greek dynasty of Bactria and compelled the abandonment of the conquest of India which that dynasty had begun a few years before. For a fascinating reconstruction of these lost chapters of Hellenistic history, see W. W. Tarn, *The Greeks in Bactria and India* (Cambridge: Cambridge University Press, 1951), pp. 183–224. Tarn's reconstruction of Antiochus IV's Eastern policy has not gone unchallenged, however. Cf. A. K. Narain, *The Indo-Greeks* (Oxford: Clarendon Press, 1959), pp. 53–57.

[42] The geographically vast fluctuations of Seleucid power in the eastern reaches of their dominions probably reflect the fact that the Hellenized cities of those parts much preferred Seleucid to any other suzerainty and willingly opened their gates to armies under the Seleucid banner. This made "reconquest" easy, whereas rivals had to reduce the cities one by one, ravaging their dependent lands and interrupting their caravans, until the city authorities reluctantly came to terms with the masters of the open countryside—Parthian, Shaka, rebellious satrap, or whomever else.

[43] In Greece itself, efforts to form federal leagues strong enough to deal with the great powers on terms of equality met with some success; but Greece as a whole never was able to unite, nor did the Greek states ever succeed in forming a common front against an outsider.

THE HELLENISTIC AGE

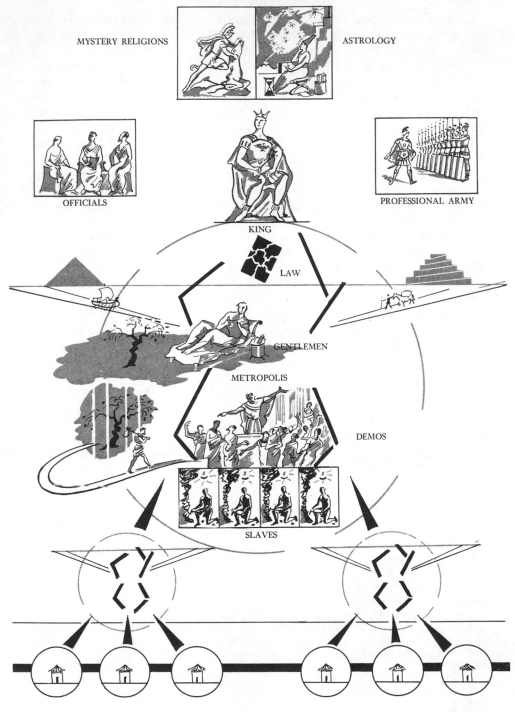

MYSTERY RELIGIONS

ASTROLOGY

OFFICIALS

PROFESSIONAL ARMY

KING

LAW

GENTLEMEN

METROPOLIS

DEMOS

SLAVES

himself "Philhellene." The kings of Parthia were certainly awake to the possibility of winning a useful income by taxing the caravan trade linking the major cities of western Asia; perhaps, too, they found something to admire in Greek culture for its own sake. At any rate, while basing their military system upon an Iranian nobility, they seem to have accorded the Hellenized cities very full autonomy. Thus Parthian overlordship of Mesopotamia (after 141 B.C.) scarcely affected the blooming city life of that region and did nothing to weaken its Hellenic stamp.

In Bactria, a somewhat similar partnership existed between Hellenized cities and a predominantly Iranian countryside, with the difference that the rulers of the Bactrian kingdom were Greek.[44] Because the history of this kingdom has been lost, an accurate assessment of the vigor of Greek culture there awaits an adequate archeological exploration of Afghanistan, Pakistan, and Russian central Asia.[45]

* * *

The military and political expansion of Hellenism, so phenomenal in the fourth and third centuries B.C., began to lose momentum after about 200 B.C. The stream of emigrant Greeks slackened and then almost ceased, due, at least in part, to a decline in the population of the homelands. Without the copious supply of hungry and eager young Greeks which had so greatly assisted the earlier Ptolemies and Seleucids, the strength of the two great Hellenistic monarchies was seriously undermined. Hellenized gentlemen of Alexandria or Antioch did not make good soldiers; and the subject peasantries of Egypt and Asia had no love for their Macedonian masters.[46]

It was not long before the growing weakness of the Hellenistic states was demonstrated on the field of battle. The Romans fastened their control upon Macedonia and Greece with remarkable ease between 200 and 146 B.C. Almost simultaneously, the Seleucids lost their easternmost provinces to raiding Shakas (between 165 and 128 B.C.), while Mesopotamia fell to the Parthians.[47] Thus soon after the middle of the second century B.C., the political bound-

---

[44] Agricultural development and incipient urbanization had started in these regions under the Achaemenids. The key factors in this eastward expansion of the civilized zone of western Asia lay, not only in pacification brought by Persian and later by Hellenistic rule, but also in the development of underground irrigation channels, which by reducing evaporation made possible the conservation of the scarce water resources of the area. Cf. R. Ghirshman, *L'Iran des origines à l'Islam* (Paris: Payot, 1951), p. 180. The technique of irrigating by means of underground channels was developed by a transfer of mining engineering to waterworks and probably was first tried in Armenia in Achaemenid times. Cf. Charles Singer *et al.*, *A History of Technology* (Oxford: Clarendon Press, 1956), II, 666. After this technical breakthrough, a new if intrinsically less wealthy Mesopotamia could and did arise on the easternmost fringes of Iran in the Oxus-Jaxartes valleys. The Greek kingdom of Bactria was the first but far from the last state to be based upon this enlarged agricultural oasis. Other oases farther east profited from this same technical advance somewhat later.

[45] Cf. W. W. Tarn, *The Greeks in Bactria and India*, pp. 225–408; A. K. Narain, *The Indo-Greeks*.

[46] The Ptolemies discovered this after the battle of Raphia in 217 B.C., which they won with the help of a native Egyptian phalanx, only to face a disastrous revolt when the victorious Egyptians returned home. Cf. the experience of the Hyksos as rulers of Egypt more than a thousand years before.

[47] Neilson C. Debevoise, *A Political History of Parthia* (Chicago: University of Chicago Press, 1938), pp. 21–28.

aries of Hellenism were pushed back behind the Euphrates; and the rump states which survived in Asia Minor, Syria, and Egypt could aspire to independence only by playing off the Romans against the Parthians. To be sure, both the Romans and the Parthians were or became sharers in the Hellenic civilized tradition. Yet their striking military successes against Hellenistic states in the middle of the second century B.C. signified the political exhaustion of the first phase of Hellenic expansion.

2. SOCIAL AND CULTURAL

The intermingling of Greeks and Orientals in the Hellenistic cities provoked complicated social and cultural changes on both sides. In the first century after Alexander's conquests, the borrowings seemed to run all in one direction —from Hellas outward. The self-confidence of the conquerors was then still undimmed; the vigor of Greek society at home remained high; Greek immigrants streamed into the East, bringing with them their characteristic style of life. The upper classes of the Hellenistic cities, whatever their origin or cultural background, wished to pass as good Hellenes and took to copying Greek ways wholesale.[48] The Greek language spread even more widely than Greek culture, for only the wealthy could afford the latter, while any tradesman could acquire the simplified common Greek, or *koine*. The *koine* replaced Aramaic in many localities as the prevailing *lingua franca* of the Middle East and became the mother tongue of many city dwellers who made no pretense of passing as Hellenes.[49]

Yet for all the apparent lopsidedness of this phase of Greco-Oriental cultural contact, it was precisely during these decades that the social structure of the Greek homeland assimilated itself to patterns that had long been normal in the East. During the Hellenistic age, the cities of Greece, like those of Asia, came generally under oligarchic control, even where, as in Athens, democratic forms were maintained. Obscure economic factors apparently favored the growth of large estates tilled by hired hands or slaves, while the old-fashioned citizen farmer with his family property disappeared by degrees. An impoverished proletariat gathered in the cities. Wages failed to rise with the general inflation of prices that followed Alexander's lavish dispersal of the imperial Persian hoard of gold; and anyone wholly dependent on wages must

---

[48] How far this process might go is vividly illustrated in passages of the Book of Maccabees, describing the conduct of the leaders of the Jewish temple community in the time of Antiochus IV Epiphanes. Of all the societies in the Hellenistic world, the Jewish was perhaps the most impermeable to outside influences; yet according to the author of Maccabees, a high priest of the Temple at Jerusalem, appropriately named Jason, "brought his countrymen over to the Greek way of living." Jason, in fact, deeply offended his more conservative countrymen by renaming Jerusalem "Antioch" and by trying to set up the usual Greek institutions. Most shocking of these was the gymnasium, where he and his fellows disported themselves "unlawfully," *i.e.*, naked, in the Greek manner. II Maccabees 4:7–15. Edgar J. Goodspeed (trans.).

[49] The best evidence for this comes once again from Jewish sources. The *Septuagint*, a Greek translation of the Hebrew Pentateuch made sometime in the third century B.C., became for the Jews of the Diaspora much what the King James translation of the Bible later became for English-speaking Christians: *the* text of Holy Writ. On the prevalence of Greek even in Palestine itself, see Salo Wittmayer Baron, *A Social and Religious History of the Jews* (2d ed.; Philadelphia: Jewish Publication Society of America, 1952), I, 185–87.

have lived very precariously.[50] Food supply, which for all the larger Greek cities had to come from abroad, was the great problem, for even slight changes in grain deliveries produced radical fluctuations in price, and a brief interruption of supply lines could produce severe local famine.

Under these circumstances, the few tended to become richer, the rest poorer. Revolutionary demands for abolition of debts and redistribution of the land were frequently heard; and a few violent uprisings gave vent to the exasperation of the lower classes, most spectacularly in Sparta in the late third century. In every case, intervention from outside suppressed such movements. Yet mere repression could not solve the ills of Greek society. Rich and poor, educated and uneducated tended to go their separate ways. Sophistication and superstition, elegant refinement and miserable poverty, lavish public works and public doles to the poor came to exist side by side within Greek cities, while the countryside was left to hired laborers and slaves.[51]

It is easy, in a democratic age, to deplore the social transformations that came to the principal cities of Greece in the Hellenistic age. The narrowing of the social circle that shared fully in the high culture of Greece was, however, a necessary corollary of the geographical spread of civilization, which made it impossible for the small Aegean center to maintain a ruthless military and mercantile exploitation of the Mediterranean coastlands like that which had provided Athens' economic sinews in its days of greatness.

The fact of the matter was that limitations of ancient technology made civilization very costly. Only when many toiled and suffered deprivation could a privileged few have the leisure and ease needful for the creation and maintenance of high culture. The social pattern of the Hellenistic age, therefore, was not new in principle, however debilitating in its altered application.

In the fifth century B.C., corporate citizen bodies—Athens above all—had collectively exploited weaker peoples, while maintaining an exhilarating sense of social cohesion and equality at home. Far from feeling compunction at the harsh treatment meted out to their victims, the Athenians and others actually took pride in the demonstrations of collective prowess through which they made good their claim to the products of others' labor. In the Hellenistic age, collective and corporate exploitation gave way to a similar (indeed on the whole distinctly milder) exploitation by private individuals of populations living closer at hand, usually in the immediate locality. In other words, unearned income now came primarily from rents, no longer from tribute; while the profits of trade, which had been of great importance in the economy of imperial Athens, became a rather disreputable alternative means of amassing the wealth needful for civilized living.

As devices for concentrating wealth into a few hands shifted to an individual and local basis, the inland march of Hellenizing culture was greatly

---

[50] Almost the only series of wages and prices for the period comes from the temple records of Delos, which have been painstakingly analyzed by several scholars. Cf. Rostovtzeff, *Social and Economic History of the Hellenistic World*, I, 235–36.

[51] For a penetrating account of social and economic conditions in the Hellenistic Greek cities, see W. W. Tarn and G. T. Griffith, *Hellenistic Civilization* (3d ed.; London: Edward Arnold & Co., 1952), pp. 79–125.

accelerated. It now became apparent that the Greek style of life was not inseparable from the peculiar and very complicated geographical and social circumstances which had produced it. It was, after all, much easier for barbarians to civilize themselves if they did not first have to build a new Athens! Instead, local landownership and suitably heavy rents, together with a little formal education, would suffice.

Conversely, however, the changed social structure of Hellenistic society meant that, even in the heart of the classical world, the barbarians were now always and inescapably within the gates. Peasants, slaves, and artisans, ministering to the comfort of their masters, but excluded from any real share in their masters' intellectual and social world, easily felt aggrieved. Under these circumstances, the cultivated upper class faced an acute moral dilemma. Some felt real compunction when confronted by the sufferings of the poor; others were eager only to make it difficult for any social upstart to gain access to the privileged circle of gentility. The geographic dispersal of the fully civilized community had a second psychologically debilitating effect. In Athens' heyday, the subjected and tributary populations had lived across the seas, while the privileged citizens had clustered in a comparatively restricted area, supporting and stimulating one another in the creative use of their wealth and leisure. When landlords, spread out far more thinly over a vastly wider area, became the heirs of Hellenic culture, the in-group was more diffuse, the individual more isolated. Only a few of the major Hellenistic cities—Alexandria, Athens, Syracuse, Pergamum, Rhodes, and later Rome—could concentrate a sufficient number of fully civilized men to provide much mutual stimulus and moral support.

Even in these great cities, the community of educated gentlemen, whose physical needs were well taken care of by slaves and who regarded a decent private income or state salary as a necessity for civilized life, lacked something which the less refined and very much more brutal Athenians of Pericles' day had possessed. The harmonic engagement of both intellect and emotion upon common enterprises was no longer possible. Reason had its role in philosophy and scientific study; emotion ran riot in uninhibited debauchery.[52] But high and serious pursuits, harnessing both the rational and the emotional sides of human personality, were far to seek in the sophisticated, urbanized, cosmopolitan, and individualist Hellenistic world. In those times (which bear interesting resemblances to our own), individuals lacked any compelling cause to which to dedicate their energies. The upper classes also lacked a religion to sustain them in times of personal crisis. They relied instead upon the rather cold comforts of rationalistic philosophy and gentlemanly "good form."

*   *   *

The rapidity with which these changes came to the Greek world should not be exaggerated. In the first flush of conquest, when Greek arms and Greek culture seemed so brilliantly to have demonstrated their superiority

---

[52] Like so many other pursuits, the art of love also became professionalized. The fame of a few courtesans rivaled the fame of the equally professional athletes and actors.

over the only civilized rival the Greeks knew, a spirit of adventure and high excitement prevailed. Not only were there new lands to administer and settle, new wealth to be won by trade or plunder, and new experiences to be sought through travel and adventure; there was also new knowledge to be gathered and digested, new songs to be sung and stories told, and a vast new audience for Greek artists of every variety—sculptors and architects, painters and actors, doctors and athletes, teachers and acrobats. The parochialism of the past, when Athens or Sparta, Corinth or Thebes had seemed to their inhabitants to be the center and apex of all that mattered, was now left behind. A spirit of cosmopolitanism took root; and a man with a good Greek education could feel at home anywhere in the civilized world.

In this busy, wide, and wealthy society, cultural activity was intense and widespread. Pergamum and Alexandria rivaled Athens as artistic and intellectual centers, where the ambitious gathered from every corner of the Greek and half-Greek world. Yet, in the estimation of later generations of classical antiquity, Hellenistic cultural achievements fell short of the heights of the fifth and fourth centuries; and for that reason moderns are largely prevented from judging the matter independently. Only a tiny fraction of the once enormous bulk of Hellenistic art and literature survives; and there is some risk in condemning an age too brusquely on such limited evidence. Nevertheless, modern taste generally concurs in the adverse judgment of late classical times.

A striking feature of Hellenistic culture was its high degree of organization. Four schools of philosophy flourished in Athens—the Academic, Peripatetic, Epicurean, and Stoic. Each offered more or less regular courses and had suitable lecture places and libraries at its disposal. The Museum in Alexandria and the Library at Pergamum were state institutions where a salaried staff carried out literary and scientific work. Almost every Hellenistic city had some sort of publicly supported educational system. Although private tutors and parents usually provided primary education, gymnasia offering more advanced training were often supported by public taxes or by private endowment. Moreover, public education, which had formerly been almost entirely devoted to military training, was supplemented by advanced general instruction in Greek manners and literature, philosophy and rhetoric.[53]

As is perhaps normal when intellectual and artistic life is so well organized, spontaneity and the wellsprings of emotion tended to dry up. Only in fields where intellect alone sufficed was the Hellenistic achievement distinguished.

In literature, a great work of editing and stabilizing the texts of classic authors was carried through, especially at Alexandria. But in proportion as the

[53] Cf. A. H. M. Jones, *The Greek City from Alexander to Justinian* (Oxford: Clarendon Press, 1940), pp. 220–26. The organization of education offers one example of the more widespread development of professional associations in the Hellenistic world. For example, the actor's profession achieved a particularly elaborate organization, so much so that Dionysiac artists sometimes treated with cities and states over matters of safe conduct and terms of employment as one sovereign body with another. These professional and trade associations seem to have reproduced in miniature most of the institutions of a Greek polis—council, magistrates, religious ceremonies, laws, etc. As the original territorial basis of the polis in-group broke apart, individuals perhaps strove to reproduce a sense of close personal identification with a larger social entity through professional associations and naturally modeled them upon the polis organization. Cf. the similar sociological character of early Buddhist monasteries, as surmised above, chap. v.

scholar's hand fixed itseif upon literature, new work tended to become artificial, full of learned references, and devoid of appeal to those who lacked a thorough literary education. Preciosity generated its antitype in the form of a scurrilous and frequently bawdy popular literature—the mime—just as within the stately halls of philosophy—but outside the schools—rude cynics poured contempt upon intellect and upon all the fine arguments and creature comforts of philosophic gentlemen.[54]

Monumental art resisted large-scale organization until about 100 B.C., when scientific, yet technically practicable, methods for making copies of statues and architectural adornments were discovered.[55] Before that time, a statue or a building had to be created especially for an occasion; and the skill with which sculptors and architects fulfilled new assignments did not decay. There was more virtuosity than before, a widened range of subject matter, and greater choice of style: a statue might be either realistic, dramatized, or idealized; a building Doric, Ionic, or Corinthian. Yet the variant styles were all unmistakably of Greek provenance; and the sculptor of such a masterpiece as the Victory of Samothrace was surely a worthy heir of even the greatest of his predecessors.

Organization of intellectual effort and widened experience of the world paid off handsomely in natural science. The Hellenistic Greeks excelled in mathematics, geography, astronomy, and medicine. Physics and chemistry—the key sciences of modern Europe—made less progress, perhaps because they involved dirty hands and the manipulation of something besides a pen—behavior which did not accord well with the code of a Hellenistic gentleman.[56]

Euclid's codification of geometry (*ca.* 300 B.C.) was completed before the savants of Alexandria gained any exact knowledge of Babylonian mathematical and astronomical achievements. But the full development of Hellenistic astronomy owed much to Babylonia, where records of the movements of heavenly bodies had been kept since the eighth century B.C. Through the use of these records, Babylonian astronomers of the fourth and third centuries B.C. discovered mathematical regularities in the observed phenomena—e.g., the periodicity of eclipses and the mathematical coordinates defining the exact path of the moon and sun.

The Babylonians themselves did not attempt to explain the observed motions geometrically. But when translations of the Babylonian observational data became available, Greek astronomers immediately set out to try to create a geometrical model that might account for the newly revealed precision of the motions of the heavenly bodies. Eudoxos, a contemporary of Plato,

[54] These antinomies of course directly reflected the polarization of Greek society between rich and poor.

[55] On the geometric principles and practical devices (three-dimensional pantographs) whereby statues were copied in classical times see the interesting discussion in Gisela M. A. Richter, *Ancient Italy*, pp. 105–16.

[56] Archimedes of Syracuse (d. 212 B.C.) constitutes a noteworthy exception to this rule, for he was both a mathematician and an engineer and formulated the hydrostatic principle of physics that still bears his name.

Musée du Louvre and Archives photographiques, Paris.

Metropolitan Museum of Art, Rogers Fund, 1909.

THE HELLENISTIC AGE

These statues portray the parting of the ways between the upper and lower classes of the Hellenistic world, and do so with self-conscious, almost nostalgic artistry. The old market woman, bowed not only by the weight of her basket but with the whole burden of life, has little in common with the magnificent Victory of Samothrace, so proud, so bold, so ethereally elated by the prospect of new worlds to conquer. The stylistic virtuosity that links the two statues is obvious; the moral attitude that made it possible to find a subject matter for high art in the ugliness of urban poverty is a further tribute to the lingering sense of civic solidarity which had once bound all polis citizens so effectively together.

was the pioneer of this attempt. After two and a half centuries of discussion, in the course of which various models (including the heliocentric)[57] were proposed and rejected, Hipparchus of Nicaea (fl. *ca.* 146–126 B.C.) elaborated the scheme that became classical. Hipparchus posited a series of crystalline (and therefore invisible) spheres, each of which revolved around the earth. Retrograde planetary motion he explained as the result of the combined motion of an earth-centered sphere and of a smaller revolving "epicycle" carrying the fiery planet with it around a point upon the (moving) surface of the first sphere. Any new refinement of observation could be explained within this system by inventing a new epicycle (if need be within an older epicycle) to describe and therefore account for the newly observed motion. The cumbersomeness of such a celestial machinery (which, of course, tended to increase across the ages) was counterbalanced by the geometrical persuasiveness with which it made the regular irregularities of planetary motion intelligible.

Perhaps the most important result of these studies was the development of more precise measurements. Certainly, it is this aspect of Hellenistic astronomy which still survives: the division of time into hours, minutes, and seconds; the analogous subdivision of a circle into degrees, minutes, and seconds; the use of spherical coordinates to locate with precision any point in the sky or on earth; and the calculation of such key astronomical quantities as the length of a day or a year, the size of the earth, the sun, and the moon, and the distances between them. In some of these calculations, Hellenistic astronomers arrived at values almost identical with those accepted today; in others, e.g., the distance of the sun and moon from the earth, they were radically mistaken. But despite such errors, and Hipparchus' fundamentally erroneous concept of celestial mechanics, astronomy attained a degree of precision and mathematical sophistication which was never afterward entirely lost.

In astrology, as in astronomy, the combination of Greek with Oriental elements proved impressively fertile. From a primary center in Alexandria, astrology spread widely throughout the Hellenistic world, and became a pervasive element in men's conception of their relation to the universe. The key idea was Babylonian: that heavens and earth corresponded to one another in such a way that predictable celestial events foreshadowed terrestrial occurrences. Hellenistic astrologers applied this age-old notion in a radically new way, by relating the predictions of the skies to individual lives. They accomplished this (1) by assuming that the conjunction of the planets and other movable celestial bodies at the time of a man's birth controlled his entire life; and (2) by developing a Greco-Egyptian mumbo-jumbo by which each such conjunction acquired particular predictive values. Astrology kept mathematical astronomy alive in the following centuries. Careful calculation to establish the positions of the planets on a day, perhaps years in the past, was needed before astrological fantasy could find data to feed upon; and there was incen-

---

[57] Aristarchus of Samos (*ca.* 310–230 B.C.) was the most famous advocate of the theory that the earth and the other planets moved around the sun. This was soon discredited on sound geometrical grounds by the absence of observable stellar parallax, but the idea was never entirely forgotten.

tive for constant rigor, since the more precise the initial calculations, the more impressive the final prescription was likely to be.[58]

Alexandria offered still another solace to the perplexed—the worship of Serapis.[59] Serapis was the city god of Alexandria, deliberately invented in the time of the first Ptolemy by combining elements from the worships of Osiris, Zeus, and Marduk. The cult offered salvation and immortal life to those who, through appropriate rituals, identified themselves with the god. Certainly the ancient mysteries of Greece contributed something to this religion; but Egyptian elements predominated, especially the doctrine of a blessed immortality. Despite its eclectic and official character, a surprising number of Alexandrians (and, in time, natives of other places as well) found it comforting to believe that an all-powerful divinity could free their souls from the web of fate and raise them to a realm of blessed eternity after death.

The worship of Serapis was not unique; for other mystery religions, some developing from older Orphic rites, others emerging from an Anatolian or Syrian background, competed with the Egyptian cult. Yet men educated in the Greek intellectual tradition could not easily surrender to the obscurantism

[58] Cf. O. Neugebauer, "The History of Ancient Astronomy: Problems and Methods," *Journal of Near Eastern Studies*, IV (1945), 1–38, for a very penetrating discussion of the subject.

[59] Serapis was in fact one of a trinity, which included the Egyptian goddess Isis and a less important figure, Anubis.

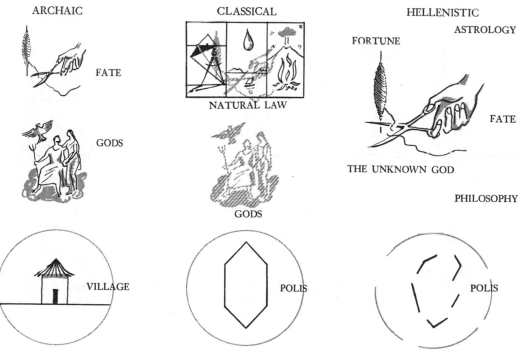

CHANGES IN THE HELLENIC WORLD VIEW

of such faiths. For them, philosophy offered an alternative to religion: a view of the world distinctly chilly to the feelings though more congenial to the intellect.

Yet there was something profoundly defeatist in the whole enterprise of Hellenistic philosophy. The two principal schools, the Epicurean and Stoic, employed the fine-tempered razor of Greek logic to arrive at conclusions discouraging the too energetic pursuit of anything, even of truth or of logic. According to both doctrines, the ideally wise man should disengage himself from the world about him so that, caring only for his own equanimity, he would remain inwardly free and invulnerable, even in the face of the severest of all moral tests—unexpected good fortune—precisely because he was committed to nothing.

This point of view was neither ignoble nor unreasonable in an age of political and social upheaval. Yet, by rejecting and endeavoring to repress the emotions, the philosophers ran against the grain of human nature. Their doctrines could appeal only to men of strong native intellect or to those favored few for whom, in fact, fortune had reserved only the best. Hellenistic philosophy thus became the upper-class equivalent of the emotionally far more powerful mystery religions. When Roman conquest disturbed the ease of the Hellenistic gentlemen, when brutal soldiers trampled their gardens, plundered their valuables, and killed their friends, gentlemanly philosophy wilted, and mystery religions of the Oriental type came fully into their own.

*　　*　　*

By 146 B.C., when Macedonia became a Roman province and Greece a Roman dependency, most of the energy with which the Greeks had begun their exploitation of the Orient had evaporated; scientific, literary, and philosophic creativity had largely worn themselves out. The Oriental view of the subordination of the individual and the nation to supernatural powers, controllable, if at all, only by prayer and ritual supplication, had come to prevail over the one-time rationalistic, curious, and restless spirit of Hellas. To be sure, the nearer Orient still wore a Hellenized garb: the splendid cities, with their gymnasia and theaters, still stood, and Greek remained the language of common use among all educated and some uneducated persons. Yet the spirit was changed. Oriental reaction had begun to manifest its massive strength behind the Greek façade. The expansive force of Hellenism had spent itself.

Roman conquest helped to bring these changes to their completion. Yet in Horace's famous phrase, the Greeks, captive, took the victors captive;[60] and Hellenism, though in modified and diluted forms, had still another, if autumnal, day to live, not only within the Roman empire, but also eastward among the Parthians, Shakas, Kushans, Indians, and even the remote Chinese.

[60] *Epistolae*, 2, 1, line 156.

CHAPTER VII

Closure of the Eurasian Ecumene 500 B.C.–200 A.D.

A. INTRODUCTION

The legionaries who in 146 B.C. sacked Corinth and demonstrated to the Greeks the abject political weakness into which their once proud cities had fallen were neither the first nor the last Roman marauders to descend upon the Greek world. For more than a century thereafter, generals, governors, tax gatherers, and adventurers of all sorts came from the west to seek fame and fortune at the expense of the Hellenistic peoples. In the process, they extended Roman rule to all the lands of the eastern Mediterranean and mulcted them of much of their accumulated wealth. Many Greek cities, especially those in the Aegean heartland of Greek civilization, suffered blows from which they never recovered. Drastic depopulation set in; and the energies which once had raised Hellenic culture so high ceased to manifest themselves.

In 128 B.C., just eighteen years after the Roman conquest of Greece, a venturesome Chinese diplomat named Chang-k'ien traveled westward to the valleys of the Oxus and Jaxartes, where he discovered—rather to his surprise—the easternmost fringes of the civilized Middle East. Thereafter, the Chinese maintained sporadic diplomatic and trading contacts with central Asia, until in 101 B.C., Chinese armies followed in Chang-k'ien's footsteps and conquered a string of oases extending as far as the Jaxartes. This enormous westward expansion of Chinese suzerainty led to the establishment of a regular caravan route between China and the Middle East—the so-called "Silk Road."[1]

[1] Cf. Albert Herrmann, *Die alten Seidenstrassen zwischen China und Syrien* (Berlin: Weidmannsche Buchhandlung, 1910), pp. 1–7 and end map. Full operation of the Silk Road depended of course upon complicated political, military, and economic conditions throughout its length; but another factor of great importance was the means of transport itself. Only the Bactrian, or two-humped, camel could carry significant quantities of goods across the inhospitable cold deserts between China and the Middle

Almost simultaneously, the sea routes of the Indian Ocean underwent decisive development. Since the barbarian invasions of the Bronze Age (1500–1200 B.C.), semi-piratical princelings established along the shorelines had strangled coastal voyaging on the Arabian Sea and the adjacent waters of the Persian Gulf and Red Sea. Despite this difficulty, sailors in the service of King Ptolemy II Euergetes of Egypt pioneered a voyage all the way to India about 120 B.C. Subsequent political disturbances in Egypt, climaxing in the Roman conquest (30 B.C.), did not prevent the newly opened route from remaining operative thereafter. Once they had gained familiarity with the regular wind patterns of the Indian Ocean monsoons, Greco-Roman sea captains gradually plucked up courage to shorten their trip to India (and escape exactions at coastal way stations) by sailing across wider and wider stretches of open water. By the first century A.D., direct voyages across the full width of the Arabian Sea, from the Straits of Aden to southernmost India, had become matters of routine. As a result, transport between the Mediterranean and Indian Ocean became vastly cheaper as well as faster; and a greatly enlarged flow of goods between these regions funneled through Alexandria by Egypt. This long-distance trade kept Alexandria prosperous even when its immediate hinterland in the Nile Valley suffered economic retrogression under Roman rule.

Once the sea captains of the Indian Ocean had mastered the art of sailing before the monsoon in the Arabian Sea, similar voyages beckoned farther east; and on the eastern shores of the Bay of Bengal, enterprising merchants established contacts with other seamen operating from the south China coast. The result was to link China with India by sea, just as the Mediterranean had (perhaps only slightly earlier)[2] been linked to India. By the second century A.D. (and possibly before), the originally separate legs of the sea journey between Roman and Chinese territory—from Egypt to south India, from south India to Malaya, from Malaya to China—merged into one more or less continuous commercial network, spanning the entire breadth of the southern seas between Africa and south China.[3]

East; and the techniques of organizing and conducting a caravan were quite as complicated as those of seafaring. There seems to be no clear information as to when Bactrian camels were first domesticated. They were known, perhaps as rarities, to the Achaemenids (cf. the Bactrian camel portrayed at Persepolis with other exotic tribute); and the Chinese also knew them in domesticated form, perhaps as early as the fifth century B.C., and certainly before 221 B.C. "The camel excels at travelling over running sands; while burdened with one thousand catties he travels three hundred li." (Translated from *T'ai ping yü lan* 901/6/*b*, by Hsio Yen Shih.)

The westward spread of the Arabian, or one-humped, camel at roughly the same time (or perhaps a little earlier) had a similar effect in opening the hot deserts of west Africa. Arabian camels were fairly numerous and important in Achaemenid Persia, but did not spread to north Africa until Hellenistic and, in the West, until Roman times. Cf. W. W. Hyde, *Ancient Greek Mariners* (New York: Oxford University Press, 1947), pp. 184–85; Stéphane Gsell, *Histoire ancienne de l'Afrique du Nord* (Paris: Hachette, 1920), IV, 139; Herodotus, VII, 83–86; and Xenophon, *Anabasis*, VI, 1.

[2] The Chinese historian Pan Ku dates the opening of sea contact with India from the reign of the emperor Wu-ti (140–86 B.C.), but does not give an exact date.

[3] Cf. Mortimer Wheeler, *Rome beyond the Imperial Frontiers* (Harmondsworth: Pelican, 1955), pp. 141–83; E. H. Warmington, *The Commerce between the Roman Empire and China* (Cambridge: Cambridge University Press, 1928), pp. 1–34; W. W. Hyde, *Ancient Greek Mariners*, pp. 169–232;

Thus, in the latter decades of the second century B.C., China consciously entered into regular contact with the other civilizations of Eurasia. Organized trade routes, both by land and by sea, soon linked the four great cultures of the continent. In addition, Eurasia's central sea of grass provided a third linkage, more sensitive to military than to mercantile enterprise. By the fourth century B.C., horse nomadry had spread to all the tribes of the steppe. The tumultuous relations of these tribes with one another and with the various civilizations lying on their southward flank regularly transmitted from one end of the continent to the other the tremors generated by any important military-political disturbance. Thus, the Eurasian ecumene was closed as never before.

This event may be compared with the far more famous closure of the global ecumene in the sixteenth to eighteenth centuries A.D., when European explorers, merchants, and missionaries systematically opened up the coasts and islands of all the world to Western enterprise. To be sure, the European expansion was on a larger geographical scale; and its political, social, and cultural consequences were more dramatic than in the earlier case. In the centuries between 200 B.C. and 200 A.D., the four major civilizations of Eurasia were very nearly on a par technologically and aesthetically, so that no very radical readjustment of established patterns of life was forced upon any one of them. Cultural borrowings arising from this first closure of the ecumene were therefore limited to those items which the recipients found desirable. Consequently, the enterprise of ancient mariners, soldiers, and caravan leaders created nothing resembling the upheaval of modern times, with its destruction of the cultural autonomy of the entire non-European world. On the contrary, the cultural balance of Eurasia remained much as it had been before.

Nevertheless, the first closure of the ecumene worked important alterations in the general pattern of Eurasian history. Two areas which had previously been marginal to the civilized world now became central points on the new trade routes: south India, and the river valleys on either side of the Hindu Kush. It is probably no coincidence that both these regions became the seats of important cultural innovations in the following two or three centuries. Southern India seems to have been the principal seedbed for the cults of Shiva and Vishnu, which between them gave a distinctive character to subsequent Hinduism; and Mahayana Buddhism probably arrived at its distinctive form in the region of the Hindu Kush.

Cultural creativity may perhaps be expected in a region where trade and urbanization permit men of diverse cultural backgrounds to meet and mingle. But neither southern India, where Aryan, Dravidian, and eastern Mediterranean cultures came together, nor central Asia, where Chinese, Indian, Greek, nomad, and Middle Eastern cultures overlapped, gave birth to any-

---

J. J. L. Duyvendak, *China's Discovery of Africa* (London: Arthur Probsthain, 1949), pp. 7–12; K. A. Nilakanta Sastri, "The Beginnings of Intercourse between India and China," *The Indian Historical Quarterly*, XIV (1938), 380–87; G. F. Hudson, *Europe and China* (London: Edward Arnold & Co., 1931), pp. 53–102; Radhakumud Mookerji, *A History of Indian Shipping and Maritime Activity* (London: Longmans, Green, 1912), pp. 116–41 and *passim*.

thing that could be called a new civilization. In these regions, the internal conservatism and external attractiveness of the ancient and well-established Eurasian civilizations soon stifled the independent growth of new styles of civilized life. Nevertheless, both southern India and central Asia were able to transmit, fuse, and work certain mutations in older cultural elements, thereby making important new motifs available to be accepted, rejected, or modified still further by the older civilized communities according to local choices.

On the whole, diffracted elements of Hellenistic civilization attracted a larger share of favorable attention. than did the achievements of any of the other cultures of the world between 200 B.C. and 200 A.D. The history of art gives the clearest evidence of this; for both Indian and Chinese art styles of the period were profoundly affected by Greek sculpture. In religion and in science, a parallel, though less striking, process may be detected. Mahayana Buddhism, for example, shows influence of Hellenistic religious conceptions, while Indian and Chinese astronomy and astrology appropriated numerous Hellenistic elements, though important local differences of course remained. The profound Hellenic imprint upon Rome and the lands of western Europe need not be argued, for in that direction the Greek cultural model had no serious rivals. Hence even after its core area around the Aegean had lost all creativity, Hellenism's cultural radiation did not cease but, like the light from a dead star, continued to propagate itself in the farther reaches of the civilized world for two or three additional centuries.

But while ideas and techniques originating in the orbit of Greek culture were spreading widely throughout Eurasia, the other great civilizations did not stand still. Indeed, the reception and transformation of elements originally Greek was in itself a sign of assimilative energy on the part of the Indians and Chinese; for no external force compelled them to accept foreign innovations. Moreover, by conquering and converting contiguous barbarians, both India and China rapidly extended the geographical area dominated by their own styles of life, while new emphases continued to emerge within their respective core areas, without, however, infringing upon the distinctive stylistic cohesion previously attained by each civilization.

Before analyzing the main line of cultural interchange resulting from the closure of the Eurasian ecumene, it will therefore be needful to survey the development of the separate civilizations of Asia and of the European Far West prior to the inception of such interchange.

B. EXPANSION AND DEVELOPMENT OF THE NON-HELLENIC CIVILIZATIONS OF EURASIA, 500–100 B.C.

1. INDIA

The most active seat of Indian civilization in 500 B.C. was in the Ganges Valley, where powerful, centralized kingdoms were in the process of destroying older tribal and aristocratic polities. The Indus Valley, part of which was then under Persian government, remained politically divided and socially conservative, although various influences from the Middle East—coined money, for example—filtered into India from that direction. The south, for which no records are available, was presumably undergoing a gradual Aryanization through contact with the culturally more advanced north.

When Alexander invaded India (327 B.C.), the Ganges kingdom of Magadha had already subdued most of northeastern India. Shortly afterward, Chandragupta Maurya (reigned 322–298 B.C.) united the Ganges and Indus valleys into a single great empire, based on the kernel of the Magadha kingdom.[4] His grandson Ashoka (reigned *ca.* 273–232 B.C.) brought the empire to its greatest extent, controlling almost all India except for a small area in the extreme south. Ashoka's heirs were unable to maintain the unity of this far-flung state, which soon disintegrated into smaller and perhaps competing units; and about 185 B.C. a usurper drove the last Maurya ruler from the throne of Magadha. Simultaneously, or soon thereafter, invaders from the northwest—first Greek rulers of Bactria, then tribes of Shakas and Kushans—gave Indian politics a new complexion. These invaders did not conquer all of India; their control only sporadically extended beyond the Punjab. To the south and east, other states, the boundaries and very names of which are often unsure, divided the Maurya heritage.

Chronological uncertainties make exact history impossible for these centuries. Nonetheless, it is clear that Indian culture continued to develop along the lines already defined. Oral transmission of literature and learning was the rule in the time of Buddha (d. *ca.* 486 B.C.); and the habit of putting texts on paper gained intellectual respectability very slowly.[5] Its oral forms gave Indian literature a wide flexibility. New ideas and emphases, glosses and omissions grafted themselves almost imperceptibly onto older materials, as one master after another passed on the wisdom of the past to his pupils. Only sacred texts like the *Vedas*, or recognized and authoritative classics like Panini's Sanskrit grammar, escaped such protean evolution across the generations.

The oral evolution of Indian literature blunts the tools of textual criticism which Western scholars are accustomed to use in analyzing the development of thought. Existing manuscripts, all of them dating from relatively recent times, represent the deposit of a centuries-long oral development; and there is no sure way to tell which passages may have survived unaltered and which are new—nor the dates of any part thereof. As a result, the chronology and authenticity of all early Indian literature is a subject of fundamentally insoluble controversy.

Despite pervasive uncertainty, surviving texts make it clear that Brahmin-

---

[4] In 305 B.C., Chandragupta induced Seleucus I to cede Alexander's Indian conquests to him. Thereafter, the two monarchs maintained cordial diplomatic relations. Chandragupta or his son probably married a Seleucid princess; and it has even been suggested that his famous successor, Ashoka, may have been the offspring of this marriage. Cf. K. H. Dhruva, "Historical Contents of the Yugapurana," *Journal of the Bihar and Orissa Research Society*, XVI (1930), 35.

[5] Sanskrit terms for "book," "pen," and "ink" are of Greek derivation. This suggests that written learning established itself in India only after Indians acquired some acquaintance with the Hellenistic book trade. Cf. A. L. Basham, *The Wonder That Was India* (London: Sidgwick & Jackson, 1954), p. 230.

ism was on the defensive from the fifth century B.C. until after the time of Ashoka. To be sure, the old Vedic learning, with its elaborations in the *Brahmanas* and *Upanishads*, continued to be studied in Brahminic schools. New commentaries and distillations of that wisdom were produced—the so-called *sutras* (literally "threads")—which attempted to apply traditional doctrine to the vast variety of sacrificial and everyday circumstances which might puzzle a pious Brahmin. Furthermore, the problem created by the growing divergence between spoken tongues and the sacred Vedic language gave rise to an impressive, if often recondite science of linguistics. The great monument of the new study was Panini's Sanskrit grammar, probably dating from the fourth century B.C. This book codified rules for "classical" Sanskrit —a language not identical with that of the *Vedas*, but derived directly from it.[6]

In general, the Brahmins seem to have found it difficult to adjust to the changing social scene in India. The rise of cities, where mercantile and artisan populations mixed together cheek by jowl with men claiming superior social status by right of birth, accorded ill with the taboos and ritual observances required by Brahminical religion. Various *sutras* expressly forbade travel by ship, for example; and there were no Vedic rituals for urban circumstances. Towns were spoken of slightingly in the *sutras* or simply neglected.[7]

Buddhist writers offer a much more variegated picture of Indian society. Merchants and their voyages to distant parts figure favorably in many of the cautionary tales and pious stories which constitute the bulk of this literature; and these works preserve only incidental traces of the pride of birth and emphasis upon ritual purity so characteristic of Brahminical writings. It seems, therefore, that Buddhism (together with Jainism) appealed particularly to urban groups in India. The fact that the early Buddhist monks preached in the language of the streets and did not cultivate a recondite and semi-archaic language like Sanskrit must have helped them to win the popular ear.

A major problem for both Buddhists and Jains was the definition of their respective orthodoxies. Surviving records contain clear echoes of disputes and schisms affecting both religions. Recognition of an authoritative canon of scripture was an obvious way of limiting doctrinal controversy; but the Indian Buddhists, with characteristic ebullience, developed several collections of sacred texts and never quite managed to close the canon, much less to determine which of a number of variant versions of a given story or sermon was the authoritative one.[8] The emperor Ashoka may have attempted to bring a modicum of order to the confusion by summoning leading dignitaries of

---

[6] In addition to learned and sacred texts, a Sanskrit heroic literature attuned to the taste of kings and warriors certainly existed in oral form. On special sacrificial occasions Brahmin priests probably recited verses derived from this lay tradition, in order to celebrate and sanctify their noble patrons' ancestors. From such a confluence of sacred and secular literary genres, India's epic poetry was later to emerge.

[7] Cf. *Cambridge History of India*, I, 237, 240, 248; A. L. Basham, *The Wonder That Was India*, p. 231.

[8] The version of Buddhist scriptures recorded in Pali, one of the vernaculars current, presumably, in Buddha's own time, probably contains more ancient and authentic material than other collections. Yet new texts and glosses were added to the Pali canon as late as 500 A.D. and ceased then only because the evolution of spoken languages in India had made Pali into a learned and therefore sacred language, no longer lightly to be tampered with.

the faith to a council; but if so, he did not see fit to mention such a council in his famous rock edicts, which constitute the sole unimpeachable source for Indian history of his age.

These inscriptions, carved on rocks and pillars at Ashoka's command, tell us that the emperor was attracted to the Buddhist path after youthful disillusionment with more violent and traditional methods of statecraft. Early in his reign, Ashoka invaded and after a bloody fight annexed the sole important Indian state that had escaped the conquests of his grandfather. Thereafter, he foreswore military operations in favor of spiritual conquests and launched a series of missions to preach Buddhism among his own subjects and in neighboring lands as well.[9] Prior to this time, Buddhism had found its main successes along the eastern and southern fringes of Aryan India, where Brahminism had only imperfectly won the assent of autochthonous peoples.[10] Ashoka's missionary enterprises established Buddhism in all parts of India and in Ceylon and gave it at least a foothold in central Asia.

The religion that thus attracted Ashoka's support, and which he did so much to propagate, was already rather different from the metaphysical pessimism and moral discipline which Gautama Buddha had (perhaps) taught. To the original core had been added a rudimentary, popular cult, centering at *stupas* (shrines) built around the relics of holy men,[11] or at other especially sacred places. Pillars, and trees commemorating the tree under which Buddha had received enlightenment, were often associated with the *stupas*.

Through such modifications, Buddhism assimilated itself to age-old local observances. Reverence for relics made it easy for holy places and spirits of the most diverse origins to assume a Buddhist garb; and the figure of the Buddha himself took on an increasingly superhuman character. The greatest shrines were those associated with the critical turning points of his life or built around portions of his ashes—divided, according to pious tradition, among several *stupas* immediately after his death, and further distributed by the piety of Ashoka, who built a large number of new *stupas* around portions of Buddha's earthly remains in diverse parts of his wide realm.

With state support and a cult accessible to the humblest understanding, Buddhism thus became a widely popular religion in India. For Ashoka himself, and presumably for most of his coreligionists, the doctrine and ritual of Buddhism were associated with a generous and comprehensive morality. The main theme of Ashoka's inscriptions was exactly this: exhortations to his

[9] Missions were sent (perhaps in 255 B.C.) to the Seleucid, Ptolemaic, Macedonian, Epirote(?), and Cyrenaic courts; but no Hellenistic record of their reception has been preserved.

[10] Nalinaksha Dutt, *Aspects of Mahayana Buddhism and Its Relation to Hinayana* (London: Luzac & Co., 1930), pp. 14–21. In addition to the original centers in the Ganges Valley, where Buddha himself had been active, it appears that early disciples established another center in western India, in the kingdom of Avanti. Perhaps it was here that the Pali canon of Buddhist scriptures principally took form. Cf. *Cambridge History of India*, I, 184–85; A. L. Basham, *The Wonder That Was India*, p. 391.

[11] The Buddhist *stupa* derived its shape and ground plan from simple burial mounds. The idea seems to have been to honor the relics of a departed holy man with a mound specially hollowed out to allow the living to gain nearer access to the source of holiness: hence a circular dome, with access through a narrow passage to a small interior room where the relics reposed. Cf. A. L. Basham, *The Wonder That Was India*, pp. 262–63.

people to conduct themselves in accordance with *dharma*. His own definition of *dharma*, as presented in the so-called Second Pillar Edict, was as follows: "Dharma is good. But what does dharma consist of? It consists of few sins and many good deeds, of kindness, liberality, truthfulness and purity."[12] More particularly, *dharma* for Ashoka required toleration and mutual respect among the various religious groups of his realm and abstention from killing animals or men. He forbade animal sacrifices, thus bringing the power of the state to bear against the old Vedic rituals which involved such sacrifice; and he himself gave up hunting and warfare, the traditional sports of kings in India, as elsewhere.

As a man of religion, Ashoka was certainly one of the most characteristically Indian personalities who ever sat a throne; but he was also an emperor with pretensions to universal monarchy; and in this capacity he appears, like his father and grandfather before him, to have deserved the epithet "philhellene."[13] The idea of universal empire may have reached India from Achaemenid Persia. Archeological investigations provide concrete evidences of affinities between the Mauryan and Persian courts, suggesting, for example, that the Maurya palace at Pataliputra was built around a great columned hall, quite in the style of Persepolis. Even more telling is the close resemblance of Mauryan sculpture to Persian (and Greek) models.[14]

The Greek notion of the supremacy of the state over all aspects of human activity probably also attracted the Mauryan monarchs; and they may have tried to establish an efficient bureaucratic administration like that of Ptolemy in Egypt. Yet the usual uncertainty prevails, for the principal evidence concerning Mauryan government—the *Arthashastra*—is itself of questionable authenticity.[15] Nevertheless, whether or not it describes real practices, the *Arthashastra* bears a strong imprint of Hellenistic ideas. In particular, its doctrine that the royal law was supreme, overriding sacred precedent and custom, was alien to older, as well as to later Indian tradition.[16] We should prob-

[12] N. A. Nikam and Richard McKeon (eds.), *The Edicts of Asoka* (Chicago: University of Chicago Press, 1959), p. 41.

[13] Bestowed upon the king of "Palibothra" (*i.e.*, the Maurya capital, Pataliputra) by Diodorus Siculus (first century B.C.), II, 60.

[14] Indeed, the artists who carved the lions atop Ashoka's columns may have been Greek or Iranian craftsmen, imported by a court wishing to introduce the techniques of stone sculpture to India. Cf. Niharranjan Ray, "Mauryan Art," in K. A. Nilakanta Sastri, *Age of the Nandas and Mauryas*, pp. 356–61. Ashoka's famous edicts, carved into rock, are also an adaptation of an Achaemenid custom; and even details of his titles conform to the famous Behistun inscriptions made by order of Darius the Great.

[15] Learned controversy on this point is sharp. The book professes to be the work of a Brahmin named Kautilya, who served as a sort of first minister to Chandragupta and, according to legend, had much to do with that monarch's successful seizure of power and subsequent victories. For a summary of the arguments for and against the Mauryan origin of this work, see K. A. Nilakanta Sastri, *Age of the Nandas and Mauryas*, pp. 190–201. Whatever its origin, the final form of the book does not appear to have been reached until about 300 A.D. Cf. A. Berriedale Keith, *A History of Sanskrit Literature* (London: Oxford University Press, 1928), p. 461.

[16] "Whenever sacred law is in conflict with rational law [or, by another translation, king's law], then reason shall be held authoritative. . . ." *Arthashastra*, III, 1, as quoted in R. Shamasastry, *Kautilya's Arthashastra* (Mysore: Wesleyan Mission Press, 1929), p. 171. The alternative translations are offered by Mr. Shamasastry.

ASHOKA'S INDIA

On the left, the brusque, mustached lions from Sarnath, India, are perceptibly different in style from the more softly contoured Rampurwa bull on the right. Both originally stood atop columns erected by the Emperor Ashoka in the third century B.C. On the lower left is a seal impression from Mohenjo-daro which suggests a continuity of motif and possibly even of sculptural idea from the ancient Indus culture. The conception and execution of the lion capital, on the other hand, has definite Middle Eastern and even Hellenistic affiliations. Yet Ashoka's sculptors found no difficulty in combining foreign with native traditions and motifs—a fact nicely illustrated by the Buddhist "Wheel of the Law" adorning the plinth on which the lions stand, and by the palmetto motif stemming from the Mediterranean that is to be found beneath the bull's feet.

ably interpret the *Arthashastra* less as a description of actual practice than as a handbook of advice to a ruler on how to maximize his power.[17] Taken in this light, the *Arthashastra*, as well as the general administrative and military effort of the Mauryas, may be thought of as an attempt to implant upon the refractory body social of India a Greco-Iranian concept of the supremacy of the state as against all other forms of human association.[18] Yet, in practice, the Mauryan administration was undoubtedly based upon older precedent within the kingdom of Magadha. And, although Chandragupta and his successors may have been dazzled by Hellenistic concepts of rulership, it was an indigenous Indian stratum that prevailed in the end.[19]

To sum up: India's development to the time of Alexander's invasion appears to have pursued lines laid down at the beginning of the fifth century or before. With the new intimacy between India and the Hellenistic world that resulted from Alexander's venture, and with the rise of the "philhellenic" Mauryan dynasty within India itself, new, though still comparatively superficial, foreign influences upon Indian society became apparent. The royal court patronized a westernizing art style, and perhaps promulgated Greco-Iranian patterns of administration and political theory. Beyond the courtly circle, however, foreign influence was probably trifling until long after Mauryan times, when prolonged and more massive military and commercial contact with the Mediterranean world allowed a deeper penetration of Hellenistic and Roman influences into Indian society as a whole.

2. CHINA

In the centuries between 500 and 100 B.C., China moved in a world of its own. Until the opening of the Silk Road in the first century B.C., communication across the land and sea spaces between China and western Asia was too slight to leave traces at either end. Yet these centuries were a time of great literary and intellectual activity in China, when the classics of Chinese thought took shape.

Written transmission of literature and learning had become normal in China even before the time of Confucius (d. 479 B.C.), so that no protean oral tradition like that of India obstructs the modern historian. From Han times onward, Chinese themselves devoted much energy to historical investigation and composition and maintained quite exact chronological records. As a result, Chinese history is vastly better known than is Indian. Yet there are real uncertainties in interpreting the old texts; and records edited and re-edited across the centuries cannot always be taken at face value. Indeed, the very bulk of the surviving materials complicates the task of ascertaining the

---

[17] Cf. Machiavelli's *Prince*.

[18] Cf. the judgment of K. A. Nilakanta Sastri: ". . . the Mauryan system of administration like Mauryan art was in some of its essentials an exotic—a parenthesis that broke the course of normal indigenous development." *Age of the Nandas and Mauryas*, p. 190.

[19] Surviving sculpture sensitively reflects the Janus-face of Mauryan society, for Ashoka's western-type lion capitals were twinned with other capitals that strikingly recall seal engravings from the ancient Indus civilization itself.

main lines of Chinese development, while giving political history an un-rivaled precision and permitting some fairly confident sociological generalization.

Between the fifth and second centuries B.C., the feudal society of earlier Chou times was destroyed; and a far more complicated social system emerged in which officials, scholars, and merchants played important roles side by side with the older peasant and landlord classes. Two key transformations seem to have occurred: (1) the rise of a new type of landholding, supplanting older feudal tenures; and (2) the elaboration of bureaucratic administrative machines in the service of the various princes. These changes were interconnected; and both may be taken as aspects of the breakdown of old social and political distinctions between the autochthonous populations and the Chou conquerors, who had initially held themselves apart from their subjects. Interwoven with both changes was the spread of a money economy, the appearance of merchants, markets, cities, and the greater social mobility associated with these phenomena.

Some recent scholars have used the phrase, "rise of the gentry," to describe the transformation of landholding that came to China between the time of Confucius and the establishment of the Former Han dynasty. The essence of the change seems to have been that a more baldly economic relationship between landlord and peasant supplanted a regime of traditional rights and duties among hierarchically ranked lords and followers. How this happened is obscure. The introduction of money and the rise of markets was undoubtedly one factor. In addition, the Chou nobles seem to have sought to consolidate their authority and increase their income by appointing agents[20] to gather rents directly from peasant families, instead of collecting a tribute through village head-men as had been traditional.

Another factor was military. The old-style feudal levies were composed of descendants of the original Chou invaders, who owed traditional but far from automatic allegiance to their lord. Thus the size and dependability of feudal armies was limited; and ambitious nobles began to supplement their forces through the recruitment of peasants. As this occurred, the Chou gradually lost their special status and merged into the general population. Conversely, the power of an energetic noble, both over his own subjects and against outside rivals, increased substantially.

But once alteration in traditional military and economic relationships was admitted, the question arose as to what level of the old feudal hierarchy should in practice reap the reward of enhanced wealth and power made available by the new administrative and other techniques. The rent collectors and recruiting sergeants of a petty nobleman constituted a bureaucracy in miniature; but near the top of the feudal pyramid, precisely the same pursuit of wealth and power impelled princes to create larger bureaucracies capable of collecting taxes and marshaling armies on a territorial scale; and, if the later

---

[20] Such agents, dealing with the members of the village as strangers and taskmasters, may often have originated among peddlers or petty merchants, whose livelihood depended upon treating buyers and sellers in just such an extratraditional and impersonal manner.

Chou emperors had not been helpless puppets, the central government might have made a similar effort. Obviously, the desire of local landlords to squeeze an enlarged flow of goods and services from the peasants conflicted directly with the desire of a prince to raise more taxes and recruit more soldiers from the same source. Accordingly, an acute collision of interest, regulated by no custom or law, utterly disrupted the old Chou feudal hierarchy. Nothing but naked force could settle the resulting quarrels.

Chronic and increasingly bitter warfare characterized these centuries, in the course of which many Chou noble families were dispossessed or exterminated. Their land came into the possession of new men—parvenus who were quite prepared to pay taxes and accept subordination to the prince and his officials, and who at the same time were free of the older chivalric and paternalistic attitudes in dealing with equals and inferiors. Thus by about 300 B.C., when such upstarts—the so-called "gentry"—emerged as a well-consolidated land-lord class, little of the former Chou noble tradition survived.[21]

The consolidation of princely administration was facilitated also by improvements in communication, above all by the construction of canals, which became important in China only after 500 B.C.[22] Canals intensified and extended agriculture by improving both drainage and irrigation; they also permitted cheap transport of large quantities of goods over considerable distances. Their net effect upon China was profound. The landscape itself was altered: agriculture had formerly been limited to scattered localities—primarily on hills and slopes—where natural drainage was good; but canals and other flood control works allowed the expansion of cultivation downslope until the older patches of farmland were gradually engulfed in a contiguous and vast carpet of fields stretching out over the flood plains of north China. The consequences for princely power were no less striking. Newly reclaimed land could be treated like newly conquered land, *i.e.*, administered outside the older feudal relationships and thus made to contribute directly to the prince's central exchequer. Moreover, as networks of canals and roads spread out over the plains, it became possible to concentrate large quantities of goods at capital cities, thus providing means of support for ever more elaborate bureaucracies and armies. Finally, improved transport promoted trade and manufacture and thus offered a new source of princely revenue in the form of taxes and tolls.[23]

---

[21] Cf. Wolfram Eberhard, *Conquerors and Rulers: Social Forces in Medieval China*, pp. 8–17; Henri Maspero, *La Chine antique*, pp. 134–37; Marcel Granet, *Chinese Civilization* (New York: Barnes & Noble, 1951), p. 234. The term "rise of the gentry" is of course borrowed from the social history of Tudor England. Parallels seem sufficiently close to make the term useful.

[22] Karl A. Wittfogel, "The Foundations and Stages of Chinese Economic History," *Zeitschrift für Sozialforschung*, IV (1935), 40–42.

[23] The weight to be assigned to water engineering in ancient China has become a matter of learned controversy. Karl Wittfogel elaborated a theory to the effect that "Oriental despotism" represents a distinct and definite type of social organization, common to India, China, and parts of the Middle East, and that this despotism is based upon hydraulic engineering—in particular upon canal construction and irrigation. Cf. his complete exposition in Karl A. Wittfogel, *Oriental Despotism: A Comparative Study of Total Power* (New Haven, Conn.: Yale University Press, 1957). Like many sweeping theories, this

When frontier principalities had shown what bureaucratic centralized government could accomplish by massive land reclamation, even the weaker and smaller states in the center of the Chinese world began to imitate the successes of their fellows. This tipped the scales decisively against local nobles, whose personal estates were not large enough to permit effective flood control measures. Nonetheless, the princes' victory was illusory; for, in proportion as they became strong at home, they found themselves engaged in an increasingly fierce struggle with rival princes. As a result, centuries of warfare eliminated one princely state after another, until in 221 B.C. Shih Huang-ti, the ruler of Ch'in, emerged as the political and military master of all China.

Ch'in enjoyed the usual advantages of a state located on the frontiers of a civilized society; and its military techniques had been tempered in the hard school of border warfare against the horse nomads of the northern steppe. Partly because the Ch'in rulers had always to spend so much energy in guarding the frontier against the nomads, they remained in themselves half barbarian. In particular, a strain of ruthlessness and a readiness to disregard Chinese social and political traditions distinguished them from their more fully civilized rivals.

In a sense, Shih Huang-ti attempted to repeat the work of the first Chou emperors.[24] He swept away old political forms and extended Ch'in institutions over all China. Some eight centuries before, the early Chou rulers had apparently proceeded in similarly drastic fashion; but in view of the state of technology and society in their day, the regime they instituted was feudal, superimposed upon a more or less autonomous village life within which variegated local custom survived for centuries. The Ch'in regime was radically different: a centralized, militarized, bureaucratized system, uniform in principle (though not quite in practice) throughout China.

Shih Huang-ti brought important and lasting reforms to China. He divided the country into provinces and prefectures, governed by civil and military officials arranged in a hierarchy of ranks. This principle, already familiar in many states besides Ch'in, was retained by all subsequent rulers of China. He imposed by decree a new system of standardized writing, modeled on the style of calligraphy familiar in Ch'in; and this reform, too, with further simplifications in later generations, set the standard for all subsequent Chinese writing.[25] Shih Huang-ti also constructed grandiose public works, the most famous of which was the Great Wall of China, while the most important was

---

seems to fall into a monocausal fallacy; and Wittfogel's ideas have been vigorously challenged, as far as China is concerned, by other scholars, e.g., Eberhard, *Conquerors and Rulers*, pp. 18–51; Henri Maspero and Jean Escarra, *Les institutions de la Chine* (Paris: Presses Universitaires, 1952).

[24] The state of Ch'in in fact centered in exactly the same region from which the Chou had originally come—the Wei Valley.

[25] Apparently the use of a brush to write with became usual at this time—a great improvement over the bamboo stylus that had been employed previously. Brush movements, however, were different from the movements of a rigid stylus; and the shape of the characters had to be altered accordingly. Cf. O. Franke, *Geschichte des chinesischen Reiches* (Berlin: Walter de Gruyter & Co., 1931), I, 239.

an elaborate road and postal system. These, too, were maintained throughout most of subsequent Chinese history.[26]

But later Chinese tradition vigorously repudiated other aspects of the Ch'in regime. Shih Huang-ti's conception of the emperor as an absolute sovereign, whose will could override all custom, decorum, or propriety, ran directly counter to the teachings of Confucius. Indeed, in order to suppress doctrines subversive of his regime, Shih Huang-ti ordered (213 B.C.) that all works by Confucius and certain other authors should be burnt, save only for official copies to be deposited in the imperial archives. Confucian scholars of later generations never forgave this obduracy and systematically blackened Shih Huang-ti's name in subsequent historiography.[27]

Presumably even so vigorous a state as Ch'in found it difficult to digest the whole of ancient China; and Shih Huang-ti's autocratic methods had made Ch'in unpopular. When he died in 210 B.C., an uncertain succession opened the gates for revolt. After a brief but violent bout of renewed warfare, Kao-tsu, a petty official turned general, emerged as supreme ruler of China and founder of the Han dynasty (202 B.C.). .

Kao-tsu at first compromised with the feudal principle, appointing or recognizing autonomous rulers in several of the old states into which China had long been divided. But gradually he succeeded in removing most such rulers; and the Ch'in principle of centralized bureaucratic government came back into its own. It was, however, bureaucracy with a difference; for the ruthless militarism and centralization of Ch'in days was not renewed. Indeed, Kao-tsu owed much of his success to a studied mildness of demeanor toward subordinates, rivals, and subjects. The core of the new Han bureaucracy consisted of Kao-tsu's comrades-in-arms who had helped him to power; but recruitment was open from the start to "men of excellent reputation and manifest virtue."[28] In practice, this meant the gentry; and within two generations it also came to mean men trained in the Confucian classics and molded according to the Confucian ideal.

No doubt a profound war-weariness assisted the new Han dynasty in establishing and consolidating its power. A unified state seemed the only way to assure tolerable peace and order among the rival polities into which China had been divided for five hundred years; and an imperial government which ruled mildly, respected learning, and accorded the landowning class a leading role in official and unofficial life was able to secure general support. Consequently, even though Kao-tsu (d. 195 B.C.) was succeeded first by a mere boy, and then by an infant, the rather crude palace intrigue provoked by

[26] The Great Wall pieced together several walls which had been built earlier and was capable, when suitably manned, of checking nomad raids from the northern steppe. Similarly, the road system linked together older roads and gave China a central nervous system, so to speak, allowing messengers and soldiers, officials and the emperor himself to travel to and fro rapidly and with comparative safety. Canals were fine for slower movement of heavy goods, but roads were required for speed.

[27] These remarks on the Ch'in unification of China depend primarily upon Derk Bodde, *China's First Unifier: A Study of the Ch'in Dynasty as Seen in the Life of Li Ssu* (Leiden: E. J. Brill, 1938).

[28] A translation of an edict of 196 B.C., as quoted in Homer H. Dubs (trans.), *The History of the Former Han Dynasty by Pan Ku* (Baltimore, Md.: Waverly Press, 1938), I, 18.

such temporary nullity of the imperial office failed to shake the authority of the Han dynasty in the country at large.

After a period of recuperation from civil strife, the Han emperors turned Chinese energies outward by attacking a nomad confederacy—the empire of the Hsiung-nu—which had meanwhile become formidable in the northwest. Weaker peoples of south China felt the force of Han military might as well.[29] During the long reign of Wu-ti (140–87 B.C.), nicknamed the "Martial Emperor," the power of a united China was demonstrated on a grand scale. Under his banners Chinese soldiers overran the oases of central Asia and opened direct contact between China and the civilized world of western Asia. By conquering part of Korea, Wu-ti prepared the way for the infusion of Chinese culture into that country and Japan. He also made contact with the Indian cultural sphere by conquests in Annam and raids into Yunnan. Indeed, as we have already seen, it was this abrupt, far-ranging expansion of Chinese power which brought about the closure of the ecumene at the beginning of the first century B.C.

The reign of Wu-ti also marked an important turning point in the cultural life of China; for it was he who made Confucianism official (*ca.* 136 B.C.).[30] The philosophy of Confucius had won increasing influence at court ever since the time of Kao-tsu, so that Wu-ti merely set the seal of imperial recognition upon a change long in the making. In the centuries to come, the conservative and humanist orientation of official Confucianism certainly proved highly congenial to the gentry of China. As heirs and successors of the Chou feudality, they were predisposed by the very tenor of their lives to a philosophy which rationalized and refined the older chivalric code of conduct. Moreover, Confucian teachers never lost sight of the founder's goal of training men to govern; and when, under the Han, an official career came to be the principal goal of ambition, a training which aimed expressly at turning out loyal and capable officials had an obvious advantage over more purely speculative or subjective schools of thought.

The return of Confucianism to favor under the Han meant that the texts proscribed by the Ch'in had to be restored. This obviously called for a careful collation of scholars' memories with surviving manuscripts.[31] The effort put into this task of reassembling and transcribing the Confucian classics set Chinese scholarship in a literary-historical mold that has lasted until the present.[32] Such an amazing continuity of learning carried penalties too, for a

---

[29] The Ch'in emperor had already shown what a united China could accomplish against its neighbors by driving the nomads north of the great bend of the Yellow River and penetrating southward to the coast. With the disruption of his government, however, Chinese power receded from these regions, until they were brought permanently within the Chinese pale by the Han. On Ch'in conquests, see O. Franke, *Geschichte des chinesischen Reiches*, I, 228–29.

[30] It was probably in this year that Wu-ti accepted the proposal of the famous scholar, Tung Chung-shu, that "all not within the field of the Six Disciplines or the arts of Confucius, should be cut short and not allowed to progress further." Fung Yu-lan, *A History of Chinese Philosophy* (Peiping: Henri Vetch, 1937), I, 403.

[31] Old Texts required re-editing in any case because the new calligraphic brush style made older writings unintelligible to ordinary scholars.

[32] Cf. Derk Bodde, *China's First Unifier*, p. 166.

somewhat antiquarian spirit, limiting itself mainly to commentaries upon established texts, dominated Chinese intellectual activity thereafter; and the more venturesome flights of thought which had characterized the immediately preceding centuries died rapidly away.

This crystallization of the learned tradition was perhaps no more than a normal response to the social and political stabilization which the Han dynasty brought to China as a whole. The chaos and distress which had nourished intellectual effort during the period of the warring states no longer afflicted Chinese society in the same degree as before. The Confucian classics were intrinsically impressive, and their mastery opened alluring careers in the service of the state. Thus the stimulus to radical or energetic intellectual innovation evaporated.[33]

But before Chinese thought thus lost its venturesomeness, it had undergone a notable flowering, comparable in the variety and sophistication of its ideas to the achievements of Greece and India. Chinese historians later distinguished six schools of Chinese philosophy: Confucian, Mohist, Taoist, Legalist, Logician, and Yin-Yang. There is an element of arbitrariness in these classifications, for a wide variety in emphasis appears to have existed within each school, and not a little borrowing occurred among them. Paraphrase of their doctrines is unusually risky; for the changes in script which came in under the Ch'in soon had the effect of making older writings unintelligible, even to the learned. The ancient philosophical texts therefore were edited and re-edited according to the fancy of Han Confucians; and original meanings, as opposed to the traditional interpretations of Confucian scholarship, are usually in doubt.[34]

It seems safe to say that Chinese thought showed a strong practical streak —though perhaps this arises from the selectivity of the Han scholars who determined which of the old texts should survive. Yet Confucians, Mohists, and Legalists all seem to have been primarily concerned with remedying the political and social ills which were so flamboyantly manifest in the period of the warring states. The Mohists organized a highly disciplined band of semi-military character, prepared to use weapons where words would not suffice;[35] and the Legalists not only provided Shih Huang-ti with doctrinal justification for his ruthless military measures, but also supplied the leading ministers who carried out his policy. Taoists and adepts of the Yin-Yang school also sought to enhance their powers, but in a quite different manner, through magical manipulation of the forces of nature. In the course of their experiments they developed elaborate (and to moderns largely unrecoverable) doctrines about cosmological, physical, and psychological phenomena. The Logicians alone seem to have indulged in intellectual activity without immediate practical ends

---

[33] Cf. the analogous transformation of Greek philosophy in Hellenistic and especially in Roman times.

[34] Cf. the astounding differences of meaning read into Taoist texts by two modern translators, as reproduced in Joseph Needham, *Science and Civilization in China*, II, 109–11.

[35] Fung Yu-lan, *A History of Chinese Philosophy*, I, 81–84.

in view, for they delighted in verbal paradoxes in a manner reminiscent of their Greek Eleatic contemporaries.

Of all these schools, only the Confucian and the Taoist survived as distinct elements in Chinese culture. In becoming official, Confucianism acquired a rudimentary cult which honored the Sage as the font of true doctrine and sometimes accorded him a more than human greatness.[36] Built around the study of the Five Classics,[37] which were erroneously attributed to Confucius himself, enriched by the Book of Mencius (371–289 B.C.), and expounded in the writings of numerous less famous scholars, Confucianism as it emerged under the early Han managed to appropriate elements from most of its rival philosophical schools and balanced the astringency of Confucius' common sense by canonizing an anthology of tellingly effective early poetry. Confucius' own political doctrine was left largely untouched, although Mencius gave it a more distinctly paternalistic tinge by arguing that the ultimate justification of rulership was the welfare of the people.[38]

Precedent, the way of the ancestors, decorum, and filial piety; an emperor who ruled by virtue and employed educated gentlemen in his service; a society in which every man had his rightful place and neither rose above nor sank beneath it: this was the ideal; and for long periods of Chinese history, reality approximated to it as nearly as human recalcitrance is ever likely to permit the realization of any ideal. The profound conservatism of Confucianism, together with the weighty reasonableness of its doctrines, the richness of its literature, and the educational and political institutions erected for its perpetuation, combined to give China a remarkable stability through all subsequent dynastic changes and made it easy to restore the imperial structure time and again. No other major civilization has had such a history.

Taoism played a quite different part in Chinese life. It was a more personal, indeed anarchical doctrine, appealing to the gentleman out of office. A man residing on his estate, with plenty of time to commune with his soul, found Taoist teachings especially attractive, for they allowed him both to understand and, hopefully, to control the mysteries of nature.[39] Among such practitioners, verbal paradox and hyperbole, together with rites intended to prolong life or induce supernatural powers, became entangled with the more philosophic aspects of the doctrine. In essence, Taoism offered a poetic alternative

---

[36] It was not, however, until 59 A.D., when the emperor ordered all schools to sacrifice to Confucius, that his cult definitely differentiated itself from the normal "ancestor worship" of Chinese families. Cf. J. K. Shryock, *Origin and Development of the State Cult of Confucius* (New York: Century Co., 1932), p. 103.

[37] These are: the *I-ching* ("Book of Changes"), *Shu-ching* ("Book of History"), *Shih-ching* ("Book of Poetry"), *Chou-li* ("Book of Rites"), *Ch'un-chi'u* ("Spring and Autumn Annals").

[38] Fung Yu-lan, *A History of Chinese Philosophy*, I, 111–13.

[39] It is possible but, in view of the uncertainty of the meaning of Taoist texts, not certain that Taoists in the period of the warring states were in some degree spokesmen for the lower classes and perhaps particularly for the lower classes of southern China, where primitive village community life survived more nearly intact than elsewhere in the country and may have seemed to offer a hopeful pattern for the reorganization of all society. Cf. J. Needham, *Science and Civilization in China*, II, 98–121, where the Taoists are portrayed as primitive Communists, lacking only a Marx to explain to them their dialectical position in world history.

SON OF HEAVEN

ANCESTORS

OFFICE

SCHOOL

PUBLIC

PRIVATE

CONFUCIANISM

TAOISM

MAGIC

CHINESE WORLD VIEWS

to the prosaic common sense and cool moderation of Confucianism. The same individual might adhere to both philosophies with no sense of strain, since Confucianism was for public occasions, Taoism for private and personal moments. The anarchic, individualist emphasis of Taoism, which made a Taoist organization something of a contradiction in terms,[40] meant that the Chinese expressed in private the sentiments which other civilized societies incorporated into organized religion; and this may explain how Chinese government was able to maintain itself for more than two millennia without more than sporadic support from a public and emotionally powerful religion. Thus despite the almost polar opposition of their emphases, Confucianism and Taoism fitted together into a whole, complementing and completing each other like the two halves of the Yin-Yang symbol.

3. THE FAR WEST: ROME AND WESTERN EUROPE, 336–146 B.C.

Westerners are so much accustomed to putting their own history in the foreground that it is perhaps well to underline the marginal character of Roman and European history between the fourth and second centuries B.C. It was only after 146 B.C. that Roman Italy or the western Mediterranean lands at large accepted more than a tincture of the civilization that was already old in the Hellenistic world; and when military conquest of the East, together with social differentiation at home, prepared the way for its reception, the grandeur of that foreign edifice was so overwhelming as to stifle independent Roman culture—though not before Latin literature had added something to the Hellenistic symphony.

The westward expansion of Hellenistic styles of life into barbarian or semi-barbarian lands was exactly comparable to similar movements that occurred at roughly the same time on the margins of other civilized societies. Thus the civilization of northern India definitely took root in the south from about the time of Ashoka (d. 227 B.C.); and in the immediately subsequent centuries, southern India showed rather more cultural independence and creativity than did western Europe. Similarly, the expansion of China southward after the establishment of the Ch'in dynasty (221 B.C.) brought vast new areas within the pale of Chinese civilization; while to the east, between the third and first centuries B.C., Korea and Japan began to construct their own variants upon Chinese cultural models. Even in the Middle East, where, civilization being older, the possibilities of expansion onto new ground were smaller, these centuries saw a significant spread of urbanization eastward into the Oxus and Jaxartes valleys—an expansion which, as we have already noted, occurred under Greek rulers and therefore bore a generally Hellenistic stamp.

Yet there was one great difference; for Rome conquered the core area of Hellenism and proceeded to overrun roughly half of the still older Oriental world as well. By comparison with the Hellenistic Far West, the Indian Far South and the Chinese Far East and Far South were politically passive. While Rome created a military power superior to all her Mediterranean rivals, the

---

[40] Taoist monasteries existed in China, but they arose only in response to the challenge to indigenous habits of thought offered by Buddhism in the early centuries of the Christian era.

converts to Indian and Chinese civilization on the Asian mainland were relatively peaceful folk who, far from conquering their civilizers, were conquered by them.[41] Thus, while each of the peripheral civilizations of Eurasia developed a duality between older heartland and new "colonial" region, the political dominance of the Hellenistic colonial area over its heartland gave the structure of that society a distinctive aspect.

The early stages of the rise of Rome may be conceived as an instance of a successful native reaction against foreign pressures. Rome's position on the margins between the centers of Greek and Etruscan power in Italy gave her a head start over a rival "native reaction" that developed among the Samnite tribes farther south. Even so, long and difficult wars with the Samnite confederacy (343–290 B.C.) formed the prelude to Roman supremacy in Italy. Defeat of the Samnites was followed by the subjugation of Etruria; and after these victories, the Romans found it comparatively easy to consolidate their control over the Greek cities of Italy, despite setbacks when they first encountered the full panoply of Hellenistic warfare, as exemplified by the armies of King Pyrrhus of Epirus (282–272 B.C.). As a result, by 265 B.C. all Italy south of the Apennines recognized Roman leadership.

The conquest and political consolidation of Italy was the key to subsequent Roman victories. For Italy was densely populated by a hardy peasantry; and Italian society was morally united up and down the social scale in a fashion conspicuously absent from the Hellenistic East. Consequently, after winning control of all Italy, Rome disposed of a dependable pool of military manpower far greater than any rival state could command. Even after the uprooting of peasant proprietors during the Second Punic War against Carthage (218–202 B.C.) brought social strife to the peninsula, the numbers and hardihood of the Italian peasant soldiery continued to give Roman generals an easy superiority over their opponents.

The contrast between the inveterate particularism of Greek cities and the relative ease with which the Romans consolidated all of Italy into a web of alliances reflected the survival in Italy of loose and comparatively flexible cantonal and tribal federations. Sovereignty having never been sharply localized in definite territorial and institutional units, like the Greek city-states, but being rather dispersed between kinship, territorial, federal, religious, and military associations, could be further consolidated into a superfederation controlled by the Senate and people of Rome without doing violence to any deep-seated Italian loyalties. The Greek cities of Italy, to be sure, could not so easily renounce their sovereign independence; and when Hannibal seemed to offer an alternative, not a few of them took the opportunity to abandon the

---

[41] The Chinese cultural frontier did, of course, also march with warrior peoples of the steppe; and the Ch'in subdued all China by using military techniques perfected in frontier warfare against the steppe peoples. The relation of Ch'in to the center of Chinese civilization was therefore very like that of Rome to the Hellenistic world; but the Ch'in empire did not outlast its founder. In Japan, too, Chinese culture came into contact with a people whose traditions (from whatever source) were quite as warlike as those of Europe. But not until the sixteenth century A.D. did Japan make any prolonged and serious effort to duplicate the Roman feat—at a time when the divergences between Chinese and Japanese cultures had become far more deeply fixed than was the case when rude Roman countrymen first gaped at the luxury of Corinth.

Roman allegiance. But when Carthage had ceased to be a serious rival to Rome (202 B.C.), the overpowering weight of the Italian populations massed together under Roman leadership gave the Italian Greeks no further opportunities to express their local discontents.

The First and Second Punic Wars (264–202 B.C.) made Rome an empire. For the first time, the Romans annexed provinces overseas which were not admitted to the Italian system of alliances. The Second Punic War, moreover, worked decisive changes within Italian society. Years of interminable campaigning pried many peasant soldiers loose from their ancestral farms; and an idle urban proletariat, which subsequently played an important political role, began to drift into Rome. Simultaneously, senators and tax farmers who collected provincial revenues became rich beyond all Roman precedent.

As Roman society thus underwent an extremely rapid economic differentiation, the upstart rich of the new capital of the Mediterranean world began to feel the attraction of the luxuries and refinements of Greece. To the horror of old-style Romans like Cato, Hellenistic urban styles began to seep into the city on the Tiber. The seepage became a flood after 146 B.C., when the spoils from the sack of Corinth—including numerous art objects—were brought home. Thus Rome, having won her first political successes as champion of a rude peasant reaction against the alien corruptions of civilization, was herself finally ensnared by the siren attractions of the selfsame civilization in its Hellenistic form. Profound irony lay in the fact that Rome's military success against the more civilized but socially and politically more divided peoples of the eastern Mediterranean resulted in the rapid assimilation of the Roman social structure to that of the effete and abject East they so despised.

Although the rise of Rome to empire was the dominating development in the Hellenistic Far West in this period, Rome was not the only expanding power of the area. North of the Alps, from a dispersal area on the middle Danube, tribes of Celts continued sporadically to overrun weaker neighbors, all the way from Asia Minor to the Atlantic face of Europe.[42] Civilized peoples first felt the power of these barbarians when they burst into the Po Valley (fouth century B.C.) and ravaged the Balkans before settling in Asia Minor (third century B.C.). But for all their formidable impetus in battle, the Celts characteristically failed to create any stable, large-scale political-military organization; and as they settled down to an aristocratic ease, based upon the exploitation of conquered populations, they soon lost their primitive military energy. Celtic mercenaries and allies serving with the Carthaginians constituted a formidable threat to Roman power as late as Hannibal's day; but with his defeat, they ceased to be a serious menace to Italy. Caught between expanding German tribes to the north, whose poverty made cattle thieves into heroes, and Roman armies to the south, whose discipline made peasants into soldiers, the aristocratic Celtic warriors found the military balance tipped decisively against them by 150 B.C.

This situation condemned Celtic culture to an early extinction, save along the westernmost Atlantic fringes of Europe, where Roman power and civili-

---

[42] Celtic conquests began in the eighth century and continued as late as the second.

zation never fully penetrated. Yet between the fourth and first centuries B.C., the Celts developed a protocivilization principally expressed in complex oral literature: partly secular, commemorating the deeds of ancient heroes; and partly sacerdotal, expounding cosmology, immortality, and other religious doctrines. Colleges of bards and priests transmitted and elaborated this literature and exercised judicial and augural functions as well. Maintaining close links across tribal boundaries, the colleges gave a degree of homogeneity to the higher aspects of Celtic culture in western Europe.[43]

The druids of Britain, Gaul, and Ireland presumably represented a fusion between Indo-European forms of worship and the older traditions of Bronze Age "megalithic" religion. A western European style of civilization might have arisen from these roots had not the civilization of the Mediterranean area been so near and so impressive. As it turned out, however, the Arthurian legends of medieval Brittany and the literary records left by the precocious Christian civilization of Ireland (fourth to seventh centuries A.D.) constitute the only surviving samples of the achievements of Celtic culture; and even these in the forms available today are much transformed by Mediterranean elements—Christianity chief among them.[44]

C. THE EURASIAN ECUMENE, 100 B.C.–200 A.D.

1. POLITICAL AND SOCIAL DEVELOPMENTS

The establishment of a Chinese garrison in the Ferghana oasis in 101 B.C. almost bridged the geographical gap which had previously separated the Chinese from their civilized contemporaries in western Asia. Less than forty years later, the Roman frontier reached the upper Euphrates, which became an almost permanent, though much disputed frontier between Rome and Parthia thereafter. Then, in the first century A.D. (or perhaps earlier), the consolidation of a Kushan empire forged a final link between Parthia and China, completing a chain of civilized empires that extended all across Eurasia, from the Atlantic to the Pacific. Throughout its length this Eurasian civilized belt confronted steppe nomads whose raids and migrations continued, like ocean waves, to break from time to time upon the fringes of civilized, sedentary societies. Indeed, the nomad challenge was sufficiently important that the

---

[43] The druids of Gaul, for example, customarily went to Britain to study the more recondite aspects of their religion. Julius Caesar, *Gallic War*, VI, 13.

[44] For these remarks on the Celts, I have consulted Henri Hubert, *Les Celtes depuis l'époque de la Tène* (Paris: Renaissance du livre, 1932), pp. 223–26; J. A. MacCulloch, *The Religion of the Ancient Celts* (Edinburgh: T. & T. Clark, 1911), pp. 293–318 and *passim;* T. D. Kendrick, *The Druids: A Study in Celtic Prehistory* (London: Methuen & Co., 1927), pp. 194–211 and *passim;* T. G. E. Powell, *The Celts* (London: Thames & Hudson, 1958).

The parallel between early Aryan culture in north India and that of the Celts of western Europe is striking and has often been remarked. The resemblances cease to be so surprising if one remembers that north India and western Europe represented two extreme wings of the Bronze Age expansion of the steppe warriors. On both these extreme flanks of the then civilized world, the Indo-European tribesmen overran archaic and in all probability priest-ruled societies—societies which in their turn had distant but real connections with the prime centers of early civilization in the Middle East. Druids and Brahmins may have resembled one another so closely because both arose from a fusion of Indo-European priesthoods with priestly traditions deriving from the megalithic and the Indus societies, respectively.

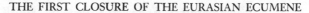

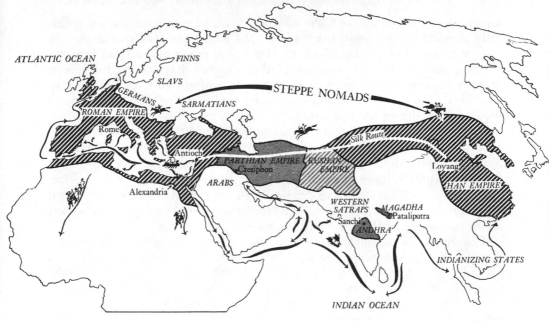

political history of the ecumene may in large part be understood as the consequence of shifting pressures brought from the steppes against the various
segments of the civilized world.

*　　*　　*

As suitable pasture lands filled up with tribes of horse nomads, struggles for
pasture rights led to the formation of loose confederations among various
tribal groups, united, when on campaign, by common obedience to a war
leader, but otherwise dispersed over the grasslands with their herds.

At the close of the third century B.C., one such confederation, based in
Mongolia, attained a size and cohesion that made it a worthy antagonist to
the Chinese empire itself. Chinese historians knew this state as the empire of
the Hsiung-nu.[45] The decisive event in its consolidation appears to have been

[45] At its height, the "empire" of the Hsiung-nu extended from Manchuria deep into central Asia
and exercised a general suzerainty over oasis dwellers of the regions all the way from China to the
Jaxartes, as well as over strictly nomad groups as far west as the Aral Sea. Many diverse linguistic and
racial groups were embraced in the federation. The ruling group probably spoke a Turkish tongue and
was probably related in some fashion to the Huns of later European history. This is an obscure and
debated issue, however, for there is a large gap, both chronologically and geographically, between the
last Chinese records of the Hsiung-nu, who departed for the West in the second century A.D., and the
appearance of the Huns in southern Russia in the late fourth century A.D. Between these dates, there
was ample opportunity for disintegration and reintegration of war bands and alliances among the small
groups into which every nomad "state" dissolved when the time came to follow the herds over the
steppe. The continuity between the political-military association known to the Chinese as Hsiung-nu
and the similar confederation known to Europeans as Huns may thus have been very slight. Cf. William
M. McGovern, *The Early Empires of Central Asia*, pp. 87–121, 467–70; E. A. Thompson, *A History of
Attila and the Huns* (Oxford: University Press, 1948), pp. 43–46; Franz Altheim, *Reich gegen Mitter-
nacht: Asiens Weg nach Europa* (Hamburg: Rowohlt, 1955), pp. 27–29.

the attacks launched by the Ch'in emperor against China's restless but politically divided nomad neighbors,[46] for in 214 B.C., Shih Huang-ti drove the groups that became the kernel of the Hsiung-nu confederacy from Inner to Outer Mongolia. In their new home, the refugees developed a formidable military organization by accepting the principle of absolute obedience to an individual war leader and by subordinating traditional tribal antagonisms to the larger loyalty of the war confederation.

No doubt their new military organization was first tested against the natives of Outer Mongolia; but with the outbreak of civil war in China after Shih Huang-ti's death (208 B.C.), the Hsiung-nu promptly recovered their former pastures in Inner Mongolia and went on to raid far into China. After a difficult and almost disastrous campaign, the first Han emperor was forced to conclude a treaty relinquishing all Mongolia to the Hsiung-nu and agreeing to pay tribute to the new barbarian state.[47]

The rise of a formidable war confederation in Mongolia constituted a serious threat to the steppe peoples farther west. The Hsiung-nu confronted no political or geographical obstacle to indefinite military expansion on the steppe itself, for a victory simply meant the addition either of new pasture lands or of new fighting men to the resources of the confederacy. Distance did set a certain limit, of course: in the absence of highly organized postal systems, the commands of a single war leader could not be effective thousands of miles away. Moreover, if a nomad empire were to achieve more than temporary cohesion, the habit of obedience to such commands could only be instilled by entrusting local leadership to men who owed their authority, not to traditional chieftainship of the tribe, but to appointment by the supreme war chief himself. These adjuncts to nomad empire developed to their fullest extent only in the thirteenth century A.D., when the Mongols not only succeeded in uniting almost all the Eurasian steppe but lapped over into the Chinese, Middle Eastern, and European agricultural zones as well. In the second century B.C., however, the "empire" of the Hsiung-nu was a much simpler and far more precarious structure. After the first burst of conquest—209–174 B.C.—successive war leaders found it difficult to control the allied tribes, whose

---

[46] Cf. the putative barbarian reaction to Sargon of Akkad's penetration of the Mesopotamian borderlands, mentioned above, pp. 91–92.

[47] The diplomatic arrangements thus concluded (200 B.C.) gave expression to what we may consider the normal relationship between China and the nomads. To be sure, this relation was interrupted from time to time either by Chinese efforts to break up nomad power, or by nomad conquest of part or all of China. The "normal" relationship, however, regularly reasserted itself. Efforts to unite the steppe and the Chinese agricultural world into a single political unit never won enduring success. One or the other half of such a composite state regularly broke away, as nomad conquerors became Sinicized and alienated their fellows who remained herdsmen, or as Chinese soldiers, compelled to live and fight like the nomads of the steppe, withdrew their obedience from a distant and alien imperial court.

The durability of this "normal" relationship was a measure of the advantages it offered to both sides. Tribute from China allowed the nomad war leader to maintain his court on princely scale and, perhaps more important, gave him the means wherewith to reward his chief followers with precious gifts—silks, metal goods, and other luxuries—and thus keep them loyal and obedient. From the Chinese viewpoint, such "gifts" were a cheap form of insurance against incursions from the steppe. Cf. Owen Lattimore, *The Inner Asian Frontiers of China* (New York: American Geographical Society, 1940), for a detailed analysis of this secular relationship and its geographical determinants.

leaders tended to obey commands only when it seemed locally advantageous to do so.

Nonetheless, the military power of this first great empire of the eastern steppe precipitated a far-ranging displacement of peoples: for the alternative to submission was flight. Many nomads submitted, but some preferred to flee toward the richer and imperfectly defended lands to the west and south. Their movements started a wave of migration that affected all Eurasia. Thus, for the first time, under the prick of Hsiung-nu political consolidation in Mongolia, the steppe gradient came fully into operation.

* * *

Iranian-speaking peoples were the protagonists of the resulting political disturbances; for Shakas and Kushans in Afghanistan and India, Parthians in Iran, and Sarmatians in southern Russia all appear to have spoken Iranian dialects. The flights of these peoples abandoned the central portions of the steppe

CHINA AND THE STEPPE

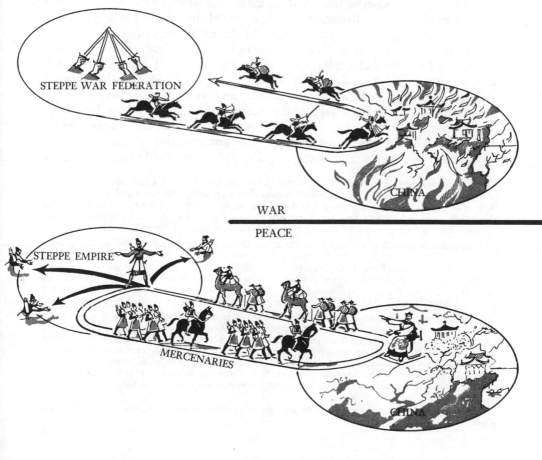

to Turkish-speaking tribes;[48] while their conquests rolled Hellenistic political frontiers back to the Euphrates.

Details and sometimes even the main outlines of these migrations and conquests are unfortunately obscure. Chronological uncertainty surrounds the central fact in the whole drama: the consolidation of the Kushan empire,[49] which temporarily closed the Iranian aperture upon the steppe against further nomad incursion and thereby created a propitious political climate for the caravan trade that came to link India, China, and the Middle East more closely than ever before. Yet the general pattern of events seems clear enough. On the extreme flanks of the ecumene, neither Rome nor China was deeply affected by the military and political events of the steppes until near the end of the second century A.D. Their evolution, therefore, proceeded along lines dictated mainly by an internal balance of forces; and the striking resemblances between Han and Roman history may be attributed to resemblances in the social structures of the two empires.

In the middle reaches of Eurasia, however, the disturbances generated by the Hsiung-nu empire were felt in drastic fashion between 165 and 128 B.C., when a massive irruption of Yueh-chi[50] and Shaka tribesmen brought a new political regime to eastern Iran. A conspicuous casualty of this movement was the Greek kingdom of Bactria.[51] Parthia survived the assault much more successfully. Although the initial shock of Shaka raids compelled the Parthian monarchs to loosen their grip on Mesopotamia (which they had but recently conquered from the Seleucids), under King Mithridates II (123–87 B.C.) this state staged a brilliant recovery. As a result, many of the Shaka princelings of eastern Iran recognized Parthian suzerainty, and on his western flank Mithridates was able to build a powerful empire that united western Iran with Mesopotamia and Armenia. A century or more later, the Kushan empire emerged on the Parthians' eastern flank. The consolidation of Kushan power dislodged Shaka bands from Bactria and drove them into India, where they

[48] The operation of the steppe gradient reversed a flow from west to east which had earlier led first peasant farmers, then charioteers, and lastly nomad horsemen across the oases and steppe lands of Asia. The linguistic drift which thus set in during the second century B.C. continued to operate for about 1600 years and brought first Turks and then Mongols far westward. The movement was then reversed again in modern times by Russian colonization and conquest of Siberia and central Asia.

[49] Scholars have ranged all the way from 80 B.C. to 278 A.D. in their estimate of the beginning of the "Kushan era." Cf. Louis de la Vallée Poussin, *L'Inde aux temps des Mauryas et des barbares, Grecs, Scythes, Parthes, Yuetchi* (Paris: E. de Boccard, 1930), pp. 343–74. The most recent study I have seen tentatively suggests that the consolidation of the empire dated from about 46 A.D.; but adequate evidence is still lacking. Roman Ghirshman, *Bégram: Recherches archéologiques et historiques sur les Kouchans* (Cairo: Institut Français d'Archéologie Orientale, 1946), pp. 118–24.

[50] Tribes known by this name to Chinese historians fled from the modern province of Kansu about 165 B.C. They settled first in the Ili River region of modern Kazakhstan and then trekked farther west into modern Afghanistan where, in all probability, elements among them constituted the core of the Kushan empire. No alternative name for the Yueh-chi has entered scholarly currency, although the Chinese term may be misleading when applied to an Iranian-speaking group. Cf. Berthold Laufer, *The Language of the Yüe-chi or Indo-Scythians* (Chicago: R. R. Donnelley & Sons, 1917); Sten Konow, "On the Nationality of the Kusanas," *Zeitschrift der deutschen morgenländischen Gesellschaft,* LXVIII (1914), 85–100.

[51] A few Greek rulers maintained themselves for more than a century afterward south of Hindu Kush.

established another series of petty states. The Kushans, however, soon pursued their defeated rivals southward and subdued a fairly wide stretch of territory in northwest India to add to their possessions north of the mountains.[52]

The consolidation of the Kushan empire had the effect of deflecting steppe migration routes northward. In consequence, bands of Sarmatians, after debouching from the gap between the Caspian Sea and the Ural Mountains, drove the partially Hellenized Scythians from the rich pasture lands of southern Russia and the lower Danube. As a result the Roman legions stationed on the Danube encountered Sarmatian practitioners of the fully developed style of steppe warfare for the first time in 172 A.D.[53] But just before this first recorded clash between Roman and Sarmatian troops took place, the ultimate source of politico-military disturbance along the steppe itself disintegrated. For the empire of the Hsiung-nu, strained by long wars with the Chinese and frayed from within by internal frictions, collapsed about 160 A.D. before another conqueror whose homeland lay north of Mongolia.[54] But the newly victorious nomad war confederation failed to outlast its founder; and the tribes of the eastern steppe reverted to a condition of military atomization which offered their neighbors respite for more than a century.

*   *   *

Two aspects of the civilized response to these steppe migrations deserve emphasis. First, the retreat of Greek rule from Mesopotamia and Iran did not eradicate the impress of Hellenistic culture upon those regions. The Parthian court itself was at least superficially Hellenized;[55] and the kings continued to pursue a "philhellenic" policy toward the cities of their empire. Even the half-barbarous Shakas, when obliged to govern a country in which city life and agriculture were firmly established, fell back upon Hellenistic precedent so far as their own rude background allowed.[56]

Second, the Parthians were able to withstand and then roll back nomad attack only because they had developed a new style of armament and tactics effective against the horse archers of the steppe. The key change was the development of a big, strong breed of horse, able to carry enough armor to

[52] Great obscurities attend these struggles, and chronology is quite unsatisfactory. Parthian as well as Shaka strains seem to have been present among India's invaders—perhaps because some of the Shakas continued to recognize Parthian suzerainty. Most of the Shaka states of India were later incorporated into the Kushan empire; but some outlying rulers (the "satraps of Ujjain") outlasted the Kushans and probably never accepted outside control in any but the most nominal sense. Cf. *Cambridge History of India*, I, 563–85; La Vallée Poussin, *L'Inde aux temps des Mauryas*, pp. 261–328.

[53] Cf. Michael I. Rostovtzeff, *Iranians and Greeks in South Russia*, pp. 113–46.

[54] This event in all probability marks the first eruption of Mongol tribes into history. Cf. René Grousset, *L'Empire des steppes* (Paris: Payot, 1939), pp. 73, 93–94.

[55] According to Plutarch, *Life of Crassus*, 33, the Parthian and Armenian kings, who had just concluded a marriage alliance, were watching a performance of Euripides' *Bacchae* when Crassus' head was thrown onto the stage by messengers from the field of Carrhae. Cf. Nelson C. Debevoise, *A Political History of Parthia* (Chicago: University of Chicago Press, 1938), p. 93.

[56] Roman survivals in Merovingian Gaul provide a rough parallel to the situation of Bactria under Shaka rule.

make both horse and rider effectively arrow-proof.[57] A force of armored horsemen could stand quietly under the harassment of galloping steppe cavalry, exchanging shot for shot, until their assailants' quivers and horses were both exhausted, when a final charge could be counted on to break the spirit and disperse the forces of the steppe raiders. Seldom could heavy armored cavalry overtake light steppe ponies; but a force of armored men could forbid any locality to the steppe bowmen and make their retreat uncomfortably hasty. The net effect, therefore, of the introduction of armored cavalry—or cataphracts, as the Byzantines later called them—was to establish a fairly exact balance between steppe and civilized warfare. Nomads could not imitate the new civilized style of armament because the open steppe lacked sufficient pasture to sustain great horses.[58] Similarly, civilized horsemen could not penetrate deeply into the steppe, without themselves adopting (as the Chinese in fact did) the nomad style of light cavalry. Hence a millennial stalemate ensued, each type of cavalry supreme in its own environment, but unable to penetrate the realm of its rival, save occasionally when the military organization and social cohesion of one or the other party to the confrontation weakened.[59]

[57] Experiments with armor as protection against horse archery had been made soon after steppe light cavalry tactics had been introduced. Herodotus reports, for instance, that the Massagetae, who inhabited very nearly the same region from which the Parthians later came, protected their horses with metal breastplates in 530 B.C. Cf. Herodotus, I, 215.

What was new in the first century B.C. therefore was not the idea but the scale upon which armor was used and the strength of the horses which allowed armored cavalry to retain vital mobility even when burdened with a heavy defensive weight of metal. One theory is that the great horse of eastern Iran developed as a result of the crossing of blood strains. Cf. W. W. Tarn, *Hellenistic Military and Naval Developments* (Cambridge: Cambridge University Press, 1930), pp. 77–83. On the other hand, the discovery that horses could be fed on harvested alfalfa, and thus nourished adequately all through the year, seems quite adequate to account for the development of a breed of large, strong horses. And it is clear from Chinese records that the marvelous "blood sweating" horses of eastern Iran, which seemed so valuable to the emperor Wu-ti that he sent an expedition to Ferghana expressly in order to secure specimens of the new breed, ate alfalfa, which was accordingly imported into China (along with the grape) by the returned expedition (101 B.C.). Cf. W. P. Yetts, "The Horse: A Factor in Early Chinese History," *Eurasia Septentrionales Antiqua*, IX (1934), 231–55.

[58] On the better-watered western portions of the steppe this was less of a limiting factor; and the Sarmatians did in fact maintain relatively large forces of the new style of cavalry. This was probably their main advantage over the Scythians.

Farther east, too, the prestige (and beauty) of the big horses made them precious items, which a chief was willing to maintain even at very considerable cost. Thus, in the Altai, where unusual climatic conditions resulted in the deposition of permanent ice in their tombs, chieftains were buried both with little scrub steppe ponies and with great horses. Examination of the stomach contents of the great horses showed that they were fed on grain—human food!—and the condition of their hooves suggested that they had been kept stabled. Cf. Tamara Talbot Rice, *The Scythians* (London: Thames & Hudson, 1957), p. 71.

[59] The full effectiveness of cataphracts depended on stirrups, to give the rider a firm seat on his horse and allow shock tactics. Cavalrymen who were able to charge with fixed lances (like the medieval knights of western Europe), putting the weight of horse and man behind the thrust, could break up any opposing formation unless it resorted to the same tactics.

This appears to have been the great medieval invention of western European warfare, where ancient prejudices against the bow continued to prevail until the time of Crecy (1346) and Agincourt (1415). Iranian and Byzantine cataphracts had no such prejudices and fought regularly with bows, resorting only occasionally to hand-to-hand combat. A Sassanian rock carving nevertheless proves that Iranian cataphracts jousted with lances. See p. 395. Perhaps, therefore, the European knight was not so

During the four centuries between 200 B.C. and 200 A.D., when the Parthians and Kushans took the lead in perfecting a civilized armament capable of coping with the military challenge offered by steppe horsemen, China enjoyed comparative stability. Despite Wu-ti's delight in the "blood sweating" horses of Iran, the Han emperors found the new style of heavy cavalry too expensive to maintain on a large scale, since the alfalfa that the great horses required could be grown only by diverting land from the production of human food. They preferred to carry the battle to the enemy by sending armies into the steppe, mounted on steppe ponies like the forces they opposed.[60]

Such border wars did not, however, deeply affect internal Chinese affairs. The political unity of the country remained unbroken; and the political and social balance which had been struck under the first Han emperors continued without important modification until 9 A.D. In that year, an unusually energetic master of court intrigue, Wang Mang, exploited marriage ties with the imperial family to usurp the throne. He then undertook an antiquarian revolution, proclaiming a return to the real or supposed precedents of the Chou as against the corruptions of the more recent Ch'in and Han regimes. Yet under the guise of such doctrinaire Confucianism, Wang Mang did not scruple to tamper with old texts by correcting or "completing" them whenever it suited his interest to do so.[61] His reforms had unexpected results; for in discrediting established institutions, he unleashed a widespread peasant rising directed against landlords, officials, and moneylenders. Before long, champions of social order and the old imperial dynasty took the field against him, and against the rebellious peasants as well. Wang Mang was quickly overthrown (22 A.D.);[62] but fourteen years of civil war intervened before China was again united under the rule of a scion of the house of Han.

---

much the result of a Western invention as of a Western failure to appropriate the entire panoply of cataphract warfare.

The question of when and where stirrups were invented is quite unclear. Lynn White, *Medieval Technology and Social Change* (Oxford: Clarendon Press, 1962), attributes the first use of stirrups to India; others (with very slender evidence) have attributed it to the steppe nomads. The only certain fact appears to be that stirrups first became common during the fifth–sixth centuries A.D. in both China and Europe. Cf. M. Rostovtzeff, *Iranians and Greeks in South Russia*, p. 130; Tamara T. Rice, *The Scythians*, p. 50; E. H. Minns, *The Scythians and Greeks* (Cambridge University Press, 1913), p. 250; Charles Singer (ed.), *A History of Technology*, II, 556–57.

[60] Cf. Berthold Laufer, *Chinese Clay Figures. Part I: Prolegomena on the History of Defensive Warfare* (Chicago: Field Museum of Natural History, 1914), pp. 218–34. As in any stubbornly contested borderland, a class of fighting men who had far more in common with one another than with civilians in the rear developed on both sides of the Chinese-Hsiung-nu frontier. Cases of desertion back and forth were not uncommon; and famous military leaders could usually count on a warm reception in the enemy camp and renewed employment against their former friends if they so desired. A code of chivalry developed among the border fighters; and a bold leader, charging at the head of his men, won admiration from both friend and foe. For incidents illustrating these points, cf. W. M. McGovern, *The Early Empires of Central Asia*, pp. 130–302.

[61] The lasting effects of Wang Mang's alterations of the Confucian texts is a matter for scholarly disagreement; but it probably left some traces upon the versions handed down in later times.

[62] He met his death sitting in full regalia upon the imperial throne, hoping perhaps (if he was, indeed, a convinced believer in Confucian doctrine) that the rude soldiers who cut off his head would be overawed by his august presence and by the correctness of his decorum.

Thus was inaugurated the Later Han Dynasty, which endured until 220 A.D. For the most part, the emperors of this period lacked the ability and energy which had distinguished the founders of the line; and intrigue and violence flourished in high places. After 184 A.D., the central administration increasingly lost control of the provinces. Rival generals manipulated puppet emperors and sought, with varying success, to build up personal power systems. Widespread popular risings, led by Taoist adepts who claimed magical powers, added to the confusion and lent an element of ideological bitterness to the civil strife. The farce of imperial unity played itself out in 220 A.D., when the last of the Han emperors officially abdicated at the bidding of a general who had already kept him in custody for several years.

Despite the intrigues which so often disfigured Han politics, and despite the miserable disorders prevailing toward the close of the dynasty, the constructive importance of the Han period as a whole can hardly be exaggerated. The ideal of a united China, governed according to Confucian precept, was indelibly implanted in the Chinese mind by the nearly four centuries during which the Han emperors (at least theoretically) upheld this ideal. During the same period, the historic frontiers of China were effectively established. In the course of generations, soldiers, officials, and teachers brought the vast region south of the Yangtze within the pale of Chinese culture; and the Han conquests in Korea, central Asia, and Mongolia directed a powerful stream of Chinese influence into these borderlands. In other words, under the Han China became China in the political and geographical sense; and to this day, the Chinese remember this fact in popular speech by calling themselves the "Sons of Han."[63]

*   *   *

To a surprising degree, Roman imperial history resembles that of Han China. Roman conquests in western Europe, by which a genteel version of Hellenistic culture was extended into a vast and semi-barbarous area, bear comparison with the conversion of south China to Confucian decorum under the Han. Roman efforts to control Arabia, Armenia, the Caucasus region, and Mesopotamia resemble the rather more successful undertakings of the Han emperors in central Asia. The northern barbarians with whom the Romans fought and traded, and whom they later hired as mercenaries and admitted as settlers within their borders, bore much the same relation to the Mediterranean world as did the Hsiung-nu to China, although the Romans never had to face a war confederacy as wide-reaching as that against which the Chinese emperors struggled.

The parallels extend to internal affairs as well. Julius Caesar's (d. 44 B.C.) extralegal and almost nakedly military hold on the Roman state closely resembled the position Shih Huang-ti had won in China almost two centuries

[63] These remarks on Han politics depend on W. Eberhard, *A History of China* (London: Routledge & Kegan Paul, 1948), pp. 71–105; O. Franke, *Geschichte des chinesischen Reiches*, I, 358–431; Pan Ku, *The History of the Former Han Dynasty*, Homer H. Dubs (trans.), 3 vols. (Baltimore, Md.: Waverly Press, 1938–55).

before. Moreover, both these upstarts set out to reorganize the power relations of their respective societies with scant regard for precedent or legal niceties; and their successors, after renewed bouts of civil war, found it prudent to veil naked military despotism behind more decorous forms. Thus Augustus (d. 14 A.D.) deferred to the political pieties of Rome by "restoring the Republic" (27 B.C.) without, however, surrendering his own supreme military control of affairs; while the first Han emperors supplemented and sustained the victories of their armies by invoking the sanctions of Confucianism.

The Roman imperial bureaucracy under Augustus' successors suffered from ills similar to those besetting the Han—palace intrigue, systematically oppressive tax collection, and an occasionally corrupt officialdom. The nostalgic classicism of the Antonine age (117–180 A.D.), with its reverence for ancient Greece, had a counterpart in China also, where Confucian scholars lavished uncritical admiration upon the Chou and still earlier dynasties. Finally, the rude militarism of Septimus Severus (197–211 A.D.), raised to the purple by civil war, resembled the regimes set up by Chinese warlords of the late Han period.

Underlying such parallels was a significant likeness in social structure. Both in the Roman empire and in China, a class of genteel landowners, living upon rents from country estates, dominated society. In both empires, this class provided the leading personnel of public administration and exhibited a declining enthusiasm for the rigors of a military career. Indeed, the way of life of a Roman gentleman of the second century A.D., residing in town, collecting taxes on behalf of the central government, entertaining at elegant banquets, dabbling perhaps in belles lettres or philosophy, and cultivating a taste for the fine arts—was astonishingly similar to that of his Chinese counterpart, if one overlooks the radical difference of the forms in which their respective cultural heritages found traditional expression. The status of peasants and townsmen—the former owing heavy rents to their social superiors, the latter catering to the tastes of wealthy landowners—was also very similar in the two empires.

There were, of course, important differences as well. The Roman empire was culturally pluralistic. In the eastern Mediterranean lands, the dominant Greek tradition mingled with a massive Oriental inheritance which rose to renewed prominence as the *élan* of Greco-Roman civilizatian decayed in the first centuries A.D.; while in the West, the Latin version of Hellenistic culture never entirely assimilated the complexities and corruptions of the Greek-speaking East. In Han China, on the contrary, a single high cultural tradition predominated throughout the empire; and regional variations had little importance.

Another vital difference concerned the role of the family. Loyalty to relatives, even of the second or third degree, stood high in the scale of Chinese virtues; and widely ramified family cliques formed the basis of much Chinese political activity. The Confucian emphasis on filial piety and on the importance of having sons to honor departed ancestors also exalted family ties and gave the Chinese gentry a comfortable social nexus in which to live. All this was absent from Roman society, where a comparatively radical individualism

MVN[...]P[...]P.P.M.
AN.XVIII

HELLENISM'S HIGH TIDE, EAST AND WEST

Demetrius, King of Bactria (*ca.* 190–160 B.C.), appears on the
right, wearing an elephant headdress to symbolize his victories in
India. The inscription on the obverse of the coin reads "King
Demetrius." The rise of the Greek kingdom of Bactria, perched
astride Hindu Kush, represented the high tide of Hellenic political dominion over central Asia. A century-and-a-half later, far
to the west, Augustus' consolidation of the Roman empire (27
B.C.–14 A.D.) in effect put a term to the military expansion of
Roman power. Just as Demetrius' portrait reflects an Indian
environment in the outlandishness of his headdress, so Augustus'
military dress reflects the Roman environment. Yet the common
core of Hellenic style is clear enough—as the resemblance between Augustus' posture of the stance of the "Zeus" on the
obverse of Demetrius' coin neatly demonstrates.

prevailed, so that private persons confronted the state with remarkably few and weak intermediary social linkages.[64]

A third important contrast between Rome and China lay in the fact that Roman agriculture was in general far less intensive than that of China. Irrigation was seldom practiced in the Roman empire, except in Egypt and other places, where it had been the basis of life for centuries.[65] Consequently, the productivity of the soil was comparatively modest; and the means for supporting the apparatus of an imperial state were correspondingly restricted. Even in Augustus' time, the peasantry of the empire bore a substantial tax burden; and with the passage of time, the number of Roman soldiers and officials increased. This gave the Roman state in its later period something of a top-heavy character and made the reconstruction of a bureaucratic, centralized regime next to impossible when once it had been broken apart by barbarian invasion. By contrast, irrigation continued to spread in China, and with it an intensive and relatively very productive style of agriculture. As a result, the Chinese could perhaps better afford an imperial bureaucracy and army. Certainly, they found it comparatively easy to reconstruct the apparatus of effective centralized government despite repeated breakdowns incident to barbarian conquests.[66]

Rome's agricultural weakness was offset by a modest commercial and industrial strength. The old pattern of exchange, whereby regions producing wine and oil exported those products to regions less favorably situated, continued to constitute the backbone of Roman commerce. First Italy and then Spain and Gaul became important centers of grape and olive culture, while Egypt and north Africa specialized in supplying the imperial capital with grain. Yet, as earlier in Greece, the spread of olive-grape agriculture to new districts meant radical decay of the prosperity of older centers of commercial agricul-

---

[64] In the countryside, immemorial status relationships and the personal ties of village community life drastically modified the individualism characteristic of Greco-Roman cities. Even within the cities, artisans and other occupational groupings formed guilds which fulfilled social as much as economic functions. Religious associations, of which the early Christian churches offer examples, were also of great importance. Hence the statement in the text really applies only to the upper classes of Greco-Roman cities. The striking failure of this class to reproduce itself biologically may be related to the decay of family and other ties, which made the procreation and nurture of children seem pointless. Other factors (disease, hot baths) may, however, have been decisive in the biological suicide of the Roman upper classes. See below, pp. 359–60.

Yet whatever the causes may have been, the crude numerical attenuation of the cultivated classes meant a weakening of the traditions of classical civilization. In the Roman empire of the second century A.D., the high culture of paganism was sustained principally by landlords and other rentiers. Chinese Confucians drew their income from similar sources; but the emphasis they placed upon family continuity meant that such privileged groups seldom failed to reproduce themselves. The survival of the Han style of Confucian culture through all the subsequent vicissitudes of Chinese history was certainly assisted by this fact, whereas the disruption of classical paganism was greatly facilitated by the demographic decay of its principal champions.

[65] North Africa constituted an exception; for skillful water engineering, pioneered in the area by the Carthaginians, was greatly extended in that province during Roman times. Cf. R. M. Haywood, "Roman Africa," in Tenney Frank (ed.), *An Economic Survey of Ancient Rome* (Baltimore, Md.: Johns Hopkins Press, 1948), IV, 48–49; Charles Singer *et al.*, *A History of Technology* (Oxford: Clarendon Press, 1956), II, 670, 678.

[66] The cultural unity of China as contrasted to the pluralism of Roman society was also of great importance in facilitating China's repeated imperial restorations.

ture. Hence at the close of the first century A.D., the irremediable economic depression which had struck Greece so hard in Hellenistic times visited Italy.[67] By contrast, the Chinese economy of Han times exhibited no very important regional specializations, so that each province enjoyed a more nearly autarchic economic life than the Roman provinces did. This gave China a greater resilience, for the delicate articulation required to sustain interregional trade was not vital to the economy, whereas without the circulation of taxes and goods from one end of the Mediterranean to the other, neither the Roman army nor the Roman bureaucracy could long survive.

Finally, the conditions beyond the frontiers of the two lands were dissimilar. The German and Sarmatian tribesmen who attacked Rome never united their forces into a single confederation like that of the Hsiung-nu; but their greater numbers made them more difficult for the Romans to assimilate. Moreover, the Parthian realm on Rome's eastern frontier was more populous and culturally more developed than any neighbor with whom the Chinese had to cope. China's steppe neighbors of course offered a real military threat; but their successes invariably resulted in their eventual incorporation into the Chinese body politic. In Rome's case, however, successful invaders were not predestined to Romanization, as Franks and Arabs later were to demonstrate.

Thus a comparison of the two great empires that flourished on the extreme flanks of the ecumene between 200 B.C. and 200 A.D. shows that the Chinese structure was a good deal more secure than the Roman. Later events, of course, proved this to be the case; but discussion of Rome's collapse and China's revival must wait until the next chapter. It remains now to consider the cultural changes that came to the Eurasian ecumene in the age of its initial closure.

2. CULTURAL GROWTH AND INTERCHANGE

ART. The difficulties of translation automatically insulate the literary and intellectual aspects of a culture from its neighbors. A deliberate effort is necessary to overcome such barriers, for the soldiers and merchants who normally pioneer contacts among divergent communities are unlikely to take much interest in letters and learning. This is less true of the visual arts; for training is not required to appreciate a strange new art style.[68] For this reason, contacts among mutually alien cultural traditions are almost certain to be reflected sooner and more obviously in the visual arts than in those arts more closely bound to language. The closure of the Eurasian ecumene in the first

---

[67] By the second century A.D., the circulation of wealth in the Roman empire may be schematized as follows: taxes from the eastern provinces maintained soldiers along the Rhine and Danube frontiers. These moneys passed from the army to landlords of Gaul and Spain who supplied the wine and oil and some of the grain required to maintain the troops. The landlords in turn spent their money on manufactures from the eastern provinces, thus completing the cycle.

[68] Full understanding of any particular art style does, of course, require an extensive knowledge of the cultural milieu from which it springs and a mastery of the symbolic meanings embodied in the conventions and subject matter of the art itself. But such knowledge is not prerequisite for admiration, imitation, appropriation—witness the impact of African sculpture upon some contemporary Western artists, who quite neglect the magico-religious beliefs which nourished that art in its original habitat.

century B.C. aptly illustrates this rule; for the most evident borrowings occurred in the realm of the visual arts, especially in sculpture; whereas the traces of similar interchanges in literature and thought are less distinct and often remain questionable.

The keystone of the ecumene was Bactria, where tendrils from the Hellenistic, Indian, Chinese, and Iranian styles of civilization met and intertwined. Greek kings ruled the country until 135 B.C.; while some of their descendants lasted on the Indian side of the mountains for a century more. The Shaka and Kushan sovereigns who followed the Greeks did not themselves add much to the remarkable cultural heritage of the territory; but in the interest of revenue, they promoted trade. Caravans traveling between China and the eastern Mediterranean, or into and out of India, could generally expect a favorable reception in Bactria. Thus men of widely differing backgrounds regularly rubbed shoulders in the cities and caravanserais of the region and made it into an active cultural center between 100 B.C. and 200 A.D.

Fairly extensive and impressive art remains have been discovered on either side of the Hindu Kush. Some of the early coins of Greek Bactria, mainly from the third century B.C., are among the most artistically successful portrait coins of all Hellenistic antiquity, and imply the presence of skilled die cutters fully in command of Hellenistic sculptural traditions.[69] Considerable quantities of statuary showing strong Hellenistic or Roman influence have also been found in Gandhara, south of the Hindu Kush. Indeed, some scholars assume the artists to have been Greeks; yet, when the subject matter can be identified, these statues frequently turn out to be portrayals of Buddhist saints and saviors. The incongruous employment of an Apollo type to represent the Buddha is seldom really successful; but the importance of Gandharan sculpture does not really depend upon its own stylistic success. The main point at issue is whether or not Indian and Chinese sculptural styles received significant stimulus from Hellenistic prototypes. The answer to this question turns upon a disputed and obscure chronology: for, if the art of Gandhara dates from the first century B.C., its influence upon Indian sculpture at large would be difficult to deny; but, if it is a phenomenon of the Kushan royal court of the first or second century A.D., it could be dismissed as a second-rate mishmash of styles already fixed. This is a much debated question, which available evidence does not suffice to settle.[70]

Yet the idea that Indian sculpture received significant stimulus from con-

[69] There are some glaring gaps in the archeological record, especially in Afghanistan, where the mound of Balkh, once capital of Greek Bactria, has never been excavated. It is likely that excavation here would reveal full-scale statuary in the same tradition.

[70] Scholars have reached diametrically opposite conclusions on this point; and their differences have been sharpened by feelings of national pride. Cf. A. Foucher, *L'Art greco-bouddhique du Gandhara* (new ed.; Paris: E. Leroux, 1951); Ludwig Bachhofer, *Early Indian Sculpture* (2 vols.; New York: Harcourt, Brace & Co., 1929); A. K. Coomaraswamy, *History of Indian and Indonesian Art* (New York: E. Weyne, 1927); Benjamin Rowland, *The Art and Architecture of India* (London: Penguin Books, 1953). W. W. Tarn, *The Greeks in Bactria and India* (Cambridge: Cambridge University Press, 1951); H. Ingholt, *Gandharan Art in Pakistan* (New York: Pantheon Books, 1957). The disagreements of these authors arise partly from the uncertainties of the Shaka and Kushan eras, but mainly from different judgments of the affinities of Gandharan sculpture with Hellenistic and/or Roman prototypes.

Victoria and Albert Museum, London.　　　　　　　　　　*Metropolitan Museum of Art, Kennedy Fund, 1926.*

GANDHARAN AND CHINESE SCULPTURAL STYLES

The head of Buddha on the left is an unusually fine example of Gandharan sculpture, in which Hellenistic and Indian styles seem to come together effectively. The date of the piece is uncertain, and some scholars put it as late as the fifth century A.D. The standing Buddha on the right, dated by an inscription to 477 A.D., is one of the earliest surviving examples of Buddhist sculpture from China. The Greco-Indian inspiration is apparent in such details as hair style and facial expression; but the Chinese or central Asian artist who made this statue transformed what had once been a naturalistic representation of folded drapery (p. 291) into a decorative pattern. Both the Gandharan and the Chinese sculptors sought to portray a beneficent deity, for which purposes the naturalistic, ultimately Hellenic, heritage was largely irrelevant. Hence the stylistic transformation which closely paralleled, both in time and spirit, the similar shift from Greco-Roman to Byzantine styles of art (pp. 407, 411) occurring in Hellenism's own Aegean heartland.

tact with Hellenistic models does not really depend on the dating of the Gandhara materials. Long before the time of Alexander, India had been connected with the Mediterranean world. In the third century B.C., Ashoka had introduced stone monuments and sculpture into India, some of which may have been carved by Iranian craftsmen. Trading connections with Hellenistic cities multiplied in the following two centuries; and the conquest of northwestern India by Greeks, Shakas, and Kushans brought a mixed Hellenistic-Iranian culture onto Indian ground. Under these circumstances, Indian stonecutters and sculptors had ample opportunity to see Hellenistic and Roman work with their own eyes, as the discovery of a fair number of imported statuettes on Indian soil makes clear.[71] Because stone sculpture in India started in Ashoka's time, no ancient and hallowed native tradition prevented Indian sculptors from responding vigorously and creatively to the stimulus which even a second-rate miniature copy of a Hellenistic masterpiece could offer beginners.

The Indian response was not slavish imitation, any more than archaic Greek sculptors had exactly reproduced their Egyptian models. Rather, as in the Greek case, contact with a fully developed and vastly impressive alien art served to accelerate the maturation of an indigenous style, the artistic success of which depended precisely upon a free departure from the foreign models. The rapidity with which an Indian sculptural style developed from the isolated beginnings of Ashoka's time to the rich proliferation of the great *stupa* at Sanchi a mere two centuries or so later seems to bear out this speculation. At Sanchi the Hellenistic imprint is not obvious: foreign stimulus had already been successfully digested into a generally naturalistic form related loosely to the Greek, yet fully distinct from it or any other alien art tradition.

The relationship of Hellenistic and Roman art to that of central Asia and China is clearer, for archeological discoveries permit scholars to follow the transmission of the Gandharan art style along the Silk Road to China. To be sure, the earliest surviving Chinese statues which show Hellenistic influence date from the fifth century A.D. But there is good reason to suppose that the art of Gandhara, being intimately associated with Buddhism, began to trickle into China with the first Buddhist missionaries who arrived as early as the

---

[71] After the second century B.C., the mass production of statuary became a regular business in the eastern Mediterranean, using mechanical methods for full-scale reproduction of famous pieces and employing molds for lesser works. This trade in statuary was, of course, mainly directed toward the Roman market in the West; but nothing prevented an enterprising merchant from trying his luck in India, too. It was probably in this way that some of the stray works of Mediterranean art which archeologists have turned up first reached India.

In the first century A.D., when Roman trade with India was at its peak, regular trading stations, inhabited by merchants from Roman territory, sprang up along the Indian coasts. One such station, adjacent to the later French trading station of Pondicherry on the southeast coast of India, appears to have had the outward appearance of a small Roman provincial town, complete with forum and temples. It therefore seems obvious that as long ago as the first century A.D. there were a few "pukka sahibs" in those parts who brought with them as much of their native way of life as possible, including minor works of art. Cf. R. E. M. Wheeler, "Arikamedu: An Indo-Roman Trading Station on the East Coast of India," *Ancient India*, II (1946), 17–124; Mortimer Wheeler, *Rome beyond the Imperial Frontiers* (Harmondsworth: Penguin Books, 1955), pp. 173–78.

Archaeological Survey of India, New Delhi.

Archaeological Survey of India, New Delhi.

Eliot Elisofon and Life Magazine.

THE GREAT STUPA AT SANCHI

The general view of the great Buddhist stupa at Sanchi, India shows how the entire structure was planned, with four elaborately decorated gateways, giving access to the central dome, wherein lay the relics of Buddha that made the place especially holy. A view of the sculptural decoration of the north gate (*lower left*) gives an idea of the richness and complexity of the composition, in part merely decorative, and in part narrative of scenes from Buddha's life. The detail of a bracket from the east gate (*lower right*) suggests the sensuousness of Indian life and religiosity that stood always in opposition to the ascetic tradition so prominent in literature.

first century A.D.[72] But Buddhist art was at first quite as alien to prior Chinese tradition as Buddhism itself, and therefore could not be assimilated at once. In Han times, the older animal-mask designs of Chinese bronzes had given way to geometrical patterns, employed characteristically to decorate the backs of bronze mirrors. Sculpture portraying human or animal figures remained by comparison quite crude. We may therefore imagine that the Buddhist art of Gandhara and central Asia, with statues life-size or larger, richly painted and adorned with gold, must have struck Chinese observers with the force of a new revelation.[73] At any rate, later Chinese art was transformed by accepting—always with a unique accent—the transcendentalized naturalism (as well as some decorative details) of Greco-Indian-Buddhist art.

Thus the sculpture of the eastern Mediterranean affected the art styles of all the civilized peoples of the ecumene during the centuries between 100 B.C. and 200 A.D. To be sure, the Greek imprint altered as it traversed Asia: conventions were misunderstood, draped togas became linear patterns pure and simple, and the all-too-human gods of Hellenistic tradition were transmuted into impassive Buddhas, whose statues expressed a vision of the universe far removed from Mediterranean paganism. In short, cultural borrowing led, as

[72] In the mid-fifth century A.D., an official persecution of Buddhism in China involved widespread and systematic destruction of Buddhist temples and art works. This may account for the failure of earlier examples of this art to survive. O. Franke, *Geschichte des chinesischen Reiches*, II, 203.

[73] Cf. the myth later employed to explain the arrival of Buddhism in China, telling how the emperor Ming-ti in the year 61 (or 65) A.D. saw a golden man in a dream and was stimulated thereby to send to India for knowledge of the Buddha. O. Franke, *Geschichte des chinesischen Reiches*, I, 407.

THE DIFFUSION OF HELLENISM

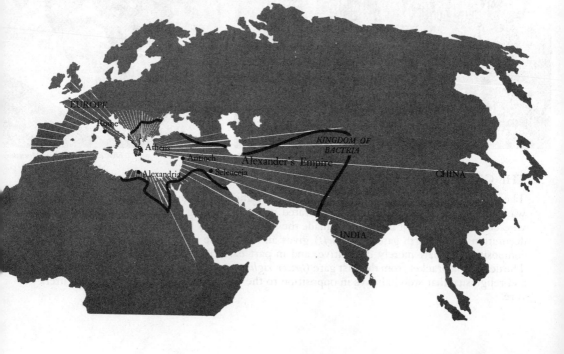

EUROPE
Rome
Athens
Antioch
Alexandria
Seleucia
Alexander's Empire
KINGDOM OF BACTRIA
CHINA
INDIA

Epstein Gallery.

SCYTHIAN AND CHINESE ANIMAL STYLES

The plaque at the top is a copy of Scythian goldsmiths' art; the two pieces below it stem from bronze casters' shops of Han China. On top are two "tigers," one Scythian, one Chinese. Their resemblance betrays the connection between steppe art and the art of China which dated back to the eighth-seventh centuries B.C. On the other hand, the miniature striding dragon shows a quite different style of animal portraiture, whose stylized angularity is more closely akin to subsequent Chinese work.

Epstein Gallery.

always, not to mechanical copying, but to metamorphosis—for as alien elements are incorporated into a new cultural environment, they inevitably acquire meanings and symbolic values different from those they had originally borne.

*　　*　　*

The steppe zone, too, transmitted art motifs throughout Eurasia. From eastern Europe to eastern Siberia, all the steppe peoples participated in an "animal style," which first appeared in the seventh or sixth century B.C., when steppe nomadry assumed its mature form. This animal style borrowed some elements from civilized traditions—e.g., the Sarmatians favored polychrome work, related to Iranian art, which in due course was communicated to European barbarians and became one of the sources of European medieval art. Similarly, Chinese and nomad art interacted in limited respects across the eastern steppe frontier. But by the nature of steppe life, nomad art could find expression only in the decoration of easily portable small objects. Full-blown monumental art could not arise from such roots.[74]

RELIGION. The civilized peoples of western Eurasia, who lived under the political domination of the Roman, Parthian, and Kushan empires, remained for the most part quite satisfied with the cultural institutions and traditional ways of life that had been built up over the generations in their respective parts of the world. The Hellenized gentlemen of the Roman towns, the baronial aristocrats of the Iranian countryside, and the Aryan upper classes of India all had rich and intrinsically attractive ways of life to defend and maintain. Each did so with general success.

Yet, to other social strata, the civilized traditions of their societies meant far less. The peasant majority of each civilized community had small share in the culture of their social superiors. But local village life and the age-old rhythm of the fields, together with magical precautions and festive observances, constitued a simpler but more stable cultural tradition than any known to the upper classes. No serious challenge to the high cultures of India, the Middle East, or Europe could come from the subject peasantries, although their exclusion from the arcana of each civilization did constitute a potential weakness.

Far more critical was the life of the cities, where large numbers of men, drawn from diverse regions, with differing social and cultural inheritances, came together. Particularly in regions where urban life was new, or newly expanded, city dwellers must often have found themselves emotionally adrift, lacking a firmly established pattern of conduct and belief to which they could naturally and unconsciously adhere. Men in such a position obviously sloughed off many of the moral commitments that normally divide mankind into separate cultural communities.

[74] On Hsiung-nu art, cf. René Grousset, *L'Empire des steppes*, pp. 59–62; on Sarmatian art, cf. Rostovtzeff, *Iranians and Greeks in South Russia*, pp. 181–208; Rostovtzeff, *The Animal Style in South Russia and China* (Princeton, N.J.: Princeton University Press, 1929).

The lost souls among the slaves and artisans of the Roman cities therefore formed part of a much larger mass of culturally dispossessed individuals, who found themselves psychologically alienated from established religious and cultural values. In this respect, inhabitants of the great trading cities of central Asia, India, Iran, and Mesopotamia, as well as of the emporia of the eastern Mediterranean and of Rome itself, were all in the same boat. Among such populations, to whom political and cultural frontiers were largely irrelevant, the great and truly world-shaking religious developments of the period found fertile ground.

Another dimension to the cultural map of western Eurasia between 100 B.C. and 200 A.D. contributed decisively to religious history. In addition to the politically ascendant Greco-Roman, Iranian, and Indo-Aryan societies and cultures of the age, there were a number of politically submerged, yet still living cultural traditions, whose adherents found themselves in some measure assimilated to the condition of the uprooted populations of the great cities. Egyptians, Jews, and Syrians in the Roman empire; Jews, Babylonians, and Greeks in Parthia; and Greeks, together with the Dravidian, Munda, and other non-Aryan populations of India, were all in some sense dispossessed by the political and social structures under which they lived. Members of such groups had the choice either of abandoning the cultural traditions of their forebears by conforming to alien ways or of experiencing the frustration of a life in which some of their most deeply held values could not find full expression. Reinterpretation and readjustment of their cultural inheritance, together with a complex process of cultural syncretism, was the inevitable response to such circumstances.

The Jews are the only politically submerged people about whom anything much is known. Yet it seems likely that the career of several other peoples during the same centuries bore a general likeness to the tribulations through which Jewry passed under the Roman and Parthian empires. To be sure, the Jews survived as a distinct people, owing to the uniqueness of their religious and literary heritage, and the extraordinary social discipline that kept Jewish communities cohesive in the midst of an alien and often hostile world. Nearly all the others sooner or later lost their separate identity—but only after prolonged travail which found mainly religious expression. These peoples, together with the slave and artisan classes of the great cities of western Asia, provided the social setting for the extraordinary religious efflorescence of the period just before and just after the Christian era.

Christianity and Mahayana Buddhism were, of course, the chief monuments of this efflorescence, but they did not stand alone. A wide variety of mystery religions flourished in the Roman empire. In India, religious sects and movements were even more various; for it was during these centuries that Hinduism began to emerge from the older Brahminism, through a revaluation of the immemorial multiplicity of local worships. Very imperfect information suggests that similar religious seeking was prevalent also in Mesopotamia, although the main manifestations of religious invention in that ancient land date from a slightly later period (third to sixth centuries A.D.).

Like Zoroastrianism, Judaism, and Orphism in earlier centuries, the new religious movements centered in regions where two or more cultural traditions met and overlapped. Thus Christianity took form in Palestine, Syria, and Anatolia, where Jewish, Greek, Iranian, and (more weakly) Indian cultures intermingled; Hinduism evolved with particular vigor in southern India, where intrusive Aryan and (much weaker) Greco-Roman cultures encountered indigenous Dravidian tradition; and Mahayana Buddhism assumed its mature form in northwest India, where Indian, Iranian, and Greek cultures met. Such multiplicity provided an ample stock of ideas and motifs of piety from which new religions might evolve.

Important resemblances between Christianity, Mahayana Buddhism, and Hinduism may be attributed to borrowings back and forth among previously more or less independent and isolated religious traditions. But parallel invention should not be ruled out, for, if the social and psychological circumstances of the submerged peoples and urban lower classes were in fact approximately similar in all parts of western Asia, we should expect to find close parallels among the religious movements which arose and flourished in such milieux. This is in fact the case; for three fundamental features shared by the major religious movements of the age distinguished them from anything that had gone before.

First, Christianity, Mahayana Buddhism, and Hinduism agreed in defining the goal of all human life as salvation. All three promised their adherents eternal life in a blissful afterworld,[75] although prerequisites for entry into such a blessed state, and theoretical descriptions of Heaven and of the mode of survival after death, differed substantially from one religion to another. The older concept of religion as necessary for maintaining cordial relations with the supernatural powers that ruled the world was not abandoned; but emphasis shifted from the short-term practical advantages that might be expected in this life to the eternal bliss of Heaven, where all the sorrows of the world would find redress.[76]

Second, all the new religions of western Asia were egalitarian in the sense that any ordinary man could perform the duties and participate in the rites which were held to be necessary for salvation. Even more important, women as well as men were admitted to full participation in religious services and deemed capable of salvation. This constituted a great source of strength; for women had almost invariably been excluded from equal franchise in earlier religious systems. The new forms of worship therefore offered them hope of escape from the inequalities and inequities under which they continued to la-

[75] This was nothing new, for Egyptian and Megalithic religion, not to mention Orphism, had held such hopes before their adherents for millennia. Yet "salvation" was new in the sense that earlier religions had viewed the afterworld as essentially a continuation of life as lived on earth, perhaps with some inescapable diminution of its fulness. The new religions of salvation, on the contrary, held that life beyond the grave involved radical change and improvement of society, so that only purged and purified spirits could share in life eternal.

[76] The psychological power of such a view of the human condition need not be emphasized. Everyone born into the tradition of one of these religions rejects only regretfully the comfort such an explanation of man's place in the universe affords.

bor in daily life. Therefore it is scarcely surprising that the most pious and energetic adherents of the new faiths were women; and through their influence upon children, they were able to assure comparatively rapid propagation of the new doctrines.

A third common feature was the concept of a savior God who was both a person and at the same time universal in his nature. Such a savior, it was held, conferred salvation upon his worshippers either by allowing them to become identified with him, thus directly sharing his power and immortality, or else by a transfer of merit or of power, more mechanically conceived, which was, however, completely adequate to assure the salvation of the recipient. The gap between universal, omnipotent, omniscient deity and the helpless human individual was bridged by the concept of a god-man, who of his own free will descended into human form to lead men toward salvation. Christ and Mithra, Vishnu and Shiva, and the innumerable Bodhisattvas of Mahayana Buddhism all shared these characteristics.

Logic may find it impossible to combine transcendent Deity with God Incarnate. Similarly, monotheism and polytheism may be logical antitheses. But in practice, such incompatibles fit well together. Christianity as well as Hinduism and Mahayana Buddhism were monotheistic in the sense that they assigned all power and glory to God the Savior, Creator, and Sustainer; yet all three cults made room for the invocation and adoration of lesser beings— saints and angels in the Christian tradition, and local gods and spirits assigned to the retinue of one or another incarnation of the supreme deity in Indian lore. In general, the Christians, as heirs of the stricter and more intolerant monotheism of Judaism, were somewhat more cautious than Hindus or Buddhists in allowing subordinate objects of devotion to distract attention from the supreme Deity. Yet, despite the scruples of theologians, early Christian piety quickly plunged into a thicket of saint worship, essentially similar to the adoration of local deities which proliferated endlessly in both Hinduism and Mahayana Buddhism. The difference, therefore, lay more in theory than in practice. But the theoretical difference did not lack important consequences, for subsequent Christian history was distinguished by recurrent efforts to purify the faith by eradicating idolatrous excrescences, whereas the Indian religions, having accorded full theoretical sanction to any and every form of local worship, however crude or strange its rites, were exempted from such crises of conscience.[77]

A pervasive historicity of outlook also distinguished Christianity from its Indian contemporaries. Christians regarded the Creation, Incarnation, and Last Judgment as unique events which gave meaning and hope to ordinary terrestrial human life. Against this historical, time-bound view, Buddhists and Hindus set a cosmological vision of innumerable worlds endlessly repeating a

---

[77] The divergence went back a long way in time. Aryan priests, too, had perhaps once tried to eradictate the worships of the land. But Brahmins soon found it preferable to compromise with village pieties and presently justified such cults with the doctrine that some portion of abstract deity inhered in every form of worship. Christian theology, on the other hand, inherited the ancient Hebrew tension between Yahweh and the baals of Canaan; and, like the Hebrews, Christians could neither exclude nor entirely approve the adoration of saints and other local cult practices.

cyclical process of creation and destruction. Divine incarnations multiplied, becoming in fact infinite in number, so that no single divine event could have the unique significance for Hindus or Buddhists that Christians assigned to the coming of Christ.

Finally, religions like Christianity and Mahayana Buddhism may be distinguished from numerous competing forms of worship by their emphasis upon ethics. Devotees of Serapis and Isis, for example, and of certain Hindu cults, were not expected to change their usual mode of life very significantly in order to qualify for salvation. Magical rites sufficed. But Buddhism and Christianity associated eternal salvation with an ethical code to be aspired after in this world and attained perfectly in the next. This ethical aspiration, together with effective ecclesiastical organizations, gave these two faiths a much firmer hold on their followers' daily lives than any merely ritualistic religion could have possibly achieved. This palpable imprint upon the everyday life of the community of believers, as much or more than any doctrinal superiority, accounted for the extraordinary successes that came to Christianity and Mahayana Buddhism.

Christianity. In the strict sense, Christianity began with the preaching and death of Jesus of Nazareth, about 27–30 A.D. Yet much of Jesus' gospel was no more than an emphatic assertion of ideas already familiar in the Judaism of his day. From the time of Antiochus IV Epiphanes (175–163 B.C.), who had stirred up revolt by trying to Hellenize Jewish worship, and of the Maccabees, who established an independent Jewish state in Palestine (168–42 B.C.), the expectation of a Messiah who would bring God's kingdom to earth had excited vivid attention among the Jews. Just what the Messiah would be like was a matter for debate. Some expected a conquering monarch who would restore the kingdom of David; others awaited a supernatural being, arriving on wings of fire at the end of time, when the skies would open to reveal God's ineffable glory.[78] Difficult conditions of life in Palestine (which came indirectly under Roman rule after 63 B.C.) convinced more and more Jews that God would not long permit such injustices to endure. Special communities arose, like that revealed by the Qumran Dead Sea scrolls, whose members held themselves in a constant state of readiness for the end of the world, seeking to avoid every form of defilement lest God should find them unworthy of his kingdom on the last day.

Connected closely with these messianic visions was the idea, championed primarily by Pharisees, that the righteous might look forward either to personal immortality or to bodily resurrection on the Day of the Lord. This doctrine, smacking of Iranian and Hellenistic notions, was resisted by other Jews, who found no basis for such beliefs in the Law and the Prophets; but lack of traditional sanction did not prevent a doctrine so attractive to men in a troubled time from taking firm root in the Jewish community.

[78] Iranian, and especially Zoroastrian, motifs were prominent in the imagery used to describe the end of the world. The Jews of Babylon may have been particularly prominent in bringing this strand of thought into Judaism, since they were most closely in touch with Iranian religious speculation.

Jews living outside Palestine laid the groundwork for Christianity in quite another fashion. Living far away from Jerusalem, they could not regularly participate in the services at the Temple. Instead, they kept alive religious practices, first developed during the exile in Babylon, that could be pursued locally. In addition to family observances, which were of great importance, the Jews of the diaspora maintained the custom of meeting at weekly intervals for public reading from the Scriptures, accompanied by exposition of the meaning of the texts. Special buildings—synagogues—housed such meetings and became public centers for Jewish community activities. These synagogues provided the cells out of which the Christian churches were to grow.

Apart from this institutional cradle, the Jewish diaspora also prepared the way for Christianity by initiating a generalized process of acculturation between Jew and Greek. The Jews of the diaspora were inevitably exposed to the ideas and habits of the Hellenized urban world. Many such Jews spoke Greek as their native language; and they admitted a fair number of pagan converts into their community. But even after accepting Judaism, such converts inevitably retained many of their old habits of thought and feeling. This situation and the over-all pressure of the environment gave many Jewish communities a semi-Hellenized character; and men were not wanting who, like Philo of Alexandria (20 B.C.–50 A.D.), sought to interpret Judaic religious belief in terms of Greek philosophy. Such rapprochement between Jew and Greek smoothed the way for Christianity's transition from the status of a Jewish sect to a religion that drew most of its converts from the pagan world.

Yet, when these anticipations and preparations for the Christian revelation have been duly taken into account, there remains a central spark that was unique. The spark was provided by a handful of very humbly situated Galileans—Jesus himself first and foremost, together with Peter and the other disciples. The personality of Jesus must have been extraordinarily vivid. His injunctions and personal example challenged his most devoted followers to live up to an utterly uncompromising ethical ideal—"Turn the other cheek"; "Love thy neighbor as thyself"; "Do unto others as you would be done by" —proclaimed initially with all the high emotion generated by an eager anticipation of the imminent end of the world. Jesus' message, "Repent, for the Kingdom of Heaven is at hand," certainly excited powerful emotions among his immediate followers and stirred the messianic hopes of a much wider group of hearers as well. Given the exacerbated state of public feeling endemic to Palestine at the time, it was not strange that Jesus' preaching should have occasioned a riot in Jerusalem, nor that he should have been arrested and crucified for blasphemy and sedition.

The really remarkable thing was that his teachings survived his death. The account preserved in Acts of how a handful of Jesus' most intimate followers gathered in an upstairs room and there suddenly felt the Holy Spirit descend upon them until they became absolutely convinced that their Master who had just died on the cross was with them still bears all the marks of authenticity. It was, after all, an event no one present could possibly forget, and sufficiently miraculous to require no embroidery in retelling. After undergoing such an emotional experience, which, moreover, was repeated subsequently, who could doubt that Jesus of Nazareth, the carpenter's son, was in truth the Messiah and would soon return in glory? And who, with such an experience behind him, could refrain from telling others, warning them of the Second Coming, helping them to prepare themselves for it, and explaining the signs and proofs of Jesus' messiahship? By preaching and teaching, and by inviting the Spirit through gatherings of the faithful, where scenes from Jesus the Messiah's earlier appearance among men were recalled and marvelled at, the small kernel of Jesus' followers that first rallied together after the crucifixion speedily began to add new members and to gain fresh confidence in their new understanding of all the shocking and wonderful experiences they had gone through together.[79]

The next great turning point in Christian history focused around the career of St. Paul. Born in Asia Minor, in the Hellenistic city of Tarsus, Paul was a man of the great world, not a simple Galilean like the twelve Apostles. A pious, educated, and energetic Jew, he was among the first to attack the ignorant and impious sectaries who had begun to preach the Risen Messiah in the streets of Jerusalem. Yet when journeying to Damascus to urge the local Jewish community of that city not to tolerate the new doctrines in their midst, Paul saw Jesus Christ in a vision and was converted to the faith he had formerly attacked. Having seen Him, Paul preached the Risen Christ; and speaking in Greek to audiences accustomed to Greek habits of thought and turns of speech, he naturally brought a markedly Hellenistic element into his doctrine. The imminent end of the world, to be accomplished by the Second Coming of Christ, remained at the center of the Christian message; but what struck a still stronger chord in the minds of gentile hearers of the gospel was the proof that Paul offered, from his own experience, that Jesus Christ had really risen from the grave. Such a savior might indeed have the power to raise others from their graves if they believed firmly in him and served him faithfully.

A question which immediately arose in the Christian communities outside Palestine was whether or not the Mosaic law remained binding. Paul's answer was that Christ had abrogated the Old Dispensation by opening a new path to salvation. Other followers of Christ held that traditional Jewish custom and law still remained in force. This issue provoked the first important doctrinal conflict in the Christian community, and, as with any dispute among men deeply convinced that they are in the right, neither Peter and James, the leaders in Jerusalem, nor Paul and Barnabas, who came from Antioch to discuss the question (40 A.D.?), could persuade the other party. Apparently it was agreed to let each group pursue the policy that seemed right to its leaders

---

[79] In subsequent Christian history, sectarian groups have repeatedly reproduced most or all of the unusual psychic manifestations that bound the first Christian community together so powerfully. Men whose ordinary lives involve persistent frustrations easily fall into collective states of excitement. In such circumstances, red-hot religion offers a surrogate for, and yet hovers on the verge of, mass violence. Popular persecutions of early Christianity and later Christian attacks upon pagans like Hypatia (d. 415) sufficiently attest the kinship between religious excitement and mob action in the Roman empire. More recent sectarian history, both medieval and modern, offers many similar cases.

—which meant, in practice, that Paul and his associates found a fertile field for their preaching among the gentiles, whereas the Palestinian Christian community remained a minor Jewish sect. For among the Jews, the discrepancies between their grandiose messianic expectations and the actual accomplishments of Jesus' life were too great to make the idea of Jesus' messiahship convincing to anyone who had not already joined the community and felt the Spirit himself.

As the apostolic generation began to grow old and die, it became obvious that their memories of Jesus' deeds and sayings should be written down. The Gospels evolved from such recollections, supplemented by pious invention designed to show how details of Jesus' life did in fact fulfil the messianic prophecies and expectations. Christian communities also found a useful and authoritative exposition of doctrine in Paul's letters sent to some of the churches he had established. Other writings were added, chief among them the apocalyptic visions of the approaching end of the world that go by the name of the Book of Revelation, until by about 200 A.D., a standard collection of Scripture had been accepted by most or all Christian communities as divinely inspired. This was the New Testament, the reading of which became an important part of Christian worship. The Jewish sacred scriptures were also retained as part of the Christian inheritance, despite attacks upon them made by some speculatively minded converts who found the anthropomorphism and moral crudity of some passages in the Old Testament offensive.

In 66 A.D., a widespread revolt broke out in Palestine, stimulated by messianic hopes similar to those Jesus had himself stirred up. Rome sent troops to restore order; and in the stubborn and most bitter war which followed, Jerusalem was captured and the Temple destroyed (70 A.D.). This upheaval dispersed or destroyed the Christian community in Palestine; and its remnants either merged into the larger Christian community abroad or else returned to the fold of Judaism. The early links between Christianity and Judaism were thereby broken; and the new faith proceeded to make its way in the Greco-Roman world in rivalry, not only with pagan religions, but with Judaism as well.

Since converts inevitably brought their pagan mentality with them into the early Christian churches, Christianity came increasingly to resemble other Hellenized religions. Yet important hallmarks stemming from the Jewish cradle of the faith were never obliterated. An emphatic intolerance of all rival creeds and a closely-knit community were among the most important of these inheritances. Much of Christianity's early success rested upon the systematic charities through which members helped one another and upon the ritual weekly meetings for scripture reading, exhortation, and (at first) a common meal commemorating the Last Supper Jesus had taken with his disciples. These too were adaptations of the ordinary practice of the synagogue, adjusted to accommodate the new Christian message. The upshot was to create a cohesive community of believers who viewed the outside world as basically alien and evil, but within their own ranks enjoyed the fellowship, the pervasive social discipline, and the burning hope for the future which had long characterized Judaism.

Christianity combined these traits with a doctrine better attuned to Greek minds, and rites freed from regulations and prohibitions which offended Greek feeling. None of the other mystery religions of the Roman empire had as much to offer. A noble ethic, sacred writings popularly written, yet backed by the sanction of ancient prophecy, a warm emotional brotherhood among the faithful, the promise of eternal and blissful life topped by a vivid expectation of an early overthrow of worldly injustices on earth: all these made a powerful appeal to the poor and dispossessed of the great cities of the Roman world, and beyond Roman borders as well.[80]

The birth of Christianity is one of the central dramas of human history. The enormous influence Jesus and a handful of humble Galilean country folk exercised upon subsequent human generations staggers the imagination. The disciples' success in overcoming the apparent defeat of all their hopes upon the cross and in reinterpreting their experiences was extraordinary in itself, but far more so in its tremendous consequences; and the new emphasis which the preaching of St. Paul gave to the Christian gospel was no less significant for the future. The actions, thoughts, and feelings of these few men profoundly affected the acts and thoughts and feelings of hundreds of millions. They continue to exercise vast influence to this day and will do so through foreseeable human time; for the living force of Christian faith, hope, and love, together with the no less powerful forces of Christian bigotry and superstition, are by no means yet exhausted.

Buddhism and Hinduism. The obscurities of early Christian history are as nothing compared to the uncertainties surrounding the evolution of Indian religions. Undoubtedly the central reason for this is the fundamental ahistoricity of all Indian thought: time and place become irrelevant to those who habitually dwell in the presence of the infinite.

The first generation of Buddha's disciples preserved the memory of their master's life and teachings, much as Jesus' disciples were later to do. But the Buddhist canon of edifying writings was never closed, so that new ideas and modifications of old ones were accepted into the faith for more than a thousand years after Gautama had passed from the scene. The same was true of Hinduism, with the difference that, having no identifiable founder, it was emancipated from history from the start. Indian sects were always numerous, but generally found it possible to live together peaceably, since there were many ways to truth and no one in the Indian cultural context was inclined to assume that he alone possessed the key to salvation. The chronically intimate interplay that resulted among all the diverse religious groups of India enormously confused religious history.

[80] Successful missionary activity in Mesopotamia, Armenia, Ethiopia, and India started very early, although some scholars doubt the dates which the legends of the churches in those regions assign to their origin. Cf. Johann Peter Kirsch, *Die Kirche in der antiken griechisch-römischen Kulturwelt* (Freiburg: Herder & Co., 1930), I, 135–38; Kenneth Scott Latourette, *A History of the Expansion of Christianity.* Vol. I: *The First Five Centuries* (New York and London: Harper & Bros., 1937), pp. 100–108.

Despite all uncertainties, it is clear that in the period 200 B.C. to 200 A.D., a popular Hinduism began to emerge from an amalgamation between sacerdotal Brahminism, immemorial village rites, and a new element: the concept of God Incarnate, strong to save. Simultaneously, it became evident that Buddhism had failed to capture the loyalty of the Indian population as a whole.

The decline of Indian Buddhism was centrally due to the fact that it never offered the Indian laity a complete religion. Early Buddhism knew no ceremonies for birth and death, marriage, illness, and other critical turns of private life; and Buddhist observances for occasions of more public moment likewise failed to develop. Only for the community of monks did Buddhism provide a complete and well-defined way of life. Ordinary folk might adhere to the faith by contributing to the support of the monks or by engaging in solemn perambulation of *stupas* and other sacred spots in order to acquire some tincture of the holiness inherent in these places. Rulers and men of wealth might build sacred structures or edify the public by commissioning sculptured monuments celebrating Buddha's career. But Brahmins were needed for all the ordinary crises of life, ready with their rites and sacred formulas to ward off danger or minimize the damage. This elemental fact assured the survival of Brahminism in India, despite the vigorous attack upon sacrifice and priestly pretention which Buddhism and Jainism had launched in the sixth century B.C.

Brahmins, in offering their services as ritual experts to the general public, gradually accommodated themselves to the views and attitudes of the people they served. The villages of India were inhabited, then as now, by peoples of many different tongues and variegated cultural backgrounds. From time immemorial, the villagers had preserved and elaborated the worship of a great variety of gods and spirits, some conceived in human and others in animal or other forms. By appropriately identifying local divinities with figures of the Vedic pantheon, the Brahmins reconciled these multiform cults with Vedic religion and grafted onto village piety some of the high metaphysical speculation that had developed from the original Aryan religion.

In the course of time, two figures—the great gods Shiva and Vishnu—gathered to themselves a complex series of traits and stories, until they became rival, yet complementary supreme deities of Hinduism. It does not appear that the myth cycles—linked together by the doctrine of *avatars*, according to which Vishnu and (probably only by imitation) Shiva were believed to have incarnated themselves repeatedly in various forms— took anything like canonical form until the fourth–sixth centuries A.D. The numerous deities designated as *avatars* of the great gods had previously existed in their own right; and Indians worshipped dozens, if not hundreds of other divinities who never won a place in the Vaishnavite or Shaivite cults. Confronted by the practical task of ministering to populations who held so many and such various deities in awe, the Brahmins validated whatever they encountered by interpreting each lesser god as a partial manifestation of the ultimate spiritual reality, corporealized in a manner suitable to the level of their worshippers' understandings. This amalgam may be called Hinduism, although the term is perhaps best reserved for a later age, when a more nearly systematic pantheon and a distinctive mystical cult had begun to give form to the pullulating confusion of local pieties.

*   *   *

In the long run, Buddhism failed to hold its own against the Hindu synthesis of high metaphysics and vulgar superstition. Nevertheless, before dissolving back into the variegated religiosity from which they had sprung, some Indian Buddhist sects underwent far-reaching changes, which adapted them to the emotional needs of laymen who could not or would not accept the more strenuous monastic regimen.

The ideal of early Buddhism had been a mental and physical discipline which culminated in mystic experience, defined as the dissolution of self, or *nirvana*. Individuals who had attained this blissful state were termed *arhats* and were believed to have escaped from the wheel of reincarnation. But during the two centuries or so after the beginning of the Christian era, a quite different conception of the highest goal of religious life won wide support among Buddhists. Certain teachers held that instead of seeking the "selfish" goals of personal dissolution and the dignity of arhatship, holy men should refrain from entering nirvana in order to help other, more sinful and misguided men to ascend the ladder of incarnation and ultimately escape from the suffering of existence. Such religious athletes were termed *Bodhisattvas* and were believed to inhabit a heaven of their own making, pending such time as they might find it suitable to make their own final incarnation and dissolve blissfully into nirvana.

The exact steps by which this radical change in emphasis arose within Buddhism are far from clear. Pressure exerted by a laity unwilling or unable to undergo the discipline required of an *arhat*, but still longing for salvation, must have been one element in the transformation. Probably another was competition offered by the rising cults of Vishnu and Shiva: certainly some details of the careers and powers later assigned to various of the Bodhisattvas seem to have been borrowed from the mythology surrounding these two great Hindu deities.

Speculative argument about the nature of the Buddha also helped to form the new doctrine. Supernatural and miraculous powers had early been attributed to Gautama Buddha, until, in time, the historical human figure of Gautama became almost unimportant. The term "Buddha" was used to designate the transcendent principle sustaining the cosmos; and Buddha-incarnations multiplied until the particular Buddha of the sixth century B.C. became only a trifling incident in a most complex Buddhology. Speculation about the kind of prior lives which might prepare a person for incarnation as a Buddha led to the concept of the Bodhisattva, or Buddha *in potentia*. Bodhisattvas in turn took on cosmic proportions, their number multiplied indefinitely, and elaborate mythologies grew up around some of them. Finally, a ritual of worship, prayer, and self-dedication to one or another Bodhisattva was admitted to

Buddhist devotions. This remodeled form of Buddhism—termed the Mahayana, or Greater Vehicle—thus became a religion offering personal salvation, fully capable of competing with other forms of worship for the attention and devotion of ordinary laymen.

Among the Mahayanists, the ideal of personal dissolution as the final aim of religious life tended to fade. To escape an embarrassing vacuum at the pinnacle of their ladder of incarnations, therefore, Mahayana theologians attributed multiple essences to incarnate Buddhas. While one essence might proceed to nirvana and dissolution in the old-fashioned way, others remained as cosmic principles to aid struggling mankind toward salvation. With typical Indian exuberance, Buddhist speculation postulated not one, but hundreds, thousands, and ultimately an infinite number of such saviors—as many as the sands of the Ganges, according to one text—whose merits might be shared by devout believers who invoked their help in prayer. Not only monks, but any man, however weak and sinful, might hope eventually to enter upon the Buddha-path and, after a suitable number of incarnations, to become a Bodhisattva and a Buddha himself.

Some of the earliest exponents of Mahayana teachings seem to have lived in southern and eastern India; but the new doctrine found its greatest scope in the northwest. Very probably Kanishka, the imperial Kushan monarch of the second century A.D., patronized Mahayana Buddhism. Certainly the faith penetrated central Asia during the first post-Christian centuries, and from there spread along the Silk Road and into China.[81]

Despite the radical differences between the Mahayana and the more conservative Hinayana (Lesser Vehicle) form of Buddhism, monks of either persuasion lived together quite peaceably, often in the same monastery. The divergent doctrines were not felt to be antipathetic to one another; and some Hinayana writings reached China in addition to the Mahayana flood. The success of the Mahayana was due, no doubt, to the warmer hope it extended to mere laymen—busy merchants or poor artisans—who, in their current incarnation, were only expected to pray for salvation and refrain from sinning whenever they could. In Ceylon and Burma, however, the older doctrine generally held the field, perhaps because in those comparatively remote regions the urbanization which elsewhere had created a rootless public thirsting for salvation had not yet advanced very far.

* * *

The transformation of Buddhism through the development of Mahayana doctrine was as radical as the change that came to Christianity when it left its Jewish cradle and launched itself upon the Greco-Roman world. Moreover, in each case the direction of the shift was the same: earlier emphases were supplemented and eventually superseded by a popular religion, offering high ethical prescripts for this world and the hope of salvation in the next. Bud-

[81] The dates at which certain Mahayana texts were translated into Chinese alone supplies a *terminus ad quem* for the rise of the Mahayana in India.

dhology, for all its multiplication of saviors, bore a general resemblance to Christology: the idea of divine incarnation was central to both.

Something more than the general similarity of social circumstances which existed in the areas where each religion took form seems needed to produce such parallelism. Nonetheless, most students of Buddhism pay only perfunctory attention to the question whether Iranian or Hellenistic ideas contributed in any important way to the rise of the Mahayana. To be sure, some details have caught scholarly attention: for example, the figure of the future Buddha, Maitreya, bears interesting resemblances to Mithra.[82] One or two of the Bodhisattvas also have specifically Iranian attributes, indicating that the Buddhist writers whose stories gave a living personality to these particular figures probably borrowed epithets and incidents from Iranian religion. But such details are not much more significant than the appearance of Buddha, under the name of Barlaam, in Christian hagiography in the seventh century A.D.

The central idea of both Christianity and Mahayana Buddhism was the concept of a divine savior or saviors, who assumed human form in order to show mankind the way to blissful life after death. It has long been recognized that Christian soteriology stemmed largely from Greek speculation; it is possible that the same was true of Mahayana Buddhism. Ample opportunity for such intermingling of Greek with Indian thought existed. For example, one of the Greek kings of northwest India named Menander (second century B.C.) gained a reputation in Indian circles as a man of philosophical learning. This is evidenced by a Buddhist religio-philosophic dialogue in which he appears as a protagonist.[83] After Menander's time, commercial contacts between Indian and the Hellenized cities of the eastern Mediterranean were close; and although merchants were not philosophers, they were fully capable of transmitting the sort of popular religious views which lay behind Christian soteriology.[84] Therefore, it is reasonable to suppose that Mahayana doctrines may have been stimulated by Hellenistic notions in a really important way. But we are likely never to know for certain, since whatever communication across cultural frontiers did occur took place among persons of humble social station

[82] The whole idea of a savior destined to come at some future time may have percolated from Iranian sources into both Judaism and Buddhism. Eschatology, however, never played a great role in Buddhist thought, for men accustomed to dwell familiarly with an infinite number of worlds and saviors could not attach any unusual importance to the approaching dissolution of the particular world in which they happened to live, or even to the next Buddha in an infinitely extended series of Buddha-incarnations.

[83] The book is called *Milindapanha*, translated as *The Questions of King Milinda* (T. W. Rhys Davids [trans.]) in F. Max Müller, *The Sacred Books of the East* (Oxford: Clarendon Press, 1890–94), Vols. XXXV–XXXVI. The holy man who answers Milinda's questions, the monk Nagasena, was probably one of the principal figures who developed Mahayana doctrines. The historicity of the dialogue is, however, out of the question.

[84] For a learned survey of the surprisingly extended traces left in Indian literature by "Yavanas," or Greeks, see Sylvain Levi, "La Grèce et l'Inde d'après les documents indiens," *Revue des études grecques*, IV (1891), 24–25. Cf. also Gauranga Nath Banerjee, *Hellenism in Ancient India* (2d ed.; Calcutta: the author, 1920); Eugene F. A. comte Goblet d'Alviella, *Ce que l'Inde doit à la Grèce* (Paris: Leroux, 1897); Richard Fick, "Die buddhistische Kultur und das Erbe Alexanders des Grossen," *Morgenland Darstellungen aus Geschichte und Kultur des Ostens*, Heft 25, 1933; K. A. Nilakanta Sastri, "Ancient Indian Contacts with Western Lands," *Diogenes*, No. 28 (1959), pp. 52–62.

—merchants, sailors, caravan attendants, and the like—who made no written records of their conversations with strangers.[85]

The history of art lends support to the hypothesis that Christianity and Mahayana Buddhism perhaps share a Hellenistic soteriological strand. The Hellenistic imprint is definitely clearer upon Buddhist art than upon Buddhist theology, for the earliest surviving portraits of Buddhas and Bodhisattvas derive directly from Hellenistic prototypes. Indeed, the Greek custom of portraying gods and heroes in human form must have served to popularize the concept of divine incarnation among uneducated and unsophisticated persons. To a cultivated Greek or Roman of the second century A.D., a statue of Apollo might be merely a beautiful work of art; to an Indian, a similar statue must have required elaborate explanation: How could a god be a man? And when Buddhas and Bodhisattvas, too, came to be carved in human shapes, the speculation that had already turned Buddha into a cosmic principle must have required re-examination and re-explanation. Mahayana doctrine may in fact have arisen very largely from such an interplay of art traditions with theological speculation.

The question must be left open, though it is worth noting that, if Hellenistic ideas did in fact play a formative role in the rise of the Mahayana, then the two major religions of our period were half-sisters, springing from Hellenistic seeds implanted in two different mothers, one Jewish, one Indian; while a bit higher up the family tree lurked an Iranian father-in-law. To be sure, fertility of religious invention has seldom been lacking in India; and most of Mahayana mythology, the fundamental timelessness of the Buddhist outlook, and the remarkable multiplicity of incarnate saviors surely derived from India alone. Greek ideas may have provided key stimuli to the development of the Mahayana concept of salvation; but its elaboration and definition took place in a predominantly Indian environment.[86]

Iran and China. The state of Zoroastrianism under the Parthians, its relation to Mithraism and other Iranian cults, and the religious policy and belief of the Parthian rulers are simply not known.[87] Certain coins suggest that

---

[85] Some of the principal figures in the development of Mahayana doctrine—Ashvaghosa, a poet, playwright, and Buddhist moralist; and Nagarjuna, a sophisticated Buddhist philosopher—are traditionally associated with the court of Kanishka. This court derived substantial income from dues levied on merchants traversing the kingdom; and the main trading centers must have seen a constant mixing of men of widely dispersed geographical origin. Cf. R. Ghirshman, *Bégram*, pp. 150–54.

[86] For these remarks on the beginnings of Hinduism and Mahayana Buddhism, I have consulted the following: Edward Conze, *Buddhism: Its Essence and Development* (New York: Philosophical Library, 1951); Edward J. Thomas, *The History of Buddhist Thought* (2d ed.; New York: Barnes & Noble, 1951); Nalinaksha Dutt, *Aspects of Mahayana Buddhism and Its Relation to Hinayana* (London: Luzac & Co., 1930); A. Berriedale Keith, *Buddhist Philosophy in India and Ceylon* (Oxford: Clarendon Press, 1923); Helmut von Glasenapp, *Die fünf grossen Religionen* (Düsseldorf-Cologne: Eugen Diederichs Verlag, 1951), Vol. I; Har Dayal, *The Bodhisattva Doctrine in Buddhist Sanskrit Literature* (London: Kegan Paul, Trench, Trubner & Co., 1932); Emil Abegg, *Der Messiasglaube in Indien und Iran* (Berlin and Leipzig: Walter de Gruyter & Co., 1928); Paul Masson-Oursel *et al.*, *L'Inde antique et la civilisation indienne* (Paris: Albin Michel, 1951); Paul Levy, *Buddhism: A "Mystery Religion"?* (London: Athlone Press, 1957); A. L. Basham, *The Wonder That Was India;* Helmut von Glasenapp, *Der Buddhismus in Indien und im Fernen Osten* (Berlin, Zurich: Atlantis Verlag, 1936).

[87] Roman Ghirshman, *L'Iran des origines à l'Islam* (Paris: Payot, 1951), pp. 228, 239–43; R. C. Zaehner, *The Dawn and Twilight of Zoroastrianism* (New York: G. P. Putnam's Sons, 1961).

CHRISTIANITY   MAHAYANA BUDDHISM   HINDUISM

some Parthian monarchs may have turned away from patronage of things Greek and emphasized native Iranian religion.[88] We do know that the cult of Mithra played an important role on Roman territory and found an early welcome among the Latin-speaking populations of the West. In the third and fourth centuries A.D., Mithraism in fact became Christianity's most formidable rival in the Roman world.

In the form known to the Romans, Mithraism was a religion promising blessed immortality; and it retained Zoroastrian dualism by recognizing an evil principle of the universe as well as a good. But Mesopotamian, Syrian, and Hellenistic motifs were added to the Iranian base of Mithraism—a syncretism that probably occurred in Anatolia in the first century B.C., about the time of the Roman conquest of that region. The greatest weakness of this religion was the exclusively masculine character of its religious brotherhood, well enough suited to a military camp, but ill-suited to society at large. Perhaps for

[88] Such alternation of policy probably reflected the tension between partially Hellenized towns and a more definitely Iranian countryside which had characterized Iran and parts of Mesopotamia ever since the Macedonian conquest. Kings who relied on town support against an always unruly Iranian aristocracy would normally patronize the still vaguely Hellenic town culture, whereas a monarch dependent directly on the support of the country squires of Iran would be likely to fall back upon Zoroastrianism or some modification of that ancient faith as sign of his Iranian identity. Similar tensions and fluctuations of royal policy became more extreme in the Sassanian period; and Sunni-Shi'a splits in Islam echoed similar social cleavages later still.

this reason, Mithraism ultimately failed to establish itself in Rome or anywhere else.

China's case was different, for there the burst of religious creativity that distinguished the rest of civilized Eurasia between 100 B.C. and 200 A.D. was conspicuously lacking. During most of this period, the political and social structure of Han China remained intact; and Confucianism and Taoism presumably continued to meet the religious needs of the population. Under the Later Han, Confucianism expanded into a doctrine embracing physical and metaphysical as well as moral teachings. The Sage came to be honored through official as well as family rituals; and Confucianism thus took on some aspects of a state religion.[89] Yet these changes were scarcely new departures. They were rather in the nature of a consolidation, whereby a number of doctrines and ideas previously developed by other Chinese schools—mainly the Ying-Yang—were folded into official Confucianism.

Only toward the end of the second century A.D., when the Han state began to totter toward its dissolution, did signs of a deeper religious unsettlement become evident in China. Taoism, for example, became associated with popular movements directed against the authorities, although no particular doctrinal development seems to have accompanied this political manifestation. At the same time, Buddhism began to make progress in China. Its major successes, however, came only after the downfall of the Han, when barbarian invasion and internal disorder had broken down the older Chinese social system and prepared men's minds for a doctrine so utterly alien to earlier Chinese thought.[90]

Summary. The religious travail of the submerged peoples and rootless populations of the cities of western Asia in the first centuries of the Christian era marks a profound change in human history. The rise of Christianity, Hinduism, and Mahayana Buddhism offered a view of the world that allowed men to face almost any sort of disaster with a modicum of cheerfulness, since, according to each of these faiths, this world was but the prelude to another. The disruption of the imperial states that had permitted the closure of the ecumene actually forwarded the progress of these religions. They throve in times of trouble, for they stood ready to offer solace to an entire society, as in their infancy they had solaced the pains of the poor and downtrodden.

Societies in earlier times had never known anything quite like these religions of salvation. Perhaps the prophetic and ecstatic religious movements of the tenth–eighth centuries B.C., as manifested in Anatolia and the eastern Mediterranean lands, were a crudely comparable reaction to the breakdown of the civilized society of those times. But the parallel only underlines how much the civilized world had developed between the tenth and first centuries B.C., since, with the important exception of prophetic Judaism, such move-

[89] Cf. Fung Yu-lan, *A History of Chinese Philosophy*, II, 7–132; John K. Shryock, *Origin and Development of the State Cult of Confucius* (New York: Appleton-Century, 1932).

[90] It was, after all, only under similar conditions that Christianity conquered the Roman empire.

ments in the earlier age did not succeed in giving birth to institutions and doctrines capable of affecting human lives over generations and centuries. Egyptian religion, with its gradual democratization of immorality, its priestly organization, and its mythological elaboration perhaps came closest to anticipating the emphases and organization of the higher religions; but the Egyptians conceived the afterlife as second best to life on earth; and the missionary impulse so characteristic both of Buddhism and of Christianity was utterly lacking. Instead, the idea that religion was tied to locality, the precious possession of a special people, gave Egyptian and nearly all other antique religions a profoundly parochial character that stood in diametrical opposition to the emphatic universalism of the religions of salvation.

Christianity, Hinduism, and Mahayana Buddhism provided perhaps the first really satisfactory adjustment of human life to the impersonality and human indifference that prevails in large urban agglomerates. Nature religions, personifying the forces of earth and sky, could meet the psychological needs of village farmers whose social ties to their fellows were personal and close. State religions were adequate for the early civilized peoples, whose cultural inheritance was nearly uniform and who maintained a close personal identification with the body social and politic. But when such uniformity and cohesion in civilized society broke down, as was bound to happen as the civilized area increased and the complexity and variety of cultures and social systems enlarged, such official, state religions could not satisfy the growing number of deracinated individuals whose personal isolation from any larger community was barely tolerable at best. We have seen how Babylonian religion failed to meet such needs;[91] and Greco-Roman religion of the polis manifested the same deficiency when local city-states ceased to be cohesive, psychologically self-contained social universes.

Something more than either nature religion or a religion of state was needed for peace of mind in a great city, where strangers had to be dealt with daily, where rich and poor lived in different cultural worlds, and where impersonal forces like official compulsion or market changes impinged painfully and quite unpredictably upon daily life. Knowledge of a savior, who cared for and protected each human atom adrift in such mass communities, and confidence in a future life where all evil and suffering of this world would be duly recompensed, certainly offered men a powerful help in the face of any hardship or disaster. In addition the religious community itself, united in a common faith and in good works, provided a vital substitute for the sort of primary community where all relations were personal, from which humankind had sprung and to which, in all probability, human instinct remains fundamentally attuned. Quite apart from any question of doctrinal truth or error, Christianity, Hinduism, and Mahayana Buddhism fitted men more successfully than ever before to the difficult task of living in a megalopolitan

[91] Cf. also the Book of Job.

civilization.[92] Perhaps, therefore, the epiphany of religions of salvation assured, as it certainly assisted, the survival and revival of megalopolitan society.

3. OTHER ASPECTS OF THE HIGH CULTURAL TRADITION OF EURASIA, 100 B.C.–200 A.D.

Despite the prevalence of religious innovation in the interstitial regions of the ecumene, the heartlands—China, India, and Rome—remained generally conservative. Foreign ideas and practices lacked all attraction for the learned men of these civilizations, who already possessed a quite satisfactory cultural heritage of their own and could afford to neglect all that failed to conform to it.

The situation was otherwise in the Middle East. The cosmopolitan civilization of that region had suffered such blows from Alexander and his successors that it tended to fall apart into its old constituent elements—Egyptian, Mesopotamian, Jewish, Iranian. Each of these cultures separately had to come to terms with the attractive disruption of intrusive Hellenism. Neither Mesopotamian nor Egyptian priestly learning survived this shock. Berossus of Babylon (*ca.* 250 B.C.), who migrated to the Aegean island of Cos, where he translated the astronomical and historical wisdom of the priests of Bel Marduk into Greek, and Manetho of Egypt, who did the same for the historical traditions of his native land at about the same time, represent almost the last gasp of intellectual energy traceable to their respective priestly traditions. No longer viable in their own right, the age-old religions of Mesopotamia and Egypt began to undergo far-reaching changes, mingling with Greek ideas and forms to become Oriental mystery religions of the sort that inundated the Roman world from the first century B.C. onward. From Egypt came the cult of Isis and Serapis; Mesopotamia produced the "science" of astrology. In such disguised and modified forms, therefore, a part of the ancient learning of the Middle East lived on; but the corporate identity of the two traditions was irretrievably lost.

On the other hand, the Jews were able to maintain the independence of their cultural tradition, even in the face of renewed political disaster. During the revolt of 66–70 A.D., Roman armies destroyed the Temple in Jerusalem and the priesthood that served it; but the scattered synagogues proved able to maintain the faith even without the center in Jerusalem. The utter destruction of the Jewish peasantry in Judea, as a consequence of a second Palestinian revolt (132–135 A.D.), likewise failed to cripple Judaism, for the urban communities of the diaspora survived. In general, the messianic excitement which had set off the disastrous revolts of 66 and 132 A.D. subsided; the Messiah's coming was no longer so imminently expected; and the high hopes of former

---

[92] In time, of course, such religions spread far beyond urban bounds, since the answers they gave to the recurrent problems of human life were just as satisfying for men whose lives were less atomized than was the case in the cities where these religions first grew up. At the same time, the existence of the higher religions made subsequent urban growth easier, surer, stronger, by reducing social frictions and maintaining moral solidarity among all ranks and conditions of men (so long as they were of the same faith) at a higher level than could have been attained without such religions.

days hardened into learned legal, philological, and polemical exegesis of scripture. Rabbinical schools replaced the Temple as the master institution of Judaism, for it was necessary to train experts in the Law and the Prophets who could expound and apply the Scriptures to the variegated circumstances of everyday life. The most important of these schools was in Galilee,[93] where the canonical text of the Hebrew Scriptures was defined during the second century A.D. Thus Judaism remained a living faith; and, under the leadership of learned rabbis, it proved quite able to resist both Hellenism and Christianity.[94]

The Iranian case was intermediate. Certainly the Persian literary tradition retained a degree of continuity from the days of Zoroaster to the revival of national culture under the Sassanids after 226 A.D. Yet there was much syncretism, too, as evidenced by the utterly obscure literary and intellectual pedigree of the *Avesta*, the sacred scripture of Sassanid Zoroastrianism.[95]

In sum, the cosmopolitanism of the ancient Middle East broke apart culturally as well as politically during the period 100 B.C. to 200 A.D. Hellenic and Indian influences played upon the region; invaders from the steppe added a fresh barbarian strand to the mixture; and the resultant cultural syncretism found a primarily religious expression.

* * *

No such fragmentation occurred in the Roman world. There, the traditions of Greek and Hellenistic civilization were maintained, though often with diminished energy. Greek philosophy, rhetoric, historiography, and belles lettres all developed Latin counterparts; and in the process the Latin language acquired a learned vocabulary capable of conveying the high culture of the Greek East to the various peoples of the western Mediterranean. The major work of translating and adjusting Greek learning to the Latin tongue and temperament was performed in the first century B.C. by Cicero (d. 43 B.C.), Lucretius (d. *ca.* 55 B.C.), and Catullus (d. *ca.* 54 B.C.). In the succeeding generation, Vergil (d. 19 B.C.), Horace (d. 8 B.C.), and Livy (d. 17 A.D.) brought Latin letters to their most perfect expression. Thereafter, the Roman peace and the comfortable life of Roman gentlemen discouraged serious intellectual or artistic work. A dilettante and sometimes archaizing spirit prevailed, relieved only by the venomous involution of Tacitus' (d. *ca.* 117 A.D.) histories.

The second century A.D. saw a modest revival of Greek letters (e.g., Plutarch, d. *ca.* 120 A.D.), and a very influential codification of Greek science in the work of Galen (d. *ca.* 200 A.D.) for medicine and of Ptolemy (d. after

[93] The population of this region was not uprooted in the great war of 132–135 A.D.

[94] Salo W. Baron, *A Social and Religious History of the Jews* (2d ed.; Philadelphia: Jewish Publication Society, 1952), II, 89–128.

[95] Jacques Duchesne-Guillemin, *Ormazd et Ahriman, L'Aventure dualiste dans l'antiquité* (Paris: Presses Universitaires, 1953), pp. 55–134; H. S. Nyberg, "Die Religionen des alten Iran," *Mitteilungen der Vorderasiatische-aegyptischen Gesellschaft*, Band 43 (Leipzig: J. C. Hinrichs, 1938); R. C. Zaehner, *Dawn and Twilight of Zoroastrianism.*

161 A.D.) for astronomy and geography. The very perfection and mathematical elegance of Ptolemy's astronomy, and the copious, yet systematic character of Galen's medicine seemed to later generations incapable of improvement and thus played a part in checking further development of Greek science. A shift of learned attention toward metaphysical and particularly theological questions contributed even more powerfully to the same result.

The laws of nature, as analyzed mathematically and descriptively by Ptolemy and Galen, bore an interesting, and perhaps not entirely accidental similarity to the law of nations and of nature, as discerned by a long succession of Roman jurists. Roman jurisprudence culminated in the work of such men as Ulpian and Papinian at the very end of the second century A.D. and the beginning of the third. The concept of an objective law applicable to human affairs, yet operating in accord with Nature and Reason and apart both from divine revelation and from human whim or passion, was peculiar to Rome and societies descended from the Roman. Other civilized peoples had laws and law codes, to be sure; but their laws were normally confined to criminal and public matters, leaving merely private relations to private or customary regulation.[96] Roman law, as developed in the cosmopolitan milieu of the empire, attempted to bring regular classification and clear rules to bear upon the confusing multiplicity of both public and private concerns. Concepts of ownership, contract, and property—matters so intimate to our daily lives that we scarcely notice their existence—were more and more precisely defined, so that particular disputes could be reduced to a legal case and settled in accordance with a published rule through a judicial process. To a complex, individualized, and urbanized society, the advantages of such a legal system are enormous, for it tends to make dealings with strangers predictable and safe, even in the absence of any firm customary consensus. No other early civilization developed a legal system of such refinement and generality. Elsewhere, local custom, group mores, family traditions retained greater scope, while the personal discretion of officials and men of power enjoyed a much wider range.

The value of the Roman law to subsequent European civilization would be difficult to exaggerate. When urbanism began to develop afresh in western Europe after the eleventh century, the imposing corpus of Roman law lay ready at hand. The models it offered for reshaping the chaotic customary law which had meanwhile grown up in Europe automatically facilitated, stabilized, and gave new scope to urban, market-oriented activity.[97]

[96] The inclusion of private relationships within the purview of Roman law was no doubt an inheritance from the totalitarianism of early polis organization, which had elevated the territorial state far above all other human ties.

[97] Moreover, the relationship between human law, natural law, and scientific laws of nature was always close. Minds accustomed to finding a law to govern one sort of activity were prone to look for laws operating elsewhere. Cf. the remarks above on Ionian speculation and polis law. Conversely, in societies where law enjoyed no such scope and dignity as it did in the Roman scheme of things, men were the less likely to expect or look for regularities in the behavior of inanimate nature. Hence it does not seem fantastic to suggest that modern science owes much to Roman law. Cf. the comparison of Chinese with European attitudes toward law, both human and scientific, in Needham, *Science and Civilization in China*, II, 518–83.

In India, the period 100 B.C. to 200 A.D. saw a vigorous development in art and literature, moving toward the "classical" expression attained in the age of the Gupta empire (320–535 A.D.). The two great epics of Indian literature, the *Mahabharata* and the *Ramayana*, were probably nearing their final form by 200 A.D.; and literary Sanskrit, based upon the grammatical precepts of Panini, had already developed into a genuine if artificial literary medium. However, chronological uncertainty makes it impossible to assign most of the monuments of classical Sanskrit art and literature to any definite period, either before or after 200 A.D. It therefore seems best to reserve their discussion until the next chapter, despite the risk of unduly slighting the achievements of pre-Gupta times.

* * *

China, at least, offers few chronological difficulties; and with the Han a remarkably successful consolidation of the multiplicity of inherited Chinese traditions under the banner of Confucianism became official. Mathematical and astronomical knowledge increased as a by-product of calendrical disputation;[98] but literary and philological scholarship occupied the center of Chinese intellectual activity. For such scholarship, textual authenticity was of primary importance; and this question accordingly provoked a weighty dispute between the "New Text" and "Old Text" schools.[99] Aside from minutiae of wording, the schools divided over the question of how freely to allow Ying-Yang and related notions to color their interpretation of Confucianism. The "Old Text" scholars decried such travesty of the teachings of the Master; the "New Text" scholars tended to read between the lines, seeing hints and symbolic significances behind the superficial (and sometimes quite trivial) meanings of the classic texts themselves. Besides learned polemics, of which there were many, this discussion led to the compilation of the first systematic Chinese dictionary, arranged, as Chinese dictionaries are still, according to the radicals of the characters.

Chinese historical writing also came to maturity under the Han. Ssu-ma Ch'ien's (145–86 B.C.) many-volumed history of China (indeed of the whole world within Chinese ken) established the frame within which Chinese history continued to be written almost until the present day. Ssu-ma Ch'ien accepted and made canonical the theory that each dynasty began with an

---

[98] Different calendrical systems became weapons in political struggles, especially at the time of Wang Mang's usurpation (9 B.C. to 24 A.D.). As a result of these factional disputes, the Later Han instituted a new calendar that was astronomically less accurate than that Wang Mang had used. Cf. Wolfram Eberhard, "Contributions to the Astronomy of the Han Period, III," *Harvard Journal of Asiatic Studies*, I (1936), 194–241. For a detailed but confusingly technical and topically arranged discussion of Chinese mathematical astronomy, cf. Joseph Needham, *Science and Civilization in China*, III, 1–461.

[99] The first of these based their interpretation of the Confucian classics upon the texts that had been reconstructed in the early Han period after the Ch'in emperor's ban upon Confucian books (213 B.C.) had been withdrawn; the Old Text scholars, on the other hand, claimed to base their views upon more authentic versions, written in the old character style and dating from before the destruction of the books.

especially virtuous ruler and then gradually dissipated that virtue until Heaven lost patience and substituted a new dynasty in its place. This idea was very ancient in China; but Ssu-ma Ch'ien was the first to fit the facts of history into such a pattern; and his success made the scheme binding for subsequent historians. In addition to a political narrative organized on this principle, Ssu-ma Ch'ien's history included treatises on such special subjects as music, sacrifices, waterworks, and military methods, describing how each had developed from the beginning to the historian's own time. Other treatises dealt with the careers of noble houses of ancient China, while the bulkiest section of the entire work comprised biographical essays about distinguished individuals. The work of Ssu-ma Ch'ien combined Herodotus' scope with Thucydides' exactness (in intention if not always in fact); and his example fixed the mold for subsequent Chinese historiography.[100] As a result, the second important historian of Han times, Pan Ku (32–92 A.D.) adhered exactly to his predecessor's model in composing the history of the Former Han dynasty.[101]

We are much less well informed about the Han intellectual underworld. It was probably inhabited by Taoist sages who pursued chemical experiments intended to produce an elixir with the power to confer long life or even immortality upon those who drank it. Part of the terminology and conceptual framework of later Arabian and European alchemy seems to have originated in this way. But the diffusion of alchemy westward, like the movement of astrology eastward, became significant only in the centuries after 200 A.D. The conservatism of learning was such that, even when commercial intercourse had made intellectual contacts possible, little serious interchange took place until severe social stress had disturbed the even tenor of the times in China, India, and Europe.

* * *

Technology was a little, but only a little, less conservative. Significant migrations of useful plants and animals did occur; but artisan skills and trade secrets diffused less readily. Thus, for example, familiarity with cotton, sugar cane, and chickens, all first domesticated in India, spread to both China and western Eurasia during this period, while China contributed apricots and peaches, perhaps also citrus fruits, cherries, and almonds to western Eurasia. In exchange, the Chinese imported alfalfa and a number of vegetable crops, as well as the Iranian great horses.[102]

[100] On Ssu-ma Ch'ien, see Burton Watson, *Ssu-ma Ch'ien: Grand Historian of China* (New York: Columbia University Press, 1958). Parts of his work have been translated by Édouard Chavannes, *Les Mémoires historiques de Ssuma-Ts'ien* (5 vols.; Paris: Leroux, 1895–1905).

[101] Homer H. Dubs has translated the section of Pan Ku's work treating the imperial annals. Pan Ku, *The History of the Former Han Dynasty*, trans. Homer H. Dubs (3 vols.; Baltimore, Md.: Waverly Press, 1938–55).

[102] Charles Singer et al., *A History of Technology*, II, 199; Roman Ghirshman, *L'Iran des origines à l'Islam*, p. 256; Alphonse de Candolle, *The Origin of Cultivated Plants* (New York: D. Appleton & Co., 1902).

It was relatively easy for travelers to bring seeds of exotic plants back with them; but the skills and secrets of manufacture could not so easily be acquired and transported. In any case, skilled artisans working for export, and merchants engaging in foreign trade, presumably had no desire to see the spread of technical information to new regions. As a result, industrial or proto-industrial technology presents geographically a nearly static picture for this period.[103]

Roman water mills and techniques of glass production seem to have been the best in the world. Indian steel attained a peculiar quality that commanded a market in the Roman empire, but could not be duplicated there; Chinese silk was exported to India, the Middle East, and Rome; but the secrets of its manufacture did not reach the outer world until the sixth century A.D.[104] Roman military technology, especially siegecraft and fortification, commanded a considerable reputation in India, and perhaps even in China;[105] and it is probable that Roman ships introduced a new level of marine architecture into Indian waters which made possible the remarkable overseas expansion of Indian culture in the early post-Christian centuries.[106]

In general, however, too little is known of the history of technology to permit a satisfactory over-all picture. Differences cannot have been very marked, the special skills and techniques of each of the civilized communities being roughly equivalent. Handicraft methods of course prevailed everywhere, for the use of inanimate power was just beginning with the introduction of water mills, used mainly for grinding grain to flour.

Everywhere in the civilized world, wealth depended primarily upon agriculture. An overwhelming majority of the population of civilized states were peasants; and perhaps the major economic demarcation lay between areas where water engineering made agriculture capable of sustaining a dense population and the more thinly populated areas of dry-land farming, where crops were at the mercy of an always erratic and sometimes excessive rainfall. Until western Europe had developed agricultural methods that could cope with waterlogged plains, farming there was perforce concentrated on hillsides and on especially well-drained subsoils (e.g., loess and chalk). Thus the far western fringe of the ecumene lagged behind the agricultural wealth of the drier Mediterranean and Middle Eastern lands; and nowhere could farming in rain-watered land approach the productivity of the irrigated valleys of China, India, and the Middle East.

[103] Chinese technical inventions may have been both particularly important and particularly immobile. Cf. J. Needham, *Science and Civilization in China*, I, 240–43.

[104] Charles Singer *et al.*, *A History of Technology*, II, 57, 322, 593–601; G. F. Hudson, *Europe and China* (London: Edward Arnold & Co., 1931), pp. 68–102, 120–22.

[105] Sir Mortimer Wheeler, *Rome beyond the Imperial Frontiers*, p. 160; Homer H. Dubs, *A Roman City in Ancient China* (London: China Society, 1957).

[106] This is hypothesis based upon praise of "the beautifully built ships of the Yavanas" (*i.e.*, Ionians, or Greeks generally) in early Tamil poetry of south India. Cf. Wheeler, *Rome beyond the Imperial Frontiers*.

All these exchanges of ideas and techniques depended on conscious human action and were correspondingly inhibited by indifference, ignorance and inattention. No such obstacles hindered the diffusion of disease germs. Infections which in earlier times had been familiar only in one or another part of the Old World could be and undoubtedly were carried with merchant ships and pack trains from one edge of Eurasia to the other and back again. But uncertainty prevails in these matters and no critical study of what information is available has been made. Hence any statements about either the history of diseases or the growth and decline of populations in the ancient world can only rest upon informed guesswork. Indian records, indeed, do not even allow sound guessing; but a survey of the ancient Mesopotamian canal system suggests that the peak of population in that important region came between the third and sixth centuries A.D.[107] Chinese and Roman records are comparatively well known and indicate an earlier population apogee, coming about the first century A.D. Severe pestilence was a major factor in the decay of both Roman and Chinese populations from the second century onward; and it is perhaps not surprising that these communities, situated on the extreme edges of the ecumene, should have suffered more seriously from new and unfamiliar diseases than did the Middle East, where traffic with the far reaches of the Old World was not new and the local populations may be presumed to have already established a degree of immunity to diseases which in the Far East and Far West were still capable of decimating biologically unprotected populations.[108]

Pestilential disease, resulting directly from the closure of the ecumene may therefore be held partially responsible[109] for the radical decay of population

[107] Thorkild Jacobsen and Robert M. Adams, "Salt and Silt in Ancient Mesopotamian Agriculture," *Science*, CXXVIII (1958), 1251; Robert M. Adams, "Agriculture and Urban Life in Early Southwestern Iran," *Science*, CXXXVI (April, 1962), 116–19.

[108] The severity a new disease may have among a biologically defenseless population was repeatedly illustrated after the European closure of the global ecumene, when sailors and others introduced such diseases as measles or even the common cold among Amerindians, Eskimos, Polynesians, for example, only to see the victims die of an infection which for a European was comparatively trifling. Obviously, European (and Asian) populations acquired their immunities only by prior exposure to these diseases; and this biological process must have passed through one of its principal phases in the early Christian centuries. On epidemics, cf. Georg Sticker, *Abhandlungen aus der Seuchengeschichte und Seuchenlehre*, Band I, erster Teil: *Die Geschichte der Pest* (Giessen: Alfred Töpelman, 1908); W. H. S. Jones, *Malaria: A Neglected Factor in the History of Greece and Rome* (Cambridge: Macmillan & Bowes, 1907); Benno von Hagen, *Die Pest im Altertum* (Jena: Gustav Fisher, 1939). On China, cf. K. Chimin Wong and Wu Lien-teh, *History of Chinese Medicine* (Shanghai: National Quarantine Service, 1936), pp. 53–138. None of these works, however, approaches the available data with the important questions in mind; and a really sophisticated survey of the history of pestilence among mankind still remains to be written.

[109] Since theoretical grasp of population phenomena remains imperfect even for modern times, when fairly exact data about what does happen is available, it would be ridiculous to suggest that the rise and decay of ancient populations can be adequately understood. Other factors besides the new severity of pestilence resulting from the wider circulation of infections incident to improved communications undoubtedly undermined Roman population. Various sexual perversions, together with the custom of bathing in very hot water (thus killing male sperm), perhaps do much to explain the failure of the upper classes to reproduce themselves in imperial Rome; and both economic and psychological conditions no doubt affected peasant and artisan reproduction rates. The relative importance and practical effect of these and still other factors simply cannot be determined.

which became a persistent problem in Roman imperial times and assumed catastrophic proportions in the third century A.D.[110] Substantial decline of the Chinese population seems also to have occurred in the late Han period;[111] and the barbarian invasions which assumed major proportions in both the Far East and Far West during the third and fourth centuries A.D. may in part be attributed to a disease-induced dearth of population behind both the Roman *limes* and the Chinese wall.[112]

[110] On the basic importance of population decay in Roman history, cf. the provocative remarks of Arnold Hugh Martin Jones, *Ancient Economic History: An Inaugural Lecture Delivered at University College, London* (London: H. K. Lewis, 1948).

[111] Cf. Hans Bielenstein, "The Census of China during the Period 2–742 A.D.," Museum of Far Eastern Antiquities, Stockholm, *Bulletin*, XIX (1947), 125–63.

[112] Drastic decline of population carried its own corrective, for the consequent decay of productivity checked when it did not halt long-distance trade, particularly since trade dealt fundamentally in luxuries. But as contacts with strange parts of the world decreased, the transmission of diseases, we may assume, correspondingly declined, thus checking one and perhaps the prime factor which earlier had decimated civilized populations at the extremes of the ecumene. The survivors, nevertheless, carried immunities in their bloodstreams which meant that renewed exposure to the diseases of distant parts of the Eurasian continent could never again have quite such lethal consequences as they probably had in the second–fourth centuries A.D.

CHAPTER **VIII**

Barbarian Onslaught and Civilized Response 200–600 A.D.

A. INTRODUCTION

By 200 A.D., Hellenism had lost almost all of its expansive energy. Neighbors and strangers no longer saw much to admire and found still less to imitate in the style of life prevailing among the genteel Greco-Roman heirs of that tradition. The Confucian tradition of China also underwent a similar, though less drastic decay. Confucianism, too, was largely confined to a class of landowners and officials; and the cool moderation and decorous conservatism of Confucian gentility ill-suited the age of internal disorder and barbarian invasion that followed the collapse of the Han dynasty.

India, on the contrary, entered upon an age of remarkable cultural expansion both at home and abroad. Under the Gupta dynasty (*ca.* 320–535 A.D.) Indian art and letters achieved a golden age; simultaneously, the transcendental religiosity long characteristic of Indian civilization exerted a powerful appeal among strangers. The spread of Mahayana Buddhism overland into central Asia, China, Korea, and ultimately to Japan was the most spectacular demonstration of the expansive power of Indian culture in this age. But an almost equally vast movement followed the seaways, for precisely during the centuries when Buddhism was winning its greatest victories north of the Himalayas, Indian maritime enterprise planted a series of states in southeast Asia and Indonesia which drew their high culture directly from India. In Iran and the eastern Mediterranean, where rival religions held the

361

ground, Indian cultural models met far greater resistance. Yet even there, Neo-Platonic and Gnostic thought exhibited definite Indian affinities; Indian ascetic discipline may have contributed to the style of mysticism that established itself among Christian monks; and the vaguer but pervasive spirit of world renunciation characteristic of early Christianity and of some of its chief rivals (e.g., Manichaeism) also owed something to the stimulus of Indian religious attitudes.

If one concentrates attention upon the movement of ideas and especially upon religious changes, India therefore appears to have played the leading role in the entire Eurasian world between 200 and 600 A.D. But if one thinks instead of military and political affairs, India's role shrinks to trifling proportions, and a quite different geographical locus becomes critical—the long frontier between civilized and barbarian peoples that ran all the way from the mouth of the Rhine to the mouth of the Amur. The balance of forces across that frontier changed decisively in the late fourth century, with the result that very considerable linguistic and population shifts occurred in widely separated parts of Eurasia.

In the Far West, barbarian war bands and migrating hordes broke into the Roman empire; and similar, though less numerous groups invaded north China. In both areas, the invaders set up a series of short-lived states and gradually acquired some of the culture of their subjects. By the sixth century, the initial impetus of these invasions had spent itself; and in China a restoration of imperial unity proved possible. But Justinian's parallel effort in the Roman West met only ephemeral success; and the empire he had partially reunited dissolved again before fresh waves of barbarian invasion. Only after Latin Christendom (ninth century A.D.) adopted the Iranian type of heavy armored cavalry could the civilized or semi-civilized) peoples of the Far West halt the barbarian tide and begin a contrary movement of expansion (tenth–eleventh centuries A.D.).

From the military and political point of view, Iran was therefore the key area of the ecumene. Long before 200 A.D., civilized Iranians had developed effective techniques of defensive cavalry warfare and had established sociopolitical institutions capable of sustaining a formidable force of armored cavalrymen scattered out across the countryside, where they were perpetually ready to mount a formidable local defense against nomad attack. Slowly and reluctantly, European societies adjusted their defenses and modified their social systems along the lines of the Iranian model. This institutional reorganization was what made Europe "medieval." Eastward, Iran's influence upon China was comparatively slight; but it was the effectiveness of the Iranian frontier guard against the steppe that secured India against invasion, thus contributing indirectly to the flowering of Indian culture in the Gupta age.

The appearance of several new civilized styles of life in regions marginal to the older culture centers of Eurasia was an important feature of the period 200–600 A.D. Ireland, Ethiopia, and Japan all became the seats of new and (at least potentially) independent civilizations. The reason is plain: as commercial links among the major Eurasian civilizations weakened, outlying areas were thrown back more exclusively on their own resources. Interruption or drastic diminution of contacts with the outer world then allowed the local peoples to elaborate their own styles of life, while making use at will of civilized elements which had come to their attention during the earlier, more cosmopolitan, and better traveled age.[1] In the same period, civilizations reminiscent of ancient Sumer arose in the New World. But whether the inhabitants of Peru and Central America, like those of Ireland, Ethiopia, and Japan, received valuable stimuli from the Old World cannot yet be determined with certainty.

*   *   *

In view of the unusually complex pattern of world history between 200 and 600 A.D., orderly presentation becomes particularly difficult. This chapter arbitrarily divides Eurasia in two, treating first the flowering and expansion of Indian civilization and its impact upon southeast Asia and China; then considering the development of western Eurasia and the transformation of social organzation and culture that came to those parts under the pressure of barbarian attack. The chapter concludes with some remarks upon changes along the fringes of the civilized world. This tends perhaps to overemphasize the division of the ecumene between Indian and Iranian fields of force and to minimize the links connecting India with the Mediterranean, and Iran with China. Nevertheless, this ordering of the subject seems the most likely to illumine, even while it distorts, reality.

B. THE FLOWERING OF INDIAN CULTURE, 200–600 A.D.

Between the third and seventh centuries A.D., and particularly during the Gupta imperial age (320–570 A.D.), the culture of India achieved an elegant and complete expression which remained ideally normative for later generations. This age saw the definitive fusion between Aryan-Brahminical cultural traditions and elements derived from the pre-Aryan populations of the land. Simultaneously, Indians responded triumphantly to the cultural stimuli they had received during the preceding centuries from the Hellenized world and from Iran. Gupta times, therefore, remind one more of the mature strength of middle age than of youth's reckless grace. It was India's golden age.

1. POLITICAL AND SOCIAL FRAMEWORK

The Kushan empire, which during the first and second centuries A.D. had constituted the keystone of the ecumene, did not long survive its own success. The vigorous military energy of Sassanid Persia (from 224 A.D.) compelled the Kushan lands north of Hindu Kush to recognize Persian suzerainty; while in northwest India, Kushan power disintegrated. Perhaps the real

---

[1] Classical Greek civilization took form under substantially the same circumstances, when the Iron Age invasions had broken down the earlier Middle Eastern cosmopolitanism that had extended at least marginally to include the Aegean.

changes were not very great: local rulers, who had long enjoyed most of the realities of sovereignty, simply withheld ceremonial deference and tribute payments from the Kushan kings.

Elsewhere in India, similar political fragmentation prevailed in the third century A.D. Yet the ideal of universal, imperial rule, as exemplified in the past by the Maurya state, remained alive—a fact which probably facilitated the rise of the Gupta empire in the following century. The kernel of the Gupta state lay in the lower Ganges plain, in or near Bengal. This region was still on the frontier of Indian society when the first important Gupta ruler, Chandra-gupta I (320–30 A.D.),[2] like many another lord marcher before and since, exploited his strategic location to consolidate authority over most of the Ganges Valley states. His successors, Samudra-gupta (330–80 A.D.) and Chandra-gupta II (380–415 A.D.), between them brought all of northern India under Gupta sway, from the Bay of Bengal to the Arabian Sea and from the Himalayas to the Deccan.

In most cases, these conquests did not involve the overthrow of pre-existing states and dynasties. The Gupta emperors usually left local rulers in office, but compelled them to attend the imperial court, pay tribute, and at least in some cases to accept an imperial agent as a sort of "resident." Areas imme-diately adjacent to the Gupta hereditary lands were directly incorporated into the imperial domain; but the Guptas did not attempt to extend their cen-tralized administration beyond the middle reaches of the Ganges Valley. No doubt this mild policy toward defeated sovereigns facilitated the Gupta ex-pansion. It had the additional advantage of conforming to the moral precepts of Brahminical political theory, which held that a righteous conqueror was bound to maintain his defeated enemy (or a member of the enemy's family) in power.[3]

All details of the military operations that built the empire have been lost; but it is unlikely that the fighting was severe. Literature attests the growth of elaborate chivalric conventions, which may have made Indian warfare of the time almost harmless to noncombatants and not very dangerous to partici-pants. Certainly the expansion of the Gupta power inaugurated a period of unusual peace in India. Save for a raid by a nomad people—the Ephthalite Huns, who broke through the Iranian frontier guard and briefly ravaged northwest India about 460 A.D.—there is no surviving record of warfare until almost the end of the fifth century. The Deccan and southern India never be-came part of the Gupta dominions; but the half-dozen or so states into which those regions were divided appear to have lived together without notable conflict; and all maintained trade and diplomatic relations with the Gupta empire in the north. Thus the fifth century A.D., which saw military disaster

[2] His name is identical in Sanskrit with that of the founder of the Maurya empire; but to minimize confusion it is conventional in English to hyphenate the name of the later imperial founder.

The year 320 A.D. marks the first year of the Gupta era, as decreed by Chandra-gupta I, probably in commemoration of his own coronation. R. C. Majumdar *et al.* (eds.), *The History and Culture of the Indian People* (Bombay: Bharatiya Vidya Bhavan, 1954), III, 2.

[3] A. L. Basham, *The Wonder That Was India* (London: Sidgwick & Jackson, 1954), p. 126.

and unusual disorder in both Europe and China, was an age of extraordinary peace in India. Sheltered by this peace, the "classical" age of Indian culture came safely and confidently into bloom.

The peacefulness of Gupta times appears strange when contrasted with the chronic violence accompanying the simultaneous fragmentation of political authority in Europe. India's peacefulness may be attributed (1) to the final taming of the fierce and barbarian war-band ethos which the Aryans had introduced into India nearly two thousand years before; and (2) to the rise of a compelling code of conduct and system of values presided over by Brahmins and conveniently called Hinduism. The two are really one, for the eclipse of the ancient warrior ideal was merely an aspect of the wider process of cultural synthesis that produced Brahminical Hinduism—a synthesis which involved the infusion of new meanings, drawn often from pre-Aryan sources, into Aryan languages and cultural forms.

A century of growingly chivalrous warfare, followed by about eighty years when chivalry sought its principal conquests in the boudoir rather than on the battlefield, is sufficiently rare in civilized history to deserve our admiration. Recognition of the fact that a major reason for this extraordinary limitation on violence was the wide dispersion of effective power within Indian society need not detract from that admiration. Who occupied which throne and paid deference and tribute to whom made remarkably little difference to the population at large, as long as barbarians like the Ephthalite Huns stayed north of the mountains. The social bonds regulating ordinary lives remained almost unaffected by the chivalry, pomp, and ceremony of kings and emperors, for the Guptas did not attempt to remake Indian political institutions on the more totalitarian Iranian and Hellenistic model, as the Mauryas perhaps had done. Instead they tolerated all the immemorial diversity of Indian society. This meant acquiescence in the drastic diffusion of power inherent in all the variegated customary rigidities of caste, sect, and locality.

The numerous self-regulating corporations which constituted the very tissue of Indian society set severe practical limits upon the authority of the central power. Indian villages usually enjoyed a wide autonomy and managed their affairs with little intervention from outside. Imperial officials taxed the harvest and sometimes obliged local populations to labor on public works; but villagers were often exempt from the control of local landlords.[4] A similarly broad autonomy made guilds, towns, monasteries, and temples immune from most outside control. The institution of caste, which apparently was fully developed by Gupta times, provided a loose but effective co-ordination among the myriad of social groupings. Order of precedence among castes was precisely defined; and customary patterns of behavior both within and with-

---

[4] The Chinese pilgrim, Fa-hsien, who visited Buddhist shrines and monasteries during the reign of Chandra-gupta II, was much surprised at the leniency and limited scope of the imperial administration and commented favorably upon the liberties and prosperity of the commoners: "The people are numerous and happy; they have not to register their households or attend to any magistrates and their rules; . . . if they want to go, they go; if they want to stay on, they stay." J. H. Legge, *Record of the Buddhistic Kingdoms, Being an Account of the Chinese Monk Fa-hsien's Travels* (Oxford: Clarendon Press, 1886), pp. 42–43.

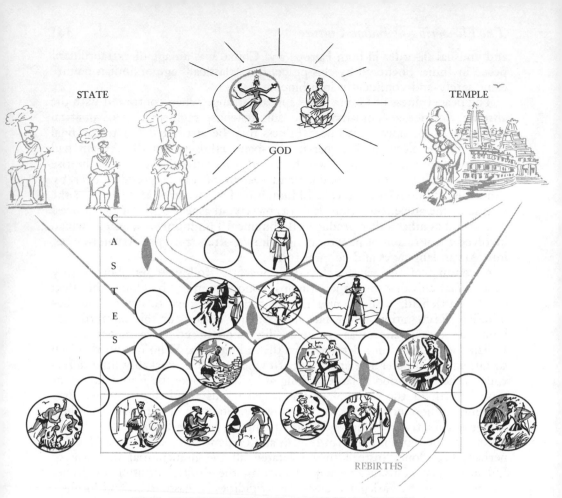

STATE

TEMPLE

GOD

C
A
S
T
E
S

REBIRTHS

THE STRUCTURE OF INDIAN SOCIETY

out each particular caste offered a reasonably clear definition of proper conduct in all ordinary circumstances of life for all the peoples of India.

The theory of caste was a central part of the doctrine of Hinduism. Hindu myth explained caste status as the consequence of *karma* accumulated in earlier incarnations. Pious behavior in this life might therefore result in reincarnation as a member of a higher caste, until the soul had earned its eventual escape from the wheel of rebirths. A series of law books, the *Dharma Shastras*, spelled out the principles of human relations more exactly, defining the duties and rights of individuals and groups in the light of Brahminical tradition and sacred texts. Indeed, these law books themselves soon became sacred texts, and their precepts established norms for individual and social behavior. The earliest and most revered of the *Dharma Shastras* was the *Book of Manu*.

It purported to contain the instructions given to the first man by the divine creator of the universe; but in fact the book evolved gradually through the accumulation of oral tradition until it became so holy (*ca.* 200 A.D.) that further changes could not be incorporated into its text. Legal thought thereupon shifted into new channels, so that four other, almost equally authoritative *Dharma Shastras*, elaborating upon and sometimes modifying the principles set forth in the *Book of Manu*, took form during the following four or five centuries.

The comparatively superficial nature of Indian governments was well illustrated by these law books. They treated religious authority and legal authority as one and the same. The highest source of law was the *Vedas*, followed in descending order by commentaries upon the *Vedas*, then the customs and examples of holy men, and at the bottom mere personal inclination. Royal edict ranked, of course, as an instance of personal inclination, although two of the later *Dharma Shastras* admitted that in practice the king's decision was final.[5]

The practical influence of the *Dharma Shastras* upon Indian society has been immense. Even today, they constitute a guide to the lives of ordinary men and a powerful check upon those in authority. Claiming divine origin, their precepts naturally took precedence over any merely human legislation and, theoretically, if not necessarily in practice, confined the arbitrary will of even the most absolute of Indian rulers within narrow bounds. Regardless of their personal piety or impiety, Indian monarchs often found it safer and wiser to conform, at least in appearance, to the principles of conduct laid down by these sacred books of law.[6]

The peculiar toughness of the infrapolitical structure of Indian society, newly strengthened by the sacred sanction of Brahminical theory, meant that the accidents of political geography could have little importance in India. It scarcely mattered to any but the immediate royal circle whether a given area fell under the jurisdiction of a particular monarch or of his rival. As a result, the rise and fall of Indian states has left remarkably few literary traces. For the history of the Gupta empire, scholars must rely upon Fa-hsien's travelogue and a few other Chinese records, together with some Ceylonese, Tibetan, and Arabic chronicles. Surviving Indian materials tell remarkably little, even when organized chronologically with the help of these foreign sources. Coins and a limited body of inscriptions provide some information; but direct mention of political events in Indian literature is as scarce for the Guptas as for far less distinguished dynasties.

[5] R. C. Majumdar *et al.*, *History and Culture of the Indian People*, II, 254–57, 335–59; M. Winternitz, *Geschichte der indischen Literatur* (Leipzig: Amelangs Verlag, 1920), III, 479–504; Arthur Berriedale Keith, *A History of Sanskrit Literature* (London: Oxford University Press, 1928), pp. 439–48.

[6] The morals of statecraft set out in the *Dharma Shastras* stand in sharp contrast to those expressed in the *Arthashastra*. Perhaps the amoral methods of maintaining power recommended in the *Arthashastra* describe the real practices of Indian kings more accurately than do the prescriptions of the *Dharma Shastras*. Too little is known about the administration of the Indian states to warrant any generalization on this point.

2. CULTURAL ACHIEVEMENTS

The literature, philosophy, religion, art, and science of the Gupta age set the mold for subsequent Indian efforts in each of these fields. Moreover, with the exception of philosophy, Gupta achievements are generally regarded, both by Indian and by foreign scholars, as constituting the highest peaks of the entire Indian cultural tradition.

It is important to realize that, even in this age of cultural creativity, innovation was not really respectable. Learning took the form of commentary upon older texts, when it did not consist in making additions or adjustments to those texts, professing, of course, to restore the original meaning. Belles lettres could not avoid deliberate creation but did prefer a learned and largely artificial language, Sanskrit, to any of the Prakrits—the literary versions of the spoken languages of the day. Important and authoritative texts continued to be transmitted orally, for it was felt that genuine mastery could only pass from teacher to pupil by means of the spoken and memorized word. The body of written learning and literature therefore was merely an accretion upon the central core of orally transmitted truths, not something complete in itself.

LANGUAGE. In the age of Gautama Buddha and for several centuries thereafter, much Indian literary activity had been aimed at a popular audience. To be sure, the Brahmins' oral treasures had never been lost, since some portion of the vast Sanskrit literature of the *Vedas, Brahmanas,* and *Upanishads* had always been studied and memorized by those who followed the priestly profession. But in addition, and in some sense in opposition, to the Brahmin Sanskrit tradition there had been Prakrit literatures. These were associated especially with Buddhists and Jains who wrote fables, sermons, and poems in languages close to popular speech.

Yet these forms of popular literature began to wither away after the second century A.D.[7] Sanskrit, once confined to the learned recesses of Brahminical society, made an extraordinary comeback, until even the Buddhists and Jains began to write their theological and philosophical works in their rivals' ancient language. From the field of learning, Sanskrit spread to administration. Mauryan government had been conducted in one or more of the Prakrits; but Gupta inscriptions and coins used Sanskrit; and presumably the language of administration was the same archaic but widely understood speech.[8]

---

[7] An exception must be made for Tamil, one of the Dravidian languages of south India. Tamil attained literary definition in the Gupta period and never ceased to be an important literary medium thereafter.

In Tamil land generally, knowledge of Aryan India and of the Hellenistic Mediterranean had penetrated as equally alien but fascinating novelties during the preceding centuries. The subsequent efflorescence of Tamil literature and art was like the springtime of youth and did not much resemble the mature cultural synthesis of Sanskrit India; though as we shall see, the Tamils contributed important strands to the civilization and especially to the religion of the rest of India, especially during the centuries between 600 and 1000 A.D. when the local cultural autonomy of southern India was being overwhelmed by the greater magnitude and maturity of the northern achievement. Cf. the relationship of Irish Christianity to Latin Christendom during the same period of time.

[8] Sanskrit literature always remained oral, so that the language had never ceased to be spoken by educated Brahmins. This meant that men who found each other's daily speech quite unintelligible could

The revival of Sanskrit after its six- or seven-hundred year banishment to the learned fringes of society was truly remarkable. It attested the prestige and weight of the Brahminical tradition and proved the effectiveness of the numerous educational institutions of the land, which trained, not only priests, but large numbers of lay folk to familiarity with the learned language of the Hindu scriptures. Perhaps not least, it reflected the gradual withdrawal of Buddhism behind monastic walls, leaving to the Brahmins the streets and by-ways where Gautama had taught. Only in Ceylon did Buddhist writers continue to use one of the Prakrits; but Pali was as much a learned vehicle in Ceylon as Sanskrit was in India. Partly for this reason, later Pali literature closely resembled the Sanskrit, taking the form of progressively more learned commentaries upon sacred texts.

LITERATURE. Many of the masterpieces of ancient Indian oral literature took final form in Gupta times. Foremost of these were the two great epics, the *Mahabharata* and the *Ramayana*. Both of these poems ultimately derived from ancient balladry and heroic verse. At some time or other, recitation of such verses became part of religious sacrifices, so that Brahmin priests fell heir to a body of poetry which presumably had had its origin among secular bards and warriors.

Various geographical and other references make clear that additions to the *Mahabharata* were made as late as 400 A.D.; but the great bulk of the poem is certainly much older; and some passages may descend intact from the second millennium B.C. Through a process perhaps analogous to that by which Greek heroic poetry coalesced around the Trojan War, the plot of this poem ostensibly crystallized around the tale of a struggle between rival claimants to the throne of a minor Indian kingdom. But the *Mahabharata* includes an extraordinary diversity of matter, most of which is only loosely attached to the central theme. Folk tales and primitive myths mingle with discourses on cosmology, theology, and the dignity of Brahmins; and from time to time, action is suspended indefinitely while lengthy narratives of events unrelated in time or space to the main story are dragged in to illustrate some particular point. Under such elaboration (the poem is roughly three-and-a-half times as long as the entire Bible) the main plot sometimes disappears from sight for hundreds of pages at a stretch. The total effect is reminiscent of one of the south Indian temples, where sculpture oozes from every crevice—utterly obscuring the structural lines of the building, but lending an eye-entrancing interest to each separate part.

The looseness of its structure has not prevented the *Mahabharata* from attaining and maintaining an immense popularity in India down to the present day. As Homer did for the Greeks, the *Mahabharata* fixed the popular Hindu conception of the gods and their mutual relations; but unlike the Homeric epics, which are structurally and theologically coherent, the *Mahabharata* offers incidents and ideas to fit every level of taste, from the crudest and most

---

often converse in Sanskrit. Cf. the role of Latin in medieval Europe or the position of English in contemporary India.

naïve of tales to the abstruse and paradoxical pantheism of the passage known as the *Bhagavad Gita*.[9]

The *Ramayana* is shorter than the *Mahabharata*, though still a very lengthy poem. It recounts the adventures and trials of the hero Rama and his wife Sita. It is comparatively coherent; indeed most of the *Ramayana* in its existing form may be the work of a single author. Like the *Mahabharata*, it is Vaishnavite, for Rama is portrayed as an *avatar* of that god. But explicit religious teachings and moral instruction are less important than the vibrant and very human portraits of the hero and his faithful wife. These have a universal appeal and have made the *Ramayana* as popular and nearly as influential as the *Mahabharata* among Indians.

The popularity of these two poems was such that epic verse became the usual form for almost all kinds of Indian didactic writing. The law books (*Dharma Shastras*) and the vast collections of legend and fable known as the *Puranas* were fixed in poetic form in Gupta times; and even so ruthlessly practical a treatise as the *Arthashastra* was rendered in the same medium.

For all these types of literature, a long process of oral transmission and transformation lay behind the versions that came to be fixed in the Gupta age. The case was otherwise with Sanskrit drama and courtly poetry, most surviving examples of which have assignable, individual authors and appear to have been put in writing from the beginning.

The origins of Sanskrit drama are unknown,[10] though it is likely that Hellenistic influence was important in bringing this art form to maturity in India. In any case, certain technical terms of Greek provenance were employed in the Sanskrit theater; and traveling bands of mimes and dancers from Alexandria were sufficiently well known to have left several notices in Indian literature. But by the time when the earliest of the surviving plays were written, the conventions of Indian drama had been fixed and did not directly mirror Greek precedents.[11]

Dramatic performances in the third and fourth centuries were courtly affairs. Indeed, some of the Gupta kings are said to have composed plays themselves; and several reputedly royal compositions survive. The *Mahabharata*

---

[9] The *Gita* is a dialogue between Arjuna, the principal hero of the *Mahabharata*, and his charioteer, Krishna, in which the latter explains the whole nature of man and the universe, reveals himself to be an *avatar* of Vishnu, and promises Arjuna salvation. Even within the relatively small compass of the *Gita*, discordant doctrines find expression; but the mystic, devotional tone of the poem provides a unity which, according to its admirers, surpasses logic. Cf. Franklin Edgerton, *The Bhagavad Gita, Translated and Interpreted* ("Harvard Oriental Series," Vols. XXXVIII–XXXIX [Cambridge, Mass: Harvard University Press, 1944]).

No satisfactory translation of the *Mahabharata* exists in English. Edward P. Rice, *The Mahabharata: Analysis and Index* (London: Oxford University Press, 1934), and S. C. Nott (ed.), *The Mahabharata of Vyasa Krishna Dwaipayana: Selections* (New York: Philosophical Library, 1956), are, however, useful in providing samples of the whole.

[10] The earliest surviving dramatic fragment, a Buddhist story of edification dealing with the conversion of two of Buddha's disciples, apparently dates from about 100 A.D. The earliest Sanskrit plays to survive complete probably date from the fourth century A.D., just before the time of Kalidasa, the acknowledged master of Sanskrit dramaturgy and courtly poetry.

[11] The nature and extent of Greek influence upon Sanskrit drama has been hotly disputed. Cf. the summary in A. Berriedale Keith, *The Sanskrit Drama* (Oxford: Clarendon Press, 1924), pp. 12–77.

and the *Ramayana* provided Indian playwrights with the source of most of their plots; but the courtly circle for which they wrote is reflected in their choice of themes: love stories, cases of mistaken identity, and the like. Kalidasa, who seems to have been associated with the court of Chandra-gupta II (380–415 A.D.), brought the Sanskrit drama to its greatest excellence. His style was simple, yet elegant, with telling metaphors, skilful characterizations, and well-contrived, if trifling plots. His lyric poetry, some of which strikes home even in translation, exhibits the same traits. For example:

> I see your body in the sinuous creeper, your gaze in the startled eyes of deer,
> your cheeks in the moon, your hair in the plumage of peacocks,
> and in the tiny ripples of the river I see your sidelong glances,
> but alas, my dearest, nowhere do I see your whole likeness.[12]

Courtly poetry and plays continued to be written after Kalidasa's time; but ornate and involuted language soon became an end in itself, so that some of the later Sanskrit poems were more akin to an acrostic puzzle than to ordinary discourse.[13]

Prose was cultivated in Gupta times in the form of romances, dealing usually with the loves and adventures of royalty. In the same period, the anonymous author of the *Pancha Tantra* developed the animal fable to a very polished art form. This collection of tales was translated into Persian in the sixth century and thence spread all over the Islamic and Christian worlds.[14]

In contrast to the courtly, polished Sanskrit literature of the Gupta age, Tamil poetry of the time was more popular and emotionally direct. The earliest surviving Tamil poems were collected into anthologies about 500 A.D. but represent the precipitate of an older bardic tradition going back several centuries. The poems of these anthologies deal with the feelings of common people—villagers and merchants, fishermen and warriors—in a quite realistic and unadorned fashion. Devices like initial rhyme at first made Tamil prosody entirely different from the conventions of Sanskrit poetry; but, in the course of the sixth century, prosodic shifts in the direction of Sanskrit, as well as a heavy importation of Sanskrit words into the Tamil vocabulary, attested the penetration of the south by Brahmin learning.

Epic poetry had such high prestige in the Sanskrit literary tradition that Tamil poets, as they became better acquainted with Sanskrit, were impelled to create a considerable body of epic poetry in their own language. *The Lay of the Anklet*, a Tamil epic of royal injustice and personal tragedy, seems (at least in translation) far more powerful and infinitely better articulated than either of the famous Sanskrit epics which may in part have inspired it.[15]

---

[12] From Kalidasa's most famous poem, "Cloud Messenger." Translated by A. L. Basham in *The Wonder That Was India*, p. 420.

[13] The poet Bhatti (seventh century A.D.) ended one of his works thus: "This poem can be understood only by a comment; it suffices that it is a feast for the clever, and that the stupid come to grief in it as a result of my love of learning." Quoted in A. B. Keith, *History of Sanskrit Literature*, p. 116.

[14] Tracing the transmission of these tales has been a *chef d'œuvre* of comparative literary scholarship. For a summary of results, see Keith, *History of Sanskrit Literature*, pp. 357–59.

[15] Translated into English by V. R. R. Dikshitar, *The Lay of the Anklet* (Oxford: Oxford University Press, 1939).

The most remarkable and widely influential Tamil poems were ecstatic hymns, composed by wandering holy men to glorify Vishnu or Shiva. Like Tamil epic poetry, these hymns arose from an intermixture of Hindu Sanskrit tradition with the Tamil bardic art. But although the gods that inspired these hymns had long been familiar to northern India, the Tamil rhapsodists voiced a distinctively new religious mood. Intense and reciprocal love between the deity and his devotee was the keynote. A sense of personal unworthiness, mingled with joyous wonder at divine grace and the bliss of the mystic vision of the Godhead, were themes of these poems that later spread from Tamil land through the rest of India and gave to mature Hinduism much of its emotional tone and vigor.[16]

RELIGION AND PHILOSOPHY.   The Hindu religion, as expressed doctrinally in such works as the *Mahabharata, Ramayana,* and *Dharma Shastras,* and reinforced emotionally by the ecstasy of the Tamil hymn writers, carried all before it in the Gupta age. The emperors themselves were adherents and patrons of the revived and revised Brahmin faith, usually of the Vaishnavite persuasion. Apparently most ordinary Indians now also found a place for themselves in the capacious Hindu system, which readily accommodated the most crudely superstitious peasants as well as the most refined scholars within itself.

As a result, even as it was winning its greatest victories abroad, in its own homeland Buddhism shrank to the status of a withdrawn, well-to-do sect. Comfortable life in richly endowed Buddhist monasteries presumably discouraged monks from preaching in public places, as Gautama and his early followers had done. Instead, if one may judge from their extant literary products, the monks of the Gupta age devoted themselves to scholastic elaboration of doctrine and lengthy polemic against their Brahmin opponents. Such activity produced recondite theological expositions that had some importance in China, where enthusiastic converts translated many such texts into Chinese and accorded a semi-canonical status to the tangle of obscurities that resulted. But in India, Buddhism isolated itself more and more from a living relationship to the population at large.

The Jains, whose popular success had never been as great as that of the Buddhists, seem to have undergone a similar evolution, although Jainism never entirely disappeared from India. Down to the present day, it has remained a minor sect, supported principally by prosperous merchant groups.

During the Gupta age a number of recognized "schools" of philosophy arose in each of the three principal religious camps. Of these, only the six schools of Hindu philosophy proved enduring, for Jain philosophy soon withered and Buddhism disappeared. Hindu philosophers, however, had plenty to do in trying to bring some sort of intelligible order to the pullulat-

---

[16] R. C. Majumdar *et al., History and Culture of the Indian People,* III, 326–40; cf. the sample translations in A. L. Basham, *The Wonder That Was India,* pp. 330–31. The contribution of Tamil emotionalism to Hindu piety offers another instance of a submerged (or semi-submerged) culture exhibiting unusual religious creativity.

ing confusion of popular cult practices. More particularly, the rising worship of Vishnu and Shiva accorded ill, at least on the surface, with the older Vedic pantheon, while the rarefied theism of the *Upanishads* had little in common with either. Various efforts were made at explaining the many discrepancies, but not until perhaps the eighth century, with the philosophy of Shankara, did something like a definitive reconciliation of the discordant elements of the Hindu heritage emerge.

SCIENCE. The most remarkable of the Indian sciences was grammar, together with related linguistic studies like lexicography and metrics. Sanskrit grammar grew out of the need for general rules to assist the Brahmins in remembering the sacred syllables of the *Vedas*. Panini (*ca.* fourth century B.C.) gave Sanskrit its classical form; but later grammarians continued to amplify and comment upon his text for a thousand years thereafter. As Sanskrit developed into a learned tongue, the study of grammar became the prerequisite for all advanced scholarship. By Gupta times, however, principles had been so well worked out that Sanskrit grammar was no longer susceptible of significant modification.[17] Attention therefore shifted to other branches of the linguistic sciences, with the development of treatises on the meters of Sanskrit poetry and the completion of a famous dictionary of the sacred language which became standard for later ages.

Indian medicine, also, had very ancient roots. From Vedic times, incantation and magic as well as medicaments and surgery played a part in Hindu medical technique; whereas philosophical doctrines concerning body and soul, together with religious notions about cosmology, demons, and deities, dominated medical theory. Three classic treatises of Indian medicine survive, one dating probably from the first century A.D., one from the fourth century, and one from the seventh or eighth. The earliest of these, by Charaka, is a rather confused and unsystematic catalogue of diseases and cures, put together from diverse and sometimes contradictory sources. Quite different was the textbook of Susruta (fourth century A.D.)—a concise, well-organized manual, which set the pattern for all later medical writing in India. Unlike Galen, Susruta recognized surgery as belonging to the doctor's art and even recommended the observation of corpses as a means of learning anatomy, although the demands of ritual purity prevented dissection.[18]

Although Indian and Greek medical ideas show certain parallels which may reflect early professional contact at the Achaemenid court, the general body of Indian medicine remained autonomous. This was not true of astronomy, however; for during the Gupta period, Greek mathematical astronomy (and the astrology associated with it) radically revolutionized Indian concepts in

[17] The two important grammars of the age were the work of a Buddhist and a Jain respectively, each of whom set out to produce a text from which objectionably Brahminical illustrative examples would be absent. Cf. R. C. Majumdar *et al.*, *History and Culture of the Indian People*, III, 319–20.

[18] Henry R. Zimmer, *Hindu Medicine* (Baltimore, Md.: Johns Hopkins Press, 1948), pp. 46–59, 175–76; Jean Filliozat, *La Doctrine classique de la médecine indienne, ses origines et ses parallèles grecques* (Paris: Imprimerie Nationale, 1949), pp. 199–215 and *passim*; A. B. Keith, *A History of Sanskrit Literature*, pp. 513–15.

these fields. Yet the new astronomy did not entirely supersede earlier animistic explanations of the heavenly movements, which remained incongruously juxtaposed to sophisticated mathematical computations in Indian astronomical texts.[19]

Indian mathematics began with a body of rules for the construction of altars and similar adjuncts of sacrifice. But no continuity is apparent between texts that set forth such rules and later, more formally mathematical treatises. The earliest surviving Indian mathematical work was written by Aryabhata in the year 499 A.D. for use in astronomical calculations. Much of Aryabhata's mathematics seems to have been borrowed from the Greeks, although he made some innovations of his own, e.g., a unique system of numerical notation. He also seems to have been familiar with the decimal place value system, as perfected by a generalized use of the zero sign; but he did not use this notation himself.[20]

In later centuries Arabs credited Indians with inventing the numerals Europeans term "arabic." In the absence of any clear evidence to the contrary, it is likely that the Arab tradition is correct and that Indian mathematicians did in fact perfect the system of numerical notation used today all round the world. The earliest known reference to the use of such a system dates from 269–70 A.D.[21]

The long-term effects of this improvement, both in facilitating the everyday transactions of the market place and in forwarding the arcane pursuits of science, can scarcely be exaggerated. Indeed, the perfecting of the decimal place system of numerical notation, which made all ordinary arithmetical calculations so magnificently simple, may properly be bracketed with the invention of alphabetic writing as one of the major milestones of human intellectual achievement.

ART.   The best surviving Gupta sculpture and painting are all of Buddhist inspiration. This may seem strange, in view of the decay of Buddhism which characterized the period. Yet it is not inexplicable, for artists commissioned

---

[19] It was not the Ptolemaic astronomy of Alexandria that reached India, but earlier, less perfected, and more various calculations. Evidence suggests that the Sassanian court played the role of intermediary. Cf. Otto Neugebauer, *The Exact Sciences in Antiquity*, pp. 160–61, 167–69, 178, 180.

[20] A cryptic and highly condensed verse form makes the interpretation of Aryabhata's meaning often a matter of uncertainty. Cf. the translation and commentary by Walter Eugene Clark, *The Aryabhatiya of Aryabhata* (Chicago: University of Chicago Press, 1930).

[21] I owe this information to oral conversation with Dr. David Pingree (1962) whose forthcoming edition of the *Yavanajataka* of Sphujidhvaja will bring this date to the attention of the learned world. The earliest reference previously known was contained in Aryabhata's treatise, dated 499 A.D. Cf. G. R. Kaye, *Indian Mathematics* (Calcutta and Simla: Thacker, Spink & Co., 1915); A. B. Keith, *History of Sanskrit Literature*, pp. 523–28.

It is worth remembering that the place value system was known to the Babylonians as early as the eighteenth century B.C. and had passed from them to Hellenistic mathematicians. Some Babylonian texts even used a dot to indicate zero, but only in a medial, not a final position, i.e., 202 could be written unambiguously, but 220 could not. The final step, therefore, which seems to have been taken in India about the third century A.D., was merely to generalize the use of a zero sign, and at the same time to free decimal notation from an awkward intermixture with a sexagesimal number system. Mingling of decimal and sexagesimal number systems had been characteristic of both Babylonian and Hellenistic astronomy, and Western mathematicians still tolerate the same awkwardness when treating circular measurement. Cf. O. Neugebauer, *The Exact Sciences in Antiquity*, pp. 3–22.

THE ART
OF GUPTA INDIA

The contrast between the finely chiseled Boddhisattva torso from Sanchi on the left and the cruder relief on the right showing Vishnu in one of his mythological incarnations symbolizes the difference between the exquisitely polished court culture of Gupta India and the still inchoate but vigorous and emotionally powerful Hinduism of the countryside. The building, also located at Sanchi, is an early example of Hindu temple architecture. Its simple lines reveal the basic (Greek-inspired?) structure which subsequent architects elaborated and obscured (p. 459).

by the wealthy Buddhist monasteries had five full centuries of artistic tradition behind them upon which to draw and at the same time commanded very skilled techniques both of carving and painting. The conjunction of wealth, artistic tradition, and skill is always rare. In Gupta India it produced such masterpieces as the paintings of the Ajanta caves and the Buddha of Sarnath, not to mention the precise elegance of the Bodhisattva torso from Sanchi, which visually matches the courtly perfection of Kalidasa's poetry.

Hindu art achieved no such stylistic success, despite the fact that Hinduism commanded the allegiance of both court and countryside. Hindu iconography lacked any ancient tradition; and the polymorphism of Hindu gods must have presented artists with formidable problems. Some fumbling was perhaps inevitable, therefore, before plastic representations of Vishnu, Shiva, and other deities achieved really satisfactory definitions. The clumsy Hindu sculpture surviving from the Gupta period seems definitely to confirm such a view.[22]

Temples played no part in early Brahminism. Aryan religious ceremonies took place out-of-doors at spots specially consecrated for the occasion; and Vedic aniconic traditions died slowly. Nevertheless, as their deities became more vividly personal, it was natural that Hindus should seek to visualize their gods through sculpture and to house such images in suitably magnificent dwellings. Hence arose temple architecture.

Hindu sacred architecture bore no apparent relation to the circular ground plan characteristic of Buddhist *stupas*.[23] Instead, Hindu temples were built around a windowless rectangular cella where the cult image was housed, to which an entrance porch gave suitably impressive access.[24] Architects later added a spire, built on top of the cella, and in time obscured the simplicity of the original form with many subsidiary decorations. Nevertheless, as with so many other aspects of Indian culture, the general plan fixed upon in Gupta times remained basic to Hindu temple architecture thereafter.   ·

OTHER ASPECTS OF INDIAN CULTURE. Ancient Indians recognized three main goals for human endeavor: *dharma* or righteousness, *artha* or practical skills, and *kama* or love.[25] This account of classical Indian culture has dealt almost exclusively with matters pertaining to the first of these three categories. To be sure, the polite literature of the Gupta age dealt with love; and special treatises were devoted to the subject. In daily life we may believe that

[22] The systematic iconoclasm of Moslem conquerors in northern India must always be borne in mind in considering Indian art history. It is possible, for example, that a more successful Hindu art existed in northern India in Gupta times than surviving monuments, mainly located in southern India, suggest.

[23] Cave temples, carved out of the living rock, antedate freestanding masonry temples in India. They are usually elongated in ground plan, with an apse at the farthest end. The resemblance to a Roman basilica is striking, but perhaps merely accidental, since the cave temples seem to have developed by uniting the circular ambulatory of a *stupa* with an entrance hall. Cf. Benjamin Rowland, *The Art and Architecture of India*, pp. 69–71.

[24] Some of the earliest buildings strikingly resemble Greek temples in general design, e.g., Temple 17 at Sanchi; and it is possible that Greek architecture had some influence.

[25] A B. Keith, *A History of Sanskrit Literature*, p. 450.

the upper classes, and perhaps the whole population, practiced the arts of love with fewer inhibitions and with at least as much absorption as the popular culture of contemporary Western society encourages today. Similarly, the practical skills of ancient India were highly developed, ranging from those of humble artisans to the subtleties of music, dancing, and government administration.

We should recognize that the practical and erotic sides of Indian culture were prominent and important parts of the whole, which was far less dominated by Brahminical and ascetic ideals than the surviving literature might suggest.[26] In turning to the remarkable geographical expansion of Indian culture which occurred during the Gupta period, it is worth remembering that part of the appeal of Indian civilization rested upon the luxury, refinement, and overt sensuality of Indian life. Ascetic religious doctrine was not everything, though it has left far more abundant traces in literature.

C. THE EXPANSION OF INDIAN CIVILIZATION
200–600 A.D.

At a time when both the Roman and Chinese empires were suffering from the ravages of barbarian attack and inner convulsion and when Iran was hard-pressed to hold back the steppe peoples, Indian civilization came into full flower. India's cultural eminence in the Gupta age perhaps encouraged merchants and missionaries to exhibit far more energy in widening the sphere of Indian influence than they had done before or would ever do again. The result was a remarkable expansion of Indian civilization into southeast Asia and a no less striking infiltration of Indian culture into central Asia and China. Even in the lands of the eastern Mediterranean, Indian ideas and practices acquired a certain importance, despite the antipathy of the Christian church to Hindu and Buddhist religion.

In one respect, the expansion of Indian culture was very different from the earlier expansion of Hellenism. Military conquest played almost no part: merchants and missionaries took the place of the armies of Macedon and Rome. Consequently, Indian expansion followed trade routes, particularly the sea route to southeast Asia and the islands of Indonesia, and the overland trail through the oases of central Asia to northwest China.

1. SOUTHEAST ASIA

Communication between India and the lands of southeast Asia was very ancient. Common elements in prehistoric remains from both areas suggest that Indians and their neighbors across the Bay of Bengal had maintained distant

[26] Unbridled sensuality may in fact have been a major factor in provoking or sustaining Indian asceticism, for extremes of indulgence and of revulsion against eroticism often go hand in hand. Indian temple sculpture adequately proves that remarkably free and explicit sexuality found recognition in public religion side by side with the asceticism so highly esteemed in literary records. The peculiar catholicity of Hinduism was illustrated by the success with which it enfolded undisguised sex into religion, in contrast to the emphatic puritanical emphases of the Christian, Moslem, and Confucian traditions.

but real connections in pre-Aryan times.[27] The earliest evidence of more extensive contacts dates from the first centuries of the Christian era, when merchant ships from Indian ports[28] began to visit the coasts of Burma, Malaya, Indonesia, Siam, and Indochina. At that time the populations of these areas were peaceable folk, acquainted with rice agriculture and familiar with boats and rafts, but without elaborate political organization or any very impressive cultural system that could withstand the blandishments of civilization. Such peoples were easily persuaded that the visitors, with their large and seaworthy vessels, their strange gods, and their practical skills, possessed a powerful magic which should be assimilated as rapidly as possible. Foundation legends of the Hinduized states of the area, which Chinese sources have sometimes preserved, suggest that Indian merchants or adventurers married into leading native families and from this vantage point readily established leadership over the native populations.

Archeologists have discovered a fair number of Sanskrit inscriptions and a variety of Indian works of art in southeast Asia. The inscriptions make clear that during the fourth and fifth centuries A.D., a series of states centering around courts whose culture and atmosphere were thoroughly Indian arose both on the mainland and in the islands. As the possibilities of winning wealth and honor in those regions became better known on the Indian mainland, not only the humbler merchant classes who had pioneered the movement, but Brahmins and warriors as well, began to migrate across the Bay of Bengal in significant numbers, and thus powerfully reinforced Indian influences in the courts and capitals of southeast Asia.

Although Buddhists had been prominent in the earliest phases of Indian penetration of southeast Asia, most royal courts there had become Shaivite by the Gupta age. Probably the ritual and concepts of this branch of Hinduism accorded well with earlier autochthonous religious ideas. In addition, by emphasizing the magical role of the ruler in bringing fertility to the fields, Shaivism probably helped local kings to consolidate their power over tribal or village chieftains. Cult statues and other works of art were imported from India to body forth these new religious-political ideas and ideals. Only after about 600 A.D. did royalty patronize local sculpture and stonemasonry and thus stimulate the development of local variations upon the Indian heritage. Materials surviving from before that date suggest a thoroughly "colonial" atmosphere in the courts of southeast Asia, where kings and courtiers sought distinction, not by encouraging local arts, but by importing the best possible reproductions of the most authentic Indian originals.

[27] G. Coedès, *Les États hindouisés d'Indochine et d'Indonesie* (Paris: E. de Boccard, 1948), pp. 23–28; H. G. Quaritch Wales, *The Making of Greater India* (London: Bernard Quaritch, 1951), pp. 47–83.

[28] Some of the pioneering voyages from Indian ports may have been made by merchant adventurers hailing from the Mediterranean world. A few Roman objects have been found as far afield as Cochin China, dating from the second century A.D.; and a Chinese history records the visit of "ambassadors" from Marcus Aurelius in the year 166 A.D., who had come by the southern sea route. Coedès, *Les États hindouisés*, p. 38. After the second century A.D., however, the trade between the eastern Mediterranean area and southern India declined with the general decline in the prosperity of the Roman world; and Indian merchants speedily took over the eastward voyaging (if they had not themselves pioneered it).

The great bulk of the population in southeast Asia was only indirectly affected by the Indian culture of the courts. Village life went on much as before, modified only by the growth of royal authority in matters such as taxation and *corvée*. But however superficial the spread of Indian styles may have been, we should nonetheless recognize that the geographical area involved—from Borneo to Sumatra and from Indochina to Burma—far exceeded that of the European territories which the Roman empire had brought within the sphere of Hellenism in an almost equally superficial fashion.

As the Indian culture-sphere expanded northward along the coastal plain of Indochina, the frontiers of Indian and Chinese civilization met for the first time. To be sure, this confrontation was short-lived; for when China recovered from the disruption following the fall of the Han and resumed imperial expansion into Annam, direct Indian influence had already begun to wane in the farthest reaches of the "Greater India" which had been built overseas during the Gupta period. The reassertion of pre-Indian cultural traditions played a part in this change; in addition, Indian commercial vigor faded rapidly after the seventh century, when Moslem competition began to drive Indian commerce from the southern seas. India's withdrawal from southeast Asia therefore created a sort of buffer zone between the Indian and Chinese culture areas. This buffer still survives, but it does so only because the initial Indian penetration stimulated the peoples of southeast Asia to lift themselves to a level of culture almost equal to that of their more anciently civilized neighbors, thus partially filling what had before been a conspicuous sociopolitical vacuum.[29]

Indian ships undoubtedly explored and traded along the coast of Africa in Gupta times; and ethnologists have detected various traces of their presence there. Indeed, the peoples of Sudanic Africa, even as far west as the Guinea coast, seem to owe important staples of their agriculture to Indian or Indonesian ships and settlers who probably introduced such crops as yams, taro, and bananas to the African continent about the beginning of the Christian era.[30]

2. EASTERN MEDITERRANEAN, IRAN, AND CENTRAL ASIA

Indian commercial and cultural penetration of southeast Asia coincided in time with a weakening of trade connections with Egypt. Impoverishment of

---

[29] In addition to books cited separately, I have consulted: R. C. Majumdar, *Ancient Indian Colonization in South East Asia* (Baroda: University of Baroda Press, 1955); Majumdar, *The History and Culture of the Indian People*, II, 651–58; III, 631–44.

[30] The fact that Madagascar is largely inhabited by people speaking an Indonesian language, whose ancestors must have migrated all the way across the Indian Ocean from Borneo or some other Indonesian island, is a striking demonstration of the capability of simple ships to carry people long distances through the equable southern seas. Probably the migrants skirted the coasts of south Asia rather than sailing all the way across the open ocean; but no unmistakable traces of their way stations—if they existed—have been discovered. Cf. George Peter Murdock, *Africa: Its Peoples and Their Culture History* (New York: McGraw-Hill, 1959), 212–71; James Hornell, "Indonesian Influences on East African Culture," *Journal of the Royal Anthropological Institute*, LXIV (1934), 325 and *passim*; G. W. B. Huntingford, "The Hagiolithic Cultures of East Africa," *Eastern Anthropologist*, III (1950), 119–33.

the Roman world through plague and war may have been the principal factor in checking the Red Sea trade; but newly formed Arab and Ethiopian states also helped to choke this commerce by exacting extravagant tolls from merchant ships attempting to pass through the Straits of Aden.[31] Yet, as direct commercial intercourse between India and the Mediterranean world declined, the learned community of Alexandria began to evince a much livelier interest in the wisdom and powers of the "gymnosophists" of India.

Reasons for this at first surprising chronological displacement between the apogee of economic and of intellectual intercourse between India and the Mediterranean are not really very far to seek. The transcendental emphasis of Indian thought, and the ascetic disciplines whereby Indian holy men invited mystic visions, offered a world-view and pattern of life as coherent and impressive as anything advocated by the gentlemanly philosophers of the Greco-Roman world. In an age when violence and disease were disrupting the social universe of the Roman world, and when religions of salvation were competing for the allegiance of the populace, the optimistic rationalism of the Greek philosophic tradition seemed utterly inadequate to account for events. How could a reasonable man accept the Stoic doctrine of the supremacy of natural law, for example, when whim and chance so obviously dominated Roman politics—distracted as the empire was by civil war, multiple usurpations, and barbarian invasions? In such times, Indian mystical philosophy, directly validated by the suprarational vision of transcendent being—a vision which each individual adept could attain through a suitable course of training and self-discipline—seemed to offer a surer avenue to truth. A key figure in bringing Greek and Indian high intellectual traditions into contact with each other may have been Ammonius Saccas (d. 242), himself perhaps of Indian origin, and who probably taught both Plotinus (d. 270), the great renovator of pagan philosophy, and Origen (d. 254?), the first systematic theologian of the Christian church. At any rate, many of Plotinus' most important doctrines seem to echo the *Upanishads;* whereas the Platonic roots of his philosophy, while real, were nevertheless distant.[32]

Within the Christian fold, traces of Indian influence are less apparent. A dogmatic religion, claiming a monopoly of truth through divine revelation, could not admit external influence. Nor is there any good evidence that Christian orthodoxy, as it slowly emerged from the doctrinal disputes of the first centuries A.D., borrowed anything of importance from Indian thought. Various of the other Oriental faiths prevalent in the Roman world—Gnosticism in particular—appear to have been much more open to Indian ideas, although the Iranian imprint upon Gnosticism was also very prominent.[33]

[31] When tolls became too high, goods could be rerouted by caravan to the Persian Gulf. The rise of Palmyra in the third century A.D. was partly due to this deflection of trade routes; but its destruction in 273 A.D., and the long wars between Romans and Persians that followed, must have interrupted trade for long periods of time even more effectually than the parasitism of the states controlling the Straits of Aden.

[32] Cf. Émile Bréhier, *La Philosophie de Plotin* (Paris: Boivin & Co., 1923), pp. 107–34; Jean Filliozat, *Les Relations extérieures de l'Inde* (Pondicherry: Institut Français d'Indologie, 1956), pp. 27–30, 51–58.

[33] Until recently, authentic sources allowing scholars to study Gnosticism through something less opaque than Christian polemic were almost lacking. After World War II an impressive manuscript

On the other hand, what might be called a "style of holiness" that strongly resembled practices and preconceptions long familiar in India did establish itself as one of the fundamentals of Christianity. Extreme manifestations of the Christian pursuit of holiness, exemplified, for instance, in the pillar saints of Syria, reveal Indian affinities in details of ascetic conduct.[34] Far more important is the question whether Christian monasticism as a whole drew any significant inspiration from the ascetic traditions of India. Documentary acknowledgment of indebtedness is not to be expected; yet popular stories about the prowess of Indian holy men may well have provided the first Christian monks with hints they found helpful in their own pursuit of sanctity and the beatific vision.[35]

* * *

In Babylonia and Iran the first Sassanian monarchs (after 226 A.D.) patronized a revived Zoroastrianism as part of a self-conscious reassertion of Persian cultural independence. As a result, Iran and Mesopotamia, unlike China, could not become flourishing Buddhist mission fields, for Persian pride would not accept Indian cultural models unless they first assumed an effective local disguise. This does nothing to clarify the cultural and religious history of Iran and Mesopotamia, which remains tantalizingly obscure, despite the efforts of modern scholars to reconstruct the tenets and organization of Sassanian Zoroastrianism and of such rival faiths as Manichaeism and Mazdakism. We may surmise, nevertheless, that Indian motifs were probably a good deal more

---

discovery in Egypt opened entirely new possibilities; but political and other obstacles prevented their full and immediate exploitation. Cf. Jean Doresse, *The Secret Books of the Egyptian Gnostics* (New York: Viking Press, 1960); Eva Meyerovitch, "The Gnostic Manuscripts of Upper Egypt," *Diogenes*, No. 25 (1959), 84–117; Robert M. Grant, *Gnosticism and Early Christianity* (New York: Columbia University Press, 1959); Hans Jonas, *The Gnostic Religion: The Message of the Alien God and the Beginnings of Christianity* (Boston: Beacon Press, 1958).

[34] Cf. Hippolyte Delehaye, *Les saints stylites* (Brussels: Société des Bollandistes, 1923), pp. cxci–cxcv.

[35] The importance of Indian influence upon monasticism and other aspects of Christian piety has been both uncritically exaggerated and unreasonably denied. Cf. the summary of learned opinions assembled by Henri de Lubac, *La Rencontre du Buddhisme et de l'Occident* (Paris: Aubier, 1952), pp. 9–27. Magnification of Indian contributions to Christianity was commoner fifty years ago than more recently. Cf. Richard Garbe, *India and Christendom: The Historical Connections between Their Religions* (LaSalle, Ill.: Open Court Publishing Co., 1959); Ernst Benz, "Indische Einflüsse auf frühchristliche Theologie," Akademie der Wissenschaften und Literatur (Mainz), *Abhandlungen der Geistes- und Sozialwissenschaftlichen Klasse*, No. 3 (1951), pp. 172–202; Mircea Eliade, *Le Yoga* (Paris: Payot, 1954), p. 412; Karl Heussi, *Der Ursprung des Mönchtums: Geistesgeschichte des antiken Christentums* (Munich: Carl Beck Verlag, 1955), I, 523–29.

Jewish ascetic communities, such as that at Qumran, and biblical accounts of ancient prophets who dwelt in the wilderness obviously offered Christian monks another and very important model. But Jewish precedents, so far as I know, never recognized that the end of ascetic discipline was the beatific vision of God, as Indian ascetics long had held. Moreover, the psychic phenomena induced by fasting and other physical deprivations did not announce themselves unmistakably as visions of the Godhead. Indian precedents for interpreting such experiences in this theological and transcendental sense may therefore have been of absolutely key importance to the first Christian mystics. In this somewhat loose, largely untraceable sense, Indian influences upon early Christianity seem to me to have probably been of great importance.

prominent in Sassanian lands than they were in Roman territory. Moreover, Buddhist monasteries continued to flourish in the eastern part of the Persian realm, as they had done under the Kushan empire and perhaps even earlier. Farther east along the Silk Road, in the oases of the Tarim Basin, Buddhism throve vigorously between 200 and 600 A.D. Under the aegis of Buddhist monasteries, a mixed culture, in which Indian elements kept the upper hand, spread across all of central Asia and lapped against the mighty mass of China itself.[36]

3. CHINA

In China the reception of Buddhism and of the Indian cultural impress that accompanied it was a complicated affair, extending across about four centuries of time and involving subtle reciprocities between Indian ideas and older Chinese traditions, particularly the Taoist. The basic circumstance that made the Chinese ready to take Buddhism seriously was a distressing breakdown of Han institutions and the apparent futility of the Confucian way which had been so effectively wedded to those institutions during the Han period. When bitter factional strife around the throne gave way first to social revolt on the part of hard-pressed peasants (beginning 184 A.D.) and then to political fragmentation as usurpers, barbarian raiders, and local warlords disputed the imperial succession, Confucian precepts seemed more and more irrelevant to political reality. Restless minds began therefore to cast about for alternative modes of interpreting the universe.[37]

Yet even when Chinese minds had been thus prepared for the reception of a religion that preached withdrawal from family and society as the highest form of holiness and held forth the annihilation of the personality as the supreme end of religious striving—doctrines that could scarcely have been more antithetical to the familial values traditional to Chinese civilization—a difficult task of translation interposed itself between Indian originals and the would-be Chinese adept. The Chinese language lacked terms capable of conveying Buddhist meanings; and not until the fifth century did a handful of scholars become sufficiently at home in both Chinese and Indian learning to be able to translate Buddhist texts into Chinese with a modicum of adequacy.[38]

On the whole, it was the Mahayana form of Buddhist teaching that attracted Chinese converts; but the sectarian differences of Indian Buddhism never loomed very large in Chinese eyes. By the end of the fourth century

---

[36] Roman Ghirshman, *Bégram*, p. 100; Sir Aurel Stein, *On Central Asian Tracks* (London: Macmillan & Co., 1933); Albert von LeCoq, *Auf Hellas Spuren in Ostturkestan* (Leipzig: J. C. Hinrichs, 1926).

[37] Various efforts to revitalize older Chinese schools of thought reflected the bankruptcy of Confucian orthodoxies of the Han even before Buddhism began to move into the vacuum that events had created within Chinese culture. Cf. the very penetrating analysis of Arthur F. Wright, *Buddhism in Chinese History* (Stanford, Calif.: Stanford University Press, 1959), pp. 20–31.

[38] As an example of the initial difficulties in domesticating Buddhist thought into China, Wright cites the fact that the Chinese term *Tao* ("Way") was used indifferently to translate *Dharma*, *Bodhi*, and *Yoga*—Buddhist terms that may be rendered in English, approximately, as "righteousness," "enlightenment," and "discipline." Arthur F. Wright, *Buddhism in Chinese History*, p. 36.

A.D., as they achieved an adequate mastery of the concepts and terms of Indian Buddhism, the Chinese began to develop schools of their own. These schools divided along lines having little relevance to Indian doctrinal disputes but did sometimes hark back to divergences present in pre-Buddhist Chinese thought. Buddhism, in short, was beginning to be thoroughly domesticated into the Chinese cultural scene. As this occurred, the novel and initially alien outlook of the Indian faith had somehow to come to terms with the various strands already woven into Chinese culture, ranging all the way from Confucian and Taoist learning to local sub-literate peasant magic. Buddhists were strikingly successful in penetrating all levels of Chinese society, from the stateliness of royal courts and the private meditations of local landowners to the humble rituals of peasants hoping merely to promote the fertility of their fields. But, while accommodating themselves to older Chinese expectations, Buddhist doctrine and practices simultaneously widened and redefined traditional Chinese sensibilities and aspirations.

Art provides the most sensitive and accessible index of the interplay within Far Eastern Buddhism between intrusive Indian and autochthonous Chinese traits. The great prestige the Chinese initially attached to the Greco-Indian art style inspired pious pilgrims to return from India and central Asia with authentic images of the Buddhas and Bodhisattvas of Mahayana mythology. By the sixth century A.D., however, a distinctively Chinese Buddhist art had arisen, in which figures with Chinese dress and Chinese faces nonetheless continued to conform to Indian conventions of gesture and ornament.[39] The result was often very effective; and the synthesis thus achieved may be taken as indicative of a wider synthesis between Buddhist and pre-Buddhist cultural styles that began to emerge in China after about 500 A.D. The splendor and repose of Buddhist monasteries, the lengthy schooling of Confucian literati, the magical manipulations of Taoist recluses, the pomp of courtly life, the discipline of army camps, and the backbreaking labor of the peasantry all entered into this revised social and cultural equilibrium which found political expression in the reunification of China under the Sui dynasty in 589 A.D.

Steppe barbarian conquerors also contributed some elements to the reorganized Chinese civilization of the sixth century A.D. The linguistically variegated tribes[40] that overran northern China after 311 A.D. did not come bare of cultural traditions, nor were they always eager to adopt Chinese ways. Indeed, in the fourth century, some of the rulers of north China perhaps patronized Buddhism as a palladium of their own cultural independence vis-à-vis the Chinese;[41] but with the gradual accommodation between Buddhism and native Chinese tradition, this ceased to be possible. In any case, by the

[39] Cf. Laurence Binyon, "Chinese Art and Buddhism," *Proceedings of the British Academy*, XXII (1936).

[40] Mongolian, Tungusic, Turkish, and Tibetan languages were all represented among the invaders of north China; and not infrequently the same war confederation comprised groups of differing speech. Cf. O. Franke, *Geschichte des chinesischen Reiches*, II, 54–117, for a summary of the very confusing political history of the age.

[41] Arthur F. Wright, *Buddhism in Chinese History*, p. 57.

sixth century the barbarian rulers of the north had become thoroughly Sinified and no longer wished to keep culturally aloof from Chinese society. Therefore, the barbarian contribution to the new cultural balance within China was limited to such subtle yet important matters as the habit of obedience to military superiors, a more autocratic definition of imperial power than Confucian propriety of the Han period had really approved, and such externals as the use of stirrups for riding horseback.

China's political fragmentation between 220 A.D. and 589 A.D. failed to prevent a substantial expansion of the geographical range of Chinese culture. The withdrawal of Han garrisons from the oases of central Asia did not really restrict China's westward reach, since receptivity to the Buddhist currents flowing eastward through these same oases actually strengthened the cultural ties between China and central Asia. Similarly, the various barbarian conquerors of northern China usually attempted to combine portions of the steppe and their new Chinese territories under one sovereignty. This, also, invited Chinese cultural penetration of the steppe on a scale at least as great as anything the Han armies had ever been able to impose. In southern China, a great work of colonization and acculturation proceeded steadily and almost unnoticed. It had the ultimate effect of bringing the Yangtze Valley for the first time fully abreast of the economic and cultural level of the north.

Eastward also, in Korea and Japan, the Chinese example began to find fertile ground as the political and social organization of those regions developed toward civilized complexity. Buddhist monks became the principal carriers of high Chinese culture to Korea and Japan; but local rulers were quick to understand that appropriation of Chinese civilized institutions might enhance their power and therefore made their courts into important centers of Sinification as well. Co-operation between rulers and missionaries therefore established Buddhism as a sort of state religion in each of the kingdoms of the Korean peninsula between 372 and 528 A.D. A similar process commenced in Japan in 552 A.D., when the first important Buddhist mission reached that archipelago. As Korea and Japan thus entered the circle of civilized peoples, they added significantly to the cultural variety of the Far East. The Chinese model, while of the utmost importance, never eclipsed the local differences that made Japan always and Korea sometimes so distinct from China as properly to constitute a separate civilization.

*   *   *

The full acculturation of Indian Buddhism to the Far East, and the revival of Chinese political and cultural aplomb that ensued, marked the end of Indian cultural expansion along the central Asian trade routes. The barbarian incursions into northwest India that damaged or destroyed some of the important centers of Buddhist missionary enterprise accelerated the reversal of cultural drift that began when the T'ang dynasty (618–907) undertook reconquest of central Asia. The internal transformation which reduced Indian

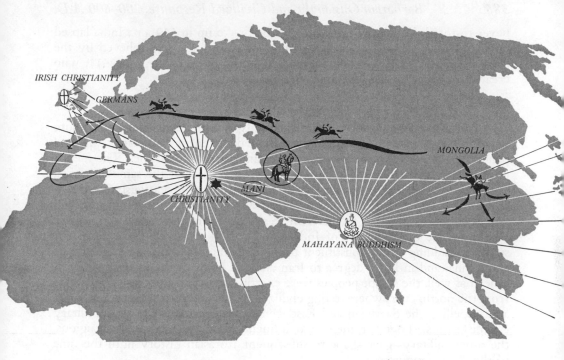

Buddhism to the abstruse speculations of comfortably insulated monks was still more important, for it cut off the font of missionary inspiration at its source.[42] Yet before the force of Indian cultural expansion had thus reached its term (about 600 A.D.), it had contributed important new elements and emphases to the cultural heritage of more than half the human race.

D. THE NORTHERN FRONTIER: BARBARIAN BREAK-THROUGH AND CIVILIZED REACTION, 200–600 A.D.

At the close of the fifth century A.D., a new barbarian irruption shattered the peace which had nourished Gupta civilization. The Ephthalite Huns[43] over-ran central Asia, invaded northwestern India, and threatened to break the overland connection between India and the Far East. We have already no-ticed their first raid into northwest India (*ca.* 455 A.D.), which had no great importance; but between about 490 and 549 A.D., the Ephthalites established an extensive hegemony in northern India, raiding far and wide, and leaving many Buddhist monasteries in ruins behind them. The Gupta empire was

[42] Cf. the loss of Hellenism's capacity to gain converts as it became a polite accomplishment of the upper classes in the Greco-Roman world.

[43] R. Ghirshman, *Les Chionites-Hephtalites* (Cairo: L'Institut Français d'Archéologie Orientale, 1948), p. 115. The usual uncertainties persist as to the linguistic affiliation of this horde. Ghirshman argues that they spoke an Iranian language; the older view labeled them "Turko-Mongol." Cf. René Grousset, *L'Empire des steppes*, p. 110.

never restored. When the Ephthalite horde broke up in 549 A.D., India lapsed into political division and disorder, punctuated but scarcely relieved by the occasional emergence of a successful conqueror like Harsha (606–41), who created an ephemeral empire in northwest India.

I. THE GREAT MIGRATIONS

The Ephthalite invasions of India were only one incident in a much more widespread movement of peoples that affected the entire Eurasian steppe and penetrated deeply into the adjacent forest and agricultural zones. The migrations of the German tribes in the Far West were part of the same upheaval, as was the barbarian occupation of north China. Only precariously were Sassanid Persia and East Rome able to resist barbarian engulfment and maintain an unconquered island of civilized life in the center of the ecumene.[44]

Thus while the influence of Indian civilization was welling up from the south and adding a new constituent to the cultural inheritance of central Asia and China, and in lesser degree to Iran and the lands of the eastern Mediterranean as well, the steppe peoples were exerting a similarly pervasive influence from the north, everywhere testing civilized defenses, overrunning weak spots, and impelling the Sassanian and East Roman states to improve their military establishments. Together these two influences—the one primarily religious, the other military—gave shape to subsequent Eurasian history until the time of the Arab conquests.

In conformity to the geographical determinants of the steppe gradient, Outer Mongolia continued to be the principal center of nomad dispersion between 200 and 600 A.D. From this region a new war confederacy, known to the Chinese as the Juan-juan, began to snowball across the steppe about the middle of the fourth century. At its height, the Juan-juan controlled a wide belt of territory extending from Manchuria as far west as Lake Balkash, or even beyond. Meanwhile, other nomad peoples had penetrated the north China plains. One of these, the Toba confederation of Turkish-speaking tribesmen, ruled most of north China between 386 and 534 A.D. (the northern Wei dynasty) and proved strong enough to withstand the outer nomads, even after the Juan-juan had organized them into a powerful confederation. The consolidation of the Toba empire blocked the comparatively short road from the steppe into China and thereby diverted subsequent nomad expansion westward along the steppe.

While these events were transpiring in the Far East, changes of similar scope occurred farther west along the frontier between barbarism and civilization. The Parthian empire had long been subject to strong fissiparous tendencies. Whenever a king of only average energy and aggressiveness occupied the throne, the rural magnates and local princelings of the Iranian countryside were likely to become restive. In 226 A.D. one such magnate, Ardashir, succeeded in challenging and overthrowing his Parthian overlord, but then, surprisingly, proved able to make his leadership effective through-

---

[44] South China and south India also remained immune from barbarian attack, but this was more by reason of geographical distance than because of local military or political strength.

out the wide realms which had before been only loosely consolidated under the Parthian monarchy. Appeals to Persian pride and the revival and reorganization of Zoroastrianism as a state religion, together with a more explicit recognition of aristocratic privilege, all contributed to the enhancement of Ardashir's power. Indeed, the success of this combination was so great that the dynasty he founded—the Sassanid—ruled for more than four hundred years and during most of that time proved conspicuously more successful than either the Romans or the Chinese in holding the steppe frontier.

While Iran and Mesopotamia therefore enjoyed relative security in the third century A.D., the internal cohesion of the Roman state showed signs of serious disrepair. The civil war between 193 and 197 A.D., which brought the first "barracks emperor" to power, was a mere prelude to the distresses of the years 235 to 285 A.D., when recurrent struggles between rival candidates for the imperial throne opened the gates to barbarian invasion accompanied by pestilential disease of unusual severity. Widespread depopulation resulted, weakening Roman powers of resistance at the same time that barbarian pressures against the frontiers were mounting.

In the Far West, along the Rhine, German tribesmen had begun to settle down to a more intensive agriculture as early as the time of Tacitus (*ca.* 100 A.D.). Their numbers correspondingly increased without at first altering the warrior ethos they had inherited from an earlier, more pastoral style of life.[45] Along the lower Danube, the Sarmatians, who had lorded it over the westernmost portions of the Eurasian steppe since the second century B.C., gave way to hordes of Goths, who migrated southward from the Baltic region toward the Black Sea in the early part of the third century. As befitted conquerors of steppe lands, the Goths (and other east German tribes) adhered to a more pastoral style of life, although they practiced some agriculture also. From a Roman point of view, however, German prowess, which now combined numbers along the Rhine with mobility along the Danube, threatened disaster.

Yet nothing like a sense of community existed among the various Germanic tribes. They fought one another as readily as they fought the Romans; and German settlers, admitted to Roman territory on a treaty basis, were ready enough to defend their new lands against fellow Germans even if it meant submission to Roman command. Divisions among the German tribes, and the existence of a real, if somewhat attenuated imperial consciousness among the populations of the empire, made it possible for soldier-emperors like Decius, Claudius Gothicus, Aurelian, and Diocletian to tame and in the end turn back the barbarian invasions of the third century A.D.

The restored fabric of the Roman state endured for more than a century (285–395 A.D.), thanks mainly to the enlarged resources which a ruthless resort to compulsion made available for state purposes in general and for the support of the army in particular. But the additional strength attainable

---

[45] Cf. the status of the Latin populations of Italy some 800 years earlier, when they, too, had but recently settled down to fixed agriculture and solved the problem of rapidly growing numbers by embarking upon a career of conquest that ultimately eventuated in the Roman empire. Considered in this light, the Roman state in the West was destroyed by the same forces that had created it.

through compulsion was limited. Even when reinforced by the supernatural sanctions of the Christian church and sustained by a rapid acculturation of German mercenaries and frontiersmen, the late Roman empire lacked resilience in the face of disaster, since most of its subjects found the government oppressive, rapacious, alien. In the fifth century, therefore, local defeats in the western provinces could no longer be made good, and Roman power disintegrated in the Latin-speaking half of the empire. Only in the Greek-speaking provinces did the continuity of the Roman state remain unbroken until 1204, thanks in no small measure to the eminently defensible capital which Constantine (d. 337 A.D.) had built on the site of ancient Byzantium.

The proximate cause of Rome's final collapse in the Far West was the sudden appearance of the Huns in eastern Europe. The original impetus which ejected this horde from the Aral region of the steppe can only be conjectured.[46] But in 374 A.D., the Huns quickly defeated the Ostrogoths on the Dnieper, terrified the Visigoths into seeking refuge south of the Danube, and proceeded to build up an extensive nomad "empire" from a center in the Hungarian plain. In the following decades, Italy and Gaul as well as the Balkan peninsula felt the scourge of Hunnic raids; and all across Europe, whole peoples submitted in terror or fled before the new conquerors. Yet following the death of Attila (453), the last great Hunnic warlord, civil dissension within the horde and a rebellion of subject peoples destroyed this nomad empire even more quickly than it had arisen. Hunnic remnants took refuge along the Roman borders or retreated eastward to the region of the lower Don, where they resumed their ancestral mode of life and became but one of many similar groups occupying the steppelands of Eurasia.

In consequence of the Hunnic devastations, the Roman government lost control of its western provinces; and a series of German "successor kingdoms" arose in Italy, Gaul, Spain, Britain, and north Africa. Like other barbarian conquerors of civilized lands, the Germans wished both to preserve their accustomed tribal organization and to ape the wealth, ease, and elegance of Roman upper class life. Thus a petty chieftain who took possession of an estate had to play the role of Roman lord and master vis-à-vis the local cultivators, while maintaining the bluff manners of a successful war-band leader vis-à-vis his German followers and fellow warriors. This was a difficult combination, for an excess of Roman hauteur would alienate the German rank and file and cause the military basis of the leader's power to crumble. Conversely, if war-band ethos were allowed free rein, plundering, idleness, and rapacious extortion were likely to disperse or destroy the peasantry, whose

---

[46] The sudden irruption of the Huns into Europe was immediately preceded by a not dissimilar irruption of the Ephthalites into the eastern marches of the Sassanid state. The first certain reference to the establishment of the Ephthalites in the agricultural regions of the upper Oxus (ancient Bactria) dates from 371 A.D. In that year, Shapur II of Persia appears to have come to an understanding with the Ephthalites, whereby the horde recognized his suzerainty and was entrusted with the defense of this portion of the Sassanid domain in return for the right to rule that still rich land. Cf. R. Ghirshman, *Les Chionites-Hephtalites*, p. 82.

The remarkable chronological coincidence suggests that displacements of peoples within the central steppe, probably emanating from the region where the Juan-juan confederacy was coming into being, pushed both Huns and Ephthalites from their accustomed pasture lands.

labor alone made the estate valuable. Similarly, the desire of tribal kings both to maintain the tax and other public powers of Roman sovereignty and to preserve their traditional tribal prerogatives within the German community proved irreconcilable. Such hybrid states were clearly transitional, and none of them lasted long.[47]

These events in Europe had interesting parallels farther east. The hybrid social structure of the German successor kingdoms resembled that of the Ephthalite empire of Bactria and northern India (371–576), where relatively crude barbarians likewise sought to rule civilized peoples on civilized principles and simultaneously to preserve their traditional war-band discipline and ferocity. In China also, the Toba empire (386–534) was constituted along substantially the same hybrid lines.[48]

Parallels extend still further, for the overthrow of these various successor states occurred at nearly the same time (mid-sixth century) in each portion of the ecumene and resulted from substantially similar processes. Everywhere three factors came into play: (1) the weakening of barbarian war-band ethos and discipline as the seductive force of civilized or semi-civilized living made itself felt; (2) resurgence of civilized imperial power, drawing at least part of its strength from a "native reaction" against foreign intruders; and (3) the rise of effective political organizations among outer barbarians who were in a position to attack the successor states on one flank while the revivified civilized empires assaulted them on the other.

The European protagonists of this drama were the Franks and the East Roman empire. Under Clovis (481–511) and his sons, the Franks formed a powerful military state based upon an increasingly dense agricultural occupation of the Rhinelands. The weight and mass of Frankish attack was therefore far greater than that which the comparative handful of Goths and Burgundians with whom they collided in Gaul could muster. Frankish encroachment from the north was matched by the emperor Justinian's (527–65) systematic campaigns intended to reunite the Roman empire. Since they included a small but formidable corps of heavily armed and armored cataphracts, Justinian's forces technically far outmatched any troops the German kings of the West could bring into the field. Instantaneous success (as in north Africa) or prolonged and piecemeal siege warfare, when his opponents sheltered behind fortifications (as in Italy) therefore characterized Justinian's campaigns in the West. By his death, Roman armies had brought north Africa, Italy, and part of Spain back to the imperial obedience, exercised, of

[47] An important geographical distinction asserted itself during the fifth century. In the northwesternmost regions of the Roman empire, the moist and cool Atlantic climate made a Mediterranean style of agriculture ineffective. There the fabric of Roman life crumbled before the invading Germans, whose agriculture was better adjusted to the climatic conditions. Thus Roman settlement was obliterated in Britain and the lower Rhinelands; and an almost purely Germanic style of life took its place. The hybrid type of society in the "successor kingdoms" prevailed only farther south, where Roman populations were much more firmly established and where the German occupation was correspondingly thinner.

[48] Wolfram Eberhard, *Das Toba Reich Nordchinas: eine soziologische Untersuchung* (Leiden: E. J. Brill, 1949).

course, from Constantine's New Rome on the Bosphorus. Most of Gaul, however, had long since (507) fallen to the Franks.

In the Far East, the Sui dynasty surpassed the achievements of Justinian by reuniting all of China in 589. Yet the victory was not won without the help of outer barbarians, who with Chinese aid destroyed the Juan-juan confederacy in 552. This passage of arms opened the way for the creation of a new nomad confederacy on the eastern steppe, led this time by Turks. The new Turkish empire was, of course, as much of a potential threat to China as the Juan-juan confederation had been. But a quarrel between two branches of the Turkish ruling family divided the horde into eastern and western halves in 572. Thereafter, Chinese diplomacy kept the eastern Turks harmless by a judicious distribution of gifts, blended with unobtrusive diplomatic encouragement of internal frictions within the horde.

In central Asia, essentially the same drama reached its crisis in 567, when the western Turks joined forces with a resurgent Sassanian empire to overthrow the Ephthalites. In the division of spoils that ensued, the western Turks acquired regalian rights in the oases east of the Oxus. This substantial accession to their wealth was among the factors stimulating the quarrel with the eastern Turks, who had enjoyed no such success and could not hope to do so as long as Chinese strength remained intact.[49]

In both the Far and Middle East, the new constellation of forces between civilized and barbarian empires which thus emerged in the second half of the sixth century endured for nearly three hundred years. To be sure, the T'ang dynasty supplanted the Sui in 618; and the Sassanians, after a series of suicidal wars with the Byzantines, gave way to the Moslems. Yet in both regions, restored and reinvigorated civilized empires held the steppe nomads successfully at bay until the tenth century A.D. This was not the case in Europe, however, where fresh waves of barbarian invasion promptly undid Justinian's work in the West and even compelled his successors to abandon control of much of the Balkan peninsula. The prime center of disturbance that provoked this new wave of migration was again located on the steppe. A new war band, fleeing from upheavals in central Asia, and known in European history as the Avars,[50] set up headquarters in the Hungarian plain in 567 and, thence, like the Huns before them, launched raids far and wide, provoking Lombards to invade Italy, Slavs to swarm into the Balkans, and allowing Bulgars, another nomad tribe, to establish themselves on the lower Danube.

2. CONSEQUENCES OF THE MIGRATIONS

The barbarian migrations of the third to sixth centuries A.D. forwarded three general processes, each of which profoundly altered styles of life throughout Eurasia. First, and not least in importance, was the effect upon the barbarian peoples themselves, who in varying degrees assimilated civilized styles of life.

---

[49] René Grousset, *L'Empire des steppes*, pp. 110–15, 124–30; Ghirshman, *Les Chionites-Hephtalites*, pp. 83–134.

[50] Scholarly opinion is divided as to whether the Avars were remnants of the Juan-juan or of the Ephthalite confederacy. Cf. Grousset, *L'Empire des steppes*, pp. 226–27.

Second, the civilized communities of Eurasia (excepting China) were impelled to modify their military, political, and social systems by introducing many of the features we are accustomed from European history to term "medieval." Third, the rise of religion to a central place in personal and public affairs gave a radically new character to the high cultural traditions of both Rome and Persia and affected Chinese civilization in a similar, though less drastic fashion. Each of these points requires some elaboration.

CIVILIZING THE BARBARIANS.   The history of civilization is a history of the expansion of particularly attractive cultural and social patterns through conversion of barbarians to modes of life they found superior to their own. Between the third and seventh centuries A.D., India and China played the role of civilizers in what we may regard as the normal fashion: India by converting barbarians without the gates, and China by civilizing tribes that had first battered their way onto anciently Chinese ground. Along the eastern marches of the Sassanian state, however, and on a more massive scale in the European Far West, the barbarian onslaught nearly overwhelmed civilized life. This is not surprising, for civilization in those regions had hitherto always been confined to a thin stratum of landowners, officials, and merchants; and, at least in Europe, the invading barbarians were comparatively quite numerous. As a result, in western Europe and central Asia, the capacity of civilized communities to absorb and convert the invaders was greatly overstrained; and the barbarian component of the end mixture was far more prominent than elsewhere.[51]

Yet even here, close contact with more advanced peoples soon modified barbarian ways of life. The Ephthalites, for example, though they persecuted Indian religions and demolished sacred edifices in their raids south of the Hindu Kush, did so in the name of their own faith—a solar religion perhaps derived from primitive Iranian sun worship. They tolerated and may even have patronized Buddhist art in the state they established north of the mountains, where they created the framework of a regular administration, issued coins, and had an eye to the advantages of trade. Indeed, had their empire not been destroyed by Turkish and Sassanian attack in the sixth century, it might well have become a close replica of the Kushan state, whose former territories it occupied.[52]

The Turks, who superseded the Ephthalites in central Asia and in the Oxus-Jaxartes region, were culturally primitive when they first demonstrated their military might to the world. Yet before the breakdown of their

---

[51] The invasions of the eighteenth to fifteenth centuries B.C., which destroyed the Indus and Minoan civilizations but merely overran the stronger civilized societies of the Middle East, offer a close parallel. The pattern was repeated, though less strongly, with the invasions of the twelfth to tenth centuries B.C., when Mycenaean, Hittite, and perhaps other less well-known marginal areas of civilized society were reduced to barbarism again.

Yet a millennium of civilized development was not without its effect, so that, between the third and seventh centuries A.D., civilized societies resisted barbarian attack more successfully, lost less ground, and revived more quickly than had been possible in the earlier ages.

[52] Cf. the rehabilitation of the Ephthalites undertaken by R. Ghirshman, *Les Chionites-Hephtalites*, pp. 115–34.

political cohesion, they appear to have absorbed elements of the Zoroastrian religion from Persia, developed trade with surrounding regions, and acquired some of the material refinements of Sassanian civilization.[53]

In the same way, the Hunnic horde brought Slavs and Germans of the north European forest into unprecedentedly close contact with the civilization of the Mediterranean. The gold and other valuables which the East Roman emperors paid to Attila in tribute tended always to filter back southward in payment for various luxury goods—for which even the fierce Huns speedily developed a taste. Roman merchants found barbarian territory an attractive field of operation when such quantities of gold had preceded them; and their progress to and fro between the Roman and the barbarian worlds tended, with the military operations themselves, to knit the two regions more closely together.[54]

The Goths, who had but recently (third century A.D.) conquered the grasslands north and west of the Black Sea, proved far more receptive to Roman civilization than were the more egalitarian west Germans of the Rhineland forests. When they first encountered the Roman style of life, the Goths were themselves still in process of adjusting their own folkways to new conditions of life on the steppes. This fact, together with the sharp differentiation between aristocrat and commoner which pastoralism encouraged, made it far easier for Roman luxuries and learning to find lodgment among the Goths than among the simpler Franks of the West. Thus, even before the Ostrogoths penetrated Roman frontiers, Bishop Ulfilas (d. 383) had converted their leading men to the Arian version of Christianity; and by translating portions of the Bible into the Gothic language, he inaugurated Germanic literacy. Not until the end of the fifth century did Clovis, king of the Franks, accept the orthodox form of Christianity and compel his principal lieutenants and followers to do the same (496); and the evangelization of Britain began a century later still (596). Franks and Goths had had roughly equal opportunities for encountering Roman Christian culture; and the lag of more than a century in their conversion to Christanity indicates how stubbornly Frankish feeling at first resisted the infiltration of foreign frippery and alien piety.[55]

However superficial the initial conversion of German princes and kings[56] to

[53] Grousset, *L'Empire des steppes*, pp. 129, 131–32.

[54] The detailed description of Attila's camp written by Priscus, who visited it as a member of a Roman embassy, allows fascinating glimpses of the impact of Roman civilization beyond Roman borders. Cf. E. A. Thompson, *A History of Attila and the Huns* (Oxford: Clarendon Press, 1948), pp. 161–83. The vivid picture of Attila's state which thus survives may serve as an archetype for dozens of other, essentially similar, nomad war-band headquarters which arose both before and after Attila's time in the steppe zones and whose military success brought them into close symbiosis with civilization, whether Chinese, Middle Eastern, or European.

[55] Cf. Old Roman resistance to Greek civilization, and the no less stalwart conservatism of the Bible belt in the United States.

[56] Barbarian kings had good reason to welcome Christian missionaries, who propounded doctrines about the sacredness and the prerogatives of rulership far exceeding anything that tribal custom allowed. A Christian chieftain could count upon the Church for enthusiastic support against conservatives who in politics sought to resist the transformation of war-band leadership into permanent, territorial kingship, and in religion remained loyal to the old gods.

Christianity may have been, baptism nevertheless brought in its train not only churches and monasteries, but literacy and a general initiation into the traditions of Roman and Christian civilization. Together with Greek and Syrian traders, Christian missionaries therefore became pioneers of civilization throughout the barbarian fringes of the Roman world.[57] Certainly the general level of culture declined in western Europe; but the very simplification and barbarization of Roman civilization allowed it to transcend the Rhine-Danube frontier which, from the time of Augustus, had marked the boundary of the Mediterranean-centered classical high culture. Simultaneously, the consolidation of Germanic states, and social differentiation within German society, prepared the way for the reception of this simplified form of Latin Christian civilization. By Clovis' time, therefore, the Rhine was no longer a terminus, but was becoming the axis of a German-Roman cultural amalgam from which Western civilization later developed.

MODIFICATION OF CIVILIZED MILITARY AND POLITICAL INSTITUTIONS IN WESTERN EURASIA. Three centuries of barbarian rule in north China altered Han political and military institutions very little. As the invaders became Sinicized, the old patterns of Chinese government and army administration reasserted themselves, partly, at least, because Ch'in and Han institutions had themselves taken form under steppe pressures and were therefore well attuned to the task of frontier guard against the nomads. The case was otherwise farther west, where Persia led the way and Byzantium reluctantly followed in adjusting inherited forms of warfare, government, and society to the requirements of defense against barbarian attack.

Iran had a long head start upon the Romans in this respect, inasmuch as the Parthian invasion (third century B.C.) had led to the development of a style of armament—the heavy armored cavalryman or cataphract—which permitted effective defense against nomad light horse. To maintain and organize a sufficient force of such troops posed a serious problem for civilized societies, for the heavy horses and elaborate armor were expensive; and cataphracts required long training to be able to handle their complex armament effectively. Probably the Parthians were the first to solve this problem in the "feudal" manner, which in time became normal in all western Eurasia. The essence of the system linked particular agricultural villages to particular warriors, who thereby acquired sufficient income and leisure to equip and train themselves and perhaps a few followers as heavy armored cavalrymen, ready at a moment's notice for local self-defense and able, when an effective central administration existed, to gather into larger bodies for major operations. But warriors on their estates might not readily answer the summons of their king, nor willingly obey their superiors in the field. The disintegration of effective central administration was therefore always a real danger for states that maintained a force of armored cavalry in this way.

[57] The phenomenon was not confined to western Europe. In Justinian's time, for example, the Caucasus region was brought within the Christian fold; and to the south, Ethiopia was Christianized as early as the fourth century.

In states with a flourishing mercantile life, taxes levied against the cities could finance a royal mercenary force capable of counterbalancing centrifugal tendencies. A standing army, equipped as well as the best of the feudal forces, could usually overawe potential rebels and keep the most ambitious local aristocrats obedient to the royal summons. Such a dual system characterized the military regime of the Sassanian empire, although the relative position of king, magnates, lesser nobles, cities, and even, in one conspicuously revolutionary episode, of peasant villagers, shifted from reign to reign.[58]

In these respects, the Sassanian regime differed little from the Parthian. But the identification of royal government with an official religion—Zoroastrianism—and with a priesthood which not only managed religious affairs but assisted actively in judicial and other functions of public administration was new and probably helped to strengthen and stabilize the central authority. The first Sassanian monarch, Ardashir (226–41), came from a family of priests. He may even have owed the rapidity and completeness of his success to active support given him by priests of the ancient Iranian cults,[59] who felt themselves threatened as never before by the inroads of Buddhism and Christianity.

Ardashir's successors on the Persian throne repeatedly indulged in religious experiments, perhaps because they found difficulty in controlling the Zoroastrian priesthood and the aristocracy to which it was closely allied. Yet in the end, the Sassanids always returned to their ancestral faith. They could not afford to antagonize too deeply the Iranian noblemen, upon whose prowess the military security of state and society fundamentally depended. The urban populations of the empire—whom the Parthians had tended to favor over the country nobles—may have been restless. The infiltration of Christianity, the flourishing condition of Babylonian Judaism, and, above all, the religious movements associated with the names of Mani and Mazdak strongly suggest urban dissatisfaction. But only when quarrels between king and aristocracy reached an unusually acute pitch was a Sassanian monarch likely to favor one or another of the urban religions of his realm. The alliance of throne and altar was too precious to discard wantonly, for it lent religious sanction to the

[58] For details see Arthur Christensen, *L'Iran sous les Sassanides* (2d ed.; Copenhagen: E. Munksgaard, 1944).

Mesopotamia was the great focus of urban life in the Parthian and Sassanian empires. Recent surveys have shown that the irrigation system and water engineering there reached their maximal elaboration under the Sassanians, with branching canal systems, elaborate sluices, and technical feats of construction such as that involved in carrying a trunk canal over lesser watercourses. Irrigation and the economic organization required to construct and maintain the system have never since reached comparable levels in Mesopotamia, not even under the Abbasids. Indeed, until the Chinese in the T'ang period opened the Grand Canal between the Yellow River and the Yangtze, no comparable feats of water engineering were known anywhere in the world. Cf. Thorkild Jacobsen and Robert M. Adams, "Salt and Silt in Ancient Mesopotamian Agriculture," *Science*, CXXVIII (1957), 1253–57.

[59] The religious situation in Mesopotamia and Iran under the Parthians is highly obscure. It is likely that when Ardashir began his conquest, no uniform Zoroastrian cult or body of doctrine was everywhere accepted in the Iranian lands. Cf. R. Ghirshman, *L'Iran des origines à l'Islam*, pp. 282–86; H. S. Nyberg, *Die Religionen des alten Irans* (Leipzig: J. C. Hinrichs, 1938), pp. 404–10.

SASSANIAN WARRIORS

The silver bowl at the top and the badly damaged bas-relief below portray Sassanian monarchs engaged in two activities that most befitted them: hunting and fighting. The weathering of centuries has badly obscured details of the cliffside carving, but enough remains to show the tactics of medieval knighthood here memorialized as early as the third century A.D. The silver bowl preserves its original clarity and shows that, like their Assyrian predecessors (p. 235), Sassanian knights lacked stirrups and, unlike their later Far Western counterparts, saw nothing undignified in bow and arrow.

ruler's power and thus gave the state a degree of stability which it could scarcely have otherwise attained.[60]

The "medieval" characteritics of Sassanian Persia are very striking to anyone familiar only with European history, and rightly so, for the over-all success with which Sassanian military forces met the challenge of nomad harassment and local raiding[61] made them a model first for Byzantium and through Byzantium for remote western Europe, where aristocratic armored cavalry became the basis of local self-defense a full thousand years after the development of a similar system in Iran.

*   *   *

Roman institutions worked badly between the third and sixth centuries. Not until the latter part of Justinian's reign (527–65) did the remnant of the Roman empire in the East approach the Persian level of stability at home and formidability abroad. In the military sphere, recurrent conflicts with the Persians and with raiders from the Danubian steppes compelled East Rome to abandon the ancient infantry tradition of the European West and to imitate Persian heavy cavalry. Large-scale conversion to the new cavalry style began only after the time of Constantine (324–27), although experiments with this form of armament had been made earlier.[62] By Justinian's day, mail-clad horsemen wielding both spears and bows had become the backbone of the Roman armies.[63]

Even after cataphracts had become the Roman fighting arm par excellence, the imperial government never really solved the related problem of numbers. Policy forbade the establishment of a military aristocracy on the land in the Persian fashion, and the practice of allowing war captains to recruit and maintain personal followings of cataphracts who lived on the spoils of successful campaigns failed to provide forces to guard the exposed landward frontiers of the empire. Even successful captains found it difficult to maintain a sufficient flow of booty;[64] and the necessity of doing so subjected them to a standing temptation of waging war, not along the barren and unattractive frontiers of

[60] The long reigns of many of the Sassanid monarchs stand in striking contrast to the series of imperial assassinations that distinguished Roman history during the third and fourth centuries. Only after the Romans, too, espoused a religion of state did the frequency of rebellion and imperial murder begin to decrease, as a religious aura came to sustain imperial might against the danger of usurpation.

[61] Small-scale raids such as those which regularly penetrated the Roman defenses along the Danube were in Iran turned back by local forces of armored noble cavalrymen. It required a major convulsion, such as the Ephthalite assault upon Bactria, to break through the local defenses of the Persian countryside.

[62] Such experiments went back to the days of Hadrian (117–38 A.D.), for Trajan's wars across the Danube had brought the effectiveness of Sarmatian armored horsemen to Roman attention. Pauly-Wissowa, *Real-Encyclopädie der klassischen Altertumswissenschaft* (Stuttgart: J. B. Metzler Verlag, 1899), s.v. *cataphracta*.

[63] For details see Robert Grosse, *Römische Militärgeschichte von Gallienus bis zum Beginn der byzantinischen Themenverfassung* (Berlin: Weidmannsche Buchhandlung, 1920), pp. 314–37 and *passim*.

[64] Belisarius, the most famous of these captains, maintained a personal following of 7,000 men, according to Procopius, *Gothic War*, III, 1, 20. His total forces for the invasion of north Africa in 533 were 15,000 men, but his 5,000 cavalrymen constituted the only really effective arm.

the empire, but in its vitals, where the imperial throne perennially beckoned and where rich cities and cultivated countryside constituted a tempting booty for their soldiers. Such a system clearly threatened to perpetuate the disease of overmighty generals from which the Western empire had perished; but when the emperor Maurice (582–602) attempted to forestall this danger by putting the army in the pay of the imperial fisc,[65] the exigencies of imperial finance and policy made it impossible to maintain adequate numbers of cataphracts on guard along the frontiers.

The Roman government's dilemma was simple, though painful. Cataphracts stationed where they could really check raids from across the frontier were bound to escape effective imperial control. The three available organizational alternatives—militarized local landowners (on the Persian model), private bands of professional plunderers working on government contract (on Justinian's model), no less than a frontier force whose pay (at least theoretically) came from the imperial government, but which in practice obeyed a particular general whose ambitions might not stop short of the imperial purple (on Augustus' model)—were all alike dangerous to the central power. The Byzantine emperors found it necessary, therefore, to leave their landward frontiers exposed to a steady process of local raiding and barbarian infiltration—a fact which accounts for the oddly inconspicuous but massive change in Balkan ethnic alignments that occurred as small Slavic bands gradually migrated southward, supplanting earlier populations bit by bit.[66]

A series of wars with the Persians (572–630) dramatically demonstrated the weakness of the Byzantine state in land warfare. Despite the handicap of operating in distant and presumably hostile country, Persian armies twice penetrated within sight of Constantinople itself (610, 626) and conquered all of Syria, Palestine, and Egypt. Yet the Byzantine empire survived long after the Sassanians had succumbed to the Moslem flood. Byzantine longevity rested squarely on sea power, which repeatedly saved the capital itself and gave the imperial land forces a limited but supremely effective strategic mobility which a purely land power like Persia could never equal. Hence, although the Byzantines were never able adequately to defend their inland frontiers, as long as their fleet remained strong enough to succor the army, the two imperial forces together always proved able to safeguard the vital centers of the state.[67]

Diplomacy and subsidy served the Byzantine government as surrogates for an adequate frontier guard. This policy may in fact often have been cheaper

[65] Steven Runciman, *Byzantine Civilization* (London: Edward Arnold & Co., 1933), p. 139.

[66] The central government was of course aware of the unsatisfactory posture of frontier defenses and did attempt to meet the problem by compelling people living near the borders to build and garrison local fortresses, on the theory that such strongholds could delay an invader until such time as the main body of mobile cataphract troops appeared to drive the marauders away. But only a really massive attack was likely to attract the emperor's household cavalry; small-scale raiders could safely bypass such barriers.

[67] The advantages of sea power were vividly demonstrated by Justinian's campaigns in the western Mediterranean, and most dramatically by Heraclius' wars with the Persians (610–30), when the emperor left his beleaguered capital, sailed along the Black Sea coast to take the Persian besiegers in the rear, and in the end compelled them to withdraw. Cf. Archibald R. Lewis, *Naval Power and Trade in the Mediterranean, 500–1100* (Princeton, N.J.: Princeton University Press, 1951), pp. 3–53.

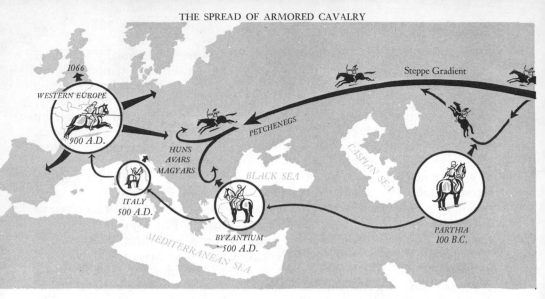

than maintaining an army sufficient to cope with external threats would have been, and it must have seemed safer to emperors who knew how many of their predecessors had met a violent death at the hands of rebellious frontier soldiery. Moreover, tribute payments to barbarians abroad allowed the unwarlike and commercially minded populations of the Byzantine cities to maintain their social dominance at home in an age when the urban classes in Mesopotamia and Iran had lost ground to the landed aristocracy.[68]

Persian influence on the Byzantine state was not confined to the sphere of military technology. From the time of Diocletian (284–305), the rulers of the Roman empire deliberately copied aspects of Persian courtly ritual and sovereign splendor. Insignia of rulership—the diadem and scepter—as well as the custom of requiring all who approached the emperor enthroned to prostrate themselves, were among such borrowings.[69] Diocletian, a peasant by birth, seems to have adopted these devices less from personal inclination than in the hope of surrounding his person with an awe that would inhibit assassination and encourage obedience; but his successors in the fourth and fifth centuries increasingly took courtly pomp and ritual seriously.

After Constantine's conversion to Christianity, all the Roman emperors except Julian (361–63) were professing Christians and therefore enjoyed the sanction of a religion whose leaders hastened to reverence Caesar as Christ's

[68] The Arab conquest of Syria and Egypt deprived the Byzantines of their wealthiest cities; and with the reign of Leo III, the Isaurian (717–41), the rural Anatolian hinterland began, in a limited sense at least, to dominate the remaining urban centers along the coasts of the Aegean and Black Seas. With this change, the Byzantine state came to resemble the Sassanian much more closely. Interestingly enough, it was only after the military reforms inaugurated by Leo that something like an effective frontier guard in Anatolia became possible, with the establishment of a landed military class under the imperial aegis, similar in character to the petty Persian nobility which had constituted the most numerous element in the royal Sassanian field army.

[69] Styles of dress, which, with art generally, constitute a sensitive indicator of cultural drift and affiliations, also became Orientalized during the fifth century, when long brocaded coats replaced the toga of Rome. Cf. Kondakov, "Les Costumes orientaux à la cour byzantine," *Byzantion*, I (1924), 7–49.

vicegerent upon earth[70] when they did not recognize him as arch-heretic and enemy of truth. This change in the imperial style, too, brought Roman institutions into line with Persian practice,[71] where church and state had embraced each other with the same strenuous ambiguity from the beginning of the Sassanian period.

In Constantine's day and for a long time thereafter, Christianity was predominantly an urban religion, without any of the aristocratic, rural affiliations that distinguished Zoroastrianism in Persia. Thus the Christianization of the empire reinforced urban dominance within Roman society. The loss of all the provinces where cities were too few and weak to sustain the burden of Roman bureaucratic administration further confirmed this balance. The Persian state, depending fundamentally upon the military support of a rural aristocracy, stood in fundamental contrast; and the established religions of the two empires reflected and supported this basic divergence.

In sum: the Persian adjustment to the military pressure from the steppe was more radical and more successful than that of Roman Byzantium. This was so, not only because the stronger and more continuous barbarian pressures along the Persian frontiers forced a more radical adjustment and did so earlier, but also because unmilitary urban populations played a greater role in Roman society. Along the Mediterranean, Aegean, and Black Sea coasts, shipping could nourish commerce on a larger scale than was possible inland, where transport was, in the nature of the case, far more expensive. As long as Byzantium held the eastern Mediterranean coasts, social leadership retained a fundamentally urban character, and urban populations could, or would, make only partial and imperfect adjustments of their military and political institutions along the lines which the Persians had so effectively pioneered.

CULTURAL CHANGES IN PERSIA AND ROME.   Time has dealt so harshly with the monuments and records of Sassanian Persia that a just estimate of that society's cultural achievement is scarcely possible. Secular literature, if there was any, has entirely vanished, and the works of art that survive have nearly all suffered severely from the ravages of time. Even religious thought, which dominated other aspects of Sassanian high culture, has disintegrated into dispersed and contradictory fragments. It is clear that the Sassanian court harked back to ancient Persia and aped the Achaemenids in religion and art and perhaps in other respects. Yet Iran and Mesopotamia could not escape their geographical location at the crossroads of the ecumene, where merchants and pilgrims from distant parts rubbed shoulders with one another in the bazaars, exchanged tall tales, and boasted of their various wisdoms and skills. The conscious archaism of the court circle was therefore islanded in a sea of cultural

---

[70] Cf. Eusebius, *Life of Constantine*, III, 10: "[Constantine] himself proceeded through the midst of the assembly, like some heavenly messenger of God, clothed in raiment which glittered as if it were with rays of light."

[71] Neither Constantine nor his successors consciously modeled their reordering of Roman religious institutions on Persian precedent. Religiosity was everywhere in the ascendant; and Constantine, like the rough soldier he was, probably figured that the Christian God had brought him victory at the Milvian Bridge (312) and therefore deserved respectful attention and all due honor.

syncretism which, at least occasionally, was equally conscious. As with other urban civilizations that lacked real roots in the countryside, the results were grand and artificial, in theology as in architecture; and Moslem conquest cut off the entire tradition in the seventh century, just as Alexander's victories had earlier disrupted the high culture of the Achaemenids.

Characteristic juxtaposition of archaism with syncretism is well reflected in Sassanian art, despite its fragmentary and ruined state. The royal palaces, which constituted the principal Sassanian monuments, used ancient Mesopotamian techniques of brick construction and in some instances revived Achaemenid decorative motifs; but the basic plan combined a domed and vaulted interior, anticipating some features of Byzantine architecture, with a Hellenistic façade of pilasters and arches bearing no relation either to the interior plan or to the constructional principles of the building. Yet cool, shimmering audience halls, offering a welcome refuge from the Mesopotamian sun and entrancing the eye with wall paintings or mosaics now lost beyond recovery may have redeemed a style apparently so incoherent and structurally clumsy.[72]

The Sassanian monarchs likewise imitated their Achaemenid predecessors by cutting gigantic rock-hewn sculptures into cliffs near Persepolis; but the style of these works betrays a strong affinity both to the sculpture of the late Roman empire[73] and to the Indo-Buddhist art of eastern Iran and central Asia.

India supplied the Sassanian grandees with two famous amusements for their leisure hours, for both chess and the animal fables of the *Pancha Tantra* had been naturalized in Persia by the sixth century. Similarly, in 529 A.D., when Justinian proved his Christian piety by closing the Academy of Athens which Plato had founded nearly a thousand years before, Chosroes I (531–79) welcomed the refugee philosophers to his court. But odd scraps of information such as these do not permit adequate reconstruction of the secular side of Sassanian culture, which had somehow to accommodate both the rude and proudly rural Iranian baronage and the sophisticated complexities of great cities like the capital, Ctesiphon on the Tigris.

In Sassanian Persia, as everywhere else in the ecumene of that day, cultural and social movements regularly took religious form. The tension between archaism, seeking to revive the Zoroastrianism of Achaemenid times, and syncretism, aspiring to unite the truths of every faith into a grand and final synthesis, dominated the religious striving of the urban populations; and the religious conservatism of the Iranian baronage, while more difficult to document, was probably of equal importance in the Sassanian religious-political balance.

As befitted the crossroads of the ecumene, adherents of each of the major

---

[72] Cf. Oscar Reuther, "Sassanian Architecture," in Arthur Usham Pope, *A Survey of Persian Art* (London and New York: Oxford University Press, 1938), I, 493 ff. Indo-Buddhist elements may also be found in a few Sassanian architectural remains.

[73] This is not surprising, for many Sassanian monuments were built by "Greeks" captured in war or otherwise induced to lend their skill to the Persian service. Cf. Steven Runciman, *Byzantine Civilization*, p. 259. For a balanced survey of the learned argument between champions of Iranian and champions of Roman primacy in the genesis of the Byzantine style, cf. O. M. Dalton, *East Christian Art* (Oxford, Clarendon Press, 1925), pp. 68–89.

religions of the age found a foothold in Mesopotamia and Iran. Buddhists were well established in eastern Iran, where important monasteries and regularly organized educational institutions flourished as they had since the time of the Kushans. The principal Buddhist missions to China passed through, when they did not originate within, the eastern marches of the Sassanian empire.

The Jews of Mesopotamia, who had experienced their share of vicissitudes since Nebuchadnezzar first planted their forefathers in the land, entered upon a period of unusual religious activity in the fourth and fifth centuries. Indeed, a group of Babylonian rabbis set their stamp upon medieval Jewry everywhere by compiling the version of the Talmud which came to be generally accepted as more authoritative than the earlier Palestinian version.[74]

The Jewish communities in Mesopotamia paved the way for Christianity, which rapidly won a substantial foothold in the urban centers of the Sassanian empire just as it was simultaneously doing in the East Roman empire. Aramaic rivaled Greek as a vehicle for Christian propaganda in Mesopotamia, as was also the case in Roman Syria. By the fifth century A.D., doctrinal disputes over the exact relation between the divine and human natures of Christ enormously exacerbated this linguistic-cultural rift. The Christians also had unending difficulty in defining their relation to the Sassanian state, which alternately tolerated, persecuted, or merely distrusted them as potential agents of the Christian (after 324 A.D.) empire of Rome. Not until the very close of the Sassanian period did definitive separation between the Christian church of Constantinople and that of Persia occur, when, as a result of internal quarrels and the gradual erosion of the Greek element in the Mesopotamian church, a loosely Nestorian doctrine[75] came to predominate among the Christians of Persia.

Buddhist, Jewish, and Christian faiths had all taken form beyond Sassanian frontiers and were therefore in some measure alien intruders. Yet during the Hellenistic period, the ancient worship of Bel Marduk had frayed out into astrology; and the ancient faith of Zoroaster had become an unhappy hodgepodge of divergent oral traditions, cast in a dead language, and maintained by temple priesthoods among whom aristocratic birth had long since supplanted intellectual culture. Ardashir, the founder of the Sassanian dynasty, came from such a priestly family himself and sought to revive the glories of Achaemenid times by promoting the faith of Zoroaster. This, however, raised the question of how to reconcile widely divergent traditions which had developed in different Zoroastrian temples. The effort (undertaken at Ardashir's behest) to collate these traditions, decide upon a canon, and then enforce uniformity of doctrine and ritual raised awkward problems of authentication. In addition, champions of the new official cult had to confront arguments and questions that adherents of other, more sophisticated faiths put

---

[74] Salo Wittmayer Baron, *A Social and Religious History of the Jews*, II, 204–9, 294–98.

[75] Initially propounded in 428 by Nestorius, a Syrian, when newly appointed Patriarch of Constantinople, Nestorianism held that Mary was mother of Jesus only in his human nature and should therefore not be addressed as "Theotokos," "Mother of God." The Council of Ephesus in 431 officially anathematized this view, which had its main support in Syria among Aramaic-speaking Christians.

to them; but the comparatively crude tenets of a rural, aristocratic, time-in-crusted Zoroastrianism, that now had the temerity to claim supremacy, offered an inadequate basis for effective rebuttal.

These problems found two interesting solutions under Shapur I (241–71), Ardashir's son and successor. On the one hand, Shapur encouraged Zoroastrian priests to repair the all too obvious defects of their intellectual inheritance by incorporating into the *Avesta* whatever selections from Greek and Indian wisdom seemed to offer valuable supplements to older Zoroastrian truths. Skilful translation and compilation along these lines might be expected to produce a sacred canon far superior to Christian and Buddhist scriptures, disfigured as they were by all sorts of logical and historical discrepancies.[76] But Shapur had a second string to his bow, for he also looked with favor upon the efforts of a new-sprung prophet, Mani (*ca.* 216–77), who with an intellectual virtuosity strikingly like that of his Gnostic predecessors preached a doctrine that boldly combined Zoroastrian, Buddhist, and Christian motifs.[77]

The core of Mani's message fell familiarly on Persian ears, for he viewed the world as a battleground between the forces of Light and Darkness and summoned his hearers to rise toward the Light. He developed this idea into an elaborate cosmology, explaining all the stages and stratagems whereby Darkness had created the world by entangling fragments of Light in the prison of matter, and tracing, with equal precision, the steps by which the two cosmic antagonists would again separate from one another, and thus bring the world to an end. In the course of his cosmogony, Mani found ample room for Zoroaster, Jesus, Buddha, and other divine helpers of mankind, each of whom, he declared, had sought to reveal the same religious truths but had been variously misunderstood by followers who through human error had produced the divergent creeds of Mani's own day.[78] Mani therefore conceived

---

[76] Practically all the encyclopedic material thus grafted onto the Zoroastrian scripture was subsequently lost, since the new texts found no liturgical use and therefore soon lapsed from memory.

R. C. Zaehner has suggested that an influx of Greek philosophy into Zoroastrian intellectual circles dated from Shapur's time. Such interesting phenomena as the elevation of Aristotle's ethical principle of the mean into an actor in the cosmic drama of creation eventuated from this process of cultural syncretism! Cf. R. C. Zaehner, *Zurvan: A Zoroastrian Dilemma* (Oxford: Clarendon Press, 1955), pp. 250–51 and *passim*. My remarks on Sassanian culture and society are based largely upon this book, as well as the same author's more comprehensive treatise, R. C. Zaehner, *The Dawn and Twilight of Zoroastrianism* (New York: G. P. Putnam's Sons, 1961), pp. 175–321; and A. Christensen, *L'Iran sous les Sassanides*.

[77] Like many of the Christian Gnostics, Mani regarded Jesus as a wholly supernatural figure; and his doctrine has traditionally been classed by Christians as a form of heresy akin to Monophysitism. Cf. F. C. Burkitt, *The Religion of the Manichees* (Cambridge: Cambridge University Press, 1925), p. 71; Hans H. Schraeder, "Der Manichäismus nach neuen Funden und Untersuchungen," *Morgenland*, XXVIII (1936), 99; H. C. Puech, *Le Manichéisme, son fondateur, sa doctrine* (Paris: Musio Guimet Bibliothèque de Diffusion, 1949), pp. 82–83 and *passim*.

Mani's revaluation of Jesus strikingly resembled the transfiguration of the historic Gautama which was introduced into Buddhism by teachers of the Mahayana. But the Indian tradition of religious tolerance simply accepted the Mahayana as a form of Buddhism, whereas Mani's teaching was from the beginning recognized by Christians as foul heresy, all the fouler for its approximation to Christian revelation.

[78] Being a highly self-conscious prophet, Mani sought to prevent any similar corruption of his own doctrine by writing out his own sacred scriptures and issuing stern injunctions against unauthorized copying. A. Christensen, *L'Iran sous les Sassanides*, pp. 198–99.

his role as one of bringing men back to the original truth which had been lost. He utterly repudiated the notion that his doctrine was in any way new.

Mani was not merely a prophet and metaphysician; he also busied himself with the practical task of founding a church. He established a definite hierarchy of religious ministrants and divided his adherents into the "elect," for whom a rigorous and ascetic discipline was prescribed, and "hearers" who supported the elect with gifts and benefited vicariously from their sanctity, secret knowledge, and religious prowess. The perspicacious prophet also prescribed appropriate rituals, including congregational hymn singing, confession of sins, and rites of absolution. Detailed ethical instructions and rules of conduct for hearers and elect completed this highly systematic religion, which Mani designed, as he himself said, to enlighten all mankind.

The wide response which Mani won during his lifetime is not surprising in view of the royal favor he enjoyed and the inherent appeal of a faith claiming to incorporate all the truths of its rivals, while purifying them of human errors and the stubborn inconsistencies of tradition. But the ancient Iranian priesthoods were not easily vanquished, and when Shapur I died, Mani lost his royal protector. An intolerant Zoroastrian orthodoxy reasserted itself at court (perhaps coupled with an aristocratic, Iranian reaction).[79] As a result, Mani died a prisoner. His followers went underground but long retained considerable influence in the cities of Mesopotamia.

These first forcible efforts to impose a redefined Zoroastrian orthodoxy upon the variegated populations of the Sassanian state could not quiet the religious anxieties of the time; and the attempt was not long maintained. Drastic fluctuations in royal religious policy reflected the ambiguous position of succeeding rulers vis-à-vis the Zoroastrian priests and the Iranian baronage with whom the doctrinally conservative priestly faction was identified. Too close dependence upon the aristocracy and priests spelled disintegration of royal independence and an alienation of the urban populations for whom a conservative Zoroastrian orthodoxy could have little appeal. But too vigorous a defiance of the Iranian priests and nobles threatened civil war or local revolt and undermined the military strength of the state.

The more energetic Sassanian monarchs therefore regularly attempted to balance the power of an often overweening Zoroastrian priesthood by making gestures in the direction of rival urban religions, even Christianity, despite its Roman coloring. King Kobad (ruled 485–98 and 500–531) made the most remarkable of these experiments. Early in his reign, Kobad attacked the intrenched power of the Iranian nobility by patronizing a radical sect known as Mazdakites, whose emphatic egalitarianism constituted a direct challenge to

---

[79] The priests of Zoroastrianism directed their wrath not only against Mani, who after all had accused them of distorting their prophet's true message, but against the Christians, Jews, Buddhists, and Brahmins as well. Cf. R. C. Zaehner, *Dawn and Twilight of Zoroastrianism*, pp. 186–90.

What may have lent an especial sharpness to the whole affair was a sectarian quarrel within Zoroastrian ranks between a more boldly speculative, syncretist wing—loosely, "Zurvanism"—and a more rigidly conservative and anti-intellectual Mazdean orthodoxy. Virulent sectarian fissiparousness was the natural consequence of unleashing the speculative theological spirit within Zoroastrianism. Christian theology of the same age demonstrated the same fertility. Cf. R. C. Zaehner, *Zurvanism*, for an ingenious reconstruction of the variant Zurvanist doctrines.

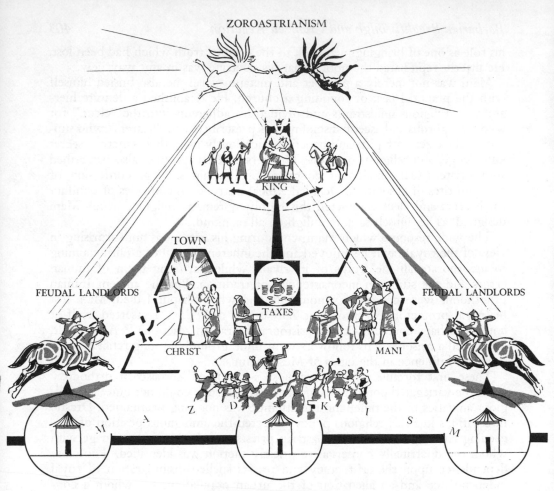

ZOROASTRIANISM

KING

TOWN

FEUDAL LANDLORDS

TAXES

FEUDAL LANDLORDS

CHRIST   MANI

M A Z D A K I S M

SASSANIAN PERSIA

the aristocratic order of Sassanian society.[80] But royal sponsorship of social revolution did not last very long, for Kobad soon broke with his erstwhile protégés, who had provoked civil war by resorting to violence in defense of their principles. His son and successor, Chosroes I (531–79), brutally suppressed the revolutionary movements, executed Mazdak, the leader of the sect, and reinstituted a conservative Zoroastrian orthodoxy. Yet seemingly the royal authority emerged from these disturbances stronger than ever. At any

[80] Mazdakites were accused by their enemies of favoring communism of property and of women. A recent student has suggested that this may mean no more than that they broke through Sassanian class and family feeling by proclaiming new marriage and inheritance laws that would break aristocratic primacy in society. Cf. R. P. de Menasse, "L'Église mazdéene dans l'empire sassanide," *Cahiers d'histoire mondiale*, II (1955), 561–62. But cf. the older view in A. Christensen, *L'Iran sous les Sassanides*, pp. 337–40, and for a Marxian interpretation see Ottokar Klima, *Geschichte einer sozialen Bewegung im sassanadischen Persien* (Prague: National Czechoslovak Academy, 1957).

rate, Sassanian armies met with their greatest successes under Chosroes; and perhaps in consequence of the prestige gained through such victories, Chosroes relaxed the rigor of Zoroastrian orthodoxy in the later years of his reign by tolerating Christians, as well as by patronizing the pagan Greek philosophers who had fled from the Academy of Athens.

Nevertheless, despite Chosroes' military victories, the ease with which, less than a century later, the Moslems were able to defeat the Persian armies and utterly destroy the Sassanian state surely means that the official Zoroastrian religion and the social regime it upheld somehow had failed to strike deep roots among the peoples of the empire. The cool calculation whereby Shapur sought to enrich the Zoroastrian heritage with the distilled wisdom of Greeks and Indians, no less than the speculative syntheses launched by Mani, and perhaps also by Mazdak all failed to generate a world religion capable of standing against Islam. This failure, by branding the thought and sectarian struggles of Sassanian times as vain and heathen noises in the judgment of later generations, renders impossible any really satisfactory appraisal of the cultural life of the empire. Nonetheless, the fact that Sassanian culture cast a long shadow abroad should dispose us to a charitable judgment of its inherent qualities. The oases of central Asia became Sassanian cultural dependencies with the slackening of Indian influence that became apparent about 400 A.D. Indeed, Persian Christians attracted a following in India itself; and in the Roman empire the two most pertinacious rivals Christianity had to face—Manichaeism and Mithraism—were both of Persian inspiration. Manichaeism retained importance even late in the fourth century, as St. Augustine's (d. 430) *Confessions* eloquently attest; and Mithraism, which had taken form in Asia Minor where Greek and Persian cultural worlds met and overlapped, kept its hold upon the Roman armies of the West as long as such forces continued to exist. A culture that exhibited such power to influence its neighbors must have had attractions we can today but speculatively glimpse.

* * *

In the Roman empire, as in the Persian, religion dominated the cultural scene during the centuries 200–600 A.D. The polite pagan culture of the Roman upper classes crumbled in the civil wars of the third century; and popular religions rose up through the debris of paganism, absorbing elements from it, but integrating old and new beliefs into a distinctive world-view and way of life. In Sassanian Persia, religious conflict brought the triumph of the somewhat archaic, and definitely aristocratic, Zoroastrianism; in the Roman empire, aristocratic religion gave way before the far more popular, and even democratic,[81] Christianity.

[81] Apart from the doctrinal point that all human souls are equally valuable in the eyes of God, the social composition of the Church in its first centuries of existence was predominantly urban and lower class. Even after state support had made the Christian faith attractive to men of wealth and ambition, groups like the Egyptian monks, who more than once defied the imperial power, retained a strong affiliation with the urban poor.

Indeed, despite the military autocracy, later Roman and early Byzantine society as a whole was

Christianity had originated as a faith whose burning conviction was not buttressed by any elaborate metaphysic or theology. But the need for defense against pagan criticism, and for settling differences within the Christian community itself, led gradually to the formulation of a precise body of dogma. Christian doctrine received its first systematic development in Alexandria, where a school for the higher education of priests was established in the second century A.D. Origen (*ca.* 182–251) and others who taught at that school inevitably fell back upon the terms and concepts of Greek philosophy when they undertook to express Christian doctrine in coherent, logical fashion and to answer objections raised against the new faith by unbelieving pagans.

A great dividing line in the history of the Church came when the emperor Constantine made Christianity a legal (313) and specially favored (324) religion. Before that time, sporadic but sometimes severe persecutions had tended to keep the Christian community together, since the general hostility of the outside world called for a common front. But when the state ceased to threaten Christians and conversion no longer involved personal risk, the pressure toward unity slackened just when men of widely differing backgrounds swarmed into the Church for reasons not always connected with religious belief. Under these circumstances, quarrels over points of theology and ritual became an avenue through which personal ambition, as well as a wide variety of social resentments, found expression. Consequently, Donatists in Africa, and Arians in Egypt and Syria, were only the first of a long series of similar dissident groups which disturbed the unity of the Christian church.

These disputes had many dimensions. Constantine himself attempted to adjudicate the Donatist and Arian controversies; and in each case brought the weight of the imperial power behind the doctrine declared to be orthodox. As a result, heresy thereafter sometimes became an avenue for the expression of covert hostility against the central government. Rivalry among the principal bishoprics of the Church—Rome, Alexandria, Antioch, and Constantinople—likewise fomented differences of theological opinion. Finally, religious dissent sometimes took on tones of social revolution or came to express the cultural self-awareness of a partially submerged people like the Berbers of north Africa or the Aramaic-speaking Syrians. But these facts should not obscure the basic and authentic theological anxiety which lay behind the urge to compel all heretics to cease and desist from spreading false doctrine, lest God himself should take the matter in hand and revenge himself both upon the false prophets and upon those who allowed them to preach.

Closely interwoven with the difficulty of defining dogma was the need to create an ecclesiastical hierarchy and to accommodate its jurisdiction within the traditional powers of the state. The earliest Christian communities appear to have managed their own affairs with only informal aid and counsel from outside. Very soon, and perhaps from the beginning, each local church lodged

---

far more democratic than the earlier Roman empire had been. Peasants repeatedly rose to the imperial purple through advancement in the army; and high officials of both Church and state were frequently recruited from humble backgrounds. Autocracy and democracy are far closer kin than at first appears, as the politics of the twentieth century should remind us.

Antike Denkmaeler, *III, 20.*

A ROMAN EMPEROR OF THE FOURTH (?) CENTURY

This colossal bronze statue in Barletta, Italy may represent the Emperor Valentinian I (364–75 A.D.), although the identification is uncertain. Like Augustus (p. 327), the emperor is shown in military dress; but the comparative crudity of details, together with the hard, haughty expression on the emperor's face, well reflect the change of Roman government from principate to despotism. To suggest majesty and power of more than human proportions seems to have been the artist's aim, whereas in Augustus' time a more naturalistic, human portrait sufficed to impart a quieter air of authority.

authority in the hands of a bishop; and bishops of the more important cities tended to exercise a vague supervision over the provincial churches in the area. As ecclesiastical jurisdiction became better defined, it tended to conform to existing political divisions, particularly after the state itself became Christian. On this principle, the Second Ecumenical Council (381 A.D.) granted to the bishop of Constantinople jurisdiction over the Church in most of Asia Minor and the Balkans on the ground that "Constantinople is New Rome."[82]

Apostolic succession constituted an alternative and theologically more impressive basis upon which authority in the Church might rest. Upon this principle, the bishop of Rome claimed primacy over the entire Church in his capacity as successor to Peter, Prince of the Apostles, and putative founder of the Christian church in that city. Pope Leo the Great (440–61) therefore felt justified in proposing his own definition of Christian truth as a solution to the doctrinal disputes that were tearing the Eastern churches apart. When the Council of Chalcedon (451) approved Leo's *Tome*, he chose to regard this as a definitive recognition of the supremacy of Rome. Eastern bishops, however, interpreted the same act as the exercise of sovereignty by a general council of the Church, in which all bishops rightfully had equal voice.

Yet this conciliar principle, which the Eastern Church never abandoned, was modified in reality by the emperor's participation in the deliberations of the councils. Constantine presided over the first council at Nicaea (325 A.D.) and dominated it completely.[83] His successors intervened frequently in theological disputes; and the power and majesty of the emperor usually insured that his will prevailed in ecclesiastical as well as secular matters.[84] Hence the emperor in Constantinople and the pope in Rome each claimed supreme authority over the Church and tended to regard councils rather as a device for ratifying their own respective decisions than as sovereign legislative bodies. The conciliar and the papal theories were never reconciled and constituted a permanent irritant in relations between the Latin-speaking churches of the West, which generally supported Rome, and the Greek-speaking churches of the East, which usually adhered to the decisions of the councils.

The alienation between Greek- and Latin-speaking Christians mirrored a more general drifting apart of the two halves of the Mediterranean world. Diocletian's (285–305) administrative reorganization had divided the empire into an eastern and a western half; but in the Balkan interior and along the Danube, the Eastern empire included important Latin-speaking areas within its boundaries. Hence Latin was heard in the streets and council halls of Constantinople long after Greek had disappeared from the West.[85] But with the

---

[82] S. Runciman, *Byzantine Civilization*, p. 109.

[83] Eusebius' account, *Life of Constantine*, III, 6–15, clearly reflects the awe most of the Christian bishops assembled at Nicaea must have felt for the majesty of the emperor.

[84] There were exceptions to this generalization. For example, Ambrose (d. 397), bishop of Milan, was able to compel the emperor Theodosius to do public penance for his crime of ordering a massacre in Salonika. Ambrose's lofty conception of priestly functions found its principal support in the West, where after the fifth century the civil power was weak or nonexistent, and bishops became by default the political as well as the spiritual leaders of their communities.

[85] Justinian, for example, spoke Latin as his native language, though born in what is today the Yugoslav town of Nish.

loss of the Western provinces to Germans and of the Balkan interior to Slavs, the Latin language faded and disappeared from the East Roman, now properly Byzantine, empire. Ignorance of each other's language became almost universal and fostered the mutual distrust and dislike between Latins and Greeks that became a conspicuous feature of medieval Christendom.

Within the Eastern empire, a second linguistic-cultural division became increasingly important in the sixth and seventh centuries. Among the populations of Egypt and Syria, where Hellenism had intruded upon an older cultural stratum, an active hostility developed both to Hellenic paganism and to ecclesiastical-political dominance from Constantinople. This spirit of separatism found expression in adherence to the Monophysite definition of Christ's nature.[86] When the Council of Chalcedon (451) declared this view heretical, the bishops and people of the "Syriac" East did not tamely surrender; and the efforts of emperors and ecclesiastical statesmen to propound a mutually satisfactory creedal formula merely added new sectaries to the dispute. Sporadic violence and persecutions embittered the struggle, until in the seventh century, the Moslem conquest of Syria and Egypt liberated these two stubbornly Monophysite countries from Constantinople's ecclesiastical and political control.

The doctrinal disputes and jurisdictional difficulties within the Church provoked a great outpouring of polemical and theological treatises, which together with hymns, sermons, ecclesiastical histories, saints' lives, and biblical commentaries formed a bulky and sometimes impressive Christian literature. The greatest Christian writer of the age was Augustine (d. 430), whose biblical commentaries, treatises on doctrine, *Confessions*, and *City of God*, taken together, provided the major intellectual framework within which Latin Christianity subsequently evolved. In the Eastern Church, no single writer was equally influential. The Greeks honored a multitude of theologians, who provided a more varied, if less authoritative interpretation of Christian doctrine.

The age was notable also for its ascetics. Saints, mystics, and holy men often commanded deep popular reverence; and the reconciliation of the sometimes eccentric inspiration of these men with orthodox doctrine constituted a serious problem for the Church's official hierarchy. Yet ascetic fires and the mystic vision could be harnessed to an orderly routine, as St. Pachomius (*ca.* 290–345) proved when he gathered desert anchorites of Egypt into monastic communities. A litle later, St. Basil (329–79) prepared a set of monastic regulations which subsequently became standard in the Greek East. The monastic movement spread more slowly in the West; and not until about 529 did St. Benedict of Nursia formulate his rule, which set the mold for subsequent Latin monasticism. The monastic life attracted many intellectually sensitive persons, for it offered opportunity in an otherwise turbulent world for a man to cultivate both his soul and his mind. With the decay of secular centers of

[86] *I.e.*, the view that Christ was wholly divine and at the Incarnation merely put on the appearance of humanity without soiling Himself with its real essence.

education, monasteries became, especially in the West, the principal refuges of learning.

In capturing the cultural life of the Roman empire so completely, Christianity rejected much of the pagan past, altered some of what it accepted, but also preserved at least a limited familiarity with the older Greek and Roman literature. The grammar of one or other of the classical languages was taught in Christian as it had been in pagan schools, so that despite the growing gap between ordinary speech and the literary forms of Latin and Greek, at least a few learned men always were able to read Homer (in the East) and Vergil (in the West). Aside from this literary continuity, the most important carry-over from the pagan past was in the sphere of law. Early in his reign Justinian ordered the codification of all the laws of the empire, and the resulting compilation, together with the commentaries upon the principles of jurisprudence, which comprise the *Corpus Iuris Civilis*, exercised an enormous influence upon subsequent European legal ideas and practices.

*   *   *

The Christian art of the East Roman empire appeals far more powerfully to modern minds than does the literature, learning, polemic, and piety of the age. Sculpture fell under Christian suspicion as tending dangerously toward idolatry; but Byzantine architecture and mosaic decoration bear comparison with any art style of the world. Byzantine artistic conceptions perhaps originated in Syria or Persia. In any case, the Hellenistic ideal of naturalistic representation was definitely abandoned. Instead, simplified drawing and rich coloring were used to achieve an immediate and emotionally powerful symbolic representation of the majesty of Christ and the saints, or of the emperor and his court. The use of mosaic technique, with glass or other colored material set (usually) against a background of gold leaf, produced a shimmering irridescence, powerfully suggestive of the transcendent eternity which Byzantine artists sought to reveal through the symbolic figures of their compositions.

Architects, like the mosaic artists, found no satisfaction in working within old Hellenistic and Roman styles. Instead of accepting the long, columned hall of a Roman basilica as fundamental for ecclesiastical architecture (as happened in the Latin West), Byzantines sought new inspiration in Syria, Armenia, and Mesopotamia. In Hagia Sophia, Justinian's great church at Constantinople, they perfected a radically new form of church building, cruciform in ground plan and dominated by a vast central dome, where the imposing figure of Christ Almighty imaged Heaven itself to the faithful multitudes gathered below.[87]

The striking transformation of the culture of the Roman world from the naturalism and rationalism of Hellenism to the transcendentalism and mysticism of the fifth and sixth centuries had no real parallel elsewhere in the ecumene. The Indian, Middle Eastern, and Chinese civilizations never underwent

---

[87] Charles Diehl, *Manuel d'art byzantin* (2d ed.; Paris: Éditions A. Picard, 1925), I, 9–23 and *passim;* O. M. Dalton, *East Christian Art* (Oxford: Clarendon Press, 1925), pp. 1–14 and *passim.*

Silvana Editoriale d'Arte, Milan.

THE EMPRESS THEODORA

This is a detail from the famous mosaic in the church of San Vitale in Ravenna, portraying the Empress Theodora and her attendants. An aloof stateliness and a gaze which seems fastened upon some far off, transcendent reality gives this portrait a peculiar power. The artist's unconcern with naturalistic portrayal of details of bodily shapes constitutes a striking reversal of the preoccupation of Hellenistic art (p. 291) with just such realistic touches.

so drastic a remodeling after their first formulation.[88] Nor did Europe's cultural instability end with the establishment of a Christian style of civilization; for modern Western culture and society are at least as different from the Christian world of the third–sixth centuries as that civilization was from its pagan predecessor. Unusual instability, arising out of a violent oscillation from one extreme to another, may in fact be the most distinctive and fateful characteristic of the European style of civilization.

E. THE OUTER FRINGES, 200–600 A.D.

With the exception of Australia and the southern parts of the African interior, where Stone Age cultures prevailed and men continued to hunt in small bands as their ancestors had done from time immemorial, all the major habitable regions of the earth began to feel the force of civilized culture, however faintly, in the period 200–600 A.D.

In east Africa, with the weakening of Roman commercial enterprise in the second century A.D., the kingdom of Ethiopia seized control of the Straits of Aden, and from this strategic position entered upon a period of commercial dominance of the trade of the Arabian and Red Seas. In the fourth century, the Ethiopians accepted Christianity; and their Nubian neighbors followed suit in the sixth. Southward along the African coast, an Indonesian immigrant population, surviving to the present in the Malagasy peoples of Madagascar, played an important trading and colonizing role; while on the other side of the continent, the kingdom of Ghana may have begun to arise in the western Sudan as early as the third or fourth century A.D. on the basis of an agricultural population and gold trade with the trans-Saharan north. Simultaneously, the rain forests of the Congo basin were in all probability being penetrated by Bantu speakers whose slash-and-burn style of cultivation depended in large part on crops derived from the tropical agriculture of distant Indonesia.[89]

The migration of steppe art styles into Germany and Scandinavia attests a similar infiltration of civilized influence into the forest and tundra zones of northern Eurasia. Jewelry recovered from graves is the principal evidence of this development; but the value of such objects is itself sufficient evidence of the emergence of a high barbarism in those parts, with incipient social differentiation and the concomitant beginnings of political consolidation.[90] In Siberia, too, grave finds at Minussinsk show that steppe art penetrated into forested country—a process which had begun centuries before, perhaps be-

---

[88] The transformation of lusty Aryan warriors into the ascetics of the *Upanishads* may have been equally drastic; but this occurred before Indian styles of life had fully transcended the barbaric level.

[89] Cf. George Peter Murdock, *Africa: Its Peoples and Their Culture History* (New York: McGraw-Hill, 1959), p. 45 and *passim*. Murdock's method of tracing agricultural crops and other culture trait diffusion is not perhaps infallible, but his book represents a great advance over earlier efforts to unravel the pre-Islamic history of Africa. Cf. Diedrich Westermann, *Geschichte Afrikas: Staatenbildungen südlich der Sahara* (Cologne: Greven, 1925), 276–301 and *passim*; E. Wallace Budge, *A History of Ethiopia* (London: Methuen & Co., 1928), I, 52–103, 204–64.

[90] M. I. Rostovtzeff, *Iranians and Greeks in South Russia*, pp. 189–91, 206–8.

AN INTERIOR VIEW OF HAGIA SOPHIA

This photograph shows the interior of Justinian's great church at Constantinople when it was in use as a mosque. Hence the medallions with quotations from the Koran and the absence of mosaic decorations which the Turks painted over as idolatrous. The structural principle which raised the dome so high over the central area is, however, clear, for one can see two of the pendentives upon which the main dome rests.

cause placer gold in the waters of the Yenesei had attracted merchants and prospectors thither.[91]

Far to the West, the Celtic fringe of Europe saw an extraordinary cultural upsurge in the fifth and sixth centuries. As with Ethiopia, on the other flank of the Roman empire, sea lanes connected the Celtic communities of Brittany, western Britain, and Ireland with one another and brought them into touch at least tenuously with the Mediterranean centers of high civilization. The life of St. Patrick (d. 461), born in Wales(?), educated in Gaul, and active in Ireland, aptly illustrates the importance of these sea connections.

The rapid development of Irish Christian culture, which made Ireland the seat of a more vigorous Christianity and of a wider learning than any which survived in Gaul itself, remains a remarkable instance of the fructifying influence of Christianity upon a society just emerging from barbarism.[92] The remote position which rendered Ireland immune from serious invasion encouraged this precocious cultural flowering in an age when Britain and the Continent were repeatedly harassed by barbarians. When the Scandinavian Vikings brought that immunity to an end, Irish civilization glimmered and died; and Ireland sank to the status of a backward outpost of Latin Christendom, where a few strange and peculiar traditions lingered. Yet before it disappeared, Irish Christian culture transmitted some of its force to Britain and the Continent. A series of missionaries, of whom the first was St. Columba (d. 597), brought Irish Christianity to Scotland and northern England; and from this vantage point other missionaries subsequently penetrated deep into northwest Europe.

*   *   *

Meanwhile, two major centers of high culture had developed in the Americas—one in the highlands of Central America, the other in the coastal valleys and uplands of Peru. These cultures were, of course, the fruit of long centuries of development. Maize, the staple food of both regions, may have been cultivated in Mexico as early as 2500 B.C.; and village life probably established itself there about 1500 B.C. Corresponding developments in Peru seem to have lagged somewhat behind: indeed, maize cultivation and other key techniques may have reached Peru from the north only about 700 B.C.[93] If so, the Peruvians, like the ancient Egyptians, compensated for their late start by a more rapid rate of development.[94] In any case, the "classic" Mayan civiliza-

[91] Cf. René Grousset, *L'Empire des steppes*, pp. 109–10.

[92] Some of the unique features of Irish Christianity probably had roots in Celtic druidism; and behind druidism lurked the ancient Megalithic religion of western Europe. For example, the high social status of Irish holy men, and the emphasis upon learning in Irish monasteries, bear suspicious resemblance to what is known of druidic (and megalithic) priestcraft.

[93] Gordon R. Willey, "Prehistoric Civilizations of Nuclear America," *American Anthropologist,* LVII, pp. 571–93; G. H. S. Bushnell, *Peru* (New York: Praeger, 1957), pp. 52–53.

[94] Peru of the Incas, *i.e.*, from the fourteenth to the early sixteenth century A.D., resembled Pharaonic Egypt also in the extraordinary centralization of political and economic control. Perhaps Stalinist Russia in the twentieth century is only the most recent of a long line of societies which have—consciously or otherwise—set out to "overtake and surpass" an older civilization by resort to centralization and wholesale compulsion.

tion seems to have emerged in the highlands of Guatemala almost simultaneously with the formulation of comparable "classic" cultures in central Mexico and Peru.[95]

All three civilizations had a good deal in common. As in ancient Sumer, priests appear to have been the principal leaders of society; for in all three areas, temples, pyramids, sacred roadways, and other appurtenances of the cult constitute by far the most conspicuous remains. Yet each society had a style of its own, both artistically, where the differences are easily verifiable, and presumably in the general sense as well.

Mayan civilization focused upon a dozen or more ceremonial centers which arose in the jungle areas of Guatemala and adjacent parts of Mexico. Some exchange of expertise among the priests of the different communities must have occurred to keep art styles and intellectual development—above all, the refinement of a very elaborate and amazingly accurate calendar—in harmony. Peasant communities were clustered around the great temple centers, subsisting upon a primitive shifting agriculture which, however, required relatively little labor to produce needed quantities of food.[96] By means unknown to us, the priests organized the farmers' spare time for labor on vast construction works and apparently also maintained a number of professional sculptors and metalworkers to produce the finer works of art. In addition, the Mayan priests developed a system of writing and arithmetical notation, which they used in connection with their elaborate astronomical and calendrical calculation.

Around the core area of Mayan civilization lay a penumbra of other societies which shared most of the Mayans' techniques. But apparently only in the plateau of central Mexico, near the present Mexico City, did a temple center comparable to those of the Mayan area develop before 600 A.D. The art and architecture of the plateau differed stylistically from the Mayan; but the social systems of the two areas were probably similar.

In Peru, geography dictated a more variegated development. Short river valleys, plunging down from the high Andes to the Pacific, offered a series of coastal sites where the earliest Peruvian high cultures flourished. These valleys were separated from one another by utter desert, and upstream abutted upon a broken topography where mountain valleys and high plateaus offered a second locus ·capable of sustaining civilized societies. Geography also prompted a really significant difference between Mayan and Peruvian development—for Peruvian agriculture depended on irrigation, whereas Mayan

[95] Mayan chronology alone allows a fair degree of certainty owing to the fact that Mayan hieroglyphs can be read well enough to decipher dates carved into ceremonial stelae; and the translation of the Mayan calendar into our own has recently been pretty well settled among the experts. Thus one can say, with satisfying exactness, that the earliest dated stela known today was dedicated on April 9, 328 A.D. Cf. J. Eric S. Thompson, *The Rise and Fall of Maya Civilization* (Norman, Okla.: Oklahoma University Press, 1954), p. 53.

[96] It has been estimated that forty-eight days' work per year can today support a Mayan and his family. Inasmuch as farming techniques in Yucatán (where the modern Mayas live) have changed very little since ancient times, a similar margin of leisure probably prevailed when the great ceremonial structures of the Mayan temple complexes were built. Cf. G. H. S. Bushnell, *Peru*, p. 41.

maize fields were watered by rain. Peruvians also used important resources from the highlands like the llama and the potato, which were quite unknown in central America.

By about 500 A.D., no fewer than three major cultures had taken "classic" form in Peru, one in the northern coastal valleys, a second in the more southerly coastal valleys, and the third in the altiplano near Lake Titicaca. In creating these cultures, the ancient Peruvians performed extraordinary feats of water engineering and built terraces as elaborate as any the world has ever seen. Priests did not have undisputed control, for in the northern coastal area (and perhaps elsewhere too), warriors played a considerable role. Political organization appears to have been highly centralized, as was perhaps inevitable in a region where life depended upon a scant supply of water, which had to be strictly controlled if each claimant were to have an equable share. But unlike the Mayans, the Peruvians did not develop any system of writing; and their sculpture was considerably more primitive and less abundant than the Mayan. Hence the glimpses of religion and mythology which Mayan stone monuments provide are not available for Peru, although pottery offers a partial substitute.[97]

In general, the level of these American civilizations in 600 A.D. was roughly comparable to that of the ancient river valley civilizations of Mesopotamia, Egypt, and the Indus about 3000 B.C. In 600 A.D., Mayan civilization was just entering upon its greatest age of artistic and intellectual development; in Peru, where chronology is far less certain, the classical period probably began at about the same time. This places the rise of American civilizations more than 3500 years behind comparable evolution in the Old World—a handicap which the New World civilizations never overcame. In addition, certain key items long familiar in Eurasia were never developed in the New World—e.g., draft animals, the wheel, iron metallurgy. This put the Amerindians at a permanent disadvantage as compared to their Eurasian contemporaries. Whatever transoceanic stimuli may have contributed to the development of New World cultures, it is clear that the American civilizations were essentially independent and belated cultural ventures. Amerindian history bore no vital relation to the contemporary scene in Eurasia until the sixteenth century A.D., when the Spaniards broke in upon the civilizations of the New World, only to decapitate them.

---

[97] In addition to books cited separately, I have consulted Sylvanus G. Morley, *The Ancient Maya* (Stanford, Calif.: Stanford University Press, 1946); Walter Krickeberg, *Altmexikanische Kulturen* (Berlin: Safari Verlag, 1956); Hans Dietrich Disselhoff, *Geschichte der altamerikanischen Kulturen* (Munich: Verlag R. Oldenbourg, 1953).

CHAPTER IX

The Resurgence of the Middle East 600–1000 A.D.

A. INTRODUCTION

For seven centuries, the line of the Syrian desert and the upper Euphrates divided the Middle East between Roman and Iranian sovereignties. This frontier proved remarkably stable. Despite innumerable wars, it underwent no permanent shift from 64 B.C., when Pompey fastened Roman control upon Palestine, Syria, and Anatolia, until 636 A.D., when Khalid ibn al-Walid defeated a Byzantine army at the battle of the Yarmuk and drove the Roman frontiers back into Anatolia. Shortly thereafter, Arab armies overran Mesopotamia (641), penetrated Egypt (642), and by 651 had even conquered Iran and extirpated the Sassanian dynasty.

The speed of these conquests was remarkable; but far more remarkable was the enduring realignment of cultural boundaries and the regrouping of peoples that followed in their wake. The ancient Middle East, where the earliest human civilizations had matured, only to be submerged under a wave of Hellenism and split politically between Iran and Rome, was united once more. Within the new political frame, a distinctive Islamic cultural synthesis soon took form, incorporating elements drawn from all the civilizations which had met and mingled at this crossroads of the ecumene for a millennium past. Regional variations of course persisted within the new Moslem empire, especially when it spread to include such distant regions as Spain (by 711) and the Indian province of Sind (by 715). Yet throughout this whole area, a common language and a common faith prevailed. Because of the central role played by religion in this extraordinary cultural synthesis, the result may best be termed "Islamic" civilization.

Yet the political and cultural reintegration of the Middle East did not quite restore the ancient primacy of that region over the other civilizations of the world. Islamic culture and society were not so obviously superior as to compel or induce the heirs of other civilized traditions to attune their traditional styles of life to the Moslem model. Nothing like the blending of elements from widely diverse regions which had produced the Gandhara art style or Chinese Buddhism occurred along the borders of the Islamic world during the period before 1000 A.D. Individuals and communities either accepted Islam or rejected it *in toto.* There was no half-way house, no liberty to pick and choose elements from the Islamic tradition and adapt them to local cultural styles. The reason, clearly, was the central and absolutely basic place which organized religion occupied, not only in Islamic civilization, but also in the civilizations of Islam's principal neighbors, Christendom and Hindustan. Civilizations built around a doctrinally developed religion demanded orthodoxy; and orthodoxy meant not only the acceptance of a single cultural model, but the rejection of all others as dangerously heretical or leading to heresy.[1]

The centrality of religion to the life of Europe, the Middle East, and India in the first centuries of the Moslem era thus gave the interrelationships of these three great civilizations a special rigidity. As long as doctrinal rigor prevailed, even prolonged and intimate commercial and military contact among men of different faiths made little impression upon anyone's cultural predilections. More nearly than at any time before or since, the civilized societies of Eurasia lived separately, each secure in the conviction that unbelievers could offer nothing of importance to followers of the true faith. Only after about 1000 A.D. did a freer cultural interchange begin to develop once again within the ecumene.

In the Far East, on the other hand, a looser-textured and less dogmatic cultural tradition survived. Under the T'ang dynasty (618–907 A.D.), China attained perhaps the most vigorous and variegated cultural efflorescence of her long history. Buddhism became thoroughly acculturated to the Chinese scene during this period and stimulated Taoist and Confucian champions of an older order partially to reinterpret and reorganize their inherited wisdom in the light of Buddhist ideas and practices. A second stimulus came from the steppe peoples, who were no longer raw barbarians, but by virtue of their geographical position were able to transmit to China elements of pre-Islamic Iranian culture. Chinese art and literature flourished under such stimuli; and Chinese influence upon Korea, Japan, Yunnan, Tibet, and the adjacent portion of the steppe became stronger than ever before.

In many ways, the efflorescence of T'ang China resembled that of Gupta

---

[1] Indian religions, of course, were less sharply defined dogmatically and far more tolerant than were either Christianity or Islam. Nonetheless, the unilateral intolerance of Islam, which at least in principle regarded all the Indian religions as "idolatry," seems to have effectually insulated Hindu from Islamic civilization until Moslem political domination reached beyond the Indus in the eleventh century.

India. Yet T'ang culture won no such reception outside its homeland as Indian culture of the Gupta age had done. The main reason, no doubt, was that the dogmatic and articulated religions of western Asia presented nearly impermeable psychological barriers to the westward diffusion of Chinese styles of life. A second factor was the reduction of traffic along the Silk Road itself after the Byzantine silk industry became well enough established to supply the Mediterranean demand.[2] Nevertheless, mercantile and military contacts continued to connect China with western Asia; and religious prejudice did not prevent the diffusion of such Chinese technological secrets as the art of paper making, which reached the Arabs via prisoners of war captured (751) in central Asia.

Islam, therefore, did not destroy the fourfold character of the Eurasiàn cultural equilibrium, although it sharpened the boundaries among the components of the balance and enlarged the relative weight of the Middle East. The initial Arab conquests constituted, in fact, a reassertion of very ancient lines of cultural demarcation[3] and transformed the balance of the ecumene into something that was both radically new and at the same time very olà. A resurgent Middle East could, indeed, be nothing else.

During the first centuries of the Moslem era, the Eurasian cultural map underwent a second major change. The age-old processes of civilized expansion widened the rather narrow belt of civilized communities which at the beginning of the period extended—not without some very slender reaches—all the way across Eurasia from the Atlantic to the Pacific. To the south, Mohammed made Arabia an integral part of the civilized world for the first time. In addition, Negro states in the west African Sudan, Moslem communities along the east African coast, and new or newly powerful states in Kashmir, Tibet, Burma, and Yunnan broadened the belt of civilized or semi-civilized communities and filled in almost all of the interstices which had previously cushioned contacts among the major civilizations of Eurasia. But except for Arabia and Tibet, each of which enjoyed a brief but brilliant imperial career, these new states on the southerly flank of the ecumene, together with older ones like Ethiopia, Nubia, and the Hindu kingdoms of southeast Asia, remained of secondary importance in the world balance.

In the northern steppe and forest zone, however, the penetration of civilization had a more important and in the long run revolutionary effect. The steppes had long been the greatest reservoir of militarized barbarism; and ever since the eighteenth century B.C., civilized societies had repeatedly felt the power of the steppe peoples. Yet the exigencies of pastoral life had been such as to preclude the development of stable political unity and the economic dif-

---

[2] Cocoons were smuggled from China into Byzantine territory between 552 and 554; and by the end of the century, the silk industry was well established there. Cf. G. F. Hudson, *Europe and China* (London: Edward Arnold & Co., 1931), pp. 120–22; R. S. Lopez, "Silk Industry in the Byzantine Empire," *Speculum*, XX (1945), 1–42.

[3] Except for Anatolia, which had once been Persian and now remained (often precariously) Byzantine, the first burst of Moslem expansion stayed almost exactly within the limit of territories which had once belonged to the ancient empires of Persia and Carthage. Half-forgotten hostilities against the intrusive Hellenism which had long overlaid the more ancient cultures of these regions undoubtedly both facilitated and delimited the initial Moslem advances.

ferentiation essential to civilized life. These limiting conditions did not disappear after 600 A.D.; yet they were modified sufficiently to permit the extension of civilized influence into the steppes on a larger scale than before. Comparatively large and stable tribal federations occupied almost the entire steppe: Avars, Bulgars, Khazars, and Uighurs, for example. Through a combination of plunder raids, tribute exactions, and peaceful bilateral trade, these peoples laid hands on increasing quantities of the goods of civilization. Income of this sort both consolidated the nomad federations, allowing the leaders to cement their followers' loyalty through suitable gifts, and at the same time spread familiarity with aspects of civilized life among a wider group of nomads than before.[4]

Trade often opened a path for more subtle infiltration from the civilized world. Religious ideas and institutions, in particular, tended to attract steppe peoples' attention. Conversions followed, although not always to the religion dominant among the civilized people closest at hand, since that might imply too great a loss of spiritual independence. Thus the Khazars became Jews and the Uighurs Manichaeans,[5] thereby asserting their independence of the adjacent civilized communities and yet gaining the advantages of civilized religion, *i.e.*, literacy and principles of political legitimacy that supplemented and went far beyond traditional tribal practice.

In the European Far West, no belt of grassland separated the northern forests from the civilized or semi-civilized country south of the Danube and west of the Rhine. But the military prowess of the European forest dwellers was comparable to that of the more easterly steppe peoples; and both groups won a place on the margins of civilized economies through essentially the same process. Indeed, plunder, tribute, and trade, together with civilized example, transformed Scandinavians, Germans, and Slavs even more effectually than they transformed the Turkish-speaking peoples of the steppes; for agriculture was possible in the forest zones. With agriculture, the full panoply of settled, civilized life took root and began to thrive after about 1000 A.D. in what had previously been a barbarous backwoods.

Thus the extension of civilization into the Eurasian steppes and forests gradually displaced the axis of military and economic power northward and laid the basis for the radical expansion in the period after 1000 A.D. of Turkish and Mongol peoples by land, and of western Europeans both by land and by sea.

B. THE MOSLEM WORLD TO 1000 A.D.

About 613 A.D., a hitherto undistinguished native of the trading city of Mecca named Mohammed (*ca.* 570–632 A.D.), began to denounce the polytheistic faith of his fellow tribesmen and to preach a new revelation. About three years previously, Mohammed, who was then a mature man of about forty,

---

[4] Service as mercenaries in civilized armies was a second and often highly important channel through which such familiarity spread.

[5] The religion of Mohammed represents a similar, though far more significant and original adaptation of civilized religion to local needs.

had begun to have strange and puzzling visionary experiences. Prolonged spiritual travail eventually persuaded him that the voice he heard in his visions was the angel Gabriel, instructing him to make Allah's will known to the Arabs. In a series of inspired and poetic utterances, Mohammed obeyed. A handful of his fellow citizens accepted his message; but most scoffed, and demanded miracles to prove the genuineness of the Prophet's mission.

Such were the modest beginnings of Islam. Yet within less than two decades, Mohammed united nearly all Arabia into a new religious-political community; and this community, having effectively suppressed divisive feuds among the tribes, enabled the Arabs in the twenty years following Mohammed's death to seize the richest provinces of the Byzantine empire and completely to destroy the Sassanian state. Never before or since has a prophet won such success so quickly; nor has the work of a single man so rapidly and radically transformed the course of world history. Through his inspired utterances, his personal example, and the organizational framework he established for Islam, Mohammed laid the basis for a distinctive new style of life, which within the space of two centuries attracted the allegiance of a major fraction of the human race and today commands the loyalty of about one-seventh of mankind.

The themes of Mohammed's early preaching were remarkably simple. He proclaimed the existence of one God, Allah, the terror of Allah's impending Day of Judgment, and the duty of each human being to obey the will of Allah as revealed by his prophet, Mohammed.

Allah was conceived as the same deity who had earlier revealed himself through Jesus and other Jewish prophets. In his first years Mohammed appears to have assumed that the adherents of Judaism and Christianity would recognize him as God's latest, last, and most authentic messenger. Only when he removed with his followers to Medina (622 A.D.) and came into close contact and conflict with Jewish tribes already settled in that oasis did he recognize the falsity of this assumption. Mohammed concluded that Jews and Christians had so corrupted and forgotten the Divine revelation as to reject undiluted truth. He thereupon declared himself spokesman for the authentic "religion of Abraham," to whom he ascribed the establishment of the ancient sanctuary, the Kaaba, which constituted one of the bases of Meccan commercial importance. Accordingly, he made Mecca and the Kaaba the central shrine of his new revelation instead of Jerusalem, which in his first prophetic period he had recognized as the primary terrestrial locus of holiness.[6]

Allah, according to Mohammed, was all-powerful, the creator and sustainer of the world. Allah was also supremely good and benevolent toward those who responded to His presence and power with a suitably humble gratitude, expressed in worship, almsgiving, and self-purification. Like the early Christians, Mohammed preached an imminent Day of Judgment, when the world would come to an end, the dead would rise from their graves, and all

---

[6] The content of Mohammed's revelations makes clear that he was familiar with certain Bible stories, which he had perhaps heard over caravan campfires in his youthful travels on trading expeditions to the borders of Palestine and Syria.

men would confront God, to be rewarded according to their deserts by consignment to Heaven or to Hell.

In Mecca, Mohammed was merely a private person, protected by the head of his tribe from the enemies his preaching aroused. The Prophet's role changed profoundly after he went to Medina in 622 A.D. Mohammed had been invited to Medina by feuding Arab farmers who desperately needed an authoritative outsider to settle their quarrels. This flight from Mecca to Medina—the Hegira—was later reckoned to be the beginning of the Moslem era, for from that date Mohammed began to exercise public authority. The community of the faithful henceforth became an autonomous and distinct political entity and began to exhibit an astounding power to transform first Arab and then Middle Eastern politics and culture.

In Medina, the Prophet confronted new problems; and his inspired utterances increasingly took on the character of law-giving. By degrees, the outlines of a new, God-centered way of life emerged—the way of Islam.[7] The heart of the Moslem discipline was prayer, prescribed five times a day. Prayer involved a ritual abasement before God, expressed by a fixed series of gestures culminating in repeated prostrations and punctuated by the recitation of set forms of praise. In addition, Mohammed proclaimed the duties of almsgiving, of fasting from dawn to dark in the month of Ramadan, and (after his return to Mecca) of pilgrimage to that city and the holy Kaaba. He also prohibited wine drinking and the eating of pork. All this, together with rules concerning inheritance, marriage, apportionment of booty, settlement of disputes among believers, and similar practical questions, quickly gave the small but growing Moslem community a character and internal discipline uniquely its own.

The Moslem aim was to serve God as He wished to be served, utterly and without reservation. In practice this meant unquestioning obedience to Mohammed, God's messenger. Military successes made such obedience easier, for the community of the faithful quickly proved itself far stronger than any Arabian rival. Ruthless hostility toward all the outer world secured the inner cohesion of the new religious community. Holy horror of idolatry certainly entered into this attitude; but the fact that the body of the faithful who had migrated with Mohammed from Mecca lacked all means of economic support within the already crowded oasis of Medina certainly helped to give a cutting edge to their religious sentiments. The pious alms of converted Medinese could not sustain the newcomers for long, so Mohammed sent his followers out into the desert to intercept the caravans passing to and from Mecca. The outraged Meccans, seriously divided among rival factions, failed in their attempts to check Moslem harassment.

When it became clear that Mohammed could not win the support of the Jewish colony in Medina, he instructed his followers to drive the Jewish farmers from the oasis. He then distributed their land among the faithful. But the community of believers grew so rapidly through the adherence of out-

[7] The term means "submission," or "resignation" (to God's will).

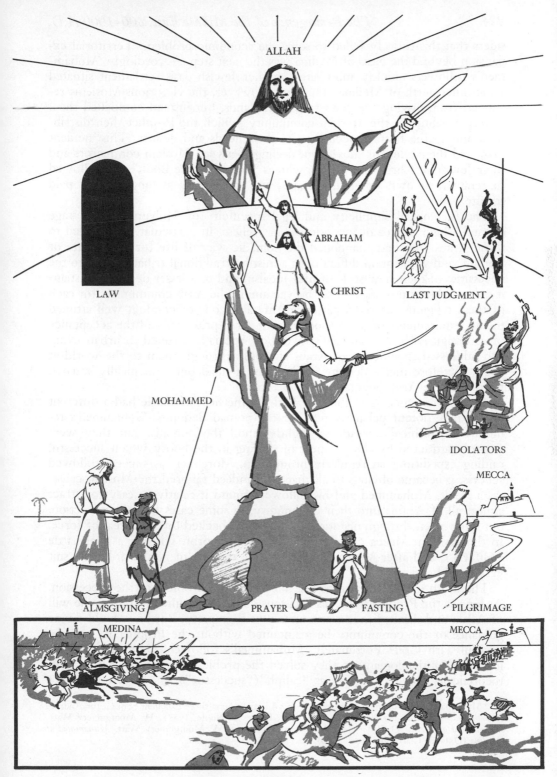

ALLAH

LAW

ABRAHAM

CHRIST

LAST JUDGMENT

MOHAMMED

IDOLATORS

MECCA

ALMSGIVING   PRAYER   FASTING   PILGRIMAGE

MEDINA   MECCA

ISLAM

siders that this entirely failed to solve the economic problem. Territorial expansion beyond the oasis of Medina was the next step. Accordingly, Mohammed's followers quickly subjugated another Jewish oasis settlement situated some miles north of Medina. This time, however, the victorious Moslems refrained from driving the Jews from their lands, but instead compelled them to pay a tribute to the Moslem community, which the Prophet then distributed among the faithful according to their needs and deserts. This incident provided the model for subsequent dealings between Moslem conquerors and their Jewish or Christian subjects, who as "People of the Book" were allowed to retain their own religion, customs, and institutions as long as they paid tribute.

The theological simplicity and legal specificity of Mohammed's message carried a high degree of intrinsic persuasiveness. In particular, it appealed to those Arabs who had abandoned the nomadic way of life for agriculture or trading, and who found difficulty in adjusting traditional tribal custom to the necessities of their new style of life. Judaism and to a lesser degree Christianity also had begun to move into this vacuum in the Arab community, for each of these religions offered a pattern of life and code of conduct well attuned to the requirements of settled society. But Arab pride resisted the acceptance of a foreign faith. Mohammed's revelation, specially attuned to urban living and addressed specifically to Arabs and only through them to the world at large, therefore met a definite need among a small but strategically situated portion of the Arab population.

The prompt success of the new faith on the field of battle had a different but equally potent persuasiveness for the nomad Bedouin. Mohammed's religious and ethical message sat lightly upon the nomads; but they were strongly attracted by the prospect of sharing in the booty which successful raiding expeditions so regularly brought in. Moreover, as success followed success, it became obvious to all that God indeed favored the Moslem cause. As a result, Mohammed and his followers found it relatively easy to attract almost all of Arabia into their community, in some cases by military action, but more often through negotiation, sometimes backed by the threat of force. In this fashion, Mecca came within the Moslem orbit without a final battle (630 A.D.); and after Mecca had capitulated, the rest of Arabia followed suit very quickly.[8]

The death of Mohammed in 632 A.D. raised the problem of the succession. As long as the Prophet lived, his decisions could be assumed to reflect the will of Allah; and disobedience was tantamount to impiety. But how could divine guidance of the community be maintained without the Prophet to link the faithful with God? Fortunately, Mohammed's followers were not yet philosophers or theologians, so they solved the problem practically, rather than theoretically, by recognizing as "caliph"("successor") one of Mohammed's

    [8] My remarks on Mohammed's career are based largely upon three excellent books: Tor Andrae, *Mohammed: The Man and His Faith* (New York: Barnes & Noble, 1957); W. Montgomery Watt, *Muhammad at Mecca* (Oxford: Clarendon Press, 1953); and W. Montgomery Watt, *Muhammad at Medina* (Oxford: Clarendon Press, 1956).

earliest converts and closest companions, Abu Bakr.[9] As caliph, Abu Bakr took over the practical leadership of the Moslem community. His general policy was in all things to adhere as closely as possible to the precedents Mohammed himself had established. This in turn required a careful husbanding of the Prophet's sayings, particularly those he had himself identified as stemming from revelation; for only through a careful weighing of such remembered utterances could the correct precedent for any particular new situation be discovered.

Many of the Arab tribes which had joined the Moslem community felt that Mohammed's death released them from the obligations they had contracted with him. To most of the nomad chiefs, their profession of faith in Allah and his Prophet Mohammed must have seemed merely an unimportant incident in the treaty negotiations. Yet backsliding, if unpunished, endangered the very existence of the Moslem community. Indeed, continued success in war was vital to the survival of what was only a precarious confederation of tribes, whose ancient quarrels were still much remembered. Only a steady inflow of

[9] Mohammed had no surviving sons. Hereditary claims to leadership of the Moslem community therefore rested upon descent from his daughter, Fatima, wife of Ali, a cousin of Mohammed and one of the Prophet's first prominent converts. Such claims became important only later, when familiarity with Persian and Byzantine ideas of hereditary rulership had penetrated the Moslem community. In pre-Islamic Arabia the hereditary principle was not regularly followed; tribal leadership was too important to be entrusted to a minor or an incompetent.

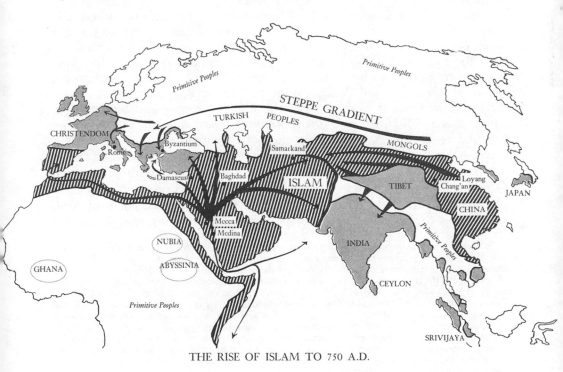

THE RISE OF ISLAM TO 750 A.D.

booty, together with the *élan* and discipline of regular campaigning in the field, could forestall renewal of intertribal feuds; for in Mohammed's last days the Islamic community had grown so rapidly that a mere handful of the faithful had as yet cultivated a really religious fervor or attained any deep religious conviction.

In this confusion, Mohammed's Medina followers threw their intense enthusiasm and conviction into the scales. This small but disciplined core sufficed once again to tip the balance decisively in favor of Islam. Two hard-fought campaigns brought the rebellious Arab tribes back to obedience; and just as Arabia was once again united, Abu Bakr died (634 A.D.).

His successor, Omar, was a man whose physical vigor, pious enthusiasm, and commanding spirit had already made him the leading figure of the Moslem community in the time of the mild and elderly Abu Bakr. Under his command the first great Moslem conquests beyond Arabia occurred. Raids had been launched toward Palestine and Syria while Mohammed was alive, but met with no notable success. Nevertheless, the precedent was clear; and when the peninsula had been united once more, Omar summoned restless elements from all Arabia to attack Byzantine and Sassanian unbelievers in the name of Allah. This time successes followed one upon another with incredible speed. Like ripe fruit, Syria (636), Iraq (637), Mesopotamia (641), Egypt (642), and Iran (651) fell to Moslem arms. Such unambiguous evidence convinced even the most skeptical Arab of Allah's greatness and power.

Long-standing disaffection against Byzantine and Persian tax gatherers in Iraq, Syria, and Egypt, and perennial restiveness against the respective religious orthodoxies of the two great imperial states, certainly smoothed the path for the first Moslem conquests. Yet this alone does not explain how Bedouin tribesmen, led by Arab townsmen, could overcome the professional armies of Byzantium and Persia. To be sure, financial stringency[10] and war-weariness prevailed in both empires, the result of a long and mutually exhausting war (606–30); and the Byzantines were simultaneously heavily engaged against the Avars on their northern frontier. Yet the fact remains that poorly equipped Arab forces, operating over very long distances and in no great numbers, defeated the best professional cataphract forces which Greeks and Persians could muster. Superior mobility and superior generalship played some part in the outcome; but surely the major determinant of Arab success was the discipline and courage inspired in the rank and file by the

---

[10] Internal tensions between aristocracy, commonalty, and monarch in Persia certainly were acute, as evidenced by the religious revolutionary movement of Mazdakism. A factor which may both have sharpened these antagonisms and seriously depleted the royal treasury was the decay of the silk trade after the end of the sixth century, when home-grown cocoons allowed the Byzantines to do without silk imported from China. The Persians had long been middlemen in this trade; and the cities of Sassanian Persia and the royal treasury had both drawn important revenues from it. Indeed, the unprecedented scale of Persian attack upon Rome in the long war of 606–30 may have been at least partly a desperate effort by the Persian king to seize as plunder wealth he could no longer gain by taxing caravans carrying silk to Syria. Without such a money income he may have been unable to maintain an adequate standing army to counterbalance the unruly feudality of Iran. The absence of Sassanian records makes any estimate of the position of the monarchy speculative; but some radical weakness seems necessary to account for the ease of Moslem conquest.

AN EARLY MOSQUE

The Dome of the Rock in Jerusalem stands on ground once occupied by Solomon's temple. Omar built a simple mosque of wood on the site immediately after his conquest of the city; but the basic lines of the existing building, photographed here, were constructed at the command of Caliph Abdul-Malik (685–705). Close affiliation with Byzantine ecclesiastical architecture is obvious, although the octagonal shape of the outer ground plan is unusual if not unique. The building has, however, been repeatedly restored. The decorative tile of the exterior was added as late as the sixteenth century, while the dome was rebuilt after a fire in the fifteenth century. Hence only the general plan of the Ummayad building survives.

certainty, confirmed with each victory, that Allah was indeed fighting on their side.[11]

Omar's life was cut short by an assassin in 644. The next caliph was Othman, a leader of the Ummayad family, which had long been prominent in Meccan affairs. He seems to have been selected as the weakest, and therefore perhaps the least dangerous, among the handful of councilors who gathered after Omar's death to decide who should succeed. In accordance with old Arab custom, Othman used his powers to advance the interests of his family, appointing kinsmen to the best posts in the new empire. But Othman, too, was assassinated in 656; and Ali, Mohammed's cousin and son-in-law, then attempted to make good his claim to the caliphate. Some five years of disorder ensued, for Ali's election was not everywhere accepted as legitimate. His main rival was the Ummayad governor of Syria, Muawiya, whose power depended on the loyalty of the Arab garrison of that province. Ali's main military support came from Iraq; but the Arabs of the two garrisons were reluctant to fight each other. The dispute therefore ended without having come to a head when one of Ali's disgruntled supporters assassinated him in 661.[12] Muawiya, as sole surviving claimant to the caliphate, then was able to establish the capital of the new Moslem empire at Damascus in Syria, from which city caliphs of the Ummayad dynasty ruled until 750 A.D.

Moslem military expansion continued until 715, although at a slower pace than in Omar's day. In time, Berber and Persian converts supplemented the Arab armies and helped to carry Moslem power to distant Spain in the West, and to no less distant Transoxiana and Sind in the East. Then followed a series of checks. In 715, Turkish intervention in the Oxus region compelled the Moslems to abandon the area for more than two decades. In 733 the Frankish leader Charles Martel defeated a Moslem raiding party near Tours; and Moslem power recoiled upon the Pyrenees. Far more significant than either of these relatively petty setbacks was the failure of the siege of Byzantium. The main Ummayad forces did indeed succeed in cutting the city off from its hinterland for an entire year, 717–18, and threatened to destroy the entire Byzantine state. Yet Byzantium survived, the siege had to be lifted, and the Moslems for the first time suffered really serious defeat.

Victorious wars, resulting in abundant booty and a flood of tribute from

---

[11] Information about the armaments, numbers, tactics, and other details of the first Arab campaigns is remarkably scarce. Cf. Reuben Levy, *The Social Structure of Islam* (Cambridge: Cambridge University Press, 1957), pp. 407–45; Friedrich W. Schwartzlose, *Die Waffen der alten Araber* (Leipzig: J. C. Hinrichs, 1886); *Encyclopedia of Islam*, s.v. "Yarmuk," "Nehawand," "Al-Kadisiya."

It is worth pointing out that daily prayers must have had much the same psychological effect upon an army on campaign as does modern close-order drill. Precise gestures and recitation of prayers conducted in unison five times daily must have inculcated sentiments of solidarity within the ranks and habits of obedience to the commander, who in the early days was also prayer leader. Such exercises no doubt did much to overcome the chronic weakness of any nomad confederacy—insubordination resulting from tribal and personal rivalries. The further conviction that death fighting in Allah's cause assured immediate access to Paradise gave an additional dash of recklessness to each warrior's charge.

[12] Later Moslem piety wove many legends around the figure of Ali and his son Husain, who was killed fighting the Ummayads in 680. In time, the principal sectarian division within Islam, that between Sunni and Shi'a, came to turn upon the question whether the caliphate rightly belonged to the heirs of Ali. Immediately after Ali's death, however, his adherents seem to have been very few.

conquered populations, had hitherto kept tribal and personal rivalries among the Arabs within relatively modest bounds; for those who lost out at the seat of power in Damascus could find ample scope for their ambition in the frontier provinces. But, when expansion stopped, the dynamic equilibrium which had held the Moslem community together ever since Mohammed's Medina days fell to the ground. Factional, tribal, and regional struggles, complicated and embittered by doctrinal and sectarian differences, broke out and flourished with quite unparalleled virulence. The upshot was the overthrow of the Ummayad dynasty and the establishment of the Abbasid caliphate in its place (750).

Two obvious rivalries exacerbated the disturbances that descended upon the Moslem world after 715. First was the jealousy between Syria and Iraq, each of which claimed first place in the state. Second was the friction between Arabs and converts to Islam recruited from other populations of the empire. More subtle and complex, but no less important, was the religious ferment that centered around the question of how the community of the faithful should be led and by what principles it should be governed. Brief comment upon each of these issues may perhaps bring out the main lines of Moslem political evolution under the Ummayads.

1) Omar it was who first established the rules according to which the victorious soldiers of Islam received their reward. Instead of assigning lands to individuals, as nearly all other conquerors of the Middle East had done, he paid his soldiers money wages and settled them in a number of special garrison cities. The most important of these garrisons were established on the edge of the desert, either at new foundations like Kufa in Iraq or Kairawan in north Africa, or on older sites, like Damascus in Syria and Basra in Iraq. This policy had obvious advantages: it conformed to precedent established by Mohammed in dividing booty and tribute among his followers; it kept the authority of the central power close and immediate over the troops, since wages could be cut off at will; and it kept the Moslem community together, an island of holiness in a sea of unbelievers.

The money Omar required to pay his soldiers came from tax income, collected at first according to the old Byzantine or Persian methods, and usually by the same personnel as before. Indeed, until almost the end of the seventh century, governmental administration remained exclusively in non-Arab hands; and even when the caliph Abdalmalik (685–705) made Arabic the official language of administration, most officials continued to belong to one or another of the subject nationalities, and often adhered to the Christian or Jewish faith. These facts implied that the old line of demarcation between Roman Syria and Persian Iraq survived the Moslem conquest. A strong sense of the difference between the two provinces among the population at large, fostered by the differences in their respective administrations, easily coalesced with long-standing rivalries among the different Arab tribes, which were now established in the garrison cities of the two areas. The result was to make Iraq chronically restless under the Syrian-centered administration of the Ummayads.[13]

2) Omar's policy of segregating the Arab conquerors in special garrison cities underlined the difference between Arab and non-Arab. Moreover, since the warriors of a particular tribe normally fought as a unit under their own chiefs and were usually stationed at one place when doing garrison duty, their concentration in a few centers helped to maintain the old tribal groupings. Indeed, the power structure of the Ummayad caliphate rested as much upon an informal confederation of Arab tribal chieftains who recognized the caliph as the first among equals as it did upon the bureaucracy of officials inherited from Byzantium and Persia. The Arabs' extraordinary successes certainly fed their pride, which tribal geneologies had long cultivated. As a result, the Ummayads made no systematic effort to convert the Christians, Jews, and Zoroastrians of the empire. Quite the contrary, when increasing numbers of the subject populations adhered to Islam, the Arabs found it an embarrassment. Such converts, of course, escaped the special tax levied on unbelievers; and this was harmful to the revenues upon which the Arab garrisons depended. Moreover, as long as the Arab tribal system provided the political framework for the Moslem community, converts from outside did not really fit. They could be admitted to the protection of a tribe and assigned the status of freedmen or "wanderers," but full rights could only come from birth. Yet Islam emphasized the equality of all true believers, since all men were the same in the eyes of God and had the same duties before him.

Here arose a strong tension between tribal and Islamic principles. Not unnaturally, converts sought in the name of the faith they had espoused to gain the full rights which Arab tribal custom denied them. As long as Ummayad power depended on the support of tribal chiefs, who commanded the garrison forces of the empire, the caliph could not satisfy the converts' demands. On the contrary, the government took steps to prevent the erosion of the state revenues by conversion and, as a last resort, even compelled Moslem converts to pay taxes. The result was to make the majority of converts eager to support revolutionary movements that offered them equality with Arab tribesmen in the name of a stricter adherence to the true principles of the Prophet.

3) Nor were Arab champions of a stricter, purer Islam wanting. A community under God, such as that which had existed in Medina during the Prophet's lifetime, was the ideal. But how to attain such a goal when Moslem power had spread so widely was not easy to decide. An obvious step was to treasure and study all authentic utterances of the Prophet. Accordingly, under Othman these were gathered into a definitive collection, the Koran. Mohammed's separate utterances were arranged according to length, thus obscuring the development of the Prophet's revelation and producing a text that reads in an oddly disjointed fashion.[14] In addition, the Prophet's acts and informal con-

[13] The fact that Ali had based himself in Iraq raised Iraqi visions of what might have been and made that area especially fertile ground for Alid sects.

[14] The Koran has been translated many times; but little of its literary power survives in English. From the standpoint of literary effectiveness, the best translation is that of A. J. Arberry, *The Holy Koran* (London: Allen & Unwin Ltd., 1953).

versation, if reported through a chain of reliable witnesses, and even the deeds and words of his intimate circle of companions, soon came to be considered as a valuable clue to godly behavior. This lore, carefully sifted for authenticity and interpreted to apply to all the varieties of circumstance that might confront a pious Moslem, became in time the basis for the *Sharia*, or Sacred Law of Islam.[15] Soon there developed a body of legal specialists, the *ulema*, centering at first mainly in Medina, who were prepared to declare what the law might be in specially difficult cases that were submitted to them by less expert Moslems.

The concern of the pious to make both their private lives and the life of the entire Moslem community a perfect image of God's will had important implications for the conduct of public affairs. Men resolved upon holiness could not neglect the old problem of succession to the Prophet; nor were they satisfied to settle on a basis of practical convenience, as the Moslem community had done when Abu Bakr and Omar held the office of caliph. A godly community required a godly head; and a mere tribal chief writ large like the Ummayad rulers failed all too clearly to fit such a prescription. One school of thought maintained that only the descendants of Mohammed's daughter, Fatima, wife of Ali, possessed the divine illumination required to lead the Moslem community; others held that Ali's descendants, whether by Fatima or by any of his other wives, could claim that dignity; still others argued that only the consensus of the Moslem community, fixing upon a man of the most perfect piety, could pick a legitimate leader; and many additional, sometimes downright anarchistic ideas also found vent in radically pious circles. Almost the only point upon which these groups agreed was that the Ummayad caliphate was a usurpation resting upon armed force and perpetuated by a hereditary principle which neither piety nor tribal custom supported.

Piety so subversive of the established government obviously had great appeal to all the discontented groups in the Ummayad state. Nor could the authorities suppress such criticism without outraging religious sentiment. Hence the Ummayads had to tolerate the agitation of religious dissidents, until in 744 a disputed succession to the throne touched off a decade of revolution and civil strife. The victor belonged to another important Meccan clan, the Abbasids;[16] and he assumed the title of caliph as arbitrarily as the first

[15] Not surprisingly, even ingenious interpretation of the Koran and the Traditions proved insufficient to give guidance in all cases. Hence Moslem jurists came to admit the consensus of the community of the faithful as a supplementary source of law, on the ground that Allah would not allow the entire community to err. In addition, legal analogy was admitted, in order to extend the range of matters that could be handled by the Sacred Law. These two supplementary principles introduced a measure of ambiguity and, therewith, flexibility, into the Moslem law that could not otherwise have been attained. Another important element of flexibility was provided by forging Traditions.

In these ways, a workable body of law, covering almost every possible contingency of life in the complex, urbanized society of the Moslem Middle East, was developed in the course of the first two centuries of Islam. Four orthodox schools of jurisprudence introduced minor variations; but this did not counteract the fact that, once a rule had found lodgment in the Sacred Law, there was no device for its repeal or modification. This proved in the long run a serious handicap to Moslem society, introducing far greater rigidity than Western legal systems have ever known.

[16] The Far West of the Moslem world, Spain, never recognized Abbasid political authority, although the scions of the Ummayad house who ruled there from 756 did not claim the title of caliph until the tenth century.

Ummayad had done. Nevertheless, the Abbasids were able to remove some of the sources of discontent which had fomented opposition to their predecessors.

First and most important, the Abbasids effectively destroyed the distinction between Arab and non-Arab Moslems. Arab tribesmen were deprived of their privileged position as a salaried soldiery by the fact of defeat in war. The main military support of the Abbasid caliphs came from Persian converts of eastern Iran, who vindicated their ancient reputation as warriors by outfighting the Arab garrisons of Iraq and Syria. Persian Moslems tended to regard the old Sassanian political patterns as a norm; and from the beginning, the Abbasid caliphs consciously modeled themselves in many respects upon Sassanian precedents. The Moslem capital was moved to Baghdad on the Tigris; and courtly pomp and ceremony, together with sedulous seclusion of the caliph's person from the outer world, replaced the manners of the shiek's tent, which had set the standard for Ummayad etiquette.

The effect was to bring all Moslems into the same subjection to an absolute sovereign. Already in the time of the later Ummayads, the segregation of Arabs into garrison cities had begun to break down; and many Arabs had stepped outside tribal relationships by acquiring property and becoming local landlords. This process of assimilation was accelerated under the Abbasids, so that the always small community of Arab conquerors was speedily absorbed into the variegated populations of the cities of the empire. Arab tribal loyalties rapidly evaporated under such circumstances, except in the deserts of Arabia itself, where the age-old Bedouin way of life continued nearly as before. In the more civilized portions of the Moslem world, tribal affiliation no longer had any political value; and the intertribal frictions which had always set limits to Ummayad power ceased to matter. The Abbasid government rested squarely upon the bureaucracy and upon a royal standing army, recruited at first primarily from among the warlike Iranian aristocracy. Arab privileges certainly suffered under the new regime; but the non-Arab Moslems had won essentially all they desired.

The initial Abbasid triumph had owed much to support from the partisans of Ali's descendants, or Shi'a.[17] Nonetheless, by strict Moslem standards, the Abbasid caliphate was no more legitimate than the Ummayad had been; and the second Abbasid caliph, al-Mansur (754–75), was obliged to put down a widespread Shi'a revolt. His successor, al-Mahdi (775–85), was then able to reach a fairly satisfactory modus vivendi with a majority of the pious radicals. In effect, al-Mahdi recognized the jurisdiction of the *ulema* over most aspects of ordinary life. Under these circumstances, the *ulema* accepted the flattering doctrine that leadership in the continuing effort to mold a human community after God's will rested upon themselves. Sitting in the market place as private yet authoritative persons, honored for their piety and learning by the rest of the community, it was they who expounded the Sacred Law and applied it to particular cases. They also became the leaders of public prayers and educators of the young. They, in short, were the true heirs

[17] The Abbasids were collaterally related to Ali and had made much of this fact in their propaganda.

THE ABBASID COMPROMISE

of the Prophet. By comparison, the role of the caliph in his palace, and of all his soldiers, tax gatherers, and officials, was trivial. The question of exactly which persons should administer the government and protect the community could therefore safely be left to considerations of practical convenience.

The Moslems who accepted this compromise came to be known as Sunnites and have constituted a majority of the Islamic community ever since. Yet they had undeniably abandoned a part of the aspiration after a perfectly godly community. Some refused the compromise and continued to aspire to a world in which the caliph and his servants would be as totally pleasing to God as in the glorious days of Medina. Such sectarians more and more put their hopes in one or another line of Ali's descendants and opposed the Abbasids on the same grounds their predecessors had used against the Ummayads.

Nevertheless, the balance of religious-political forces which established itself under the first Abbasids lasted for about a century. The freer mixing of peoples of differing origins provoked a flowering of Islamic culture, most notably around the caliph's court in Baghdad. A powerful economic upsurge accompanied a relatively high level of peace and order. Merchants and artisans ministered to the refined tastes of the wealthy at home and developed trade with most of the lands of Eurasia.[18] Moslem traders visited India and China and penetrated deep into the steppe and forest zones of the north. Christendom too entered the circle of Moslem trade, mainly through Jewish intermediaries, who were able to maintain connections on either side of the religious frontier.

* * *

The effort to remake human life according to the will of Allah, which had such important effects in politics, was equally significant in the cultural sphere. In its extremest form, radical piety entailed suspicion of any activity not directly serving the ends of religion. Truth and beauty resided in the Koran; any other respository, being merely human, distracted men from the pursuit of holiness. This implied the rejection of all cultural achievements antedating Mohammed, including the Hebrew and Christian scriptures, which in the Moslem view contained distorted versions of true revelation. Thus the scope of orthodox Moslem culture remained remarkably narrow: study of the Koran, of the Traditions about Mohammed and his friends, and of Arabic, the language of the Koran, became the sole legitimate intellectual pursuits.

Yet the past could not be erased so completely as piety required. The Arab conquerors continued to prize the highly stylized art of Arabic poetry, which descended from pagan times and centered around praises of noble deeds and lineages. By Abbasid times, the essentially aristocratic nomad ideal expressed in such poetry coalesced with the Persian courtly tradition to produce a secu-

[18] By the tenth century, a banking system, managed by Jews, permitted the transfer of funds by letter of credit over long distances; and the financial requirements of the caliphs were met by loans from the great bankers of Baghdad on the security of anticipated revenues from entire provinces. Cf. Walter Fischel, "The Origin of Banking in Medieval Islam," *Journal of the Royal Asiatic Society* (1933), pp. 339–52, 569–604.

lar, aristocratic, and genteelly warlike style of life that stood in basic opposition to the puritanical zeal of radical piety. Some knowledge of Greek philosophy and science also survived, though only marginally in restricted professional circles. Nevertheless, the Greek emphasis—whether pagan or Christian—upon logical argument and syllogistic reasoning constituted a standing challenge to a faith based solely upon the Koran and the Traditions. Finally, a generous measure of unorthodox piety and mysticism added to the discrepancies within Islamic culture.

In Ummayad times, pious Moslems, seized with the vision of a perfect society under God, had managed to insulate themselves from the other cultural traditions of the Middle East. A mere handful of learned men had determined the principles of the Sacred Law through oral discussion among themselves, mainly at Medina; and their pupils and followers elsewhere in the empire had simply proclaimed the ideal so defined, uncompromisingly and in total ignorance of all competing intellectual and moral systems. All this changed under the Abbasids. When the majority of the *ulema* came to terms with the regime and accepted major responsibility for directing daily life in the great world of the caliphate, they could no longer entirely disregard the Persian and Greek cultural inheritances. Yet radical piety made only limited concessions to its rivals. During the first century of Abbasid rule, the four great canonical systems of the Sacred Law, differing on minor points but all recognized as orthodox, were put into permanent written form. This codification of the Sacred Law gave rigidity to the pious program for human life at the very moment when Moslem men of learning were obliged for the first time to take seriously the logic and abstract argument of the Greeks and when the political compromise with the Abbasids made it no longer possible to denounce the members of the polished, Persianate courtly circle as traitors to Islam.

The pious did not relax their claims to the total man; but in practice, individuals who perversely preferred to follow either the gentlemanly or the philosophic-rationalistic ideal were assigned appropriate and restricted niches in society, where they were free to risk their immortal souls. The caliph's court and the high society which took its cues from the court became the main citadels of these discordant traditions. Elsewhere, except insofar as superstition and remnants of ancient beliefs survived on a subliterate level, Moslem piety and the Sacred Law prevailed.

Moslem gentlemen did not find it difficult to reconcile the pagan with the Islamic elements of their cultural ideal. Cultivation of the nuances and refinements of the Arabic tongue constituted the center of their education; but a good knowledge of the Koran and passable familiarity with the Sacred Law also ranked as appropriate genteel accomplishments. Such training differed only in emphasis from the pious ideal, for learned *ulema* too required a thorough knowledge of Arabic grammar and vocabulary in order to understand the Koran correctly. But the gentlemanly cultivation of an elegant literary style, including suitable references to odd bits of knowledge about history, geography, natural science, and, above all, to pagan Arabic poetry, encouraged a very different spirit from that prevailing among the *ulema*. The luxurious life available to landlords and courtiers likewise tended to seduce them from the pursuit of holiness, although asceticism, which Mohammed had explicitly repudiated, was not part of the Moslem ideal. In this respect, too, the clash between genteel and pious standards was therefore tangential rather than head-on.

The case was otherwise with the "philosophers," some of whom maintained a distinctly reserved attitude toward revealed religion and regarded Mohammed as at best a vulgarizer of the truth, who had dressed metaphysics in meretricious rags to win the support of the ignorant. The pious repaid such attitudes with a radical distrust of the philosophers' Reason, yet in practice admitted that such men might have their uses as astrologers and healers. In these capacities, even religiously suspect Moslems, not to mention Christians and Jews, found protection in the retinues of the great men of the empire, and from such vantage points added their speculation and studies to the general stream of Moslem culture.

Yet the disturbing impact of the Greek inheritance[19] could not be bottled up entirely in such an innocuous fashion. Like the early Christians, pious Moslems felt impelled to defend their faith through reasoning. Systematic theology thus found some scope in early Islam, although it never won the pre-eminence it enjoyed among Christian intellectual pursuits. Most Moslem believers preferred to rest doctrine directly upon the literal text of the Koran and the Traditions and distrusted any theological formulation that went beyond the letter of sacred texts and precedents.[20]

A seeming paradox lies in the fact that Islamic culture before 1000 A.D. was effectually isolated from its civilized neighbors despite constant and comparatively quite intimate contact across Moslem frontiers. Yet the paradox has an easy explanation. In the provinces, the *ulema* prevailed; and their emphasis upon the Sacred Law, the Koran, and Traditions of the Prophet could make no appeal to anyone who was not a Moslem, or ready to become one. By contrast, the world of cultivated literary gentlemen and of philosophers was largely restricted to courtly circles, first in Baghdad and, later, as the caliphate began to break up (after about 861), also at a number of local

---

[19] This inheritance was mediated through Christian theology and polemic against Islam, as well as directly through pagan philosophy. Cf. Louis Gardet and M. M. Anawati, *Introduction à la théologie musulmane, essai de théologie comparée* (Paris: Librairie Philosophique, 1948), pp. 37 ff.

[20] The key doctrinal issue in Abbasid times was whether or not the Koran was the uncreated word of God and thus an integral part of the divine essence, or whether it had originated in time and was therefore a creature of God, not part of his essence. Until the middle of the ninth century, the caliphs supported the latter view; but popular piety, expressed on occasion by street riots in Baghdad, won out; and the extreme position that the Koran was indeed an integral part of the divine essence thereafter became official.

In some measure, this doctrinal turning point represented a defeat for the more rationalistic theology of earlier days, which had been willing, for example, to explain away anthropomorphic passages in the Koran on the ground that God, being one, eternal, and transcendant, could in logic share no human traits. Gardet and Anawati, *Introduction à la théologie musulmane*, pp. 47–60.

courts whose rulers modeled their entourage on the caliphal example.[21] But before 1000 A.D., such limited, if brilliant circles scarcely affected the Moslem world at large, far less Christendom, Hindustan, or China. Instead, Islam presented to the outer world an uncompromising legal-theological system, of which no part could be taken without accepting the whole.

Despite these limitations, the polished elegance of Arab courtly poetry and rhymed prose, and the bulky scientific and philosophical treatises composed by the "philosophers" of the Moslem courts, command an honorable place in the history of mankind, the more so because nowhere else in the world of the ninth and tenth centuries A.D. was the spirit (and a great deal of the detailed knowledge as well) of Hellenic science and philosophy kept alive.

Unfortunately, Arabic literature, like the Koran itself, suffers drastically in translation. Pre-Islamic poetic conventions were very rigid; and Mohammed had not looked with favor upon the pagan poets. Hence the Moslem conquest failed to find the epic voice it deserved. Later, in the new luxury of the caliphal court, poetry returned to favor. The old pagan poetic conventions were modified; and graceful lyrics in praise of love and wine reflected the leisured, luxurious circle for which such poetry was composed. By the tenth century, this "new" style had in turn become highly elaborate; and loosely rhymed prose stories, essays, and eulogies tended to supplant poetry as the favorite medium for polite composition.[22]

Of Ummayad and Abbasid art little survives, for the major cities of that period have been continuously inhabited ever since and frequently destroyed and reconstructed. Nonetheless, it is clear that Byzantine and Sassanian styles continued to dominate the architecture and decoration of Moslem palaces, and even of mosques. Mosaics and frescoes which could easily be mistaken for Hellenistic work have been found in Ummayad residences in Syria and Iraq. The prohibition of representational art was in this early period no more than a pious program, not a governing principle, and it was only in the tenth century that human figures began to disappear from Moslem art. In general, the triumphs of a distinctive Moslem art style lay still in the future in 1000 A.D.[23]

Arab science and philosophy derived directly from the Greek, with some immixture of Indian ideas. Until near the end of the ninth century, the main

[21] The narrow dependence of secular literature, philosophy, and science upon courtly patronage goes far to explain the otherwise puzzling geographic distribution of Arab learning and belles-lettres. Both tended to cluster at the extremes of the Moslem world, in eastern Iran and in Spain, from the tenth century onward. These were the regions where independent courts and local patronage arose earliest and remained most stable.

[22] Cf. H. A. R. Gibb, *Arabic Literature, an Introduction* (London: Oxford University Press, 1926), pp. 14–81; R. A. Nicholson, *A Literary History of the Arabs* (Cambridge: Cambridge University Press, 1930). A remarkable pastiche of English translations, Eric Schroeder, *Muhammad's People* (Portland, Me.: Bond Wheelwright Co., 1955), gives a vivid idea of the character and variety of early Arabic literature and of Moslem society as well.

[23] Cf. George Marcais, *L'Art de l'Islam* (Paris: Larousse, 1946), pp. 19–60; M. S. Dimand, *A Handbook of Muhammedan Art* (2d ed.; New York: Metropolitan Museum of Art, 1944), pp. 7–25, 85–91, 132–35; Ernst Diez, *Die Kunst der islamischen Völker* (Berlin: Akademische Verlagsgesellschaft Athenaion, 1917), pp. 7–70.

task of Arab scholarship was the appropriation of the Hellenistic heritage. Official patronage greatly aided this effort. Caliph al-Mamun (813–33), for example, established a "House of Wisdom" at Baghdad, and organized the large-scale translation of Greek, Persian (Pahlavi), and Sanskrit writings into Arabic. This work continued until most of the extant treatises of Greek philosophy and science, as well as some important Sanskrit and Syriac texts, had been rendered into Arabic. New compositions were limited at first to commentaries upon authorities like Aristotle, Galen, or Ptolemy, and to encyclopedic compilation of scientific information.

By the close of the ninth century, however, savants began to produce original works very much in the ancient Hellenistic spirit. The fusion of Indian and perhaps Babylonian[24] with Hellenistic ideas stimulated fresh discoveries and the development of some important scientific devices, such as accurate balances, the astrolabe, and alembics. The mathematician al-Khwarizmi, in the early ninth century, became the first to use Indian (our "Arabic") numerals[25] to develop new forms of calculation. The doctor al-Razi (d. *ca.* 925), who wrote a vast medical encyclopedia and many smaller works, conducted chemical experiments which were remarkably free from the usual baggage of alchemical preconceptions. More surprising were the radical speculations of the polymath al-Farabi (d. 952), who explicitly rejected all forms of revealed religion and made the reconciliation of Platonic and Aristotelian philosophy his life work.

Geography and history were less suspect than science or philosophy in the eyes of pious Moslems; and by the tenth century both had reached a high level of sophistication. The principal geographer of the time was al-Masudi (d. 957), who drew upon extensive personal travels as well as the reports of others to write a descriptive geography of the world. The universal history of al-Tabari (d. 923) surveyed all the world from creation to 915 A.D. To the delight of modern scholars, religious piety required al-Tabari painstakingly to preserve conflicting traditions about early Moslem times.

Thus, a theoretically unresolved but pragmatically effective compromise between the orthodox *ulema* with their Sacred Law, the polished gentlemen with their elegant literature, and the philosophers with their rationalistic curiosity provided the framework for the first great flowering of Arabic culture under the Abbasids. Yet as the early aspiration after a life totally devoted to God faded into the humdrum application of a codified Sacred Law to the variety of daily affairs, it was natural that strenuous seekers after godliness should turn to other channels. Mohammed had quite explicitly rejected monasticism as a path to God, so early Islam lacked any convenient institutional

[24] A community of learned pagans survived into Moslem times at Harran in northern Mesopotamia and may have transmitted to Moslem science a mathematical tradition that descended from the ancient Babylonian learning. Cf. A. Mieli, *La Science arabe* (Leiden: E. J. Brill, 1938), pp. 84–85.

[25] These numerals were referred to as early as 662 by a Syriac Christian bishop; and a translation of the Sanskrit Siddhanta into Arabic made in the time of Caliph al-Mansur (754–75) brought the Hindu method of arithmetical notation to the attention of the Moslems a generation before al-Khwarizmi put the numerals to new uses. Cf. George Sarton, *Introduction to the History of Science*, I (Washington: Carnegie Institute of Washington, 1927), 493–530.

niche for religious athletes who refused to live by the Law alone. On the other hand, the ascetic ideal cultivated by Christian and Buddhist monks remained a living force in the Middle East long after the Moslem conquest; and parallel movements soon began to assert themselves within Islam. Organizational forms developed only slowly; but individual mystics appeared even in Ummayad times. Mystics became more prominent under the Abbasids and began to introduce a new theme into Moslem piety—a personal and immediate sense of God's love. In the Koran, Allah appeared as splendid, awesome, great, but only incidentally as an object of man's love or as a lover of mankind. As a result, the early Moslem mystics hovered on the edge of heresy, claiming, on the basis of their mystic experiences, a familiarity with Allah that went far beyond anything authorized by the pages of the Koran.

Nevertheless, mystical religious practices—or Sufism, as they came to be called in Islam—corresponded to deep psychological needs and gained power in proportion to the encapsulation of orthodoxy in a closed system of law and learning. Individual mystics acquired bands of disciples and popular reputations as "saints" who walked familiarly with God. Some of them were venerated after their deaths, so that saints' tombs gradually became as important in Islam as they had long been in Christianity.[26] Not until the twelfth century A.D. was the tension between Moslem orthodoxy and Sufism diminished by the elaboration of a theology that found room for the private, mystic approach to God as a supplement to the ordinary path offered by the Koran, the Traditions, and the Sacred Law.

The suspect orthodoxy of early mysticism meant that Sufi teachers associated closely with the heterodox sects of Islam. Despite a marked fissiparous tendency, these sects achieved a fairly coherent organization in the second half of the eighth century. Enthusiasts and malcontents who rejected the Abbasid compromise developed the idea that in each generation a supernatural authority descended upon some particular member of Ali's house. The holder of this authority—the "imam"—was the sole rightful head of the Moslem community. Disagreement developed over who in fact was the real imam; and the various Shi'a sects which took form after 765 were distinguished from one another by their recognition of different claimants to that dignity.

One extreme Shi'a group, the Isma'ilis, permitted allegorical interpretation of the Koran and thereby opened wide the gates to all sorts of departures from orthodoxy. The Isma'ili movement went underground and developed a graded system of initiation into the secrets of the faith. The higher circles of the sect recognized both Christianity and Judaism as valid revelations of divine truth; and the innermost circle seems to have taught the imperfections of every revealed religion. Isma'ili missionaries became remarkably active in all parts of the Moslem world. They throve on social and ethnic discontents and soon became a serious threat to the established order. By the late ninth century, several Isma'ili leaders rose to power in outlying regions of the empire; and

---

[26] On Sufism, cf. A. J. Arberry, *Sufism: An Account of the Mystics of Islam* (London: Allen & Unwin, Ltd., 1950).

chronic Isma'ili revolts, centering apparently among urban craftsmen, affected Mesopotamia and Syria as well.[27] The Fatimids of north Africa (909–72) and Egypt (968–1171) were the most successful of the Isma'ili sectaries and were the first to break the theoretical political-religious unity of Islam by defying the authority of the caliph in Baghdad and claiming his title for themselves in 909 A.D.[28]

The other major group of Shi'a recognized a different descent from Ali as the line of the true imams and kept far closer to orthodox doctrine. Nor did they ever take up arms in active revolt. When the last of their imams died in 873 without an heir, these "Twelvers"[29] confined themselves to bewailing the corruption of the times, which did not allow a legitimate head of the Moslem community to remain upon earth.[30]

These sectarian movements certainly weakened the position of the Abbasid caliphs. In addition, after the middle of the eighth century, strong-armed rebels in outlying districts began to set up what were in fact, though not in theory, independent governments. The Syrian-Iraqi heartland of the empire remained (somewhat precariously) subject to Baghdad until 945 A.D.; but Baghdad itself was controlled by Turkish slave-soldiers, who from the time of the caliph Mutasim (833–42) became the principal pillar of caliphal authority. Such a government could neither force sectarians to orthodoxy nor rebels to submission. In the end, the decay of the central government permitted first Persian (945) and then Turkish (1055) adventurers to seize authority at Baghdad, while dozens of other states, divided by both religious and ethnic antipathies, disputed the imperial Abbasid inheritance.

But political disintegration did not interrupt the development of Islamic culture. Rather, the establishment of a multiplicity of courtly centers increased the patronage available to men of letters and learning, while the decentralization of scholarship, and the loss of its privileged seclusion within the caliph's palaces, helped to provoke an effort to bring philosophy, science, and letters into closer harmony with theology, law, and mysticism. Simultaneously, the infusion of Turkish tribesmen from the northern steppe gave Islam a new military energy, which soon became manifest along the frontiers dividing the

---

[27] The rapid spread of a distinctive type of craft guild, which on occasion became politically important in the Moslem world from the tenth century onward, may perhaps be taken as an outward indication of the spread of these Shi'a movements. Cf. Bernard Lewis, "The Islamic Guilds," *Economic History Review*, VIII (1937), 22–26. The obscure history of Sassanian religious revolutionary movements—Manichaeism and Mazdakism—must be borne in mind as background for the rise of these Islamic sects.

[28] The Fatimid family claimed descent from Fatima, Mohammed's daughter and Ali's wife, and on the strength of their putative ancestors claimed to be imams of the true faith. At the time of their rise to power in north Africa, the whole Isma'ili sect recognized Fatimid leadership. Later, when the responsibilities of power led to compromises in defiance of the more antinomian aspects of Isma'ili teaching, purists broke away. For Isma'ilism in general, cf. Bernard Lewis, *The Origins of Isma'ilism* (Cambridge: W. Heffer & Sons, 1940).

[29] So called because they recognized twelve imams after Ali.

[30] Ritual mourning for Ali's son Husain, who had died in 680 revolting against the Ummayad regime, became central to Twelver piety. Details closely resembled much older forms of Middle Eastern religion, which had mourned a dying and rising god of vegetation.

Moslem world from Christendom and Hindustan. Thus in both the cultural-religious and the military-political sense, Islam entered upon a new phase of its development about the year 1000 A.D.[31]

C. CHRISTENDOM

During the first six centuries of its existence, Christianity had spread outward in roughly concentric fashion from its cradle-land in Palestine. Expansion westward into Europe and north Africa paralleled a somewhat less massive expansion eastward into Mesopotamia, Armenia, and the Caucasus, and southward into Nubia and Abyssinia. The rise of Islam, followed in due course by widespread conversions from Christianity to Mohammedanism, entirely altered this geographical distribution and threatened to confine Christianity to scattered refuge areas on the periphery of the Moslem world. Christianity did indeed retreat from its oldest centers; for only on the extreme flanks of the Levant—in the highlands of Abyssinia and of the Caucasus—did homogeneously Christian societies long survive the Moslem conquest.[32]

Had Constantinople fallen to Moslem arms, as it twice seemed on the verge of doing,[33] European Christendom might have suffered a similarly drastic dispersal. Driven from the Mediterranean, homogeneously Christian societies could have survived only in the remote forests and scattered fields of northwestern Europe. In fact, however, the walls of Constantine's capital on the

[31] In addition to books cited separately, I have consulted the following authorities on the early history of Islam: H. A. R. Gibb, *Mohammedanism: An Historical Survey* (New York: Mentor Books, 1953); H. A. R. Gibb, *The Arab Conquests in Central Asia* (London: Royal Asiatic Society, 1923); Bernard Lewis, *The Arabs in History* (2d ed.; London: Hutchinson, 1954); Alfred Guillaume, *Islam* (Harmondsworth: Penguin Books, 1954); Ignac Goldziher, *Vorlesungen über den Islam* (2d ed.; Heidelberg: Carl Winter, 1925); Gustave E. von Grunebaum, *Medieval Islam: A Study in Cultural Orientation* (2d ed.; Chicago: University of Chicago Press, 1953); G. von Grunebaum (ed.), *Unity and Variety in Muslim Civilization* (Chicago: University of Chicago Press, 1955); G. von Grunebaum, *Islam: Essays in the Nature and Growth of a Cultural Tradition* ("American Anthropological Association Memoirs," No. 81 [April, 1955]); Carl Brockelmann, *History of the Islamic Peoples* (New York: G. P. Putnam's Sons, 1947); Edward G. Browne, *A Literary History of Persia* (Cambridge: Cambridge University Press, 1956); T. W. Arnold, *The Preaching of Islam* (2d ed.; London: Constable & Co., 1913); T. W. Arnold, *The Califate* (Oxford: Oxford University Press, 1924); Berthold Spuler, *Iran in früh-Islamischer Zeit* (Wiesbaden: Franz Steiner Verlag, 1952); A. J. Wensinck, *The Muslim Creed* (Cambridge: Cambridge University Press, 1932); Maurice Gaudefroy-Demombynes, *Muslim Institutions* (London: Allen & Unwin, Ltd., 1950); M. Gaudefroy-Demombynes, *Le Monde musulman et byzantin jusqu'aux Croisades* (Paris: E. de Boccard, 1931); Louis Gardet, *La Cité musulmane, vie sociale et politique* (Paris: J. Vrin, 1954). The principal debt I owe, however, is to an as yet unpublished "Manual of Islamic Civilization," prepared by Marshall G. S. Hodgson for a course, "Introduction to Islamic Civilization," at the University of Chicago.

[32] To be sure, Christians continued to exist in significant numbers within Islam's dominion; yet in Abbasid times they became a minority, often restricted to special occupations and subject to a variety of social disabilities. Although the commercial and intellectual prominence of the Christian minorities was often disproportionate to their numbers, such submerged fragments of Christendom survived not as integral societies, but as mere sects within the Islamic body social.

[33] Between 673 and 680, the caliph's fleet blockaded Constantinople from a base inside the Sea of Marmora itself. Only the use of "Greek fire" (a highly combustible compound whose exact chemical composition is uncertain today, and which perhaps was then newly invented) compelled the Moslem fleet to withdraw. As we have already seen, in 717–18 the Moslems again blockaded Constantinople, this time both by land and by sea. The city was saved only after internal convulsions brought a capable general, Leo III, to the imperial throne.

Bosphorus held. Consequently, European Christendom survived as a geographically and culturally significant rival to Islam.

Nevertheless, the Moslem assault provoked radical readjustments. Until the critical turning point in 717–18, the Byzantines fought a life-and-death struggle against the Ummayad caliphs for control of the sea. Three increasingly massive Moslem attempts to win sovereignty of the Mediterranean failed; thereafter, with the transfer of the Moslem capital to Baghdad, the Abbasid caliphs renounced further maritime efforts. In the meantime, however, Moslems had broken into the western Mediterranean, driven the Byzantines from their last stronghold in north Africa (698), and conquered most of Spain and part of Narbonese Gaul (by 717).

While Christendom thus with difficulty and incomplete success staved off the Moslems, another wave of nomad migration threatened on the north. The formation of the Turkish confederacy in Mongolia and the Altaic-Ural region between 552 and 565 pushed a great horde of refugees, known to European history as Avars, into southern Russia, where they joined forces with earlier inhabitants of the region. In 567 the Avars invaded the plain of Hungary, annihilated one Germanic tribe—the Gepids—and forced another—the Lombards—to flee southward. In the following century, Avar horsemen spread havoc deep into the Balkans and repeatedly appeared under the walls of Constantinople itself. These raids provoked two lasting ethnic changes: the occupation of Italy by the Lombards (568), who in turn drove the Byzantines from the interior of that peninsula; and the retreat of the Latin- and Greek-speaking peasantries of the Balkan peninsula to refuge areas in the mountains or along the coasts. Slavs took their places, supporting themselves by a primitive migratory type of agriculture not technically much different from the style of life the Dorians had brought to Greece some 1500 years before.[34]

Internal quarrels, fomented by Chinese diplomacy, led to the breakup of the great Turkish confederacy shortly after 630. But some of its western-

---

[34] How completely the Slavs displaced (or replaced) the earlier Balkan populations has been a matter of learned dispute ever since. J. P. Fallmerayer, *Geschichte der Halbinsel Morea während des Mittelalters* (Stuttgart: J. G. Cotta, 1830), argued that there had been a complete slavicization of the peninsula. Cf. summary of the arguments pro and con in A. A. Vasiliev, *History of the Byzantine Empire* (new ed.; Madison, Wis.: University of Wisconsin Press, 1958), I, 176–79.

Generally, it seems true that whenever Slavic settlement penetrated zones of Mediterranean climate, Hellenization (or along the Adriatic coast, Latinization) speedily set in. This was probably due to the fact that the distinctive social unit of the primitive Slavs, the *zadruga*, was ill-adapted to carry on even a semi-commercial style of agriculture such as prevailed in the wine-olive regions of the Balkan peninsula. The *zadruga* involved sharing losses and gains among its members, *i.e.*, among several small families, usually united by descent from some common ancestor. This sort of social unit probably brought real advantages when it came to subsistence farming, under conditions of near anarchy, when life and limb were in constant peril. In such a time, a single family farming enterprise, which Roman law had made customary among the older Balkan populations, might easily be wiped out by the loss of a single adult male; whereas a similar loss to a family belonging to a *zadruga* would involve no comparable disaster, since the other *zadruga* members would support and protect widow and children as a matter of course.

On the *zadruga*, cf. Philip E. Mosley, "The Peasant Family: The Zadruga, or Communal Joint Family in the Balkans, and Its Recent Evolution," in Caroline F. Ware (ed.), *The Cultural Approach to History* (New York: Columbia University Press, 1940), pp. 95–108.

most components promptly established lesser, though nonetheless formidable political structures in the region between the Caucasus and the lower Volga. The Bulgar and the Khazar confederacies—both of them dominated by Turkish-speaking tribes, though doubtless including other linguistic groups—were the most important of these states. Sometime in the mid-seventh century, the Khazars apparently defeated the Bulgars, forcing some of them to submit to Khazar overlordship and others to flee westward to the lower Danube region, where they appeared in 679. For about a century thereafter, the western steppe enjoyed comparative stability.[35]

Byzantine diplomacy did what it could to use the Khazars as a counterweight to both Bulgars and Moslems. The emperors fostered trade relations with the Khazars and did not disdain marriage alliances with Khazar princesses. Nevertheless, the Byzantines were unable to prevent the western Bulgars from building a powerful state in their new home on the plain of the lower Danube. In time, the Bulgars intermarried with the Slavs they had subdued and adopted Slavic speech. The effect was to give the dispersed Slavic tribes of the eastern and central Balkans a centralized political-military structure such as they had not previously known. The relatively abundant military manpower thus folded into the Bulgar state made it Byzantium's most formidable rival in the ninth and tenth centuries.

Meanwhile, a comparable, if less drastic movement of peoples took place in western Europe. The Frankish kingdom that Clovis (d. 511) had founded continued to be ruled by his descendants until 751; but in fact after 638 the kings of the ruling Merovingian house were all nonentities. The kingdom was divided between the two branches of the royal family; but real power rested in the hands of a tumultuous local nobility. The principal political plum was the office of mayor of the palace; for the mayors wielded whatever royal rights the nobles had not already usurped. In 687 Pepin of Heristal made good his claim to serve as mayor of the palace to both branches of the royal house and thereby effectively reunited the Frankish state. More than that, he confiscated the estates of his opponents, who resided principally in the former Roman province of Gaul and awarded them to his own personal followers fresh from the German Rhinelands. This amounted to a second wave of German invasion; for the earlier Frankish lords of Gaul had by this time become at least partially Latinized.[36]

---

[35] The Khazars were heavily engaged against the Moslems; and for a brief moment their khan was even compelled to profess Islam (737) after suffering a severe defeat. The disturbances incident to the Abbasid revolution (744–51) meant a relaxation of Moslem pressure; and it appears to have been at this time that the ruling circles among the Khazars espoused Judaism, thereby asserting their spiritual independence vis-à-vis both the Moslem and Christian worlds.

My remarks upon the history of the western steppe in this period are based on René Grousset, *L'Empire des steppes* (Paris: Payot, 1939), pp. 124–42, 226–38; D. M. Dunlop, *The History of the Jewish Khazars* (Princeton, N.J.: Princeton University Press, 1954), pp. 41–170.

[36] In 732 Charles Martel, Pepin's son and successor, found it convenient to extend his father's confiscations to the Church lands in Gaul; but in piety he allowed the prelates to retain nominal ownership and merely required the bishops and abbots to assign the income from such lands to suitably stout fighting men. The men enriched by such benefices were supposed to come at Charles's summons

While the Franks were attempting with only indifferent success to maintain Roman administrative and cultural traditions in Gaul and simultaneously to develop the purely Germanic society of the Rhinelands toward civilization, a remarkable work of conversion and acculturation was carried through in the British Isles. The Celtic Christian culture of Ireland reached its apogee in the sixth and seventh centuries. Successful Irish missionary enterprise in Scotland and northern England was extended to the continent by St. Columban (d. 615), who established three famous and influential monasteries at Luxeuil in Burgundy, St. Gall south of Lake Constance, and Bobbio in Italy. A second missionary thrust reached the British Isles from Rome in 597, when Pope Gregory the Great dispatched St. Augustine to Kent. The result was that two somewhat divergent forms of Christianity, one stemming from Rome, the other from Ireland, contended for primacy in Britain. At the Synod of Whitby in 664, the English Church decided in favor of the Roman version of the faith. Thereafter, the Anglo-Saxon kingdoms of England, especially Northumbria, where the Irish imprint had been strongest, rapidly assimilated the cultural traditions of Latin Christendom.[37] By the eighth century, Anglo-Saxon learning and piety far surpassed that of Gaul.

* * *

After 750, Christendom enjoyed a respite from foreign attack and invasion. In the East, the Byzantines used their sea power to cut off Moslem Syria and Egypt from commercial contact with the rest of the Mediterranean. In consequence, trade routes shifted northward. Byzantium's Crimean ports became important centers for trade running north along the rivers into the Russian forests and east across the open steppes to the Volga or beyond. Trebizond, on the southern shore of the Black Sea, became the authorized port of entry for goods originating in or coming through Baghdad from ports of the Persian Gulf. The Abbasid caliphs were not averse to such readjustments; for the new Byzantine trade regulations had the effect of enhancing the importance and prosperity of Iraq, while reducing that of the old Ummayad strongholds in Syria and Egypt.[38]

---

equipped as heavy armored cavalry. In this fashion, a substantial force of cataphracts, or to give them their familiar European name, knights, was for the first time created on Frankish soil.

The technical advance over earlier German foot soldiery was enormous. Mounted troops enjoyed superior mobility both on the battlefield and in getting to it. This had been the case since men first began riding horseback. More significant was the new shock power which came with the use of stirrups and of tactics based on charging the foe with lance fixed. This put the full weight of man and horse behind the lance head; and nothing but a similarly equipped cavalryman, charging in the opposite direction, could hope to stand against such force. The drawback was that long training and extremely expensive equipment were required before such tactics could be effective. Hence Charles Martel's confiscations. Cf. Lynn White, *Medieval Technology and Social Change* (Oxford: Clarendon Press, 1962), 1–38, which effectively sums up and supersedes earlier discussion.

[37] Theodore of Tarsus, Archbishop of Canterbury 669–90, was largely responsible for bringing the English Church fully into the Roman fold. His career, starting from St. Paul's birthplace in Asia Minor and moving thence first to Rome and then to Canterbury, illustrates the real unity of Christendom in this age, despite its political fragmentation.

[38] Archibald Lewis, *Naval Power and Trade in the Mediterranean 500–1100*, pp. 89–131, argues that it was Byzantine economic warfare, initiated in 693, but made effective only after 718, when Byzantine

In western Christendom, Pepin of Heristal's victory over his rivals led in due course to the establishment of the Carolingian empire. His grandson, Pepin the Short, first made official the power he and his predecessors had wielded by assuming the title of king in 751. His son and successor, Charlemagne (768–814), carried Frankish arms to the farthest limits they ever attained. In Charlemagne's day, the Frankish army, composed of peasant footsoldiers stiffened by a professional cavalry force, went on campaign nearly every year. It subdued the Saxons in northwest Germany, pushed across the Elbe into Slavic territory, and even destroyed the Avar encampment in Hungary. To the south, the Franks annexed the Lombard kingdom in Italy and pushed the Moslems back beyond the Pyrenees. These military successes led Charlemagne to challenge the imperial prerogatives of Constantinople directly by allowing the Pope at Rome to crown him "Emperor of the Romans" on Christmas Day, 800 A.D.

Charlemagne and his predecessors brought all the Germanic peoples of Europe (except Scandinavia) within the circle of Christendom. Frankish swords converted the stubborn Saxons; and the peaceable missionary efforts of men like St. Willibrord (d. 738) and St. Boniface (d. 754) brought Christian worship and an organized Christian church to such peoples as the Frisians, Bavarians, and Thuringians. The Frankish rulers generously supported these enterprises, permitting, for example, the consignment of broad lands for the support of newly founded monasteries and bishoprics. The Christian faith, therefore, together with increasing social differentiation, tended by degrees to assimilate the Germanic tribes to the Latinate society of more southerly lands.[39]

Thus we see how Christendom's relative security from foreign attack during the latter half of the eighth century enabled both Byzantines and Franks to push considerably deeper into continental Europe. Byzantine penetration proceeded mainly by means of trade, the Frankish through military conquest and religious conversion; but in both East and West, the geographic base and social weight of Christendom were significantly enlarged.

Yet, from the viewpoint of Christendom as a whole, this achievement was

---

fleets again could patrol the seas, that cut Frankland off from its economic ties with the Levant. These ties had been maintained through Merovingian times on the basis of an exchange of slaves and forest products for Eastern manufactures. Byzantium had slaves and forest products at hand north of the Black Sea and needed nothing from Gaul: hence Byzantine sea power proved damaging to the Frankish as well as to the Syrian economy. Moreover, political rivalry between Franks and Byzantines in Italy gave no incentive to Byzantine authorities to encourage trade that would tend to strengthen the Carolingian state by offering the Frankish upstarts a supplementary source of revenue.

Thus Lewis turns Pirenne's famous thesis upside down, putting responsibility for the decay of trade between Syria and Frankland not on the Arab conquests, as Pirenne did, but on Byzantine mercantilistic policy. Cf. Henri Pirenne, *Mohamet et Charlemagne* (7th ed.; Paris: Félix Alcan, 1937); Robert S. Lopez, "East and West in the Early Middle Ages: Economic Relations," *Relazioni del X Congresso Internationale di Scienzi Storiche*, III (Florence: G. C. Senisoni, 1956), 113–63; Bryce Lyon, "L'Œuvre de Henri Pirenne après vingt-cinq ans," *Le Moyen Age* (1960), 437–93.

[39] Christianity forwarded the process of social differentiation within Germanic society: for Christian doctrine both exalted the powers and sacrosanctity of the king and, by virtue of the very principle of hierarchical ecclesiastical organization, introduced a new, non-tribal, and authoritarian concept of social organization into the backwoods.

counterbalanced by the outbreak of acute friction between the Latin and Greek halves of the Christian world. The Byzantine emperor, Leo III the Isaurian (717–41), precipitated the controversy in 726 by banning the images of Christ, the Virgin, and the saints from Christian churches. Such interference with widespread custom provoked resistance at home, especially from monastic circles; it also alienated the papacy and all of Latin Christendom. Nevertheless, the Byzantine government maintained the prohibition until 787, when a Church council restored the use of images; then in 815 the emperors again embraced iconoclasm, until the dispute finally ended with a second reversal of imperial policy in 843.[40]

The iconoclastic controversy brought into the open a fundamental shift in papal relations with Byzantium. After the fall of the imperial Roman government in the West, the popes had frequently found themselves in need of military or diplomatic support from Constantinople against Arian Ostrogoths and barbarous Lombards. This had drastically limited papal independence. By the eighth century, however, the presence of a revivified Frankish monarchy north of the Alps enabled the popes to maneuver between the two great states of Christendom. Pope Stephen II took spectacular advantage of this situation in 754 by journeying to the court of Pepin the Short and consecrating him King of the Franks—thus sanctifying the title Pepin had usurped three years earlier. Pepin returned the favor by invading Italy, defeating the Pope's Lombard enemies, and presenting the papacy with title to a stretch of territory extending across Italy from Ravenna to Campania. When this alliance between the Frankish monarchy and the papacy culminated in Pope Leo's coronation of Charlemagne as Roman Emperor (800), there was nothing the affronted Byzantines could do.[41]

*   *   *

Soon after Charlemagne's death, however, the widening rift between Eastern and Western Christendom was dwarfed by massive new attacks upon both parts of the Christian world. First of all, Christendom's southern flank suddenly became vulnerable when the Byzantines lost control of the narrow seas to new-sprung Moslem states of north Africa. This was demonstrated in 827, when Moslem freebooters conquered Crete, while others invaded Byzantine Sicily. A generation later, Rus warrior-traders descended the Russian

---

[40] Just what forces lay behind iconoclasm are unclear. Leo III was a soldier, native to eastern Asia Minor, and came to power in the crisis of the great Ummayad siege of Constantinople (717–18). His iconoclasm may have been inspired by personal religious conviction or by a desire to forestall Moslem criticism of Christian "idolatry"; he may have sought to conciliate puritanical feelings endemic in eastern Asia Minor, whence were recruited the most valuable fighting men of the Byzantine army; he may also have wished to strip the monasteries of some of their power and wealth. There certainly was significant popular support for the imperial policy, especially in the army; but evidences have been so thoroughly doctored by the victorious iconodules that reconstruction of the motives and arguments on the iconoclastic side is next to impossible. Cf. A. A. Vasiliev, *History of the Byzantine Empire*, I, 251–58, 263–64; P. J. Alexander, *The Patriarch Nicephorus of Constantinople: Ecclesiastical Policy and Image Worship in the Byzantine Empire* (Oxford: Clarendon Press, 1958), 111–25, 214–25.

[41] In 812, in return for the cession of a considerable territory along the northeast Adriatic coast, the Eastern emperor recognized and thereby legitimated Charlemagne's title.

rivers to challenge Byzantine maritime supremacy in the Black Sea and in 860 actually attacked Constantinople itself. The weakened Byzantine fleet could neither cope effectively with the Rus, nor prevent Moslem pirates and adventurers from raiding the entire Mediterranean coast.[42]

Moslem enterprise thus rendered Byzantine trade restrictions ineffective and stimulated a rapid development of the prosperity of the entire north African coast. Commerce across the Sahara brought gold and slaves to the Mediterranean littoral and stimulated the rise of the first important Negro states of the sub-Saharan regions. Moslem Spain, too, entered upon its golden age only after Byzantine domination of the Mediterranean had thus been broken.

The fact that from the early ninth century both the Byzantine and Frankish states were heavily engaged on their landward flanks helps to explain these Moslem successes on the sea. The relaxation of Ummayad pressure upon the Khazars after 744 allowed that confederacy to expand in all directions. Khazar war bands raided south of the Caucasus, brought a broad, if undefinable stretch of territory in southern Russia under their domination—and set off another wave of nomad migration westward. Probably in 893, the Khazars with the help of allies from Siberia defeated the Pechenegs, who had been occupying territory between the Volga and the Ural rivers; the Pechenegs fled westward and fell upon the Magyars, a mixed Finno-Ugrian-Turkish tribal confederation, which as a subject-ally of the Khazars was then probably in possession of the mid-portion of the Russian steppe. The Magyars in turn fled westward and in 895 reached the farthest extremity of the European steppe—the plain of Hungary. The Pechenegs did not follow them but remained in the region between the lower Danube and the Dnieper.[43] Both these new neighbors of Christendom proceeded to raid and plunder far and wide, though on occasion the Byzantines were able to use the wild Pechenegs against the now semi-civilized Bulgarians, who took advantage of the precarious condition of Byzantine military power to renew their attacks on Constantinople (913–24).

While the Khazars were thus driving flotsam and jetsam across the steppe to the distress of an ill-defended Christendom, a second powerful center of

[42] In 904, the second city of the Byzantine empire, Salonika, was seized and sacked by Moslem sea raiders. Only the capture of Constantinople itself could have offered a more dramatic demonstration of the erosion of Byzantine sea power.

A. Lewis, *Naval Power and Trade in the Mediterranean*, pp. 120–31, has advanced interesting opinions upon the reasons for this decay of the Byzantine fleet. He attributes it fundamentally to the restrictive trade policy which the empire had adopted in the early eighth century; a policy which Lewis thinks damped down Greek maritime enterprise, as well as freezing out Syrian and Egyptian commerce. As the Greek merchant marine decayed, yielding place to the semi-piratical enterprise of North African and Italian "poachers" who could not be adequately controlled from Constantinople, the material and manpower base of Byzantine naval power shrank, until the slow shift of commercial sea power was dramatically demonstrated by an abrupt alteration of the naval balance in the Mediterranean in the year 827. This interesting thesis may be both suspiciously consonant with modern liberal trade principles and true.

[43] Geographical details are quite unclear. But cf. D. M. Dunlop, *History of the Jewish Khazars*, pp. 196–204; C. A. Macartney, *The Magyars in the Ninth Century* (Cambridge: Cambridge University Press, 1930); George Vernadsky and Michael de Ferdinandy, *Studien zur ungarischen Frühgeschichte* (Munich: Verlag R. Oldenbourg, 1957).

disturbance developed in Scandinavia. Beginning in the late eighth century, but reaching full force only in the ninth and tenth, Viking ships' crews spewed from the Scandinavian fjords, spreading fire and rapine across all of western Christendom. The shallow draught of their ships permitted the Vikings to sail far up the rivers of the north European plain, so that even inland regions became vulnerable to their depredations. Eastward, the Russian rivers offered even more extensive possibilities; and Scandinavian river pirates soon established political control over the Russian waterways.[44] The expanding power of the Rus, as these Scandinavians came to be called, soon collided with the Khazars in the southeast. In the end it was the Rus who prevailed. About a century after establishing a supreme military and commercial command post on the middle Dnieper (862), they were able to seize and plunder the Khazar capital on the Volga (965). Khazar power never entirely recovered from this blow, perhaps because much of the lucrative trade between the northern forest lands and the civilized world of the south had already passed from Khazar into Rus hands.[45]

The Carolingian state disintegrated miserably under Viking, Magyar, and Arab assault. But Byzantium survived, partly by a clever diplomacy which often succeeded in playing one enemy off against another, partly by virtue of financial strength arising from her commerce, and partly thanks to reserves of hardy military manpower in Asia Minor. The revival of Byzantine fortunes became apparent after 867, when a capable general came to the throne, and as Basil I, founded the Macedonian dynasty.

Even more significant for the fate of eastern Christendom was the conversion of the Slavs. In 863 St. Cyril and St. Methodius ventured deep into central Europe to preach Christianity among the inhabitants of Bohemia and

---

[44] Sassanian, Ummayad, and Abbasid coin finds in Scandinavia prove the existence of an important commerce between the Middle East and Scandinavia from surprisingly early times. Rus penetration of the Russian waterways may have begun in the late eighth century; but it appears that, about 840, native peoples drove them out, only to recall them on terms a generation later (862), when the need for the military prowess of the northmen as protection against the expanding Khazar (or perhaps the associated Magyar) power made itself felt. Cf. George Vernadsky, *A History of Russia* (new rev. ed.; New Haven, Conn.: Yale University Press, 1944), pp. 19–30; Archibald R. Lewis, *The Northern Seas: Shipping and Commerce in Northern Europe, A.D. 300–1100* (Princeton, N.J.: Princeton University Press, 1958), pp. 270–74; S. F. Cross, "The Scandinavian Infiltration into Russia," *Speculum*, XXI (1946), pp. 505–14; F. Dvornik, *The Making of Central and Eastern Europe* (London: Polish Research Center, 1949), pp. 5, 61–64.

[45] The Rus success may have rested in good part upon manpower superiority, for the Scandinavian warriors quickly assimilated themselves, as the Bulgars had done before, to the Slavic community over which they ruled. The weight of a fairly massive farming population was thereby put behind the Rus state, whereas the Khazars probably rested their power almost entirely upon a nomad society, intrinsically far less populous.

The tactics and strategy of river war and commerce remain entirely obscure. If hand-to-hand combat and boarding tactics prevailed, then the standing superiority of nomad to agricultural warfare was largely irrelevant to the struggle for control of the waterways and of trade. Nomad horsemen could harass a convoy of ships by shooting arrows from the banks but could scarcely halt navigation by such tactics, unless rapids made a continuous journey impossible, or portage from one river system to another had to be made. Most portages lay in the forest zone, near the headwaters of the Russian rivers, and thus beyond easy nomad control. Rapids, like those of the Dnieper near modern Dniepropetrovsk, therefore constituted the most critical strategic areas where nomad domination of the open steppes and Rus control of the riverways clashed directly.

Moravia.[46] To facilitate their labors, St. Cyril adapted the Greek alphabet to suit the peculiarities of local speech and thus inaugurated literacy among the Slavs. Unlike the Roman church, which made Latin the sole legitimate liturgical and administrative language, the Greek hierarchy was prepared to allow the use of native languages for ecclesiastical purposes. Accordingly, when Bulgaria was converted to Christianity (after 865), bringing massive Slavic-speaking populations within the pale of Christendom, a new literary language, Old Church Slavonic, directly based upon Bulgarian speech, developed for their use. By the close of the ninth century, therefore, eastern Christendom had become a duality, combining Greek and Slavic populations, just as the Christian West had long rested upon a duality between Latin- and German-speaking peoples. In the following century, the conversion of the Slavs of Russia (989) extended Christendom to the northern forested zone of eastern Europe and added a considerable weight to the Slavic element in the Greco-Slavonic cultural amalgam which eastern Christianity thus became.

For a time, the Slavs, converted, seemed about to conquer Byzantium itself. Acceptance of Christianity did not prevent the Bulgarian monarchs from aspiring to the imperial throne of Constantinople: on the contrary, a growing familiarity with the refinements of Byzantine civilization sharpened Bulgar ambitions. Consequently, in the ninth and tenth centuries, the two empires fought a series of increasingly violent wars, culminating in the Emperor Basil II's conquest and annexation of Bulgaria in 1014. During the tenth century, Byzantine armies were also able to recover northern Syria (968) and Armenia (1020) from the Moslems, although these successes perhaps resulted more from Moslem political disruption than from any real increment to Byzantine strength. A limited restoration of Byzantine naval power also allowed the reconquest of Cyprus and of Crete, although Moslem and (presently) Italian pirates and merchants never acknowledged Byzantine maritime supremacy.

Western Europe was slower to recover from the barbarian and Moslem assault of the ninth century. Yet by the second half of the tenth century, its recovery was unmistakable. Viking raids diminished as regularly constituted kingdoms began to take shape in Scandinavia. These kingdoms were in turn Christianized and thereby at least partially civilized during the later tenth and early eleventh centuries. Simultaneously, the Magyars were crushingly defeated in battle by Otto the Great of Germany (955) and in the next generation accepted Christianity (1000). These extensions of the realm of Latin Christendom, paralleled by the simultaneous expansion of Orthodox Christianity into the Balkan interior and to Russia, meant that by the year 1000 nearly all of Europe had been brought at least superficially within the circle of Christian culture. Only a relatively small area south of the Baltic remained a pagan preserve, where a simpler tribal style of life survived until the thirteenth century.

We may say, therefore, that under Moslem pressures, European Christendom recoiled from the Mediterranean between 800 and 1000 A.D. That sea,

---

[46] Cf. Matthew Spinka, *A History of Christianity in the Balkans: A Study in the Spread of Byzantine Culture among the Slavs* (Chicago: American Society of Church History, 1953), pp. 22–56.

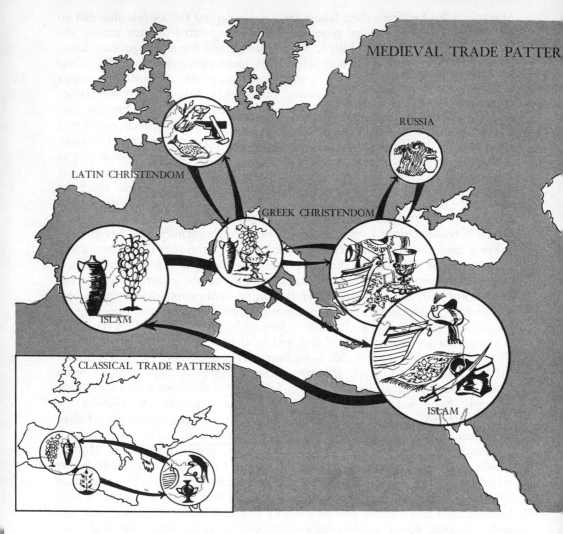

MEDIEVAL TRADE PATTER

RUSSIA

LATIN CHRISTENDOM

GREEK CHRISTENDOM

ISLAM

CLASSICAL TRADE PATTERNS

ISLAM

around which classical civilization had centered, became a no-man's zone, where Moslem and Christian (not to mention Moor and Egyptian, Frank and Greek) plundered and traded and in doing so began to intermix their diverse cultures. But while surrendering domination of the Mediterranean, Christendom found new and spacious ground for its future development in the north, a gain which in the long run more than compensated for its losses in the south.

Up to the year 1000, Christendom's displacement from the Mediterranean was less marked in the east, for the Byzantines were at no time entirely driven from the sea. Nevertheless, under the Macedonian dynasty (867–1054), social and military power shifted decisively away from the seaboard and toward the interior regions of Anatolia and the Balkans. Princely landowners arose, especially in Asia Minor, whose obedience to the central government was precarious at best. Such landholders maintained armed retinues, equipped and trained in the best techniques of the day, *i.e.*, as heavy armored cavalry. As a result, the Macedonian emperors were able both to defend and to extend their landward frontiers as Justinian had never been able to do. But the price of these successes, as earlier in the Parthian and Sassanian states, was an uncertain imperial control over the armed resources of the society as a whole. In his untried youth, for example, Basil II, the "Bulgarslayer," was twice nearly overthrown by armed rebellions organized by magnates of Anatolia; and after his death (1025) the erosion of the central power was painfully demonstrated in the course of a confused clash between rural and urban aristocracies, each of which sought to control the imperial government.

Under the Macedonian emperors, therefore, the structure of Byzantine society came closely to resemble that of Sassanian Iran. Cities and a money economy did not disappear from the Byzantine scene; yet the urban element underwent a comparative retrogression with the decay of naval power, while the dispersal of land forces throughout the countryside in effect magnified the power of the provincial aristocracy. Thus the vastly improved frontier guard which permitted spectacular territorial expansion under the Macedonian dynasty depended on structural shifts within Byzantine society which in the end proved fatal to the imperial bureaucratic power.

The geographical and social displacements within the Latin half of Christendom were far more radical. In the eighth century, the littoral of the North Sea and the English Channel replaced the Mediterranean region as the most active center of the Latin West, both politically and culturally. The conversion of England, the rise of the Frankish state, and the severance of commercial ties with the Levant all contributed to this result. In addition, notable improvements in European shipbuilding (e.g., the stern post rudder)[47] permitted navigators gradually to overcome the terrors of wind and tide which had made travel on the northern seas painfully precarious in Roman times. As this occurred, the northern and western face of Europe began to enjoy advantages comparable to those the Mediterranean had long conferred upon the south. Commerce and contact across long distances and among diverse regions became easy and cheap. Indeed, the number of navigable rivers flowing northward across the European plain greatly extended the inland reach of sea commerce compared with anything possible in the Mediterranean regions, where only the Nile and the Russian rivers offered comparable inland access routes.

Before the year 1000, however, these geographical advantages were still largely potential. Economic life in northern Europe remained primitive; and the products of various regions differed too little from one another to offer any substantial inducement to trade. Moreover, the first fruit of these navigational improvements was the outbreak of wholesale piracy, in which the Scandinavian Vikings played the foremost part. Yet precisely during this period of

[47] Lynn White, "Technology and Invention in the Middle Ages," *Speculum*, XV (1940).

cultural stagnation, political disintegration, and economic backwardness, tech-niques and institutions were created which in time produced the extraordinary upsurge of medieval Europe and gave the Latin West a character quite differ-ent from that of classical or of Byzantine society. Three facets of this emergent social order deserve emphasis: (1) agricultural advance; (2) mili-tary advance; and (3) the special role of piratical trade.

1) In Roman times, swamp and forest covered most of the north European plain, and farmers confined their cultivation to well-drained slopes and espe-cially permeable soils. The wetness of the Atlantic climate and the poor nat-ural drainage of the flat-lying plains kept the land waterlogged for so much of the year that the methods of tillage developed in the dry climate of the ancient Middle East and Mediterranean proved impractical, except on a few specially favored soils, mainly chalk and loess. The drainage problem was eventually solved by the use of a heavy moldboard plow, which in turning over the fur-rows created artificial ridges and hollows in even the flattest field and thus drained surplus water from lands otherwise unusable. A few Germans may have used such devices in Roman times; but heavy moldboard plows did not come into widespread use until after the fifth century and were not gen-erally established as the essential basis of west European agriculture until the tenth.[48]

The long delay in the establishment of this type of plow, in spite of its obvious advantages on the wet and clayey soils which prevailed on the north European plain, was due to the fact that a team of four (or more) oxen was needed to pull it. Moreover, heavy moldboard plows could not work effec-tively in small, squarish fields such as were usual in the older agricultural parts of Europe. Few peasants could put a complete team into the field; and only a pooling of draft animals (together, often, with a reorganization of field shapes and shift of land-ownership rights) could sustain the improved type of cultivation. It was, therefore, in times when rapine and robbery destroyed established relationships on the land that men became willing to pool their resources and redistribute land rights according to new patterns. In circum-stances such as these, the introduction of the more efficient plow and the establishment of co-operative tillage had everything to recommend them. Thus it was precisely in the ninth and tenth centuries, when northwestern Europe was most cruelly harried by Viking and Magyar raids, that the type of agriculture known as "manorial" achieved the technical basis that soon made it possible for European peasants to produce a considerable grain surplus on lands that had lain waste in earlier ages.[49] The solid occupation of the

---

[48] The principal evidence for these statements rests upon the study of field shapes; for the heavy moldboard plow was difficult to turn and could work well only in "long acre" fields. For details, cf. Marc Bloch, *Les Caractères originaux de l'histoire rurale française* (Paris: A. Colin, 1952); Lynn White, "Technology and Invention in the Middle Ages," 141–59; *Cambridge Economic History of Europe,* I, 127–32; Charles Singer (ed.), *A History of Technology,* II, 86–93.

[49] The fact that manorial history has usually been studied from a legal point of view has disguised the fundamental technical change that came to European agriculture in the ninth–tenth centuries. Rela-tions of dependence upon a landlord descended from Roman times and were preserved in the new order; but instead of the cultivation of small fields by independent peasant householders, or exploitation

north European plain by peasant farmers was thereby assured; and medieval Europe attained an agricultural base broad enough to sustain both a numerous military aristocracy and a vigorous town life.[50]

This conquest of the northern European plain, together with the conquest of the northern seas, laid the economic basis for the rise of northwestern Europe to a level of wealth, power, and culture surpassing that of the older Mediterranean centers of civilization. The northward shift of the political and cultural center in the West thus proved, not a passing accident of the political geography of the seventh to tenth centuries, but a permanent feature of European society.

2) The military advance of northwestern Europe in the ninth and tenth centuries depended directly upon the agricultural surplus which the newly developed manorial system made possible. For it was dues and rents collected from the peasants that supported the rise of a formidable class of professional fighting men, equipped and trained for battle according to the best technical models of the time, *i.e.*, as heavy-armed cavalrymen. Because the tastes of this class were at first simple, and the new type of agriculture was comparatively very productive, even a thinly populated and commercially primitive Europe became able to support relatively large numbers of knights.

This social pattern was far from new in the world: Iran had developed a similar system for local defense against steppe raiders nearly a thousand years earlier; and we have just seen that, under the Macedonian dynasty, contemporary Byzantium moved in the same direction. Nevertheless, the rise of knighthood profoundly altered the position of Latin Christendom vis-à-vis its neighbors. When a hard crust of professional knights formed atop the agricultural community of northwestern Europe, raiders and pirates soon lost their accustomed easy superiority. Their depredations consequently slackened and soon ceased. To be sure, bands of knights sometimes ravaged one another's lands; and this sort of local war became endemic as the feudal system

---

of larger areas by gangs of slaves, the mature medieval manor had a quite different technical basis in the heavy moldboard plow, whose operation required a pooling of draft animals and the cultivation of long, narrow strips in open fields. My understanding of the technical basis of medieval manorialism is derived largely from the excellent and eminently sensible discussion in C. S. and C. S. Orwin, *The Open Fields* (Oxford: Clarendon Press, 1938). Cf. also Lynn White, *Medieval Technology and Social Change*, pp. 39 ff.

[50] The equable climate and moist summers of northwestern Europe—a gift of the Gulf Stream—permitted both fall and spring plantings of grain. This in turn meant that the markedly seasonal character of Mediterranean grain tillage could be mitigated. A Mediterranean farmer can plow during only three or four months of the year; a medieval plowman of northwestern Europe kept his plow running most of the year, halting only in winter when lack of adequate fodder for his animals weakened them for heavy work and frozen soils impeded work in the fields. In summer, when other fields were under crops, the fallow required plowing as preparation for the sowing of winter grain; in the fall and early spring the spring grain fields required the same attention.

The result was to multiply the area an average peasant family could keep in tilth, from the five to ten acres estimated as average for an Athenian family of the fifth century B.C. to the thirty-acre virgate of medieval England. Moreover, because labor could now be applied more evenly throughout the year, a single peasant family could produce a far greater grain surplus than had been attainable in classical times. Grain supply for towns and cities had always been a problem for the ancient Greeks and Romans; only in the event of local crop failure was provisioning of the towns a problem in medieval Europe. This permitted a far more intensive urbanization than had been possible in classical times.

spread across western Europe from its locus of origin in northern France.[51] Even so, such local disorder was far less destructive than barbarian raids; and before long, restless members of the knightly class found outlet for their prowess in foreign conquest and adventure. The expansion of Europe thus found a new and very effective basis in military technology, for European knights proved themselves on the whole superior to the military forces of every adjacent society.[52]

3) Obviously enough, piracy rapidly lost its charm when the intended victims developed means to resist or even overcome the attacker. But when it was no longer safe to seize valuables by main force, trade offered an alternative way of getting possession of foreign goods formerly acquired through piracy. Oscillation between raiding and trading has certainly occurred repeatedly in history[53] and was all the easier because even successful pirates seldom got the right assortment of booty for their own use and normally found it convenient to trade booty surpluses for such essentials as weapons or food.[54]

Hence, with the development of an effective local self-defense in western Europe, pirate ships and raiding parties predictably gave way to merchant shipping and pack trains. The important point here is the continuity of ethos between piratical raider of the ninth and European merchant of the tenth centuries. Undoubtedly, pirate-traders often shifted from one role to the other as local circumstances suggested; but even when trading became prudent in more and more circumstances, bands of itinerant merchants still expected, like their piratical predecessors, to manage their own affairs and look after their own defense. They also tended to treat peasants and lords of the land as strangers—potential victims of sharp practice, if no longer often of the sword.

[51] The utter collapse of royal authority in this area in the ninth century facilitated the development of local systems of defense. The more or less fictional hierarchy of lord and vassal, descending downward from the king, gave a legal dress to what were at the time very brutal realities. Another reason for the early development of feudalism in northern France was that here the peasantry, largely descended from Roman coloni, had long lost the habit of self-defense and had no tradition of tribal solidarity to hinder the acceptance of some strong-armed, and often self-appointed warrior as lord.

In the purely German regions to the east, tribal solidarity was still close to the surface; tribesmen did not easily reconcile themselves to dependent and subordinate status; and it was correspondingly difficult for tribal dukes (or German kings) to find the means to support any numerically important body of knights. But peasant foot soldiery, of the style familiar in Charlemagne's army, was little use against mobile striking forces—Magyar horsemen, Viking ships' crews, or presently, French-style knights. Hence the "old-fashioned" military establishment of the Saxon emperors (919–1024) gradually gave way to enfeoffed knighthood. But the spread of feudalism into Germany also involved the disappearance of most of the effective power of the German kingdom, as had happened earlier in France.

[52] This superiority was due to the unique manner in which Europeans exploited the shock potentialities of stirrups and lance, despising the bows which elsewhere continued to be the principal cavalry weapons. Cf. Lynn White, *Medieval Technology and Social Change*, 1–38. Frankish preference for the crushing blow and hand-to-hand combat carried forward into the high Middle Ages an antique bias of European warfare, extending back at least to the Mycenaeans. The necessity of fighting in terrain where trees were so numerous as to interfere with arrows may account for this otherwise inexplicable European disdain for missiles. See above, pp. 107, 237.

[53] As an example of a contrary shift, cf. the career of Mohammed's early followers, recruited from the fringes of a trading city, who initiated raids and conquest with conspicuous success.

[54] For instructive remarks on Viking trade, cf. A. R. Lewis, *The Northern Seas*, pp. 282–86 ff.

AN IRISH GOSPEL

This is the title page of the Gospel according to St. Luke in the Book of Kells, painted in the eighth century A.D. in Ireland. It thus stems from a time when Irish Christian culture was attaining its greatest elaboration, on the eve of the Viking raids which destroyed nearly all that had been achieved by the Irish monasteries. The wonderful geometric precision and complexity of the line drawing of this page, so ebullient as even to break through the heavy outer margins with a series of playful whirlygigs and curlicues, suggests the delicate precocity of Irish civilization between the fifth and ninth centuries A.D.

Eventually, such merchant communities began to establish themselves permanently at some convenient location—often near a bishop's seat or, more rarely, under the walls of an abbey or feudal castle. From such nuclei, the towns of northern Europe took form. The growth of towns occurred mainly after 1000; but the central and essential psychological and institutional forms of north European urban life were shaped in the chaotic age when piracy transmuted itself into trade.

In Byzantium, the Middle East, India, and China the ethos of townspeople contrasted fundamentally with that of the reformed pirates of northwestern Europe. Merchants and artisans of the other civilizations of Eurasia were primarily caterers to the tastes of their social superiors: officials, landlords, rulers. They were accustomed to regulation and taxation from above; in return they relied upon the political authorities for protection. The aggressive, ruthless, and self-reliant ethos of western European merchants was profoundly different. The distinctive characteristics of subsequent Western history arise largely from this fact; for in Europe, as elsewhere in the civilized world, towns became the principal centers and sustainers of high culture once the brute problems of economic and military survival had been solved.

* * *

Before 1000 A.D., Christian culture, like Christian society as a whole, was generally on the defensive, seeking to preserve fragments from the past and rarely venturing upon anything fresh, distinctive, or capable of attracting other civilized peoples. Irish culture was perhaps an exception; for, until Viking raiders snuffed out the monasteries of the island in the eighth and ninth centuries, the Irish effectively combined Celtic oral literary traditions with Latin and even Greek learning. Equally, the heroic poetry of Scandinavia in the Viking age and its Christianized equivalents, the *chansons de geste*, gave evidence of a rude vigor which appeals to modern taste. Yet these were marginal to European Christendom; the backward-looking learning of Byzantium, which fixed its admiration upon the Christian fathers of the Church with an occasional side glance at pagan classical antiquity, and the naïve miracle tales and superstition of Pope Gregory the Great's sermons, are more representative of the cultural life of Christendom as a whole.

Thus, despite sporadic scintillations, Christian culture was at low ebb between 600 and 1000 A.D., being almost entirely insulated from the Moslem world by religious prejudice, and in the West by the disparity of cultural level between half-barbarous Franks and the increasingly urbane Moslems of Spain.

D. INDIA

The Moslem explosion of the seventh–eighth centuries surrounded and isolated the Indian world but actually lopped off only the marginal province of Sind on the lower Indus River. A Moslem victory over the Chinese at the Talus River (751) added the central Asian oases north of Hindu Kush to the sphere of Islam and thereby interposed an almost impermeable barrier athwart the land route between India and China. Moslem shipping likewise soon gained a leading position in the Indian Ocean (eighth century)[55] and sharply restricted Indian sea contacts with the Hindu-Buddhist colonial area of southeast Asia and with China. But although Islam thus nearly circumscribed Hindustan, both by land and by sea, the northern Himalayan borderlands remained beyond Moslem reach. Here Indian expansion continued uninterruptedly. Kashmir and Bengal became powerful states soon after 600, deriving their religion and high culture from India. Moreover, after Chinese rebels massacred the Moslem community of Canton in 879, Moslem dominance of the southern oceans began to decay. Indian shipping revived correspondingly; but by this time the cultures of southeast Asia had attained a degree of individuality which checked their further assimilation to Indian patterns.

The consolidation of powerful states along the northern marches gave Indian politics a new character. No one of these new states proved sufficiently strong to unite the north Indian plain; yet each was able to prevent any other from doing so. This balance of power resulted in a remarkably confused political kaleidoscope. Frontier guard against Islam presented no serious problem once the initial Moslem conquest of Sind had been completed (712), so Indian rulers remained free to pursue their quarrels with scant regard to foreign pressures.

Because Indian states had such shallow roots in the body social, political fragmentation and consequent chronic warfare had small effect upon the population at large. Cities flourished; and Indian culture continued to develop along the lines laid down in the Gupta period. The revival of Hinduism proceeded: indeed, most of the Tamil hymn writers who did so much to reinvigorate ancient Hindu worship became active only after 600; and the canon of their works, adjusted to liturgical use in temple ceremonies, was not compiled until the late tenth century.[56]

Institutionally, Hinduism organized itself more and more definitely around temples, which offered a more accessible, popular counterpart to the monasteries which had been the principal centers of Buddhism. Temples, indeed, became foci of the most diverse aspects of cultural activity. Not only priests, architects, and artists, but dancers, singers, teachers, and writers all tended to cluster within the temple precincts. Royal courts seem to have played only a subordinate cultural role after the temples of Hindu India established themselves. The court-centered culture of Gupta times underwent a corresponding transformation: religion and the gods came more to the forefront, and nonreligious intellectual pursuits like mathematics and astronomy, which had made such a promising start under the Guptas, lost most of their vigor.[57] By

[55] Cf. George Fadlo Hourani, *Arab Seafaring in the Indian Ocean in Ancient and Early Medieval Times* (Princeton, N.J.: Princeton University Press, 1951), pp. 51–84.

[56] K. A. Nilakanta Sastri, *A History of South India from Prehistoric Times to the Fall of Vijayanagar* (Madras: Oxford University Press, 1955), pp. 361–63.

[57] There is no evidence of friction between temple and court. The great temples were royal foundations supported by generous grants of land or other sources of income and perhaps built to express as much the glory of the ruler as of the god.

the tenth century, some of the temples had attained a vast size and become extremely ornate. Their central feature was an elaborately decorated tower, rising above the sanctuary which contained the image of the god; but subsidiary buildings, courtyards, and walled enclosures extended the temple complex and gave scope for a truly extraordinary richness of decoration throughout.

The rise of temples as the primary loci of Hindu cultural expression may have been stimulated by the assimilation of pre-Aryan attitudes and ideals to the high culture of India. The role of these temples certainly resembles the putative role of similar institutions in Indus society, not to mention the Sumerian temple organizations which perhaps lay ultimately behind both.[58] In the realm of doctrine, the rise of Tantrism appears similarly atavistic, representing the emergence of immemorial village superstitions to the level of literate culture; while magical and libidinous Tantric cult practices probably derived directly from Neolithic fertility rites. The complicated theories which Hinduism and Buddhism built around even the grossest Tantric crudities, in order to fit such practices into the path of salvation, exhibit the extraordinary catholicity of Indian religion.[59]

Tantric ideas began to gain prominence about the fifth century A.D., but came to full flower only in the seventh–eighth centuries. By that time, a variety of charms, spells, and rituals, designed to control both the human body and the physical world and ultimately to induce personal identification with divinity, became the most prominent aspect of Indian piety. In a sense, these Tantric practices cheapened earlier religious values by promising to ordinary people the miraculous powers which Indian holy men had long sought in asceticism. But like the democratization of immortality in Egyptian religion centuries before, the attraction of such new ideas was irresistible; and with their spread, monasticism and the older ascetic life lost much of their *raison d'être*.

As popular Hinduism thus reached out to embrace within its already enormous variety the magic-hungry mentality of the most primitive villager, the

---

[58] According to K. A. Nilakanta Sastri, *A History of Southern India*, pp. 57–59, the Dravidians came into India from the Caspian-Iranian area from which the Sumerians perhaps also came. On the probability of relations between Mesopotamia and the Indus civilization, see above, p. 85.

Village piety and cult practice may conceivably have preserved elements of Indus or other very ancient traditions, e.g., temple prostitution, even on a very humble scale. Wooden temple structures would leave no trace for archeologists but may have provided the social—not the architectural—model around which Hindu temples of the sixth and subsequent centuries were elaborated.

[59] European witchcraft presents some interesting parallels to Tantrism and may have a similar background in Neolithic religion. Cf. Henry T. F. Rhodes, *The Satanic Mass: A Sociological and Criminological Study* (London: Rider & Co., 1954); Margaret A. Murray, *The Witch Cult in Western Europe* (Oxford: Oxford University Press, 1921); Elliott Rose, *A Razor for a Goat: A Discussion of Certain Problems in the History of Witchcraft and Diabolism* (Toronto: University of Toronto Press, 1962).

Tantric doctrine has been little investigated, despite (or perhaps because of) a bulky literature. Until recently, at least, European moral feeling was repelled by Tantric rites; and many Indian scholars, too, felt embarrassed at its more extreme manifestations. For a summary of Tantric doctrine, cf. Mircea Eliade, *Le Yoga* (Paris: Payot, 1954), pp. 205–73; Edward Conze, *Buddhism*, pp. 174–99.

Eliot Elisofon and Life Magazine.

HINDU TEMPLES

The temple at the top was erected about 1000 A.D., by which time the simplicity of the earliest structures (p. 375) had been quite overwhelmed by the elaboration of exterior ornament, above all by the development of a massive tower rising high above the dark central room where the god's image resided. The eye-entrancing richness of detail is shown by the photograph below, which portrays the tower of another temple, erected a little earlier.

Atlantis Verlag, Zurich.

elaboration of philosophical theology simultaneously enriched and in some degree stabilized its theoretical aspects. The most famous and influential Hindu religious philosopher was Shankara (fl. *ca.* 800). Shankara sought his central inspiration in the *Upanishads*, tried to reduce their variety to an intellectual system, and to superimpose that system upon the multiplicity of the popular pieties of his day. The basis of his philosophy was an uncompromising monism, which reduced all change and multiplicity to the status of mere illusion. Popular cults ranked as aspects of the illusion, justifiable because they might assist humbler intellects upward toward recognition of the Absolute behind all appearances. Other schools of Hindu philosophy competed with that graced and crowned by Shankara; but the mainstream of Hindu speculation has tended ever since to flow along paths he defined.[60]

The net result of the development of Tantrism and of Hindu philosophy was to undermine the separate existence of Buddhism in India. The fact that Tantrism flourished within both Buddhism and Hinduism tended to blur the distinction between them. In addition, the monastic life lost much of its meaning in a society where Tantric short-cuts to the supernatural had won general acceptance,[61] and where the venerated figure of Buddha had long since been admitted to the Hindu pantheon as an incarnation of Vishnu. Buddhism therefore gradually merged back into the wider field of Indian religiosity from which it had sprung and survived as a distinct organization and doctrine only on the fringes of the Indian world, in Ceylon, Burma, and Tibet.[62] But in India itself, Buddhism had become an empty shell by the end of the tenth century, and when Moslem conquerors plundered the surviving monasteries, no one cared to rebuild them. The Moslems thus definitively eradicated Buddhism from the land of its birth.[63]

[60] Cf. Surendranath Dasgupta, *A History of Indian Philosophy* (Cambridge: Cambridge University Press, 1951), I, 429–39.

[61] To be sure, individuals remained who rejected the easier path; and it is interesting to note that Shankara undercut Buddhism, not only through his intellectual synthesis of Hindu tradition, but also by introducing monasticism into Hinduism. Previous Brahmin teaching had held that only in old age, after fulfilling family duties, should a man devote himself entirely to the pursuit of sanctity; and this must have had the effect of diverting at least a few impatient, religiously incandescent young men into Buddhist monasteries. Shankara provided an institutional refuge for such individuals within Hinduism by founding no less than three Hindu monasteries. Nevertheless, monasticism never became of serious importance in Hinduism.

[62] In southeast Asia, Buddhism survived side by side with Hindu cults much longer than in India itself. Cf. G. Coedès, *Les États hindouisés d'Indochine et d'Indonesie* (Paris: E. de Boccard, 1948), pp. 205–7. As in Tibet, important native elements gave the Hinduism and Buddhism of this region a somewhat individual character. Cf. H. G. Quaritch-Wales, *The Making of Greater India* (London: Bernard Quaritch, Ltd., 1951), who particularly emphasizes the native elements which Coedès largely disregards.

[63] The Jains of India resisted the Tantric movement in large degree and thereby preserved their identity, but only as a sect whose members were confined largely to special occupations and concentrated principally in southern and western India. An even more distinct group were the Parsis, followers of Zoroaster who came to India as refugees from Moslem conquest between the eighth and tenth centuries. They have survived as a very small community until the present day, mainly in the region around modern Bombay.

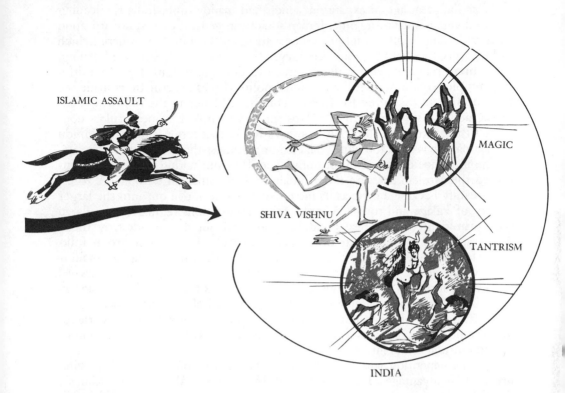

ISLAMIC ASSAULT

MAGIC

SHIVA VISHNU

TANTRISM

INDIA

The evolution of Indian religion and culture as a whole during the seventh and eighth centuries systematically hardened Hindu opposition to Islam. To be sure, the Moslems had taken the initiative, attacking India both with weapons and with words in the name of an intolerant religion which recoiled in horror from Indian idolatory. Consequently, Moslem intolerance tended to provoke Indians into regarding everything foreign as hostile. But the Moslem culture incorporated the same Iranian and Greek elements which in an earlier age had done so much to quicken Indian art and literature. The Hindu reaction was defensive: to fall back upon autochthonous tradition and reject those aspects of their earlier culture that had been most transparently affected by foreign influences. This meant in practice the admission of much that was very primitive and ancient to the circle of literary culture. It also meant that Hinduism came to present a more nearly seamless whole to the outer world than ever before, since the humblest villager and the most erudite Brahmin could now alike find scope for their very different mentalities in the capacious Hindu heritage.[64]

[64] The power of the unique Hindu combination of atavistic ritualized emotion with the most rarefied metaphysical subtlety is well conveyed in the final section of the novel by E. M. Forster, *Passage to India* (London: Edward Arnold & Co., 1924).

After the great age of expansion which had made Gupta India the leading civilized community of its time, Indian society in general turned inward upon itself and clung with a stubborn conservatism to the Hindu synthesis which had emerged by about the ninth century. High artistic skill, intricate learning, and vibrant religious feeling all continued to flourish, sustained by a wealthy and complex economy. Yet the perennial political weakness of India made the subcontinent an easy prey for foreign conquest. Hence in the following centuries, political subjection first to Moslem and then to European rulers confirmed this attitude of culturally conservative introspection and made Hindu India a passive area in the world balance until almost the present day.[65]

The influence exercised by primitive peoples from within powerfully reinforced the Moslem pressure upon Indian civilization from without. A forest tribe readily became a caste as its members began to move out into the larger society of village and town. Whereas other civilizations regularly assimilated such primitive communities, Hinduism modified but did not destroy them. The result was to perpetuate an immense variety of divergent group folkways, loosely federated into the caste system and the Hindu religion. Doubtless it was the caste principle of Indian society that permitted the long survival and eventual revival of the atavistic religious notions that found expression in Tantrism. The same principle of requiring minimal alteration of local habits certainly facilitated the folding of south India and the Himalayan borderlands into the body of Hindu society, as it had earlier allowed the vast extension of Indian cultural styles into southeast Asia.

Yet in competition with the other Eurasian civilizations, India was inevitably at a disadvantage. The looseness of India's internal social cohesion set drastic limits upon the proportion of energy and resources that could be directed into any given enterprise. Hence India's perennial military-political weakness. And in the face of foreign challenge, the appropriate psychological counterpart to India's peculiar social structure was a prevailingly passive, indrawn attitude, similar to that characteristic of primitive peoples everywhere when suddenly thrust into the confusing circle of civilized society.

E. CHINA AND THE FAR EAST

In appropriating the outward aspects of Chinese civilization, the Turkish and Mongol invaders of north China nonetheless retained their nomadic propensity for war. Therefore following the reunification of China in 589 under a new dynasty, the Sui, China's military energies soon proved themselves far greater than at any time in the preceding six centuries. A tax-gathering bureaucracy constructed on the ancient Confucian model, supporting a military establishment imbued with the spirit and techniques of steppe warfare, proved formidable indeed and carried Chinese arms rapidly westward, until early in the eighth century the servants of the Son of Heaven collided with the followers of Mohammed in the region east of the Oxus.

The Sui dynasty, which unified China, failed to reap the imperial fruits of

---

[65] Cf. the analogous career of Egyptian civilization from about 1100 B.C. until Roman times.

this dramatic success; for the second Sui emperor was also the last. Peasant discontent at the government's ruthless conscription of labor for public works conspired with the strain of an unsuccessful war against Korea (612–14) to bring about the downfall of the newly established line. Rebellions broke out in many parts of the country; but in 618 one of the rebel leaders gained effective supremacy and founded the T'ang dynasty. The next T'ang emperor, T'ai Tsung (627–49), was the first to carry China's new-found power deep into Asia. In 630 the eastern Turkish confederacy recognized his suzerainty; twelve years later most of the tribes east of the Caspian Sea did likewise. Soon afterward, T'ai Tsung fastened his control upon the oases of central Asia, and in 668 his heirs finally succeeded in conquering Korea.

During the next several decades, a series of palace coups coincided with Turkish revolts and the abrupt rise of a new military power in Tibet to cause a temporary disruption of Chinese power. But after 715, the stabilization of the T'ang regime under the emperor Hsuan Tsung (712–56) enabled China, through her Turkish allies, to inflict important setbacks upon the Moslems in Transoxiana.[66] Between 747 and 749, Chinese troops campaigned on the frontiers of India and claimed lordship over both Kabul and Kashmir, then, after 751, when Moslems annihilated a Chinese expeditionary force in the battle of the Talas River, T'ang control of central Asia collapsed. In the same year, a Chinese invasion of Yunnan failed; and a new nomad confederacy, the Kitai, defeated yet a third imperial army on the northeast frontier. These events set the stage for a great military rebellion which broke out in 755 and paralyzed China for eight years.[67]

The T'ang dynasty survived but owed its preservation to the intervention of Turkish (Uighur) forces.[68] The later T'ang emperors remained politically dependent on Uighur goodwill. They gave up the effort to dominate China's borderlands by military power and instead kept the nomads quiet by tribute payments and diplomacy. This policy perhaps in part reflected a waning aptitude for war among Chinese populations, as the descendants of earlier nomad conquerors became more thoroughly acculturated. It also reflected the internal political weakness of the later T'ang; for during and after the great rebellion of 755–63, the central government lost effective authority over the provinces. Various local warlords rose to power, fought among themselves, and ruled their domains with only occasional deference to the wishes of the emperors.

The ultimate disappearance of the T'ang dynasty in 907 had only symbolic importance, for effective imperial power had vanished long before. Renewed invasions of north China between 936 and 960 repeated on a lesser scale the

[66] The Chinese did not engage their own forces against the Moslems until 751. In 715 they merely encouraged their Turkish allies of the central steppe to support local princes who were revolting against the Arabs.

[67] For a persuasive analysis of the social forces operating in this rebellion, cf. Edwin G. Pulleyblank, *The Background of the Rebellion of An Lu-shan* (London: Oxford University Press, 1955).

[68] An internal convulsion in 743–44 had substituted a tribe known as Uighurs for the older leaders of the eastern Turkish confederacy; but the peoples belonging to the two confederacies were substantially the same.

disorder which had followed the collapse of the Han; but the renewed danger of barbarian conquest probably facilitated the unification of all south and central China by the Sung dynasty after 960. Through a moral regeneration of the bureaucracy, the early Sung emperors were able to secure loyal servants who put an end to the local warlords surviving from late T'ang times. The Sung failed, however, to recover the northern tier of provinces, which remained in barbarian hands until the time of the Ming dynasty (1368–1644).

* * *

Far-reaching changes in the Chinese economy made possible the military successes of the early T'ang emperors and sustained the brilliant luxury of T'ang culture. In earlier centuries, the valley of the Yellow River (with some of its tributaries) had constituted the primary center of Chinese society. The lush vegetation and moister climate of the south had presented serious obstacles to Chinese farmers, accustomed to the loess soils of the north, so that, even after the extension of imperial rule into south China by the Han dynasty, the potential wealth of the region remained undeveloped. But during the troubled times between 200 and 600 A.D., refugees from the more exposed northern provinces migrated southward in considerable numbers and, little by little, accomplished the laborious work of clearing the luxuriant jungle and of building the indispensable irrigation and drainage ditches. Carpets of paddy fields began to spread out from the banks of rivers and lakes where they had first concentrated, until by the beginning of the seventh century, the Yangtze Valley not only sustained a large population, but was also capable of producing a substantial food surplus.

A similarly vast work of land reclamation had been carried through about a thousand years before in the valley of the Yellow River itself by merging previously separated patches of fertile ground into a single irrigated continuum. Indeed, it was the patient toil of these Chinese peasants that provided the Ch'in and Han rulers with the agricultural base and economic *raison d'être* of their empires, for a single centralized administration was needed to keep such elaborate irrigation works in order throughout the length of the entire valley. The Sui and T'ang rulers differed from their imperial predecessors in having a double base, one in the Yellow River Valley and a second, and even more productive one, in the valley of the Yangtze.

Effective utilization of the new surpluses of the south demanded a well-developed system of internal transport. Accordingly, the Sui and T'ang emperors built many large canals, of which the most important was the Grand Canal joining the Yangtze with the Yellow River. This vast engineering enterprise was completed in 611 by the conscript labor of literally millions of peasants. It made possible the shipment of vast quantities of rice and other goods from the south to the imperial capitals of Chang'an and Loyang in the north. Granaries were set up in convenient places to store and distribute the grain and other goods which were thus put at the government's disposal; and management of the collection, transport, and distribution of such goods became the prime function of the imperial bureaucracy. This vast network for the circulation of imperial wealth reached full efficiency in the eighth century.[69]

In a year of normal harvests, however, full efficiency provided the imperial court with more grain and other foodstuffs than it could use. By about the middle of the eighth century, therefore, imperial officials began to exchange surplus grain for various luxury goods,[70] for which the consuming capacity of the court was virtually unlimited. The effect, therefore, was to create or vastly to expand a market for the most highly skilled artisan wares—fine silks, porcelains, lacquer work, and the like—in all regions of China. Provincial officials, finding themselves with grain surpluses on hand, became eager to exchange food for local artisan specialties, which were both easier to transport and more welcome at the court than crude agricultural produce. A substantial enlargement of the artisan and merchant classes naturally ensued. Towns in China (except for the imperial capitals) do not seem to have been previously very important. But T'ang times saw an extensive urban growth, thanks to the extensive food surpluses of the south and to the circulation of goods which imperial and official convenience dictated.

The spread of a money economy accompanied the growth of provincial towns. Although coins had been known in China for centuries, they came into widespread use only after the convenience of converting tax income into a standard and easily transportable measure of value became apparent. Official figures show, for example, that in the year 749 only 3.9 per cent of the government's income took cash form, whereas by 1065 this figure had risen to 51.6 per cent of a greatly enlarged income.[71]

Easier transport and a money economy of course promoted regional specialization, according to the distribution of raw materials or of special artisan skills. Merchants found new scope as intermediaries between the court and the actual producers of goods and, in time, supplemented the official commodity circulation with an extensive private trading network.[72] The partial

[69] On the development of south China and the canal system, cf. Ch'ao-ting Chi, *Key Economic Areas in Chinese History* (London: Allen & Unwin, Ltd., 1936), pp. 133–30 and *passim;* Pulleyback, *Background of the Rebellion,* pp. 27–28, 32–38; Hans Bielenstein, "The Census of China during the Period 2–742 A.D.," Museum of Far Eastern Antiquities, Stockholm, *Bulletin,* XIX (1947), 125–62, and especially the population maps appended to this article.

[70] The *Old T'ang History (Chiu T'ang Shu,* 84.1.*b)* informs us, for example, that in 742 the commissioner for land and water transport ordered "that coarse grain in the Public Granaries in the prefectures and counties should be sold for light goods." Quoted from Pulleyback, *Background of the Rebellion,* p. 36.

[71] Edward A. Kracke, *Civil Service in Early Sung China, 960–1067* (Cambridge, Mass.: Harvard University Press, 1953), p. 13.

[72] On the rise of trade and cities, cf. Stefan Balasz, "Beiträge zur Wirtschaftsgeschichte der T'ang Zeit," *Mitteilungen des Seminars für orientalische Sprachen zu Berlin,* XXXIV (1931), 21–25; XXXV (1932), 37–73. The role of Buddhist monasteries in the development of a money economy and of non-official trade was very important. These institutions accumulated substantial wealth from gifts of the pious and set out on a smaller scale to duplicate the activities of the imperial court itself, seeking luxury goods for the cult (and for the monks' own consumption) where they could be found. Money-lending also became an important monastic activity. Cf. *Mitteilungen des Seminars für orientalische Sprachen zu Berlin,* XXV (1932), 15–21; Jacques Gernet, *Les Aspects économiques du Bouddhisme dans la société chinoise du Ve au Xe siècle* (Saigon: École Française d'Extrême-Orient, 1956), pp. 149–84.

Buddhism, of course, had entered China via the trading cities of the central Asian oases. Hence the

breakdown of the centralized bureaucracy in the later T'ang period allowed even greater scope for private enterprise; and the establishment of regional capitals by the great warlords of late T'ang times accelerated the rise of provincial cities that could bear comparison with the imperial capitals.

Changes on the land are more obscure but were probably of great importance. In early T'ang times it appears that a considerable proportion of the peasantry were independent landholders, particularly in the more northerly provinces where numerous barbarians had settled during the preceding centuries. The army of the first T'ang conquerors was composed primarily of a peasant militia, supplemented by Turkish auxiliaries and commanded by professional officers. But the militarized free peasants of early T'ang times seem gradually to have lost their land, perhaps through foreclosure on debts. At any rate, in 737 the emperor converted the army into a professional force, largely recruited from and commanded by barbarians.

The great rebellion of 755–63, launched by a frontier general commanding a barbarian force whose only loyalty was to himself, soon demonstrated the weakness of such a system. The uprising was suppressed only by calling in still wilder barbarians from the outer fringes of the Chinese world, who thenceforth held the T'ang emperors more or less at ransom. Toward the end of the T'ang dynasty, when recurrent military disorder had been superadded to the exactions of landlords and moneylenders, peasant distress found expression in a series of bitter rebellions (notably 874–83). Yet the political and military disorder of the early tenth century seems not to have shaken the hold of the gentry-landlords upon the Chinese peasantry; and when the Sung dynasty restored a modicum of peace to central and southern China after 960, the peasants remained firmly under the thumb of their social superiors.[73]

* * *

By the year 1000, Chinese society had attained what may be termed its "modern" form. Until the twentieth century, further development enlarged the scale but failed to alter the main lines of the social structure which had emerged by that date. This gave Chinese civilization a head start over its Far Western counterpart, as Marco Polo's awe at the wonders of Cathay aptly illustrates. In the longer run, however, drawbacks in the Chinese system eventually allowed Europe to spurt far ahead of the Far East. Brief comparison with medieval Europe will make the limitations of China's "modern" order of society clearer.

commercial and financial activities of the Buddhist monasteries in a sense simply brought into China patterns of economic exchange which had long been familiar in western Eurasia, and then adjusted these patterns to the peculiar institutional organization of China. Cf. the way in which Buddhist art styles were first imported raw and then adjusted themselves to Chinese aesthetic sensitivities. The economic contribution of Buddhism to Chinese life may have been just as important in its field as was the more obvious contirbution of Buddhism to Chinese art.

[73] Cf. Pulleyblank, *Background of the Rebellion*, pp. 27–29, 61–74; J. Gernet, *Aspects économiques du Bouddhisme*, pp. 126–38; S. Balasz, "Beiträge zur Wirtschaftsgeschichte der T'ang Zeit," XXXIV (1931), 61–92; Denis Twitchett, "Lands under State Cultivation under the T'ang," *Journal of the Economic and Social History of the Orient*, II (1959), 162–204.

BUDDHA

MERCENARIES

Yellow River

Yellow Sea

COURT

MANDARIN

ARTISAN

TRADERS

Grand Canal

MONASTERY

ARTISAN

Yangtze

ARTISAN

MONASTERY

THE STRUCTURE OF T'ANG SOCIETY

First, by 1000 A.D. European agriculture had come to depend upon the relatively large concentrations of animal draft power required to drive the heavy moldboard plow through moist and clayey soils. Such extravagant use of animal power necessitated a relatively extensive style of cultivation and allowed a single cultivator to produce comparatively large food surpluses. By contrast, Chinese cultivation of the moist lands of the Yangtze Valley put the main burden of field labor directly upon human muscles. Chinese agriculture supported far denser populations and assured much higher calorie yields per acre than any Europe knew; but it resulted also in lower productivity per capita, since Chinese farmers mostly did without the animal power that magnified the efforts of European peasants.[74] The European type of agriculture therefore implied the possibility (not necessarily realized) of a higher standard of living for the common people, since the margin between bare subsistence and production per agricultural head was wider in Europe than in China.[75]

Second, the comparatively low level of peasant consumption in Chinese society tended to restrict the market for artisan products to the official and landlord classes. The important role of the government and of the courtly circle in organizing the transportation system and initiating the demand for artisan specialties emphasized this tendency and tended to concentrate artisan skills upon the luxury products which persons in high places desired. In marked contrast, early European manufacturing emphasized comparatively crude products like woolen cloth, smoked herring, or iron and steel tools and weapons,[76] which were designed for a socially much wider market.

Third, merchants were disreputable in China. Confucius had ranked them at the bottom of the social scale, together with soldiers and other practically necessary but ideally superfluous occupational groups. The fact that many of the early merchants in China were foreigners—Sogdians, Persians, Arabs, Uighurs—both reflected and confirmed this traditional judgment. Moreover, the character of the Chinese economy tended to confine merchants to the role of obsequiously catering to the tastes of the court, of officials, and of landlords; for these groups possessed the only significant purchasing power. Under such circumstances, it is not surprising that government policy seldom took much account of merchants' interests, nor that successful merchants tended rather to invest their capital in land than in industry and to assimilate themselves into the gentry class. All this inhibited the development of a really massive mercantile capital and diverted Chinese attention from the active pursuit of trade abroad.[77]

The nub of the difference between the Far East and the Far West lay in the fact that despite the development of great cities, of a significant regional

[74] The differences between European and Chinese agriculture were not so fully developed in T'ang times as they came to be later. Rice was just coming to pre-eminence among the cereal crops of China; and only rice culture gave the intensive, garden style of farming its full scope. Yet in 624 the official norm for a peasant holding in China was defined as the equivalent of twelve acres, less than half the thirty acres of a European virgate. Scattered statistics seem to show that actual holdings did not vary much from this norm. Cf. S. Balasz, "Beiträge zur Wirtschaftsgeschichte der T'ang Zeit," XXXIV (1931), 44–52.

[75] Climate was a second and very important factor working to differentiate the agricultural living standards of Europe from those of China. The expansion of European agriculture during the early Middle Ages into the northwest brought a region of comparatively low temperatures within the circle of civilization. Mere biological survival in such regions required a greater food intake and more elaborate housing and clothing than was required in a warmer climate. Chinese agricultural expansion during the same centuries went from a severe toward a warmer climate, where lower levels of food consumption, housing, and clothing were compatible with survival.

[76] Again, a geographical difference between China and western Europe reinforced the contrast; for China seems always to have suffered a metal shortage (especially of iron) as against the comparative abundance of iron and other metals in western Europe. Cf. Balasz, "Beiträge zur Wirtschaftsgeschichte der T'ang Zeit," XXXV (1932), 23–25.

[77] Cf. Ping-ti Ho, "Salt Merchants of Yang-chou: A Study of Commerical Capitalism in 18th Century China," *Harvard Journal of Asiatic Studies*, XVII (1954), 130–68.

specialization, and of a highly skilled artisan class, these features of "modern" Chinese life were successfully encapsulated within older agricultural social relationships. The commercial and artisan classes of China never developed a will and self-confidence to challenge the prestige and values of the bureaucracy and landed gentry; whereas in northwestern Europe the evolution of merchant communities from the pirate bands of the ninth–tenth centuries gave them from the start a sense of independence from—indeed of hostility toward—the landed aristocrats of the countryside. European merchants did not cater to anyone: they sought to become powerful in their own right and soon succeeded in doing so. Indeed, by the thirteenth century in Italy, and by the sixteenth century in critically active centers of northern Europe, merchants had captured the state and bent it to their own purposes to a degree utterly inconceivable in Confucian China.

The net effect of the weakness of the Chinese mercantile class was to blunt (or control?) the social and political impact of a number of important technological developments in which China conspicuously led the world during the period before 1000 A.D. Inventions like paper and porcelain, printing and gunpowder, were not entirely without effect upon Chinese society as a whole;[78] but the full and reckless exploitation of these inventions was reserved for the looser, less ordered society of western Europe, where no overarching bureaucracy and no unchallengeable social hierarchy inhibited their revolutionary application.

*   *   *

Naturally enough, the structure of Chinese society deeply affected the character of Chinese culture under the T'ang. The emperor and his court always constituted a major patron of the arts; in addition, Buddhist or Taoist monasteries and private gentlemen as well frequently possessed both the means and the inclination to patronize or create works of piety, thought, and art. The bulk of the art and literature surviving from the period stemmed from one or more of these sources and catered to the refined tastes of the educated and leisured classes. Before 1000 A.D., only the smallest beginnings of a more popular, urban, middle-class literature found lodgment within the massive Chinese literary heritage.

The religious policy of the first T'ang emperors was one of toleration. Imperial patronage was reserved for Buddhists, Taoists, and Confucians; but Manichaeans, Nestorian Christians, Zoroastrians, and Moslems all mingled in the mercantile communities of the great imperial capitals, Chang'an and Loyang. The presence of such foreigners no doubt contributed to a continuing, if subdued tension between the ancient Chinese schools of thought and

[78] Paper had first been manufactured in Han times; porcelain-making achieved full technical maturity in T'ang times; printing in China started in 756; chemical explosives were first recorded for military uses in 1000 A.D. Cf. T. F. Carter, *The Invention of Printing in China and Its Spread Westward* (2d ed.; New York: Ronald Press, 1955), pp. 82–85; L. Carrington Goodrich and Feng Chia-sheng, "The Early Development of Firearms in China," *Isis*, XXXVI (1946), 114–23.

the intrusive religions of salvation. But in the T'ang period the general tendency was for free interaction between Taoism, Confucianism, and Buddhism to bring each to resemble the others more closely than before.

Until about the middle of the seventh century, translation of Indian texts into Chinese continued. Thereafter, with the decay of Buddhism in India, Chinese Buddhists more and more had to rely upon their own theological resources. The most significant expression of Chinese Buddhism's emancipation from Indian influence was the growth of the Ch'an (in Japanese, Zen) sect in the second half of the eighth century. Ch'an Buddhists rejected the elaborate metaphysical speculation of other schools and insisted that salvation came by instantaneous enlightenment or not at all. At least some of its practitioners adopted a deliberately paradoxical mode of expression and a somewhat surly anti-intellectualism.[79]

While Buddhism in the Chinese environment was thus shedding part of its alien garb, both Taoism and Confucianism, in differing ways, incorporated elements of Buddhist thought. Taoists developed a monastic organization and compiled a canon of sacred texts with which to rival the Buddhists. Confucianism had no need for such institutional bulwarks: it was already secure in its hold on officialdom through the revived examination system. But the sophistication of Buddhist argumentation and Buddhist allegorical methods of finding the hidden meanings of a text had much to offer an earnest student of the Confucian classics who sought to make them relevant to the T'ang age. Accordingly, the pioneers of Neo-Confucian thought, who began to be active about 800, freely borrowed techniques of textual interpretation as well as certain doctrinal positions from the Buddhists. Then in early Sung times, when the Neo-Confucian movement got seriously under way, a heavy infusion of Taoist doctrine penetrated Confucianism through the application of originally Buddhist methods of interpretation to old Confucian texts.[80]

Such blending and borrowing among the three major intellectual traditions of China did not lead to any rapprochement among their respective adherents. On the contrary, Neo-Confucians reinterpreted Confucian classics in order better to refute the Buddhists; and Taoists developed their organization with a similar end in view. The more aggressive spirit of remodeled Confucianism[81] and Taoism naturally tended to weaken the position of Chinese Buddhism, which in the sixth and early seventh centuries had seemed on the verge of becoming a state religion. Other factors also helped to undermine Buddhism: a growing secularism in courtly circles and, indeed, in some of the wealthy Buddhist monasteries as well; and a powerful xenophobia, which gained

---

[79] Fung Yu-lan, *A History of Chinese Philosophy*, II, 385–406. The popularity of Ch'an Buddhism perhaps reflects a basic uncongeniality between the rarefied abstractions of Indian speculation and both the Chinese and Japanese temperaments. Chinese and Japanese intellectual temperaments may, in time, mainly result from the concrete references continually implicit in an ideographic script.

[80] Fung Yu-lan, *A History of Chinese Philosophy*, II, 407–33.

[81] The main line of attack on Buddhism was well expressed in a famous essay by Han Yu (768–824): "Being sons, they do not treat their fathers like a father, and being subjects, they do not treat their ruler like a ruler. . . . They elevate the rules of the barbarians above the teachings of the early kings, thus becoming almost the same as barbarians themselves." Quoted from Fung Yu-lan, *A History of Chinese Philosophy*, II, 410.

A CHINESE BODHISATTVA

This statue, which was made between 550 and 577 A.D., shows the effective appropriation of foreign Buddhist stimulus by Chinese sculptors. Indian and central Asian prototypes for the treatment of hair and drapery, as well as for the pose itself, are clear and unmistakable. A comparison with a similar statue, cast a century earlier (p. 331), shows how much more Chinese the later work has become, owing not merely to changes in facial expression and proportions but to a more purposeful treatment of the lines of folded drapery. What had been a decoratively misunderstood naturalistic convention in the earlier statue has now become a deliberately stylized patterning which suggests monumental solidity behind the flimsy drapery.

University Museum, University of Pennsylvania.

strength as a Chinese military power vis-à-vis the barbarians waned after 755. Indeed, the very success with which Buddhism had transformed itself from a religion of the poor and humble into a semi-official faith richly endowed with land and official privilege tended to sever its popular roots.[82]

The upshot of these changes was a great outburst of religious persecution in China between 843 and 846, precipitated by the collapse of the Uighur state in 840 under the attack of outer barbarians. The ruling groups among the Uighurs had professed Manichaeism since 762 and had used their military power to protect Manichaeans in China, while simultaneously exacting tribute from the Chinese. When, therefore, the Uighur power collapsed, the Chinese reaction was to rid themselves of all Manichaeans, who in any case were mostly merchants of Uighur or other alien origin and had long lorded it over the Chinese on the strength of their foreign protector. Other religious intruders—Nestorians, Zoroastrians, and Moslems—soon suffered similar persecution; and in 845 the rich Buddhist monasteries were also suppressed, perhaps more for fiscal reasons than in the narrowly xenophobic spirit of the first persecutions. Official annals record that no fewer than 44,600 Buddhist religious establishments were destroyed, 260,500 monks and nuns put back onto the tax lists, and 150,000 of them enslaved.[83] Chinese Buddhism never recovered from this blow. Having forfeited much of its initial appeal to the public by acquiring great wealth and having then lost its material possessions when the government took back its own, Buddhism found itself rather abruptly reduced to comparative insignificance in China. Rites and blessings to protect humble folk from evil spirits became the chief Buddhist stock in trade—a public service for which the Taoists were on the whole better equipped. Chinese Buddhism survived mainly in its Ch'an form, for the most part in the remoter provinces and especially beyond the limits of the Chinese state in Japan and Korea.[84] The ebullition of Indian speculation died away completely; and Buddhism ceased to be an important element in the high culture of China.

Hence, after 845 no alien religion seriously challenged Confucianism and Taoism in China; and by Sung times (after 960), Neo-Confucianism had absorbed so much of Taoist language as to blur the age-old opposition between those two traditions. Thus, in the same way that Confucianism had successfully digested Legalist, Mohist, and other rival schools in Han times, so in the later Sung, *i.e.*, after 1000 A.D., Neo-Confucianism, having absorbed important elements from Buddhism and Taoism, emerged unchallenged as the

---

[82] J. Gernet, *Les Aspects économiques du Bouddhisme*, pp. 240–98, describes the changing social role of Buddhism in a most penetrating and persuasive fashion. A very similar decay had weakened Indian Buddhism some centuries before. See above, p. 372.

[83] O. Franke, *Geschichte des chinesischen Reiches*, II, 498. These statistics may be exaggerated.

[84] Manichaeism survived for a few more centuries among the Uighurs, who succeeded in establishing a rump kingdom in the Tarim basin after having been driven from the high steppe. (This, incidentally, marks the point at which Turkish replaced the earlier Indo-European languages of the central Asian oases.) Zoroastrianism practically disappeared, and Nestorian Christianity lingered as a minority faith in the central Asian oases; but in central Asia the future lay with the still expanding religion of Mohammed.

official intellectual system of China. This was a victory for the gentry as against mercantile and military intruders; a victory, too, for autochthonous Chinese tradition against the metaphysical religions of salvation of western Asia. The rejection of Buddhism, with its ineradicably alien aspect, assured Chinese civilization of a degree of continuity and coherence which none of the other Eurasian civilizations came near to equaling. Yet the monolithic nature of the Neo-Confucian synthesis tended to set narrower limits to the future evolution of Chinese culture than any imposed by the more variegated intellectual inheritances of the Islamic and Christian worlds.[85]

In China the natural sciences, especially astronomy, mathematics, and medicine, seem to have remained remarkably immune from foreign influences in T'ang times, even though Indian scientific works were known and, indeed, a few Indian astronomers held high positions in the imperial service. Chinese astronomers made various refinements in their observations during this period, as well as notable improvements in instruments for measuring the movements of the heavenly bodies. But the close connection between astronomy and divination—astronomers existed officially only to interpret the will of Heaven as manifested by eclipses and other unusual occurrences—perhaps sufficed to safeguard traditional methods against subversive notions from abroad.[86]

The evolution of the fine arts in China between 600 and 1000 parallels the intellectual and religious history of the epoch. In early T'ang times, Buddhist sculpture and painting still often modeled themselves upon Indian and central Asian prototypes.[87] By the eighth century, however, distinctively Chinese styles of Buddhist art had emerged; and some of the statues of the period clearly reflect a waning of religious enthusiasm before a more secular spirit. After 845, Buddhist art survived only in peripheral regions of China, where the religious persecutions had been less severe.[88]

The abrupt termination of Buddhist artistic production which resulted from the suppression of the monasteries in 845 did not bring the influence of

[85] If Indian cultural development in this period may correctly be described as dominated by atavism toward pre-Aryan and precivilized roots, Chinese consolidation around a much modified Confucianism might be considered a less drastic but not dissimilar atavism, aiming not at a precivilized but nonetheless at a vanished, "purer," more limited age of the past. Deliberate constriction of the cultural tradition of China through a Confucian renaissance became clearer in later centuries, when critical Chinese scholarship discarded many of the Neo-Confucian reinterpretations of Confucian classics. The strikingly contrary consequence of the equally atavistic European Renaissance and Reformation will be considered in a later chapter.

[86] An Indian astronomer, who was appointed as director of the Royal Astronomical Office in the first half of the eighth century, translated Indian texts in which the decimal place notational principle, sine tables, and other adjuncts of Indian mathematical astronomy were explained; but these novelties were disregarded by the Chinese. Cf. Kiyoshi Yabuuchi, "The Development of the Sciences in China from the Fourth to the End of the Twelfth Century," *Cahiers d'histoire mondiale*, IV (1958), 337–39.

[87] The famous Chinese pilgrim Hsuan-tsang brought back from India in 645, not only Sanskrit texts, but also "authentic" images of Buddha. Sassanian styles, as domesticated in the central Asian oases, also left clear marks upon some Chinese Buddhist work.

[88] Cf. Ludwig Bachhofer, *A Short History of Chinese Art* (New York: Pantheon, 1946), pp. 63–80; Lawrence Sickman and Alexander Soper, *The Art and Architecture of China* (Harmondsworth: Penguin Books, 1956), pp. 53–77.

Buddhist art in China to an end. On the contrary, just as Neo-Confucianism won its eventual victory only after adopting certain Buddhist traits, so also Chinese secular art came into its own only after borrowing much from Buddhist prototypes. This was especially evident in painting, the foremost art[89] of later Chinese civilization. In sharp contrast to the fantastic, semi-geometric portrayals of the earliest Chinese styles, Buddhist painting sought to represent human figures and scenery in a visually unambiguous fashion and to tell a story that could be "read" even by the unlettered. The technical problems of doing this had on the whole been satisfactorily solved in the eighth century, when the earliest masters of Chinese painting flourished. By the ninth and tenth centuries, Chinese painters had learned also to indicate space as a unified and unifying whole, although not by means of linear perspective—fifteenth-century Europe's solution to a comparable problem. Chinese landscapes were projected instead from a shifting aerial point of vision, conveying a sense of vast spatial vistas, yet at the same time suggesting a mood, and delighting the eye with an elegantly decorated surface. This highly sophisticated, delicate, and suggestive style fixed the broad character of all subsequent Chinese painting, although later artists continued to modify details.[90]

In the realm of literature and music, the classical forms of composition modeled on Han precedents were supplemented by wide-ranging innovations during the early T'ang period. Although the unique nature of Chinese writing and the normal barriers of language assured belles-lettres of comparative immunity from foreign influence, court histories mention dances, songs, and music derived from the steppe invaders of previous centuries.[91] In addition, the popular, and initially somewhat disreputable, song and story of the streets provided inspiration for a series of innovating poets. Li Po (701–62) and Tu Fu (712–70) were among the earliest and most famous gentlemen poets who developed verse forms derived from these vulgar sources into effective, if sometimes mannered art.

By a supreme paradox, the poetic conventions these and others made respectable became sterilized after the tenth century by the fact that every educated gentleman perforce became a poet. For when the imperial civil service examinations came to require the composition of a poem according to strict rules and with a prescribed subject matter, poetry became so well regulated that it could not flourish, although vast quantities of polished verse continued to be produced. Lyricism, which for a few generations had broken through older conventions to strike a highly personal, often autobiographical note,[92] was thus safely recaptured by the Confucian learned tradition.

[89] Perhaps the major reason for this fact was that painting was closely allied with calligraphy, both being the work of the brush. A gentleman-scholar could therefore become a painter with no loss of dignity; indeed, a great painter was highly respected. Beginning about 500 A.D., a learned literature dealing with the lives and works of notable painters morticed the art of painting firmly into the Confucian literary tradition.

[90] Cf. Osvald Siren, *Chinese Painting* (New York: Ronald Press, 1956–58).

[91] E. D. Edwards, *Chinese Prose Literature of the T'ang Period* (London: Arthur Probsthain, 1937), I, 30–40, 60–72.

[92] Cf. the biography of Li Po, based in large degree upon his poems and inferences from them, by Arthur Waley, *The Poetry and Career of Li Po* (London: Allen & Unwin, Ltd., 1950).

THE POMP AND ELEGANCE OF IMPERIAL CHINA

The statuette at the top, dating from the Sui dynasty (581–618 A.D.), and the wall painting copied from a cave in western China, dating from the later T'ang period (618–912 A.D.), below, indicate something of the dignity and delicacy of courtly life in China. The slender hauteur, elaborate dress, and whispered sensuality of the statuette reveal what the shuttered palanquin of the painting hid from vulgar eyes: the high artifice of a courtly beauty. The painting records a festive procession centering around the local governor and his wife, who are shown accompanied by jugglers, dancers, and horsemen to express the pomp of their office. Buddhists first brought to China the idea of using art to tell a story in this manner (two further panels not reproduced here complete the procession); but the secular subject and gay worldliness of this painting show how thoroughly the Chinese had digested this particular foreign influence by the T'ang period.

Other literary forms persisted in full, if not always inspired production. The histories, essays, collections of miscellaneous information, and commentaries on classic texts which engaged the energies of the literati still constitute a formidable mass, even though many of them have disappeared over the intervening centuries.[93]

Another important dimension of T'ang and early Sung culture was its elegant night life. Professional actors, musicians, and dancers entertained the court and the gentry and, on a cruder level, ministered to the pleasures of merchants and other less respectable groups. Ceramic figures of court beauties still impart some suggestion of the elegance of vanished evenings when sing-song girls exhibited their captivating arts. Popular poetry and love stories, characteristically telling of the extravagant attachment of a gentleman for a low-born sing-song girl, convey a similar image of luxury, refinement, and delicacy stopping just short of debauchery.

* * *

The enrichment and refinement of Chinese civilization in the T'ang and early Sung periods constituted something of a golden age in China's long history, although the continuity and general conservatism of Chinese tradition deprives the age of any towering pre-eminence. Moreover, Islam's dogmatic imperviousness to pagan achievements meant that T'ang culture failed to influence its civilized Eurasian contemporaries as Hellenism and Gupta India earlier had done. As a result, the powerful attractiveness of China's mature civilization was effective only within the narrower circle of the Far East, until the Mongol conquest of the thirteenth century brought some of China's skills to the attention of the rest of the civilized world.

Chinese influence upon Japan, Korea, and the barbarian borderlands was of course nothing new; and, between 600 and 1000 A.D., Chinese expansion in these regions continued much as before. The major area added to the sphere of Chinese culture was Yunnan, where an independent state successfully resisted Chinese arms but in doing so surrendered to the spell of Chinese culture.[94] During these same centuries, the Indianized states of southeast Asia expanded inland from the coastal plains and river banks where they had first arisen.[95] Thus, for example, the lower valley of the Mekong River became the center from which an extensive state pushed its frontier northward to the border of Yunnan by the end of the ninth century. This brought an Indian satellite culture directly into contact with a state just won to cultural depend-

[93] My remarks on Chinese literary developments are based on E. D. Edwards, *Chinese Prose Literature of the T'ang Period;* James R. Hightower, *Topics in Chinese Literature* (Cambridge, Mass.: Harvard University Press, 1950); Herbert A. Giles, *A History of Chinese Literature* (New York: D. Appleton & Co., 1901).

[94] O. Franke, *Geschichte des chinesischen Reiches*, II, 448–51, 501–4. Yunnan remained politically independent until the thirteenth century.

[95] Great temples and other religious structures were built, some of them impressively decorated with sculpture in the Indian tradition; but the social system sustaining this high art was comparatively fragile. Cf. G. Coedès, *Les États hindouisés d'Indochine et d'Indonesie*, pp. 202–9.

ency upon China.[96] Similar contact eastward along the Indochina coast and westward across the Burmese-Yunnan border had been made earlier. The result was to produce a more or less continuous frontier between the penumbral zones of the two great civilizations of southeast Asia. Primitive life of course survived, islanded in the interstices of a growingly dense network of civilized and semi-civilized societies.

Along the northern semi-circle of the Chinese frontier, however, civilized expansion increasingly transcended the geographic boundary between steppe and sown which had long confined Chinese styles of life to irrigable land. The Turkish confederacies which bordered China on the north—especially the Uighur state, which lasted from 745 to 840—were no longer mere barbarian hordes. Like the Khazars, their counterparts on the other extreme of the Turkish world, the Uighurs appropriated many of the traits of civilized society, including literacy, a higher religion, and a fairly stable administrative bureaucracy. Like the Khazars also, they supplemented traditional nomadic styles of animal husbandry with riverine and caravan trade. Such trade not only traversed the steppe in an east-west direction, but also moved north-south to bind the forest zones of the Eurasian north to the civilized centers of the south. To be sure, the severer climatic conditions in the eastern steppes made civilization more fragile there than in the more favorable milieu of southeastern Europe during the same period; yet the enlarged cultural impress of China and of the central Asian oasis populations upon the forests and steppes of Manchuria and eastern Siberia was unmistakable.

Analogous developments brought Tibet within the circle of semi-civilized life, beginning rather abruptly in the early seventh century with the unification of that land into a militarily formidable kingdom. When Chinese power in central Asia collapsed in the mid-eighth century, Tibetan raiders disputed the spoils of the oasis cities with the Moslems of eastern Iran. The success of the Tibetans was such that they soon built an empire reaching from the mouth of the Ganges and the upper Indus northward to Lake Balkash and east to the great bend of the Yellow River. By 860, the outlying regions of this empire had broken away; but the nucleus of the Tibetan state survived.

For the most part, the Tibetans borrowed their religion from India, their secular culture from China, and colored both with their own native traditions. Under Buddhist auspices, systematic and remarkably massive efforts to translate useful knowledge from Sanskrit into Tibetan began in 632, when the king of Tibet sent one of his ministers to India expressly for the purpose of making, or finding, a script for the Tibetan language. A "native reaction" between 836 and 842 threatened to uproot Buddhism from Tibet; but by the mid-tenth century, a fairly stable synthesis of Buddhism with the native Bon religion had been achieved. This amalgam is usually known as Lamaism.[97] Culturally intermediate between India and China, and secure behind towering mountains, Tibet easily retained its political independence.

---

[96] Cf. G. Coedès, *Les États hindouisés d'Indochine et d'Indonesie*, pp. 167–78, 188–201.

[97] Cf. Helmut Hoffmann, "Tibets Eintritt in die Universalgeschichte," *Saeculum*, I (1950), 258–79.

To the northeast, Chinese influence had no competition from Indian or Iranian cultural traditions; hence while diverse native elements—language in particular—were never eliminated, the civilizations of Korea and Japan came to bear a more purely Chinese stamp than was the case along China's other borderlands.

Korea had entered marginally into the circle of Chinese culture in pre-Han times and had long served as intermediary between China and Japan. Migrations from the north—analogous to those that brought various barbarian peoples into north China between the third and sixth centuries A.D.—led to the establishment of a powerful and warlike state in northern Korea. Having successfully resisted invasion by the Sui emperors, internal faction led the Koreans to acknowledge Chinese suzerainty in 668; but the T'ang emperors, for the most part, contented themselves with a more or less fictional authority.

Radical difference between the Korean and the Chinese languages was a major reason for the preservation of a separate Korean cultural identity. Although Chinese characters, like our familiar numerical notation, are ideographs which can be read in any language, in the seventh century Korean scholars found it useful to invent supplementary symbols representing specifically Korean inflections and connectives.[98] Used at first as marginalia to Chinese texts, these symbols eventually developed into an independent Korean script. This assured Korea of a distinct literary tradition.

Renewed political disorders in Korea paralleled the collapse of the T'ang dynasty in China. By 935, however, a new Korean dynasty had united the entire peninsula; and when China in turn re-emerged as a powerful state under the Sung (960), the two countries renewed their political-cultural relations. Yet Korea was now definitely less dependent upon China than she had been in T'ang times. The need to conciliate the Kitan state, which bordered both Korea and China on the north, prevented the Sung from overtly exercising political sovereignty over Korea. In addition, the Buddhist faith professed by the new Korean dynasty served to emphasize local cultural autonomy and protected Korea from the Neo-Confucian orthodoxy of Sung China in much the same fashion that Manichaeism had formerly protected the Uighurs from the unmitigated weight of Chinese cultural superiority.[99]

Japan seems to have received her first impulses toward civilization from contact with Korea. A major landmark was the reception of Buddhism in 552; but the new religion did not achieve a secure status in Japan before 587. From this point on, the consolidation of central authority and an eager appropriation of Chinese civilization proceeded hand in hand. Direct relations between the Chinese and Japanese courts were opened for the first time in

---

[98] Chinese lacks grammatical particles and endings; but these parts of speech were of critical importance in languages like Korean and Japanese. Hence the need for a supplementary notation, from which, in due course, syllabaries and eventually alphabetic notations developed. The development of a fully alphabetical script in Korea was facilitated, and perhaps caused, by the Sanskrit studies undertaken by Buddhists who sought to master the pure sources of their religion.

[99] M. Frederick Nelson, *Korea and the Old Order in Eastern Asia* (Baton Rouge, La.: Louisiana State University Press, 1945), pp. 28–57; Homer B. Hulbert, *The History of Korea* (2 vols.; Seoul: Methodist Publishing House, 1905).

607; and Japan sent special missions at frequent intervals thereafter. Artists and craftsmen as well as scribes, interpreters, and diplomatic dignitaries accompanied these missions and systematically brought back whatever aspects of Chinese culture they felt might be useful at home.

As a result, during the Nara period, 646–794,[100] Japan developed a somewhat precocious courtly culture. Poetry and painting in the Chinese style flourished almost as in China itself; administration, court ranks, and imperial protocol all were modeled closely on T'ang examples. By the tenth century, however, a more distinctively Japanese version of this culture began to take form. A syllabary simplification of Chinese characters allowed phonetic writing of the Japanese language for the first time;[101] and the authority of the Japanese imperial court began to give way before the ruder strength of border barons who shared only slightly in the Sinified culture of the capital. The most remarkable monument of Japan's cultural emancipation from Chinese models was the romance, *Tales of Genji*,[102] written by Lady Murasaki, a lady in waiting of the imperial court in the early eleventh century. Written in Japanese, with only an occasional intrusion of Chinese words, *Tales of Genji* is a masterpiece of world literature: a lively love story, portraying the elegant sensibility of the courtly circle. But the imperial power waned soon afterward; and Lady Murasaki found no worthy successor among the denizens of the court, which shortly became little more than a gilded cage.[103]

*   *   *

The net result of the expansion of the Chinese cultural sphere in the T'ang and early Sung periods, together with the simultaneous expansion of Indian and Moslem[104] civilizations, was to fill in nearly all the gaps which had previously separated the major civilizations of Asia from one another. The border zones filled up with states and peoples that were culturally only semi-independent of the major civilizations of the continent. Characteristically, these peoples—Uighurs, Khazars, Tibetans, Koreans, and others—used the literacy, religion, and political-military organization they had borrowed to resist assimilation into the body politic of any of their greater neighbors.[105] Whereas in earlier periods, cultural absorption had been the normal fate of

[100] So called because the imperial capital was then at Nara.

[101] Japanese had been written in Chinese characters ever since the fifth century, with equivalences being based on the identity of meaning. This system, however, was no better suited to Japanese than it was to Korean.

[102] Translated by Arthur Waley, *The Tale of Genji* (Boston, New York: Houghton Mifflin Co., 1935).

[103] These summary remarks about Japan are based on G. B. Sansom, *Japan: A Short Cultural History* (rev. ed.; New York: Appleton-Century, 1943), pp. 64–255.

[104] The Moslem penetration of the western and central steppe will be described in the next chapter; it had begun before 1000, but its major consequences ripened only after that date.

[105] The Kitan empire, which controlled the northernmost provinces of China from 907, offers a good example of how consciously this policy could be pursued. The internal dualism of this state, which seems deliberately designed to allow the Kitans to preserve their social and cultural identity against the Chinese, has been painstakingly analyzed by Karl A. Wittfogel and Feng Chia-sheng, *History of Chinese Society, Liao (907–1125)* (Philadelphia: American Philosophical Society, 1949).

limitrophic barbarians, now the cross-currents among the various civilizations of Eurasia were strong enough to offer barbarian peoples choice among divergent styles of civilization. The possibility of such a choice provoked increased barbarian resistance to complete assimilation into any existing civilization. This gave the Eurasian continent a rather novel cultural physiognomy, comparable on an enlarged scale to the complexity created by the rise of the semi-satellite cultures around Mesopotamia and Egypt in the second millennium B.C.

F. THE OUTER FRINGES

The expansion of the Eurasian ecumene between the seventh and tenth centuries A.D. brought a wide and nearly continuous belt of territory from the Atlantic to the Pacific and from the Indian Ocean to the forest zones of the north within the range of Old World civilizations. By the year 1000 A.D., only a thin and dispersed population of hunters and reindeer herdsmen on the extreme northern face of Eurasia remained still almost unaffected by the extension of agriculture and commerce which had brought the steppe and much of the forest zone of the Eurasian continent into touch with one or more of the styles of civilized life.

During the same centuries, traders effectively broke through the Saharan barrier to the south. An increasing use of camels, which had been introduced into north Africa in Roman imperial times, allowed a wider-ranging caravan trade than before. The magnets which chiefly attracted caravan leaders to risk the dangers of the desert crossing were gold, and next to gold, slaves. Heavier traffic across the Sahara in turn stimulated the elaboration of more complicated Negro societies. Chiefs and their agents sought to monopolize the supply of gold and slaves and, in the process, tended to develop the production of both commodities on a more systematic and larger scale. Ghana, the earliest state organized along such lines, seems to have come under the control of a new dynasty in the eighth century, an event which may signify the transfer of authority from Berber to Negro rulers. Simultaneously, in adjacent parts of west Africa, the village communities of the region began to support other, rival foci of political-commercial power. Such states offered enlarged scope for mining, military, and craft specialists, thereby inaugurating a shadowy protocivilization that extended across a far wider territory than Ghana ever controlled.[106]

In east Africa also, the early Moslem period saw a substantial expansion in the geographical range of civilized mercantile enterprise. By the eighth century A.D., Arab shipping had supplanted earlier traffic along the African coast; and a series of settlements as far south as Sofala speedily took on a

[106] Cf. E. W. Bovill, *Caravans of the Old Sahara: An Introduction to the History of the Western Sudan* (London: Oxford University Press, 1933), pp. 43–47, 59–63; Diedrich Westermann, *Geschichte Afrikas, Staatenbildungen südlich der Sahara* (Cologne: Greven Verlag, 1952), pp. 72–76; J. D. Fage, *An Introduction to the History of West Africa* (Cambridge: Cambridge University Press, 1955); George Peter Murdock, *Africa: Its Peoples and Their Culture History* (New York: McGraw-Hill, 1959), pp. 72–73; J. Spencer Trimingham, *A History of Islam in West Africa* (London: Oxford University Press, 1962), pp. 20–22.

Moslem aspect. In these coastal stations, Arab merchants in co-operation with native chieftains brought gold, slaves, and ivory from the interior for shipment to the various ports of the Indian Ocean. Yet with the dubious exception of Zimbabwe,[107] this trade apparently led neither to state building nor to any important modifications of traditional social organization in the east African highlands.[108]

Until after 1000 A.D., the central rain forest of Africa and the semi-arid south remained almost unaffected by the progress of civilized men. To be sure, Bantu-speaking tribesmen, who practiced a primitive slash-and-burn type of agriculture, continued to spread their settlements through the forests of the Congo basin. But farther south and east, primitive hunters roamed as their forefathers had done for untold millennia. The same conservatism prevailed in the other great refuge area of the Old World, Australia.

During these same centuries, the wide Pacific became the scene of one of the most remarkable human dispersals of all history. Remote coral atolls and isolated volcanic cones, sometimes separated from the nearest land by hundreds of miles of trackless ocean, became sites of human habitation; and in some cases, even extremely remote islands sustained quite complex societies. Such communities were propagated from one island group to another by accidental drift voyages; for, if a storm or other mischance prevented a boat's crew from making its intended landfall, wind and wave might easily carry their vessel hundreds or even thousands of miles beyond its intended destination. Many crews were probably exclusively male and could therefore not found any lasting new settlement; but when women happened to be on board, new island communities could and did arise through a process not unlike the scattering of dandelion seeds before the wind. The puzzling variety of Micronesian and Melanesian settlements arose from such dispersals, beginning long before 600 A.D.; but the most spectacular and far-ranging sea migration, that of the Polynesians, seems to have occurred mainly between 600 and 1000 A.D.[109]

Polynesians probably never undertook deliberate voyages of more than 200 or 300 miles, for their methods of navigation were too primitive to allow a reasonable chance of successful landfall at greater distances. But the fact that voyages of even that length were undertaken meant that far longer acciden-

---

[107] The date to be assigned to the extensive stone structures in Rhodesia, of which there are remains on several sites, is a matter of debate. G. P. Murdock, *Africa: Its Peoples and Their Culture History*, pp. 209–11, says that the Zimbabwe remains date from the seventh century A.D. G. Caton-Thompson, *The Zimbabwe Culture* (Oxford: Clarendon Press, 1931), argued for a ninth–tenth century date. D. Westermann, *Geschichte Afrikas*, pp. 412–16, and H. A. Wieschoff, *The Zimbabwe-Monomotapa Culture in Southeast Africa* (Menosha: George Banta, 1941), believe that these structures were built in the fourteenth century. All agree that gold mining was the economic basis for the rise of these urban or semi-urban centers.

[108] On the beginning of civilized penetration of east Africa, cf. R. Coupland, *East Africa and Its Invaders* (Oxford: Clarendon Press, 1938), pp. 1–41; Zoë Marsh and G. W. Kingsnorth, *Introduction to the History of East Africa* (Cambridge: Cambridge University Press, 1957), pp. 1–12.

[109] One may hazard the guess that it was the development of efficient outrigger floats that made the extraordinary Polynesian voyages possible. An outrigger canoe, properly provisioned and handled, can survive even a severe storm and sail or drift indefinitely.

tal ones were bound to occur whenever a boat lost its way. Occasional contacts with the Americas as well as with the Asian mainland certainly occurred in this haphazard fashion, so that the Polynesians established a slender but real cultural continuum across the entire Pacific. Cases in which such accidental voyaging had any important consequences were certainly rare. Only if chance brought a boat crew to a fertile and uninhabited island, or precipitated the castaways upon a shore where the local population was willing and able to acquire something of cultural value from the newcomers, could such voyages leave any lasting trace. By far the most common cultural exchange occurred when a canoe from some distant place carried a locally unfamiliar type of plant or animal as part of its food supply. The erratic and complex distribution of cultivated plants and domestic animals among the Pacific islands therefore offers a sensitive indicator of the range and variety of sporadic contacts that linked the shores and islands of the Pacific before Europeans arrived to complicate local ecologies still further by introducing still other kinds of new plants and animals.[110]

In the New World, the so-called "classic" period of the Amerindian civilizations continued in full bloom for several centuries after 600 A.D. In Guatemala and adjacent parts of Mexico, classic Mayan cult centers increased in number and complexity. Then, about the middle of the ninth century, Mayan temples began to be abandoned, one by one, and jungle grew back over the vast courtyards, roadways, and step pyramids. Yet there is no reason to suppose that the Mayan populations abandoned the region. Perhaps raids from the north destroyed the prestige of gods who failed to protect their people from merely human enemies. Or invaders[111] may have captured and sacrificed the corps of ritual experts, thus preventing the continuance of the old elaborate cults, even if the common people still retained full faith in them. But, in view of the absence of any signs of violence at the deserted sites, it is more probable that the priestly specialists simply failed to prevent the spread of a simpler, popular religion that allowed individual farmers to assure the fertility of their maize fields by appropriate private ceremonies, thus rendering the priests' costly ritual services otiose. In the sixteenth century, European intruders found just such a private cult among the Mayan peoples, which (whenever it was introduced) obviously made the elaborate temple centers of an earlier age permanently unnecessary.

Farther north, the course of events is less clear. The Mexican plateau and some districts on the coast saw a rise and fall of monumental cult centers that

---

[110] Andrew Sharp, *Ancient Voyagers in the Pacific* (Wellington, N.Z.: Polynesian Society, 1956) has effectively disposed of earlier misapprehensions about the character and range of Polynesian seafaring. An impressive array of records of accidental drift voyages which occurred during the first decades of European presence in the southern seas sufficiently proves his point: that deliberate voyages were always of relatively short range but gave scope, by accident, for the long-range travels which account for Polynesian settlement. Thor Heyerdahl, *American Indians in the Pacific* (Stockholm: Bokförlaget Forum AB, 1952), however interesting, is among those whom Sharp effectively refutes; but cf. Heyerdahl's modified views as presaged in *Aku-Aku* (Chicago: Rand McNally, 1958), pp. 371–77.

For plant dispersals and the puzzles these create for botanists, cf. George F. Carter, "Plants across the Pacific" ("Society for American Archaeology Memoirs," No. 9 [1953]), pp. 62–72.

[111] There are traces of alien "Mexic" motifs in some of the last Mayan carvings.

may have been roughly contemporaneous with the Mayan temple complexes. Almost certainly, an irruption of more warlike, barbarous tribes from the north destroyed the Mexican temples. At any rate, later sites show palaces rivaling temples as monumental centers; and sculptural remains suggest that a far more bloodthirsty cult gained ground at the expense of the emphasis upon astronomy and vegetable fertility characteristic of earlier religion. Toward the end of the tenth century, an offshoot of this Mexican style of civilization penetrated into the Mayan area and established a major religious and political center at Chichen-Itza in Yucatan. Older Mayan art motifs mingled with newfangled Mexican ones in the monuments of Chichen Itza; but compared to the classic Mayan style, both the precision of stone carving and the exactitude of astronomical and calendrical knowledge declined.

In Peru, chronology is wildly uncertain. Sometime between 500 and 1000 A.D.,[112] an art style associated with Tiahuanaco, a vast cult center in the Andes, spread over most of the Peruvian area. Whether this attests political conquest and the establishment of a great empire, or some religious movement which upset older pieties, cannot be said with certainty. An increase in warlikeness seems to have occurred; and the level of artistic excellence declined as compared with what had gone before.[113]

Just as in the Old World, the cultural achievements of Peruvian and Mexican societies affected more backward peoples within range of the civilized core areas. All details of this diffusion are unclear. Yet agricultural villages, more or less permanently settled in one spot, certainly spread through large parts of both North and South America; and modest beginnings of cult centers reminiscent of those of Mexico probably began to appear by 1000 A.D. in regions as far afield as what is now the southeastern United States.

[112] There are experts who argue for each of these extreme dates.

[113] Gordon R. Willey, "The Prehistoric Civilizations of Nuclear America," *American Anthropologist*, LVII (1955), 571–93; J. Alden Mason, *The Ancient Civilizations of Peru* (Harmondsworth: Penguin Books, 1957), pp. 12–107; Wendell C. Bennett and Junius B. Bird, *Andean Culture History* (New York: American Museum of Natural History, 1949), pp. 153–201; G. H. S. Bushnell, *Peru* (London: Thames & Hudson, 1956), pp. 65–102; Walter Krickeberg, *Altmexikanische Kulturen* (Berlin: Safari Verlag, 1956), pp. 283–487; J. Eric S. Thompson, *The Rise and Fall of Maya Civilization* (Norman, Okla.: University of Oklahoma Press, 1954), pp. 56–118; G. C. Vaillant, *The Aztecs of Mexico* (Harmondsworth: Penguin Books, 1950), pp. 65–82.

The parallels that seem to hold between Central and South American developments may be attributed to direct (seaborne?) or indirect contacts; but the remarkable likenesses between the general development of the American civilizations and that of early Mesopotamia raise far more fundamental questions. The militarization and artistic-intellectual retrogression of the Amerindian civilizations between 600 and 1000 A.D. reminds one of the age in Mesopotamian history inaugurated by Sargon of Akkad; and the parallel becomes more remarkable still if one accepts the hypothesis that an irruption of marginal barbarians into the old civilized centers preceded the respective "imperialist" periods.

Do such parallels suffice to define a general law of ecological succession in the history of civilized human social structures?

CHAPTER X

Steppe Conquerors and the European Far West

1000–1500 A.D.

A. INTRODUCTION

Two major occurrences decisively affected the balance of the ecumene during the half-millennium that began about the year 1000. One was the outpouring of Turkish, Mongolian, and Tungusic peoples from the Eurasian steppe, reaching a climax in the thirteenth century with the conquests of Genghis Khan and his successors. The second was the rise of a vigorous civilization in western Europe.

Of the two, the movements of the steppe peoples were by far the more conspicuous. Infiltration or cataclysmic conquests at the hands of those barbarians affected almost the entire civilized world. Only outliers of the ecumene—Japan, part of southeast Asia, the southernmost tip of India, and the European Far West—escaped political domination by warriors deriving directly or indirectly from the steppe. In geographic scope, the conquests of the bronze-wielding charioteers of the eighteenth to fifteenth centuries B.C. alone can compare with this inundation.[1] Thus Indo-European barbarians at the beginning of steppe history, and Altaic barbarians at its climactic close, share pride of place as conquerors whose victories reverberated throughout the entire Eurasian continent.

---

[1] The *Völkerwanderungen* of the third to sixth centuries A.D. did not much affect India; and the Iron Age invasions of the eleventh to ninth centuries B.C. left no clear trace in either India or China. These movements, therefore, while comparable on a restricted scale, failed to exert a truly ecumenical influence upon the civilizations of Eurasia.

484

The Mongol invasions, extending from China to eastern Europe, and from the fringes of the Siberian forests to Java, Burma, and the Punjab, intermixed elements drawn from all the major civilizations of the Old World more intimately than ever before. Long before that climax, Turkish warriors, by first infiltrating the heartlands of Islam and then pushing beyond onto Christian and Indian ground, forwarded interaction among the three civilizations of western Eurasia. When the Mongols superadded Chinese elements to this mixture, cross-fertilization among the high cultures of the Old World reached its geographical limit.

Cultural immixture and borrowings across the ecumene were not, however, the most important consequence of the Turkish and Mongol conquests. The ancient, massive, and profoundly impressive structures of Islamic, Indian, and Chinese civilizations could not be more than incidentally enhanced by such additions. Only in the Far West of Eurasia, where Latin Christendom had not yet established a fixed and hallowed pattern of life, were men malleable enough psychologically to incorporate techniques derived from distant China with more massive borrowings from their Moslem and Byzantine neighbors and make the amalgam fundamental to their expanding civilization. This was Europe's good fortune. Western Europeans could and did welcome innovations from abroad as the more settled and anciently civilized societies of Asia (and of southeastern Europe) could not. Yet, among the older civilizations, reactions to the new barbarian conquests were by no means uniform. In brief, Islam civilized the new masters of the Middle East; China and Russia first endured and then expelled their alien rulers and proceeded to encapsulate themselves within the psychological protection of a "native reaction"; while India and Byzantine Christendom, unable to expel, had to accommodate to the rule of Islamized Turks.

Thus, through a reversal of roles not uncommon in history, Islamic civilization, which suffered most from nomadic infiltration and conquest, was able to profit most from the upheaval of old relationships which the steppe invasions brought in their wake. To be sure, a far-reaching internal transformation of Islamic civilization was necessary before a more or less satisfactory modus vivendi was established between the new Turkish (or Mongol) rulers and the older civilized peoples of the Middle East. Yet, when this had been accomplished, the prowess of the Islamized steppe peoples, together with the new missionary energy generated by the Sufi movement, led to a most remarkable expansion, which carried Islam beyond its classical borders into Asia Minor, eastern Europe, sub-Saharan Africa, most of India, southeastern and central Asia, and even to parts of China.

We are so accustomed to regard history from a European vantage point that the extraordinary scope and force of this Islamic expansion, which prefigured and overlapped the later expansion of western Europe, often escapes attention. Yet an intelligent and informed observer of the fifteenth century could hardly have avoided the conclusion that Islam, rather than the remote and still comparatively crude society of the European Far West, was destined to dominate the world in the following centuries. Latin Christendom in the fifteenth century was still restricted to a comparatively small portion of the globe; its powers of expansion had been only intermittently demonstrated; and its arts and culture were only beginning to reach a level of refinement and polish comparable to that long familiar in Asian civilizations. Yet our imaginary observer would have been radically in error. Not Islam but western Europe turned out to be the agent that upset the fourfold balance of the Eurasian ecumene and brought the Americas, southern Africa, and Australia into the circle of Old World civilization.

Wise after the event, the historian may hope to detect some of the peculiarities of western European civilization that made this astounding career possible. Medieval Europe undoubtedly deserves special attention as the proximate cradle from which the world-girdling civilization of modern times arose, even though, at the time, Europe gave small sign of the potential that lay within it. Yet the growth on formerly semi-barbarian territory of a civilization comparable in most respects to any in the world constituted in itself an alteration in the balance of the ecumene. As such, the rise of western Europe deserves to rank as a distant second behind the movement from the steppe as a major disturber of the Eurasian cultural balance between 1000 and 1500 A.D.

B. INFILTRATION AND CONQUEST FROM THE STEPPE

By 1000 A.D. the steppe gradient had been in full operation for thirteen or fourteen centuries, sporadically impelling one tribe after another to seek better pastures in more favorable western environments. The effect was to establish a linguistic drift across Asia, as first Indo-Europeans, then Turks, and lastly Mongols migrated westward. Yet, while languages changed, in all that time the essential economic, political, and military patterns of horse nomadry altered very little.

Nonetheless, knowledge of civilized ways had penetrated with a new intensity among the tribesmen of the steppe in the centuries just before 1000 A.D. A closer symbiosis with agricultural and urban populations always had great attraction for nomad groups, since cereals, textiles, metals, and trinkets offered a welcome supplement to the sparse resources which pastoral and hunting life provided. Hence, as more frequent trade contacts and mercenary service in civilized armies[2] gave the steppe populations an enhanced awareness

---

[2] A striking feature of Islamic society was the widespread use of slave soldiery to support the personal power of a ruler. The germ of the institution lay in the concept of a private household staffed largely by slaves; and a ruler whose control over the state was challenged by unruly landowners or other elements of society found it tempting to expand and arm his household until his personal slaves became a standing army. Apparently the first to take this step was the caliph Mutasim (833–42), who found the landed classes of Khurasan, whence his Abbasid predecessors had drawn their bodyguards, insufficiently obedient, and hit upon the device of substituting Turkish slaves in their place. Cf. Reuben Levy, *The Social Structure of Islam* (Cambridge: Cambridge University Press, 1957), pp. 417–18. The supply of Turkish slaves was presumably assured by tribal wars on the steppe itself—captives from such wars being sold by the captors to Moslem merchants. Nothing like this existed in China, where mercenary service with the Chinese government characteristically involved not individuals but whole tribes or even tribal confederations, and where the institution of slave soldiery was unknown.

of the wealth and wonders of the southerly civilizations, the gravitational pull of China, the Middle East, and Byzantium upon the formidable horsemen of the steppe inevitably increased.

The infiltration of nomad groups into settled regions was easiest in the Middle East, where the agricultural land of eastern Iran shaded off by almost imperceptible degrees into parched grassland. There the nomads could continue their accustomed mode of life on the margin of settled society and graze the stubble after harvesting, while also enjoying the luxuries attainable through trade or tribute relationships with farming and urban populations. At the same time, urban or proto-urban centers moved far out into the steppe, arising around trading posts where nomads came to exchange furs, animals, and slaves for the goods of civilization. Thus the line between steppe and sown became increasingly blurred; and in the course of time, Turkish-speaking groups extensively interpenetrated Iranian populations, pushing the frontier of Turkish speech well to the south of the Aral and Caspian seas. These Turks accepted the Moslem faith and took on something of Islamic manners; but they did not entirely lose themselves in the Moslem world. A sense of superiority, based upon pride in their military prowess, kept them from full assimilation; and they retained their language, together with much of the warlike ethos of the steppe.[3]

Two other adventitious factors facilitated Turkish assimilation into the Moslem world as a distinct, yet scarcely alien people, and contributed decisively to the Turkish military and political success in the Middle East. One was the fact that at the time the Turks first emerged as a formidable element within the Islamic body politic, Shi'a rulers were dominant almost everywhere. Consequently, when Turkish leaders espoused Islam, they tended to opt for its Sunnite form, thereby asserting their spiritual independence against the civilized authorities closest to them. But Sunnite doctrine had been the orthodoxy of the great days of the early caliphate and was still the faith of

---

[3] Cf. W. Barthold, *Turkestan down to the Mongol Invasion* (2d ed.; London: Oxford University Press, 1928), pp. 235–58, 391–93; W. Barthold, *Histoire des Turcs d'Asie centrale* (Paris: Maisonneuve, 1945), pp. 47–124.

The permeability of the Iranian aperture upon the steppe in the tenth and subsequent centuries stands in striking contrast to the general success with which the Parthians and Sassanians had held that frontier in earlier ages. There was no change in military technology to account for the difference: armored cavalry still had a limited superiority over steppe archers as aforetime. What seems to have happened was that the rough country squires and nobles of the Iranian frontier regions, whose strong right arms had held the steppe peoples at bay in the early Christian centuries, were no longer very formidable fighting men. The growth of towns in Khurasan and Transoxiana had been a marked characteristic of the Moslem period; presumably many landowners had moved to town to enjoy the comforts and cultivation of town life. By doing so, they lost the military habits of their ancestors and no longer could or would effectively take the field against the Turks. The changed ethos of the Iranian gentlemen is accessible to us through Persian poetry of the tenth century and after, a poetry which breathes elegance and refinement but is notably lacking in martial vigor. Cf. the analogous transformation of Celtic aristocrats of Gaul from warriors to Roman gentlemen as town life spread into that province between the second century B.C. and the second century A.D. As Barthold argues, economic and political factors, saddling landowners with debt, or in other ways making landholding precarious or unprofitable, and giving merchants the upper hand in the cities of Khurasan and Transoxiana may have hastened the decay of the Iranian landed gentry. Cf. Barthold, *Turkestan down to the Mongol Conquest*, pp. 307–8. Moreover, Moslem piety required urbanization, for religious duties could not be adequately fulfilled by men living in remote country houses, far from mosques and experts in the Sacred Law.

the majority of Moslems. Hence, in submitting to Turkish rule, many Moslems felt that they were overturning foul heresy and, hopefully, harking back to the glories of the past.[4]

The second adventitious factor was the Islamic concept of "holy war" waged by *ghazis, i.e.*, special champions of the faith whose courage in battle constituted a sort of sanctity. Warfare across the frontiers of Islam therefore offered rude Turks a highly honorable role that was tailor-made to their warrior traditions. And if plunder and heroic self-aggrandizement played a greater role in most Turkish minds than piety and the service of Allah—for the Turks were never inclined to take very earnestly the ideal of building a society in conformity to the divine will—the same could be said of many of Omar's best fighting men. In general, the Turkish nomadic background closely resembled that of the first Arab conquerors. This made it comparatively easy to find an honorific niche for such doughty, if barbarous warriors within Islam and allowed civilized Moslems to deflect the brunt of Turkish military enterprise against their Christian and Hindu neighbors.[5]

The net result of these geographical, religious, and cultural circumstances, therefore, was to permit the massive incorporation of Turkish society into Islam. Turks provided a majority of the Moslem rulers and soldiers from the eleventh century onward and constituted the cutting edge of Islamic expansion into both Christendom and Hindustan.[6]

In China, the sort of gradual barbarian infiltration and subsequent seizure of power from within which occurred in the Islamic world after the tenth century was utterly impossible. Neither the Confucian nor the Buddhist tradition of China afforded a very honorable place to soldiers; and the Tibetan form of Buddhism which the Mongols tended to favor as early as the time of Genghis Khan (d. 1227) and firmly adopted during the sixteenth century[7] could not appeal to any Chinese group as a restoration of ancient orthodoxy and vanished glories. Even more to the point, the Gobi Desert intervened between Outer Mongolia and the agricultural land of China. This tended to limit the zone of piecemeal interpenetration between Mongols and Chinese to Inner Mongolia; while in Outer Mongolia, where a much larger steppe population was always located, the severity of the climate dictated an almost pure nomadry, supplemented by hunting. Such populations remained inescapably alien to Chinese civilization, even when well aware of its attractions.[8] The

---

[4] Cf. the analogous Frankish advantages over those German tribes that had become Arian Christians.

[5] For the importance of the tradition of "holy war" in the early growth of the Ottoman empire, cf. P. Wittek, *The Rise of the Ottoman Empire* (London: Royal Asiatic Society, 1938), pp. 42–43.

[6] Cf. the relationship between German barbarians and the Latin Christians from the fourth century.

[7] René Grousset, *L'Empire des steppes* (Paris: Payot, 1939), pp. 592–93.

[8] Cf. B. Vladimirtsov, *Le Régime social des Mongols* (Paris: Maisonneuve, 1948), pp. 39–56. No Gobi Desert hindered the penetration of Chinese influence northeastward; and from the tenth century a geographically extensive intermingling of nomad and sedentary populations established itself in Manchuria. Cf. Karl A. Wittfogel and Feng Chia-sheng, *History of Chinese Society: Liao, 907–1125* (New York: Macmillan Co., 1940), pp. 53–58, 115–25. The depth and socio-economic character of this penetration of the Manchurian area seems quite similar to that which occurred across the Iranian-Turkish border during the same centuries.

policy of every Chinese government, within the limits of its power, was to keep such outer barbarians at arm's length. Nomad tribes could fit into the bureaucratic patterns of Chinese society only as submissive, distant clients; and any group that declined to accept this subordinate status could enter the Chinese world only by armed force.[9]

The relative impermeability of the Chinese frontier made nomad intrusions upon China very different from the Turkish infiltration into Iran. Before a nomad confederation could develop sufficient striking power to batter down Chinese defenses, it had first to attain a rather high degree of internal organization and discipline. When such a confederation did succeed in seizing Chinese territory, the nomad leaders had every reason to try to maintain the instrument through which they had conquered. Their power depended upon the military force of a tribal confederation; and a too-enthusiastic assimilation of Chinese ways by the conquerors would be sure to destroy the basis of nomad rule. Hence a long succession of foreign conquerors made explicit efforts to insulate nomad and Chinese styles of life from one another, even when the two had become geographically intermingled. Chinese efforts to keep the nomads in their place were thus fully reciprocated by those nomads who succeeded in conquering the Chinese.[10]

Such an effort to resist the attractions of Chinese culture ran against the grain of human nature, yet must have seemed vital just because the conqueror's own "nativist" policy implied the preservation of a subordinate Chinese administration to govern and exploit the Chinese population for the benefit of the conquerors. This in turn meant that the power instrument for the reassertion of an almost "pure" Chinese government and society lay always at hand. Ease and wealth meant an all but inevitable decay of the conquerors' military prowess and political cohesion; and, when such decay had proceeded far enough, native reaction under Chinese leadership, inspired by the natural dislike of a subject population for foreign overlords, was comparatively easy to organize. Such was the origin of the Ming dynasty (1368–1644), which ended Mongol rule in China. In expelling the hated conquerors, the Ming systematically and successfully eradicated nearly every trace of the Mongols' hundred-year encampment in the midst of Chinese society.

Turkish domination of the Middle East had far more permanent and fundamental effects. Before the Turks attained political power, they had already lived for many years on the fringes of the Islamic world and had become

[9] Byzantine relationships with the nomads of south Russia and the Danubian plains more nearly resembled the Chinese than the Iranian pattern; but since no massive nomad breakthrough of Byzantine defenses took place after the ninth century—thanks perhaps to the southward deflection of steppe migration routes into Islamic territory—we can neglect Byzantine dealings with Pechenegs, Cumans, and others. For interesting details of this frontier history, cf. F. Dvornik, "Byzantium and the North," in Michael Huxley (ed.), *The Root of Europe: Studies in the Diffusion of Greek Cultures* (London: The Geographical Magazine, 1952).

[10] Wittfogel and Feng, *History of Chinese Society, Liao, 907–1125*, point out differences in the degree to which nomadic and Chinese elements were kept separate by successive conquerors. Thus the Jurchen rulers (1115–1234) allowed more blurring of lines between Chinese and barbarian elements than did the Kitan (907–1125) who had preceded them in north China; and the Manchus (1616–1912) were similarly more open to Sinification than the Mongols (1206–1368) had been. These differences modify but scarcely invalidate the generalization of the text.

Moslem in religion. Thus they were not alien to their subjects in the degree that the conquerors of China were alien. Nor could they so easily be expelled. No ready-made, non-Turkish power system comparable to the Chinese bureaucracy existed within the Islamic states;[11] and any decay in the military effectiveness of one group of rulers simply opened a path for fresh bodies of Turks, more recently come from the steppe, to rise to power.

*   *   *

The rhythm of events can best be grasped by distinguishing three phases of the nomad expansion: (1) the rise of Turks to political domination over the Islamic world, with an accompanying breakthrough against both Hindustan and Christendom (1000–1200 A.D.); (2) the Mongol conquests, initiated by Genghis Khan (1206–27), which extended almost across Eurasia and temporarily checked Moslem expansion; and (3) the recovery of Turkish dominance over the Middle East and resumption of Islamic expansion into India and Europe (1300–1500).

1) The various Turkish states that arose on Moslem ground in the eleventh and twelfth centuries were for the most part ephemeral. One of the most stable, the Seljuk sultanate, maintained its coherence for only half a century (1037–92) before breaking up into dozens of warring fractions. More successful was the consolidation of Egypt, Syria, and Iraq under Saladin (1169–93), which was aided by Moslem reaction to the Frankish victories in the First Crusade (1097–99). The failure of the Third Crusade (1189–92) demonstrated the effectiveness of Saladin's work; and after the last of his dynasty died in 1250, the Turkish slave soldiery of Egypt, known as Mamelukes,[12] established a remarkable oligarchic regime which successfully maintained control of most of Saladin's empire until 1517.

The major landmark of the Turkish advance against Christendom was the battle of Manzikert in 1071, by which the Seljuks decisively defeated the Byzantines and consolidated their hold upon the central Anatolian plateau.[13] On Islam's other flank, the self-appointed son of a Turkish slave soldier, Mahmud of Ghazni, raided far and wide in the Punjab and upper Ganges Valley (998–1030) from a base in modern Afghanistan. His successes paved the way for Moslem occupation of all northern India. But the power exercised by various Moslem upstarts and adventurers south of the Himalayas did

[11] In the Moslem world, underground "resistance" movements took sectarian religious (Shi'a) form. Thus the Assassins, who exercised a strange power as a dispersed and secret state within a state from 1090 to 1256, did their best to overthrow Seljuk rule. They may have appealed to anti-Turkish as well as to anti-Sunnite sentiment. Cf. Marshall G. S. Hodgson, *The Order of Assassins* (Gravenhage: Mouton, 1955).

[12] A. N. Poliak, "Le Caractère colonial de l'état mamelouke dans ses rapports avec la Horde d'Or," *Revue des études islamiques*, IX (1935), 231–48, advances the interesting thesis that the Mameluke regime was in reality an overseas colonial empire of Circassian and Turkish merchants and warriors based north of the Black Sea, displacing in the Levant a similar "Frankish" colonial regime.

[13] Claude Cohen, "Le Problème ethnique en Anatolie," *Cahiers d'histoire mondiale*, II (1954–55), 347–62, points out that Turks had infiltrated Anatolia before Manzikert, so that the battle sealed an accomplished fact, rather than opening a new region to Turkish expansion.

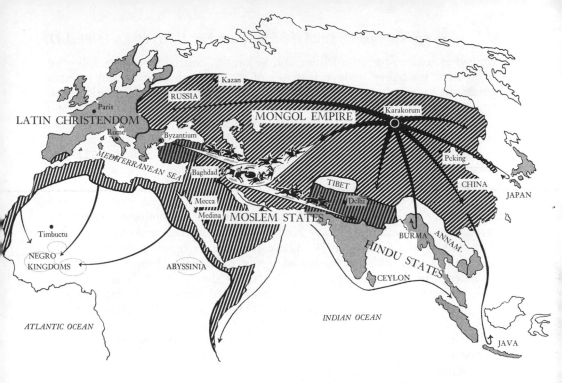

THE MONGOL EXPLOSION TO 1300 A.D.

not achieve any sort of stability until 1206, when the first of a line of Turkish slave kings ascended the throne of Delhi and inaugurated a regime resembling the government later established in the Levant by the Mamelukes.[14]

2) The military convulsion that engulfed most of Eurasia in the thirteenth century, centering upon the high steppe of outer Mongolia, constituted a second wave of the nomad expansion. It was profoundly different in character from the earlier Turkish infiltration of the Middle East, for the Mongols came as a horde of fierce and barbarian warriors, prepared to treat their human victims as they treated animals rounded up in their annual great hunts: domesticating or slaughtering them as circumstances might dictate.

The career of the great Mongol leader, Genghis Khan (1206–27), is the most dramatic example in all history of the potentialities of nomad warfare. In youth a fugitive and once even helplessly imprisoned by his enemies, he was able by dint of personal prowess, wiliness, and luck to create a great tribal confederacy and to impose a rigorous discipline upon the fighting men who thus came under his command.[15] Early victories allowed him to fold erst-

[14] By an interesting coincidence, these two polities alone among the Moslem states withstood the Mongol storm that burst upon the Islamic world in the thirteenth century.

[15] B. Vladimirtsov, Le Régime social des Mongols, pp. 56–158, argues that the Mongols were in process of transition from a clan and tribal society toward what he calls a "feudal" system, whereby wealth and leadership devolved, not so much upon hereditary clan and tribal leaders, as upon appointees and close relatives of the ruling house. Clearly, it was only by breaking through older clan lines and or-

while enemies into his own forces; and as long as unbroken success followed his banners, the booty-hungry warriors of the steppe had no reason to rebel against the severe discipline he exercised over them. In quick succession, his armies launched vast raids against those parts of China, the Middle East, and Europe lying nearest the steppe. Superior generalship, mobility, and what today would be called staff work gave the Mongols superiority over every enemy they encountered. Consequently, when Genghis Khan died in 1227, his armies were undefeated; and the entire steppe from the Volga to the Amur had been welded into a single vast military confederacy.[16]

Under Genghis Khan's successors, booty raids by degrees gave way to a more regular exploitation of the conquered lands. But conquests continued: eastern Europe became tributary after 1241; Persia, Iraq, and Anatolia after 1258; and all of China by 1279. Thereafter, the Mongols' military *élan* diminished. In 1260, the Mamelukes of Egypt defeated a Mongol-led force in the Palestinian desert and proceeded to expel the Mongols from Syria. In 1281, the failure of an invasion of Japan checked the eastward expansion of Mongol power; and between 1285 and 1303, the sultans of Delhi repelled a series of Mongol raids into India, though not without sacrificing control of part of the Punjab. As late as 1292, a Mongol expedition against Java met temporary success; and in 1297 an army overran Burma; but Mongol power in these distant regions did not last long and made no deep impression.

3) Genghis Khan's three elder sons confronted the task of ruling vast ap-

---

ganizing his armies upon a hierarchic principle that Genghis Khan created his instrument of conquest. But the term "feudal" seems an inept epithet to describe Mongol political relationships. In addition to native traditions, Uighur (*i.e.*, ultimately Sassanian?) and Chinese bureaucratic models helped to inspire Genghis Khan's military and territorial administration. Cf. Barthold, *Turkestan down to the Mongol Conquest*, pp. 386–93; George Vernadsky, *The Mongols and Russia* (New Haven, Conn.: Yale University Press, 1953), pp. 92–137.

[16] No technical improvement in weapons was associated with the Mongol conquests. Genghis Khan's army did, however, show itself adept in making use of new military machines, wherever encountered. Thus catapults constructed by Moslem artisans battered down Chinese city walls for the Mongol commanders and Chinese gunpowder may have been used in Hungary.

Basically the Mongol striking force was cavalry; but the light cavalry archers, native to Mongolia, were early supplemented by heavy armored "cataphracts," thus combining firepower with shock. The normal tactic was encirclement, modeled on the annual hunt which was a regular feature of Mongol tribal life. For this hunt, all the men of the tribe rode forth to form a great circle, which then gradually closed, driving the game into a limited "battlefield" where it could be conveniently slaughtered for winter meat supplies. This called for co-ordination of movements over long distances without loss of contact or control and constituted the best sort of "staff" training for Mongol commanders and soldiers, since huntsmen and soldiers were one and the same.

Generally, the superiority of the Mongols over civilized armies lay not in numbers (they were often inferior) nor in armament, but in mobility and co-ordination of movements over very long distances. The Mongols were capable of moving in widely dispersed columns over all sorts of terrain, while maintaining communication between the separate columns so as to assure concentration of all forces at the decisive time and place. Subotai, the general in charge of the invasion of Europe in 1241, thought nothing of co-ordinating columns operating in Poland with others pressing into Hungary, despite the Carpathian barrier between them. No comparable feats of co-ordination over such distances were achieved by European armies until the late nineteenth century. What made it possible was an excellent courier service, elaborate advance and flank scouting, and the extraordinary hardihood of both horses and men who had grown up under the bleak and harsh conditions of the Mongolian steppe. For a convenient summary of Mongol military organization and tactics, see H. Desmond Martin, *The Rise of Chingis Khan and His Conquest of North China* (Baltimore, Md.: Johns Hopkins Press, 1950), pp. 11–47.

panages carved from their father's empire without the support of the Mongol army, which was concentrated under the command of their youngest brother.[17] Consequently, in all the western portions of the Mongol empire, Turkish peoples came quickly to the surface again. Turks of the steppe had been folded into the Mongol military system from the start; and their superior numbers led to a rapid decay of the Mongol language among the ruling groups everywhere west of Mongolia proper. This linguistic transformation paralleled a wider process of acculturation, for once the initial devastation of the Mongol storm had passed, the old process of assimilation between Islamic society and nomad overlords resumed operation. As early as 1257, the khan of the Golden Horde on the Volga began to favor Islam and allied himself with Mameluke Egypt against the Mongol khan of Persia.[18] In 1295 the khans of Persia espoused the Moslem faith; and during the following century, Islam became dominant in the ancient oases of the Tarim basin and penetrated the central steppe itself. Under these circumstances, the tumultuous struggles which laid low the Mongol dynasty of Persia (1349) and raised various Turkish and Mongol-Turkish successors to ephemeral power made little difference. The chaotic political processes which sustained Moslem expansion against Christian Europe and Hindu India at the cost of perpetual disorder in the core areas of Islam reasserted itself.

Throughout the central steppe and in the Middle East and northern India, new Islamic states rose and fell with kaleidoscopic rapidity, depending upon the success of one or another military captain. The most remarkable of these captains was Tamerlane (1360–1404), a Turk and a Moslem who posed as heir and successor to Genghis Khan and imitated Mongol ruthlessness as a matter of deliberate policy. Only the Mameluke empire of Egypt and Syria (whose rulers were recruited after 1382 from Circassian rather than from Turkish slaves) and the Ottoman Turkish state (1284–1921) maintained internal stability and cohesion.

Cultural and economic life certainly suffered damages from the unceasing political disorder of the Moslem core area; yet it did not check the expansion of Islam. Quite the contrary. Incessant warfare in the Moslem heartlands produced a continual stream of skilled soldiers who, having met only hard knocks in Iran and central Asia, were eager to try their fortunes as warriors for the faith against Hindustan or Christendom. Thus the political disorder at the center of Islam acted like a great winnowing fan, sucking warlike groups and individuals from the steppe into the Moslem heartlands and then driving survivors pell-mell toward the frontiers.

The main beneficiaries of this military migration were the Moslem rulers of

---

[17] According to a Moslem historian, only 4,000 Mongols were assigned to each of Genghis Khan's elder sons. By contrast, the youngest son commanded 129,000 men. Barthold, *Turkestan down to the Mongol Conquest*, p. 404. Such lopsided distribution of authority had the virtue, however, of maintaining an effective if loose unity to the entire empire until 1294, when Kublai Khan, Genghis' grandson, died.

[18] The khan of the Golden Horde had quarreled with the khan of Persia over possession of Azerbaijan and the Caucasus region. Grousset, *L'Empire des steppes*, pp. 475–76; B. Grekov and A. Iakoubovski, *La Horde d'Or* (Paris: Payot, 1939), pp. 76–82.

India and the Ottoman sultans. By 1500, most of India had submitted to Moslem rule.[19] By the same date, the Ottomans had united Asia Minor and all the Balkan Peninsula south of the Sava-Danube line, save for a few Venetian strong points on the Adriatic coast and in the Peloponnesus. Nevertheless, by 1500 the military tide had turned against the steppe peoples. Firearms were becoming the decisive weapons of war, and it was because of their willingness and ability to make full use of these new weapons that the Ottoman armies achieved their most brilliant victories after about the middle of the fifteenth century.[20] But as soon as firearms became decisive on the battlefield, steppe peoples found themselves at a tremendous disadvantage. Such complicated weapons could only be produced by civilized communities with access to fuels, metals, chemicals, and artisan skills which nomads could never attain. Moreover, centuries of attachment to the arts of horse archery made the steppe peoples extremely loath to experiment with the new weapons, even when civilized traders put them expensively within the nomads' reach. Their reluctance was reinforced by the fact that the invention of firearms reversed the long-standing balance of forces between cavalry and infantry.[21] In due course, when civilized infantry, equipped with firearms, became able to view the charge of even the fiercest and best disciplined steppe horsemen with complete equanimity, the military and historical importance of the nomads came to an end.[22]

[19] The last of the militarily formidable Hindu states, Vijayanagar, founded 1335, was not destroyed until 1565.

[20] The famous Janissary corps, a military slave corps recruited after 1438 mainly from Christian subjects of the Ottoman sultan, was equipped with muskets about 1500. The Ottomans had an efficient artillery as early as the siege of Constantinople in 1453. Cf. David Ayalon, *Gunpowder and Firearms in the Mamluk Kingdom* (London: Vallentine, Mitchell, 1956), Appendix II. On guns in India, cf. Syed Abu Zafar Navdi, "The Use of Cannon in Muslim India," *Islamic Culture, the Hyderabad Quarterly Review*, XII (1938), 405–18.

[21] Until the late sixteenth century, hand guns were too heavy and clumsy for cavalry use. Even when horse pistols became available, they were puny and ineffective by comparison with infantry muskets.

It is ironic that the greatest steppe victory of history, the Mongol conquests, probably hastened the age of gunpowder. Chinese experiments with explosives and primitive cannon antedated similar beginnings in Europe and elsewhere; and it is highly likely that some knowledge of Chinese successes along these lines started European gunsmiths and artillerists on their even more successful career. Yet without the Mongol empire of Asia, such stimulation might have been long delayed or never have occurred at all.

For Chinese pioneering in firearms, see L. Carrington Goodrich and Feng Chia-sheng, "The Early Development of Firearms in China," *Isis*, XXXVI (1946), 114–23; Wang Ling, "On the Invention and Use of Gunpowder in China," *Isis*, XXXVII (1947), 160–78. Wang adduces evidence to suggest that the Mongol invasion of eastern Europe in 1240–41 may have first introduced Europeans to gunpowder in the form of explosive grenades hurled by catapults. The seeming identity between the earliest recorded cannon shapes of Europe (see, e.g., Charles Oman, *A History of the Art of War in the Middle Ages*, Vol. II [Boston and New York: Houghton Mifflin Co., n.d.], Pl. XXIX) and the Chinese weapon of 1221 which was "cast in the shape of a gourd of pig iron two inches thick" (Goodrich and Feng, p. 117) certainly suggests that European artisans somehow learned of other uses the Chinese had found for gunpowder during the decades that followed the great Mongol conquests, when, as Marco Polo's *Travels* prove, movement across Eurasia was relatively easy.

[22] While the central drama of world history was thus turning upon the spectacular deeds of Turks and Mongols, an analogous drama played itself out in north Africa and Spain, where a succession of

C. ISLAMIC REACTION TO THE PRESSURES FROM THE STEPPE

I. POLITICAL AND SOCIAL

The Turkish infiltration of the Moslem world, together with the catastrophic Mongol conquest, upset the compromise reached under the early Abbasids between the religious ideal of a holy community under God and the practical requirements of governing an empire. When the Mongols overthrew the Baghdad caliphate (1258), even the pretense of political unity disappeared.[23] Moreover, the chicane and violence characteristic of successful Turkish adventurers, and the aversion to Islam typical of the first Mongol rulers, made a miserable laughingstock of any effort to bring day-to-day political realities into harmony with religious principles. Effective government within the new states derived partly from old Persian models, partly from tribal and steppe institutions, and partly from the ruthless suspicion of hard-pressed adventurers who trusted no one in a world where no binding moral commitments cushioned the naked struggle for power.

Yet the early ideal of a godly community lingered like a ghost from the past to haunt Moslem hearts. Upon occasion, reformers and armed prophets like the Almoravid (1056–1147) and Almohad (1130–1269) rulers of north Africa and Moslem Spain seriously set out to realize the pious aspirations of their followers. But such efforts to revive the spirit of the early Moslem community regularly failed. Religious fervor wilted as the need to consolidate political authority obliged the leaders to compromise their religious principles. Yet on a sub-political level, the Moslem community survived and flourished, despite profound political disappointment.

Even the most irreligious of rulers allowed scope to the teachers and administrators of Islamic Sacred Law. No other legal system existed within the Moslem community for the setlement of private disputes.[24] Hence study of the Sacred Law continued despite all political vicissitudes; and an expert in the Law might hope to find honorable reception and even high office under

---

nomad barbarian conquerors from the fringes of the Sahara overwhelmed and reorganized the political system of the Moslem Far West. But these Berber tribesmen were in contact with only one high civilization and therefore could not assume the role of cultural cross-fertilizers which their Turkish and Mongol counterparts played in Eurasia. Only in relation to the Negro communities of the western Sudan was Berber violence mitigated by a civilizing by-product.

Cf. Ibn Khaldun, *The Muqaddimah: An Introduction to History*, Franz Rosenthal (trans.) (3 vols.; New York: Pantheon, 1958), in which he attributes the decadence of the native north Africa in his time (fourteenth century) to a cycle of nomad conquests.

[23] A scion of the Abbasid house escaped to Egypt and was recognized as caliph by the Mameluke rulers of the land; but this "caliph" was never widely recognized in other Moslem states. Cf. T. W. Arnold, *The Califate* (Oxford: Clarendon Press, 1924), pp. 87–120.

[24] Even in their shamanist-Buddhist days, the Mongol rulers of Iran allowed the jurists of Islam to judge and direct the affairs of the Moslem community. Cf. Bertold Spuler, *Die Mongolen in Iran* (Berlin: Akademie Verlag, 1955), pp. 375–76.

any of the rulers of the Moslem world.[25] The pilgrimage to Mecca and the prestige of study at Medina brought students and teachers from every corner of Islam into close contact with one another, and thereby maintained a trans-governmental body of jurists and theologians which effectively bound the entire Moslem world together.

Yet in proportion as the Sacred Law became a complicated collection of rules for everyday living, religious persons tended to repudiate a discipline of holiness so mechanically conceived. The Sufi path of mystic communion with God therefore tended to supplant the earlier effort to regulate every detail of daily activity according to divine instructions. Despite the inherently private character of the experience, Sufi orders—the dervishes or fakirs—successfully institutionalized the mystic striving and channeled it into congregational forms. A famous saint, a few enthusiastic disciples, and a more or less distinctive ritual and pattern of life sufficed to bring a new Sufi order into existence. Such orders proliferated endlessly all over the Moslem world in the eleventh and twelfth centuries, although only a few of them attained either long life or a wide geographical scope.

Craft guilds or other urban "brotherhoods" often made Sufi exercises the central act of their association. Such groups occasionally succeeded in arousing the local population to resist some petty tyrant fastened upon the community through the chances of war. But this sort of political counterpoise to the military superiority of Turkish soldiery failed to develop into stable town government. A few Anatolian and Iranian towns in the fourteenth century appear to have enjoyed an autonomy approaching that of the free towns of Europe during the same age; but such situations remained exceptional. Permanent power structures could scarcely be based upon groups dedicated first and foremost to ecstatic communion with God. When a temporary crisis had passed, the Sufi adepts naturally returned to preoccupation with the supreme end of human striving—the cultivation of the mystic vision—to the neglect of ordinary administration and self-defense. Hence government was left to the armed minority; and the guilds, brotherhoods, and dervish orders acted only as an intermittent, if sometimes effective check upon arbitrary power.[26]

Lack of scholarly studies makes any general assessment of economic conditions within the Islamic world before 1500 A.D. impossible.[27] Violence surely interfered with trade; many great and wealthy cities were sacked; and some suffered complete destruction. Moreover, Moslem shipping lost control of the

[25] The career of the famous traveler Ibn Batuta (1304–69?) strikingly illustrates the international character of Moslem learning and jurisprudence. Born in Morocco, he held judicial office in such distant regions as India and the Maldive islands and attained the same dignity upon returning to his native Morocco at the end of his life. Despite the variety of government and custom, the same Sacred Law, at least in principle, applied throughout the realm of Islam and an expert in the Law was therefore qualified to hold office anywhere. Cf. Ibn Batuta, *Travels in Asia and Africa*, H. A. R. Gibb (trans.) (London: George Routledge & Sons, 1929).

[26] Cf. Franz Taeschner, "Beiträge zur Geschichte der Achis in Anatolien (14–15 Jht)," *Islamica*, IV (1929), 1–47; Bernard Lewis, "The Islamic Guilds," *Economic History Review*, VIII (1937), 20–37.

[27] Cf. Claude Cohen, "L'Histoire économique et sociale de l'Orient musulman medieval," *Studia Islamica*, III (1955), 93–115.

Mediterranean to the rising Italian towns after the tenth century. Nonetheless, city life in the Islamic world continued strong. Losses in one region were offset by the rise of new capitals, enriched by plunder and adorned by artisans transferred from their former homes at the bidding of mighty, if evanescent conquerors. Prolonged misrule, as in Egypt under the Mameluke regime of the fifteenth century, certainly produced economic retrogression; but on the other hand, the rise of relatively stable new states like the Ottoman empire probably encouraged trade and increased wealth.

In view of these contradictions, no generalization about economic advance or retrogression within Islam between 1000 and 1500 A.D. is possible. It seems, however, that Iraq and Syria, the economic and political heartlands of earlier Islam, lost ground relatively, and perhaps also absolutely, while Iran and Anatolia attained much greater importance than before. In particular, the irrigation system of Mesopotamia fell upon evil days when Turkish upstarts and plunderers began to quarrel over political supremacy in the ancient flood plains. Failure of elaborate and skilful maintenance of the canal system spelled disaster. As a result, salt pans and swamps, barren desert and scant grazing lands had begun to encroach upon formerly cultivated fields a century or more before the Mongol conquest (1258).[28] Such decay at the old center, even when offset by an upsurge of prosperity in Anatolia and the Balkan lands after the consolidation of the Ottoman empire, augured ill for the socio-economic health of Islam as a whole.[29]

* * *

As political fragmentation became normal within Islam, and conformity to a minutely defined Sacred Law ceased to be the pre-eminent hallmark of a believer, the limits of orthodoxy expanded to admit far wider doctrinal variations than before. Sufism went from strength to strength and incorporated many traits deriving directly from Christian, Zoroastrian, Hindu, and shamanist cults. Indeed, it was only with the rise of Sufism, and of the cult of saints connected therewith, that Islam finally reached out to embrace nearly all Christians of the Middle East. Sufism, in fact, attached the countryside firmly to Islam for the first time, for it represented, among other things, an accommodation within what had before been a distinctly urban religion to

[28] Cf. Thorkild Jacobsen and Robert M. Adams, "Salt and Silt in Ancient Mesopotamian Agriculture," *Science*, CXXVIII (1958), 1257. The critical problem was the raising of fields above canal levels as a result of centuries of silting. Failure to dig out canal channels at frequent intervals could and did wreak drastic damage; but this hazard had been present from the earliest days of Mesopotamian irrigation and could always be repaired with a season's hard work. Not so the more basic problem created by rising field levels, which could only have been solved by vast new canal construction, on a scale and with a technical complexity which only a centralized administration could possibly carry through. Modern Iraq is only now, in the second half of the twentieth century, beginning to undertake the massive engineering necessary to re-establish agriculture on the scale which had been attained in that ancient land in the early Christian centuries.

[29] The classical Greco-Roman world passed through a similar evolution, whereby economic decay at the older centers coincided with the rise of formerly peripheral regions to new prosperity. The history of sugar plantations in the Caribbean later recapitulated the same pattern. Yet the technical factors in these three instances seem to have nothing whatever in common.

the ideas and aspirations of ordinary countryfolk. Simultaneously, the missionary attraction of Islam beyond its classical borders increased greatly when, not conformity to a rigorous Sacred Law, but simple reverence for holy men who walked familiarly with God, became the first and most important step in conversion to the faith of Mohammed.

As new peoples accepted Islam and as Sufism increased the internal variety of the faith, important divergences from region to region became evident. Variation in detail became almost infinite. The vast Sufi missionary successes therefore created an even vaster task for the *ulema*—the experts in theology and law—who set out to make the thoughts and habits of the converts conform to the legal, classical definition of Islam. Only very slowly did the Sacred Law make headway against the immemorial variety of local custom and legal practice; yet it did make headway as individuals and whole communities modified local custom to bring it into closer conformity with the Sacred Law. As a result, Islam as a whole was able to maintain a certain balance between the antinomian tendencies of Sufi mysticism and the old-fashioned legalism of the *ulema*.

Amid the religious flux and political fragmentation that characterized Islam, the stability and wide dominion of the Ottoman state constituted a conspicuous exception. Unfortunately, the origins of this state are most obscure. Arising on the frontier between Islam and Byzantine Christendom, it seems in its early days to have drawn most of its strength from *ghazi* frontiersmen. Turkish recruits to the wars steadily percolated into the frontier region from farther east, urged onward by settled governments glad to rid themselves of troublesome elements so cheaply. In addition, large numbers of local Christians went over to the Moslems, finding more in common with them than with distant Byzantine officialdom. Sufi saints and brotherhoods played their usual role in such conversions;[30] so did a rough and ready egalitarianism, fostered by the *ghazi* tradition and by the brotherhoods and guilds which played a conspicuous part in early Ottoman society.

When, however, the Ottoman state became a territorially substantial empire, the *ghazi* leader, or sultan, faced the usual problem of holding his conquests together. His fighting men were intractable subjects, who could be kept from mischief at home only by annual campaigns against Christendom. The sultans therefore fell back upon the familiar Moslem institution of a slave family to provide the sinews of regular government; but they skilfully reconciled this instrument of autocracy with the *ghazi* tradition by turning their slave family into a vast educational establishment for the conversion of Christian boys into champions of Islam. The system does not appear to have

---

[30] The Bektashi Order of dervishes, which came to be closely associated with the Ottoman slave army corps of Janissaries, was remarkable even among Sufi orders for its latitudinarian doctrines. The Bektashi taught that Islam, Christianity, and other religions were essentially alike—all of them only imperfect efforts to express and thereby to imprison the mystic experience of the Godhead. Such doctrines, obviously, facilitated conversion to Islam, since, not the repudiation of Christianity, but of Christianity's claim to exclusive truth, was alone at issue. Cf. J. K. Birge, *The Bektashi Order of Dervishes* (Hartford, Conn.: Hartford Seminary Press, 1937); F. Hasluck, *Christianity and Islam under the Sultan* (Oxford: Clarendon Press, 1929), I, 159–66.

assumed regular form before the 1430's. Thereafter, the Ottoman sultans possessed in their slave family a powerful counterpoise to the unruliness of their freeborn Moslem subjects.

Little by little the importance of the original *ghazi* freebooters declined, while that of the slave family increased. Yet until the end of the sixteenth century, hard-bitten Moslem cavalrymen, living on their estates in winter and joining the sultan's standard for each summer's campaign, constituted by far the largest single element in the Ottoman armies.[31] As long as the Moslem fighting class and the slave family counterbalanced each other, the Ottoman state went from strength to strength. The succession to the throne always presented a crisis; yet a long line of vigorous rulers of the House of Osman proved able to keep a rough equilibrium between the two facets of their military power, and thereby to remain sovereigns in fact as well as in name.

In attempting to convert a freebooters' frontier principality into a great Moslem empire, the early Ottoman sultans also called upon the *ulema* for help.[32] This had two curious effects. On the one hand, by enhancing the place of the Sacred Law in Ottoman life, the *ulema* widened the breach between Moslem and Christian ways of life—a breach which had been minimal in the beginning phases of Ottoman expansion. Second, the Sacred Law itself inculcated toleration for People of the Book and forbade forcible interference with Christian or Jewish religion, thus checking *ghazi* habits of headlong attack upon any and all infidels. Hence as the rude frontiersmen of early Ottoman history gave ground before the slave family, on the one hand, and before the orthodox *ulema* of Sunni Islam, on the other, conversion of Christian subjects almost ceased, save through the limited channel of the slave family itself.[33] Only in remote and mountainous regions like Bosnia, where the prevalence of Bogomilism probably facilitated the reception of Islam, or in Albania, where continuous local warfare fostered a spirit resembling that of the old *ghazis*, did mass conversion from Christianity to Islam occur after the mid-fourteenth century.

When Mohammed II, the Conqueror, captured Constantinople in 1453, he therefore proceeded to regularize a double regime, entrusting wide judicial and other powers over his Christian subjects to the Orthodox patriarch. The Christian clergy became a mirror image of the *ulema* itself, bearing an authority over Christians comparable to that which the legal experts of Islam exercised over Moslems. Conversely, the sultans took a leaf from the Christian

---

[31] Christian auxiliaries, fighting under their own princes, also played a considerable role in early Ottoman armies. The Rumanian provinces remained under such a regime but elsewhere the sultans extended direct Turkish administration to one region after another and assigned estates in the new provinces to Moslem fighting men, who thus displaced their Christian predecessors. Consequently, after about 1450 Christian auxiliaries no longer were important in Turkish armies.

[32] In Brusa and Nicaea, the first important towns captured by the Ottoman Turks (1326 and 1331), institutions of higher religious learning were established immediately after the conquest, presumably in order to supply an adequate number of judges and teachers for the new state. Cf. Abdulhak Adnan, *La Science chez les Turcs Ottomans* (Paris: Maisonneuve, 1939), pp. 9–11.

[33] A notable reinvigoration of Orthodox Christianity also reduced the appeal of Sufism to Balkan Christians. See below, p. 522.

ALLAH

LAW MOHAMMED LAST JUDGMENT

SULTAN

TIMARIOTS

JANISSARIES

DERVISH ULEMA

MONK BISHOP MAGNATE

FRANKS

TAXES

THE PEOPLE OF THE BOOK

THE STRUCTURE OF THE OTTOMAN EMPIRE

book by organizing a regular hierarchy among the *ulema* and subjecting them to a more rigorous state control than any previous Moslem ruler had done.

Nowhere else did a Moslem state approach the success of the Ottoman regime. In Spain, the Moslems of Andalusia proved unable to stem the Christian advance from the north and lost their last foothold in Granada in 1492, at a time when the Ottoman power was just approaching its apogee. In central Asia, Iran, and India, a long succession of military adventurers failed to establish long-lasting states, perhaps because they lacked the support of the *ghazi* tradition which had nourished the early Ottoman regime and which continued to constitute a significant element in its mature structure, even after 1500 A.D.[34]

2. CULTURAL

Political fragmentation and Turkish overlordship did not at once alter the intellectual and artistic climate of the Moslem world. Until about the end of the eleventh century, the tripartite division between the sacred sciences of Islam, the rationalistic philosophy and science of the Greeks, and the belles-lettres of cultivated courtiers continued much as before. Even rough conquerors like Mahmud of Ghazni, the pillager of India, patronized men of letters and learning on a lavish scale, going so far as to kidnap particularly shining lights from rival courts. Prolonged violence and upheaval, therefore, did not seriously interfere with the pursuit of learning. Political fragmentation merely supplied a larger number of ambitious rulers eager to patronize the famous. Indeed, the three greatest figures of Moslem science and philosophy all lived amid scenes of political turmoil: the doctor and theologian Ibn Sina (Avicenna, 980–1037) spent most of his life in eastern Iran, where Turkish pressure was greatest, as did the polymath and student of Indian thought al-Biruni (Alberuni, 973–1046); while at the other end of the Moslem world, Ibn Rushd (Averroes, 1126–89) survived the conquest of Spain by the fanatical Almohades. The work of these and dozens of lesser men brought the corpus of received knowledge to a level of complexity and systematic cohesion equal or superior to that of Hellenistic Alexandria.

Generally speaking, by the twelfth century A.D., Moslem savants had mastered the learning of their Greek and Indian predecessors; fitted a body of fresh knowledge into the older framework, especially in the fields of mathematics, medicine, chemistry, and optics; and adjusted the whole in some degree to Moslem doctrine. The great systematizers of Greek learning—Aristotle, Galen, Euclid, Ptolemy—provided the basic framework for Moslem investigations; but numerous details and a few principles of Moslem science went beyond anything known to these ancient preceptors.[35]

[34] My remarks on the Ottoman polity depend primarily upon the elegant little book by Paul Wittek, *The Rise of the Ottoman Empire* (London: Royal Asiatic Society, 1957). Cf. also A. H. Lybyer, *The Government of the Ottoman Empire in the Time of Suleiman the Magnificent* (Cambridge, Mass.: Harvard University Press, 1913); Franz Babinger, *Mehmed der Eroberer und seine Zeit* (Munich: F. Bruckmann, 1953).

[35] Cf. George Sarton, *Introduction to the History of Science* (Washington: Carnegie Institution, 1931), I, II; Aldo Mieli, *La Science arabe* (Leiden: E. J. Brill, 1939), 90–216.

Presumably, the tension between rationalistic thought and the sacred sciences of Islam could not have endured indefinitely, since on a number of points, e.g., whether the world had been created or was eternal, the arguments of philosophers and the dogma of religion directly collided. Logically, one or the other approach to truth had to yield; and this was, it so happened, what did in fact occur. Rationalistic thought bowed to dogma, but not without a struggle, nor before the sacred science of theology had taken over many of the philosophers' logical weapons wherewith to demonstrate the vanity of human reason. The decisive factor in the triumph of the sacred sciences was their alliance with popular religious feeling, manifest in the Sufi movement. This alliance was sealed by the life and writings of one of the greatest and by all odds the most influential theologian of Islam, al-Ghazali (1058–1111).

Under the Abbasids, angry Baghdad mobs and distrustful Islamic jurists had joined forces to defeat the first Moslem effort to construct a rationally argued theology. Yet by the time of al-Ghazali's youth, the need to rebut philosophical logic had led even conservative experts in the Sacred Law onto the slippery ground of theological debate. In their hands, Aristotelian logic served to demonstrate the inadequacy of reason to discover theological truth. Al-Ghazali was trained in this tradition; but in the midst of a brilliant career as professor of theology at Baghdad, he underwent a profound personal crisis and began to doubt everything. At length a mystic experience came to his rescue: he resigned his position at Baghdad and became a simple Sufi, cultivating the rapture of personal absorption in God. In his old age, al-Ghazali began to write and teach once more, strong in the conviction that men could in fact attain certain knowledge of God. Theological argument, he now felt, was merely a useful device to point men toward the mystic path by showing up the errors of philosophers and other irreligious teachers.[36]

Al-Ghazali's radical distrust of human reason became standard for all subsequent Moslem theology. Systematic anti-intellectualism gave ample scope to Sufi mysticism and allowed the *ulema* to muster popular support for their struggle against rationalistic free thinking. In such an inhospitable climate of opinion, the radical daring and sweep of Ibn Rushd's revived and revised Aristotelianism was virtually neglected in the Moslem world.[37] Indeed, the history of Moslem science and philosophy from the twelfth to the fifteenth

---

[36] Al-Ghazali wrote a brief autobiography, translated by W. Montgomery Watt, *The Faith and Practice of Al-Ghazali* (London: Allen & Unwin, Ltd., 1953), pp. 19–85. Cf. also Louis Gardet and M. M. Anawati, *Introduction à la théologie musulmane* (Paris: J. Vrin, 1948), pp. 67–76; A. J. Wensinck, *La Pensée de Ghazzali* (Paris: Maïsonneuve, 1940).

The manner in which Pope Innocent III succeeded in harnessing the enthusiasm of the Franciscan movement to the official hierarchy of the Roman Catholic Church about a century later bears an interesting parallel to the work of al-Ghazali, although perhaps one should point rather to St. Bonaventura, the mystical theologian of Franciscanism, as al-Ghazali's Christian equivalent.

[37] Averroes' importance for the history of ideas lay in his stimulating effect upon Latin Christian theologians, who knew him as a fascinating and heretical, but far from negligible, thinker. Aristotle, of course, had always been known to Moslem philosophers; but his doctrine had, from late Roman antiquity, been curiously disguised by a Neo-Platonic garb. Averroes' great intellectual achievement was to abstract Aristotle from this alien dress, thus permitting the theologians of Paris to start their revolution of Christian philosophy from a more or less authentic Aristotelian basis.

century might almost be epitomized in the titles of three books: al-Ghazali's *The Destruction of Philosophy;* Ibn Rushd's *Destruction of the Destruction,* in which he claimed greater scope for human reason than al-Ghazali had allowed; and a much inferior work, *The Destruction of the Destruction of the Destruction,* written by one Hodja Zada (d. 1487 or 1488) at the command of Sultan Mohammed II, who instructed his servant to settle the argument in al-Ghazali's favor.

The net result of this intellectual evolution, therefore, was to throttle almost all innovation in Moslem science and philosophy. The need for training expert doctors and astrologers, which in early Abbasid times had stimulated the incorporation of the Greek and (later) Indian intellectual heritages into the corpus of Moslem learning, was no longer a problem. Authoritative and exhaustive handbooks were readily available and summed up all a professional man needed to know. With Ibn Sina's *Canon* of medicine at hand, what more could any doctor require? After all, when the mystic experience was valued above all else, mere human reason ceased to have much importance; and since nothing really important remained to be discovered, wanton tampering with established truths and accepted doctrines could only justify the distrust with which official theology already regarded science and philosophy.[38]

Thus by a curious and fateful coincidence, Moslem thought froze into a fixed mold just at the time when intellectual curiosity was awakening in western Europe—the twelfth and thirteenth centuries A.D. The rote memorization and congregational recitation of authoritative texts which prevailed in Moslem institutions of higher learning, the *madrasas,*[39] presented a remark-

---

[38] Yet even within the Sufi tradition, reasoning could not be entirely avoided. Systematic expositions of doctrine and of the steps and stages of the mystic path were attempted, drawing heavily upon Neo-Platonic language and metaphors and in some cases assuming a highly intellectualized, abstract form. Cf. Reynold Alleyne Nicholson, *Studies in Islamic Mysticism* (Cambridge: Cambridge University Press, 1921), pp. 77–142; A. J. Arberry, *Sufism,* (London: George Allen, 1950), pp. 93–105.

The upsurge of mysticism in Islamic society may be compared with the intellectual currents of India in the seventh–sixth centuries B.C. and of the Roman world in the first Christian centuries. Anyone who is not himself a mystic is likely to seek explanation for such a phenomenon in some sort of frustration of human striving in this world: and it is tempting to attribute this profound transformation of Islamic thought to the failure of the original grand ideal of a totally God-directed society on this earth. When political realities made it impossible even to pretend to citizenship in a society constructed according to divine ordinances, Moslems clearly refused the leap into secularism which many intellectual leaders of western Europe were later to make and took refuge in an essentially personal, private mysticism instead.

The difficulties of life in urban milieux, when the impersonal uncertainties of market relationships were exacerbated by irregular, violent interventions of brutal soldiers, may go far to explain the psychological attraction of the mystic path. If from the eleventh century urban prosperity suffered a decline in large areas of the Moslem world, economic suffering and disappointment may have fed the flame of mysticism. Information about Moslem economic history is, however, too scant to give such an explanation any secure basis in fact.

[39] These institutions were first introduced into Iran and Iraq in the eleventh century, supplementing and institutionalizing the informal schools of law and theology which had previously formed around famous men of learning. It appears, however, that such institutions had a prior history in the Moslem East—a fact which helps to account for the intellectual distinction of such towns as Bokhara. According to W. Barthold, *Histoire des Turcs d'Asie centrale* (Paris: Maisonneuve, 1945), p. 48, the *madrasa* was an adaptation to Moslem use of Buddhist educational institutions which had flourished from perhaps the second to eighth centuries in Transoxiana. And behind Transoxianan Buddhism lay Indian schools harking back ultimately to the forest retreats of the *Upanishads.*

able contrast to the intellectual tumult of the universities of western Europe. The existence of hundreds of *madrasas*, sometimes liberally endowed and well staffed, merely fastened the dead hand of authority more securely upon Moslem minds. Only in fields remote from the sacred sciences—notably history and geography—did something of the old brilliance of Moslem intellectual culture survive, as the writings of Ibn Batuta (d. 1369?) and Ibn Khaldun (d. 1406) attest.

To be sure, theosophical speculation continued to proliferate in Sufi circles, outside and in some measure in opposition to the orthodox learning of the *madrasas*. Perhaps, therefore, it would be more correct to say that, after the twelfth century, the intellectual energies of Islam were divided between an increasingly rigid scholasticism of official learning and a looser, amorphous, but still evolving mystical tradition. This tradition, however, found more congenial and impressive expression in poetry than in more pedestrian forms of discourse. Perhaps for this reason, poetry and literature in general continued to flourish in Islam long after science and philosophy had withered.

The Sufi inspiration fructified Persian more than Arabic poetry; yet Arabic literature too continued vigorous. In Andalusia, for example, new poetic forms based upon rhymed stanzas arose in the eleventh century and later spread to other parts of the Arabic-speaking world. Beginning in the thirteenth century, popular tales redolent of the bazaars and caravanserais of the Moslem world acquired the dignity of literary form in such collections as the *Thousand and One Nights*, recounting the doings of rogues and merchants, princes and fair ladies, in an essentially secular spirit.[40]

But the real glory of Moslem literature was the work of Persian poets. Persian began to emerge as a literary language in the ninth–tenth centuries, deriving from an unbroken oral tradition and from works written in the earlier Pahlavi script. The first great Persian poet was Firdausi (d. 1020), whose principal work was a long epic poem celebrating the heroes of the Persian nation from the beginning of time to the Moslem conquest. Firdausi's poetry was patriotic rather than pious; but his successors centered their supremely polished verses around an elaborately ambiguous simile between human and divine love. Their poems may therefore be interpreted either as allegories of the Sufi mystic experience or as hedonistic glorifications of the delights of the flesh. In some cases the religious intent is clear, as in the poems of Rumi (d. 1273), founder of one of the most important dervish orders of Anatolia. In other cases hedonism is explicit and can scarcely be interpreted away, as in the verses attributed to Omar Khayyam (d. 1123).[41] Between such extremes lie the poems of Sa'di (d. 1291) and Hafiz (d. 1390), the latter in particular gaining a peculiar power through the persistent ambiguity of his praise of love.

[40] H. A. R. Gibb, *Arabic Literature*, pp. 60–114. Cf. the parallel appearance of the European fabliaux and of urban "middle class" tales under the Sung dynasty in China.

[41] Omar Khayyam was a mathematician and astronomer, chiefly noted for his remarkably accurate reform of the calendar under the Seljuk sultan Malik Shah (1072–92). He may well have written verses, but it appears that the collection attached to his name gravitated thither because of Omar's reputation as a freethinker in an age when such views were coming more and more under attack. Cf. Edward G. Browne, *A Literary History of Persia* (Cambridge: Cambridge University Press, 1956), II, 246–59.

No analytic paraphrase can convey the importance of Persian poetry to the Moslem world. The achievements of the Persian poets displaced Arabic from pride of place as the language of poetry par excellence. Under the Turks, Arabic came to be increasingly confined to the sacred sciences; Turkish was reserved for administration and war; while Persian became the tongue of belles-lettres and courtly intercourse. The gentlemanly ideal of earlier Moslem society was thereby recast into Persian form, intertwined with Sufi mysticism, and suffused with the delicacies of carnal and or spiritual love.

In a sense, therefore, Moslem culture of the eleventh–thirteenth centuries successfully synthesized traditions which had been separate and conflicting in earlier times, for the triumphant mystic way of Sufi holy men suffused the sacred sciences of the *ulema*, spiritualized the manners of the gentlemen, and superseded the reasoning of the philosophers. The world of politics remained apart; yet even there, Sufism inflamed the *ghazi* spirit and sustained the urban brotherhoods which played a central part in building so important a structure as the Ottoman empire.

But as Ottoman power emerged to supremacy in the Middle East, even the Sufi spirit began to flag; and the Moslem world as a whole began to live upon its cultural capital from the past. Perhaps the labyrinthine paths of mysticism had been pursued to their ultimate limits; perhaps vulgarization of the mystic experience into congregational exercises and saint worship deprived the Sufi way of its earlier intellectual venturesomeness; perhaps political and social pressures for conformity to the outward decencies and conventions of Islam sapped the vitality of the Sufi movement; or perhaps a restoration of urban prosperity under the Ottoman peace removed an important stimulus sustaining the mystic effort to transcend disappointments of the everyday world. However this may be, it is clear that just at the time when western Europe was beginning its greatest adventure, Islam found itself imprisoned in twin mausoleums—the official structure of the Sacred Law with its ancillary disciplines, and the para-official Sufi tradition. Neither the one nor the other housed much intellectual vitality; yet their imposing mass and infinite complexity inhibited any new start. The articulation of the two wholes was so exact that any change threatened to bring down the entire structure. Total repudiation was unthinkable, since it would have meant total apostasy and a loss of cultural identity. Hence, the very success with which the Sufi mystics of the eleventh to thirteenth centuries synthesized discordant elements of the Moslem cultural inheritance helped to induce the languid and ultimately disastrous immobility that has characterized subsequent Islamic thought until almost our own time.

* * *

The visual arts entirely escaped paralysis. In both architecture and painting, active and successful innovation continued until well after 1500. Instead of neglecting foreign influences, as scholars and writers tended to do, Moslem artists proved themselves alert and eager to adapt aspects of Chinese and European painting to their own use; and architects found much to appropriate from their Byzantine and Indian predecessors.

The history of Moslem architecture is both complicated and unclear. Early buildings have mostly disappeared with the destruction and rebuilding of the major Islamic cities. Many of the Moslem military adventurers of the tenth to fifteenth centuries were great builders; and where a considerable number of mosques survives, as in Cairo, the artistic excellence and the technical skill of construction tended to increase even after 1500.[42] Ottoman, Persian, and Indian Moslem architecture exhibited a similar vigor and wide stylistic variety as late as the seventeenth century.[43]

Architecture was the great public art of Islam, if only because mosques, *madrasas*, palaces, and fortifications were vital both to the religious and to the secular life of Moslem society. Sculpture and painting, so prominent in the Western artistic tradition, occupied a very different place, for they both fell under Mohammed's ban upon images. Sculpture, indeed, was so closely identified with idolatry that it was little practiced in Moslem countries at any time. Painting survived despite the religious suspicion attached to it, but only as a semi-secret vice, patronized by a handful of rulers and wealthy courtiers in the privacy of their libraries and baths. As such, Islamic painting really belongs among the domestic arts with furniture-making, ceramics, and carpet- or textile-weaving. All these attained an extraordinary elegance and refinement in the centuries between 1000 and 1500;[44] and many exquisite pieces were produced well after the latter date.

Moslem wall frescoes have nearly all been destroyed together with the palaces they once adorned; but a substantial body of manuscript illustrations survives to give a partial idea of the development of Islamic painting. The most important tradition was Persian, building directly on Sassanian, Manichaean, and Buddhist precedents. Persian artists also imitated aspects of Chinese styles after the Mongol conquests of the thirteenth century and experimented eagerly with perspective and other techniques of the European Renaissance. During the fourteenth century, they developed a distinctive stylistic synthesis of their own, which reached its apogee during the fifteenth and sixteenth centuries. The brilliant colors, sharp, clear lines, and incredibly minute elaboration of Persian miniatures rank them with the greatest artistic achievements of the world. Such paintings usually illustrated books of Persian poetry and therefore penetrated all parts of the Islamic world where that poetry was appreciated.[45]

[42] Cf. R. H. C. Davis, *The Mosques of Cairo* (Cairo: Middle East Publications, n.d.).

[43] Cf., e.g., Georges Marcais, *L'Art de l'Islam* (Paris: Larousse, 1946), pp. 109–89; Percy Brown, *Indian Architecture: Islamic Period* (Bombay: D. B. Taraporevala Sons, 1942); Ernst Diez, *Die Kunst der islamischen Völker* (2d ed.; Berlin: Akademische Verlagsgesellschaft Athenaion, 1917), pp. 71–185.

[44] A useful conspectus may be found in M. S. Dimand, *A Handbook of Muhammedan Art* (2d ed.; New York: Metropolitan Museum of Art, 1944).

[45] Moslem India was particularly affected by Persian painting and developed a derivative yet distinct school of its own in imitation of Persian work. Cf. T. W. Arnold, *Painting in Islam* (Oxford: Clarendon Press, 1928); Laurence Binyon, *The Spirit of Man in Asian Art* (Cambridge, Mass.: Harvard University Press, 1936), pp. 105–43; Arthur Upham Pope, *A Survey of Persian Art* (London: Oxford University Press, 1958).

DOME OF A CAIRO MOSQUE

This elaborately decorated dome was erected to shelter the tomb of an unimportant Mameluke sultan of Egypt, Kait Bey (1472–74). Continuity of basic design from the Dome of the Rock (p. 427) is obvious, and bespeaks Islam's rigid conservatism when once the codification of the Sacred Law had been completed. Yet the precise, intriguing patterns of the arabesque carvings which adorn the dome suggest an impressive level of cultivated vigor, being neither too elaborate to allow decipherment of the pattern from a distance, nor so simple as to be comprehensible without prolonged scrutiny.

D. INDIANS, CHRISTIANS, AND JEWS UNDER MOSLEM RULE

I. THE MOSLEM HEARTLANDS

Despite the religious attractions of Islam and the practical advantages which conversion to the dominant faith might bring, the toleration which the Koran prescribed for "People of the Book" allowed substantial Christian and Jewish populations to survive in the Middle East for centuries after the Moslem conquest. Even the Crusades, whose initial success (1099) called Moslem military supremacy briefly into question and sharpened the collision between the two faiths in the Levant, did not lead to wholesale persecution of Christians by the Moslem states. In the thirteenth century, however, the repercussions of the Mongol invasions drastically upset the long-established modus vivendi among the religious communities of the Middle East.

Before encountering Islam, the Mongols had met both Buddhism and Nestorian Christianity among the Uighurs and other eastern Turkish populations. Duly impressed by the claims of these civilized religions, Mongol chieftains characteristically took the precaution of enlisting the religious services of Buddhist and Christian experts in the supernatural to supplement their ancestral shamanist rites. As a result, when they became rulers of the Middle East, the Mongols at first favored the Christians as against the Islamic majority. No doubt this policy seemed wise on political grounds, for Moslems resented their infidel masters, and the loyalty of grateful Christians therefore constituted a valuable political asset.[46]

The conversion of the khans of Persia to Islam (1295) therefore unleashed long-pent and bitter Moslem indignation against the traitorous Christian minorities. Massive expulsions, massacres, and forced conversions resulted, in consequence of which the Christian communities of Iraq and Syria lost their importance. Only a few mountainous refuge areas remained solidly Christian after about 1300.[47] In Egypt, which escaped Mongol conquest, and in Anatolia, where Mongol policy failed to arouse serious religious hostility, Christians survived as an important minority into modern times; but in the Syrian-Mesopotamian heartland of the Moslem world, the Christian communities ceased to be numerically significant after 1300.[48]

---

[46] When the first fright aroused by the Mongol incursion into central Europe (1241) subsided, Latin Christendom entertained great hopes of capitalizing upon the Mongol inclination toward Christianity; and Westerners organized several missionary efforts to convert the Great Khan. Reports of some of these missionary journeys survive and constitute a major source for the history of Asia in the thirteenth and early fourteenth centuries. Cf. W. W. Rockhill (ed. and trans.), *The Journey of William of Rubruck . . . with Two Accounts of the Journey of John of Pian de Carpine* (London: Hakluyt Society, 1900); Christopher Dawson (ed.), *The Mongol Mission* (London and New York: Sheed & Ward, 1955); Leonard Olschki, *Marco Polo's Precursors* (Baltimore, Md.: Johns Hopkins Press, 1943).

[47] Economic motives probably played a part in fostering this religious persecution; for the Christians had tended to specialize as traders, money lenders, and shopkeepers. This, of course, exposed them to the hostility of peasant and proletarian. Cf. the traditional role of Jews in European society. Moreover, if we assume that the military disorders of the thirteenth and subsequent centuries led to serious economic dislocations, economic motivation for attacks upon Christians clearly increased.

[48] Cf. Pierre Rondot, *Les Chrétiens d'Orient* (Paris: J. Peyronnet, n.d.), pp. 78–79, 144–45, 154–55; William H. Shedd, *Islam and the Oriental Churches* (Philadelphia: Presbyterian Board of Publications, 1904), pp. 196–204 and *passim*.

The Jews of the Moslem world survived more successfully than the Christians were able to do, despite the fact that they, too, suffered from persecution and mob violence in the thirteenth and fourteenth centuries. Until the Mongol period, Mesopotamia remained the chief intellectual, religious, and economic center of Jewry, as it had been since Sassanian times. Thereafter, no one center enjoyed a clear pre-eminence, although the various Jewish communities maintained connections across political frontiers as before.

The Copts, Jacobites, Nestorians, and other Christian sects of the Levant cherished their own traditions so exclusively as to disregard the currents of thought and feeling that prevailed in the larger context of Moslem society. Not so the Jews. Although they continued to elaborate their unique heritage— the Law as applied and interpreted by generations of learned rabbis[49]—this did not prevent a man like Moses Maimonides (1135–1204) from bringing fresh winds of doctrine into the rather dusty recesses of rabbinical lore. Maimonides was a doctor by profession and wrote on medical subjects; but his fame rests largely upon his work as a theologian and philosopher, in which capacity he sought to reconcile the rationalism of Aristotle with religious revelation. His work thus strikingly resembles that of his Moslem contemporary and fellow Andalusian, Ibn Rushd (d. 1198). But whereas later Moslem theologians turned their backs upon Ibn Rushd's astringent rationalism, Maimonides' *Guide for the Perplexed* played an important part in subsequent Jewish (and Latin Christian) thought.

Despite intimate contacts with the larger Moslem world round about, Judaism proved able to retain a separate social, intellectual, and literary existence. The ancient Hebrew language remained alive as a medium of philosophy and belles-lettres[50] and gave birth to a vigorous poetry as well. Moreover, Jewry extended well beyond the limits of Islam, penetrating Christendom and boasting at least a few outposts in India and China. Jewish merchants and men of learning maintained close communication across the Moslem-Christian borders, so that Jews found themselves in a peculiarly strategic position to mediate aspects of Moslem civilization to western Europe, once Europe was ready to receive them.

2. INDIA

Increased religious uniformity of the Moslem heartlands was fully counterbalanced by the massive new alien communities which rapid military expansion brought under Islamic dominion. In eastern Europe, the relationship between Moslem overlords and their new Christian subjects fell into wellestablished patterns; but India was different. In Moslem law, Hindus and

---

[49] The close resemblance between the general character and aims of the Jewish and Moslem Sacred Law may have made it easier for Jewish thinkers to participate in the intellectual life of the Islamic world. On the resemblance between the Jewish and the Moslem Sacred Law, cf. S. D. Goitein, *Jews and Arabs* (New York: Schocken Books, 1955), pp. 59–61; Abraham I. Katsh, *Judaism and Islam: Biblical and Talmudic Backgrounds of the Koran and Its Commentaries* (New York: New York University Press, 1954).

[50] Maimonides himself wrote in Arabic; but his works were translated into Hebrew almost immediately and attained their principal diffusion in that language.

Buddhists were not "People of the Book," but idolaters, and as such excluded from the traditional limits of toleration. Moreover, some of the Indian temples and monasteries had accumulated vast treasures that made them tempting objects of plunder. Hence Moslem penetration of India first took the form of holy wars, in which religious horror of idolatry inspired the victorious Moslem armies to despoil and destroy the main religious centers of northern India.[51] As we have already seen, Buddhism collapsed under this attack; but Hinduism, firmly rooted in the daily routine and piety of the Indian population, survived the loss of its temples and successfully withstood sporadic persecution at Moslem hands.

Almost two centuries elapsed between the conquests of Mahmud of Ghazni (998–1030) and the establishment of a more or less stable Moslem state in northern India following the crushing victories won by Mohammed of Ghur (1175–1206). Thereafter Moslem advance was rapid, until by 1313 Moslem states had arisen throughout most of India. About 1335, a "native reaction" found political embodiment in the Hindu kingdom of Vijayanagar, which rolled back the Moslem power in the south; but all of northern and central India remained subject to an unstable constellation of Moslem rulers.

Clearly, some modification of the Moslem conception of "idolater" was prerequisite to any modus vivendi between the conquerors and their Hindu subjects. In practice, Moslem rulers in India quickly accorded Hindus a toleration analogous to that enjoyed by Christians, Jews, and Zoroastrians in other Moslem states. Moreover, since the Moslem overlords were always few in proportion to their subjects, substantial numbers of Hindu landowners were allowed to retain their possessions; and some of them even served in Moslem armies. Conversely, the Hindu kings of Vijayanagar maintained a corps of Moslem mercenaries and found allies as well as enemies among the Moslem rulers to the north.[52]

During the first centuries of their rule in India, the Moslems made remarkably little impression upon the cultural traditions of their subjects. Presumably the bulk of the Indian population treated the Moslems as just one more caste and simply neglected the challenge which Islam offered to their inherited religious and social system.[53] Yet alien rule inevitably made some changes in the Indian scene. For example, the destruction of temples in north India checked the tendency for Hinduism to crystallize around cult ceremonies. This cleared the way for simpler sectarian pieties, organized around particularly holy, charismatic, and God-intoxicated men. Such groups soon pervaded northern India with the sort of ecstatic devotion to a personally conceived deity which had already become prominent among the Tamils of south India before 1000 A.D. A parallel movement in philosophy, of which the greatest proponent was Ramanuja (*ca.* 1100), challenged the abstract impersonality of

[51] Moslem attitudes and behavior interestingly recapitulated Aryan reaction to the religious rites of the Indus civilization. See above, pp. 88–89.

[52] B. A. Saletore, *Social and Political Life in the Vijayanagara Empire* (Madras: B. G. Paul & Co., 1934), I, 395–414.

[53] Cf. A. B. M. Habibullah, *The Foundation of Moslem Rule in India* (Lahore: S. Muhammed Ashraf, 1945), pp. 272–308.

Shankara's metaphysical monism by offering elaborate arguments in favor of a theistic universe. This alternative thereafter continued to rival Shankara's views within the dominant Vedanta school of Indian philosophy.[54]

Moslem rulers were generally not much interested in converting their Indian subjects to Islam, if only because conversions diminished their tax income. Nevertheless, in time Sufi holy men persuaded significant numbers of Indians to profess the Moslem faith. The urban lower classes were particularly susceptible to Sufi missionary appeals. Among such populations, village custom and status relationships had been weakened so that Hindu doctrine, which condemned them to membership in the lowest castes, could not easily compete with a faith that officially declared every human soul to be equal before God. Islam also won numerous converts in Bengal, where primitive peoples in the process of entering into the Indian cultural world frequently preferred the religion of Mohammed to a Hindu system that placed them near the bottom of the caste hierarchy.

Such converts, of course, tended to maintain their old ways of life even after entering the Islamic community. Hence efforts to enforce conformity to the Sacred Law met with only limited success even among the orthodox Sunnis of India; while heretical Shi'a sects, building upon their mystic and antinomian tradition, carried accommodation to Indian customs and ideas very far indeed. One Indian branch of the Isma'ilis, for example, held that Ali was an incarnation of Vishnu.[55] The Sufi orders of India took on many of the characteristics traditional to Hindu asceticism and gave rise to a group of individual holy men who wandered about the country without the restraint of any definite discipline or regularly constituted order.

As Islam thus gradually penetrated the tissues of Indian society, thoughtful Hindus found it more and more difficult to neglect the central challenges which the Moslem faith presented: the reproach of idolatry and the repudiation of caste distinctions.[56] Beginning in the fifteenth century, a number of Indian religious thinkers attempted to purge Hinduism of these defects and to find a common ground between the rival religions. The first great reformer to act along these lines was Ramananda (*ca.* 1400), a popular preacher who discarded the Sanskrit integument of Hinduism by resorting to the Hindi vernacular. He also disregarded caste rules and made the god Rama the object of vibrant personal devotion. A still more famous religious thinker was Kabir (mid-fifteenth century), who may have been one of Ramananda's disciples. Kabir went much farther than Ramananda in rejecting Indian tradition. He denied reincarnation and criticized all outward forms of religiosity, whether the circumcision of the Moslems or idol worship of the Hindus. He declared

---

[54] Cf. M. Hiriyanna, *The Essentials of Indian Philosophy* (London: Allen & Unwin, Ltd., 1949), pp. 175–99; S. Dasgupta, *A History of Indian Philosophy* (Cambridge: Cambridge University Press, 1956).

[55] Marshall G. S. Hodgson, *The Order of the Assassins*, pp. 277–78; J. N. Hollister, *The Shi'a of India* (London: Luzac & Co., 1953), pp. 356–57.

[56] Islamic monotheism as opposed to Hindu polytheism was not a serious issue, since Indian philosophy had long since reduced the multiplicities of the traditional pantheon to mere aspects of an ultimate reality—a doctrine which was not very different from the Sufi version of Islam.

that Hindus and Moslems really worshiped the same God and attracted a considerable following in northern India from both religious communities. The Sikhs trace their origin to Kabir, although their distinctive religious organization and detailed doctrine developed only two or three generations later under the leadership of Nanak (d. 1538).[57] The thread of historical continuity between Kabir and Nanak cannot be reconstructed; yet the Sikhs may justly claim to be the true heirs of Kabir in the sense that they, like him, sought to unite Moslems and Hindus into a single religious community.

But Indian traditional religions were too deeply entrenched in the everyday habits of the population to be easily transformed. In the end, efforts at rapprochement between Hinduism and Islam did not prevail. The rich profusion of Hindu sects and deities survived the Moslem destruction of the northern temples; and the principal effort to meet the religious and intellectual challenge of Islam simply gave rise to one more sect, the Sikhs.

3. ORTHODOX CHRISTENDOM

In the first two decades of the eleventh century, Orthodox Christendom appeared to be in a stronger position than at any time since the age of Justinian. Byzantium, having successfully staved off the Moslem attack upon its Aegean heartlands, even launched a modest but successful counter-offensive in northern Syria and Armenia. In 989, the conversion of the Russian prince of Kiev to Christianity had opened the vast hinterland north of the Black Sea to the full force of Byzantine civilization; and in 1018, the emperor Basil II succeeded in overthrowing the rival Bulgarian empire, thus uniting Greeks and Slavs of the Balkan Peninsula into an imposing imperial structure. These achievements, together with the political fragmentation of the Moslem world and the general backwardness of Latin Christendom, seemed to render the Byzantine state secure on every side.

Yet the four centuries following the death of Basil II (1025) brought a long series of disasters. We have just seen how the Moslem world acquired new military energies by absorbing Turks and Mongols; and Orthodox Christendom was one of the principal victims of this second great surge of Islamic expansion. No less dangerous to Orthodoxy was the rapid rise of Latin Christendom after 1000 A.D. The "Franks"—to use the term Byzantines applied to all Latin Christians—were even more detestable enemies than the Moslems; for they insisted upon substituting their own creed and rites for Orthodoxy, whereas Moslem rulers allowed the Orthodox church to manage its own affairs, subject only to payment of taxes and recognition of Moslem political supremacy.[58] Under the circumstances, whenever Orthodox Christians had to

---

[57] Several other religious groups, some Moslem, some Hindu, also claimed Kabir as their founder. Cf. Charles Eliot, *Hinduism and Buddhism* (London: Edward Arnold & Co., 1921), II, 262–66.

[58] John of Damascus (d. *ca.* 752), the leading Christian apologist of his time and himself a subject of the caliphate, had classified Islam as a Christian heresy; and this remained the standard view of the Orthodox Church. Hence, from a strict doctrinal point of view, there was little to choose between Moslem heretic and Latin schismatic. Both had recklessly tampered with the Truth; and if the *filioque* clause of the Latin creed seemed less conspicuous than the Koran, this simply made Latin error more insidious, therefore more dangerous.

DANCING SHIVA

By the twelfth to thirteenth centuries, when this statue of Shiva was made, Hindu iconography had found traditional and effective forms. (Compare the awkwardness of the plate on p. 375 [*center*].) The softly molded contours of the torso betray descent from Gupta (p. 375 [*left*]) and perhaps even from the ancient Indus art traditions (p. 87 [*left*]). Such resonances with the Indian past illustrate how successful the Indian response to the Moslem challenge could be. Even after systematically repudiating everything felt to be alien within older Indian cultural traditions, a rich and impressive residue remained, here bodied forth in bronze.

choose between Turkish (or in Russia, Mongol) rule and Western domination, an overwhelming majority regularly opted against the Franks—a fact which did much to assure Turkish success in the Balkans and helped to stabilize Mongol power over the Russian principalities.[59]

The decline of Byzantium and of the Kievan state in Russia was as much a consequence of internal weakness as of Turkish, Mongol, or Frankish strength. The disintegration of the Kievan state into a dozen or more rival principalities in the eleventh century made it comparatively easy for nomads from the Caspian and Volga regions to penetrate the Black Sea steppe and drive the Russians back into the northern forests. When the last powerful ruler of Kiev died in 1054, effective sovereignty of the Ukrainian steppes therefore passed to bands of Kipchak Turks. This cut off the surviving Russian principalities from easy communication with Byzantium, and divided the Orthodox world in two.[60] A generation later, Orthodox Christendom suffered an even more serious blow when Byzantium finally lost control over the Anatolian plateau to another branch of the Turkish people, the Seljuks.

The Turkish pincers north and south of the Black Sea which were thus closing in on Byzantium in the eleventh century were matched by a similarly double offensive from the West. Norman adventurers seized Byzantium's Italian possessions between 1042 and 1071,[61] went on to take Sicily from the Moslems (by 1090) and to launch a major attack upon the Balkan Peninsula (1081–85). Simultaneously, the Venetians gained a stranglehold upon Byzantine trade, partly through their commercial enterprise, partly by their political and naval strength. In exchange for Venetian naval help against the invading Normans, the Byzantine emperors in 1082 granted Venetian merchants far-

[59] Westerners at least sometimes reciprocated the bitterness of a family quarrel. Petrarch, for example, wrote: "The Turks are enemies, but the Greeks are schismatics and worse than enemies." Quoted from A. A. Vasiliev, *A History of the Byzantine Empire* (new ed.; Madison, Wis.: University of Wisconsin Press, 1952), p. 671.

[60] The Kipchaks were called Polovtsi by the Russians, Cumans by the Byzantines, Kipchaks by themselves. They later became incorporated into the Mongol state (the Golden Horde) and in this capacity were known as Tatars or Tartars. Cf. R. Grousset, *L'Empire des steppes*, p. 242.

The irruption of the Kipchaks into the Russian steppe should be compared with the Magyar invasion of Hungary in the ninth century, which cut Byzantium off from the western Slavs and in the end nullified the missionary work of SS. Cyril and Methodius in Moravia. The establishment of the Kipchaks in the Ukraine pushed other nomad groups ahead of them into the lower Danube plains (Pechenegs, Ghuzz, and others). These migrations therefore erected an unbroken barrier between the heartland of Orthodox Christendom and its northern "colonial" regions. The pagan newcomers might soon have been smoothly incorporated into the Orthodox world by conversion to Christianity had not the Mongol conquest with subsequent Islamization supervened, for a few Kipchak chieftains had already professed Orthodoxy before the Mongols appeared. But as part of the Golden Horde, the Kipchaks became Moslem in the fourteenth century. This effectually sealed the division of Orthodox Christendom into two separate parts, one Byzantine, one Russian.

[61] Papal patronage of the Normans as a makeweight against both German and Byzantine emperors helped to make the schism of 1054 between the papacy and the ecumenical patriarch final. Earlier schisms between Rome and Byzantium had all been patched up eventually; but every effort to compromise the dispute over the *filioque* clause of the Latin creed failed. The fact that the Byzantine emperor no longer held territory in Italy meant, in effect, that the papacy had little to gain from any compromise. All concessions therefore had to come from the Orthodox side—a fact that made any bargain the popes would agree to almost automatically unacceptable to the majority of Orthodox Christians.

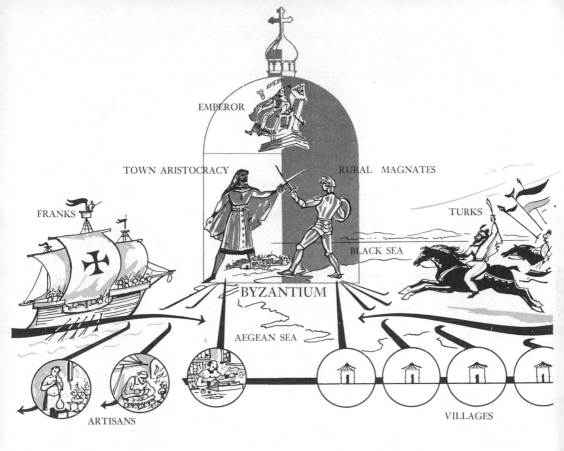

EMPEROR

TOWN ARISTOCRACY

RURAL MAGNATES

FRANKS

TURKS

BLACK SEA

BYZANTIUM

AEGEAN SEA

ARTISANS

VILLAGES

BYZANTIUM IN DECLINE

reaching commercial privileges, including exemptions from tolls. Thereafter, Byzantine subjects were unable to compete commercially against the privileged Italians, and later attempts to loosen the Venetian stranglehold by making similar concessions to Genoa (1155) and other Italian cities merely tended to make Byzantium a pawn of rival Italian commercial imperialisms.[62]

Such military ineffectiveness contrasted strikingly with the Byzantine successes of the preceding century. One source of weakness, clearly, was the growth of large estates enjoying partial or complete exemption from normal taxation.[63] Especially in Asia Minor, owners of such estates had developed into a semi-militarized aristocracy with private armed retinues to support their chronic insubordination to the central government. Thus the Byzantine empire in the eleventh century was threatened with the same sort of political disintegration which had disrupted the Abbasid caliphate in the tenth.[64] As great estates grew, the military smallholders who had constituted the backbone of

[62] Cf. Peter Charanis, "Economic Factors in the Decline of the Byzantine Empire," *Journal of Economic History*, XIII (1953), 412–24.

[63] Cf. George Ostrogorsky, *Pour l'histoire de la féodalité byzantine* (Brussels: L'Institute de philologie et d'histoire orientales et slaves, 1954).

[64] Cf. similar evolutions within the Parthian, Sassanian, and Carolingian monarchies.

Byzantine armies under the Macedonian emperors disappeared or transferred their allegiance to local magnates. The central government was compelled therefore to rely more and more exclusively upon mercenaries.

This might not in itself have been particularly disastrous if the emperors had been able to secure sufficient tax monies to maintain a formidable army and fleet. But such was not the case in the eleventh century. Adequate studies of Byzantine urban history have yet to be made; but it seems plausible to believe that important changes in the character of town life lay behind the failure of mercantile and artisan enterprise to supply the imperial fisc with sufficient funds to keep the empire strong. In Constantinople itself, an urban aristocracy, drawing its income mainly from the perquisites of office and secondarily from ground rents, came to dominate the scene; and some historians have argued that the palace coup d'états which disfigured Byzantine history after the death of Basil II (1025) reflected a struggle for power between the rural and semi-militarized landowners of Asia Minor and the urban office holders and rentiers of Constantinople.[65]

Mercantile and artisan enterprise should probably not be expected to flourish in communities dominated by rentiers and office holders, if only because successful traders or other economic entrepreneurs are prone to withdraw from risky and troublesome ventures and use their funds to buy an office in the government or to invest in sound rent-producing properties. In extreme cases, when fiscality becomes an unchecked principle of administration, speculative capital is likely to find far richer rewards through the purchase of governmental office than in any economically productive venture. Yet such offices are lucrative only because they permit their holders to ambush the money and goods of the public at large. Government becomes, in effect, a great siphon concentrating wealth in the hands of a small group of insiders, whose cultured luxury may disguise the rapacity of the regime which sustains them. Taxation easily becomes confiscation, and tax gatherers soon begin to resemble marauding robbers. Economic devolution and a radical retrogression of trade and industry may be the unintended result.

To what extent such a parasitic cycle came into operation in Byzantium after 1000 A.D. cannot be said. It is clear, however, that Italians came to dominate the trade first of the Aegean and then of the Black Sea during the eleventh and twelfth centuries. Apart from the loss of revenues from tolls and the diversion of middlemen's profits to Italy, this shift of trading patterns meant an irremediable decay of Byzantine sea power; for the merchant marine was the necessary base of the navy. Hence long before Latin Crusaders seized Constantinople in 1204, the Byzantine empire had been reduced to economic dependence upon the West.

As these processes worked themselves out, therefore, the Byzantine emperors lost first an obedient and dependable soldiery in the countryside and

---

[65] Cf. Richard Busch-Zantner, *Agrarverfassung, Gesellschaft, und Siedlung in Südosteuropa* (Leipzig: Otto Harrassowitz, 1938), pp. 60–61; George Ostrogorsky, *History of the Byzantine State* (Oxford: Basil Blackwell, 1956), pp. 280–333; A. A. Vasiliev, *History of the Byzantine Empire*, pp. 351–54.

O. M. *Dalton*, Early Christian Art.

BYZANTINE WARRIORS

These two carvings adorn the top and front of an ivory casket. Carved in Byzantium, perhaps in the eleventh century, it was probably plundered by one of the Franks of the Fourth Crusade and brought to France, where it now reposes among the treasures of the Cathedral of Troyes. Observe the stirrups and armor of the fully developed cataphract (cf. pp. 235, 395) and the alternative forms of his armament: spear, sword, or bow. Most striking of all, however, is the conscious archaism of these panels. Not only is the motif of lion hunting purely an artistic convention, descended from Assyrian times when kings did in fact hunt lions, but the helmet of the bowman is modeled on classical Greek and the armor of all four figures on ancient Roman patterns. Like the rest of Byzantine society, the artist evidently felt it more important to preserve (indeed revive) the glories of the past than to imitate or record the current scene.

then the money income needed to maintain an adequate mercenary force to take the place of the vanished peasant-soldiery. Debasement of the coinage and tortuous negotiations with rulers of Latin Christendom, aimed at securing military aid from that quarter, were the result. But Western aid was two-edged: it might indeed roll back the Moslem frontier in Asia Minor and the Levant, as in the First Crusade (1097–99); but it could also, as in 1204, lash out against Constantinople itself.

Nevertheless, the Byzantine empire died slowly. Periods of partial recovery, such as that between 1081 and 1180 under the energetic Comneni emperors, resembled the spectacular recoveries of earlier Byzantine history; but in the long run the social and economic processes undermining the power of the central government proved more than even the most resolute emperors could overcome. During the twelfth century, first Serbia (from 1167) and then Bulgaria (from 1187) broke away from Byzantine sovereignty. A more crippling disaster was the capture of Constantinople by Western Crusaders in 1204. Frankish adventurers held the city until 1261 and carved out duchies for themselves from the richest Byzantine territories of Europe, although they failed to overrun northwestern Asia Minor, where Greek rule and the imperial title survived. Even after the Greek emperor regained his capital, the territories he ruled consisted only of dispersed fragments, owning little more than a nominal allegiance to Constantinople.

By the fourteenth century, the political weakness of the Byzantine state, compounded by religious and social strife,[66] was patent to all. The only question was whether a Serbian empire based upon a rural aristocracy and open to Latin influence, or an Ottoman empire, drawing strength from a more urban, rudely egalitarian tradition and glowering menacingly at the West across the chasm of infidelity, would inherit the Byzantine lands. The Turks settled this question in 1389 by overwhelming the Serbian chivalry at the battle of Kossovo. More often than not, Greek, Serb, and Bulgarian peasants welcomed the conquering Turks as liberators from the oppression of Christian rural aristocrats.[67] This made Turkish victories irreversible, their setbacks, temporary. The capture of Constantinople in 1453 had great psychological and symbolic repercussions; but long before that time, Turkish power completely dominated the Balkans.

---

[66] Signs of bitterness between the upper and lower classes of the Byzantine state are not wanting from the twelfth century onward. At first the conflict tended to take an ecclesiastical form—conflicts between the "Zealots" and the "Politicians" within the Church. The Zealots were led by monks who wished to keep the Church free of all secular control; the Politicians, controlled by the cultured ecclesiastics and officials of the urban upper classes, preferred the traditional subordination of Church to state; and some of them were even prepared to come to terms with the papacy in order to secure military and diplomatic support from the West. Questions of theological doctrine—the Hesychast controversy—later came to be associated with the quarrel; and by the fourteenth century, full-scale social revolution broke out in several cities, most notably in Salonika, where from 1342 to 1349 a radically democratic republic under a Zealot regime successfully defied Constantinople. The Ottoman Turks took Salonika just eleven years after this revolutionary movement was suppressed. Cf. Vasiliev, *History of the Byzantine Empire*, pp. 659–84.

[67] Cf. F. Braudel, *La Méditerranée et le monde méditerranéen à l'époque de Philippe II* (Paris: A. Colin, 1949), pp. 509–11.

In the Balkan countryside, the immediate result of Ottoman conquests was to substitute Turkish warriors for the older landed classes. Turkish demands upon the peasantry were initially very much less burdensome than those of the Christian gentry had been. Turkish cavalrymen expected to live as much on booty as on rents and were normally away on campaign during the summer months, leaving the peasants largely to their own devices.[68] Town populations grew markedly, for the consolidation of the Ottoman state seems to have provoked a rise in commercial and manufacturing activity, if only because it brought a higher level of peace to the countryside and ended the economic tutelage formerly exercised by privileged Italians.[69]

The Christian populations of the Balkans certainly acquiesced in Turkish rule, preferring it to the only apparent alternative after the Serbian defeat: subordination to the Latin West. Mohammed the Conqueror met his Orthodox subjects halfway by according extensive power and privilege to the Orthodox Church which, having rejected all compromise with Roman Catholicism, became the principal bearer of Orthodox self-consciousness.[70]

* * *

The other great segment of Orthodox Christendom, Russia, collapsed politically in the thirteenth century before the Mongols, yet emerged in the fifteenth century as a strong, united, and economically vigorous society at the very time when the Byzantine state was in its death agony.

When in the thirteenth century the Orthodox principalities of Russia found themselves caught between the expanding forces of the Latin West, represented by the Teutonic Knights,[71] and the onrush of the Mongols, the majority of the Russian princes preferred Mongol overlordship.[72] They had reason for this choice. In contrast to the religious intolerance of the Knights, the Mongols allowed the Orthodox Church complete doctrinal liberty and exempted churchmen and church lands from taxation. In addition, the khans bolstered the power of the princes—so long as they were duly submissive to

---

[68] Richard Busch-Zantner, *Agrarverfassung, Gesellschaft, und Siedlung in Südosteuropa*, p. 63.

[69] Cf. Omer Lufti Barkan, "Essai sur les données statistiques des registres de recensement dans l'empire Ottoman aux XVe et XVIe siècles," *Journal of the Economic and Social History of the Orient*, I (1958), 9–36.

The considerable migration of Jews from Spain and other parts of Europe into the Ottoman empire was perhaps both a sign and a cause of urban prosperity. Spanish-speaking Jews became very prominent in the commercial activity of the Ottoman empire by the sixteenth century. Cf. I. S. Emmanuel, *Histoire des Israelites de Salonique* (Paris: Librairie Lipschutz, 1935); M. Franco, *Essai sur l'histoire des Israelites de l'empire Ottoman depuis les origines jusqu'à nos jours* (Paris: Librairie A. Durlacher, 1897).

[70] Under the Turks the Orthodox Church enjoyed wider autonomy and far greater internal peace than under the later Byzantine emperors, who from 1274 onward had repeatedly tried to force religious agreement with Rome in the hope of last-minute rescue from the West.

[71] A Crusading order established on the Baltic coast in 1229.

[72] Alexander Nevsky (d. 1263), who won his sobriquet by defeating Western invaders in a series of actions between 1237 and 1242, but who submitted to the Mongols, represented this frame of mind. Later, during the fourteenth and fifteenth centuries, the current tended to reverse direction, for, with the expansion of Lithuania-Poland into western Russian lands, many nobles opted for the Western world by becoming Catholic and Polonized.

their Mongol overlord—as against both nobles and commoners, who in Kievan Russia had shared in political authority.

The Russians made great advances during the Mongol period. At first the Mongol (or Tartar)[73] rulers collected taxes through their own agents; but in the early fourteenth century they began to entrust this function to Russian princes, who thereby developed subordinate but effectively autonomous administrative machines of their own. A vast work of cutting the forests and taming the land for agriculture proceeded steadily, so that the Russian population ceased to be concentrated principally along the river banks, as it had been in Kievan times, with hinterlands left largely to hunters and fur trappers. Again, although the first effect of the Mongol conquests was to reduce many Russian cities to empty shells and to transfer the river trade of Russia to Moslem merchants from central Asia, Russian traders soon resumed operations and, by the late fourteenth century, again controlled the Volga commerce.[74] Thus when the Golden Horde began to disintegrate (after 1419), its broken fragments confronted a number of well-consolidated and vigorous Russian principalities, of which the chief was the Grand Duchy of Moscow.

By 1480, when Ivan III of Moscow (1462–1505) formally renounced allegiance to the crumbling Tartar power, overwhelmed the rival Russian principalities, and assumed the title of Tsar, the Russians had already reversed the balance of forces between the forest and steppe zones of eastern Europe. A unified and centralized state, a numerous agricultural population, a vigorous trade, and artisans capable of manufacturing firearms enabled the Muscovites to extend their power deep into the steppe and across Siberia within an amazingly short time.[75] The Russians also held their own, though with greater difficulty, against renewed encroachment from western Europe, represented

---

[73] Tartar is the name usually given to the Turko-Mongol populations of the Golden Horde, which was in its turn one of the four appanages into which the Mongol empire was subdivided among the sons of Genghis Khan. Relatively close co-operation between the Great Khan in China and the rulers of the Golden Horde continued to exist into the fourteenth century, largely as a result of common enmity toward the rulers of the central portions of the vast Mongol dominion. Russian conscript troops, for example, were regularly dispatched to supplement the armed forces of the Great Khan and as late as 1332 a casual reference proves the existence of a special Russian detachment at the court in Peking. George Vernadsky, *The Mongols and Russia*, p. 87. On the Golden Horde, see also B. Grekov and A. Iakoubovski, *La Horde d'Or* (Paris: Payot, 1939).

[74] Cf. George Vernadsky, *The Mongols and Russia*, p. 343.

[75] Use of firearms in Russia is first recorded in 1376. In that year, a Muscovite army confronted the new weapons when attacking the town of Bolgary. Four years later, Moscow itself was defended by cannon, perhaps imported from Bohemia. By 1450, arsenals equipped to manufacture cannon and smaller guns existed in both Moscow and Tver. According to Vernadsky, *The Mongols and Russia*, p. 278, the fact that Tamerlane raided the territories of the Golden Horde between 1391–95, destroyed their principal cities, and dispersed the artisans who had lived there put the Tartars at a crippling disadvantage when it came to exploiting the potentialities of firearms. The skilled craftsmen needed to make guns had been carried off to Samarkand or elsewhere just when the new weapons were being introduced, whereas the Muscovite artisan communities remained untouched. This may have hastened the reversal of the balance between the Russian and Tartar states. Another element in this reversal was the introduction of hand guns, which made infantry more than a match for the Tartar nomad cavalry and brought the superior numbers of the agricultural Russian society to bear against the comparatively limited numbers of Tartar horsemen. Cf. the overthrow of Bronze Age charioteers by the infantrymen of the Iron Age, discussed above, p. 117–18.

in the fifteenth and sixteenth centuries by Sweden and the aristocratic Polish-Lithuanian state.

The religious life of Russia had long been linked with Byzantium through the subordination of the Russian church hierarchy to the patriarch at Constantinople. But Russian churchmen refused to accept the far-reaching concessions made by the patriarch in his treaty of union with Rome in 1439. The Russian church therefore became autocephalous. Soon afterward, Constantinople fell to the Turks. Popular piety in Russia saw in this event the judgment of God against the Greeks who had betrayed Orthodoxy in the vain hope of succor from the schismatic West. Gradually the idea gained currency that Moscow, the only remaining repository of Orthodoxy, had inherited the mantle of Christian empire from Constantine's New Rome on the Bosphorus. Accordingly, in 1492 the Metropolitan Zossima publicly hailed Moscow as "Third Rome" for the first time.[76]

* * *

The presumption (as well as the plausibility) of Moscow's claim to rank as the "Third Rome" arose from the fact that the crude life of the Russian towns and countryside had little in common with Constantinople's cultivated brilliance. As the Byzantine empire decayed, the intellectual and artistic life of the capital flourished as seldom before. Perhaps this cultural efflorescence resulted from the concentration of wealth and power in the hands of urban officials and rentiers, among whom a lively sense of kinship with the classical past quite appropriately took root. At any rate, Byzantine art and letters underwent a vigorous Hellenic Renaissance during the eleventh century.

Historical scholarship, inspired directly by Herodotus and Thucydides, was perhaps the most admirable result of this classical revival;[77] but philological works as well as a great variety of poetry and prose also poured forth from the busy pens of the Byzantine educated classes. Efforts to compose in the language of the ancients and a flamboyant display of learned allusions to classical literature form an obstacle to modern appreciation of these literary efforts. They much resembled, and indeed helped to stimulate, the work of Italian humanists of the fourteenth and fifteenth centuries.

In all this erudite literary activity there was a large element of artificiality. Far different was the popular epic, *Digenes Akritas,* composed (or compiled) probably in the eleventh century on the basis of ballads celebrating the deeds of borderers fighting against the Moslems. This poem faithfully reproduces the ethos of the military frontiersmen who provided the sinews of the imperial army in the time of the Macedonian emperors.[78]

[76] The fact that Ivan III married the niece of the last emperor of Constantinople gave color to the claim that Moscow was indeed the true heir of fallen Byzantium. Cf. V. O. Kluchevsky, *A History of Russia* (London: J. M. Dent & Sons, 1912), II, 16–23; William K. Medlin, *Moscow and East Rome* (Geneva: E. Droz, 1952), pp. 78–80.

[77] Cf. Karl Krumbacher, *Geschichte der byzantinischen Literatur* (Munich: Carl Beck Verlag, 1891), pp. 78–107.

[78] For a convenient summary of Byzantine literature, see Norman F. Baynes and H. St. L. B. Moss, *Byzantium: An Introduction to East Roman Civilization* (Oxford: Clarendon Press, 1948), pp. 221–52.

If *Digenes Akritas* breathes the popular spirit of the frontier regions, theological controversy voiced the concerns of populations living nearer the center of the empire. Monks were the pre-eminent spokesmen for the Byzantine man in the street. Many monks were of humble social origins and without much formal education, but were nonetheless able to find assurance of salvation in mystical religion and a new ascetic discipline that spread among the monks of Mount Athos and elsewhere in the fourteenth century. A few of the educated elite of Byzantine society also adhered to the new piety. Thus St. Gregory Palamas (d. 1360) defended the authenticity of monkish visions of God with great learning and dialectical subtlety. He wrote with the energy of personal conviction, for he personally practiced the breathing exercises and other ascetic disciplines and knew the ineffable vision of God at first hand. Inspired to an utter conviction by such experiences, Palamas and others like him carried through a remarkable renovation of Orthodox theology and drastically reformed the hierarchy of the Orthodox Church.[79]

The success won by the mystical movement identified the hierarchy of the Orthodox Church with popular sentiment far more effectively than before, when cultivated ecclesiastics, members of the office-holding aristocracy of Constantinople, had ruled the Church as well as the state. Moreover, the mystic vision of God, shared by thousands, imparted to Orthodoxy an emotional power capable of sustaining individual believers through any sort of personal crisis. This popularization of the Orthodox faith may account for the otherwise puzzling fact that few Christians were attracted to Islam in the European provinces of Turkey, whereas, only a short time earlier, wholesale conversions had been common in Anatolia.[80]

Art, more clearly than literature, reflected the interaction between Byzantine, Italian, Armenian, and Persian cultures. In the eleventh century, at the

[79] A lasting consequence of the Hesychast controversy, as the struggle between monkish mysticism and politically minded prelates is termed, was the capture of the patriarchate and of all the higher offices of the secular church by monks. Until the fourteenth century, it was usual for secular clergy (or even on occasion a hastily consecrated layman) to rise to the episcopal and patriarchal dignity. But after the Hesychast controversy had been won by the mystical monkish party, the high offices of the Church were filled only from monastic ranks. This became one more distinguishing mark dividing the Orthodox from the Latin Church. Cf. Vasiliev, *History of the Byzantine Empire*, pp. 656–76; Baynes and Moss, *Byzantium*, pp. 114–16.

[80] In Asia Minor, popular discontent was channeled into Sufi paths by Moslem holy men; in Europe, Christian monks performed an analogous service, forestalling Moslem mysticism by only a few decades; for the monks of Athos supported by the mob of the capital won their victory over the Politician party and gained control of the patriarchate just at the time when the Turks, who also profited from popular discontents against the landowning and official classes of Byzantium, were establishing their rule on the European side of the straits. Moreover, important interrelations existed between Moslem and Christian mysticism. The Byzantine mystics seem to have employed techniques—breath control and prolonged repetition of the divine name—which had earlier been staples of Sufism and, before Sufism, of Indian asceticism. Moreover, the association of laymen with the Hesychast movement bears close analogy to the lay followings built up by dervish communities in Anatolia. Cf. L. Gardet, "Un problème de mystique comparée: la mention du Nom divin—dhikr—dans la mystique musulmane," *Revue Thomiste*, 1952, pp. 642–79; 1953, pp. 197–216; G. G. Arnakis, "Gregory Palamas among the Turks," *Speculum*, XXVI (1951), 104–16; Jean Meyendorff, *St. Grégoire Palamas et la mystique orthodoxe* (Paris: Editions du Seuil, 1959), pp. 64, 85, 108–9, and *passim*. The social and economic background from which the Orthodox mystical movement emerged remains, however, as obscure as the comparable background of the Sufi movement. Economic suffering, especially among the urban lower classes, may have helped to provoke both.

OUR LORD AND SAVIOR JESUS CHRIST

This icon, painted in Novgorod, Russia, about 1500, seems somehow to capture the mystic aspiration dominating the Orthodox churches from the fifteenth century. Echoes of pagan antiquity, such as can be detected in the preceding plate (p. 517), no longer interest the artist. Yet the principle that art imitates the past has not been abandoned; the preferred model has simply been transferred to the mosaics of the early centuries of Byzantine Christian art. Nevertheless, the use of shading to suggest three-dimensionality around the eyes and nose betrays the impact of Italian Renaissance artistic models. In this icon, therefore, we may see Holy Russia already toying with Western techniques in order to assert her difference from the West more emphatically.

height of the Hellenic literary renaissance, a notably naturalistic style of painting appeared, attesting the abiding power of classical models. Thereafter, a number of regional schools arose, among which may be counted the early Renaissance painters of Venice and Siena. Icon painting in Russia and Crete, church frescoes in Serbia, Macedonia, and Italy, as well as some secular painting and mosaics, gave vigor and variety to the art of the Orthodox world. The Turkish conquest put an end to such activity in the Byzantine heartlands; but on the periphery, in Venetian Crete[81] and in Russia, a vigorous development continued into the sixteenth century.[82]

Even more abrupt was the quietus the Turkish conquest brought to Byzantine literary activity and religious controversy. The learned officials and their hangers-on, who had constituted the literary class of Constantinople, ceased to exist; only the Church remained, and the Church was well content with its inheritance. The energy of the mystics waned even more rapidly than it had mounted as the Orthodox communities of the Balkans settled down under Ottoman rule. And the Russians, busy building and defending a vast state, had little energy either for literary and intellectual creation or for religious controversy. Thus save for an afterglow in the artistic field, the high culture of Orthodox Christendom dimmed until it could no longer hold its own against the vigorous upthrust of western European civilization. The strength of the Ottoman and Muscovite states commanded respect in the West; but after 1500 the culture of the Orthodox world, which in the early Middle Ages had so far surpassed that of the half-barbarous lands of Latin Christendom, could no longer exert a living influence upon its western neighbors.

E. THE FAR EAST

I. CHINA

The traditional organization of Chinese history by dynasties fits awkwardly into the periodization of this chapter, for the years 1000 and 1500 of the Christian calendar both cut arbitrarily through important Chinese dynasties. To be sure, one of the main factors making the five centuries between 1000 and 1500 A.D. seem cohesive in the history of western Eurasia also affected the Far East, for China was exposed to Turkish and Mongol conquest from the steppe just as were Islam, Orthodox Christendom, and (one degree removed) Hindustan. But China had been exposed to similar dangers ever since the fourth dynasty B.C.; and the fluctuations between native dynasties and dynasties from the steppe during the period 1000–1500 fitted into a long series of dynastic upheavals which had begun in Han times and continued into the twentieth century.

Nevertheless, the date 1000 A.D. appropriately symbolizes a deeply significant change in Chinese social history. For about that time, when the bureaucratic reorganization of the first Sung rulers had taken full effect, China's

---

[81] Domenicos Theotocopoulos (El Greco, d. 1614) was the most notable luminary trained in the Cretan school.

[82] Cf. O. M. Dalton, *East Christian Art* (Oxford: Clarendon Press, 1925), pp. 234–47 and *passim;* N. P. Kondakov, *The Russian Icon* (Oxford: Clarendon Press, 1927).

social and economic structure attained a new and, as it proved, lasting balance between rural and urban elements—that is, between officials, landlords, and peasants on the one hand and merchants and artisans on the other.

Chinese social development during the ensuing centuries may be viewed as a sort of race between landed interests on the one hand and urban interests on the other. Townsmen had made conspicuous headway in the late T'ang period, when the central government had been chronically disorganized. But the whole weight of Chinese imperial tradition favored the landed and official classes; and after 960, the Sung restoration of centralized bureaucratic government greatly strengthened that side of the balance. Yet not until the Ming dynasty established itself firmly in all of China (*ca.* 1450) was the supremacy of a centralized, Confucian bureaucracy, recruited largely from the landowning class, definitely secured. Between 1000 and 1450, China's social structure teetered on the verge of a fundamental change analogous to the rise of the bourgeoisie in medieval and early modern Europe. Yet the transformation never quite came off, and in the end the social order assigning predominance to the landed and official class, as organized under the Sung and restored by the Ming, became China's modern system of society, lasting until the twentieth century.

The first notable tremor in the balance between China's commercial and landed interests occurred after the Sung emperors lost north China to Jurchen invaders (1127). Thrown back upon the traditions and resources of the south, China in the later Sung period saw a notable development of riverine and maritime trade. Great cities arose on the south China coast and along the Yangtze; and growing numbers of merchant vessels set sail for southeast Asia and the Indian Ocean.[83] The development of maritime commerce provoked and was in turn sustained by important improvements in naval architecture—cotton sails in place of bamboo slats, an adjustable centerboard keel, and a notable increase in the size of vessels, together with the invention of the compass.[84]

These improvements made oceanic voyages a reasonable risk even in foul weather and allowed Chinese vessels gradually to displace Moslem shipping, which had long dominated the trade of the southern oceans. During their campaigns in south China, the Mongols (Yuan dynasty, 1260–1371) learned to appreciate Chinese naval potentialities, as their attempted invasions of Japan and Java prove. Moreover, the comparatively high status enjoyed by mer-

---

[83] Cf. Jung-pang Lo, "China as a Sea Power," *Far Eastern Quarterly*, XIV (1955), 489–503. The development of Chinese navigation between the twelfth and fifteenth centuries perhaps built upon ancient pre-Chinese maritime traditions of the south China coast. If so, the rise and fall of Chinese sea power may be viewed as an ultimately unsuccessful assertion of indigenous southern tradition against the more specifically Chinese, land-centered tradition of the north.

[84] The compass is first mentioned in Chinese sources of the late eleventh century. The Chinese not only discovered the direction-finding properties of a magnetized needle but also developed a series of mountings, from a simple float in a dish of water to the pivoted compass mounted over a compass card. Cf. Li Shu-hua, "The South-Pointing Carriage and the Mariner's Compass," *Tsing-hua Journal of Chinese Studies*, n.s., I (1956), 63–113. For Chinese compass cards, cf. W. Z. Mulder, "The Wu Pei Chih Charts," *T'oung Pao*, XXXVII (1944), 1–14.

chants in the Mongol scheme of things encouraged the shipowners of south China to develop a flourishing trade with southeast Asia and India. Official efforts to restrict this trade on the ground that it sent too much metal currency out of the country were apparently only sporadic and quite ineffectual.[85]

The Ming (1368–1663) established far stricter state control over sea trade. Between 1405 and 1433 a series of great maritime expeditions, led or directed by the court eunuch Cheng-ho, established Chinese hegemony over the key commercial centers of the Indian Ocean—the Malacca Straits, Ceylon, Calicut—and asserted a less definite suzerainty over Hormuz at the mouth of the Persian Gulf. Chinese fleets also visited the coast of east Africa.[86] Some 250 vessels and thousands of men participated in these expeditions—a truly imperial scale of operations that far eclipsed the first efforts of Europeans in the Americas and the Indies a century later. Nevertheless, despite the success of Cheng-ho's expeditions in bringing back giraffes and similar wonders, and in forcing the rulers of Ceylon and other distant lands to pay him homage, the emperor in 1424 abruptly ordered the suspension of such enterprises.[87] Thereafter, apparently as a by-product of intrigue at court, even the memory of these extraordinary expeditions was effectively suppressed. The government went so far as to forbid the construction of seagoing vessels, presumably because in private hands many of them indulged in piracy or smuggling and could not be properly controlled by a land-fast officialdom. The result was to deliver the coasts of China into the hands of Japanese and Malay pirates, who from the fifteenth century onward made the China Sea unsafe for peaceable commerce.

The Chinese certainly possessed the technical resources[88] to have anticipated the Portuguese in the Indian Ocean. World history would surely have taken a far different turn if Vasco da Gama had discovered a powerful Chinese overseas empire in possession of the principal ports and strategic gateways of the Indian Ocean in 1498. If the mercantile communities of south China had been left to their own devices, still more if the imperial government had supported and encouraged their activities, such an empire might well have confronted the Portuguese explorer. But the Ming court lived far away from the south China coast whence the armadas of the early fifteenth century sailed and was far more concerned with the danger of a renewed Mongol attack on the northwest frontier than with any advantages which might have accrued

[85] W. W. Rockhill, "Notes on the Relations and Trade of China with the Eastern Archipelago and the Coasts of the Indian Ocean during the Fourteenth Century," *T'oung Pao*, XIV (1913), 473–76; XV (1914), 419–47; Jung-pang Lo, "China as a Sea Power." The rise of important Chinese mercantile and artisan communities in southeast Asia dates from Mongol times.

[86] J. J. L. Duyvendak, "The True Dates of the Chinese Maritime Expeditions in the Early Fifteenth Century," *T'oung Pao*, XXXIV (1938), 341–412.

[87] This order was subsequently modified to permit one last voyage. J. J. L. Duyvendak, "The True Dates of the Chinese Maritime Expeditions," pp. 388–90.

[88] In 1393 an imperial order prescribed that each naval vessel should carry four guns with "muzzles the size of rice bowls," twenty guns of smaller caliber, ten bombs, twenty rockets, and a thousand rounds of shot. Jung-pang Lo, "China as a Sea Power," p. 501.

from a vigorous exploitation of the new techniques of seamanship.[89] At the critical moment, therefore, the Chinese government not only abdicated from an active maritime role but actually prohibited private ventures on the sea.

Another dimension of Chinese social evolution during these centuries goes far to explain how old values and a fundamentally agricultural frame of society proved strong enough in Ming times to prevail so strikingly over the mercantile and urban interest. For agriculture, too, acquired vast new resources from the eleventh century onward. Nameless peasants discovered new varieties of rice that ripened in sixty days or less, allowing two crops to be grown in a single season on the same land. Moreover, these early ripening varieties required less water than others, so that terraced hillsides where irrigation was possible only during the spring run-off could now successfully be turned into paddy fields. This permitted an enormous extension of the area under intensive cultivation, particularly in the hills of south China.[90] The result was to multiply several times over the food-producing capacity of Chinese agriculture, permitting a great growth of rural population and a corresponding multiplication of landowners, who were therefore able to maintain or even to increase their weight in Chinese society as a whole.

This reinforcement of the landed interest meant that the gentry class, which from Han times had been the principal carrier of the Confucian tradition and the champion of everything distinctively Chinese, was more easily able to hold its own against merchants and other upstarts. The crisis came under the Mongols, who, like all nomads, traditionally assigned an honorable place in society to traders. Genghis Khan and his successors freely accorded special privileges and high office to foreign merchants like Marco Polo. Many of these strangers combined mercantile activity with tax farming and other fiscal operations, none of which endeared them to the Chinese public at large. Hence when the Mongols were ejected from China in 1368, gentry officials had wide support for their effort to reassert the Confucian principle which classified merchants among the necessary evils of society. In practice this meant fastening close official supervision and control upon all mercantile ac-

---

[89] Duyvendak, "The True Dates of the Chinese Maritime Expeditions," pp. 395–99, attributes the defeat of a project to resume voyaging to the Indian Ocean, advanced sometime between 1465 and 1487, to the hostility of the mandarins of the court against eunuchs, who by virtue of Cheng-ho's feats were identified with a forward policy on the seas. Cf. Jung-pang Lo, "The Decline of the Early Ming Navy," *Oriens Extremus*, V (1958), 149–68.

Clique rivalries may have been a major determinant of imperial policy, but the decision was not irrational, for the mandarins had good arguments against dissipating imperial resources overseas. In 1421 the Ming capital was moved north to Peking and the government launched a series of campaigns into Mongolia to forestall the rise of a new Mongol confederacy. Yet in 1449 the Mongols captured the emperor himself. Renewal of the age of Genghis Kahn seemed at hand. In face of such dangers, how could resources be spared for unnecessary ventures on the seas? For events across the Chinese-Mongol frontier, see D. Pokotilov, *History of the Eastern Mongols during the Ming Dynasty from 1368 to 1634*, Rudolf Loewenthal (trans.) (Chengtu: Chinese Cultural Studies Research Institute, 1947).

[90] Ping-ti Ho, "Early Ripening Rice in Chinese History," *Economic History Review*, IX (1956–57), 200–218. The new varieties were apparently developed by cross-breeding with rice brought from Indochina because of its drought resistance. This foreign rice was first noticed by Chinese writers in 1012, when it was introduced into the lower Yangtze Valley from Fukien. Thereafter, this rice and the new early-ripening varieties derived from it spread gradually over most of China.

THE SHIFTING BALANCE OF CHINESE SOCIETY

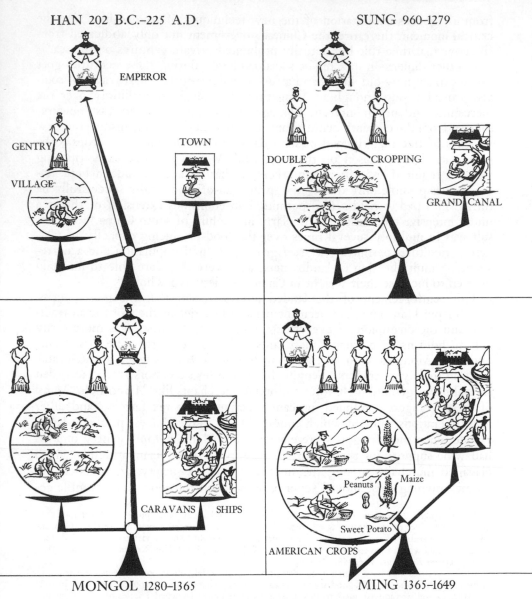

HAN 202 B.C.–225 A.D.

SUNG 960–1279

EMPEROR

GENTRY

VILLAGE

TOWN

DOUBLE

CROPPING

GRAND CANAL

CARAVANS

SHIPS

Peanuts

Maize

Sweet Potato

AMERICAN CROPS

MONGOL 1280–1365

MING 1365–1649

tivities—witness Cheng-ho's naval expeditions to the Indian Ocean—and completely subordinating mercantile interests to the presumed interests of the state —witness the abrupt termination of such naval enterprise after 1438.

The victory of the official and landed interest in China was sealed by the persistent moral weakness of a merchant class that had no arguments with which to rebut the Confucian charge of social parasitism. Even more insidious was the Confucian principle that made social leadership depend on learning and moral excellence, for this opened wide the gates to any man who secured a good education. Successful merchant families therefore tended to buy land, abandon trade for a rentier's life, and use their resultant leisure to master the Confucian classics. In this manner, families whose neighbors had regarded them as blood-sucking social parasites might become thoroughly respectable members of the gentry class within a single generation. The urge to follow such an upward path was certainly strong, and thousands of families climbed high upon the Confucian ladder of success.[91] But the very openness of Chinese society at the top tended to decapitate mercantile communities and effectually checked the development of large-scale trade and manufactures, for which in 1000 A.D. China had been technically far better prepared than any other part of the civilized world.[92]

* * *

On the political and cultural levels, a similar challenge to old Chinese tradition reached its crisis under the Mongols and then quickly receded under the Ming. The Mongols brought China into far closer touch with western Eurasia than ever before. During the first decades of their rule, the Great Khans conscripted multitudes of strangers from central Asia, the Middle East, Russia, and even from western Europe for service in China. As long as the capital remained at Karakorum in Mongolia, north China was partitioned among deserving Mongol captains, who governed their new possessions as they saw fit. Since the Mongol magnates were liable to nearly continual military service, they could not superintend their estates themselves. Instead, they normally entrusted the task to corporations of central Asian merchants (Uighurs and others) who paid over lump sums for the right to collect rents and taxes from the Chinese.[93] But after 1264, when the capital was transferred to Peking, Kublai Khan decided to restore the old Chinese tax machinery.[94] This involved the re-establishment of a centralized imperial bureauc-

---

[91] Edward A. Kracke, "Sung Society: Change within Tradition," *Far Eastern Quarterly*, XIV (1955), 479–88; Ping-ti Ho, *The Ladder of Success in Imperial China* (New York: Columbia University Press, 1962).

[92] Contrast the social exclusiveness of European and Japanese aristocracies, whose social eminence rested upon a presumed superiority of ancestry. As Toynbee eloquently pointed out, penalized minorities, like the European burghers of medieval and early modern times, sometimes reap unexpected rewards.

[93] Cf. the role of Moslem merchants from western Asia as tax farmers and traders in Russia during the first decades of Mongol rule there.

[94] Herbert Franz Schurmann, *Economic Structure of the Yüan Dynasty* (Cambridge, Mass.: Harvard University Press, 1956), pp. 2–8.

racy and the recruitment of Chinese officials in the traditional manner through examinations based on the Confucian classics. The Chinese, however, were usually confined to relatively subordinate positions, while upstart outsiders like Marco Polo, stemming from the most varied origins, continued to hold most of the top government jobs. Clearly the Mongol emperors did not entirely trust their Chinese servants; but in practice, the bulk of the native population, dealing only with lower-ranking officials, was again ruled by Chinese in the Chinese fashion.

For millions of Chinese, therefore, the reconstitution of the bureaucracy in north China and the extension of Mongol administration into south China after 1279 simply meant that life resumed its wonted course. Since the number of Mongols and of other strangers[95] was always small in proportion to China's millions and since most of them were culturally inferior to the Chinese, the society and culture of China underwent surprisingly little lasting alteration as a result of the Mongol regime. When the conquerors lost their military hardihood after about three generations of battening upon the wealth of China, a native-led revolt established a new Chinese dynasty, the Ming. Thereupon, the Chinese deliberately repudiated foreign ways; and only in fringe areas like Yunnan, which had never been wholly incorporated into Chinese society, did enduring traces of foreign influence survive.[96]

The real importance of the denser communications across Asia which the Mongol conquests opened up therefore lay not in any effects upon China, but in the penetration into Moslem and Christian lands of certain key elements of Chinese technology, notably gunpowder, the compass, and printing.[97] The importance of these devices for western European history can

---

[95] In 1270, when the conquest of China was almost complete, and when the number of invaders perhaps stood at or near its peak (*i.e.*, before intermarriages had diluted the alien character of the military establishment), there were about 390,000 "military" households in China. This amounted to about 3 per cent of the Chinese population, as measured by the first census taken under the Mongols in 1290, which showed no less than 13,000,000 taxpaying households. Cf. Herbert Franke, *Geld und Wirtschaft in China unter der Mongolen-Herrschaft* (Leipzig: Otto Harrassowitz, 1949), pp. 128–29.

[96] The hitherto independent kingdom of Nan Chao in Yunnan was conquered by the Mongols in 1253 and incorporated in due course into their Chinese state. From 1274–79, Kublai entrusted this area to a Moslem governor, who seems to have been responsible for the firm establishment of Islam in this area. Cf. Marshall Broomhall, *Islam in China* (London: Morgan & Scott, 1910), pp. 123–25. The comparable establishment of Islam in eastern Bengal, along the fringes of the Indian world, took place during the same centuries; and both areas have since remained stubbornly distinct from the surrounding Chinese and Indian cultural worlds.

[97] No documentary proof of the transmission of these inventions from China has been discovered and probably never will be, since artisans and merchants did not normally write books. If Marco Polo had not been taken captive by the Genoese and used his time in prison to dictate an account of his career at the court of Kublai Khan, nothing whatever of his extraordinary adventures would be known to us. Yet both before and after the Polos, many thousands of artisans and merchants moved to and fro across the Mongol dominions; and the tales of some who returned may well have included useful hints or even precise information about the special skills of the Chinese.

The case for a reasonably speedy diffusion of both gunpowder and the compass from China to Islam and Christendom is sufficiently clear. Both Moslems and Christians were manufacturing and using gunpowder before the middle of the fourteenth century; and the mariner's compass reached the Mediterranean nearly a century earlier, having traveled through the southern oceans, not overland, as did gunpowder.

The case of printing is more difficult. Not only was the invention made much earlier in China (block

scarcely be overestimated; yet in China their impact was comparatively modest. Printing helped to sustain the scholarly and literary efflorescence of the later T'ang and Sung periods and facilitated the elevation of such popular literary forms as the drama and the novel to the dignity of written (printed) form. Yet the fabric of Chinese society was stable enough to inhibit any widespread expression of new thoughts such as those which stormed into print in Europe from the sixteenth century onward. Printing in China simply spread old ideas more widely and thereby fastened the ancient Chinese intellectual heritage all the more securely upon society at large by widening the circle of those who might participate in the republic of letters.

Gunpowder too failed to revolutionize Chinese life. Quite the contrary. When guns gave the emperor power to batter down even the most elaborate fortifications within a comparatively short time, the rise of local warlords like those who had distracted the country in late T'ang times became more difficult, and the ancient ideal of a united state obedient to a single ruler became much easier to realize. The effect of the new weapons therefore was to sustain the ancient ideal rather than to bring in something new.[98] And, as we have already seen, the compass and associated improvements in naval technique failed to transform China's relations with the rest of the world in any lasting fashion, despite the extraordinary episode of Cheng-ho's voyages to the Indian Ocean.

* * *

The failure of technological improvements and of foreign contacts to do more than ruffle the surface of Chinese life between 1000 and 1500 A.D. was partly the consequence of the Chinese habit of mind that classified all foreigners as barbarians; partly, too, it reflected the real superiority of Chinese numbers, wealth, and skill over those of any other part of the globe. Likewise, Chinese literary and intellectual culture was quite as impressive as—and on the basis of its presumed antiquity obviously superior to—anything to be found in other civilized lands. Thus Chinese cultural evolution serenely pursued its own paths, oblivious to the world outside.

---

printing in the eighth or ninth century, movable type in the eleventh century), but its reception in Christendom was delayed until the fifteenth century, and in Islam (where learned prejudice long forbade printed reproduction) until the eighteenth. The key to this delay seems to lie not in ignorance— the Moslems certainly were well acquainted with printing for centuries before they accepted it; and Christians had ample opportunity to learn of the technique long before Gutenberg printed his famous Bible in 1456. Rather, the delay apparently was caused by the slowness with which knowledge of how to manufacture paper spread from China through the Moslem world to western Europe. Before a cheap material with which to reproduce a printed text became available, printing offered little or no advantage over hand reproduction. It has been calculated, for instance, that each copy of Gutenberg's Bible, printed on parchment, required the skins of 300 sheep. Thomas Francis Carter, *The Invention of Printing in China and Its Spread Westward* (New York: Columbia University Press, 1925), p. 204. But the secrets of paper manufacture did not reach the Rhineland until the fourteenth century. *Ibid.*, p. 85.

[98] From the time of the Mongols until the twentieth century, China retained political unity and avoided prolonged lapse into local anarchy such as had recurrently visited the land in earlier times. This was a remarkable achievement in a country as large and diverse as China. Confucianism plus guns made it possible.

禮部侍郎致仕王渙九十歳

CHINESE SAGES

The elderly Chinese gentleman
on the left, decorously deferential to his superiors and expecting appropriate deference from
his inferiors, contrasts force-
fully with the liberated spirit
portrayed on the right, whose
communion with nature charms
precisely because it frees him
from the obligations of society.
Both paintings date from the
eleventh century. They suggest
the complementary polarity between the Confucian and Taoist
ways that dominated Chinese
intellectual life from the ninth to
the nineteenth century. The calligraphy on the right, an integral
part of the work of art, tells the
office, name, and age of the man
portrayed.

Konchi, Kyoto, Japan.

The elaboration of Neo-Confucian philosophy which had begun before 1000 was carried to completion during the twelfth and thirteenth centuries. Philosophers discussed such metaphysical questions as the relation of form and matter, movement and rest; but always in the forefront of Chinese thought was the practical problem of how to lead a good and wise life—an emphasis which descended from Confucius himself and seldom yielded more than momentarily to purely abstract discussion. The Buddhist and Taoist motifs prominent in the earlier stages of Neo-Confucianism faded into the background as philosophers like Chu Hsi (1130–1200), the brightest star of the Neo-Confucian firmament, developed a well-reasoned ideal of life capable of competing, both intellectually and emotionally, with Buddhist and Taoist myth and metaphysics.[99]

Chinese literature in the Sung and Mongol periods was enriched by the appearance of drama[100] and fiction, written in everyday language and reflecting in some degree the bustling outlook of city life. Yet these "popular" literary forms speedily came to be dominated by literati trained in the Confucian tradition; and Confucian precepts thereafter set fairly narrow limits to the range of sentiment and sorts of ideas communicated by Chinese plays and novels.[101]

Art underwent no comparable enlargement of themes or subject matter. Painting remained an avocation for gentlemen, a profession for a few. The practice of modeling new paintings upon masterpieces of the T'ang and early Sung assured a close continuity of style, so much so that modern scholars often have difficulty distinguishing genuine early paintings from later copies.[102] Refinement, elegance, and specialization (some men painted only bamboo twigs) were characteristic of the subschools and individual artists of the Mongol and Ming periods. But all were content to remain within the molds set by the ancients, thereby reflecting faithfully the cast of mind which dominated all the life and activity of the Chinese scholar class.

As long as that class remained supreme within Chinese society, little change could be expected, and little change there was. Despite the substantial breaches during the Mongol period in the geographical barriers which previously had always prevented more than sporadic contact with the other great civilizations of Eurasia, China remained, by her own choice, a world apart.

[99] Fung Yu-lan, *History of Chinese Philosophy*, II; J. Percy Bruce, *Chu Hsi and His Masters* (London: Arthur Probsthain, 1923).

[100] Chinese plays were sung and more nearly resembled the European opera than European drama.

[101] Cf. Herbert A. Giles, *A History of Chinese Literature* (New York: D. Appleton & Co., 1901), pp. 256–91; J. R. Hightower, *Topics in Chinese Literature*, pp. 84–102; Adolf Zucker, *The Chinese Theater* (Boston: Little, Brown, 1925), pp. 3–42.

[102] The dominating spirit was well expressed in a colophon written by Chao Meng-fu (1254–1322), a prominent official under Kublai Khan and his four successors: "The most important quality in a painting is the spirit of antiquity. If this is not present, the work is not worth much, even though it is skilfully done. . . . My paintings may seem to be quite simply and carelessly done, but true connoisseurs will realize that they are very close to the old models and may therefore be considered good. This is told for real connoisseurs and not for ignoramuses." Quoted by Osvald Siren, *Chinese Painting* (New York: Ronald Press, 1958), IV, 19.

2. CHINA'S OUTLIERS

The massiveness and grandeur of Chinese civilization had long provoked both admiration and imitation among China's neighbors. Between 1000 and 1500, Korea and central Manchuria, together with Annam and Yunnan, developed increasingly close relations with Chinese metropolitan culture. To be sure, these regions did not quite lose their special identity. From the Mongol period onward, Manchuria and Yunnan were administered as integral parts of China, yet the special military regime in Manchuria, where Chinese, Tungusic, and Mongol populations intermingled,[103] and the prevalence of Islam in Yunnan marked off these frontier zones from the main body of Chinese society. Korea remained a client kingdom, accepting the overlordship of whichever dynasty ruled north China. Language remained the principal barrier to Korea's total cultural absorption into China; but the Korean upper classes did their best to overcome this obstacle by eagerly imitating all the latest modes and refinements of the Chinese court.[104] Annam in the south was more recalcitrant and acquiesced in client status only when the Mongol and Ming dynasties were at the height of their power. Nonetheless, Chinese cultural models dominated even the politically independent periods of Annamese history.

Severe geographical conditions made anything more than a protocivilization impossible in Tibet and Mongolia. This, together with the desire to remain spiritually independent of China, accounts for the very limited penetration of Chinese styles of life into these areas. Lamaists of Tibet, for example, remained always conscious of the Indian Buddhist origins of their faith, thus in effect opposing Sinification by appealing to the tradition of a rival great civilization. The moral energy of Lamaism increased in the fourteenth century when a reform movement captured many of the monasteries of the country and instituted a more rigorous intellectual and ascetic discipline among the monks. This reformed "Yellow Church"—so called from the color of the monks' robes—became dominant in later Tibetan history.[105]

Geographically, Japan offered far better ground for the building of a civilization, as the successful transplantation of Chinese patterns of court life and high culture to the islands during the Nara period (646–794) had shown. Yet the Japanese were not long content with wholesale borrowing. Instead of hastening, like the Koreans, to adopt the latest nuance of Chinese styles, the

[103] Franz Michael, *The Origin of Manchu Rule in China* (Baltimore, Md.: Johns Hopkins Press, 1942), pp. 12–58.

[104] M. F. Nelson, *Korea and the Old Order in Eastern Asia* (Baton Rouge, La.: Louisiana State University Press, 1945).

[105] Kublai Khan had favored the Tibetan form of Buddhism; and Lamaism remained the official Mongol religion in China throughout the remainder of the dynasty's existence. When the Mongols were expelled from China, however, the religion of the Great Khans seems to have lost all official standing in Mongolia and was only reintroduced in the sixteenth century at the initiative of Mongol princes who were then striving to centralize and confirm their power over unruly clan chieftains. Cf. D. Pokotilov, *History of the Eastern Mongols during the Ming Dynasty* (Chengtu: Chinese Cultural Research Institute, 1947), pp. 135–37. On Tibetan Buddhism, cf. L. Austine Waddell, *The Buddhism of Tibet* (London: W. H. Allen, 1895), pp. 5–76.

Japanese between 1000 and 1500 built a society and culture of their own. No longer a mere provincial copy of China's imperial splendor, the new Japanese civilization was nonetheless closely related to and largely derived from the Chinese.

Between the ninth and twelfth centuries, Japan's precocious imperial and bureaucratic government, modeled on the institutions of T'ang China, gave way to a military regime in which power depended upon rights over land and upon personal loyalties between lords and vassals. Resemblances to European feudalism were fairly close. A professional fighting class, the *samurai*, came to dominate Japan and developed a code of honor enforcible privately with the sword in cases beyond the scope of a superior lord's court. Adherence to this code marked the *samurai* off from the rest of the population. Local violence became chronic, punctuated by larger-scale warfare between rival coalitions of lords and vassals. In such a milieu, the military life acquired high prestige, in direct contrast to Chinese disdain for soldiering.

By the fourteenth century, towns had become important elements of Japanese society. In addition to artisans who served local markets, such towns attracted considerable numbers of footloose *samurai*, who, having lost their lands in the disorders of the countryside, took to the sea as pirates and merchants. Clearly, towns sheltering such formidable entrepreneurs as the Japanese pirates differed radically from the comparatively civil and submissive cities of China, India, and the Middle East. Only in the remote Far West could similarly rude and self-assertive townsmen be found.[106]

Buddhist monasteries, especially those of the Zen sect, constituted a social link between the urban population and the *samurai* of the countryside. The monks shared the militarism of the age, sometimes themselves taking to arms. As important landholders, the monasteries were continually entangled in the military-political struggles among the feudal lords. Yet these same monasteries also played a pioneering role in organizing early Japanese ventures overseas and offered a haven for defeated or aging *samurai* alternative to and more reputable than any of the urban occupations open to a warrior. On the intellectual plane, Zen doctrine afforded the *samurai* a much needed supernatural sanction and supplement to the rather bleak ethical injunctions of their peculiar moral code.

A society so different from the Chinese inevitably found itself cramped by the borrowed forms of Chinese cultural expression and soon developed new forms of its own. Yet the Japanese never lost their admiration for Chinese cultural models. Hence a sort of duality developed within Japanese culture. Small circles in metropolitan centers and at the imperial court continued to cultivate distinctively Chinese arts like poetry and painting, while the politically dominant provincial *samurai* and townsmen oscillated between scorn of such effete sensibility and submission to its charms.

By the fifteenth century, the rise of provincial towns gave high cultural activity a somewhat broader base. In the urban setting, native Japanese and

---

[106] European townsmen of the fourteenth century differed from their contemporaries in Japan in having piracy some centuries behind them.

imported Chinese styles rubbed off on one another much more effectually than had formerly been possible when such interplay had been almost entirely confined to the imperial court. Maturation of Japanese painting and drama resulted. The former remained heavily under the impress of Sung styles, though artists nonetheless developed a touch distinctively Japanese. Drama, on the other hand, was quite independent of Chinese prototypes, drawing its themes from legends and stories about the *samurai* heroes of Japan, and its conventions from autochthonous ritual dances and popular poetry.

Japan's religious development reflected the same mixture. The various sects of Japanese Buddhism derived from Chinese analogues and forerunners; yet on Japanese soil they developed a character and emphasis of their own. In the twelfth and thirteenth centuries, a number of great religious leaders arose who preached a reformed, or Pure Land Buddhism that dispensed with priestly mediation and even criticized monasteries as an obstacle to salvation. The Pure Land sects were organized on a congregational pattern and appealed primarily to the poor and humble. Occasionally these sectarians provoked violent friction with older Buddhist monasteries; and in the fifteenth century they stimulated widespread popular risings, which for a few decades even challenged the supremacy of the *samurai*.

Zen Buddhism, established in Japan soon after 1200, shared some of the qualities of the Pure Land sects, inasmuch as it too rejected the paraphernalia of monastic learning and ritual. But Zen differed from the more popular sects in its greater emphasis upon "sudden enlightenment" and mystic experience and in a preference for individual rather than congregational discipline and devotions. The emotionalism of congregational assemblies was entirely alien to the Zen tradition, which became closely identified with the *samurai* class.

Buddhism in such forms was only distantly related to Chinese or Indian prototypes, even where doctrinal affiliations can be traced. The uniqueness of Japanese religious life was further illustrated by the survival of the autochthonous Shinto cult of the sun goddess. After a long period of near-oblivion,[107] Shinto gained a firmer foothold again in the fifteenth century, when priests of the principal temple of the goddess developed a pantheistic interpretation of traditional mythology, and thus equipped Shintoism with a doctrinal content comparable in sophistication to the theology of the Buddhist sects. Instead of being a narrowly imperial rite confined to the emperor and his immediate court, as in earlier centuries, Shinto now began to appeal to wider circles of the population. Moreover, by emphasizing the uniqueness of Japan, the sun goddess' favorite and first-created land, popularized Shinto was in a position to appeal to a growing sense of Japanese national identity.[108]

Thus in religious life, as in other fields of cultural expression, Japan became

[107] The fact that the emperor was held to be descended from the sun goddess and that he therefore, in the spirit of Chinese filial piety, was obliged to maintain a shrine to his divine ancestor was perhaps the principal means by which Shinto survived the initial flood of Chinese ideas.

[108] These remarks on Japanese culture are largely based on G. B. Sansom, *Japan: A Short Cultural History* (New York: Appleton-Century, 1943), pp. 256–400.

independent of China in the fourteenth and fifteenth centuries. From this time onward, two separate, if closely related civilizations existed in the Far East; and China was no longer the undisputed center and font of high culture in eastern Asia. This marked a fundamental change in the physiognomy of the Eurasian ecumene, a change comparable, though on a smaller scale, to the rise of an independent and markedly individual civilization on the other extreme flank of Eurasia, in western Europe.

F. THE FAR WEST

1. INTRODUCTORY

Compared to the civilized societies of Asia, European civilization exhibited marked instability. Rising to an extraordinary peak in classical times, it declined in equally extraordinary fashion following the fall of the Roman empire in the West. By contrast, Chinese, Indian, and even Middle Eastern history presents a far smoother curve. Despite marked changes in modes of religious, artistic, and intellectual expression, the civilized peoples of Asia always maintained a fairly stable institutional base on the local level. Complex social structures, involving both economic and cultural specialization, survived all the disturbances of time from the second millennium B.C. onward (from the third millennium in the Middle East). Save perhaps on the easterly face of the Iranian plateau, such complex societies never retreated for any long period of time from any extensive geographic area. On the contrary, the geographical and sociological base of Asian civilizations tended persistently to expand, though at varying rates of speed.

In Europe, however, the wide expansion of Hellenic civilization was followed by drastic withdrawal, so that in the eighth and early ninth centuries A.D. civilized social structures were restricted to an area not much greater than the original Aegean cradle from which classical Greek culture had sprung 1400 years before. From this low point, the Macedonian emperors restored Byzantine military power; and, as we have just seen, cultural revival ensued. Thereafter, the cultural life of Byzantium flourished despite political and military disaster, until the Turks took Constantinople in 1453. But the very richness of Byzantium's Christian and classical heritage constituted a heavy burden and repressed new creation. Due to their knowledge of and reverence for the ancients, both Christian and pagan, Byzantine writers and artists proved unable to attain the freshness, vigor, and *élan* which formerly had characterized the Greeks, and again characterized the Latin West in the centuries after 1000 A.D.

By comparison, the European wild West of the eleventh century was in an especially advantageous position. While elements of the classical, Byzantine, and Moslem civilizations lay readily within reach, the men of western Europe directly inherited a society in which nearly all the overburden of civilized institutions had crumbled into agrarian simplicity. Europeans could therefore build anew, utilizing elements from the variegated cultural inheritances of their neighbors according to choice. Moreover, the universal claims of the Roman Catholic Church, together with the military success that Frankish arms soon attained on every frontier, gave western Europeans a secure sense of superiority that ruled out both slavish imitation of their more civilized neighbors and the fear that any borrowing whatever would endanger their spiritual independence. A society remarkably open to innovation thus emerged—sure of itself, interested in the wonders of the civilized world, and eager to seize wealth, fame, and learning wherever they could be found. As a result, within a period of two or three centuries, Europe rose to a level of civilization comparable to that of any other part of the world.

Western Europe also enjoyed important geographical advantages which the technical developments of the so-called Dark Age (500–900 A.D.) brought into play for the first time. Broad and fertile plains cultivated by the mold-board plow, an indented coast line, numerous navigable rivers traversed by ships capable of withstanding the perils of Atlantic wind and tide, and an abundance of metals, especially of iron, and of timber, all contributed essential elements to western Europe's abrupt ascendance.

The barbarian inheritance—both from the remote Bronze Age invasions of the second millennium B.C. and from the more immediate Germanic, Scandinavian, and steppe invasions of the first millennium A.D.—made European society more thoroughly warlike than any other civilized society on the globe, excepting the Japanese. But it was the Greco-Roman and Judaeo-Christian inheritances, however attenuated during the Dark Age, that provided the fundamental frame for the elaboration of high medieval and modern European civilization. This inheritance was shot through with contrariety. Europeans confronted unresolved and unresolvable tensions between the primacy of the territorial state as the "natural" unit of human society and the claim of the Church to govern human souls; tensions between faith and reason, each claiming to be the pre-eminent path to truth; tensions between naturalism and metaphysical symbolism as the ideal of art. The barbarian ingredient of European tradition introduced still other contradictions—violence vs. law, vernacular vs. Latin, nation vs. Christendom. Yet these polar antitheses were built into the very fundament of European society and have never been either escaped or permanently resolved.

Quite possibly western civilization incorporated into its structure a wider variety of incompatible elements than did any other civilization of the world; and the prolonged and restless growth of the West, repeatedly rejecting its own potentially "classical" formulations, may have been related to the contrarieties built so deeply into its structure. Coming late to the scene and inheriting such incompatibles, the high civilization of the Far West has not yet come to rest but has revolutionized itself three times over. No other civilized society has ever approached such restless instability, nor exerted such drastic influence upon its fellows all round the world. In this, far more than in any particular intellectual, institutional, or technological expression that western Europe has from time to time put on, lies the true uniqueness of Western civilization.

2. THE STRUGGLE FOR POLITICAL ORDER

In the tenth century, western Europeans succeeded in turning back the tide of barbarian invasions which had sporadically distracted their political and economic life for more than five hundred years. By the year 1000, expansion was unmistakably under way. Yet the reversal of the balance of power between Latin Christendom and the bordering Moslem, Orthodox, and barbarian peoples did not bring peace and order to European society. Indeed, the cure for barbarian invasion—local self-defense conducted by strong-armed and often insubordinate knights[109]—was only slightly more tolerable than the disease. Relaxation of outside pressure simply freed local lords to attack one another with all the savage energy they had formerly employed in repelling barbarian assault.

Analysis of the confused and almost incessant fighting of ensuing centuries reveals a four-cornered struggle among incompatible levels of political integration, each of which adhered to the totalitarian traditions of the Greek political order by laying claim to the whole loyalty of the inhabitants of a more or less well-defined territory. At one extreme stood the ideal of (1) Christendom, meaning in practice only Latin Christendom, ruled by a "Roman" emperor and/or a Roman pope. Opposed to such universalism were (2) national monarchies; (3) feudal principalities, both lay and clerical; and (4) city-states. At each level, every political unit strove to increase its power; and the most varied alliances and alignments among them produced an almost infinitely complex and ever shifting balance of power.

Until 1059, the primary axis of this balance of power was the alliance between the "Roman" emperor—*i.e.*, the most powerful prince of central Europe—and the prelates of the Church in Germany and (sporadically) in Italy. This alliance was directed against the secular lords of Germany[110] and against the Byzantine power in Italy. A penumbra zone—northern Spain, France, England, Scandinavia, Poland, and Hungary—was only marginally connected to this political system. These countries, for the most part, evolved separately, but in contrasting directions. In France and northern Spain, political devolution prevailed, as local lords consolidated new principalities for themselves from the welter of local warfare.[111] In the more backward regions to the

---

[109] For the tenth century this description applies primarily to northern France. Only in the following century did knighthood become a master institution in immediately neighboring countries like England, Germany, and Spain. Such lands as Scandinavia, the Celtic fringe of Great Britain, and the Mediterranean littoral never saw knighthood really flower, because this ground was held too strongly by a wide variety of other social-political-military institutions.

[110] In any quarrel, some secular lords of Germany were bound to adhere to the emperor's standards, since the feudality was riven by local rivalries. In the consequent confusion, the emperor's power of appointment to high office in the Church was calculated to assure the loyalty of most bishops and abbots to the imperial cause, making the emperor, on most occasions, more than a match for his unruly secular vassals.

[111] A French kingship, tracing descent from Charlemagne, survived in theory, but from 987, when the first Capetians ascended the French throne, the kings of France became in fact merely one of a score or so of local rulers, whose claims to suzerainty over all France were honored only when it suited local convenience. In Spain, on the other hand, no single crown survived the Moslem conquest, so the dispersal of sovereignty was theoretical as well as real in practice.

north and east, however, England, Denmark, Norway, Sweden, Poland, and Hungary witnessed a gradual political consolidation as tribal states and confederations merged into new national monarchies.[112]

The overthrow of this political constellation of Europe began when a powerful reform movement within the Church, prompted by the monasteries of the Congregation of Cluny (founded 910), captured the papacy. The reformers' central idea was that the Church must win independence from lay control in order to perform its spiritual function properly. Accordingly, in 1075 Pope Gregory VII directly threatened the basis of imperial power in Germany by demanding that the emperor give up his traditional right to appoint bishops. To enforce such a program, the papacy had to ally itself with the German feudality and with local Italian states,[113] both of which had old grievances against imperial efforts at consolidation and centralization. Despite stubborn efforts by a succession of emperors to save or even extend their power, by the middle of the thirteenth century the imperial administration lay in utter ruin, and the papacy emerged as the sole exponent of the political ideal of a united Christendom.

The papal government, however, lacked any important military strength of its own. Supernatural sanctions were certainly important, and many a man must have hesitated to defy a papal command for fear of condemning his soul to eternal torment. Yet the terrors of interdict and excommunication proved a poor substitute for physical force when papal commands collided with the political interests of national monarchies, which were far more strongly rooted in local feeling than a "Roman" empire exercised by Germanic kings had ever been.

Open collision between the popes and national monarchies was postponed until 1296, in part because unusually pious kings ruled both France and England throughout the middle years of the thirteenth century. Nevertheless, the first decades of that century brought a fundamental change in Europe's political balance, when Philip Augustus of France (1180–1223) and his son Louis VIII (1223–26) seized half a dozen of the most powerful feudal principalities of the kingdom and proceeded to administer them directly. The main loser was the king of England, whose predecessors had, largely through marriage alliances, won title to about half the fiefs of France. The result was to create relatively homogeneous and comparatively powerful national kingdoms in both France and England at the very time when the final collapse of imperial

---

[112] An interesting antitype of the land-based Holy Roman Empire was the short-lived sea empire centered in Denmark, which disintegrated after the death of King Canute (1035) into the separate kingdoms of England, Denmark, Norway, and various lesser districts on the Baltic coast.

[113] In northern Italy, the papacy became the champion of city-states against both imperial and feudal rivals; in southern Italy, a strongly centralized Norman kingdom had arisen through the successful brigandage of Robert Guiscard and his sons; and the popes allied themselves with this upstart government, much as in earlier times Pope Stephen II had allied himself with the upstart Carolingian house. The Norman conquest of southern Italy not only gave the popes a useful military counterweight to invading German armies from the north; it also dissipated permanently any prospect of Byzantine intervention in Italy, thus freeing the popes from their earlier dependence on the German emperors as makeweights against Constantinople.

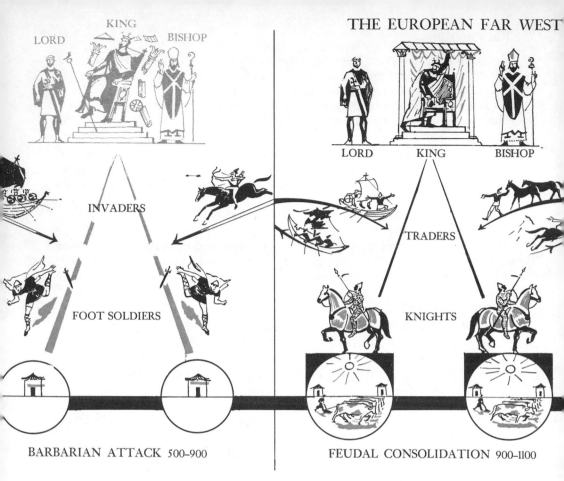

BARBARIAN ATTACK 500–900   FEUDAL CONSOLIDATION 900–1100

power in Italy and Germany reduced those countries to an assembly of small territorial and city-states.

When the kings of France and England began to collect new tax monies from the clergy of their realms, a direct conflict of interest arose between the papacy and the newly consolidated national monarchies. The attempt of Pope Boniface VIII (1294–1303) to forbid such trespass upon clerical immunity met with utter failure; and from 1305 the papacy itself, having transferred its seat from Rome to Avignon, compromised its claims to independent jurisdiction by becoming an open collaborator with the French monarchy.

The secret of the new strength of the French and English monarchs lay largely in their informal alliance with townsmen of the realm, who agreed to contribute tax monies to the royal exchequer in return for guaranties of their corporate liberties and protection against local feudal lords. Royal protection, even when it involved a degree of control over town affairs, seemed far more attractive to French and English burghers than the local anarchy prevailing in much of Italy and Germany. Anarchy had its compensations nonetheless, for the breakdown of central authority in Italy and Germany allowed the

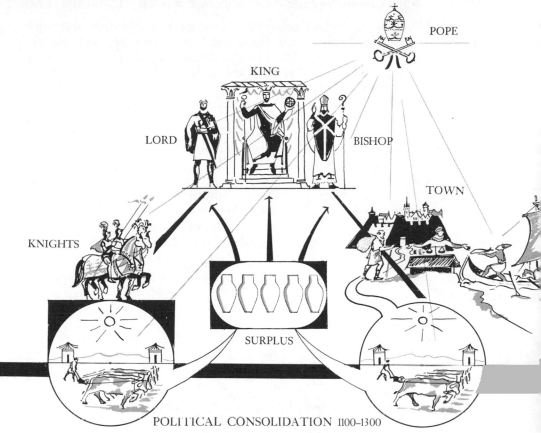

POPE

KING

LORD

BISHOP

TOWN

KNIGHTS

SURPLUS

POLITICAL CONSOLIDATION 1100–1300

towns of those regions to establish themselves as fully sovereign entities. In Scandinavia, Poland, and Hungary, where urban life was less well developed, the national monarchies were correspondingly weaker; yet there, too, essentially the same political alliance between king and townsmen prevailed. Spain was a special case. The long warfare against the Moslems of southern Spain, ending only in 1492, sustained a greater solidarity between monarchs and feudality than elsewhere in Europe; and the few important Spanish towns tended to oppose kings and lords alike, striving for complete autonomy on the Italian model. When royal intermarriages resulted in the union of all the states of the peninsula except Portugal under a single dynasty, Spain too emerged as a powerful national monarchy, but one in which friction between burghers and monarch was far more usual than co-operation.

The national states which had thus emerged in part of Europe by the fifteenth century had a long and brilliant future ahead; yet the city-states which had meanwhile established themselves in northern Italy, southern and western Germany, and along the North Sea and Baltic coasts were the principal seats of both cultural and economic leadership in the fourteenth and fifteenth centuries. Even in war and politics, where brute size counted, federal leagues of free cities like the Lombard and Hanseatic leagues, together with modifications of the federal pattern like the Swiss cantons and the later Dutch republic, could sometimes meet even nation states on even terms. As a result, from about 1300 until 1494, when the French invaded Italy and crushingly demonstrated their military superiority over the Italian city-states, the political balance of Europe lay between economically backward national states around the periphery and the constellation of smaller but exceedingly vigorous leagued city-states near the center of western Christendom.

Although the political variety and instability of western Europe brought chronic warfare in its train, this did not prevent rapid cultural and economic growth.[114] On the contrary, it was one of the factors in that growth. Unending competition among rival polities kept society fluid and encouraged innovation by putting a special premium on any novel mode of exercising power. Indeed, if medieval Europe had been reduced to political peace and

[114] Certain other societies have experienced a similar first bloom amid the alarms of war: e.g., the Sumerian cities at the beginning of the third millennium B.C., the Chinese warring states of the eighth–third centuries B.C., the Greek city-states of the sixth–fourth centuries B.C.

POLITICS OF WESTERN CHRISTENDOM

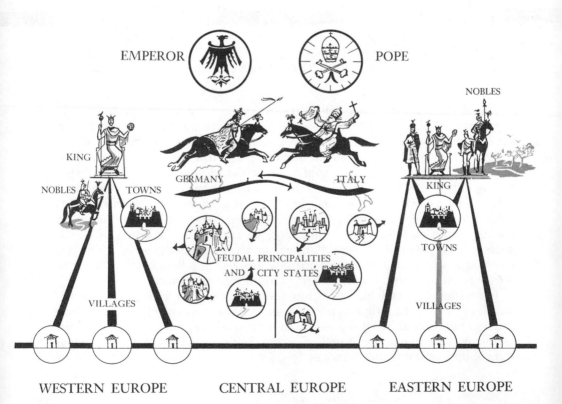

EMPEROR   POPE

NOBLES

KING

NOBLES   TOWNS

GERMANY   ITALY

KING

FEUDAL PRINCIPALITIES
AND CITY STATES

TOWNS

VILLAGES

VILLAGES

WESTERN EUROPE   CENTRAL EUROPE   EASTERN EUROPE

order either by a strong and successful emperor or by a victorious papacy, it is hard to believe that the pulsating growth of European civilization would not have been stunted and attenuated by confinement within either of these institutional frames. Chronic warfare arising from persistent political multiplicity has long been one of the painful, but powerful mainsprings of the West's vitality.

3. THE EXPANSION OF WESTERN EUROPE

Throughout the eleventh, twelfth, and thirteenth centuries, a great and peaceable task of internal colonization proceeded in western Europe. Fertile fields replaced forests and swamps; new villages and towns arose; population grew rapidly. Church parish organization, market relationships, and a variety of often competing systems of law—manorial, princely, royal, ecclesiastical— affected an ever-larger proportion of the population, and an ever-widening spectrum of daily activity. This internal development created a growingly complex network of relationships that bound all Western society into an interacting whole and enabled Latin Christendom to mobilize larger and larger energies—whether in the form of wealth and manpower or in the subtler forms of intellectual and artistic creativity—for common ends.

This internal consolidation of western European society sustained important territorial expansion. Between the eleventh and fourteenth centuries, the conversion of Hungary, Poland, Denmark, Norway, Sweden, and Lithuania to Christianity brought a wide belt of territory on the northern and eastern flanks of Germany within the pale of Latin civilization. In these lands, the establishment of an ecclesiastical hierarchy on the Roman model meant both an entering wedge for western European culture and the strengthening of royal prerogatives by the introduction of Roman law concepts of sovereignty. Commercial development followed, as impecunious kings sought the revenue that more westerly princes gained through taxing towns and accordingly offered favorable terms to merchants and artisans (recruited mainly from Germany) in order to induce them to settle in their territories.[115]

In Hungary, Poland, and Lithuania, acceptance of Western civilization was stimulated by mingled fear and admiration of the military prowess of Western princes, who from the time of Charlemagne had maintained an intermittent pressure upon the Slavic marchlands beyond the Elbe. The last pocket of Slavic paganism in the region between Poland and Saxony disappeared beneath the tread of German knights in the twelfth century. From 1229, when the Teutonic order gave up the crusade against Islam in favor of a crusade against Baltic paganism, the eastward expansion of Latin Christendom became a sustained, organized, and deliberate enterprise. By 1285, the Order

[115] Scandinavian towns were in part indigenous; and in Poland, military collision with German princes who were at work conquering Slavic lands east of the Elbe made German townsmen more or less suspect. Hence the welcome afforded to Jewish immigrants who brought urban skills and something of German culture, yet who could not be suspected, after the pogroms which had disgraced the Crusading movement in Germany, of any yearning after German political overlordship.

had almost exterminated the pagan Prussians and brought in German settlers and townsmen to take their place. After 1237, the Teutonic Knights, through amalgamation with the Knights of the Sword, extended their activity into Livonia and proceeded to reduce that region to Christian obedience by main force, but without entirely exterminating the native society. Their attempt to penetrate Russia was, however, turned back by Alexander Nevsky in 1240–42.

The most dramatic, and for European culture the most important, aspect of Western expansion was the penetration of the Mediterranean. In the Iberian Peninsula, the slow and checkered advance of the Christian principalities against the Moslem power resembled the German advance beyond the Elbe. The struggle was almost entirely confined to land, and neither ships nor cities played any important part in the Christian victories. The same was true of the Norman conquest of southern Italy (1041–71), and even of the First Crusade (1096–99) which won the Levant coast from the Moslems after a long and precarious march overland. Yet at a critical moment during the siege of Antioch, Italian ships came to the support of the Crusaders; and the Italians were quick to bargain for valuable trading concessions from their victorious fellow Christians.

From that time until the late fifteenth century, when the Ottoman Turks set about building a navy, Italian ships dominated the waters of the Mediterranean. The later Crusading forces, from the Third Crusade (1189–92) onward, traveled from Italy to the Levant by sea; and when a host of Crusaders captured Constantinople itself in 1204, Italian naval and mercantile operations penetrated the Black Sea also. The prosperity of Venice and Genoa and, to a lesser degree, of other Italian and even of some trans-Alpine cities came to rest very largely upon trade with the Levant. Without the economic underpinning and the artistic and intellectual stimuli arising from this trade, the flowering of city-state culture in Italy which we call the Renaissance could not have occurred.

Yet the more anciently civilized peoples of the eastern Mediterranean, whether Moslem or Orthodox, deeply resented Frankish dominance; and this resentment contributed to the success of the Ottoman state in uniting Anatolia and the Balkans against the Latin West. By the time the Turks captured Constantinople in 1453, Italian cities had everywhere lost their privileged status in the Levant, save in a few islands still held by Frankish forces. Soon thereafter, naval war between Turkey and Venice, 1465–79, ended in the loss by Venice of most of her territories in the Aegean.[116] Local competition, both commercial and naval, revived when the Italian yoke was lifted; and before long, Moslem pirates operating from the north African coasts challenged Italian control even of the western Mediterranean.

---

[116] Venetian diplomacy salvaged something even from defeat, for the Turks confirmed Venetian rights to trade in the Levant by the treaty. Cf. W. Heyd, *Histoire du commerce du Levant au Moyen-Âge* (Leipzig: Otto Harrassowitz, 1885), II, 324–26.

Thus western Europe's first overseas empire[117] collapsed before the Turks. Yet the riposte to this setback carried European explorers, merchants, missionaries, and soldiers all round the globe and made the oceans of the world the highroad of Western overseas expansion. The success of this second, oceanic phase of European expansion dwarfed the scale of the first Baltic and Mediterranean ventures and inaugurated a new era in world as well as in European history.

4. CULTURAL GROWTH: THE HIGH MIDDLE AGES

The unruly energy of Western military, economic, and political enterprise carried over into thought and art. Avid absorption of those aspects of Moslem and Byzantine culture that interested Western minds was but prelude to a phenomenal burst of creativity, instinct with all the freshness of youth. The reckless spirit of adventure characteristic of Western men-at-arms had its analogue in the no less reckless intellectual adventures of St. Anselm (d. 1109) and Peter Abelard (d. 1142); while the soaring heights of Gothic cathedrals constitute a visual expression of the same high vaulting venturesomeness.

Three phases may be distinguished in the cultural growth of western Europe between the eleventh and fifteenth centuries. First came a period when the confluent energies of the Church and of the rising towns provided a basis for eager and systematic appropriation of suitable elements from the high civilizations of Islam and Byzantium, together with adaptation of this inheritance to the special conditions and interests of the West. This period reached its climax and crisis in the thirteenth century, between the time of Pope Innocent III (1198–1216) and Pope Boniface VIII (1294–1303). Then followed a time when tension between churchmen and burghers replaced the earlier harmony, when the Church's effort to control cultural activity became rather a restraint than a stimulus, and when a more purely secular spirit began to find expression in urban circles. North of the Alps, this period of tension and transition lasted throughout the fifteenth century; but in Italy, a third phase of development became apparent much earlier. Italian towns were stronger and in closer touch with the non-Christian world than were their counterparts north of the Alps; hence it is not surprising that a secularized style of life, for which Christian doctrine and practice became increasingly irrelevant, began to prevail in Italy long before it penetrated to the more northerly regions of Europe. By the end of the fifteenth century, this "Renaissance" culture pervaded the innermost circles of the papacy itself and had begun to influence the courts and capitals of northern Europe.

---

[117] This phrase overlooks the Viking empire of the northern seas, which embraced not only Scandinavia and the British Isles, Normandy, and the Russian river system, but also extended tentacles into the Atlantic to Iceland (settled *ca.* 874), Greenland (settled 985), and North America (discovered 1000). But the Vikings can scarcely be counted as sharers in Western civilization at the time they established their empire; and when Scandinavia came within the circle of Latin Christendom, the restless energy of the Vikings quickly evaporated. Nevertheless, Iceland and Greenland became Christian; and the settlement in Greenland persisted, though in a parlous and poverty-stricken state, until the fifteenth century. Small bands of Norse adventurers seem also to have penetrated North America as far as the Great Lakes, but in doing so lost touch with European society and appear to have left no perceptible trace upon the Indian inhabitants of the continent.

During the first phase of this cultural evolution, everything seemed possible; and the pre-eminent center of cultural energy lay in northern France, where not only European feudalism but scholastic philosophy and Gothic architecture first took form.

The impoverishment of the Dark Ages had precluded monumental building in stone; but, with the eleventh century, first monastic and then cathedral churches began to arise all over western Europe as visible symbols of the reform and revivification of the Church. Byzantine-type churches, featuring a central dome, had found reception in western Europe from Carolingian times; but in the eleventh century, this was repudiated in favor of the old Roman basilica church, the central feature of which was a long columned hall. The addition of a transept to the basilican archetype produced a cruci-' form ground plan, which, together with free embellishment of the façade with towers and sculpture, created the style known as Romanesque.

The structural principles of the Romanesque style set definite limits to the width and loftiness of the central nave, since any increase in the weight of the roof and superstructure required an increase in the thickness of the walls or additional rows of columns. Moreover, as long as the walls constituted the sole support of the roof, windows could not be made large enough to admit much light. The Gothic style, which originated in northern France during the twelfth century, solved both these problems by concentrating the weight of roof and superstructure at selected points, from which great buttressed piers of masonry carried the thrust to the ground. The bracchiating pattern of the ribs which conducted the thrust of the roof to the piers produced an effective decorative pattern, the more striking because the large windows permitted by these structural principles allowed light to illuminate details of the interior.

Gothic architecture spread rapidly to England, Germany, and the adjacent Slavic lands, and to a lesser degree into Italy and Spain. Adjacent towns attempted to outdo one another by building ever higher-roofed and more magnificent churches in the new style. Most of the great European cathedrals were begun in the twelfth and thirteenth centuries; but many were not completed until later, when a taste for ornate detail obscured the original simplicity of Gothic structural lines under an incrustation of flamboyant decoration.

The other great monument of the age was scholastic philosophy—an attempt to explain and define Christian doctrine. The pioneers of this effort—men like St. Anselm and Peter Abelard—drew on the Latin intellectual inheritance as filtered through the early Church. This they supplemented in radical and daring fashion through the use of their own reasoning powers. Such an approach to questions of theology and metaphysics generated a tremendous excitement among the curious and unfettered minds that clustered in Paris and other centers of scholastic instruction and debate.

Once their intellectual curiosity had been aroused, Westerners discovered that the Moslems possessed a sophistication of mind and richness of learning far surpassing that available in Latin. Regular schools of translators therefore

THE HOLY CATHOLIC CHURCH

The topmost register of this stained glass window from Poitiers cathedral shows God the Father in Heaven, flanked by angels and adored by the saints. In the center and dominating the whole composition is the Crucifixion; at the bottom the martyrdom of St. Peter, Prince of the Apostles and founder of the Holy Catholic Church. Thus the artist found it possible to present the fundamental doctrines of the medieval Church in the design of a single window.

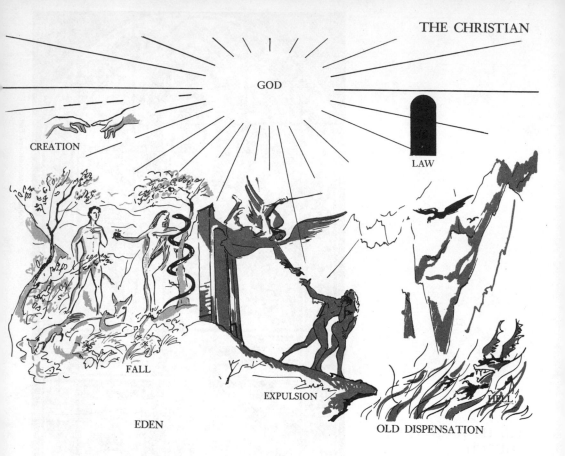

GOD

CREATION

LAW

FALL

EXPULSION

HELL

EDEN

OLD DISPENSATION

set eagerly to work to bring the treasures of Arabic learning to the Latin world. Toledo became the principal seat of this activity; but parallel work was done also in Sicily and, on a smaller scale, at Salerno, Salamanca, and Venice. The translators sought useful knowledge and were little concerned with belles-lettres. Hence they concentrated on works of medicine, mathematics, astronomy, optics, philosophy, and encyclopedic collections of information about the natural and supernatural world.

In the twelfth century, Ibn Rushd (Averroes) and Maimonides had revivified Aristotle's philosophy. The doctors of Islam, who cherished their own well-tried patterns of thought and honored other sources of authority, paid no attention; but in the Latin West, where men were only beginning to explore the subtleties and complexities of intellectual life, the logical method and systematic reasonableness of Aristotelian philosophy had all the force of fresh revelation. Aristotle offered a world-view that rivaled the traditional Christian (for the Latin West, basically Augustinian) outlook; a pagan philosophy, to be sure, yet one so impressive, so fascinating, and so appealing to the powers of reason that it could not casually be neglected. Some ecclesiastics

LAW

INCARNATION

RESURRECTION
CRUCIFIXION

GOD

CHURCH

POPE

SINNERS

HELL

NEW DISPENSATION   LAST JUDGMENT

feared the new thought and attempted to outlaw its study. But even papal pronouncements could not suppress the lively curiosity and reckless desire to
know which had taken hold in the universities.

Two consciously rival intellectual traditions arose in the thirteenth century
as a result of the infusion of Aristotelianism into Western thought. The one
Christianized Aristotle by asserting the superiority of revealed truth over any
mere human reasoning—thus preserving central Christian doctrines which
could not be demonstrated—but trusted enthusiastically in reason insofar as it
did not contradict Christian truth. The Dominican friars, Albertus Magnus
(d. 1280) and St. Thomas Aquinas (d. 1274), were the greatest exponents of
this school of thought. Others, among whom Franciscan friars were conspicuous, clung more closely to the Augustinian and ultimately Platonic intellectual tradition of the Church. Distrusting the abstract syllogistic reasoning of
Aristotelianism, Franciscans preferred the certainty of divine things gained
through contemplation and mystical exercise, and the humbler but useful
knowledge of the sensory world that could be derived better through experiment and observation than through abstract reasoning. St. Bonaventura (d.

1274) emphasized the mystical side of the Franciscan distrust of Aristotelianism; Robert Grosseteste, Bishop of Lincoln (d. 1253), and the friar Roger Bacon (d. *ca.* 1292) emphasized experimental distrust of the long chains of syllogistic reasoning so confidently constructed by Aristotle's Dominican admirers.

In his monumental *Summa Theologica*, St. Thomas Aquinas provided a massed array of authoritative opinions and carefully reasoned answers to questions of faith and morals. Within a short time this book acquired semiofficial status as the most authoritative exposition of Christian theology. St. Thomas' remarkable success in using Aristotelian logic and terminology to expound Christian doctrine left little for his followers to do except to admire his learning and the elegance of his demonstrations.[118] Those who attacked Aristotelianism showed greater variety and vigor. Franciscans like Duns Scotus (d. 1308) and William of Ockham (d. *ca.* 1349) kept philosophical and theological controversy alive in the fourteenth century; yet already in their time, the elaboration and refinement of the questions under discussion prepared the way for the humanists' hostile caricature of scholasticism as a preserve for meretricious verbalism and futile triviality.

The medieval synthesis of faith and reason was clearly fraying out in the fourteenth century; and the verbal extravagances of late scholastic philosophy —"How many angels can dance on the head of a pin?"—resembled the flamboyant overdecoration of late Gothic architecture in a more than metaphorical sense. In both cases, the structural lines and central purpose became obscured by a façade of excessive ornament and exhibitionistic virtuosity. Yet while the two principal expressions of Christian culture were thus degenerating into triviality and excess, previously shrouded tensions between sacred and secular—between the ecclesiastical, Christian ideal and an at first almost unformulated this-worldliness—came clearly to expression in the vernacular literatures and popular religion.

*   *   *

This tension was evident even amid the majestic technicalities of the law. Roman law, codified by Justinian in the Latin tongue, had never been entirely forgotten in the West; but it acquired a new importance early in the twelfth century when Irnerius (d. *ca.* 1130) inaugurated systematic study of Justinian's Code at Bologna. The Roman law provided reasoned and consistent principles of jurisprudence, as well as ready-made classifications of social relationships and rules for the settlement of disputes. This cut with the grain of a society in process of rapid transition to a more impersonal basis. Undoubtedly the pre-existence of this system of law, so superior to the tangle of local customary law which had grown up everywhere in Europe, greatly facilitated and speeded the restoration of civilized complexities to western European life.

The Roman law had other functions in medieval Europe. First and fore-

---

[118] In this, St. Thomas resembled Aristotle himself, whose systematic completeness oppressed his intellectual heirs by its very perfection.

most, as a legal system believed to embody universal principles of natural and divine law, it became a most effective instrument of political centralization. The papacy was the first to exploit this possibility by developing a body of canon law closely modeled upon the Roman code and a hierarchy of ecclesiastical courts to enforce its provisions. The jurisdiction of the canon law was not confined to clergymen; for cases of faith and morals, together with disputes arising in connection with Church property, all fell within its scope. The rise of papal power between the eleventh and thirteenth centuries rested squarely upon the work of the canonists, who all across Europe brought myriad circumstances of private and public life under ecclesiastical jurisdiction.

But rational and systematic law was a two-edged weapon. Secular rulers, too, could use it to extend their power over their subjects. Collision with the ecclesiastical courts was inevitable; and although the papacy was able to defeat the attempt of the German emperors to avail themselves of the centralizing force of the Roman law, papal legality could not prevail against the newer-sprung legal and administrative systems of the French and English monarchies. Yet even after Boniface VIII had been humiliated by the king of France (1302), the legal and administrative system of the Church did not dissolve. Rather, kings and popes agreed in effect to divide jurisdiction over clergy and laity between them, while combining their forces to override feudal and municipal jurisdiction. This compromise between the secular and the sacred uses of law lasted until the Reformation.

Vernacular literature, by its very nature, reflected the concerns of a wider proportion of the population than the Latin learning of the Church and universities could do. Norse and Anglo-Saxon sagas and French *chansons de geste* expressed the heroic ideals of the warrior classes; and the earliest of them show little trace of Christianity. But heroic poetry gave way to romances, in which knighthood was Christianized and the rude vigor of the warrior was clothed in courtesy and gentle manners. Yet at the same time, a rival tradition expressed in the songs of the troubadours maintained in a new form the old antithesis between pagan and Christian ideals by praising adultery, lovely ladies, and the hedonistic worldliness of the courtier.

Burghers, too, early found a voice in vernacular literature. Many *fabliaux*, for example, celebrated the cleverness of commoners and, not infrequently, held priests up to ridicule. Yet townsmen were not insensitive to the claims of Christianity; and some of the miracle plays, designed for a town audience, embody simple, unquestioning piety. With Dante (d. 1321), townsmen found a literary voice that rose far above the crudity of *fabliaux* and the naïveté of miracle plays. Dante's Italian sonnets constitute a Christianized version of the courtly love of the troubadours; while his great epic, the *Divine Comedy*, presents the magnificent paradox of a strongly anticlerical, yet deeply Christian and vastly learned poem.

Popular religious movements illustrated the tension between churchmen and townsmen in the clearest and most immediate sense. In the late twelfth century, a variety of heresies spread through northern Italy and southern France, finding their primary reception among weavers and other artisan groups. The most prominent such heretics were the Cathari,[119] religious rigorists who put Christians to shame by strict asceticism and a strongly congregational piety. When argument and preaching failed, the Cathari were brutally suppressed by the so-called Albigensian Crusades (1208–29).

But force alone scarcely sufficed to meet the challenge which heretical sects offered to the Church. Dominican and Franciscan friars therefore took up the task of maintaining a Christian and Catholic spirit among the townspeople of Europe. By their preaching, charity, and pious example, the friars strove to communicate to townsmen a better understanding of Christian faith and conduct. Pope Innocent III hesitated long before sanctioning the lay brotherhood that gathered around St. Francis of Assisi (d. 1226), for the mystic visions, miracle-working powers, and eccentric disregard of social conventions vouchsafed to the saint—himself a layman—bypassed both the ordinary sacramental channels of grace and the authority of the official apostolic hierarchy. Moreover, St. Francis' mendicancy challenged, not explicitly but by implication, the princely style of life affected by the prelates of the Church. Yet in the end the pope did give his blessing to the new order and thereby captured for the Church the tremendous outpouring of religious enthusiasm St. Francis and his order generated.

The very intensity of Franciscan religiosity created constant problems for officials of a Church whose many compromises with the world deeply offended religious rigorists like the so-called "Spiritual" Franciscans of the fourteenth century. The principal issue dividing these friars from the hierarchy of the Church was fraught with broad and emotionally explosive implications; for the "Spirituals," making explicit what had earlier been only implicit in the Franciscan movement, claimed that possession of property was incompatible with the example set by Christ and the Apostles, whose successors the bishops claimed to be. This doctrine constituted a direct assault upon the worldly wealth and practical power of the Church; it also called into question the legitimacy of the entire ecclesiastical establishment, for how could men who had strayed so far from the apostolic example be trusted in any matter whatsoever? The Church therefore anathematized the doctrine of apostolic poverty; yet stubborn extremists refused to acknowledge the authority of their judges, and some were silenced only by execution. But even severe persecution could not suppress criticism of the wealth and worldliness of the clergy entirely, though it did drive the religious rigorism of the Spirituals (as earlier of the Cathari) underground, whence it reappeared in full spate only with the Reformation.

Even more subversive to official religion than outright heresy was the spirit of religious indifference or scepticism which found lodgment in some urban circles from the thirteenth century onward. Skeptics did not usually parade their lack of religious conviction or offer any open challenge to the Church.

[119] The Cathari (also known as Albigenses in southern France) appear to have drawn their doctrines from the Bogomils of the Balkans and ultimately, perhaps, from Manichaeism, which had survived covertly, despite persistent persecution, in Iraq and bordering regions from Sassanian times.

Instead, they devoted themselves to the "finer things of life," whether these were defined in terms of wealth, power, or beauty. As such attitudes gained ground, especially in Italy, the prelates of the Church frequently fell in with worldly values—sometimes enthusiastically—and reduced their religion to little more than ritual gesture and lip service to familiar phrases. This inner decay of the Italian Church, in juxtaposition to the continuing vitality of religious rigorism in northern Europe, set the stage for the explosion of the Reformation in the sixteenth century.

Before that drastic and dramatic break in European religious unity occurred, the secularizing spirit of Italian townsmen found an attractive style of expression in the culture of the Renaissance. From the fourteenth century onward, a few men of letters set out to revive classical Latin in all its Ciceronian purity. Their emphasis upon language shifted attention from Arabic and classical didactic works, which had so entranced European scholars of the twelfth and thirteenth centuries, and put belles-lettres in the forefront. Such interests brought Italian humanists, as they called themselves, into close harmony with contemporary Byzantine literary circles, whose preoccupation with their own classical literature directed the attention of a few Italians to the riches of the Greek literary inheritance—an inheritance which had been almost forgotten in western Europe since the fourth century. But Latin and Greek letters opened the vision of a life unencumbered by revealed religion; and before the end of the fifteenth century, some of the more daring humanists had consciously broken with Christianity. A few, like Niccolo Machiavelli (d. 1527), flaunted their irreligion. Others, like Pico della Mirandola (d. 1494), sought to preserve their faith by modifying traditional Christian dogma in a pantheistic direction.

Chronic inability to refrain from classical allusions and other proofs of literary learning make the writings of most humanists thoroughly unattractive to contemporary taste. No comparable blight affected the visual arts. Classical examples of painting were lacking; and in sculpture and architecture, Renaissance artists inadvertently transcended their (mostly second-rate) classical models. The initial effort of Italian painters was toward a more perfect naturalism. Masaccio (d. 1428) introduced shading—subsequently elaborated into aerial perspective—to suggest three-dimensionality; and about 1435 Leon Battista Alberti (d. 1472) formulated a geometrical method for calculating linear perspective. This allowed painters to organize their figures within an illusory space which receded infinitely toward a vanishing point. By the end of the fifteenth century, the changes had been rung on both these new techniques; and artists were already straining beyond naturalism toward dramatic exaggeration and distortion—presaging the Baroque.

This truly remarkable definition of a new and distinctively Western style of painting involved a sophisticated mathematization of space and an intellectual reorganization of intuitive optical experience. Italian painting thus presaged the mathematical development of natural science that came to full expression only in the seventeenth century.

The art and worldliness of Renaissance Italy, redolent of fresh ventures into the unknown, found an echo north of the Alps before 1500, especially in court circles. But in general, northwestern Europe was caught betwixt and between. In the fourteenth and fifteenth centuries, men in France, England, and Germany increasingly chafed against the rigidities of the institutional and intellectual framework which their forefathers had constructed with such brilliance in the twelfth and thirteenth centuries; but they were not able, or perhaps willing, to discard or break through the limits implicit in that inheritance. Indeed, during the fourteenth and fifteenth centuries medieval European civilization seemed to show promise of an incipient stabilization in its principal cradle land north of the Alps. Yet this potentially "classical" definition of European society and culture had no sooner begun to emerge than the twin revolutionary forces of Renaissance and Reformation utterly disrupted it.

Prior to that disruption, however, diverse aspects of transalpine society suggest that the medieval frame of European society had stuck at dead center. The growth of towns, for example, underwent a drastic check, partly due to the ravages of the Black Death (1348–50)[120] and the Hundred Years' War (1337–1453), but also because of other factors. Most towns of northwestern Europe had fallen under the domination of tight little oligarchies, living upon traditional monopolies and rents, and quite disinclined to launch new ventures of any sort, economic, cultural, or political. Only toward the fringes of Latin Christendom, along the Baltic coast and in previously little-developed regions like southern Germany, did vigorous expansion of urban life continue in the fourteenth and fifteenth centuries.

Discontent with this confining social system was variously expressed. Peasant revolts were matched by risings of the lower classes in the towns; but all such movements failed, at least partly because the rebels lacked any well-considered program of reform. Psychological alienation from the established order may be glimpsed in the Lollard heresy in England, inspired by John Wyclif's (d. 1384) criticisms of ecclesiastical practices, and in the related Hussite movement of Bohemia. The tale of *Piers Plowman* (*ca.* 1370) breathes something of the same spirit. And even outwardly orthodox expressions of mystical piety, like those of the Brethren of the Common Life in the Low Countries, surely reflect disenchantment with the world and dissatisfaction with formal religion and the apparatus of the Church.

Yet it would be wrong to suggest that transalpine Europe entered upon a state of cultural catalepsy after 1300. Many of the cathedrals begun earlier were completed in the fourteenth and fifteenth centuries; scholastic logic and

---

[120] The severity of the demographic effects of the Black Death deserves emphasis. A recent study estimates population loss at no less than 50 per cent in Provence and finds recovery delayed until 1470. Cf. Edouard Baratier, *La démographie provençale du XIIIe au XVIe siècle, avec chiffres de comparison pour le XVIIIe siècle* (Paris: S.E.V.P.E.N., 1961). Cf. also Josiah Cox Russell, "Late Medieval Population Patterns," *Speculum*, XX (1945), 157–71.

The Black Death bears roughly the same chronological relationship to the opening of easier and more frequent communication across the Eurasian ecumene by the Mongol conquests of the thirteenth century as did the great plagues of the second century A.D. to the "closure of the ecumene" discussed above in chapter vii. Perhaps the stabilization and revival of European population under the ravages of the plague was possible in the fourteenth–fifteenth centuries A.D. because of the prior exposure of European populations to the diseases which had caused the plagues of the second century.

A FLEMISH BURGHER

The self-assurance, luxury, and quiet ostentation of these representatives of the middle class indicates one of the key differences between the Far West and the other civilizations of the world. Jan van Eyck painted this portrait of Jan Arnolfini and his wife in 1434. In that same year, he became a salaried artist at the court of Philip the Good of Burgundy. The fact that a man of the market place could patronize the same artist whom a prince like Philip of Burgundy employed also suggests the uniquely high status European merchants enjoyed.

mystical piety competed uneasily for men's minds; popular unrest simmered unceasingly; while the florid chivalry of the court of Philip the Good (d. 1467) of Burgundy or the quieter elegance of Flemish burghers as portrayed in the paintings of the van Eycks were not entirely unworthy of comparison with the greater brilliance and daring of contemporary Italian culture. Yet clearly, except in Italy, these centuries do not rank among Europe's great ages.

5. UNIQUE CHARACTERISTICS OF WEST EUROPEAN CIVILIZATION

In view of the revolutionary role that European civilization played in the world after 1500, it is worth asking how medieval Europe differed from its contemporaries elsewhere. Two observations suggest themselves.

First, from the eleventh century onward, western Europeans entered upon' the inheritance of the classical, Moslem, and Byzantine worlds relatively uninhibited by their own past. The ease and eagerness with which they appropriated these alien inheritances has perhaps no equal in civilized history, unless it be the Greek assimilation of Oriental civilization in the sixth century B.C. The speed and single-mindedness with which Europeans learned what more anciently civilized neighbors had to teach them perhaps permitted the European novices to carry further than their Asian contemporaries the effort at rationalization of human effort—an effort toward which their share in the Greek inheritance predisposed them. Roman law, Greek science and philosophy, and the ecclesiastical encouragement of reasoning about doctrine and the world all forwarded this development. Apt and important symbols of the new possibilities which such an attitude opened for Europeans were the mathematization of space in Renaissance art, and of time with the invention of the mechanical clock (thirteenth century). No other civilization achieved such precise tools for the co-ordination of human sensibility and effort.

Second, popular participation in economic, cultural, and political life was far greater in western Europe than in the other civilizations of the world. The staples of European commerce were not luxury goods designed for the wealthy few, as tended to be the case in the Asian civilizations, but such common items as grain and herring, wool and coarse cloth, metals and timber —all destined for a much wider class of consumers. Culturally, the aspirations of a wide variety of social groups—clergy, nobility, burghers, and to some degree even peasants—found literary expression in medieval European society, whereas only passing crises in the other Eurasian civilizations brought anything comparable to the surface. Despite the dominance of aristocracy in the European countryside and of oligarchy in the towns, a larger proportion of the total population participated in the war and politics of medieval Europe than was true of any of the civilized Asian societies, with the possible exception of contemporary Japan. Thus, for example, pikemen recruited from the towns of northern Italy and later from the villages of Switzerland challenged the military supremacy of aristocratic knights from the twelfth century onward, while in the fourteenth century, the cream of French chivalry could not prevail against English bowmen, recruited originally from the poverty-stricken Welsh marchlands. As for politics, such representative institutions as the English Parliament, the French Estates-General, and the Ecumenical Councils of the Church, all brought varied social groups into the highest arenas of the political process.

The result was to mobilize greater human resources within European society than was possible within the more rigidly hierarchical societies of the other civilized lands. The Greek democratic polis of the classical age had shown for a brief period the potentialities of a small community of free men and citizens. Western Europe was neither so free nor so intensely creative; yet there, too, we can perhaps detect the stimulating effect of circumstances that called forth conflicting energies of a larger proportion of the total population than could ever find expression in a society dominated by just a few individuals of comparatively homogeneous, though much more refined, outlook.

G. THE FRINGES OF THE ECUMENE

By 1000 A.D., most of central and northern Eurasia had been brought within the circle of civilized commerce. Only the Arctic tundra, the home of reindeer nomads and of fishers and hunters, remained untouched. During the ensuing five centuries, agricultural occupation of the forest zones of northern Europe advanced very significantly, especially in Russia. An analogous though less massive agricultural expansion into the northern forested zone of the Far East, in Manchuria, the Amur Valley, and northern Japan, also occurred. During the same period, as this chapter has tried to show, the high barbarism of the steppes, closely bound to the civilized societies of the south by commercial and military relationships, played a critically important role in the history of all Asia and of eastern Europe.

On the southern flank of the Eurasian civilizations, a much wider belt of territory remained little affected, or even absolutely untouched, by civilized influence down to 1000 A.D. This was true of all south Africa and Australasia; and limited pockets of primitive life survived in the rain forests of the Mekong and adjacent river valleys. Australasia continued to be a world apart; but in Africa and southeast Asia, civilized military and commercial penetration drastically transformed the cultural map between 1000 and 1500. Islam was the principal agent of this transformation—a consequence of the fact that Moslems controlled the trade of the Indian Ocean and of the Sahara between 1000 and 1500 A.D.

In southeast Asia, civilized states had existed since about the beginning of the Christian era. In 1000 A.D., three Indianized states, the sea empires of Srivijaya (Sumatra) and Majapahit (Java) and the river empire of the Khmers (lower Mekong) divided the political stage with the Sinified state of Annam. Enormous and magnificent temples, adorned with elaborate and sometimes exceedingly beautiful sculpture, remain as monuments to the wealth, skill, and piety of the peoples of these three states. However, in the thirteenth century, barbarian Thai tribesmen disrupted the Khmer empire;

and, simultaneously, Buddhist monks from Ceylon and Moslem missionaries from India began to undermine the older religious systems. On the whole, the Buddhists were successful inland and converted the Thai to their version of Indian culture (fourteenth century), while Islam won the coasts and islands, even as far afield as Mindanao in the Philippines (fourteenth to fifteenth centuries).[121]

Three major transformations occurred in Africa between 1000 and 1500 A.D. First, in west Africa Moslem states replaced the pagan Negro kingdom of Ghana after the sack of that kingdom by the Almoravids (1076)—a puritanical Islamic sect turned conqueror. Ghana's most important successor was Mali, a Negro Moslem kingdom that reached its apex early in the fourteenth century and disappeared (1488) before still another Moslem conqueror, based this time in Morocco. Agriculture was the economic basis of Negro society in the west African savanna; and trade connections through the Sahara with the north African coast were always important. Organized mining produced large quantities of gold dust—so much, indeed, that when a ruler of Mali made a pilgrimage to Mecca in 1324, his lavish distribution of gold is reputed to have depressed the value of that metal in Arabia for a decade afterward.

The second transformation of the African scene was the migration of Bantu-speaking pastoral peoples southward along the spine of east Africa and into the central rain forests of west and central Africa. This movement began well before 1500 A.D. and may have been reinforced by the migration of tribes fleeing from Moslem pressures in the northwest. The process resembled the much earlier expansion of cattle and horse nomads through the Eurasian steppe (the Bantu, however, lacked horses) and may have resulted from an analogous stimulus, *i.e.*, acquisition of the arts of cattle husbandry from more civilized neighbors (perhaps in Nubia), followed by the development of a warlike ethos to accord with their new pastoral mode of life. At any rate, the Bantu enjoyed an easy military supremacy over the earlier inhabitants of east central Africa, reaching the Zambesi River by the end of the fifteenth century; while other pagan Negro peoples penetrated to the Guinea and Dahomey coasts, where they founded a number of small states. Arab trade inland from the coastal ports of east Africa declined; for the Bantu, with their military prowess, proved less amenable to commercial exploitation than earlier inhabitants of the African hinterland had been.[122]

The third major landmark in African cultural history was the consolidation of Islam in the northeast. The critical event in this process was the Moslem conquest and conversion of the Christian kingdom of Nubia, completed by the beginning of the fifteenth century. Moslems also won control of all

---

[121] The rise of Islam in southeast Asia was connected with the shift of sea power and commercial dominance to a new state, Malacca, founded probably in the fourteenth century and converted to Islam in the fifteenth. Cf. D. G. E. Hall, *A History of South East Asia* (New York: St Martin's Press, 1955), pp. 37–186; J. C. van Leur, *Indonesian Trade and Society* (The Hague: W. van Hoeve, 1955), pp. 44–117; G. Coedès, *Les États hindouisés d'Indochine et d'Indonesie* (Paris: E. de Boccard, 1948).

[122] The abandonment of the Zimbabwe towns and mines may have been caused by Bantu conquest, though some scholars believe it was their arrival in Rhodesia that started large-scale mining! See above, p. 481.

the Red Sea coast, confining Christians to the Ethiopian highlands. Yet the very effort required to resist Moslem encroachment and to escape the fate of Nubia induced an Ethiopian "golden age" between the late thirteenth and early sixteenth centuries, when Amharic literature and the fine arts flourished as never before or since in that culturally isolated society.

Thus by the time Europeans began to explore the coasts of Africa, most of that continent had already felt the transforming touch of civilized influences. West Africa was a marginal province of Islam; the high barbarism of Bantu tribal society occupied the central spine; and in the northeast, Islamic states divided the landscape with Christian Ethiopia. Only in the far south and in parts of the Congo rain forest did truly primitive peoples survive.[123]

* * *

In the Americas, the most important change in the civilizations of Mexico, Central America, and Peru between 1000 and 1500 was the development of large urban agglomerations out of the earlier cult centers. Yet the socio-economic patterns of Amerindian civilizations always differed widely from the patterns familiar in the Old World. Market relationships were little developed. In the highly integrated Inca empire, for example, the exchange of goods was politically controlled; officials collected food and artisan products from the producers and in turn distributed these goods as compensation for specified military, administrative, or labor service. Petty barter between artisans and peasants did occur; but no class analogous to the professional merchants of Eurasian civilizations seems ever to have developed in the New World.

Politically, the history of the New World becomes for the first time comparatively clear. In Mexico, a number of rival and warlike "city-states" arose as heirs of the Toltec priest-state. One of these, Tenochtitlan, in alliance with two lesser cities, gained military predominance in the early fifteenth century. In the following decades, through annual military expeditions aimed partly at plunder and land-grabbing, but justified at least theoretically by the need for supplying the gods with an adequate diet of human hearts, this Aztec city fastened its power upon a fairly wide belt of territory in central Mexico. The Aztecs did not destroy local tribal and city-state organizations, however; and the imperial sway of the warriors of Tenochtitlan was in fact very insecure when Cortez invaded their domain in 1519.

In the Mayan area, political fragmentation replaced the earlier unity. The political supremacy of Chichen-Itza, established shortly before 1000, was overthrown about 1200, to be replaced by the analogous hegemony of the rival city of Mayapan. This new hegemony in turn dissolved about 1450,

---

[123] C. W. Bovill, *Caravans of the Old Sahara* (London: Oxford University Press, 1933), pp. 4–183; Diedrich Westermann, *Geschichte Afrikas* (Cologne: Greven Verlag, 1952), pp. 356–62, 382, 390–91, and *passim*. A. H. M. Jones and Elizabeth Monroe, *A History of Ethiopia* (Oxford: Clarendon Press, 1955), pp. 44–79; J. C. de Graft-Johnson, *African Glory* (London: Watt & Co., 1954), pp. 68–126; R. Coupland, *East Africa and Its Invaders* (Oxford: Clarendon Press, 1938), pp. 2–43; G. P. Murdock, *Africa: Its Peoples and Their Culture History* (New York: McGraw-Hill, 1959).

leaving Yucatan and the Mayan areas of Guatemala politically divided between petty rival states when the Spaniards appeared on the scene.

Peru was the seat of the only really well-consolidated and extensive state which confronted the Spaniards in the New World. There, in the fifteenth century, the Incas overran previously independent city-states and petty territorial units to create a centralized empire. They imposed an amazingly comprehensive and systematic administration upon the conquered lands, concentrating all authority in the hands of the Great Inca and his immediate relatives. Impressive feats of engineering—especially road-building—proved the capacity of the regime to organize and control the labor of its subjects; but the system faltered in 1527 when a disputed succession paralyzed the whole administrative machine. By mere chance,[124] this was the year when Pizarro launched his freebooting expedition against Peru.

Neither in art, nor in technology—the only aspects of Amerindian civilizations easily accessible to modern examination—was there any notable advance between 1000 and 1500. Most judges, in fact, detect a decline in artistic excellence as military rule replaced the earlier priestly dominance over society. Certainly, none of the New World civilizations was in a politically sound condition when the Spaniards appeared; and the potential strength of the Amerindian peoples was never really brought to bear against the handful of European invaders. Nor does it appear that the cultural life of the Indian civilizations was especially flourishing or had deep hold upon the loyalties of the common people. The remarkably rapid success of Spanish missions in converting the Amerindians to at least the superficial aspects of Christianity could not have occurred had the mass of the population been really deeply attached to the priestly and imperial traditions of their erstwhile rulers. The loss to human culture involved in the Spanish extirpation of Amerindian civilizations does not therefore seem very great. Over centuries and millennia, who can say what might have arisen? But in 1500 A.D., the actual achievements of the New World were trifling as compared to those of the Old.[125]

---

[124] Or perhaps not. A smallpox epidemic, resulting from the arrival of the Spaniards in the New World, may have devastated Inca lands and created the dynastic crisis which so greatly aided Pizarro.

[125] G. C. Vaillant, *The Aztecs of Mexico* (Harmondsworth: Pelican, 1950); Walter Krickeberg, *Altmexicanische Kulturen* (Berlin: Safari Verlag, 1956); J. Eric Thompson, *The Rise and Fall of Maya Civilization* (Norman, Okla.: University of Oklahoma Press, 1954), pp. 84–130; J. Alden Mason, *The Ancient Civilizations of Peru* (Harmondsworth: Pelican Books, 1957), pp. 93–230; Hans Dietrich Diesselhoff, *Geschichte der Altamerikanischen Kulturen* (Munich: Verlag R. Oldenberg, 1953), pp. 76–201, 303–48.

PART III

The Era
of Western Dominance
1500 A.D. to the Present

General Introduction

The year 1500 A.D. aptly symbolizes the advent of the modern era, in world as well as in European history. Shortly before that date, technical improvements in navigation pioneered by the Portuguese under Prince Henry the Navigator (d. 1460) reduced to tolerable proportions the perils of the stormy and tide-beset North Atlantic. Once they had mastered these dangerous waters, European sailors found no seas impenetrable, nor any ice-free coast too formidable for their daring. In rapid succession, bold captains sailed into distant and hitherto unknown seas: Columbus (1492), Vasco da Gama (1498), and Magellan (1519–22) were only the most famous.

The result was to link the Atlantic face of Europe with the shores of most of the earth. What had always before been the extreme fringe of Eurasia became, within little more than a generation, a focus of the world's sea lanes, influencing and being influenced by every human society within easy reach of the sea. Thereby the millennial land-centered balance among the Eurasian civilizations was abruptly challenged and, within three centuries, reversed. The sheltering ocean barrier between the Americas and the rest of the world was suddenly shattered, and the slave trade brought most of Africa into the penumbra of civilization. Only Australia and the smaller islands of the Pacific remained for a while immune; yet by the close of the eighteenth century, they too began to feel the force of European seamanship and civilization.

Western Europe, of course, was the principal gainer from this extraordinary revolution in world relationships, both materially and in a larger sense, for it now became the pre-eminent meeting place for novelties of every kind. This allowed Europeans to adopt whatever pleased them in the tool kits of other peoples and stimulated them to reconsider, recombine, and invent anew within their own enlarged cultural heritage. The Amerindian civilizations of Mexico and Peru were the most conspicuous victims of the new world balance, being suddenly reduced to a comparatively simple village level after the directing classes had been destroyed or demoralized by the Spaniards. Within the Old World, the Moslem peoples lost their central position in the ecumene as ocean routes supplanted overland portage. Only in the Far East were the effects of the new constellation of world relationships at first unimportant. From a Chinese viewpoint it made little difference whether foreign trade, regulated within traditional forms, passed to Moslem or European merchants' hands. As soon as European expansive energy seemed to threaten their political integrity, first Japan and then China evicted the disturbers and closed their borders against further encroachment. Yet by the middle of the nineteenth century, even this deliberate isolation could no longer be maintained; and the civilizations of the Far East—simultaneously with the primitive cultures of central Africa—began to stagger under the impact of the newly industrialized European (and extra-European) West.

The key to world history from 1500 is the growing political dominance first of western Europe, then of an enlarged European-type society planted astride the north Atlantic and extending eastward into Siberia. Yet until about 1700, the ancient landward frontiers of the Asian civilizations retained much of their old significance. Both India (from 1526) and China (by 1644) suffered yet another conquest from across these frontiers; and the Ottoman empire did not exhaust its expansive power until near the close of the seventeenth century. Only in Central America and western South America did Europeans succeed in establishing extensive land empires overseas during this period. Hence the years 1500–1700 may be regarded as transitional between the old land-centered and the new ocean-centered pattern of ecumenical relationships—a time when European enterprise had modified, but not yet upset the fourfold balance of the Old World.

The next major period, 1700–1850, saw a decisive alteration of the balance in favor of Europe, except in the Far East. Two great outliers were added to the Western world by the Petrine conversion of Russia and by the colonization of North America. Less massive offshoots of European society were simultaneously established in southernmost Africa, in the South American pampas, and in Australia. India was subjected to European rule; the Moslem Middle East escaped a similar fate only because of intra-European rivalries; and the barbarian reservoir of the Eurasian steppes lost its last shreds of military and cultural significance with the progress of Russian and Chinese conquest and colonization.

After 1850, the rapid development of mechanically powered industry enormously enhanced the political and cultural primacy of the West. At the beginning of this period, the Far Eastern citadel fell before Western gunboats; and a few of the European nations extended and consolidated colonial empires in Asia and Africa. Although European empires have decayed since 1945, and the separate nation-states of Europe have been eclipsed as centers of political power by the melding of peoples and nations occurring under the aegis of both the American and Russian governments, it remains true that, since the end of World War II, the scramble to imitate and appropriate science, technology, and other aspects of Western culture has accelerated enormously all round the world. Thus the dethronement of western Europe from its brief mastery of the globe coincided with (and was caused by) an unprecedented, rapid Westernization of all the peoples of the earth. The rise of the West seems today still far from its apogee; nor is it obvious, even in the narrower political sense, that the era of Western dominance is past. The American and Russian outliers of European civilization remain militarily far stronger than the other states of the world, while the power of a federally reorganized western Europe is potentially superior to both and remains inferior only because of difficulties in articulating common policies among nations still clinging to the trappings of their decaying sovereignties.

* * *

From the perspective of the mid-twentieth century, the career of Western civilization since 1500 appears as a vast explosion, far greater than any comparable phenomenon of the past both in geographic range and in social depth. Incessant and accelerating self-transformation, compounded from a welter of conflicting ideas, institutions, aspirations, and inventions, has characterized modern European history; and with the recent institutionalization of deliberate innovation in the form of industrial research laboratories, universities, military general staffs, and planning commissions of every sort, an accelerating pace of technical and social change bids fair to remain a persistent feature of Western civilization.

This changeability gives the European and Western history of recent centuries both a fascinating and a confusing character. The fact that we are heirs but also prisoners of the Western past, caught in the very midst of an unpredictable and incredibly fast-moving flux, does not make it easier to discern critical landmarks, as we can, with equanimity if not without error, for ages long past and civilizations alien to our own.

Nevertheless, an attempt must be made to treat European and world history in the modern era with the same broad brush employed hitherto in this book, if the artistic proportions of the entire essay are not to be lost. Fortunately, a noble array of historians has traversed the ground already, so that it is not difficult to divide Western history into periods, nor to characterize such periods with some degree of plausibility. A greater embarrassment arises from the fact that suitable periods of Western history do not coincide with the benchmarks of modern world history. This is not surprising, for Europe had first to reorganize itself at a new level before the effects of its increased power could show themselves significantly abroad. One should therefore expect to find a lag between the successive self-transformations of European society and their manifestations in the larger theater of world history.

I have therefore divided the following chapters along cleavages that seem appropriate to the history of the world; but each chapter will go back in time to consider some of the transformations of European life which antedated and in large degree provoked the new phase of world development. Thus the chapter dealing with the two centuries 1500–1700 will consider European developments only to 1650, by which time Europe had painfully outgrown its medieval mold. The chapter dealing with the period 1700–1850 on the world scale will, however, treat of Europe and the extra-European

West under the Old Regime, 1650–1789; and the final chapter, touching upon developments during the years 1850–1950, will consider the West from 1789 to 1917. The conclusion will then discuss what seem to be the key transformations of Western society since 1917 and venture a few speculations upon the likely consequences for world history that lie still in the future.

Compensation for the inherent awkwardness of such a scheme may perhaps be found in the manner in which it emphasizes the central dynamic of modern history.

CHAPTER XI

The Far West's Challenge to the World 1500–1700 A.D.

A. THE GREAT EUROPEAN EXPLORATIONS AND THEIR WORLD-WIDE CONSEQUENCES

Europeans of the Atlantic seaboard possessed three talismans of power by 1500 which conferred upon them the command of all the oceans of the world within half a century and permitted the subjugation of the most highly developed regions of the Americas within a single generation. These were: (1) a deep-rooted pugnacity and recklessness operating by means of (2) a complex military technology, most notably in naval matters; and (3) a population inured to a variety of diseases which had long been endemic throughout the Old World ecumene.

The Bronze Age barbarian roots of European pugnacity and the medieval survival of military habits among the merchant classes of western Europe, as well as among aristocrats and territorial lords of less exalted degree, have already been emphasized in this book. Yet only when one remembers the all but incredible courage, daring, and brutality of Cortez and Pizarro in the Americas, reflects upon the ruthless aggression of Almeida and Albuquerque in the Indian Ocean, and discovers the disdain of even so cultivated a European as Father Matteo Ricci for the civility of the Chinese,[1] does the full force

---

[1] "Running away is no dishonour with them [Chinese soldiers]; they do not know what an insult is; if they quarrel, they abuse one another like women, seize each other by the hair, and when they are weary of scuffling become good friends again as before, without wounds or bloodshed." From a letter, written in 1584, as quoted by G. F. Hudson, *Europe and China* (London: Edward Arnold & Co., 1931), p. 248.

of European warlikeness, when compared with the attitudes and aptitudes of other major civilizations of the earth, become apparent. The Moslems and the Japanese could alone compare in the honor they paid to the military virtues. But Moslem merchants usually cringed before the violence held in high repute by their rulers and seldom dared or perhaps cared to emulate it. Hence Moslem commercial enterprise lacked the cutting edge of naked, well-organized, large-scale force which constituted the chief stock-in-trade of European overseas merchants in the sixteenth century. The Japanese could, indeed, match broadswords with any European; but the chivalric stylization of their warfare, together with their narrowly restricted supply of iron, meant that neither *samurai* nor sea pirate could reply in kind to a European broadside.

Supremacy at sea gave a vastly enlarged scope to European warlikeness after 1500. But Europe's maritime superiority was itself the product of a deliberate combination of science and practice, beginning in the commercial cities of Italy and coming to fruition in Portugal through the efforts of Prince Henry the Navigator and his successors. With the introduction of the compass (thirteenth century), navigation beyond sight of land had become a regular practice in the Mediterranean; and the navigators' charts, or *portolans*, needed for such voyaging showed coasts, harbors, landmarks, and compass bearings between major ports. Although they were drawn freehand, without any definite mathematical projection, *portolans* nevertheless maintained fairly accurate scales of distances. But similar mapping could be applied to the larger distances of Atlantic navigation only if means could be found to locate key points along the coast accurately. To solve this problem, Prince Henry brought to Portugal some of the best mathematicians and astronomers of Europe, who constructed simple astronomical instruments and trigonometrical tables by which ship captains could measure the latitude of newly discovered places along the African coast. The calculation of longitude was more difficult; and, until a satisfactory marine chronometer was invented in the eighteenth century, longitude could be approximated only by dead reckoning. Nevertheless, the new methods worked out at Prince Henry's court allowed the Portuguese to make usable charts of the Atlantic coasts. Such charts gave Portuguese sea captains courage to sail beyond sight of land for weeks and presently for months, confident of being able to steer their ships to within a few miles of the desired landfall.[2]

[2] The most striking application of the new techniques of scientific navigation was the route chosen by Vasco da Gama for his voyage to India in 1497. He sailed far out into the Atlantic (and must indeed have come close to the coast of Brazil) before turning east at the appropriate latitude and steering for the Cape of Good Hope, which had been discovered by Bartholomew Diaz only eleven years before. This route cut through the difficult tropic calms by the shortest possible route, far from any shores, where coastal currents or tides might endanger ships struggling for steerage in calm weather; it also took advantage of the westerlies of the southern Atlantic for the eastward leg. Da Gama's fleet was out of sight of land for 96 days and traveled about 4,500 miles between landfalls—a vastly greater voyage than Columbus' 2,600 miles in 36 days without sight of land. Moreover, Da Gama reached the coast of Africa within about 130 miles of the Cape for which he had steered—a remarkably precise feat of navigation considering the difficulty of taking sights of the sun on a pitching ship with the primitive instruments of the time. Cf. K. G. Jayne, *Vasco da Gama and His Successors, 1460–1580* (London: Methuen & Co., 1910), p. 40; Boies Penrose, *Travel and Discovery in the Renaissance, 1420–1620* (Cambridge, Mass.: Harvard University Press, 1955), pp. 50–51; Henry H. Hart, *Sea Road to the Indies* (New York: Macmillan Co., 1950), pp. 128–29.

The Portuguese court also accumulated systematic information about oceanic winds and currents; but this data was kept secret as a matter of high policy, so that modern scholars are uncertain how much the early Portuguese navigators knew. At the same time, Portuguese naval experts attacked the problem of improving ship construction. They proceeded by rule of thumb; but deliberate experiment, systematically pursued, rapidly increased the seaworthiness, maneuverability, and speed of Portuguese and presently (since improvements in naval architecture could not be kept secret) of other European ships. The most important changes were: a reduction of hull width in proportion to length; the introduction of multiple masts (usually three or four); and the substitution of several smaller, more manageable sails for the single sail per mast from which the evolution started. These innovations allowed a crew to trim the sails to suit varying conditions of wind and sea, thus greatly facilitating steering and protecting the vessel from disaster in sudden gales.[3]

With these improvements, larger ships could be built; and increasing size and sturdiness of construction[4] made it possible to transform seagoing vessels into gun platforms for heavy cannon. Thus by 1509, when the Portuguese fought the decisive battle for control of the Arabian Sea off the Indian port of Diu, their ships could deliver a heavy broadside at a range their Moslem enemies could not begin to match. Under such circumstances, the superior numbers of the opposing fleet simply provided the Portuguese with additional targets for their gunnery. The old tactics of sea fighting—ramming, grappling, and boarding—were almost useless against cannon fire effective at as much as 200 yards distance.[5]

The third weapon in the European armory—disease—was quite as important as stark pugnacity and weight of metal. Endemic European diseases like smallpox and measles became lethal epidemics among Amerindian populations, who had no inherited or acquired immunities to such infections. Literally millions died of these and other European diseases; and the smallpox epidemic raging in Tenochtitlan when Cortez and his men were expelled from the citadel in 1520 had far more to do with the collapse of Aztec power than merely mili-

[3] Cf. Charles Singer *et al.*, *A History of Technology* (Oxford University Press, 1958), III, 471–93.

[4] By the sixteenth century, European ships' walls were of oak, about two feet thick, with double planking on either side of heavy ribbing.

[5] Shipbuilding in the Indian Ocean had achieved a very considerable sophistication and economy by 1500. Light vessels, whose timbers were sewn together by vegetable fibers, proved so well adapted to the regular winds and weather of the southern seas—maneuverable, fast, and easy to beach in small harbors, etc.—that they have survived for fishing and coastal uses to the present. Yet as fighting vessels they were helpless against the Portuguese ships, built to withstand the North Atlantic; and the radical differences of construction, together with the difficulty of supplying the massive quantities of metal required by European naval architecture inhibited Moslem shipbuilders from imitating the Europeans, although apparently some efforts at such imitation were made in the very early days before Portuguese control of the Indian Ocean was secure. Cf. W. H. Moreland, "Ships of the Arabian Sea c. 1500," *Journal of the Royal Asiatic Society* (1939), pp. 63–74, 173–92. Chinese junks were far larger and more massively built than the Moslem ships of the Indian Ocean and might have offered a real challenge to European shipping on the high seas had metal shortages and the profound indifference—not to say hostility—of Chinese and Japanese political authorities toward naval enterprise prevented it. Even so, private piratical fleets in the south China sea long rivaled the almost equally piratical but publicly organized enterprise of the first European ships in those waters.

tary operations. The Inca empire, too, may have been ravaged and weakened by a similar epidemic before Pizarro ever reached Peru.[6]

On the other hand, diseases like yellow fever and malaria took a heavy toll of Europeans in Africa and India.[7] But climatic conditions generally prevented new tropical diseases from penetrating Europe itself in any very serious fashion. Those which could flourish in temperate climates, like typhus, cholera, and bubonic plague, had long been known throughout the ecumene; and European populations had presumably acquired some degree of resistance to them. Certainly the new frequency of sea contact with distant regions had important medical consequences for Europeans, as the plagues for which Lisbon and London became famous prove. But gradually the infections which in earlier centuries had appeared sporadically as epidemics became merely endemic, as the exposed populations developed a satisfactory level of resistance.

[6] P. M. Ashburn, *The Ranks of Death: A Medical History of the Conquest of America* (New York: Coward McCann, 1947), pp. 82–87.

[7] These and other diseases of the Old World tropics also ravaged the Amerindian populations when brought across the Atlantic on slave ships and seem to have made such regions as the Amazon basin and the Caribbean lowlands almost uninhabitable. Syphilis may have constituted a partial revenge of the American Indians upon their European conquerors; but medical opinion is divided as to whether or not syphilis did in fact have an American origin. P. M. Ashburn, *The Ranks of Death*, pp. 98–140, 175–90.

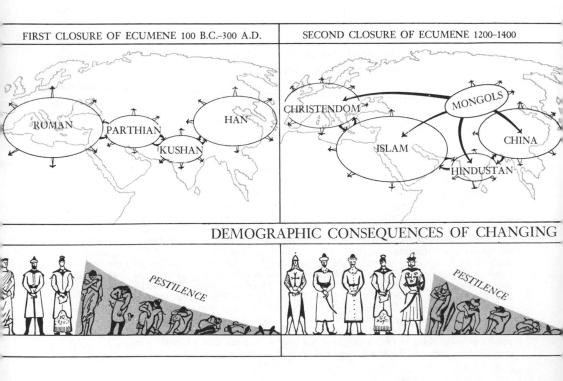

FIRST CLOSURE OF ECUMENE 100 B.C.–300 A.D.   SECOND CLOSURE OF ECUMENE 1200–1400

DEMOGRAPHIC CONSEQUENCES OF CHANGING

Before 1700, European populations had therefore successfully absorbed the shocks that came with the intensified circulation of diseases initiated by their own sea voyaging. Epidemics consequently ceased to be demographically significant.[8] The result was that from about 1650 (or before), population growth in Europe assumed a new velocity. Moreover, so far as imperfect data allow one to judge, between 1550 and 1650 population also began to spurt upward in China, India, and the Middle East.[9] Such an acceleration of population growth within each of the great civilizations of the Old World can scarcely be a mere coincidence. Presumably the same ecological processes

[8] Roger Mols, *Introduction à la démographie historique des villes d'Europe du XIVe à XVIIIe siècle* (Louvain: Publications universitaires de Louvain, 1955), II, 452. The last great plague in western Europe ran from 1663–84; there were later outbreaks in eastern Europe, and a local epidemic in southern France as late as 1724. Cf. Georg Sticker, *Abhandlungen aus der Seuchengeschichte und Seuchenlehre*, Band I, Erster Teil: *Die Geschichte der Pest* (Giessen: Alfred Töpelmann, 1908), pp. 175–236.

[9] L. Carrington Goodrich, *A Short History of the Chinese People* (3d ed.; New York: Harper & Bros., 1959), pp. 198–99, dates the upturn in China from the 1570's. G. Findlay Shirras, "The Population Problem in India," *Economic Journal*, XLIII (1933), p. 61, estimates Indian population at 80 million in 1650 and at 130 million in 1750. Fernand Braudel, *La Méditerranée et le monde méditerranéen à l'époque de Phillippe II* (Paris: A. Colin, 1949), pp. 353–57, finds rapid growth of populations subject to Ottoman rule in the sixteenth century. The population of Anatolia, for example, increased by 41 per cent between 1528 and 1580 according to Omer Lufti Barkan, "Essai sur les données statistiques des registres de recensement dans l'empire Ottoman aux XVe et XVIe siècles," *Journal of the Economic and Social History of the Orient*, I (1958), 30.

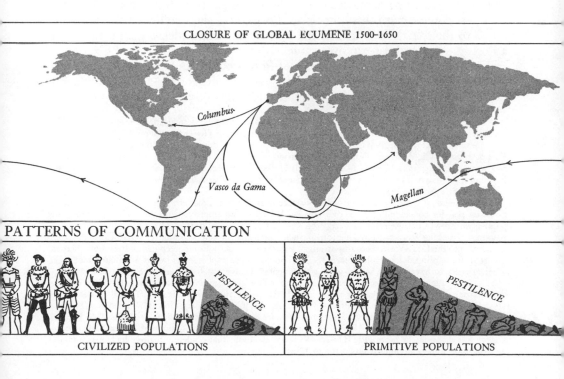

CLOSURE OF GLOBAL ECUMENE 1500-1650

Columbus

Vasco da Gama

Magellan

PATTERNS OF COMMUNICATION

PESTILENCE

PESTILENCE

CIVILIZED POPULATIONS

PRIMITIVE POPULATIONS

worked themselves out in all parts of the ecumene, as age-old epidemic checks upon population faded into merely endemic attrition.[10]

The formidable combination of European warlikeness, naval technique, and comparatively high levels of resistance to disease transformed the cultural balance of the world within an amazingly brief period of time. Columbus linked the Americas with Europe in 1492; and the Spaniards proceeded to explore, conquer, and colonize the New World with extraordinary energy, utter ruthlessness, and an intense missionary idealism. Cortez destroyed the Aztec state in 1519–21; Pizarro became master of the Inca empire between 1531 and 1535. Within the following generation, less famous but no less hardy conquistadores founded Spanish settlements along the coasts of Chile and Argentina, penetrated the highlands of Ecuador, Colombia, Venezuela, and Central America, and explored the Amazon basin and the southern United States. As early as 1571, Spanish power leaped across the Pacific to the Philippines, where it collided with the sea empire which their Iberian neighbors, the Portuguese, had meanwhile flung around Africa and across the southern seas of the Eastern Hemisphere.

Portuguese expansion into the Indian Ocean proceeded with even greater rapidity. Exactly a decade elapsed between the completion of Vasco da Gama's first voyage to India (1497–99) and the decisive Portuguese naval victory off Diu (1509). The Portuguese quickly exploited this success by capturing Goa (1510) and Malacca (1511), which together with Ormuz on the Persian Gulf (occupied permanently from 1515) gave them the necessary bases from which to dominate the trade of the entire Indian Ocean. Nor did they rest content with these successes. Portuguese ships followed the precious spices to their farthest source in the Moluccas without delay (1511–12); and a Portuguese merchant-explorer traveling on a Malay vessel visited Canton as early as 1513–14. By 1557, a permanent Portuguese settlement was founded at Macao on the south China coast; and trade and missionary activity in Japan started in the 1540's. On the other side of the world, the Portuguese dis-

---

[10] Population estimates for past ages are notoriously imprecise; yet demographers seem to agree that the remarkable increase in world population which is still in progress dates from about 1650. This opinion may merely reflect the beginning of something like population statistics at about that time in some European cities. Cf. Walter F. Willcox, "Population of the World and Its Modern Increase," in *Studies in American Demography* (Ithaca, N.Y.: Cornell University Press, 1940), pp. 22–52; United Nations Population Division, *The Past and Future Population of the World and Its Continents* (World Population Conference, paper No. 243, 1954).

Nevertheless, if these calculations are anywhere near the mark, modern population increase among civilized peoples considerably antedated any really significant improvements in medicine. The new population growth can therefore scarcely be credited to scientific control of disease. Increased food resources resulting from the introduction of such American products as maize, potatoes, and sweet potatoes into the Old World were important in some areas; and political pacification may have played a part in forwarding democraphic increase. Yet none of these explanations seems adequate to explain what appears to have been a world-wide phenomenon. I have not found any demographers who attribute the change to an increased level of immunity to disease among civilized populations resulting from closer contact throughout the ecumene. Cf. Raymond Pearl, *The Natural History of Population* (New York: Oxford University Press, 1939); A. M. Carr-Saunders, *World Population* (Oxford: Clarendon Press, 1936); Marcel R. Reinhard, *Histoire de la population mondiale de 1700 à 1948* (Paris: Editions Domat-Montchrestien, 1949). Yet the very painstaking investigations of Roger Mols, *Introduction à la démographie historique*, II, 426–59, leave no doubt that epidemic disease had been a major control upon European populations prior to 1700.

PORTUGUESE IN JAPAN

This handsome, brightly colored screen records the impression a visiting Portuguese ship made upon a Japanese artist in the late seventeenth century. The ship is shown on arrival, with men still scrambling in the rigging and others preparing to go ashore. In the foreground, the waiting Japanese dignitaries are almost engulfed in a great cloud of smoke, the result, no doubt, of a gun salute. This great billowing tongue of gunsmoke, running inland from the Europeans' floating gun platform, aptly symbolizes the initial phase of the European impact upon the rest of the world in the era of the great oceanic discoveries.

covered Brazil in 1500 and began to settle the country after 1530. Coastal stations in both west and east Africa, established between 1471 and 1507, completed the chain of ports of call which held the Portuguese empire together.

No other European nations approached the early success of Spain and Portugal overseas.[11] Nevertheless, the two Iberian nations did not long enjoy undisturbed the new wealth their enterprise had won. From the beginning, the Spaniards found it difficult to protect their shipping against French and Portuguese sea raiders. English pirates offered an additional and formidable threat after 1568, when the first open clash between English interlopers and the Spanish authorities in the Caribbean took place. Between 1516 and 1568 the other great maritime people of the age, the Dutch, were subjects of the same Hapsburg monarchs who ruled in Spain and, consequently, enjoyed a favored status as middlemen between Spanish and north European ports. Initially, therefore, Dutch shipping had no incentive to harass Iberian sea power.

This naval balance shifted sharply in the second half of the sixteenth century, when the Dutch revolt against Spain (1568), followed by the English victory over the Spanish armada (1588), signalized the waning of Iberian sea power before that of the northern European nations. Harassment of Dutch ships in Spanish ports simply accelerated the shift; for the Dutch responded by despatching their vessels directly to the Orient (1594), and the English soon followed suit. Thereafter, Dutch naval and commercial power rapidly supplanted that of Portugal[12] in the southern seas. The establishment of a base in Java (1618), the capture of Malacca from the Portuguese (1641), and the seizure of the most important trading posts of Ceylon (by 1644) secured Dutch hegemony in the Indian Ocean; and during the same decades, English traders gained a foothold in western India. Simultaneously, English (1607), French (1608), and Dutch (1613) colonization of mainland North America, and the seizure of most of the smaller Caribbean islands by the same three nations, infringed upon Spanish claims to monopoly in the New World, but failed to dislodge Spanish power from any important area where it was already established.

*   *   *

The truly extraordinary *élan* of the first Iberian conquests and the no less remarkable missionary enterprise that followed closely in its wake surely mark a new era in the history of the human community. Yet older landmarks of that history did not crumble all at once. Movements from the Eurasian steppes continued to make political history—for example, the Uzbek con-

[11] Both English and French expeditions vainly explored barren and forbidding segments of the North American coast in the hope of finding a northwest passage to the wealth of the Orient. Similar efforts to explore a northeast passage led to the opening of commercial relations between England and Russia via Archangel in 1553. English traders presently sailed down the Volga and through the Caspian Sea all the way to Persia.

[12] Portugal was ruled by Spanish sovereigns 1582–1640, a fact which exposed Portuguese imperial possessions to a double danger: encroachments by Spaniards being in Portuguese eyes no less offensive than those of Spain's Dutch, French, and English enemies.

quest of Transoxiana (1507–12) with its sequel, the Mogul conquest of India (1526–1688); and the Manchu conquest of China (1621–83).

Chinese civilization was indeed only slightly affected by the new regime of the seas; and Moslem expansion, which had been a dominating feature of world history during the centuries before 1500, did not cease or even slacken very noticeably until the late seventeenth century. Through their conquest of the high seas, western Europeans did indeed outflank the Moslem world in India and southeast Asia, while Russian penetration of Siberian forests soon outflanked the Moslem lands on the north also. Yet these probing extensions of European (or para-European) power remained tenuous and comparatively weak in the seventeenth century. Far from being crushed in the jaws of a vast European pincer, the Moslems continued to win important victories and to penetrate new territories in southeast Europe, India, Africa, and southeast Asia. Only in the western and central steppe did Islam suffer significant territorial setbacks before 1700.

Thus only two large areas of the world were fundamentally transformed

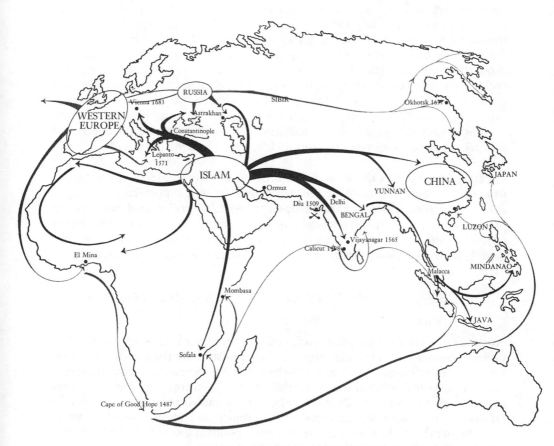

MOSLEM vs. EUROPEAN EXPANSION, 1000–1700 A.D.

during the first two centuries of European overseas expansion: the regions of Amerindian high culture and western Europe itself. European naval enterprise certainly widened the range and increased the intimacy of contacts among the various peoples of the ecumene and brought new peoples into touch with the disruptive social influences of high civilization. Yet the Chinese, Moslem, and Hindu worlds were not yet really deflected from their earlier paths of development; and substantial portions of the land surface of the globe—Australia and Oceania, the rain forests of South America, and most of North America and northeastern Asia—remained almost unaffected by Europe's achievement.

Nevertheless, a new dimension had been added to world history. An ocean frontier, where European seamen and soldiers, merchants, missionaries, and settlers came into contact with the various peoples of the world, civilized and uncivilized, began to challenge the ancient pre-eminence of the Eurasian land frontier, where steppe nomads had for centuries probed, tested, and disturbed civilized agricultural populations. Very ancient social gradients began to shift when the coasts of Europe, Asia, and America became the scene of more and more important social interactions and innovation. Diseases, gold and silver, and certain valuable crops were the first items to flow freely through the new transoceanic channels of communication. Each of these had important and far-reaching consequences for Asians as well as for Europeans and Amerindians. But prior to 1700, only a few isolated borrowings of more recondite techniques or ideas passed through the sea lanes that now connected the four great civilizations of the Old World. In such exchanges, Europe was more often the receiver than the giver, for its people were inspired by a lively curiosity, insatiable greed, and a reckless spirit of adventure that contrasted sharply with the smug conservatism of Chinese, Moslem, and Hindu cultural leaders.

Partly by reason of the stimuli that flowed into Europe from overseas, but primarily because of internal tensions arising from its own heterogeneous cultural inheritance, Europe entered upon a veritable social explosion in the period 1500–1650—an experience painful in itself but which nonetheless raised European power to a new level of effectiveness and for the first time gave Europeans a clear margin of superiority over the other great civilizations of the world.

B. THE TRANSMUTATION OF EUROPE, 1500–1650 A.D.

1. POLITICS

An ancient bias of European civilization, going back at least to classical Greece, emphasized territorial organization into states at the expense of alternative types of human association. Perhaps for this reason, it is comparatively easy to grasp the political aspect of the sixteenth–seventeenth century transmutation of European civilization, when the localisms of towns and feudal estates together with the universalism of empire and papacy went down in ruins before the middle term of the medieval political hierarchy, the territorial —and in the most successful cases, the national—state.

The consolidation of relatively large territorial states was achieved by importing into northern and western Europe administrative devices and moral attitudes which had first developed in the smaller city-states of Italy between the thirteenth and fifteenth centuries. Apart from their exemplary role in details of tax management, chancery procedures, and the like, Italian cities showed that it was possible to unite landed aristocracy and urban bourgeoisie into an effective territorial-political community, held together partly by the sentiment of patriotism and partly by a professional bureaucracy. In northern Europe, town and countryside had generally remained at arms' length prior to 1500. Burgher, noble, and peasant distrusted or despised each other, while the connecting link provided by royal or imperial government had been too weak and tenuous to do much to bridge the gap. But by the mid-seventeenth century, territorial governments had vastly increased their authority in most of Europe, undermining the particularism of the towns and curbing aristocratic habits of violence. Secular rulers also brought ecclesiastical administration largely within their scope and made even the peasantry feel the power of royal law, as administered by a professional bureaucracy. In short, the states of modern Europe fused the medieval estates to create nations in the north and west, and dynastic empires in the central and eastern parts of the continent. As a more orderly political framework imposed itself upon the medieval maze of corporate and private jurisdictions, the rival governments of Europe became able to mobilize ever larger concentrations of manpower and wealth, both for warlike and (less spectacularly) for peaceable undertakings. The upshot was a great increase in European power, particularly military power.

The appearance of a limited number of comparatively clearly defined sovereignties within Europe implied both less and more social and political variety. The enormous multiplicity of strictly local customs, laws, and institutions which had dominated the lives of most Europeans in the Middle Ages tended within each territorial state to develop toward a common norm. In this sense variety was reduced. But the simultaneous weakening of the papacy and empire meant a sharper differentiation from region to region and from state to state. Different states struck different balances among the competing classes and interest groups. Each such balance, enshrined in national or territorial institutions, tended to mark off and divide the populations of Europe more sharply than had been the case in medieval times. The retreat of Latin as a lingua franca and the use of local vernaculars for more and more purposes hastened such differentiation; but it was undoubtedly the religious variety introduced by the Reformation and enhanced by the subsequent divisions within Protestantism that most powerfully supported the partition of the population of the European body politic into distinct, competing segments.

From the sixteenth century onward, the most successful and influential states of Europe were located along the Atlantic coast. The first great power of modern Europe was Spain, where Ferdinand of Aragon (1479–1516) availed himself of his marriage with Isabella of Castile to weld the two kingdoms into a new and formidable power. Ferdinand's most effective instrument for reducing the separate kingdoms and estates of his realm to obedience was the Spanish Inquisition. This was a system of ecclesiastical courts designed to suppress heresy and therefore empowered to override local immunities and every form of special privilege. Since opposition to the royal will might also indicate religious heterodoxy, a really punctilious Inquisitor was obliged to arrest and interrogate such contumacious individuals. If their religious opinions proved above reproach, they were, of course, released; but the prospect of a few days, weeks, or sometimes years in the hands of the Inquisition very effectually overawed Ferdinand's domestic opponents.

Intimate alliance with the Catholic church was not the sole source of Spanish political greatness. American treasure, together with a hardy professional soldiery, also contributed essential sinews to the strength of Spain. Yet that strength proved insufficient to bear the burdens which dynastic ambition and accident put upon it. For when the young Charles of Hapsburg made good his claim to succeed his grandfather Ferdinand on the Spanish throne (1516), he brought with him the Hapsburg lands of Germany, together with the Burgundian inheritance in the Low Countries, and presently added the claims and aspirations of Holy Roman emperor (1519) to this array of dignities. Thereafter, Spanish national policy became inextricably entangled with the pan-European dynastic interests of the Hapsburgs and married itself to the glamorous but moribund imperial ideal. Catholic fervor, Spanish blood, and American silver did not suffice to sustain such a burden. Even after Charles V abdicated (1556) and the imperial title passed to his brother in Austria, thus leaving his son Philip II (d. 1598) free to concentrate Spain's strength upon the support of only one of the two universal institutions of the medieval past—the papacy—Spaniards still proved unable to overcome Dutch (from 1568) and English harassments.

Nevertheless, the Spanish crusade won real successes in Italy, where it put iron into Catholic reform and gave a cutting edge to the Counter Reformation.[13] The cause of the medieval empire was indeed utterly lost, degenerating by 1648 into the *Hausmacht* of the Austrian branch of the Hapsburg line; but the papacy and Catholicism made a spectacular comeback from the religious slackness and political weakness of the early sixteenth century, thanks very largely to Spanish religiosity and to Spanish policy. By almost eliminating Protestantism from southern and eastern Europe and by checking its progress in central Europe, the Spanish-Hapsburg-papal power cluster put a lasting imprint upon the religious and cultural map of the continent.

*   *   *

Leadership of Europe moved north to France, England, and Holland in the seventeenth century. In France, Henry IV (1589–1610) restored the monarchy to authority after a long bout of civil and religious wars. The state remained officially Catholic; but French national interests were kept carefully distinct from the cause of the papacy or of international Catholicism. Effec-

---

[13] Spanish domination over Italy was not easily won. Some popes resisted bitterly and with arms, though vainly in the end. Yet even at the height of Spanish influence, the papacy never quite became a mere Hapsburg chaplaincy and always commanded springs of power that were inaccessible to any merely secular ruler.

tive royal control of the Church in France dated back to the fourteenth century and was vigorously and successfully maintained against the revivified papacy in the sixteenth and seventeenth centuries.[14] Thus Richelieu, chief minister of the French king and a cardinal of the Church, did not hesitate to intervene on the Protestant side in the Thirty Years' War when it suited French interests to do so.

During the reign of Louis XIII (1610–43), Richelieu used the king's armies to destroy castles and subdue towns that resisted centralized administration. Royal power then became genuinely effective in all parts of France for the first time; but only after the failure of the confused uprising known as the Fronde (1648–53) did the French style of absolute monarchy definitely emerge as the pre-eminent model of modern government for Europe as a whole.

By that time, French power had come to rest squarely upon a professional bureaucracy recruited mainly from the middle classes and upon a standing army. These familiar instruments enabled the French government to exercise a stricter control over a larger and wealthier population than any other European government could do. Moreover, the administrative unification of the country was supported by a widespread pride which made Frenchmen glory in belonging to the most powerful and civilized kingdom of Europe. Yet public attachment to the regime rested also upon a delicate balance between a theoretically absolute royal prerogative and the traditional privileges of nobles, the interests of townsmen, and the rights of peasants.

The king rarely suppressed antique political institutions. More frequently, he allowed them to fade gracefully toward the inanity of pageantry and ceremonial, while the real business of government shifted to new administrative channels created expressly to circumvent intractable local customs and laws. This cautious policy often gave the appearance of administrative confusion; but as long as the French king was served by energetic, capable officials, the system proved eminently workable despite (perhaps indeed because of) its incrustation with illogical survivals from the medieval past.

Holland, with its federal form of government deriving from a league of autonomous medieval towns, and the no less archaic English parliamentary style of government were both eccentric to general European political development. Yet despite outward archaism, both these governments gave greater scope to the middle classes than did the French monarchy. In Holland, indeed, wealthy burghers tended to dominate the town governments and, through them, the entire state. In England, landed aristocrats always balanced and usually outweighed the urban interest represented in parliament; but the representation of town and country was sufficiently close to the realities of power

---

[14] Indeed, the prior existence of something resembling a French national church within the Catholic fold was a principal reason—perhaps *the* principal reason—for the ultimate failure of Protestantism in France. In proportion as the Protestant movement tended to become identified with turbulent noblemen and stubborn townsmen, ready to defend their rights and immunities against the central government by armed force, not only the weight of royal authority, but the pressure of French national feeling and the general desire for peace and order turned against the Protestants. Henry IV, who had begun his career as a Protestant champion, sensed these facts and therefore found it politic to change his religion.

within English society to make parliament a formidable element in all domestic affairs. Victory in the English Civil Wars (1640–49)[15] against an aspiring royal absolutism allowed parliament to make good its right to supervise government finances and through its control of the purse parliament became able to control administration in general. This gave the gentry and merchants of England a far more active and direct role in high policy-making than their counterparts in France could achieve under absolute monarchy.

The eccentricity of the English and Dutch governments in western Europe was matched in central Europe by the federal league of urban and rural Swiss cantons, which also combined outward archaism with an unusual inner flexibility. In eastern Europe, the aristocratic republic of Poland turned its back upon French models of modern government by weakening royal power with each election to the throne. By a fateful chance, Poland's eastern neighbor, Muscovy, departed from the European norm in the opposite sense; for there the autocracy of the tsars eclipsed the rights of every social class, and under Ivan the Terrible (1533–84) precipitated something close to social revolution from above.[16]

Despite these and many other anomalies and local peculiarities, and despite all the confusion of wars and diplomacy—indeed, in large part *because* of military needs—administrative consolidation inched ahead in nearly all the states of Europe. This meant that the power of the European state system as a whole advanced very rapidly as against the rest of the world, where traditional political systems confronted far less rigorous pressures. The most obvious manifestations of the new European state power were military. European armies were trained to mechanical drills and massed maneuvers, all carefully designed to maximize firepower even in the excitement of battle; and similar principles, applied to naval warfare, allowed fleets operating as effective units to add additional weight to the already formidable effect of single-ship cannonades. Man for man, European armies and navies clearly became more formidable instruments of violence than any possessed by other civilized peoples, except possibly the Japanese.

These developments in military organization and control were part of the general increase in the effectiveness of political administration. As European armaments became more elaborate and expensive, monarchs could more easily monopolize organized violence within their states, thus strengthening domestic sovereignty. Yet even when secure at home, rulers found small surcease from innovating effort; for foreign rivals, rising to power by the same means,

---

[15] The Cromwellian dictatorship proved to be only an interlude in English history, its principal effect being to provoke a revulsion against military government—even, or perhaps especially, a government of "saints." In the context of subsequent European history, however, Cromwell's government has a special interest and importance, for it was one of the earliest examples on a national scale of a "party" dictatorship emerging from a social revolution and mobilizing hitherto unequaled energies for foreign wars. The earlier regime of the Sea Beggars in the Dutch provinces, and the later French and Russian Revolutions offer interesting parallels despite the great differences in successive revolutionary ideals. Cf. Crane Brinton, *Anatomy of Revolution* (New York: W. W. Norton, 1932).

[16] Russia should not be counted as a real participant in European civilization before the time of Peter the Great. Remarks upon Russian developments between 1500 and Peter's accession will therefore come in a later section of this chapter.

constantly challenged even the most powerful states to elaborate still further the military technology upon which their power and security so clearly depended.

2. ECONOMICS

The economic development of Europe proceeded hand in hand with political consolidation and differentiation. As larger sovereignties emerged and as state regulation supplemented or superseded guild and municipal regulation, economic enterprise could operate more freely over wider territories. Hence merchants, miners, and manufacturers were often able to extend the geographical scale of their activities without running afoul of local discrimination against outsiders or entangling themselves in mutually contradictory systems of law. Further, the responsiveness of most European governments to mercantile and financial interests, and the direct initiative many governments took to establish new manufactures and skills within their territories, probably accelerated economic development. To be sure, governmental economic policies were usually inspired by fiscal and military ends; and war, as always, was economically destructive. Yet by the seventeenth century, European statesmen had firmly grasped the notion that a flourishing commerce and industry was a direct asset to the state. Official efforts to encourage trade and manufacture did not always secure the desired results, but the contrary policy of discouraging commercial activity by official harassment—a policy followed with much success in contemporary China—became unusual in Europe.

Governments in other parts of the civilized world exhibited no comparable solicitude for the prosperity of urban populations, perhaps because the social gap between ruling cliques and the merchant and artisan classes was so great. The gap was real enough in Europe too, but not nearly so impassable as elsewhere. European townsmen had behind them a tradition of local self-government and effective self-assertion against all comers; and even when folded into the larger framework of the national or dynastic state, the burghers of Europe retained much of their former political influence. Indeed, in those states which enjoyed the greatest political success in the seventeenth century, the middle classes secured a firm niche within the machinery of government and exerted direct pressure upon high policy. Merchants' sons entered the royal service and rose to high positions; and many an impoverished nobleman swallowed his pride to marry a well-dowered banker's daughter. In ways like these, the gap between merchants and aristocrats was bridged; and despite the fact that the new bureaucracies usurped many of the liberties and rights once proudly exercised by townsmen and noblemen, both classes found a more or less satisfactory place in the transformed body politic.

Although most governments tried hard to manipulate the flow of trade and particularly of specie, the European exchange economy was never effectively caged within the separate compartments of rival political jurisdictions. Interregional European commerce intensified during the sixteenth and seventeenth centuries and was supplemented by an increasing volume of transoceanic trade. At first, long-distance trade staples continued to be items of high value in proportion to their bulk. Overland portage from northern Italy to the entrepôts of southern Germany constituted no insuperable obstacle to such trade, which had long constituted a mainstream of European commerce. Consequently, profits accumulated in Italy and southern Germany, so that, when money-lending became a semi-reputable occupation,[17] international banking firms, which played an important role in developing European mining and other economic activities, tended to locate their head offices in cities along this route, e.g., in Florence, Genoa, Venice, Augsburg, and Ulm.

This pattern of trade and finance was supplemented and, by the seventeenth century, eclipsed in importance by international exchanges centering in the Low Countries. Bulk commodities transported by sea—grain, herring, codfish, lumber, metals, woolens, coal, etc.—constituted a more important part of this northern commerce than the trade in spices and specie, although these and other staples of the older trade also passed through Dutch and Flemish hands.

Even in the Middle Ages, the indented coastline and navigable rivers of northwestern Europe had permitted a considerable development of long-distance trade in bulk commodities; but financial pre-eminence had remained with the luxury trade centering in Italy. In the seventeenth century, however, bulk trade in cheaper commodities definitely surpassed the older style of commerce; and the European exchange economy thereby definitively attained the vulgar character that distinguished it from trade patterns elsewhere. On the one hand, this meant that, compared to the rest of the ecumene, a far wider segment of the total population entered actively into the market by purchasing commodities of distant origin. The corollary of such broadened participation in market relationships was that price changes began to affect a widened segment of everyday activity, impelling Europeans to expand some and contract other traditional occupations and to launch some totally new enterprises. A comparatively radical rationality was thereby introduced into the European economy. As men shifted resources from one field to another in accordance with the dictates of the market, it became possible to mobilize wealth and effort for particularly attractive projects—e.g., trade with the Indies—more rapidly and more massively than any other civilized community was able to do. The growth of European wealth and power was thereby still further accelerated.

Agriculture, too, reflected the expansion and intensification of the commercial economy. In the most active centers of European life, calculations of price and profit began to introduce modifications in crop rotation and methods of tillage and in the balance between animal husbandry (sheep raising) and cultivation. Even land and rents were sometimes treated as commercially negotiable commodities. As a result, perhaps for the first time in

---

[17] Ingenious casuistry gradually softened the ecclesiastical reprobation of usury, which, being based squarely upon Old Testament denunciation of money-lending, was unusually difficult to explain away. Only when Christian principles ceased to have a fully binding force in the community did a profession openly based upon usury become possible.

all civilized history, an absolute majority of the population ceased to find their lives circumscribed by an immemorial round of traditional agricultural tasks. Instead, they faced the troubling ups and downs of an unpredictable market economy in which some few grew rich, some prospered, while many became paupers; and all, rich and poor, suffered inescapable uncertainty as to the future.

The cost, especially for the poor, was certainly great; yet the growingly intricate market economy of Europe, supported by cheap water carriage of bulk commodities, constituted a potent lever for raising European power and wealth far above the levels attained elsewhere. Technical advances in mining, manufacturing, and transportation generally brought financial reward, so that the persuasive hope of profit counterbalanced and often overcame traditional resistances to change; while a genuinely mass market gave the European exchange economy a momentum, flexibility, and scope unequalled elsewhere.

Finally, a rapid advance in prices, strongly reinforced by the unexampled influx of gold and silver from the Americas, acted as a powerful solvent to all traditional economic and social relationships. When prices doubled, trebled, or even quadrupled within a century, rentiers and wage earners, together with governments, suffered a serious erosion of real income, while entrepreneurs of all sorts tended to benefit. This "price revolution" helps therefore to explain the rise of the middle classes to political eminence in northwestern Europe, although the contrary course of events in Spain shows that a rise in prices alone could not achieve such a result. More than this: the price revolution introduced a systematic distortion of all traditional social relationships and put a severe strain upon the traditional expectations of nearly every rank of society. The consequent distress and uncertainty besetting men's minds in an age when nothing any longer seemed sure does much to account for the peculiar violence of religious and political controversy in the sixteenth and early seventeenth centuries.

3. CULTURE

The twin movements of Renaissance and Reformation tore apart the fundamental fusion between Hellenic and Judaeo-Christian elements in the cultural heritage of Europe. The extreme champions of each, by insisting upon the sole validity of their chosen outlook, rejected the delicate compromise between this world and the next, reason and faith, sense enjoyment and spiritual cultivation which had been struck by the thinkers and artists of the high Middle Ages.[18] Yet the relationship between these two movements was extraordinarily complex and often paradoxical. The Protestant reformers set out to achieve a radical sanctification of all human endeavor before God, but, in fact, after the lapse of a couple of generations, provoked in parts of Europe a disciplined application to the business of making money such as the world had scarcely seen before; while the Jesuits, who set out to win souls for Christ

---

[18] Cf. Ernst Troeltsch, "Renaissance and Reformation," *Historische Zeitschrift*, CX (1913), 519–56.

RENAISSANCE AND REFORMATION

These three paintings powerfully suggest the complex linkages and tensions that tied the European movements of Renaissance and Reformation together. Botticelli's "Birth of Venus" is self-consciously pagan and classical; Dürer's portraits of the four evangelists hark back to biblical times in a no less conscious fashion. Each of the paintings shares the naturalistic ideal of art and employs techniques of perspective in order to create an illusory third dimension in which their figures become free to move, as it were, in the round. Yet Botticelli's "Venus" is not really at ease without her clothes, as a pagan goddess of love ought to be; and Dürer's evangelists, serious, intent, and intellectual though they be, lack the transcendent vision and certainty of things divine which characterized contemporary Russian icons (p. 523). Thus the immensely fertile uncertainties of European culture in the sixteenth century betray themselves in these three works of art.

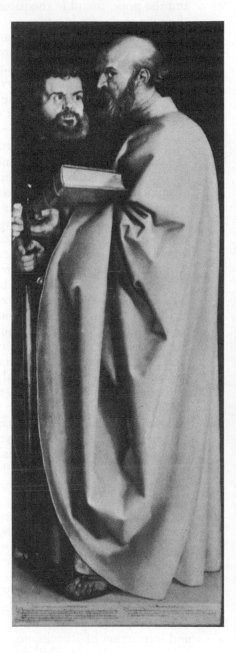

Original in the possession of the Bayerische Staatsgemäldesammlungen, Munich.

and the pope, found in the pagan learning of the humanists one of their most effective tools of education.

In such confusion and contrariety, perhaps all one can say by way of general summary is that both religion and secularism acquired a new energy from their mutual jostling. In a world full of intellectual novelties and inflamed by religious passions, casual lip service to Christianity or its easy repudiation became as difficult as the dogmatic conviction of the adequacy of Christian doctrine to guide men in all things whatsoever.

When passions subsided after 1648, the intellectual novelties remained, but so did an enhanced and deepened popular commitment to one or another form of Christian orthodoxy, a commitment which was sustained by much expanded and ecclesiastically controlled educational systems. The new climate of opinion which manifested itself during the second half of the seventeenth century in the most active centers of European culture allowed reason and faith to pursue gradually divergent ways. The ambition of discovering and imposing a total Truth, by force if need be, lost its hold on men's minds and ceased to be a question of practical statecraft. Under these circumstances, a growing autonomy of separate intellectual disciplines tended to dethrone theology from its accustomed primacy among the arts and sciences without ever directly challenging the traditional prerogatives of religion.

This upshot of the tumultuous struggles of the sixteenth and early seventeenth centuries was clearly contrary to the intention of almost all who took part in them. It was the failure of Europeans to agree upon the truths of religion, within as well as across state boundaries, that opened the door to secularism and modern science. In states where the religious aspirations of the Reformation age came closer to success, *i.e.*, where lay and ecclesiastical officials joined forces to impose an almost perfect religious conformity, something close to intellectual stagnation ensued—redeemed, sometimes, by artistic brilliance. Thus the political diversity of Europe thwarted the heart's desire of nearly all the intellectually sensitive men of the time[19] by making impossible the construction of a single authoritative, definitive, and (as almost everyone also desired) enforcible codification of Truth.

Yet, ironically, the failure to construct a world-view commanding general assent was the great achievement of the age. Europeans inherited from the passionate and anguished strivings of the sixteenth century a high seriousness in the pursuit both of knowledge and of salvation. They inherited also a range of unsolved problems and new questions which assured the continuance of rapid intellectual and artistic development. Neither the intellectual dilettantism toward which the Italian Renaissance had tended to descend in the fifteenth century, nor the volcanic dogmatism of the Reformers of the sixteenth century, could cope with the problems each raised for the other. The collision and interaction of Renaissance and Reformation, by heightening the tensions between the incompatible inseparables at the core of European culture—the

---

[19] Mathematically-minded rationalists like Descartes were quite as earnest as theologians in seeking for an absolute, unquestionable truth. Since they were in a tiny minority, I am not aware that any of them suggested use of state authority to enforce their Truth, however.

Hellenic pagan and the Judaeo-Christian heritages—increased the variety, multiplied the potentialities, and raised the intellectual and moral energies of Europe to a new height.

*   *   *

It is easier to understand than to share the theological passions of the Reformation period. When human affairs conform more or less to common expectation, intellectual hypothesis and new doctrine may excite attention among a limited circle of professionals but will pass almost unnoticed by the great majority of the population. This had been the case in the fourteenth and fifteenth centuries, when radical ecclesiastical reform programs had won only׳ local and limited followings, when heretical notions about the nature of God and man had been freely promulgated in Italian intellectual circles, and when humanistic scholars had increasingly held scholastic theology and philosophy up to scorn. It ceased abruptly to be true in 1517, when an obscure friar in a remote German university town posted ninety-five theses on the door of the castle church of Wittenberg in the best tradition of medieval academic controversy. Instead, all Germany took fire. With explosive speed, preachers and printers promulgated the increasingly radical views of Martin Luther, until presently not only Germany but all of northern Europe was caught up in bitter religious controversy. A full generation elapsed before the rulers of the Catholic church in Rome took real heed of the Reformation challenge; but once the Roman church had reorganized itself, the dedication of its agents, above all of the Jesuits, equalled the religious fervor and surpassed the organized discipline of the Protestants. By 1648, a century of dubious battle had accomplished a lasting division of the continent between Catholic and Protestant states. Most of Germanic Europe became Protestant, but almost all of Latin Europe, together with the Slavic, Magyar, and Irish fringes of medieval Christendom, remained loyal to Rome.

Complex doctrinal differences between Protestant and Catholic, and among the various Protestant churches, sprang to life in the tumultuous wake of the Lutheran movement. Nuances of creed, such as precise definition of the essence and accidents of the Eucharist, or the evidences for infra- as against supralapsarianism, seemed absolutely vital at the time, though they no longer excite much attention. Yet the most fundamental point of difference between Protestants and Catholics, the question of the nature and sources of religious authority, remains crucial. Luther, Calvin, and their followers taught the priesthood of all believers, thereby extending to all Christians religious functions and powers which medieval theology had reserved for the professional caste of ordained clergy. These reformers held that clerical office implied special duties and responsibilities but did not confer special powers to dispense or withhold the saving grace of God. Grace descended instead directly from God himself to those whom he chose to save from the damnation they deserved; and God's own word, recorded in the Bible, was the sole authentic authority in matters of religion. The task of the clergy was to expound and explain God's word, to invite the faith of the laity, and await in hope the miracle of God's grace.

To be sure, as Lutheran and Calvinist churches took form, the practical consequences of these beliefs ceased to be very apparent. The doctrines and ceremonies which Lutheran and Calvinist divines derived from the Bible differed in numerous details from the creed and liturgy of the Roman church. Yet all were doctrines expounded dogmatically by men who allowed themselves no doubts in theological matters and who were prepared to impose their views by force whenever political circumstance allowed. Nevertheless, in denying the professional clergy a monopoly of supernatural powers, Protestant theologians found themselves in a difficult position when others drew different conclusions from Holy Writ. Hence the multiplication of sects and schism, which was a pronounced characteristic of Protestantism from the beginning. And when a few men's minds withdrew from the struggle after unassailable religious truth, preferring to study the world and its wonders with no very compelling theological presuppositions, Protestant clergymen might thunder from their pulpits against such divagation from man's eternal concerns, but were, at least logically, in terms of their own definition of clerical powers, in no position to forbid it.

In sum, the anarchic, personal, and private confrontation of the believer with his God which lay close to the heart of the Protestant movement at its beginning (1517–25) was quickly healed over by the establishment of orthodox Protestant churches that were as authoritarian as the Catholic hierarchy and in some respects more totalitarian in their demands upon the faithful. Yet an individualistic weakness remained beneath the surface of the Protestant establishments and appeared openly whenever Protestant minorities defied constituted religious authority on the basis of the same Bible to which all Protestants appealed. The difficulty of establishing consensus on a biblical basis tended therefore to widen the areas of tolerance within Protestant states. The scope for toleration was distinctly smaller in Catholic lands just because the supreme religious authorities—the pope and canon law—were less ambiguous than Protestantism's Holy Writ.[20]

Whether or not the Reformation forwarded intellectual variety and toleration within Protestant states, there can be no doubt that by dividing Europe

---

[20] The affinity of sixteenth- or even seventeenth-century Protestantism with liberalism and individualism as they developed in the eighteenth and nineteenth centuries is easy to exaggerate. The German Protestant states remained bound to rigid orthodoxy at a time when Holland and England had both found room for divergent opinions; and conversely, France, for all the state's Catholicism, was the seat of much religious and intellectual variety in the seventeenth century as later. Only where the Spanish and Jesuit imprint upon the Counter Reformation was allowed free scope, as in Italy, Austria, and Poland, did Catholicism become as rigid as my text suggests.

In general, the regions where urban middle classes attained the greatest weight in society became the most diverse intellectually and religiously; and this, perhaps, goes farther to explain the evolution of Holland, England, and France than the religious alignments of their respective governments. Even the case of Italy, which seems best to illustrate the blighting power of the Counter Reformation upon free intellectual adventure, may also be accounted for as a reflection of prior decay of urban enterprise in Italian towns.

On the other hand, Max Weber's famous thesis attributed the political and social rise of a middle class in transalpine Europe to the moral discipline of Calvinism.

into opposing camps, Protestantism promoted a new range of religious variety within the circle of European civilization. Such variety raised doubts as to the perfect adequacy of any particular religious or intellectual system, a situation far more challenging to further thought than any likely to arise as long as the fabric of the Church remained unbroken.

In the political sphere, both the Protestant and the Catholic Reformations contributed directly to the advance of the secular power at the expense of the papacy and of the empire. Protestant rulers confiscated much ecclesiastical property and often reduced the clergy to the status of salaried appointees of the state. Even in Catholic countries, where the Church retained most or all of its possessions, the papacy was forced to concede very extensive powers to local rulers in such matters as ecclesiastical appointments, taxing powers over Church property, and judicial authority over clergymen. As a result, fairly distinct national or state churches tended to form even within the universal frame of Catholicism. Although international agencies like the Jesuit order acted to check the fragmentation of the Church along national lines, even the Jesuits had to come to terms with secular rulers and as a matter of deliberate policy secured some of their most brilliant successes by winning the confidence of kings.

Protestantism served also as a rallying cry for the resistance of German princes to the efforts of the Hapsburg emperors to dominate Germany. Strictly religious alignments affected but did not really govern the alliances which succeeded in frustrating imperial ambitions in the Thirty Years' War (1618–48). Thus Catholic France allied herself with heretics and Turks when common enmity to the Hapsburgs dictated such a move; and individual Protestant princes in Germany more than once chose the Hapsburg side for reasons of their own. By the close of the war, the territorial princes of Germany had become effectively sovereign, not so much because of their own local strength as owing to the intervention of Sweden, France, and other foreign powers against the Hapsburgs. Thus the definitive collapse of the medieval ideal of imperial unity (and incidentally the frustration of incipient German nationalism) no less than the disruption of the Church Universal may be attributed to the German Reformation.

* * *

The thundering voices of the Reformation and Counter Reformation contrast sharply with the slender siren song of the Renaissance. Yet the siren song was piercing, too. Even in the midst of the volcanic passions and violent upheavals provoked by religious strife, it could still be heard, tantalizing many of those whom it could not win over. Beauty created by human imagination and skill for its own sake, and truth pursued by an unfettered human reason independent of all external authority, had a seductive charm even for men striving desperately after religious and moral certainty. Once such ideals had found clear and uncompromising expression, as occurred in Italy in the fifteenth and in northern Europe in the early sixteenth century, they could never be dismissed. Individuals made their choice between such concerns and the clamorous demands of religion, sometimes painfully, as in the cases of Erasmus (d. 1536), Pascal (d. 1662), or Milton (d. 1674), sometimes with a welcome sense of release, as in the cases of Loyola (d. 1556), Calvin (d. 1564), and Descartes (d. 1650), and sometimes without any apparent inner struggle, as in the cases of Shakespeare (d. 1616), Cervantes (d. 1616), and Francis Bacon (d. 1626).

Perhaps because so many of the fundaments of older European society and civilization had been called into question, the age was amazingly fertile in arts and letters and gave birth to exact natural science. No subsequent time has been more revolutionary, nor raised European culture so distinctly to a new level.

Cultural advance proceeded in two apparently contradictory directions. Art and letters tended to differentiate into distinct national schools, whereas the sciences and practical arts remained pan-European while manifesting a growing professional independence and intellectual autonomy. Both developments had the effect of insulating Europe's cultural leaders from the dominion of any over-all philosophical-theological world-view, thus making explicit the innumerable discrepancies in the European cultural inheritance and achievement.

The vernacular languages of Spain, Portugal, France, England, and Germany all found lasting literary definition in the sixteenth and seventeenth centuries. Cervantes (d. 1616) and Lope de Vega (d. 1635) in Spain, Camoens (d. 1580) in Portugal, Rabelais (d. 1553) and Montaigne (d. 1592) in France, Luther (d. 1546) in Germany, Shakespeare (d. 1616), Milton (d. 1674), and the translators of the King James (1611) Bible all gave their respective languages definitive literary form. In Italy, where the vernacular tongue had earlier achieved literary definition, these centuries were of only secondary importance; whereas in central and eastern Europe, literary vernaculars withered when the Counter Reformation brought the full weight of Latin, German, and Italian letters to bear against the still tender and uncertain shoots put forth by the various local Slavic languages.

In the visual arts, language barriers could not operate to isolate national schools from one another; and the persuasive example of Italian styles in painting and architecture therefore had a wide influence beyond the Alps. Yet here, too, painters in Holland, Germany, and Spain developed distinct national schools of their own, even though such magistral techniques as mathematical and aerial perspective, chiaroscuro, and the idea that painting should so imitate nature as to suggest an illusion of optical experience—techniques and ideas that had originated or found their fullest flowering in fifteenth- and sixteenth-century Italy—gave a general coherence to all the separate schools of European painting. Architecture in northern Europe was more conservative. The Italianate baroque was generally limited to Catholic lands; in Protestant countries variations upon the older Gothic style persisted until the second half of the seventeenth century.

The evolution of science, technology, and the practical arts in Europe proceeded, not by regional or national differentiation, but by a process of differentiation into special subject matters and skills. Nonetheless, borrowings and cross-stimuli among the emergent specialties were important. Mathematics in particular tended to rise to the place of queen among the sciences which had once been occupied by Aristotelian logic. Thus mathematical geography and cartography, mathematical physics, mathematical astronomy, and (with Descartes) mathematical philosophy all made their appearance. Latin continued to be the usual language of scholarship, so that the republic of learning, focused especially in Italy but with a strong secondary center in Holland, easily transcended national and local linguistic barriers.

The key to the rapid progress of the natural sciences in Europe lay very largely in a growing habit of testing theories against careful measurement, observation, and upon occasion, experiment. Such procedures implied a disrespect for the authority of inherited learning; and some of the manifestations of the new spirit—e.g., dissection of the human body and practical experimentation in physics and optics—also defied a long-standing prejudice among the learned against dirtying their hands with anything but ink.[21]

In an age when experimental method has achieved the dignity of dogma, it is worth emphasizing that astronomers and physicists undertook closer observations and more exact measurements only after Copernicus (d. 1543) had put an alternative to traditional Ptolemaic and Aristotelian theories before the learned world; and Copernicus did so, not on the basis of observations and measurements, but on grounds of logical simplicity and aesthetic symmetry. His heliocentric hypothesis appears to have been suggested partly by the knowledge that some of the ancients, most notably Aristarchus, had advocated such an explanation of the celestial movements and partly by the vogue for Pythagorean number mysticism and "sun worship" which was prevalent in Italian intellectual circles during his student days at the University of Padua.

Copernicus' intellectual affinities were not mere individual eccentricities, for the Pythagorean-Platonic tradition influenced many, perhaps most, of the pioneers of modern mathematical science down at least to Newton's (d. 1727) day. Indeed, it is scarcely an exaggeration to say that what opened the door in seventeenth-century Europe for detailed measurements and observation of natural phenomena was friction between the scholastic orthodoxies of Aristotelian physics and the heterodoxies of a revived Pythagorean-Platonic mathematical mysticism. With alternative hypotheses in the field, careful measurements of the planetary motions and elaborate mathematical calculations based upon such observations made sense as a means of deciding between rival theories. Moreover, because advocates of Pythagorean-Platonic ideas undertook to overthrow an established body of scientific doctrine, it was they who took the lead in gathering new data. Johannes Kepler (d. 1630), for example, was inspired to a lifetime of laborious computation by the hope of reducing

[21] Accurate observation and ingenious experiment carried conviction to ordinary, uninstructed men, and to some men of learning also. Yet there were rigorous minds that stoutly resisted conclusions based upon fallible sense impressions, on the ground that such conclusions lacked the logical certainty of theories carefully deduced from self-evident first principles. In cases of conflict, it seemed plain enough which sort of argument was to be preferred. The Italian astronomers who refused to sully their minds by looking through Galileo's telescope were not therefore irrational—merely rigorously logical.

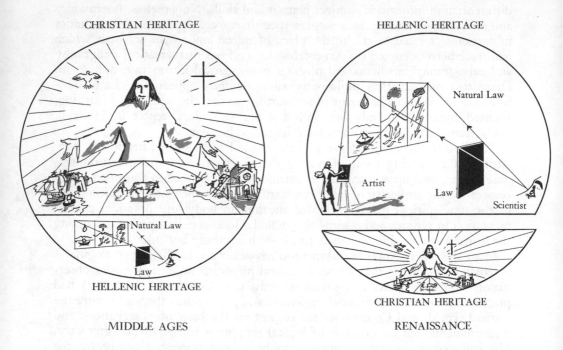

CHRISTIAN HERITAGE

HELLENIC HERITAGE

Natural Law

Artist

Law

Scientist

Natural Law

Law

HELLENIC HERITAGE

CHRISTIAN HERITAGE

MIDDLE AGES

RENAISSANCE

the music of the spheres to mathematical formulae. By extraordinary chance, he found part of what he was looking for in the simple elegance of his laws of planetary motion, even though he failed in his central quest: the discernment of the harmonic ratios of the planetary orbits.

Yet measurement and observation did not enter altogether by the back door. The progress of the practical arts—mining, water engineering, shipbuilding, printing, gun casting, glassmaking, etc.; the geographical discoveries, bringing new plants and animals to European attention; and the arrival in Europe of strange products of foreign skills like Chinese porcelains or Indian cottons suggested to Francis Bacon (d. 1626), for example, that nature had yet further secrets which observant minds might discover and put to practical use if they would only take sufficient pains to observe, record, and compare the facts of nature. Such optimistic empiricism found congenial ground in medicine, where elementary anatomical and clinical observation disproved a number of received ideas about physiology and the treatment of diseases and wounds. Yet even in medicine, the bombast of Paracelsus (d. 1541), which was centrally inspired by Neo-Platonic mysticism and a flamboyant egotism, helped to clear a path for the detailed labors of Vesalius (d. 1564) in human anatomy and of William Harvey (d. 1657) in physiology. By challenging the age-old prestige of Galen, Paracelsus put an alternative theory in the field, as his contemporary, Copernicus, did for astronomy.

A second key to the success of exact science was the rapid evolution of instruments which enhanced the natural powers of the human eye and other senses. Such devices as the telescope (invented *ca.* 1608), microscope (in-

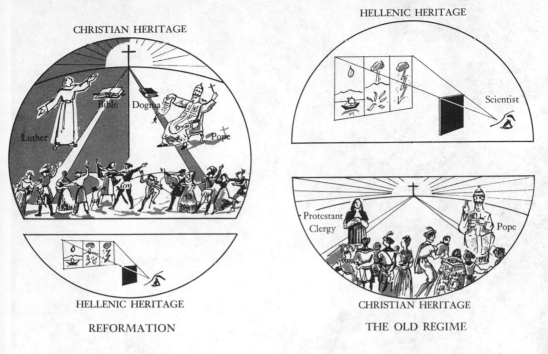

CHRISTIAN HERITAGE

HELLENIC HERITAGE

HELLENIC HERITAGE

CHRISTIAN HERITAGE

REFORMATION

THE OLD REGIME

vented *ca.* 1590), thermometer (invented *ca.* 1592), barometer (invented *ca.* 1643), and pendulum clock (invented *ca.* 1592) gave a new range and precision to observation and measurement of physical phenomena.[22] The invention of new symbols for mathematical notation had a similar effect in facilitating calculation. Even more important, increasingly generalized symbols often suggested new operations and new relationships that had been effectually hidden by the clumsiness of earlier notations or by the complication of earlier methods of calculation. Similarly, the use of woodcuts and engravings to illustrate botanical, geographical, medical, and similar treatises made it possible to record and transmit the observations of a single man with an accuracy unattainable through mere words.

The habit of testing theories empirically, the use (and invention) of improved instruments, and the mathematicizing mental bias derived from Pythagorean-Platonic tradition all came together in the person of Galileo Galilei (1564–1642), who more than any other single man deserves to be called the father of modern European science. Galileo's laws of terrestrial motion, his striking telescopic discoveries (sunspots, the moons of Jupiter), his ingenious experiments and careful measurements, together with his ranging (and sometimes erroneous) theoretical explanations of what he found, launched European physical science on a path of discovery which has not yet been exhausted or abandoned. Despite the condemnation of his astronomy by the papal Inquisition, the European intellectual world was permanently transformed by his

[22] Cf. A. Wolf, *A History of Science, Technology, and Philosophy in the 16th and 17th Centuries* (New York: Macmillan Co., 1935), pp. 71–120.

595

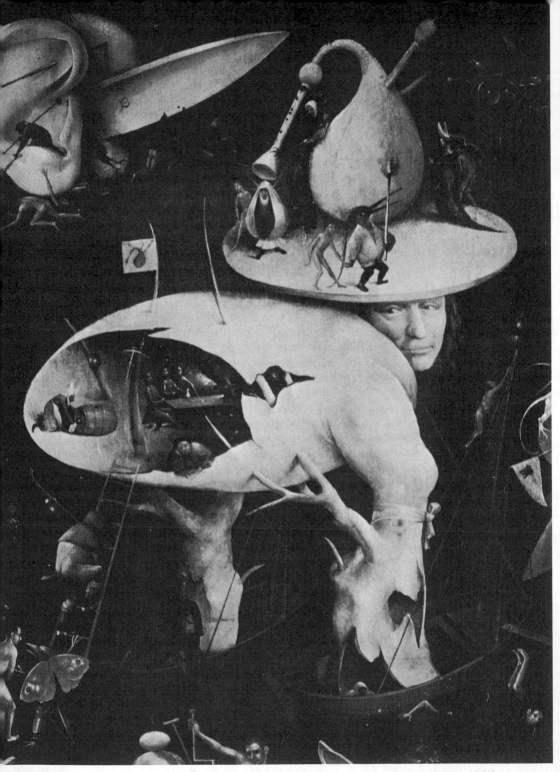

NEW HEIGHTS AND DEPTHS

The detail from a painting of Hell by Hieronymus Bosch (d. 1516) on the left and the head of St. John the Baptist by El Greco (d. 1614) on the right suggest contrasting aspects of the European search for certainty in the face of the unprecedented social and cultural upheaval that brought on the modern age. Bosch here portrays the sins of the senses, with a sort of fascinated revulsion. Such painting is redolent of the subconscious depths of the human psyche, depths which came un- usually close to open expression during the troubled transition from Europe's medieval to its mod- ern mold. El Greco's portrait, on the other hand, embodies the fusion of worldly splendor and other- worldly aspiration that established itself in Catholic Europe in the seventeenth century. El Greco here uses the exquisite skills of the Italian Renaissance painter to express the renewed religious vision of the Catholic Reformation. He achieves his effect by departing freely from the ideal of optical exactitude, elongating his figures, enlarging their eyes, and in other ways creating an image reminiscent of the Cretan-Byzantine art style he had known in his youth. Such a mingling of Greek mannerisms, Italian techniques, and Spanish religiosity admirably exemplifies the cultural openness of western Europe—an openness wherein lay both the secret and measure of its enhanced vigor in early modern times.

work, not least because of the literary art and polemical skill with which he advanced his ideas.

By Galileo's time, the medieval hierarchy of the sciences, integrated by logic and theology into a coherent world-view, had been dissolved by the restless investigations of specialists. No new authoritative synthesis emerged—although the laws of Newton came close to doing so in the field of astronomy and physics. Unlike their medieval forerunners, the scientists and technicians of the sixteenth and seventeenth centuries were content with striving to understand only a small segment of reality at a time, leaving the great questions of religion and philosophy to one side. Rapidly expanding data, derived increasingly from observation and experiment, continually challenged the adequacy of old concepts and provoked the emergence of new ones. Thus a self-sustaining circle of growingly recondite professional activity established itself within half a dozen or more separate sciences. Under these circumstances, all efforts to confine scientific theory within one or another authoritative frame were doomed to failure, even when supported by the august procedures of ecclesiastical authority, by the most strenuous appeals to the inerrancy of Scripture, or by the austerely radical discipline of Cartesian doubt and a priori deduction.

*   *   *

The magnitude of European cultural achievements in the sixteenth–seventeenth centuries, together with the violence and scale of the religious, political, economic, and social changes of the age, arouses a sense of wonder and amazement. Old human relations, old habits of thought, and old patterns of sensibility and piety lost their normal rigidity, and individual genius correspondingly enlarged its scope as seldom before in civilized history. In any particular situation, use and wont lost their former comforting accuracy in defining what was to be thought and in circumscribing what should be done. Instead, individuals and groups had to choose. The result was to bring an extraordinarily wide range of human potentialities into play. The heights and depths of the human spirit found unusually varied expression when raw human capacities confronted untoward and inescapable uncertainties. Yet Europeans brought all the advantages of a rich cultural inheritance, an elaborate technology, and the stimulus of contacts literally all round the world to the solution of problems created by the rapid disintegration of the social and cultural frame of their medieval past.

In the ancient world, the civilizations of the Roman empire and of Han China, when confronted by a disordering of traditional society, had responded by religious revolution—the rise of Christianity. In the sixteenth century, Hindu India and Europe both responded religiously to the breakdown of their respective cultural worlds—in India by an emotionally revivified and popularized Hinduism, in Europe through the Reformation and Counter Reformation. Yet Europe also reponded to the breakdown of its medieval order with the creation of exact science and secular literatures, baroque art and rationalistic philosophy; and in these lay the germs of the leap into secularism which was to become a dominant characteristic of subsequent European history.

The basic duality of the European cultural inheritance helps to explain the diversity of reaction to Europe's social and cultural crisis of the sixteenth–seventeenth centuries. But such duality was not unique. China, too, enjoyed a dual cultural inheritance after the Buddhist inundation; and interplay between Confucianism and Buddhism certainly constituted a major growth point for later Chinese culture. The Moslem world also from its beginning exhibited a cultural duality between Hellenic and Oriental heritages. Yet the interaction between these discrepant cultural strands in China and in the Middle East was usually confined to small intellectual circles, remained comparatively genteel, and conspicuously lacked the passion and violence, the extremism and recklessness of the European adventure. Doubtless the generally stable social pattern of Chinese and Middle Eastern society, based always upon a polarity between landowners and peasants, and encapsulating suitably obsequious urban populations, helps to explain this contrast.

Yet all such explanations leave out the factor of individual genius and the catalytic role which single personalities may play in critical situations. The Reformation without Luther, the Jesuits without Loyola, or modern science without Galileo are really unthinkable. It is a defect of historical essays such as this that the unique individual career and the strategic moment of personal thought or action can easily be obliterated by the weight of inexact generalizations.

When all propitious circumstances and conditions have been duly considered, there still remains always an element of incalculable surprise in human affairs. This element finds peculiarly wide scope in situations such as confronted Europeans in the sixteenth and early seventeenth centuries, when human greatness as well as human depravity throve on pervasive moral uncertainty. Wonder and amazement at such demonstrations of the range of human potentiality constitute a fitting acknowledgment of the personal and collective limitations within which all men must live. We, and all the world of the twentieth century, are peculiarly the creatures and heirs of a handful of geniuses of early modern Europe, for it was they who defined the peculiar and distinctive modern bent of European, presently of Western, and now to a very substantial degree, of world civilization.

C. EUROPE'S OUTLIERS: THE AMERICAS AND RUSSIA, 1500–1650

I. THE AMERICAS

Interaction between European and Amerindian civilizations in the sixteenth and seventeenth centuries was remarkably one-sided. Spaniards found little to admire in the native American cultures; and except for such indigenous American food plants as maize, tobacco, and potatoes,[23] they borrowed little from the peoples they had subdued. From the Indian side, however, the mili-

---

[23] Even these crops became important in Europe only after 1650.

tary superiority of the conquerors was enormously magnified by the moral collapse of native leaders, who found their inherited institutions and skills utterly inadequate to cope with Spanish ideas, Spanish diseases, and Spanish power. Hence the higher political and cultural organization of the Aztec and Inca empires disappeared almost overnight when the priests and warriors who had sustained these structures lost faith in their inherited social and cultural systems. Instead of stubbornly clinging to familiar ideas and institutions, the Indians numbly submitted to the leading strings imposed by Spanish missionaries and officials. They proved so docile that Christianity was imprinted upon Mexico and Peru within little more than a generation.

Missionaries became the pioneers of Spanish America when the gold fever of the conquistadores subsided. Since they were seeking souls, not gold, Jesuits, Dominicans, and Franciscans were eager to penetrate comparatively primitive regions like Paraguay and the Orinoco Valley, where they erected a series of remarkable missionary principalities. The impressiveness of European technology[24] and of Catholic ritual and doctrine, the devoted (though sometimes self-interested) energy of thousands of priests and friars, and the remarkable plasticity of Amerindian mentality in the face of almost total disruption of their pre-existing social systems all contributed to the success of the Spanish missions. By the end of the seventeenth century, pockets of unadulterated heathendom within the limits of Spanish control were few and far between. Every considerable town boasted vast and architecturally impressive churches; and the Indians retained only remnants of their former religions, disguised, sometimes quite consciously, in Christian dress.[25]

The establishment of Spanish institutions and secular culture went hand in hand with the spread of Christianity. Legal and political relationships above the village level were speedily made over on Spanish models; and within the more accessible Indian villages, new economic patterns imposed by Spaniards soon encroached upon traditional subsistence agriculture. Semi-compulsory labor for Spanish masters in mines and on ranches ate into the manpower of the villages, so that by the close of the seventeenth century autonomous villages of the pre-Columbian type had been relegated to isolated areas in mountains, desert, or jungle.[26]

The home government of Spain and many missionaries on the scene conscientiously tried to protect the rights of the Indian populations under Spanish rule. Spanish entrepreneurs were less scrupulous and found means of securing Indian labor for their mining and agricultural operations with or without formal legal authorization. Unaccustomed and sometimes very severe

[24] Cf. Alfred Métaux, "The Revolution of the Ax," *Diogenes*, No. 25 (Spring, 1959), pp. 30–31, for interesting remarks on the role of metal tools and weapons in Spanish missionary success.

[25] The success that came to Christian priests may itself have constituted a survival from pre-Columbian times, inasmuch as the Indian rank and file may simply have transferred to the new masters of the supernatural the obedience they formerly had tendered to Inca, Aztec, or other native priesthoods. In this oblique sense, the pagan carry-over was of basic importance in shaping the social patterns of Spanish America.

[26] Charles Gibson, "The Transformation of the Indian Community of New Spain, 1500–1810," *Cahiers d'histoire mondiale*, II (1954–55), 581–607.

working conditions may have killed off some of the Indian conscripts; but the continued ravages of European diseases were far more serious. Ironically, the effort to relieve the labor shortage by importing Negro slaves from Africa simply compounded the problem by introducing African diseases also. The result was radical depopulation. According to one calculation, a central Mexican population of about eleven million in 1519 had shrunk to a mere 2.5 million by 1600; and depopulation continued until a low point of about 1.5 million was reached in 1650.[27] Such figures, if at all accurate, go far to explain the demoralization of native communities and the ease with which an always numerically small Spanish minority[28] imposed its cultural and economic forms upon them.

Toward the fringes of the Spanish empire of the New World, Indian societies suffered less sudden and drastic disruption. In Chile, the Araucanians withstood Spanish military pressure for twenty years before succumbing; and warlike tribes in northern Mexico gave the Spaniards occasional trouble throughout the seventeenth century. Still more insulated communities, like the Pueblos of New Mexico, suffered no drastic alteration in old ways even after falling within the penumbra of Spanish authority.

On the great plains of North America, however, where Spanish power never established itself, the spread of horsemanship worked a rapid social transformation. Tribes which had lived on or near the grasslands took to buffalo hunting from horseback, thus acquiring a much enlarged supply of food as compared to what hunters on foot had been able to secure. This was only the beginning of radical cultural readjustment, for tribes that migrated into the high plains and took to life on horseback had also to alter and adjust a wide range of social customs to fit the necessities of a warlike, semi-nomadic style of life.[29]

[27] S. F. Cook and L. B. Stephens, "The Population of Central Mexico in the 16th Century," *Ibero-Americana*, XXXI (1948), 1–48. Earlier estimates both of the initial population and of the decline were not so great. Cf. Angel Rosenblat, *La Población Indígena de América desde 1492 hasta la Actualidad* (Buenos Aires: Institución Cultural Española, 1945), pp. 57, 92, for Mexico; and summary table for the entire New World, p. 109.

[28] The Spanish population (including mestizos) was estimated at only 114,000 in central Mexico in 1646 by Woodrow Borah, "New Spain's Century of Depression," *Ibero-Americana*, XXXV (1951), p. 18. Borah points out that, as the size of the Indian community decreased, the Spanish-mestizo population grew, being comparatively unaffected by the epidemics that destroyed Indian populations; and this in turn meant a progressively more intensive exploitation of Indian labor in order that the officials, ecclesiastics, landowners, and mine operators of Spanish descent might continue to enjoy the immunity from manual labor which the first Spanish settlers had arrogated to themselves. This in turn required the destruction of native village communities and town organization, which it had been the policy of the Spanish government to maintain in the first decades of their rule in Mexico. Instead, *latifundia*, worked by debt peons, and mines, worked also by compulsory labor, became the dominant economic and social organizations, while even the upper classes of the towns descended into genteel poverty. Resemblances to the transformations of late Roman society are very striking and may represent a common response to population decay, resulting in both cases from the shattering impact of new diseases.

[29] There is a curious irony in the fact that the popular image of Indian life that prevails in the United States and in much of the rest of the contemporary world is a caricature of the culture of the plains Indians, who were themselves still in process of adjusting to the novelties of their new life when cowboys with a fuller share in Western civilization behind them intervened with crushing effect.

One of the most interesting features of the spread of horsemanship among the plains Indians is the manner in which it recapitulated the development of horse nomadry in Eurasia. See above, pp. 234–38.

NORTHERN EUROPE MEDITERRANEAN EUROPE

AT HOME

OVERSEAS

FAMILY PATTERNS AND RACE MIXTURE

When French, English, and Dutch settlements began to flourish along the Atlantic coast of North America in the seventeenth century, the Indians of the eastern woodlands became exposed to the same diseases and demoralization that had so seriously hurt their fellows in Spanish America. The French, like the Spaniards, put considerable effort into missionary work among the Indians of Canada; whereas the Dutch and English left such enterprise to eccentric private individuals and for the most part treated the Indians either as enemies or as gullible trade partners. Thus on the whole the French enjoyed better relations with the Indians than did their English rivals; but French diseases were no less destructive for being communicated by men who wished the Indians well. Strong liquor added to the demoralizing influence of military defeat, economic exploitation, and disease. Consequently, native Indian social organization crumpled into sullen apathy, punctuated by sporadic and vain rebellion along both the French and English lines of frontier settlement.

Racially mixed societies arose in most of Spanish and Portuguese America, compounded in varying proportions from European, Indian, and Negro strands. Fairly frequent resort to manumission mitigated the hardships of slavery in those areas; and the Catholic church positively encouraged marriages between white immigrants and Indian women as a remedy for sexual immorality. However, in the southern English colonies and in most of the Caribbean islands, the importation of Negro slaves created a much more sharply polarized biracial society. Strong race feeling and the servile status of nearly all Negroes interdicted intermarriage, practically if not legally. Such discrimination did not prevent interbreeding; but children of mixed parentage were assigned to the status of their mothers. Mulattoes and Indian half-breeds were thereby excluded from the white community. In Spanish (and, with some differences, Portuguese) territories a more elaborate and less oppressive principle of racial discrimination established itself. The handful of persons who had been born in the homelands claimed topmost social prestige; next came those of purely European descent; while beneath ranged the various racial blends to form a social pyramid whose numerous racial distinctions meant that no one barrier could become as ugly and impenetrable as that dividing whites from Negroes in the English, Dutch, and French colonies.[30]

In Argentina and in the more northerly English and French colonies, the Indians were too backward and too few in numbers to provide a significant source of labor power; and plantation agriculture based on Negro slavery was impractical. Hence in New England and the middle Atlantic colonies, the hard work of clearing the forests and tilling the fields had to be done by the settlers themselves; while in Argentina the lighter labor of ranching in the pampas fell likewise to immigrant Europeans. Hence solidly European societies arose in these regions, loosely resembling the parent societies of the Old World in their basic institutions and values. The most obvious difference be-

---

[30] The contrast between Iberian and English attitudes toward race mixture may have been slightly affected by divergences in legal and religious heritages; but a far more important factor was the ratio of white women to white men. Because Spanish and Portuguese custom required rigid supervision of unmarried girls, few women emigrated to the colonies. In England, on the other hand, much looser family customs at home allowed unmarried women to follow the first pioneers to the colonies in sufficient numbers to make good the principle that a white man could contract a respectable marriage only with a white woman. The fact that white women were always in short supply meant that comparatively heavy penalties in the form of social disapproval and ostracism had to be invoked to check the ever present tendency for surplus males to marry Indian or Negro women. The result was the peculiarly sharp color line and remarkably emotion-charged race prejudice in matters of sex which characterized the southern United States and other slaveholding English colonies.

The history of the color bar in India offers a good test case. Until British women came to India in significant numbers, there was no color bar in India at all. But British wives in India made it their business to fasten an acute color consciousness and narrow social discrimination upon the British community in India. The entire *raison d'être* of the coterie of white women, expensively imported from England to live idly in a distant and alien country, depended upon the establishment of just such a bar against the social acceptability of native women as wives.

Anyone who has observed either American or British soldiers overseas will not easily believe that anything in Anglo-American culture, law, or prejudice creates any sort of race discrimination in matters of sex that noticeably affects behavior—*in the absence of white females.*

tween these Old and New World societies was the weakness or absence of an aristocratic class in the Americas, except in the slave-holding areas. No less important was the more variegated religious pattern of the New World; for the English government permitted religious minority groups to emigrate freely to the colonies. However, the French, like the Spaniards, restricted immigration to reliable Catholics and maintained a rigorous religious conformity in their colonial possessions.

The French and Spanish governments kept their colonies strictly dependent upon the homeland, both politically and economically. By contrast, the English authorities permitted colonial self-government to develop a broad scope, partly because the constitutional difficulties and civil wars of mid-seventeenth-century England distracted attention from American affairs. In the absence of close supervision and control from the homeland, the tendency toward an egalitarian social pattern latent in any society where men are scarce and land abundant came to the surface and imbued the English colonial governments with a distinctly democratic tinge.

In the long run, the looser, more chaotic, and more democratic patterns of the English colonies offered greater scope for growth. Nonetheless, in the sixteenth and seventeenth centuries the solicitude of Spanish authorities for their American possessions brought handsome returns. The crude life of New England could not compare with the splendor of Lima or Mexico City. The refinement of the viceregal courts of Mexico and Peru, the magnificence of the baroque churches of provincial Mexico, and the educational and charitable activities of the Spanish missions had no counterpart in the Massachusetts backwoods. Yet such achievements had their price. In the short run, demographic and economic decay undermined the grandeur of Spanish colonial life; and the economic recovery of later centuries failed to redress the situation. Cribbed, cabined, and confined by priests, officials, lawyers, and landowners, and kept always in leading strings from Madrid, Spanish-American society entered upon a bitter travail when the self-appointed guardians of the Hispano-Indian-Negro society of the Americas quarreled among themselves, and the subject classes ceased to accept tutelage with the unquestioning docility of the first two centuries.[31]

2. RUSSIA

European exploration and discovery in the sixteenth and seventeenth centuries were not confined to the high seas. During the same decades when Spanish explorers conjured a New World from the Atlantic mists, Italians,

[31] In addition to books cited separately, I have consulted the following on Latin American history: C. H. Haring, *Trade and Navigation between Spain and the Indies in the Time of the Hapsburgs* (Cambridge, Mass.: Harvard University Press, 1918); C. H. Haring, *The Spanish Empire in America* (New York: Oxford University Press, 1947); Julian H. Steward and Louis Faron, *Native Peoples of South America* (New York: McGraw-Hill, 1959); William Lytle Schurz, *This New World: The Civilization of Latin America* (New York: E. P. Dutton, 1954); Philip Ainsworth Means, *Fall of the Inca Empire and the Spanish Rule in Peru, 1530–1780* (New York: Scribner's Sons, 1932); Herbert Ingram Priestley, *The Coming of the White Man* (New York: Macmillan Co., 1929); John Collier, *The Indians of the Americas* (New York: W. W. Norton, 1947); H. A. Wyndham, *The Atlantic and Slavery* (London: Oxford University Press, 1935).

Germans, Dutchmen, and Englishmen engaged in a comparable enterprise of discovering Russia to western Europe. Although the Russian Orthodox principalities had, of course, been neighbors of Latin Christendom since the thirteenth century, and Hansa traders had maintained important settlements in Novgorod and some other Russian cities from the fourteenth and fifteenth centuries, such contacts had been limited in scale, and deep penetration of the Russian hinterland had been rare. But as Moscow became the political center of a geographically vast state, Russia's furs and forest products attracted venturesome merchants from the West, just as the mineral wealth of the New World simultaneously prompted the Spanish explorations.

The Russians, of course, were not nearly so weak vis-à-vis western Europe as were the Amerindians. Autochthonous Russian institutions and culture easily survived the fall of Moscow to Polish invaders in 1610, whereas the civilization of the Aztecs and Incas crumbled irretrievably under the tread of Spanish conquistadores. Despite this difference, Russia, like the Americas, became an outlier of western Europe from the sixteenth century onward, not merely in a geographical sense, but also because the most critical issues confronting Russian society came to turn upon the question of how to cope with the intrusive Europeans and their civilization.

The sovereigns of Muscovy at first welcomed Western traders and adventurers, valuing the skills and technical knowledge they brought. Yet from the beginning there was an arcanum of Russian thought and feeling which vigorously repelled foreign influence in the name of Orthodoxy and autocracy. In proportion as their superiorities to Russian civilization became obvious, a painful ambivalence began to characterize Russian attitudes toward the Western nations. Antagonistic attitudes often struggled for primacy within a single individual, so that every commitment to the West was tentative and every repudiation of Western influence qualified. In the sixteenth century, when contact with western Europe was still slender and before the Western threat to Orthodox culture and society had become apparent, Russians on the whole were ready enough to appropriate whatever foreign skills and knowledge seemed superior to their own; but in the first half of the seventeenth century, after Polish attack had demonstrated the danger from the West, reaction set in and the impulse to withdraw behind the distinctive Russian past came strongly to the fore.

A profound irony, rooted in military urgency, blunted the force of all Russian efforts to appropriate Western skills. The Russian government could never safely neglect the threat inherent in an ever changing Western military technology. Yet efforts to transplant the full panoply of Western armament to Russian soil required rapid transformation of existing social relations and practices. This, in turn, invited if it did not require wholesale resort to legal compulsion, as the shortest way to make people do what the leaders of the government found necessary. Yet while it narrowed the technical gap between Russian and Western societies, massive use of force to compel the population at large to do what the rulers deemed necessary simultaneously widened the breach between Russia's social institutions and those of Western nations.

Hence Russia's urgent efforts to imitate Western technology made full and complete assimilation of Western culture impossible. Moreover, the government's wholesale use of legal compulsion to attain ends largely incomprehensible to the Russian peasantry sustained a strong anarchistic streak among the majority of the Russian people, who, even when constrained to submit bodily, never entirely reconciled themselves in spirit to the heavy bondage imposed by the state.

These dilemmas began to emerge during the reign of Ivan III (1462–1505), who opened diplomatic relations with several of the Western powers and inaugurated a policy of importing foreign artisans and architects (mainly from Venice) to beautify Moscow with stone-built palaces and churches. Ivan IV, the Terrible (1533–84), welcomed English merchants arriving via Archangel and gave them special trade privileges; and even in the seventeenth century, when reaction against the West was at its height, the first Romanov tsar, Michael I (1613–45) invited a Dutchman to set up armaments works in Tula in order to secure a better supply of weapons for his troops.

Yet while the superior skills of the West could never be a matter of indifference, it generally remained true that the artisans and entrepreneurs whom the Russians imported or admitted into their territory were made to serve distinctly Russian purposes. The success with which the Westerners were kept in check depended upon the vigor of the two central institutions of Russian society: the Orthodox church and the Muscovite autocracy. Yet the requisite vigor was not easy to maintain in the face of an ever mounting Western challenge. Both the Russian church and the Russian state had therefore to make radical adjustments to the pressures of the West and, doing so, did not escape severe intestine troubles.

*   *   *

The Russian church was torn by bitter controversy at the end of the fifteenth and beginning of the sixteenth century. Emphatic defenders of every jot and tittle of existing forms of Russian Orthodox ritual and belief clashed angrily with others who desired radical reformation. The reformers acted at first in private and more or less in secret and were stigmatized by their opponents, probably with more vituperation than exactness, as "Judaizers." Their doctrines were no sooner anathematized than a new controversy broke out over the question of whether or not churches and monasteries could legitimately own landed estates.[32] On this issue, the rulers of Moscow took an ambiguous stand, for they were torn between the attraction of confiscating the vast properties of the Church, as proposed by the radicals, and the emphatic glorification of princely power which was a keynote of the conservative camp. This controversy brought to expression diametrically opposed views of the proper function of the Church. The critics of the Orthodox

---

[32] Cf. the contemporary Protestant policy of confiscating most Church property and the crisis provoked by "Spiritual" Franciscans two centuries before. Relations between the Russian reformers and German Protestantism, if any, are obscure.

hierarchy aspired toward a clergy dedicated to the imitation of Christ and the apostles, living humbly and in poverty close to the people, whereas their opponents desired a Church staffed with pious and competent prelates who would discipline and educate the rank and file of the clergy and make the Church a first line of defense against foreign heresy and error. In the end, Vasili III (1505–1533) opted for the conservative side and set his soldiers and officials the task of hunting down and suppressing critics, radicals, and reformers.

Yet this policy had its pitfalls also. Russian liturgical books and practices varied considerably from place to place, for over the centuries numerous translators' and copyists' errors had crept into Church manuals. Standardization seemed requisite; but the authentic standard could not be discovered without critical textual scholarship of which the Russian clergy were not then capable. Importation of foreign scholars seemed a necessary recourse; yet this ran counter to the deep conviction, nourished ever since the fall of Constantinople (1453), that Russia alone had preserved the Orthodox faith in its entire purity. Hence when a party within the Church invited an Italian-trained scholar known as Maxim the Greek to come to Russia in order to bring Russian church manuals into accord with Greek originals, a new storm arose, and the unfortunate scholar ended his days (1556) as a prisoner in a remote monastery.

The problem became acute after 1568, when the Jesuits, armed with the full scholarly resources of the Counter Reformation, became active in Poland-Lithuania. They won rapid successes against Polish Protestants, and then turned their attention to the numerous adherents of the Orthodox church. The learning and piety of the Orthodox hierarchy of the Ukraine (most of which was then attached to the Polish-Lithuanian state) was at a low ebb. As a result, the Orthodox clergy were quite unable to reply effectively to the Jesuit challenge, backed as it was by the full weight of the Polish crown and nobility. Accordingly, in 1595 most of the Orthodox bishops of the Ukraine and of Lithuania accepted union with Rome, on condition that they be allowed to retain a Slavonic ritual. Thus the so-called "Uniate" church came into existence. It roused deep fear and hostility among Russian Orthodox clerics who saw in the Uniate compromise with the papacy a renewal of the apostasy (Union of Florence, 1439) which had led to the downfall of Constantinople.

Nevertheless, Roman Catholic arguments and scholarship were difficult to refute, especially when obvious textual errors could be pointed out in the official Russian liturgical handbooks, as was the case. But Orthodoxy had one great resource that seemed proof against Latin attack: the superior antiquity of Greek Christianity. Resumption of the effort to reorganize Russian ecclesiastical practices and liturgical books in accordance with Greek models therefore seemed necessary; and in 1653, the patriarch Nikon[33] officially launched

---

[33] The Metropolitan of Moscow had been elevated to the patriarchal dignity after negotiations (1588–90) with the four ancient Orthodox patriarchates of Constantinople, Antioch, Alexandria, and Jerusalem.

such a program of reform. Nikon's purpose of confuting Jesuit critics required him to "spoil the Egyptians" by employing the techniques of textual criticism in which the Roman Catholics excelled. Worst of all, in the eyes of his Orthodox opponents, the men who were capable of using such techniques had all been trained, at Kiev or elsewhere, in circles tainted by close contacts with the heretical West.

A lasting schism within Russian Orthodoxy resulted, for the domineering personality of Nikon and the equally stubborn and fanatical spirit of his opponents[34] brooked no compromise. Even after Nikon himself had quarreled with the Tsar and been deposed from office, his policy was maintained by church and state. Flights and exiles attendant upon official persecution of the communities of "Old Believers," as those who rejected Nikon's innovations were commonly called, simply spread dissent throughout the length and breadth of Russia. Old Believer sects went underground, where they nourished a stubborn opposition to their oppressors, whom they regarded as agents or even incarnations of Antichrist. Thus the Russian Orthodox church withstood Western attack only at the cost of a serious schism, provoked by the effort to assimilate in one stroke the learning which had been acquired gradually across some four or five centuries in the West.

* * *

Like the Church, the Russian state suffered violent stresses and strains as it strove to cope with foreign attack and internal anarchy. In 1564 Tsar Ivan IV[35] launched a terroristic revolution against the hereditary aristocrats of Russia, confiscated their landed possessions, and granted suitable estates to men who undertook military and other forms of state service in return. In this way the Tsar sought to build up an army and administration capable of overcoming his foreign enemies. In the East he was extremely successful: Russian forces began to occupy Siberia and opened the Volga to Russian trade by conquering the khanates of Kazan and Astrakhan (1552, 1558). But against the Poles and Swedes, the Russians won no more than occasional victories and during Ivan IV's reign actually lost some territory to their Western neighbors.

After Ivan's death, an incompetent son and a series of usurpers brought on a period of disturbances traditionally known in Russian history as the "Time of Troubles" (1584–1613). It was compounded of ruthless intrigue among the high nobility, Cossack greed for plunder, and blind anger welling up from

---

[34] Cf. the enlightening autobiography of the archpriest Avvakum, who became the principal leader of the "Old Believers," *The Life of the Archpriest Avvakum by Himself*, trans. Jane Harrison and Hope Mirrlees (London: Leonard & Virginia Woolf, 1924). According to James H. Billington (oral conversation, 1962), contagion from the Jewish communities of Russia, where Sabbatai Sevi's claim to be the Messiah created intense excitement in 1666–67, was an important source of messianism among the Old Believers. On Sabbatai Sevi, see below, p. 639.

[35] Ivan IV was the first officially to assume the title of "tsar," though it had been used before his time unofficially. The title was, of course, a form of the Roman "Caesar" and implied that Moscow was the imperial successor to Rome and Constantinople.

Department of Art, University of Chicago.

TWO VIEWS OF THE CATHEDRAL OF ST. BASIL, MOSCOW

Ivan IV the Terrible (1533–84) built this church in commemoration of his conquest of the khanates of Kazan and Astrakhan. Old Muscovy here stands before us: Church and state wedded in the very conception of a cathedral built by an autocrat to celebrate military success. Byzantine, Persian, Italian, and medieval Russian architectural traditions all contributed to the oddly concordant and splendidly colorful result. This architectural tour de force expresses in brick and mortar the no less remarkable political tour de force by which Ivan and his immediate predecessors pressed Tartar and European foreigners into the Russian service and used their technical skills to sustain and extend the Muscovite autocracy.

the oppressed peasantry,[36] capped by a confused, yet massive rally to the Orthodox Russian past against Polish Catholic invaders. The patriarch of Moscow, Filaret, and his son, Michael Romanov, were the principal beneficiaries of this public reaction, which carried Michael to the Russian throne (1613–45) and re-established the autocracy and the service nobility as rulers of the Russian state.

In the sixteenth century, Russian rulers experimented with semi-autonomous local governments and with national meetings of advisory bodies representing officials, nobles, townsmen, and clergy; but these institutions all faded away under the first Romanovs. Their analogues in France, the provincial assemblies and the estates-general, were simultaneously giving way to the centralizing power of absolute and bureaucratic monarchy. Thus in outward form, the political development of Russia approximated closely to that of the most advanced country of western Europe. But instead of the complex balance between crown, nobility, and bourgeoisie which lay behind French absolutism, the Russian autocracy was raised upon a servile, suppressed, and generally discontented peasantry, and rode roughshod over townsmen and ecclesiastics. Only the creatures of the autocracy, the service nobles, were in a position to make their will felt in the state; and even that group, indispensable though it was to the government, could be made to dance to the tune of a strong-willed ruler. Thus despite superficial resemblances, Russian autocracy and French absolutism were in fact very different.

Under the first Romanovs, Russia sought to exclude foreign influences as far as was compatible with safety. This meant that, while foreigners were needed as army drillmasters and as armaments makers and while foreign merchants were required for the export trade in furs, which brought the treasury substantial revenue,[37] nevertheless all strangers were kept so far as possible at a safe distance. Enclosed within special ghettoes in Moscow and other towns, they were treated with general suspicion as dangerous heretics. The lively curiosity and rather capricious favor with which Ivan the Terrible had greeted the first Englishmen to visit Russia had vanished; yet Russia's long and exposed land frontier against the West made it impossible to exclude the troublesome foreigners completely, as the Japanese, for example, were able to do. Despite all efforts to escape, Russia found herself inextricably entangled

[36] A corollary of Ivan's effort to mobilize maximal forces against external enemies was the restriction of the right of ordinary peasants to move about the country. Land granted to a member of the new "service" nobility was useless without cultivators, so the government was compelled to try to keep peasants working for their new masters. This was achieved by one legal device or another—stricter definition of debt and labor contracts, imposition of collective responsibility for taxes upon the villagers, edicts prohibiting one landlord from bidding against another for the services of a peasant family, etc. By the middle of the seventeenth century, when this evolution came to completion, an oppressive serfdom verging upon slavery had been fastened upon the majority of Russian peasants. The severity of the laws was provoked by the very ease with which a discontented peasant could slip away across one of the open land frontiers of the Russian state and take up life under pioneer conditions in Siberian forests or on the open steppe of the south, where Cossack bands stood ready to welcome such recruits to their ranks.

[37] Raymond H. Fisher, *The Russian Fur Trade, 1550–1700* (Berkeley, Calif.: University of California Press, 1943), p. 122, estimates that profits from state trading in furs and taxes on private fur traders amounted to about 10 per cent of the entire revenues of the state in the seventeenth century.

in the toils of an expanding, dangerously powerful, and vastly attractive western European civilization.

At the same time, the militarized autocracy of Russia was in a very favorable position on its southern and eastern frontiers, for the efforts required to stand off Western attack imparted to the Russian military and political machine a definite superiority over all rivals in Siberia and permitted Moscow to annex most of the Ukraine from the disintegrating Polish state during the second half of the seventeenth century.[38] Russia's ambiguous and painful relationship with western Europe thus offered enormous compensations along other frontiers and indeed made of Russia a quasi-Western state vis-à-vis the more backward peoples of the forest and steppe zones of northern Asia.[39]

D. THE CHANGING BALANCE OF THE ECUMENE 1500–1700 A.D.

1. THE MOSLEM WORLD

By the end of the fifteenth century, Islamized steppe warriors, aided by Moslem missionaries, merchants, and local converts to Islam, had engulfed the old heartland of Orthodox Christendom, driven deep into India, and established the Moslem faith and culture in outlying provinces of China. Even in sub-Saharan Africa and southeast Asia, well beyond the range of the steppe warriors' bowshot, merchants and missionaries had won numerous peoples to Islam by 1500. The springs of Moslem expansion did not decay when a few Europeans rounded Africa and asserted their naval predominance in the Indian Ocean. Moslem warriors and merchants together with sufi saints and learned *ulema* continued, as in the centuries before 1500, to win new territories and new converts throughout the sixteenth and seventeenth centuries; and while Moslem military victories became few after 1700, peaceable propaganda and conversions have not ceased even in our own day.

Moreover, the social instrumentalities which sustained Moslem expansion before 1500 continued to operate, almost unmodified, for some two centuries after that date. Thus between 1507 and 1515, Uzbek nomads fresh from the central Asian steppe overran the cities of Transoxiana, as many a tribal confederation had done before them. Survivors of the former ruling clique of the region—Persianized Turks, quarreling heirs to Tamerlane's power—fled southward to the plains of northern India, where they established the Mogul

[38] The fact that most of the Cossacks were of Orthodox extraction and disliked the Catholic policy of the Poles was an important element in bringing the Ukraine into the Muscovite camp. If free Cossack communities could not survive as sovereign bodies—and the seductions of landlord status offered to the Cossack leaders by both Poland and Russia made this impracticable—then most Cossacks preferred association with Orthodox Russia rather than with Catholic Poland.

[39] I have relied mainly upon Michael T. Florinsky, *Russia: A History and an Interpretation* (New York: Macmillan Co., 1955), Vol. I, for these remarks on Russian developments. In addition to the books cited separately, I have also consulted S. Platonov, *Histoire de la Russie* (Paris: Payot, 1929), pp. 167–487; W. E. D. Allen, *The Ukraine: A History* (Cambridge: Cambridge University Press, 1940); Gunter Stökl, *Die Entstehung des Kosakentums* (Munich: Isar Verlag, 1953); Frederick C. Conybeare, *Russian Dissenters* (Cambridge, Mass.: Harvard University Press, 1921); James Mavor, *An Economic History of Russia* (2d ed.; London and Toronto: J. M. Dent & Sons, 1925), Vol. I; Serge Bolshakoff, *Russian Nonconformity* (Philadelphia: Westminster Press, 1950).

empire.[40] Almost simultaneously, in 1565 a coalition of Moslem rulers in southern India, who recruited much of their fighting manpower from Iran and Turkestan, combined to overthrow Vijayanagar, the last strong Hindu state. The prestige of victorious Islam was felt also in Java, where sometime between 1513 and 1526 a coalition of Moslem coastal states overthrew the Hinduized monarchy of the interior and began to propagate their faith inland. Other islands and coasts of southeast Asia, especially those where trade was active, similarly came within the circle of Islam at various dates between the fourteenth and the eighteenth centuries.[41]

Substantially the same missionary processes operated in the west African Sudan, where itinerant merchants and holy men, supported by a series of Moslem imperial states—Timbuctu, Kano, Bornu, Morocco—sporadically en-' larged the realm of Islam even while fighting among themselves.[42] In east Africa, Moslem trading cities generally submitted to Portuguese domination after 1500; but Moslem tribal nomads spearheaded a deep penetration of the hinterland (mainly in the north), despite Christian control of the coastline.[43]

Even in Christian Europe, where both cultural and military resistance to Islam was far more vigorous than in Africa or Asia, the Ottoman state expanded at Christian expense until nearly 1700. Ottoman armies conquered most of Hungary between 1526 and 1543 and established a ring of client states all round the Black Sea. Following a time of troubles (1579–1623), when the weaknesses of the Ottoman system for determining succession to the throne provoked paralysis at the center, a new sultan (1623–40) resumed victorious war—but this time against a rival Moslem imperial power based in Persia. After a second period of incompetent leadership, a vigorous and violent grand vizier, Mohammed Koprulu, initiated (1656) the last phase of Ottoman military expansion in Europe, which came to a climax in 1683 with a second siege of Vienna.[44] Such a history seemed to carry forward the process

[40] The rise of a strong Persian state was also in part provoked by the Uzbek danger. All this strictly accorded with very ancient precedents but has the distinction of being the last time in history when steppe peoples of western Asia were able to overturn civilized governments and set in motion a chain reaction of state building in India and the Middle East. In the eastern steppe the Manchu conquest of China in the next century enjoys the same distinction.

[41] Malacca was the principal focus of this mercantile-missionary enterprise before 1511, when the Portuguese captured the place; and multiple secondary centers became seedbeds of Islam after that date. Cf. D. G. E. Hall, *A History of South East Asia* (New York: St Martin's Press, 1955), pp. 176–85; G. Coedès, *Les États hindouisés d'Indochine et d'Indonesie* (Paris: E. de Boccard, 1948), pp. 382–86, 398–411. These Moslem achievements of mercantile-missionary state building in southeast Asia closely resembled the earlier activities of Hindus and Buddhists in the same area. The Moslem geographical range was greater, extending as far as Borneo and Mindinao, but Moslem missions were themselves bracketed by the Christian missions to Japan and Luzon.

[42] J. Spencer Trimingham, *A History of Islam in West Africa* (London: Oxford University Press, 1962), pp. 93–103, 121–47.

[43] George Peter Murdock, *Africa: Its Peoples and Their Culture History* (New York: McGraw-Hill, 1959), pp. 138–41, 320–24.

[44] This revival of Ottoman power under the Grand Vizier Mohammed Koprulu not only secured for the sultans sovereignty in Crete (1669) and Podolia (1676); it also brought long-standing client states —Transylvania (from 1661) and Moldavia and Wallachia (from 1658–59)—back to effective Turkish obedience. Austrian efforts to make good the loss of Hapsburg influence in Transylvania led only to an inconclusive war, 1661–64, which was settled to the Turks' advantage. Polish efforts to check the Ottoman advance resulted in the loss of Podolia to the Turks.

of Moslem expansion at the expense of Christendom which dated back to the very inception of Islam. All good Moslems could feel confident, at least until the Austrian victory at Zenta in 1697, that the thousand-year ebb and flow of frontier fighting against Christendom was tending still, as in the past, to favor the Moslem cause.

Yet despite these impressive continuities with earlier centuries, Moslems suffered three important setbacks in the early sixteenth century from which they never recovered. These were (*a*) the Iberian crusade against Islam in the Mediterranean, the Atlantic, and the Indian Oceans; (*b*) the administrative consolidation of Muscovy, with the result that the Moslem khanates of the western steppe could no longer stand up against Russian military strength; and (*c*) the violent split between Sunni and Shi'a Moslem sects, consequent upon the imperial conquests of Shah Ismail Safavi.

The last of these setbacks certainly seemed the most critical to Moslem contemporaries; and the subsequent transformations within Islam which the Shi'a-Sunni quarrel provoked or strengthened perhaps bear out this judgment. Wars with the Spaniards and Portuguese engaged a significant proportion of the Ottoman forces; but by the close of the sixteenth century, the Turks could congratulate themselves upon their success in defeating the Iberian challenge. Meanwhile, the Moslems of the Indian Ocean—not without Ottoman help—had effectively circumvented the Portuguese threat to their political and commercial position in southern Asia. Against the Russians, however, the Islamic world failed to organize any adequate riposte. The prosperity of Islam on the western steppe was indelibly linked to the fate of the Turkish horsemen, whose age-old military superiority against sedentary populations disappeared with the introduction of firearms. Until 1676, however, when Russian and Ottoman frontiers for the first time became contiguous, remnants of older steppe empires interposed a broad cushion between the centers of Moslem and of Russian power. Hence, for the time being, the great empires of Islam were able to neglect with apparent impunity the new, but still distant rival in the north.

THE IBERIAN CRUSADE AND MOSLEM RESPONSE. Crusading began earlier and lasted longer in Spain than in any other part of Europe; and even before the last Moslem state of the peninsula was crushed in 1492, both Spaniards and Portuguese had carried the war overseas into Africa. The Portuguese established a foothold opposite Gibraltar as early as 1415 and continued to hold various sections of the west African coast until 1578. A main aim of the entire Portuguese enterprise around Africa was to outflank the Moslems and link Christian Europe with the legendary Christian kingdom of Prester John. Although Prester John's realm shrank rather disappointingly to the proportions of a half-barbarous Ethiopia (visited by envoys from Portugal as early as 1493 overland, and in 1520 via the southern sea route), Portuguese naval successes in Indian waters permitted them to disrupt Moslem trade routes in the southern oceans. Simultaneously, the Spaniards resumed operations against the Moslems, first conquering Granada (1492), and presently carrying the war into north Africa (1509–11). When Charles V added the Spanish lands to his

Hapsburg inheritance in Germany and the Low Countries, Spain became indirectly involved on still a third front against the Moslems—this time on the Danube.

The Ottoman empire responded vigorously to this Hapsburg threat. On land, Suleiman the Lawgiver (1520–66) pushed the Ottoman frontier to the Carpathians. In the Mediterranean, a long and indecisive struggle ended in 1578 when a peace between Spain and the Turks, intended as a mere breathing space, became a lasting *modus vivendi*, owing to Spain's financial exhaustion and involvement on other fronts. Despite the Christian victory at Lepanto (1571), the Turks could justly claim an over-all success, for they kept at least nominal control of Tunis and Algeria and maintained the naval predominance in the eastern Mediterranean they had won from the Venetians in the fifteenth century.

Islam won no comparably decisive successes in the Indian Ocean. Although Ottoman admirals overcame severe geographical obstacles[45] to mount three large-scale expeditions against the Portuguese (1536, 1554–56, 1585–89), they failed to destroy Portuguese naval supremacy in the southern oceans.[46] By the second half of the sixteenth century, however, the initiative of local Moslem seafarers had restored Moslem commerce to nearly its former proportions in south Asia. By avoiding ports under Portuguese control and by carrying sufficient armament to discourage casual attack, Moslem vessels found it easy to slip through Portuguese patrols. From the Moslem point of view, therefore, Portuguese efforts to exert their naval supremacy shrank to the proportions of bearable piratical attrition. Indeed, the Moslems were so successful in evading their control that before the end of the century the Portuguese opened their ports to Moslem ships, finding harbor tolls more lucrative than piracy and war.[47]

In both the Mediterranean and in the Indian Ocean, the Dutch, French and English gradually supplanted the Iberian sea hegemony. These northern powers owed their success in large part to the official favor of Moslem rulers, who looked upon them as a valuable counterweight to the Spaniards and Portuguese. In 1536, for example, the French secured commercial concessions in the Ottoman empire as part of the Franco-Ottoman military alliance against the Hapsburgs which was concluded in that year. The English Levant Company acquired comparable privileges in 1580; while the Dutch appeared in the eastern Mediterranean in 1597 (under the French flag until 1612) and quickly became effective commercial rivals of both the French and the English.[48] Similarly, Dutch and English trade penetrated India under the aegis

[45] Shipbuilding in the Red Sea was crippled by lack of wood. Hence Turkish vessels had to be constructed of materials transported overland via Egypt from Asia Minor or Syria.

[46] The last of these expeditions operated along the coast of east Africa, where it permanently rolled back Portuguese power from the northern portion of that coast. The final disruption of the Ottoman fleet (near Mombasa) was the result of native revolt as much as of Portuguese naval strength. Cf. F. Braudel, *La Méditerranée et le monde méditerranéen à l'époque de Philippe II*, p. 1019. Braudel's work is a fundamental guide to the Iberian-Moslem struggle, especially in its latter half-century.

[47] B. Schrieke, *Indonesian Sociological Studies* (The Hague: W. van Hoeve, 1955), I, 45.

[48] Braudel, *La Méditerranée*, pp. 483–502; Paul Masson, *Histoire du commerce français dans le Levant au XVII siècle* (Paris: Hachette, 1896), pp. xi–xxxiii.

of treaties concluded with the Mogul emperors and other Moslem rulers. Moreover, in view of their initial dependence upon Moslem good will, the Protestant powers deliberately eschewed the missionary activity which had been a very prominent feature of Iberian expansion.[49]

Yet French, Dutch, and English mercantile activity in Moslem lands, though usually subject to the complaisance of local rulers, laid the groundwork for later European dominion. This was most clearly the case in India and the East Indies, where even in the seventeenth century Dutch and English commercial enterprise began to work significant changes in the Asian economies. The great Dutch and English trading companies assiduously cultivated European demand for oriental products like Indian indigo, cotton goods, and saltpeter, Chinese silks, tea, and porcelains, Arabian coffee, and Persian carpets; and the growing market for such goods in Europe soon had a significant effect upon the production patterns of Asia.

Dutch and English merchants were not content to limit themselves to trade between Europe and the Asian lands but sought actively and persistently to develop the commerce and industry of the "Indies." Gain from local and intra-Asian trade was the aim, for the European companies badly needed to generate profits within Asia in order to limit the outflow of gold and silver from Europe which home governments viewed with perennial alarm. Export of specie from Europe could not be checked (short of stopping the importation of the new oriental products) until Asians developed a taste for European goods. But until the second half of the seventeenth century, European products were usually ill-suited to Asian markets and often appeared coarse and crude by comparison with local manufactures. Even after European craftsmen had imitated some of the Asian skills and invented improved methods of production, the Asian market for European goods remained very limited, so that the pressure upon the trading companies to make money in Asia itself remained very strong.

The consequences for Asian economies were sometimes spectacular. The Dutch, for example, rationalized agriculture in Java and adjacent islands on a large scale, setting Javanese peasants to work raising tea and sugar cane as well as spices. Similarly, the English gradually established a loose managerial control over the textile workers of western India. After advancing small sums to weavers on account, English agents could prescribe the type of goods to be produced, while the scale of loans soon served to regulate the quantity of cloth coming onto the market. Goods so produced were then offered for sale by European middlemen, not merely in Europe, but all along the African and south Asian coasts as well as in Japan and China—wherever, in short, profitable markets could be discovered. Previously backward regions like the Philippines and the eastern shores of the Bay of Bengal developed rapidly under this economic regimen. Everywhere, European traders, organized into

---

[49] It was symptomatic of the early symbiotic relationship between Protestant trading companies and Moslem rulers that the Dutch captured Malacca from the Portuguese in 1641 only with the help of land forces provided by the sultan of Johore. On the other hand, in Java and other East Indian islands where the Dutch acquired sovereignty, they provoked an ineffectual but bitter "counter crusade" from the Moslem side. Cf. D. G. E. Hall, *A History of South East Asia*, pp. 252–82.

powerful, armed companies, gained more and more decisive control of large-scale commerce, while native enterprise was gradually pushed back toward petty local traffic.[50]

European economic penetration of the Ottoman empire proceeded far more slowly. Yet here, too, by the close of the seventeenth century, French, English, and Dutch vessels were carrying most of the long-distance trade from Ottoman ports. The pattern of exchanges—Ottoman raw materials for European manufactures—tended to reduce the Levant to economic passivity. The unfavorable social status of the commercial populations of the Ottoman empire, subjected as they were to a military and official class which was generally indifferent or hostile to their interests, made it difficult and in the end impossible for the sultan's subjects to sustain large-scale commercial activity in competition with European traders. Middleman's profits on commodities originating in Asia had been sharply reduced by the European conquests of the oceans; and after this setback to the Middle East's traditional economic position in the ecumene, indigenous manufacturing and mercantile enterprise proved inadequate to sustain a leading part in the world's commerce. Nevertheless, until after 1700, European merchants scarcely penetrated beyond Ottoman ports; internal exchanges remained in the hands of local merchants; and after 1592 the commerce of the Black Sea became an Ottoman preserve.[51]

In 1700, no one could foresee the ultimate consequences of European commercial power. The Iberian crusade had been turned back in the Mediterranean and blunted in the Indian Ocean; and the political implications of Dutch, French, and English commercial penetration of Islamic lands were not yet apparent. Moslems therefore had seemingly good grounds for expecting that close adherence to ancestral patterns of life would serve as well in future as they had in the past. Western Europe's assault upon Islam had failed—to all appearances—just as the Crusades of the Middle Ages had failed. There seemed no cause for alarm, no reason for reform, no basis for doubting the essential superiority of Moslem ways.

[50] Cf. W. H. Moreland, From Akbar to Aurangzeb: A Study in Indian Economic History (London: Macmillan & Co., 1923); Bal Krishna, Commercial Relations between India and England, 1601–1757 (London: George Routledge & Sons, 1924); J. C. van Leur, Indonesian Trade and Society (The Hague: W. van Hoeve, 1955), pp. 159–245.

[51] I have been unable to discover any satisfactory economic history of either the Ottoman or the Safavi empire. But cf. Paul Masson, Histoire du commerce français; A. C. Wood, A History of the Levant Company (London: Oxford University Press, 1935); H. A. R. Gibb and Harold Bowen, Islamic Society and the West (London: Oxford University Press, 1950), Vol. I, Part I, pp. 294–313. Braudel, La Méditerranée, pp. 616–43, tentatively suggests that a "seigneurial reaction" extended throughout the Mediterranean from Spain through Italy to Turkey and speaks of the "trahison de la bourgeoisie," who preferred investment in land to the uncertainties of trade and manufactures. Traian Stoianovich, "The Conquering Balkan Orthodox Merchant," Journal of Economic History, XX (1960), 234–62, on the other hand, finds evidence of rising commercial energies among Ottoman subjects from the fourteenth to the eighteenth centuries.

Until further work has been done in Ottoman economic history, it would be premature to venture definite statements about the social and economic transformations of the Middle East which may have forwarded the decay of its trading position vis-à-vis Europe in the sixteenth and seventeenth centuries. Yet the resemblances between the "colonial" position of Byzantium after the twelfth century in relation to the Italian trading cities and the economic relationship of the Ottoman lands to northwestern Europe after the last decades of the seventeenth century seem remarkably close.

THE RISE OF RUSSIA AND ITS CONSEQUENCES FOR ISLAM. When Ivan III of Moscow asserted his political independence of the Golden Horde in 1480, the Tartars were so weakened by internal feuds as to be incapable of responding with more than an ineffectual military demonstration. As a result, by 1517 Muscovy and Poland-Lithuania between them had annexed all of the Russian principalities formerly subject to the Tartars; and both these powers began to expand rapidly southward into the steppe.

In the sixteenth century, independent Cossack communities in the southern steppes organized unruly republics which for a short while seemed capable of forming power centers rivaling Warsaw and Moscow.[52] But in the seventeenth century, Russian, Polish, and Turkish advances into the steppe made Cossack independence increasingly insecure. The leaders of the Cossack hordes found it advantageous to ally themselves with one or another of these neighboring governments, receiving in return subsidies for military service and securing from Poles and Russians (but not from the Turks) recognition as landlords over their followers. After some complicated maneuvering between Rusisa, Poland, and Turkey, the Cossack communities definitely opted for the Russian connection in 1681, and thereafter "registered Cossacks," *i.e.*, men inscribed on special military rosters, formed a useful auxiliary to the Russian armed forces. Betrayed by their own leaders, the rest of the Cossack rank and file was reduced to serfdom. Thereupon the rude egalitarian lawlessness of the first Cossack communities went underground, to reappear in the form of wild peasant revolts in the seventeenth and eighteenth centuries.

Long before consolidating their power in the Ukraine, the Russians overthrew the khanates of Kazan (1552) and Astrakhan (1556), opening the entire Volga region to Russian settlement and trade. Shortly thereafter, pioneer traders and adventurers crossed the Ural Mountains and began to establish Russian power on the upwaters of the Ob (1579–87). Fratricidal quarrels within the Moslem khanate of Sibir made the Russian victory comparatively easy. Beyond lay a vast expanse of forest and tundra, inhabited mainly by primitive and unwarlike peoples, and by ermine and other fur-bearing animals. Russian agents found it easy to compel the natives to trap furs and yield them as tribute. Hence as soon as they had mastered techniques of sledding along frozen rivers and of portage from river to river, Russian explorers and adventurers met no insurmountable obstacle in traveling all the way to Okhotsk on the Pacific coast which they reached in 1638.[53]

These Russian successes in the western steppe and in the Siberian forests,

---

[52] The Cossack hordes constituted the equivalent on land of the pirate communities which in the same age established themselves in the West Indies, the South China Sea, and along the "Barbary" coast of North Africa. Like the Cossack strongholds, pirate nests were situated where the strength of organized governments could not reach. The fundamental dependence of the Cossacks upon supplies (arms and gunpowder) coming from the settled agricultural communities was precisely analogous to the pirates' dependence on similar supplies from civilized ports.

[53] John F. Baddeley, *Russia, Mongolia, and China* (2 vols.; London: Macmillan & Co., 1919), I, lxix, lxxiii; Robert J. Kerner, *The Urge to the Sea: The Course of Russian History* (Berkeley and Los Angeles, Calif.: University of California Press, 1946), pp. 66–88; Raymond H. Fisher, *The Russian Fur Trade, 1550–1700* (Berkeley and Los Angeles, Calif.: University of California Press, 1943).

together with the progress of Lamaism in the central[54] and eastern steppe, combined to roll back the northern frontier of Islam very substantially in the sixteenth–seventeenth centuries. The great Moslem powers made no serious efforts to check this trend of events.[55] Persia, the natural guardian of the gate upon the central steppe, was heavily engaged against the Ottoman empire and had no energy to spare; while the Uzbek empire of Bokhara, by espousing a rigid and narrow Sunni orthodoxy, effectively repressed the Sufi missionary spirit which in previous centuires had won for Islam its main successes among the steppe peoples. The steppe itself was poor and unpromising, all the more so after overland caravan routes across Asia had lost most of their importance to new sea and river-portage routes that ran far to the south and north of central Asia. Civilized Moslems therefore found little occasion for penetrating the wilds of the steppe. The cultural and religious vacuum thus created was duly filled by Tibetan Lamaism.

It was therefore in the steppe lands of eastern Europe and central Asia that Islam suffered its first serious setbacks, at a time when in regions directly exposed to Western assault the Moslem empires were still victoriously advancing their frontiers.

THE SUNNI-SHI'A CONFLICT AND ITS CONSEQUENCES FOR ISLAM.   The two and seventy jarring sects which Moslem learning somewhat arbitrarily discerned within the community of the faithful were divided on the ancient issue of the legitimacy of the succession to the Prophet into two main groupings: the Shi'a, who held that the succession rightfully descended only through Mohammed's son-in-law, Ali; and the Sunni, who recognized the legitimacy of Abu Bakr, Omar, Othman, and their successors in the caliphate. With the rise of the numerous Sufi orders, brotherhoods, and other religious congregations, this basic divergence of allegiance was vastly complicated. The sharpness of its lines tended to blur with the proliferation of heterodox religious groups that drew elements from Shi'a piety while remaining Sunni in the sense of admitting the legitimacy of the first three caliphs. Confusion was compounded by the fact that although the Shi'a remained a minority in most parts of the Moslem world, their practice of simulating Sunni orthodoxy while revealing hidden truths only to trusted initiates made possible the spread of a wide variety of Shi'a groups throughout the Moslem lands. On this basis, an uneasy balance among the sects of Islam had long prevailed, subject to recurrent local disturbance whenever a particularly holy man won a strong following or some fanatical leader arose to preach the damnation of all who differed from his theological principles.

[54] This constituted a notable failure of Moslem missionary energy. The region around the Ili River, where the Kalmuk power centered, had once been Moslem; but Islam receded when the Uzbeks of that region pushed south and west into Transoxiana and gave ground to the then still pagan Kalmuks.

[55] The Ottomans did send one expedition in 1659, aimed at repelling Russia from the lower Volga and at uniting forces with the central Asian khanates in order to take the Shi'a Persian state in the rear. However, a mutiny of the Janissaries and disputes with the khan of the Crimea, who perhaps feared for his autonomy if Ottoman power should establish itself firmly on his landward flank, persuaded the Ottomans to abandon the enterprise. For interesting comments upon the importance of this rather half-hearted effort and its failure cf. A. J. Toynbee, *A Study of History*, VIII, 225–27.

The political instability of the Moslem lands after the tenth century, and the frequently precarious grasp on power enjoyed by the Turkish war lords who divided sovereignty over the realm of Islam, contributed to the maintenance of this religious balance, since few rulers cared or dared to risk rebellion by insisting too strenuously upon religious conformity. The Ottoman state was no exception; for although the sultans came around to the support of Sunni orthodoxy, making it a religion of state in the fifteenth century, they did not thereby break relations with the heterodox dervish communities whose religious enthusiasm had contributed so greatly to early Ottoman expansion.

The religious and political equilibrium of Islam was therefore drastically disturbed when in 1499 a fanatical Shi'a sect, whose leaders had for some centuries been domiciled near the southern end of the Caspian Sea, began to win a series of startling victories. Beginning with only a scattered remnant of fervent followers, the leader of the sect, Ismail Safavi, rapidly built up a fanatical and formidable army while still a mere boy and within a year had captured Tabriz and crowned himself shah (1500). Victory followed victory, until by 1506 the entire Iranian plateau was united under the new conqueror. In 1508, Ismail asserted his power over Baghdad and most of Iraq, and in 1510 he administered a drastic defeat to the Uzbeks of Transoxiana, thereby securing his eastern frontier.

The secret of these successes was the religious fanaticism of Ismail's soldiers, which several generations of underground Shi'a propaganda, capped by their own spectacular victories, fostered very effectively. In accordance with the energy of his Shi'a sentiments, Ismail persecuted all Sunni Moslems who fell within his grasp and supported a vigorous Shi'a propaganda both within and beyond the frontiers of his new state. Moreover, Ismail's victories emboldened numerous Shi'a sympathizers to come out into the open in various parts of the Moslem world, especially in eastern Anatolia, where they presented a challenge the Ottoman sultan could not overlook. Indeed, in 1514 when a massive Shi'a revolt broke out against the Ottomans in Anatolia, the sultan had to muster the full strength of his armies to suppress it. After quelling the heretics at home, the Ottoman forces advanced eastward against the source of infection itself. At Chalderan near Tabriz, Ottoman artillery prevailed over Safavi fanaticism (1514); but unrest among the Janissaries compelled the sultan to retire without destroying Ismail's power.[56]

Throughout the sixteenth century, the Safavi empire remained a profoundly disturbing force in the Moslem world, dedicated to the defense and propagation of Shi'a doctrines at home and abroad. This policy implied a normal state of hostility with the Ottoman empire, punctuated only briefly by periods of peace. By the seventeenth century, however, when the Safavi empire reached

[56] The Janissary corps was closely associated with the Bektashi order of dervishes; and it may be that their sympathy with that heterodox, crypto-Shi'a religious community made them reluctant to see a crushing victory for Sunni orthodoxy. I know of no direct evidence to support such an idea; yet in general, the doctrinal latitudinarianism characteristic of the Bektashi order predisposed its initiates to sympathy for earnest seekers after God along whatever path. Cf. John K. Birge, *The Bektashi Order of Dervishes* (Hartford, Conn.: Hartford Seminary Press, 1937).

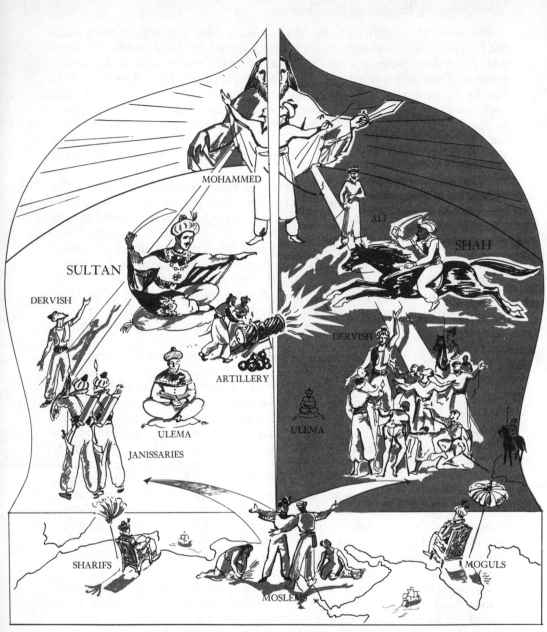

SUNNI-SHI'A SPLIT WITHIN ISLAM

its apogee under Shah Abbas the Great (1587–1629), the fanaticism of the Shi'a revolution had faded, at least in court circles; and a lasting peace with the Ottomans was concluded in 1639.[57]

The violent duel between Shi'a and Sunni, which thus divided the heartland of Islam for more than a century, echoed throughout the Moslem world and became an inescapable political issue for every Moslem ruler. The previous uneasy symbiosis among the Moslem sects threatened everywhere to break down into bitter civil strife, as religious opinion tended to become the criterion of political loyalty. In general, the more extreme manifestations of Shi'a enthusiasm were confined to the Safavi realm, while in the Ottoman lands the sultans' vigorous and effective countermeasures checked Shi'a heresy before it attained political dominion. But beyond the Ottoman reach, toward the margins of the Moslem world, local rulers fluctuated uneasily between the Sunni and Shi'a camps.

After failing in 1514 to eliminate the font of the whole disturbance, the Ottoman sultans' next move was to conquer the Mameluke kingdom of Egypt and Syria. Selim the Grim achieved this victory in a single campaign, 1516–17, thanks to the same artillery superiority he had employed against Shah Ismail. His victory forestalled an incipient alliance between Shah Ismail and the Mamelukes. It also gave the Ottomans control of the religiously strategic holy cities, Mecca and Medina, which had long been dependencies of the Mameluke power.

Second, Selim extended his reach along the coast of north Africa, partly to counter the Spanish threat to Moslem north Africa and partly to check the expansion of a second insurgent Shi'a power, the Sa'di Sharifs of Morocco. The Sharifs had by 1511 organized a powerful state among the tribal and urban populations of the Moslem Far West on the strength of a religious propaganda similar to that which was simultaneously winning such dramatic successes in Persia and Iraq.[58] In the same year, Ottoman naval squadrons first became active off the Algerian coast—thus provoking long-drawn-out naval wars with Spain that lasted through most of the sixteenth century.

The indecisiveness of the naval conflict with Spain did not prevent the Turks from achieving their aim: to forestall both Spaniards and Moroccans in Algeria.[59] Common enmity to the Iberian Christians helped to prevent any

[57] This Ottoman-Safavi struggle was of great significance for Europe. From 1606 until 1639, the Ottomans concentrated upon their war with Persia and correspondingly relaxed their pressure against Christian Europe—thus, in effect, permitting the Thirty Years' War. By mutual consent, the Hapsburgs and the Ottomans turned their backs upon each other in order to concentrate on what turned out to be vain efforts to exterminate heresy within their respective religious communities. Each was so exhausted by the effort that Moslem-Christian wars in Danubian Europe were not seriously resumed until late in the seventeenth century, when in 1683 the Turks advanced to the second siege of Vienna.

[58] Holy war against Portuguese and Spanish encroachments upon the African coast was a major stimulant to the Sa'di movement, which needed no prompting from the Safavids. Nonetheless, from the Ottoman viewpoint the simultaneous appearance of powerful Shi'a states on east and west at a time when Shi'a sympathizers within Ottoman boundaries were moving toward open rebellion was certainly ominous. On this passage of Moroccan history, sadly divorced from the wider Moslem context, however, cf. Coissac de Chavrebière, *Histoire du Maroc* (Paris: Payot, 1931), pp. 268–94.

[59] The Turks also claimed suzerainty over Morocco itself; but this was an agendum for future action rather than a reality. Cf. Braudel, *La Méditerranée*, p. 995.

direct clash between the Ottoman and Moroccan states; and when the Iberian pressure was removed (after 1578), Moroccan ambitions turned southward against the Negro kingdom of Timbuctu (captured 1591), while Ottoman forces continued to be fully engaged on other fronts.[60]

The Safavi revolution provoked rather more complicated political changes in the Moslem East. The new Uzbek power naturally enough took up the cudgels of Sunni orthodoxy against the neighboring Safavi heretics; while in India, the Mogul emperors walked a delicate tightrope between Sunni and Shi'a until the time of Aurangzeb (1659–1707). At low points in their stormy careers, both Babur (d. 1625), the founder of the Mogul state, and his son Humayun publicly professed the Shi'a faith in order to secure much needed Safavi support; but, when the opportunity came, each signified his political independence by conforming instead to Sunni forms of piety. Yet this was not entirely satisfactory either, for the Ottoman sultans claimed an ill-defined leadership over the entire Sunni community in rebuttal to the Safavi championship of the Shi'a.[61]

Hence a family that traced its descent from Genghis Khan and Tamerlane and regarded both the Ottoman and Safavi ruling houses as mere upstarts could not feel perfectly at ease in either the Sunni or the Shi'a camp. Accordingly, as soon as the emperor Akbar (1556–1605) had secured the Mogul power by establishing a firm and effective administration over all of northern India, he laid claim to an independent religious authority himself.[62] Akbar's son Jahangir was little interested in religious questions and therefore maintained far better relations with the doctors of Islam than his father had done.

---

[60] Alphonse Gouilly, *L'Islam dans l'Afrique occidentale française* (Paris: Larousse, 1952), pp. 62–63.

[61] The title "caliph," *i.e.,* "successor" to the Prophet as leader of the faithful on earth, had lost the sharpness of its original meaning by the sixteenth century. Sunni jurists inclined to the view that the true caliphate had disappeared in the thirteenth century, when the Mongols destroyed the remnants of the Abbasid state. Hence the sporadic appearance of the title "caliph" among the various official titles of the Ottoman sultans is of no great importance; other Moslem rulers had been and continued to be addressed in the same fashion. Nonetheless, Moslem political theory, whether Sunni or Shi'a, called for the unification of the faithful into a single political community; and any ruler claiming religious legitimacy, as the Ottoman rulers assuredly did, was impelled to aim at universal dominion within Islam, however vaguely such dominion might be conceived. On the caliphate and its relation to the Ottoman sultans, see H. A. R. Gibb and Harold Bowen, *Islamic Society and the West*, Vol. I, Part I, pp. 26–38; T. W. Arnold, *The Caliphate* (Oxford: Clarendon Press, 1924), chap. xi.

[62] The exact nature of Akbar's religious policy and the motives which inspired it are matters of debate. Personally, Akbar seems to have been an open-minded seeker after religious truth who listened with interest to champions of every faith that came within his purview, without being entirely convinced of the adequacy of any one of them. He gathered around himself a band of intimates and experimented with rites and observances drawn from diverse sources. Akbar very likely regarded this group as a sort of Sufi order with himself as founder and guide. Such eclectic and semi-secret practices scandalized strict Moslems and tantalized expectant Christian missionaries but would have seemed perfectly natural to any Hindu. Cf. F. W. Buckle, "A New Interpretation of Akbar's 'Infallibility Decree' of 1579," *Journal of the Royal Asiatic Society* (1924), pp. 590–608; M. L. Roychourdouri, *The State and Religion in Mughal India* (Calcutta: Indian Publicity Society, 1951), pp. 67–118 and *passim;* Sri Ram Sharma, *The Religious Policy of the Mughal Emperors* (Oxford University Press, 1940), pp. 15–69; Arnulf Camps, *Jerome Xavier S.J. and the Muslims of the Mogul Empire* (Schöneck-Beckenried, Switzerland: *Nouvelle Revue de Science Missionaire*, 1957), pp. 51–91; Aziz Ahmad, "Akbar, Hérétique ou Apostat?" *Journal Asiatique*, CCXLIX (1961), 21–35.

Yet outward conformity to Sunni orthodoxy did not prevent governmental policy from remaining distinctly noncommittal as between the rival claims of the Sunni and Shi'a *ulema* until the emperor Aurangzeb (1659–1707) militantly espoused the Sunni cause. His armies overthrew the Shi'a rulers of southern India, thus bringing the Mogul empire to its greatest territorial extent. Yet in the long run Aurangzeb's religious enthusiasm weakened the empire, for his attacks upon Hindu idolatry roused a widespread guerrilla in central India; while the Moslem community had become so bitterly divided between Sunni and Shi'a as to be no longer able to act in concert against the Hindu challenge.[63]

Azerbaijan, Persia, and Iraq were most strongly affected by the Shi'a revolution; for in these lands Ismail and his followers made a serious effort to remodel society according to their religious principles. Difficulties quickly arose when they set out to organize their new regime, for like many another revolutionary before and since, the Safavids soon discovered that raw sectarian enthusiasm was by itself an inadequate basis for government. Ismail therefore assembled learned doctors of the Shi'a law from the odd corners of the Moslem world where they had found refuge and proceeded to employ them (as the Ottoman sultans had employed Sunni jurists under somewhat analogous circumstances almost two centuries before) to define the rules by which his followers and subjects ought to live. Religious rivals, including Sufi brotherhoods, dervish orders, and of course all Sunni religious institutions were rigorously suppressed—an action quite as drastic as the nearly simultaneous suppression of the monasteries in Protestant Europe. Not surprisingly, it proved easier for the court and the Shi'a doctors to agree upon what should be suppressed than upon details of positive doctrine. The shahs were reluctant to surrender any of their prerogative, even to men of religion; and Shi'a purists found it hard to forgive the remaining imperfections of even the most sympathetic regime. Quarrels with the court, however, only reinforced the energy with which Shi'a propagandists of the "Twelver" persuasion sought to indoctrinate the population in the principles of their faith.[64] Acquiring a reputation for miraculous powers and familiarity with God's will, these Shi'a doctors

[63] Personal religious belief may, as in Akbar's case, have entered into the determination of Aurangzeb's policy. Yet it is worth pointing out that, by the time he came to the throne of India, the Ottoman power was in disarray, so that Aurangzeb could hope to displace the sultan as principal head of the entire Sunni community. Aurangzeb's conquests in southern India at the expense of unbelievers and heretics clearly qualified him for the role of authentic caliph and commander of the faithful and may have been undertaken in part for this very reason. He was in fact accorded this title by learned jurists even outside his political dominion. H. A. R. Gibb and Harold Bowen, *Islamic Society and the West*, Vol. I, Part I, p. 35. Cf. also the excellent and penetrating essay by Aziz Ahmad, "Moghulindien und Dar-al-Islam," *Saeculum*, XII (1961), 266–90; John Norman Hollister, *The Shi'a of India* (London: Luzac & Co., 1953), pp. 126–40.

[64] Simplified handbooks of doctrine played the role of the "shorter catechisms" in the Christian churches of western Europe. For an account of Shi'a theological literature and paraphrase of a typical doctrinal handbook, cf. E. G. Browne, *History of Persian Literature* (Cambridge: Cambridge University Press, 1920), IV, 368–411.

ISLAM IN THE SEVENTEENTH CENTURY

These miniatures were painted at the court of the Mogul emperor Jahangir (1605–27). On the left, Jahangir is shown embracing the Safavi shah, while beneath their feet the lion and the lamb lie down together. The artist thus celebrated a politic and passing reconciliation of the Sunni-Shi'a, Indian-Iranian rivalries. On the right, the emperor is shown seated on his throne, receiving a book (the Koran?) from a Moslem man of religion in the presence of two Europeans and a Hindu. The prayerful attitude of the dark, bearded European indicates perhaps that he has come to seek permission to trade (or some other favor) from the mighty Moslem ruler of India.

attained great influence over the people at large, until their opinions came to constitute a fairly effective check upon the actions of the shah himself.[65]

Secular administration and military organization evolved more slowly. Not until the time of Shah Abbas the Great was the tribal basis of Ismail's army[66] and government supplemented and counterbalanced by the creation of a standing army, recruited mainly from Georgian and Armenian converts to Islam on the model of the Ottoman Janissary corps.[67]

The drastic reforms carried out by the Safavids had no counterpart in either the Ottoman or the Mogul empires. Sunni orthodoxy had long reconciled itself to religious heterodoxy; and no popular movement of Sunni fanaticism arose to sustain a religious revolution such as that which transformed the Persian scene in the sixteenth century. Heterodox dervish orders were too firmly interwoven with the fabric of the Ottoman state to be safely suppressed;[68] and after the revolt and massacres of 1514, the Shi'a, so far as they survived in Ottoman territories, took their traditional refuge by conforming outwardly to Sunni observances. With open provocation thus removed, the complaisant temper of the Sunni community made drastic counter-reformation like that just starting in Catholic Europe out of the question. The Ottoman sultans, therefore, contented themselves with administrative precautions. Suleiman the Lawgiver (1520–66) perfected and extended the hierarchical organization of the *ulema* of the empire, subsidized Sunni educational institutions, and generally put the weight of the government squarely behind a more strictly conceived Sunni orthodoxy. As a result of his careful legislation, the religious and political institutions of the Ottoman empire attained a form which endured virtually unchanged for more than two centuries.[69]

Mogul institutions attained a comparable definition under the emperor Akbar (1556–1605). Akbar organized his court and central administration along Persian lines but allowed local custom to prevail in village and town. He permitted some Hindu clan and territorial lords—the "Rajputs"—to exercise local jurisdiction; but Moslems remained heavily preponderant in the higher administration. Religious diversity within the empire remained a delicate

---

[65] Unless one discounts the language of his Turki poems, Ismail appears to have claimed that he was, as the Turkish tribesmen who rallied to his banners probably believed him to be, nothing less than God incarnate. This, however, was not the official "Twelver" view, which held that the Safavids were merely descendants of the seventh of the twelve legitimate imams, and as such presumptively a bit closer to God than ordinary men. Cf. Hans Robert Roemer, "Die Safawiden," *Saeculum*, IV (1953), 31–33.

[66] Seven Turkish tribes from Azerbaijan constituted the core of the original force.

[67] Sir Percy Sykes, *A History of Persia* (2d ed.; London: Macmillan & Co., 1921), II, 175–76; Laurence Lockhart, *The Fall of the Safgvi Dynasty* (Cambridge: Cambridge University Press, 1958), pp. 18–22. Until Abbas' time, the Persians had lacked artillery and infantry firearms; Abbas secured these advantages through the mediation of European merchants and adventurers, most notably a pair of Englishmen named Robert and Anthony Sherley.

[68] The Janissaries, for example, could be counted upon to defend their spiritual advisers, the Bektashi dervishes; and other dervish orders had similarly strategic affiliations with urban guilds in the capital and with regional communities, especially in Anatolia.

[69] A. H. Lybyer, *The Government of the Ottoman Empire in the Time of Suleiman the Magnificent* (Cambridge, Mass.: Harvard University Press, 1913). Despite the title, H. A. R. Gibb and Harold Bowen, *Islamic Society and the West*, offer by far the best analysis of Ottoman religious policy for this period with which I am acquainted.

A. U. Pope, Introduction to Persian Art. *London: Peter Davies Ltd., 1930.*

A PERSIAN MOSQUE AND MADRASA

These buildings both adorn the city of Isfahan, the Safavi capital. The mosque above was erected in 1621 by Shah Abbas the Great; the madrasa on the left was erected in 1710, proof of the continuing vitality of Persian art until comparatively very recent times. The exterior setting of both buildings is an important part of the whole; indeed Isfahan in its entirety is a garden city designed for the royal pleasure. Numerous reflecting pools, such as that in the foreground on the right, and spacious squares for polo and other public ceremonies like that in front of the mosque attest both their designers' skill and the shah's autocratic power that could so effectively order a new city into existence.

problem. In the seventeenth century, Sufi mysticism and various syncretisms between Hinduism and Islam gained momentum among the poorer classes, who sought in such creeds an escape from the disadvantageous social status accorded them by Hindu doctrine. The enormous gap between these lower-class Moslems and the thin layer of officials and soldiers surrounding the emperors helps to explain the failure of Aurangzeb's effort to confine Indian Islam within an official, Sunni mold.[70]

* * *

The religious and political transformations of Islam consequent upon the Shi'a revolt involved some drastic changes in Moslem high culture. In literature, Persian poetry dried up at its source; for an intolerant fanaticism could not be reconciled with the delicate sensuousness and religious ambiguity of classical Persian poetry. Familiarity with the great Persian poets and imitation of their style remained an essential ingredient of every Ottoman and Mogul gentleman's education; but when it came to original compositions, courtly poetasters allowed verbal cleverness and ornate clichés to supplant the authentic subtlety of their models.

The decay of Persian letters was compensated for in some measure by the literary development of Turkish (both in its Ottoman and central Asian forms) and of Urdu—a Persianate Hindi used at the Mogul court. As vehicles for poetry, these newer literary languages were heavily influenced by Persian prototypes; but some Turkish prose, for example the delightful memoirs of Babur, comes like a breath of fresh air amid cobwebs of conventional verbosity.[71]

The rise of great imperial Moslem courts in Turkey, Persia, and India meant a more stable and lavish patronage for architects and luxury craftsmen of all sorts: painters, calligraphers, carpet makers, and others. Although much of the product of this latest age of Islamic artistic greatness has disappeared, enough remains to give an overwhelming impression of splendor and elegance, extraordinary workmanship, and brilliant coloring. Painting, of course, was religiously suspect and ranked for Moslems among the minor arts; but in the sixteenth and seventeenth centuries, court painters in both Persia and India tended to emancipate themselves from their traditional roles as manuscript illuminators and bathroom muralists and branched out into portraiture, historical and even religious (!) scene painting. Stimulus from China and from Europe may have assisted this development; at any rate, both Chinese landscape motifs and European linear perspective became familiar to Moslem court artists and found imitators among them. But the painters who played

[70] Cf. Jadunath Sarkar, *Mughal Administration* (Calcutta: M. C. Sarkar & Sons, 1920); W. H. Moreland, *India at the Death of Akbar* (London: Macmillan & Co., 1920), pp. 31–94; R. C. Majumdar et al., *Advanced History of India* (London: Macmillan & Co., 1958), pp. 554–65; J. N. Hollister, *The Shi'a of India*, passim.

[71] These memoirs are translated into English by Annette S. Beveridge (4 vols.; London: Luzac & Co., 1912–21). On Turkish and Urdu literatures cf. the perhaps overenthusiastic descriptions and extensive translations in E. J. W. Gibb, *A History of Ottoman Poetry*, II, III (London: Luzac & Co., 1902, 1904); Ram Babu Saksena, *A History of Urdu Literature* (Allahabad: Ram Narain Lal, 1940).

with these importations did not surrender a stylistic integrity of their own, in which brilliant colors and a lavish wealth of minute detail united to produce a gorgeous and eye-entrancing result.

Architecture remained the great art of Islam during the sixteenth and seventeenth centuries; and a burst of building activity ran all across the Moslem world as the rulers of the new empires sought to commemorate their piety and greatness in stone. Persian and Mogul buildings sometimes attained extraordinary refinement and beauty, both in detail and in general plan. The Taj Mahal of India, built for the emperor Jahan between 1632 and 1653, and the royal mosque of Isfahan, built for Shah Abbas the Great some two decades earlier, are world-famous examples of the skill and taste of the architects and craftsmen these rulers gathered around them. Persian and Indian buildings were often set in the midst of formal gardens constructed around reflecting pools and adorned with cypresses and flowers. Such gardens offered islands of coolness, color, and elegance in hot and dusty landscapes and were as integral to the total work of art as the building itself. Ottoman architecture was characteristically more solid and severe and carried on Byzantine structural traditions. This meant emphasis upon an enclosed interior, whether for mosque or palace; whereas the Persian and more particularly the Indian styles tended to concentrate decorative and dramatic effects upon the exterior and the setting. Constantinople's comparatively severe climate thus conspired with the severity of Sunni orthodoxy to sustain a monumental and massive architectural style in Ottoman lands which contrasts strikingly with the more splendid but almost effeminate elegance of Persian and Mogul buildings.[72]

Anyone who acquaints himself with Moslem art of the sixteenth and seventeenth centuries, reflects upon the variety of the court cultures each substyle mirrors forth, and recognizes both the intermingling of Persian, Turkish, Arab, Hindu, Chinese, and European elements and the successful syntheses of distinctive art styles from such diversity will not easily believe that Moslem culture and civilization were in a stage of decay from 1500 onward. Moslem literature, dominated in belles-lettres by an admiration for word play and freighted down with a heavy mass of theological and legal lore enlivened only by venomous recrimination between Sunni and Shi'a doctors, is certainly less attractive to a Western taste; yet here, too, the rise of new vernaculars as literary media may perhaps be taken as a sign of continuing capacity for growth.

Indeed, by any standard except the only one that mattered—the standard set by the contemporary growth of European civilization—Islam was in a flourishing condition; and as the acerbity of religious conflict faded away

[72] On Moslem art of this period I have consulted: E. B. Havell, *Indian Architecture from the First Mohammedan Invasion to the Present Day* (London: John Murray, 1913); Heinrich Glück and Ernst Diez, *Die Kunst des Islam* (Berlin: Propyläen-Verlag, 1925); Arthur Upham Pope, *An Introduction to Persian Art* (London: Peter Davies, 1930); Arthur U. Pope (ed.), *A Survey of Persian Art* (6 vols.; London: Oxford University Press, 1938-39); Sir Thomas W. Arnold, *Painting in Islam* (Oxford: Clarendon Press, 1928); Percy Brown, *Indian Painting under the Mughals* (Oxford: Clarendon Press, 1924); L. A. Mayer, *Islamic Architects and Their Works* (Geneva: Albert Kundig, 1956); Hermann Goetz, *Bilderatlas zur Kulturgeschichte Indiens in der Grossmogulzeit* (Berlin: Dietrich Reimer & Ernst Vohsen, 1930).

A PERSIAN CARPET AND AN INDIAN WINDOW

The delicate tracery and precise decoration of these two sixteenth-century examples of Moslem art show an amazing refinement, the product of centuries of skilled workmanship. On this level of elegance, Europe of the sixteenth and seventeenth centuries still lagged perceptibly behind.

during the seventeenth century, Moslems could legitimately feel that they had successfully weathered the storms that at the beginning of the sixteenth century had threatened their society from within and from without. The result was sublime smugness vis-à-vis the world of unbelievers, European or otherwise, and at home an adamant conservatism bent upon discarding all novelties.

The basically backward-looking character of Islamic law and piety certainly predisposed the Moslem world to such rigidity. Yet the harsh collision between Shi'a and Sunni in the sixteenth century may have fastened Moslem minds more strongly to ancient formulae of truth and encouraged the neglect of those elements in the Islamic intellectual heritage which might have permitted them more nearly to keep pace with Europe's extraordinary series of cultural and economic revolutions.[73] Something like the spirit of the Italian Renaissance had been abroad in the courts of Mohammed the Conqueror[74] and Akbar; but Selim the Grim and Suleiman the Lawgiver undertook to suppress dangerous thoughts in the Ottoman empire; and Aurangzeb attempted to do the same in India. Suleiman was so far successful that no revival of the inquiring, innovating spirit which in seventeenth-century Europe gave birth to modern literature and science ever occurred in the Ottoman empire (or in any other Moslem state). Herein, far more than in the loss of middlemen's profits from the spice trade, lay the central failure of Islam in modern times.

The social structure of the Islamic world contributed powerfully to this result. New notions found uncongenial soil in states built upon a small class of officials and soldiers raised far above a tax-burdened peasantry. The servility of townsmen toward officials and landlords had been a persistent feature of Middle Eastern society from the second millennium B.C.; and the Ottoman and Mogul empires, by the very splendor of their imperial organization, confirmed this social pattern. Only in the Safavid empire, where propaganda on behalf of Shi'a doctrines brought a limited popular element into the political balance and where the survival of Turkish tribalism counterpoised the royal bureaucracy, did politics achieve a somewhat broader social base.

The sixteenth-century religious split in Islam between Sunni and Shi'a did not create this dominant sociological character in Islam. Nonetheless, by impelling the sultans to a more vigorous espousal of Sunni orthodoxy, it may have helped to widen the gap between rulers and townsmen. In the Ottoman em-

[73] The dreadful abyss of religious uncertainty which had briefly confronted the Sunni community of Islam was escaped by institutional rather than intellectual invention. Having balked at meeting the intellectual challenge of heresy by anything more than bald reaffirmation of the past, a paralyzing precedent inhibited any more constructive response to subsequent intellectual challenges. More than that, most pious and educated Sunni Moslems came to feel that an uncritical acceptance of religious truth was the only safe intellectual posture—and the more uncritical the better. But in the absence of controversy, intellectual vigor rapidly died away in the Ottoman empire; and the *ulema* became less and less perfect masters even of their own intellectual inheritance. Such intellectual flabbiness was a high price to pay for the protection of Sunni orthodoxy against the challenge of heresy. Interestingly, Moslem intellectual energy remained distinctly higher in Persia and India, where religious controversy, particularly in India, remained strong.

[74] Cf. Abdulah Adnan-Adwar, "Interaction of Islamic and Western Thought in Turkey," in T. Cuyler Young (ed.), *Near Eastern Culture and Society* (Princeton, N.J.: Princeton University Press, 1951), pp. 121–22.

pire, at any rate, artisans and tradesmen tended in the seventeenth and eighteenth centuries toward various forms of religious heterodoxy; and the dervish orders, divorced as they were from state-endowed educational institutions and from Moslem higher learning, became more and more imbued with vulgar superstition and thaumaturgy.[75]

By driving a wedge between the Sunni establishment and ordinary townsmen and commoners, the repression of the Shi'a revolution contributed to this result. Thus in this respect, as well as in its more immediate political and cultural consequences, the Shi'a-Sunni split constituted the central feature of Islamic history in the seventeenth and eighteenth centuries. By comparison, the collision with Europe remained merely marginal.

2. THE SUBJECT RELIGIOUS COMMUNITIES IN THE MOSLEM WORLD

HINDU INDIA AND BUDDHIST SOUTHEAST ASIA. Despite the political eclipse of Hinduism in the sixteenth century, the overwhelming majority of Hindus remained faithful to their ancestral religion and way of life. Ordinary villagers and townsmen were scarcely affected by the Mogul conquest and simply treated the Moslems among them as one more caste. The royal government's principal point of contact with the populace—its revenue-collecting branch—was largely staffed by Hindus, who alone were familiar with the intricacies of traditional land systems and tax registers. Moreover, in many regions Hindu nobles retained their properties; and, as we have seen, the emperor Akbar even admited Rajputs into his official military and administrative hierarchy. Hence the Moslem political domination of India did not seriously interfere with the continuance of Hindu life in all its immemorial antiquity.

Nevertheless, the transfer of political power to an alien religious group tended to impoverish Hindu high culture. The construction of Hindu temples, for example, had been financed by state revenues and therefore came to a halt wherever Moslems took over the government. Only in the far south, where Moslem political control was never more than nominal, did some architectural activity continue. Moreover, the Hindu upper classes tended to acquire a veneer of the Persianate culture of their Moslem overlords, even while remaining true to their own religion. Rajput painting was the most distinguished product of this cultural blending; for Persian artistic techniques applied to the portrayal of Hindu gods and heroes soon produced an art stylistically distinct from its prototype and endowed with a real charm of its own.

As we have seen before, religious syncretism between the Hindu and the Moslem traditions long antedated the Mogul conquests. The Sikhs, the most important of the sects which sought to reconcile the two faiths in a higher revelation, underwent a remarkable transformation in the seventeenth century. Their canon of sacred writings was officially closed in 1604. Soon thereafter, the Sikh leaders fell afoul of the Mogul authorities; and the community took to arms with such effect that, as the imperial power disintegrated during the eighteenth century, the Sikhs emerged as the most important heir to the Moguls in the Punjab. Yet this success was dearly bought; for the transforma-

[75] Gibb and Bowen, *Islamic Society*, I, Part II, 179–206.

tion of the Sikh community into a warrior state meant in effect the renunciation of the universalist ambition of earlier Sikh teachers. The polymorphous piety of the Hindu tradition and the elaborate legal prescriptions of Islam could not be reduced to the slender thread of obedience to the Sikh *gurus,* no matter how impressively their teaching was validated by success in battle.

Far more significant for the Hindu community at large were popular religious and literary movements that resisted doctrinal definition but induced a powerful emotional exaltation among their adherents. Before 1500, the vast variety of local Hindu observances had existed for the most part on a simple customary level, with little in the way of formal literary expression or definition. The ancient learning of the Brahmins, while never abandoned, had little meaning for the unlearned, to whom Sanskrit was unintelligible; and Brahminical pretensions to social privilege, based upon the Sanskrit tradition, did not always win an easy acquiescence among the low-born castes. In the sixteenth century, however, Hinduism underwent a vital reformation. Holy men and poets not only relocated the foci of popular piety, but also brought the vernacular tongues of northern India to a literary expression and used these languages as vehicles for a vastly intensified religious aspiration. Hinduism thereby secured an emotional power which has assured its continued hold upon the loyalties of the great majority of Indians down to the present time.

Three men stood out in this development: the saint and revivalist Chaitanya (d. 1534), and the Hindi poets Tulsi Das (d. 1627) and Sur Das (d. 1563). The writings of the poets and the sect which gathered around the charismatic figure of Chaitanya agreed in concentrating a highly emotional devotion upon one particular divine incarnation, although they differed in their choices from among the myriad incarnations available in traditional Hindu mythology.

Chaitanya was an unusual figure, even in the context of the Indian ascetic tradition. In early manhood, under the stress of extraordinary personal experience of the power and glory of Krishna, he abandoned the Brahminical life to which he had been born and became an itinerant holy man. His easy ecstasy and utter emotional abandon, expressed through violent physical contortions and endless ejaculations of praise, gave unfriendly critics good reason to think him mad; but the crowds which gathered in his presence saw instead a man who actually embodied the divinity he worshipped. God in the flesh was no common thing, even in India; and the religious excitement generated among Chaitanya's followers wiped out caste and other social distinctions and imparted to them a poignant sense of the immediacy of divinity.[76]

---

[76] Chaitanya was active principally in Bengal, where in his time a variety of formerly primitive peoples were in process of being folded into the Indian body social. Such tribes were usually assigned places very near the bottom of the Hindu caste hierarchy, being ritually unclean in some of their customs. This had made possible the success of Islam in Bengal before Chaitanya's time; but the movement that sprang up around him effectively stopped the progress of Islam in those parts. Men who had once experienced the emotional surge of crowd excitement when confronted by deity in the flesh were bound to find the ritual and creed of Islam, even in its Sufi forms, a pallid and unsatisfactory substitute. And because caste distinctions were vigorously repudiated among Chaitanya's followers in the early phases of the movement, one of Islam's chief appeals was radically undercut.

Cf. the manner in which the victory of monastic and popular piety in the Hesychast controversy within Orthodox Christianity checked the progress of Islam in the Balkans, discussed above, p. 522.

The poet Tulsi Das, on the other hand, directed all his devotion to another divine incarnation, Rama, and wrote voluminously of the deeds and glories of his hero. Although he quarried most of his material from the *Ramayana,* his poems were far more than mere translations from Sanskrit into Hindi. He edited and elaborated the episodes he selected, always seeking to enhance the divine element in the God-man he glorified. The poems of Tulsi Das became widely popular and of enormous importance for the moral and religious education of later generations of Hindus.

In a very similar manner, Sur Das took the myths of Krishna's childhood, particularly the episodes of his youthful love-making among the milkmaids, and turned them into allegories of divine love for mankind. In later life, Sur Das enjoyed an entree to Akbar's court; and his religious thought and feeling closely resembled the ambiguous interpenetration of divine and carnal love that had long pervaded Persian poetry and Sufi mysticism. Perhaps partly because of this foreign taint, his influence upon subsequent Hindu religious sensibility was less strong than that of Tulsi Das.

According to Hindu tradition, both Rama and Krishna were *avatars* of Vishnu; and Chaitanya was accepted by his followers as yet another incarnation of the same deity. Thus the groups which arose under the influence of Chaitanya and the two great Hindi poets were doctrinally quite compatible; for each could assert that in fact they all worshipped the same divine reality though in different manifestations. Yet each group, by focusing almost exclusive attention upon its chosen form of the deity, did in practice build up a distinct sect, with a liturgy and literature of its own, and relegated other dimensions of the variegated Hindu heritage to the background. Shiva lost some of his following; and the various Tantric magic spells and modes for compelling divine assistance tended to melt away in the white heat of personal devotion to and identification with a very human, yet at the same time an utterly divine being, whether invoked by the name of Rama, Krishna, or Chaitanya.

To each of these sects, Brahminical learning and piety were largely irrelevant. Nonetheless, the ancient Sanskrit tradition persisted and was held in high respect by all except Chaitanya's followers; and Brahmins were still employed for family ceremonies at birth, marriage, death, and all the other crises of ordinary life. Yet because the treasures of Sanskrit learning were closed to the great majority, Hinduism as a working religious system came to center about the new vernacular devotional literature and around family ceremonies, public processions, and other festive manifestations of religious devotion.[77]

This evolution rendered popular Hinduism proof against the charms and criticisms of Islam. The warmth and color of a religion built around a God-

[77] Cf. K. B. Jindal, *A History of Hindi Literature* (Allahabad: Kitab Mahal, 1955), pp. 52–155; Dinesh Chandra Sen, *History of Bengali Language and Literature* (Calcutta: University of Calcutta, 1911), pp. 398–565; F. E. Keay, *A History of Hindi Literature* (Calcutta: Association Press, 1920), pp. 19–72; Surendranath Dasgupta, *A History of Indian Philosophy* (Cambridge: Cambridge University Press, 1922–55), IV, 384–95; Melville T. Kennedy, *The Chaitanya Movement* (Calcutta: Association Press, 1925).

ALLAH

MOHAMMED

SIKHS

DERVISH

MOGUL EMPEROR

ULEMA

BRAHMAN

CHAITANYA SUR DAS TULSI DAS

ISLAM

HINDUISM

THE REVIVAL OF HINDUISM

man, with whom, in moments of religious exaltation, the poor and insignificant as well as the rich and powerful might feel personal identification, scarcely needed the prop of formal theology. The vivid, personal experience of millions, sustained and indeed generated in vast public ceremonies usually held out-of-doors, had a validity of its own. Neither the rigidity of Brahminical lore nor the routine of temple ritual confined Hinduism any longer; popular piety was rescued from the triviality and occasional sordidness of its Tantric manifestations. Men who had once had personal and direct experience of the Living God of Hinduism, clothed in whatever form, were thereafter immune to Moslem, Christian, or any other alien religious propaganda. Hinduism thus escaped the decay and disruption which had overtaken Indian Buddhism some five hundred years earlier.

But no such transformation invigorated Hinduism overseas; and Islam therefore supplanted the Shaivite cults of southeast Asia, save in the remote island of Bali. Buddhism, on the contrary, survived in Ceylon, Burma, and

Siam. From ancient times Ceylon had been the seat of an especially holy Buddhist shrine; and the metropolitan role of the temple at Candy in relation to the Buddhism of all southeast Asia may have helped to maintain the faith in Ceylon. More important was the fact that Buddhism became a palladium of Singhalese cultural identity, as opposed to the Hindu faith of Tamil intruders from the Indian mainland. Similar forces acted to preserve Buddhism in Burma and Siam, for those peoples were attached to their religion by the very fact that it set them apart from the Moslem communities besetting their borders. The appearance of European traders and missionaries introduced a new and disturbing element into Burmese, and more spectacularly, into Siamese affairs. But after a period of imperial expansion and mutual rivalry in the sixteenth century, both countries retreated inward upon themselves, restricted contacts with foreigners, and sought by a policy of isolation to minimize the pressures Moslems and Europeans had begun to exert upon them.[78]

CHRISTIANS UNDER MOSLEM RULE. Only small encapsulated communities of Syriac and Coptic Christians survived into the sixteenth century in the heartlands of Islam. Living as peasants in remote hill regions or confined to special occupations in the cities, they played a very minor role in Ottoman society. Much larger Christian communities survived in Georgia, Armenia, and the Balkan Peninsula. Georgia maintained political autonomy under native princes, who fluctuated precariously between Ottoman and Persian suzerainties; and until the later part of the seventeenth century, Transylvania and the Rumanian provinces of Moldavia and Wallachia were often only nominally subject to Ottoman control; but the Armenians of Anatolia as well as the Greeks and Slavs of the Balkans submitted to the regular Ottoman administration. This did not imply complete loss of autonomy, however, for the prelates of the Greek, Serbian, and Armenian churches performed many of the functions which in western Europe were reserved to governments. Christian ecclesiastics adjudicated disputes among their coreligionists when village custom did not suffice; they also served as intermediaries between the Christian community and the Ottoman authorities. Tax farmers, many of whom were Christian, represented a second major link between Ottoman officialdom and the Christian subject population.

Commercial agriculture became increasingly important in the Balkans during the seventeenth century. Cotton, tobacco, wheat, and maize were the staples of this tillage; and the traditional patterns of peasant cultivation were forcibly modified, especially in the fertile plains of the eastern half of the

---

[78] Siam withdrew from the world only after an extraordinary episode of flirtation with the French. A Greek adventurer, who went by the name of Phaulcon, played the central role in this affair. A native of the island of Cephalonia, he had come to the East in the service of the British East India Company but later transferred his allegiance to the French and became a Roman Catholic convert. In Siam he gained the confidence of the king and for a few years almost controlled Siamese foreign policy. He used his position to bring a French force of soldiers and missionaries to Siam, and for a while hopes were high in the court of King Louis XIV that the entire kingdom of Siam would shortly be converted to Christianity. A palace coup d'état cost Phaulcon his life in 1688, and soon thereafter the French withdrew. Cf. W. A. R. Wood, *A History of Siam* (London: T. Fisher Unwin, 1926), pp. 189–216; D. G. E. Hall, *A History of South East Asia*, pp. 297–315.

Balkans, by agricultural entrepreneurs who were interested in maximizing their money income from the land. In general, commercial farming seems notably to have increased the landlords' share of the total crop yield, while hurting peasant interests.[79]

A second change of vital importance to the Christian peasantry was the discontinuance after 1638 of the Ottoman practice of recruiting Christian boys as slaves to be trained for positions in the sultan's official household and army. This meant the end of a form of tribute that peasant families had often resented. But for Ottoman society as a whole it implied a disastrous loss of social mobility. In consequence, the gap between Christian and Moslem, landlord and peasant, village and town, widened markedly in the seventeenth century and thereafter. As long as all the state officials of the Ottoman empire were men who had spent the first twelve to twenty years of their lives in Christian villages, and who regularly retained a certain distant sympathy for their former nation and faith,[80] administrative policy could not reflect solely the interests of the Moslem landlord and urban groups of society. When, on the contrary, the armed forces and officialdom came to be recruited from sons of Moslems, and mainly among sons of those already within the administrative or military hierarchy, no such restraint applied. The Christian peasantry became fair game for oppression, both within and outside the law. Restless and energetic peasant boys who in earlier times might have risen to high office in the state were driven into banditry; and a sullen, if normally repressed hostility between Christian peasant and Moslem master, which had been conspicuously absent from earlier Ottoman history, began to divide and weaken the society as a whole. This perhaps more than any other single factor undermined and eventually destroyed the Ottoman polity; but its effects only began to appear in the seventeenth century.

Cultural creativity reached low ebb among the Christians of the Ottoman empire in the sixteenth and seventeenth centuries. Ecclesiastical dignitaries and the handful of urban merchants, bankers, and tax farmers who constituted the leaders of the Christian populations remained in general content with the privileges assigned to them by the Ottoman regime. Indeed, they often rivaled Turkish landlords and officials in oppressing their fellow Christians. Echoes of the religious controversies which so agitated western Christendom in the Reformation period were faintly felt among the Orthodox. But long-standing popular prejudices against the Latin heretics reinforced the

---

[79] The change meant a radical decay of military landholding and a corresponding shrinkage of the Turkish cavalry contingent in Ottoman armies. The new landlords were Moslems, mostly of urban background, who owed their estates, typically, to some personal connection with strategically placed officials. The legality of many titles was distinctly suspect. Cf. Richard Busch-Zantner, *Agraverfassung, Gesellschaft und Siedlung in Sudosteuropa* (Leipzig: Otto Harrassowitz, 1938), p. 63; Jovan Cvijic, *La Péninsule balkanique: géographie humaine* (Paris: A. Colin, 1918); L. S. Stavrianos, *The Balkans since 1453* (New York: Rinehart, 1958), pp. 138–42; Traian Stoianovich, "Land Tenure and Related Sectors of the Balkan Economy, 1600–1800," *Journal of Economic History*, XIII (1953), 398–411.

[80] The Grand Vizier Mohammed Sokolli, who governed the Ottoman empire from 1560 to 1579, used his authority to re-establish the Serbian patriarchate of Ipek and appointed his brother to be the first occupant of the new office.

moral and intellectual indifference of corrupt intriguers who dominated the official hierarchy of the Orthodox church in an age when office was openly purchased from the sultan or his grand vizier. Hence the efforts of the patriarch Cyril Loukaris to fight Catholicism more effectively by reforming Orthodoxy in a Calvinist direction were successfully checked when his opponents persuaded the sultan to execute him on a trumped-up charge (1638). Thereafter, the leaders of the Greek church concentrated on cultivating the favor of the Ottoman authorities by spurning everything Western as heretical.

Yet while the urban cultural traditions of Balkan Christians stagnated in this fashion, a vigorous peasant culture flourished in the mountainous wild west of the peninsula, where cycles of heroic balladry told of the defeat of the Serbian chivalry at Kossovo (1389) and the deeds of outlaw Robin Hoods. But Balkan Christians produced practically nothing on a more sophisticated level, either in literature, art, or scholarship. Only a few monasteries preserved some tatters of past Byzantine, Serbian, and Bulgarian splendors in the form of neglected libraries and decaying churches.[81]

JEWS IN MOSLEM LANDS. The sixteenth century appears to have been something of a golden age for Ottoman Jewry. Many Jews found refuge in the Ottoman empire from the persecution of the Spanish and Portuguese governments. Bringing with them not only capital but also mercantile connections and the habit of enterprise, they quickly attained a very prominent place in Ottoman economic life. One of their number, Joseph Nasi, rose high in the confidence of the sultan and played an important role in the finance and diplomacy of the Ottoman government for more than two decades (1553–74).[82]

The seventeenth century, however, brought a sharp setback; for the decline of Ottoman commercial prosperity affected the Jews more directly than it did other communities. Economic hardships in turn provided the background for the extraordinary career of Sabbatai Sevi, whose claim, announced in 1666, to be the long-awaited Messiah stirred frantic excitement among Jews throughout the Ottoman empire as well as beyond its borders. The effect was to discredit all Jews in the eyes of the sultan, who no longer felt confident of their political loyalty. This permitted Greeks and Armenians to take over strategic functions in Ottoman society formerly exercised mainly by Jews. In particular, Christians became the financiers of the Ottoman regime, advancing funds Turkish pashas required for the purchase of office and reaping a rich reward in the form of compound interest, a wide variety of official favors, and profitable tax-farming contracts. Greeks also became the principal interpreters and intermediaries for the Turks in their dealings both with their Christian subjects and with western Europeans. Hence in the second half of the seventeenth century, the bulk of the Jewish community came to consist

[81] The Turks were peculiarly hostile to Christian architectural enterprises and refused as a rule to permit construction of new church buildings. They also obstructed repairs to old structures by requiring official permits.

[82] Cf. Cecil Roth, *The House of Nasi: The Duke of Naxos* (Philadelphia: Jewish Publication Society of America, 1949).

of depressed traders, distressed artisans, distrusted bankers, and discarded dragomen. Little indeed was left of the favored and powerful position their forefathers had enjoyed.[83]

3. THE FAR EAST

CHINA.   From the vantage point of Peking, the "south sea barbarians" from Europe who began to appear sporadically in the ports of southern China from 1513, and set up a permanent base at Macao by 1557, were among the least of the concerns that increasingly distracted the Ming imperial majesty. For the central government slowly lost control of the country before being supplanted, in the course of some sixty years (1621–83), by a barbarian conqueror issuing from the Manchurian forests and steppes to the northeast. Such upheavals were scarcely new to China. Indeed, the Manchu conquerors of the seventeenth century were more nearly Sinified before entering China proper than most of their barbarian predecessors had been. Consequently, Chinese life and institutions were less affected than in previous periods of barbarian invasion.

Yet despite the massive continuity of things Chinese, the new regime of the seas, heralded by the first arrival of Portuguese merchants at Canton in 1513, did have important repercussions within Chinese society, and before the close of the seventeenth century, the new maritime contacts had injected ferments into Chinese life which eventually ate deeply into traditional structures. But this was not at once apparent. On the contrary, China in 1700 was again strong and prosperous, its ancient institutions, arts, and customs in good working order.

The transition from Ming to Manchu rule adhered closely to historic precedent, as the usual problems of a long-established Chinese dynasty progressively undermined Ming authority. Heavy and inequitable taxation combined with the fears and ambitions of officials out of favor at court to provoke revolts in the provinces; and the imperial military establishment, while always large and occasionally formidable, lost cohesion when its leaders sank into a morass of court intrigue.[84]

As a natural corollary to such internal weakness, barbarian raids gained momentum. China's ancient enemies, the Mongols and the Manchu tribes of the northeast, were supplemented by Japanese and European sea pirates; and Chinese rebels frequently assisted them both. At the end of the sixteenth century, China's weakness enticed the Japanese, newly united under the war lord Hideyoshi, to follow up local piratical successes with a massive invasion of the mainland. But after seven years of victorious but inconclusive military operations in Korea, Hideyoshi's death (1598) led the Japanese to withdraw. No such fortuitous event forestalled the advance of the Manchus. United

[83] Traian Stoianovich, "The Conquering Balkan Orthodox Merchant," *Journal of Economic History*, XX (1960), 244–48.

[84] For a striking story of how a successful naval commander, who had made a good start toward re-establishing Chinese authority in coastal waters, lost his office and his life through such intrigue, see C. R. Boxer, *South China in the 16th Century, Being the Narratives of Galeote Peireira, Fr. Gaspar da Cruz, Fr. Martin de Rada (1550–77)* (London: Hakluyt Society, 1953), pp. xxvi–xxix.

into a strong confederacy after 1615, they proceeded to overrun Chinese settlements in southern Manchuria (1621) and seized Peking by *coup de main* in 1644. The Manchu armies had entered Peking as allies of a "loyal" Ming general; but once in possession of the capital they refused to acknowledge Ming lordship and proclaimed a new dynasty, the Ch'ing. Not until 1683 were the last champions of the Ming vanquished or persuaded to surrender. Thereafter, peace and order returned to China; and the ground was cleared for a new period of prosperity, security, and stability.

The Manchus re-established Chinese administration for all civil purposes but kept military affairs in their own hands. Field units of the army, known as banners, were stationed at suitable points throughout the empire; and while Manchu soldiers were supplemented by Mongol and by some Chinese troops, the high commanders were all Manchu. Conscious efforts were made to keep the traditions, clothing, and manners of the Manchu soldiery distinct from those of the Chinese; and for some generations, the barbarian vigor and military discipline of the new masters of China permitted them to hold Tibet and Mongolia in awe, if not always in perfect obedience.

All this was strictly conformable to precedent. Every new Chinese dynasty had attempted to police the western and northern borderlands; and all barbarian conquerors had, sooner or later, recognized the advantages of re-establishing a Chinese administration for the Chinese heartland. It was, however, symptomatic of the weakening of the steppe as against the organized armed establishments of civilized states that the Manchus faced a new rival for influence over the steppe nomads: the Russians. Cossack pioneers had extended tentacles of Russian state power throughout the Siberian forests early in the seventeenth century and then sought, not without some success, to extend their influence southward into the steppe lands of central and eastern Asia. But the centers of Russian power were distant; and Russian armies were fully engaged in the West; so after some sparring between the two empires, they agreed by the Treaty of Nerchinsk (1689) to delimit their respective zones of influence in the Far East and to regulate the caravan trade between Siberia and Peking. By this settlement, Outer Mongolia and the central steppe remained a no-man's land. Chinese armies subsequently penetrated deep into central Asia; and by the Treaty of Kiakhta (1727), the Russians were forced to recognize Peking's jurisdiction over these last major strongholds of nomad political power.[85] No earlier Chinese dynasty had ever secured the Chinese frontier against the steppe so successfully.

But strict adherence to traditional methods no longer sufficed to defend China's coasts. Japanese piracy and European sea power were of a far greater magnitude than anything which former Chinese governments had confronted; and a sea empire such as that created off the south China coast by the pirate king Koxinga[86] represented a challenge which the traditional armed estab-

---

[85] Cf. John F. Baddeley, *Russia, Mongolia and China;* Michel N. Pavlovsky, *Chinese-Russian Relations* (New York: Philosophical Library, 1949), pp. 4–41.

[86] Koxinga is the Portuguese transliteration of Cheng Ch'eng Kung (d. 1662). He was the self-appointed champion of the cause of the Ming, and founder of a "piratical" state based on the islands and inlets of the south China coast (especially Fukien) and, after 1662, on Formosa, which he con-

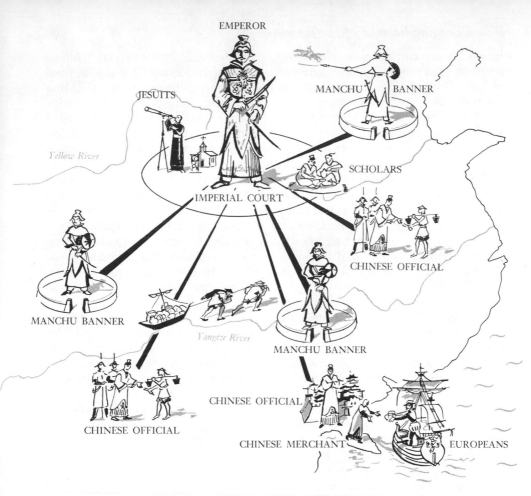

EMPEROR

JESUITS

MANCHU BANNER

Yellow River

SCHOLARS

IMPERIAL COURT

CHINESE OFFICIAL

MANCHU BANNER

Yangtze River

MANCHU BANNER

CHINESE OFFICIAL

CHINESE OFFICIAL

CHINESE MERCHANT

EUROPEANS

CHINA UNDER THE MANCHUS

lishment of China could not easily meet.[87] Divide and rule had, however, long been a central principle of Chinese diplomacy; and by coming gracefully to terms with importunate European sea merchants, both the Ming and the Manchus secured a useful naval counterpoise to local piratical forces.[88] Far

quered from the Dutch just before his death. On Koxinga, see Arthur W. Hummel (ed.), *Eminent Chinese of the Ch'ing Period* (Washington, D.C.: U.S. Government Printing Office, 1943–44, s.v.); Henri Cordier, *Histoire générale de la Chine* (Paris: Paul Genthner, 1920), III, 262–65.

[87] Chinese naval power was sporadically effective, and Chinese war vessels even won some engagements against Portuguese ships, e.g., in 1520–22. But the inveterately land-minded court never sustained naval efforts for long; and a disbanded navy inevitably provided recruits for piratical enterprise, thus confirming the court's worst suspicions. Cf. P. A. Tschepe, *Japans Beziehungen zu China seit den ältesten Zeiten bis zum jahre 1600* (Jentschoufu: Verlag der katolischen Mission, 1907), pp. 216–307.

[88] Macao seems to have been established through an agreement between local Chinese officials and the Portuguese, by which the latter agreed to use their ships against local piracy. Cf. Boxer, *South China in the 16th Century*, pp. xxxv–xxxvi; Tien-tse Chang, *Sino-Portuguese Trade from 1514 to 1644* (Leyden: E. J. Brill, 1934), pp. 86–93.

It is worth noticing that the Chinese agreement with the Russians, formalized by treaty in 1689, and the local and less formal agreements in south China made with Portuguese, Dutch, and British traders conformed essentially to the same pattern. In both cases, the Chinese elected to come to terms

more important in reducing the danger from the sea was the policy of the Japanese government, which became increasingly hostile to the sea rovers who had for more than a century made the Japanese name a terror in the China seas. In 1638 this turn of policy was crowned by a decree which formally prohibited Japanese from leaving the home islands and forbade the construction of seagoing ships. The principal source of manpower and supplies for local piratical enterprise accordingly disappeared; and the Chinese were thereby spared the task of adjusting their traditional armaments to cope with a form of attack for which centuries of concentration upon guarding a land frontier against horse nomads had left them but ill prepared.

Thus largely by chance—for the Japanese decision against sea roving arose from internal political circumstance—and partly by diplomatic guile, the Chinese government was able to reduce the threat from the sea to nuisance level. After 1683, when Koxinga's grandson surrendered Formosa to the Manchus, thus eliminating the last public adherent of the Ming, the sporadic depredations of pirate junks and the occasional depredations of European merchant-pirates could be and were treated as merely local ʼffairs of the south China coast. Until 1759, China's main military strength continued to be directed toward the western borderlands, where the traditional task of subduing and policing nomad societies was pursued in traditional ways but with more than the usual success.

Unlike Genghis Khan's Mongols, the Manchus were quite untainted by contacts with any civilization other than the Chinese. Hence, as they overran China, they assumed with minimal awkwardness the full panoply of Chinese culture. Yet beneath the seemingly unruffled surface, slow and largely unnoticed changes, deriving from European trade and discoveries, began to work within the Chinese body politic. Until long after 1700, these innovations fitted smoothly enough into the edifice of Chinese civilization and far from weakening tended rather to strengthen the empire. European novelties which did not accord easily with Chinese tradition were simply rejected as unworthy of attention.

The most important transformation attributable to the European conquest of the oceans was the introduction of American food crops into China. During the sixteenth and seventeenth centuries, the sweet potato, being tolerant of poor soils and highly productive when intensively cultivated, made it possible to push farmlands up the hillsides and into other marginal areas where rice could not grow.[89] The social effect of this, together with the introduction of other, less valuable new crops (maize, peanuts, tobacco, "Irish" potatoes, and others) was analogous to that which had followed the introduction of early-ripening rice in the eleventh to thirteenth centuries. Large new areas, especially in southern China, could now be cultivated successfully. This in turn sustained the weight of the landlord interest in Chinese

with a more distant force in order to make it possible to bring more immediate, local threats to peace and order under control. From a Chinese viewpoint, therefore, the European toeholds on the south China coast represented nothing more than a standard application of time-honored methods of diplomacy to the perennial problems of border guard.

[89] Cf. Ping-ti Ho, "The Introduction of American Food Plants into China," *American Anthropologist*, LVII (1955), 191–201.

society as a whole—a matter of critical importance in an age when manufacturing and mercantile activity was also markedly on the upgrade.

A second major transformation which became apparent in the latter half of the seventeenth century was the growth of population. American food resources and the pacification of China through the Manchu victories certainly contributed to this growth; probably an enhanced immunity to epidemic disease did likewise. By 1600, the population of China stood at about 150 million, two-and-a-half times what it had been at the beginning of the Ming period (1368). Although the prolonged political disturbances and warfare of the seventeenth century led to population decline, most of the loss had been made good by 1700, when the total population of China again reached about 150 million.[90]

Chinese trade and manufactures also expanded during the sixteenth and seventeenth centuries. Chinese exports found new markets in Europe and the Americas (via the Philippines); and in some trades at least, e.g., porcelain manufacture, something like mass production for the overseas market was organized. An influx of Mexican silver relieved China's long-standing shortage of metals for coinage. These developments enriched a few Chinese merchants and must have enlarged the artisan class; yet they brought no perceptible change in the social status of either group. As long as agriculture expanded *pari passu* with urbanism, there was nothing to upset the ancient subordination of merchant and artisan to the landowning and official class; and all Chinese tradition, government policy, and even the ultimate values cherished by the townsmen themselves tended to sustain this social hierarchy.

*   *   *

Chinese cultural activity accurately mirrored the vigorous stability of Chinese society at large. Novelties, so long as they fitted smoothly into existing patterns of thought and sensibility, were welcomed eagerly, whether they sprang from the city streets, as did the picaresques prose tales that found lodgment in Chinese literary culture in the seventeenth century, or from the European barbarians, as did much interesting new mathematical, astronomical, and geographical information. Some Chinese painters also experimented with European linear perspective and chiaroscuro; and imperial courtiers much admired the chiming clocks and other mechanical toys Jesuit missionaries in Peking distributed as gifts.

Yet these manifestations of interest in things foreign were remarkably sterile of consequences. Alien thoughts and techniques remained no more than piquant curiosities, quite incapable of disturbing the complacency with which educated Chinese viewed their cultural inheritance. The main task, after all, was to sustain that high heritage by faithful adherence to the ancients, whether in art or in scholarship. Neo-Confucianism remained the official doctrine of the state; and although the literati differed strenuously among themselves upon points of Confucian interpretation, all agreed that the

---

[90] Such estimates are subject to wide margins of error, and scholars have arrived at widely divergent conclusions. I follow Ping-ti Ho, *Studies on the Population of China, 1368–1953* (Cambridge, Mass.: Harvard University Press, 1959), pp. 10, 264–66.

major effort should be to get closer to the "Han classics" by stripping off Buddhist and Taoist accretions. Such self-conscious archaism[91] scarcely constituted a break with the Neo-Confucian ideal; it merely restricted somewhat the boldness of earlier interpretations of the classics by concentrating attention upon careful analysis of words and their meanings.[92]

By 1700, therefore, European commercial, military, and missionary pressures upon the traditional Chinese style of life had been successfully contained within the restored imperial fabric of the Middle Kingdom. Intellectual challenges inherent in the new breadth of the ecumene had been largely passed by; China's political problem had been successfully solved along traditional lines; and economic changes seemed only to strengthen and solidify Chinese society.

JAPAN. Despite the survival of a phantom imperial authority, Japan in 1500 was divided into numerous feudal jurisdictions; and civil war was endemic. Warlike communities of monks challenged the power of the clans of professional warriors; and under the leadership of Buddhist sectaries, even ordinary peasants occasionally took successfully to arms. Sea roving, organized by the lords of coastal principalities and by companies of urban adventurers, was the maritime counterpart to this domestic disorder. Pirate bands

[91] The energy with which Chinese scholars of the Ch'ing (Manchu) period sought to purify ancient learning may have been partly motivated by a psychological recoil from the new and unplumbed vistas opened by European learning and science. The identical defense reaction, seeking to repair defects in local cultural armor by an appeal to ancient correctness, took place in Russia under the Patriarch Nikon at exactly the same time; and Siam, Burma, and Japan each reacted to the European pressure in a generally similar fashion—by reasserting the value of their own, ancient, and immemorial culture. The Chinese alone extracted some net gain from such a basically negative and escapist attitude by sharpening the tools of their literary scholarship to a point scarcely equaled by the best European philologists.

[92] J. R. Hightower, *Topics in Chinese Literature* (Cambridge, Mass.: Harvard University Press, 1950), pp. 68–70; Fung Yu-lan, *History of Chinese Philosophy*, II, 592–672; Osvald Sirén, *A History of Later Chinese Painting* (London: The Medici Society, 1938), II, 70–77 and *passim*; Cyrus H. Peake, "Some Aspects of the Introduction of Modern Science into China," *Isis*, XXII (1934–35), 173–77. The role of the Jesuit mission which penetrated China in 1582 and established headquarters at the imperial court itself in 1601 is difficult to assess. On the one hand, members of the mission held high rank in the official hierarchy; and Adam von Schall, who headed the mission from 1640 to 1664, exercised a remarkable personal ascendancy over the first Manchu emperor, who mounted the dragon throne as a mere boy and found in the Jesuit both a friend and mentor. Alfons Väth, *Johann Adam Schall von Bell, S.J., Missionar in China, Kaiserlicher Astronom und Ratgeber am Hofe von Peking, 1592–1666: Ein Lebens und Zeitbild* (Cologne: J. P. Bachem, 1933), p. 192, goes so far as to suggest that von Schall was the real ruler of China from 1651 to 1660, since the emperor himself cared little for statecraft.

Yet for all their entree at court, their usefulness to the government as astronomical, engineering, and mathematical experts, their earnest preaching of Christian doctrine, and their efforts to accommodate Christian practice to Chinese custom, Jesuit ideas and skills seem to have remained merely an exotic curiosity in the eyes of cultivated Chinese and never took root beyond a very small circle. Perhaps traditional education was so well organized that ordinary men had no time to spare for novelties that could not help on the imperial examinations. Cf. Arnold H. Rowbotham, *Missionary and Mandarin: The Jesuits at the Court of China* (Berkeley and Los Angeles, Calif.: University of California Press, 1942). Jesuit critical techniques may have helped to stimulate the "school of Han learning" in its attack upon Buddhist accretions to Confucian texts. Cf. Herrlee G. Creel, *Confucius, the Man and the Myth* (New York: John Day Co., 1949), pp. 258–59. But the relationship may have been rather reversed, with Jesuit missionaries availing themselves of Chinese scholarly attacks upon Buddhist elements in Confucianism as a useful weapon against elements inimical to Christianity in traditional Chinese culture. Cf. Kenneth Scott Latourette, *A History of Christian Missions in China* (New York: Macmillan Co., 1929), pp. 196–97.

spread havoc deep into China, even ascending the Yangtze to besiege Nanking in 1559; and Japanese vessels occasionally penetrated the Indian Ocean. In the course of the sixteenth century, growingly elaborate alliances among the *samurai* clans increased the scale of warfare; and the superior skill and organization of these professional soldiers soon drove the Buddhist monks and their peasant militias from the field. Nor did military consolidation[93] stop with the victory of the *samurai* class, for by 1590 all the military clans had been forced to acknowledge the leadership of a self-made warlord, Hideyoshi (d. 1598). After an interlude when Hideyoshi vainly but stubbornly attempted to expand the Japanese piratical enterprise into full-scale conquest of China, his successors, the Tokugawa shoguns, eliminated the only remaining locus of independent military strength by outlawing seafaring and prohibiting shipbuilding (1626–28).

Peace and order thus returned to Japan. A great burst of economic prosperity followed, which, ironically, permitted the merchant classes to regain much of what they had earlier lost on the battlefield. The *samurai*, deprived of their occupation by the new peace, devoted themselves to extravagance and fell hopelessly into debt. Financiers and merchants in turn used their wealth to support a middle-class urban culture, which was both vigorous and sensuous and stood in self-conscious opposition to the austere code of the *samurai*. Thereby the cities took over the cultural role played earlier in Japanese history by the imperial court—*i.e.*, they offered a cultural challenge and an alternative to the way of life reverenced, though not always lived up to, by the militarized aristocracy of the land.

So rapid and drastic an evolution of Japanese society did not proceed without important back eddies and side currents; and the play of personalities among the rulers who succeeded one another in supreme control of the country had much to do with the way things turned out. Hideyoshi, who began his career as a stable hand and ended as a despotic war lord whose writ ran unquestioned throughout Japan, maintained a restlessly aggressive policy throughout his life. Ieyasu, founder of the Tokugawa shogunate, was a man of very different stamp; and his policies were much less grandiose than those of his friend and predecessor. His concern and the concern of his heirs was to secure power at home against all possible rivals rather than to spread Japan's greatness abroad. Hideyoshi had attempted to combine *samurai* traditions with the equally bloodthirsty traditions of the sea pirates. Ieyasu preferred to use his power over those among the *samurai* whom he invested with rights to collect heavy rents from the peasantry against the sea pirates and all other unauthorized military adventurers. Thus the expansive, outward-looking, self-confidence of Hideyoshi's time shrank into a narrower concern of the "ins" to maintain their favored position in Japanese society against all conceivable rivals. It took time for this transformation to work itself out. Not until 1636–38 did Tokugawa precautionary policy reach its logical conclu-

---

[93] The introduction of European-type firearms had much to do with the victory of a central authority in Japan, for the supply of muskets and cannon was far easier to monopolize than the supply of swords had been. Cf. Delmer M. Brown, "The Impact of Firearms on Japanese Warfare," *Far Eastern Quarterly*, VII (1948), 236–53.

sion, when the third shogun closed Japan to the outside world and prohibited Japanese seamen from leaving home waters or building seagoing ships.[94]

The activities of Christian missionaries helped to provoke this policy of seclusion. Portuguese adventurers first reached Japan in 1542 or 1543; and missionary activity began with the arrival of St. Francis Xavier in 1549. Xavier's saintly and imperious personality, the courage, learning, and persistence of his fellow Jesuits, and the attractiveness of Christian ritual and doctrine help to explain the success which attended the missionaries' propaganda. Yet in other parts of civilized Asia, similar missions made little impression. Hence the peculiar success of the Christian mission in Japan, as well as its later destruction, must be attributed to local circumstances.

The political chaos and multiple sovereignties prevailing throughout Japan when the Jesuits first arrived favored their early efforts. If one lord rejected the missionaries' overtures, his neighbor was automatically predisposed in their favor, all the more when he saw an opportunity of gaining superior weapons or other advantages through trade with the Portuguese. Unlike the Chinese, the Japanese immediately appreciated the technical superiority of European warfare and soon extended their admiration for muskets and cannon to other aspects of Portuguese civilization. Thus a fashion for European dress accompanied a widespread vogue for baptism; and for a few decades, the Jesuits in Japan could congratulate themselves upon what seemed the imminent evangelization of the entire nation.

The rise of an effective central authority in Japan did not at first seem prejudicial to Christian missionary efforts. Nobunaga (d. 1582), who began, and Hideyoshi, who completed the unification of the country, were both very friendly toward the missionaries, sharing with them a strong distaste for the Buddhist monks who constituted almost as formidable an obstacle to the policies of the war lords as they did to the aspirations of the Jesuits. Yet Hideyoshi was a religious skeptic and distrusted Christians as actual or potential agents of a foreign power. Hence in 1587 he issued a decree banishing foreign missionaries from Japan; but he then forebore from enforcing it, probably because he wished to maintain the Portuguese trade uninterrupted.[95]

Unlike Hideyoshi, Ieyasu was a practicing Buddhist and shared his predecessor's distrust of the political affiliation of Christian missionaries to the full. Moreover, the appearance of the Dutch in Japanese waters after 1609 opened an alternative source for guns and other Western goods and rendered con-

[94] Cf. the repression of Viking enterprise by the rising monarchies of Scandinavia in the eleventh century. In both societies, a really successful pirate automatically became too much of a rival to the central authorities to be tolerated. The fact that Japan had too many warriors for the available fiefs added a special edge to the shogun's policy; for landless warriors were obviously predisposed to hostility against the regime, and found a natural outlet for their ambitions in piratical enterprise abroad. Hence the extreme measures against sea roving made sense to those in possession of the coveted fiefs.

[95] Portuguese merchants operating from Macao enjoyed a peculiarly strategic position throughout the second half of the sixteenth century. Official relations between Japan and China were broken off because of the Japanese piratical attacks on the China coast; and peaceable trade between the two nations was therefore—at least officially—impossible. Yet Chinese silks and other luxury items were indispensable for the outfit of a Japanese gentleman; and Japanese silver was always welcome in China. The Portuguese therefore became go-betweens, carrying goods between the two nations, and earning very handsome middleman's profits from the trade. Cf. C. R. Boxer, *Fidalgos in the Far East, 1550–1770* (The Hague: M. Nijhoff, 1948).

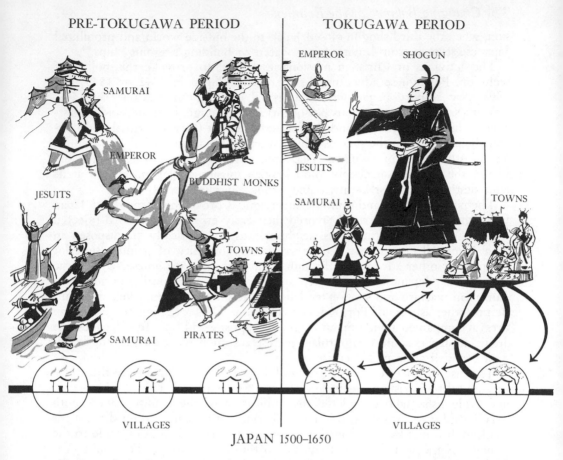

PRE-TOKUGAWA PERIOD | TOKUGAWA PERIOD

EMPEROR   SHOGUN

SAMURAI

EMPEROR

JESUITS

BUDDHIST MONKS

JESUITS

SAMURAI   TOWNS

TOWNS

SAMURAI   PIRATES

VILLAGES   VILLAGES

JAPAN 1500–1650

ciliation of the Portuguese unnecessary. The result was to unleash sporadic
persecution of the Christian communities. Most of the Japanese territorial
lords who had accepted baptism abandoned the Christian faith; a few lost
their lands. But some among the humbler ranks of society remained stead-
fastly Christian even in the face of mounting persecution. Such stubbornness
ended by rousing the frantic fears of the third Tokugawa shogun, who interpreted the religious fervor of Japanese Christians as an open defiance of his
authority. Revolt broke out in Kyushu in 1637; and this confirmation of the
shogun's foreboding sealed the fate of the entire Christian enterprise in Japan.
Yet more than a year passed before the shogun's forces succeeded in capturing the last Christian stronghold. Wholesale massacre and systematic hunting
down of Christians throughout Japan accompanied the struggle. Foreign
missionaries were tortured and executed along with their Japanese converts;
and relations with the Portuguese were entirely broken off. Henceforth
foreign trade was reduced to a minimum and put under rigid surveillance to
prevent any recurrence of the disturbance which Europeans in general and
Roman Catholics in particular had brought to the contrived political order
of Tokugawa Japan.

Japanese high culture during the sixteenth and seventeenth centuries underwent changes as dramatic as those that transformed the social scene. The great war captains who united Japan were social upstarts, with little appreciation for the refined and muted sensibility of the Sinified tradition of courtly art. Hideyoshi was a great builder; and the structures raised at his command were distinguished by vastness of bulk and flamboyance of decoration. But under the Tokugawa shoguns, the older aesthetic restraint reasserted itself. *Bushido*, the ethical code of the warrior, was given precise definition by formal edict in 1615; and gradually an aesthetic canon clothed the activities befitting the *samurai* with a suitably spare elegance. Rituals like the "tea ceremony"—the core of which was display and appreciation of antique and beautiful utensils used in brewing and serving tea—or the stylized "No" drama, set the tone of this newly defined *samurai* aesthetic.

Yet the vigorous vulgarity of Hideyoshi's age persisted in the rising urban centers, where professional entertainers—geisha girls, puppet masters, miming "Kabuki" actors, acrobats, and others—catered to the tastes of wealthy townsmen. Poetry, prose, drama, and painting all took new forms, reflecting the luxury and license of the growing cities. Traditional moral standards were seldom explicitly rejected; yet this art and literature exhibited a spirit of irreverence, gaiety, and occasionally of explicit sexuality which accorded ill with the restrained decorum of the older, aristocratic Japan. Such delights readily seduced the *samurai* from the austerely disciplined conduct befitting men whose profession was violence.

The shogun's government distrusted these novelties and strove by sumptuary regulations and censorship to restrict the more flagrant expressions of the new spirit. The government patronized Neo-Confucian studies; and a number of distinguished scholars tried, not without some success, to popularize Confucian ideals. Buddhism, politically crippled in the wars of the sixteenth century, became culturally dormant; while Shinto, the ancient worship of the sun goddess, became a rallying ground for heterodox scholars who rejected the officially accredited Neo-Confucian doctrines. Since Shinto tended to elevate the prerogatives of the imperial descendant of the sun goddess at the expense of the shogun's authority, such ideas could not escape official reprobation. They were, however, usually advanced with such arcane learning and scholarly caution as to make violent persecution unnecessary.

Thus after the exclusion of the Europeans and the suppression of Christianity, Japan achieved a curious cultural duality. The official world of *Bushido*, Neo-Confucianism, and Sinified art styles confronted an innovating, irreligious, urban culture, whose uninhibited sensuality and spontaneous vigor stood in marked opposition to the officially approved decorum and restraint. Yet such seeming discrepancies did not prevent the contrived balance of Japanese society and culture, as worked out under the early Tokugawa shoguns, from surviving for more than three centuries.

TIBET, MONGOLIA, AND THE CENTRAL ASIAN STEPPE. While Japan was thus pursuing an independent evolution on the sea flank of China, an interesting and tantalizingly obscure transformation of Tibetan and Mongol soci-

ety was also underway. The central phenomenon was the missionary extension of reformed "Yellow Church" Lamaism among nearly all the Mongol
peoples. The Yellow Church dated back to the fourteenth century and was
characterized by insistence upon celibacy and a stricter monastic discipline.
Early in the sixteenth century, the Yellow Church won control of the Tibetan government when its leader, the Grand Lama of Lhasa, became a sort of
mayor of the palace and assumed political as well as religious authority in the
land.

Toward the end of the sixteenth century, various Mongol tribes began to
acknowledge the authority of the Yellow Church; and by the early seventeenth century, most of them had been won to the faith. The Chinese government attempted to establish diplomatic influence over the leaders of this
church, but it is uncertain how successfully they did so. The religious hierarchy of Lamaism, for example, may have had a hand in consolidating the formidable Kalmuk confederacy, which from its headquarters on the Ili River
challenged the best military efforts of the Chinese government until 1757,
when a smallpox epidemic finished what Chinese armies had begun and wiped
the stubborn nomads from political existence. Thereafter, Tibet itself abandoned the ambiguous deference of preceding decades and submitted to the
victorious Chinese.

Whatever the true political role of Lamaism within the nomad communities
of the sixteenth and seventeenth centuries may have been, the religion seems to
have served to protect the horsemen of the steppe from the spiritual domination of their more highly civilized neighbors, even in an age when the development of military technology was depriving Asian nomads of their wonted
importance in world history.[96]

4. AFRICA

Until 1500, sub-Saharan Africa knew the civilized ecumene almost solely
through Moslem intermediaries; for the isolated Christian states of Ethiopia
and Nubia were barely able to withstand Moslem pressure upon their own
borders and could not rival Islam as an influence upon Africa at large. This
situation altered after the Portuguese rounded the Cape of Good Hope and
established trade and naval stations at suitable points along the African coast.
Thereafter, the African peoples found themselves caught between the European and Moslem worlds; and they were sometimes able to choose between the
two. Both Moslems and Christians took active part in the slave trade; and
more than once, the depredations of slavers undid the work of missionaries
among African tribes and kingdoms. Thus paganism survived and not infrequently revived even after a period of official conversion to Christianity or
Islam.

Until after 1700, European penetration of Africa remained very superficial.
In west Africa, where Islam had long been established and where shifting
constellations of local states and empires had existed for centuries, Europeans

---

[96] Cf. John F. Baddeley, *Russia, Mongolia, and China*, I, lxxiv–lxxxiii. Manichaeism among the
Uighurs and Judaism among the Khazars had once served the same function.

merely occupied a few coastal stations from which to carry on the slave trade. Farther south, the Portuguese discovered territorially extensive kingdoms, located in the Congo basin and between the Zambesi and Limpopo rivers of east Africa. But these states were comparatively weak; and even the conversion of their rulers to Christianity apparently had slight consequences. At any rate, both the kingdom of the Congo and the empire of Monomatapa in east Africa disintegrated or lost nearly all their importance in the course of the seventeenth century despite (perhaps because of) Portuguese support.

Africa underwent two important economic changes in the sixteenth and seventeenth centuries. First, animal husbandry and nomadism spread into many parts of the continent where they had been absent or unimportant before. Throughout the northern parts of the Sudan, from the horn of east Africa to the Moroccan coast, nomadic tribes expanded their habitat, sometimes at the expense of settled agricultural communities. These nomads were Moslem, although on a fairly primitive level; and their expansion signified the penetration of Islam deeper into Africa. In addition, pagan Bantu-speaking tribes continued to follow their herds of cattle southward through the east African highlands toward the Cape of Good Hope. Their advance drove primitive hunters—Bushmen and Hottentots—into refuge zones; and unlike the nomadic expansion farther north, represented a net gain in the technical level of exploitation of the environment.

Second, a number of American crops were introduced into Africa, presumably via ships provisioned in the New World for the slave run. Maize, manioc, sweet potatoes, peanuts, squash, and cacao quickly became staples of west African agriculture; and the first three spread rapidly over wide stretches of the continent. Presumably the resemblance of the African climate to that of Central and South America facilitated the rapid acceptance of these new crops, as did the shifting "garden" type of cultivation prevailing in Africa; for no fixed rotation or established agricultural routine inhibited experimentation with new plants.

The appearance of large territorial states in central and east Africa, the spread of cattle nomads and semi-nomads over wide ranges of the continent, and the adoption of American food plants all signified the closer incorporation of Africa into the ecumene. The great link was the slave trade, which assumed far larger proportions after American plantations and mines, having exhausted Amerindian labor supplies, found a substitute in African slaves. Both Moslem and European slavers operated deep into the continent, rudely breaking in upon immemorial village and tribal isolation to seize hundreds of thousands of helpless victims. The operation was brutal; yet without such cruel harrowing, African societies would not so quickly have been shaken from their primitive slumber. Perhaps the ability of African peoples to withstand the impact of European political and economic domination in the nineteenth century was founded upon the fact that their forefathers had already experienced and survived the violent disruption of their native social patterns at the hands of the slavers.[97]

[97] G. P. Murdock, *Africa*, pp. 284–327, 364–68, 392–405, 410–21; and *passim;* D. Westermann, *Geschichte Afrikas*, pp. 94–208, 211–75, 288–92, 390–97, 412–16, and *passim;* J. Spencer Trimingham, *A History of Islam in West Africa*, 141–47 and *passim.*

E. CONCLUSION

Between 1500 and 1700, the Eurasian ecumene expanded to include parts of the Americas, much of sub-Saharan Africa, and all of northern Asia. Moreover, within the Old World itself, western Europe began to forge ahead of all rivals as the most active center of geographical expansion and of cultural innovation. Indeed, Europe's self-revolution transformed the medieval frame of Western civilization into a new and vastly more powerful organization of society. Yet the Moslem, Hindu, and Chinese lands were not yet seriously affected by the new energies emanating from Europe. Until after 1700, the history of these regions continued to turn around old traditions and familiar problems.

Most of the rest of the world, lacking the massive self-sufficiency of Moslem, Hindu, and Chinese civilization, was more acutely affected by contact with Europeans. In the New World, these contacts first decapitated and then decimated the Amerindian societies; but in other regions, where local powers of resistance were greater, a strikingly consistent pattern of reaction manifested itself. In such diverse areas as Japan, Burma, Siam, Russia, and parts of Africa, an initial interest in and occasional eagerness to accept European techniques, ideas, religion, or fashions of dress was supplanted in the course of the seventeenth century by a policy of withdrawal and deliberate insulation from European pressures. The Hindu revival in India and the reform of Lamaism in Tibet and Mongolia manifested a similar spirit; for both served to protect local cultural values against alien pressures, though in these cases the pressures were primarily Moslem and Chinese rather than European.

A few fringe areas of the earth still remained unaffected by the disturbing forces of civilization. But by 1700 the only large habitable regions remaining outside the ecumene were Australia, the Amazon rain forest, and northwestern North America; and even these latter two had already felt tremors of social disturbance generated by the approaching onset of civilization.

At no previous time in world history had the pace of social transformation been so rapid. The new density and intimacy of contacts across the oceans of the earth assured a continuance of cross-stimulation among the major cultures of mankind. The efforts to restrict foreign contacts and to withdraw from disturbing relationships with outsiders—especially with the restless and ruthless Westerners—were doomed to ultimate failure by the fact that successive self-transformations of western European civilization, and especially of Western technology, rapidly increased the pressures Westerners were able to bring against the other peoples of the earth. Indeed, world history since 1500 may be thought of as a race between the West's growing power to molest the rest of the world and the increasingly desperate efforts of other peoples to stave Westerners off, either by clinging more strenuously than before to their peculiar cultural inheritance or, when that failed, by appropriating aspects of Western civilization—especially technology—in the hope of thereby finding means to preserve their local autonomy.

CHAPTER XII

The Tottering World Balance 1700–1850 A.D.

A. INTRODUCTION

By 1700, the wealth and power at Europe's command clearly surpassed anything that other civilized communities of the earth could muster; and European society had attained a precarious equilibrium resting upon intensification as well as extension of enterprise at home and abroad. The New World offered the greatest single field for European expansion, although no part of the habitable globe entirely escaped attention. Between 1700 and 1850, such vast regions as northern Asia, Australia, South Africa, India, and the Levant all in varying degrees became satellites of the European political-economic system. Only in the Far East did massive civilized societies retain full autonomy; and even there, China and Japan began to experience creeping internal crises that prepared the way for a definitive collapse of the traditional social order in the Far East shortly after 1850.

The millennial balance of the ecumene among the civilizations of the Middle East, India, China, and Europe did not decisively collapse until about the middle of the nineteenth century. By that date, when the enhanced power which accrued to the West with the Industrial Revolution was superadded to the older energies of European expansion, the leaders of the other peoples and civilizations of the earth began to feel that something was radically lacking in their own pasts. Before that time, however, Moslems and Hindus could, and with few exceptions did, believe that the precious traditions of their respective civilizations must be preserved intact, even in the face of evident European military and economic superiority; while in the Far East, the problem of how to react to the West was not yet really pressing. The policy of holding Europeans at arm's length seemed to work well enough; and the Chinese and Japanese accordingly felt no need to modify their inherited institutions and traditions in order to cope with the West. The period 1700–1850 is therefore a middle stage in the rise of the West, when Europeans began to dominate the bodies, but had not yet made much impression upon the minds, of most of the inhabitants of the globe.

This phase of world history overlapped the Industrial and Democratic[1] Revolutions in Europe's own history. These two revolutionary movements violently disrupted the compromises of the European Old Regime, thereby inaugurating a convulsive self-transformation within Western civilization that resembled the earlier disruption of Europe's medieval institutions and ideas by the twin movements of Renaissance and Reformation. Assuredly, both the Industrial and Democratic Revolutions had begun to work deep changes within Western society before 1850; and the enhanced wealth and power which they imparted to men of European culture had already started to affect the rest of the world. Yet these were comparatively weak anticipations of the future: until after the middle of the nineteenth century, the European imprint upon the other peoples of the earth was largely an aftermath of the Old Regime. Railroads and other devices of the new mechanically powered technology began to transform even European society only after 1850; and the new ideas of political loyalty and responsibility proclaimed in 1776 and 1789 by the American and French Revolutions penetrated the non-Western world more slowly still.

Hence in this chapter, as in the preceding one, Europe and its outliers will be treated within a chronological span offset from that of the rest of the chapter. An account of the expansion of European-type societies onto new ground and an analysis of the European Old Regime (1650–1789) will precede discussion of the impact of the European Old Regime upon the Moslem, Hindu, and Far Eastern civilizations (1700–1850).

B. THE OLD REGIME OF EUROPE, *1650–1789 A.D.*

The Peace of Westphalia which ended the Thirty Years' War (1648), together with its sequels, the Peace of the Pyrenees between France and Spain (1659) and the restoration of the Stuart monarchy in England (1660), mark a new era in European history. In the latter part of the seventeenth century, religion became a more nearly private concern; and statecraft began to turn upon more naked, but also more moderate, struggles for wealth and power. A series of tacit compromises softened or disguised the earlier conflicts of principle; and new or newly strengthened institutions balanced, adjudicated, or repressed the conflicts of interest which remained, vigorous enough, within the European body politic.

This changed atmosphere was a victory of common sense and moral ex-

---

[1] This term is borrowed from R. R. Palmer, *The Age of the Democratic Revolution: A Political History of Europe and America, 1760–1800* (Princeton, N.J.: Princeton University Press, 1959), to describe the changes in political ideas and practices that came to the Western world in the late eighteenth and early nineteenth centuries. The American and French revolutions were, of course, the most conspicuous but by no means the sole expressions of this transformation.

haustion in the face of the stubborn variety and incongruities of the European cultural landscape. Relaxation of the effort to discern and then to enforce true doctrine was in turn vastly facilitated—perhaps made possible—by the fact that Europeans were able to direct their restless energies outward. East and west, overland and overseas, frontiers lay open. Everywhere opportunity beckoned the enterprising with grandiose visions of wealth to be acquired, territory to be settled, adventures to be undertaken. Thus Europe had a safety valve ready at hand. Restless spirits could often escape from the trammels of their station in life by venturing far afield; and a generally rising curve of prosperity meant that the uncertainties resulting from market fluctuations were tolerable, if not exactly comfortable, for those who stayed at home.

Under these circumstances, the striving for absolute truth which had been so widespread and impassioned in the sixteenth and early seventeenth centuries ceased to disturb public order and became once more the concern of professional intellectuals. Differences in approach and emphasis between theologians and scientists were adequately compromised, not by all-embracing logical systematization, but by giving each profession a secure institutional niche within society and allowing individuals to discuss their differences more or less freely. Established churches, officially intolerant of heresy, existed in every European state; and official censorship of publications remained in effect even in France. Yet the law and the facts tended increasingly to diverge, despite an occasional recrudescence of pious persecution like that which accompanied Louis XIV's revocation of the Edict of Nantes (1685).

Comparably illogical but effective compromises between monarchy, aristocracy, the commercial classes, and poor common folk embodied themselves in reasonably stable political institutions in all the states of Europe; while in economics, the innovating, engrossing, rationalizing activity of capitalists and chartered companies interpenetrated older forms of guild organization without provoking violent counteraction. Thus the untidy illogic of the Old Regime, so scorned by a later generation of rationalists and social theorists, emerged piecemeal and unplanned. It proved, all the same, a workable and highly effective system of society.

The most obvious measure of the effectiveness of the Old Regime was its successes vis-à-vis the non-European world. As European institutions and ideas settled toward an effective equilibrium, governments were less distracted at home; and those suitably located at or near the periphery of Europe became correspondingly freer to devote attention to frontier and colonial expansion. This, in effect, unleashed the power of the new forms of economic and military organization which Europeans had developed in the sixteenth and early seventeenth centuries—especially, joint stock companies and standing armies and navies. With such organizations as spearheads, Europeans worked their way deep into the tissues of weaker societies in almost all parts of the globe.

Expansion abroad assisted, perhaps even sustained, comparative stability within Europe; and stability at home reinforced the European outward thrust. The upshot of this circular process was to transform Europe by the end of the eighteenth century into a giant society straddling the Atlantic, reaching deep into the Eurasian steppe, and extending to the antipodes. This expanded Europe became the center of a vast political-economic power system, engulfing most of the Moslem and Hindu worlds and lapping round the edges of the Far Eastern citadel itself. Europe, in short, became the West.

The only comparable event in world history was the rise of a cosmopolitan civilization in the Middle East between 1500 and 500 B.C. Then, too, a series of outward thrusts from the Mesopotamian base brought what had earlier been essentially independent civilizations and cultures into a great melting pot. Egypt, Anatolia, and Iran, together with fringes of the Greek and Indian worlds, lost their autonomy and were merged into a Mesopotamian-centered cosmopolitanism. Yet the analogy is imperfect. European expansion was not achieved by a succession of imperial conquerors but worked multifariously from a politically divided center; and the fact that European enterprise impinged upon a number of previously thinly settled and weakly organized regions allowed massive migration and settlement, thus incorporating vast and often distant areas into an expanded "Western" body politic. Phoenician and Greek colonization of the ancient Mediterranean offers a parallel in miniature. Yet except in Sicily, Phoenician and Greek superiority over autochthonous populations was never so great as to induce destruction of the host societies. European colonization, by contrast, often led to this result, more perhaps because of the devastating effect of unfamiliar diseases upon primitive populations than from deliberate policy.

For the sake of clarity, it seems best to treat successively (1) European expansion onto new ground; (2) intensification of European influence in the American and Russian outliers of European civilization; and (3) the compromises of the Old Regime at home. Such separation is, of course, artificial. The reader must bear in mind the intimate interdependence between expansion abroad and the precarious equilibrium of the center.

1. EUROPEAN EXPANSION TO NEW GROUND

The multifarious aspects of European expansion in the seventeenth and eighteenth centuries may, without unduly drastic schematization, be reduced to three types of exploitation of the lands and peoples with which Europeans came in contact. First and farthest-ranging, Europeans continued to penetrate regions where readily available local products had value for European or other civilized markets. Furs from the frozen northlands of Asia and America plus gold and diamonds from the Brazilian jungles were the most important such products in the period 1650–1789. Second, in certain tropical and subtropical lands, especially the West and East Indies, Europeans reorganized local economies to produce commodities in demand upon the world market. This involved drastic interference with pre-existing social relationships, for European enterprise was based upon slavery or other forms of forced labor and sometimes involved massive population transfers. Third, in temperate regions, primarily in North and South America and in the western parts of the Eurasian steppe, European settlements developed from crude beginnings

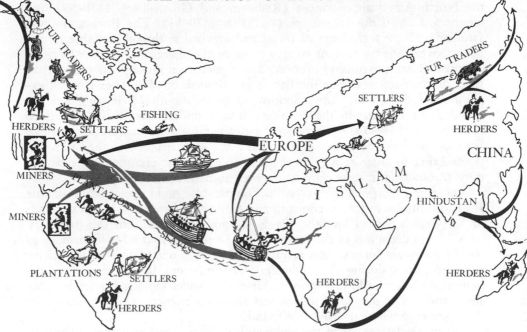

into genuine transplants of a European style of society, even when separated from the heartland of Europe by thousands of miles.

EXPLORATION, TRADE, AND NATIONAL RIVALRIES. In 1650, oceanic exploration had almost ceased, despite the fact that vast reaches of the Pacific remained untouched. By that date, first the Iberians and then the Dutch and English had explored the richest and commercially most worthwhile parts of the earth. Probing voyages along the coasts of North America or in the direction of Australia revealed only unpromising and undeveloped regions where no valuable trade could be expected. Ships could therefore be better employed along already established trade lanes than in risking hazardous, uncharted, and unprofitable voyages. In addition, European navigation in the seventeenth century labored under important technical limitations. The absence of any method for accurately determining longitude meant that even when a ship blundered off course and sighted new lands—as certainly happened more frequently than surviving records show—there was no sure way of repeating the landfall. Because long voyages involved also the certainty of scurvy—the result of a vitamin-deficient diet on shipboard—cruising in vast ocean spaces like the Pacific was a very risky business which only the assurance of handsome profit from trade could justify.

On land, however, the pursuit of furs pushed Russian, French, and (after 1670, when the Hudson's Bay Company was organized) British trading posts rapidly forward. From their headquarters at Quebec, the French penetrated the Great Lakes area, and then moved west of Lake Superior into the heart of the North American continent (Radisson and Grosseilliers, 1658–59) and southward down the Mississippi (La Salle, 1679–83). The British, not yet familiar with the techniques of travel and survival in the inhospitable Arctic North, were at first content to stay close to the shores of Hudson Bay. By contrast, Russian expansion proceeded at a pace even more phenomenal than the French. After reaching the Pacific at Okhotsk in 1639, later Russian expeditions followed the Amur southward to its mouth (1649–53) and descended the Kolyma to the Arctic, thence rounding the tip of Siberia to Kamchatka (1648–56).[2] Thereafter, a distinct pause in exploration ensued; for the handful of adventurers who had made such strides into the unknown needed time to organize native fur collection and to overcome the extraordinary transport difficulties they confronted in marketing their pelts.

Not furs, but gold, motivated a comparably rapid penetration of the Brazilian interior in the seventeenth and eighteenth centuries. Initially, bands of half-breeds pushed into the jungle looking for slaves; but the discovery of gold and diamonds in the interior (1695) precipitated a "gold rush" into the Amazon rain forests. As a result, Brazil became one of the world's major gold producers during the eighteenth century; and bands of prospector-explorers crisscrossed the interior as far as the Andes looking for fresh minefields and establishing small settlements along the numerous tributaries of the Amazon, even where no gold was found.[3]

During the latter part of the eighteenth century, improvements in seamanship together with national rivalries among the major European powers stirred up a fresh burst of exploratory activity. Exploration became a matter of government policy rather than of individual filibuster or local improvisation, as had earlier been the case. Official agents of the Russian, British, and French governments, backed by the naval resources of their home fleets, and inspired partly by scientific curiosity and partly by a desire to claim new territories for their respective sovereigns, renewed exploration by sea. Captain Vitus Bering of the Russian navy was the first such official explorer (1728, 1741), while Captain James Cook of the British navy was the most successful and far-ranging (1768–79). Cook's voyages were also significant for two technical breakthroughs. He banished scurvy by feeding his sailors sauerkraut;[4] and on his second voyage he tested the first model of a marine chronometer which was sturdy and accurate enough to permit precise calculation

[2] Raymond H. Fisher, *The Russian Fur Trade* (Berkeley and Los Angeles, Calif.: University of California Press, 1943), pp. 43–45. There is doubt whether this last expedition proceeded by land or by sea. If the latter, Bering Strait must have been discovered—though not recognized as a strait—three-quarters of a century before Bering made his first voyage.

[3] National rivalries between Portuguese and Spaniards in the south and between Portuguese and French in the north also induced the Portuguese to extend Brazilian coastline settlements. Cf. Bailey W. Diffie, *Latin-American Civilization: Colonial Period* (Harrisburg, Pa.: Stackpole Sons, 1945), pp. 652–81; Felix Reichwein, *Sugar, Gold, and Coffee: Essays on the History of Brazil* (Ithaca, N.Y.: Cornell University Library, 1959), pp. 88–117.

[4] Cf. Christopher Lloyd, *Captain Cook* (New York: Roy Publishers, n.d.), pp. 93–95, 120. Captain Cook more than once resorted to the cat-o'-nine-tails to make his reluctant sailors consume such an outlandish novelty. The more effective lime juice came into use in the British navy only a generation later.

of longitude. The result was to make Cook's charts of the coastlines and islands of the North and South Pacific far more reliable than those of his predecessors and to bring even tiny islets of the south seas within easy range of European navigation.

National rivalries likewise stimulated new exploration overland in the latter part of the eighteenth century. Russian fur traders speedily followed up Bering's discoveries in Alaska by establishing trading posts, first in the Aleutians and later on the mainland. News of this Russian advance led fur traders based in Montreal to explore and thus lay claim to the far reaches of the Canadian Northwest (Alexander Mackenzie's voyage to the Arctic, 1789); and the same news inspired the Spaniards to advance their line of settlement northward from Mexico along the Pacific coast into California (San Francisco founded 1775) and British Columbia (Nootka founded 1789). Thus by the end of the eighteenth century, Russian fur traders and explorers traveling eastward had met British fur traders (heirs to the French in Canada after 1763) at the general line of the Canadian Rockies. Between them, they had girdled the Arctic and brought the tundra and forested zones of the circumpolar lands within the circuit of civilized trade. Simultaneously Spaniards and Russians did the same to the entire Pacific coast of the Americas.

By 1800, therefore, when organized expeditions equipped by European navies had explored the chief features of the world's oceans, save for the ice-covered regions of the poles, only the interior of sub-Saharan Africa and of Australia remained terra incognita to Europeans. Within all the vastly enlarged circuit of this known world, European traders and seamen everywhere ravaged and disrupted primitive societies with the diseases and goods of civilization.

PLANTATIONS AND THE CONSCIOUS TRANSFORMATION OF TROPICAL AND SUBTROPICAL ECONOMIES. However drastic the impact of Europeans upon the hunters of the Arctic North or upon the fishermen and gardeners of Oceania may have been, it was in a sense merely accidental. The intruders were interested only in gathering furs or in provisioning their ships and refreshing their crews after the strain of a long ocean voyage, not in transforming the economy and culture of the local populations.

In other parts of the world, this was not the case. The Dutch in the East Indies were perhaps the pioneers in using native labor to sustain a rationalized plantation agriculture, cultivating crops specifically for transoceanic markets and periodically adjusting the scale of production in order to maximize profits.[5] But commercial spice-growing was already ancient in the East Indies when the Dutch first arrived on the scene; and their efforts to monopolize and rationalize the trade did not therefore involve a radical break with the

---

[5] Banda, Amboina, and Ternate, the principal clove producers of the East Indies, were conquered by the Dutch between 1621 and 1657; and when Macassar became a serious rival, it too was overwhelmed in 1669. The islanders were thereupon required to produce only as many cloves as the market in Europe, India, and China could absorb—a policy which required alternate expansion and contraction of plantation. Cf. J. H. Parry, *Europe and a Wider World, 1415–1715* (New York: Hutchinson's University Library, 1949), pp. 154–56; B. H. M. Vlekke, *Nusantara: A History of the East Indian Archipelago* (Cambridge, Mass.: Harvard University Press, 1943), pp. 138–39, 145.

local past. In the New World, on the contrary, plantation agriculture could not draw upon any pre-established labor force or local skills. Portuguese sugar growers emigrating from the Madeira Islands[6] to Brazil brought the first canes to the Americas about 1520; and the crop did so well that Spaniards soon imitated their example in some of the Caribbean coastlands. But these beginnings were far eclipsed in the second half of the seventeenth century by the rapid development of sugar plantations in the islands of the Caribbean, where first the English, then the French, and to a lesser extent the Dutch, established a rigorously rationalized commercial agriculture based upon Negro slavery.

The development of Caribbean sugar production created a remarkably profitable transatlantic trade; for vessels could carry cheap textiles and other manufactures from Europe to the coast of Africa, barter them for slaves, which brought a handsome profit in the Caribbean islands or on the mainland, and then return home with a cargo of American sugar and rum for sale in Europe. West Indian long-staple cotton and indigo were less valuable, though nonetheless important items in this triangular trade. Moreover, the cod of Newfoundland and the timber and grain of New England and the Middle Atlantic colonies found important markets in the sugar islands of the Caribbean, where agriculture rapidly became so specialized that basic food crops were neglected. Thus both sides of the Atlantic came to be bound together by a vigorous commerce, all centering around the tiny Leeward and Windward Islands of the Caribbean.[7]

Less profitable, yet important plantations dependent upon Negro slavery also extended into the southern English colonies on the American mainland and along the Brazilian coast. On the other side of the globe, from the early eighteenth century onward, the Dutch in the East Indies put increasing emphasis upon agriculture as a supplement to their mercantile enterprise. New products, above all coffee, constituted the backbone of this cultivation. It was supervised sometimes by Dutch planters, sometimes by immigrant Chinese entrepreneurs, but for the most part by native princelings, who were required to yield fixed quantities of coffee or other crops to the Dutch as a sort of tribute. Labor in the East Indies was not as a rule formally enslaved; but the

---

[6] Sugar became an important crop in the Madeiras in late medieval times, having come to European attention via the Moslems from the Indian Ocean area.

[7] The eighteenth-century economic importance of these minute specks of land is amazing. As late as 1773, official records showed that British trade with the West Indies was more valuable than trade with the mainland colonies of North America; and the whole Far Eastern trade likewise lagged behind the value of commerce with these same small islands. Cf. tables compiled by Eric Williams, *Capitalism and Slavery* (Chapel Hill, N.C.: University of North Carolina Press, 1944), pp. 225–26.

Sugar cultivation, as conducted in the seventeenth and eighteenth centuries, mined the fertility of the soil, so that the islands which first took up sugar cultivation gradually found it impossible to produce as cheaply as new areas more recently brought into cultivation. The result was the weakening of the British sugar islands before French competition toward the end of the eighteenth century, followed in the nineteenth by the eclipse of the French (and in Haiti, ex-French) sugar islands by Cuba and Puerto Rico, which had remained Spanish. Thus sugar moved through the chain of Caribbean islands like a golden plague, leaving behind exhausted soil, impoverished populations, and seriously disjointed societies. Abolition of slavery in the nineteenth century did little to relieve the social problems this process created.

local "regents" of Java nonetheless often used force to compel their subjects to cultivate the coffee trees and other new tribute crops.[8]

THE SPREAD OF EUROPEAN SETTLEMENT. In diverse parts of the earth, European settlers produced a series of mutations from the social patterns of their homelands. The rigorous slavery of a West Indian sugar plantation and the rude egalitarianism of a New England frontier community represent extremes of a spectrum along which many intermediate social forms may be discerned. The harsh slavery of Barbados shaded into the less rigorous conditions of servitude that prevailed on Spanish or Portuguese plantations in Central America and Brazil. The neo-serfdom of eastern Europe and the forced labor exacted from the Indians of Spanish America represented a milder form of compulsory service, in law if not always in fact; and once again the Spanish case was milder, if only because the weight of government regulation stood on the side of Indian rights. Workmen indentured for a term of years—a common practice in early Virginia—and felons transported to Australia or Siberia occupied midpoints in the spectrum. Finally, the free settler of a proprietary colony, owing quitrents to a noble lord, and the small New England farmer, owning his land in fee simple, enjoyed a personal freedom inferior only to the ultimate anarchy of such diverse types as the American frontiersman, the Siberian or Canadian fur trader, the Brazilian bandiera, the gaucho of the Argentine pampas, the Ukrainian Cossack, or the buccaneer of the Spanish Main.

On any advancing frontier, labor shortage is always a major problem. Diametrically opposite solutions offer: drastic compulsion to sustain social stratification; or equally drastic liberty with concomitant regression toward an egalitarian neo-barbarism. Each policy has advantages and drawbacks. Drastic compulsion may be required to sustain specialists who are needed if the society is to exist at all. Thus without hard-driving economic entrepreneurs, plantations could not arise; and without a professional military class, agricultural settlements on the western parts of the Eurasian steppelands could not have been defended. Moreover, an upper class sustained by compulsory labor may rapidly attain a comparatively high degree of culture and lend the society as a whole a veneer of elegance otherwise unattainable. Such achievements are easily underrated in a democratic age, when men are more likely to sympathize with the slave or serf than with his master. Yet civilization first arose only through the direction of the labor of one group by another; and by a similar process, civilized societies repeatedly were able to transcend constricting geographical barriers—whether long ago in Hittite Asia Minor and Roman Gaul, or more recently in Spanish America and Russian Ukraine. Yet the drawback to such forcible propagation of civilization is always serious; for a culture which excludes the great majority of the inhabitants remains necessarily precarious.

We are far more likely to admire the other alternative of the frontier: drastic egalitarianism. Yet the rough violence of such communities, directed against helpless natives and breaking out in drunken brawls among the

[8] B. H. M. Vlekke, *Nusantara*, pp. 179–85.

frontiersmen themselves, meant a degeneration of erstwhile civilized populations toward barbarism. Though armed with the guns of civilized workshops, European frontiersmen sloughed off nearly all the legal and cultural restraints of civilized society. To be sure, civilized life gradually arose in the wake of rude pioneers through social differentiation, education, and technical advance. Moreover, this process undoubtedly worked itself out more rapidly and regularly than the comparable process of cultural filtering down from a cultivated aristocracy. In this lay the real superiority of anarchic frontier liberty as against its alternative of wholesale compulsion. But during the seventeenth and eighteenth centuries the advantages of the plunge toward anarchism remained almost wholly potential, while the shorter-range successes of compulsion were evident and undeniable. Assuredly, the cultivated elegance of aristocratic Virginia, New Spain, Hungary, and Russia—based in each case upon compulsory labor—far overbalanced the modest beginnings of civilization along the New England seaboard.

Yet the New England and Middle Atlantic colonies of North America compensated for their cultural crudity by the comparatively large number of European (or rather ex-European) settlers they accommodated. Nowhere else in the world did such large and compact agricultural communities arise. Nonetheless, the eighteenth century saw a substantial growth of Spanish population in the La Plata region of Argentina; and in southern Brazil, Portuguese settlers pre-empted wide territories. But in both these regions, ranching

ALTERNATIVES OF THE FRONTIER

was more prominent than agriculture, so that settlement remained comparatively thin. In Canada, French farmers remained close to the banks of the St. Lawrence; and backwoods farming began to develop only toward the end of the eighteenth century, in large part through the initiative of Tory refugees from the American Revolution. In South Africa, Dutch colonists landed at Capetown in 1652. When the British took over the colony in 1795, Dutch ranchers had penetrated far inland; while near the Cape itself a fairly substantial farming community had taken root. In 1789 the first English settlers landed in Australia. Thus except for New Zealand, first colonized in 1840, all the major overseas centers of European population had begun their development by the end of the eighteenth century.

The movement of European settlers across the world's oceans was spectacular and pregnant for the future; but the simultaneous settlement of the western Eurasian steppelands probably involved a more massive migration and was no less significant in changing the cultural balance of the world. In the sevententh and eighteenth centuries, millions of pioneers broke the vast grasslands lying between central Hungary and western Siberia to the plow. At the extreme edges of this eastward movement, anarchic frontier conditions arose comparable to those of the New World. Russian settlers in Siberia, for example, escaped all but nominal control and lived rough lives as hunters, fishers, and agriculturalists much like those of American frontiersmen. This was, however, atypical. In the western steppe massive European settlement could occur only after the Austrian and Russian military establishments had driven Moslem herdsmen and warriors from the region. This occurred in Hungary after 1699; but it was not until the annexation of Crim Tartary to Russia in 1783 that Moslem state power was eliminated from the area of the Ukraine.

After their victories over the former Moslem overlords of the western steppe, the Austrian and Russian governments were free to apportion their newly conquered but thinly inhabited lands in whatever manner they saw fit. Settlement of the western steppe took three forms. In most of Hungary and the Ukraine, large tracts of land were assigned to great noblemen with influence at court, who could populate their new estates, at least in part, with serfs from their more thickly settled lands elsewhere. Along the Ottoman and Persian borders, however, both the Austrian and Russian governments opted for militarized, free peasant communities under special imperial jurisdiction. Such populations could be relied upon to guard their own properties against border raids; and in any case, neither the Russian Cossacks nor the Austrian "Grenzers," accustomed as they were to bearing arms in irregular warfare across Tartar and Ottoman frontiers, could easily have been reduced to serfdom. Thus the Serbs, Croats, Rumanians, and others who populated the Austrian military frontier, and the "registered" Cossacks of southern Russia, continued to enjoy personal freedom in return for obligatory military service in special regiments.[9] A third alternative was to attract settlers from abroad by

---

[9] The British combined these approaches in order to tame the Scottish highlands after the rebellion of 1745. Like their contemporaries among the Russian and Hungarian nobility, Scottish clan chieftains

offering land on especially favorable terms. The Austrians adopted this policy in the Banat, as did the Russians in a few special districts of the Ukraine. As the empty land filled up, both the military settlements and the free peasant communities which had been set up under imperial auspices tended to fall under landlord control. In some cases, internal differentiation among the settlers themselves led to this result, as in the case of the Cossacks; but sometimes a formal government grant assigned hitherto free communities to the not very tender mercies of a court favorite.[10]

In one notable case, however, European overseas settlement met with very imperfect success. The colonization of Ireland by Cromwell and his predecessors entirely failed to extend English society across St. George's Channel. The wild Irish, driven to subsist upon the potato, could work more cheaply for the new landowners of the country than English or even Scottish settlers were willing to do: hence they prevailed demographically, but at the price of a miserable economic bondage to a culturally alien aristocracy.[11] Although legal forms differed, the social patterns of eighteenth-century Ireland resembled those of eastern Europe and the southern colonies of North America in being sharply polarized between a privileged body of landowners who shared in European civilization, and a culturally deprived, psychologically alienated mass of agricultural laborers.

2. ACCULTURATION IN THE OLDER OUTLIERS OF EUROPE: AMERICA AND RUSSIA

The expansion of European civilization after 1648 proceeded, not only by occupation of new ground, but also by acculturation to European styles of life in outlying regions already within Europe's sphere of influence. By 1789, this process had brought large parts of Russia and the New World to full membership in what henceforth must be called Western, rather than merely European civilization. This addition of America and Russia to the Europe-centered body politic of the West increased the variety and diluted or perhaps even debased the quality of Western civilization. Yet despite persistent differences between the old centers of European civilization and the outliers, a basic community of culture more and more united the American, western

---

were granted large estates; and all competing "native" claims upon the land were brusquely disregarded by the English law. Simultaneously, numerous clansmen were enrolled in special Highland regiments, used, however, not for local guard, as were their Russian and Austrian counterparts, but rather for British imperial purposes all round the world. But, since Russian Cossack and Austrian Grenzer regiments also served in wars far from the frontier they normally guarded, the difference was actually small.

[10] Cf. Henry Marczali, *Hungary in the Eighteenth Century* (Cambridge: Cambridge University Press, 1910), pp. 46–61; W. E. D. Allen, *The Ukraine* (Cambridge: Cambridge University Press, 1940), pp. 206–32; Boris Nolde, *La Formation de l'empire russe* (2 vols.; Paris: Institut d'études slaves, 1952–53), *passim;* Konrad Schünemann, *Oesterreichs Bevölkerungs-Politik unter Maria Theresia* (Berlin: 1935).

[11] Cf. W. H. McNeill, "The Influence of the Potato on Irish History" (unpublished Ph.D. dissertation, Cornell University, 1947).

European, and Russian peoples, and set them off from the civilized communities of the rest of the world.

The acculturation of Russia and the Americas to a European style of civilization proceeded by remarkably different paths. Russians had first to cast off much of their peculiar cultural heritage—a violent and painful process—before they could embrace the West. By contrast, the American descendants of European immigrants were merely reclaiming what their ancestors had in varying measure sloughed off by succumbing to rude conditions of frontier existence; and no deep psychological strains were involved in once again sharing more fully in European civilization.

In Russia and in America, acculturation was the work of relatively small minorities. But in America the cultural leaders commanded fairly willing support—or at least passive acceptance—from the rest of the population; whereas in Russia, the imposition of European technology, art, and fashions bred a sullen resentment among the majority, who understood little or nothing of the new cultural world in which their masters moved. In addition, acculturation in the Americas proceeded without conscious plan, by the spontaneous action of individuals and groups who found personal stimulus and enrichment through a fuller participation in European civilization; whereas in Russia, this process took the form of a strenuous campaign consciously organized by the government and initially aimed nakedly at the acquisition of military power.

The results differed as greatly as the methods of acculturation had done. By the close of the eighteenth century, America and Russia confronted Europe with new extremes of liberty and despotism. Each extreme challenged the illogical compromises standing at the heart of the European Old Regime; and in their different ways, both contributed to its overthrow.

SPANISH AMERICA. The decay of Spanish hegemony among the powers of Europe was symbolized by Portugal's successful reassertion of national independence after 1640 and by the unfavorable terms of the Peace of the Pyrenees concluded in 1659. Yet the Spanish empire in Europe maintained itself until 1713–14; and the empire overseas remained almost intact until the nineteenth century. Dynastic accident and the conservative action of balance-of-power diplomacy combined with the inherent strength and imperial traditions of Spain to secure this result.

The twin institutions of a hierarchical church and a centralized bureaucracy, directed in both cases by appointees of the Spanish crown, kept Spanish-American society within strict and traditional bounds until the third quarter of the eighteenth century. The Amerindian populations remained submissive, lacking either cultural or political leaders who could effectively challenge Spanish dominion.[12] Yet even within this carefully controlled and seemingly immobile society, far-reaching changes were under way. First and most basic:

---

[12] This seems generally true, despite the fact that Indian revolts broke out sporadically. The most important occurred in Peru, 1780–81, led by a man who claimed descent from the Inca royal family. More primitive tribes "reduced" in a mission often attempted to withdraw from their new dependence; but Spanish agents usually were able to compel them to return without massive exertion of force.

the paralyzing decay of Indian populations ceased to undermine the prosperity of Mexico and probably also of Peru after about 1650. Presumably Amerindians had by then begun to acquire a better immunity to European and African diseases, while disease-resistant mestizos had increased in numbers until they constituted a major element in the total population. The reversal was slow at first; but by the closing decades of the eighteenth century, very rapid population growth had set in. This in turn sustained a remarkable upsurge of economic activity: mines became more profitable than ever before; and both agriculture and trade flourished.[13]

Economic expansion was facilitated by widespread administrative reforms initiated in the eighteenth century by the new Bourbon monarchy of Spain[14] and especially by a drastic liberalization of trade regulations. In 1774, the Spanish colonies were allowed to trade freely among themselves for the first time. Four years later, supplementary decrees permitted twenty-four Spanish-American ports to trade with any port in Spain, thus terminating the exclusive rights of Cadiz on the Spanish side, and of Cartagena, Porto Bello, and Vera Cruz in America, to handle ships carrying goods between the colonies and the mother country.

Freer trade and the general economic upsurge in the Spanish colonies meant that a considerable class of merchants, petty retailers, and professional men began to flourish as never before. This growth of a middle class gave a new timbre to the intellectual and cultural life of the colonies. Despite the fact that elaborate educational institutions existed in Spanish America throughout the seventeenth and eighteenth centuries, and some of them had introduced modern curricula, including the study of such authors as Descartes, Leibniz, and Newton,[15] learning had remained sterile, limited to a few savants. Toward the close of the eighteenth century, however, wider circles of Spanish-American society began to interest themselves in new ideas from Europe; and as elsewhere, merchants and professional men led the way in exploring the novelties of the Enlightenment. These intellectual pursuits made such men increasingly critical of the society around them. They particularly resented the Spanish government's systematic discrimination in awarding high colonial offices exclusively to peninsular Spaniards.

With the appearance of a significant middle class and the beginning of an intellectual effervescence extending beyond the circle of professional savants, Spanish America became much more truly Europeanized than before. The continued retreat of purely Indian cultures before the missionary activity of the Church contributed to the same result. Racial plurality of course marked the new society off from its European model. The prevalence of large estates,

---

[13] Cf. statistics assembled in Bailey W. Diffie, *Latin-American Civilization, Colonial Period* (Harrisburg, Pa.: Stackpole Sons, 1945), pp. 381, 439–40, 450–55, and *passim;* R. A. Humphreys, "The Fall of the Spanish American Empire," *History,* XXXVII (1952), 213–27.

[14] For a detailed and very interesting study on how governmental initiative from Spain affected Mexican mining, cf. Clement G. Motten, *Mexican Silver and the Enlightenment* (Philadelphia: University of Pennsylvania Press, 1950).

[15] C. H. Haring, *The Spanish Empire in America,* pp. 235 ff.

the widespread resort to compulsory labor—whether debt peonage or outright slavery—and the extraordinary economic[16] and cultural importance of the Church continued to distinguish Spanish America from some parts of Europe; but these features of American society resembled conditions in Spain itself and had close analogues on Western civilization's other flank—eastern Europe.

BRAZIL AND NORTH AMERICA. Portuguese Brazil and the British colonies in North America had several points in common that distinguished them from the Spanish empire of the New World. Politically, both were radically decentralized; and serious domestic troubles in the home countries (the English Civil War, 1642–49, and the Portuguese revolt against Spain, 1640–59) threw the colonists very much upon their own resources in the middle years of the seventeenth century.[17] A plantation economy based upon slave labor dominated Brazil as well as the southern English colonies; and in both areas, a group of rough-and-ready frontiersmen sometimes accepted and sometimes defied the political leadership of the plantation owners of the coasts.

Yet on the whole, the resemblances between the two societies were more illusory than real. The Brazilian aristocracy, proud of its military and sexual prowess, disdaining both hard work (the fate of slaves) and intellectual cultivation (the province of priests), differed fundamentally from the landowners of Virginia or South Carolina. Despite governmental reforms initiated in the late eighteenth century by the despotic and "enlightened" Portuguese minister, the Marquis de Pombal, and despite a substantial economic growth, Brazil remained to the end of the century strongly differentiated from other societies. In particular, both Indian and Negro cultures, although intertwined with Portuguese tradition, retained a degree of vigor which was not matched elsewhere in the New World.[18]

Even at the end of the eighteenth century, the English, ex-English and French colonies lagged far behind Spanish America. Mexico City, with 112,926 inhabitants in 1793,[19] eclipsed anything to the north and indeed surpassed in size any city of contemporary France and England except Paris or London. Indeed, the population of Mexico exceeded by a substantial margin that of all thirteen English colonies together; and the splendor, elegance, and

[16] The Church held lands in its own right and also made loans to improvident landowners. The result was that, according to one estimate, as much as four-fifths of the land in the central part of New Spain was owned by or mortgaged to the Church. C. H. Haring, *The Spanish Empire in America* (New York: Oxford, 1952), pp. 190–91. In addition, such organizations as the Jesuits had become very prominent economic entrepreneurs and merchants, since they had to dispose of the products of their Indian missions, some of which, as in Paraguay, had become flourishing and numerically very substantial societies.

[17] The Brazilians, for example, evicted the Dutch from their country through a long guerrilla, 1643–54. At first the Brazilian insurgents disobeyed the Portuguese home government, which in 1641 had recognized the Dutch possession of Brazil in order to secure Dutch support against Spain. Cf. C. R. Boxer, *The Dutch in Brazil, 1623–1654* (Oxford: Clarendon Press, 1957).

[18] On Brazil I have consulted Diffie, *Latin-American Civilization*, pp. 633–753; Gilberto Freyre, *The Masters and the Slaves: A Study in the Development of Brazilian Civilization* (New York: Alfred A. Knopf, Inc., 1946); Lawrence F. Hill, *Brazil* (Berkeley and Los Angeles, Calif: University of California Press, 1947); Gilberto Freyre, *Brazil: An Interpretation* (New York: Alfred A. Kopf, Inc., 1947).

[19] Diffie, *Latin-American Civilization*, p. 453.

cultivation of the Spanish colonial upper class surpassed anything yet achieved along the Atlantic coast of North America.

Yet the culturally laggard New England and Middle Atlantic colonies of North America represented the most thoroughgoing translation of European-type society to new ground to be found anywhere in the world. These English colonies developed rapidly from the small and isolated coastal lodgments of the early seventeenth century into a more or less continuous band of settlements stretching from New Hampshire to Georgia and, by the time of the American Revolution, extending inland to the Appalachians. Population grew very fast, partly by immigration but mainly through natural increase. By 1790, when the first United States census was taken, it totaled four million, not far short of half the population of Great Britain.

Numbers brought a fuller approximation to the conditions of European and, specifically, of English political and cultural life. To be sure, New England had no aristocracy, and the monarchical power was far away and usually quite ineffective. Moreover, the continued accessibility of an open frontier made land easy to come by and maintained uniquely egalitarian farming communities. But in older settlements and especially in the seaports, an oligarchy of successful merchants and men of property began to develop in the eighteenth century very much along English lines. The habit of business enterprise was firmly planted in New England and the Middle Atlantic states, arising in large part from the same Puritanical background which gave England many of her most successful entrepreneurs. In particular, New England shipping had begun to penetrate distant seas. Abundant, cheap timber and crews disciplined to hard living and hard work by Calvinist doctrine and stony soils permitted the Yankee merchant marine to undercut every rival. Industrial development, on the other hand, remained rudimentary until after the American Revolution.

Social mobility and political liberty prevailed in the English colonies to an unusual degree. A clever and energetic man could rise fast and far, as the career of Benjamin Franklin (1706–90) showed. Even in the South, the plantation slave economy was in some measure counterbalanced by backwoods farming communities which resembled New England frontier settlements in all but the intensity of Calvinist religious discipline. Indeed, the English colonies in a sense enjoyed the best of two worlds: for the cultivated Virginia aristocrat, familiar with common law and acquainted with John Locke, dabbling in French authors, speculating in western lands, active in local government, and devoting his main energies to the management of his plantation, provided a sophisticated leadership for the backwoods without so completely dominating the scene as to fasten oligarchic rule upon the community. In similar fashion, merchants, shipowners, and businessmen of the northern colonies could retain their political leadership only so long as the rural hinterland would follow them. A comparatively broad suffrage permitted a large segment—in some colonies an absolute majority—of the adult male population to register its will in politics. This created an atmosphere strikingly different from the passive submission of the Latin American and French

Canadian rank and file to the leadership of their bureaucratic, oligarchic, and ecclesiastical masters.

Religious variety constituted a pervasive solvent to ecclesiastical and theological rigidity. Diversity of religious establishment from colony to colony was taken entirely for granted; and no one dreamed of imposing a single faith upon all of British North America. Moreover, as the eighteenth century advanced, within each religious community individuals increasingly turned away from the theological enthusiasms of their fathers, even in Puritan Massachusetts, and shared in the secularization of opinion which was simultaneously transforming Europe. This did not prevent revivalist preachers from stirring up extremes of religious emotion; yet deists and freethinkers, Anglicans, Congregationalists, Presbyterians, Quakers, Roman Catholics, Methodists, Baptists (not to mention groups springing from outside the English tradition like Mennonites and Dutch Reformed) had somehow to get along with one another. Thereby, colonial society necessarily pried itself loose from the domination of any single church or doctrine.

As long as the English colonies were hemmed in by the French and their Indian allies to the north and west, and exposed to attack by French ships of war or privateers, the protection of the British navy, and on occasion of regular British troops, was essential. But when the British annexed Canada after their victory in the Seven Years' War (1756–63), the French threat dwindled to insignificance and the relation of the colonies to the mother country changed accordingly. The attempt of the British government to collect additional taxes, to station troops in the colonies, to regulate the New England trade, and to restrict the powers of colonial legislatures roused a storm of opposition. The liberties of Englishmen were called upon to justify colonial resistance to the decrees of the British parliament. Organized defiance of British laws and authorities, however, precipitated a popular upheaval, sanctified by the rights not merely of Englishmen but of Man, as conceived by the most radical theorists of the day. Nevertheless, occasional outbursts of mob violence against "Tories" did not prevent the revolutionary movement from following generally legal paths, as the Patriot party rewrote the laws of the various colonies and experimented, at first rather unhappily, with federal union. When British troops attempted to quell disorder and disobedience, their action provoked progressively more extreme opposition; and by 1775, relations between the colonists and the British government had degenerated into open war. After many vicissitudes, the revolutionary cause triumphed in 1783, more because of bitterly divided counsels in the British government and the intervention of the French (who declared war on Great Britain in 1778) than because of the victories won by George Washington's tattered armies.

Thus the American Revolution achieved its fruition within the nexus of European power politics and war, while the American revolutionary leaders justified their actions by drawing upon the stock of radical political ideas which had recently become current in Europe. The same radical ideas, tempered by experience, inspired the men who drew up the Constitution of the United States. Theoretical principles of the division of powers among legislative, executive, and judicial branches of government, and of the distribution of governmental functions between local and federal authorities, were reduced to a workable constitution, while the principles of individual liberty and government by consent of the governed were proudly trumpeted to all the world.

Herein lay a powerful challenge to the Old Regime of Europe. Americans seemed to have wiped the slate clean of outmoded institutions in order to construct a rational system of government. Though some might doubt the stability or deny the principles of the new regime, nowhere in the Western world could the American experiment be regarded with indifference. Thus the former English colonies, however much they lagged behind Spanish America in outward state, and however crude their life might be when compared to that of European aristocrats, entered with a vengeance into the mainstream of European thought and action. Indeed, the American revolutionary example was a potent factor in stimulating the French Revolution which brought down the Old Regime of Europe.[20]

RUSSIA. The consolidation of a militarized, modernized, and autocratic government in Russia offered a very different sort of challenge to the Old Regime of Europe. It was not so drastic and immediate as the ideological challenge of the American Revolution. Yet the rise of a great new military empire, disposing of vast territory and population, and (at least in principle) channeling all human and material resources to the service of the state, clearly did challenge a politically fragmented and socially divided old Europe. Only by tapping new resources and finding new bases of power by continued self-transformation could comparative pygmies like France and Britain hope to meet the new Russian giant on anything like an equal footing. The fact that during the nineteenth century the Democratic and Industrial Revolutions did create new bases for power and wealth in western Europe, leaving Russia far behind for more than a century, has tended to obscure the nature of the Russian challenge as presented in the last decades of the eighteenth century. In effect, the Russian threat to Europe's traditional multiplicity was thereby postponed until our own time.

Until 1698, when the youthful Peter the Great returned from his famous tour of western Europe to inaugurate revolution from above, Russia jogged along under the policy and polity adopted by the first Romanovs. The effort was to maintain the peculiar Russian heritage intact by minimizing contacts with foreigners. This policy worked well in the seventeenth century. For example, Russia's role as champion of Orthodoxy helped the Tsars to secure title to the eastern Ukraine (1667) after a long war with Poland; for the Cossacks preferred an Orthodox to a Catholic master, if master there must be.

Peter, however, cared nothing at all for Orthodoxy and found the rude and boisterous manners of the foreign ghetto of Moscow far more to his taste than the ritualized life of the Russian court. Yet his intimate association with

---

[20] The relationship between the two revolutions is curiously symbolized by a chronological accident: George Washington was inaugurated as first President of the United States on April 30, 1789, on the very morrow of the day set for the Estates-General to convene at Versailles.

SCIENCE

ORTHODOXY

TECHNIQUE

TSAR

FOREIGN GHETTO

MANNERS

PEASANTS

ART

COSSACKS

TURKS

THE WEST

RUSSIA

RUSSIA UNDER PETER THE GREAT

foreigners remained merely a private idiosyncracy for nearly a decade after he became undisputed ruler of Russia. But when the revolt of a military unit in Moscow (1698) precipitated revolutionary action, Peter persevered until his dying day in a frenetic effort to make the clique of boon companions and adventurers he had gathered around himself into the masters of the Russian state.

One after another, old landmarks disappeared: beards and caftans were prohibited, the Julian calendar was introduced, the alphabet simplified, female seclusion abolished at court, and a new capital built at St. Petersburg on the Gulf of Finland. Peter routed the Russian nobles from their country estates and put them either in barracks or behind government desks. He turned Russian administration topsy-turvy in a wholesale effort to make it conform to Swedish models, and even dared to subject the Holy Orthodox Church to a lay procurator. Everywhere, the restless and capricious energy of the Tsar drove and hectored his reluctant people along new paths. Like Ivan the Terrible before him and like Stalin afterward, Peter's individual will effectually transformed Russian society and institutions within a quarter of a century.

Terror and wholesale violence helped to stamp Peter's reforms ineradicably into the Russian body politic, as did the vicissitudes of a long and difficult war with Sweden (1700–1721). Yet Peter and his friends could not have ridden roughshod over Russian customs and institutions with impunity had not the loyalty to Old Russia already been greatly weakened. Limited but prolonged exposure to the palpable superiorities of European civilization had undermined secure and unthinking confidence in the old traditions; and the official Church had been profoundly shaken by the secession of the Old Believers. Only the autocracy remained; and when it fell into the hands of a revolutionary who spurned the Russian past and chose to imitate aspects of European civilization, no rallying point of effective resistance remained.

At the center of all Peter's tumultuous activities was a remarkably single-minded drive for enhanced military power. His governmental reforms were dominated by the goal of recruiting, equipping, and maintaining an army and navy equal or superior to the forces of Western nations. This required, not only men and money, but also industrial establishments and shipyards, mathematics and practical skills, broader literacy, and a lavish resort to compulsion up and down the social scale. Peter conscripted serfs for the army, for his new armaments factories in the Urals, and for the construction of St. Petersburg; he conscripted nobles with an almost equal ruthlessness to serve wherever needed, and enrolled their sons in his regiments of Imperial Guards. In addition, he ordered merchants to transfer their activities from Archangel to his new capital at St. Petersburg, assigned Swedish prisoners of war to administrative duties in the Russian provinces, and imported hundreds of Dutch or other foreign artisans to establish new skills in Russia. Peter himself, driven by an almost demoniac restlessness, divided his time between erratic attention to detail, sudden drastic decisions, wild drinking bouts, and violent, unreasoning rages.

Peter's administrative reforms remained chaotic, and covert resistance to his innovations in all ranks of society did much to blunt his plans. Yet Peter re-made Russia. He won the war against Sweden, despite the prowess of his antagonist Charles XII, and annexed a substantial band of territory on the Gulf of Finland—his famous "window on the West." Wars with the Turks were less successful. Victory in 1696 secured access to the Sea of Azov; but this victory was canceled in 1711 when a second expedition ended in disaster, forcing the Tsar to surrender all the gains of the preceding campaign. As par-tial compensation, at the very end of his reign, Peter's armies won a war against Persia and advanced the Russian frontier to the southernmost shores of the Caspian.

Peter's extraordinary talents and unstable personality made his work pos-sible. The secret of his extraordinary success lay in the fact that he organized an informal but highly effective training system for turning out young men who would serve his revolutionary purposes. Peter's educational institutions were the Imperial Guards regiments, built around a core of his childhood playmates whom he had dragooned into military formations. When the revo-lution from the top got underway, the Tsar drew upon the Guards for the army officers, administrators, diplomats, and other helpers he needed. He then replenished the depleted ranks of the regiments by requiring the Russian nobles to send their sons to serve as privates. As a result, Peter quickly created a powerful ruling clique that was loosely but effectively united by the com-mon experience of a period of service in the Guards. Moreover, that fact that the new masters of Russia, having scornfully rejected much of the Russian past, were at first no more than a tiny garrison in an alien land gave them all a compelling reason to prevent the popular attachment to pre-Petrine Russia from finding any political expression that would endanger their power. Hence the fierce quarrels which characterized the ruling clique during the eighteenth century always stopped short at sudden palace coups d'état. Any lasting party factionalism might have opened a door to violent mass reaction against all who had betrayed the old Russian ways.[21]

After Peter's death, the history of Russia turned upon the history of the revolutionary clique he had built around the Imperial Guards regiments. Feuds and alliances among its members found expression in a remarkable series of palace revolutions, as one autocrat succeeded another without benefit of any settled line of succession or clear principle of legitimacy. The most extraordinary coup d'état was that which overthrew Peter II in 1762 and brought his wife, an obscure German princess, to the throne. Yet the usurper,

---

[21] The striking resemblances of the Imperial Guards to the Ottoman slave family system seem not to have been explored by historians. Although the soldiers of the Guards were not legally enslaved, they were subject to the same sort of regimen as Ottoman Janissaries and the palace staff had been in the days of Ottoman greatness. Moreover, the conversion of mind, manners, and morals involved in leaving a country estate in rural Russia and coming to serve in one of the Guards regiments was nearly as drastic as the conversion of Christian peasant boys into Ottoman pashas. Like the Turks, Peter al-lowed men of the most miscellaneous backgrounds to enter his regiments; but it was foreigners and sons of the Russian nobility who predominated. Few peasants cared to serve "Antichrist," even if they could have escaped from their masters to do so. The Communist party of Russia in our own time shares some important traits with both these older institutions.

as Catherine II, maintained her imperial position until her death in 1796 and raised Russian power to hitherto unparalleled heights.

Catherine preserved her throne by cultivating the Guards and by satisfying the noble class at large. Even before she came to the throne, the crude amoralism which had distinguished the roughnecks Peter gathered around himself had already been brought under some control by French governesses and German tutors imported into noble households to train children in the languages and manners of the European aristocracy.[22] But as familiarity with European aristocratic life spread, Russian nobles began to demand the privileges and status of their counterparts farther west. In particular, they wished to be relieved of the necessity of government service. Catherine's hapless husband granted this privilege in 1762, whereupon thousands of nobles left the army and bureaucracy to take up residence on their estates. Catherine improved upon this concession by providing legal safeguards against confiscation of noble properties and other arbitrary punishment. She also confirmed and enhanced the nobility's legal powers over their serfs and authorized the provincial nobles to form corporate organizations for specified and limited purposes.

Catherine could afford to relax the pressures upon the nobility, because Russia now had a fairly adequate supply of reasonably well-trained persons who were willing, and indeed eager, to occupy government and army posts. Economic development had reached a point where the autocracy disposed of sufficient tax income to pay its officials some sort of salary, so that the old form of payment by grants of land was no longer necessary.[23] Government service remained a ladder for social advancement, for, by definition, the attainment of a certain rank in either army or civil service carried with it an automatic grant of nobility, with all the legal privileges of that rank.

But at the bottom of the social scale, the serfs saw no improvement in their condition and indeed were more aggrieved than before. After the nobles were relieved of their obligation to serve the state, the peasants naturally thought that they, too, should be freed of their obligation to serve the nobles. A great peasant uprising centering in southern Russia gave expression to this conviction (1773–75) but was brutally suppressed by the authorities. Thereafter, peasant discontent was diverted from direct expression into chiliastic sectarianism and widespread drunkenness.

Russia thus divided into two increasingly alien communities more sharply

[22] Cf. Émile Haumont, *La Culture française en Russie, 1700–1900* (Paris: Hachette, 1913), pp. 85–90. Only slowly did regular schools establish themselves, the most important becoming the Corps of Pages (established 1731), which allowed young nobles to qualify for a commission in the army (or in government service) without serving in the ranks of the Guards, as had been obligatory in Peter's time.

[23] Economic development under Catherine was phenomenal. Urban population rose from about a third of a million at the end of Peter's reign to something between 1.3 and 2.3 million at Catherine's death. Cottage industry as well as large manufacturing enterprises multiplied; and exports increased from about 30 million rubles in 1773 to over 81 million at Catherine's death. These figures are from Michael T. Florinsky, *Russia: A History and an Interpretation* (New York: Macmillan Co., 1955), pp. 561–64. For an overview of the economic boom in southern Russia and adjacent areas, cf. Traian Stoianovich, "The Conquering Balkan Orthodox Merchant," *Journal of Economic History*, XX (1960), 234–313.

than ever before. The privileged nobility, whose wealthier members had become completely acclimated to the thought and manners of French salons by the end of the eighteenth century, moved in a world totally divorced from the harsh ignorance and brutishness of peasant life. The more civilized and cultivated the Russian aristocrats became, the less they had in common with their peasants.

Here of course lay a great source of future weakness. But in the eighteenth century itself, the social fissures between aristocracy and commonalty in western Europe were nearly as great; and for the time being, Russia's social structure constituted no great handicap vis-à-vis the Western powers. Moreover, mere massiveness told powerfully in Russia's favor. Catherine not only annexed about half of Poland through three successive partitions of that unhappy country (1772–95) but also pushed Russia's frontiers to the Black Sea, where she secured for Russian ships the right to navigate what had been a closed Ottoman lake and to pass the straits freely (1774, 1783). Dreams of destroying the Ottoman empire entirely and of substituting a restored and dependent Greek empire on the Bosphorus remained unfulfilled. Nevertheless, the military power inherent in a state so vast as Russia had been unambiguously demonstrated. Russia had announced herself as a European great power under Peter; she arrived under Catherine.

3. THE COMPROMISES OF THE OLD REGIME IN EUROPE

France emerged as principal victor from the Thirty Years' War and rapidly became the cynosure of all Europe. The pomp of Louis XIV's court (1643–1715) bespoke power and wealth, refinement and elegance. Aristocrats, tamed by attendance at court, gave up older habits of violence. The French countryside therefore experienced a new profundity of peace while the king's armies marched and countermarched beyond French borders, where they gave his diplomats leverage to expand those borders toward the Rhine. German princelings, so far as they could afford it, and Charles II of England (1660–85), so far as he dared, sought to imitate the glories of the French monarch; and if Louis XIV's armies were difficult to match, being so expensive, at least it was easy to find rivals to his mistresses. To be sure, French military predominance waned after 1715, as England on one flank and Austria on the other enhanced their power. But French thought and letters, already impressive in the seventeenth century, acquired in the eighteenth a prestige that transcended political or linguistic boundaries and irradiated all Europe, as well as America and Russia.

Since the breakdown of medieval Latin Christendom, Europe's social and cultural cohesion had never been so great. The contrarieties of the European inheritance, so violently at odds with one another in the sixteenth century, were reconciled in the sevententh by a series of quite illogical but nonetheless effective compromises, extending from politics and society to thought and, less distinctly, to the arts. The resultant equilibrium never ceased to change, varying from time to time and from region to region; moreover, from its inception it contained the seeds of its nineteenth-century dissolution. Yet it is possible to characterize some of the main lines and more lasting features of the Old Regime of Europe.

POLITICAL AND SOCIAL COMPROMISES. The Old Regime of Europe was built upon a multiplicity of territorial states, each jealously guarding its sovereignty. Recognizing no superior without, the rulers of such states likewise acknowledged no indefeasible limits to their authority within their own territories. Yet in practice even the most absolute monarchs were obliged to accommodate their conduct to the interests of towns, provinces, chartered companies, guilds, the Church, and other privileged corporations at home; while the balance of power confined their actions abroad to fairly narrow limits.

Sovereignty was also restricted by conventions of propriety. Chastened by the furor of religious wars, the rulers of Europe forswore direct appeal to the deeper springs of human action and regarded doctrinaire enthusiasm inspired by a vision of religious or any other form of truth as ridiculous, naïve, and downright dangerous. Rulers instead found it wise to widen the scope of professionalism, which could be trusted to work tepidly but effectively within well-worn and familiar paths. Professional lawyers, doctors, merchants, courtiers, landowners, bureaucrats, army officers, and by the eighteenth century, even writers, trained in the techniques and conformable to the conventions of their calling, remolded the life of Europe bit by bit as the decades advanced, and did so with only rare appeals to the depths of human passion or to the heights of human aspiration. Even a theoretically absolute, energetic, and ambitious ruler like Louis XIV was therefore limited, not only by the alliances of foreign powers that checked his aggressive wars, but also by a less formal but far more durable alliance of autonomous or semi-autonomous professional bodies and privileged corporations within France, each of which, adhering stubbornly to its rights, procedures, and accustomed routine, acted as a stabilizing force in society. Conventions and decorum backed by the weight of massive institutions prevented even the most absolute of kings, not merely from revolutionizing society, but from even conceiving the possibility of doing so. Theoretically absolute sovereignty, therefore, remained entirely theoretical.

International war and diplomacy well illustrated the checks upon sovereignty inherent in the Old Regime. For a brief period at the beginning of Louis XIV's reign, French power exceeded that of its continental rivals; but the balance was restored when England joined the ranks of the Grand Alliance against France in 1689. Thereafter, even such drastic operations as the dismemberment of the Spanish empire in Europe (1700–1714), the overthrow of the Swedish empire of the Baltic (1700–1721), and the partitioning of Poland (1772–95) were carried through with careful regard for the balance of power among the major European states.

During most of the eighteenth century, this balance was maintained by parallel processes of expansion. In the west, France and Britain throve upon trade and overseas ventures; while in eastern Europe Austria, Prussia, and Russia grew powerful by incorporating weakly organized and partially empty regions on the landward frontier of European society. Ultimately, the advantage lay with the powers farthest removed from the European center. Thus insular Britain won a decisive victory in the Seven Years' War (1756–63) and acquired the French empire in India and America. To the east, Austria enjoyed a comparable advantage in the late seventeenth and early eighteenth centuries when Hapsburg armies drove into Hungary (1683–99) and the Balkans (1714–18) and opened the westernmost extremity of the Eurasian steppe to resettlement by Hapsburg subjects. After about the mid-eighteenth century, however, Russia replaced Austria as the principal gainer from the continuing process of expansion along the landward frontier of Europe.

Yet the peripheral powers of Europe had their weaknesses too. Subduing, settling, and civilizing the borderlands taxed the diplomacy and the resources of distant central governments; and the very extent of the British, Austrian, and Russian empires with their variegated peoples and customs frequently placed demands upon the center to which it was unequal. Scottish rebellions (1715, 1745), the American Revolution (1775–83), risings in Hungary (1703–11, 1789), and the inchoate armed protests led by Stenka Razin (1670–71) and Emilian Pugachev (1773–75) in Russia illustrated the difficulties and illuminated some of the shortcomings of the British, Austrian, and Russian home governments in their respective borderlands.

Within each European state, the weight of different elements in the system of checks and balances varied from time to time. In seventeenth-century France, the rationalizing, centralizing pressure of the civil and military bureaucracies tended to encroach upon other elements in French society. The aristocracy, in particular, saw its independence undermined, as much by the distribution of royal pensions and favors as by direct usurpation of noble rights. Later, in the eighteneth century, the aristocracy reclaimed some of its autonomy—but did so with pen, not sword in hand, through legal argument (the *parlements*) and theoretical disquisition (e.g., Montesquieu).

In Austria, by contrast, the Church retained a greater independence and a more inclusive authority than in Gallican France. The middle classes were definitely weaker; and the separate crown lands remained distinct entities, only loosely united by a comomn fealty to the Hapsburg monarch. Administrative centralization, which had been carried forward so successfully in seventeenth-century France, became the major agenda before the Austrian bureaucracy from the middle of the eighteenth century onward, only to be interrupted far short of completion by the French Revolution. Spain and Portugal adhered generally to the rhythm of Austrian Hapsburg development, attempting, in effect, to borrow French techniques of political and military greatness during the middle years of the eighteenth century.

Sweden and Poland, which had played a role as great powers in the seventeenth century, lost this status in the eighteenth, as much because of failure to establish the sort of administrative concentration and social balance achieved in seventeenth-century France as because of any inherent limits to their human or natural resources.[24] Holland likewise declined in political importance in the eighteenth century. Located as it was near the heart of European civilization, its scant natural resources and relatively small population were inadequate to support the status of a great power. The positions once occupied in European war and diplomacy by Sweden, Poland, and Holland were taken over by two polities, Britain and Prussia, which diverged strikingly from the

[24] Sweden, though thinly populated at home, had a rich and extensive Baltic empire *in potentia* at the close of the Thirty Years' War. The Swedish nobility, however, preferred liberty at home on the Polish model, while the countervailing forces of king, bureaucracy, and middle classes were inadequate to check the resultant erosion of state power. In 1772 a royal coup d'état saved Sweden at the last moment from becoming, like Poland, a helpless pawn of Russia and/or Prussia.

THE OLD REGIME IN THEORY AND PRACTICE

norm of the Old Regime. By remarkable coincidence, the years 1640–88, which witnessed revolution from above in Prussia and from below in Britain, were decisive in defining the peculiar constitutional and social balance of each.

In 1640, when Frederick William of Hohenzollern, the Great Elector, came to power in Brandenburg, Prussia was a poor and remote province which he held in fief from the Polish crown, while his other territories lay scattered widely through the Germanies. But when the Great Elector died in 1688, Brandenburg-Prussia had become a garrison state, in which all available resources were concentrated upon the task of sustaining a large and efficient standing army. Frederick William and his officials allowed nothing to stand in the way of this goal. Noble privileges, provincial and town immunities, guild and even village customs all were co-ordinated, adjusted, and if need be suppressed in order to produce the greatest possible military strength. As a result, what had been poor, weak, and disparate territories were knitted into an administrative unity which proved capable not only of defending itself, but also of providing an effective base from which the authority of the house of Hohenzollern could be extended to new lands.[25]

The Great Elector's successors were capable rulers and proved remarkably single-minded in advancing the power and increasing the territories of their state. By the time of Frederick II, the Great (1740–86), Prussia had become equal to France on the battlefield, rival to Austria in the Germanies, and partner with Russia and Austria in the partitioning of Poland. Success softened the almost Spartan rigor of the Prussian polity; and a modest prosperity, carefully fostered by a government aware that armies throve on taxes, added urban complexity and privileged occupational groupings to Prussian society. As a result, by the end of Frederick's reign, Prussia differed less from the other states of continental Europe than had earlier been the case.

England's development was different. The English Revolution (1640–88) established the authority of parliament even against the crown and fastened an oligarchical government upon the nation. Subsequent developments, such as the emergence of cabinet government, merely widened the distance between British and continental institutions. In the seventeenth century, parliament looked like an archaic survival from medieval times, provoking domestic disturbance with its factiousness and thwarting modern, efficient govern-

[25] The fact that Brandenburg had been repeatedly devastated during the Thirty Years' War, and that the population of most of the Elector's territories had suffered from Swedish and other foreign occupation over long periods of time, certainly facilitated the clean sweep of old obstructions to centralizing authority which the Great Elector carried through. Towns were still small and few, so that the multiplex corporate structure of French society did not exist to oppose revolution from above. Moreover, any policy, no matter how radical, which aimed at preventing repetition of the experiences of the Thirty Years' War could command widespread assent.

Yet, as in the case of Peter the Great of Russia, the personality of the ruler cannot be left out of account. Much of Germany had suffered devastation similar to that which afflicted the Hohenzollern lands; and urban life was likewise weak in many parts of Germany. But only in the Hohenzollern realms did these conditions provoke or permit radical militarization of society and government. The will and judgment of the Great Elector, capitalizing upon the military traditions of the Teutonic Knights and of the entire German *Drang nach Osten*, determined this result.

ment with its parsimony. By the mid-eighteenth century, however, Britain's newfangled cabinet government, responsible to parliament, began to impress even continental observers with its capacity to wage successful wars abroad while maintaining liberty and order at home. Above all, the British parliament stood for the notion that property owners had the right to take active part in making the laws, in formulating governmental policy, and in administering local affairs. Some of the aristocrats of France, reduced to a largely decorative function at court, and leading French merchants and professional men, who sometimes chafed at the rigidity of royal regulations, began to feel that French greatness had been dearly bought by the surrender of their political liberties. Particularly after parliament's able handling of the Seven Years' War (1756–63), many Frenchmen began to suspect that some reordering of their own institutions in the direction of British parliamentarianism would be advantageous.

The British government, like the French, rested upon a closely meshed tangle of legal corporations and looser associations, whose conservative weight restrained parliament almost as effectively as their counterparts in France restrained the absolutism of the king. Yet the parliamentary system allowed a more constant, and more sensitive, adjustment among the interests of these groups than was possible within the more rigid framework of a royal, bureaucratic government. As their wealth and numbers increased, new interests like the West Indian sugar planters, the Bristol slavers, the improving landlords of Norfolk, and even the plebeian upstart cotton manufacturers of Manchester could make their weight felt in parliament. Such groups were then in a position to see to it that government policy was adjusted to suit their needs, within limits set by competing interests also represented in parliament. On the other hand, French, Austrian, and even Prussian regulations, generated within a bureaucracy, were far less responsive to the shifting constellation of economic interests and tended to remain in force even after conditions had changed. The result was to retard or even inhibit economic and technical innovations to which the looser British system gave free scope.

Perhaps the most fundamental difference between the social patterns of Britain and the Continent (apart from Holland and some of the Swiss and German free cities) was the greater prestige and autonomy which merchants and financiers enjoyed. In France, and on the Continent generally, a successful businessman made haste to leave his past behind, either by direct purchase of a royal patent of nobility or by sending his sons into government service where they might hope to win or purchase the ennoblement that went with high office. This required withdrawal from the degrading associations of the market place. In England, however, nobles regularly trespassed upon the market place by investing in commercial ventures; and successful merchants who bought country estates and set themselves up as gentlemen did not necessarily abandon their mercantile activities, though they were likely to become financiers rather than active entrepreneurs. Under these circumstances, the spendthrift habits of an idle nobility tended in France and elsewhere to disperse commercial capital more thoroughly than was the rule in England. Converse-

UPPER AND LOWER CLASSES OF THE OLD REGIME

Thomas Gainsborough's portrait of the Honourable Frances Duncombe with its classical reminders and rural setting contrasts forcibly with William Hogarth's sketch of a London street scene. Prior to the Industrial Revolution, all civilization had been built upon a comparable cultural displacement between rich and poor, cultured and uncultured, masters and servants. Yet recognition of the gap and a sense of its injustice, such as stands behind Hogarth's drawing, had seldom been paralleled elsewhere and previously. Perhaps the changeability of the Old Regime, the growth of a few really large cities, and the corresponding shift from status to market relationships uprooted habitual patterns of deference, and made men at each level of the social hierarchy more acutely aware of the treacherousness of the ground beneath their feet than could be the case in more purely agrarian societies. The Hellenistic parallel above (p. 291) stemmed from a similarly megalopolitan social setting.

ly, the easy availability of relatively large quantities of capital which resulted from this interpenetration of the landed nobility and the merchant class much facilitated the remarkable economic growth of Great Britain in the seventeenth and eighteenth centuries.

Tolerance of religious nonconformity likewise contributed to England's economic development. After 1689, Puritans and adherents of various more radical religious sects enjoyed limited rights, including that of engaging in business, although election to parliament and admission to the universities and learned professions were denied them. The nonconformist community, with an ethos shaped by evangelical religion and legal disabilities, became a nursery for many of England's most hard-driving entrepreneurs; and its members often led the way in economic innovation. In France, on the contrary, Louis XIV's determination to uproot heresy from his kingdom disrupted the community of Huguenot merchants and manufacturers who had played a similar economic role. French industry and commerce suffered; but the Huguenot refugees correspondingly enriched lands like England and Prussia, where they found welcome.

George III (1760–1820) was the last English king to challenge parliament by attempting to rule in his own right. The "patriot" king availed himself of his power of making official appointments to build a royal following in parliament, hoping thereby to transcend the incessant factional bickering which was the life and essence of the parliamentary method of adjusting the complex interests constituting British society. The attempt failed, discredited by successful American rebellion (1775–83) and by the king's intermittent insanity (after 1788). On the eve of the French Revolution, therefore, parliamentary supremacy, responsible cabinet government, and oligarchic domination of the country were firmly implanted in Britain. The liberties of Englishmen, expressed in the chronic effervescence of parliamentary and extra-parliamentary debate, and confirmed by economic and imperial success, provided a sharp contrast to the deferential obedience which the absolute monarchs of the Continent expected from their loyal subjects.

In most of the larger territorial states of Europe, the Old Regime endowed the central authority, whether parliament or monarch, with far more formidable instruments of military and economic power than ever before. The general wealth of Europe increased to a point where tax income could pay and equip comparatively large and formidable standing armies and professional navies. New or newly expanded financial devices, like the British national debt and the Bank of England (chartered 1694), allowed mobilization of economic resources on a new scale by tapping private capital for state uses. Such devices, together with the chartered joint stock companies, which had been introduced at the beginning of the seventeenth century, gave Europeans the means of continued economic expansion and increased their military power in all parts of the world.

Although the poor and propertyless had small share in Europe's enhanced power and prosperity, yet individuals of energy and ability frequently climbed up a rung or two on the social ladder, and, even among the most poverty-stricken, survival became more frequent. Professionalization checked the ravages of war; new crops (especially potatoes and maize), better tillage, and improvements in transportation checked famine. Even disease became less of a scourge, as acquired immunities and improvements in medical diagnosis and treatment made cures more frequent than before. As a result, Europe's population spurted upward. Despite appalling conditions in cities like London, where cheap gin for a while supplanted epidemic disease as a prime destroyer of human life, Europe's poor as well as the middle and upper classes throve as seldom before under the political and social compromises of the Old Regime.

INTELLECTUAL COMPROMISES. The antagonism between secularized reason and religious faith, so vehemently expressed in the clashing ideals of Renaissance and Reformation, found a practical, if not a theoretical resolution under the Old Regime. In effect, the effort to attain logical consistency in society as a whole was given up. More and more, the states of Europe allowed old laws requiring religious conformity to fall into disuse and permitted individuals to follow their own religious inclinations. A decent respect for the conventions was expected; blasphemy and all extreme sectarian manifestations continued to be outlawed in every European state. But the note of desperation so prominent in sixteenth-century struggles for theological and metaphysical certainty, together with the ruthless demand for orthodoxy in word, thought, and deed, rapidly died away after the close of the Thirty Years' War. By the eighteenth century, the intellectual leaders of Europe tended to concentrate their attention on science and rationalistic philosophy rather than on theology and no longer concerned themselves overmuch with making their conclusions conform to Christian doctrine.

The phenomenal successes of rationalistic thought and of natural science in the seventeenth century partly explain this altered intellectual climate. René Descartes (d. 1650) boldly set himself the task of reasoning out a complete science from self-evident first principles that would explain metaphysical, physical, biological, and psychological reality with all the certainty of a geometrical demonstration. His contemporaries, Baruch Spinoza (d. 1677) and Thomas Hobbes (d. 1679), were also fascinated by the apparent certainty and precision of mathematical reasoning, and like Descartes, attempted to apply the methods of mathematics to things human and divine. Gottfried Wilhelm Leibniz (d. 1716) did likewise a generation later. Despite the widely divergent conclusions to which their mathematical mode of reasoning led, these and other seventeenth-century thinkers agreed in extending the realm of law and regularity to numerous new phenomena and in reducing or entirely eliminating the sphere of caprice, accident, chance, and miracle. For example, both Descartes and Hobbes asserted that animals were automata governed by definite laws, and Descartes outlined the principles of a world machine to explain all phenomena of both heavens and earth. The reasoning of Spinoza and Leibniz was more abstruse; but both were also gripped by the vision of a world subject to laws and regularities which could be grasped and expounded by the unaided power of human reason.

Descartes attracted a larger following than other philosophers, perhaps because his theories were both more comprehensive and more comprehensible than theirs. Indeed, in the second half of the seventeenth century, Cartesian philosophy became fashionable in French intellectual circles and won numerous adherents in other countries as well. Yet the vogue did not last, for Cartesianism as a whole could not long survive the collapse of Descartes' physics when confronted by the elegant demonstrations of Sir Isaac Newton's *Philosophae Naturalis Principia Mathematica* (1687). The great strength of Newtonianism lay in its empirical validation and the simplicity with which it reduced the movements of the moon and of the planets to mathematical formulae, which, wonder of wonders, also described the behavior of objects moving on the earth. Such radical simplification of the apparent diversity of natural phenomena exalted the mind. What philosophers had long sought to prove now seemed to have been verified beyond all doubt: law, simple, clear, and beautiful in its mathematical precision, did indeed govern the universe, a law so ineluctable and universal that it controlled alike the future movements of the heavenly bodies and of cannon balls. At first some critics boggled at the occult nature of gravitational force acting at a distance; but doubts were soon drowned in a chorus of admiration as new observations confirmed the accuracy of Newton's mathematical expression of the laws of motion.

Mathematics had indeed been vindicated. It was easy to infer that God himself, the architect of the universe whose laws had now been discovered, was a master mathematician, who could show his wisdom and the excellence of his creation only by retiring from active supervision of the world machine he had made. Interference with the natural order of events would obviously infringe divine laws and thereby confess their inadequacy. The Being who had created such a complex, yet wonderfully simple machine could not be expected to spoil his own handiwork by arbitrary intervention on behalf of mere human beings. Such ideas about Nature, God, and Man stood in radical opposition to Christianity. No room was left for divine grace, providence, or original sin; and in a Newtonian universe it was also difficult to find a suitable location for Heaven and Hell as traditionally conceived.

Moreover, it was logical to suppose that God had also laid down laws for human behavior, which, if they could be recognized, might establish a harmony among mankind as wonderful as the harmony of physical nature. Another Newton who would unravel the tangled skein of human phenomena and discover the natural law of society might therefore be expected to raise earth to the heavens and bring Heaven to earth, as Newtonian physics had already, quite literally, done for the world of inanimate objects.

Such a hope amounted to a radical secularization of Christian eschatology. Instead of waiting upon the Second Coming of Christ, Reason boldly essayed the task of saving mankind from all the miseries, crimes, and follies of the past. Despite persistent vagueness about all details concerning the ultimate earthly perfection of humanity, manly strides along the road of progress now seemed assured, for had not mankind at long last emerged from its infancy and awakened to the voice of Reason?

Despite the plausibility of such "deist" views, the great majority of Europeans continued to adhere to traditional Christianity. Conservative inertia was in part responsible: yet the deist outlook had a serious defect which did much to strengthen orthodox religion. God the clockmaker and master mathematician had little appeal to the heart and offered no present help in time of trouble. Intelligent and subtle-minded men shuddered at the thought of a dead, mechanical universe of infinite spaces and natural law. Most famous of these was Blaise Pascal (d. 1662), who reaffirmed with all the force of new conviction the vital importance of personal confrontation and communion with God.

Perhaps just because the silent emptiness of Newton's infinite space threatened to engulf and utterly lose so petty a planet as earth, the seventeenth and eighteenth centuries were particularly prolific of new religious movements and sects, all emphasizing a direct, emotionally charged experience of God. Within the Protestant tradition, the Quakers and Methodists in England and the pietists in Germany had wide appeal; and in Catholic countries, Jansenism and Quietism might likewise have grown to great proportions had not papal condemnation led to forcible suppression of both.

What was remarkable about European society in the eighteenth century was that such widely discordant views were permitted to exist side by side more or less peaceably, dividing the loyalty of the population with each other and with a frequently somnolent official ecclesiastical establishment. Champions of religious orthodoxy, for example Bishop Bossuet (d. 1704) of France, publicly expressed their deep mistrust of the new science. But others, like Bishop Sprat (d. 1713) in England, enthusiastically championed the scientific spirit. In general, theologians and scientists tended to go their separate ways, each adhering faithfully to the standards and conventions of their increasingly divergent intellectual traditions. Many persons, like Newton himself, combined new science with old faith, either by establishing separate criteria of truth for religion and science or by various and ingenious schemes designed to make room for biblical cosmology in the new world of science or for the new scientific universe in older Christian cosmologies.

Not only natural scientists, but also lawyers, doctors, writers, philosophers, musicians, painters, and savants of every kind were now free to elaborate the technicalities and traditions of their chosen profession with little regard for the religious orthodoxy of their results. With this, the modern pluralistic age of intellect began. New institutions, like the Académie Française (founded 1635) or the Royal Society of England (founded 1660) stimulated and sheltered literary and intellectual activities; while learned professional journals, together with books and pamphlets popularizing scientific results, communicated new ideas and data to all who might be interested. Less formal groupings, such as the habitués of Dr. Johnson's favorite coffee house in London or the visitors to the intellectual salons of Paris, also played a great part in stimulating and sustaining the variety and vigor of European intellectual and artistic life.

Never since has the Western world as a whole seriously tried to establish a single, all-embracing truth and doctrine, although segments of that world—Communist Russia, Nazi Germany, and Fascist Italy—have made the attempt. Memories of their predecessors' bloody and futile struggles to discover and then impose an all-embracing truth played their part in reconciling men to the illogic of multiplicity. More pervasive and more permanent was the autonomy of the various professions and associations which sustained wide divergence of thought and belief. Finally, and perhaps most vital of all, the general prosperity and success of European society under the political and social compromises of the Old Regime made it comparatively easy to tolerate differences even on important questions.

Under these conditions, European thought achieved extraordinary fertility and variety. With an unending stock of new data coming in, whether from more careful observation, better instruments, more elaborate analysis, or from penetration of new regions of the earth, the intellectual leaders of Europe faced a tremendous task in merely validating, cataloguing, and ordering their expanding fund of knowledge. These were, in fact, the great tasks of natural science in the eighteenth century. In physics, the astronomer Pierre Simon Laplace (d. 1827) and French artillerists carried on Newton's work by applying his celestial and terrestrial mechanics to new phenomena. In botany and zoölogy, the Swede Linnaeus (d. 1778) and the Frenchman George Louis Leclerc de Buffon (d. 1788) undertook to classify and catalogue the forms of plant and animal life of the entire world. Only in chemistry did the eighteenth century see a major new theoretical breakthrough, when Joseph Priestley (d. 1804) and Antoine Lavoisier (d. 1794) worked out a new theory of combustion, and Lavoisier formulated the principle of the conservation of matter in chemical reactions.

Needless to say, the application of reason to human affairs met with less success. Yet the effort was boldly made and was not without its victories. Empiricism and rationalism were brilliantly combined in the study of history, for example. During the seventeenth century, scholars painfully reconstructed a fairly firm chronological frame for Europe's classical and medieval past from the confusion of old records and calendrical systems. In addition, the Benedictine monk Jean Mabillon (d. 1681) developed sophisticated techniques for validating old manuscripts and assigning them approximate dates. As a result of these and similar labors in the eighteenth century, monumental historical narratives such as Edward Gibbon's *Decline and Fall of the Roman Empire* could be constructed on the basis of the detailed critical work of hundreds of scholars.

But while the study of history was advancing to new levels of accuracy and venturing upon bold synthetic interpretations, metaphysics underwent a remarkable deflation. John Locke's *Essay Concerning Human Understanding* (1690) cast doubt upon the possibility of achieving universally valid knowledge; Bishop George Berkeley (d. 1753) and David Hume (d. 1776) took up the epistemological questions Locke had raised and pointed out new difficulties in achieving certainty. Immanuel Kant (d. 1804), however, rescued philosophy from the impasse in which Hume's criticism had left it by accepting the impossibility of knowing things in themselves, but asserting that careful examination of the structure of the human intellect itself yielded universally valid truths concerning all possible objects of human experience. Kant in turn opened the door for the revival in nineteenth-century Germany of grandiose systematic philosophies based upon confident efforts to anatomize the Spirit, whose active role in defining reality he had so impressively pointed out.

Epistemological and metaphysical difficulties certainly did not prevent publicists and self-styled philosophers of the eighteenth century from criticizing existing society in the name of reason. By and large, customary practices and established institutions fared badly under this scrutiny. In France, Voltaire (d. 1778) held up to ridicule the superstition and bigotry of organized religion; and in Scotland, Adam Smith argued in *The Wealth of Nations* (1776) that economic production and exchange would automatically find their most efficient forms if human nature, inspired by rational self-interest, were allowed free scope. On this view, state interference with economic processes as universally practiced under the Old Regime was merely an impediment to the general welfare.

The basis of all political authority obviously required reconsideration by men who no longer believed that God personally intervened in human affairs. Without Divine Providence, divine-right monarchy became mere usurpation. An alternative basis for legitimizing government was found in the notion of a social contract; but the terms of such a contract were subject to widely differing formulations. Thomas Hobbes (d. 1679) used the notion of social contract to argue the necessity of absolute monarchy; whereas John Locke (d. 1704) and Jean-Jacques Rousseau (d. 1778) both justified revolution by appropriate redefinition of the contract's terms. Rousseau's *Social Contract* was indeed a thoroughly revolutionary book; for it advanced a democratic theory of sovereignty and held that rebellion was justified whenever a government failed to satisfy the people it ruled. Such theories, demanding in effect a clean sweep of established institutions and the substitution of a rationalized order of human society, were utterly subversive of the Old Regime and all its tattered compromises.

Yet critics who took their principles so seriously as to repudiate existing patterns of life were always a small minority. If confidence in reason and progress, a vague belief in the essential goodness of human nature, and a generally more secular outlook penetrated comparatively broad strata of the European populace in the eighteenth century, it remained true nonetheless that the great majority remained faithful to older patterns of belief and conduct. Whatever incompatibility they may have felt between Christianity and the new notions, most men refrained from pursuing such incompatibilities to any logical conclusion, whether in word or in deed. Thus the institutional irrationality which so offended enlightened critics had its intellectual analogue among a majority of the critics themselves.

COMPROMISES IN THE ARTS. The pluralism of European society and thought under the Old Regime was also manifest in the arts. In England in the latter part of the seventeenth century, the high seriousness of John Milton's epic *Paradise Lost* (1667) and the bawdiness of Restoration comedy overlapped; while a century later, the elaborate urbanity of Samuel Johnson's prose (d. 1784) jostled the artful rusticity of Robert Burns (d. 1796). It is customary to distinguish a classical followed by a romantic tendency in European letters; and art historians recognize three successive styles in architecture and painting: baroque, rococo, and classical. These classifications are

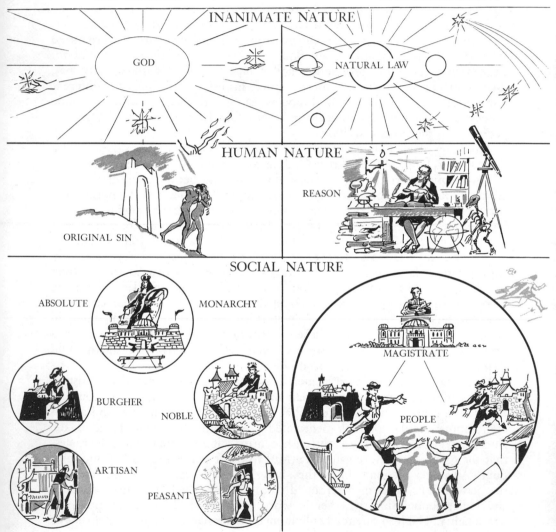

INTELLECTUAL CHALLENGES TO THE OLD REGIME

useful, so long as one does not press them too hard; but they scarcely fit such a writer as Daniel Defoe (d. 1731) or the Dutch school of painting, and we should always remember that shifting standards of fashion and taste never displaced literary classics like Shakespeare from the English stage or Luther's Bible from German homes.

On the surface, the late seventeenth and early eighteenth century showed a remarkable cohesion in art and letters, as the prestige of French culture spread "classicism" throughout Europe. The great classical dramatists of France, Pierre Corneille (d. 1684), Molière (d. 1673), and Jean Racine (d. 1699) took rules of correctness seriously, both in diction (following the *Dictionnaire* of the Académie Française) and in composition (the "three unities"). In subsequent decades, lesser men assiduously followed their example, both in France and abroad; and French became the language of belles-lettres throughout much of Europe. Only English literature remained fully independent, while sharing in the classical norms of restraint, elegance, precision, and wit with writers such as Joseph Addison (d. 1719) or Alexander Pope (d. 1744). Yet an enormous variety coexisted with this high, cosmopolitan, self-conscious literary culture—running the gamut from the hectic visions of George Fox (d. 1691), founder of Quakerism, to the ponderous learning of the German jurist Samuel Pufendorf (d. 1694).

The French classical ideal clearly began to lose its force in the second half of the eighteenth century. Particularly in England and Germany, writers turned away from French models and sought inspiration rather in the heritage of classical Greece or in their own national and medieval pasts. Bishop Percy's *Reliques of Ancient English Poetry* (1765), a collection of popular ballads, and Johann Gottfried Herder's (d. 1803) impassioned pleas for an authentic German literature rooted in the language and feeling of ordinary folk were landmarks of this development. Romanticism proclaimed spontaneous expression of feeling to be the sole source of great literature and emphasized national, local, and personal genius. Such views stimulated (or merely coincided with?) a sudden efflorescence of German literature. Friedrich von Schiller (d. 1804) and Johann Wolfgang von Goethe (d. 1832) were the two central figures of the German literary revival, although particularly in Goethe's case, the term romanticism is inadequate to encompass the variety of his work.

In architecture, similarly, the successive fashion for baroque, rococo, and classical styles did not prevent wide variations in actual performance. Indeed, baroque and rococo strove self-consciously for new and unexpected effects, so that each term embraces a tremendous variety of structures. Exotic architectural styles were often deliberately juxtaposed in the eighteenth century. Thus, for example, an English half-timbered country house might well find itself surrounded by a "Gothick" ruin (built to the owner's specification, since no authentic castle lay at hand) and situated to lour suitably across the greensward upon a grotto, whose rude exterior effectively set off an elaborate rococo interior. These piquancies might be further enriched by a "Chinese" tea house or Indian pagoda; while in the nearby village, thatched or slated cottages clung faithfully to an immemorial and strictly local tradition of construction.

Painting reflected less of the variety and restlessness of European culture. Techniques remained essentially those of the high Italian Renaissance; and the usual subject matters, whether aristocratic portraiture, classical allegory, or religious stories likewise stayed within older traditions. However, landscape painting, in which human figures were dwarfed or entirely absent, provided a significant addition to the repertory of European painting.

In music, Europeans came into possession of a wide gamut of new or newly perfected instruments in the early eighteenth century, as the relation between sound waves and musical tones came to be better understood. Johann Sebastian Bach's (d. 1750) well-tempered clavichord—a stringed keyboard instrument capable of playing in different keys—and the modern violin, perfected by such craftsmen as Antonio Stradivari (d. 1737), were the most conspicuous of the numerous additions to the musical resources of Europe. The result was to open a new world of instrumental music in which older principles of harmony could be applied and enlarged to take into account the differences of tone and timbre among the various instruments. The challenge of working out the possibilities inherent in this new complexity, and of uniting instrumental with vocal music, occupied European musicians for the rest of the eighteenth century. Bach, Christoph Willibald Gluck (d. 1787), Wolfgang Amadeus Mozart (d. 1791), and Franz Joseph Haydn (d. 1809) worked within well-defined rules, like the contemporary classical writers. But the rules of harmony were not yet confining, as tended sometimes to be the case in literature. Rather, they guided composers and public in their energetic exploration of the possibilities inherent in the new instruments and their various combinations. The result was one of the great ages of European music.

ELEMENTS OF INSTABILITY IN THE OLD REGIME. As the memory of the wars of religion faded and as confidence in reason and belief in progress grew, impatience with the numerous inequities of European society mounted. The nobles of France were so much dissatisfied with their political insignificance that in the decades immediately preceding the outbreak of the French Revolution they became leaders of the agitation against monarchical absolutism. Their discontents found a ready echo among the professional and business classes, who easily persuaded themselves that they deserved greater political importance and social eminence. Ideas about liberty, the rights of man, the dignity of the individual, and even the sovereignty of the people fomented discontent with the existing state of affairs. Yet the interlocking of vested interests made change difficult, even dangerous, as such diverse personalities as the reforming zealot, Joseph II of Austria (1780–90), and that persistent gadfly of the English legal profession, Jeremy Bentham (d. 1833), discovered.

But ideas were not the only, nor perhaps the chief, solvent of the Old Regime. The advance of technology, which gathered speed throughout the seventeenth and eighteenth centuries, played a more direct and tangible role in remaking society. Technology affected men's lives bit by bit, without any over-all plan or deliberate purpose of reordering society. Yet some thinkers proclaimed a firm faith in the beneficent effect of just such piecemeal technical change. The English empirical tradition proved particularly hospitable to such an outlook; for such men as Francis Bacon (d. 1626) and the founders of the Royal Society (1660) looked forward with complete confidence to the benefits they expected to arise from technical improvements arrived at through careful observation and experiment. Yet, in fact, it was only slowly that scientific theory came to have much bearing upon the processes of economic production. Until chemistry achieved a precision which it lacked in the eighteenth century, abstract science had little to contribute to the industrial arts. But theory was not really needed. Rough-and-ready empiricism, finding expression in a general willingness to reconsider traditional practices, to tinker with new devices, and to try different procedures, materials, or tools, was quite enough to work cumulatively enormous changes in European technology; and the rate of such advance was vastly accelerated by the new custom of recording, measuring, comparing, and publishing results in professional journals.

Most basic of all economic activities was agriculture; and here such simple procedures as systematic selection of seed, careful breeding of animals for specific traits, and the introduction or spread of new crops like clover, turnips, potatoes, maize, cotton, and tobacco worked enormous increases in the productivity of farm land. Deliberate tests to discover the best shapes for plowshares and other implements promoted the efficiency of cultivation. Gentlemen farmers systematically and enthusiastically explored the benefits of repeated tillage, elimination of weeds, tile drainage, and application of manures and other fertilizers. England took the lead in this development; for English landowners were in a position to impose new methods upon farm laborers; whereas in most other parts of Europe, a routine-bound peasantry continued to adhere to old methods and only slowly adopted improved agricultural techniques.

Road and canal construction were much improved by the same trial-and-error procedure, although here government initiative was far more important than it was in agricultural development. France led the way in constructing tolerable all-weather roads and a canal system that linked the major rivers of the country into an interlocking pattern of navigable waterways. England followed suit only toward the close of the eighteenth century, while the rest of Europe (except Holland) lagged appreciably behind. Ship, wagon, and passenger coach construction improved steadily; and railroad cars, drawn either by men or by horses, came into general use for short hauls of heavy or bulky materials.

As in earlier times, mining constituted a major growth point for technology. By the eighteenth century, English coal mines took over the technical leadership formerly held by Germans. As shafts were sunk deeper into the ground and the scale of coal mining increased, the need for heavy machinery for hoists and for pumps to keep the pits from flooding taxed engineering ingenuity. The need for powerful prime movers spurred experiments with steam engines. As a result, Thomas Newcomen's engine (1712) led to the first practicable use of coal to energize pumping systems for the mines. During the following decades, the usefulness of these engines increased with improvements in details of their construction and a rapid increase in their size and power. Then in the 1760's, James Watt revolutionized steam engine design by driving a piston with live steam.[26] He patented his invention in 1769; but in the following decades diversifications of design, together with the adaptation of his engine for uses other than pumping, greatly increased its value.

The practical success of steam engines depended upon techniques for shaping metal accurately, so that piston and cylinder walls could be made to match closely enough to prevent serious loss of pressure. These and other technical problems were solved practically, rather than theoretically, by a small band of ingenious artificers and mechanics with little or no formal scientific training. Nevertheless, the routine of the workshop itself constituted a type of training, and in fact the co-ordination of human activity necessary to the large-scale production of such a complicated piece of machinery as a steam engine was at least as significant as technological details of the new invention. Scores and soon hundreds of men had to be disciplined to make a large variety of metal parts that would ultimately fit together into an engine: this required precise measurement at every stage of manufacture and the skilful use of file and calipers until just the right dimensions had been achieved. Ancient individual artisan skills of hand and eye were, in effect, linked together to produce an end result that no single man could achieve without an extravagant expenditure of time. And this linkage was itself created by an unprecedentedly abstract and precise mesh of dimensional specifications for the separate parts—valves and valve seats, pistons and cylinders, rods and bearings—that, when assembled, made a steam engine that really worked.

Metallurgy also underwent fundamental development, again primarily in England, where the shortage of wood for charcoal had long hindered steelmaking. During the second half of the eighteenth century, the use of coke as a substitute fuel solved this problem for the steel industry. Other technical improvements permitted a more uniform quality and increased scale of production; and as steel became cheaper, it found new uses in bridge building and structural work as well as for machinery. Thus England and Scotland were already plunging headlong toward the age of coal and iron when the French Revolution began.

The most spectacular technical development, however, was reserved to the textile trades, where a series of inventions, from John Kay's flying shuttle (1733) to Samuel Crompton's spinning mule (1774), made possible the mechanization of spinning and weaving and thereby enormously multiplied rates of output while cheapening the finished cloth. The cotton industry, which was new in England and thus uninhibited by long artisan tradition, most readily adopted these new processes. As a result, by the last decades of

[26] Rather than relying, as Newcomen had done, upon atmospheric pressure to push a piston into the partial vacuum created by the condensation of steam in a cylinder.

the eighteenth century, English cotton cloth was beginning to undersell the products of Indian looms, even in India itself.

England and Scotland thus began to surge ahead of the rest of Europe in important branches of technology. The Industrial Revolution, which was to remake the face of Europe and of the world, had begun. Prior to 1789, however, the clanging mills and busy coal pits were only beginning to show their power of transforming human society. Europe as a whole remained overwhelmingly rural, and even in Great Britain the preponderance of agriculture was not yet in question.

* * *

Not the progress of the Industrial Revolution, nor the prevalence of radical political ideas, but the French Revolution was what brought down the European Old Regime; and the causes of the French Revolution were as manifold as the society it convulsed. Yet the Revolution and the wars which ensued could not have taken the drastic form they did without the inspiration of radical ideas which had become familiar in the last decades of the Old Regime; nor could the Revolution have had such permanent effects had not the laws, wars, and property shifts which it involved helped to unleash the power of the machine. The political events of the Revolution (with its American precursor) served as a catalyst, activating the elements of instability in the Old Regime and magnifying their effect so as to transform European society. Without all the details of the shifting political kaleidoscope in France—Louis XVI's indecision, the rigidity of the French tax system, aristocratic insubordination, popular discontent—neither radical ideas nor new technical processes could have transformed European society so rapidly and so fundamentally. Thus even in its death agony, the Old Regime illustrated its complex, subtle multiplicity.

C. MOSLEM CATALEPSY, 1700–1850 A.D.

The Treaty of Carlowitz of 1699, by which the Ottoman empire surrendered most of Hungary to the Austrians, marked a definite turning point in the military balance between the Islamic world and Europe. A mere sixteen years earlier, in 1683, the Turks had amazed and frightened the West by besieging Vienna; after Carlowitz, the Ottoman state regularly found itself on the defensive, chronically unable to equal the armed strength of adjacent European empires. Growingly serious internal disorders exacerbated this military weakness, as local governors defied the sultan's authority, while bands of brigands harried the countryside. During the same period, the other two great Moslem empires also suffered dramatic collapse. Aurangzeb's death in 1707 left India in a state of turmoil, as Hindu, Sikh, Moslem, French, and British forces struggled over the prostrate body of the once proud and formidable Mogul state. Just two years later, in 1709, the Safavid empire was crippled by an Afghan revolt; and for the next two decades utter confusion prevailed as Turks, Russians, Afghans, and Uzbeks grabbed at parts of the former Safavid territory.

Political disorder within the Moslem heartlands presumably had adverse effects upon economic prosperity. In addition, changing trade patterns, in particular an increasing sale of European textiles and other factory-made goods, tended to depress the tradition-bound handicraft industries of Moslem towns. Crushing European economic superiority, attained through the cheapness of machine-made goods, came only with the nineteenth century and became definitive about 1830. Only after that date did the traditional structure of Moslem urban life break down. But throughout the eighteenth century, Moslem economies (save in fringe areas of Africa and remote islands of southeast Asia), like Moslem polities, were everywhere shrinking and crumbling before the European onslaught.

Nothing in the past prepared the Moslem world for such disasters. Until the end of the seventeenth century, the age-long conflict between Islam and Christendom had generally tended to favor the Moslem cause. Nothing less could be expected by followers of Allah, whose Prophet had declared victory in battle against unbelievers to be clear and distinct evidence of divine favor. Therefore the abrupt reversal of the trend of history, setting in so unmistakably and massively with the beginning of the eighteenth century, presented Moslems with a desperate and insoluble puzzle. Had Allah deserted them? And if so, why? And no matter what the shortcomings of the community of the faithful might be, how was it conceivable that God should favor Christian dogs and unbelievers?

Political disasters had not been unknown in Moslem history before 1699; but they had always been transitory. Even the Mongol invasion of Iraq and the destruction of the Abbasid caliphate had soon been followed by the conversion of the khans to the true faith and a resumption of Moslem expansion on all fronts. Hence, the prevailing Moslem reaction to the disasters of the eighteenth century was to wait patiently for the storm to blow over, meanwhile remaining true to the past so far as circumstances allowed.

When the storm failed to blow over, however, two opposed responses began to assume importance in Moslem societies. On the one hand, reformers argued that Islam had been seriously corrupted over the centuries. In particular, pure monotheism had been obscured by the saint worship and reverence for holy men which Sufism had infused into the faith. It followed that only a strenuous and rigorous reassertion of the pristine truths of religion, as preached by Mohammed himself, could restore Allah's favor, and thereby put the world back on its proper course. The most significant movement of this type originated in central Arabia with the preaching of Mohammed ibn Abdul Wahhab (1703–92). Wahhabi influence was felt only gradually beyond the Arabian desert but remains to this day an important strand in Moslem reaction to the dilemma posed for pious believers by the history of the last two centuries.

The second response was to try to appropriate those aspects of European civilization which seemed responsible for the Europeans' successes. The most obvious such aspect was military technology; and from 1716 onward, Ottoman officials embarked upon sporadic efforts to make the Turkish armed forces over on European models. But, for more than a century, the adamant conservatism of the Janissaries and *ulema* of the empire made all such efforts abortive. Changes initiated by a reforming sultan or minister were repeatedly undone by popular riots in the capital, supported by Janissary mutinies. Even after 1826, when the sultan employed artillerists trained in the European style to destroy the insubordinate Janissaries of Constantinople, resistance to reform remained pervasive and deep-seated within the Ottoman empire. Recurrent foreign complications, compounded by rebellion at home and by repeated disaster in war against the European powers, distracted the sultans from the effort needed to strengthen their military establishment. No vigorous, overpowering personality ascended the Ottoman throne to carry through a revolution from above; consequently, reform remained stillborn. As for the Mogul empire of India, its rulers scarcely made the attempt to save themselves by imitating European military methods, while the various usurpers who supplanted the Safavis in Persia were impelled by their precarious tenure of power to maintain a conservative social and political system. Even in the Ottoman empire, reform appealed to very few. The vast majority of Moslems remained in a state of catalepsy, unable to cope either intellectually or practically with the new conditions created by European military and cultural superiority. A blind conservatism, clinging to the crumbling landmarks of a vanishing social order, dominated the Moslem world until well past the middle of the nineteenth century.

1. OTTOMAN REFORM AND CHRISTIAN REBELLION

The numerous fissures within Ottoman society greatly complicated efforts at reform. In the European provinces of the empire, a majority of the population was Christian and more or less consciously opposed to its Turkish masters. The Arabs, constituting a major bloc in the Asiatic portion of the empire, were marked off from the Turks by linguistic and to some extent by cultural differences. Likewise, a sharp gulf existed between town and village, and between those villages subject to landlords and the free villages of mountainous or other remote regions. Finally, pastoralists constituted an important segment of the population in both the European and the Asiatic provinces of the empire. Sometimes organized tribally, sometimes operating from more or less settled villages, such peoples were always freer of official control than the cultivators of the plains could hope to be.

Pastoralists and semipastoralists constituted a pool of manpower chronically ready and willing to engage in brigandage. Given a cause to make robbery respectable and leaders who knew how to combine preaching with pillage, brigandage could speedily snowball into a formidable military rebellion. The first Wahhabi "empire" of Arabia arose in this fashion in the mid-eighteenth century, growing rapidly until a well-equipped expeditionary force from Egypt suppressed it in 1818.[27] Analogous occupational groups in

---

[27] Cf. H. St. J. B. Philby, *Arabia* (London: Ernest Benn, Ltd., 1930), pp. 8–102. Precisely the same social mechanism operated in the formation of Mohammed's empire as in the growth of the Wahhabi state. The major difference lay in the separation of the prophetic from the political roles in the Wah-

the Balkans—shepherds, muleteers, mountaineers—also played a significant part in the history of the Serbian (1803–13) and Greek (1821–30) revolts; for the military leadership and the best fighters of both movements came from brigand bands organized to serve the new ideal of nationalism. The preachers and teachers of this ideal were not, as in the Wahhabi case, reactionary radicals, but revolutionaries tainted in one degree or another by knowledge of and admiration for the West. In the short run, this foreign taint hampered the Serbs and Greeks by dividing leaders from followers. But in the longer run, inoculation with the virus of Western ideas gave a longer political viability to the national enterprises of the Balkan Christians than any reactionary appeal to the Orthodox heritage analogous to the Wahhabi movement in Islam could have done.

Yet the appeal of sanctified brigandage was by no means the sole cause of Christian and Arab rebellion against their Ottoman overlords. In fact, the Wahhabi movement began to win adherents among intellectuals and city dwellers precisely after its divorce from booty-raiding; and Wahhabism became a powerful force beyond Arabian borders only after its military defeat.[28] The restlessness of the Ottoman Christians was more complex in origin. Simply by virtue of their religion, they were far more open to European ideas than the Arabs or Turks could be, especially after Orthodox Russia began to challenge the Ottomans in the Black Sea. Russia's successful self-revolution made it seem practicable to hope for a similar rebirth among the Orthodox communities of the Balkans; and from the early eighteenth century, Russian agents sporadically but quite successfully inculcated dreams of restoring a Christian empire in the Balkans under Russian auspices. When a Russian fleet appeared in the Mediterranean in 1770 and the day of ultimate reckoning with the Turks seemed at hand, revolt did break out in the Peloponnesus but was soon suppressed.

Internal changes within the Balkan Christian community supplemented incitement from abroad to increase the Christians' discontent. In the eighteenth century, merchant communities began to flourish in Greece and Serbia. Initially, muleteers from the Balkan mountains prospered by providing newly settled villages of the Hungarian, Rumanian, and Ukrainian plains with petty trade goods. This sort of caravan portage increased in scale as the export of grain from these potentially very productive regions became better organized. By the close of the eighteenth century, however, shipping had far outstripped overland commerce in importance. By the Treaty of Kuchuk Kainardji (1774), the Turks for the first time allowed Russian merchant ships to

---

habi movement, for the religious revivalism of Abdul Wahhab found its sword in princes of the house of Sa'ud. The different military result arose from the fact that, by the nineteenth century, Arab nomad warriors faced artillery and muskets rather than the dispirited cataphracts who had confronted Mohammed's immediate successors.

[28] Intellectual repudiation of the synthesis of Sufi mysticism with Sunni legalism which had assumed a more or less official character within the Ottoman empire fed the Wahhabi movement, as did a rising sense of rival ethnic identities as between Arab and Turk. Cf. the penetrating analysis of A. Hourani, "The Changing Face of the Fertile Crescent in the XVIII Century," *Studia Islamica*, VIII (1957), 89–122.

sail on the Black Sea and to pass the straits. The initial total lack of Russian ships and seamen in these waters was made good by Russian consuls stationed in the Balkans, who freely accorded Greeks and other Christians the right to fly the Russian flag. As a result, the carrying trade of the eastern Mediterranean, Aegean, and Black Seas was soon mainly in Greek hands.[29] These merchants, together with a smaller company of professional men, inevitably encountered western European ideas and constituted a slender but effective transmission belt between Orthodox Balkan society and western Europe. They, more than any other group, provided the ideals and voiced the slogans for the Serbian and Greek revolts.[30]

Yet the Christians of the Ottoman empire were not united in opposition to their Moslem masters. From the late seventeenth century, Phanariot[31] Greeks had gained important positions in Ottoman administration, acting as interpreters and go-betweens for the Turks in their dealings both with European powers and with the Christian subjects of the empire. The Phanariot power was partly financial: bankers among them regularly financed Turkish pashas in the purchase of office and secured important privileges in return, e.g., lucrative tax-farming contracts. In addition, Phanariot families firmly controlled the Orthodox patriarchate of Constantinople and took pains to extend its jurisdiction over the formerly autocephalous Serbian and Bulgarian churches in the mid-eighteenth century.[32] Finally, from 1711 onward, the Turks entrusted the government of the Rumanian provinces to Phanariots, who modeled their courts at Bucharest and Jassy on half-forgotten Byzantine imperial etiquette and dreamed discreetly of an eventual restoration of Greek power on the Bosphorus.[33] Yet with such a substantial stake in the Ottoman regime, the Phanariots were of two minds about attempting to overthrow it. Some of them supported the merchant groups in cautious negotiations with the Russians, toyed with the ideas of the French Enlightenment,[34] and dreamed of reviving the glories of ancient Byzantium. The majority held back, only to see their power destroyed after 1821, when the Greek revolt made the Turks doubt the loyalty of all Greeks.[35]

The overthrow of the Phanariots (1821–30) opened the way for a small

---

[29] Cf. Traian Stoianovich, "The Conquering Balkan Orthodox Merchant," *Journal of Economic History*, XX (1960), 234–313.

[30] Cf. L. S. Stavrianos, "Antecedents to the Balkan Revolutions of the Nineteenth Century," *Journal of Modern History*, XXIX (1957), 335–48.

[31] So called from the fact that they lived in a quarter of Constantinople near the lighthouse, or phanar.

[32] Cf. Ladislas Hadrovics, *Le peuple serbe et son église sous la domination Turque* (Paris: Presses universitaires, 1947).

[33] Cf. L. Sainéan, "Le régime et la société en Roumanie pendant le règne des Phanariotes, 1711–1821," *Revue internationale de sociologie*, X (1902), 717–48, for an interesting account of the Byzantine-Ottoman mingling in Phanariot courts.

[34] Cf. Nicholas Jorga, "Le despotisme éclairé dans les pays Roumains au XVIIIe siècle," *Bulletin of the International Committee of Historical Sciences*, IX (1937), 110–15.

[35] Cf. the analogous disaster that afflicted the Jewish communities of the Ottoman empire after Sabbatai Sevi's messiahship (1666).

group of Westernized Turks to take over some of the official functions formerly exercised by Greeks.[36] Moslem reformers could hope to penetrate the innermost recesses of the Ottoman state, as unbelievers could never do; and when Reshid Pasha in 1839 proclaimed wholesale political and social reforms on the European model, it appeared that the Westernizers had in fact captured the springs of power. But Reshid's promises remained unfulfilled, for very few Ottoman officials were as yet prepared to believe in the wisdom or

[36] Turks had scarcely studied Western society and techniques (beyond the narrowly military) before 1792, when the sultan for the first time established regular diplomatic missions in some of the principal European capitals. Cf. Bernard Lewis, "The Impact of the French Revolution on Turkey," *Cahiers d'histoire mondiale*, I (1953), 111–12.

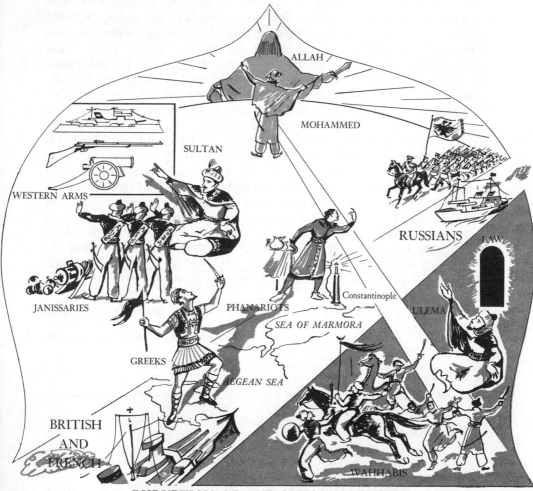

DISRUPTION OF THE OTTOMAN EMPIRE

necessity of implementing such radical departures from Ottoman and Moslem traditions. Until after the Crimean War (1853–56), the reluctance or positive hostility with which most Turks viewed any change whatever effectively nullified almost all the reforms initiated by the sultan.

Insubordinate local despots were sometimes more successful in breaking through the cake of custom that so firmly bound Ottoman society. By very brutal methods, directly aimed at maximizing their military power, such war lords often became far more efficacious agents of Europeanization than the sultan and the central government. The most spectacular and successful of these military adventurers was Mehemet Ali of Egypt (d. 1849). An Albanian who had risen by ruthless intrigue to be Ottoman governor of Egypt, Mehemet Ali in 1811 massacred the Mameluke military garrison and emerged as absolute master of the country, although he still remained nominally subject to Constantinople. He proceeded to Europeanize his army, reform the administration, and build up the commercial economy of Egypt. He employed numerous Europeans (especially Frenchmen) in his service and ruthlessly exploited the native Egyptians. Nor did his ambition stop at Egypt's frontiers: he extended his control into Arabia (Wahhabi War, 1811–18), the Sudan (1820–22), Crete (1823), and Greece (1825–28). Combined British, French, and Russian naval forces interrupted this empire-building by destroying Mehemet Ali's fleet in the harbor of Navarino (1827); and Western diplomats then compelled him to evacuate Greece, thus ensuring the success of the Greek war of independence. When he took Syria from the Ottoman sultan in 1832–33, the European powers once again snatched away the fruits of victory, forcing him to settle for hereditary rule over Egypt and the Sudan.[37]

Intervention against Mehemet Ali stepped up the scale of European interference in Ottoman affairs; for the great powers of Europe had come to consider the preservation of the Ottoman empire as essential to the maintenance of the balance of power. In a sense, European support of the Ottoman regime prepared the way for more thorough and effective internal reforms in the second half of the nineteenth century. Yet the mere fact that the sultan depended upon foreign diplomatic and military support tended to alienate spontaneous enthusiasm among Moslems for reform programs which appeared merely as devices for fastening European power more firmly upon the community of the faithful.[38]

[37] Henry Herbert Dodwell, *The Founder of Modern Egypt: A Study of Mohammed Ali* (Cambridge: Cambridge University Press, 1931). Other war lords had similar though less spectacularly successful careers, as for instance Ali Pasha of Janina (d. 1822) and Ahmed Jezzar (d. 1804) of Acre. For a summary of the disturbed political history of the Arab provinces of the Ottoman empire and penetrating observations about the social effects of private mercenary armies upon which the power of the local warlords depended, cf. H. A. R. Gibb and Harold Bowen, *Islamic Society and the West*, Vol. I Part I, pp. 200–234.

[38] By 1841 the Ottoman empire had lost Algeria to the French, the Black Sea coast as far as the Pruth to the Russians, and the southern part of the Balkan peninsula to the independent kingdom of Greece, which enjoyed the protection of Britain, France, and Russia. In addition, Serbia was an autonomous principality, Egypt was independent in all but name; the Rumanian provinces had become autonomous principalities under Russian protection; while in the East, Iraq, Kurdistan, and Arabia

In view of the distressing political circumstances of the Ottoman empire, it is scarcely surprising that the sultan's subjects were culturally uncreative. In language and literature, however, important changes were introduced, for by a striking coincidence, Turks, Greeks, and Serbs all developed new literary languages for themselves between 1750 and 1850. In the eighteenth century, Turkish poetry emancipated itself from Persian models, though it was perhaps impoverished and vulgarized in the process; and Turkish prose found a new and simpler vocabulary and style with the work of Akif Pasha (1787–1847).[39] Literary Turkish has since been largely based upon Akif's reformulation of the language.

The Serbian and Greek languages underwent a parallel and even more self-conscious transformation. Dositej Obradovich (d. 1811) and Vuk Karadjich (d. 1864) used the peasant dialect of Herzegovina[40] as the basis for literary Serbian; and by the mid-nineteenth century, their creation had replaced the older literary standard based upon Church Slavonic. Similarly, Adamantios Korais (d. 1833) created a new Greek literary medium, designed to emphasize connections with the classical tongue and to purify common speech from its heavy infiltration of Italian and Turkish words. These labors bore little fruit until after 1850. The new literary vehicles were shaped not by anything indigenous to Serbian or Greek culture but by philological and national ideas developed in western Europe, especially in Germany. Hence the appearance of the new languages in the early nineteenth century was more a manifesto for the future than an indication of local cultural achievement.

Nevertheless, the old structure of Ottoman society, with its elaborate articulation between religious, occupational, and locally autonomous groupings, was irremediably and definitively broken by 1850. The fact that Turks, Arabs, and Christians were all dissatisfied with the resultant confusion guaranteed further upheavals.

2. IRAN AND TURKESTAN

When the Safavid dynasty was finally snuffed out in 1736, a new conqueror, Nadir Shah (1736–47), supplanted Ismail's heirs. Nadir had been the power behind the Persian throne for a decade before assuming the diadem, during which time his victories rescued Persia from the Afghans. After indecisive wars with the Turks, Nadir launched a spectacular invasion of India (1738–

---

were very imperfectly controlled from Constantinople. Yet the old core of the empire in Europe and Asia Minor, with an outlier in Syria, had been brought back under the administration of Constantinople through the elimination of a large number of insubordinate pashas and local warlords. In this sense, Ottoman reform did win real successes in the first half of the nineteenth century.

[39] Cf. E. J. W. Gibb, *A History of Ottoman Poetry* (London: Luzac & Co., 1902–05), IV, 3–14 and *passim*.

[40] The choice of Herzegovina was designed to make it easy for the Serbian and Croatian languages to converge, thus opening Serbia more fully to the Western connection long enjoyed by Croatia. Unlike most such schemes, this one actually worked and made modern Yugoslavia a possibility. Alternative rapprochement between Serb and Bulgar around, e.g., the Macedonian dialect would have produced a very different national and cultural configuration among Balkan Slavs.

39), defeated the Mogul army, and occupied·Delhi. Then, with the onset of hot weather, he unexpectedly reinstated the Mogul emperor and returned northward after demanding the cession of all territories north and west of the Indus. Victorious campaigns in Transoxiana in 1740 carried Nadir's career to its zenith; but revolts and renewed wars with the Turks soon began to disrupt the new empire. On his assassination in 1747, it shattered into fragments,[41] many of which were soon gathered up by a new Afghan conqueror, Ahmed Shah Durrani (1747–73). The empire of Ahmed Shah extended from the Aral Sea southward into India; but it likewise disintegrated shortly after the death of its founder. Yet the career of Ahmed Shah had considerable importance in Indian politics; for the battle he fought at Panipat in 1761 against the Maratha confederacy permanently weakened the Hindu armies and left India far more vulnerable than before to English encroachment.[42]

Unstable governments and chronic factional warfare built around ethnic rivalries between Afghans, Persians, and Turks continued to disturb the peace of Iran and central Asia after the disappearance of these two great conquerors. This perennial strife invited Chinese incursions into eastern Turkestan in the eighteenth century; and persistence of political disorder provoked comparably extensive Russian encroachments in the Caspian and Caucasus area in the nineteenth. In 1835 the Shah himself entered into close relation with Russia, to the dismay of the British, who in their more imaginative moments felt nervous for their position in India. To forestall the Russians, a British force invaded Afghanistan (1839), only to be ignominiously driven back when supplies gave out. A second punitive expedition burnt the Afghan capital (1842) and then withdrew.

In general, the ancient warlike tradition of Iran and Turkestan continued almost unchanged prior to 1850. But wild horsemen, however hardy and brave, were no longer a match for armies organized and equipped in either the European or the Chinese style. Consequently, China from the east, Russia from the north, and Britain from the south ineluctably restricted the former range of action of the Moslem cavalrymen. Subsidies and supplies of powder and shot sufficed to make or break local princes; and as European manufactures gained a wider market, the indigenous artisan and merchant classes lost ground. This economic decay correspondingly reduced whatever possibility remained of building a stable political regime upon local resources. Hence the old-fashioned society of Iran and Turkestan, despite its remoteness from Eu-

---

[41] Nadir Shah's religious policy was a curious one. On his accession he repudiated the Shi'a faith, which since 1500 had deeply penetrated Persian life. He later attempted a crude assimilation of Shi'ism into Sunni Islam by trying to persuade or compel the Sunni doctors to admit Shi'ism as a fifth system of orthodox law. This policy was an utter failure, since neither Sunni nor Shi'a divines would agree to such a politic burying of their differences.

Nadir perhaps was aiming at a pan-Islamic empire, hoping to unite Turkey and India into one gloriously restored caliphate; and he may have thought it necessary to reconcile the two hostile factions of Islam as an essential preparation for the achievement of this ideal. In personal life he appears to have been completely, almost naïvely, irreligious. Cf. L. Lockhart, *Nadir Shah* (London: Luzac & Co., 1938), pp. 99–100, 278–79.

[42] Cf. W. K. Fraser-Tytler, *Afghanistan* (London: Oxford University Press, 1950), pp. 60–69.

rope, was as unable to cope with European military and economic power as was the geographically more exposed Ottoman empire. Cultural stagnation or outright retrogression accompanied such political and economic weakness.[43]

3. DISINTEGRATION OF THE MOGUL EMPIRE IN INDIA

Chronic revolt began to undermine Mogul power even during the reign of the emperor Aurangzeb (1658–1707). From the hill country southeast of Bombay, a group of Marathas led by Shivaji (d. 1680) began a career of pillage and guerrilla harassment which the emperor's armies proved unable to prevent. Consciously championing the cause of Hinduism against Islam, the Marathas attracted into their ranks a wide variety of Hindu adventurers and eventually founded a state of their own. By the mid-eighteenth century, they had established a loose hegemony over all of central India and had clearly become the leading contenders within India for succession to the weakened Mogul power.

Following Aurangzeb's death (1707), the Sikhs of the Punjab likewise threw off Mogul and Moslem control and created their own state. In addition, rebellious Mogul governors set up a patchwork of independent principalities in various parts of India. The most stable such principality was Hyderabad in the Deccan, which derived an effective discipline from the need for constant defense against the neighboring Marathas. Finally, a series of invaders from Iran and Afghanistan, together with Gurkha raiders from Nepal, added to the confusion of Indian politics. The Mogul empire survived in name until 1858; but a series of weak and debauched emperors made the imperial authority more often than not a fiction, even in the immediate environs of the capital.

These political conditions increasingly forced the European trading companies in India upon their own resources. Like the provincial officials of the Mogul empire itself, local company agents gradually acquired a practical sovereignty, subject to no effective control from distant Paris or London. Military as well as commercial affairs came within the purview of the companies' servants; for the raids and exactions of Indian warlords made necessary the erection of forts and an increase in the garrisons safeguarding the European establishments. Because native Indians could be employed more cheaply than Europeans, company agents filled the ranks of their armed forces with local recruits but put them under European command. By the eighteenth century, even small bodies of such "sepoys," trained and equipped in European style, were able to overcome numerically much superior Indian forces.[44] This fact

---

[43] Cf. W. Barthold, *Histoire des Turcs d'Asie centrale* (Paris: Maisonneuve, 1945), pp. 188–97; Mary Holdsworth, "Turkestan in the Nineteenth Century" (mimeographed; Central Asian Research Center, Oxford, 1959); Lockhart, *Nadir Shah*, pp. 276–78. A perceptible revival of Islamic studies in Bokhara, tending in the direction of Wahhabi fundamentalism, occurred toward the middle of the nineteenth century on the very eve of Russian conquest of the region. In addition, on the northwesternmost fringes of Islam, Chinese Moslems underwent an ill-understood religious upheaval—a "New Teaching"—which first attracted the attention of Chinese officialdom in 1762 and led to open revolt against Chinese authority in 1781 and 1783. Cf. H. M. G. D'Ollone, *Recherches sur les Musulmans chinois* (Paris: Leroux, 1911).

[44] Mogul troops had lost both mobility and discipline; and even the Marathas began to suffer from similar weaknesses, since luxurious living and factional quarrels among their leaders rapidly under-

was not lost upon local Indian rulers, who began themselves to employ European adventurers in the hope of acquiring similarly formidable armies of their own. From the European viewpoint, this offered compelling reasons for intervening in local Indian politics, since a Frenchman in command of the armies of an Indian prince might be expected to favor the French company, and an Englishman could be counted on to do the same for English trade.

Neither the French nor the English home companies were eager to pursue such adventures; for profits were likely to suffer from a too ambitious military policy. The obvious solution was to make military enterprise pay for itself by conquering territory and using local tax income to pay military costs. The French under the leadership of Marquis Joseph François Dupleix pioneered this policy in 1749, when in return for intervention in a local struggle, they received a substantial grant of territories near Pondicherry. The English soon followed the French example; and the outbreak of war between the two nations in 1756 gave impetus to their competition. The English had a decisive advantage against the French, for the British navy controlled the sea and could reinforce and transport British forces, while preventing the French from doing the same. Such strategic mobility, fully exploited by Robert Clive, allowed the British to drive their rivals from most of southern India and Bengal by 1757.[45] The treaty which concluded the Seven Years' War in 1763 sealed the French defeat in India, as well as in Europe and America.

This British victory in India almost coincided with the battle of Panipat (1761), when, as we have just seen, the Marathas suffered a crushing defeat at the hands of invading Afghans. Their speedy subsequent collapse in effect created a military and political vacuum in India. No native force could stand against the troops of the East India Company; and pretexts for intervention in Indian politics were easy to find. Indeed, once the Company had become a territorial sovereign, problems of border security and the need to forestall the rise of inimical neighboring princes conspired with the greed of the Company's servants to extend the areas of India under British control very rapidly.

The directors of the East India Company continued to resist wholesale annexation of new territories; and public criticism of its servants' rapacity and extortion in India may sometimes have retarded the Company's territorial advance. But neither parliamentary objections, nor a series of administrative reforms which restricted the opportunities for individual enrichment at Indian expense, prevented sporadic involvement of British forces in the affairs of the various Indian states. Except in the northwest, where Afghan and other war-

---

mined their military qualities. Iranians and Afghans were far more formidable, as their successes in northern India showed; but the unstable political order of their homelands prevented them from establishing any sustained occupation of India.

[45] The small size of the European units that fought and won decisive engagements in these wars is truly amazing. Clive had a force of 200 Europeans and 300 Indian sepoys for his march on Arcot in 1751, which destroyed the French position in the Madras-Pondicherry area. Similarly, by the standards of eighteenth century warfare, in Europe, the battle of Plassey (1757), which gave the British their first important territorial toehold in Bengal, was scarcely more than a skirmish.

like tribesmen offered stubborn resistance, the British military interventions met little opposition, until by 1818, when the Marathas were finally crushed, the East India Company attained unquestioned supremacy throughout the entire subcontinent. Yet even by that date, Company officials administered only a small part of India directly. The rest was controlled through alliances with local princes, whose policies were kept under surveillance by British residents appointed to their courts.

Two facts help to account for the ease of the British conquest. First, the Moslem rulers of India were never able to unite against the English. Threatened by Afghan raids from without and by Hindu revolt from within, many of them considered English protection a good bargain. Second, the Moslem rulers commanded no widespread support among their subjects, most of whom were Hindus. Even the Moslem lower classes felt no strong loyalty to their masters and contributed little to the struggle against the Europeans.

Nevertheless, Indian Moslems did resent their loss of power and status. This found veiled expression in a reformed and revitalized Islam, approximating to the Wahhabi model,[46] which won wide response and prepared the way for overt expression of Islamic discontent in the sepoy mutiny of 1857. The mutiny temporarily shook the British position in India, but ended with the defeat of the mutineers and the simultaneous abolition of the Mogul empire and of its heir, the East India Company.[47]

4. ISLAM IN AFRICA AND SOUTHEAST ASIA

Disorders within the old centers of Moslem civilization did not interrupt the progress of Islam in Africa. On the contrary, the pace of Islamization increased, especially in the nineteenth century. Conversion was partly the work of traders and holy men, partly of local conquerors who built their states around Islamic institutions. Partly too, the progressive breakup of tribal routines of life through the slave trade opened a door for Islam in previously pagan areas; for individuals deprived of older cultural traditions often found in Islam an attractive reordering of their mental and moral universe. Particularly in east Africa, the fierce effort toward religious purity characteristic of the Wahhabis of Arabia aroused strong echoes among pastoral and semi-pastoral populations. Elsewhere, looser forms of the faith, admitting saint worship and various compromises with pagan customs, were more in evidence.[48]

[46] Cf. Murray T. Titus, *Indian Islam* (London: Oxford University Press, 1930), pp. 178–93.

[47] Remarks on the Moslem collapse in India are based on *Cambridge History of India* (Cambridge: Cambridge University Press, 1929), IV, V; R. C. Majumdar et al., *An Advanced History of India* (London: Macmillan & Co., 1958), pp. 645–783; *Oxford History of India* (Oxford: Clarendon Press, 1958), pp. 455–672; Holden Furber, *John Company at Work* (Cambridge, Mass.: Harvard University Press, 1948).

[48] Cf. John Spencer Trimingham: *Islam in the Sudan* (London: Oxford University Press, 1949), pp. 102–4; *Islam in Ethiopia* (London: Oxford University Press, 1952), pp. 104–17; *History of Islam in West Africa* (London: Oxford University Press, 1962), pp. 155 ff.; J. N. D. Anderson, "Tropical Africa: Infiltration and Expanding Horizon," in Gustav E. von Grunebaum (ed.), *Unity and Variety in Muslim Civilization* (Chicago: University of Chicago Press, 1955), pp. 261–83.

In southeast Asia, too, a doctrinally more strenuous assertion of Islamic principles made itself felt. Although collision with the English, Dutch, and Spaniards cost Moslems some crippling setbacks,[49] a gradual process of conversion of upcountry populations and more distant islands continued to widen Islam's geographical range in that part of the world.

D. HINDU AND BUDDHIST ASIA, 1700–1850 A.D.

From the eleventh century, the militancy of expanding Islam in India and southeast Asia together with the xenophobia of Neo-Confucianism in China and Japan had put Hindu and Buddhist cultures generally on the defensive. Hence the Hindus and Buddhists had already had long practice in withstanding alien cultural and political pressures before European power manifested itself in Asia. These precedents remained binding in the eighteenth and early nineteenth century. Hindus retained some of the mental flexibility and emotional vigor first evidenced in their response to Moslem pressure in the sixteenth century. Buddhists, on the contrary, retreated behind the safeguards of a hallowed routine, seeking to minimize all disturbing contacts with outsiders.

The ostrich policy pursued by Buddhists everywhere could at best only stave off decline. In the Far East, increasing isolation behind monastic walls caused Chinese Buddhism to fade gradually in importance,[50] while Japanese Buddhism underwent comparatively precipitous decay. In southeast Asia, matters were more complex. There Buddhism had become the palladium of both Burmese and Siamese ethnic identities, so that the fate of the religion was inextricably intertwined with the fate of these two nations. Burmese imperial ambitions provoked prolonged and bitter war with Siam that lasted throughout most of the second half of the eighteenth century; but except for an episodic Chinese intervention in northern Burma (1765–70), these struggles attracted little attention from outside. The policy first adopted in the seventeenth century of restricting foreign contacts kept Europeans at a safe distance—no great achievement when all available European energies and resources were employed in subjugating India.

In the nineteenth century, however, as the East India Company climbed to paramountcy, British relations with India's Buddhist neighbors took on a new aspect. In Ceylon, frictions with the British[51] led to the destruction of the

---

[49] Two Moslem revolts, inspired by fanatical revivalist movements, occurred in the East Indies—one in 1750 in Java and a second in the 1820's in Sumatra. Both were defeated by the Dutch, not without difficulty. Comparable movements in Africa met no check from European arms until the late nineteenth century; and the greater success of Islam in Africa is surely related to this fact. On Islamic movements in the East Indies, cf. B. H. M. Vlekke, *Nusantara*, pp. 201, 263; G. W. J. Drewes, "Indonesia: Mysticism and Activism," in G. E. von Grunebaum (ed.), *Unity and Variety in Muslim Civilization*, pp. 284–310.

[50] A partial exception to this statement must be made for a variety of secret societies, some of them tinged with Buddhist (and Taoist) ideas, which began to manifest active and sporadically formidable popular discontents in the latter eighteenth and early nineteenth centuries. Cf. B. Favre, *Les Sociétés secrètes en Chine* (Paris: Maisonneuve, 1933), pp. 89 ff.

[51] When the French overran Holland during the revolutionary wars, the British took over Dutch possessions in Ceylon and in the Indies. The peace treaties of 1815 returned only the latter to the Dutch.

Buddhist kingdom of Candy in 1815. Between 1768 and 1824, the British also infringed upon Siam's sovereignty by acquiring a foothold in Malaya through treaty arrangements with local Moslem princes.[52] Even imperial Burma lost most of its seacoast to the same intruder after a war in 1824–25. Yet these demonstrations of British power did not lead Buddhist rulers or religious leaders of southeast Asia to attempt any serious readjustment of their traditional way of life. European contact was still too new and Buddhist cultural traditions too rigid to allow any such reaction. Like the Moslems, the Buddhists remained physically bruised but mentally almost unaffected by European expansion up to 1850.[53]

* * *

The Hindu communities of India, and particularly of Bengal, showed themselves distinctly more resilient under European pressure. To be sure, the great mass of the population was but little concerned with the change from Moslem to Christian overlordship, even in those regions directly under British administration. Theistic devotionalism, which had found such impassioned expression in the sixteenth century, continued to attract nearly all Hindus; and the caste system allowed even the most pious and scrupulous to accommodate easily to the European presence in India. Ceremonial cleansing after contact with a European, as prescribed by immemorial custom, sufficed to make room for one more alien community in the midst of all the fissiparous Hindu castes.

Until the beginning of the nineteenth century, these time-tested methods of dealing with foreigners served the Hindus well enough. As the Turkish-Persian-Afghan power sank, that of the English and French rose. From the Hindu viewpoint, one foreigner merely replaced another, as had often happened before. Until 1818 or even later, it seemed as though the European imprint upon India could be confined to the comparatively superficial levels reached by earlier invaders.[54]

Following the decisive defeat of the Maratha power by the British in 1818, all prospect of the emergence of a powerful Hindu state and of a coherent Hindu culture from the ruins of the Mogul empire disappeared. Instead, British officials confronted the task of ruling a vastly enlarged and remarkably variegated empire in India. Many of them were convinced that a mere hand-

---

[52] When France annexed Holland during the Napoleonic period, the British occupied the East Indies to forestall the French. Sir Thomas Stamford Raffles acted as Lieutenant Governor of Java and its dependencies from 1811 to 1816, where he introduced sweeping liberal reforms, hoping to attach the Javanese permanently to the British empire. His subsequent ventures in Malaya were, in a sense, a second-best substitute for the Indies, which had been returned to the Dutch in 1816.

[53] These remarks on Buddhism in southeast Asia are based on D. G. E. Hall, *A History of South East Asia* (New York: St Martin's Press, 1955), pp. 315–460; John F. Cady, *A History of Modern Burma* (Ithaca, N.Y.: Cornell University Press, 1958), pp. 3–86; Lennox A. Mills, *Ceylon under British Rule, 1795–1932* (Oxford: Oxford University Press, 1933), pp. 1–205.

[54] Cf. *Cambridge History of India*, IV, 426–27. The rise of independent and formidable Hindu states, like that of the Marathas, in the interstices between Mogul and European power seems to have afforded no important stimulus to Hindu culture. In secular affairs the Maratha leaders were in general content to imitate the luxuries and administrative forms of their Mogul predecessors, while conforming to traditional Hindu ritual observances in matters of religion.

ful of Britishers could control the vast subcontinent only by respecting and even promoting traditional Hindu and Moslem customs and institutions. Others held that British rule could be confirmed only by liberal reforms, designed to win the sympathy of the common people by offering them a higher level of justice than they had previously known. The conservative policy of maintaining the customs of the land intact conformed to the will of the overwhelming majority of Indians; and, so long as the British hold upon India was insecure, this policy dominated British councils, subject only to such modification as military or financial stringencies might dictate.

Toward the end of the eighteenth century, a small number of Englishmen, of whom Sir William Jones (d. 1794) was the most eminent, began to investigate Indian languages and literature. Early in the next century, British authorities started to devote official funds to the patronage of such researches and to the training of Indians in both Moslem and Hindu educational institutions. Yet even while intending to preserve native learning, the alien hand of men brought up in the traditions of European scholarship could not avoid transforming many familiar landmarks. For example, European scholars soon focused attention upon the earliest monuments of Hindu literature, largely because the philology of the day sought to determine the original forms of European speech through a study of Sanskrit. But such investigations pointed up innumerable discrepancies between Vedic and contemporary religious practices and beliefs. Intellectually inclined Hindus therefore found it quite impossible to escape the question of how to reconcile popular pieties and superstitions with their ostensible Vedic base.[55]

Thus the idea that the Hindu religion required reformation gained telling arguments from the very effort to inculcate and restore knowledge of its roots. This view, moreover, easily coalesced with the principles of English liberals, who demanded humanitarian modifications of Indian institutions and customs. A further impetus toward reform was provided by Christian missionaries, who became increasingly numerous in India after 1813, when the act of parliament renewing the East India Company's charter required their free admission to the country.[56] Few Indians ever espoused Christianity; but the missionaries nevertheless played an important part in stimulating Indian response to Western civilization. Missionaries were the first Europeans to teach, preach, and publish in Indian vernaculars. They also established schools, in which secular subjects supplemented religious instruction; and thereby

[55] Hindu efforts to master the origins of their religion may have had non-European roots also. Archaism is indeed a normal response for any threatened culture, and it is interesting to note that a precisely parallel reaction occurred among Indian Moslems, for whom the effort to return to the undefiled religion of the Koran meant an attack upon Sufi and Hindu practices. The Moslems did not need European stimulus here. The Wahhabis of Arabia, whom pilgrims to Mecca encountered, had attempted precisely this epuration without waiting upon Western scholarship.

[56] The East India Company, having first established itself in India by coming to terms with Mogul authority, originally adopted a strict policy of forbidding Christian missionary work under the Company's aegis. Nevertheless, with the evangelical revival in England, missionaries began to penetrate India from the last decade of the eighteenth century, operating at first either clandestinely or under the protection of Danish trading stations.

they brought not only specifically Christian but also more generalized European ideas and knowledge to the attention of the literate Indian public.

In the first decades of the nineteenth century, therefore, British liberal and missionary groups agreed in attacking various facets of Hindu custom and demanded legal prohibition of such practices as suttee—the custom of burning widows on their husbands' funeral pyres. The issue did not, however, rest entirely with the British. A small but vocal group of Hindus, located chiefly in Calcutta, also began to press for reforms of the Hindu law and custom; and it was only after such radical views had been voiced by Indians themselves that the liberal, reforming policy won a clear predominance in official British circles.

The most distinguished of the Indian radicals was a Bengali Brahmin, Ram Mohan Roy (d. 1833). Trained as a boy in both Hindu and Moslem learning,[57] he later acquired thorough familiarity with English and at least a smattering of Greek, Latin, and Hebrew as well.[58] Such linguistic training allowed him to bridge the cultural gap that separated Indian from European civilization, as only a handful of European Orientalists had previously been able to do. After giving up an official career in the English service early in life, Ram Mohan Roy devoted his principal efforts to questions of religion. His investigations of Christianity, Hinduism, and Islam led him to conclude that all three faiths conveyed essentially the same message—an ethical monotheism reminiscent of the nineteenth-century Unitarianism of Britain and America. From his world-encompassing point of view, details of ritual and divergences of doctrine sank to insignificance.

Such a radical reinterpretation of religion obviously challenged Christian as well as Hindu tradition. Ram Mohan Roy, therefore, engaged in polemics against both Christian missionaries and Hindu conservatives. He finally established a religious society of his own, the *Brahma Samaj*, through which he hoped to promote the spread of his ideas. Although his converts were few, Roy's influence served to stimulate the reform of Hindu laws and institutions. He waged a literary campaign against suttee and urged the British authorities to prohibit the custom a full decade before they actually did so (1829). Likewise, he petitioned the British to establish schools for Indians that would teach European sciences and learning. Nor was he content to wait for official action but devoted his own time and money to setting up schools privately for the propagation of his reforming ideas.

In a sense, Ram Mohan Roy was an isolated forerunner of the Anglicized upper-class Indians who were subsequently to play an important part in Indian history. Although the direct influence of the organizations he established was never widespread, some of his followers held strategic social posi-

---

[57] Until 1835 the British continued to employ the Mogul language of administration, *i.e.*, Persian. Any Indian aspiring to an official career had therefore to learn Persian and through that language was inevitably exposed to Moslem culture at large.

[58] His native tongue was Bengali; and Ram Mohan Roy's polemical writings in that language constitute a major landmark of Bengali literary development. He was the first to use Bengali as a medium for serious prose composition and gave it a form which later writers generally accepted. Cf. J. C. Ghosh, *Bengali Literature* (London: Oxford University Press, 1948), pp. 98–115.

tions and were able to flatter British authorities into believing that the English had a moral obligation to bring the benefits of European civilization and knowledge to the Indian peoples. The great landmark of this effort was the British decision (1835) to set up government schools teaching a European curriculum to Indian students in the English language. The establishment of such schools, and after 1857 of European-style universities as well, assured a supply of Indians who combined, as Ram Mohan Roy had done, a familiarity with both Indian and European cultural traditions. The importance and attractiveness of such education increased enormously after 1844, when English became the language of administration, so that any young Indian hoping for government employment now had to learn English.

The repercussions of this policy were felt mainly after 1850. Before that date only the groundwork for full-scale interaction between European and Hindu cultures had been laid. The overwhelming majority of Indians remained firmly enmeshed in an immemorial round of custom, loyal to their traditional faiths, and disinclined to look beyond the limits of their hereditary castes.[59]

[59] I have consulted R. C. Majumdar, *Advanced History of India*, pp. 812–26; Upendra Nath Ball, *Rammohun Roy: A Study of His Life, Works, and Thoughts* (Calcutta: U. Ray & Sons, 1933); Sophia Dobson Collet, *The Life and Letters of Raja Rammohun 'Roy* (London: H. Collet, 1900); Sahitya Akademi, *Contemporary Indian Literature*, (2d ed.; Calcutta: Ministry of Information and Broadcasting, 1959); J. N. Farquhar, *Modern Religious Movements in India* (New York: Macmillan Co., 1915), pp. 1–45.

INDIAN WORLD VIEW ABOUT 1850

E. CREEPING CRISIS IN THE FAR EAST, 1700–1850 A.D.

I. CHINA

Measured by any traditional yardstick, the eighteenth century was one of China's great ages. Political stability at home and imperial expansion into the borderlands accompanied a striking growth of agriculture, trade, and population. Peace and prosperity sustained a massive scholarly and artistic effort and lent weight to the remarkable cultural impress of China upon such distant barbarians as the Europeans. The great imperial ages of Han and T'ang could alone compare with these Manchu achievements.

Yet the very success with which Manchu policy reproduced the achievements of its ancient predecessors contained the seeds of the eventual and utter dissolution of the traditional Chinese social and political regime, when institutions and attitudes which had raised China high above the level of surrounding barbarians in earlier ages suddenly in the nineteenth century lost their efficacy against Europeans. Nevertheless, until the 1850's the crisis of Chinese society remained primarily internal and, like all aspects of the Manchu polity, conformed closely to ancient patterns. Only after slow processes acting to increase bureaucratic corruption, peasant unrest, and military slackness had prepared the way for thoroughly traditional collapse did the Chinese really begin to feel the drastically disruptive effects of European civilization. Until that time, China's history continued to be only marginally affected by contact with Europeans.

The K'ang Hsi emperor brilliantly consolidated Manchu rule over China during his long reign (1662–1722). The great task of his successors was to chastise and regulate the outer barbarians. Accordingly, through a long series of difficult campaigns, Chinese administration was extended to Tibet, Mongolia, and Chinese Turkestan between 1688 and 1757. Following the last important Chinese victory in central Asia—the destruction of the Kalmuk confederacy (1757)—the Manchu government adopted the policy of sealing off the northwestern frontier, even to the extent of removing population from near the border.[60] China's other frontiers had far less military significance. Diplomacy rarely had to be backed by military action (as in Burma, 1765–70) in order to forestall threats from southeast Asia or Korea; and most of these states maintained a tributary relationship to China—*i.e.*, a ceremonial recognition of dependence.[61]

---

[60] China also frequently interrupted Russian trade, despite the provisions of the Treaty of Kiakhta (1727) which called for a triennial Russian caravan to Peking and regular trade at the border town of Kiakhta itself. After 1762, Russian caravans ceased to come to Peking; and until 1792, when more regular and amicable relations were again established, even the border trade was repeatedly suspended by the Chinese. On Chinese-Russian relations and Chinese policy in central Asia, see Michel N. Pavlovsky, *Chinese-Russian Relations* (New York: Philosophical Library, 1949), pp. 18–40.

[61] Since Chinese protocol classified any diplomatic or trading relationship as "tribute," the term was very elastic. Burma continued to be officially regarded as tributary despite the Chinese military defeat of 1769; and Britain fell into the same class. The Russians alone, heirs to former empires on China's northwest frontier with which the Chinese had been compelled to deal as equals, escaped this classification. As a corollary of this unique status, the Russians alone had the right of maintaining a permanent diplomatic and trade mission in Peking from 1727.

On the seaward frontier, European activities were restricted by rigid regulations which minimized direct contact between Chinese and foreigners and fixed responsibility for any untoward consequences of the European presence upon persons who were suitably at the mercy of local officials. Indeed, the court at Peking regarded relations with the European merchants as too trifling to be regulated by formal treaties and, consequently, allowed local officials to manage relations with the foreigners. Moreover, since direct involvement in commercial questions was deemed degrading to a Confucian mandarin, even the local officials erected a barrier between themselves and the Europeans. This took the form of a Chinese merchant guild, which from 1720 had the responsibility of dealing with all European ships that came into Canton. In 1757, the emperor declared Canton to be the sole port for such trade, confirming officially a monopoly which the city had enjoyed practically for some time before.[62]

Until 1834, when the British parliament terminated the East India Company's exclusive right to trade between England and China, these arrangements worked quite smoothly, for both the Company and the merchant guild at Canton profited from their respective monopolistic positions. To be sure, the Chinese monopoly was far more secure than the Company's: for other European nations as well as British interlopers competed for the Canton trade. On various occasions, Europeans sought to secure more favorable terms of trade for themselves by enlarging the Chinese merchant ring in Canton or by breaking its monopoly; but such efforts uniformly failed. European merchants therefore had recourse to smuggling in order to counterbalance the Chinese monopolists' legal advantages. After 1800, when the Chinese government forbade the importation of opium but proved unable to enforce its decree, this illegal trade became big business. As a result, the Canton trade in the nineteenth century lost the legal and carefully controlled character which the Chinese authorities had imposed upon it in the eighteenth; and the irregular and sporadically violent patterns typical of the earliest European mercantile operations on the China coast reasserted themselves.

The importance of the foreign trade at Canton for the Chinese economy as a whole is impossible to estimate. Certainly it increased rapidly in scale. Tea became the largest single Chinese export; but silk, lacquered wares, porcelain, and various curios were also in great demand in Europe. Cotton cloth from India was the principal Chinese import, until the habit of opium smoking took hold in China during the eighteenth century.[63] Produced mainly in

[62] The British East India Company opened Canton to trade in 1699, as a supplement to the older European foothold at Macao. Based largely upon the sale of Indian and southeast Asian goods in China, the British trade thereafter rapidly expanded, eclipsing older Portuguese and newer European rivals. Correspondingly, Canton outstripped Macao as the primary locus of Chinese-European contact.

[63] Opium had long been known in China and elsewhere; but it was treated as a curative drug, taken internally. In 1689, the smoking of opium was mentioned by a Dutchman in Java where it was mixed with tobacco. Toward the end of the eighteenth century, opium smoking (omitting the tobacco) became widespread in China. Large quantities of the drug were produced in China itself, despite an imperial decree issued in 1729 which forbade its sale. Demand for opium developed so rapidly that the importation of the drug through Canton rose from 5,000 chests in 1821 to no less than 30,000 in 1839. Cf. L. C. Goodrich, *A Short History of the Chinese People* (3d ed.; New York: Harper & Bros., 1959), pp. 222–23.

India, opium provided European merchants for the first time with a commodity which the Chinese were eager to have in quantity. As a result, the drain of specie from Europe to pay for Chinese goods diminished steadily, until the balance of trade turned in favor of the Europeans and an outflow of Chinese silver began. In proportion as European trade came to center upon opium, any stimulating effects which an enlarged export of Chinese manufactures may have had upon the artisan and mercantile communities were counterbalanced by the social destructiveness of the opium habit. Moreover, it appears likely that various forms of "squeeze" siphoned off most of the profits of foreign trade into the hands of officials, who were always able to keep the Canton merchants and, through them, the artisan producers of export goods firmly under control.

Christian missions constituted Europe's other arm in China. Missionary influence decayed drastically in the eighteenth century, largely because of disputes among the missionaries themselves concerning the proper translation of Christian theological terms into Chinese and the extent to which Chinese converts might retain their ancestral customs. From the inception of their activity in China, the Jesuits had maintained that family rites honoring ancestors and public celebrations honoring Confucius were civil ceremonies which did not necessarily conflict with Christian belief. Other missionaries, particularly the Dominicans, considered that such accommodation to Chinese practice was inconsistent with Christian faith. National and personal frictions inflamed this "Rites Controversy"; and its complexities increased further when the disputants appealed both to the pope *and* to the Chinese emperor for adjudication. After initial hesitation, the pope in 1715 decided against the Jesuits, to the intense indignation of the Son of Heaven, who had meanwhile endorsed the Jesuit position.[64]

This controversy had important effects both in China and in Europe. In 1708 the Chinese emperor decreed that all missionaries must accept the Jesuit view or leave the country; and when obedient Catholics could no longer sustain that position, Christian missions in China could only operate in defiance of the law of the land. Missionaries did indeed continue to slip into China, and their congregations never entirely disappeared; but Christianity was reduced to the level of a secret society.[65] As such, it appealed almost entirely to the poor and dispossessed, and suffered at best official neglect, at worst sporadic persecution.

The imperial court nevertheless allowed the Jesuits to remain at Peking; and the Ch'ien Lung emperor (1736–95) regularly employed them for such purposes as designing palaces and building water fountains, clocks, and other mechanical devices. Jesuits also retained official positions as astronomers and calendar makers until the pope dissolved their order in 1773, after which time the Lazarist Order assumed these duties. But any real meeting of minds

---

[64] Beginning as early as 1628, this controversy did not finally subside until 1742, when a papal bull once again and most emphatically forbade Jesuit compromises with Chinese custom.

[65] Chinese society was riddled with similar groups, which characteristically clothed social discontents in religious garb.

or serious interest in European knowledge and civilization, of which there had been little enough in the seventeenth century, became less and less apparent in the eighteenth. The Chinese literati were too well assured of the success of Chinese institutions and too firmly convinced of the self-sufficiency of their own cultural world to spare time and attention for the pursuit of barbarian trifles.

In Europe, by contrast, the Rites Controversy provoked a vivid curiosity about China among broad circles of the intellectual elite. The fact that the Jesuits in France were deeply involved in disputes with Jansenists and Gallicans sharpened the debate over the legitimacy of Jesuit proceedings in China. Information about China was accordingly sought, not only for its own sake, but to provide ammunition for controversies having other origins and aims. Yet the knowledge of China which percolated into Europe as a by-product of the quarrel had significant side effects. Enthusiasm for *chinoiserie* flavored the whole rococo art style that spread widely through Europe from about 1715. The picture of virtuous Chinese sages, whose morality did not depend upon revealed religion, appealed to deists; and such aspects of Chinese society as its civility (which Ricci in an earlier generation had despised), the absence of a hereditary aristocracy, and the principle of appointment to government office on the basis of public examination all chimed in with radical movements of thought that gathered way, especially in France, during the eighteenth century. China became, for Voltaire and some other *philosophes*, a model to be held up to Europe. After all, was not the Celestial Empire— whose Confucianism might be construed as a working and only slightly shopworn model of rational religion—great, prosperous, and peaceful without benefit either of clergy or of hereditary aristocracy?

Such partisan admiration for China, though arising from intellectual and artistic developments internal to Europe, nonetheless constituted a noteworthy departure from the dislike, fear, and disdain that normally prevail among men of differing civilizations. The handful of Europeans who explored the intricacies and elegancies of Chinese civilization in a sympathetic spirit in the eighteenth century were pioneers of a new and more open contact between cultures. Their attitude stood in striking contrast to the sublime disinterest in things foreign which prevailed among the corresponding intellectul circles of China.[66]

[66] The vogue for things Chinese faded out after about 1770 almost as suddenly as it had arisen. In the early nineteenth century, European merchants, soldiers, and missionaries on the China coast returned to a more normal disdain for "corrupt" Chinese ways; and their attitudes communicated themselves to Europe at large. Yet as European admiration for China faded, India tended to fill the gap, thanks to the exciting discovery of the Indo-European linguistic relationships and initial exploration of the echoing vastnesses of ancient Indian philosophy and mysticism. What China had been to the *philosophes* of the eighteenth century, India became for the romantics of the early nineteenth. Thus European curiosity and sympathy for alien civilizations shifted focus but was never entirely intermitted from the time when Ricci in China and less famous Jesuit missionaries in India like Roberto de Nobile (d. 1656) first embarked upon the adventure of trying to understand another civilized tradition in its own terms. It is curious, though perhaps not surprising, that Europe's closest neighbor and traditional rival, Islam, was the latest to receive serious European study; and even today, historians habitually treat Islamic development since 1256 primarily in terms of its relation to Christendom and modern Europe. Crusade and counter-crusade die hard just because European and Moslem civilizations have so much in common.

Yet the very richness and variety of China's literary and artistic heritage, the lifetime of effort required to master it, and the high rewards entailed by success on the provincial and imperial examinations adequately explain the Chinese indifference to foreign learning. Traditional forms of scholarship continued to flourish under the Manchus on a massive scale. Vast compilations, systematizations, and summaries of earlier knowledge were completed under official patronage. Carefully edited texts and authoritative commentaries crystallized the long tradition of Chinese learning and provide most of the raw materials for modern Sinology.

Poetic composition and essay writing remained part of the official examinations and continued to be cultivated with pedestrian assiduity. Imaginative prose literature constituted a more impressive genre of Chinese belles-lettres, for under the Manchus novels attained respectability despite their popular origin. *The Dream of the Red Chamber*, written in the late eighteenth century, remains by common consent the greatest Chinese novel,[67] though it was but one of many.[68]

Chinese painting remained prolific, skilled, and various. Chinese taste of the age itself praised painters for their faithfulness to old masters, while modern Chinese and Western scholars tend to prize the artists' individual accent and stylistic innovation. There was much for both to admire in eighteenth-century Chinese painting; yet, rather ungratefully, both Chinese and Western critics of the twentieth century seem to agree that the real greatness of Chinese art lay in the past.[69]

Thus to all appearances, Chinese civilization and the Chinese state were flourishing in the eighteenth century. Yet the same mechanisms which had caused the downfall of earlier Chinese dynasties were already at work and manifested themselves in public events during the last quarter of the century. The basic problem was rising peasant distress. The growth of rural population caused excessive subdivision of land, until in a bad season the tiny farms which resulted could no longer sustain a family.[70] Hopeless peasant indebtedness and

[67] The great length of this novel has discouraged translation; but cf. Tsao Chan, *Dream of the Red Chamber*, Chi-chen Wang (trans.) (New York: Twayne Publishers, 1958), for a translation of the first chapter and summary of the rest.

[68] Cf. Ou Itai, *Le Roman chinois* (Paris: Editions Vega, 1933).

[69] Cf. Osvald Siren, *A History of Later Chinese Painting*, II, 152–227; Laurence Sickman and Alexander Soper, *The Art and Architecture of China*, pp. 188–204. The low appreciation of the works of more recent painters seems to me to result from an undue idolization of the antique, much of which in fact is known or inferred mainly through modern copies.

Chinese painting, unlike Chinese literature of the eighteenth century, occasionally reacted to and experimented with Western techniques. In addition, individual Europeans, like the Jesuit Giuseppe Castiglione (d. 1766), were accorded high honor as painters by the Ch'ien Lung emperor. Castiglione achieved his repute by bringing a Western naturalism to bear within a generally Chinese style of composition. A few Chinese followed his example, thus illustrating once again the comparative ease with which artistic motifs and techniques may diffuse from one culture to another, since linguistic barriers are largely irrelevant.

[70] Ping-ti Ho, *Studies on the Population of China, 1368–1953*, pp. 270–78, estimates that China's population of about 150 million in 1700 rose to 313 million by 1794 and reached 430 million in 1850, on the eve of the vastly destructive Taiping rebellion. He suggests that "optimum conditions" under the technology of the time were reached between 1750 and 1775, after which time the continued growth of population led only to greater destitution and discontent.

AN EIGHTEENTH-CENTURY ARISTOCRAT

This Chinese lady communing with nature to the sound of a flute represented a way of life vastly older, more deeply rooted, and apparently far more secure than that embodied by European aristocrats of the same age. When this picture was painted, Chinese armies were winning victories in central Asia, where they had not penetrated since T'ang times; and the strenuous effort to remain true to the ancients in word and thought seemed to be producing most excellent results. Exquisite refinements of sensibility, touched perhaps with just a whiff of vague disquiet against submission to the measured decorum of Chinese society, may perhaps be read into this painting— a quality unkind critics call decadent. Decadent or no, the artist seems faithfully to mirror the conservative gentility of Chinese culture under the Manchus.

sporadic foreclosure was the inevitable result. Land therefore accumulated in the hands of moneylenders of the gentry class, who were often able to escape normal tax payments on the land and thereby shifted an ever-increasing share of the tax burden to the remaining peasant properties. Simultaneously, mounting bureaucratic corruption and the decay of military hardihood among Manchu bannermen, accustomed to an easy garrison life in Chinese cities, weakened the regime just when discontent and despair mounted among the mass of the peasantry.[71]

Opium smoking and peasant rebellion were the two principal responses to these unhappy circumstances. A widespread rising in 1774 started a long series of similar movements which culminated in the cataclysmic Taiping rebellion of 1850–64. Such violence worsened the economic condition of the country as a whole, forcing the government to raise additional revenue for retaliatory military action, and this in turn fed peasant discontent.

The vicious circle into which the government thus floundered did not entirely escape official attention. Well-intentioned decrees against opium smoking and exhortations to official probity were ineffectual; but a parallel effort to control dangerous thoughts may have met with somewhat greater success. At any rate, between 1772 and 1788 the government carried through a vast epuration of Chinese literature, burning books that contained disparaging remarks about the Manchus or their forebears. Some of the books condemned in the course of this inquisition appear to have permanently disappeared.[72]

A similar fear of independent thought perhaps lay behind changes (1792) in the imperial examinations which made them tests of memory, calligraphy, and routine facility in writing essays and poems on fixed subjects according to strict rules. Since preparation for the examinations dominated most Chinese intellectual endeavor, these changes tended to narrow the minds of the leaders of Chinese society by restricting their thoughts to politically innocuous channels.[73] The effort was strikingly successful, for almost to a man the educated class of China remained loyal to the Manchu regime even into the twentieth century.

Until 1850, when the Taiping revolt shook the empire to its foundations, the government's countermeasures seemed on the whole adequate to sustain the imperial fabric against domestic dangers. No basic changes seemed called for; and deliberate emphasis upon ancient and authoritative Chinese precedents might plausibly be expected to stave off the threatened dissolution of

---

[71] Chung-li Chang, *The Chinese Gentry: Studies on Their Role in Nineteenth Century Chinese Society* (Seattle, Wash.: University of Washington Press, 1955), pp. 70–141, offers interesting data on the increase in the number of the gentry in the nineteenth century. Cf. also Wang Yu-Ch'uan, "The Rise of Land Tax and the Fall of Dynasties in Chinese History," *Pacific Affairs*, IX (1936), 201–20; and Maurice Meissner, "The Agrarian Economy of China in the Nineteenth Century" (unpublished Master's thesis, University of Chicago, 1955).

[72] Cf. L. C. Goodrich, *The Literary Inquisition of Ch'ien Lung* (Baltimore, Md.: Waverly Press, 1955).

[73] Cf. Chung-li Chang, *The Chinese Gentry*, pp. 174–82; David F. Nivison and A. F. Wright (eds.), *Confucianism in Action* (Stanford, Calif.: Stanford University Press, 1959), pp. 4–24.

the empire. Chinese self-assurance, therefore, received a tremendous shock between 1839 and 1842, when a few British gunboats and marine landing parties proved able to penetrate Chinese military defenses almost at will.

The occasion for this demonstration of British military might was a dispute over the administration of justice;[74] but fundamental discrepancies of viewpoint, giving rise to unending local frictions, lay behind the quarrel. In 1834 the British government had deprived the East India Company of its former control of and responsibility for the China trade and, by throwing the trade open to all comers, had attempted to bring commercial relations with the Chinese into the legal framework normal between European nations. This required the overthrow of the elaborate restrictive rules which for more than a century had enveloped commercial dealings between Europeans and Chinese. As it happened, this change in British policy came at a time when the Chinese government was intent upon restricting and controlling foreign trade even more rigorously than before. In 1839, a special imperial commissioner arrived at Canton with instructions to suppress the illegal opium trade. His energetic efforts in this direction resulted in the confiscation of no less than 30,000 chests of the drug from British and other European merchants. Grievances on both sides became acute;.and the dispute over correct legal procedures offered only the occasion for war.

Chinese military ineffectiveness soon compelled the imperial government to make peace on British terms. By the Treaty of Nanking, 1842, four new ports were opened to British trade and Hong Kong was ceded to the victors. Other European nations and the United States quickly made similar treaties and indeed improved upon the initial British terms by securing exemption from regular Chinese jurisdiction for their nationals and a guaranty of official toleration for Christian missionary activity in the "treaty ports."

Such privileges were utterly incompatible with traditional Chinese attitudes toward foreigners and merchants. The indignities embodied in this treaty and the military helplessness it betokened vis-à-vis Western gunboats certainly discredited the Manchu regime in Chinese eyes; yet no significant body of Chinese opinion arose to advocate departure from old ways. Educated Chinese found it all but impossible to believe that the Celestial Empire had anything important to learn from foreign barbarians. Indeed, the impressive successes that China had so recently attained within the thoroughly conservative frame of Manchu policy made adjustment to the new realities of world affairs uniquely difficult. It was therefore not until the twentieth century that the Chinese seriously undertook the task of remodeling their society in order to cope with the West.[75]

[74] A British sailor committed murder; and when the guilty individual could not be identified, the Chinese, in accordance with their practice of holding the community responsible for infractions of law and order, demanded that an Englishman—any Englishman—be turned over to them for punishment. No apter instance of the conflict between European and Chinese outlooks could have offered itself; for both sides naturally felt themselves completely in the right.

[75] In addition to books cited separately, I have consulted the following in connection with these remarks on China: G. F. Hudson, *Europe and China*, pp. 258–357; Henri Cordier, *Histoire générale de la Chine* (Paris: Librarie Paul Genthner, 1920–21), III, IV, *passim*; Kenneth Scott Latourette, *A History of*

2. JAPAN

The history of Japan in the eighteenth and early nineteenth centuries contrasts remarkably with that of China during the same period. While Chinese armies surged into central Asia, Japan remained continually at peace. While China's population more than doubled, that of Japan remained stable or even declined after about 1730. Most basic of all, Chinese culture was virtually monolithic, closed to outside influences, whereas that of Japan was torn between incompatible tendencies at home and became increasingly responsive to alien winds of doctrine blowing from across both the high and narrow seas. The official policy of Sinification sought, not without success, to transform warriors into gentlemen but failed to repress the licentiousness of popular culture. Simultaneously, a small but strategically placed group of Japanese intellectuals explored such alternatives to Neo-Confucian orthodoxy as native Shinto religion and Western science, while artists faithfully mirrored the cross-tensions between divergent autochthonous, Western, and Chinese styles.

In view of the hurried and changeable course of Japanese history both before and after the Tokugawa period, the policy of rigorous isolation and domestic stabilization which the shoguns maintained so successfully for over two hundred years appears as a remarkable tour de force. Powerful economic, political, and intellectual forces were at work throughout the eighteenth and early nineteenth centuries in Japan, undermining the delicately poised political system with which the first Tokugawa shoguns had sought to strengthen and protect their power. Yet the system remained intact until 1853; and even after the entire machinery of the shogun's government had been swept away by the "restoration" of the emperor in 1867, the militarized aristocrats who had ruled Japan under the shoguns continued to dominate and direct the nation.

The shoguns' most pervasive difficulties arose from the growing discrepancy between the loci of political and economic power. The politically dominant *samurai* class became economically dependent upon merchants and moneylenders, who ranked officially at the very bottom of the social hierarchy. The shoguns' policy of requiring all their own followers and the semi-

---

Christian Missions in China (New York: Macmillan Co., 1929), pp. 120–302; A. H. Rowbotham, *Missionary and Mandarin*, pp. 119–301; Antonio Sisto Rosso, *Apostolic Legations to China of the Eighteenth Century* (South Pasadena, Calif.: P. D. & Iona Perkins, 1948); H. B. Morse, *The Gilds of China, with an Account of the Gild Merchant or Co-Hong of Canton* (Shanghai: Kelly & Walsh, 1932); B. Favre, *Les Sociétés secrètes en Chine* (Paris: Maisonneuve, 1933); J. R. Hightower, *Topics in Chinese Literature*, pp. 102–13; Ssu-yu Teng and John K. Fairbank, *China's Response to the West* (Cambridge, Mass.: Harvard University Press, 1954), pp. 1–45; John K. Fairbank, "Synarchy under the Treaties," pp. 204–34, in John K. Fairbank (ed.), *Chinese Thought and Institutions* (Chicago: University of Chicago Press, 1957); L. Petech, *China and Tibet in the Early Eighteenth Century* (Leiden: E. J. Brill, 1950); Marshall Broomhall, *Islam in China*, pp. 129–30, 147–51; Grace Fox, *British Admirals and Chinese Pirates, 1832–69* (London: Kegan Paul, Trench, Trubner & Co., 1940); Adolf Reichwein, *China and Europe: Intellectual and Artistic Contacts in the Eighteenth Century* (New York: Alfred A. Knopf, Inc., 1925); Lewis A. Maverick, *China: A Model for Europe* (San Antonio, Texas: Paul Anderson Co., 1946); Donald F. Lach, *Contributions of China to German Civilization, 1648–1740* (Chicago: University of Chicago Press, 1944); Virgile Pinot, *La Chine et la formation de l'esprit philosophique en France, 1640–1740* (Paris: Librairie Paul Genthner, 1932); Earl Pritchard, *Anglo-Chinese Relations during the 17th and 18th Centuries* (Urbana, Ill.: University of Illinois Press, 1929).

independent "outside" lords to reside part of the time in urban centers contributed to this situation; for when they left their estates even the great magnates had to convert rice income into money by selling to merchants, and were strongly tempted to indulge in extravagant urban living. Moreover, the very success of the Tokugawa shoguns in ending foreign and domestic warfare gave the *samurai* less and less occasion to interrupt their luxurious idleness with the exercise of the military art.

Both lords and peasants suffered from the radical fluctuations in agricultural prices entailed by the penetration of a money economy into the countryside; and their discontents mounted with their debts. Peasant distress found expression in sporadic riots, which became increasingly frequent from the end of the eightenth century, and constituted significant evidence of growing social instability.[76] The *samurai*, with the help of the Tokugawa government, made more sophisticated, though scarcely more successful efforts to escape from their indebtedness. Debasement of the currency, price controls, moral exhortations to parsimony, sumptuary legislation, repudiation of debts, and on occasion, outright confiscation of merchant fortunes all were tried.[77] But the success of such measures was temporary at best; for the same impersonal and ill-understood economic forces soon brought both government and *samurai* back into financial dependence upon the despised merchant class.

Other responses to the financial difficulties of the *samurai* class proved more significant for the future. Some of the lords promoted more intensive agriculture on their estates and in a few cases organized mines and new industrial enterprises. Sericulture in particular expanded markedly, so that in the first quarter of the nineteenth century, Japan ceased to depend upon imports of silk from China.[78] Second, penniless noble families sometimes adopted the son of a merchant, thereby improving the family finances and securing to the merchant the advantages and prestige of *samurai* rank. In these ways the distinction between *samurai* and commoner upon which the Tokugawa legal system was predicated lost some of its sharpness. A vast acceleration of these processes of economic expansion and blurring of distinctions between the

[76] Widespread infanticide, though officially frowned upon, kept the population of Japan more or less stable and undoubtedly helped to save the Japanese peasantry from utter destitution. Cf. Ryoichi Ishii, *Population Pressure and Economic Life in Japan* (Chicago: University of Chicago Press, n.d.), pp. 3–16.

[77] Cf. George Sansom, *The Western World and Japan* (New York: Alfred A. Knopf, Inc., 1950), pp. 144–95. Schemes for an "ever-normal granary" managed by the government were attempted as a solution to price fluctuations; but neither the honesty of officials nor the needful commercial skill for management of such a program was forthcoming, so that all such efforts failed ignominiously. Price regulation by fiat and through currency manipulation were also theoretically discussed but without permanent success in practice. But restriction of the export of metals, especially silver and copper, put into force between 1715 and 1742, did succeed in reducing both Dutch and Chinese trade to minor proportions, as had been intended. Cf. Takao Tsuchiya, *An Economic History of Japan* (Tokyo: Asiatic Society of Japan, 1937), pp. 206–7.

[78] Improvements in irrigation—treadmills and Dutch pumps for raising water—and some new implements for cultivation and for hulling and grinding rice were introduced. New crops like sugar cane, sweet potatoes, potatoes, peanuts, maize, and some European vegetables also were added to the Japanese economy. Likewise, under the inducement of special tax remission offered by the government, a considerable amount of new land was brought into cultivation. Cf. Takao Tsuchiya, *An Economic History of Japan*, pp. 154–57.

ranks of society stood at the very center of the social changes that came to post-Tokugawa Japan. They had, however, started long before.

The weakness inherent in a regime resting upon a proud but impoverished warrior class, an oppressed and discontented peasantry, and a wealthy but politically insecure merchant-financial oligarchy, was compounded by the ancient political fissures which had only been papered over by the Tokugawa shogunate. Powerful "Outside Lords" continued to hold large areas of Japan; and recollections of their ancestors' rivalries with the victorious Tokugawa family never disappeared. As the prestige and morale of the Tokugawa administration declined, these "Outside Lords" became foci of a potentially formidable military opposition to the regime. Problems of foreign relations likewise began to loom larger in the nineteenth century, as Russian, British, French, and American ships began to skirt the Japanese coast. With increasing frequency, such vessels defied the law by putting in at Japanese harbors when in real or pretended distress, and occasionally secured compliance with their demands by threat of force.

Small but important groups of Japanese intellectuals were vividly aware of the weakness of their country and strove in different and conflicting ways to elaborate programs that would solve the difficulties they detected. The Neo-Confucian official ideologists of the regime sought to inculcate loyalty and obedience in all ranks of society. Moral reprimand and sumptuary legislation were the answers that came readiest to their minds as means for righting the wrongs of the age; but even their own official Neo-Confucianism had treacherous political pitfalls for the Tokugawa regime. If loyalty to one's superiors were the supreme virtue, how could the shoguns' treatment of the emperor be justified? Historical investigation, launched under official auspices in a Confucian spirit, led to equally or even more embarrassing questions, for no adjustment of the record could make the power of the shogun look like anything but usurpation. Hence, groups of good Confucians arose who challenged the regime on the basis of its own principles.

More important in the long run were others who rejected Confucianism and the official policy of Sinification entirely. Such men in turn divided into two groups: those attached to native Japanese traditions who sought to revivify and purify them, and those who admired Western civilization and advocated the adoption of Western knowledge and techniques. Despite what might seem a fundamental collision between their views, men from these two camps often found it possible to co-operate, for both had the same opposition to overcome: the official establishment and the weight of Chinese tradition. After all, Western medicine, geography, astronomy, and mathematics could be welcomed not only for themselves, but also as proofs of hitherto unsuspected defects in Chinese learning.

Among the anti-Confucian traditionalists, historical and antiquarian researches into the Japanese past provided raw materials for the definition and elaboration of the ancient Shinto cult into a religion that might bear comparison with anything derived from China or, for that matter, from the West.[79] Because the imperial family, descended from the sun goddess, was central in Shintoism, the cult inevitably drew men's minds away from loyalty to the shogun and his minions and turned it toward the rigorously secluded person of the emperor. Out-and-out devotees of Shinto remained comparatively few before 1850; yet by that date its doctrine and rituals had been refurbished and defined. Shinto was thus ready in the wings, fully prepared to displace Neo-Confucianism as the favored religion of state when the Tokugawa regime disappeared.

The energetic efforts of a handful of men to penetrate the secrets of European learning were even more impressive and proved equally pregnant for the future. Linguistic difficulties and the very restricted opportunities for meeting educated Europeans greatly hindered this task. Yet it was undertaken with dogged determination and enthusiasm. By the end of the eighteenth century, a few Japanese had not only mastered the Dutch language, through which they acquired familiarity with European learning, but had also published books in Japanese setting forth Western ideas in such fields as medicine, anatomy, astronomy, and geography.[80] Some Japanese also realized the superiority of Western military technology. When in 1842 the British humbled China's pride, such men drew the obvious lesson, not with the panic surprise which afflicted the shogun and his circle, but with a sense of personal vindication. They had long believed that Japan could not afford to neglect the knowledge and arts of the "red-haired" barbarians; events had now proven them correct.

Notions so subversive of the established order naturally provoked counteraction. In 1790, for example, the shogun's government prohibited the teaching of any but the officially approved Neo-Confucian philosophy and imprisoned or executed a few individuals for infringing this and similar legislation. Yet such measures proved no more effective than those taken to control economic processes. Private individuals, sometimes protected by one of the semi-independent "Outside Lords," continued to pursue the forbidden learning, to oppose the regime, and to elaborate alternative policies for Japan which they believed better suited to the realities of the time. Hence in 1853, when the shogun reluctantly agreed to open Japan to Western commerce, a small but strategically placed group of Japanese had already developed fairly definite ideas to guide the necessary reordering of Japanese society.

The richness and variety of the Japanese artistic and literary activity in the

---

[79] Even in this arcanum of Japanese national piety, the linkage between patriotism and Westernization may have operated, for the men who remodeled Shinto seem to have borrowed ideas of ecclesiastical organization and other notions from Christianity. Cf. Donald Keene, *The Japanese Discovery of Europe* (New York: Grove Press, 1954), pp. 110–11.

[80] "Dutch learning" in Japan during the eighteenth and early nineteenth centuries had the same adventitious attractiveness that Sinology had in France in the early eighteenth century. In both cases, by studying a distant and dimly apprehended outer world, criticism of the society at hand, which might have been dangerous if voiced directly, found indirect expression. Cf. the remarks of Thomas C. Smith, *Political Change and Industrial Development in Japan: Government Enterprise, 1868–1880* (Stanford, Calif.: Stanford University Press, 1955), p. 2.

eighteenth and early nineteenth centuries matched the complexity of these intellectual crosscurrents. Pictorial styles derived from the Chinese—of various periods—coexisted and sometimes intermingled with autochthonous and Western styles. Color prints, usually with a strongly naturalistic, if stylized, quality were the most novel achievement of Japanese art in this period. A witty, colloquial, and often salacious genre of poetry also flourished, as did play- and novel-writing. As in the seventeenth century, actors and geisha girls continued to inspire poetry and art in rivalry with the officially approved, more severe and traditional modes which drew their inspiration from China. But just as the class barriers of Tokugawa Japan began to lose their sharpness in the nineteenth century, so also in art the stylistic distinctions which had been pronounced at the beginning of the eighteenth century tended gradually to blur, as artists combined elements drawn from popular and official canons of taste, or even experimented with such alien Western techniques as oil painting.

Art, like thought, thus faithfully reflected the social confusion and tensions which underlay the apparent immobility of the Tokugawa regime. Under the circumstances, the duration of that regime seems more surprising than its collapse. To be sure, the peasantry remained a massive, stable element in Japanese society, living on the margin of subsistence, respectful to their betters, and inaccessible to strange new ideas. But the precariousness of the shoguns' domestic position was shown by the rapidity and scale of the changes that occurred in Japan as soon as the country had been officially opened to foreigners. Foreign pressure was merely a trigger releasing the internal forces that precipitated revolutionary reorganization of Japanese society after 1853.[81]

F. THE RETREAT OF BARBARISM, 1700–1850 A.D.

The rapid expansion of civilization, especially of Western civilization, had its corollary in the diminution of the geographic scope and political importance of simpler societies. In the Old World, the eighteenth century saw the definitive collapse of the political power of steppe peoples. Russia and China partitioned the steppe between them, China taking the eastern portion, Russia the richer western portion, with the Hungarian plain falling to Austria. The Chinese victory over the Kalmuk confederation in 1757 marked the final

---

[81] In addition to books cited separately I have consulted the following in connection with this section on Japan: George B. Sansom, *Japan: A Short Cultural History*, pp. 441–524; E. Herbert Norman, *Japan's Emergence as a Modern State* (New York: Institute of Pacific Relations, 1940), pp. 3–35; C. R. Boxer, *Jan Compagnie in Japan, 1600–1817* (The Hague: Martinus Nijhoff, 1936); George Alexander Lensen, *The Russian Push towards Japan: Russo-Japanese Relations, 1697–1875* (Princeton, N.J.: Princeton University Press, 1959), pp. 9–306; Masaharu Anesaki, *Religious Life of the Japanese People* (Tokyo: Kokusai Bunka Shinkokai, 1938); Noritake Tsuda, *Handbook of Japanese Art* (Tokyo: Sanseido Co., 1936), pp. 218–80; Peter C. Swann, *An Introduction to the Arts of Japan* (Oxford: Bruno Cassirer, 1958), pp. 159–213; D. C. Holm, *The National Faith of Japan: A Study in Modern Shinto* (London: Kegan Paul, Trench, Trubner & Co., 1938), pp. 44–52; Robert N. Bellah, *Tokugawa Religion* (Glencoe, Ill.: Free Press, 1957).

雪舟筆

Tokyo National Museum.

Charles P. Swann, An Introduction to the
Arts of Japan. Frederick A. Praeger, Publisher.

THREE JAPANESE PAINTINGS

The stylistic variety of modern Japanese painting is suggested by the sharp contrasts between these three paintings. At the upper left, a winter scene by Sesshu (1420–1506) reproduces a Chinese landscape in a style thoroughly Chinese, although experts can detect distinctive personal traits to his brush work that give the painting an individual character. The comparatively crude portrait of a peasant below dates from the eighteenth century and was made by a humble "folk" artist. Its vigor nevertheless suggests the energy of the Japanese peasantry. On the right, Hiroshige's (1797–1858) witty spoof, showing a monkey fishing the moon's reflection from the sea, offers us a gay caricature of Japan's own long-armed reach, first after Chinese and more recently after Western styles of civilization.

coda to an era in world history—the last time civilized armies confronted a serious rival on the steppe.[82]

Definitive destruction of barbarian and savage styles of life in the Americas and in Oceania occurred only in the latter part of the nineteenth century; yet, with Western frontier expansion in full swing throughout the eighteenth and early nineteenth centuries, the final disruption of Amerindian and Australian tribal societies clearly was only a matter of time. Even the smaller islands of the Pacific suffered widespread social disturbance in the wake of visits by whalers, copra merchants, and missionaries. The tropical rain forests of South America, southeast Asia, and the larger islands of the southwest Pacific offered geographically more extensive refuge zones for primitive societies; yet even these were precarious, for gold and slave hunters from the civilized world penetrated such recesses freely, if not very frequently.

By 1850, sub-Saharan Africa constituted by far the largest single barbarian reservoir left in the world; yet here, too, civilized and semi-civilized societies were encroaching rapidly. Moslem pastoralists and conquerors continued sporadically to extend their political control along the northern fringes of the Sudan from the Niger to the Nile, and southward below the horn of east Africa as well. Simultaneously semi-civilized Negro kingdoms based in the rain forests of west Africa extended and consolidated their power, largely through organized slave raiding and various other forms of commerce with the European traders of the coast. European political control had begun by 1850 to extend laterally along the coast and inland along the rivers; but these footholds were still minute as measured against the geographical vastness of the African continent.[83]

In east Africa, Portuguese power north of Mozambique disappeared by 1699, yielding before a combination of local revolt and armed intervention from Oman in southern Arabia. In the eighteenth century, a new mercantile power, based on Oman and its colony of Zanzibar, dominated the trade of east Africa. Slaves seized in the African interior, together with ivory and cloves from Zanzibar itself, became the export staples of this mercantile state. After 1822, however, British naval superiority in the Indian Ocean forced the sultan of Zanzibar reluctantly to accept various and progressively more

---

[82] Russian annexation of the Ukraine and lower Volga has already been noticed. Farther east, Russian suzerainty over the Kazaks was asserted through a series of treaties signed at various times between 1730 and 1819 with the four hordes into which that nation divided. No heavy fighting was involved. The fate of the Kalmuks convinced the Kazaks that it was necessary to come to terms with one or another of the great agricultural empires of Asia, and Russia was the nearer of the two. Cf. E. B. Bekmakhanov, *Prisoedinenie Kazakhstana k Rossii* (Moscow: Izdatelstvo Akademii Nauk, 1957). Read for me by George W. Smalley.

The destruction of the Kalmuk confederacy had the further effect of persuading both Mongols and Tibetans to desist from long-standing intrigues aimed at throwing off Chinese control. Cf. above, p. 650.

[83] The effort to halt the slave trade was one of the main impulses behind European political encroachment in West Africa. Missionary enterprise, closely linked with the humanitarian antislavery movement, was also an important factor. Cf. J. D. Fage, *An Introduction to the History of West Africa* (Cambridge: Cambridge University Press, 1959), pp. 98–133.

severe limitations upon the slave trade, so that his power ceased to be entirely autonomous.[84]

In the southern part of the African continent, Bantu war confederacies like the Zulu (from 1818) and the Matabele (from 1835) disputed the grasslands with Dutch-speaking pioneers (the Boers). Seeking new pastures for their animals and freedom from British administrative control at the Cape, the Dutch in 1835 began a massive migration northward into the veldt, where they pre-empted almost all suitable land for ranches or farms, and through their military prowess secured an abundant supply of Negro forced labor.[85]

Thus the simple farmers and pastoralists of the African interior found themselves beleaguered. From every direction Moslem, African, and European communities, possessing either superior political-military organization or superior technology or both, pressed in upon them. The old simplicities stood no chance against such opponents. Only the obstacles of geography, reinforced by African tropical diseases and by political rivalries among the European powers, preserved a degree of autonomy and cultural independence for African barbarian and savage communities into the second half of the nineteenth century.

[84] Cf. Zoe Marsh and G. W. Kingsnorth, *An Introduction to the History of East Africa* (Cambridge: Cambridge University Press, 1957), pp. 16–24.

[85] Cf. Leo Marquard, *The Story of South Africa* (London: Faber & Faber, 1955), pp. 74–155.

CHAPTER XIII

The Rise
of the West:
Cosmopolitanism
on a Global Scale
1850–1950 A.D.

A. INTRODUCTORY

Four events clustering near the midyear of the nineteenth century aptly symbolize the irremediable collapse of the traditional order of each of the major Asian civilizations. In China the Taiping rebellion broke out in 1850, and as it ate its way deep into the social fabric during the following fourteen years, return to the erstwhile imperial policy of deliberate insulation from the outer world became more and more impractical. Simultaneously, Japan emerged from the contrived social rigidities of the Tokugawa shogunate by means of a less violent but nonetheless drastic revolution from the top, begun in 1854 with the opening of Japan to limited foreign commerce. In India, the mutiny of 1857–58 played the role of grave-digger to the older order of society. After it had been suppressed, schools and railroads made it more and more impossible for Indians to regard the Westerners as just one more caste of conquerors, to be endured until a successor came along; and growing numbers of Indians began to discard the integuments of their inherited traditions. Finally, the Crimean War (1853–56), in which the Turks with the potent help of French and British allies won a victory over the Russians, turned out to be far more disruptive of Ottoman institutions than earlier defeats had been. The Sultan's empire, indeed, never recovered from such war-born innovations as a sizable public debt owed to European investors and railroads built by European engineers, not to mention a formal guaranty of equal liberties to all Ottoman subjects, promulgated in 1856 on the demand of the British, French, and Austrian ambassadors.

Thus in each of the great Asian civilizations, revolt either from above or from below rather suddenly discredited or subverted old ways and values; and, in each instance, disruptive influences were enormously stimulated by contacts and collisions with the industrializing West. Indeed, it seems scarcely an exaggeration to say that within the decade of the 1850's the fundamental fourfold cultural balance of the ecumene, which had endured the buffets of more than two thousand years, finally gave way. Instead of four (or with Japan, five) autonomous though interconnected civilizations, a yeasty, half-formless, but genuinely global cosmopolitanism began to emerge as the dominant reality of the human community.

The remarkable coincidences which funneled so great a change in world history into the space of less than ten years were not entirely accidental. The Japanese who opened their country to foreign contacts knew of China's contemporary difficulties; and the mutinous Indian soldiers were well aware of Britain's involvement in the Crimean War; while from the European side, the forward policy in China in 1858–60 was a translation to the Far East of

THE RISE OF THE WEST

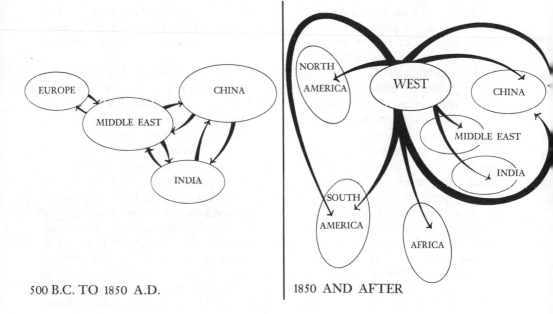

500 B.C. TO 1850 A.D.   1850 AND AFTER

Anglo-French collaboration first tested in the Crimea. In general, the density, speed, and regularity of world transport and communication had reached such a point by the mid-nineteenth century that no civilized part of the earth was isolated by more than a few weeks from any other; and instantaneous communication by means of the electric telegraph, although it became intercontinental only after oceanic cables had been laid (1867), was already by 1850 a reality in much of Europe and North America. The spread of railroads, which required a much more elaborate initial outlay, lagged behind the telegraph, but only by a decade or so; while on the oceans, steamships displaced sailing vessels for standard cargo runs between the 1870's and 1890's.

These revolutionary improvements in transport and communication were part of the entire complex of the West's rapidly evolving technology; and during the second half of the nineteenth century, technology, in turn, entered into systematic and enormously fruitful relation with theoretical science, which was itself evolving at a hitherto unparalleled pace. Moreover just as the revolution in communications which so drastically changed the relationship among the great civilizations of the world rested upon a wider matrix of technology, and technology upon science, all three depended upon the propitious environment offered by a particular set of European institutions and attitudes, without which communications, technology, and science could not have acquired their world-transforming force. Yet technological change transformed old social relationships in unforeseen and unforeseeable ways; and in some sense it seems true to say that, in the first decades of the twentieth century, side effects arising from the enormous successes of modern technology (which on a really massive scale is not yet much over a century old, even in the pioneer country of Great Britain) disrupted the older civilized tradition of the West just as the Asian civilizations had been disrupted sixty to seventy years earlier.

It is arguable that the marriage of science with technology has twisted *all* the civilizations which constituted the social landscape of former centuries from the articulations of two hundred years ago, substituting a new, "modern," cosmopolitan culture for the debris of older, parochial civilizations. Indeed, in view of the enormous changes in daily life and outlook brought by the lapse of even a single twentieth-century generation, the continuities uniting the life of the megalopolitan masses of our time with the isolated rural communities of the recent past appear slender indeed. Yet in another sense, the "disruption" of Western civilization that became palpable in the first part of the twentieth century was not a disruption at all but simply a further stage of its own inner evolution. Throughout history, drastic instability has distinguished the Far West from the other great civilizations of Eurasia; and one may view the recent history of the world as yet another instance of this long-standing proclivity for revolutionary reorganization, in which not solely Westerners but all mankind has this time been entangled.

For persons who feel themselves the heirs of Western civilization, choice between these alternative interpretations of the history of the recent past depends largely upon personal taste and temperament; whereas the heirs of other cultural traditions generally prefer the view that "modern" civilization differs from all older styles of life in more important respects than it resembles any one of them. Agreement under these circumstances cannot be expected; and men of the twentieth century obviously lack the time perspective needed for an emotionally neutral and perspicacious assessment. The fact that all the cultural variety of mankind is now embraced within the bounds of an intimately interacting whole may have entirely unforeseeable consequences; and even the very best observers of the twentieth century may well turn out to be as limited in their insight into the world around them as were the cultivated Greco-Romans of the first century A.D. who remained entirely insensitive to the future importance of the tiny Christian communities of their time. But these are limits inherent in the human condition, which we necessarily share with our heirs and successors as well as with former generations.

Operating therefore cheerfully enough within confines imposed by time, milieu, and temperament, two themes seem paramount in the history of the past century: (1) the growth of human control over inanimate forms of energy; and (2) an increasing readiness to tinker with social institutions and customs in the hope of attaining desired goals. In terms more familiar to historians, these developments reduce to industrial and political-social revolutions; while in the language of a (perhaps old-fashioned) social philosopher, the two themes might be subsumed under a single head: the progress of human reason applied to nature and to man. Progress there has most certainly been in science and technology; progress also, it seems to me, in many important aspects of human relations. And the supreme ironies of our own time, whereby the reasonings of philosophers have uncovered the impossibility of knowledge, the reasonings of psychologists have discovered the irrationalities of human nature, and the reasonings of anthropologists, sociologists, economists and other observers of society have pointed out the incommensurability of social phenomena with human calculations—not to mention the unanimous chorus of all thinking men asking whither and toward what goals? according to what values? and at whose direction does all the contemporary hustle and bustle of humanity proceed?—all these ironies should not provoke despair. However weak the reed, human reason has yet a rapier point; and centuries hence, the intellectual dilemmas of our time may appear just as interesting, and just as irrelevant, as the theological polemics of sixteenth-century Europe appear today.

If one takes advances in the deliberate manipulation of (1) inanimate and of (2) social energies as the master themes of recent history, Europe and the West are thrust into the center of attention even more emphatically than before, since all the principal innovations in technology and in social organization that kept humanity in turmoil during the nineteenth and first half of the twentieth century arose within the Western, and in most cases within the specifically European, context.

As in the immediately preceding chapters, it seems wise to juxtapose European developments of an earlier time with those on the world scene of a few decades later. The "New Regime" that came tumultuously to Europe after 1789, compounded as it was of French political and of British industrial experimentation, gave new shape and tone to the rapidly expanding West. But the West's expansion helped to precipitate decisive breakdown of older styles of civilized life in Asia about the middle of the nineteenth century. For a full hundred years thereafter, the non-Western world struggled to adjust local cultural inheritances in all their variety and richness to ideas and techniques originating in the European nineteenth century. Newer intellectual and moral dilemmas, arising from newer types of social and political manipulation, together with the technological wonderland of electronics, atomic energy, and rocketry of the mid-twentieth century, have scarcely yet been domesticated beyond the borders of the Western world. This does not mean that other peoples have been unaffected by such changes; it does mean that such peoples as the Indians, Chinese, and Moslems of the Middle East—in common with the overwhelming majority of Western mankind—had no active part in shaping the novelties that promise to give the second half of the twentieth century its special historical character.

Accordingly, this chapter will analyze European and Western developments from 1789 until 1917, reserving a few cursory observations upon the most recent period of Western history for the conclusion. This will be followed by an effort to discern landmarks in the processes of cultural interplay between the Western and non-Western worlds down to 1950. Nor does the date 1950 have any special significance: its virtues as a cutoff point are merely arithmetical. Future historians may well prefer 1945, or a year still in the future, when seeking to divide twentieth-century world history into meaningful periods.

B. THE WESTERN EXPLOSION, *1789–1917 A.D.*

I. TERRITORIAL EXPANSION

At the outbreak of the French Revolution in 1789, the geographical boundaries of Western civilization could still be defined with reasonable precision. By the time of the Russian Revolution in 1917, this was no longer the case. Western history had merged into world history; but simultaneously and by definition, the same fate overtook all the other civilizations, savageries, and barbarisms of mankind.

In this amalgamation, the peoples of the West had a distinct advantage over all others. Firm belief in the value of their own inherited institutions, together with burgeoning numbers, the world's most powerful weapons, and most efficient network of transport and communication, permitted Westerners easily to overcome whatever opposition their activities aroused among other peoples.

Consequently, within a few decades settlers of European origin or descent were able to occupy central and western North America, the pampas and adjacent regions of South America, and substantial parts of Australia, New Zealand, and South Africa. Similarly, the frontier of Russian settlement in Siberia, central Asia, and the Caucasus continued to advance throughout the nineteenth century. But Western political and economic penetration extended far beyond the areas of European-type settlement. By 1914, almost all of Africa, southeast Asia, and Oceania had come under European political control. Mines and plantations were opened in many new parts of the world, often at places remote from European or any other sort of civilization. New products like tea and rubber, nickel and oil, together with old ones like gold, were eagerly pursued in jungles, deserts, and Arctic forests, as well as in more hospitable regions of the earth. Even the fur traders of the eighteenth century found their analogue in the whalers of the nineteenth, who hunted the seven seas and harassed primitive populations of oceanic islands with their diseases and gewgaws just as fur traders had earlier hunted and harassed the animal and human populations of the circumpolar lands.

These movements of men and goods enormously altered the older distribution of populations and cultures in the world. Neither natural nor manmade obstacles sufficed any longer to halt the spread of Western technology and ideas anywhere on the habitable globe. Yet despite its significance for world history, the geographical expansion of Western civilization in the nineteenth century seems to have had no critical importance for the historical development of Europe itself. Europe's history between 1789 and 1917 was dominated by industrialism based upon the use of inanimate power, and by political revolution based upon a new evaluation of human rights and duties. Both were rooted deep in Europe's local past and neither in inception nor in their development to 1917 bore more than an adventitious external relation to the wider world.

Until very nearly our own time—and perhaps even today—cultural exchanges precipitated by the cosmopolitan mixing of men from all the diverse regions of the earth have tended to run strongly in one direction: from Western to non-Western. As a result, contemporary higher culture and thought owe little to non-Western cultural traditions. Indeed, as conviction of the inherent superiority of their own civilization took firmer hold upon Western minds—a conviction conveniently sustained by repeating rifles and naval gunboats—educated Europeans became less accessible to alien cultural influences and in that sense more parochial than their forefathers of the eighteenth century had been.[1]

2. INDUSTRIALISM

In the nineteenth century, industry went through two fairly distinct phases, dividing about the year 1870. Each had a distinctive technology and distinctive organizational forms and ideals. The first phase centered very conspicu-

[1] Even systematic study of primitive peoples and of other civilizations, which always attracted some scholars, tended to become an investigation of interesting social specimens, from which even the most sympathetic observer, armed as he was with scientific curiosity, necessarily held himself aloof. Such scientific social distance inhibited ordinary cultural interaction far more effectively than earlier religious dogma had ever done.

ously in Great Britain; the second was more diffused, with both the United States and Germany, but especially the latter, serving as pioneers and exemplars.

THE FIRST OR BRITISH PHASE. The technical aspect of the first phase of modern industrialism can be summed up in two words: coal and iron. This style of technology achieved full expression by about mid-century, when railroads, cotton mills, and hundreds of other new or improved machines and devices had been put to work. The Great Exposition of 1851 in London displayed and aptly symbolized the technological transformation that had come to fruition in Great Britain by that time.

The use of coal and iron for industrial as well as for household purposes was hardly new in nineteenth-century England. Thomas Newcomen had used coal to drive an engine as early as 1712; and iron had been a standard material for tools for three thousand years. The innovation in nineteenth-century Britain was the scale upon which these two basic materials were used. As innumerable new applications of steam power to iron machinery were found, changes in scale pyramided into changes in kind. Wooden looms and spinning wheels, powered by human muscles and dispersed in country cottages, bore litle resemblance to the thousands of spindles and scores of steam-driven looms concentrated in an early Victorian cotton mill; and the cheapness, uniformity, and above all the quantity of the product far exceeded that which could be produced by hand. Changes almost as radical in other traditional trades like metallurgy or printing, and the rise of new occupations like engineering and railroading, drove the new technology deep into the fabric of British society by 1850.

By that time, a few imaginative minds (Henri Saint-Simon, d. 1825; Auguste Comte, d. 1857; Robert Owen, d. 1858) had begun to glimpse the possibility of a future economy of abundance, in which the massive application of inanimate power to industrial processes would put an end to human want. Majority opinion, however, continued to hold that poverty was ineradicable and that any increase in goods would be rapidly absorbed by an increase in numbers. Certainly population grew spectacularly in nineteenth-century Britain, increasing by about 34 per cent in the twenty years from 1801 to 1821. For the century as a whole, British population rose from about 10 million in 1801 to 37 million in 1901.[2]

From the perspective of the 1960's, it looks as though the industrial transformations which began in England about two hundred years ago and reached really massive proportions only a little more than a century before our time constituted a mutation in the economic and social life of mankind comparable in magnitude with the Neolithic transition from predation to agriculture and animal husbandry. In Neolithic times, farmers' techniques for deliberately remodeling the natural environment multiplied the food and power resources available to mankind several times over, supported a radical increase in human numbers, and made possible the concentration of compara-

---

[2] Data are conveniently assembled in "Report of the Royal Commission on Population," Cmd. 7695 (1949), Table III.

tively massive populations into cities where specialization of occupations could develop the skills and sophistication of civilized life. Through all of recorded history (down even to our own day) the majority of men have lived out their lives within a frame established by the daily and yearly routines of tillage, subject to the chances and disasters of weather, war, or pestilence, and disciplined by the obvious relationship between harvest and hard work in the fields.

Modern industry may yet establish a comparably pervasive framework within which the majority of men will exist far into an unforeseeable future; but the social, political, and cultural possibilities inherent in such a change in the elemental rhythm and routine of human life have not yet been more than partially and perhaps fumblingly explored. It is difficult, therefore, to exaggerate the historical consequences flowing from the pioneer work of a small circle of inventors, enginers, and promoters in a few provincial towns of Great Britain in the later eighteenth and early nineteenth centuries.

It was, however, and perhaps still is, very easy to exaggerate the lasting importance of the institutional and intellectual framework within which Great Britain's modern industrialism arose. Possibly such metaphysical entities as the "Protestant ethic," the "nonconformist conscience," and the "capitalist spirit" were vital and necessary ingredients of pioneer industrialism; though it is worth pointing out that, in a country like Hungary, neither Calvinism nor nonconformity had industrial consequences. Certainly Britain was favored by easy availability of beds of coal and iron ore, a labor force that could be constrained to accept new routines of work, and a class of innovators and entrepreneurs willing to develop new ideas and able to acquire the money or credit needed to embody them in new machines and procedures.

A pervasive looseness in the texture of British society perhaps stimulated inventiveness and helped to give Britain a commanding lead over other nations in the first phase of modern industrialism. This looseness had been inherited from parliament's angry dismantlement of the aspiring absolutism of the early Stuarts in the mid-seventeenth century. But, between 1756 and 1815, the parliamentary archaism of the English Old Regime was rather thoroughly shaken up by the strains and exigencies of war with the French.[3] Abrupt changes in overseas trading patterns, depending on the momentary constellation of naval forces; equally abrupt changes in government orders for the manifold sinews of a growingly complicated and massive warfare;[4] and drastic fluctuations in money supply and price levels all weakened traditional resistances to economic innovation. Under these conditions, the financial rewards accessible to a lucky or skilful promoter were so conspicuous as to induce hundreds of other ambitious or greedy individuals to attempt to dupli-

[3] From 1756 to 1815 Britain was at war with France (and various other states) during all or part of 37 years and at peace during only 22 years.

[4] According to one calculation, Britain had a total of 1,062,000 men under arms in 1814, counting militia and volunteers as well as regular forces. Even minimal equipment for such numbers required a very great effort for a country of about 12 million inhabitants. Cf. W. W. Rostow, *British Economy of the Nineteenth Century* (Oxford: Clarendon Press, 1948), p. 13.

cate his feat.[5] Quite possibly, in a better regulated society, a more energetic official control of individual initiative and war profiteering would have prevented the rapid transformation of Britain's industrial plant which in fact occurred in the late eighteenth and early nineteenth centuries.

But no catalogue of general conditions can ever entirely account for a massive change in human affairs. Individual persons, inspired by diverse motives, made decisions and acted in ways that in sum began to transform the life of England. Pride in skilful workmanship and the wish to achieve respect among fellow mechanics may have been as potent a stimulus to invention in some cases as the desire for money was in others. The man who patiently filed down a metal thread to make it fit the nut smoothly and tight, regulating the bite of his file by thoroughly traditional skills of hand and eye, was just as necessary for the success of the new machinery as was the capitalist who ordered the machine built and paid operators to tend it; while an inventor who was not, like James Watt, both mechanic and capitalist himself, depended upon the co-operation of both before his idea could be embodied in moving iron.

The important thing to grasp, in any consideration of the institutional setting of early industrialism, is that the older framework of British society, though it was certainly strained and extended by the technical innovations which came so thick and fast in the first half of the nineteenth century, did not at any time give way.[6] This was neither a necessary nor a stable state of affairs, however. The fact that early industrialism appeared and flourished in an institutional setting which was at once commercial and rural, aristocratic and parliamentary, insular and individualistic, does not prove that institutions of this type have any inherent, long-range affinities with industrialism. The assumption of a necessary connection between the growth of industrialism and the institutions and attitudes peculiar to Britain (and, at one degree removed, to western Europe and North America generally) is an intellectual error common to Marxian dogmatists, nineteenth-century liberals, and twentieth-century conservatives.

Nevertheless, this assumption was plausible until about 1870, when industrial leadership in the world began to shift from Britain to Germany and the United States. Adam Smith (d. 1790) and similarly minded philosophers developed an elaborate and impressive body of economic theory showing that the rational action of free individual judgment in buying and selling would produce maximal satisfaction of human wants. Because British institutions seemed to give unusual scope to just such individual pursuit of private interest, the conclusion seemed obvious that Britain's extraordinary industrial advance was directly due to the rationality of British laws in refraining from interference with the freedom of individuals in the market. This philosophy of

[5] Cf. Robert Owen, *The Life of Robert Owen* (2 vols.; London: E. Wilson, 1857–58), for a vivid account of how rapidly an energetic and lucky man could make a killing in cotton in the first decades of the nineteenth century.

[6] Jane Austen's novels are a wholesome reminder of how faintly wars and revolutions—industrial or otherwise—echoed in rural society. And rural Britain, until after the middle of the nineteenth century, remained numerically preponderant, prosperous, and socially as well as politically important.

laissez faire became a fundamental article of the liberal creed in the mid-nineteenth century, and in many European countries provided a rallying cry for those who attacked legal and other obstacles to the development of industrialism in their own localities.

Yet even in the nineteenth century, the facts were otherwise. Technology rapidly outran liberal institutions and found lodgment in societies of very different stamp. The industrialization of Japan was the most striking instance of this phenomenon; but even within the Western world, the rise of industry in Germany after 1870 and in Russia two or three decades later brought the full panoply of contemporary industrial technology into societies where the liberal tradition was weak or politically negligible. Yet industry flourished under the nurture of government and corporation officials whose stake in the success of the enterprise, when measured by the yardstick of personal enrichment through a share in the profits, was often slight or entirely absent.

Moreover, while industry was advancing rapidly in Germany and Russia, the British captains of industry tended to rest on their laurels. Sons of successful industrialists were powerfully attracted to the cultivated style of life prevailing among the landed and leisured class. Owners affecting such a style of life were often loath to authorize heavy new capital expenditures—why interfere with a good thing? In addition, gentility required withdrawal from active daily management of mill or factory—indeed, often required a town house in London or at least in Manchester, and if possible a place in the country, far away from the grime and clangor of the industrial process. All this inevitably and enormously widened the gap between factory management and workingmen. The easy and technologically fruitful interplay between an entrepreneur and his hired hands which had existed in the more modest workshops of earlier days tended therefore to disappear. Ingenious mechanics still existed; but few of them were inclined to use their ingenuity to enrich a socially distant capitalist, especially when doing so might put fellow employees out of work.

A second reason for Britain's loss of industrial leadership was the lack of any deliberate and systematic link between theoretical science and technological invention.[7] To be sure, industrialists sometimes consulted theoretical scientists when particular difficulties arose. Thus mine owners commissioned Sir Humphry Davy in 1815 to design a safety lamp for use in coal mines; and a professor of natural philosophy, Charles Wheatstone, became a partner in the first successful British telegraph company (1837) because the entrepreneurs needed his knowledge of electromagnetism in their initial experimentation.[8] In the following generation, Lord Kelvin, a professor at Glasgow, solved certain difficulties hindering the transmission of transoceanic telegraphic messages and also designed a compass that would work on the new

[7] Cf. Sir Eric Ashby, *Technology and the Academics: An Essay on Universities and the Scientific Revolution* (London: Macmillan & Co., 1958), pp. 1–49 and *passim*.

[8] Cf. Charles Singer *et al.*, *A History of Technology* (Oxford: Oxford University Press, 1958), IV, 95–96, 656–57.

iron ships produced in Glasgow shipyards.[9] But such confrontations between scientific theory and technological practice remained haphazard: an emergency affair more often than not, broken off by mutual agreement as soon as a particular problem had been solved.

The fundamental expectation of men engaged in the industrial process remained static. Workingmen and owners alike tended to assume that once a new technique had been tried out—machinery built, labor skills acquired, and a market for the finished product established—then the process should go on indefinitely without further important change. To be sure, the facts never much resembled this ideal. In the early days, when initial capital costs were still comparatively small, a rival armed with new patents on improved machinery might easily disrupt a going concern by cutting costs and prices; and the rough jolts of the business cycle did even more to weed out inefficient or technically obsolescent enterprises.

Yet, despite all experience to the contrary, both the British industrialists and workmen characteristically expected or hoped for stability. As the growing complexity of machinery and the elaboration of manufacturing processes resulted in increased initial capital costs, disturbance from domestic competition declined; but competition from abroad eventually proved no less disruptive.[10] The notion that technical improvement was an unending process found no real lodgment among practical men in Britain before 1914. They found it hard to believe that perfectly good machines might become obsolete while still in excellent working order. The paradoxical idea that a firm should add to its current costs by financing research aimed specifically at superseding the industrial processes of its own plants was only grudgingly admitted in a few British industries before World War I.

British national power and wealth may perhaps have suffered through such social and moral-intellectual obstacles to technological advance. Yet from another point of view, this incipient (and abortive) stabilization of industrialism proved the vigor and adaptability of the older patterns of British society. Successful capitalists and scientists assimilated traditional upper-class outlooks and manners, while at the other end of the social spectrum, British industrial laborers showed rather more originality by constructing a tolerable moral universe for themselves around new institutions like the pubs, trade unions, and Methodist chapels.

Had Britain been left to its own devices, the extraordinary burst of inventiveness and technological transformation which reached a crescendo in the first half of the nineteenth century would probably have died down, and a much slower rate of technical evolution taken its place. But Britain was not

---

[9] *Encyclopaedia Britannica, s.v.* "Kelvin."

[10] The history of the aniline dye industry is a case in point. After a brilliant start in Britain in the 1850's, this industry was largely taken over by Germans in the 1860's. The close linkage between German research chemistry and the dye and chemical industries contrasted sharply with the attitude of British firms which, secure behind a patent, sought only to exploit a good thing. This contrast, more than any other single factor, gave the Germans pre-eminence in the dye industry before World War I. For the British beginnings of the aniline dye industry, cf. Singer *et al., A History of Technology*, V, 269–74 and 281.

left to its own devices. Instead, industrialism, reacting with divergent attitudes and institutions in other lands, acquired a second impetus, even more powerful than the first; and the British, like everyone else in the world, had to adjust themselves accordingly.

THE SECOND OR GERMAN AND AMERICAN PHASE (TO 1917). The technology of the second phase of modern industrialism embraced a wider variety of materials and tapped new sources and forms of energy; but the primacy of coal and iron was not really disturbed in the period before World War I. The diversification inherent in the rise of the electrical, chemical, petroleum, and light metals industries, with their derivative products like automobiles, radios, airplanes, and synthetic textiles, had only begun. Yet coal and iron, the two kings of earlier nineteenth-century technology, were themselves significantly transformed. Coal found other than crude fuel uses; tars derived from its distillation were transformed by suitable chemical manipulation into products as diverse as aspirin, dyes, and explosives. Iron, too, underwent notable chemical diversification after the invention of the Bessemer converter (1856) allowed mass production of steel. Steel itself, being a chemical mixture of iron with carbon and other elements, was capable of indefinite variation. Chemists and metallurgists learned to standardize and diversify their product by a more exact control of its components and discovered that minute variations in ingredients and their proportions produced steels with widely different qualities of hardness, resilience, rust resistance, and tensile strength. The term "steel" thus came to cover a wide range of special types of metal suited to particular uses. Hence, although coal and iron still reigned supreme among industrial materials between 1870 and 1917, in reality, by the end of the period chemists and metallurgists had transmuted the twin monarchs of earlier industrialism into a complex array of entirely new substances.

The development of special steels and of coal tar derivatives exemplified a more general trend in the technology of the later nineteenth century. The new uses of coal and iron took advantage of properties developed through deliberately induced changes occurring at molecular and submolecular levels. Indeed, as chemists swarmed into the forefront of technological advance and made industrial engineers their pupils,[11] the range of the older technology, which had centered upon macro-material manipulations performed by moving iron machines, was enormously expanded by a drastic miniaturization of the natural forces tapped by industrial processes. Deliberate manipulation of molecular, atomic, and (with electricity) subatomic particles, forces, and properties gave a vast new range, a subtle flexibility, and an unparalleled precision to human control of both matter and energy. The flip of a switch replaced boiler-stoking as the way to turn on local power supplies; and electricity proved able to energize a wide variety of machines which mere drive wheels could not even begin to operate. If the stationary steam engine, with

[11] The career of Justus von Liebig, professor of chemistry at Giessen and Munich 1824–73, aptly symbolizes the marriage between theoretical chemistry and technology. Aside from his own discoveries, the most famous of which was the measurement and analysis of the chemical requirements for plant growth, Liebig taught a surprising number of the industrial and commercial chemists of the mid-nineteenth century.

its ponderous rocker beams, heaving pistons, humming drive shafts, and clouds of steam and smoke was the mechanical archetype of the first phase of modern industrialism, the "machine" in which motion perceptible to the human senses has been transcended—a radio, a transformer, an electrolytic vat, a photographic plate, or an electric furnace—is a fitting symbol of its second phase.

The new technology of course did not entirely replace older processes, any more than the invention of the steam engine had caused the abandonment of animal and water power. In fact, new developments in the older style of technology were sometimes of great importance. Increasing size of blast furnaces, locomotives, steamships, printing presses, and the like brought important economies; and the invention of automobiles and airplanes presaged transformations of human society comparable to those wrought earlier by the railroads. Yet these improvements, though obvious and impressive to the men of the age, rather fulfilled the promise of the first phase of industrialism than pioneered its second phase—a phase in which we of the 1960's are still immersed.

*   *   *

The social organization and ideals basic to the industrial organization of the United States before World War I closely resembled those of England. The United States shared or exaggerated most of the peculiarities of British society, being even more insular, entrusting public officials with minimal economic and social functions, and lacking, at least in the north, a clear differentiation of social classes. Long before the American Revolution, pecuniary calculation and the cunning of the market place had been firmly implanted in the society of New England and the Middle Atlantic states; and Yankee mechanical ingenuity equaled any in the world. In such a community, modern industrialism easily took root, especially when railroads and river navigation made available the extensive iron and coal deposits of Pennsylvania and other inland regions. The enormous natural resources of the United States, and the comparatively thin but rapidly growing population meant that until and even after World War I the United States preserved a boom atmosphere very like that which had prevailed in industrial circles in England between 1790 and 1850. Moreover, the individualistic ideals and competitive practice of American industrialists were cut from nearly the same bolt of cloth which had covered the crudities of early Victorian industry with a veil of public decency. The careers of mechanics and entrepreneurs like Thomas Edison (d. 1931) and Henry Ford (d. 1947) recapitulated the earlier achievements of men like Richard Arkwright (d. 1792) and James Watt (d. 1819) on an enhanced financial scale suitable to the enlarged dimensions of the American landscape and domestic market.

The industrialization of the United States was vastly accelerated by massive and variegated immigration. By 1914 the American people had become an ethnic league of nations, with European elements predominating, yet with a substantial Negro minority and at least token representation of all other major stems of mankind. The cultural plurality resulting from this mixture added a distinctive note to the social and psychological strains inherent in industrialism's shift from rural to urban living. The American solution was to emphasize the English cultural inheritance and political precedents, thereby obscuring, at least for a few decades, the diversity which immigrants brought to the country and providing a comparatively flexible common ground upon which cultural discrepancies among diverse segments of the population might interact.

The industrialization of the United States differed from its British prototype also in the fact that corporations quickly became the normal organizational form for American business enterprise. The tendency for corporations to become private bureaucracies in which power depended on office rather than on ownership clearly pointed away from the rugged individualism which had prevailed in Britain during the first phase of industrialism. Public regulation of private business also demonstrated that powerful companies, like John D. Rockefeller's Standard Oil, sometimes grew beyond the dimensions tolerable to a strictly private sovereignty, even in the United States. But these tendencies were more fully developed in Germany, where the traditions of the Prussian government encouraged broad action in economic as in other matters and where the commonalty viewed officials not as hogs at the public trough, greedily consuming the taxes paid by honest men, but as representatives in the flesh of that transcendent entity, the State, in which—at least in principle, if not always in fact—conflicting private interests were suitably sublimated into the common good.

*   *   *

German industrial development closely paralleled that of the United States in time, partly because both countries required railroads to unlock mineral wealth previously cut off from exploitation by the difficulties of transport from inland locations. But the relatively rigid class system of Germany, especially in the east; the powerful and popular mystique of state, army, and bureaucracy; the excellence of German education; and the wide distribution of handicraft skills and even of guild organization—all assured that modern industry in Germany would exhibit a different social and moral character from that known in England or the United States.

The Germans' most important innovation was to extend the scope of deliberate, conscious management in the industrial process. This was done along several different lines, which may be termed (1) technical, (2) financial, and (3) human engineering.

1) In the sphere of technique, the Germans organized invention, making it a deliberate, expected, normal affair. The fact that large-scale German industry came to the scene just as chemists were beginning to achieve an adequate theoretical understanding of their subject no doubt helped to establish the notion that technique was subject to indefinite improvement. At any rate, German chemical and electrical companies pioneered the creation of indus-

trial research laboratories, staffed by university-trained chemists and physicists, whose investigations and experiments were conceived, not as a sort of emergency auxiliary to normal operations, but as an integral and permanent part of the enterprise. Thus a few German corporations institutionalized technical invention by establishing a reliable link between the high theory of scientific research and the humdrum routine of factory practice. The payoff was dramatic, for by the turn of the century German chemical and electrical industries led the world.

2) In finance, the German government extended the zone of deliberate management by abrogating or controlling the free market, which at least in theory had guided the decisions of British industrialists. Thus tariffs and, above all, minutely adjusted railway rates were used to encourage particular enterprises and industries necessary for national defense. Before but even more emphatically after 1866, when the Prussians first demonstrated how to achieve strategic surprise by transporting troops by rail, the railroads themselves were laid out with an eye to potential military use. The needs of speedy deployment along a threatened frontier became more important than any prospective financial return in dictating the nature and location of new railroad construction. Yet in thus abrogating market considerations, Germany as a whole gained not only a significant military advantage but a remarkably coherent and—especially after 1879, when state purchase of privately owned railroads became official policy—also an unusually efficient transport network.

Government agents were not the only officials bent upon controlling the development of German industry. Under the umbrella of the state, half a dozen or so "private" bureaucracies arose that had an extraordinarily pervasive influence upon the growth of the German economy. These "private" hierarchies were called banks. Their power arose from the fact that they financed German industry with generous long-term loans on a scale which British bankers, loath to lock up too much money in machines and buildings under someone else's private control, refused to do. The availability of such easy credit vastly accelerated the upsurge of German industry after 1870; but there was another side to the coin, for the banks insisted upon having a voice in controlling the firms they so lavishly financed. This was done chiefly by insinuating bank representatives onto boards of directors. When a single bank thus established intimate symbiosis with several industries and with numerous enterprises, the ostensible independence of separate firms became largely fictitious. A bankers' point of view, national or even international in scope, and pecuniary in its angle of vision, tended to dominate management decisions.

The cartel became the characteristic expression of the cohesion of German industrial management arising from the co-ordinating role played by the great banks. The general aim of a cartel was to control the supply and sale price of a particular group of products in a manner that would maximize profit for the industry as a whole and minimize fluctuations in the flow of goods and services through the industrial establishment. Agreements to share the market among all cartel members according to some negotiated proportion were usual; price-fixing was almost universal; and frequently the same product was offered to different classes of customers at different prices. Details varied from industry to industry; and in the case of products which could not easily be standardized, the cartel principle usually broke down. But in coal and steel and many other major industries, the German cartels met with outstanding success.

Through cartels, German financial and industrial managers controlled the market (within limits), instead of being controlled by it. During the first phase of industrialism, men had simply assumed that the fluctuations of prices on a free market were natural, and they adjusted their activities to the recurrent pattern of boom and bust as best they might, much as farmers had for centuries adjusted themselves to the violence or beneficence of the weather. The German cartels did not, of course, escape entirely from the fluctuations of world-wide markets in the pre–World War I years;[12] but by introducing planned production and a measure of deliberate rigidity into prices they did achieve a hitherto unparalleled control over the financial climate.

3) Even in Germany, progress in human engineering was uneven before 1914. Nevertheless, German trade and technical schools prepared men for specific jobs more effectively than any others in the world; and Bismarck's social insurance laws also introduced a new element of conscious management into millions of human lives. Likewise, Bismarck's behind-the-scenes manipulation of the press was a preliminary step toward the sort of thought control which has become widespread in our time.

More important than these rather feeble beginnings on the nation-wide scale was the manner in which individual owner-entrepreneurs rapidly gave way to a corps of professional managers who not only operated the factories, firms, cartels, and banks entrusted to them with exemplary efficiency but also ordered the conditions of their own existence by creating a managerial elite with a strong internal discipline and an *esprit de corps* quite different from the individualistic and nakedly pecuniary ethos common among British businessmen of the early nineteenth century. Members of the German industrial and commercial elite ranged themselves into tidy bureaucratic hierarchies and were rewarded for success and conformity to the ethos of their clique by promotion to higher posts with broader authority. Money in itself—the reward and measure of success in the market place—must often have been of lesser importance to such men than the prestige accruing from their rank in the business community.

Clearly, a rather narrow oligarchy, recruiting its members by co-option from the top and disciplining candidates for promotion through a lifetime of rigorous supervision, closely resembled the pyramid of governmental bureaucracy; and as a matter of fact, the industrial and governmental bureaucracies overlapped extensively. Public servants managed railroads, mines, telegraph, and telephone services in the German states; while the pervasive, if rather aloof benevolence of most governmental officials toward private cor-

---

[12] With the co-operation of French, Dutch, English, and other bankers and industrialists, the cartel principle was extended beyond merely national borders to regulate the world supply of a few commodities before World War I.

porations reached its culmination in the active and close collaboration between key industrial suppliers and the Prussian General Staff.

Indeed, the really impressive achievements of human engineering concentrated in the military sphere during the nineteenth century; and here Germany's lead was conspicuous. In the post-Napoleonic period, Prussia pioneered among European states by making universal military training (at least in principle) normal in peacetime; and the success which came to Prussia's citizen soldiers, operating upon a plan of campaign which had been carefully drawn up in advance by professional officers, amazed all Europe. After the Prussian victories against Austria in 1866 and against France in 1870–71, all the continental powers of Europe hastened to follow the Prussian example. As a result, the first weeks of World War I presented the amazing spectacle of vast human machines, complete with replaceable parts, operating in a truly inhuman fashion and moving at least approximately according to predetermined and irreversible plans. The millions of persons composing the rival machines behaved almost as though they had lost individual will and intelligence. As a result, in August, 1914, human beings in their tens of thousands met death rejoicing at their escape into the automatism of a somnambulant heroism.

The war years which followed brought about a gigantic merger of all the different elements in German society which had been so vigorously expanding the limits of conscious control over social action. By 1917, after three years of war, the various groups and bureaucratic hierarchies which had been operating more or less independently of one another in peacetime (and not infrequently had worked at cross purposes) were subordinated to one (and perhaps the most effective) of their number: the General Staff. Military officers controlled civilian government officials, the staffs of banks, cartels, firms, and factories, engineers and scientists, workingmen, farmers—indeed almost every element in German society; and all efforts were directed in theory and in large degree also in practice to forwarding the war effort.

By 1917, rationing and priorities had replaced market prices as regulators of the distribution of all important commodities. Calculations of the availability of labor, raw materials, power, and transport had taken precedence over financial controls and calculations. Scientific talent had been mobilized for such emergency programs as the fixation of atmospheric nitrogen, without which Germany would soon have lacked explosives as well as fertilizer. The war organization of imperial Germany also extended, though less perfectly, to adjacent territories allied with or conquered by the German armies. A national concentration of power for national ends thus became, within limits set by Austrian *Schlamperei*, Belgian sulkiness, and Balkan backwardness, a transnational totalitarianism. During World War I, the Germans achieved a greater concentration and smoother co-ordination of human and mechanical resources for the war than any other nation, did so sooner, and stood the strain longer. Defeat in 1918 involved the dismantlement of the military-administrative machine which had lain at the heart of the entire power complex. Yet the revelation of what was possible when resolute, ruthless, and intelligent men, inspired by a strong *esprit de corps* and organized into a tight hierarchy of authority, set out to focus the energies and resources of an entire nation upon the achievement of ends which the ruling clique had itself defined remained to haunt the minds of some, to inflame the ambitions of others, and to herald the advent of a new era in world history.[13]

Each Western nation had its own nuances of style in industrialism as in everything else; and just as British precedents and models had been received with a difference on the continent in the first half of the nineteenth century, so also the German model of the latter part of the century combined vari-

[13] Thorstein Veblen, *Imperial Germany and the Industrial Revolution* (New York: Macmillan Co., 1915) did perhaps more to shape my conceptions of the peculiarities of German industrialism than any other book. Data from J. H. Clapham, *The Economic Development of France and Germany, 1815–1914* (Cambridge: Cambridge University Press, 1951) were also helpful.

THE INDUSTRIAL REVOLUTION

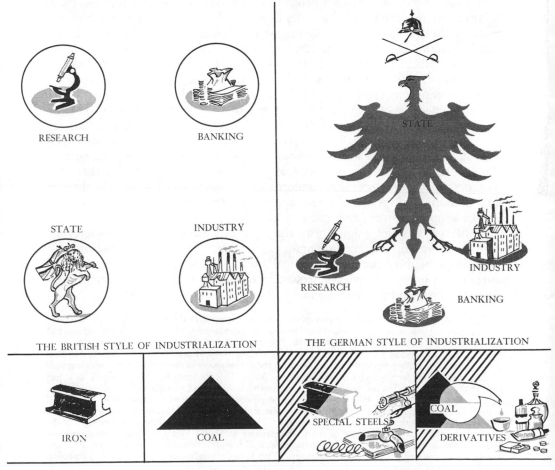

ously with local traditions, skills, and resources, and competed with the slightly variant models offered by Britain and/or France, to initiate the industrialization of eastern and southern Europe. But in 1917, industrialism had barely begun to take root beyond western Europe and the northeastern United States. Despite its great impact upon the peoples of the globe, industrialism was still an exotic local growth when World War I rudely shattered Europe's New Regime.

3. THE DEMOCRATIC REVOLUTION

In 1789 the French Estates-General, having transformed itself into the National Assembly, proclaimed the Rights of Man and set out to embody these rights in a new constitution. Thereby the Democratic Revolution, which had found its first conspicuous expression in the British colonies of North America, was transferred across the Atlantic and planted, with fanfare and panache, in the very heart of western Europe. The fanfare of the first few days was followed by more than twenty years of fireworks, in the course of which the ideas of the Revolution were broadcast over most of Europe and inflamed South America as well. Thereafter, until World War I, the major agenda for European politicians was to adjust inherited political varieties to the eternal verities newly discovered in France, *i.e.*, to secularize, rationalize, and reform existing institutions in the light of democratic principles.[14]

The French Revolution itself was a tissue of contrarieties. Quite apart from the inescapable compromises of practice, revolutionary theory, summed up in the slogan "Liberty, Equality, Fraternity," was shot through with ambiguities. But ambiguity was and is the essence of all good political slogans, since it allows men of diverse viewpoints to rally for effective action despite their differences. In this respect, the revolutionary movement of France embraced human motives as various as those tapped by any of the earlier great upheavals of European history, even the Reformation.

"Liberty," after all, might mean the right of a majority to override every obstacle to its will. By an easy paradox, liberty might even mean the right of a clique to enlighten the people, using exhortation and threat as normal stock-in-trade but in case of necessity resorting openly to violence in order to convince doubters and prevent enemies of the people from spreading the poison

---

[14] The violent emotions and deeds precipitated by the French Revolution, together with the position, power, and importance of France in the Western world at large, tended to obscure the influence of the earlier North American example after 1789. For this reason, it seems best to concentrate here entirely upon France and to forgo consideration of the vicissitudes and triumphs of the democratic ideal in the United States. During the nineteenth century, the development of the United States was markedly *sui generis*, owing largely to its frontier position. American experience became parochial, as it had been in the seventeenth but had not been in the eighteenth century and was not to be in the twentieth.

Even the American Civil War, 1861–65, had very little effect beyond the borders of the United States. Slavery and serfdom had been abolished in the other parts of the Western world earlier than in the United States, with only a few exceptions like Cuba or Brazil; and the military technology of the Civil War, which anticipated some of the characteristics of World War I battles, went almost unnoticed. Within five years after the end of the American war, the Prussians twice demonstrated how to win a war in a single well-planned campaign. With Prussian models before their eyes, the professional military of Europe and the rest of the world saw little reason to study the massive bungling of American civilians in uniform.

of deceit. But liberty might also mean the exact opposite: the right of individuals to do whatever they liked within the broadest practicable limits, even when their conduct displeased or offended a majority. In short, liberty might mean either a radical extension or a rigorous restriction of governmental authority; and the word was regularly invoked to justify both policies.

"Equality" and "Fraternity" embraced equally drastic contraries. Did equality mean equality before the law, so that all men should pay the same taxes, conform to the same restrictions, and enjoy the same liberties? If so, was a rich man really the equal of a poor starveling wretch ready to sell his birthright for a square meal? Or did true equality also require equalization of

AMBIGUITIES OF THE FRENCH REVOLUTION

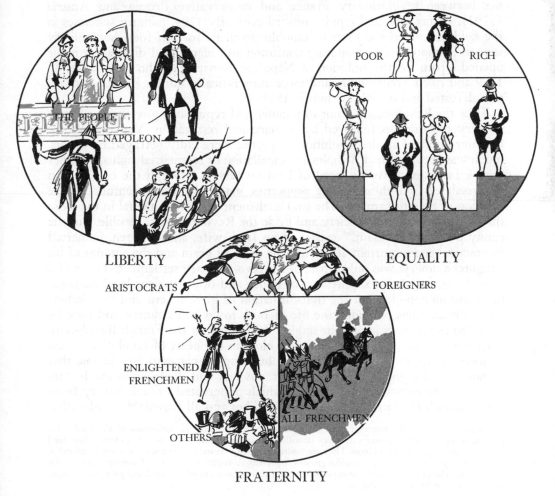

THE PEOPLE

NAPOLEON

LIBERTY

POOR   RICH

EQUALITY

ARISTOCRATS   FOREIGNERS

ENLIGHTENED
FRENCHMEN

OTHERS   ALL FRENCHMEN

FRATERNITY

economic status and redistribution of property? And if the latter, then were rich men equal before the law, or were they enemies of the people, to be subjected to special punitive legislation? As for "Fraternity," were all men brothers, or only all Frenchmen? Or perhaps were all right-thinking men brothers surrounded by unenlightened or evil-minded enemies? Or was it only a hardy band of virtuous and right-thinking Frenchmen who were really brothers, while men of lesser nations, even when their thoughts were of the right sort, fell somehow short of full brotherhood? These opposing meanings were implicit in the Revolution from its start and became more or less clearly explicit as faction split from faction within the revolutionary ranks.

The intricacies of party strife and the shifting constellations of power within France and beyond French borders during the revolutionary period need not be recapitulated here. Suffice it to say that, after the breakdown of the constitution drawn up by the National Assembly and the outbreak of hostilities between revolutionary France and conservative Prussia and Austria (1792), events mounted rapidly toward crisis. By 1794, military successes in the field had saved the French Republic from its foreign foes; but military success juxtaposed to a mounting confusion and ideological disarray at home opened a path for the ambition of Napoleon Bonaparte, who took power in 1799 and ruled France more and more autocratically until a European coalition defeated and overthrew him in 1814–15.

Thus the Revolution led not to popular and republican government but to military dictatorship followed by monarchical restoration. Yet, though the brighter hopes of all the revolutionary parties were sadly betrayed by events, much was accomplished. Wholesale cancellation of seigneurial rights, together with a fairly extensive dispersal of land ownership through the confiscation and resale of Church and noble properties, made nineteenth-century France a nation of peasant farmers. The land settlement was fundamental in the sense that it stabilized French society and made the Revolution irreversible. But the canny propertied peasant,[15] master of his land, wife, and children, immersed in practical and important affairs like the price of grain and the amount of his daughter's dowry, was only a part of the revolutionary settlement. Town life, too, changed with the suppression of guilds and other ancient legal corporations and monopolies; but the transformation of government and its relationship to individuals pervaded the life of both town and country and may be regarded as the most important single achievement of the French Revolution.

Changes in the political realm struck close to the heart of revolutionary aspiration. It was to make a government befitting a great and free people that millions had fought and hundreds of thousands had died—or so the leaders said. And the constitutional juggling which punctuated French history from 1790 through 1815 proved by practice and beyond all reasonable doubt what

---

[15] Economic foresight, together with the egalitarian testamentary prescriptions of the Code Napoleon, made French peasants extremely unwilling to confront the necessity of dividing their land among large numbers of children. They therefore commonly restricted the size of their families. A comparatively slow rate of population growth, inhibiting a really rapid rate of industrialization for France, was therefore one of the unexpected long-term consequences of the legal and property changes wrought by the French Revolution.

had before been merely a radical theory: that governments were indeed artifacts not of God nor even of Nature but of men. To be sure, conservatives
and liberals differed sharply as to whether the revolutionary constitutional
experiments also proved that man-made governments could serve the people
better than the Old Regime had done. But it was undeniable that the French
had succeeded, first under the republic and then under Napoleon, in mobilizing hitherto undreamed-of energies and channeling them into the service of
the nation-state. This aspect of the French Revolution made it a mighty twin
brother to the Industrial Revolution, inasmuch as each enormously enhanced
the range of power effectively at the disposal of Western peoples and governments.

Viewed in this light, the French Revolution looks suspiciously like a renewal of the thrust toward centralization and consolidation which had resided
in the French monarchy since medieval times. But the revolutionaries acted in
the name of a new and peculiarly absolute monarch: the People. The theory
which declared the People sovereign, while professing to confer new rights
and dignities upon the ordinary man in the fields or streets—and in some measure really doing so—also made it easier for the Sovereign People through its
official agents to demand new services and greater sacrifices from the people
severally. For the people—citizens and masters in their own right, no longer
subjects and servants of kings and nobles—were now directly responsible for
the fate of the nation. Any laggard who did not recognize his duties could
rightfully be reminded of them. Perverse individuals might even have to be
forced into freedom.

Hence, the revolutionary French government, armed with democratic theory and spurred by urgent need of men, money, and goods, casually overrode
the customary restrictions and countervailing powers which had hedged in
the absolute monarchy of France under the Old Regime. Previously indefeasible privileges, rights, and immunities were swept away on the hectic night of
August 4, 1789, never to be restored. Soon thereafter, oligarchic town and
aristocratic provincial governments, together with a tangled skein of para-
governmental bodies, disintegrated almost of their own accord, to be replaced
first by various emergency committees and eventually by a neatly tailored,
uniform, rational, and above all centralized bureaucratic administration.

Of all the corporate bodies and privileged groups which had mediated between the central authority and the individual subject under the Old Regime,
only the Church offered effective resistance to the usurpations of the revolutionary government. The Church lost its landed properties (1790), and in return the clergy were salaried by the state. But this did not make the Church a
branch of the government bureaucracy, for the authority of priests and bishops did not derive from popular sovereignty nor from the state but from their
claim of apostolic succession. Radical attempts to supplant Christianity by a
rational religion to match the rationalized revolutionary government failed
completely; and the effort to democratize Church government by making
ecclesiastical appointment depend upon the will of the people expressed
through free elections met with small success. Indeed, the Civil Constitution

of the Clergy, when it became the law of the land in 1790, opened a fissure in French society which has not yet really healed. Those who repudiated and those who sympathized with the effort to make the Church conform to democratic principles found it quite impossible to agree. Each side commanded strong emotions justified by theories which, being intellectually coherent elaborations of contradictory premises, were utterly incompatible.

The Concordat of 1801, by which Napoleon made peace with the papacy, papered over but did not resolve the rift. In the immediate post-Napoleonic years, the Roman Church everywhere appeared as a pillar of reaction, rivaled in its stalwart conservatism only by the Protestant state churches. Nevertheless, in the course of time the Democratic Revolution achieved a sort of backhanded victory, even among clerical reactionaries. In most of Catholic Europe, before the nineteenth century was over, defense of the claims and prerogatives of the Church was undertaken not solely or even principally by prelates and monarchs, fearful of revolution, but by political parties and lay associations—Catholic trade unions for example—which aimed to attract wide popular support, and in many cases participated directly in the parliamentary process.

In the first flush of the revolutionary dawn, such an intellectually confused, if practically effective, resolution of the conflict between democratic and Catholic doctrine smacked too much of the slack irrationalities of the Old Regime to have been even conceivable. Rather, the whole cut and thrust of the Revolution aimed at destroying the tissue of legal associations intervening between the individual citizen and "his" nation-state. Such mediate corporations were what the revolutionaries usually meant by "privilege." Therefore, in destroying privilege, the Revolution in effect polarized French society far more nakedly than before between a centralized bureaucracy, which in practice wielded nearly all of the extensive powers and functions arrogated to itself by the nation-state, and the millions of free, equal, and presumably fraternal citizens of France.

The obligatory military service demanded of all citizens by the French revolutionary governments was the greatest single transgression upon what in an earlier day would have been regarded as the "liberties" of a free subject. The *levée en masse* was first decreed as an emergency measure in 1793 when the Revolution was in urgent danger. It was later organized by Napoleon's prefects and police until France was almost drained of military manpower for the upstart emperor's last, disastrous campaigns. What had been instituted as a desperate last resort, based upon a frantic appeal to sentiment, thus became a Moloch-like machine, seizing upon the bodies of the citizens willy-nilly and feeding them into the French armies on a scale that made these armies the terror of all Europe for nearly two decades.

Yet millions of Frenchmen served willingly enough under the victorious banners of Napoleon and his marshals; and nearly all of them felt a thrill of pride in belonging to the mighty nation that bestrode Europe like a colossus from Campo Formio (1797) to Waterloo (1815). Hence, when Napoleon's constitutional tinkerings had reduced the legislative machinery of government to obedient impotence—thus choking off the avenue through which, according to democratic theory, the popular will should find expression—most Frenchmen scarcely missed what few had ever admired. Elected legislators, during the brief periods when they were free to speak their minds, had made the voice of liberty sound more like the shrill and irresponsible quarreling of schoolboys than like the solemn accents of the Sovereign People so confidently anticipated by followers of Rousseau.

Yet neither Napoleon's police and prefects, nor those of his Bourbon successor, could put the relation between government and people back on the prerevolutionary basis. The people of France in their millions had been told that the government belonged to them; and enough believed what they had heard to make a complete disregard of their opinions impossible. To be sure, rulers had always had to take some account of the will and wishes of their subjects. But in most times and places, reasonably precise conventional definitions of the respective roles of ruler and ruled had allowed each to leave the other in a state of salutary neglect, as long as fixed formalities of intercourse were observed—traditional tax payments, ceremonial deferences, royal largesses, and the like.

Even under the Old Regime customary definitions of political roles had weakened. Kings and ministers had shown what their colleagues of other times and places would have regarded as a bizarre interest in such unkingly concerns as fostering commerce and industry, while merchants and other commoners had presumptuously interested themselves in government affairs and had sometimes even influenced official policies. Yet for all the blurring of traditional relationships under the Old Regime, the monarch still remained king by grace of God, and his subjects remained subjects by God's will.

By proving that men could consciously make and unmake the political order, the French Revolution irremediably shattered this conventional basis of government. When men, not God, were held at least proximately responsible for political relationships, rulers could no longer safely rely upon automatic unthinking acceptance of their accustomed status. Instead, they had continually to justify themselves to the public with principles, programs, and promises. Yet this policy had its pitfalls, for promises unrealized and principles betrayed had a nasty way of haunting the men who had risen to power or kept it on the strength of incautious words. On the other hand, conservative rulers who refused to have any truck with newfangled notions of taking the public into closer partnership with government allowed others to seduce subjects from their loyalty and therefore ran the risk of open revolt, as the events of 1830 and 1848 showed. The only successful rulers were those who succeeded in rousing strong loyalties, enthusiastic support, and voluntary sacrifice from substantial numbers of men, whether through parliamentary, plebiscitary, or charismatic devices. Without intimate reciprocity between government and public, stable administration became difficult; with it, European governments could command a much greater proportion of the total energies of the population than ever before.[16]

A new intimacy between people and government was, indeed, the real secret of the French Revolution. Only when the monarchs of Europe had learned from that Revolution how to rally massive and intense public sentiment to their side were they able to gather forces adequate to overthrow Napoleon's power. And try as they might to dissociate themselves from the subsequent embarrassment of too close a popular embrace, the kings and ministers of Europe were never again able to neglect this new dimension of successful statecraft.

Governments, therefore, were either greatly strengthened or seriously weakened through their nineteenth-century inoculation with democratic principles and pretenses. On the one hand, a government might find itself harried and half-paralyzed by uncontrollable popular factionalism, as happened in Austria-Hungary. In other cases, a minister or monarch might play so skilfully upon the sentiments of the public as to stimulate extraordinary effort, as Bismarck was sometimes able to do. It was mainly in northwestern Europe that governments strengthened themselves. To the east and south, democratic ideas proved divisive and disruptive, weakening relatively, if not absolutely, the power of the great empires Austria and Russia had built along the landward frontier of Europe during the eighteenth century.[17]

The reason why east European empires were on the whole unsuccessful in tapping new energies from their people, whereas the states of western Europe were able to do so with remarkable success, lay largely in the activities and attitudes of the urban middle class, which was much more strongly developed in northwestern Europe than elsewhere. Professional men and storekeepers, merchants and financiers, factory owners and genteel rentiers acted as the principal transmission belt between government and whatever wider public cared to overhear official discussions. Where such groups were numerous, rich, and self-confident, they were able to achieve an effective partnership between government and people—meaning in practice principally themselves— in the course of the nineteenth century. Where such groups were weak and timorous in the presence of their social betters, no such partnership arose. Instead, officials and aristocrats continued to exercise power, even when, as in Austria after 1867 or in Russia after 1906, the trappings of parliamentarianism were imposed upon the bureaucratic state. Such half-measures quite failed to establish effective co-operation between rulers and ruled in the Austrian,

[16] A few city-states in classical antiquity and late medieval times had attained integration between people and government equal or superior to anything attained by the European nation-states in the nineteenth century. It is noteworthy that some French revolutionary leaders, idolizing the republican virtue celebrated in the pages of the Latin historians, had desired to model France upon the ancient city-state of Rome.

[17] This, together with the geographical incidence of modern industrialism, reversed for a century or longer the balance of power between the states of western and of eastern Europe—a balance which, in the last decades of the Old Regime, as Russia drew abreast of the political organization of other European states, had seemed on the verge of tipping decisively eastward. The Crimean War (1853–56), in which French and British expeditionary forces defeated the Russians on their own ground, dramatized this reversal.

Russian, and Ottoman empires. Instead, in the name of linguistic nationalism, popular political movements tore the social and political fabric of eastern Europe to shreds in the latter nineteenth century.[18]

* * *

After about 1870, the New Regime inaugurated by the French and Industrial revolutions began increasingly to resemble the Old Regime it had supplanted. In western Europe, the middle classes occupied the foreground of society and politics, dividing power with officialdom (recruited largely from the middle class) and making deferentially decorative accommodation for the remnants of the landed aristocracy. The ideological clashes of the French Revolution were everywhere muted by pragmatic compromises. Parliamentary bodies came to include Catholic political parties, formed with papal approval; and even imperious and conservative noblemen like Bismarck learned to play the parliamentary game. Social extremes which had once seemed irreconcilable thus found a meeting ground.

Simultaneously, a new cluster of privileged corporations began to wax great in the form of limited-liability stock companies. The powers of such corporations were often enormous; and some of the largest became virtually *imperia in imperio*. Labor unions also began to exert or at least aspire toward a semi-sovereign authority over their members; and some of the more ideological political parties, most notably the German Social Democrats, developed organization into a way of life. Such multiplication of quasi-autonomous bodies within the framework of the national state emphatically hedged in the exercise of political sovereignty. The series of pragmatic and illogical compromises among rival interests and ideologies became so complex that almost any change threatened to upset the whole structure. This was exactly what had happened among a different array of interests and ideas under the Old Regime. Moreover, under the strain of World War I and the Russian Revolution, these compromises broke apart, just as the equilibrium of Europe's Old Regime had earlier been shattered by the French Revolution and, as earlier still, Europe's medieval frame had been overthrown by the Reformation.[19]

[18] Free and democratic government does not necessarily require that linguistic, patriotic, and administrative frontiers coincide, as German-speaking Frenchmen of Alsace and French-speaking Belgians and Swiss suffice to prove. Yet in central and eastern Europe, where the geographical intermingling of diverse linguistic groups was particularly complex, the idea that linguistic and political frontiers should coincide won wide support.

Pervasive uncertainty arising from the breakdown of immemorial rural routines—in large measure a by-product of the spread of industrialism—lent special emotional intensity to late nineteenth-century nationalism. Cf. the force of similarly unsettled customary ·social relationships in the Reformation period. Incandescent nationalists of eastern Europe were in effect attempting to project their idealized memories of tight-knit village life upon an entire nation. The total failure of national self-determination to achieve any such idyll after World War I, and the passing of the acute phase of initial adjustment to an industrializing world, may account for the remarkable fading of linguistic nationalism as a live issue in European politics since World War II. The virulent and sometimes politically disruptive nationalisms of Africa and Asia since 1945 seem, in this respect, to recapitulate the earlier European experience.

[19] Perhaps Bertrand de Jouvenel, *Du Pouvoir: histoire naturelle de sa croissance* (Genève: Éditions du cheval ailé, 1945) has contributed more centrally to this analysis of the French Revolution and its sequels than any other single work.

In retrospect, it is already easy to detect critical weaknesses in the political equilibrium which seemed to be emerging in Europe between 1870 and 1914, for despite all the elaborate counterbalancings of interests and compromises of principle, two strategically placed groups were left out. The smaller but more articulate of these was the educated minority of eastern Europe, which, having tasted Western learning and speculation, found itself profoundly alienated from the social universe of its birth. The extreme and remarkably various social views nourished by the sense of isolation and frustration such men felt kept volcanic revolutionary ardors seething just below the surface of the east European empires, particularly in Russia.

Simultaneously, in the more industrialized countries of western Europe, factory hands were not always willing to accept the political lead of the middle class. From the mid-nineteenth century, Marxians and others offered the industrial working class a vision of society made over in its own image and interest. Hence it is not surprising that from the 1870's socialist arguments and appeals began to command a considerable public, especially in Germany. Yet for all the verbal thunder with which Marxians repudiated capitalism and bourgeois government, in a fundamental sense they still adhered to the values and patterns of the democratized, compromised, and publicized nation-state as it had emerged from the fusion of French revolutionary with older political traditions. The unanimity with which all but the Russian socialists marched to war in 1914 stands as evidence of this judgment.

However, a fateful coincidence distinguished the political evolution of Russia from that of the lands farther west. During the 1890's, the ideological extremism long endemic in Russia found congenial expression in Marxism. Simultaneously, the breakup of immemorial village routines and the beginnings of modern industry modified the massive peasant immobility which had been the despair of so many sensitive and educated Russians earlier in the nineteenth century. The initiative of officialdom in abolishing serfdom and building railroads, and the initiative of landowners who introduced various technical and other improvements in agriculture, combined with a growing population pressure in parts of rural Russia to set the countryside in motion. When this happened, the intelligentsia, so long frustrated by the "dark and deaf" peasantry, confronted instead a blindfolded angry giant, anxious to be led to the light. Urban conditions were also provocative, so that the Tsarist regime, which had never come to terms even with the French Revolution, found itself simultaneously challenged by liberal and by socialist discontents rooted both in town and country. Unsuccessful war, first with Japan and then on a far greater scale with the Central Powers, brought these strains within Russian society to the surface, resulting in the revolution of 1905–6 and the far greater revolutions of 1917–22.

4. ARTISTIC AND INTELLECTUAL ASPECTS

The artistic and intellectual activity of Western men between 1789 and 1917 is impressive, indeed overwhelming, in its bulk and variety. In questioning assumptions hitherto unquestioned, and questing after new certainties only to

Rodin (*Phaidon edition*).

EUROPE'S NEW REGIME

Georges Seurat's urban idyll (painted 1884–86) at the top mirrors the midsummer of Europe's New Regime, when the middle classes of France and the rest of western Europe could afford to take their ease of a Sunday, proud and well content with the unparalleled heights of civilization they saw around them. Seurat's technique of forming shapes from innumerable multicolored dots was conceived as a scientific experiment, based upon new theories of vision and the nature of light and color. But in abandoning the optical precision of the older European tradition, Seurat also gave vent to a sense of growing restlessness within inherited art forms.

Rodin's bust of Georges Clemenceau (made on the eve of World War I in 1911) suggests a far wider range of uncertainty and restlessness. Rough-hewn, "unfinished" sculptural forms are here employed to portray an infinite weariness of spirit that arose as the once revolutionary verities of "Liberty, Equality, Fraternity" lost their clarity and force.

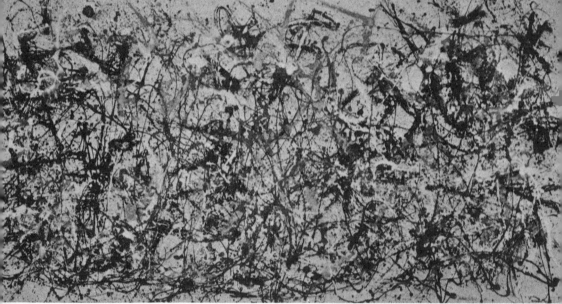

ANGRY UNCERTAINTY OF THE TWENTIETH CENTURY

Picasso's disjointed caricature of optical experience and Jackson Pollock's abstract daubs of paint agree in an emphatic repudiation of the techniques and conventions of European art and share a restless violence of mood paralleled, if at all, in the European past only by the disturbed fancies of a painter like Hieronymus Bosch (p. 596). The experiences of the sixteenth century, when the European Far West emerged painfully into modernity, constituted the sharpest shock to Europe's cultural order before the thoughts and deeds of the twentieth century dissolved so many old certainties into the torn and tangled web of doubt and fear, expressed visually by these two pictures.

discover fresh working hypotheses, Europeans weakened or destroyed many of the old coherences which had organized and guided their art and thought for centuries or millennia. Or so it now seems from the perspective of the 1960's.

On the other hand, the cultural coherence of distant epochs may be partly illusory. Much variety and confusion is simply lost and forgotten, for, to survive at all, art and thought must always be filtered through meshes imposed by the tastes of later generations. Moreover, and more significantly, lengthening time perspectives often reduce the irreconcilabilities of an age to facets of a larger unity, much as the view from a high-flying plane, by blurring details, can turn the intricacies of a landscape into a map. Some centuries hence, therefore, the main lines of artistic and intellectual development of the nineteenth and twentieth centuries may appear as straightforward as those of any other epoch.

Lacking such perspective, it is easier to detect the disruption of familiar cohesions and values than to apprehend the emergence of new ones—if they are in fact emerging. Surely, the disruption of (or liberation from) the Western past is obvious enough. By 1917, leading painters had rejected the perspective frame within which European artistic vision had operated since the fifteenth century. Physicists had modified the Newtonian laws of motion within which European scientific thought had moved since the seventeenth century. Even the special hallmark of nineteenth-century intellectual achievement—the evolutionary world-view—seemed, by undermining all traditional moral and aesthetic standards, to reduce Western thought to the level of a wounded hyena, gnawing at its own exposed and grisly guts. Yet the explosive energies that went into such destruction were also liberating, though it remains to be seen whether and when new artistic, scientific, and philosophical styles comparable in power and persuasiveness to those rejected in the early twentieth century will emerge.

* * *

In painting, techniques of linear and aerial perspective for creating three-dimensional illusion had been thoroughly explored long before 1789; and little that was vital or impressive—at least to current taste—came from the brushes of those who continued to uphold these conventions. Experiments with light and color gave the impressionists of the mid-nineteenth century a new technical range; but only in the following generation did Vincent van Gogh (d. 1890), Paul Gauguin (d. 1903), Paul Cézanne (d. 1906) decisively break through the restrictions imposed by rules of perspective and naturalistic coloring. Full and explicit rejection of the Renaissance techniques for producing an illusion of three-dimensionality occurred in the next generation, just before World War I, when a few avant-garde artists in Paris abandoned well-established public visual conventions in favor of new, private angles of vision, semi-intelligible even to the initiated, and often enough dependent upon nothing more important than momentary fad or playful experiment.

Nevertheless, as great art perhaps always does, painting in the decade before World War I created a remarkable visual symbolism of trends lying at the core of the cultural universe of Western man. The clearest case is offered by the handful of painters who in the decade before 1914 arbitrarily displaced fragments of visual experience from familiar contexts and then deliberately composed them into new patterns bearing no particular reference to any outer reality. But such fragmentation of familiarly ordered experience, resulting in an arbitrary, often incongruous juxtaposition of dismembered parts, was exactly what happened in the lives of millions of men during and after World War I. It therefore seems as though a few unusually sensitive spirits had sensed in advance the impending breakup of the no longer New Regime of Western civilization in such a way as to symbolize the future in their art.

In retrospect it now seems obvious that the institutional frame of Western society, as imperfectly readjusted during the nineteenth century to accommodate modern industrialism and democratic notions, had begun to heave and crack even before 1914. The war of 1914–18 set great chunks of habit and custom adrift like Arctic sea ice in the spring: each floe solid and recognizable in itself, like the wine bottles and guitars of a Picasso painting, and each one liable to drift—like the same wine bottles and guitars—into quite extraordinary juxtapositions with other shifting fragments of the distintegrating past. No new freeze has yet set in, nor soon seems likely; and the efforts of totalitarian dictatorships to reorganize a cultural universe by arbitrary force and deliberate fiat have so far met with only limited success. The arbitrary and deliberate efforts of twentieth-century painters to reorganize visual reality, though ever so exuberantly pursued, seem also as yet to have failed of any lasting stylistic success—in this too, perhaps, true to the society their art so mysteriously mirrors.

Music stood at an opposite pole among the arts; yet its development between 1789 and 1917 bore some striking resemblances to the history of painting. When the period began, musicians had not yet exhausted the harmonic possibilities of the eight-tone scale as applied to a wide variety of instruments, capable of playing together in any number of combinations and themselves undergoing rather rapid development. Ludwig van Beethoven (d. 1827), Johannes Brahms (d. 1897), and Richard Wagner (d. 1883), with many less famous names, exploited these possibilities brilliantly. Yet by the eve of World War I a few obscure European composers had begun to experiment with scales and harmonies beyond the domain of received convention; while in obscure American whore-houses, other musical experiments, bringing African rhythms and Western sound-making together, constituted an equally drastic, though rather less deliberate, break with the classical tradition of Western music. Atonality and jazz, though generated from opposed musical extremes of intellectuality and sensuality, nevertheless tended (like opposite ends of a straight line infinitely extended in non-Euclidean space) to meet at a point in polar opposition to the rules of harmony and rhythm as defined in Europe early in the eighteenth century.

The various branches of belles-lettres and such other major arts as sculpture and architecture fell somewhere between the extremes represented by the precocious enthusiasm with which painters abandoned old rules of their craft and the lofty unconcern with which nearly all European musicians viewed the pre-World War I experiments with jazz and atonality. Forerunners of radical departures are not difficult to find. It is enough to recall such literary monuments as Marcel Proust's (d. 1922) novels, Arthur Schnitzler's (d. 1932) plays, or Alexander Blok's (d. 1921) poems, or to remember Auguste Rodin's (d. 1917) rough-hewn statues and the drastically simplified forms of Constantine Brancusi's (d. 1957) early sculpture. Similarly in architecture, the curvilinear fantasy of Antoni Gaudi's (d. 1926) cast cement and the soaring loftiness of Louis Sullivan's (d. 1926) steel-framed skyscrapers agreed, though in very different ways, in rejecting traditional limits which had been imposed partly by taste and partly by the technical nature of older building materials and methods. But until after World War I, such men remained exceptional. In the western European lands, the main stream of literature, sculpture, and architecture continued to run within well-worn channels dating back for the most part to the fifteenth-sixteenth centuries, when national literary languages and the repertory of Renaissance sculptural and architectural themes first became fixed.

In Russia, however, a very powerful literature, of which the first major luminary was Alexander Pushkin (d. 1837), came to maturity during the nineteenth century. Nearly all of the great Russian writers displayed a profoundly ambivalent attitude toward the cultural traditions of western Europe.[20] The fact that many Westerners since 1917 have begun to feel similar ambiguities toward their cultural inheritance means that nineteenth-century Russian writers (like Thucydides in fifth-century B.C. Athens) sometimes sound a strikingly contemporary note. Fëdor Dostoevsky (d. 1881), for example, anticipated much that seems characteristic of the twentieth century. This is not so surprising as it first seems, for the breakdown of Russia's cultural autonomy, resulting from (or expressed by) Peter the Great's revolutionary reforms, put Russians psychologically ahead of Western nations, whose cultural certainties lasted longer. Hence, at a time when few western Europeans doubted the intrinsic superiority of their cultural inheritance, Dostoevsky's generation of Russian intellectuals found it impossible easily and automatically to accept any single cultural universe. Dostoevsky and many others like him wished to reject and yet to appropriate Western civilization, while simultaneously prizing and despising the peculiarities that marked Russia off from the West. Such tensions could only be relieved by conscious efforts to put a cultural universe together, more or less arbitrarily. But deliberate affirmation after agonized choice—at best an unsatisfactory psychological surrogate for the unquestioning belief of an undisturbed cultural transmission—may nevertheless be extremely fertile of high art and deep thought. Russian letters of the nineteenth century reflected the advantages

[20] The same was true, though in rather less acute form, of some American writers, e.g., Mark Twain (d. 1910).

and disadvantages of such a position and, from the similarities of their cultural position with our own, anticipated many of the characteristics of Western literature in the twentieth century.

*   *   *

Western science was as restless as Western art. Between the French and Russian revolutions, physicists and their scientific associates elaborated a world-view of extraordinary power and austere beauty—a world-view which combined an enormous scope with a marvelous precision of detail and which was, moreover, validated by experiment and ratified in ever new technologies. The main lines of this scientific structure had been established in the seventeenth century, when modern physics, centering around careful measurements of matter in motion, first took its classical form. But during the nineteenth century, the range and power of this theoretical system were so enormously enlarged that men dreamed of making over all knowledge in its image.

Scientific knowledge expanded in two directions: (1) by recognizing new "laws" that made what had before seemed to be unrelated events into special cases of some larger uniformity; and (2) by applying already familiar laws of physics to new classes of phenomena. Under the first of these heads came such achievements as James Joule's (d. 1889) recognition of the equivalency between heat and work, and the mathematical generalizations of James Clerk Maxwell (d. 1879), which united the various forms of radiant energy then known (light, radiant heat, etc.) into a continuum of electromagnetic radiation. Under the second came the application of methods and concepts of experimental physics to such diverse sciences as chemistry, astronomy, biology, genetics, and geology—in each instance with conspicuous and convincing success.

These achievements tended to reduce events to quantified occurrences within a mathematically constructed universe defined by four basic terms: matter, energy, space, and time. Until the publication of Albert Einstein's (d. 1955) first paper on relativity in 1905, space and time remained the mathematically uniform and absolute entities assumed by Galileo and defined by Newton. The concept of matter, on the other hand, underwent a notable elaboration, until toward the end of the nineteenth century it began, rather embarrassingly, to lose its solidity. Early in the nineteenth century, chemists distinguished molecules from atoms and, from about the middle of the century, learned how to analyze the atomic structure of molecules with growing precision. Toward the end of the century, physicists and chemists joined forces to penetrate the atom, which had hitherto been defined as the ultimate, impenetrable constituent of matter. By the first decade of the twentieth century, electrons ("discovered" in 1897 by John Joseph Thompson [d. 1940]) had supplanted atoms as the ultimate building blocks of matter, while the erstwhile "solid" atoms had become miniature solar systems, with planetary electrons orbiting around a "solid" (or at least comparatively dense) nucleus.

The manner in which scientists of the nineteenth century dissipated ordinary, solid, common-sense matter into clouds of successively more minute and always widely dispersed particles was matched by the way in which they made energy ever more solid. The term "energy" itself acquired quite new meanings. Careful measurements[21] established energy equivalences between such apparently diverse events as chemical reactions, movements of sensible bodies, molecular and electron motions, heat, sound, light, magnetism, and newly discovered types of radiation like radio waves or X-rays. The principle of the conservation of energy through any and all changes of physical state was speculatively advanced by Hermann Ludwig Ferdinand von Helmholtz (d. 1894) as early as 1847. Every discovery during the next half-century seemed to confirm and add fresh instances to the principle.

The transmutations of an indestructible matter, which chemists had so successfully learned to control, seemed thus to parallel transmutations of an equally indestructible something called energy, which had become the physicists' special concern. The intersections of matter with energy in space and time constituted the physical world of nineteenth-century science. It was a comfortable world intellectually, if a bit chilly to the emotions. Carefully defined terms and carefully performed measurements, mathematical reasoning and experimental verification of mathematically framed hypotheses were all elegantly articulated into a closed and logically self-consistent system, which neatly and adequately explained all physical events—with just a few, admittedly puzzling, exceptions.

Yet about the turn of the nineteenth century, these puzzling exceptions began to multiply and the very categories basic to the concepts of classical physics began to blur. Energy appeared in some contexts rather like an emission of particles, appearing only in fixed "quanta"—a notion propounded by Max Planck (d. 1947) in 1900. Matter was discovered to disintegrate spontaneously in special cases and, in the process, to emit powerful radiation—a phenomenon first observed by Antoine Henri Becquerel (d. 1908) in 1896. Even more difficult for laymen and for not a few physicists to comprehend was the linkage of time and space into a space-time continuum. This was first proposed by Albert Einstein (d. 1955) in his special theory of relativity (1905) to account (among other things) for the uniform velocity with which light appeared to travel in any direction, even when measured from a rapidly moving platform of observation like a spot on the surface of the rotating and orbiting earth. This uniform velocity was observed as early as 1887 by Albert Michelson (d. 1931) and his colleague Edward Williams Morley (d. 1923). It seemed fundamentally incompatible with Newtonian conceptions of absolute space and time, for by all ordinary logic, light rays launched from the earth in the same direction as the earth's own motion should travel faster through space than rays going in the opposite direction, since in one case the earth's velocity should be added and in the other subtracted from the absolute speed of the rays.

[21] Plus some purely metaphysical inventions like the "potential" energy assigned to a book poised casually on a mantelpiece in order to have something to draw upon to balance the energy equations if the book should happen to fall.

The unexpected upshot of these discrepancies, therefore, was to dissolve the elegant clarity of nineteenth-century physics. Matter, energy, time, and space, the four basic terms upon which the entire structure had rested, seemed no longer able to bear the burden classical physics had laid upon them. As a result, by the time World War I broke upon Europe, an imperfectly understood matter-energy system seemed to be mysteriously immersed in any one (or why not in more than one?) of several diverse space-time coordinates—Euclidean, hyperbolic, or spherical.

Moreover, the ontological status of matter-energy was far from clear. The electron, born to science in 1897, rapidly spawned a brood of other subatomic particles; Planck's energy-quanta were equally prolific; and the two merged into one another as wave particles and particle waves in a manner that defied translation into any ordinary three-dimensional imagery. Even more doubtful was the applicability to the actual universe of mathematical coordinate nets designed to measure space-time, since the mode of measurement seemed likely a priori to affect (perhaps even to invent) what was being measured.

To an outsider, therefore, it looked as though metaphysics and mysticism, having unobtrusively transferred their residence from the chancel to the laboratory, had deftly reasserted their ancient dominion over mathematics. Yet what looked to any sane layman like cabalistic nonsense, contradicting everything he intuitively knew about the material world, nevertheless continued to generate technological wonders. Here magic joined forces with mathematics, for what greater magic can be conceived than this: that the universe should obey the rules of human thought, as disciplined to the rigor of mathematical logic?[22]

A more extraordinary revolution in style of thought, passing from the rather smug finalities of late-nineteenth century physics to the confused uncertainties of the twentieth century, could scarcely be imagined, even though the new vistas opened up by physicists in the first decade of the twentieth century did not really overthrow classical theory but merely made it into a special case, applicable only within certain ranges of scale.

Physical science was of course not the only active strand of intellectual endeavor in the years between 1789 and 1917. Indeed, there is a sense in which the mathematical physicists' style of thought was merely an unusually vigorous anachronism in the nineteenth century, for the presuppositions behind the scientists' search for universal and eternal laws smacked strongly of

---

[22] The notion common to the seventeenth, eighteenth, and nineteenth centuries, that sense perception (sharpened by instruments for measuring, visually magnifying, or otherwise sensitizing human faculties) provided a check upon the free theorizing of scientists and tied theory to the real world, seems less and less applicable to recent scientific research. Experiments seeking to penetrate the subsensible and suprasensible realms of atomic physics and astronomy bring to human senses phenomena only remotely related to what may have occurred at the levels in which scientists are interested. A long and fragile chain of inference and assumption lies between a trace on a photographic plate, for example, and any "real" subatomic event it may be interpreted as having recorded. Even more to the point, what the scientist "sees" on his photographic plate is predetermined by the mathematical and other expectations he has already—expectations derived from a body of theory which more and more nearly approaches the biblical definition of Christian faith: "the substance of things hoped for, the evidence of things not seen" (Hebrews 11:1).

the naïve mathematical biases of the seventeenth century. Moreover, such presuppositions were scarcely compatible with the unique vision of reality that came sharply into focus for the first time in the nineteenth century itself and saw all things—whether laws of physics or of human societies—in process of unending development. Yet the idea of development stimulated soaring philosophers as well as humbler historians to find in temporal sequences and successions an intellectual beauty, rather less shapely than the simple symmetries of physics, but also less austere, and for some minds all the more charming because of unexpected irregularities, disjunctures, and tangled continuities.

History had, of course, been a recognized branch of European letters since the time of Herodotus. But history had traditionally concerned the deeds of men, and most historians had restricted themselves to political and military affairs. Before the nineteenth century, men had seldom taken seriously the obvious proposition that all things in the universe, and the universe itself, for that matter, have a history. But early in the nineteenth century, this traditional limitation upon the domain of history was energetically discarded. Georg Wilhelm Friedrich Hegel (d. 1831) and other philosophers raised to the level of a cosmic principle the notion that development through time was unique, making some things possible at any given moment which had been impossible before and might (or might not) be impossible ever after. This gave historians a new agenda—not merely to record the unusual event set against the basically unchanging human and natural order, as Gibbon, for example, had done, but to attempt to comprehend the entire evolution of human thought and society, being ever on the alert to detect new potentialities as they emerged in the course of time.

Karl Marx (d. 1883) was the most influential social theorist who met the challenge of Hegel's developmental philosophy by advancing a simple yet plausible schematization of human history and destiny. Marx's vision of the stages of the human past and future—from slavery to serfdom to the financial exploitation of the free market and on to the perfect freedom of socialist and communist society—appealed both to the self-righteousness of industrial workers and to the rebellious idealism of intellectuals who found the confusion of things as they were hard to bear. Marxism thus quickly became a religion, whose strongest appeal was to populations emerging abruptly from age-old rural routines into the uncertainties of urban and industrial living.

The historical point of view also had particularly explosive implications when applied to traditional religion. Juxtaposed to the mystery religions of the Roman empire, Christianity lost some of its uniqueness; and the Bible, if subjected to the same critical canons which historians applied freely to other texts, ceased to be the word of God, dictated to a series of faithful amanuenses, and became instead a human product, replete with textual errors. The accuracy and adequacy of Christian doctrine had repeatedly been challenged in European history; so this in itself was nothing new. But by abandoning high philosophical grounds and concentrating on textual details and particular historical events, the new "higher criticism" offered a more formidable antagonist than Christian theologians had ever before faced. Religious "modernism," which saw human comprehension of the divine and God's self-revelation to man as complementary and progressive processes through time, represented one extreme reaction to the new spirit. Emphatic repudiation of the results of the "higher criticism" and reassertion of the plenary authority of traditional dogma represented the other.

The fertility of the developmental-historical point of view was not limited to the humanities and social sciences. Biology was revolutionized when Charles Darwin (d. 1882) brought together the scattered evidences for biological evolution which he and other naturalists had already accumulated and drew compelling conclusions from this data in his famous book, *The Origin of Species* (1859). Darwin's theories brought all living things within the scope of a single evolutionary process. Organic evolution of course required enormous spans of time; but geologists had already proposed such a terrestrial time scale to account for the deposition of sedimentary rocks; and paleontologists proceeded, both before and after the publication of Darwin's book, to fill gaps in the enormous vista of earthly time that now opened so awesomely beneath men's feet. Human life and history were dwarfed by the immensity of geological and biological time; but it was not solely this uncomfortable shrinkage of the human universe that provoked controversy over Darwinian evolution. For Darwin's picture of evolving biological species made no exception of man.[23] By reducing human beings to the level of other animals, subject to the same laws of natural selection and struggle for survival, Darwin seemed to have undermined, not only the very foundation of religion and of the social order, but all refinement of human culture as well. Nor were disciples lacking who drew conclusions from which Darwin himself refrained and used the concepts of natural selection and survival of the fittest to justify both a rugged economic individualism at home and a ruthless collective imperialism abroad.

The historical vision, turned first upon man and his works, then extended to all living things and to the solid earth itself, thus brought profoundly disturbing issues to public attention. A crowning effort to apply the same point of view to the cosmos—an effort barely begun in 1917—had a force comparable to the effect of the earlier Copernican revolution. For astronomers, seeking to comprehend the evolution of the universe, coolly presumed the formation and snuffing out of innumerable stars, casually assumed the existence of innumerable replicas of the solar system in all stages of formation and dissolution, asserted without qualm the indefinite reduplication of the galaxy, and speculated freely upon superorderings that might unite clusters of galaxies or clusters of clusters into larger and larger wholes. Such an evolutionary view shrank sun, earth, life, and man—not to speak of the lives of individual persons—to proportions almost inconceivably minute and strained even a mind already attuned to the Copernican-Newtonian scale of being.[24] Such a change

[23] In his *The Descent of Man*, published in 1872, Darwin made explicit what had only been implicit in his first great work.

[24] G. J. Whitrow, *The Structure and Evolution of the Universe: An Introduction to Cosmology* (New York: Harper Torchbooks, 1959), provides the basis for much of this paragraph.

of scale, imposed by the cumulative work of historians and archeologists, who had brought the ancient civilizations of the Middle East to life, of biologists, geologists, and paleontologists who had set mankind against a panorama of biological evolution, and of astronomers and mathematicians who moved familiarly with the all but infinite, put a new urgency into old questions about the value and significance of human affairs, under stars so unimaginably remote, on an earth so immemorially old, and among men whose bestial ancestors and primitive forebears appeared comparatively so very close.

Such macrocosmic enormities were only one aspect of the crisis which confronted the evolutionary world-view toward the close of the nineteenth century. Like contemporary "classical" physics, the evolutionary viewpoint, which had been so confidently propounded at the beginning of the century, began just before World War I to suffer sharp microcosmic critique from philosophers and psychologists. Philosophers found it increasingly difficult to persuade themselves that Kant had satisfactorily solved the problems of knowledge; but efforts to improve upon his anatomy of the powers and limitations of reason led merely to a growing obsession with epistemology and a tendency to deny the possibility of knowing anything at all. Scientists and historians, however, went blithely on their way, so that the philosophical dilemmas of the age remained more or less private to the profession. Not so the problems raised by psychologists, who employed both resolute reason and extravagant poetic imagination to challenge reason's rule over the human faculties. Sigmund Freud (d. 1939) was by far the most influential pioneer. From study of behavior in abnormal states, Freud concluded that the ruling drives of mankind resided in an unconscious level of the mind. Consciousness accordingly became superficial, a distorting and distorted mirror of the reality beneath, its faculties and skills used as often to hide as to reveal the truth.

Such views did indeed link men with beasts and lower forms of life, as Darwin had done. They collided frontally with the optimistic estimate of human nature and rationality which the Democratic Revolution had proclaimed and assumed. They also raised from a somewhat different vantage point the simple question which was bothering philosophers: how can men know? For if the mind is fed, forced, and twisted about by instinctive drives, manifesting themselves sporadically as uncontrollable impulses, what remains of the capacity to seize upon external reality and hold it fast?

Freud was by no means the only contributor to the dethronement of reason. Social theorists as diverse as Friedrich Nietzsche (d. 1900), Georges Sorel (d. 1922), or Vilfredo Pareto (d. 1923) arrived quite independently at a similar denigration of rationality; and leaders of men—above all the officers of the more efficient European armies—had always known that the rule of reason had a very narrow scope when it came to human actions en masse. Painters, likewise, in rejecting the conventions of their art, were rejecting a remarkably rational system for reducing three dimensions to two; and the devices and conventions they substituted were redolent of the unconscious depths which Freud had tried to plumb, which politicians and soldiers had long exploited, and which social theorists had barely begun to recognize as something more than pagan survivals or primitive traits to be outgrown with the progress of civilization.

*   *   *

A survey such as this is always liable to underestimate the enduring continuities and stabilities of the social scene and to overemphasize the elements of novelty and disruption. Yet even with this bias understood, and making due allowance for the millions upon millions of persons whose lives were entirely undisturbed by the technicalities of science and whose minds were quite unencumbered by thought; recalling also the respectable multitudes who neither knew nor cared what a handful of disreputable artists were doing in run-down neighborhoods of Paris and other cities; remembering the ability of institutions and habits to survive divorce from the intellectual and social setting of their birth and even to thrive in an alien or apparently hostile environment—it still seems correct to believe that Western civilization had come to an unusually critical pass in the first decade of the twentieth century, even before plunging into the open abyss of war and revolution. When art and thought, economics and politics simultaneously pressed so hard against familiar molds, the range of the possible began to display more of its enormous variety than ever before. The inertia of the millions who lived their lives by routine surely set a limit upon the virtuosity of political or economic ambition; but when the cultural leaders of Western civilization had so uniformly cut loose from old moorings, it was only a matter of time before popular inertia would be overcome and mass energies directed into new paths. World War I and the Russian Revolution perhaps accelerated but assuredly did not create the crisis. The "New Regime" inaugurated by the French Revolution had indeed become old. It remained to be seen what new reordering of Western (or more plausibly, of world) society and culture might emerge—or whether confusion and uncertainty would prevail indefinitely.

C. THE NON-WESTERN WORLD, 1850–1950 A.D.

Disruption of traditional styles of life occurred almost simultaneously in the Moslem, Indian, Chinese, and Japanese worlds in the mid-nineteenth century. In this respect, sub-Saharan Africa and the West itself lagged behind the Asian peoples by roughly half a century, for both tribal African and middle-class Western styles of life failed to confront a general crisis until the very end of the nineteenth century and the beginning of the twentieth. At least in the proximate sense, the initial disruption of each of the non-Western cultures was largely the work of Western technology. Only when the semi-impervious shell of familiar custom and belief had been fractured, so that Asian and African minds became sensitive to alien winds of doctrine, did ideas from the West begin to rival technology as transformers of the local cultural scene.

Institutions, being the embodiments of custom and crystallizations of tradition, were strongholds of conservatism and pillars of whatever stability ex-

Art Institute of Chicago. Gift of Mr. and Mrs. Arnold H. Maremont.

PRIMORDIAL WOMAN

This reclining figure, carved by Henry Moore (b. 1898) in 1957, gives visual form to primordially primitive, inchoate dimensions of human femininity. Presumably the artist intended to penetrate beyond optical appearances in order to achieve an imagery capable of resonating within the observers' subconsciousness. Artistic universality may thus seem within reach, for all men perhaps inherit a common core of subconscious propensities. Such an aim obviously emancipates the sculptor from Western and every other art tradition. It brings—or attempts to bring—the highest intellectual sophistication into direct touch with the dark hidden springs of human life underlying all the cultural variety of historical mankind. In such a statue, therefore, our twentieth-century scientific emancipation from the cultural parochialisms of the past finds concise visual embodiment.

isted in the disturbed social landscapes of the earth. But institutions were always local, so that their interactions with the cosmopolitan novelties of the recent past must be studied region by region. Before undertaking this task, it seems appropriate to dwell upon the factors that affected all, or nearly all, the world, constituting the net by which primitive cultures and ancient civilizations alike were caught up into the global cosmopolitanism of the years 1850–1950.

I. THE CHANGING SHAPE AND STYLE OF THE ECUMENE

During the century 1850–1950, changes in mode of transport literally transformed the shape of the ecumene. Distances shrank, routes of travel and communication altered, and the centers of real and potential political power shifted. This was of course only one aspect of the general technological revolution of the recent past, but it was of peculiar importance. By defining who neighbored whom, transport and communication have always provided the basic frame within which human societies must exist. Hence only the scale was new. But scale can be decisively important; and with the enormously enhanced range of modern mechanical transport and instantaneous communication, the necessity, as well as the possibility, of global cosmopolitanism was created.

Each improvement in mechanical transport meant shrinkage of effective distances between separate parts of the earth and also redistributed the culturally (and militarily) strategic regions of the globe. Thus, the development of power-driven ships, constructed first of iron and then of steel, reinforced the importance of the ocean lanes by making sea transport cheaper and more dependable than before. The great interoceanic canals across the isthmuses of Suez (1869) and Panama (1914) worked in the same direction; but the canals also renewed the importance of old routes of travel.[25] The Suez Canal in particular, by restoring to the Middle East much of its former importance as the pre-eminent crossroads of the Eastern Hemisphere, abruptly altered the geopolitics of the Old World. The Panama Canal also affected the world balance, though less spectacularly, by strengthening the military posture of the United States.

Mechanically powered sea transport became a global reality after the 1870's; but even before that time, the possibilities of long-distance mechanized land transport had become apparent. The mills that turned out plates for iron ships also supplied the materials to build the snorting horses of iron that began as early as 1869 to clang across whole continents. Nor were railroads the only new devices: telegraphic communication antedated rail transport by a decade or two in most parts of the earth; and, after the first big railroad boom in the 1850's, further impovements in both transport and communication came thick and fast: automobiles, trucks, and pipelines as well as telephone, radio, and television.

[25] For all normal purposes, Spanish colonial administrators had preferred mule portage across the Isthmus to the long voyage around Cape Horn, just as caravan routes in the Middle East had connected the Indian Ocean with the Mediterranean long before the Atlantic route around Africa had been discovered.

In the short run, improvements in land transport reinforced the primacy of western Europe within the ecumene. Most of the new devices were invented in Europe, where the technical and financial capacity to build and operate them also concentrated. The first users of the new means of transport and communication, even in the extra-European parts of the world, were therefore often of European origin. Westerners thereby acquired a new and very powerful instrument for penetration inland from the seacoasts and ports where their earlier contacts with other peoples had usually centered.

On a longer view, however, the opening up of continental interiors to rapid, cheap, and dependable transport clearly tended to dethrone western Europe from its onetime primacy in the world. The rise of American and Russian power to their contemporary dimensions would have been inconceivable without the integration of large continental areas by a network of mechanically powered land transport. South Americans, Africans, and Asians have not yet built a truly continental transport net. Political, financial, and geographical obstacles stand in the way of any such achievement; but the technical possibility is now clear. Should it ever be realized, Europe's onetime primacy over the earth and the recent pre-eminence of ocean traffic may come to seem as extraordinary in retrospect as they would have seemed incredible in prospect to a man of the Middle Ages.

Air travel and transport, which came of age on a global scale only with improvements in aircraft design made during World War II, may in future offer a third alternative to the land-centered and ocean-centered ecumenes of the past. The ease with which airplanes surmount surface obstacles gives Great Circle routes global, not merely oceanic importance. Furthermore, since the overwhelming majority of mankind lives in the Northern Hemisphere, all the major centers of population and power on earth are now interconnected with their most distant fellows by transarctic air routes. As a result, the strategic zones of the earth have migrated northward. The Arctic may therefore become what the Middle East has been through most of recorded history—the world's principal crossroads.

Changes in transport routes and corresponding shifts of strategic loci were perhaps less important than the over-all shrinkage of the globe, which made all peoples comparatively close neighbors. To be sure, interstices and refuge zones remained almost unaffected by the new conditions of transport; but neither the jungle of New Guinea nor the desert of southwest Africa, the rain forest of the upper Amazon nor the tundra and sea ice of the Arctic shoreline seem in the least likely to sustain great human cultures. And if such isolated and remote regions should in future become the seats of anything that seemed significant to the outer world, then the tentacles of modern transport and communication would promptly and automatically close in upon them, engulfing their peoples inexorably into the cosmopolitanism of the age.

A second pervasive effect of modern technology has been to accelerate population growth in almost all parts of the earth. Numerical decay of primitive and semi-primitive populations when exposed to the weapons, germs, and psychological-social disruption brought by civilized men was transitory. Such

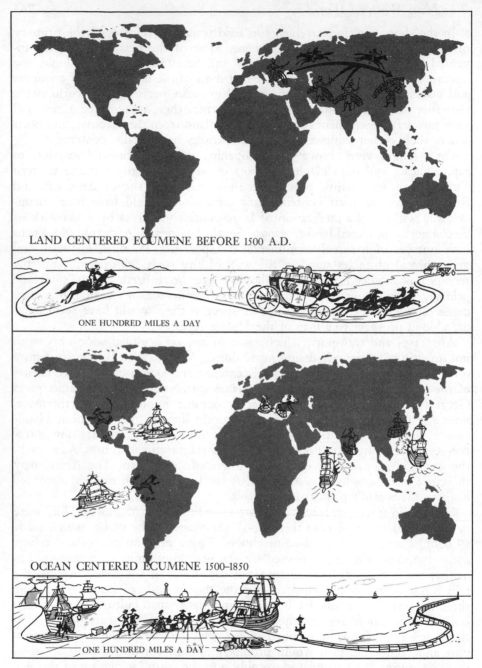

LAND CENTERED ECUMENE BEFORE 1500 A.D.

ONE HUNDRED MILES A DAY

OCEAN CENTERED ECUMENE 1500–1850

ONE HUNDRED MILES A DAY

THE SHRINKING WORLD

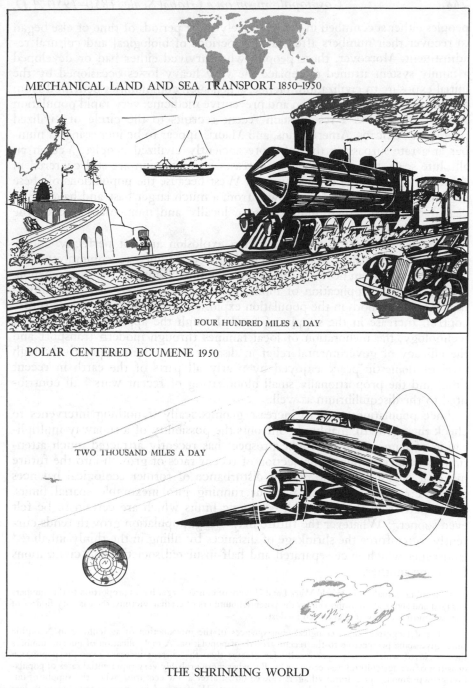

MECHANICAL LAND AND SEA TRANSPORT 1850-1950

FOUR HUNDRED MILES A DAY

POLAR CENTERED ECUMENE 1950

TWO THOUSAND MILES A DAY

THE SHRINKING WORLD

peoples either succumbed in comparatively short periods of time or else began to recover their numbers after varying periods of biological and cultural readjustment. Moreover, those peoples who survived either had or developed a family system attuned to replace the very heavy losses occasioned by the initial exposure to civilization. Hence, when such communities benefited from a modicum of public sanitation and preventive medicine, very rapid population growth ensued. As a result, such recent recruits to the circle of civilized peoples as Africans, Amerindians, and Maoris appear to be increasing in number at a rate surpassing that of more anciently civilized peoples. Yet on an absolute scale, the really massive increases in population are still centered in Asia, Europe, and the extra-European West because the populations of these regions started their modern growth from a much larger base and have never ceased to increase their numbers, save locally and momentarily, since the seventeenth century (or before).

Causes of the world-wide population explosion are not perfectly understood and presumably vary in detail from community to community. Yet general factors seem necessary to explain the universality of the phenomenon. Presumably, the application of modern medical technology was one important ingredient, both in the population explosion and, hopefully, for its future control. Increase in the supply of food through the application of modern technology, the melioration of local famines through modern transport and the efficacy of governmental relief in disaster areas, the comparatively high level of domestic peace enjoyed by nearly all parts of the earth in recent times and the proportionally small bloodletting of recent wars[26] all contributed to the disequilibrium as well.

Since populations tend to increase geometrically if nothing intervenes to check their growth, mankind confronts the possibility of a runaway multiplication of human numbers. The prospect has recently attracted much attention and concern. Simple projection of recent rates of growth into the future makes it obvious that the present disturbance of former ecological balances cannot continue very long without running into inexorable spatial limits, quite apart from the social and economic limits which are certain to be felt even sooner.[27] Whatever the future may bring, population growth tends currently to reinforce the shrinkage of distances by filling in the thinly inhabited landscapes which once separated and half-insulated societies and civilizations from one another.

[26] Absolute casualties in World Wars I and II were of course large; but in proportion to the numbers engaged and above all in proportion to the potential numbers of civilian victims, the casualty figures of our two most recent wars have been modest.

[27] The demographic and ecological consequences of the introduction of agriculture in Neolithic times give some perspective to the recent growth of population. A multiplication of human numbers then occurred which was proportionally far greater than the current increase over the population densities of our agricultural past can ever be. But what were probably very rapid initial rates of population growth among agricultural villagers slowed down after a few centuries, when the supply of unoccupied and easily cultivable land began to run short. Warfare and infanticide, together with less violent customary restraints upon procreation, then began to operate, within the absolute limits set by disease and famine, to maintain a rough balance between population and available means of subsistence.

These aspects of modern technology and human ecology together with the obvious but always important circulation of uniform factory-made goods over wide areas of the world therefore acted to entangle the segments of mankind irrevocably each with all.

* * *

Ideas also spread throughout the world with increasing velocity and volume as communications increased. To be sure, political and language barriers sometimes obstructed the flow of ideas; religious or sectarian commitments likewise checked their infiltration into particular groups; and differences of local or class customs, of ancestral cultural traditions, or of personal taste all affected their transmission round the world and sometimes resulted in rank misunderstanding or grotesque exaggeration.[28] Yet certain branches of thought (particularly the natural sciences) and of the practical arts (particularly engineering) were sometimes genuinely shared by men of very different cultural backgrounds and personal predilections.

There is another complication in the fact that many of the most highly educated and subtle-minded men of the earth no longer are sure of themselves, since they carry more than one universe of meanings and values around in their heads and can never be entirely sure which will come to the top in moments of stress. Characteristically, infants are fitted into a traditional mold—Moslem, Hindu, Confucian, or Christian as the case may be—and then in later life encounter rationalist, secularist, critical, and relativist elements of recent thought. Having made both a part of themselves, they thereafter find it impossible entirely to repudiate either one or really to reconcile the two successive phases of their experience.

This need not be a particularly distressing or disadvantageous state of mind. A man may carry two quite separate cultural worlds about with him so long as it is easy to draw the line between situations where one set of judgments and behavior patterns is appropriate and those in which the other set should be employed. But clear discrimination is not always possible. Indeed, the imperatives of one system may in critical circumstances conflict with those of the second to produce sudden shifts in individual behavior having incalculable and sometimes puzzling consequences for all concerned.[29] In the mass, this sort of unstable individual behavior may resonate within an excited crowd to induce blind outbursts of sudden violence.

Yet the state of the world is not quite so dismal as these remarks may suggest. The secularist hopes and theories of the West which have won partial hold over men's minds all round the globe are remarkably generous ones. Like the ideals of earlier religions, they may yet demonstrate a staying power even in the face of repeated disappointment and failure. At the least, it is clear that

[28] It would be strange if such were not the case. Even within the western European world, differences of language make perfect translation impossible. Indeed, anyone who has read reviews of his own writing is likely to conclude that accurate communication between men of the same profession and native tongue seldom occurs.

[29] Cf. the subtle study of this phenomenon in E. M. Forster, *A Passage to India*.

men of nearly all nations, having once been exposed to the notions of liberty, equality, and fraternity, in any of the versions and with any of the accents which have been put upon these ideals, find them hard to forget and impossible to neglect. The vision of a free, well-fed, well-clothed, well-housed, and well-educated human being, member of a free and peaceable society, exerting his proportional share of influence to determine the mild and equable policies of "his" government, and himself contributing to the general welfare to the best of his abilities, holds a vast attraction for almost everyone. It has the further advantage that it may be vulgarized or specified in almost any manner to prescribe almost any line of conduct and appeal to almost any audience.

Persons who embrace the vision of future perfectibility of mankind enthusiastically find themselves wrestling with the appalling gap between ideal and reality. The gap is so wide that practical action in the imperfect world of fact may appear simply hopeless or else may seem to require such violent action against vested interests as to turn the pursuit of good into the perpetration of evil. Yet because it is not easily achieved, the secularized vision of a future heaven upon earth does not lose vibrancy. On the contary, an ideal easily realized would soon lose its power to inspire action, whereas an unrealizable aspiration for which men must and will fight both asserts and in many cases actually reinforces its power amid the brutalities of battle. In the heat of such struggle, the standing discrepancy between ends and means will trouble only the most critical minds; and even they can never be sure that the end does not indeed justify what "has to be done."

Even a cursory consideration of the wars and revolutions, of the political and social reform movements, and of the activities of the great multitude of charitable, social service, welfare, and missionary agencies during the century since 1850 will show that many men have proved ready, even eager, to labor, to suffer, and if need be, to die in the struggle to bring the heavenly city to earth. Liberals, nationalists, socialists, and communists each have pursued their own version of the ideal on the political stage; and countless others have dedicated private efforts to the task of remodeling one or another corner of the social scene in the hope that, through the voluntary actions of innumerable individuals, a better approximation to the free, equal, and brotherly society of their dreams might in time be achieved.

The end is not yet, and cannot be foretold. Eventually men will no doubt turn away to pursue other visions; but in the meantime, however imperfectly the secular ideal of social bliss has come or ever will come to embodiment in human societies, it remains true that the universality and power of this vision among men of the late nineteenth and early twentieth centuries was a leading characteristic of the initial age of global cosmopolitanism. The spread of industrialism and the effects of mechanical transport and communication upon the ecumene were more palpable; yet the change in men's ideas of what could and ought to be done with industrialism's enhanced wealth and power was no less important. Thus the twin forces which dominated Western history from 1789 to 1917—the Industrial and Democratic revolutions—also struggled for the allegiance of the entire world between 1850 and 1950 and will probably continue to do so into the future.

DEMOCRACY AND COMMUNISM

Since 1917, the Western world has wrestled with tensions and contradictions between the movements launched by the French and the Russian revolutions. Elsewhere this is not really the case—at least not yet. Where "Liberty, Equality, Fraternity" were not written into more or less effective institutions but remained an agenda to be striven after, the Russian reformulation of the slogans of the French Revolution—"Peace, Land, Bread"—sounded more like simple glosses upon the older formula than like contradictions and challenges to it. The dilemmas of liberty, which appear so critical to Westerners, who are both heirs of the French and skeptical of the Russian Revolution, seem far less pressing to men who have yet to make much real progress toward the social transformations inculcated by Europe's two modern political upheavals.

At least until the middle of the twentieth century, therefore, the revolutionary currents in the non-Western world constituted a single, if variegated intellectual force. Everywhere the programs of action derived from French-Russian revolutionary aspiration collided with older principles of social hierarchy and challenged older ideas of the nature and destinies of human life. Individuals took widely divergent points of view, often fluctuating from extreme to extreme within a single lifetime. As a result, societies all round the globe lost the sharpness of their earlier cultural and institutional self-definition. In every quarter of the globe—Europe included—responses ranged from (1) emphatic, even hysterical reassertion of old codes of conduct and revealed certainties to (2) strenuous efforts to reform the present by a return to a more or less fictitious primitive purity of thought, act, and institution; (3) passivity in the face of painful confusion of will, punctuated, perhaps, by bursts of frantic activity; (4) frenetic conspiracy in the form of secret societies living in intimate symbiosis with the secret police; (5) utterly ruthless pursuit of personal power or wealth by persons emancipated from all scruple; or (6) dedication to a cause, even to the neglect of all the ordinary amenities. Saints, villains, cowards, and heroes as well as more ordinary persons: men, in short, in all their temperamental variety, experienced an unparalleled multiplicity of stimuli and achieved no stable, coherent pattern of response. It follows that generalizations about wide areas of the world become more than usually unsatisfactory. Accordingly, it seems best to restrict the remarks which follow to very cursory proportions.

2. THE MOSLEM WORLD

The current of history, which had so sorely tried the faith and patience of good Moslems in the eighteenth and early nineteenth centuries, continued after 1850 to run against the grain of pious expectation. Christian infidels, faithless even to their own religion, continued to bewilder the world with their ever-growing wealth and power. Conversely, the strength of Islam vis-à-vis the West continued to diminish, until such time as Moslem states in one degree or other abandoned Moslem precedent in order to appropriate political and economic techniques from Western unbelievers.

Until after World War I, the territorial retreat of Islamic political sovereignties continued apace. The entire eastern portion of the Moslem world was caught between the pressure of British power extending northward from India and Russian might pressing southward from the central Asian steppe.[30] By 1907, when the two powers reached an entente, all Moslem territory east of the Ottoman border had either been subjected to foreign administration or partitioned into spheres of influence which left little real authority to the surviving local shahs of Afghanistan and Persia. The Western reaches of the Islamic world suffered a similar fate at the end of the nineteenth century and beginning of the twentieth, when the European powers completed the partition of Moslem as well as pagan Africa into colonies and protectorates. Long before that date, the Ottoman empire itself—traditional guardian of the Moslem world against Christendom—had become a ward of the European great powers. World War I gave the empire its death blow. With British encouragement, an Arab revolt broke out against the Turks; and after 1918 the Turks themselves, through an abrupt revulsion of feeling, repudiated the Ottoman and imperial ideal in favor of a strictly Turkish nationalism.

A modest political recovery became apparent soon after World War I. Nationalist Turkey and Saudi Arabia won real independence in the years 1919–25 by successfully defying British imperial policy. Persia and Afghanistan likewise widened their effective independence by shaking off both Russian and British influence. During the 1930's, a limited retreat of European authority in the Arab countries continued; but not until World War II and after did such countries as Morocco, Tunis, Egypt, Pakistan, and Indonesia achieve formal independence.[31]

Reassertion of Moslem political independence reflected real increases in the effectiveness of Moslem political organization. Modern bureaucracies, modern armies, and modern sentiments about the right of the people to rule themselves were all successfully introduced into Moslem lands. The political will of Arabs, Turks, and other Moslem peoples thus became a factor to be reckoned with in international and still more in domestic Moslem politics. Yet the trappings of modern statehood were a sort of borrowed finery, fitting awkwardly upon the ancient Islamic body politic and in most states commanding a loyalty flawed by profound nostalgia for an irrecoverable past.

In effect, the Moslem peoples have in the past hundred years been simultaneously exposed to the force of the Democratic and Industrial revolutions and to the no less drastic revolution signified in European history by Renaissance and Reformation. This was not accidental. At the beginning of Europe's modern age, the Moslem peoples recoiled from heresy and innovation, preferring the shelter of authoritative doctrine and established hierarchy. When in the nineteenth century the institutions which had been perfected to guard orthodoxy lost their effectiveness—that is, when the Ottoman and Per-

[30] The Moslem communities of China also suffered severe damage when revolts in Yunnan and in Turkestan and Kansu were violently suppressed by the Chinese imperial authorities in the second half of the nineteenth century. Systematic massacre, especially in Yunnan, probably much reduced Moslem numbers in China. Cf. Martin Hartmann, *Zur Geschichte des Islams in China* (Leipzig: Wilhelm Heims, 1921); G. Cordier, *Les Musulmans du Yunnan* (Hanoi: Imprimerie Tonkinoise, 1927).

[31] By 1962, when the French regime in Algeria ended, only the Russians and Chinese in central Asia held empire over massive Moslem populations.

sian states and the Sunni and Shi'a *ulema* ceased to be able to command men's bodies and men's minds—Moslems had to pay the price of their earlier intellectual and moral abdication by confronting within a single century the entire complex of ideas and techniques which Europe had developed in the course of some four hundred years. Small wonder that confusion reigned in public as well as in private affairs!

Islam meant, above all, conformity to the Sacred Law which claimed to be the sole authentic instrument for regulating human affairs in accordance with the will of God. But a rigid and fully worked-out code of law and conduct could not easily be reconciled with a social order changing rapidly under the impact of Western technologies; nor did such claims easily withstand the secularism of much nineteenth- and twentieth-century thought. Indeed, the very energy and perspicacity which the early doctors of Islam had devoted to the elaboration of the Sacred Law deprived modern Moslem generations of the ambiguities they desperately needed for plausible reinterpretation and altered applications of a code which could no longer command acceptance of its every jot and tittle.[32] Few expressly repudiated the religion which gave them their cultural identity; yet most educated men felt uneasy within the rigid framework of traditional Islam.[33]

At a personal level, the usual reaction to the incompatibility between Islamic orthodoxy and modern thought has been a rigorous compartmentation of mind.[34] Lip service to Islam and to such Western ideals as democratic government, combined with systematic failure to conform to the precepts of either faith, is the public equivalent of the private duality of mind most educated Moslems now inherit. Efforts to escape from such an intrinsically embarrassing posture have indeed been made. Radical secularization of the state

[32] Reinterpretation has of course been attempted, but as yet without winning either wide acceptance or deep commitment. Theological, or rather legal, "modernists," of whom Mohammed Abduh (d. 1905) of Egypt was the most prominent, and more radical philosophical restatements of the meaning of Islam, such as those associated with the Indian thinker, Mohammed Iqbal (d. 1938), have entered the field, however, and offer alternatives to the rigid conservatism of the orthodox Islamic learned tradition. Cf. Mohammed Iqbal, *The Reconstruction of Religious Thought in Islam* (Oxford: Oxford University Press, 1934), which was composed in English. G. E. von Grunebaum, "Attempts at Self-Interpretation in Contemporary Islam," in *Islam: Essays in the Nature and Growth of a Cultural Tradition* (American Anthropological Association, Memoir No. 81 [April, 1955]), pp. 185–236, offers a useful analysis of these and a number of similar efforts to reorganize older conceptions of Moslem religion and society. Cf. also Wilfred Cantwell Smith, *Islam in Modern History* (New York: Mentor Books, 1957).

[33] How far down the social scale this weakening of Islamic convictions reached cannot be said; but a priori it seems all but certain that the peasants of Turkey, Iran, and the Arab-speaking countries remained more at home within ancient formulae and pieties than their urban fellows, and far more so than their educated fellow countrymen.

Toward the fringes of the Moslem world, mainly in Africa, but also to some degree in southeast Asia, Islam retained its accustomed aplomb. In these regions Islam offered peoples emerging from tribal and strictly local societies a way of life attuned to civilized living, doubly attractive since it opposed the Christianity of the ruling Europeans. Cf. the essays on tropical Africa and Indonesia in Gustave E. von Grunebaum, *Unity and Variety in Muslim Civilization* (Chicago: University of Chicago Press, 1955), pp. 261–310; Jean-Paul Roux, *L'Islam en Asie* (Paris: Payot, 1958), pp. 251–74; Alphonse Gouilly, *L'Islam dans l'Afrique occidentale française* (Paris: Larousse, 1952), pp. 267–92.

[34] The formal educational system of Egypt reflected this compromise, entrusting religious instruction to teachers trained at the ancient Moslem university of el-Azhar, while assigning "new" subjects to other teachers trained in Western-type colleges.

in Turkey and in Russian central Asia took place with the Kemalist (1919–23) and Bolshevik (1917–22) revolutions. Persia, too, embarked upon a rather less doctrinaire but definitely secularist policy after the accession of Reza Shah in 1925. At the other extreme, Wahhabi puritans, who aspired toward a radical Islamization of all human affairs through a return to the patterns of the primitive Moslem community, came to power in most of Arabia with the victories of Abd al-Aziz Ibn Sa'ud (1919–25).

Results of these experiments remain to be seen. Reaction in Turkey against Mustafa Kemal's irreligion became apparent in the 1950's; but information about the Russian and Chinese Moslem communities is too imperfect to allow judgment as to what may have occurred there. Equally, the religious fire of the Wahhabi movement in Saudi Arabia, having been drenched in oil since the 1930's, flamed less brightly than before. Perhaps most interesting of all is the case of Pakistan. This country came into existence in 1947 as a Moslem state whose entire *raison d'être* was the Islamic faith of the majority of its citizens. Moreover, thanks to the schools and army of British India, a substantial number of Pakistanis had acquired a far more intimate acquaintance with Western culture than any comparable body of Moslems elsewhere had done. Here, if anywhere, a fusion between Western and Islamic ideas and practice seemed possible. To date, however, success has not been conspicuous. Pakistan, like the other Moslem states of the world, seems to have found the Sacred Law of classical Islam both indigestible and inescapable—at least for the present.[35]

Industrialism made even smaller inroads upon the Moslem world than the Democratic Revolution did. Western machine-made goods disrupted old handicraft almost everywhere; and Western entrepreneurs introduced some important new extractive industries—oil above all. But in the absence of stable, persistent, and perspicacious Moslem political leadership in economic and industrial matters, Moslem entrepreneurs accomplished remarkably little toward establishing modern industry in Islamic lands before 1950. Even when the state undertook forced-draft industrialization, as in Kemalist Turkey, success came slowly among a people who by long tradition had left commerce and economic administration to despised religious minorities—Jews, Armenians, and Greeks.[36]

[35] Cf. Leonard Binder, *Religion and Politics in Pakistan* (Berkeley, Calif.: University of California Press, 1961).

[36] In addition to books cited separately, I have consulted the following in connection with the above remarks on Moslem affairs: Wilfred Cantwell Smith, *Modern Islam in India: A Social Analysis* (London: Victor Gollancz, 1946); George E. Kirk, *A Short History of the Middle East* (London: Methuen & Co., 1948); George Antonius, *The Arab Awakening* (London: Hamish Hamilton, 1938); T. Cuyler Young (ed.), *Near Eastern Culture and Society: A Symposium on the Meeting of East and West* (Princeton: Princeton University Press, 1951); H. A. R. Gibb (ed.), *Whither Islam?* (London: Victor Gollancz, 1932); H. A. R. Gibb, *Modern Trends in Islam* (Chicago: University of Chicago Press, 1947); Richard N. Frye (ed.), *Islam and the West* ('s Gravenhage: Mouton, 1957); A. J. Arberry and Rom Landau, *Islam Today* (London: Faber & Faber, 1943); Alfred Bonne, *State and Economics in the Middle East* (London: Kegan Paul, Trench, Trubner & Co., 1948); David S. Landes, *Bankers and Pashas: International Finance and Economic Imperialism in Egypt* (London: Heinemann, 1958); Richard A. Pierce, *Russian Central Asia, 1867–1917* (Berkeley, Calif.: University of California Press, 1960); Vincent Monteil, *Les Musulmans soviétiques* (Paris: Éditions du Seuil, 1957); Olaf Caroe, *Soviet Empire: The Turks of Central Asia and Stalinism* (London: Macmillan & Co., 1953); Walter Z. Laquer, *Communism and Nationalism in the Middle East* (New York: Praeger, 1956).

3. HINDU INDIA

The acceptance of Western ideas and practices proved on the whole far easier for Hindus than for Moslems. No age-old hostility divided Hindustan from the West; indeed, the Hindu majority was not displeased to witness the overthrow of Islamic power in India by British arms. The absence of doctrinal definition in their religion made it easier for Hindus to consider Western culture on its own merits or at least to avoid such a paralyzing collision as occurred between Western notions and the rigidities of the Islamic Sacred Law.[37] In addition, the Western presence in India was more intense and extensive than in any other part of Asia, for in the course of the nineteenth century, India acquired many of the trappings of the contemporary West— an educational system cast in British molds, the famed Indian Civil Service, modern law codes, armies, police, economic enterprises, and communications. Such institutions enormously enhanced the opportunities for Europeans and Indians to learn something of each other's culture.

The mere existence of the British power in India worked a pronounced inversion in Indian society by simultaneously opening a way for westernization and putting a special premium upon it. The British progressively reduced native Indian rulers and old ruling cliques to the status of figureheads or displaced them entirely. Administrative authority, under British supervision, devolved instead upon new men rising through the British-style educational system from quite varied backgrounds. Other Indians were recruited in the same way for the new professions required by the British political order, particularly law. Such men, whose work often put them into frequent contact with Englishmen and whose careers often depended upon how effectively they conformed to the expectations of their foreign supervisors, obviously had strong motives for a broad personal assimilation of Western ways. The further fact that a growingly wide range of real administrative power was bestowed upon those Indians who assimilated Western manners most effectually gave the Anglicized clique an influence far out of proportion to its numbers or to the weight it might have exerted in India without British patronage and support.

For these, and perhaps for other reasons, Hinduism, which of the four major civilized traditions of the world was the most battered and torn at the beginning of the modern era, responded more resiliently to the challenge inherent in Western civilization than either the Moslems or (at least until 1950) the Chinese were able to do. Both the Industrial and the Democratic revolu-

---

[37] Various Hindu customs and pieties did, of course, conflict sharply with the views and attitudes of the West. Nonetheless, the iconoclastic student who lived a secularized and semi-Westernized, if often poverty-sticken, life in Calcutta or London had a way of conforming again to local, family, and caste customs whenever circumstances thrust him back into a traditionally Hindu environment. By contrast, the Moslem law claimed universal validity and was therefore independent, at least in theory, of locality and social circumstances such as those which defined Hindu rites. Islam could not therefore be doffed and donned like a garment, whereas Hinduism could without the least logical inconsistency be applied to the social circumstances to which it was attuned and neglected at other times and places where it lacked all traditional applicability.

tions of Europe had their analogues in India; and by mingling British with autochthonous Indian traits, both of them acquired a distinctive and peculiarly Indian tenor.

* * *

The industrial and economic development of India from 1850 to 1950 was dominated by a conflict between political practice and principle. Political practice turned upon the overarching authority and prestige of the British administrative machine, embodied in the Indian Civil Service and, as time went on, in a series of subordinate provincial services. But British political principles circumscribed the limits of governmental activity rather narrowly, emphasizing the maintenance of peace and order at home and defense abroad, while leaving the rest largely to private enterprise. Obviously, a combination of nineteenth-century British liberalism with an efficient, centralized, and fundamentally authoritarian bureaucracy resembling those which east European empires had developed during the eighteenth century implied some striking anomalies; and of these India had its full share.

Generally, the supermodern came regularly to be juxtaposed to an immemorial antiquity, with which the modernizing government, on principle, refused to tamper. Those economic and technological developments which were considered to be within the legitimate province of government tended to be introduced early and systematically, often on a scale and with a degree of rationality surpassing anything attained in England. The outstanding example of this sort of supermodernism was the Indian railway system. Large-scale railway construction proceeded in accordance with an over-all plan approved by the governor general in 1853. Despite tergiversation between private and public ownership, and the unfortunate introduction of two separate gauges, official supervision of the Indian railroads remained very close and made the railroad net remarkably comprehensive. By the end of the nineteenth century, some 50,000 miles of track bound the subcontinent together as had never before been remotely possible.[38] Irrigation works, especially in the Punjab, constituted the other field in which the British administration engaged in economic action; while roads, port facilities, and urban utilities straggled variously behind.

On the other hand, the private sector of the economy remained generally backward. Village custom prevented the vast majority of Indians from fully exploiting possibilities opened by the new transport and technology. Most Indians utterly lacked the economic habit of mind presupposed by the liberal theory of British administration. Even the monied and commercial classes usually preferred old-fashioned usury or direct investment in land to ventures into industrial or other untried forms of economic activity. As a result, those modern enterprises which did arise were mostly controlled by Europeans, Parsis, or other foreigners. Liberal economic principles, which worked well

[38] The transfer of the capital from Calcutta to New Delhi in 1911 was a symbol of the new basis of power and the new principle of economic and political cohesion introduced by the railroads. Seaports like Calcutta, Bombay, and Madras no longer seemed convenient nor adequate as a base from which to govern the vast Indian hinterland.

enough in Britain where an enterprising economic class was firmly rooted, did not work nearly so well in India, where a galloping multiplication of village population tended to keep up with, if not to overtake, the substantial increases in agricultural and industrial productivity which did occur. Nevertheless, factory industry established a real, if comparatively modest, presence in India from the 1880's onward. Textiles, both cotton and jute, were the first important modern industry, followed in due course by metallurgy (steel from 1913, aluminum from 1944) and other types of mills and factories.[39]

Famine and war modified the antinomy between an efficient bureaucracy which on principle left most economic undertakings to private persons and a lethargic or indifferent public which, save in a few instances, could not imagine or begin to act upon untried economic potentialities. Humane principles impelled British officials to make special preparations against the recurrent danger of famine, which invariably threatened whenever a weak monsoon cut rainfall below normal levels. A special famine code, drawn up in 1883, prescribed the steps to be taken to prevent severe loss of life in seasons of crop failure. According to this code, officials undertook to import and distribute food in famine areas and to organize work projects that would justify payment of wages to the populations threatened with starvation. The result was to relieve some of the traditional severity of famine in India, despite a growing shortage of land which became more and more apparent from the 1870's onward.

World Wars I and II involved a rather more significant departure from accustomed governmental practices. Both conflicts brought home the vulnerability of India; for even a temporary interruption of normal supply channels from England had unpleasantly vivid consequences for the Indian army and government. Officials therefore launched emergency programs to develop or increase local supplies of thousands of items—briefly and without extended success during World War I and far more systematically and with greater success during World War II. This required official intervention in order to encourage, cajole, or entice private persons into new lines of economic action, when it did not seem easier to organize state enterprises directly.

By the close of World War II, therefore, when India became politically independent, the older restraint upon governmental action in the economic sphere had been largely discarded in favor of a mixed type of economy, in which both private and public enterprises functioned within a system of governmental regulations intended to facilitate or even compel economic and especially industrial expansion. After the initial emergencies of the partition had been met, the new Indian government undertook to revive and enlarge the system of official stimulation and direction of economic growth which had arisen during the war. Whether or not the growth of population will outstrip India's best efforts to increase economic production remains to be seen.

---

[39] By one count, indeed, India ranked as the sixth greatest industrial state in the world at the close of World War II. Vincent A. Smith, *The Oxford History of India*, Percival Spear (ed.) (3d ed.; Oxford: Clarendon Press, 1958), p. 835.

Parsis and Englishmen, with a sprinkling of Greeks and Levantines, had pioneered the introducton of modern industry into India; but Bengalis, soon followed by Gujeratis, Marathas, and others from the neighborhood of Bombay took the lead in introducing the ideas of the Democratic Revolution. As we saw, Ram Mohan Roy (d. 1833) showed the way at the beginning of the nineteenth century; the gradual consolidation of a school system on the English model in the years after 1835 provided human material; and the failure of the mutiny in 1857–58 discredited older social-political ideals. Then a preparatory generation elapsed during which thousands of individuals were schooled to accept European notions of political rights, before the new winds of doctrine found organized and overt expression through the Indian National Congress (founded 1885); and yet another generation passed before polite remonstrance, protest, and petition came to be supplemented by mass demonstrations, demagogic excitement, and secret terrorism.

Yet the secret cells, passwords, and activities of revolutionary student societies in Calcutta of the 1905–7 period, like the parliamentary procedure of the Indian National Congress itself, were patterned after foreign examples and were only dimly affected by their Indian environment. The first modern and at the same time authentically Indian political movement arose after World War I under the leadership of Mohandas Karamchand Gandhi (d. 1948). His charismatic blend of Indian with Western saintliness and cunning won him the title of "Mahatma," *i.e.*, "great soul"; and the agitation he directed, uniting resolute civil disobedience with emphatic non-violence, won India its independence in 1947.

Gandhi's thought and action effectively fused Hindu asceticism with Christian pacifism and democratic secularism. Comparably diverse points of view, sometimes combined within single individuals, sometimes embodied in separate persons or groups, mingled to form the Indian nationalist movement and the Congress party. Such an intimate blending between autochthonous Indian and exotic Western ideas and practices was a new phenomenon. Likewise, a mass movement commanding the loyalty of the great majority of urban Indians of every class and affecting even villagers had never previously been able to sustain itself for extended periods of time and at a comparatively high but usually well-controlled emotional pitch.

These achievements made a reality of the democratic theory according to which ordinary individuals should have some voice in political affairs. Yet Gandhi's followers were far more firmly united in opposition to British rule than in support of any positive policies. Efforts to revive handicraft industry did not appeal to the economic planners of the new Indian government; and indeed, in the cold light of calculation, Gandhi's spinning wheel could offer no solution to India's poverty. Again, Gandhi's campaign against untouchability stirred deep opposition among religious conservatives—an opposition which his assassination at the hands of a Hindu fanatic silenced more effectually than any less dramatic sacrifice could have done. In addition, the very mass character of Gandhi's movement frightened Indian Moslems and provoked their somewhat desperate and belated but nonetheless successful demand for the creation of the separate, specifically Moslem state of Pakistan.

It remains to be seen how the humane and generous ideals of Gandhism will wear over time, and how well or ill the democratic, parliamentary frame of Indian government will accord with the benevolent despotism of bureaucratic planning, with the passions arising from linguistic and religious diversities, and with the economic hardships inherent in the disproportion between population growth and economic development. Yet the pitfalls of the future are scarcely greater than the obstacles of the recent past which Indians have in fact surmounted. On a scale only rivaled by China, the government and society of India offer an example of the interpenetration of Western and autochthonous ideas, techniques, and institutions. Time alone will reveal the upshot; but from the viewpoint of the 1960's, distinctively Western elements seem to be gaining ground within India. Since 1947, the twentieth-century social revolution of the West seems to have been merging with the Indian "nationalist" revolution, making India at once a province and a partner in a world-wide, cosmopolitan, West-centered social process.

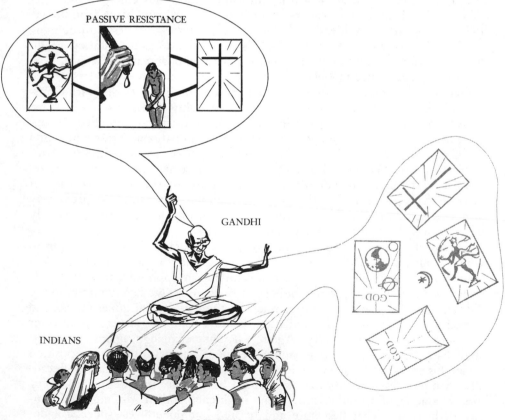

GANDHI'S MESSAGE

The emergence of India as a participant in twentieth-century cosmopolitanism has been but fitfully announced through the arts. Rabindranath Tagore (d. 1941), whose poetry mingled European, Sanskrit, and Bengali literary forms and ideas, was the single figure who achieved world reputation. It is not yet possible to tell whether the vogue for his work will subside or whether his literary reputation will maintain itself indefinitely.[40]

4. CHINA

Developments in China from the outbreak of the Taiping rebellion in 1850 until the establishment of Communist control over the country in 1949 much resembled earlier transitions from one imperial dynasty to another. Many of the remoter dependencies of the Manchu empire broke away from the Chinese connection, while a long series of internal rebellions and successful foreign aggressions convulsed the heartlands of China proper. All this conformed closely to precedent. The foreign policies of the Chinese Communist government since 1949, involving the reassertion of Chinese influence in outlying regions like Tibet, Korea, and Annam also adhered to familiar imperial patterns.

Moreover, the Communist hierarchies of party and government came close to duplicating the former Confucian hierarchies of scholars and officials, even to the manner in which they interpenetrated one another in the practical exercise of power. Indeed, totalitarian state socialism, as manifested in European countries since 1917 under both Marxian and Nazi banners, exhibited remarkable affinities with traditional Chinese bureaucratic practices, principles, and prejudices. The practice of entrusting broad discretionary powers to an educated and specially selected elite, the principle of using state power for the benefit of the people at large and of justifying even severe oppression thereby, together with prejudice against such assorted evils as profiteers, foreigners, and the superstitions of religion, were common to good Confucians, pious Communists, and dedicated Nazis.

The other master institution of traditional Chinese society, the family, also survived the century 1850–1950, just as it had survived many other periods of economic hardship and political upheaval. The vociferous repudiation of Confucian family pieties which became a prominent feature of the Chinese intellectual scene after 1917 induced unfilial conduct in large numbers of educated young Chinese; and in some regions of China, incipient industrialization

[40] In addition to books cited separately, I have consulted the following in connection with these remarks upon recent Indian history: Abdullah Yusuf Ali, *A Cultural History of India during British Rule* (Bombay: D. B. Taraporevala Sons, 1940); Nirad C. Chauduri, *The Autobiography of an Unknown Indian* (New York: Macmillan Co., 1951); Romesh Chunder Dutt, *An Economic History of India in the Victorian Age* (2d ed.; London: Kegan Paul, Trench, Trubner & Co., 1929); J. N. Farquhar, *Modern Religious Movements in India* (London: Macmillan & Co., 1929); Atulchandra Gupta, *Studies in the Bengal Renaissance* (Jadavpur: National Council of Education, Bengal, 1958); J. C. Ghosh, *Bengali Literature* (London: Oxford University Press, 1948); Percival Griffiths, *The British Impact on India* (London: Macdonald, 1952); Percival Griffiths, *Modern India* (London: Ernest Benn, Ltd., 1957); R. C. Majumdar *et al.*, *An Advanced History of India*, pp. 829–1004; Lewis S. S. O'Malley, *Modern India and the West* (London: Oxford University Press, 1941); K. M. Panikkar, *A Survey of Indian History* (3d ed.; Bombay, Calcutta, New Delhi, Madras: Asia Publishing House, 1956); William Theodore de Bary, *Sources of Indian Tradition* (New York: Columbia University Press, 1958).

put more persistent, if less obvious, strains on old familial relationships.[41] Yet the traditional attitudes and obligations, which continued to be instilled into the overwhelming majority of young Chinese even after 1917, were peculiarly tough and elastic. Family ties often reasserted themselves even among those who had in youth explicitly rejected the Confucian formulation of filial duty.

Nevertheless these impressive continuities do not justify the judgment that China merely passed through another of her traditional political cycles in the nineteenth and twentieth centuries. Since 1917, the Chinese educated minority has with increasing unanimity and energy repudiated the entire Confucian frame of life, with its age-old definitions of decorum in manners, morals, and politics. In the long run, the character of Chinese life is bound to be radically affected by so drastic a transfer of loyalties, all the more since the intellectual elite has been able to utilize ancient Chinese political institutions to further its new purposes.

The ideals espoused by China's educated classes in the twentieth century were all derived directly from the cosmopolitan culture of the West. Even in the nineteenth century, the Taiping rebellion (1850–64), which shook the Manchu empire to its core, proclaimed an ideal of Christian brotherhood, though Taoist and Buddhist elements mingled with Christian motifs from the start and became more prominent as the rebellion prospered.[42] After China suffered humiliating military defeat at the hands of the Japanese in 1895, a generation of revolutionary leaders, of whom Sun Yat-sen (d. 1925) was the most eminent, undertook an almost panic search for new talismans of power and national salvation. The obvious models were the world powers, for Western nations and now the Japanese had clearly been able to organize their societies far more successfully than the Chinese seemed to be doing. Accordingly, Sun Yat-sen and other revolutionaries quarried Western political and economic thought (often filtered through Japan) for suitable ideas. They did so with an indiscriminate naïvete, showing themselves to be masters neither of the classical Chinese nor of the Western cultural tradition. After 1917, the Russian Revolution offered another and very attractive[43] source of alien in-

[41] Cf. Hsiao-tung Fei, *Peasant Life in China: A Field Study of Country Life in the Yangtse Valley* (New York: Oxford University Press, 1946), pp. 233–35 and *passim;* Chow Tse-tsung, *The May Fourth Movement: Intellectual Revolution in Modern China* (Cambridge, Mass.: Harvard University Press, 1960), pp. 257–59.

[42] Cf. Eugene Powers Boardman, *Christian Influence upon the Ideology of the Taiping Rebellion, 1851–64* (Madison, Wis.: University of Wisconsin Press, 1952).

[43] The appeal of Marxist-Leninist doctrine in China was basically the same as the appeal of earlier heterodox religions to peoples emerging into civilization along the fringes of one or another of the established high cultures of the ecumene. Just as the Uighurs preferred Manichaeism or the Khazars Judaism to any of the orthodoxies of their civilized neighbors, so the Chinese and other proud neophytes in the contemporary West-centered cosmopolitanism might have been expected to prefer communism to any of the established orthodoxies of the West. Only so can the neophyte both defy his preceptors and acquire their skills.

In proportion as communism has itself become an established orthodoxy, first in Russia and now in China, the Marxist-Leninist doctrine of course loses this advantage; for the uncommitted peoples of the world are no more anxious to be caught in a Communist than in a liberal-capitalist net. Intellectual as well as political independence has particular charms for peoples who feel themselves at a disadvantage.

spiration; and since 1949 Communist ideology has successfully asserted an intellectual and political monopoly in mainland China.

Yet all this ideological volatility flourished against a backdrop of comparatively modest institutional change. Until the turn of the century, the policy of the government and of the Confucian gentry, who provided social leadership in the Chinese countryside, was to minimize whatever changes the Western presence in China made necessary. After 1842, when British warships first compelled Chinese authorities to conform to foreign commercial and diplomatic practices, and still more emphatically after 1858–60, when renewed Western and Russian intervention in China enlarged foreign privileges, the rulers of China could no longer even pretend to confine the powerful barbarians to their proper tributary status. Yet most of the mandarins chose to overlook this gross breach of etiquette, for the naïve ethnocentric universality of Confucianism prohibited the recognition of any alternative and equal—still less of a superior—system of society and civilization.

The rigors of checking and then defeating the Taiping rebellion did indeed bring a handful of energetic and far-sighted reformers to key positions within the Chinese government. Some of these tried to equip China with the arsenals, armies, and navies which seemed to form the basis for Western power. Yet official reforms languished once the emergency of the Taiping rebellion had passed, partly because innovations raised suspicion in more conservative minds but mainly because the reformers themselves were half-hearted. Their whole purpose was to sustain the old order; and when innovation threatened that order, they opposed it. To give China the armies, armaments, industries, and communications with which to defend herself adequately would have required a greater modification of the existing Chinese social structure than the reformers of the 1860's themselves desired.[44]

In the last years of the nineteenth century, therefore, events began once more to close in upon the tottering Confucian regime. Japanese victory in 1895, followed by the failure of the Boxer risings (1900–1901) and the imposition of additional humiliations upon China, convinced even those most reluctant to abandon the ancestral ways that drastic transformation was indeed required. Reform took many directions. Prolonged tampering with the machinery of government, both before and after the abdication of the last Manchu emperor in 1912, was usually hasty and, for a full half-century at least, was always ineffective in strengthening China. In education, however, change was both drastic and dramatically effective in transforming the whole intellectual climate of the country. Abolition of the imperial examinations based upon the Confucian classics in 1905 abruptly cut off the avenue through which the clique that had managed China for more than two millennia renewed itself. As a result, the ambitious young men who in any earlier age would have studied the classics of ancient China all their lives suddenly flooded into institutions of Western learning. Ideological clamor and confusion, wholly cut loose from any traditional anchor, inevitably ensued, as

[44] Cf. Mary Clabaugh Wright, *The Last Stand of Chinese Conservatism* (Stanford, Calif.: Stanford University Press, 1957).

thousands of Chinese whose childhood and early schooling had been thoroughly traditional found themselves plunged into a maelstrom of alien and often only half-understood ideas.[45] But for anyone who had experienced such profound discrepancies in youth, any moral, political, or intellectual commitments made in later life were bound to have a certain inner awkwardness and secret fragility. As a consequence, even the most emphatically expressed conviction could yield abruptly to new winds of doctrine if only the novelty promised speedier salvation from the tortures of indecision in thought and ineffectiveness in act. The bandwagon surge into the ranks of the Kuomintang in the 1920's and the more recent Communist consolidation in China both were possible only because of this sort of intellectual volatility.

But the Western origin of the ideas argued so passionately among Chinese intellectuals and politicians in the twentieth century easily obscures the comparative superficiality of the Western impact upon China before 1950. The great mass of the Chinese peasantry, some 80 per cent of the entire population, was like a great ocean into which rivulets of Western goods and streams of missionary exhortation flowed, without noticeably changing its level or much deflecting its waves and tides. The temporary success of the Taiping and other revolts; the persistent weakness of the Manchu regime; the rise and fall of the Kuomintang; and the success of the Communists in the 1930's and 1940's—all turned upon an axis of peasant disaffection against their rent-, tax-, and interest-collecting social superiors, most of whom resided in towns for mutual edification and protection.[46] But this was exactly the sort of thing that had happened in earlier Chinese history toward the end of each dynasty. The violence, famine, and disease which prevailed over wide regions of the Chinese countryside in the first half of the twentieth century was likewise nothing more than the traditionally efficacious, if brutal, means of redressing accumulated disproportions between land, rent, taxes, and population. The availability of Western machine-made manufactures, e.g., cotton cloth and kerosene, may have exacerbated the woes of the peasantry in some parts of China by undercutting or destroying traditional handicrafts; and town artisans may have suffered as tastes of the wealthy few turned toward exotic Western manufactures. On the other hand, new or expanded trades, like the production of tung oil, tungsten, tea, and silk for Western and world markets, tended to enlarge the possibilities of livelihood for these same classes.

Modern machine-power industry made a modest first appearance in China in the 1840's but gained significant headway only after 1895, when a provision of the treaty ending the Sino-Japanese War allowed foreigners to erect factories on Chinese soil and still enjoy most of the trade privileges already

---

[45] One calculation finds as many as 10 million Chinese exposed to some form of Westernized education by 1917. Cf. Chow Tse-tung, *The May Fourth Movement*, pp. 379–80. It is strange to think that a man like Mao-tse Tung (b. 1893) began life in a completely Confucian environment and espoused Marxism only as a grown man of twenty-seven. Other leaders of the Chinese Communists also bridge the gap in their personal lives between the old and the new regimes, a fact which helps to guarantee a massive carry-over from the Chinese past into whatever future Chinese communism may create.

[46] Cf. the emphatic but penetrating essays collected in M. P. Redfield (ed.), *China's Gentry: Essays in Rural-Urban Relations by Hsiao-tung Fei* (Chicago: University of Chicago Press, 1953).

conferred upon goods imported from abroad. World War I cut off European supplies and gave a temporary fillip to Chinese manufacture, especially of cotton cloth; but Japanese competition, together with financial and other instabilities of the interwar period, severely checked the advance of modern industry in China. Such great modern cities as Shanghai and Tientsin did not become major industrial complexes but remained primarily mercantile and financial centers dominated in considerable degree by foreign businessmen.

Railroads, likewise, played no such role in China as they did in India. Large-scale construction began only in the first decade of the twentieth century; and no coherent network spanning the whole country arose from the furious intrigues among the rival European financial interests which provided most of the capital required for railroad building in China. Moreover, even where railroads were built, they often operated only sporadically, owing to financial and administrative disorders and to recurrent military disturbances.[47]

A really massive and sustained effort to create both modern industry and modern transport in China had to await the appearance of a government strong enough to impose peace. This seemed about to happen in 1929, when the Kuomintang emerged to authority in China, only to be confronted by fresh Japanese attack (1931) and renewed domestic broils. Peace came again only in 1949. Hence, until then the Industrial Revolution had touched only the fringes of China. The fabric of older economic relationships in both village and town remained essentially intact. The Western presence in China had indeed provoked an unusual effervescence in the Chinese economy like that which the Mongols had brought in the thirteenth century; but, for all this, there was as yet no fundamental transformation.

Only *after* China had completed the traditional cycle of transition from one strong political regime to another could the West-centered cosmopolitanism of the twentieth century really begin to confront traditional Chinese institutions on a massive scale. As long as traditional social disproportions within Chinese society provoked traditional responses of violence and disorder, the cutting edge of Western economic penetration was blunted; and all the heated debates among the educated minority—while thoroughly Western in outward form and profoundly important for China's long-run future —had little immediate applicability. Really intimate and decisive confrontation between Chinese and Western civilizations therefore lies still in the future. It promises to generate the most important cultural interaction of the twentieth and perhaps of the twenty-first century.

In an age of such sharp vicissitudes, when moral as well as economic and political standards were in flux, high and serene cultural creativity ought not to be expected. Important reforms, especially of literary conventions, were projected, for example Hu Shih's movement (1919) to substitute a more nearly popular speech as a standard for writing or the more recent Communist proposal for alphabetizing written Chinese. The rigorous intellectual and scholarly tradition of the country facilitated the introduction of Western

---

[47] Cf. E-tu Zen Sun, "The Pattern of Railway Development in China," *Far Eastern Quarterly*, XIV (1955), 179–99.

science and learning into China, partly through missionary efforts, partly by means of students sent abroad to study at Western universities. Especially in the field of Sinology, the cross-stimulation of Chinese with Western methods and presuppositions of scholarship often proved strikingly fertile. Yet measured against the greatness of the past, the century 1850–1950 clearly represented a low point in Chinese cultural achievement.[48]

5. JAPAN

Japanese civilization exhibited a remarkable duality under the Tokugawa shoguns, balancing itself precariously—one is tempted to say artificially—between contrary extremes. Thus the moral ideal of the warrior with all its spartan rigor confronted the unabashed sensuous indulgences of the "Floating World"; and no *via media* offered between these moral codes. Japan was officially closed to the outside world; yet lively curiosity about Dutch learning overcame enormous obstacles. Or again, the personal, hereditary ties of Japanese "feudalism" disguised but did not really hide the lineaments of bureaucratic administration in each of the sixty-odd "fiefs" or clan territories into which Japan was divided. Even more troublesome was the separation between political and economic power, permitting despised merchants to prosper, while peasants and warriors—their superiors in the traditional scale of society —suffered recurrent want. Thus the strained, yet stabilized relationship between emperor and shogun aptly symbolized the duality that ran through all Japanese life. A holy and powerless sovereign, revered as the font of all authority and immured in a web of ritual, somehow tolerated and was tolerated by the heirs of an unusually successful swashbuckler of the early seventeenth century, the Tokugawa shoguns, who ruled Japan with heavy hand through a corps of officials, spies, and soldiers, artfully balancing man against man, class against class, and clan against clan.

Only a sustained act of will emanating from the shogun's palace sufficed to maintain equilibrium amid such seeming incompatibilities. When that will faltered, as it did in the 1850's owing to conflicts among rival cliques over the succession to a childless ruler, even the relatively modest emergency created

[48] In addition to books cited separately, I have consulted the following in connection with these remarks on China: George C. Allen and Audrey G. Donnithorne, *Western Enterprise in Far Eastern Economic Development: China and Japan* (London: Allen & Unwin, Ltd., 1954); G. E. Hubbard, *Eastern Industrialization and Its Effect on the West* (London: Oxford University Press, 1938); Kuo-heng Shih, *China Enters the Machine Age* (Cambridge, Mass.: Harvard University Press, 1944); Li Chien-nung, *The Political History of China, 1840–1928* (Princeton, N.J.: Van Nostrand, 1956); E. R. Hughes, *The Invasion of China by the Western World* (London: Adam & Charles Black, 1937); Ssu-yu Teng, *New Light on the History of the Taiping Rebellion* (Cambridge, Mass.: Harvard University Press, 1950); Siang-tseh Chiang, *The Nien Rebellion* (Seattle, Wash.: University of Washington Press, 1954); Meribeth E. Cameron, *The Reform Movement in China, 1898–1912* (Stanford, Calif.: Stanford University Press, 1931); Hu Shih, *The Chinese Renaissance* (Chicago: University of Chicago Press, 1934); F. F. Liu, *A Military History of Modern China, 1924–49* (Princeton, N.J.: Princeton University Press, 1956); Étienne Balazs, "Les Aspects significatifs de la société chinoise," *Asiatische Studien*, VI (1952), 77–87; Franz H. Michael and George E. Taylor, *The Far East in the Modern World* (New York: Henry Holt & Co., 1956); Kenneth Scott Latourette, *A History of Christian Missions in China* (New York: Macmillan Co., 1929); Chiang Monlin, *Tides from the West: A Chinese Autobiography* (New Haven, Conn.: Yale University Press, 1947); Y. Chu Wang, "The Intelligentsia in Changing China," *Foreign Affairs* (1958), 315–29.

by the appearance of Commodore Perry's "black ships" (1853–54) triggered far-ranging, deep-going transformations of Japanese society and civilization.

Until World War II, Japan's political and economic reorganization provided an unparalleled instance of successful response to Western stimuli—successful, that is, in terms of national capacity first to withstand and then to repel the Western nations whose ships and trade had precipitated the breakdown of the Tokugawa regime. Yet a policy that appropriated Western techniques so massively and rapidly did not escape internal contradictions and hidden tensions comparable to those which had characterized Tokugawa Japan. On the contrary, the success with which the Japanese borrowed aspects of Western civilization—especially its war-making and industrial techniques—depended upon yet another juggler's feat of ingenious balancing between old and new elements. Briefly put, the survival, almost intact, of an old-fashioned, sharply graded, and distinctively Japanese social hierarchy, with appropriate deferential patterns of conduct between the separate ranks of society, allowed a small group of leaders within a single generation to carry through profound changes in military and economic institutions and to remodel the political system of Japan along superficially Western lines.[49]

* * *

Severe psychological tensions, sometimes resulting in abrupt changes of conduct quite incomprehensible to an outsider, were built into Japanese life long before the ending of seclusion in 1854. The eagerness with which Japanese first received and then repudiated the Portuguese, the far earlier enthusiasm with which the Japanese imperial court appropriated Chinese civilization in the sixth and subsequent centuries A.D., and the abrupt reversals of Japanese attitudes and actions toward the United States and other foreign nations in this century all seem of a piece and suggest that a capacity for radical and sudden changes of conduct has long been a latent feature of Japanese psychology.[50]

[49] China's ideological volatility against a background of comparatively great institutional stability was therefore the antithesis of the situation in Japan. Yet, paradoxically, Japan's ideological stability was only preserved by the radical, organized instability of institutions that made the country strong and justified *samurai* leadership. Reciprocally, the rapidity of institutional change was itself possible only because traditional values and refurbished myths and symbols maintained social discipline.

Cf. Europe's radical revolutions of the Reformation period, carried through in the name of a restoration of ancient orthodoxies.

[50] Ruth Benedict, *The Chrysanthemum and the Sword* (Boston: Houghton Mifflin Co., 1946) and Robert N. Bellah, *Tokugawa Religion: The Values of Pre-Industrial Japan* (Glencoe, Ill.: Free Press, 1947) are two interesting efforts to apply different theoretical schemes to elucidate peculiarities of Japanese life that may "explain" the abruptnesses of Japanese history.

In Western history the customs of the duel offer an illuminating parallel to recent Japanese national behavior. Recognition of the points of resemblance may even make the recent drastic fluctuations of Japanese conduct toward other nations more nearly intelligible. After all, duelling in early modern times was reduced to an unwritten but binding code of behavior by swordsmen whose traditional place in society was rapidly becoming otiose. The arbiters of manners who created the Code Duello in effect sought to adjust themselves and their fellow fighting men to an increasingly alien, urbanized, and organized world by reducing the emotional extremes of their situation to a ceremonial of quarrel and reconciliation. Japanese *samurai*, swordsmen too, faced equally or more severe readjustments of their mode of life during the past century. Unlike their European counterparts, however, they were able to carry

Quite apart from internal peculiarities of Japanese society, the fact that Japan had borrowed most of its higher culture and technical skills from China over a period of more than a thousand years greatly facilitated the acceptance of Western ideas and techniques in the nineteenth and twentieth centuries. Their forefathers had already acknowledged the fact of foreign superiority in some things; hence the discovery that Europeans had knowledge and skills superior to their own was no particular shock to Japanese self-esteem. Faithful conformity to the example set by their forefathers actually required the heirs of Sinophile Japanese to become enthusiastic Westernizers.

Finally, certain congruences between Japanese and Western civilizations facilitated the acceptance of Western models in Japan. By the nineteenth century, the raw, barbarian warlikeness both of the West and of Japan had been organized (and in Japan almost suppressed) by bureaucratic governments. But the Japanese way of the warrior, with its sense of honor and social precedence, had almost exact analogues in European life. What was perhaps even more decisive, in both societies the values and attitudes of the professional warriors were in considerable degree shared and admired by other ranks and classes. Peasants and townsmen in Japan, like their counterparts in Europe, were more inclined to follow than to cringe from aristocratic specialists in violence.

Japan therefore offers the interesting paradox of a land where ideological (and emotional) conservatism served as the principal instrument to organize radical institutional transformation. As a consequence, the Industrial and the Democratic revolutions of modern times had very different degrees of success there; for, although Japanese technology leaped ahead from about 1885, the Democratic Revolution scarcely affected traditional deference hierarchies of Japanese society before 1945, despite outward constitutional forms.

*   *   *

After a shaky start in the 1880's, mechanically powered industry and transport made it possible for Japanese manufactures to compete with European or American goods all over the Far East by the time of World War I. Between the wars, the Japanese extended their sphere of commercial operations still further and in the 1930's found markets all over the world. Even more to the point, the industrial base required by modern armies, navies, and air forces developed rapidly, both in Japan proper and in her newly won empire in Korea (1910) and Manchuria (1931–32).

Japan's industrialization did not follow European patterns. The state played a far more central and critical role than it had done in any European country. As a result, entrepreneurial decisions were always affected by the requirements of national military power. In these respects, Japanese industrialization

---

the entire nation with them in adherence to a Japanese equivalent of the Code Duello. Perhaps the very rapidity of Japanese emergence from a "feudal" to a cosmopolitan social environment made the *samurai*'s feat possible, whereas a slower evolution, like that of Europe, might have split Japanese society in such a way as to prevent all classes from accepting the *samurai*'s code for the nation as a whole.

interestingly foreshadowed Russian communism. But unlike later Communist governments, the Japanese gave free rein to a multitude of small entrepreneurs who operated within traditional artisan and family relationships. Two changes were made to adjust these ancient patterns of industry to modern conditions. Light power tools, driven by electric motors, replaced or supplemented hand tools and vastly increased output. Second, the marketing of the product of small artisan shops and factories was usually entrusted to much larger firms—or to put the relationship the other way round, large marketing enterprises "put out" much or all of the work of production to small shops.

Since they needed substantial loans to tide over the gap between purchase and sale, such marketing organizations were in their turn caught up into a close network of really large-scale economic enterprises: banks, metallurgical and other heavy industries, mining enterprises, shipping companies, and a few large-scale factories. These instruments of modernity were controlled by a rather narrow economic oligarchy which was a mirror image of the political oligarchy that controlled the Japanese government. Relations between the holders of economic and political power always remained close; and individuals often married across the lines of the two elites. Indeed, the great entrepreneurial families, like the Mitsui and Mitsubishi, acquired their importance in the latter decades of the nineteenth century by taking over the management of enterprises that had been launched by official action. Small or sometimes merely token payments were asked by the state for plants which had been very costly to build; but the new "private" owners maintained a correspondingly close and continuing sense of responsibility toward the political leaders of the nation and considered it part of their duty to undertake new enterprises necessary or useful to the state.[51] As a result, the consolidation of a powerful and wealthy economic oligarchy reduced the need for direct state economic action, although state arsenals continued to produce some types of armament, especially the newer or still experimental models.

In sum, while the techniques of machine production were Western, the socio-economic organization which put the new machine technology to work was almost wholly Japanese. This meant, in particular, observing strict rules of probity and propriety as between superior and inferior in economic as in other social relationships. The Industrial Revolution in Japan therefore had a distinctive social character, which, at least in the short run, deprived modern industrialism of what students of European history often consider its "normal" partner, the Democratic Revolution.[52]

The survival of a strongly hierarchical social structure in Japan made an accumulation of capital for industrial investment comparatively easy. The government itself financed the first steps in industrial modernization by direct taxation, thereby in effect making the peasants pay for investment which could otherwise scarcely have originated from domestic Japanese sources.

[51] This was explicitly recognized in the house rules drawn up by the founder of the Mitsubishi fortune. Article 4 read: "Operate all enterprises with the national interest in mind." Cf. Bellah, *Tokugawa Religion*, p. 187.

[52] Cf. the interesting analysis in James C. Abegglen, *The Japanese Factory: Aspects of Its Social Organization* (Glencoe, Ill.: Free Press, 1958).

Later, when the financial-industrial oligarchy had taken form under the guiding hand of government, monopolistic and oligopolistic prices at home and abroad concentrated substantial financial resources into a few hands. These monopolists were, however, eager entrepreneurs, who lived modestly themselves and thereby encouraged others to refrain from conspicuous consumption, thereby stimulating capital formation up and down the social scale.[53]

* * *

A democratic revolution in the Western sense never occurred in Japan. The lords and warriors who overthrew the Tokugawa regime in 1867 and "restored" the Emperor Meiji were certainly not advocates of popular government. Even when in 1889 the Japanese introduced a Western-type written constitution, complete with an elective diet, a cabinet of ministers, and an independent judiciary, the political weight of the rank and file was carefully curtailed by appropriate limitations upon the legal powers of the diet. Indeed, the realities of politics, turning as they did upon "clan" and other long-standing local and family solidarities, were even further removed from democratic practice than the outward legalities of the Meiji constitution revealed.

With the passage of time, clan loyalties weakened and the traditional social hierarchy of Japan lost some of its rigidity. Hence, although the Meiji constitution survived until 1945, the inner realities of Japanese politics gradually became more complex. Universal male suffrage (1925) expanded the electorate and allowed upstarts to rival old established families in the inner political leadership; and in the 1930's, military cliques began to exert an independent influence upon government policy. Yet despite these challenges to their traditional primacy, rather narrow oligarchic circles continued to dominate Japanese politics from behind the scenes until 1945.

After their defeat in World War II, the Japanese for a time were forced to yield control of their country to American occupation forces. The new Japanese constitution promulgated under American auspices in 1947 was thoroughly democratic—United States style. Yet it remains doubtful whether Japanese conceptions of self, society, and status relationships, together with all the recognized proprieties of social conduct between unequals, really permit more than lip service to the egalitarian, individualistic, and fundamentally alien political ideals so carefully enshrined in that constitution.[54]

---

[53] The principal families of the economic oligarchy were of *samurai* origin and carried over into their economic management a generous dose of the spartan personal ethic of the *samurai* code. Making money, either as an end in itself or as a means to permitting some form of personal conspicuous waste, was never an acceptable motive in Japan. The collective conspicuous waste of war was, of course, another matter.

[54] Such a cavalier treatment of Japanese political evolution over the century 1850–1950 is scarcely adequate to its fascinating complexities. From the 1870's there were always a few Japanese who advocated Western liberal ideas, and, in the first decade of their existence and again in the 1920's, men of this persuasion played a limited role in affairs, if only the negative one of stimulating their opponents to more drastic, energetic, risky action. Marxism, in either its Russian Communist or Western socialist forms, seems to have played a comparable role as *agent provocateur* since the end of the American occupation.

Although nothing plausibly resembling the Democratic Revolution of other nations occurred in Japan, two semi-revolutionary changes in the form of Japanese government did take place. The first of these, the "restoration" of the emperor, was ostensibly a reactionary coup d'état, carried through by a self-appointed group of young *samurai*, many of whom had started life in humble circumstances and some of whom had had official experience within local administrations before transferring their energies to the national stage. These were the men who, wishing to restore the emperor and evict the foreigner, initiated the industrial modernization of Japan. They also worked important administrative changes, uniting all the "fiefs" of Tokugawa Japan under the central government and eliminating the legal bases of "feudalism" by buying off the rights of lords and *samurai* with government bonds. In a real sense this simply carried to its logical fulfilment the incomplete bureaucratic centralization upon which the early Tokugawa shoguns had built their power and which their successors had allowed to stand almost unchanged for more than two centuries.

Drastic reorganization of Japan's military establishment constituted a very important aspect of the Meiji restoration. Haughty *samurai*, rude peasants, humble merchants, and even the former outcastes of Japanese society were all conscripted into a new European-style army, where they were obliged to treat their officers with all the deference formerly reserved for local, hereditary social superiors. This transfer of deference from a traditional to an office-holding basis was remarkably successful. Whatever a man's origin, once commissioned as an officer of the imperial army he acquired the nimbus of command which had been burnished through the centuries by the disciplined brutality lordly masters and warriors had exercised against the rest of Japanese society. The army, therefore, became a great social escalator, especially for peasants' sons, who by dint of professional accomplishment were able to gain a status once reserved to hereditary *samurai*.[55]

One result of this situation was that the junior officers of the army became a sounding board for hotheads and radicals who were dissatisfied with the government's policies. Expressing the sentiments of large segments of the Japanese rural population, the army extremists constituted the one important group able to challenge the squabbling oligarchs who controlled party politics. In this sense they represented a democratic element in Japanese politics. Moreover, they were prepared to work outside of established social hierarchies in order to accomplish their purposes. The opposition of this military faction, backed by the threat of a popular uprising and expressed in assassination and similar deeds of violence, restricted the freedom of maneuver of Japanese politicians in the later 1930's and played a great part in driving Japan into war with China and ultimately into World War II. This was perhaps the nearest Japan came to a democratic revolution before World War II.

The results of Japan's second semi-revolution from the top, accomplished between 1945 and 1952 by General Douglas MacArthur and his minions, both American and Japanese, cannot yet be foreseen. It seems unlikely that

[55] The officer corps of the Japanese navy, by contrast, remained far more aristocratic.

the hierarchical structure of Japanese society will disappear, although it may have crumpled a bit under the impact of the war experiences, the discredit which military defeat brought to the former regime, and the disruptive effects of postwar American example and exhortation. It is also still uncertain whether the Japanese combination of Western technology with an almost unchanged social structure can strike a reasonably stable balance, or whether in the long run the Industrial Revolution will require a general and drastic reorganization of Japanese society. The question is whether indeed the Industrial and Democratic revolutions of Europe's nineteenth and twentieth centuries are connected by some necessary inner relationship, or whether the two may be effectually separated for an indefinite length of time, as the Japanese assuredly did separate them during the sixty years before 1945.

*   *   *

The social and psychological obstacles which disrupted traditional cultural expression in China and among other non-Western peoples operated less strongly in Japan because the Japanese proved able to maintain their political and spiritual independence of the West. The bulk of Japanese artistic and literary production therefore remained large. Yet the traditional arts of Japan tended either to fossilize into repetitive routine or else to decay; while imported novelties, whether architectural, scientific, or literary, did not, by the common judgment of our age, achieve real greatness. Japan, therefore, like most of the rest of the world, passed through a comparatively low period of cultural creativity between 1850 and 1950. Indeed, the Japanese achievement appears to have differed from the cultural state of the less happily situated civilized peoples of Asia chiefly in the democratization of literary culture through genuinely universal literacy.[56]

6. OTHER PARTS OF THE WORLD

Of the several thousand culturally distinct human societies existing in the middle of the nineteenth century, a good many have since been destroyed or dis-

[56] In addition to books cited separately, I have consulted the following in connection with these remarks on Japan: Hugh Borton: *Japan's Modern Century* (New York: Ronald Press, 1955); George B. Sansom, *The Western World and Japan;* Thomas C. Smith, *Political Change and Industrial Development in Japan: Government Enterprise, 1868–1880* (Stanford, Calif.: Stanford University Press, 1955); William W. Lockwood, *The Economic Development of Japan: Growth and Structural Change, 1868–1938* (Princeton, N.J.: Princeton University Press, 1954); E. Herbert Norman, *Japan's Emergence as a Modern State* (New York: Institute of Pacific Relations, 1940), and *Soldier and Peasant in Japan: The Origins of Conscription* (New York: Institute of Pacific Relations, 1943); Jerome B. Cohen, *Japanese Economy in War and Reconstruction* (Minneapolis, Minn.: University of Minnesota Press, 1949); F. C. Jones, *Japan's New Order in East Asia: Its Rise and Fall, 1937–45* (London: Oxford University Press, 1954); Inazo Nitobe *et al., Western Influences in Modern Japan* (Chicago: University of Chicago Press, 1931); Fujii Jintaro, *Outline of Japanese History in the Meiji Era* (Tokyo: Obunsha, 1958); Charles David Sheldon, "Some Economic Reasons for the Marked Contrast in Japanese and Chinese Modernization," *Kyoto University Economic Review*, XXIII (1953), 30–60; Yukio Yashiro, *2000 Years of Japanese Art* (London: Thames & Hudson, 1958); George M. Beckmann, *The Making of the Meiji Constitution: The Oligarchs and the Constitutional Development of Japan, 1868–1891* (Lawrence, Kan.: University of Kansas Press, 1957); Shibusawa Keizo, *Japanese Society in the Meiji Era* (Tokyo: Obunsha, 1958); Irene B. Taeuber, *The Population of Japan* (Princeton, N.J.: Princeton University Press, 1958).

solved into larger groupings of mankind. Yet the total number of different societies remained large even in the middle of the twentieth century and embraced an enormous variety of institutions and attitudes. Each society, great or small, continued as in times past to respond in its own way to new stimuli, opportunities, and dangers. What made the years since about 1850 unusual was the rough uniformity of critical outside stimuli encountered by each society; for the West-centered cosmopolitanism arising from the Industrial and Democratic revolutions left no important region of the earth untouched.

Tremendous multiplicity, enough to delight the most eager anthropologist, continues to variegate the life of mankind. The retreat of European (and American) colonial empires since World War II has made the variety of the human social condition far more spectacularly obvious than it was when colonial administrative cadres gave an outward appearance of uniformity to wide areas of the globe. Twentieth-century revolutionary movements in some Latin American countries have also emphasized the continued existence of the Amerindians as a significant social entity. Indeed the Mexican artistic movement, stimulated by the revolution of 1911, incorporated old Amerindian motifs into very sophisticated painting and architecture and thereby succeeded in injecting a New World primitivism into the repertory of contemporary cosmopolitan art.[57] But no other fusion between Western and local art or thought seems yet to have attracted wide attention or been able to offer significant enrichment to the already perhaps overburdened cosmopolitanism of the twentieth century.

[57] José Orozco (d. 1949) and Diego Rivera (1880—) at least liked to pretend to be the heirs of the Aztec and Toltec as well as of the European past. By contrast, Old World primitivism, primarily west African, was "discovered" by Europeans just before World War I.

Conclusion

In the spring of 1917 the United States became a belligerent in World War I. In the fall of the same year, Bolsheviks overthrew the tsarist government in Russia and withdrew that country from the war. These events make the year 1917 a serviceable landmark from which to date a new phase in Western and world civilization, marked by the Communist transformation of Russia, the rise of the United States to world power, the eclipse of western Europe as undisputed center and arbiter of Western civilization, and by enormous advances in men's ability to manipulate human as well as inanimate energies.

The most obvious and perhaps also the most important changes associated with this landmark were in (1) the scale and (2) the scope of politics after 1917.

A. SCALE OF POLITICS

Two superpowers, measured by the standard of western European nation-states, announced themselves in 1917 by proclaiming rival panaceas for the ills of the corrupt, imperialist, and war-ridden world which Europe's no longer "New Regime" had made. By 1945 both Wilsonism and Leninism had lost the dazzle of their new-minted brightness. But enhanced weight of metal, by which measure the United States and the Soviet Union far eclipsed all rivals, amply compensated for a generation's accumulation of ideological tarnish. At the close of World War II, only these two giants could sustain the elaborate panoply of modern war on the basis of their home resources. As armaments grow in complexity and expense, the possibility correspondingly decreases of restoring the sear and shrunken sovereignties of the separate nations of western Europe or of rendering the sovereignty of any small countries really secure.

The rise of the United States and the Soviet Union to world pre-eminence since World War II was, indeed, only another instance of a familiar historical phenomenon: the migration of military-political power from more anciently civilized but less effectively organized heartlands to regions nearer the frontier. Machine technology, which within recent memory carried western

Europe to the apex of its world domination, seems now, like Zeus of ancient fable, to have turned ruthlessly upon its parent. Since 1917, and more particularly since 1945, the extractive, transport, processing and distribution complexes of modern industrialism no longer fit easily within the narrow frontiers of the old west European nation-states. In 1945, the elbow room of half a continent gave both Russia and the United States a more or less satisfactory basis for military power; yet even this semicontinental scale is sure to become inadequate if any one center of power should succeed in effectively uniting the resources of still greater areas. Modern industrialism and transport, in short, have begun extravagantly to reward mere geographical extent.

A logical terminus to this expansion of political scale would be the creation of a single world sovereignty. Any world war fought in the near future, while only two superpowers are in the ring, would likely lead to such a settlement.[1] Certainly the technical means for asserting effective world sovereignty lie ready at hand. Monopolization of especially powerful "capital" weapons by an organized force obedient to a reliably united central authority would suffice of itself to supersede organized warfare among separate political sovereignties. Such a development seems a distinct possibility, even within the near future.

On the other hand, the shift in political scale from great powers the size of France, Britain, or Germany to superpowers of semicontinental scale may provide a basis for a future balance of power like that of the European Old Regime. A new family of world powers may define itself, in which China and India and perhaps Brazil or some as yet unformed political units of semicontinental scale (e.g., a United Europe or, less plausibly, a United Middle East or a United Africa) would share the leading roles with the two superpowers already on the scene.

B. SCOPE OF POLITICS

The changed scope of politics which has emerged from the two world wars and from the Communist and other totalitarian revolutions of the twentieth century seems as massive and irreversible a feature of the social landscape as is the expanded political scale. What the German General Staff contrived in 1917–18 as an emergency response to the multifold problems of bringing all possible resources to bear upon the tasks of waging war became, in effect, for Russian Communists a norm applicable indifferently to peace and to war. The

---

[1] Total extermination of humanity and all higher forms of life through pollution of the atmosphere with radioactivity now is apparently a real possibility. On the other hand, even the most formidable modern weapons, despite their almost unimaginable destructive powers, have their own peculiar vulnerability. The more complex weaponry becomes, the more difficult supply and control also become. Armies and whole nations become more liable to sudden paralysis through failure of supply or of command. In other words, transport and communication are the Achilles' heel of modern armed establishments; and total victory and total defeat would be likely to come, as they did in World War II, long before the population or the productive plant of the loser was entirely or perhaps even extensively destroyed. Modern armed power has to be purchased at a high cost in fragility, for the same reason that higher organisms and complicated machinery have to purchase their efficiency at the cost of vulnerability to all sorts of disorders that cannot afflict simpler structures whose functioning does not depend upon the exact co-ordination of so many parts.

revolutionary conspirators who came to power in Russia in 1917 took over
not merely the traditional apparatus of the state—army, police, and bureaucracy—but extended their control also to banks, factories, farms, and the various media of communication together with labor unions, political parties, and
associations of every sort. The revolutionary state even resorted to forced
labor when exhortation and wage inducements failed to distribute manpower
as desired.

Economics thus dissolved back into politics, which, indeed, became almost
coterminal with human life itself, since, at least in principle, art, letters,
thought, recreation, and family life were all harnessed to the pursuit of the
Communist goal as defined through changing times and circumstances by
appropriate and authoritative manipulations of the "party line."

Countries which escaped Communist revolutions did not experience quite
so rapid and radical an expansion of the scope of politics, although in most
European nations (and in Japan, too), socialist, nationalist, and fascist movements advanced rapidly in this direction during the interwar years. Hitler's
Germany lagged only slightly, if at all, behind Stalinist Russia in subordinat-

POLITICAL REALIGNMENTS 1918–1950

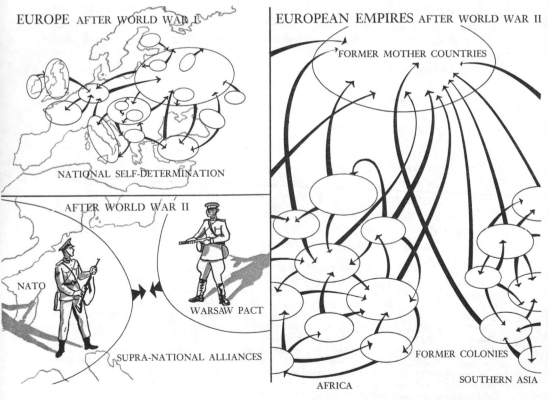

EUROPE AFTER WORLD WAR I

NATIONAL SELF-DETERMINATION

AFTER WORLD WAR II

NATO

WARSAW PACT

SUPRA-NATIONAL ALLIANCES

EUROPEAN EMPIRES AFTER WORLD WAR II

FORMER MOTHER COUNTRIES

FORMER COLONIES

AFRICA

SOUTHERN ASIA

ing all human activity to political ends. During World War II, even the most conservative democracies, where liberal scruple traditionally hedged in the power of the state in time of peace, found it wise to subordinate economic and many other aspects of social activity to the war effort, *i.e.*, to the service of politically defined goals not basically different in kind from those the German Nazis and Russian Communists were simultaneously pursuing by more violent, ruthless, and totalitarian means.

Just as the nineteenth-century distinction between politics and economics has collapsed in some countries and is blurring elsewhere, so also the much older distinction between peace and war has everywhere lost its erstwhile clarity. The normal (*i.e.*, peacetime and wartime) practices and organizational patterns developed by the Russian Communists and by the German Nazis strikingly resembled Anglo-American economic-political-military collaboration during World War II. Careful strategic and economic planning characterized all three power systems. Human engineering "machined" individuals and groups (the platoon, the division) into interchangeable parts, while industrial engineering turned out tanks and airplanes, proximity fuses and atabrine, trucks and K-rations according to priorities and production schedules keyed to a strategic over-all plan. Finally, an enveloping atmosphere of haste, emergency, and crisis sustained a psychological buoyancy and sense of excited venture among the managers and manipulators of the newly found and furbished springs of power.[2]

Wartime patterns of social organization did not, of course, prevail in the United States after 1945–46, when the machinery of American mobilization was dismantled. Yet the experience of World War II undoubtedly left important traces behind. Notions that would have seemed preposterous a decade before were accepted after the war as perfectly normal. Thus governmental responsibility for maintaining economic prosperity, for subsidizing scientific research, for developing atomic technology, and for assuring an adequate supply of engineers, was taken almost for granted. In each of these cases and in many more, government action inspired by military-political considerations encroached upon or entirely superseded the old sovereignty of the free market postulated by liberal economic theory. An enormous expansion in the size of the United States' armed forces and an extraordinary elaboration of their equipment operated powerfully in the same direction, for with the growth of the armed services, principles of military hierarchy and fiscal

---

[2] Cf. more extended remarks on this point in W. H. McNeill, *America, Britain, and Russia: Their Cooperation and Conflict, 1941–46* (London: Oxford University Press, 1954), pp. 747–68. Some, perhaps most, of these observations apply to Japan as well as to the United States, Russia, and (perhaps to a lesser extent) Germany and Great Britain. However, the Japanese war planning depended mainly upon careful preparation in advance—the Prussian formula for victory in 1866 and 1870—and upon a bulldog tenacity in holding what had been so secured. Shipping and other shortages from 1941 onward made even the maintenance of existing Japanese industry and armed forces difficult, so that Japanese planners and administrators scarcely had a chance to show what they could do. German war planning also shared some of the Japanese conservatism; for the German General Staff counted upon a short war, fought as in 1866 and 1870–71 with stocks on hand at the beginning of each new campaign. This lag offers an interesting example of how the heirs of a great past are prone to hesitate in changing their methods to accommodate changed conditions.

bureaucratization have been fastened upon a significant segment of the population and a substantial portion of the economy.

After World War II, when even a conservative country like the United States rapidly extended the scope of political-military jurisdiction over its citizens, the Communist dictatorship of the Soviet Union perceptibly recoiled from the extreme revolutionary effort to regiment the whole variety of Russian thought and action. Autonomy for specialists, each free in his own field from more than lip service to the pieties of Marxism-Leninism, had advanced a long way within the Soviet Union even before Stalin's death in 1953. Since

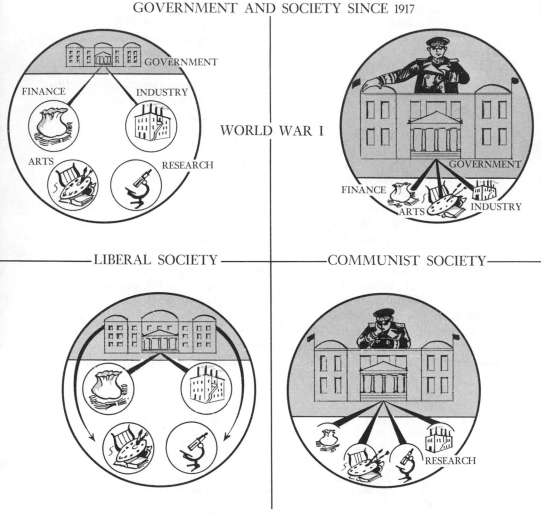

GOVERNMENT AND SOCIETY SINCE 1917

WORLD WAR I

LIBERAL SOCIETY ———— COMMUNIST SOCIETY

SINCE WORLD WAR II

that time, some gestures have also been made toward freeing writers and other artists from the shackles of the official party line. If such developments continue, as might be expected to follow from the growing wealth, complexity, and subtlety of Russian society, the second half of the twentieth century may see a gradual convergence between Russian and American social systems, each of them balancing a bit uneasily between the conflicting demands of welfare and warfare.

Such an evolution would recapitulate the nineteenth-century interplay between the French Revolution and the European Old Regime. A gradual softening of doctrinal rigor must, indeed, be the fate of all successful revolutions; for human variety is always incommensurate over time and in detail with any single ideal. But it seems equally certain that the export of successful revolution can only be prevented by those who are ready and able to borrow from the revolutionaries at least some of the practical secrets of their power. This, surely, was the history of nineteenth-century Europe. The pattern of revolutionary challenge and conservative accommodation seems likely to be repeated within the larger circle of the Western world in the twentieth century.[3]

There is a second sense in which the Russian Revolution resembled and, indeed, carried the logic of the French Revolution another step forward. The essence of the French Revolution was the sweeping away of ancient vested interests and corporate obstacles to the concentration of political power in the hands of the People, whose amorphous majesty of necessity delegated the practical exercise of authority, whether to a parliament, cabinet, committee, or dictator. Likewise, the essence of the Russian Revolution, it now appears, was the sweeping away of ancient vested interests and corporate obstacles to the concentration of a much wider range of power—political, economic, moral—into the hands of the same apotheosized abstraction, the Sovereign People. And as before, the People delegated power—or so their self-appointed leaders declared—to a corps of ideological and managerial technicians organized into a hieratic and hierarchic party. If the French Revolution proved that political institutions and authorities were in truth man-made, the Russian Revolution seems to have demonstrated by the same unimpeachable logic of act that social and economic institutions were just as much man-made as political ones and might likewise undergo wholesale and deliberate reconstruction. In remodeling Russian society, the Communists gleefully trampled upon eighteenth-century natural rights of property and ruthlessly suppressed nineteenth-century civil liberties as well. Yet the Nature in which liberal theorists had once put so much trust, abetted by the human nature of scores of mil-

---

[3] The fact that a convergence between the internal social orders of the protagonists of the mid-century cold war cannot occur in a vacuum but will happen, if it happens at all, in the midst of a world where numerous other peoples are simultaneously struggling for power, wealth, security, and in many instances for life itself, will complicate, but may hasten, the process. Hungry and aggrieved outsiders, the Chinese for example, may someday drive Russia and the United States into each other's arms, as the Germans did in World War II. This would create a potentially much more explosive political lineup, dividing the world along racial-cultural lines far more sharply than the Russo-American ideological polarity of the 1950's ever did.

lions of Russians, supinely yielded to Communist manipulations, much as
divine-right monarchy had crumpled in revolutionary France a century and
a quarter before.

Clearly, the Russian Revolution succeeded in concentrating power on a
hitherto unexampled military-political, economic-psychological scale, just as
the French Revolution had done in its day. Yet in both cases there was room
for disagreement as to whether the new conditions of life under revolutionary,
rationalized, and arbitrarily created institutions were in fact more satisfying
than they had been under the older, more various and idiosyncratic prerevolutionary regimes. In both cases also, old moral dilemmas achieved a poignancy which had been unknown in former times, when the power at human
disposal had been smaller and alternatives pressing upon human decision had
been correspondingly less drastic.

C. DILEMMAS OF POWER

Save in a loose and metaphorical sense, the people never really controlled
"their" government in the United States or anywhere else, despite the fact
that in the days of Jefferson and Jackson, official powers and duties were
restricted and the recognized political alternatives were narrowly defined by
nineteenth-century liberal principles. As for the administrative Molochs of
the mid-twentieth century, they can with difficulty be controlled by full-time
professionals. Even in countries where governmental monpoly of public
communication does not exist, governments more often than not can lull or
wheedle the public into acquiescence or whip it into enthusiasm for official
acts and plans.

Yet the dependence of modern democratic governments upon skilful
manipulation of public opinion nonetheless sets real and valuable limits upon
tyrannical exercise of official authority. Not everyone, after all, can be persuaded to commit suicide. Official lethargy or uncertainty backed by public
ignorance or indifference may sometimes result in a happy muddling through.
But though a government fearful of offending special interests and pressure
groups may indeed refrain from tyranny at home, it is also prone to be slow
in settling upon any new course of action. Anything of importance which has
not been done before is sure to offend someone and to provoke overt or
covert counterpressures. From the point of view of forthcoming elections,
politicians may calculate quite correctly that it is not safe to override even
quite small minorities. Under such circumstances, democratic political leaders
are strongly tempted to settle for the path of least resistance, either by post-
poning action or by compromising, even illogically, between incompatible
alternatives.

As long as domestic institutions remain in good working order, masterly in-
activity may often serve as a passable substitute for wisdom. But when real
crisis looms, then the stalemates and postponements arising from the pulling
and hauling of the democratic process of government as developed in the
United States and other liberal societies may become truly disastrous. Too

little and too late makes a sorry epitaph; yet one may hope all the same that the very slowness and imprecision with which a loosely controlled and directed people responds to the prods of circumstances and of official, semi-official, and unofficial voices may preserve a saving flexibility and versatility in thought and act.

A further dilemma of democratic government in our time arises from the fact that techniques for appealing to subrational and even to subconscious levels of human motivation are still in their infancy when applied to politics. Liberal democratic theory assumed human rationality and discounted the passions; but psychologists and social scientists no longer believe that men are ruled by reason, while advertisers and military men know they are not. The prospects of a royal road to power through clever and unscrupulous exploitation of the non-rational elements of human nature are far too bright to permit a facile optimism as to the future of democracy.

Yet discrepancies between theory and fact, ideal and reality, also afflict Communist regimes, and perhaps in even more acute form. Marx and Lenin assumed that once the revolution had swept away private ownership of the means of production, human rationality and benevolence would take over automatically, after only a brief period of transition. Yet as the Russian Revolution approaches its fiftieth anniversary, the onset of the Communist idyll is not much in evidence. Instead, Communist governments have regularly defied popular wishes, repressed popular movements, and oppressed individual citizens, claiming all the while to know better than the people themselves what was good, right, proper, and necessary. It is perhaps a Communist misfortune that Marxist-Leninist scriptures include rather more than their share of ardent denunciation of oppression, together with magnificently utopian anticipations of a free, leisured, and abundant material future. Given the harsh realities of initial Communist practice—compulsory saving and high rates of investment requiring a ruthless exploitation of the peasantry in order to provide capital for industrial construction—the discrepancies between rosy dream and drab fact, between generous aspiration and ugly practice become peculiarly sharp, and difficult to sustain over prolonged periods of time. Clearly, the Russians already feel this strain. An aging and prospering revolution cannot indefinitely justify failures to attain the promised land of communism by pointing to the dangers of capitalist encirclement.

Moral dilemmas such as these are aspects of basic questions of social hierarchy and human purpose which haunt all men in an age when inherited institutions and customary relationships no longer appear natural, inevitable, immutable. Hierarchy and control remain as vital as ever, perhaps even more so; for the complex co-ordination of human effort required by modern industry, government, and warfare make it certain that some few men will have to manage, plan, and attempt to foresee, while a majority must obey, even if retaining some right to criticize or approve the acts of their superiors. But who has the right to manage whom? And toward what ends should human capacities be directed?

The wider the range of human activities that can be brought within the

ALL FOR ONE AND ONE FOR ALL

THEORY AND PRACTICE OF MODERN DICTATORSHIP

scope of deliberate management, the more fateful these questions become. Or perhaps a really tough-minded critic of twentieth-century society would have to say: The wider the range of human activities brought within the scope of deliberate management, the more irrelevant questions of social hierarchy and managerial goals become. Admittedly, as the managerial elite of any particular country gathers experience and expertise, reduces new areas of human activity to its control, and integrates partial plans into a national (or transnational) whole, the bureaucratic machine exercising such powers becomes increasingly automatic, with goals built into its very structure. The administrative machine, like other specialized instruments, can only do what it was built to do. Scientific personnel classification allows, nay, requires, interchangeability of parts in the bureaucracy; hence individual appointments and dismissals make remarkably little difference so long as they do not achieve too massive a scale or too rapid a rate. The administrative totality, its over-all structure and functioning, and even the general lines of policy remain almost unaffected by changes of elected officials. Even energetic reformers, placed in high office and nominally put in charge of such vast bureaucratic hierarchies, find it all but impossible to do more than slightly deflect the line of march.

A really massive bureaucracy, such as those which now constitute every major modern government, becomes a vested interest greater and more strategically located than any "private" vested interest of the past. Such groupings are characterized by a lively sense of corporate self-interest, expressed through elaborate rules and precedents, and procedures rising toward the semi-sacredness of holy ritual. These buttress a safe conservatism of routine and make modern bureaucracy potentially capable of throttling back even the riotous upthrust of social and technical change nurtured by modern science. Consequently, as the corporate entities of government bureaucracies grow and mesh their activities more and more perfectly one with another, both within and among the various "sovereign" states of our time, use and wont—the way things have "always" been done—may become, bit by bit, an adequate surrogate for social theory. By sustaining an unceasing action, administrative routine may make rational definition of the goals of human striving entirely superfluous.

If and when the possibility of international war ceases to agitate mankind and no longer spurs officialdom within the separate political sovereignties of the earth to ever greater effort, we should expect a heavy weight of bureaucratic routine to fasten itself upon all parts of the globe. Within a comparatively short time, the unutterable but far from impracticable slogan: "Bureaucrats of the world, unite, you have nothing to lose but your jobs," could be counted upon to set powerful brakes upon the dizzy pace of change which gives men vertigo today. The cautious principle: "Whatever is is right—or at least convenient," and the regulation that says: "This action requires a permit, filled out in triplicate on the proper form and can only be issued after a committee at the next higher level has reviewed the proposal," would everywhere come into effect, without requiring formal legislation. Under such a regime, the theoretical dilemmas and moral issues that trouble the mid-twentieth century would fade from men's minds as the Cheshire cat faded from Alice in Wonderland's sight.

Much depends on how soon—if ever—stability through bureaucracy sets in. Perhaps the next step beyond the level of social and human engineering already pioneered·by the Russian Revolution will be genetic tinkering with human germ plasm to produce suitably specialized subhuman and superhuman biological varieties. Present-day theoretical knowledge probably would allow this sort of management of human evolution. The potential results in enhanced efficiency and social discipline, thereby further increasing the possibility of concentrating power, seem enormous. Any revolution which made its way by rationalizing and accelerating human evolution might, therefore, like previous revolutions, compel others to imitate at least some of its techniques. If this should ever happen, men of the future may come to differ from those alive today as much as modern domestic animals differ from their wild ancestors; and such a posthuman population might itself become as specialized in function and various in type as the social insects are now.

One may hope that some saving refractoriness of human nature and society —if not of human genetics—may make such a further extension of the realm of deliberate management forever impossible. The fact that even the best laid plans for directing human affairs still often fail may turn out to be humanity's saving grace. Alternatively, the period of grace may prove merely transitional, as human societies pass from their hitherto wild state into a future domesticated condition. Until men have been tamed, we cannot know for sure; for any failure in a first, second—or thousandth—attempt to rearrange human germ plasm according to plan would not prove that the feat was inherently impossible. This sword of Damocles may therefore hang over humanity indefinitely. Like every other important new exercise of power, it raises the old questions Who? Whom? and Wherefore? to a new order of magnitude. After all, "Who tames whom?" differs from the familiar "Who controls whom?" only in the degree of distance assumed between the two parties to the relationship.

The two-edged nature of power is nothing new in human affairs. All important new inventions have both freed men from former weakness and deficiency and enslaved them to a new regimen. The hardy hunter surely despised the first farmers, bowed down by the heavy labor of the fields; and through long subsequent centuries barbarian freemen regularly scorned the servile habits of their civilized contemporaries. Yet these repugnances never for long arrested the spread of agriculture or of civilization. Civilized history, likewise, as this book has tried to show, may be understood as a series of breakthroughs toward the realization of greater and greater power—including under this rubric the delicate but altogether real power of beauty in art and thought as well as power's cruder, ruder forms.

It seems unlikely, therefore, that recent and prospective enlargement of human capacities to organize and exert power will be permanently arrested by scruples against its use. The brash adventurers who first make good an attempt to organize new springs of power can always confront even reluctant

Photo by Louis Laniepce, Paris. Museum of Modern Art, New York, and Musée Nationale d'Art Moderne, Paris.

THE END AND THE BEGINNING

The haunting witticisms of this headboard for a double bed (carved by Georges Lacombe in 1892) juxtapose the super-sophistication of European intellectual efforts to probe human subconsciousness with artful echoes of the Christian myth of Eden and original sin. Simultaneously, the artist chose to resort to forms reminiscent of primitive African art. Yet this multiple visual pun effectively expresses an important predicament of civilized men in the twentieth century. For the great snake, making a human face emerge from the contortions of his body as he writhes with the pain of feeding upon his own tail, is strangely like the intellectuals of our time who, having used their conscious and rational faculties to discover the dark realms of the unconscious psyche—realms that tie them willy-nilly to the primitive—can no longer trust rationality, but instead make reason feed upon itself by rationally arguing the helplessness of reason.

neighbors with the choice of succumbing or of doing likewise. Power, in short, ingests weaker centers of power or stimulates rival centers to strengthen themselves. This fact—and it amounts to no more than a definition of the term "power"—has dominated the whole history of mankind. Politically, economically, socially—and perhaps, but let us hope not, also biologically—the elaboration of power structures seems in our time to be moving swiftly toward a climax. The globe is finite and if the rival political-social-economic power systems of our time coalesce under an overarching world sovereignty, the impetus now impelling men to develop new sources of power will largely cease. Naturally, great tasks of social and economic betterment will remain, and delicate adjustments between population and developed resources will be required, all subsequent, perhaps, to extensive reconstruction of war damages. But for this, application of already familiar methods on sufficient scale and with a store of resolution and intelligence already well within human reach should suffice. And once these initial adjustments have successfully been made, a stalwart, more than Chinese bureaucratic immobility would, in all probability, soon define the daily life of cosmopolitan world society.

More interesting and more promising for the remoter future are the unresolved, and in our time sometimes oppressively confused, problems of aesthetic power. So long as men remain within the human nature known to history, they may be expected to seek beauty in art and in thought. Even in the most efficiently bureaucratized world that a twentieth-century imagination can conceive, there would remain scope, perhaps even abundant scope, for imaginative and intellectual play. Religion, maybe wearing some new guise as yet undreamed, might come into its own again as an agent sustaining personal security and promoting social solidarity. Fine art and belles-lettres might also flourish if a stabilized pattern of life allowed established meanings and symbolisms to unite artists and writers with their audiences more closely than now seems to be the case. Science too might be expected to continue theoretical elaboration; but a stoutly conservative bureaucratized social order would be most unlikely to rush scientific discoveries into new technology. Technological and perhaps also scientific progress would proceed far more slowly, if only because compelling motives for taking the trouble and provoking the dislocation caused by technological innovation would weaken or disappear.

What such a vision of the future anticipates, in other words, is the eventual establishment of a world-wide cosmopolitanism, which, compared with the confusions and haste of our time, would enjoy a vastly greater stability. A suitable political frame for such a society might arise through sudden victory and defeat in war, or piecemeal through a more gradual encapsulation of a particular balance of world power within a growingly effective international bureaucracy. But no matter how it comes, the cosmopolitanism of the future will surely bear a Western imprint. At least in its initial stages, any world state will be an empire of the West. This would be the case even if non-Westerners should happen to hold the supreme controls of world-wide political-military authority, for they could only do so by utilizing such originally Western traits as industrialism, science, and the public palliation of power through advocacy of one or other of the democratic political faiths. Hence "The Rise of the West" may serve as a shorthand description of the upshot of the history of the human community to date.[4]

Historical parallels to such a stabilization of a confused and chaotic social order are not far to seek. The Roman empire stabilized the violences and uncertainty of the Hellenistic world by monopolizing armed might in a single hand. The Han in ancient China likewise put a quietus upon the disorders of the warring states by erecting an imperial bureaucratic structure which endured, with occasional breakdown and modest amendment, almost to our own day. The warring states of the twentieth century seem headed for a similar resolution of their conflicts, unless, of course, the chiliastic vision that haunts our time really comes true and human history ends with a bang of hydrogen nuclei and a whimper from irradiated humanity.

*   *   *

The burden of present uncertainties and the drastic scope of alternative possibilities that have become apparent in our time oppress the minds of many sensitive people. Yet the unexampled plasticity of human affairs should also be exhilarating. Foresight, cautious resolution, sustained courage never before had such opportunities to shape our lives and those of subsequent generations. Good and wise men in all parts of the world have seldom counted for more; for they can hope to bring the facts of life more nearly into accord with the generous ideals proclaimed by all—or almost all—the world's leaders.

The fact that evil men and crass vices have precisely the same enhanced powers should not distract our minds. Rather we should recognize it as the inescapable complement of the enlarged scope for good. Great dangers alone produce great victories; and without the possibility of failure, all human achievement would be savorless. Our world assuredly lacks neither dangers nor the possibility of failure. It also offers a theater for heroism such as has seldom or never been seen before in all history.

Men some centuries from now will surely look back upon our time as a golden age of unparalleled technical, intellectual, institutional, and perhaps even of artistic creativity. Life in Demosthenes' Athens, in Confucius' China, and in Mohammed's Arabia was violent, risky, and uncertain; hopes struggled with fears; greatness teetered perilously on the brim of disaster. We belong in this high company and should count ourselves fortunate to live in one of the great ages of the world.

---

[4] The rise of the West, as intended by the title and meaning of this book, is only accelerated when one or another Asian or African people throws off European administration by making Western techniques, attitudes, and ideas sufficiently their own to permit them to do so.

Index of Proper Names